Judicial Remedies in Public Law

Sir Clive Lewis
A Justice of the High Court, Queen's Bench Division
Bencher of Middle Temple

Contributor: C.J.S Knight

SWEET & MAXWELL

THOMSON REUTERS

First Edition	1992	by Clive Lewis
Second Edition	2000	by Clive Lewis
Third Edition	2004	by Clive Lewis
Fourth Edition	2009	by Clive Lewis

Published in 2015 by Thomson Reuters (Professional) UK Limited trading as Sweet & Maxwell, Friars House, 160 Blackfriars Road, London, SE1 8EZ (Registered in England & Wales, Company No 1679046.

Registered Office and address for service: 2nd floor, Aldgate House, 33 Aldgate High Street, London EC3N 1DL)

For further information on our products and services, visit *www.sweetandmaxwell.co.uk*

Typeset by Letterpart Limited, Caterham on the Hill, Surrey, CR3 5XL.

Printed and bound in Great Britain by CPI Group (UK) Ltd, Croydon, CR0 4YY.

No natural forests were destroyed to make this product; only farmed timber was used and re-planted.

A CIP catalogue record of this book is available for the British Library.

ISBN: 978-0-41404-535-4

Thomson Reuters and the Thomson Reuters logo are trademarks of Thomson Reuters.

Sweet & Maxwell ® is a registered trademark of Thomson Reuters (Professional) UK Limited.

Crown copyright material is reproduced with the permission of the Controller of HMSO and the Queen's Printer for Scotland.

100731268 9

To my Father
And in memory of my Mother.

Preface

This work focuses on the judicial remedies available to ensure the proper application of public law. Public law concerns the principles governing the activities of public bodies and those performing public functions. Claims for judicial review remain the primary method of determining and enforcing those public law principles. In addition, statutory appeals and applications and habeas corpus exist to ensure the principles of public law are observed. This work deals with the current scope, procedure and practice of judicial review and other public law remedies. In addition, this work considers the specific principles governing damages claims against public bodies and the enforcement of rights derived from the European Convention on Human Rights and the law of the European Union. I am grateful to Christopher Knight who contributed Chapter 10 on Judicial Review and the Upper Tribunal and Chapter 16 on the Human Rights Act 1998.

This edition has the same two aims as previous editions. First, it seeks to offer a description and analysis of the different public law remedies. Secondly, it seeks to describe the current approach of the courts to public law remedies. I have tried to set out the law as at September 1, 2014.

Clive Lewis
Royal Courts of Justice
November 16, 2014

Preface

TABLE OF CONTENTS

CONTENTS

CONTENTS

CONTENTS

CONTENTS

CONTENTS

11. Standing

12. The Discretion of the Court to Refuse a Remedy and the Exclusion of Judicial Review

CONTENTS

CONTENTS

CONTENTS

CONTENTS

CONTENTS

TABLE OF CASES

TABLE OF CASES

TABLE OF CASES

TABLE OF CASES

TABLE OF CASES

TABLE OF CASES

TABLE OF CASES

TABLE OF CASES

TABLE OF CASES

TABLE OF CASES

TABLE OF CASES

TABLE OF CASES

TABLE OF CASES

TABLE OF CASES

TABLE OF CASES

TABLE OF CASES

TABLE OF CASES

TABLE OF CASES

TABLE OF CASES

1

TABLE OF CASES

TABLE OF CASES

liii

TABLE OF CASES

TABLE OF CASES

TABLE OF CASES

TABLE OF CASES

TABLE OF CASES

TABLE OF CASES

TABLE OF CASES

TABLE OF CASES

TABLE OF CASES

TABLE OF CASES

TABLE OF CASES

TABLE OF CASES

TABLE OF CASES

TABLE OF CASES

TABLE OF CASES

TABLE OF CASES

TABLE OF CASES

TABLE OF CASES

TABLE OF CASES

TABLE OF CASES

TABLE OF CASES

TABLE OF CASES

TABLE OF CASES

TABLE OF CASES

TABLE OF CASES

xcii

TABLE OF CASES

TABLE OF CASES

TABLE OF CASES

TABLE OF CASES

TABLE OF CASES

TABLE OF CASES

c

TABLE OF CASES

TABLE OF CASES

TABLE OF CASES

TABLE OF CASES

TABLE OF CASES

TABLE OF CASES

TABLE OF CASES

TABLE OF CASES

TABLE OF CASES

TABLE OF CASES

TABLE OF CASES

TABLE OF CASES

TABLE OF STATUTES

TABLE OF STATUTES

TABLE OF STATUTORY INSTRUMENTS

TABLE OF CIVIL PROCEDURE RULES

SUPPLEMENTARY TABLE OF PRACTICE DIRECTIONS

TABLE OF CIVIL PROCEDURE RULES

TABLE OF INTERNATIONAL AND EUROPEAN TREATIES AND CONVENTIONS

TABLE OF EUROPEAN SECONDARY LEGISLATION

Regulations

Directives

CHAPTER 1

Introduction

A. PUBLIC LAW

Public law concerns the law governing relations between the individual[1] and public bodies, and relations between different public bodies, such as central and local government. The courts have developed a body of substantive principles of public law to ensure that public bodies do not exceed or abuse their powers and that they perform their duties. Thus, the courts will review an exercise of power to ensure that the public body:

1-001

(a) has not made an error of law;
(b) has considered all relevant factors, and not taken into account any irrelevant, factors;
(c) has acted for a purpose expressly or impliedly authorised by statute;
(d) has not acted in a way that is so unreasonable that no reasonable public body would act in that way[2]; and
(e) that the public body has observed statutory procedural requirements and the common law principles of natural justice or procedural fairness.

These grounds were summarised by Lord Diplock as illegality, irrationality and procedural impropriety.[3] It is not, however, possible to fit all the grounds of review into water-tight compartments. Other grounds of review exist: such as those designed to ensure that a public body does not fetter its discretion[4]; or unlawfully delegate its powers[5]; or reach a decision on no evidence[6]; or those enabling the court to determine whether jurisdictional facts exist.[7] Where reasons for a decision have been given, either because there is a statutory duty to give

---

[1] This includes legal and natural persons.

[2] The "*Wednesbury* principles", named after *Associated Provincial Picture Houses v Wednesbury Corp.* [1948] K.B. 223, where Lord Greene M.R. enunciated them. See, generally, the standard textbooks on judicial review such as H.W.R. Wade and Forsyth, *Administrative Law*, 11th edn (2014); de Smith, *Judicial Review*, 7th edn (2013); and Auburn, Moffatt and Sharland, *Judicial Review* (2013).

[3] In *Council of Civil Service Unions v Minister for the Civil Service* [1985] A.C. 374 at 410.

[4] See, e.g. *R. v Secretary of State for Foreign and Commonwealth Affairs Ex p. Everett* [1989] Q.B. 811.

[5] *Ellis v Dubowski* [1921] 3 K.B. 621.

[6] See, e.g. *Gavaghan v Secretary of State for the Environment* (1989) 60 P. & C.R. 515.

[7] *R. v Secretary of State for the Home Department Ex p. Khawaja* [1984] 1 A.C. 74. See also *R. (A) v Croydon LBC (Secretary of State for Home Department and another intervening)* [2009] 1 W.L.R. 2557 (whether a person was a child, i.e. a person aged under 18, was an objective fact which, as a matter of statutory construction, was for the courts ultimately to determine).

reasons or they are required in the particular circumstances of the case,[8] such reasons must be adequate and intelligible and deal with the principal points at issue.[9] Other grounds of judicial review have also been developed or are in the process of emerging. The courts have recognised, for example, that a clear, unambiguous and unqualified representation[10] or a previous course of conduct[11] by a public authority may give rise to legitimate expectations. Such expectations may give rise to procedural rights, such as the right to be consulted before a decision is taken, or the existence of such expectations may be a relevant consideration which a decision-maker must take into account when reaching a decision, or in exceptional circumstances, the expectation may give rise to a right to enjoy a substantive benefit which it would be unfair and an abuse of power to frustrate.[12] The public authority may need to establish that there is an overriding interest requiring a departure from the representation and that it would not, in all the circumstances of the case, be unfair to do so.[13] The courts are still developing the law governing legitimate expectations.[14] The courts have held that, in certain contexts at least, a material error of fact may be a ground for judicial review.[15] Such a ground will require a mistake as to a fact existing at the time of the decision, that the fact is uncontentious and objectively verifiable, that the mistake occurred otherwise than as a result of the fault of the claimant or his advisers and played a material part in the decision-maker's reasoning.[16] Proportionality is a recognised ground for review in cases involving EU law or the European

---

[8] The House of Lords held in *R (Doody) v Secretary of State for the Home Department* [1994] 1 A.C. 531 that there was no general duty to give reasons for administrative action but recognised that there may well be circumstances in which such a duty will be imposed. In addition, statutory provisions may impose a duty in relation to a particular decision.

[9] *South Buckinghamshire DC v Porter (No. 2)* [2004] 1 W.L.R. 1953 [36].

[10] *R. v Commissioners of Inland Revenue Ex p. MFK Underwriting Ltd* [1990] 1 W.L.R. 1545; *R. (Patel) v General Medical Council* [2013] 1 W.L.R. 2801. See also *Paponette v AG of Trinidad and Tobago* [2012] 1 A.C. 1 and also *R. (Bancoult) v Secretary of State for Foreign and Commonwealth Affairs (No 2)* [2009] A.C. 453 at [60].

[11] *R. v Commissioners for the Inland Revenue Ex p. Unilever Plc* [1996] S.T.C. 681; *R (Davies) v Revenue and Customs Commissioners* [2011] 1 W.L.R. 2625 (especially at [49]). See also *Council of Civil Service Unions v Minister for the Civil Service* [1985] A.C. 374.

[12] See *R. v North and East Devon Health Authority Ex p. Coughlan* [2001] Q.B. 213 and *R. (Patel) v General Medical Council* [2013] 1 W.L.R 2801. See also *Paponette v Att-Gen of Trinidad and Tobago* [2012] 1 A.C. 1.

[13] *Paponette v Att-Gen. of Trinidad and Tobago* [2012] 1 A.C 1 at [37]–[45].

[14] See, e.g. *R. (Patel) v General Medical Council* [2013] 1 W.L.R. 281L, *The Times*, June 21, 2013. *Nadarajah v Secretary of State for the Home Department* [2005] EWCA Civ 1363, *The Times*, December 14, 2005.

[15] *R. v Criminal Injuries Compensation Board Ex p. A* [1999] 2 A.C. 330 (the House of Lords preferred, ultimately, to base their decision on the ground that there had been a breach of natural justice). See also the dictum of Lord Slynn in *R. (Alconbury Developments Ltd) v Secretary of State for the Environment, Transport and the Regions* [2002] 2 A.C. 295 at [53] and *E. v Secretary of State for the Home Department* [2004] 1 Q.B. 1044.

[16] *E. v Secretary of State for the Home Department* [2004] 1 Q.B. 1044 at [63]–[66]. There the Court of Appeal was dealing with a ground of challenge on an appeal on a point of law from a tribunal but the same reasoning applies to claims for judicial review. The error must be as to a fact existing at the time of the decision not one established by reference to material or evidence coming into existence subsequently: see *R. (Clays Lane Housing Ltd) v The Housing Corporation* [2005] 1 W.L.R. 2229 and see also *MT (Algeria) v Secretary of State for the Home Department* [2008] 2 W.L.R. 159 at [65]–[70] and *IA (Iran) v Secretary of State for the Home Department (United Nations High Commissioner for Refugees Intervening)* [2014] 1 W.L.R. 384 at [54]–[55].

Convention on Human Rights[17] but the Court of Appeal has held that, in purely domestic law cases, proportionality is not a free-standing ground of review and the appropriate test is whether the public body has acted irrationally, that is whether it acted in a way that no reasonable public body would act. The Court of Appeal recognised that there were strong arguments in favour of accepting proportionality as a separate ground for review but considered that that was a matter for the Supreme Court.[18] Other grounds of judicial review may emerge over time or existing grounds may be extended to accommodate new bases of challenge.[19]

There are two other major sources of challenges to legislation or the actions of public bodies. First, claims may allege that legislation or administrative action is incompatible with the rights derived from the European Convention on Human Rights which was incorporated into domestic law by the Human Rights Act 1998. Judicial review is one of the primary mechanisms for bringing claims alleging that a Convention right has been violated.[20] Secondly, many areas of modern life are regulated or influenced by EU law. Claims that legislation or administrative action is incompatible with directly effective rights derived from EU law have been brought by way of judicial review for many decades.[21]   **1–002**

This work is primarily concerned with the judicial remedies by which these public law principles are enforced. In particular, this book is concerned with the avenues by which decisions of public bodies may be challenged before the higher courts. The book is not concerned with appeals brought before inferior courts or tribunals (although it will consider the ways in which decisions of inferior courts and tribunals may themselves be challenged) nor is it concerned with the internal mechanisms that frequently exist in public organisations to remedy grievances.   **1–003**

B.   THE CLAIM FOR JUDICIAL REVIEW

The primary method by which the courts exercise their supervisory jurisdiction over public bodies to ensure that those bodies observe the substantive principles of public law is by way of a claim for judicial review.[22] The relevant rules are   **1–004**

---

[17] See *R. (Daly) v Secretary of State for the Home Department* [2001] A.C. 532, at [27]; and *R. (Countryside Alliance) v Att-Gen* [2008] 1 A.C. 719.

[18] *R. (ABCIFER) v Secretary of State for Defence* [2003] Q.B. 1397 at [32]–[37]. See also the dicta of Lord Mance in *Kennedy v Information Commissioners* [2014] 2 W.L.R. 808 at [54].

[19] See, e.g. the development of certain common law "rights" such as the right to access to a court which cannot be overridden except by specific statutory provisions: *R. v Lord Chancellor Ex p. Witham* [1998] Q.B. 575 and *R. (Daly) v Secretary of State for the Home Department* [2001] A.C. 532 and, possibly, a concept of equal treatment whereby like cases are treated alike: *R. (ABCIFER) v Secretary of State for Defence* [2003] Q.B. 1397 at [83]–[86]. Conspicuous unfairness on the part of a public body may give rise to a claim that its decisions are irrational but does not constitute a free-standing head of review enabling a court to substitute its view of the merits of a decision for that of the decision maker: *R (London Borough of Lewisham and others) v AQA, Edexcel and Ofqual* [2013] EWHC 211 (Admin) at [110]–[111].

[20] See paras 2–053 to 2–055 and Chapter 16 below.

[21] See paras 2–056 to 2–060 and Chapter 17 below. For convenience, the law derived from the Treaty of European Union, the Treaty on the Functioning of the European Union, and any subsequent treaties is referred to in this work as EU law.

[22] S.31 of the Senior Courts Act 1981 refers to an application for judicial review. The CPR refers to a claim for judicial review and the latter terminology is more common and is used in this book.

now contained in Pts 8 and 54 of the CPR, read together with s.31 of the Senior Courts Act 1981.[23] In addition, the Upper Tribunal now has jurisdiction to hear claims for judicial review in certain categories of cases.[24] A claim for judicial review is a specialised procedure by which the courts may grant one of the prerogative remedies, namely a quashing order (formerly called certiorari), a mandatory order (formerly called mandamus) or a prohibiting order (formerly called prohibition)[25] and alternatively, or in addition, a declaration or injunction.[26] Damages or restitution or recovery of money may also be awarded if one of those five remedies is granted *and* damages or restitution would have been available if claimed by an ordinary claim.[27] Part 8 of the CPR, as modified by Pt 54, replaces the former RSC Ord.53, introduced in 1977, which first set out a comprehensive set of rules for making claims for judicial review.

1–005   Prior to 1977, the procedures governing the prerogative remedies and the ordinary remedies (of declaration or injunction) were entirely separate. A claimant could either apply for a prerogative remedy, using the specialised procedure that existed for such remedies, or he could proceed by ordinary claim by way of writ or originating summons for a declaration or injunction. It was not possible before 1977 to combine a claim for one of the prerogative remedies with a claim for a declaration or an injunction, or damages. The prerogative remedies were subject to a specialised procedure contained in the old Ord.53. Different procedural provisions therefore governed the prerogative remedies as compared with the ordinary remedies of declarations and injunctions. The claimant needed the permission[28] of the court to apply for a prerogative remedy whereas no such requirement existed in relation to the ordinary remedies. A stricter time-limit applied to claims for the prerogative remedies. Disclosure of documents and cross-examination were automatic in ordinary claims but were unavailable, in practice, in claims for prerogative remedies. The standing requirements were, however, more liberal for the prerogative remedies than declarations or injunctions.

1–006   The purpose of the 1977 reforms was to introduce a procedure whereby the prerogative remedies and declarations and injunctions (and in appropriate circumstances damages) could be claimed in one claim. On a claim for judicial review, the courts may therefore grant any of those remedies. The rules for judicial review also introduce uniform provisions governing disclosure; interlocutory orders for further information and cross-examination; standing and time-limits. Further reforms were made to the judicial review procedure following a review of the work of the Administrative Court Office and the relevant rules are now contained in CPR Pts 8 and 54 and the Practice Direction on Judicial Review. The relevant rules governing the bringing of claims for judicial review in the Upper Tribunal are contained in Part 4 of the Tribunal Procedures (Upper Tribunal) Rules 2008.

---

[23] As amended by the Civil Procedure (Modification of Supreme Court Act 1981) Order 2004.

[24] See ss. 15 to 19 of the Tribunals, Courts and Enforcement Act 2007 and the directions made under s.18 of that Act.

[25] See Senior Courts Act 1981 s.29 as amended by the Civil Procedure (Modification of Supreme Court Act 1981) Order 2004.

[26] See Senior Courts Act 1981 s.31 and CPR r.54.1.

[27] Senior Courts Act 1981 s.31(4) as amended.

[28] Formerly called leave.

C. SIGNIFICANCE OF THE CLAIM FOR JUDICIAL REVIEW

The prerogative remedies can now only be claimed by way of judicial review. They are, broadly speaking, only available in public law matters. The definition of what constitutes a public law matter, for this purpose, is at the heart of judicial review and is considered in detail in Chapter 2. Declarations or injunctions are available by way of judicial review as an alternative to, or in addition to, the prerogative remedies in a public law matter. The House of Lords has held that,[29] in public law cases, declarations and injunctions should normally be sought by way of judicial review and it will generally be an abuse of the process of the court to seek these remedies by way of the ordinary process of making a claim.[30] The result is the creation of a specialised procedure designed to deal with public law issues, in which all the necessary remedies are available. A distinction has therefore emerged at the remedial level between public law and private law.

1–007

Much of this book is concerned with the claim for judicial review. The early chapters of the book deal with the definition of public law and the circumstances in which judicial review is available and when it must be used. The range of measures against which judicial review is available is discussed in Chapter 4. The consequences of a finding that a public body has acted unlawfully in the public law sense are considered in Chapter 5. Chapters 6 to 8 deal with the individual remedies and their uses and any rules specifically applicable to a particular remedy. The machinery of making a judicial review claim in the High Court is then considered in Chapter 9 and in the Upper Tribunal in Chapter 10 followed by the rules dealing with standing in Chapter 11. In Chapter 12, the discretion of the court to refuse a remedy, even if the claimant has made out a case that the public body has acted unlawfully, is discussed.

1–008

Standing is seen as performing a dual function. First, it acts as a threshold issue, relevant to whether that person can even bring judicial review proceedings. Secondly, it is seen as relevant to whether the particular claimant is entitled to claim the remedy that he is seeking and so is related closely to the discretion of the courts on whether to grant that particular claimant a remedy.[31] As such, it seems appropriate to place the discussion on standing between the machinery for instituting proceedings and the discussion of the remedial discretion of the courts.

1–009

Substantive principles of public law are primarily, but not exclusively, enforced through the judicial review machinery. Avenues of challenge other than judicial review exist in which public law issues may arise for determination.

1–010

---

[29] *O'Reilly v Mackman* [1983] 2 A.C. 237, and see Chapter 3. Declarations continue to be available in ordinary actions to enforce private law rights. They will be available to enforce public law rights in situations which form an exception to the rule in *O'Reilly v Mackman* and, probably, if the Attorney-General grants his consent to relator actions.

[30] There are rare occasions when the substantive principles of public law may be enforced against a body which is not susceptible to judicial review and so is not, from the remedial point of view, a public body. This may be the position with domestic tribunals: see para.2–070.

[31] *R. v Secretary of State for Transport Ex p. Presvac Engineering Ltd* (1991) 4 Admin. L.R. 121 at 145E–146B and see below at para.11–002.

D. HABEAS CORPUS

1–011 The prerogative remedy of habeas corpus is still available as a means of challenging the legality of the detention of an individual by a public body. Habeas corpus is subject to its own specialised procedure and this is considered in Chapter 13. Despite its historical and constitutional significance, the practical importance of habeas corpus has declined over the years.

E. STATUTORY MECHANISMS OF CHALLENGE

1–012 Statute may provide a means by which the legality of decisions of public bodies may be challenged in the courts. A variety of procedures such as rights of appeal or appeal by case stated or statutory applications to quash have been created in a diverse range of areas. These are considered in Chapter 14.

F. DAMAGES AND RESTITUTION

1–013 Public bodies, like private individuals, are capable of committing tortious acts. In general, the same principles apply to public bodies as to individuals. In practice, the scope for imposing liability will frequently need to take account of specific factors relevant to public bodies. The extent to which a public body owes a duty of care, for example, may be influenced by the statutory background against which the public body is operating. There is also one tort, misfeasance in a public office, which applies uniquely to public bodies. By that tort, a public body which commits an ultra vires act, either maliciously or knowing that the act is ultra vires, which causes loss, may be liable in damages.[32]

1–014 Public bodies may have power to enter into contracts. There may be an overlap between public law principles governing the exercise of power and the ordinary principles of contract law. Restitutionary claims may also be made by, and against, public bodies. While the normal principles governing restitution will apply, the actual application of these principles will frequently need to take account of the fact that different considerations may apply in the case of claims involving public bodies as opposed to claims between two individuals. Damages may, in certain circumstances, be available where a public authority acts incompatibly with a Convention right.[33]

1–015 The application of the ordinary principles of tort, contract and restitution and to public bodies is considered in detail in Chapter 15. The special position of the Crown is also considered there.

---

[32] See below at para.15–097.
[33] See s.8 of the Human Rights Act 1998.

G. EUROPEAN CONVENTION ON HUMAN RIGHTS

The Human Rights Act 1998 provides that it is unlawful for a public authority to act in a way which is incompatible with certain of the rights contained in the European Convention on Human Rights.[34] Persons who claim that a public authority has acted in a way which violates their Convention rights can bring a claim in an appropriate court or tribunal. In practice, a claim for judicial review brought in the High Court is frequently the appropriate method for bringing such a claim.[35] In addition, the High Court must seek to interpret primary legislation in a way that is compatible with Convention rights, so far as it is possible to do so,[36] and, if it is not possible to do so, may declare that provisions of the legislation are incompatible with a Convention right.[37] The procedural provisions governing claims involving Convention rights and the remedies available, including damages, are discussed in Chapter 16.

1–016

H. EU LAW

One of the most far-reaching legal developments has been the accession of the UK to the EU. Provisions of the Treaty on the Functioning of the EU Treaty[38] and of Regulations and Directives made under the Treaty may, in certain circumstances, be directly effective in that they confer rights and impose duties which the national courts are required to protect. Such rights and duties may well circumscribe the exercise of statutory power by public bodies or impose duties on public bodies to do certain acts. As such, issues of EU law are in certain circumstances classed as public law. Damages for breach of EU law may, in certain circumstances, be available for breach of EU law by a public body. In other circumstances, EU law may confer rights on individuals which are enforceable against other individuals as well as public bodies. In such circumstances, the courts may seek to integrate the principles of European Union law with English private law. The relationship between EU law and English law and the appropriate remedies to enforce EU law rights is considered in Chapter 17. The special procedure by which questions of EU law may be referred to the Court of Justice of the European Union in Luxembourg for a preliminary ruling on the issue of EU law is considered in Chapter 18.

1–017

---

[34] See s.6 of the Human Rights Act 1998.

[35] See, generally, the standard texts, such as Clayton and Tomlinson, *The Law of Human Rights*, and Lester and Pannick, *Human Rights Law and Practice*, for a detailed description of the substantive law on Convention Rights.

[36] Human Rights Act 1998 s.3 and see *Re S (Minors) (Care Order: Implementation of Care Plan)* [2002] 2 A.C. 291 on the proper approach to interpretation.

[37] Human Rights Act 1998 s.4.

[38] There were initially three Treaties creating three Communities (the Coal and Steel Community, the European Atomic Energy Community and the European Economic Community). The most important was the 1957 Treaty of Rome which created the European Economic Community. Subsequent Treaties amended the founding Treaties. The relevant Treaties now are named the Treaty on European Union and the Treaty on the Functioning of the European Union.

CHAPTER 2

The Availability of Judicial Review

A. INTRODUCTION

Judicial review describes the process by which the courts exercise a supervisory jurisdiction over the activities of public authorities in the field of public law. The primary method by which this control is exercised is through the application for judicial review. This procedure is generally regarded as a public law remedy.[1] More accurately, the claim for judicial review is a specialised procedure by which an applicant can seek one or more of the existing prerogative remedies which can now only be claimed by way of an application for judicial review and, in appropriate circumstances, declarations and injunctions and damages.[2]   **2–001**

The judicial review jurisdiction only operates in the field of public law. Public law has traditionally been defined by reference to the scope of the prerogative remedies: this is reflected in s.31 of the Senior Courts Act 1981, which ties the availability of judicial review to the scope of the prerogative orders. More recently, the language used in Pt 54 of the CPR reflects the fact that the scope of judicial review depends not only on the scope of the prerogative remedies but also upon the nature of the functions being performed by the body under challenge.[3] Against that background, the courts have elaborated a more generalised definition of what constitutes a "public law issue" which may be resolved by way of a claim for judicial review.   **2–002**

Judicial review is only available against a body exercising public functions in a public law matter. In essence, two requirements need to be satisfied. First, the body under challenge must be a public body or a body performing public functions. Secondly, the subject-matter of the challenge must involve claims based on public law principles, not the enforcement of private law rights. In the past, the courts focused primarily on the source of the power in determining whether a body was a public one subject to judicial review. Bodies created by statute or exercising powers derived from the prerogative were seen as public bodies amenable to judicial review. Now, however, the modern approach is to consider whether the exercise of a power, or performance of a duty, involves a "public element, which can take many different forms, and the exclusion from the   **2–003**

---

[1] See, e.g. the dicta of Sir John Donaldson M.R. in *R. v East Berkshire Health Authority Ex p. Walsh* [1985] Q.B. 152 at 162; "the remedy of judicial review is only available where an issue of 'public law' is involved."

[2] For injunctions and declarations in judicial review, see paras 2–174 to 2–179. Habeas corpus is not available in judicial review proceedings but is subject to its own procedure: see Chapter 13.

[3] See CPR r.54.1 and *R. (Heather) v Leonard Cheshire Foundation (A Charity)* [2002] 2 All E.R. 936 at [37].

jurisdiction of bodies whose sole source of power is a consensual submission to its jurisdiction".[4] The source of a power or duty remains an important indication of the public law nature of a body and bodies created by statute or acting under powers derived from the prerogative will usually be public law bodies for the purposes of judicial review. Other non-statutory bodies may, however, be performing public functions and may be subject to judicial review in respect of those functions. Factors such as the nature of the function, the extent to which there is any statutory recognition or underpinning of the body or the function in question and the extent to which the body has been interwoven into a system of governmental regulation may indicate that the body performs public functions and is, in principle, subject to judicial review in respect of those functions.[5] The principal exclusion from the scope of judicial review now is bodies who acquire jurisdiction over individuals by virtue of contract. These are seen as private not public bodies.

2–004   The second requirement is that the subject-matter of the claim being pursued in the judicial review claim involves matters of public law not private law. Public bodies (like private bodies) may enter into contracts or commit torts. Individuals may only be seeking to enforce essentially private law rights. Judicial review is not available to enforce purely private law rights.

B.   SOURCE OF THE POWER

Statute

2–005   Judicial review has been and remains principally concerned with the activities of bodies deriving their authority from statute. Where an individual seeks to challenge the exercise of a power derived from statute, or seeks to compel the performance of a statutory duty, the presumption is that such an issue raises a matter of public law suitable for resolution by judicial review.[6] That presumption

---

[4] *R. v Panel on Take-overs and Mergers Ex p. Datafin (Norton Opax Intervening)* [1987] Q.B. 815 at 838E–F.

[5] See *R. v Association of British Travel Agents Ltd Ex p. Sunspell Ltd (t/a Superlative Travel)* [2001] A.C.D. 88, and *R. v Insurance Ombudsman Ex p. Aegon Life* [1994] C.O.D. 426. S.6 of the Human Rights Act 1998 recognises that public authorities may either be "core" public authorities, all of whose actions must comply with Convention rights, and "hybrid" bodies, i.e. those bodies certain of whose functions are public and which, in respect of those functions (but not their other functions), they must comply with Convention rights. Some assistance may be derived from the case law on whether a body's functions are sufficiently public so as to be subject to judicial review in deciding whether the body is also performing public functions and so is public authority for the purposes of the Human Rights Act 1998. Given that the definition of public authorities in the Human Rights Act 1998 is intended to achieve a particular purpose, that is, ensuring that those bodies for whom the UK would be liable for any breach of the Convention before the European Court of Human Rights comply with the Convention, the scope of the domestic case law on judicial review is unlikely to be determinative of the meaning of public authority in s.6 of the Human Rights Act 1998: see *Aston Cantlow Parochial Church Council v Wallbank* [2003] 3 W.L.R. 283, esp. at [52] (per Lord Hope), [87] (per Lord Hobhouse) and [163] (per Lord Rodger); see also *R (Weaver) v London & Quadrant Housing Trust* [2010] 1 W.L.R. 363 per Elias LJ at [37] and see also *Poplar Housing and Regeneration Community Association Ltd v Donoghue* [2002] Q.B. 48, esp. at [65].

[6] *Mohit v D.P.P. of Mauritius* [2006] 1 W.L.R. 3343 at [21]. See also *R. v General Medical Council Ex p. Colman* [1990] 1 All E.R. 489 (affd. the decision of the Divisional Court: see *The Times*,

may, on rare occasions, be displaced. The courts have, on occasions, approached the matter as involving a three-fold test, namely whether the public body was exercising statutory powers, whether the function in question was a public or a private function and whether the body was performing a public duty owed to the individual in the particular circumstances of the case.[7] In general, however, if the body is exercising statutory powers, and if the challenge is to the exercise of those statutory powers (rather than seeking to enforce some private law right against the body), such a challenge may be brought by way of judicial review.[8]

There is a vast array of bodies and individuals performing a wide range of statutory functions. These include central and local government; inferior courts, such as magistrates' and coroners' courts; statutory tribunals, such as admission appeal panels in the education field and regulatory bodies such as those regulating utilities—all of which have been the subject of judicial review claims. Judicial review has extended into areas such as the health service, immigration, the criminal justice system, local authority social services and town and country planning, all of which are regulated on a statutory basis. Some, such as the decisions of local authorities in the field of community care and the activities of immigration officials, make frequent appearances in the law reports, whilst others have in the past appeared more rarely, such as the duties of the Secretary of State[9] and the various health authorities[10] in relation to the NHS. Current trends, however, indicate an increase in actual or threatened challenges to decisions in the health field such as decisions refusing access to certain treatments or drugs[11] or reducing services at hospitals.[12] New statutory bodies exercising statutory functions are created from time to time and the exercise of their statutory functions will be amenable to judicial review.[13]

2–006

December 14, 1988, and [1989] C.O.D. 313), and dicta of Lord Goddard C.J. in *R. v National Joint Council for the Craft of Dental Technicians* (*Disputes Committee*) *Ex p. Neate* [1953] 1 Q.B. 704 at 707. See also *R. v Kidderminister District Valuer Ex p. Powell, The Times,* July 23, 1991.

[7] See, e.g. *R. (Tucker) v Director-General of the National Crime Squad* [2003] I.C.R. 599 at [24] at 607; *R. (Hopley) v Liverpool Health Authority* [2003] P.I.Q.R. 10.

[8] But see paras 2–011 to 2–012 below on instances where the courts have held that the third criterion is not met and so the decision is not amenable to judicial review.

[9] See, e.g. *R. v Secretary of State for Health Ex p. Keen* [1990] C.O.D. 371.

[10] See, e.g. *R. v Hillingdon Health Authority Ex p. Goodwin* [1984] I.C.R. 800 and *R. v Tunbridge Wells Health Authority Ex p. Goodridge, The Times,* May 21, 1988 (decisions to close hospitals quashed); *R. v North and East Devon Health Authority Ex p. Coughlan* [2001] Q.B. 213 (decision to close a purpose-built disabled facility quashed).

[11] See, e.g. *R. (Rogers) v Swindon NHS Primary Care Trust* [2006] 1 W.L.R. 2649. See also *R. v North West Lancashire Health Authority Ex p. A.* [2000] 1 W.L.R. 977 (court reviewed policy of refusing to fund gender re-assignment operations).

[12] See, e.g. *R. (London Borough of Lewisham, Save Lewisham Hospitals Campaign Limited) v Secretary of State for Health* [2014] 1 W.L.R. 514 (decision to close an accident and emergency unit, and other units, at a hospital quashed).

[13] See, e.g., the Office of Qualifications and Examinations Regulation, created in 2010 which is subject to judicial review. An unsuccessful claim was brought in *R. (London Borough of Lewisham) v AQA* [2013] EWHC 211 (Admin). See also the Security Industry Authority, established by the Private Security Industry Act 2001, which was also the subject of an unsuccessful claim for judicial review in *R. (Nicholds) v Security Industry Authority* [2007] 1 W.L.R. 2067.

Non-statutory bodies exercising statutory powers

2–007   Many public bodies are created by statute and exercise statutory power. However, the important feature is the source of the power that a particular body is exercising rather than the fact that the body was set up by statute. Statutory powers may be conferred, or duties imposed, on bodies which are, in origin, non-statutory, private bodies. In relation to the exercise of its statutory powers, judicial review will be available. This arrangement reflects the haphazard development of public law in the UK: functions once carried out by private individuals or charitable bodies become matters of public concern. Rather than dismantle the existing structure, statute frequently adds a super-structure of powers or duties, or otherwise incorporates existing bodies within the statutory framework within which such activities are performed.

2–008   In the field of education, for example, religious schools were incorporated into the statutory framework of education and maintained by local authorities. In so far as they exercise statutory powers, such bodies are subject to judicial review. Thus, a foundation-governor of a school administered under a trust deed was able to challenge the exercise by the trustees of a statutory power to dismiss him from office.[14] Professional bodies incorporated by Royal Charter may have statutory powers conferred on them. In the disciplinary field, statute frequently provides for statutory powers of discipline, often exercisable by a statutory committee grafted on to the existing structure of the chartered body, and the exercise of such powers is subject to judicial review.[15] The Law Society, a body created by charter, has a large number of disciplinary and regulatory functions conferred upon it by statute and the exercise of these statutory powers is amenable to judicial review.[16]

Situations where judicial review is inappropriate

2–009   The trend is to regard all statutory powers exercisable by public authorities as amenable, in principle, to judicial review. There are situations where judicial review may be inappropriate. Here, the courts have generally held that they have jurisdiction to entertain a claim for judicial review and have dealt with arguments that review is inappropriate in a particular case by the use of their discretion not to grant permission to apply for judicial review or to refuse a remedy. Thus, the courts have accepted that they have jurisdiction to review a decision to postpone a heart operation but have stressed that the jurisdiction must be used very sparingly in the realm of discretionary allocation of resources in this area.[17] Permission to challenge a decision not to operate on a child was accordingly

---

[14] *R. v Trustees of the Roman Catholic Diocese of Westminster Ex p. Andrews* [1990] C.O.D. 25.
[15] *R. v Statutory Committee of the Pharmaceutical Society of Great Britain Ex p. Pharmaceutical Society of Great Britain* [1981] 1 W.L.R. 886; *R. v Committee of Lloyd's Ex p. Posgate, The Times,* January 12, 1983, DC; *R. v General Medical Council Ex p. Gee* [1987] 1 W.L.R. 564.
[16] See, e.g. *R. (Thompson) v Law Society* [2004] 1 W.L.R. 2522 (statutory powers to consider complaints about the provision of inadequate professional services); *R. v Law Society Ex p. Reigate Projects Ltd* [1993] 1 W.L.R. 1531; *R. v Law Society Ex p. Mortgage Express Ltd* [1997] 2 All E.R. 348 (statutory powers to administer compensation scheme for those suffering loss as a result of dishonest solicitors).
[17] *Re Walker's Application, The Times,* November 11, 1987. See below at para.4–086.

refused.[18] Similarly, the House of Lords refused to be deterred from holding that the disciplinary decisions of prison governors were subject to judicial review by arguments that to do so might undermine the authority of prison governors and lead to the courts being flooded with frivolous claims. Such considerations should be dealt with by the use of the court's discretion to refuse a remedy rather than by denying the availability of judicial review altogether.[19] Furthermore, the courts may discourage claims by indicating that, whilst an exercise of a particular statutory power may, in principle, be reviewable, there will only be relatively few occasions when a claim will succeed given the limited grounds upon which a judicial review court may intervene. A particular statutory power may confer a very broad discretion or the nature of the subject-matter involved may make it inherently unlikely that the courts will find that a particular decision is irrational or displays an error of law. In a challenge to a decision of a Chief Constable as to the number of officers that he would deploy to deal with protests against the export of veal, for example, the House of Lords stressed that the Chief Constable knew the local situation, the availability of officers, his financial resources and the other demands on his force. They indicated that it was generally undesirable to intervene too readily in challenges to the exercise of discretion as to the use of limited resources.[20] A decision to institute a criminal prosecution is, in principle, amenable to judicial review but the courts have emphasised that judicial review of such decisions is generally inappropriate and challenges to such decisions should be considered in the context of the underlying criminal proceedings and not in judicial review proceedings.[21] In *R. v Lord Chancellor Ex p. Maxwell*,[22] the courts accepted that the exercise by the Lord Chancellor of a statutory discretion on allocating judges to hear trials could, in principle, be reviewed. Given the width of the discretion, and the limited grounds upon which the courts could intervene, the vast preponderance of such claims were likely to fail and so should be critically examined at the permission stage.

Rationale for judicial review of statutory powers and duties

The concentration on the statutory source of the authority's power reflects the **2–010**
underlying basis of the courts' supervisory control. The basis of judicial control over public authorities has traditionally been the doctrine of ultra vires. Statutory bodies are only able to do those things expressly or impliedly authorised by statute; actions not authorised are regarded as ultra vires and of no legal effect.

---

[18] *Re Walker's Application* note 17, above. See also *R. v Cambridge District Health Authority Ex p. B.* [1995] 1 W.L.R. 898 at 906 and see *R. (Pfizer Ltd) v Secretary of State for Health* [2002] Eu.L.R. 783 at [8]–[9] (decision to restrict the availability of a particular drug as that treatment had a lower priority than other treatments also funded by the NHS not unlawful on domestic public law grounds).
[19] *R. v Deputy Governor of Parkhurst Prison Ex p. Leech; R. v Deputy Governor of Long Lartin Prison Ex p. Prevot* [1988] A.C. 533. But see *R. (Tucker) v Director-General of The National Crime Squad* [2003] I.C.R. 599.
[20] *R. v Chief Constable of Sussex Ex p. International Trader's Ferry Ltd* [1999] 2 A.C. 418.
[21] See, e.g. *Sharma v Brown-Antoine* [2007] 1 W.L.R. 780 at [14](5) and [30]–[36]; and see also *R. (Corner House Research) v Director of the Serious Fraud Office* [2008] 3 W.L.R. 568 at [30] and see below at para.4–023.
[22] [1997] 1 W.L.R. 104 at 112G–113b. See also *R. (Hunt) v Criminal Cases Review Commission* [2001] 2 W.L.R. 319 at [16] (court should not allow the Commission to be drawn into judicial review proceedings in inappropriate cases, thereby distracting it from its statutory duty).

Judicial review is concerned with ensuring that statutory bodies do not exceed the limits of the statutory powers conferred upon them. The courts have also developed general principles governing the exercise of discretionary power. These principles can be incorporated into the ultra vires doctrine by assuming that Parliament intended statutory bodies to observe them in the exercise of their statutory functions. In reality, the doctrine of ultra vires does not play a dominant role in judicial thinking today and it is not now the sole basis of judicial review.[23] The important question is whether a body is sufficiently "public" to merit judicial supervision. The fact that such a body was created by statute or is exercising statutory powers is relevant because the courts normally regard this as sufficient to warrant treating the body as a public body, and therefore amenable to judicial review.

Statutory bodies performing a non-public function

2–011   The courts have generally accepted that the exercise of statutory powers is amenable to judicial review. Occasionally, there have been suggestions that, notwithstanding the statutory origin of a body and its powers, the functions that the body is performing may not be sufficiently "public" in nature to merit subjecting the body to judicial review or, in the particular circumstances of the case, the body was not performing a public duty owed to the individual concerned.[24] The courts have on occasion suggested that particular decisions of a statutory body are "commercial" decisions, not public law decisions. In one case, the court refused to grant certiorari to quash a decision to close a colliery. The court indicated that such activities were not public functions as a decision to close a colliery was "an executive, or business decision in exactly the same category as a decision in similar circumstances made by a public company".[25] That decision has subsequently been disapproved by the Divisional Court which followed the traditional approach that where statute imposes duties or confers powers on a public body, those duties are to be regarded as public duties amenable to judicial review. Thus, failure to comply with the statutory obligations imposed on the National Coal Board to consult prior to taking a decision on whether to close a colliery was a matter of public law susceptible to judicial review.[26] In some areas, particularly in the case of statutory powers to contract or in employment matters, the courts do on occasion consider whether there is a sufficient public element to

---

[23] See Craig, "*Ultra Vires* and the foundations of Judicial Review" [1998] C.L.J. 63; Oliver, "Is the *Ultra Vires* Rule the Basis of Judicial Review?" [1987] P.L. 543. But see also C. Forsyth, "Of Fig Leaves and Fairy Tales" [1996] C.L.J. 122 for the contrary view. The rival arguments are contained in Forsyth (ed.), *Judicial Review and the Constitution* (Hart, 2000). See also C. Forsyth and M. Elliott "The Legitimacy of Judicial Review" [2003] P.L. 286. See below at para.5–003.

[24] *R. (Tucker) v Director General of the National Crime Squad* [2003] I.C.R. 599.

[25] *R. v National Coal Board Ex p. National Union of Mineworkers* [1986] I.C.R. 791 at 795B. For a similar attempt to claim that the exercise of a statutory power by a public body was in fact "managerial and commercial" and so outside the scope of judicial review, see *R. v Birmingham City Council Ex p. Dredger* (1993) 91 L.G.R. 532. The court found that the decision was amenable to judicial review but on the grounds that the decision affected the traders' common law rights to earn a living rather than simply on the statutory origin of the power.

[26] *R. v British Coal Corporation Ex p. Vardy* [1993] I.C.R. 720 at 751F–G; see also *R. v Post Office Ex p. Association of Scientific, Technical and Managerial Staff (Telephone Contracts Offices' Section)* [1981] I.C.R. 76.

make the exercise of power subject to judicial review.[27] Most of these cases are likely now to be resolved by asking whether the actual subject-matter of the challenge involved claims based on ordinary public law principles or whether, on analysis, the individual was claiming that some private law right had been violated. If the claimant is complaining about the way in which the statutory power has been exercised (for example, claiming that the public body has exercised the statutory power to contract on the basis of irrelevant considerations or unfairly or irrationally) that will normally be a public law claim concerning the exercise of statutory power which can be dealt with by way of judicial review.[28] If the claimant is, in reality, complaining about a breach of the terms of a contract, that involves private law not public law claims and so would not normally be the subject of judicial review. This issue is considered in detail below.[29]

In some instances, however, the courts have still held that a particular exercise of power by a public body is not amenable to judicial review, even though no private law rights are in issue, because they consider that the particular acts of a public body do not involve a sufficiently public element. In *Tucker*,[30] for example, the Court of Appeal held that a decision to terminate the secondment of a police officer to the National Crime Squad was not subject to judicial review. The National Crime Squad was created by statute and had statutory powers to appoint officers on such terms and conditions as it considered appropriate. Secondment was dealt with under those terms and conditions of service. Those conditions were not contractual and there was no question of the police officer seeking to enforce private law rights. The Court of Appeal held that this was an operational or management decision relating to a particular officer which did not involve any public law element. Consequently, the Court held that judicial review was not available. A better approach would have been to recognise that such decisions are in principle subject to judicial review, just as disciplinary decisions relating to police officers are. However, the public law obligations applicable to decisions relating to secondment or transfer of officers may need to be modified to reflect the nature of the decision and, further, the nature of the decision may render judicial review inappropriate in most (but not necessarily all) cases. Such an approach would ensure that judicial review, and the substantive principles of public law so far as appropriate, are available in principle but would not subject such decisions to an inappropriate level of judicial supervision.[31]

2–012

A number of nationalised industries have been privatised. They have ceased to be statutory corporations exercising statutory powers and have usually become ordinary limited companies. At the same time, however, statutory regulatory

2–013

---

[27] See, e.g. *R. v Legal Aid Board Ex p. Donn & Co.* [1996] 3 All E.R. 1 (whether statutory power to award contract amenable to judicial review; *R. v Bolsover District Council Ex p. Pepper* [2001] L.G.R. 43 (whether exercise of statutory power to sell land subject to judicial review).

[28] See, e.g. *R. v Midlands Electricity Board Ex p. Busby: R. v Midlands Electricity Board Ex p. Williamson, The Times,* October 28, 1997 (whether terms of a contract were ultra vires the statutory powers of an Electricity Board). See also *R. v British Coal Corporation and Roo Management Ex p. G. C. Whittaker (Properties) Ltd* [1989] C.O.D. 528.

[29] See below at paras 2–135 to 2–136.

[30] *R. (Tucker) v Director General of the National Crime Squad* [2003] I.C.R. 599.

[31] As is the case, e.g. in other similar situations: see *R. (Galligan) v University of Oxford* [2002] E.L.R. 494 paras 19–23 at 501–502 and the discussion in *R. v Lord Chancellor Ex p. Maxwell* [1997] 1 W.L.R. 104 and *R. v Deputy Governor of Parkhurst Prison Ex p. Leech* [1988] A.C. 533.

bodies have been created to regulate their activities.[32] These statutory bodies are amenable to judicial review as they are exercising statutory powers to regulate the activities of the companies concerned. In one case,[33] for example, the courts quashed a decision of the Director of Water Services not to ban the use by water companies of pre-payment devices for the supply of water. These devices involved the supply of water through a machine which automatically cut off the supply of water when the pre-paid credit ran out. The court concluded that these machines should not be used to cut off supply without first serving notice of the unpaid liability. The likelihood in future is that challenges of this sort will be made by means of a claim for judicial review of the decision of the statutory regulator to act or not to act, rather than directly seeking to challenge the privatised body itself. It is possible that some privatised industries may (at least in respect of some of their activities) remain public bodies amenable to judicial review, although that would be because of the public nature of their functions or the fact that there is a degree of statutory underpinning to some of their activities.[34] In many instances, however, the fact that the body is not now statutory or does not exercise statutory powers will mean either that it will not be seen as a public body at all or that the particular functions under challenge will not involve questions of public law. In one case, a privatised railway granted a franchise to a particular taxi company to provide services to the railway station. That decision was held not to be amenable to judicial review. It was not a decision taken in the exercise of any statutory power, nor could it be said that there was any public law or statutory underpinning to the decision.[35] A similar approach has emerged in relation to the analogous question of whether a privatised company is performing public functions for the purposes of s.6 of the Human Rights Act 1998 and so was itself obliged to act compatibly with the European Convention on Human Rights. The High Court has held that a privatised company, which had ceased to have statutory responsibility for the safety of the railway infrastructure, was not exercising "public functions" for these purposes.[36] It was a commercial company whose directors were appointed by the company and were not subject to governmental influence or control. The company was not funded by the state. It possessed no special powers over individuals. Responsibility for rail safety was placed on other governmental bodies. In those circumstances, the privatised company was not exercising public functions for the purposes of the Human Rights Act 1998.[37] The likelihood is, therefore, that the bulk of challenges in the field of privatised industries will be

---

[32] See, e.g. s.1A of the Water Industry Act 1991; s.15 of the Railways and Transport Safety Act 2003; s.1 of the Utilities Act 2000; s.1 of the Telecommunications Act 1984.

[33] *R. v Director General of Water Services Ex p. Oldham Metropolitan Borough Council* (1998) 96 L.G.R. 396. See also R. v Director of Passenger Rail Franchising Ex p. Save Our Railways, *The Times*, December 18, 1995 and R. (London & Continental Stations & Property Ltd) v Rail Regulator [2004] A.C.D. 13.

[34] See, e.g. *Mercury Ltd v Electricity Corporation* [1994] 1 W.L.R. 521; *R. v Great Western Trains Co. Ltd Ex p. Frederick* [1998] C.O.D. 239 and see below, paras 2–078 to 2–106.

[35] *R. v Great Western Trains Co. Ltd Ex p. Frederick* [1998] C.O.D. 239.

[36] *Cameron v Network Rail Infrastructure Ltd* [2007] 1 W.L.R. 163. The High Court recognised that prior to 2000 the position would have been different as, at that earlier stage, specific functions for rail safety were imposed on the company by primary and delegated legislation: see [32].

[37] [2007] 1 W.L.R. 163 at [29]–[30].

by way of a claim for judicial review of the activities of the statutory regulator rather than challenges to the actions of the privatised companies themselves.

Statutory bodies and private law

Not every act of a statutory body necessarily involves an exercise of statutory power. Statutory bodies, like private individuals, may have powers to contract or deal with property, and the enforcement of rights created in the course of such transactions may raise no issue of public law.[38] Statutory bodies are also subject to common law rules on tortious liability. Such issues may raise issues of private law to which public law, and hence judicial review, is irrelevant.[39]

Statute seeks to regulate relationships between ordinary individuals and to create or modify their private law rights. In so far as a public body is affected by such statutes, it is affected in its private capacity not its public capacity. Thus, the legislation governing business tenancies regulates the private law rights of landlord and tenant. In so far as a public body happens to be a landlord or a tenant it will be governed by the legislation in its private capacity and no question of judicial review or public law arises.[40]

Statute may impose a duty on a public body only. Generally, such duties are public law duties only enforceable by judicial review.[41] Occasionally, however, such duties may still create private rights in favour of individuals enforceable by ordinary claim as well as imposing public law obligations enforceable by way of judicial review.[42] As an added complication, the courts have in the past held that a statutory duty involves a two-tier process. The decision as to whether on the facts and the law a duty is owed to a particular person is a public law decision that can only be challenged by way of judicial review. If the public body determines that a duty is owed, that duty may create a private law right enforceable by ordinary action.[43] That approach to public law duties has, however, been disavowed by the House of Lords. The House of Lords rejected an argument that a private law right could arise from a decision acknowledging the existence of a duty even though no such duty was previously owed.[44] That reasoning makes it far less likely that a court would find that a decision

2–014

2–015

2–016

---

[38] See paras 2–135 to 2–136.

[39] See paras 2–161 to 2–169.

[40] See Landlord and Tenant Act 1954. See, e.g. *Tollbench v Plymouth City Council* (1988) 56 P. & C.R. 194. see also dicta in *R. (Molinaro) v Royal London Borough of Kensington and Chelsea* [2002] L.G.R. 336 at [66].

[41] See, e.g. *R. v Kensington Borough Council Ex p. Kutjim* [1999] L.G.R. 761 (duty of a social services authority to provide residential accommodation for certain persons in need of care and attention enforceable by way of a claim in judicial review for a mandatory order or a declaration; no private law right to damages).

[42] See, e.g. *Ettridge v Morrell* (1987) 85 L.G.R. 100. See, e.g. *R. v Deputy Governor of Parkhurst Prison Ex p. Hague* [1992] 1 A.C. 58 at 155E–G (whether prisoner had a cause of action for breach of prison regulations on the grounds of breach of statutory duty or false imprisonment; that was matter of private law and did not raise public law issues).

[43] See *Cocks v Thanet District Council* [1983] 2 A.C. 286. See also *Cato v Minister for Agriculture Fisheries and Food* [1989] 3 C.M.L.R. 513.

[44] *O'Rourke v London Borough of Camden* [1998] A.C. 188 and see below, paras 3–038 to 3–043.

recognising a duty or conferring some benefit upon an individual created a private law right rather than a public law claim enforceable by way of judicial review.

2–017 It is also theoretically possible for a duty imposed on a public body alone to give rise only to private law rights, and not to be enforceable by judicial review at all. In practice, the courts tend to regard duties imposed on public bodies alone as primarily public law duties, and the only issue is whether the duty additionally creates private law rights super-imposed on the public law duty.

Prerogative

Availability of judicial review

2–018 Powers derived from the royal prerogative are classed as public law powers and, to the extent that such powers are reviewable at all, are reviewable by way of a claim for judicial review. The Court of Appeal established in 1967 that in principle certiorari lay to quash the decisions of the Criminal Injuries Compensation Board for error of law.[45] The scheme for making *ex gratia* payments to those suffering personal injury as a result of a criminal offence was not statutory but was set up by the Government with money voted by Parliament. The court held that the scheme had been created by virtue of the prerogative, but saw "no reason why the remedy by way of certiorari cannot be invoked to a body of persons set up under the prerogative".[46] The House of Lords has confirmed in *Council of Civil Service Unions v Minister for the Civil Service*[47] (the *G.C.H.Q.* case), that powers derived from the prerogative are public law powers and their exercise amenable to the judicial review jurisdiction provided that the particular exercise of prerogative power is justiciable.

Definition of the prerogative

2–019 The prerogative includes the powers, duties, rights and immunities of the Crown. There is a dispute over the precise scope and definition of the prerogative. On one definition, only those powers which are unique to the sovereign are properly regarded as prerogative powers. Thus the term "can only be applied to those rights and capacities which the king enjoys alone, . . . and not those which he enjoys in common with any of his subjects".[48] On another definition, the prerogative only includes those powers that are unique to the sovereign *and* which also produce legal effects at common law.[49] This definition would exclude acts such as the granting of passports and even the making of treaties as these acts do not affect any rights or duties at common law. However, the courts have never

---

[45] *R. v Criminal Injuries Compensation Board Ex p. Lain* [1967] 2 Q.B. 864.

[46] [1967] 2 Q.B. 864 per Lord Parker C.J. at 881.

[47] [1985] A.C. 374. And see also *R. (Youssef) v Secretary of State for Foreign and Commonwealth Affairs* [2014] Q.B. 728 at [23].

[48] Blackstone, *Commentaries on the Laws of England* (8th edn, 1778) Book 1, p.239 and see *R. (Hunt) v Criminal Cases Review Commission* [2001] Q.B. 319 at [23].

[49] See H.W.R. Wade, *Constitutional Fundamentals* (1980), pp.46–53 and "Procedure and Prerogative in Public Law" (1985) 101 L.Q.R. 180.

adopted this definition and have always regarded acts such as the issuing of passports[50] and the making of treaties as part of the prerogative.[51]

On a third definition, the prerogative:

2–020

> "... is the name for the residue of discretionary power left at any moment in the hands of the Crown, whether such power be in fact exercised by the Queen herself or by her Ministers. Every act which the executive government can lawfully do without the authority of the Act of Parliament is done in virtue of this prerogative."[52]

The courts have, on occasions, adopted this third definition of the prerogative[53] and treated all non-statutory acts of the central government as exercises of the prerogative. This approach would bring within the ambit of the prerogative acts such as the making of ex gratia payments[54] and even the dissemination of information.[55] On other occasions, the courts have recognised that the Crown not only has certain specific powers, recognised by the courts as being derived from the prerogative, but also has the same ability to act, at common law, that any ordinary individual has and has not treated the latter type of actions as an exercise of the prerogative.[56]

In summary, therefore, the present position is that the courts recognise that public law powers may be derived from statute. Further, the Crown, acting through government ministers, has powers derived from the prerogative, in the sense of a group of powers unique to the sovereign and which may include powers enabling it to alter the legal position of individuals. Thirdly, the Crown has the capacity or freedom to do any act that a natural person could do provided that that act does not involve interference with the rights of others or the doing of acts prohibited by law.[57]

2–021

In terms of the availability of judicial review, the distinction is not of great importance.[58] If powers are classed as prerogative, then the presumption will be that they are public law powers for the purposes of judicial review. To the extent that they are simply regarded as the exercise of ordinary common law powers, or

2–022

---

[50] See *R. v Secretary of State for Foreign and Commonwealth Affairs Ex p. Everett* [1989] Q.B. 811.

[51] *Blackburn v Att-Gen* [1973] 1 W.L.R. 1037.

[52] Dicey, Introduction to the Study of the Law of the Constitution, 10th edn (1959) at p.425.

[53] See, e.g. *R. (Bancoult) v Secretary of State for Foreign and Commonwealth Affairs (No.2)* [2009] 1 A.C. 453 at [69] (per Lord Bingham) and *R (GI) v Secretary of State for the Home Department* [2013] Q.B. 1008 at [11] per Laws LJ.

[54] See, e.g. *R. v Secretary of State for the Home Office Ex p. Harrison* [1988] 3 All E.R. 86; *R. v Criminal Injuries Compensation Board Ex p. Lain* [1967] 2 Q.B. 864. The Criminal Injuries Compensation Scheme has now been placed on a statutory footing: see Criminal Injuries Compensation Act 1995 s.1. The power to pay *ex gratia* compensation to persons who suffer as a result of a miscarriage of justice, which supplements the statutory powers that exist for this purpose, has been seen as an exercise of prerogative power: see *R. (Christofides) v Secretary of State for the Home Department* [2002] 1 W.L.R. 2770 at [7].

[55] *Jenkins v Att-Gen* (1971) 115 S.J. 674.

[56] *R. v Secretary of State for Health Ex p. C* [2000] 1 F.C.R. 471. See also *R. (New London College Ltd) v Secretary of State for the Home Department* [2013] 1 W.L.R. 2358.

[57] See Harris: "The 'Third Source' for Government Action Revisited" [2007] 123 L.Q.R. 225 and see below at para.2–047.

[58] See particularly, the dicta of Lord Diplock in *Council of Civil Service Unions v Minister for the Civil Service* [1985] A.C. 374 at p.409, doubting the relevance of such issues in determining the availability of judicial review.

covered by the maxim that anyone, including the Crown, may do anything that is not unlawful,[59] they are likely to be sufficiently "public" to bring them within the ambit of the judicial review jurisdiction.[60]

Scope of judicial review

2–023   The House of Lords in the *G.C.H.Q.* case also removed limitations on the scope of judicial review of the prerogative. Judicial control was traditionally limited to inquiring into the existence and the extent of prerogative powers, and whether the power had been superseded or limited by statute: the courts could not review the manner of the exercise of power in the way that they could if the power was statutory.[61] The House in the *G.C.H.Q.* case held that the manner in which prerogative powers were exercised was not immune from judicial review simply because the powers were derived from the prerogative, rather than statute. The only limitation on judicial review concerned the justiciability of the issue. Only where the issues raised were inherently unsuitable for judicial resolution—such as questions involving the prerogative power over the disposition of the armed forces—would judicial review not be available. In the words of Lord Scarman: "... the controlling factor in determining whether the exercise of prerogative power is subject to judicial review is not its source but its subject-matter."[62]

2–024   In addition, it is not the case that a prerogative power has to be either fully reviewable or not reviewable at all. An exercise of a prerogative power may be reviewable in certain circumstances but not in others. It is the subject-matter and the suitability of judicial review on the facts of a particular case which will determine whether, and to what extent, an exercise of prerogative power is reviewable. The courts can in certain circumstances, for example, ensure that the Secretary of State considers whether or not to exercise his discretion to make representations to a foreign state on behalf of a UK national who is allegedly suffering an injustice. The actual decision as to whether or not to make representations, and the foreign policy considerations relevant to such a decision, are not matters that are, generally, justiciable. Whether the court would be able to require more than due consideration to a request for assistance will, therefore, depend on the facts of a particular case.[63] A decision removing a civil servant's

---

[59] This was the basis on which Megarry V.-C. decided, in *Malone v Metropolitan Police Commissioner* [1980] Q.B. 49, that the tapping of telephones by the Post Office was lawful, since there was nothing to make it unlawful—as the activity there did not involve violation of a recognised right such as trespass or breach of confidence. See now the Interception of Communications Act 1985.

[60] See *R. v Civil Service Appeal Board Ex p. Bruce* [1988] I.C.R. 649 (affd. by the Court of Appeal [1989] I.C.R. 171) ; *R. v Secretary of State for Health Ex p. C* [2000] F.C.R. 471 (the Secretary of State was subject to the normal principles of public law in maintaining a list of persons about whom there were doubts as to their suitability to work with children) and *R (Sandiford) v Secretary of State for Foreign and Commowealth Affairs* [2014] 1 W.L.R. 2697 (power to provide assistance to nationals facing criminal charges abroad subject to judicial review whether described as a prerogative power or a common law power). And see below at para.2–047.

[61]   *Att-Gen v De Keyser's Royal Hotel Ltd* [1920] A.C. 508.

[62]   per Lord Scarman in *Council of Civil Service Unions v Minister for the Civil Service* [1985] A.C. 374 at 407. See also *R. (Abbasi) v Secretary of State for Foreign and Commonwealth Affairs* [2003] U.K.H.R.R. 203 and *R. v Secretary of State for the Home Department Ex p. Fire Brigades Union* [1995] A.C. 513; *R. v Criminal Injuries Compensation Board Ex p. P* [1995] 1 W.L.R. 845 at 855F–858A.

[63]   *R. (Abbasi) v Secretary of State for Foreign and Commonwealth Affairs* [2003] U.K.H.R.R. 76.

positive vetting clearance may not, for example, be reviewed where to do so would involve the courts reviewing decisions based on national security. Such decisions may, however, be reviewed on grounds such as breach of procedural fairness as that may not raise problems of national security.[64] Furthermore, some of the substantive grounds of judicial review developed in the context of the review of statutory powers may not be readily applicable to the exercise of prerogative powers. The nature of the prerogative is such that it is a matter for the Crown to determine whether and how to exercise the prerogative; there is no prohibition on the Crown adopting a policy of not exercising particular powers and no principle, analogous to that applicable to statutory powers, that the Crown cannot fetter its discretion.[65] Judicial review of a statutory power is likely to be governed by a consideration of the wording and purpose of the Act of Parliament. In the context of a prerogative power, there is no Act of Parliament against which an exercise of prerogative power can be measured. In such circumstances, judicial review of the exercise of a prerogative power will be based on standards developed by the common law.[66] In particular, ensuring procedural fairness and ensuring that the decision-maker has regard to any criteria that it has laid down in advance are more likely to feature significantly in challenges to the exercise of prerogative power. It may be more difficult to establish that irrelevant considerations have been taken into account or that the prerogative power has been used for an unauthorised purpose, given the absence of any statutory framework to assess such issues and the nature of the subject-matter concerned. The courts may need to review particular action or a refusal to act to determine whether the conduct complained of involves a breach of a specific right, such as the right not to be the subject of unlawful discrimination,[67] or a failure to act compatibly with the European Convention on Human Rights.[68]

One further point concerns the fact that the power in the *G.C.H.Q.* case was **2–025** one delegated by Order in Council to the minister. Lord Fraser and Lord Brightman preferred to limit their judgment to holding that the exercise of a power delegated to a minister was reviewable, and left open the question of the reviewability of a direct exercise of the prerogative. The majority clearly accepted that a direct exercise of prerogative power was reviewable. The House of Lords has held that direct exercises of the prerogative power, such as the making of an Order in Council legislating for an overseas territory, are amenable

---

[64] *R. v Director of Government Communications Headquarters Ex p. Hodges* [1998] C.O.D. 123.

[65] *R. (Sandiford) v Secretary of State for Foreign and Commonwealth Affairs* [2014] 1 W.L.R. 2697 at [60]–[66] and [78]–[83].

[66] *R. (Youssef) v Secretary of State for Foreign and Commonwealth Affairs* [2014] Q.B. 728 at [23].

[67] *R. (Al Rawi) v Secretary of State for Foreign and Commonwealth Affairs* [2007] 2 W.L.R. 1219 at [65]–[87] (court considered but rejected a claim that a decision not to make representations to a foreign government about the detention abroad of non-UK nationals normally resident in the UK involved discrimination contrary to the Race Relations Act 1976); *A. v Secretary of State for the Home Department*[2005] 2 A.C. 265 (court determined whether derogation from right not to be detained without due process was compatible with the Convention).

[68] *R. (Gentle) v Prime Minister* [2008] 1 A.C. 1356 (court considered but rejected a claim that art.2 of the European Convention on Human Rights required an inquiry to be held on whether the United Kingdom government had taken reasonable steps to be satisfied that the invasion of Iraq was lawful under international law).

to judicial review provided the subject matter is justiciable.[69] The courts have, on other occasions, also interpreted the decision in *G.C.H.Q.* as permitting judicial review of direct exercises of prerogative power.[70]

Prerogative powers that are reviewable

2–026   Some prerogative powers have already been held to be reviewable. The residual prerogative powers of the Home Secretary in the immigration field have been held to be reviewable,[71] as has the prerogative power to issue passports.[72] Prerogative powers to make ex gratia payments in the context of the Criminal Injuries Compensation Scheme were held to be reviewable.[73] A similar power to pay ex gratia compensation to the victims of miscarriages of justice has been held to be reviewable on certain grounds at least.[74] The power to grant a Royal Charter has been held to be reviewable.[75] The power to "tap" telephones was held to be a prerogative power which was subject to judicial review to ensure that the Home Secretary observed the established criteria governing the grant of warrants to intercept telephone communications[76]: this power has now been placed on a statutory footing.[77]

Prerogative powers to regulate the civil service

2–027   The power to regulate the conditions of the civil service, which is generally regarded as an exercise of prerogative power, is suitable for judicial review. The courts have held that a decision of general application applicable to all civil servants or a particular group is justiciable and amenable to judicial review. In the

---

[69] *R. (Bancoult) v Secretary of State for Foreign and Commonwealth Affairs (No.2)* [2009] 1 A. C. 453. The Divisional Court had previously held that the making of an ordinance in the exercise of powers conferred by an Order in Council made under the prerogative was amenable to judicial review: *R. (Bancoult) v Secretary of State for Foreign and Commonwealth Affairs* [2001] Q.B. 1067.
[70] See, e.g. *R. v Secretary of State for the Home Department Ex p. Bentley* [1994] Q.B. 349; *R. v Secretary of State for Foreign and Commonwealth Affairs Ex p. Everett* [1989] Q.B. 811 and also, *R. v Secretary of State for the Home Department Ex p. Ruddock* [1987] 1 W.L.R. 1482 at 1497 (Taylor J. accepted direct exercises of prerogative power reviewable but the Crown reserved right to argue point if case went further).
[71] *R. v Secretary of State for the Home Department Ex p. Beedassee* [1989] C.O.D. 525.
[72] *R. v Secretary of State for Foreign and Commonwealth Affairs Ex p. Everett* (see above, fn.70).
[73] *R. v Criminal Injuries Compensation Board Ex p. Lain* (see above, fn.54).
[74] *R. (Christofides) v Secretary of State for the Home Department* [2003] 1 W.L.R. 223 and see *R. (Tawfick) v Secretary of State for the Home Department* [2001] A.C.D. 171. The Divisional Court had earlier technically left the point open: see *R. v Secretary of State for the Home Department Ex p. Harrison* [1988] 3 All E.R. 86. The Divisional Court has also earlier held that the refusal of an ex gratia payment was not reviewable because there were no published rules governing the scheme: *R. v Secretary of State for the Home Department Ex p. Chubb* [1986] Crim. L.R. 809. The reviewability of the power also arose in *R. (Mullen) v Secretary of State for the Home Department* [2003] 2 W.L.R. 835 but the Court of Appeal did not need to consider the prerogative power as compensation had wrongly been refused under the parallel statutory powers conferred by the Criminal Justice Act 1988 s.133 (see also the decision of the House of Lords [2004] 2 W.L.R. 1140).
[75] *R. (The Project Management Group) v The Minister for the Cabinet Office* [2014] EWHC 2438 (Admin).
[76] *R. v Secretary of State for the Home Department Ex p. Ruddock* [1987] 1 W.L.R. 1482. cf. *Malone v Metropolitan Police Commissioner* [1980] Q.B. 49.
[77] Interception of Communications Act 1985.

G.C.H.Q. case,[78] it was held that an oral instruction issued by the minister by virtue of powers delegated to her by the Sovereign, by Order in Council, which sought to vary the terms of employment of civil servants at G.C.H.Q. was, in principle, reviewable on the grounds of procedural impropriety as the unions had a legitimate expectation that they would be consulted before terms of employment were altered. On the facts of the case, however, this legitimate expectation was overridden by considerations of national security and the unions were refused relief.

Similarly, where a disciplinary tribunal is set up under the prerogative, the decisions of such tribunals are justiciable and may be subject to judicial review.[79] In other cases, there may be a contract of employment between the civil servant and the Crown and the individual may be seeking to enforce the terms of that contract.[80] That is a private law claim not a public law claim. The claim cannot, therefore, be brought by way of judicial review, but that is because it does not raise a public law issue not because it is a prerogative decision which is not justiciable. The precise boundaries between claims that raise public law and private law issues are considered in detail below.[81]

Powers relating to the defence of the realm

Matters relating to defence such as the decision to take military action or deploy troops are not justiciable by the courts.[82] The Divisional Court could not, therefore, consider whether it would be a breach of international law and United Nations Resolution 1441 for the UK to engage in military action in Iraq without a further UN resolution as that would involve the courts in considering matters relating to defence.[83] The Court of Appeal would not review the merits of the possession of nuclear weapons in order to determine whether authorisations granted for the decommissioning of such weapons were lawful.[84] Even in the field of defence, however, some issues may be justiciable.[85] The courts have accepted, for example, that a policy decision that servicemen and women with a homosexual disposition should be discharged is justiciable and amenable to judicial review.[86]

2–028

2–029

---

[78] [1985] A.C. 374.
[79] See *R. v Civil Service Appeal Board Ex p. Bruce* [1989] I.C.R. 171 as interpreted by *R. v Lord Chancellor's Department Ex p. Nangle* [1991] I.C.R. 743. See also *R. v Civil Service Appeal Board Ex p. Cunningham* [1992] I.C.R. 816.
[80] *R. v Lord Chancellor's Department Ex p. Nangle* [1991] I.C.R. 743 and see in the context of statutory rather than prerogative powers *McClaren v Home Office* [1990] I.C.R. 824.
[81] See paras 2–131 to 2–160.
[82] *Council for Civil Service Unions v Minister of Civil Service* [1985] A.C. 374 at 418 per Lord Diplock; *R. (Campaign for Nuclear Disarmament) v The Prime Minister of the United Kingdom* Unreported, December 17, 2002. See also *R. (Marchiori) v The Environment Agency* [2002] Eu. L.R. 225. But see the decision of the Canadian Supreme Court in *Operation Dismantle v R.* (1985) D.L.R. (4th) 481 and see Walker, "Review of the Prerogative: The Remaining Issues" [1987] P.L. 62.
[83] *R. (Campaign for Nuclear Disarmament) v The Prime Minister of the United Kingdom* Unreported, December 17, 2002 at [47](ii) (per Simon Brown LJ), [49] (per Maurice Kay J.) and at [59]–[60] (per Richards J.).
[84] *R. (Marchiori) v The Environment Agency* [2002] Eu. L.R. 225 at [33]–[42].
[85] See, generally, *Secretary of State for the Home Department v Rehman* [2003] 1 A.C. 153.
[86] *R. v Ministry of Defence Ex p. Smith* [1996] Q.B. 517 at 539E–G (the Court of Appeal proceeded on the basis that the issue was justiciable).

Prerogative powers in foreign affairs

2–030   Matters relating to conduct by the government of foreign policy and relations with other states are not generally justiciable.[87] The fact that the ability of the government to conduct its international relations could be compromised by a court ruling on the lawfulness of military action against Iraq under international law was a further reason for the court not to entertain a claim for judicial review as to the proper construction of a UN resolution on the matter.[88] Similarly, a claim that particular action, or a refusal to act, is unreasonable in the public law sense or involves a failure to have regard to relevant considerations may not be justiciable if the matters complained of relate to the conduct of foreign relations.[89] The courts have recognised that such decisions are essentially matters for the elected government, which has greater information and expertise in such matters, and the law accords the government wide discretion as to what considerations are relevant and how to weigh those considerations.[90] Even in this field there may be instances where a particular matter is justiciable on certain grounds at least. Judicial review is available to protect a person's legitimate expectation that the government would at least consider whether or not to make representations to a foreign state if that state was apparently violating his human rights.[91] The decision as to whether or not to make any representations and, in particular, whether foreign policy considerations outweighed the interests of the individual concerned were, however, ultimately matters for the government.

2–031   The courts have considered whether the refusal to make representations on behalf of non-UK nationals detained abroad involved unlawful discrimination contrary to the Race Relations Act 1976, notwithstanding that the issue arose in the field of foreign relations.[92] The courts have similarly accepted that it may be necessary for the courts to determine whether a particular right arises under the European Convention on Human Rights and, if so, the principle of non-justiciability will not prevent courts from giving effect to that right. The fact that a claimed right would involve consideration of matters normally regarded as non-justiciable and which are matters for the executive not the courts may, however, militate against the existence of such a right.[93] Thus, the House of Lords

---

[87] *Council for Civil Service Unions v Minister of Civil Service* [1985] A.C. 374 at 418 per Lord Diplock; *R. (Campaign for Nuclear Disarmament) v The Prime Minister of the United Kingdom* Unreported, December 17, 2002; *R. (Abbasi) v Secretary of State for Foreign and Commonwealth Affairs* [2003] U.K.H.R.R. 203 at 90–91 paras 37–38; *R. v Jones (Margaret)* [2007] 1 A.C. 136 at [30] and [65]–[66].

[88] *R. (Campaign for Nuclear Disarmament) v The Prime Minister of the United Kingdom*, Unreported, December 17, 2002.

[89] *R. (Al Rawi) v Secretary of State for Foreign Affairs* [2008] Q.B. 289 at [131]–[141]. Nor will the courts rule on the legality, validity or acceptability of the sovereign acts of a foreign state as a matter of domestic or international law and will decline to enter domestic claims which, in substance at least, would require the courts do so: *R (Khan) v Secretary of State for Foreign and Commonwealth Affairs* [2014] 1 W.L.R. 872 at [25] and [36].

[90] *R. (Al Rawi) v Secretary of State for Foreign Affairs* [2008] Q.B. 289 at [140]–[141] and [147]–[148].

[91] *R. (Abbasi) v Secretary of State for Foreign and Commonwealth Affairs* [2003] U.K.H.R.R. 203 at [80]–[108].

[92] *R. (Al Rawi) v Secretary of State for Foreign and Commonwealth Affairs* [2008] Q.B. 289.

[93] *R. (Gentle) v Prime Minister* [2008] 1 A.C. 1536, see per Lord Bingham at [8](2) and Baroness Hale at [60].

has held that art.2 of the European Convention on Human Rights did not confer a right to have an inquiry into whether the government had taken reasonable steps to be satisfied that the invasion of Iraq was lawful under international law.[94] The Court of Appeal has also held that there is no duty imposed by the European Convention on the authorities in the United Kingdom to make representations of behalf of the families of persons detained abroad. In reaching this decision, the Court of Appeal again recognised that, whilst the courts retained responsibility for ensuring the protection of human rights, the elected government had special responsibility in strategic areas of policy such as the conduct of foreign relations and matters of national security and the court's supervisory role necessarily needed to reflect that consideration.[95] One important prerogative power which may be exercisable in a variety of circumstances is the treaty-making power of the Crown. The courts have traditionally adopted the view that, as a general rule, neither the making of a treaty nor the performance of the obligations under the treaty can be reviewed by the courts.[96] There is much to be said for not reviewing a decision to enter into a treaty. Such a decision will involve highly political considerations unsuitable for judicial review. In addition, treaties will normally have no legal effect within the UK until legislation implementing the treaty is enacted so will not normally give rise to justiciable issues. In *Blackburn v Att-Gen*,[97] the court declined to entertain an action for, inter alia, a declaration that it was ultra vires the power of the Crown to accede to the Treaty of Rome creating the European Community. The court pointed out that the treaty-making power lay with the Crown not the courts, and an exercise of the power could not be challenged in the courts. The courts would take no notice of a treaty until it was embodied in legislation enacted by Parliament. The Divisional Court doubted that the question of whether two treaties, the Constitutional Treaty and the Treaty of Lisbon, both concerned with reforms to the European Union, were materially similar was a justiciable issue for the courts to determine as such a question depended on matters of political judgment and perspective.[98]

There are exceptions to the general rule that the courts will not review the exercise of the treaty-making power or performance of treaty obligations unless the treaty has been incorporated into domestic law. Judicial review is available to establish whether statute has expressly or impliedly placed limitations on the making of treaties or the performance of treaty obligations.[99] In *Laker Airways v Department of Trade*,[100] for example, the Court of Appeal held that there was an implied statutory fetter on the prerogative power of the Crown arising under a treaty between the UK and the US to withdraw the designation of an airline as a suitable airline to operate on a particular route. In *Ex p. Molyneaux*,[101] Taylor J.

2–032

---

[94] *R. (Al Rawi) v Secretary of State for Foreign and Commonwealth Affairs* [2008] Q.B. 289 at [147]–[148].

[95] *R. (Gentle) v Prime Minister* [2008] 2 W.L.R. 897 at [84].

[96] *Rustomjee v R.* (1876) 2 Q.B.D. 69; *J.H. Rayner (Mincing Lane) Ltd v Department of Trade and Industry* [1990] 2 A.C. 418. See also *R. v Lyons* [2002] 3 W.L.R. 1562.

[97] [1971] 1 W.L.R. 1037. See also *J.H. Rayner (Mincing Lane) Ltd v Department of Trade and Industry* [1990] 2 A.C. 418.

[98] *R. (Wheeler) v Office of the Prime Minister and the Secretary of State for Foreign and Commonwealth Affairs* [2008] EWHC 1409 (Admin).

[99] See generally, *Att-Gen v De Keyser's Royal Hotel* [1920] A.C. 508.

[100] [1977] Q.B. 643.

[101] [1986] 1 W.L.R. 331.

considered whether Art.6 of the Union with Ireland Act 1800 or s.12 of the Northern Ireland Constitution Act 1973 restricted the power of the Crown to enter into an agreement with the Irish Republic and concluded that they did not. The domestic courts may also interpret treaties where that is necessary for the purpose of determining a person's rights or duties under domestic law. Thus, where a statutory power permitted the removal of an asylum seeker to another country, provided that that country would not send him to a third country otherwise than in accordance with obligations under the Geneva Convention on the Status of Refugees, the courts had to determine the meaning of the Convention in order to determine whether that other country would act in accordance with the Convention. The proper interpretation of the Convention was therefore necessary to determining whether the statutory power to remove the person was exercisable.[102]

2–033   It is also possible, but unlikely, that the courts could consider the compatibility of treaties with the common law (or, even more speculatively, convention). In *Molyneaux*, Taylor J. considered the legality of the establishment of the intergovernmental conference under the terms of the agreement but concluded that "its establishment did not contravene any statute, any rule of common law or any constitutional convention".[103] He also considered whether the agreement fettered the statutory powers and duties of the Secretary of State for Northern Ireland and so violated the common law principle that it is unlawful to fetter the exercise of discretionary powers although he concluded that the agreement did not do so. This could be taken to imply that the courts might have jurisdiction to grant a remedy by way of judicial review if a treaty did violate some rule of common law. However, this view needs to be set against the dictum later in Taylor J.'s judgment that "it is not the function of this court to inquire into the exercise of the prerogative in entering into such an agreement or by way of anticipation to decide whether the method proposed of implementing the agreement is appropriate".[104] Further, in *Blackburn v Att-Gen*,[105] the Court of Appeal held that they did not have jurisdiction to entertain an application for a declaration that, if the UK were to accede to the Treaty of Rome creating the European Economic Community, that would constitute a partial surrender of sovereignty which would be incompatible with the common law rule that the sovereignty of Parliament could not be fettered. The Court of Appeal also declined to consider granting a declaration as to whether there was a

---

[102] *R. v Secretary of State for the Home Department Ex p. Adan* [2001] 2 A.C. 477; see generally, on the question of when international treaties or international instruments are justiciable, *R. (Campaign for Nuclear Disarmament) v The Prime Minister,* Unreported, December 17, 2002, esp. at [36] and see *R. (Corner House Research) v Director of the Serious Fraud Office* [2008] 3 W.L.R. 568 at [43]–[47] and [65]–[68] and see Sales and Clement, "International Law in Domestic Courts: the Developing Framework" [2008] 124 L.Q.R. 388.

[103] [1986] 1 W.L.R. 331 at 335.

[104] [1986] 1 W.L.R. 331 at 336. On the justiciability of constitutional conventions, see the decision of the Supreme Court of Canada in *Reference re Amendment of the Constitution of Canada (Nos 1, 2 and 3)* (1982) 125 D.L.R. (3rd.) 1.

[105] See above, n.97. In *R. v Secretary of State for Foreign and Commonwealth Affairs Ex p. Rees-Mogg* [1994] Q.B. 552, the Divisional Court did consider whether entry into the Maastricht Treaty, which was intended to create a mechanism for establishing a common foreign and security policy among the Member States of the EU, involved an impermissible attempt to transfer the prerogative power in the field of foreign affairs to the EU rather than merely dismissing the claim as non-justiciable.

constitutional convention that no Act of Parliament would be enacted giving effect to a treaty which involved constitutional changes without there first being a referendum on the issue.[106]

Powers to legislate for overseas territories and Crown Dependencies

The Crown retains a prerogative power to legislate for certain British overseas territories.[107] The prerogative power extends to making arrangements for the exercise of legislative, executive or judicial functions in respect of certain of the overseas territories, usually by the making of Orders in Council.[108] Such orders may, in turn, confer powers on others to exercise such functions in respect of the territory. Certain issues, such as the extent of the prerogative, do raise justiciable issues upon which the courts can adjudicate. The Divisional Court has quashed the provision of an ordinance expelling islanders from the territory, purportedly made in the exercise of powers conferred by an Order in Council. The Court held that the power to make provision "for the peace, order and good government" of the territory did not include power to exclude the population from the territory.[109] The fact that the exclusion of the islanders was connected with the conduct of foreign relations and military security did not prevent the courts from ruling on the lawfulness of the ordinance. In that case, the issue essentially concerned the question of construing the scope of the ordinance-making power conferred by the Order in Council and determining whether the ordinance fell within the scope of those powers. As such, the matter should, in principle, be regarded as justiciable. The exercise is, in principle, the same as determining whether subordinate legislation made in the exercise of powers conferred by Act of Parliament is within the scope of the powers conferred by the statute.[110]

2–034

Subsequently, the courts have had to consider the extent to which powers to exclude the islanders from the territory could be contained directly in an Order in Council itself. The courts held that the power of the sovereign to legislate for an overseas territory was no longer unfettered and could in appropriate circumstances be subject to judicial review. The precise extent of the prerogative power and the circumstances in which the exercise of power is reviewable remain undecided. All three members of the Court of Appeal held that the Order in Council in the present case was unlawful in so far as it included provisions removing the right of abode from the islanders as that breached a legitimate expectation created by the government that they would be allowed to return and no justification had been advanced as to why that expectation should now be

2–035

---

[106] *R. (Southall) v Secretary of State for Foreign and Commonwealth Affairs* [2003] Eu. L.R. 832 (permission to apply for judicial review was refused).

[107] There are presently 14 overseas territories: see s.51 and Sch.6 to the British Nationality Act 1981 as amended by the British Overseas Territories Act 2002.

[108] See *Halsbury's Laws of England*, 4th edn (2003), Vol.6, [823] discussed in *R. (Bancoult) v Secretary of State for Foreign and Commonwealth Affairs* [2009] 1 A.C. 453. The prerogative power extends to those territories which were conquered or ceded to the Crown but not those acquired by settlement. In other cases, statute confers power to make arrangements for the government of the territory: see, e.g. s.2(1) of the Cyprus Act 1960 dealing with the power to make arrangements for the Sovereign Base Areas of Akrotiri and Dhekalia.

[109] *R. (Bancoult) v Secretary of State for Foreign and Commonwealth Affairs* [2001] Q.B. 1067.

[110] *R. (Bancoult) v Secretary of State for Foreign and Commonwealth Affairs* [2001] Q.B. 1067.

breached.[111] Two members of the Court also held that the Order was invalid as the decision-maker did not have proper regard for the interests of the islanders in deciding whether to exclude them from the territory.[112] In the House of Lords, a majority held that the Order in Council was lawful. They held that it was rational to take into account the interests of the United Kingdom and the feasibility of resettlement of the islanders, as well as the interests of the islanders themselves. They further held that there had been no breach of a legitimate expectation.[113]

2–036　　The question of whether the power to legislate is limited to a power to make provision for the peace, order and good government of the territory, or is a broader power encompassing the interests both of the population of the territory and the wider interests of the United Kingdom, is in principle an issue of law capable of resolution in the courts. Similarly, the question of whether or not the prerogative power can as a matter of principle extend to excluding the population for reasons unconnected with their well-being raises a discrete question of law capable of resolution in the courts. Such issues may be difficult to decide in the absence of any pre-existing constitutional or other framework indicating the limits on the power to legislate. In principle, however, the question of the existence or extent of a particular prerogative power is one that the courts ought to be able to adjudicate upon.[114] Depending on the precise width of the prerogative power, it may be far more difficult to determine whether any particular exercise of the power is lawful. The broader the power, the more difficult it will be for the courts to determine that any exercise of that power is unlawful. In particular, if the prerogative power permits the United Kingdom to take account of the wider strategic, military and political interests of the United Kingdom, any decision that such interests call for the exclusion of an indigenous population may not be justiciable or apt for resolution in the courts. If, as a matter of law, however, the prerogative power is more limited and focuses on the interests of the territory in question, it may be more feasible for the courts to police the limits of that power and ensure that any exercise of power respects the common law limits placed upon that power. Logically, the courts should consider the scope of the prerogative power first before deciding whether any particular exercise of that power violates an applicable principle of public law.

2–037　　As a matter of principle, it would appear that the power to legislate for overseas territories is broad enough to include considerations of the United Kingdom interests as well as those of any resident population. By way of example, it is difficult to anticipate that the power to legislate for the Sovereign Base Areas in Cyprus should be limited to considerations affecting the resident population (comprising British military personnel and Cypriot nationals). It may be that the interests of any resident population are so obviously a material consideration that the United Kingdom should have regard to their interests and the effect of any legislation upon the resident population. The precise balancing of such considerations is unlikely to be a matter that is justiciable. The majority of the House of Lords in *Bancoult* considered that the power to legislate for a colony did enable the Crown to consider the interests of the United Kingdom as

---

[111] [2008] Q.B. 365.

[112] [2008] Q.B. 365 per Sedley LJ at [68]–[71] and the Master of the Rolls at [122]–[123].

[113] *R. (Bancoult) v Secretary of State for Foreign and Commonwealth Affairs* [2009] 1 A.C. 453.

[114] See *Att-Gen v De Keyser's Royal Hotel Ltd* [1920] A.C. 508 discussed above at para.2–023.

well as the interests of the former residents. The majority considered that such questions, raising matters concerning the expenditure of public resources and security and diplomatic issues, were peculiarly within the competence of the executive and were not ones where the courts would readily review the rationality of the decision.[115]

The Channel Islands, consisting of Jersey and Guernsey, are Crown Dependencies but are not colonies or overseas territories.[116] Legislation is made by the legislature for the Island in question and then submitted for approval by Order in Council of the Privy Council.[117] Such Orders in Council are amenable in principle to judicial review by the courts of England and Wales, although, in appropriate cases it might well be thought more appropriate for the courts of Jersey or Guernsey to review the laws with an appeal to the Privy Council.[118]

2–038

The prerogative power to grant a pardon

Important prerogative powers in relation to the administration of justice still exist. One such power, mentioned by Lord Roskill in the *G.C.H.Q.* case as unlikely to be suitable for judicial review,[119] is the prerogative of mercy—that is the power to grant a free or conditional pardon to a convicted criminal. In 1971, the Court of Appeal refused to consider the actions of the Home Secretary in 1962 in refusing to pardon a convicted murderer.[120] This case, however, involved a claim for damages for negligence, on the grounds that the Home Secretary failed to consider alibi evidence that came to light after the conviction. Lord Denning M.R. based his view, that the court could not entertain the action, on the ground that the Home Secretary as a matter of public policy should enjoy the same immunity from negligence actions as did judges and advocates. The judgment does not necessarily support the view that judicial review of the exercise of the prerogative of mercy is never available. Salmon LJ took the then orthodox view that exercises of prerogative power could not be considered by the courts, but that judgment may need to be reconsidered in the light of *G.C.H.Q.* The Privy Council, however, had in the past stressed the purely discretionary nature of such a power, and suggested that a convicted person has no entitlement even to have his case considered.[121]

2–039

In principle, a failure to consider exercising the power to grant a pardon should be reviewable, at least if an individual can demonstrate that there is some reason why the Home Secretary should consider the case. It is also difficult to see why a decision to refuse a pardon should not also be reviewable in appropriate circumstances, for example, where the allegation is that there has been a failure to

2–040

---

[115] *R. (Bancoult) v Secretary of State for Foreign and Commonwealth Affairs* [2009] A.C. 1453 (per Lord Hoffman at [58], Lord Rodger at [109] to [113] and per Lord Carswell at [132]).

[116] See *R (Barclay) v Lord Chancellor* [2010] 1 A.C. 464 at [9]–[10] of the judgment of Lord Collins.

[117] See in relation to Guernsey, *R. (Barclay) v Lord Chancellor* [2010] 1 A.C. 464 at [17]–[21] of the judgment of Lord Collins and *R (Barclay) v Secretary of State for Justice* [2014] U.K.S.C. 54.

[118] *R. (Barclay) v Lord Chancellor* [2010] 1 A.C. 464 at [45] of the judgment of Lord Collins. *R. (Barclay) v Secretary of State for Justice* [2014] U.K.S.C. 54.

[119] In *Council of Civil Service Unions v Minister for the Civil Service* ([1985] A.C. 374.

[120] *Hanratty v Lord Butler of Saffron Walden* (1971) 115 S.J. 386. See A.T.H. Smith, "The Prerogative of Mercy, The Power of Pardon and Criminal Justice" [1983] P.L. 398.

[121] *De Freitas (Michael) also called Malik (Michael Abdul) v Benny (George Ramovtar)* [1976] A.C. 239.

consider relevant material, or a failure to act in accordance with any relevant guidelines, or if there is an error of law as to the elements of the offence for which the pardon was sought.[122]

2–041   In the *Bentley* case,[123] the Divisional Court accepted that there could be occasions when the prerogative of mercy might be reviewable. There, the applicant had been campaigning for a pardon for her brother who had been convicted of murder and sentenced to death. The sentence was carried out. The Home Secretary refused to grant a free pardon as he was not satisfied that Bentley was innocent. The Divisional Court concluded that the Home Secretary had power to grant a full or free pardon and he might, in appropriate circumstances, reserve the grant of such pardons to cases where he considered that the accused was innocent. The prerogative of mercy could also be exercised by the grant of a conditional pardon where the sentence imposed is removed on condition that a lesser sentence is served. In the present case, the Home Secretary had failed to consider whether he should grant a conditional pardon, whereby a sentence of life imprisonment was substituted for the death penalty, to reflect the circumstances of the case and in particular the arguments that Bentley should not have been executed but should have served a lesser sentence. Similarly, the Divisional Court granted judicial review of a decision to decline to consider granting a free pardon where the Secretary of State, erroneously, considered that he had no power to grant such a pardon in respect of a person sentenced abroad but serving the sentence in the United Kingdom.[124]

2–042   The Privy Council has held that the power to grant a pardon or to commute a death sentence is justiciable and is subject to judicial review.[125] The Privy Council held that the prerogative of mercy should be exercised according to procedures that were fair and proper and to that end at least the power was subject to judicial review. A condemned man was therefore entitled to know the date when an application for clemency would be considered, to be provided with copies of material put before the relevant authority and to be given the opportunity to make representations to that authority before the decision was taken. The Privy Council has also been prepared to consider whether the grant of a pardon was invalid and held that it was. In that case, the pardon was extracted as part of the negotiations surrounding the ending of a state of insurrection in Trinidad.[126] The Privy Council considered that a pardon related to an offence which had already been committed at the time that the pardon was granted. The power to pardon could not, therefore, be used to grant a pardon for future crimes, thereby granting in effect an immunity from the criminal law in respect of future actions. This suggests that there is nothing inherently non-justiciable about such matters. A decision to grant a pardon raises additional considerations—not least because the only person with standing to challenge the decision would normally be the recipient of the pardon, who is unlikely to seek to impugn his good fortune.

---

[122] See the judgment of Watkin LJ in *R. v Secretary of State for the Home Department Ex p. Bentley* [1994] Q.B. 349 at 362 where this passage was cited with approval.

[123] [1994] Q.B. 349.

[124] *R. (Shields) v Secretary of State for Justice* [2010] Q.B. 150.

[125] *Lewis v Att-Gen of Jamaica* [2000] 3 W.L.R. 1785 (departing from its earlier decisions of *Reckley v Minister for Public Safety and Immigration (No.2)* [1996] A.C. 527 and *De Freitas v Benny* [1976] A.C. 239.

[126] *Att-Gen of Trinidad and Tobago v Phillip* [1995] 1 A.C. 396.

In addition, it is difficult to imagine the courts quashing a pardon and thereby effectively requiring an individual to return to prison to resume his sentence. There may be exceptional circumstances, however, in which the validity of a pardon may be considered, as in *Att-Gen v Phillip*.[127]

Prerogative power to consent to relator action

The House of Lords has held that the decision of the Attorney-General to give or refuse his consent to the bringing of a relator action is unreviewable.[128] This decision may need to be reconsidered in the light of the ruling in *G.C.H.Q.* that some prerogative powers are amenable to review. The importance of relator actions in public law cases has declined with the relaxation of rules on standing in the context of judicial review, allowing individuals to apply in their own right rather than depending on the Attorney-General's fiat. The relator action could still be relevant in ordinary claims, particularly where an individual is seeking, as in *Gouriet v Union of Post Office Workers*,[129] to obtain an injunction restraining a private individual from breaking the criminal law. It is unlikely, given the views expressed by the House of Lords in *Gouriet*, that an improper refusal or a delay in giving consent could be reviewed, nor is it likely that the grant of consent could be reviewed, for example on the application of an aggrieved defendant in the main proceedings. On a number of occasions, the courts have also held that judicial review is not available in respect of the exercise by the Attorney-General or the Solicitor General of their statutory powers to institute proceeding on the grounds that such decisions generally are not justiciable.[130]

2–043

It is difficult, in principle, to see why the exercise of statutory or prerogative powers to institute proceedings is not justiciable and open to review in appropriate circumstances. Analogous common law and statutory powers to initiate or refuse to initiate proceedings are reviewable.[131] Judicial review is available to review the exercise of statutory powers by the Director General of Public Prosecutions to consent to the bringing of proceedings[132] and to take over

2–044

---

[127] [1995] 1 A.C. 396. Even then, however, the Privy Council left open the possibility that the institution of criminal proceedings in respect of the events to which a pardon related might be an abuse of process. On the facts of the case, the individuals had before the judge of first instance been granted an order of habeas corpus on the grounds that the pardon was valid. That order could not be appealed against and, given the existence of that order, it would have been an abuse of process to seek to commit the individuals concerned for the offences.

[128] *Gouriet v Union of Post Office Workers* [1978] A.C. 435. See also *Att-Gen ex rel. McWhirter v Independent Broadcasting Authority* [1973] Q.B. 629. See Hough, "Judicial Review where the Attorney-General Refuses to Act: Time for a Change" [1988] 8 Legal Studies 189.

[129] [1978] A.C. 435.

[130] See, e.g. *R. v Solicitor-General Ex p. Taylor* (1995) 8 Admin. L.Rep. 206 (statutory power to institute proceedings for contempt not justiciable); *R. v Att-Gen Ex p. Ferrante* [1995] C.O.D. 18 (statutory power to apply for an order that an inquest be held not justiciable).

[131] *R. v General Council of the Bar Ex p. Percival* [1990] 3 W.L.R. 323 (power of Professional Conduct Committee to initiate proceedings for misconduct reviewable). See also the dicta of Lawton LJ in *R. v Race Relations Board Ex p. Selvarajan* [1975] 1 W.L.R. 1686 at 1697 and the Privy Council in *Teh Cheng Poh* (*alias Char Meh*) *v Public Prosecutor, Malaysia* [1980] A.C. 458. However, given the nature and the width of such discretions, the chances of success are limited; *Turner v DPP* (1978) 68 Cr.App.R. 70; *Raymond v Att-Gen* [1982] 1 Q.B. 839.

[132] *R. v DPP Ex p. Kebilene* [2000] 2 A.C. 326 (power to consent to criminal proceedings under the Prevention of Terrorism (Temporary Provisions) Act 1989.

criminal proceedings with a view to discontinuing them although a successful challenge is likely to be rare.[133] The statutory power of local authorities to initiate civil proceedings, which has been described as a power to act in the public interest of people within the locality (which is a supplement to the power of the Attorney-General to act in the national public interest), is reviewable.[134] This suggests that there is nothing inherently non-justiciable in such powers. The existence of a statutory framework providing a context for judicial review in the case of the local authorities' power, and the fact that decisions of the Attorney-General involve national issues which might raise more difficult and more highly political matters suggests in any event that there would be less frequent opportunity in practice to review the prerogative power exercised by the Attorney-General and applications would rarely succeed.

Prerogative power to stop criminal proceedings

2–045   The Attorney General has a prerogative power to enter a *nolle prosequi*, to stop criminal proceedings for indictable offences where they are not in the public interest, and the exercise of this power is unlikely to be reviewable. The Privy Council has accepted that analogous statutory powers are amenable in principle to judicial review and may be reviewable in certain circumstances.[135] However, in that case, the Privy Council referred to the earlier decision of the House of Lords holding that this prerogative power was not subject to judicial review. This, therefore, remained a binding statement of the law of England and Wales until it is reviewed or modified in the light of the decision in *G.C.H.Q.* indicating that a prerogative power was not immune from review simply because it derived from the prerogative.[136] The Privy Council also drew attention to the fact that the power in England is derived from the prerogative not statute and the Attorney General is answerable for the exercise of the power to Parliament. In principle, however, there is no reason why judicial review should not be available to review the exercise of the prerogative. In practice, however, judicial review is unlikely to be appropriate given the nature of such an exercise of discretion, the range of policy and public interest factors that apply and the consequences of a successful judicial review quashing the decision and possibly requiring criminal proceedings to be resumed.

Miscellaneous prerogative powers

2–046   Other prerogative powers of greater or lesser significance exist.[137] In the *G.C.H.Q.* case, Lord Diplock expressed the view that the powers to grant

---

[133] *R. (Gujra) v Crown Prosecution Service* [2013] 1 A.C. 484 (at [44] approving the approach of the Divisional Court in [2012] 1 W.L.R. 254 at [41]–[42]).

[134] *Stoke-on-Trent City Council v B. & Q. (Retail); Wolverhampton Borough Council v B. & Q.; Barking & Dagenham London Borough Council v Home Charm Retail* [1984] A.C. 754. See para.8–059.

[135] *Mohit v Director of Public Prosecutions* [2006] 1 W.L.R. 3343.

[136] [2006] 1 W.L.R. 3343 at [14]. The House of Lords held in *Gouriet v Union of Post Office Workers* [1978] A.C. 435 that the power to discontinue proceedings was not subject to supervision by the courts.

[137] See *Halsbury's Laws of England*, 4th edn, Vol.8(2), [801]–[834].

honours, dissolve Parliament and appoint ministers were not justiciable and were not subject to judicial review.[138] The dissolution of Parliament and ministerial appointments clearly involve such politically contentious issues that the courts are unlikely to intervene. A prerogative power to take steps to maintain peace within the realm has been recognised.[139] This prerogative power included the power to supply equipment to police forces which was reasonably necessary for the more efficient discharge of their duties. Given the open-ended nature of this newly discovered prerogative, it is possible that circumstances might arise where a particular exercise might be reviewable. If the Home Secretary indicated, for example, that he would consult police authorities before taking certain action under this prerogative power, then the courts might well review a decision reached without consultation. Or, if guidelines were issued laying down criteria governing the supply of equipment, then a departure from the criteria may be subject to judicial review. Where the exercise of the prerogative power was intimately linked to the operational decisions of the Chief Constable – such as a decision that particular equipment was needed in a particular situation—the courts would be likely to maintain their traditional reluctance to review such decisions.[140]

Common law powers of the Crown

The courts have recognised that the Crown, acting through central government ministers, derives powers not only from statute and the prerogative but also has power to do acts which do not involve any infringement of the rights of others or which are not prohibited by law.[141] The basis for these common law powers is usually said to flow from the fact that the Crown, as a corporation possessing legal personality, has the same capacity as a natural person and may therefore do all those things that a natural person may do. Thus the Crown, or more accurately ministers of the Crown, may do anything so far as they do not involve acts which would amount to a tort or other interference with the private law rights of other individuals or would involve doing something prohibited by law. **2–047**

The common law powers of the Crown therefore enable central government to make ex gratia payments of money[142] or to disseminate information.[143] The **2–048**

---

[138] *Council for Civil Service Unions v Minister of the Civil Service* [1985] A.C. 374 at 418. The duration of a Parliament is now fixed by the Fixed-Term Parliaments Act 2011.

[139] *R. v Secretary of State for the Home Department Ex p. Northumbria Police Authority* [1989] Q.B. 26. Statutory and prerogative powers exist concurrently in this area.

[140] See para.4–084.

[141] *R. v Secretary of State for Health Ex p. C* [2000] F.C.R. 471; *R. (Shrewsbury & Atcham Borough Council and Congleton Borough Council) v Secretary of State for Communities and Local Government* [2008] 3 All E.R. 548; and *R. (New College Ltd.) v Secretary of State for the Home Department* [2013] 1 W.L.R. 2358 at [28] per Lord Sumption (but see dicta of Lord Carnwarth at [34]). See Harris "The 'Third Source' of Authority for Government Action Revisited" [2007] L.Q.R. 225.

[142] *R. (Hooper) v Secretary of State for Work and Pensions* [2005] 1 W.L.R. 1681 (common law power to make ex gratia payments to widowers); *R. (Elias) v Secretary of State for Defence* [2006] 1 W.L.R. 3213 (common law discretionary power to make ex gratia payments to former prisoners of war). It is not always clear whether ex gratia payments are made under a prerogative power or in the exercise of a common law power. In *Re McFarland* [2004] 1 W.L.R. 1289, there was a challenge to the exercise of a power to make ex gratia payments to victims of miscarriage of justice; the House of Lords did not identify the source of the power; the majority of their Lordships referred simply to the

courts have also recognised that the common law powers of the Crown extend to undertaking acts preparatory to introducing legislation or taking steps to prepare for the introduction of anticipated legislation such as inviting and consulting upon proposals for changes to the structure of local government.[144] The courts have previously recognised the power of the Crown to maintain a list of persons considered unsuitable to work with children in the absence of express statutory authority.[145] Similarly, the courts previously recognised that tapping of telephones by the Post Office was lawful as that did not at that stage involve the violation of any recognised domestic law or individual private law right such as trespass or breach of confidence.[146] In both instances, the powers are now regulated by statute[147] and the exercise such of powers today would also be likely to raise issues of potential contravention of rights derived from the European Convention on Human Rights. The underlying principle, that the Crown, acting through central government ministers, has power to do anything which could be done by a natural person provided that it does not involve the violation of the rights of others or the doing of an act prohibited by law remains valid.

2–049   The exercise of such common law powers by the Crown is amenable to judicial review.[148] Whilst the justification for the existence of the power may be that the Crown has the capacity or power to do acts which any ordinary individual may do, the fact that the power is being exercised by or on behalf of the Crown is usually sufficient to provide the "public" element necessary to make the exercise of power a matter of public law for the purposes of judicial review. The fact that the power is exercised by central government is, of itself, usually sufficient to make the exercise of power a public function and so subject to judicial review. In general, therefore, the usual public law principles governing abuse of power apply to the exercise of such common law powers. Furthermore, ministers cannot act incompatibly with any rights conferred under the European Convention on Human Rights and incorporated into the United Kingdom by the Human Rights Act 1998. The existence or exercise of such common law powers may also be expressly or impliedly excluded by statute. The precise circumstances in which

---

power to make ex gratia payments; Lord Scott referred to the scheme involving an exercise of prerogative power. In *R. (Mullen) v Secretary of State for the Home Department* [2004] 2 W.L.R. 1140 (involving a challenge to the statutory and ex gratia payments of compensation for victims of miscarriage of justice) and *R. (Raissi) v Secretary of State for the Home Department*[2008] 3 W.L.R. 375 (involving a challenge to the ex gratia powers) the source of the power to make ex gratia payments was not considered. In any event, there would need to be Parliament authority for the appropriation of money either specifically for particular purposes or generally to enable a department to discharge its functions, including any decision to make ex gratia payments: see the judgment of the Court of Appeal in *R. (Hooper) v Secretary of State for Work and Pensions* [2003] 1 W.L.R. 2623 at [130]–[134].

[143] See, e.g. *Jenkins v Att-Gen* (1971) 115 S.J. 674.

[144] *R. (Shrewsbury & Atcham Borough Council and Congleton Borough Council) v Secretary of State for Communities and Local Government* [2008] 3 All E.R. 548.

[145] *R. v Secretary of State for Health Ex p. C* [2000] 1 F.C.R. 471; *R. (Shrewsbury & Atcham Borough Council and Congleton Borough Council) v Secretary of State for Communities and Local Government* [2008] 3 All E.R. 548.

[146] *Malone v Metropolitan Police Commissioner* [1980] Q.B. 49.

[147] See Protection of Children Act 1999 and Interception of Communications Act 1985.

[148] *R. v Secretary of State for Health Ex p. C* [2000] 1 F.C.R. 471; *R. (Shrewsbury & Atcham Borough Council and Congleton Borough Council) v Secretary of State for Communities and Local Government* [2008] 3 All E.R. 548; *R. v Civil Service Appeal Board Ex p. Bruce* [1988] I.C.R. 649 (affd. by the Court of Appeal [1989] I.C.R. 171).

the existence of statutory powers occupy a particular field of activity and thus prevent the use of common law powers in that field is not always easy to identify in practice.[149] In *Hooper*,[150] the House of Lords had to deal with the power to make ex gratia payments. Statute provided a scheme for payments to widows but there was no statutory provision for the payment to widowers. The House left open the question of whether the exercise of a common law power to make ex gratia payments to widowers would be consistent with the statutory scheme. The decision in *Shrewsbury & Atcham Borough Council*[151] concerned the process of local government reorganisation. There was a statutory framework by which such reorganisations could be effected. New legislation was anticipated providing additional powers to make re-organisation. The government sought to take steps in anticipation of those powers by inviting and consulting upon proposals for re-organisation. No changes would be made, and no steps having legal effect taken, unless and until the new legislation was enacted. The majority of the Court of Appeal considered that the use of common law powers would be inconsistent with the statutory scheme. The minority judgment held that there is nothing inconsistent in the government taking non-binding steps in advance of legislation. The minority view seems preferable. Parliament could provide new machinery for local government re-organisation. There is no reason why the government cannot take steps in preparation for the enactment of that legislation. That is not acting inconsistently with the existing legislation; it is preparing for the implementation of new legislation.

Whilst the exercise of common law powers by the Crown is generally amenable to judicial review, the Divisional Court has held on one occasion that judicial review was not available in respect of a decision by the Lord Chancellor to award a contract for court reporting services where it was alleged that the tendering exercise leading to the award of the contract was flawed. The court held that this involved a common law power to contract and that there was no element of statutory underpinning nor any other public law element in the award of the contract and so judicial review was not available.[152] This reasoning reflects the approach found in other cases dealing with statutory powers to contract. There is a reluctance to find that the exercise of powers to enter into contracts (whatever the source of the power) is amenable to judicial review unless there is some superadded public law element present. A better approach would be to recognise that the exercise by the central government of the power to enter into contract (whatever the source of the power) is amenable in principle to judicial review without the need for some superadded element. However, given the commercial context in which such powers are exercisable, it may be that the full range of

2–050

---

[149] See, e.g. *R. (Hooper) v Secretary of State for Work and Pensions* [2005] 1 W.L.R. 1681 (uncertain whether common law powers to make ex gratia payments remained available given specific statutory scheme providing for payments to widows only); *R. (Shrewsbury & Atcham Borough Council and Congleton Borough Council) v Secretary of State for Communities and Local Government* [2008] 3 All E.R. 548 (whether the use of common law powers to take preliminary steps for introducing a new structure of local government, in advance of legislation, inconsistent with the existence of a different statutory scheme for bringing about local government reorganisation under pre-existing Act).

[150] *R. (Hooper) v Secretary of State for Work and Pensions* [2005] 1 W.L.R. 1681.

[151] *R. (Shrewsbury & Atcham Borough Council and Congleton Borough Council) v Secretary of State for Communities and Local Government* [2008] 3 All E.R. 548.

[152] *R. v Lord Chancellor Ex p. Hibbet and Saunders, The Times*, March 12, 1993.

public law principles cannot be applied to such actions and the scope of the public law obligations may need to be modified to reflect such considerations.[153]

2–051   The use of common law powers in this way is restricted to the Crown, or more accurately, to central government ministers exercising powers on behalf of the Crown. It has long been recognised that bodies created by statute, such as local authorities, only have the powers expressly or impliedly conferred upon by them statute and do not have any wider, common law powers.[154]

2–052   Concern has been expressed about the use of common law or non-statutory powers. Given the realities of modern government, the possession of such powers by central government would seem a necessary incident of government. It is unlikely to be possible to anticipate all the situations in which government may be called upon to act and to provide specific legislative authority in advance. There are limitations on the use of such common law powers. They do not enable the executive to act in a way which involves infringing recognised private law rights. The incorporation of the European Convention on Human Rights further limits the possibility of the unacceptable use of such powers as the executive will be obliged to exercise these powers in a way that is compatible with Convention rights. Nor can the common law powers be used to alter or qualify existing statutory powers. There is a further degree of protection in that some at least of the principles of public law will apply to the exercise of such powers. That said, there may be occasions when the freedom or capacity of the executive to act in a particular way may have significant consequences for individuals. The power of the Crown to contract can have significant consequences for individuals. In the past, for example, the Crown has used the power to refuse to contract as a means of seeking to ensure that companies or individuals comply with government policy. So far as this is considered unacceptable, the preferable route would be statutory or other controls on the use of common law powers in this way, rather than the removal or the denial of the existence of such common law powers.

European Convention on Human Rights

2–053   The European Convention on Human Rights is not a source of power. It is, however, unlawful for a public authority to act in a way that which is incompatible with certain rights derived from the European Convention on Human Rights.[155] A person claiming that a public authority has acted, or failed to act, or proposes to act in a way which is incompatible with a Convention right may bring proceedings in the appropriate court or tribunal.[156] A claim for judicial

---

[153] See below at para.2–143.

[154] *Hazell v Hammersmith and Fulham London Borough Council* [1992] 2 A.C. 1 at 22; *Credit Suisse v Allerdale Borough Council* [1997] Q.B. 306.

[155] Human Rights Act 1998 s.6. A public authority does not act unlawfully for the purposes of s.6 if, as a result of primary legislation, the public authority was required to act in a way which was incompatible with a person's Convention rights: see Human Rights Act 1998 s.6(2) and see *R. (Bono) v Harlow District Council* [2002] 1 W.L.R. 2475.

[156] Human Rights Act 1998 s.7.

review will, usually, be an appropriate procedure for enabling a person to enforce his Convention rights against a public authority.[157]

Public authorities for the purposes of the Human Rights Act 1998 include **2–054** "standard" or "core" public authorities such as government departments, which must always comply with a person's Convention rights and "hybrid bodies" or "functional public authorities" some of whose functions are public and some are private.[158] These hybrid bodies must comply with a person's Convention rights when exercising their public functions (but do not have to comply with the Convention in respect of acts which are private in nature). It is not easy to define what constitutes a public authority for the purposes of s.6 of the Human Rights Act 1998. There is no single test of universal application for determining whether functions are public ones.[159] Among the factors that may indicate that the function is a public one is whether it involves the exercise of statutory powers, whether the body exercising the function is publicly funded or is performing functions that would otherwise be performed by central or local government.[160] The fact that the body concerned has a range of coercive statutory powers that it exercises points towards the function it performs being a public one[161] although the fact that the activity is regulated by statute is unlikely to be sufficient to render it a public function for the purposes of s.6(3)(b) of the Human Rights Act 1998.[162] The fact that a function is performed by a private company, under contract to a local authority, is an indication that the function is not public at least in the absence of strong countervailing factors.[163] Conversely, the termination of a tenancy by a housing trust did involve an exercise of public functions. The fact that the body concerned was a registered social landlord and relied significantly on public subsidy provided in order to achieve governmental objectives in the form of the provision of subsidised housing to certain sections of the community did indicate that it was exercising a public function.[164] The reference to a body performing public functions is reminiscent of the test used in deciding whether a body is performing functions which have a sufficiently public element to make them subject to judicial review.[165] The fact that a function is, or is regarded as, a public function amenable to judicial review may therefore be an indication as to

---

[157] Except in the case of superior courts where judicial review is not available (see below at para.2–122). In this situation, a superior court, such as the High Court, would be obliged to act in accordance with the Convention and, if it did not do so, the appropriate mechanism for challenging its decision would be an appeal.

[158] See Human Rights Act 1998 s. 6(3) and *Aston Cantlow PCC v Wallbank* [2004] 1 A.C. 546 at [6]–[11] and [35] and see *R. (Weaver) v London & Quadrant Housing Trust* [2010] 1 W.L.R. 363 at [35]–[37] (per Elias LJ) and at [101] (per Lord Collins).

[159] See *Aston Cantlow* [2004] 1 A.C. 546 at [10] and *Weaver* [2010] 1 W.L.R. 363 at [35](5) to (6).

[160] See *Aston Cantlow* [2004] 1 A.C. 546 at [10] and *Weaver* [2010] 1 W.L.R. 363 at [35](7).

[161] See, e.g. *YL v Birmingham City Council*[2008] 1 A.C. 95, per Baroness Hale at [69] and per Lord Neuberger at [167]. The actual decision in *YL* will be reversed by s.145 of the Health and Social Care Act 2008.

[162] [2008] 1 A.C. 95 per Lord Mance at [116] and per Lord Neuberger at [134]. A contrary view was taken by Lord Bingham who considered that a high degree of statutory regulation of a function may indicate that it was public in nature: see [17].

[163] *YL v Birmingham City Council* [2008] 1 A.C. 95.

[164] *R. (Weaver) v London and Quadrant Housing Trust* [2010] 1 W.L.R. 363 at [68]–[72] and [101]–[102].

[165] See *Poplar Housing Association v Donoghue* [2002] Q.B. 48 esp. at [65]; *R. (Beer) v Hampshire Farmers' Market Ltd* [2004] 1 W.L.R. 233 at [25].

whether or not the function is a public function for the different purpose of s.6(3)(b) of the Human Rights Act 1998 but is unlikely to be determinative.[166] In particular, the House of Lords has emphasised the importance of bearing in mind the case law of the European Court of Human Rights in deciding whether a body is a public authority for the purposes of the Human Rights Act 1998.[167] Given that the purpose of s.6 of the Human Rights Act 1998 is to determine which bodies, exercising which functions, are obliged to comply with the European Convention on Human Rights, it is possible that the range of bodies that are public authorities for the purposes of the Human Rights Act 1998 might be different from, and arguably narrower than, the range of bodies whose activities are sufficiently public to make them subject to judicial review and obliged to observe domestic public law principles in the exercise of those functions. In any event, if a body is exercising a public function for the purposes of the Human Rights Act 1998, judicial review would be available against those bodies in respect of that function to ensure that they complied with their Convention rights and they will also normally be a public body for the purposes of judicial review and will have to observe the usual principles of domestic public law.[168]

2–055   The courts can also grant a declaration that provisions of legislation are incompatible with a Convention right.[169] A claim for judicial review is a common method of seeking such a declaration.[170]

European Union Law

2–056   The law of the European Union is an important source of rights and obligations. Such rights may be derived from the Treaty on the Functioning of the EU[171] or from regulations or directives adopted under that Treaty by the European institutions. These rights may be enforceable in legal proceedings in the courts of each Member State.[172] Section 2(1) of the European Communities Act 1972 incorporates these directly enforceable rights and obligations into English law.

---

[166] *YL v Birmingham City Council* [2008] 1 A.C. 95 esp. per Lord Neuberger at [156]. The fact that the activities of a private company in providing care to elderly persons under a contract was not a public function amenable to judicial review was a factor taken into account by the majority: see per Lord Mance at [120] and Lord Neuberger at [160]. *R. (Weaver) v London and Quadrant Housing Trust* [2010] 1 W.L.R. 363 at [37].

[167] *Aston Cantlow and Wilmcote with Billesley Parochial Church Council v Wallbank* [2004] 1 A.C. 546. See Oliver "Functions of a Public Nature under the Human Rights Act" [2004] P.L. 329.

[168] *R. (A) v Partnerships in Care Ltd* [2002] 1 W.L.R. 2610 at [9] and see *R. (Weaver) v London and Quadrant Housing* [2008] EWHC 1377 (Admin) at [64].

[169] Human Rights Act 1998, s.4. The courts must interpret legislation, so far as it is possible to do so, in a manner which is compatible with the Convention, but can grant a declaration of incompatibility if that is not possible: see Human Rights Act 1998, s.3.

[170] The issue of whether legislation can be interpreted in a way that is compatible with a Convention right or, if not a declaration of incompatibility should be granted, can also arise in the course of criminal proceedings (see, e.g. *Barnfather v London Borough of Islington* [2003] 1 W.L.R. 2318) or civil proceedings (see, e.g. *Bellinger v Bellinger* [2003] 2 A.C. 467).

[171] This Treaty was formerly known as the EC Treaty (or the Treaty of Rome) and was renamed by the Treaty of Lisbon. The European Union is based upon the provisions of the Treaty on European Union and the Treaty on the Functioning European Union.

[172] Case 26/62 *N.V. Algemene Transport-en Expediti Onderneming van Gend & Loos v Nederlandse Belastingenadministratie* [1963] E.C.R. 1.

EU law will frequently raise issues of public law. Action taken by public bodies exercising public law powers which violate EU law will be ultra vires and invalid, and judicial review will be available to quash or declare invalid such action.[173] The duties imposed and powers conferred upon public authorities by EU law may similarly be classed as public law powers and duties and so subject to judicial review.[174]   **2–057**

Not all EU law provisions are intended to restrict the scope of activity by public bodies alone. Some provisions of EU law, notably those dealing with competition,[175] or equality in employment,[176] are intended principally to regulate relations between ordinary individuals. Judicial review is not available against ordinary individuals. Such rights will therefore be classed as private law rights enforceable by such private law remedies as are appropriate, for example, by treating the breach of EU law as akin to the English tort of breach of statutory duty.[177] Private law remedies may also be available against public bodies that happen to carry out activities to which such provisions also apply.[178]   **2–058**

There are situations where a right derived from EU law may be analysed as a private law right and cannot normally be enforced by way of judicial review. Thus, a woman's claim for equal treatment with a man in respect of a right to a redundancy payment is a private law right not enforceable by way of judicial review.[179]   **2–059**

Breaches of EU law may give rise to a claim for damages, as well as being enforceable in public law by way of judicial review, where the breach displays a manifest and grave disregard by the authorities of EU law.[180] This topic is fully considered in Chapter 17.   **2–060**

Sporting bodies and other bodies deriving jurisdiction from contract

Domestic tribunals

The prerogative remedies were not available to control the activities of bodies which derived their jurisdiction over individuals solely from contract. The clear dividing line lay between bodies set up by statute (and subsequently the prerogative) where certiorari was available, and those bodies set up or exercising jurisdiction by virtue of the agreement of the parties. "Private or domestic   **2–061**

---

[173] See, e.g. *R. v Secretary of State for the Home Department Ex p. Dannenberg* [1984] Q.B. 766 and see generally Lewis, *Remedies and the Enforcement of European Community Law* (London: Sweet & Maxwell, 1996), Ch.6.

[174] *R. v Minister of Agriculture, Fisheries and Food Ex p. Bell Lines and An Bord Bainne Co-operative (Irish Dairy Board)* [1984] 2 C.M.L.R. 502.

[175] Arts 101 and 102 TFEU.

[176] Art. 157 TFEU.

[177] *Garden Cottage Foods v Milk Marketing Board* [1984] A.C. 130.

[178] [1984] A.C. 130 where the defendant happened to be a statutory body performing a non-governmental function.

[179] *R. v Secretary of State for Employment Ex p. Equal Opportunities Commission* [1995] 1 A.C. 1; see also *R. v Secretary of State for Employment Ex p. Seymour-Smith* [1997] 1 W.L.R. 473.

[180] Joined cases C-6/90 and C-9/90 *Francovich v Italian Republic* [1991] E.C.R. I-5357; Case 48/93 *R. v Secretary of State for Transport Ex p. Factortame Ltd (No.4)* [1996] Q.B. 404 (decision of the ECJ); see *R. v Secretary of State for Transport Ex p. Factortame Ltd (No.5)* [2001] A.C. 524 (decision of the House of Lords).

tribunals have always been outside the scope of certiorari since their authority is derived solely from contract... ".[181] Certiorari did not therefore lie against the decision of an arbitration body to whom the parties to an agreement, relating to an apprenticeship, had agreed to refer any disputes arising from that agreement.[182]

2–062   Decisions of private or domestic tribunals reached in the exercise of a contractual jurisdiction remain outside the ambit of judicial review. Claims for judicial review can only be made in respect of matters of public law. Tribunals who derive their jurisdiction over individuals solely from contract are still regarded as private bodies regulated by private not public law. In *Law v National Greyhound Racing Club*,[183] the Court of Appeal held that a challenge to a decision of the club, which was a company limited by guarantee, and whose sole jurisdiction over individuals derived from their agreement to be bound by the rules of the club, was a matter of private law which could be dealt with by originating summons, and was not a matter of public law suitable for judicial review. The Court of Appeal rejected the arguments that the subject-matter of the dispute—the alleged abuse of the discretion conferred on the club by the rules—or the public concern at the way that the club performed its regulatory functions injected a sufficient "public" element into the dispute to render it susceptible to judicial review.

2–063   Two issues have arisen in the light of the decision in *Law*. First, the question arose as to whether the jurisdictional position that such bodies were not amenable to judicial review needed to be reconsidered in the light of the decision in *R. v Panel on Take-overs and Mergers Ex p. Datafin Plc*.[184] Secondly, the precise ratio decidendi of *Law* has been the subject of differing opinions. The issue is whether a tribunal which usually derives its jurisdiction from contract is a domestic tribunal whose decisions can never be subject to judicial review or whether *Law* only excludes judicial review in respect of those decisions which are expressly or impliedly authorised by the contract. This second interpretation would leave open the possibility of judicial review being available in respect of the non-contractual decisions of such bodies, providing that the decision in question was sufficiently public to attract judicial review.

2–064   In *Datafin*, the Court of Appeal held that the source of a body's power was only one of the factors relevant to determining whether a body was performing public functions and so amenable to judicial review. However, the judgment in *Datafin* proceeded on the basis that judicial review is not available in relation to bodies whose sole source of power was consensual submission to their jurisdiction. The Court of Appeal has now held that the decisions of bodies who acquired jurisdiction over individuals by contract are excluded from the ambit of

---

[181] per Lord Parker C.J. in *R. v Criminal Injuries Compensation Board Ex p. Lain* [1967] 2 Q.B. 864 at 882.

[182] *R. v National Joint Council for the Craft of Dental Technicians (Disputes Committee) Ex p. Neate* [1953] 1 Q.B. 704. See also *R. v Industrial Court Ex p. A.S.S.E.T.* [1965] 1 Q.B. 377.

[183] [1983] 1 W.L.R. 1302. See also *Mullins v Mcfarlane and The Jockey Club* [2006] EWHC 986 Q.B. at [34]. *R. v Football Association of Wales Ex p. Flint Town Football Club* [1991] C.O.D. 44 and *R. v Association of British Travel Agents Ltd (t/a Superlative Travel)* [2001] A.C.D. 16. See Beloff, "Pitch, Pool, Rink,... Court? Judicial Review in the Sporting World" [1989] P.L. 95.

[184] [1987] Q.B. 815.

judicial review. In the *Aga Khan* case,[185] the Court of Appeal had to consider the powers of the Jockey Club. Under the Rules of Racing, the Jockey Club had power to disqualify a horse from a race if a prohibited substance was found in its urine. A committee of the Club found that there was a prohibited substance in a horse owned by the Aga Khan and disqualified the horse and fined the trainer £200. The Aga Khan contended that the hearing was vitiated by procedural unfairness. The issue for the Court of Appeal was whether the decision was subject to judicial review. The Court of Appeal found that the Jockey Club was not a public body. Although it had a Royal Charter and its rules had to be approved by the Privy Council, it was not in fact woven into any system of governmental control of racing. The Jockey Club acquired its powers over individuals by virtue of the fact that they agreed to be bound by the Rules of Racing and, as such, the source of the Jockey Club's power was contractual and so was not subject to judicial review. The Jockey Club acquired its jurisdiction to make the decision in the present case by virtue of the agreement to be bound by the Rules of Racing and that decision could not be challenged by way of judicial review.

The question still arises as to whether a decision which did not derive from any agreement or contract could be subjected to judicial review. In one earlier case,[186] the Divisional Court held that judicial review did not lie against a decision of the Jockey Club not to include the applicant's name on the list of people qualified to act as chairmen at race meetings. The court concluded that the case was indistinguishable from *Law* and that the Jockey Club acquired jurisdiction over the applicant by contract.[187] Neil LJ considered that no decision of a body which acquires its jurisdiction over individuals by means of contract is susceptible to judicial review. Roch J. expressly left open the possibility that if the authority to take a particular decision did not derive from contract, then judicial review might be available in relation to that decision provided that the body could be regarded as performing a public function. **2–065**

The question arose again in *R. v Jockey Club Ex p. RAM Racecourses Ltd.*[188] There the Jockey Club refused to grant the applicant 15 race fixtures for his racecourse during 1991. The applicant sought judicial review claiming that the decision was invalid as it conflicted with his public law legitimate expectation that he would be granted the 15 fixtures. There was no contractual relationship between the applicant and the Jockey Club. In the event, the Divisional Court **2–066**

---

[185] *R. v Disciplinary Committee of the Jockey Club Ex p. Aga Khan* [1993] 1 W.L.R. 909. See also *R. v Football Association Ltd Ex p. Football League Ltd* [1993] 2 All E.R. 833 to the same effect. In a different context, see also *R. (West) v Lloyd's of London* [2004] EWCA Civ 506 (judgment given on April 27, 2004); *R. v Lloyd's of London Ex p. Briggs* [1993] 1 Lloyd's L. Rep. 176 (Lloyd's acquired jurisdiction over individuals in the present dispute by means of agreement and so its decision was not amenable to judicial review); *R. v Fernhill Manor School Ex p. Brown* (1992) 5 Admin. L.Rep. 159 (relationship between a private school and those attending it was founded upon the contract with the parents; decisions to expel a student were therefore matters of private law not amenable to judicial review); *R. v Thames Valley University Students' Union* [1997] EWHC 340 (Admin) (students' union was a voluntary association of members and was not amenable to judicial review) and *R. (Moreton) v Medical Defence Union Ltd* [2006] A.C.D. 450 (rights of members of medical defence union derived from the union's association and from company law not public law).

[186] *R. v Jockey Club Ex p. Massingberd-Mundy* [1993] 2 All E.R. 207.

[187] Although Stuart-Smith LJ doubted that any contract did exist in this case: see dicta in *R. v Jockey Club Ex p. RAM Racecourses Ltd* [1993] 2 All E.R. 225.

[188] [1993] 2 All E.R. 225.

concluded that the applicant had no legitimate expectation and the application was dismissed. Their lordships did, however, go on to consider whether judicial review was available to challenge the decision. Stuart-Smith LJ held that the decisions of domestic tribunals could never be subject to judicial review whether or not any contractual basis existed for the decision under challenge. Simon Brown J. considered that there were occasions when there was no contractual basis for the exercise of jurisdiction. In such circumstances, judicial review would be available provided that the particular decision was sufficiently public. The licensing functions of a monopoly body such as the Jockey Club were sufficiently public to hold that judicial review was available.

2–067   The issue surfaced again in a renewed application before the Court of Appeal for permission to apply for judicial review. The applicant applied for permission to challenge a refusal of the Royal Life Saving Society, a body created by Royal Charter, to undertake a formal inquiry into allegations made against the applicant. The Court of Appeal did not consider the jurisdictional issue in depth but indicated, *obiter*, that if the decision was not based on contract and if it raised a public law issue, judicial review might be available.[189] In the event, the court considered that the applicant was seeking to remedy a private grievance in that she had suffered harm to her reputation by the action of the body in question and was not therefore raising a public law claim. Her application for permission was dismissed.

2–068   The jurisdictional issue arose again but was not settled in the *Aga Khan*[190] case, where the Master of the Rolls and Farquharson LJ expressly left open the question of whether a decision of the Jockey Club could ever be reviewed. Hoffmann LJ took the view that as the Jockey Club was a private body, acquiring jurisdiction over persons by contract, it could never be subjected to judicial review. The Jockey Club might, in fact, be able to exercise power with practical consequences for individuals, even though no contract existed between the Jockey Club and the individual. That, however, did not alter the fact that the Jockey Club was exercising private power and was not subject to the rules of public law. Any control had to be found in private law concepts such as contract, restraint of trade or other specific statutory mechanisms. He was prepared to accept that there may be cases where the remedies available in private law were inadequate, particularly where there was no contract between the individual and such a body,[191] but again he did not view that as a justification for subjecting a private body to public law rules. Rose J. expressed a similar view in *R. v Football Association Ltd Ex p. Football League Ltd*.[192] There, the Football League was a limited company which acquired jurisdiction over others by reason of contract. The Football League was contractually bound to comply with the Football Association's rules. Rose J. also considered that, although it had virtually monopolistic powers and its decision were of importance to many members of the public with whom it had no contract, it remained a private body and there was no governmental underpinning to its activities. The Football Association was

---

[189] *R. v Royal Life Saving Society Ex p. Heather Rose Mary Howe* [1990] C.O.D. 440.

[190] [1993] 1 W.L.R. 909.

[191] Such persons may have no private law cause of action against the body concerned. However, there is a possibility that the courts might exercise a limited degree of supervision over such bodies even where there is no contract: see para.2–070 below.

[192] [1993] 2 All E.R. 833.

therefore a private body which was not susceptible to judicial review "either in general or, more particularly, at the instigation of the League, with whom it is contractually bound".[193]

As a matter of principle, much depends on the way in which the issue is approached. If the body is seen as not possessing sufficient characteristics to make it a public body, applying the tests discussed below, there is considerable force in the analysis of Hoffmann LJ in *Aga Khan*. If the body simply does not meet the test for establishing that it is a public body, then its decisions will not be public law decisions whether or not they owe their immediate origins to any contract between the individual concerned and the body. Alternatively, however, the situation could be analysed as one where the body is a public body which is, in principle, subject to judicial review but those decisions which derive from a contractual source are excluded from judicial review. That would in one sense mirror the situation that frequently occurs when an undoubtedly public body (such as a statutory corporation) enters into a contract. The enforcement of rights derived from the contract is seen as a private law matter; controls over the exercise of other powers remain subject to judicial review. At the level of pragmatism, there is also much to recommend this solution. It is unattractive to leave bodies performing effectively regulatory functions, and exercising substantial, often monopolistic, powers with serious consequences for individuals without there being any method of controlling the exercise of such powers. There may, however, be a logical difficulty in the approach of the majority in the *Aga Khan* case. They appeared to accept that the Jockey Club was not a public body for reasons unconnected with the fact that it normally acquired jurisdiction by contract. If that were the case, then it might appear to be difficult to treat the body as a public body for certain purposes (i.e. reviewing non-contractual decisions) but not a public body for others. The answer might lie in the fact that the majority of the Court of Appeal were considering whether the body's *functions* were public and it is perfectly possible for a body to be private in origin but to be performing public functions in particular respects.[194] A body may be private in origin and some of its functions may be private; some functions, however, may be public.

Judicial control of domestic tribunals

Although the activities of such bodies are not amenable at the procedural level to judicial review, it is now likely that such bodies might still be required to observe substantive principles of public law such as natural justice[195] or reasonableness[196]

2–069

2–070

---

[193] [1993] 2 All E.R. 833 at 848h.

[194] See, e.g. the discussion at paras 2–007 to 2–008 above: bodies such as the Law Society or voluntary schools may be private in origin but have particularly statutory functions conferred upon them. The bodies are reviewable in respect of those functions.

[195] See, e.g. *Edwards v Society of Graphical and Allied Trades* [1971] Ch. 354 (trade union could not expel a member without a hearing); *Wright v Jockey Club, The Times*, June 16, 1995 and *Jones v Welsh Rugby Football Union, The Times*, March 6, 1997 (interlocutory injunction to restrain suspension from rugby football where suspected breach of natural justice; discharged on other grounds: see *The Times*, January 6, 1998); *Korda v ITF Ltd (trading as International Tennis Federation)* [1998] T.L.R. 85 (declaration granted that the ITF was not entitled under its rules to appeal to the Court of Arbitration for Sport against the decision the ITF anti-doping appeals committee; decision reversed on merits by the Court of Appeal March 25, 1999) and *Modahl v British*

or proportionality.[197] There may be an express contract between the individual and the sporting authorities[198] or the courts may infer the existence of such a contract from the fact of membership of a club and participation in sporting competitions on the basis that the participants will abide by the rules governing such competitions.[199] Alternatively, submission to the disciplinary jurisdiction of a body with the implied agreement to accept its findings may lead to the inference that there is a contract.[200] The need to observe such principles can be viewed as an implied term of the contract under which the domestic tribunal acquires jurisdiction. In such circumstances it may be possible to obtain a declaration or injunction by way of an ordinary claim, to restrain the contractual body from acting contrary to these implied terms or preventing the implementation of a decision which is contrary to the implied terms.[201] Even where a body refuses to contract with an individual, the courts may still exercise a limited degree of supervisory control over the body through ordinary claims for declarations or injunctions, even though the fiction of enforcing implied terms in a contract cannot operate at this stage. This is particularly likely to occur if the body has an effective monopoly over an activity and the actions of the body prevent the individual from pursuing his livelihood,[202] although the courts have also left open the possibility of lesser interests justifying judicial intervention.[203] If this approach were endorsed, the courts may still exercise a supervisory jurisdiction over sporting and other domestic tribunals to ensure that the body concerned acts fairly, in accordance with its rules[204] and proportionately[205] and the courts may seek to ensure that its rules do not constitute an unreasonable restraint on trade,[206] even though there was no private law cause of action, such as breach of contract, upon which the claim could be based. Irrespective of the basis upon which the

---

Athletic Federation Ltd [2002] 1 W.L.R. 1192 (individual entitled to a fair hearing, including an unbiased tribunal, but the procedures, including the appeal procedures, ensured a fair hearing overall).

[196] See, e.g. *Cowley v Heatley, The Times*, July 24, 1986 (construction of constitution of Commonwealth Games Federation).

[197] *Bradley v The Jockey Club* [2005] EWCA Civ 1056 (claim that the penalty was disproportionate failed on the facts).

[198] *Korda v ITF (trading as International Tennis Federation)* [1998] T.L.R. 85 (the existence of a contract was not disputed in the Court of Appeal).

[199] *Modhal v British Athletic Federation Ltd* [2002] 1 W.L.R. 1192 at [50] (per Latham LJ) and at [105] (per Mance LJ).

[200] See dictum of Mance LJ in *Modahl v British Athletic Federation Ltd* [2002] 1 W.L.R. 1192 at [105]. See also *Law v National Greyhound Racing Club Ltd* [1983] 1 W.L.R. 1302.

[201] See, e.g. *R. v British Broadcasting Corp. Ex p. Lavelle* [1983] 1 W.L.R. 23; *McLaren v Home Office* [1990] I.C.R. 824. See Ewing and Grubb, "The Emergence of a New Labour Injunction" (1987) 16 I.LJ 145.

[202] *Nagle v Fielden* [1966] 2 Q.B. 633 (refusal of trainer's licence); *McInnes v Onslow-Fane* [1978] 1 W.L.R. 1520 (refusal of boxing manager's licence).

[203] See *Mullins v McFarlane and The Jockey Club* [2006] EWHC 986 (QB). *Fisher v National Greyhound Racing Club*, July 31, 1985, unreported (Court refused to strike out claim that Club wrongfully refused to register a greyhound even though owner did not earn a living from racing). But, see *Currie v Barton, The Times*, February 12, 1988 (doubting whether natural justice applied to a ban on a tennis player when not a question of livelihood). See also the observations of Hoffmann LJ in *R. v Disciplinary Committee Ex p. Aga Khan* [1993] 1 W.L.R. 909.

[204] See dicta of Latham LJ in *Modahl v British Athletics Federation Ltd* [2002] 1 W.L.R. 1192 at [43]–[47].

[205] *Bradley v The Jockey Club* [2005] EWCA 1056.

[206] *Stevenage Borough Football Club v The Football League* (1996) 9 Admin. L.R. 109; *Newport Association Football Club v Football Association of Wales Ltd* [1995] 2 All E.R. 87.

courts exercise control over sporting bodies, the courts have emphasised that their role is essentially supervisory. The courts do not take the primary decision as to what would be the appropriate course of action in the circumstances. Rather, they consider whether the primary decision-maker has operated within lawful limits very much as they do in relation to judicial review of a public body.[207] The only practical difference in terms of the degree of supervision over such bodies would lie in the private law remedies available. Damages could be awarded in cases where a contract was inferred; in other cases, the courts would be limited to granting a declaration or injunction.

There may be real practical difficulties in granting any meaningful remedy. In *Mullins*, a horse came first in an important horse race but was disqualified for having a prohibited substance in its body. The horse which finished second was awarded the Gold Cup. The trainer of the disqualified horse sought a declaration that the disqualification was unlawful as the Jockey Club had subsequently established a threshold level for the drug in question and should have applied that level to this race. The court dismissed the claim on the basis that no threshold level had been established and, in any event, not applying any threshold level to earlier races was not arbitrary or unfair. If the claimant had succeeded, however, it is not easy to see what the consequence of a declaration that the disqualification was unlawful would be. In particular, would the disqualified horse be entitled to be recorded as the winner and the Gold Cup awarded to the other horse handed over to the owner of the disqualified horse? Or would he be entitled only to damages in respect of the prize money which he would have received had his horse not been disqualified?

2–071

Criticism of the existing position

Criticism has been directed at the refusal of the courts to entertain applications for judicial review in relation to such bodies. The courts clearly perceive a need to control the potential abuse of power by a body exercising control over individuals, and to prevent the body going beyond the limits conferred by the rules. This is, in essence, the same rationale as underlies the desire to subject statutory and prerogative powers to judicial review. The argument for treating domestic and statutory tribunals in the same way acquires even greater force when the same substantive principles are to be applied to domestic and statutory bodies and where the courts apply the same standard of review.[208] It is not entirely clear whether all the principles of judicial review apply or apply with the same force to domestic tribunals, and there are statements urging the courts not to be anxious to intervene in the activities of such bodies.[209] This again may only reflect the fact that the degree of judicial control and the discretion that the courts exercise in deciding whether to review and to grant a remedy differ according to the context and the interests involved rather than indicating a difference in kind between domestic and statutory tribunals. More recently, the court has described the approach to the task of supervising such bodies as essentially similar to the

2–072

---

[207] *Bradley v Jockey Club* [2005] EWCA Civ 1056 at [17] and [18].
[208] *Mullins v McFarlane and The Jockey Club* [2006] EWHC 986 (QB).
[209] See dicta of Megarry V.C. in *McInnes v Onslow-Fane* [1978] 1 W.L.R. 1520 at 1535.

task it carries out on reviewing public bodies.[210] It has also been pointed out that, if domestic tribunals are to be obliged to observe public law principles, then they should have the benefit of the public law protections such as the need for permission and the short time-limits which are built into the judicial review procedure.[211] Such domestic tribunals may, however, be reluctant to submit to the judicial review jurisdiction. There is concern that the courts might insist that such tribunals observe the whole body of substantive public law principles and that this would impose unduly onerous burdens on them. This need not be a necessary concomitant of holding such bodies subject to judicial review. The courts could adapt the principles of public law as required to meet the real and justified needs of such tribunals. There is also concern that the more liberal test of standing applicable in judicial review proceedings might result in too wide a range of people being entitled to challenge decisions of domestic tribunals.[212]

Public bodies acquiring jurisdiction by contract

2–073 The exclusion from judicial review of exercises of discretionary power derived from contract may apply even where one of the parties to a contract is a public body. The fact that one party is a public body does not automatically mean that any powers it exercises over individuals must be derived from statute or prerogative. Public bodies with corporate personality can enter into contracts and hold property as can any private individual. A contract can operate as the source of a particular power of a public body over an individual in much the same way that statute can provide such powers. The courts have on occasions considered whether a public body is exercising powers derived from statute or whether the source of its powers in a particular case is contractual. If the source is contractual, the courts may hold that judicial review is not available.

2–074 This approach can be seen in *R. v Independent Broadcasting Authority Ex p. Rank Organisation*.[213] The I.B.A. had statutory duties to perform in relation to broadcasting. It also entered into contracts with individual programme contractors for the provision of programmes in particular areas and had entered into such a contract with a company, Granada Limited. The I.B.A. refused Rank permission to exercise voting rights in respect of more than 5 per cent of its shareholding in Granada. The Court of Appeal held that the power to refuse permission was derived from the Articles of Association of Granada (which in legal terms constituted a contract between the shareholders of Granada) not from statute, and thus was a matter of private law not public law. The decision could not therefore be challenged by way of judicial review.

2–075 The articles of association of some of the privatised industries also confer special powers on government. One device is to confer a special share on the government, and to require the consent of the special shareholder—that is the government—before certain actions can be done. The Articles of the former Association of the British Airports Authority, for example, provided that the

---

[210] *Bradley v The Jockey Club* [2005] EWCA 1056 at [17]–[18].

[211] See Beatson, " 'Public' and 'Private' in English Administrative Law" (1987) 103 L.Q.R. 34 at 47–48.

[212] See dicta in *R. v Jockey Club Ex p. Massingberd-Mundy* [1993] 2 All E.R. 207 at 218c–d.

[213] March 26, 1986, Unreported. The decision of Mann J., which was affirmed by the Court of Appeal, is reported in *The Times*, March 14, 1986.

disposal of airports requires the consent of the special shareholder. In the case of certain privatised industries, the disposal of more than 25 per cent of the assets requires the consent of the special shareholder. Adopting the approach in *Rank*, these powers would be derived from private law not statute and be outside the ambit of judicial review. Yet, in reality, they are powers conferred on the government as a means of controlling the activities of certain strategic companies in the public interest. The fact that the powers are exercised through the medium of the articles of association reflects a change in the status of the company and should not become a way of shielding the regulatory actions of government from judicial scrutiny.

Other cases involving decisions of public bodies could be analysed in terms of the immediate source of the power being contractual not statutory: this is particularly true of some of the employment cases involving the dismissal of employees of public bodies. If the power to dismiss can be seen to stem from the contract of employment rather than any statutory or prerogative source, then the issue can be viewed as simply a private law contractual matter not a public law matter.[214] If the powers to dismiss derive from statute or the prerogative, or if the restrictions on the power to dismiss are derived from a public law source, then questions of public law might arise.[215] **2–076**

Analysing the availability of judicial review by reference to the source of the power is not, however, an entirely satisfactory approach to situations where a public body relies in part on common law contractual or property ownership powers, nor is it one universally adopted by the courts. There is often a complex inter-relationship between private law, statutory powers and duties, and the common law substantive principles of public law, which defies analysis in terms of looking simply for the source of power for any particular decision. Public bodies are not necessarily free to exercise their contractual powers in the way that individuals are usually free to do so. Public bodies are meant to be acting on behalf of the general public interest in the performance of their functions and not simply pursuing private interests.[216] Therefore, the fact that one party to a dispute is a public body can be extremely important in deciding whether the substantive principles of public law apply to its contractual activities, and, if so, whether these principles can be enforced by public law remedies. The relationship between contractual principles and substantive principles, and the availability of the judicial review procedure to resolve these issues, may be better analysed in terms of the subject-matter of the dispute rather than seeking to identify the formal source of the power. Then the question becomes whether the subject-matter of the dispute is the enforcement of contractual rights, in which case the matter is one of private law to be dealt with by ordinary claim, or **2–077**

---

[214] *R. v East Berkshire Health Authority Ex p. Walsh* [1985] Q.B. 152; *R. v British Broadcasting Co Ex p. Lavelle* (see above, fn.20).

[215] *R. v Secretary of State for the Home Department Ex p. Benwell* [1985] Q.B. 554; *R. v Civil Service Appeal Board Ex p. Bruce* [1989] I.C.R. 171.

[216] See dicta in *Jones v Swansea City Council* [1990] 1 W.L.R. 54 at 71, 85. The House of Lords decided the case on other grounds but see the dicta of Lord Lowry [1990] 1 W.L.R. 1453 at 1458–1459. See also *R. v Derbyshire County Council Ex p. The Times Supplements Ltd* [1991] C.O.D. 129.

whether questions of public law are involved in which case judicial review is appropriate. This question is considered in more detail below.[217]

C. NATURE OF THE FUNCTION

Bodies performing public functions

2–078   The source of the power is not now the only test for determining whether the acts or decisions of a particular body are susceptible to judicial review. The Court of Appeal in *R. v Panel on Take-overs and Mergers Ex p. Datafin plc*,[218] one of the landmark decisions in public law, accepted that the nature of the function as well as the source of the power could found the jurisdiction of the courts to entertain a claim for judicial review. Bodies performing public duties or exercising powers that could be characterised as "public" may be subject to judicial review in respect of those powers and duties even though the powers are not statutory or prerogative. Given the wide and disparate range of bodies that operate in the administrative landscape, and given a revitalised approach on the part of the courts to judicial review and the need to control potential abuses of power, a large number of non-statutory bodies have been brought within the ambit of public law and judicial review. The difficulty is to identify exactly what it is that makes a particular function "public."

2–079   The *Datafin* case involved the Panel on Take-overs and Mergers, a self-regulatory body. The panel was an unincorporated association comprised of a chairman and a deputy chairman, appointed by the Governor of the Bank of England, and 12 members representing various bodies active in the financial and business world. The panel had no statutory, prerogative or common law powers. Notwithstanding its lack of actual legal authority, the panel exercised considerable de facto power in drawing up and administering the City Code on Take-overs and Mergers. A finding by the panel that there had been a breach of the Code could lead to the withholding of the admission of shares to the Official List of the Stock Exchange (the listing of shares was a statutory function performed under subordinate legislation implementing an EEC Directive). A breach of the Code was also an act of misconduct under the Stock Exchange rules. The Department of Trade and Industry stated that the government would not seek to have legislation enacted to regulate take-overs since it was considered better to rely on the flexibility and effectiveness of the self-regulatory mechanism of the panel. The final important point was that the panel did not owe its jurisdiction to any contractual source. The code and rulings applied to all those who wished to make a take-over, not simply those who were members of bodies represented on the panel—so it could not be said that its jurisdiction was the result of contractual arrangements entered into with those whom it regulated.[219]

---

[217] See below, at paras 2–131 et seq.

[218] [1987] Q.B. 815.

[219] It was apparently not clear from the evidence whether there was a contract between the members of the panel or between the Bank of England and the bodies represented on the panel; see per Nicholls LJ [1987] Q.B. 815 at 850. Even if there were, it is not clear whether this would bring about a contractual relationship between the individual members of the representative bodies and the panel.

For those reasons, the panel was considered to be performing a public function and was amenable in principle to judicial review. The position was summarised by the Master of the Rolls[220]:

> "As an act of government it was decided that, in relation to take-overs, there should be a central self-regulatory body which would be supported and sustained by a periphery of statutory powers and penalties wherever non-statutory powers and penalties were insufficient or non-existent or where EEC requirements called for statutory provisions."

The Court of Appeal then considered the substantive application for review, but dismissed the application on the grounds that the panel had not acted unlawfully.

Two approaches to the definition of "public" can be discerned in the *Datafin* case.[221] First, there is the extent to which the body operates under the authority of the government or was established by the government or, presumably, by some other recognised public authority. Secondly, there is the extent to which a particular function is performed against a background of statutory powers even though there is no specific statutory or prerogative authority for the power which it is sought to review. Both these approaches involve some link between the government, or the legislature, and the body in question. Another element in the *Datafin* case was a reluctance to accept that bodies exercising de facto authority over individuals (which could not be controlled by private law mechanisms of contract or tort) should fall outside the control of the courts. Other approaches to the definition of "public" are also likely to emerge now that the *Datafin* case has broken the link between the origin of the power and the availability of judicial review. One feature that will continue to preclude the availability of judicial review, even after *Datafin*, is the presence of a solely contractual basis for the exercise of the power. The current approach of the courts is to consider whether the body is woven into the fabric of public regulation or governmental control of an activity or is integrated into a system of statutory regulation or, but for its existence, a governmental body would have assumed control over the activity regulated by the body under challenge.[222]

2–080

Government or public authority involvement

The existence of some direct involvement by the government or other public body in the exercise of a function will lead to a greater likelihood of a function being classified as "public." Direct action by the government can take a number

2–081

The panel also had jurisdiction over individuals who were not members of any of the representative bodies or had no contractual relationship with the panel; in that instance at least, the panel had no contractual power.

[220] [1987] Q.B. 815 at 835.

[221] See *R. v Chief Rabbi of the United Hebrew Congregation of Great Britain and the Commonwealth Ex p. Wachman*, [1992] 1 W.L.R. 1036 (no judicial review of decision of the Chief Rabbi as no element of government involvement and no statutory support for decision). *R. v Imam of Bury Park Jame Masjid, Luton Ex p. Sulaiman Ali, Independent*, September 13, 1991 (no judicial review of decision of Imam on who could vote in elections for a mosque's executive committee). See also *R. v The Provincial Court of the Church in Wales Ex p. Williams* [1999] C.O.D. 163 (no judicial review of Church in Wales following disestablishment).

[222] *R. v Association of British Travel Agents Ex p. Sunspell Ltd (t/a as Superlative Travel Ltd)* [2001] A.C.D. 88, following *R. v Insurance Ombudsman Ex p. Aegon Life, The Times*, January 7, 1994.

of forms: the clearest example of governmental involvement is the deliberate creation of a body to perform a certain function. In *R. v Criminal Injuries Compensation Board Ex p. Lain*,[223] for example, the compensation scheme was set up on the initiative of the government with money provided by Parliament. The court described this as an exercise of prerogative power but perhaps a better approach would be to regard the function as "public" because of the degree of governmental involvement in the scheme. Other compensation schemes established by central government in the exercise of common law, rather than prerogative powers, have been regarded as amenable to judicial review.[224] A common technique of government is the creation of a body on a non-statutory basis to advise a minister in the exercise of his own statutory powers. The special panel to advise the minister on the desirability of deporting aliens on national security grounds was one such example.[225] The Home Secretary has also established a non-statutory prison and probation ombudsman to investigate complaints from prisoners and those under the supervision of the probation service and to make recommendations to her and the prison and probation authorities. Such bodies are likely to be public bodies subject to judicial review. Bodies may also be set up by the government to operate on a non-statutory basis pending the enactment of legislation placing the body on a statutory basis. The Home Secretary set up the Broadcasting Standards Council to consider, inter alia, complaints about the level of sex and violence depicted in television.[226] The Council was placed on a statutory basis in 1990.[227] The activities of such bodies are likely to be "public". Following *Datafin*, all such bodies are likely, in principle, to be amenable to judicial review, since they are created by the deliberate act of government and are intended to perform functions properly seen as falling within the responsibility of the State.

2–082   A company which was created by a local authority to carry out functions previously carried out directly by the authority itself (the organising of markets on public land) was subject to judicial review. The company owed its existence to the local authority, it performed the same functions as the local authority had previously performed and the local authority had assisted it, to a certain extent, by providing facilities and finance. A decision of the company excluding an individual from participating in the markets was therefore capable of being subjected to judicial review.[228]

2–083   There may be a lesser degree of involvement or connection between the government, or some other public body, and the body whose decision is under challenge. This lesser degree of involvement will be a relevant, if not conclusive, factor in determining whether the body is performing a "public" function amendable to judicial review. The fact that the government appoints members to a body may be an indication that the body is a "public" body for the purposes of judicial review. In *Datafin*, the court referred to the fact that the chairman and the

---

[223] [1967] 2 Q.B. 864.
[224] *R. (Elias) v Secretary of State for Defence* [2006] 1 W.L.R. 1289 (scheme for making ex gratia payments to former prisoners of war); and see above at para.2–048.
[225] *R. v Secretary of State for Home Affairs Ex p. Hosenball* [1977] 1 W.L.R. 766.
[226] See H.C. Deb., Vol.133, Col.685 (April 16, 1988).
[227] Broadcasting Act 1990 s.151.
[228] *R. (Beer) v Hampshire Farmers' Market* [2004] 1 W.L.R. 233.

deputy chairman of the panel had been appointed by the Governor of the Bank of England as a relevant factor in deciding whether the panel was a public body.[229]

Difficult questions of degree could arise where some members of a particular body are appointed by the government (or other public body), especially if the governmental nominees do not form a majority or do not exert a significant influence over the activities of the body. The use of public funds, as in *Lain*,[230] may be another example of direct government or state involvement in a particular activity, although it may not be a conclusive factor. In one case, it was conceded that decisions of an unincorporated association, funded by central government grant as part of the government's strategy to promote regeneration of deprived areas, to remove members of its board for breach of the association's code of conduct was amenable to judicial review.[231] The extent to which bodies follow ministerial guidance in the discharge of functions may be another relevant factor. The integration of a system of voluntary self-regulation with a system of statutory regulation, together with government participation in the drafting of the codes of practice to be administered by the self-regulating body, provides a further example of government involvement rendering the activities of the self-regulating body public and so amenable to judicial review.[232]

2–084

Active involvement in the activities of a particular body is not, however, essential in making the body "public". There may be a deliberate decision by the government to abstain from action in a particular area precisely because there is an adequate non-governmental body performing the task. This was the case in *Datafin*, where the government took a positive decision not to subject take-overs to legislation but to leave the matter to the Panel.

2–085

A recognition that a particular function is governmental or has become suitable for legislation may be enough to render bodies actually performing that function susceptible to judicial review, even though the bodies are not set up by the government. The government proposed the creation of a statutory licensing authority to license institutions to carry out fertilisation treatment.[233] Pending the enactment of legislation, a voluntary licensing authority was set up by the Medical Research Council and The Royal College of Obstetricians. Given that the function that the voluntary authority performed had been recognised as one that properly belonged to the sphere of government, it was arguable that it be regarded as public and the authority subject to judicial review. In the event, legislation was finally adopted,[234] and the question of the availability of judicial review prior to it being placed on a statutory footing was never determined by the courts.

2–086

Conversely, a body regulating an activity may not be regarded as public where there is no suggestion that the government has deliberately abstained from

2–087

---

[229] The Governor of the Bank of England is a Crown appointment: see Bank of England Act 1998 s.1. Absence of any government appointed member may be a factor pointing against the body being public: see dictum of Sir Thomas Bingham M.R. in *R. v Disciplinary Committee of the Jockey Club Ex p. Aga Khan* [1993] 1 W.L.R. 909 at 923G–H.

[230] [1967] 2 Q.B. 864.

[231] *R. (Oyeyi-Effiong and Campbell) v The Bridge NDC Seven Sisters Partnership Board* [2007] EWHC 606 (Admin).

[232] *R. v Code of Practice Committee of the British Pharmaceutical Industry Ex p. Professional Counselling Aids Ltd* (1990) 10 B.M.L.R. 21.

[233] Human Fertilisation and Embryology; A Framework for Legislation, Cmnd. 259 (1987).

[234] Human Fertilisation and Embryology Act 1990.

regulating the particular activity in favour of the body concerned or where there is no evidence to suggest that the government would consider it appropriate to intervene to regulate the activity if the body actually undertaking the task ceased to do so. Thus, the courts have expressed the view that the fact the government would not seek to regulate the affairs of the Jewish Community,[235] the Football League[236] or horseracing[237] is an indicator that the bodies regulating those affairs are not amenable to judicial review.

2–088   The position in relation to regulation of the press is complex. There is provision, established by Royal Charter on Self-regulation of the Press, for a Recognition Panel to grant recognition of independent bodies established by or on behalf of publishers to regulate their activities. The intention is that the actual regulation of the press, including adjudicating on alleged breaches of a code of standards, will be carried out by the recognised bodies themselves. This structure was intended to ensure a degree of self-regulation on the part of the press whilst ensuring some oversight of the regulators. Decisions of the Recognition Panel are likely to be regarded as public functions and amenable to judicial review. The activities of recognised independent bodies regulating the press are also likely to be regarded as involving public functions amenable to judicial review. Given that recognised independent regulators are woven into, and underpinned by, the system of recognition provided for by royal charter, it is likely that they will be regarded as performing a public function amenable to judicial review. The body previously responsible for dealing with complaints about the press was the Press Complaints Commission, a voluntary, self-regulatory body.[238] The system of recognised independent regulators is said in the preamble to the charter to be intended to replace the Press Complaints Commission. The reviewability of the Press Complaints Commission arose in one case. The court proceeded on the assumption that the body was amenable to judicial review and considered and dismissed the application on the merits.[239] There is no obligation on publishers to become members of a recognised independent body and an alternative structure has been established for those who do not wish to participate in the chartered system. A private legal entity, a community interest company, known as the Independent Press Standards Organisation, has been established. It may contract with publishers of newspapers or magazines. The contract provides for the Organisation to deal with complaints about the printed media and to ensure the

---

[235]   *R. v Chief Rabbi of the United Hebrew Congregation of Great Britain and the Commonwealth Ex p. Wachman* [1992] 1 W.L.R. 1036 at 1041H–1042A; and see *R. v London Beth Din Ex p. Bloom* [1998] C.O.D. 131. Oddly, ecclesiastical courts in the Church of England are subject to judicial review: see below, para.6–013. The Church in Wales is not subject to review because, following disestablishment, it exists as a voluntary organisation whose authority arises from the consensual submission of its members to its jurisdiction with no statutory or governmental function: see *R. v The Provincial Court of the Church in Wales Ex p. Williams* [1999] C.O.D. 163.

[236]   *R. v Football Association Ltd Ex p. Football League Ltd* [1993] 2 All E.R. 833 at 848j.

[237]   *R. v Disciplinary Committee of the Jockey Club Ex p. Aga Khan* [1993] 1 W.L.R. 909, per Farquharson at 930B-C and per Hoffmann LJ at 932B–C; the Master of the Rolls went even further and indicated that, although he was prepared to accept that the government would regulate horseracing if the Jockey Club did not, that still did not make the Jockey Club a public body: at 923F–H.

[238]   This was established in January 1991 following the report by the Calcut Committee which was established by the Home Secretary and which recommended that one last attempt be made at effective self-regulation.

[239]   *R. v Press Complaints Commission Ex p. Stewart-Brady* (1997) 9 Admin. L.R. 274.

maintenance of press standards. It is less clear whether this alternative system of self-regulation by the press would be amenable to judicial review. On the one hand, it performs functions which are similar in nature to those carried out by recognised independent regulators. If the latter are public functions, then, arguably, the former also are public functions amenable to judicial review. Furthermore, ensuring an adequate system of control of press abuses is seen, in part, as a public function. On the other hand, however, the system operates on the basis of contract and those involved will have deliberately opted out of the chartered system. Those factors might be seen as pointing to a purely private law mechanism for dealing with press complaints and consequently as not being amenable to judicial review. Given the recognition that there is a legitimate public interest in the regulation of the press, the preferable view is that even voluntary self-regulating bodies are performing public functions amenable to judicial review.

One final point to note is that the public nature of the function might also be a **2–089** useful peg on which to hang the judicial review jurisdiction of the courts in relation to the activities undertaken directly by the government or other public body even though there is no specific statutory authority for the activities. One obvious example is the issuing by the government of circulars or advice without statutory authority, as in *Gillick v West Norfolk and Wisbech Area Health Authority and the DHSS*.[240] This could be regarded as a public function and therefore susceptible to judicial review. Such an approach would seem preferable to the rather artificial device of treating the power to issue information as an exercise of prerogative power.[241]

Statutory recognition

The presence of a degree of statutory recognition of a body is another indication **2–090** of its "public" nature, albeit that the powers it exercises are not derived from statute. Statutory recognition can arise in a number of ways and a certain amount of litigation is likely to be inevitable in establishing what degree and what form of statutory recognition is likely to lead to classification of the body as public. A non-statutory body may be woven into a system of statutory regulation. The activities of such bodies are likely to be treated as involving the exercise of public functions amenable to judicial review. The Office of the Independent Adjudicator, for example, was established as a company limited by guarantee and appointed adjudicators to review complaints by students against higher education institutions. Statute subsequently provided for the designation of bodies operating such schemes provided that they complied with certain statutory conditions and the Office of the Independent Adjudicator was designated under these provisions.[242] Statute also provided that institutions governed by the scheme had to comply with obligations imposed upon them under the scheme. The Court of Appeal held that the decisions of Office of the Independent Adjudicator were

---

[240] [1986] A.C. 112.
[241] As was held to be the case in *Jenkins v Att-Gen* (1971) 115 S.J. 674. See also paras 2–018 to 2–021.
[242] Higher Education Act 2004 Pt 2.

subject to judicial review.[243] That was clear from the statutory context in which the scheme operated and also the nature of the functions being performed. As to the latter, the purpose of the Act was to create a system for the speedy resolution of student complaints by persons experienced in higher education. The scheme could not be equated with a scheme of arbitration or mediation established by institutions but was intended to perform public functions.[244]

2–091   One important feature is likely to be the extent to which statutory sanctions are used to reinforce the decisions of non-statutory bodies. In *Datafin*, a significant factor was that the statutory powers of the Stock Exchange in relation to the listing of shares provided a means of giving effect to the decisions of the panel since a finding by the panel that a breach of the Code on Take-overs and Mergers had occurred would be a ground for withholding the admission of shares to the Official List.[245] The Advertising Standards Authority provides another example of statutory backing. The Authority is a company limited by guarantee which regulates advertising standards on a voluntary basis. The system now forms part of a wider legal framework operating in accordance with the requirements of European Union law.[246] Complaints of misleading advertising may be investigated by the Authority in the first instance. Failing a satisfactory resolution, the Director-General of Fair Trading has statutory powers to seek an injunction to restrain misleading advertisements. Decisions of the Advertising Standards Authority are subject to judicial review.[247]

2–092   Similarly, independent schools are not generally amenable to judicial review as the relationship between those attending and the school is based on a contract with the parents and there is not sufficient statutory underpinning to render the decisions amenable to judicial review.[248] The decision of an independent school to expel a child was not amenable to judicial review simply because the child had been placed in the school by a local education authority. The power to admit and exclude pupils was derived from the school's trust deed and was not regulated by statute. The relationship between the authority and the school was purely contractual and did not confer any statutory power or impose any statutory duty on the school.[249] Voluntary schools may, however, be amenable to judicial review as their articles of government are made under statute.[250] Similarly, city technology colleges which were maintained under an agreement with the Secretary of State made under express statutory powers were also amenable to

---

[243] *R. (Siborurema) v Office of the Independent Adjudicator* [2008] E.L.R. 209.

[244] [2008] E.L.R. 209 esp. at [49], [69] and [73].

[245] See dicta in *Datafin* [1987] Q.B. 815 at 834 and 852.

[246] Dir. 84/450 [1984] O.J. L250/17 which had been implemented in the UK by the Control of Misleading Advertisements Regulations 1988 (SI 1988/915).

[247] *R. v Advertising Standards Authority Ltd Ex p. The Insurance Service Plc* [1990] C.O.D. 42. See also *R. v Code of Practice Committee of the British Pharmaceutical Industry Ex p. Professional Counselling Aids Ltd*, *The Times*, November 7, 1990.

[248] *R. v Fernhill Manor School Ex p. Brown* (1992) 5 Admin. L.R. 159.

[249] *R. v Muntham House School Ex p. R* [2000] L.G.R. 255 esp. at 263B–F.

[250] *R. v Board of Governors of the London Oratory School Ex p. Regis*, *The Times*, February 17, 1988.

review.[251] Independent schools were also reviewable in respect of decisions on assisted places as these were regulated by statute which defined the admissions criteria and were publicly funded.[252]

Other forms of statutory underpinning may be found. The Institute of Chartered Accountants has been held to be performing public functions because of its important responsibilities under the Companies Act 1989.[253] A regulatory body will not, however, be subject to judicial review where it acquires jurisdiction solely by reason of agreement with its members and where it is not connected with any system of statutory or governmental control.[254] The British Board of Film Censors is a non-statutory body established and financed by the film industry rather than the Government. The Board censors films and the recommendations of the Board are heavily relied on by local authorities in the exercise of their statutory licensing powers. The Court of Appeal has accepted that by virtue of s.3 of the Cinematograph Act 1952, (see now the Licensing Act 2003) the statutory licensing authority can treat the Board as an advisory body on the licensing conditions to be attached to the showing of films, providing the authority retains the final power of decision and does not delegate its responsibilities to the Board.[255] It is likely, given the statutory background, that there could be judicial review of the activities of the Board itself. Similar arrangements apply in relation to video recordings where the Secretary of State may designate a person responsible for determining the classification of video recordings and it is an offence to supply an unclassified video recording.[256] The person designated must have suitable appeal arrangements in place.[257] The British Board of Film Classification has been designated and it appoints an independent video appeals committee to hear appeals against its decision. That committee is subject to judicial review.[258]

2–093

Private bodies discharging functions on behalf of public bodies

A more recent feature of the administrative landscape is the use of contractual arrangements by public bodies to discharge their functions. Legislation may permit a public body either to discharge certain functions itself or may permit the public body to enter into arrangements with a private sector body under which that private body undertakes responsibility for performing the relevant functions.

2–094

---

[251] *R. v The Governors of Haberdashers' Aske Hatcham College Trust Ex p. Tyrell* [1995] E.L.R. 350.

[252] *R. v Cobham Hall School Ex p. S* [1998] E.L.R. 389.

[253] *Andreou v Institute of Chartered Accountants* [1998] 1 All E.R. 14, 19h–j; and see *R. v Institute of Chartered Accountants in England and Wales Ex p. Brindle* [1994] B.C.C. 297.

[254] *R. v Insurance Ombudsman Bureau Ex p. Aegon Life Assurance Ltd* [1995] 1 Lloyd's L.Rep. 101. See also *R. v Lloyds of London Ex p. Briggs* [1993] 1 Lloyd's L. Rep. 176 and *R. (West) v Lloyd's of London* [2004] EWCA Civ 506, judgment of April 27, 2004; *R. v Panel of the Federation of Communication Services Ex p. Kubis* [1998] C.O.D. 5; *R. v Association of British Travel Agents Ltd Ex p. Sunspell Ltd (t/a Superlative Travel)* [2001] A.C.D. 16.

[255] *R. v Greater London Council Ex p. Blackburn* [1976] 1 W.L.R. 550.

[256] Video Recordings Act 1984 s.4 and 9.

[257] Video Recordings Act 1984 s.4(3).

[258] *R. (British Board of Film Classification) v Video Appeals Committee of the British Board of Film Classification* [2008] 1 W.L.R. 1658.

2–095   If a public body discharges functions itself, for example, by providing residential care of the elderly or accommodation for persons in need, the public body is subject to judicial review and will need to comply with the obligations imposed by public law. The public body will also be subject to judicial review in respect of any policy[259] it adopts relating to the use of the power to enter into arrangements with the private sector and, probably, in relation to any specific exercise of the power to enter into such arrangements.

2–096   The real difficulty arises where a public body has entered into arrangement with a private sector body. An individual may wish to challenge the way in which the private sector body is carrying out the discharge of the functions. The issue, then, is whether that private sector body is discharging a public function so that, in respect of that function, judicial review is available and, more importantly, the private body must comply with the substantive principles of public law. The question arose in *R. v Servite Houses Ex p. Goldsmith*.[260] There, a local authority had a statutory duty to provide residential accommodation for the elderly. It had power to enter into arrangements with other providers and did so with a private sector company. The arrangements between the local authority and the private service provider were purely contractual. The residents had no contractual relationship with the service provider. Subsequently, the private service provider terminated the contract with the local authority and wished to cease providing accommodation. The residents alleged that judicial review was available against the private sector provider and, in particular, that they had a public law legitimate expectation that they would be provided with accommodation at the particular home for life. The High Court held that the private sector provider was not amenable to judicial review. Unlike the education cases,[261] the statutory provisions in the present case did not impose any additional statutory obligation on the private sector body. Rather, they merely conferred authority on the public authority to enter into ordinary commercial arrangements with a private sector provider. The private sector provider was not acting as the agent or delegate of the local authority. Consequently, there was no sufficient statutory underpinning, or any other factor, to indicate that the private sector provider was discharging public functions which were amenable to judicial review and in respect of which they were obliged to act in accordance with public law principles. The majority of the House of Lords has reached a similar conclusion in deciding that a private service provider was not a public authority, as it was not discharging public functions, and so was not obliged to comply with the Human Rights Act 1998.[262]

2–097   There will, therefore, be a need for some additional element to make the activities of an ordinary private sector provider sufficiently public before it will be amenable to judicial review in respect of those functions. It is not easy to determine the precise demarcation line between situations which are and which are not public for these purposes. A private sector body will be likely to be discharging public functions, and so be subject to judicial review, where it has, in

---

[259] See, e.g. *R. v Cleveland County Council Ex p. Cleveland Care Homes Association*, *The Times*, November 26, 1993.

[260] [2001] L.G.R. 55. For criticism, see Craig "Contracting Out, the Human Rights Act and the Scope of Judicial Review" (2002) 118 L.Q.R. 551.

[261] See above para.2–085.

[262] *YL v Birmingham City Council* [2008] 1 A.C. 95. The specific decision was reversed by legislation.

fact, been created or established by the public body and simply assumes the responsibilities previously carried out by the public body and continues to receive assistance from the public body. Thus a private company established by a local authority to operate markets which the local authority had itself previously operated and which received finance and other facilities from the local authority was amenable to judicial review.[263] Similarly, a housing association was discharging public functions and it was, therefore, a public authority for some purposes under the Human Rights Act 1998.[264] Although in form a private body it had been created by a local housing authority to take a transfer of the local authority's housing stock. The local authority appointed five of the association's board members and provided guidance in relation to the discharge of its functions. Certain tenants were tenants at the time of the transfer and the association simply assumed the role formerly discharged by the local authority. In those circumstances, the housing association's actions in relation to such tenants were public functions and it was a public authority for those purposes. Similarly, the fixing of fees for residential care homes was done pursuant to a contract between a local authority and a private body. However, the activity was done in the context of the authority's obligations to provide care pursuant to its statutory functions and was governed in part by statutory guidance. In those circumstances, the decision fixing the fees involved the exercise of public functions and was amenable to judicial review.[265] Similarly, the activity of grading students who sat GCSE's by a private company and a charitable body was seen as involving a very significant public interest and as essentially a contracting out of a public function which remained amenable to judicial review.[266]

The problem posed by the contracting-out of services is not an easy one. On the one hand, there is understandable concern that individuals who formerly enjoyed the protection of the substantive principles of public law or the Human Rights Act 1998, may cease to do so because of the privatisation of service provision. There is also concern that some services, at least, because of their very nature should not be provided by bodies immune from some degree of judicial supervision. These concerns can support an argument for extending the scope of judicial review to anybody capable of affecting the rights and interests of individuals.[267] Traditionally, public law has not extended that far. There are arguments that it would not, in general, be reasonable to subject private sector bodies operating in the commercial sector to public law obligations in addition to the private law contractual obligations that they have assumed to the contracting public authority. Furthermore, to do so might well lead to increased costs or a disinclination on the part of private bodies to undertake certain forms of activity. That may be considered undesirable for other reasons.[268]

2–098

---

[263] *R. (Beer) v Hampshire Farmers Market Ltd* [2004] 1 W.L.R. 233.

[264] *Poplar Housing Association v Donoghue* [2002] Q.B. 48. The correctness of this decision was doubted in *YL v Birmingham City Council* [2008] 1 A.C. 95. But see *R. (Weaver) v London and Quadrant Housing Trust* [2008] EWHC 1377 (Admin).

[265] *R. (Bevan & Clarke LLP) v Neath Port Talbot Council* [2012] EWHC 236 (Admin).

[266] *R. (Lewisham Borough Council) v Assessment and Qualifications Alliance* [2013] EWHC 211 (Admin).

[267] See the discussion in *Servite Homes* [2001] L.G.R. 55 at 78–81 and 85.

[268] See the discussion in Craig "Contracting Out, the Human Rights Act and the Scope of Judicial Review" (2002) 118 L.Q.R. 551.

2–099   It may also be the case that there is no one solution to the issues posed by the greater privatisation of service provision. In some instances, it may be that the answer to the problem lies in imposing greater control over public authorities at the time that they first enter into contractual arrangements. In other cases, the solution has been found in creating regulatory bodies to control the private sector providers and to subject the regulator, but not the service providers, to judicial review. There may be some instances where the nature of certain services or the consequences for individuals may be such that the courts will feel obliged to apply some public law principles to control those activities.[269] The running of prisons may be one such example. That approach would, in essence, involve a value judgment on the part of the courts as to what types of activity should be subject to judicial control. In other instances, the fact that services may be provided by private sector bodies which are not subject to public law obligations may simply be a feature of current methods of service delivery. In the absence of some specific reason to subject those service providers to public law supervision, there is nothing objectionable, of itself, in the fact that such private sector providers are not subject to judicial review.[270]

The nature and importance of the function

2–100   There may be instances of de facto power being exercised which affect interests which the courts regard as sufficiently worthy of protection. The courts may then consider that the body should be required to observe the substantive principles of public law and be subject to judicial review, particularly if no other mechanism of judicial control is available.

2–101   Decisions taken by the managers of private psychiatric hospitals who were caring for patients under arrangements made with statutory health authorities were subject to judicial review. The nature of the functions, namely the need to ensure care and treatment for patients, particularly those detained by compulsion under s.3 of the Mental Health Act 1983, were sufficiently public to bring them within the ambit of judicial review.[271] Decisions of local authorities to include individuals on a register of child abusers, to which certain groups had access, are subject to judicial review.[272] Although the operation of the registration system is considered to involve the exercise of non-statutory powers, the de facto consequences for the individual in that the registration could affect his employment prospects or relations with the local authority justified the availability of judicial supervision. Schiemann J. has held that a non-statutory ethical committee of a hospital, set up to provide a forum for discussion and to give advice on ethical issues relating to fertilisation treatment, could be subject to

---

[269] See below at paras 2–100 to 2–102.

[270] That was the view of the majority of the House of Lords in respect of the issue of the applicability of the Human Rights Act 1998 to such private service providers: see *YL v Birmingham City Council* [2008] 1 A.C. 95.

[271] *R. (A) v Partnerships in Care Ltd* [2002] 1 W.L.R. 2610 at [24]–[25].

[272] *R. v Norfolk County Council Ex p. M.* [1989] Q.B. 619. See also *R. v Lewisham London Borough Council Ex p. P.* [1990] 1 W.L.R. 308. But see also *R. v Harrow London Borough Council Ex p. D* [1989] 3 W.L.R. 1239 (recourse to judicial review should be rare due to the informal nature of the process and the paramount need to protect child and preferably reserved for rulings on points of principle).

judicial review in certain circumstances.[273] Schiemann J. even refused to rule out the possibility that decisions of hospital consultants might be subject to judicial review. The performance of regulatory functions by a body is likely to attract judicial supervision, particularly if the body exercises monopolistic powers and takes decisions which may affect the livelihood of individuals and if the public generally has an interest in the way that the body performs its functions.[274] The grading of GCSEs was described as having a very significant public importance and affecting the life chances of the students concerned and was amenable to judicial review.[275]

The question of what powers are important enough to merit judicial supervision, or what constitutes a "public" function, will ultimately depend upon a value judgment of the court. The considerations outlined above may provide a framework for discussion but is unlikely to provide a comprehensive test in all cases. Nor is the definition of public authority in other contexts likely to provide much guidance and certainly will not be conclusive, particularly given the changed modern climate within which judicial review operates. 2–102

The absence of private law mechanisms of control

One of the concerns underlying the *Datafin* case was the belief that the exercise of power affecting important interests of individuals should not be left outside the scope of judicial control. In strict terms, the absence of any private law remedy to control the exercise of such power is not relevant to the question of whether or not a public law remedy is available.[276] In practice, the absence of any clear means of control by private law mechanisms for preventing an abuse of power may influence a court considering whether judicial review ought to be available to control the exercise of power although it is not decisive. In *Datafin*, for example, the court considered that abuses of power by the Panel on Take-overs and Mergers could not be controlled by contract or tort.[277] Given the perceived need to ensure that such power was not abused, the absence of any other remedy probably had some influence in persuading the court that judicial review was available to control the Panel. 2–103

---

[273] *R. v Ethical Committee of St Mary's Hospital Ex p. Harriott* [1988] 1 F.L.R. 512. Schiemann J. did not state which factors indicated that the body was public: two members were appointed by the health authority which is a statutory body; and the framework of the health service, within which the treatment would be given, is largely statutory suggesting that the body could be fitted into the *Datafin* criteria. For criticism see Grubb and Pearl, "Access to IVF Treatment – Professional Judgment or Judicial Control?" [1988] C.L.J. 167.

[274] *R. v Jockey Club Ex p. Massingberd-Mundy* [1993] 2 All E.R. 207.

[275] *R (Lewisham Borough Council) v Assessment and Qualifications Alliance* [2013] EWHC 211 (Admin).

[276] *R. v Code of Practice Committee of the British Pharmaceutical Industry Ex p. Professional Counselling Aids Ltd* (see above, fn.247); *R. v Royal Life Saving Society Ex p. Howe* [1990] C.O.D. 440.

[277] See *Datafin* [1987] Q.B. 815 at 839. See also dicta of the Master of the Rolls in *R. v Disciplinary Committee of the Jockey Club Ex p. Aga Khan* [1993] 1 W.L.R. 909 at 924C–E and see dicta in *R. (Tucker) v Director-General of The National Crime Squad* [2003] I.C.R. 599 at 606 at [18].

Common law powers of certain bodies

2–104   There are other non-statutory powers—some classified as common law powers—which are recognised as subject to judicial review. Some of these have long been recognised as subject to control by the prerogative writs and would now be subject to judicial review. Although these were treated as anomalies in the past, they can now be generalised as examples of "public functions" amenable to judicial review.

2–105   Judicial review is available to supervise the non-statutory duties and discretionary powers of the police. The courts have held that chief constables have a legal duty to enforce the law, and mandamus is available to enforce that legal duty, as they are public officers performing public duties.[278] The courts will control unlawful policy decisions of chief constables, such as a decision not to enforce certain laws,[279] and have been prepared to determine whether the police have certain legal powers[280] or whether action they have taken was lawful, as where the House of Lords considered whether intercepting coaches and sending them back to London and away from an anticipated demonstration was lawful.[281] The courts are prepared to consider whether the exercise of powers by the police infringe an individual's rights under the European Convention on Human Rights, although they have emphasised that they would not readily interfere with the authorities' assessment in the absence of clear evidence of a breach.[282] The courts have also been reluctant to grant a remedy ordering the police to take particular action in particular cases.[283] The courts have also held that the statutory powers of arrest exercised by constables confer an executive discretion subject to judicial review on normal public law principles.[284] The police also have common law powers of arrest or to take steps necessary to prevent a breach of the peace[285] and these, too, are subject to judicial review.[286]

2–106   A public body has a common law power to exclude members of the public from a meeting where it reasonably appears that there might be disruption which would prevent the public body from transacting business. Judicial review is available to control the exercise of this power.[287] A councillor has a common law right, enforceable by mandamus, of access to documents of the council if he can establish that access is reasonably necessary to enable him to perform his

---

[278]   *R. v Commissioner of Police of the Metropolis Ex p. Blackburn* [1968] 2 Q.B. 118.

[279]   [1968] 2 Q.B. 118.

[280]   *R. v Chief Constable of Devon and Cornwall Ex p. Central Electricity Generating Board* [1982] Q.B. 458.

[281]   *R. (Laporte) v Chief Constable of Gloucestershire* [2007] 2 A.C. 105.

[282]   *R. (Gillan) v Commissioner of Metropolitan Police* [2006] 2 W.L.R. 537 (dealing with statutory powers of the police in relation to terrorism but similar principles apply to the common law powers of the police).

[283]   *R. Chief Constable of Devon and Cornwall Ex p. Central Electricity Generating Board* [1982] Q.B. 458.

[284]   *Mohammed-Holgate v Duke* [1984] A.C. 437.

[285]   *Albert v Lavin* [1982] A.C. 546.

[286]   *R. (Laporte) v Chief Constable of Gloucestershire Constabulary* [2007] 2 A.C. 105. The House of Lords in *Mohammed-Holgate v Duke* [1984] A.C. 437 restricted their judgment to statutory powers and had left the point open. Individual citizens possess similar statutory and common law powers of arrest; see Police and Criminal Evidence Act 1984 s.24, and *Albert v Lavin*, above. It is an interesting point as to whether the exercise of such powers by a citizen would be subject to judicial review.

[287]   *R. v Brent Health Authority Ex p. Francis* [1985] Q.B. 869.

duties.[288] The decision as to whether a councillor has good reason for access is primarily a matter for the council but that decision of the council is subject to judicial review.[289] The power of ministers to delegate decision-making powers has been classed as a "common law constitutional power" and is subject to judicial review.[290]

D. MISCELLANEOUS BODIES

Chartered corporations

Bodies may be created by Royal Charter granted under the prerogative. A Royal Charter grants corporate capacity on a body, and consequently confers all the powers of a natural person on the chartered body. A chartered corporation has not traditionally been subject to the ultra vires rule as the charter does not grant limited statutory power on the body, but simply grants corporate capacity. Actions inconsistent with the charter have not in the past been regarded as void but bind the chartered corporation.[291] However, action by the chartered corporation which was inconsistent with the terms of the charter was a ground for proceeding by way of *scire facias* to have the charter repealed.[292] More importantly in practical terms, a member of the corporation could seek an injunction to restrain the chartered body from doing an act which could lead to the revocation of a charter.[293] The question now arises as to whether the activities of chartered bodies are subject to control by judicial review to ensure that they do not act inconsistently with their charter, and whether the substantive principles of public law might also apply to the exercise of powers derived from the charter.

2–107

The Court of Appeal has held that powers derived from a charter cannot be regarded as derived from the prerogative, notwithstanding the fact that the charter is itself granted by the prerogative.[294] Thus, chartered bodies cannot automatically be classed as public bodies by applying the "source of power" test. The Court of Appeal, however, has indicated, *obiter*, that relief by way of judicial review is available to restrain a chartered corporation from carrying out unauthorised acts.[295] An earlier case[296] also held that the prerogative remedies lay

2–108

---

[288] *R. v Barnes Borough Council Ex p. Conlon* [1938] 3 All E.R. 226.

[289] *R. v Birmingham City District Council Ex p. O.* [1983] 1 A.C. 578; *R. v Lancashire County Council Police Committee Ex p. Hook* [1980] Q.B. 603.

[290] *R. v Secretary of State for the Home Department Ex p. Oladehinde; R. v Secretary of State for the Home Department Ex p. Alexander* [1990] 2 W.L.R. 1195. (Decision affd. by the House of Lords, [1990] 3 W.L.R. 797 although the precise basis of power to devolve was not specifically considered).

[291] *Sutton's Hospital Case* (1612) 10 Co.Rep. 1. This decision was described as "largely incomprensible in 1990" but was not overruled by the House of Lords in *Hazell v Hammersmith and Fulham London Borough Council* [1992] 2 A.C. 1 at 39F. See generally *Halsbury's Laws of England*, 4th edn (1974), Vol.9, [1332].

[292] *Jenkin v Pharmaceutical Society of Great Britain* [1921] 1 Ch. 392.

[293] [1921] 1 Ch. 392.

[294] *R. v Disciplinary Committee of the Jockey Club Ex p. Aga Khan* [1993] 1 W.L.R. 909. See also the dicta of Lord Diplock in *Swain v The Law Society* [1983] A.C. 598 suggesting that powers derived from a charter are not public law powers.

[295] *Hazell v Hammersmith and Fulham London Borough Council* [1990] 2 Q.B. 697 at 770D–771H. The House of Lords decided the case on other grounds: see above, fn.29. See also the dicta of Farquharson LJ *Ex p. Aga Khan*, fn.294 above at 930E–G.

against a chartered university, but this decision has been doubted on the grounds that the university acquired its disciplinary jurisdiction over students by virtue of contract.[297]

2–109   Even if chartered corporations are not automatically classed as public bodies, it is possible that for certain purposes they may be regarded as performing a public function, and therefore amenable to judicial review in respect of those functions. The fact that a body is acting under a charter may be a relevant factor in establishing that the body is performing a public function,[298] but it is unlikely to be a factor of much significance.[299]

2–110   Statute may specifically authorise the grant of a Royal Charter. The extent of the chartered body's powers then depend upon the true construction and intent of the statute.[300] In particular, it is a question of statutory construction as to whether the corporation is essentially a statutory corporation able to act only within the scope of its statutory powers and subject to the ultra vires principle or whether the corporation has all the powers of a corporation at common law to act as a natural person.[301] Thus, the House of Lords has held that, where statute authorised the incorporation of London boroughs by Royal Charter, it was intended that such boroughs would be statutory corporations and would only be entitled to exercise those powers expressly or impliedly conferred upon them by statute.[302] Statute did not authorise the boroughs to enter into a particular type of financial transaction and the transactions were therefore ultra vires and unlawful. The boroughs could not claim that they were chartered corporations and possessed all the powers of a natural person including the power to enter into such financial transactions. Judicial review would be available to restrain a corporation from acting ultra vires its statutory powers.

2–111   Statute may, on occasion, confer additional statutory powers on a body. Judicial review is available in respect of the exercise of these specific statutory powers applying the source of power test. Thus, the Law Society formerly had statutory powers in the field of legal aid, and these were subject to review.[303] Professional bodies set up by charter may have statutory disciplinary powers conferred upon them, and such powers are reviewable.[304] Conversely, a chartered body may acquire jurisdiction over individuals by way of contract. Judicial review would not be available in respect of decisions deriving from the exercise of the contractual jurisdiction of such a body. Thus, judicial review is not available in respect of disciplinary decisions taken by chartered corporations who acquire their disciplinary jurisdiction over their employees by contract.[305]

---

[296]   *R. v Aston University Senate Ex p. Roffey* [1969] 2 Q.B. 538.

[297]   *Herring v Templeman* [1973] 3 All E.R. 569. But see paras 2–116 to 2–117.

[298]   See judgment of Roch J. in *R. v Jockey Club Ex p. Massingberd-Mundy* [1993] 2 All E.R. 207.

[299]   *R. v Royal Life Saving Society Ex p. Howe* [1990] C.O.D. 440.

[300]   *Hazell v Hammersmith and Fulham London Borough Council* [1992] 2 A.C. 1.

[301]   [1992] 2 A.C. 1 and *Bonanza Creek Gold Mining Co. Ltd v The King* [1916] A.C. 566 at 577.

[302]   *Hazell v Hammersmith and Fulham London Borough Council* (see above, fn.300).

[303]   See, e.g. *R. v Law Society Ex p. Gates, The Times,* March 31, 1988.

[304]   See, e.g. *R. v General Medical Council Ex p. Gee* [1987] 1 W.L.R. 564; *R. v Statutory Committee of the Pharmaceutical Society of Great Britain Ex p. Pharmaceutical Society of Great Britain* [1981] 1 W.L.R. 886; *R. v University of Liverpool Ex p. Caesar-Gordon* [1991] 1 Q.B. 124 (statutory duty imposed on chartered universities and colleges, to ensure freedom of speech, enforceable by judicial review).

[305]   *R. v British Broadcasting Corp. Ex p. Lavelle* [1983] 1 W.L.R. 23.

The British Broadcasting Corporation

One of the most significant chartered corporations is the British Broadcasting **2–112** Corporation. The BBC was created by Royal Charter and operates under the terms of the Charter and an agreement made between it and the Government.[306] The precise status and method of judicial control of the activities of the BBC is a matter of doubt. The present charter sets out the structure of government for the BBC but there are relatively few specific duties imposed on the BBC which are likely to give rise to dispute, although some, such as the provisions for the removal of members of the BBC Trust, could conceivably do so. There is a possibility that the courts could hold that the charter imposed implied duties on the BBC, the most obvious candidate being a duty of impartiality. The courts in Northern Ireland have, however, held that there is no such duty of impartiality in the charter, and have refused to accept that a voluntary policy of impartiality gave rise to a legally enforceable duty of impartiality.[307] At that stage, however, neither the charter nor the agreement included any specific obligation on the BBC to act impartially. The current agreement does impose such an obligation and it is likely that *Lynch* will either be distinguished or not followed.[308] There is also the possibility that claims could be made that the BBC was acting in a way that failed to conform with the objects set out in the charter, or that the BBC was acting contrary to its declared policies. In any event, there are strong arguments that if regulatory functions are to be imposed on the BBC, then such functions are inherently public and similar in kind to the express statutory duties imposed on the regulatory authorities in respect of independent television.[309] The present Charter contemplates that judicial review is available in relation to the exercise of functions under the Charter and the agreement as it notes that the courts may have an appropriate role in exercising judicial review.

The position in relation to the agreement under which the BBC operates is **2–113** more complex. Two separate questions arise. First, there is the question of which remedies are available against the Secretary of State when he takes action under the terms of the agreement. Secondly, there is the question of which remedies are available against the BBC if it fails to conform with the duties imposed by the agreement; such as the duty to provide party political and referendum broadcasts and not to broadcast its own opinion on political matters, or to treat controversial subjects with due accuracy and impartiality. In *R. v Secretary of State for the Home Department Ex p. Brind*,[310] journalists sought judicial review of a direction issued by the Home Secretary under both cl.13(4) of a previous agreement between the BBC and the Secretary of State and virtually identical statutory powers under s.29(3) of the Broadcasting Act 1981 in relation to independent television. The direction prohibited the broadcasting of spoken words by members of banned organisations. The House of Lords and the courts below

---

[306] The BBC is not a Crown Servant and cannot take advantage of the rule that legislation does not bind the Crown unless it expressly or impliedly applies to the Crown: *British Broadcasting Corp v Johns* [1965] Ch. 32 (BBC not exempt from taxation). This is not conclusive on the different question of whether the BBC may be subject to judicial review.

[307] *Lynch v British Broadcasting Corp.* [1983] N.I.J.B. 193.

[308] *R. v British Broadcasting Corp. Ex p. Referendum Party* (1997) 9 Admin. L.R. 553 at 569–571.

[309] See now the duties imposed by the Broadcasting Act 1996.

[310] [1991] 1 A.C. 696.

considered the claim on its merits and dismissed the application as the direction was not unlawful. The arguments were concentrated essentially on the legality of the exercise of statutory powers in relation to the I.B.A. and the specific position of the BBC was not considered.[311] Given that one direction had been issued under both the licence and the statute, it would have been odd if different principles applied to each. It would certainly be absurd if judicial review were available in respect of independent producers but not the BBC.

2–114   So far as remedies against the BBC itself is concerned, *Brind* is not directly relevant. There must be a strong argument, however, that just as the powers exercisable by the Secretary of State under the agreement are subject to judicial review so too are the powers exercisable by the BBC. Further, in so far as the powers and duties under the agreement are similar to those imposed by statute on the body that regulates independent broadcasting (which are treated as a matter of public law[312]), the enforcement of the obligations or supervision of the powers contained in the licence should also be seen as a matter of public law. The matter has come before the courts on a number of occasions. The fullest discussion came in *R. v British Broadcasting Corporation Ex p. Referendum Party*,[313] where a political party sought judicial review of the allocation of time for party political broadcasts during a general election, contending that the allocation breached the agreement which provided that the BBC was to treat matters of political controversy with due accuracy and impartiality. The Divisional Court observed that the BBC and the statutory Independent Television Commission were exercising almost identical public duties, that the function was a public function of great importance and that it was possible that the obligation included in the agreement could be regarded as governmental as it reflected the government's policy on an issue of public concern. The Divisional Court, however, did not finally resolve the question of whether the BBC was susceptible to judicial review and left the question to be resolved on another occasion. In *R. (ProLife Alliance Ltd) v British Broadcasting Corporation*,[314] the BBC refused to transmit an election broadcast which they considered offended good taste and decency. The agreement between the BBC and the Secretary of State imposed an obligation on the BBC to do all it could to ensure that broadcasts did not contain such material. Similar obligations were imposed by statute on the independent television companies.[315] It was accepted, without argument, that the decision of the BBC was amenable to judicial review.[316]

2–115   The alternative, but unlikely, possibility is that the agreement simply constitutes a contract between the Secretary of State and the BBC governed by the private law of contract, and as such falls outside the ambit of judicial review. The Secretary of State (but not interested individuals) might be able to seek

---

[311] See, however, the judgment of Lord Ackner [1991] 1 A.C. 696 at 754H, where he referred to "the contractual powers of the Secretary of State".

[312] *R. v Independent Broadcasting Authority Ex p. Whitehouse*, *The Times*, April 4, 1985. But not all its decisions are statutory: see *R. v Independent Broadcasting Authority Ex p. Rank Organisation*, *The Times*, March 14, 1986 discussed above at para.2–074.

[313] (1997) 9 Admin. L.R. 553.

[314] [2003] 2 W.L.R. 1403.

[315] See now Communications Act 2003.

[316] See in the Court of Appeal [2002] 3 W.L.R. 1080 at 1083 [3]. There was no suggestion in the House of Lords that the BBC was not subject to judicial review in respect of such decisions: see [2003] 3 W.L.R. 1040.

contractual remedies against the BBC, such as an injunction to restrain action inconsistent with the agreement. Ofcom also has certain regulatory functions, including the power to require payment of a penalty for breach of certain provisions of the agreement.[317] There is also the possibility that some of the provisions of the agreement are not justiciable and the only "remedy" for breach might be the exercise by the Secretary of State of any implied power to terminate the agreement that he may have.[318]

Universities and colleges

A small number of universities have been created or recognised by statute.[319] The exercise of statutory powers by these universities are amenable to judicial review.[320] The majority of the older universities, and the Oxford and Cambridge colleges, are chartered bodies.[321] The courts have held in the context of non-chartered universities that a student both has a contract with the university and is able to seek judicial review to ensure that that a university acts in accordance with its own rules and regulations.[322] A similar conclusion is likely to be reached in relation to chartered universities. In one case,[323] the Court of Appeal did assume that an order for certiorari (now a quashing order) was available to control the actions of a chartered university which sought to exclude a student from continuing his studies at the institution although the point was not argued. In any event, the courts will normally, as a matter of discretion, require students to use the complaints machinery set up under the auspices of the Higher Education 2004 Act before seeking judicial review of decisions of higher education institutions.[324]

2–116

---

[317] See clause 94 of the July 2006 agreement between the BBC and the Secretary of State for Culture, Media and Sport Cm 6872 and s.198 of the Communications Act 2003.

[318] This point was expressly left open in *Lynch v British Broadcasting Corp* [1983] N.I.J.B. 193.

[319] See, e.g. the Universities of Oxford of Cambridge (as opposed to the individual colleges which were created by royal charter); see Oxford and Cambridge Act 1571; the University of London, see University of London Act 1978 and the University of Newcastle-upon-Tyne: see Universities of Durham and Newcastle-Upon-Tyne Act 1863. See generally, D.J. Christie, "The Power to Award Degrees" [1976] P.L. 358.

[320] See, e.g. *R. v University of Cambridge Ex p. Persaud* [2001] E.L.R. 480 (postgraduate student challenging the refusal of a degree); *R. (Galligan) v University of Oxford* [2002] E.L.R. 494 (exercise by Vice-Chancellor of power to appoint an inquiry amenable to judicial review). Matters governed by a member of staff's contract of employment are not amenable to judicial review; see *Evans v University of Cambridge* [2003] E.L.R. 8.

[321] Formerly, chartered institutions had a Visitor whose jurisdiction was exclusive and ousted that of the courts: see *Thomas v Bradford University* [1987] A.C. 795; *R. (Hull University Visitor Ex p. Page* [1993] A.C. 682 and *R. v Her Majesty in Council Ex p. Vijaytunga* [1988] Q.B. 322. That jurisdiction was abolished by s.20 of the Higher Education Act 2004 and is now of historic interest only in relation to student complaints.

[322] *Clark v University of Lincolnshire and Humberside* [2000] 1 W.L.R. 1988.

[323] *R. v Aston University Ex p. Roffey* [1969] 2 Q.B. 538.

[324] See, e.g. *R. (Carnell) v Regents Park College and Conference of Colleges Appeal Tribunal* [2008] E.L.R. 798; *R. (Peng Hu Shi) v King's College London* [2008] A.C.D. 177. The relevant scheme is operated by the Office of the Independent Adjudicator whose decisions are amenable to judicial review: see *R. (Siborurema) v Office of the Independent Adjudicator)*[2008] E.L.R. 209 and see para.2–090 above. The time taken in bringing a complaint to the OIA may also justify an extension of time for bringing a judicial claim against the university after the expiry of the normal time limits.

2–117   More recently, institutions of higher education have also gained university status but by a different route. Higher education corporations will normally have been incorporated and designated as eligible to receive higher education funding by the exercise of powers conferred by statute.[325] They will be carried on in accordance with instruments and articles of government made pursuant to statute.[326] Some institutions may, in fact, be companies (usually companies limited by guarantee). They too may be designated as eligible to receive higher education funding and they will be required to make instruments and articles of government.[327] The Privy Council may, by order, specify that an institution of higher education may award degrees or diplomas and may, with its approval, use the word "university" in their title.[328] The courts have recognised that new universities are statutory bodies with public law functions and are amenable to judicial review. A student seeking to challenge the validity of decision of such a university may challenge that decision by way of judicial review.[329] In addition, students usually have a contract of membership with the university and, in appropriate cases, and proceedings may be brought by way of an ordinary claim for breach of contract.[330] In such cases, therefore, the student has both public law rights enforceable by way of judicial review and private law rights arising out the contract of membership.[331] Challenges alleging that a decision of a university is flawed because it has not interpreted its statutes or regulations correctly or has failed to follow its procedures properly or has failed to act fairly would more appropriately be brought by way of judicial review than a contractual claim.[332] However, the courts will normally require the student to use the alternative complaints procedure operated by the Office of the Independent Adjudicator under the Higher Education Act 2004 before seeking judicial review.[333] Claims that a university has failed to comply with an agreement to offer a place to a student[334] or has provided inadequate tuition[335] are, in essence, claims arising in private law and are more appropriately brought by ordinary claim.

---

[325] Education Reform Act 1988 ss.121, 124 and 129.

[326] Education Reform Act 1988 ss.124 and 129A.

[327] Education Reform Act 1988 ss.129 and 129B.

[328] The Further and Higher Education Act 1992 ss.76 and 79.

[329] See *Clark v University of Lincolnshire and Humberside* [2001] 1 W.L.R. 1988 at [15] per Sedley LJ and at [29] per Lord Woolf M.R.

[330] [2001] 1 W.L.R. 1988 at [12] per Sedley LJ and at [38] per Lord Woolf MR.

[331] See generally, McManus, *Education and the Courts*, 3rd edn. (Bristol: Jordans, 2012), Ch.8; Lewis, "The Legal Nature of a University and the Student-University Relationship" [1983] Ottawa Law Review 249.

[332] See, e.g. *R. v Liverpool John Moores University Ex p. Hayes* [1998] E.L.R. 261: *R. v Manchester Metropolitan University Ex p. Nolan* [1994] E.L.R. 380; *R. v Board of Governors of the Sheffield Hallam University* [1995] E.L.R. 267; *R. v University of Central England Ex p. Iqbal Sandhu* [1999] E.L.R. 121.

[333] *R. (Carnell) v Regents Park College and Conference of Colleges Appeal Tribunal* [2008] E.L.R. 798. The decision of the OIA is subject to judicial review: *R. (Siborurema) v Office of the Independent Adjudicator)* [2008] E.L.R. 209 and see para.2–090 above.

[334] See, e.g. *Moran v University College Salford University (No.2)* [1994] E.L.R. 187.

[335] See, e.g. *Sammy v Birkbeck College, The Times,* November 3, 1964 (affd. *The Times,* May 20, 1965); *D'Mello v Loughborough College of Technology, The Times,* June 17, 1970. The circumstances in which the courts will find that there has been such a failure are likely to be rare. The courts are particularly unlikely to want to determine whether a student would have graduated if proper tuition had been provided; if there were a successful claim, damages would be likely to involve recovery of fees and possible wasted expenses during the currency of the course, not damages for future loss.

The position in relation to academic staff is more complex. The question of whether a university lecturer has only a contract of employment enforceable by ordinary private law remedies, or whether he also has a status protected by public law has never finally been decided by the courts.[336] The better view is that the relationship is governed by contract in any event and does not give rise to public law rights capable of enforcement by way of judicial review.[337] At common law, the exclusive jurisdiction of the Visitor applied to academic staff and excluded the jurisdiction of the courts so far as both judicial review and contract were concerned but did not exclude jurisdiction in respect of statutory rights arising under the employment protection legislation.[338] The Education Reform Act 1988 empowers University Commissioners to modify university and college statutes in order to provide for appeal procedures in respect of dismissal of academic staff.[339] Once the University Commissioners made new statutes for a university or college providing for an appeals procedure in respect of academic employment, the Visitor ceased to have jurisdiction in such matters.[340] The precise status of the disciplinary process and the appeal tribunal remains uncertain.[341] The disciplinary procedures may be regarded as incorporated into the contract of employment of academic staff and be enforceable by way of an ordinary contractual action.[342] It may be that the disciplinary rules will be seen as deriving from the Education Reform Act 1988, or from the exercise by the University Commissioners of their statutory powers to modify the university or college statutes. If so, they may have a sufficient statutory under-pinning to make any action taken under the rules a matter of public law thereby rendering the action susceptible to judicial review.

2–118

The Inns of Court

The decisions of judges, sitting as Visitors to the Inns of Court, are subject to judicial review. These decisions include hearing appeals from the disciplinary tribunal which adjudicates on allegations of professional misconduct by barristers.[343] The precise origin of the visitatorial jurisdiction is unclear. The Inns of Court are not corporations nor are they founded by royal charter. Rather they are seen as voluntary societies which, in fact, exercise disciplinary control over their members. The judges sit as Visitors, controlling the affairs of the Society and, in that capacity, hear appeals against disciplinary decisions of the Inns, such

2–119

---

[336] The Privy Council, in *University Council of the Vidyodaya University of Ceylon v Silva* [1965] 1 W.L.R. 77, held that a lecturer was an employee only. In *Thomas v Bradford University* [1987] A.C. 795 the claim was framed in contract, but it was assumed that a lecturer also had a coterminous status.
[337] *Evans v University of Cambridge* [2003] E.L.R. 8.
[338] *Thomas v Bradford University* (see above, fn.321).
[339] Education Reform Act 1988 ss.203, 204.
[340] Education Reform Act 1988 s.206(1). In the transitional period prior to the making of new statutes, the Court of Appeal held that the university or the member of staff could still refer a matter to the Visitor and, at that stage, the Visitor's jurisdiction would then oust the jurisdiction of the courts: see *Pearce v University of Aston in Birmingham (No.1)* [1991] 2 All E.R. 461 and see *Hines v Birbeck College (No.2)* [1992] Ch.33.This issue is now of historic interest only.
[341] Education Reform Act 1988 s.206(3).
[342] By analogy with *R. v East Berkshire Health Authority Ex p. Walsh* [1985] Q.B. 152, and see para.2–135.
[343] *R. v Visitors to the Inns of Court Ex p. Calder* [1994] Q.B. 1.

as a decision barring a person from being a barrister.[344] As such, the judges, sitting as Visitors, are amenable to judicial review in respect of their decisions. The scope of judicial review is at present restricted in respect of these visitatorial decisions. [345] The courts will consider whether the judges as Visitors exceeded their jurisdiction or acted in breach of the rules of natural justice or abused their powers or whether the Visitors have failed to comply with any statutory requirement governing their appointment as Visitors[346]; they will not intervene in respect of decisions on the construction and application of the law applicable to these disciplinary issues. The initial disciplinary stage in relation to complaints against barristers was formerly carried out by the Professional Conduct Committee of the Bar which investigated complaints and determined whether to prefer a charge of professional misconduct to a disciplinary tribunal. The Divisional Court has held that the decision of that Committee on whether or not to prefer disciplinary charges was subject to judicial review.[347] The Divisional Court held that the visitatorial jurisdiction over disciplinary decisions did not oust the judicial review jurisdiction over the actions of the Committee.[348]

Parliament

2–120 The courts will not engage in judicial review of the internal workings of either House of Parliament.[349] Thus the courts will not engage in judicial review if that would involve considering whether the internal procedures of Parliament were properly followed in enacting legislation[350] or whether a bill should be introduced before Parliament.[351] The courts will not consider matters relating to membership

---

[344] See *In re S* [1970] 1 Q.B. 160; *R v Council of Legal Education ex p. Eddis* (1994) 7 Admin. L.R. 357. Disciplinary powers over barristers are presently vested in the Council of the Inns of Courts with provision for appeals to the judges as Visitors: see *Russell v Bar Standards Board* judgment of the Visitors of 12 July 2012. The Visitors are to act as an appellate court, and should not normally limit their jurisdiction to a purely supervisory role: *R. v Visitors to the Inns of Court Ex p. Calder* [1994] 1 Q.B. 1.

[345] *R. v Visitors for the Inns of Court Ex p. Calder* [1994] 1Q.B. 1 applying the decision of the House of Lords in *R. v Hull University Visitor Ex p. Page* [1993] A.C. 682 (judicial review of the decisions of the Visitor to a University was restricted).

[346] *R. (Leathley, Mehey and Hayes) v Visitors to the Inns of Court and the Bar Standards Board* [2013] EWHC 3097 (Admin).

[347] *R. v General Council of the Bar Ex p. Percival* [1991] 1 Q.B. 212.

[348] [1991] 1 Q.B. 212 at 228G to 229B.

[349] *Bradlaugh v Gossett* (1884) 12 Q.B.D. 271. *R. (Wheeler) v Office of the Prime Minister and Secretary of State for Foreign and Commonwealth Affairs* [2008] EWHC 1409 (Admin) at [49]–[51], discussed below, para.7–046 and *R v Chaytor* [2011] 1 A.C. 684 at paras [76]–[77].

[350] *British Railways Board v Pickin* [1974] A.C. 765. The Supreme Court has left open the question of whether this principle would be abrogated by the requirement to ensure supremacy of EU law, or whether the provisions of the European Communities Act 1972 are themselves subject to the need to protect fundamental constitutional principles, such as the principle, enshrined in Art.9 of the Bill of Rights Act 1969, that the courts will not review internal proceedings in Parliament. In the event, the Supreme Court held that that the relevant provisions of EU law, properly construed, did not require the national courts to review the adequacy of internal proceedings in the legislature: see *R. (Buckinghamshire County Council and others) v Secretary of State for Transport* [2014] 1 W.L.R. 324 at [202]–[211]. See below at 4-066.

[351] *R (Wheeler) v Office of the Prime Minister and the Secretary of State for Foreign and Commonwealth Affairs* [2008] EWHC 1409 (Admin).

or other internal matters of either House.[352] Nor will the courts review the Parliamentary Commissioner for Standards. He is an officer appointed by the House of Commons under their standing orders to investigate complaints about the conduct of members of Parliament and report to the House of Commons Select Committee on Standards and Privileges. He was one of the means by which the Select Committee carried out its functions. His activities were, therefore, connected with proceedings in Parliament and were not subject to judicial review.[353]

Charities

Certain charities may be public bodies performing public functions. The National   2–121
Trust is arguably such a body given that it has been created and is regulated by statute and performs functions of public importance.[354] Charity proceedings are governed by the Charities Act 1993. Charity proceedings are proceedings brought under the court's jurisdiction with respect to charities or the administration of a charitable trust.[355] Such proceedings may be brought by the charity trustees or any person interested in a charity, that is any person with a greater interest in the administration of the charity than an ordinary member of the public.[356] Section 33(2) of the Charities Act 1993 provides, however, that charity proceedings may only be brought with the consent of the Charity Commissioners or, if that is refused, with the consent of a judge of the Chancery Division. The courts will normally require proceedings seeking to challenge the actions of charities, even if they are public bodies, to be brought by way of an ordinary claim in the Chancery Division, rather than by way of judicial review.[357] There may be cases where it is appropriate to proceed by way of judicial review, providing that the charity is a public body,[358] for example if a person had sufficient interest for the purposes of judicial review but not for the purpose of bringing charity proceedings.[359] Such proceedings might still fall within the definition of charity proceedings,

---

[352] See, e.g. *Baron Mereworth v Ministry of Justice* [2012] 2 W.L.R. 192 and *Bradlaugh v Gossett* (1884) 12 QBD 27. The criminal courts will consider whether actions relating to the administration of Parliament, such as the making of allegedly fraudulent expenses claims, give rise to a criminal offence even though judicial review would not be available to review such matters: *R. v Chaytor* [2011] 1 A.C. 684.

[353] *R. v Parliamentary Commissioner for Standards Ex p. Al Fayed* (1998) 10 Admin. L.Rep. 69; and see *R. v Chaytor* [2011] 1 A.C. 684 at [74]–[78].

[354] *Scott v National Trust for Places of Historic Interest or Natural Beauty* [1998] 2 All E.R. 705 at 716f–h; *Ex p. Scott* [1998] 1 W.L.R. 226.

[355] Charities Act 1993 s.33(8).

[356] See Charities Act 1993 s.33(1) and see generally, *Re Hampton Fuel Allotment Charity* [1989] Ch.484 and *RSPCA v Att-Gen* [2002] 1 W.L.R. 448.

[357] *Scott v National Trust for Places of Historic Interest or Natural Beauty* [1998] 2 All E.R. 705.

[358] Not all charities are public bodies amenable to judicial review. While the National Trust is probably a public body (see *Scott v National Trust for Places of Historic Interest or Beauty* [1998] 2 All E.R. 705), the RSPCA was not: see *RSPCA v Att-Gen* [2002] 1 W.L.R. 448. The Leonard Cheshire Foundation is not a public authority for the purposes of the Human Rights Act 1998 and is unlikely to be a public body for the purposes of judicial review: see *R. (Heather) v Leonard Cheshire Foundation* [2002] 2 All E.R. 936.

[359] See *RSPCA v Att-Gen* [2002] 1 W.L.R. 448.

depending on the circumstances, so that the permission of the Charity Commissioners or a judge sitting in the Chancery Division would be required to institute the claim for judicial review.[360]

Superior courts

2–122 Judicial review is not available against certain of the superior courts.[361] These include the Supreme Court. The Court of Appeal and the High Court form part of the senior courts,[362] and decisions of these courts are not amenable to judicial review.[363] It is only the decisions taken in the exercise of their jurisdiction as superior courts that are immune from judicial review. Thus, where a judge or other officer of the court is not acting as a superior court but is exercising some other statutory function, judicial review will be available in respect of a decision taken in the exercise of those statutory powers. A decision of the Master of the Rolls exercising statutory powers to hear appeals from decisions of the solicitors' disciplinary tribunal may be challenged by way of judicial review.[364] The decision of a taxing master assessing costs under the Legal Aid Regulations has similarly been held to be reviewable.[365] The statutory designation of a court or tribunal as a superior court of record is not, however, sufficient of itself to render such a court or tribunal immune from judicial review. Thus, the Upper Tribunal, which hears appeals from the First-tier Tribunal, is designated as a superior court of record[366] but is still subject to judicial review in respect of decision taken in the exercise of its appellate functions.[367] Judicial review will generally be refused as a matter of discretion where there is a possibility of appealing a decision to the Court of Appeal. Judicial review will only be granted in respect of an unappealable decision, such as a decision refusing permission to appeal to the Upper Tribunal, if the case raises an important point of law or there is some other compelling reason for allowing a claim for judicial review.[368] In principle, it is possible that other courts are to be regarded as superior courts whose activities are not subject to judicial review by the High Court. In practice, the modern approach is to regard courts and tribunals exercising a limited jurisdiction

---

[360] *Ex p. Scott* [1998] 1 W.L.R. 226; *Scott v National Trust for Places of Historic Interest and Natural Beauty* [1998] 2 All E.R. 705 at 716f–g. See also *R. v Leonard Cheshire Foundation* [2002] 2 All E.R. 936 at [2].

[361] *R. v Oxenden* (1691) 1 Show. K.B. 217 and see *Suratt and Others v Att-Gen of Trinidad and Tobago* [2008] 2 W.L.R. 262 at [49].

[362] Senior Courts Act 1981 s.1.

[363] *Re Racal Communications* [1981] A.C. 374.

[364] See, e.g. *R. (Law Society) v Master of the Rolls* [2005] 1 W.L.R. 2033 and *R. v Master of the Rolls Ex p. McKinnell* [1993] 1 W.L.R. 88.

[365] *R. v Supreme Court Taxing Office Ex p. Singh & Co* [1995] 7 Admin.L.Rep. 849, not following the obiter dicta of the Divisional Court in *R. v Shemlit (Taxing Officer) Ex p. Buckley* [1998] C.O.D. 40 that the decisions of a Master of the Supreme Court were not reviewable.

[366] See Tribunals, Court and Enforcement Act 2007 s.3(5).

[367] *R. (Cart) v Upper Tribunal* [2012] 1 A.C. 663. Similarly, the Special Immigration Appeals Commission is designated a superior court of record but is amenable to judicial review. See the decision of the Divisional Court in *R. (Cart) v Upper Tribunal (Public Law Project Intervening)* [2011] Q.B. 120 (there was no appeal against this aspect of its decision and its reasoning, in relation to the Upper Tribunal, was affirmed by the Supreme Court).

[368] *R. (Cart) v Upper Tribunal (Public Law Project Intervening)* [2012] 1 A.C. 663; and see now CPR 54.7A.

conferred by statute as amenable to judicial review. Thus, a parliamentary election court was subject to judicial review even though it was given the same power, jurisdiction and authority as a High Court judge. The powers of the court were still derived from, and were subject to, the provisions of the Representation of the People Act 1983. The judges were not exercising their powers as High Court judges; rather they were exercising the powers of a court of limited jurisdiction and, in that capacity, their decisions were amenable to judicial review.[369]

The Crown Court is part of the senior courts,[370] but s.29(3) of the Senior Courts Act 1981 provides that the High Court does have jurisdiction to issue the prerogative orders against the Crown Court except in matters relating to trial on indictment. In other words, judicial review, whether by way of the prerogative remedies or by way of a declaration,[371] is not available in respect of decisions of the Crown Court relating to trial by indictment.[372] It is only orders of the Crown Court that are excluded from the ambit of judicial review by reason of s.29 of the Senior Courts Act 1981. Decisions of other bodies, such as that of the Director of Public Prosecutions consenting to the institution of proceedings by way of indictment, are not excluded from the ambit of review by this section.[373]

2–123

The leading decision on the definition of a matter relating to trial on indictment is the House of Lords decision in *Re Smalley*.[374] There, the applicant entered into a recognisance of £100,000 to guarantee the attendance of his brother at his trial on indictment. Following the failure of the brother to attend for trial, the trial judge ordered that the recognisance be estreated. The House held that the order did not relate to the trial on indictment, and was subject to judicial review. Lord Bridge, with whom the other Lords agreed, stated that it was not possible to prescribe a precise test which would in all cases determine whether a decision of the Crown Court was reviewable. The exception in s.29(3) of the 1981 Act excluded judicial review of decisions "affecting the conduct of a trial on indictment"[375] or which formed " . . . an integral part of the trial process . . .".[376] Matters are part of the integral process of trial if they involve the Crown Court making a decision in the light of what it has learned of the nature of the case during the trial and in the light of the conduct and outcome of the trial.[377] The

2–124

---

[369] *R. (Woolas) v Parliamentary Election Court* [2012] 1 Q.B. 1. The Court of Appeal had previously left open the question of whether a local election court was a superior court: *R. v Cripps Ex p. Muldoon* [1984] Q.B. 686 (the Divisional Court having held that it was an inferior court amenable to judicial review: [1984] 1 Q.B. 68).

[370] Senior Courts Act 1981 s.1.

[371] *R. v Chelmsford Crown Court Ex p. Chief Constable of the Essex Police* [1994] 1 W.L.R. 359 and *R. (Faithfull) v Crown Court at Ipswich* [2008] 1 W.L.R. 1636 at [41].

[372] In *R. v Crown Court at Maidstone Ex p. Harrow London Borough Council* [1999] 3 All E.R. 542, the Divisional Court held that s.29(3) may not exclude judicial review in relation to an order of the Crown Court which would normally be treated as a matter relating to trial on indictment because the challenge to the individual decision was based on a lack of jurisdiction on the part of the Crown Court rather than a challenge to the quality of the decision. That reasoning is at variance with the approach exhibited in the existing case law and appears wrong as a matter of principle.

[373] *R. v Director of Public Prosecutions Ex p. Kebilene* [2000] 2 A.C. 326.

[374] [1985] 1 A.C. 622. See Ward, "Judicial Review and Trials on Indictment: s.29(3) of the Supreme Court Act 1981" [1990] P.L. 50.

[375] *Re Smalley* [1985] 1 A.C. 622.

[376] *Re Sampson* [1987] 1 W.L.R. 194.

[377] [1987] 1 W.L.R. 194.

House of Lords has also subsequently observed that the decisions of the Crown Court which have been held to be reviewable are those in which either the order was made under a wholly different jurisdiction from the jurisdiction exercisable in trying an indictment (such as binding over an acquitted person or a third person) or the order sought to be reviewed has been made against someone other than the accused.[378] Consequently, the House of Lords identified another question that could assist in determining whether a decision of the Crown was made in a matter relating to trial by indictment, namely "Is the decision sought to be reviewed one arising in the issue between the Crown and the defendant formulated by the indictment (including the costs of such an issue)?"[379] If the answer is in the affirmative, then the matter is probably related to the trial by indictment and so excluded from judicial review.

2–125   The courts may also be influenced by practical considerations such as whether there is a means by which the order can be challenged if judicial review is refused, or whether judicial review of an order would delay the trial process.[380] The Divisional Court has also added a further qualification in respect of the extent to which judicial review is excluded.[381] In *R. v Maidstone Crown Court Ex p. London Borough Council*,[382] the Crown Court made a supervision and treatment order in respect of an accused person who pleaded not guilty by reason of insanity under s.5 of the Criminal Procedure (Insanity) Act 1964. Such an order could only be made where a jury had returned a special verdict of not guilty by reason of insanity; the Crown Court could not make such an order simply following a plea of not guilty by reason of insanity. The Divisional Court held that an order made under s.5 would normally be a matter relating to trial on indictment and so would not normally be subject to judicial review. Where, however, the Crown Court had no jurisdiction to make the order in the narrow sense of not having power to make an order at all, judicial review was not excluded by s.29(3) of the Senior Courts Act 1981. The exclusion applied to the manner in which the Crown Court exercised its discretion; it did not remove the ability of the court to review those matters which purported to be an the exercise of a jurisdiction in a matter relating to trial on indictment but where the Crown Court had no jurisdiction at all in the matter. The Divisional Court was influenced by the fact that to reach any other conclusion would mean that a decision of the Crown Court, made without jurisdiction in the narrow sense and where no other remedy such as an appeal was available, would otherwise remain uncorrected. The Divisional Court has also granted judicial review of the making of a hospital order under s.51 of the Mental Health Act 1983, following a direction that a verdict of not guilty be entered, on the grounds that the judge had misdirected himself as to the proper test to be applied and therefore acted without jurisdiction.[383] These cases do not, however, establish any wider principle that to quash any sentence that exceeds the jurisdiction of the sentencing court is permissible. Rather, they are special cases where there had been no trial on

---

[378] *R. v Manchester Crown Court Ex p. Director of Public Prosecutions* [1993] 1 W.L.R. 1524.

[379] [1993] 1 W.L.R. 1524 at 530E–F.

[380] These considerations underlay Lord Bridge's definition in *Re Smalley* [1985] 1 A.C. 622.

[381] *R. v Maidstone Crown Court Ex p. Harrow London Borough Council* [2000] Q.B. 719; *R. (Kenneally) v Crown Court at Snaresbrook* [2002] Q.B. 1169.

[382] [2000] Q.B. 719.

[383] *R. (Kenneally) v Crown Court at Snaresbrook* [2002] Q.B. 1169.

indictment. The usual position where there has been a trial on indictment and the judge makes an error as to his powers when sentencing is that such an error is a matter relating to trial on indictment which cannot be the subject of a claim for judicial review.[384]

The exception clearly prevents review of the verdict and the sentence.[385]   **2–126**
Decisions affecting the conduct of the trial and which are not reviewable include:

(a) orders requiring disclosure of criminal convictions of jury members[386];
(b) witness summonses[387];
(c) orders that charges lie on the file and cannot be proceeded with except with the leave of the court[388];
(d) adjournments[389];
(e) refusals to grant legal aid for a trial[390];
(f) orders relating to costs made at the conclusion of a trial[391] including following acquittal[392];
(g) refusals to direct a verdict of not guilty[393];
(h) orders prohibiting the publication of the names of witnesses[394];
(i) an order that a defendant pay a contribution to his legal aid costs[395];
(j) quashing an indictment[396];
(k) staying the whole or part of an indictment[397];
(l) reinstating an earlier legal aid certificate by revoking an earlier decisions discharging the earlier legal aid certificate[398];
(m) issuing a warrant of imprisonment alleged to be incorrectly drawn up as it did not reflect the sentence passed[399];
(n) listing the order in which trials are to take place[400]; and

---

[384] *R. (Crown Prosecution Service) v Crown Court at Guildford* [2007] 1 W.L.R. 2886.

[385] [2007] 1 W.L.R. 2886. Sentences include confiscation orders and compensation orders: see *R. (Faithfull) v Crown Court at Ipswich* [2008] 1 W.L.R. 1636.

[386] *R. v Sheffield Crown Court Ex p. Brownlow* [1980] 1 Q.B. 530 (the result, although not the reasoning, was approved in *Re Smalley* (see above, fn.354).

[387] *Ex p. Rees, The Times*, May 7, 1986. But, in *R. (B) v Crown Court at Stafford* [2007] 1 W.L.R. 1524 a prosecution witness was permitted to seek judicial review of a witness ordered to produce the claimant's medical record.

[388] *R. v Central Criminal Court Ex p. Raymond* [1986] 1 W.L.R. 710.

[389] [1986] 1 W.L.R. 710.

[390] *R. v Chichester Crown Court Ex p. Abodunrin* (1984) 79 Cr.App.R. 293.

[391] *Re Meredith* [1973] 1 W.L.R. 435.

[392] *Hunter v Crown Court at Newcastle-upon-Tyne* [2014] 1 W.L.R. 918. An order that the defence pay costs at a plea and case management hearing before the start of the trial does not relate to trial on indictment: *R. (Crown Prosecution Service) v Crown Court at Bolton* [2013] 1 W.L.R. 918.

[393] *R. v Preston Crown Court Ex p. Fraser* [1984] Crim. L.R. 624. See also *Hunter v Crown Court at Newcastle upon Tyne* [2013] 3 W.L.R. 918.

[394] *R. v Central Criminal Court Ex p. Crook* (1985) 82 L.S. Gaz. 1408.

[395] *Re Sampson* (see above, fn.376) and see *R. (Regentford Ltd) v Canterbury Crown Court* [2001] A.C.D. 40.

[396] *R. v Manchester Crown Court Ex p. DPP* above, fn.378.

[397] *Re Ashton* [1994] 1 A.C. 9. (overruling *R. v Central Criminal Court Ex p. Randle* [1991] 1 W.L.R. 1087 and *R. v Norwich Crown Court Ex p. Belsham* [1992] 1 W.L.R. 54).

[398] *R. v Isleworth Crown Court Ex p. Willington* [1993] 1 W.L.R. 713.

[399] *R. v Lewes Crown Court Ex p. Sinclair, The Times*, July 23, 1992.

[400] *R. v Southwark Crown Court Ex p. Ward* (1994) 7 Admin. L.Rep. 395 (not following the decision in *R. v Southwark Crown Court Ex p. Commissioners for Customs and Excise* [1993] 1 W.L.R. 764

(o)   a decision refusing to dismiss a charge on the ground that the evidence is not sufficient for a jury to convict.[401]

Matters which do not relate to trial on indictment include orders:

(a)   made in respect of persons other than the accused forfeiting property[402];
(b)   estreating the recognisance for bail[403];
(c)   binding over the person[404];
(d)   for a permanent stay of criminal proceedings rather than enter a verdict of not guilty following a prosecution decision not to offer evidence[405]; and
(f)   a decision refusing bail,[406] at least where there is no trial in progress.[407] A refusal of bail once a trial has started does relate to a trial on indictment and judicial review is not available.[408]

There is uncertainty as to the availability of judicial review in respect of a decision to dismiss charges under s.6 of the Criminal Justice Act 1987 prior to arraignment on the grounds that the evidence was insufficient for a jury properly to convict. On one occasion, the Divisional Court has held that such a decision does not relate to trial on indictment and may be judicially reviewed.[409] Subsequently, the Divisional Court doubted that that decision properly reflected the law and concluded that analogous decisions under para.2 of Sch.3 to the Crime and Disorder Act 1998 were not amenable to judicial review.[410]

2–127   The courts have been divided on the question of whether an order under s.39 of the Children and Young Persons Act 1933 allowing or prohibiting the publication of particulars identifying a young person relates to a trial on indictment. The Divisional Court has held that it does not and the order is reviewable.[411] The position in relation to decisions to arraign is also uncertain. On two occasions, the Divisional Court has had to consider decisions arraigning a person which were intended, or had the effect to circumvent the statutory provisions requiring a person to be given bail if he is not brought to trial within the custody time limits and no extension has been granted. The effect of the

---

which held that listing decisions did not relate to trial on indictment. The court in the later case considered, it is submitted correctly, that the earlier decision did not survive the reasoning of the House of Lords in *Re Ashton* above, fn.397).

[401]   *R. v (Snelgrove) v Crown Court at Woolwich* [2005] 1 W.L.R. 3223.
[402]   *R. v Maidstone Crown Court Ex p. Gill* [1986] 1 W.L.R. 1405.
[403]   *Re Smalley* [1985] A.C. 622.
[404]   *R. v Swindon Crown Court Ex p. Singh (Pawittar)* [1984] 1 W.L.R. 449.
[405]   *R. v Central Criminal Court Ex p. Spens, The Times,* December 13, 1993 (although it is doubtful if this decision can survive the dicta in *Re Ashton* [1994] 1 A.C. 9).
[406]   *R. (Malik) v Central Criminal Court* [2007] 1 W.L.R. 2455.
[407]   *R. (S) v Crown Court at Northampton* [2012] 1 W.L.R. 1 at [5].
[408]   *R. (Uddin) v Crown Court at Leeds* [2014] 1 W.L.R. 1742.
[409]   *R. v Central Criminal Court ex p. Director of the Serious Fraud Office* [1993] 1 W.L.R. 949 (the House of Lords in *R. v Manchester Crown Court Ex p. D.P.P.* [1993] 1 W.L.R. 1524 did not express a view on the correctness of this decision).
[410]   *R. (Snelgrove) v Crown Court at Woolwich* [2005] 1 W.L.R. 3223.
[411]   In *Re H. In Re D, The Times,* August 13, 1999. See also *R. v Cardiff Crown Court Ex p. M, The Times,* April 28, 1998, *R. v Lee* [1993] 1 W.L.R. 103 and *R. v Leicester Crown Court Ex p. Lee* [1993] 1 W.L.R. 111. The Divisional Court in *R. v Winchester Crown Court Ex p. B* [1999] 1 W.L.R. 788 reached the opposite conclusion and held that such orders were not reviewable.

arraignment was that the statutory provisions requiring the grant of bail did not apply after arraignment so that the accused could be detained in custody. On both occasions, the Divisional Court held that a decision to arraign when there was no trial date in prospect for the purposes of evading the effect of the expiry of a custody time-limit was susceptible to judicial review.[412] In the alternative, the Divisional Court held that the applicant was entitled to habeas corpus to determine the validity of the arraignment and that remedy remained available irrespective of the limits on the grant of judicial review.[413] On a third occasion, the Divisional Court considered that the arraignment of a defendant was a matter relating to the trial on indictment and was not amenable to judicial review.[414] The approach in the earlier cases is understandable as it is unattractive for a person to be detained in custody in circumstances which may be unlawful and yet to have no remedy. The better approach, it is submitted, is to treat the remedy of habeas corpus as the appropriate remedy since, as a matter of statutory construction, an arraignment does appear to relate to the trial on indictment.

The Crown Court also has jurisdiction in a wide variety of matters unconnected with trials in the Crown Court itself. These include appeals from magistrates' courts and other administrative bodies.[415] Judicial review is available against decisions in such matters. **2–128**

Inferior courts

Judicial review is, in principle, available in relation to the acts and omissions of inferior courts such as the county court[416] or magistrates' courts.[417] In practice, the availability of judicial review is likely to be limited by the availability of other methods of challenge such as appeals. Judicial review will not normally be permitted if there are adequate alternative remedies available.[418] There are rights of appeal against decisions of district judges and county courts, for example. Where the possibility of an appeal to a higher court exists, that route is the appropriate method of challenging the original decision rather than a claim for judicial review unless there are exceptional circumstances justifying bring a claim for judicial review.[419] **2–129**

Permission to appeal to a higher court is required in relation to most such decisions. There can be no appeal if permission is refused. The courts retain jurisdiction to entertain a claim for judicial review of the decision refusing permission to appeal but have held that it is only in exceptional circumstances that judicial review should be used to challenge a refusal of permission to appeal.[420] In relation to the county court, review was said to be limited to cases **2–130**

---

[412] *R. v Maidstone Crown Court Ex p. Hollstein* [1995] 3 All E.R. 503; *R. v Maidstone Crown Court Ex p. Clark* [1995] 1 W.L.R. 831.
[413] See *R. v Maidstone Crown Court Ex p. Clark* [1995] 1 W.L.R. 831, per Glidewell LJ at 842G–843D and per Curtis J. at 844C–E; in *R. v Maidstone Crown Court Ex p. Hollstein* [1995] 3. All E.R. 503, the Divisional Court also granted habeas corpus.
[414] *R. v Leeds Crown Court Ex p. Hussain* [1995] 1 W.L.R. 1329.
[415] See generally, Chapter 14.
[416] *R. (Sivasubramaniam) v Wandsworth County Court* [2003] 1 W.L.R. 475 at [33].
[417] See, e.g. *R. v Hereford Magistrates' Court Ex p. Rowlands* [1998] Q.B. 110.
[418] See generally the discussion on alternative remedies in Chapter 12.
[419] *R. (Sivasubramaniam) v Wandsworth County Court* [2003] 1 W.L.R. 475 at para [46]–[48].
[420] [2003] 1 W.L.R. 475 at [49]–[55].

where there was a jurisdictional error or a procedural irregularity of such a kind as to constitute a denial of the applicant's right to a fair hearing.[421] The Supreme Court subsequently disapproved of that approach in the context of challenges to decisions of the Upper Tribunal refusing permission to appeal and considered that judicial review should only be available where there is a challenge to a refusal by the Upper Tribunal to grant permission to appeal in cases involving an important point of principle or practice or where there is some other compelling reason to permit judicial review.[422]

E. SUBJECT-MATTER OF THE CLAIM

2–131   Judicial review is only available against public law bodies in public law matters. There are occasions when the body in question is undoubtedly a public body which is in principle amenable to judicial review but where the particular issue under consideration does not involve any public law matter but rather involves private law rights.

2–132   Public authorities may exceed or abuse their statutory, prerogative or other powers, or may fail properly to perform their statutory duties. These issues raise questions of public law, suitable for resolution by way of judicial review. Their activities may also raise issues of private law and an individual may be seeking to enforce some private law right against a public body. Public authorities may enter into contracts and there may be disputes as to whether the public authority has breached the terms of the contract. In the course of exercising statutory powers, public bodies may commit torts such as negligence, nuisance or trespass. In so far as these acts are not authorised by statute, the public authority may be liable in damages to the individual concerned. In addition, certain statutory duties give rise to liability in damages in the event of a breach of that duty. These cases, involving as they do allegations of contractual liability or tortious conduct, are matters of private not public law. They could arise in a dispute between two private individuals or in a dispute between an individual and a public body. The fact that one of the parties to the dispute happens to be a public authority is incidental to the nature of the dispute. The individual will be seeking to enforce a private law right against the public body and will not be trying to enforce any right derived from public law. As such, the subject-matter of the claim is private law and so not amenable to judicial review.

2–133   It is, however, useful to note that claims against public bodies will often arise against a backcloth of statutory powers. It is perfectly possible for questions of public law and private law to arise in relation to one dispute. It is also possible for situations to arise where the courts will superimpose onto a private law question (for example, has there been a breach of contract) an obligation to observe principles derived from public law. The courts have not always been clear or consistent in determining when circumstances generate public law or private law obligations. The dividing line between public and private law issues is not always

---

[421] See *R. (Sivasubramaniam) v Wandsworth County Court* [2003] 1 W.L.R. 475 at [56].

[422] *R. (Cart) v Upper Tribunal* [2012] 1 A.C. 613. See also *PR (Sri Lanka) v Secretary of State for the Home Department* [2012] 1 W.L.R. 73 and *JD (Congo) v Secretary of State for the Home Department* discussing how these criteria operate in the analogous context of applications for permission to appeal to the Court of Appeal from decisions of the Upper Tribunal. See generally Chapter 10.

clear and there are "cases where it is not immediately clear whether the rights which the plaintiff claims and which he claims have been infringed by a public authority, are truly to be classified as rights under public law or rights under private law".[423] There "is no universal test which will be applicable to all circumstances which will indicate clearly and beyond peradventure as to when judicial review is or is not available".[424]

There are occasions when the courts have specifically had to consider whether a particular claim raises issues of private or public law, and whether the claim may be pursued through judicial review. More frequently, the courts have had to deal with claims that an issue brought by way of ordinary claim is, on a proper analysis, an issue of public and not private law. The defendant will then seek to have the ordinary claim struck out, relying on the rule established in *O'Reilly v Mackman*,[425] that it is an abuse of the process of the court to bring a public law matter by way of ordinary claim rather than judicial review. Even if the courts hold that certain types of disputes involving public authorities can be dealt with by ordinary claim, that does not conclusively deal with the question of whether judicial review is available. In some cases, only private law issues are raised and judicial review cannot be used. In other cases issues of private and public law may be intermingled and an individual may have a choice between making an application for judicial review or bringing an ordinary claim. This area and this topic are considered in detail in Chapter 3.

2–134

Contract

The courts have drawn a distinction between rights derived from contract which are classed as private law rights, and rights derived from public law. By "public law" rights, the courts generally mean the ability to invoke the supervisory jurisdiction of the courts to ensure that public authorities perform their statutory duties and properly exercise their statutory (or sometimes prerogative) powers. This includes ensuring the observance of the principles developed by the courts to control the exercise of discretionary power. Judicial review is concerned with the protection of rights derived from public law. Judicial review is not, however, available to enforce private law rights. Such rights can only be enforced by way of an ordinary claim for damages, a declaration, or an injunction. Thus, in *R. v East Berkshire Area Health Authority Ex p. Walsh*,[426] the Court of Appeal held that they did not have jurisdiction on a judicial review application to enforce rights derived from a contract of employment. Such rights were private law rights and the appropriate machinery for enforcing such private law rights was an ordinary contractual action for wrongful dismissal.[427]

2–135

The distinction between private and public law rights is clear in principle but may be difficult to apply in practice. Much depends on the precise definition

2–136

---

[423] per Dillon LJ in *McClaren v Home Office* [1990] I.C.R. 824 at 829F.

[424] per Woolf LJ in *R. v Derbyshire County Council Ex p. Noble* [1990] I.C.R. 808 at 814F.

[425] [1983] 2 A.C. 237.

[426] See *R. v British Broadcasting Corp Ex p. Lavelle* [1981] 1 W.L.R. 23. Before the introduction of the judicial review procedure, the courts had held that certiorari was not available to enforce rights derived from a contract of employment; *R. v Post Office Ex p. Byrne* [1975] I.C.R. 221.

[427] Or an application to an employment tribunal to enforce statutory rights relating to unfair dismissal.

given to private and public law rights. Clearly private law rights include the enforcement of specific terms and conditions included in a contract and any implied terms.[428] Claims that a contract does in fact exist also raise a private law issue.[429] However, questions of public and private law are often intermingled and cannot easily be separated. Questions of public law arise in a number of ways including the following.

Statutory restrictions on the power to contract

2–137   Statutory provisions may expressly or impliedly impose restrictions on the exercise of contractual power by a public body. Judicial review will be available to determine whether a contract violates such statutory restrictions. In this instance, the courts would be performing their public law supervisory role of ensuring compliance with the statutory limitations on the powers of public authorities, and would not be dealing with the private law issue of what the terms of the contract were and whether they had been broken. Thus, in *Walsh*,[430] the Court of Appeal accepted that if Walsh had been seeking to enforce statutory restrictions on the power of the health authority to dismiss him, that would have involved questions of public law appropriate for judicial review. However, in *Walsh*, statute only required the authority to incorporate certain terms in the contract of employment which they had done. Once incorporated, the matter became one of enforcing the rights under the contract, which was a private law issue not amenable to judicial review. If the authority had failed to observe the statutory requirements then judicial review would have been available to force the authority to perform its statutory duty of contracting on the stipulated terms. There are other instances where the courts have recognised that judicial review is available to ensure that specific statutory provisions governing the exercise of a power to contract are observed. Thus statutory provisions requiring an authority to tender for contracts for the disposal of waste and prohibiting the making of arrangements in any other ways were enforceable by way of judicial review.[431] The Court of Appeal declared, in judicial review proceedings, that certain provisions of a contract breached provisions of the Public Contracts Regulations and principles of EU law governing the award of contracts.[432]

2–138   Other cases could be classified as instances of the courts enforcing statutory restrictions on contractual power, although they could also be described as cases where the courts held that the public body had no power to enter the particular contract in question as discussed in the following section. The Court of Appeal, for example, has considered whether a local authority had the necessary statutory authority to insert restrictive covenants in a contract for sale of land, and whether

[428] See, e.g. *R. v East Berkshire Area Health Authority Ex p. Walsh* [1985] Q.B. 152.

[429] *McLaren v Home Office* [1990] I.C.R. 824.

[430] *R. v East Berkshire Area Health Authority Ex p. Walsh* (see above, fn.406). See also *R. v Tower Hamlets London Borough Council Ex p. Thrasyvalou* [1991] C.O.D. 123 (judicial review available in relation to a claim that public body unlawfully delegated its statutory housing duties but not in relation to a claim arising out of parties' contractual dealings).

[431] *Mass Energy Limited v Birmingham City Council* [1994] Env. L.R. 298.

[432] *R. (Law Society) v Legal Services Commission* [2008] 2 W.L.R. 803. A person who has tendered for a contract governed by the Public Contracts Regulations 2006 may find that the courts require him to use the remedies provided in those regulations rather than seeking judicial review: see *R. (Cookson & Clegg) v Ministry of Defence* [2005] EWCA Civ 811.

the inclusion of such covenants would constitute an unlawful fetter on the exercise of other of its statutory powers.[433] In one case, Schiemann J. considered by way of a claim for judicial review a claim that a particular term of contract between an electricity board and a customer was ultra vires the statutory powers of the board.[434] Similarly, claims that draft contract clauses violated restrictions imposed on the local authorities by the Local Government Act 1988 were dealt with by judicial review.[435]

Power to contract

The courts have been prepared to grant judicial review of decisions of public   2–139
bodies to enter into contracts. They have also considered on judicial review applications whether contracts of public authorities are outside the scope of their statutory powers.[436] Statutory bodies, such as local authorities, only have power to do those things expressly or impliedly authorised by statute.[437] Statute may confer a specific or a general power to contract[438] or it may be implicit in the statute that the body may contract in order to discharge its functions. The public body may only enter into contracts where it is specifically or impliedly authorised to do. The courts will determine whether the contract is within the scope of the public body's statutory powers. Furthermore, the courts will also ensure that, in exercising the statutory power to contract, the public body has properly observed the relevant public law principles governing the exercise of statutory power such as ensuring, for example, that the power is exercised for a proper not an improper or unauthorised purpose. The exercise of such a statutory power is, in principle, subject to the same degree of control as any other statutory power.

There are numerous examples of such cases. Judicial review has been granted   2–140
to determine whether local authorities have power to contract to sell goods and materials to other bodies or enter into agreements whereby they arrange for goods to be supplied in return for the payment of commission fees.[439] Judicial review has been used to determine whether a local authority had statutory power to dispose of land subject to a non-building covenant[440] or whether it was entitled to

---

[433] *R. v Hammersmith and Fulham London Borough Council Ex p. Beddowes* [1987] Q.B. 1050.

[434] *R. v Midlands Electricity Board Ex p. Busby; R. v Midlands Electricity Board Ex p. Williamson,* *The Times,* October 28, 1987.

[435] *R. v Islington London Borough Council Ex p. Building Employers Confederation* [1989] I.R.L.R. 38d.

[436] Such issues may also be raised as a defence in private law proceedings. One party may be seeking to enforce the contract and the other may be saying that the contract is ultra vires and unlawful as it is outside the scope of the public body's statutory powers: see, e.g. *Credit Suisse v Allerdale Borough Council* [1997] Q.B. 306.

[437] See, e.g. *R. v Yorkshire Purchasing Organisation Ex p. British Educational Suppliers Association* (1997) L.G.R. 727 at 730; *Credit Suisse v Allerdale Borough Council* [1997] Q.B. 306 per Neill LJ at 316F–H and Hobhouse LJ at 348D–350D and *Stretch v West Dorset District Council* (1997) 10 Admin. L.R. 129 at 131 (local authority could only dispose of property through the exercise of statutory powers).

[438] For local authorities, see now Local Government (Contracts) Act 1997, s.1. See generally Arrowsmith, "Judicial Review and Contractual Powers" [1990] 106 L.Q.R. 277 and Bailey, "Judicial Review of Contracting Decisions" [2007] P.L. 444.

[439] *R. v Yorkshire Purchasing Organisation Ex p. British Educational Suppliers Association* fn.437.

[440] *R. v Westminster City Council and the London Electricity Board Ex p. Leicester Square Coventry Street Association* see also *Stretch v West Dorset District Council* (1999) 77 P. & C.R. 34d;

enter into factoring arrangements, whereby the authority agreed to sell expected receipts from future sales of land[441]; or whether statutory water companies were entitled, prior to privatisation, to buy shares in other water companies.[442] In *R. (Structadene Ltd) v Hackney London Borough Council* a decision to enter into a contract to sell land was quashed as, amongst other things, the council had failed to have regard to its fiduciary duty and acted unreasonably when accepting a lower offer for the land.[443] More unusually, the court quashed a decision to award a catering contract to a contractor, and declared the contract to be void, where, in breach of the relevant regulations, parent governors were not allowed to vote at the meeting where the decision was taken.[444]

2–141   The courts have also entertained applications for judicial review to determine whether a decision to enter into a contract violated one of the substantive principles of public law developed by the courts to control abuse of power. In *R. v Port Talbot Borough Council Ex p. Jones*,[445] a decision to grant a tenancy was quashed and the purported tenancy declared void on the grounds that there had been an unlawful delegation of the power to grant a tenancy and that the decision was based on irrelevant considerations.

2–142   Occasionally, the public law issues arise in the context of a defence to a claim that there has been a breach of contract rather than in an application for judicial review. One party may seek to enforce a contract; the other may contend that the decision is ultra vires the powers of the statutory body and so void.[446]

2–143   The process whereby a statutory body determines how to award a contract ought similarly to be subject to judicial review. Again, this type of case involves an attempt to ensure that the public body observes any statutory limitations placed upon it, together with the usual public law principles, in exercising its statutory power to contract. There are numerous examples of such decisions being reviewed. The courts have held that a general decision of a local authority to boycott Shell products, which in effect amounted to a decision as to how they would exercise their contractual purchasing powers, was unlawful as it constituted an attempt to put pressure on Shell to change its trading policy on South Africa.[447] Challenges have been made to acts of a public body before any

---

[441] *R. v Wirral Metropolitan Borough Council Ex p. Milstead* (1989) 21 R.V.R. 66.

[442] *R. v Southern Water Authority Ex p. Water Companies Association*, *The Times*, December 30, 1988.

[443] [2001] 2 All E.R. 225. See also *R. v London Borough of Barnet Ex p. Pardes House* [1989] C.O.D. 512; more debatable is the decision in *R. v Leeds City Council Ex p. Cobleigh* [1997] C.O.D. 69 (decision not to sell land had no statutory underpinning; in this case the Council was, as a minimum, still performing its normal public law duty to consider whether or not to exercise its statutory power and it is difficult to see why, in principle, such a decision is not amenable to judicial review).

[444] *R. (Transport and General Workers Union) v Walsall Metropolitan Borough Council* [2002] E.L.R. 329.

[445] [1988] 2 All E.R. 207. The Housing Act 1985 s.21, conferred general powers of management in relation to housing on the local authority although the judgment does not expressly refer to the statutory source of the power to grant a tenancy.

[446] See, e.g. *Credit Suisse v Allerdale Borough Council*, above, fn.437 (Court of Appeal held that a contract of guarantee, whereby a local authority guaranteed certain loan payments, was ultra vires as the local authority had no power to enter into any such guarantees and had, in any event, decided to do so for an improper purpose).

[447] *R. v Lewisham Borough Council Ex p. Shell U.K.* [1988] 1 All E.R. 938. See also *R. v Lancashire County Council Ex p. Telegraph Stations, The Times*, June 15, 1988 (certiorari issued to quash a decision of sell land, as the local authority had failed to investigate the possibility of a higher bid

contract has actually been entered into. Judicial review has been used to challenge the legality of draft clauses prepared by a local authority,[448] and to quash a decision to remove a contractor from a list of approved contractors,[449] where these actions violated statutory provisions regulating the exercise of local authority contractual powers. The decision to put the work out to competitive tender rather than perform it within the authority itself is reviewable.[450] In general, the process of tendering involves the exercise of statutory powers, as the "statutory element, if nothing else, brings the case within the scope of our public law jurisdiction".[451]

The courts, however, have not at present adopted the view that a tendering **2–144** exercise involves the exercise of statutory powers and so is amenable to judicial review. Rather, the prevailing view at present is that tendering exercises involve a commercial dispute between the successful and unsuccessful tenderer. Judicial review will not normally be available to review the carrying out of a tendering exercise unless there is some specific statutory requirement that the tendering exercise be carried out in a particular way or unless there is some other additional element which gives the dispute a sufficient public law element.[452] One of the earliest cases to cast doubt upon the availability of judicial review over tendering exercise did not in fact involve the exercise of a decision made pursuant to a statutory power. In *R. v Lord Chancellor Ex p. Hibbet and Saunders*,[453] the court was dealing with the common law power of the Crown to contract and was not contracting pursuant to a statutory power. In those circumstances, the court considered that there was nothing to suggest that the decision to contract was underpinned by statute or involved any other public law element sufficient to make the decision amenable to judicial review. Waller J., in particular, considered that judicial review would have been available if the body had been acting pursuant to a specific statutory power; in such circumstances, the courts would not only enforce any specific statutory restrictions but they would also enforce any implied obligation such as the duty to act fairly. While the decision in *Hibbet and Saunders* that there was no public law element to the tendering exercise can be criticised, the decision itself is not authority for saying that a statutory power to contract cannot be reviewed on normal grounds. Similarly, other cases refusing judicial review involve situations where there was no specific statutory power to

---

being made) and *R. v Derbyshire County Council Ex p. The Times Supplements Ltd* [1991] C.O.D. 129 (decision not to advertise in Times Group newspapers unlawful as authority acting in bad faith).

[448] *R. v Islington London Borough Council Ex p. Building Employers Confederation* [1989] C.O.D. 432.

[449] *R. v Enfield London Borough Council Ex p. T.F. Unwin (Roydon) Ltd* [1989] C.O.D. 466. Standing orders authorised under the Local Government Act 1972 s.135 may also be enforced by way of judicial review: see *R. v Hereford Corp. Ex p. Harrower* [1970] 1 W.L.R. 1424.

[450] *R. v Walsall Metropolitan Borough Ex p. Yapp* (1993) 92 L.G.R. 110. See also Arrowsmith "Protecting the Interests of Bidders for Public Contracts" [1994] C.L.J. 104.

[451] *R. v Walsall Metropolitan Borough Ex p. Yapp* (1993) 92 L.G.R. 110 at 113 per Nolan LJ.

[452] See *Mass Energy Limited v Birmingham City Council* [1994] Env. L.R. 298 at 306 and 313–314; *R. (Cookson and Clegg) v Ministry of Defence* [2005] EWCA Civ 811 at [18] ; *R. (Gamesa Energy UK Ltd) v National Assembly for Wales* [2006] EWHC 2167 (Admin) at [66]–[68] and *R. (Menai Collect Ltd and others) v Department for Constitutional Affairs* [2006] EWHC 727 (Admin); *R (Law Society) v Legal Services Commission* [2008] Q.B. 737 (judicial review available to ensure compliance with provisions of domestic regulations and EU law relating to tendering for certain contracts.).

[453] *The Times*, March 12, 1993.

contract, as, for example, where a body had been privatised and ceased to be a statutory corporation and so was not exercising statutory powers and was not limited to doing only those acts expressly or implied authorised by statute.[454]

2–145   However, the courts have taken a similar approach even in cases involving statutory powers to contract and the carrying out of tendering exercises to determine who should be awarded the contract. The courts have held that judicial review is available where there are statutory restrictions on the way in which the powers to contract are exercised in order ensure that those statutory restrictions are observed.[455] The courts also recognise that judicial review may be available in cases where it was alleged that there was bad faith or corruption or the award of a contract pursuant to an unlawful policy.[456] Absent such factors, however, the current case law indicates that challenges to a tendering exercise will normally be seen as a purely commercial dispute between the successful and unsuccessful tenderers. Judicial review will not be available unless there is some sufficient element of public law. Thus in the *Gamesa*[457] case, the High Court held that judicial review on grounds of unfairness or irrationality was not available to challenge a tendering exercise. The fact that the body in question was exercising a statutory power and spending public money was not, of itself, sufficient to render the process amenable to judicial review. The public body was entitled to adopt a tendering exercise to identify suitable candidates. The criteria to be used were a matter for the public body. The exercise involved the application of the same criteria to all tenderers. In those circumstances, the complaints of irrationality and unfairness were concerned with the operation of that system and the effect on the individual claimant. There was no sufficient public law element to such a challenge rendering the tendering process amenable to judicial review. Similarly, in the *Menai Collect* case,[458] the court indicated that a tender evaluation process was essentially a commercial process and that where the challenge was essentially to the fact that the contract had been awarded to one bidder rather than another, indicated that there was no relevant public law obligation in issue. The precise situations in which a tendering exercise will be amenable to judicial review is unclear. On one occasion, Ognall J. had to consider whether the tendering process adopted by the Legal Aid Board leading to the award of a contract to do legal work was reviewable. There, the Legal Aid Board was specifically empowered by statute to achieve its objects by contract where the Lord Chancellor had so directed as he had done in the instant case. That of itself would seem clearly to make the tendering exercise leading to the award of a contract amenable to judicial review on normal principles. Ognall J., however, preferred to consider the matter on the basis of whether the process involved some sufficient public law element (other than the statutory element). He found

---

[454] *R. v Great Western Railway Ltd Ex p. Frederick* [1998] C.O.D. 239.

[455] See para.2–137 above.

[456] *R. (Cookson and Clegg) v Ministry of Defence* [2005] EWCA Civ 811 at [18]; *Mercury Energy Ltd v Electricity Corporation of New Zealand* [1994] 1 W.L.R. 521; and *R. (Menai Collect Ltd and others) v Department for Constitutional Affairs* [2006] EWHC 727 (Admin) at [42] and [47].

[457] *R. (Gamesa Energy UK Ltd) v National Assembly for Wales* [2006] EWHC 2167 (Admin) at [66]–[79]. For criticism of this line of authority, see Bailey "Judicial Review of Contracting Decisions" [2007] P.L. 444.

[458] *R. (Menai Collect Ltd and others) v Department for Constitutional Affairs* [2006] EWHC 727 (Admin).

that it did and that the process of considering the tenders had been procedurally unfair in that case and quashed the decision to award the contract.[459] The decision would appear correct although the better view would be that the statutory element itself rendered the decision amenable to judicial review; the case is certainly not authority for the view that a power to contract derived directly from statute is not reviewable.

The courts have also differed over whether the decisions of a local authority to dispose of land are subject to judicial review simply because the source of the authority's power to sell is derived from statute. The preferable view is that the fact that a local authority is exercising a statutory function ought to be sufficient, in itself, to justify the availability of judicial review to determine whether any of the recognised principles of public law, designed to prevent the abuse of power, have been breached. The precise scope of the public law obligations may need to be adapted to reflect the context in which a claim for judicial review arises, but the fact that the local authority is performing a statutory function is sufficient, of itself, to render the function public for the purposes of judicial review. That was the view taken by the High Court in *R. (Molinaro) v Royal London Borough of Kensington and Chelsea.*[460] **2–146**

In *R. v Bolsover District Council Ex p. Pepper*,[461] however, the High Court held that the fact that the local authority was exercising a statutory power when it decided to sell was not sufficient to make its decision a public law matter. The Court considered that a decision by a local authority to sell or not to sell land is normally to be seen as a private law matter unless a public law element is introduced into the decision-making process. The reason given for that conclusion was that, in such cases, a local authority was acting as a landowner and was not performing a public law function. A decision would only be a public law matter if some public law element were introduced into the decision-making process, for example if the authority had a policy governing sales or if some statutory requirement was breached. In that case, a claim that a person had a public law legitimate expectation that the Council would sell land, or alternatively, that he would be given the opportunity to make representations before the Council decided whether to sell, failed. **2–147**

The decision ultimately reached in *Ex p. Pepper* appears to be correct. The reasoning, however, is open to debate. There was no doubt that the court in *Ex p. Pepper* considered that a power to contract was amenable to judicial review if some public law element was present. The real issue concerns the extent to which the courts ought to assume that the public law principles apply to the exercise of a power to sell. The court in *Ex p. Pepper* took the view that those principles did not apply simply because the power to sell was derived from statute; hence the need to find some additional element making the matter a public law matter and thereby engaging the courts' supervisory jurisdiction. The better view is that the public law principles do, generally, apply to such decisions because of the statutory origins of the power and the fact that, as a public body, a council ought to exercise its statutory powers in accordance with the principles designed to **2–148**

---

[459] *R. v Legal Aid Board Ex p. Donn & Co.* [1996] 3 All E.R. 1.
[460] [2002] L.G.R. 336.
[461] [2001] L.G.R. 43 and see *ISE Lodge Amenity Committee v Kettering Borough Council* [2002] E.G. 148.

prevent abuse of power.[462] The preferable basis for the decision in *Ex p. Pepper* is that, on the facts, no legitimate expectation arose. The local authority and the other party had been negotiating over the sale of land and the correspondence had been marked subject to contract. It was clear that the parties did not, therefore, regard themselves as bound to sell until a contract was entered into and they regarded the transaction as being regulated by ordinary contractual principles rather than one involving public law legitimate expectations. If however, the approach in *Ex p. Pepper* is followed, a number of factors have been identified as introducing the additional public element into the decision-making process and so rendering it subject to judicial review. These include the fact that an authority is operating in accordance with a general policy governing disposals, or that there are statutory procedural or other requirements that need to be observed in relation to a particular disposal,[463] or that the authority is using its contractual powers not simply as a private owner but in order to achieve some other purpose such as giving effect to its planning policy.[464] The fact that an authority was proposing to dispose of land that had been given to the authority for use as a public open space, that the decision to sell involved a change of policy on the part of the authority and that the authority had accepted the need to consult on disposals, thereby recognising the public interest in the matter, was also sufficient to render the decision to sell the land a public law matter for the purposes of judicial review.[465]

Public law principles regulating the exercise of contractual power

2–149   The courts have also accepted that the substantive public law principles developed by the courts to control power—such as reasonableness, relevancy, purpose and procedural fairness—may be relevant to the exercise of contractual power by a public authority. The courts have not yet comprehensively considered the relationship between the principles governing the exercise of discretionary power and contractual power. In the past, they have looked for some factor suggesting that the issue raises more than a simple question of the enforcement of contractual rights between the parties, and has a "public" element suggesting the need for the courts to intervene to control the exercise of power.

2–150   In a number of cases involving the termination by a local authority of a contractual licence to use land as a market stall for trading, the exercise of the power was held to be subject to judicial review on the usual administrative law grounds.[466] In one case[467] the public element attracting the application of public law principles was found in the fact that the authorities were effectively performing a licensing function in determining who should and should not be allowed to trade in a public place. That went beyond simple contractual

---

[462] The approach taken by Elias J. in *R. (Molinaro) v Royal London Borough of Kensington and Chelsea* [2002] L.G.R. 336.

[463] See *R. v Bolsover District Council Ex p. Pepper* [2001] L.G.R 43 at [33].

[464] See, e.g. *R. (Molinaro) v Royal London Borough of Kensington and Chelsea* [2002] L.G.R. 336 at [63]–[64].

[465] *ISE Lodge Amenity Committee v Kettering Borough Council* [2002] E.G. 148.

[466] *R. v Basildon District Council Ex p. Brown* (1981) 79 L.G.R. 655; *R. v Wear Valley District Council Ex p. Binks* [1985] 2 All E.R. 699.

[467] *R v Wear Valley District Council Ex p. Binks* [1985] 2 All E.R. 699.

agreements between two parties, and involved the exercise of discretionary power that the courts should control. In another case, the court simply regarded it as axiomatic that a public authority established by statute and exercising statutory powers could be judicially reviewed to ensure that it had properly interpreted its own regulations and had not acted unfairly in terminating a licence.[468] In a third, the court appeared to base its decision that judicial review was available on the fact that underlying the relationship was the common law right to trade.[469] In another case, involving a resolution by a local authority banning an individual from access to council premises, the courts drew a distinction between premises to which the public did have access and those to which they did not. There was a public law element in relation to decisions denying individuals access to premises to which the public generally had access, and such decisions could be subject to judicial review. The issue would only be a matter of private law if the local authority was relying on its powers as a landowner in relation to premises where the public had no right of access.[470]

This readiness to apply public law principles alongside the contractual provisions has continued after *Walsh*.[471] The courts have been prepared to superimpose public law principles onto contractual situations, and to ensure the observance of those principles by way of judicial review. They are prepared to do this even if the effect of granting a public law remedy is to vary the rights existing under a contract as, for example, where a decision to terminate a contract is quashed and the contractual provisions then revived. In *R. v Hertfordshire County Council Ex p. NUPE*[472] the council decided to terminate the contracts of employment of school dinner ladies and offer them new contracts of employment on less favourable terms. The Master of the Rolls held that if it could be established that such a decision was unreasonable in the public law or "*Wednesbury*" sense—that is, so unreasonable that no reasonable local authority could have come to the decision—then questions of public law would arise, and the courts could deal with the matter by way of judicial review. On the facts, no

2–151

---

[468] *R. v Basildon City Council Ex p. Brown* (1981) 79 L.G.R. 655 per Lord Denning M.R. at 661; and per Templeman LJ at 667; Dunn LJ considered that the particular dispute only involved contractual rights as it involved the giving of notice under the terms of the licence and so was not reviewable; even Dunn LJ, however, appeared to consider that the authority was subject to the control of the courts and if the decision to terminate was shown to be ultra vires or taken in bad faith or in breach of natural justice, he would have held that judicial review was available, see at 672 and 674–675. See also *R. v Barnsley Metropolitan Borough Council Ex p. Hook* [1976] 1 W.L.R. 1052. See also *R. v Durham City Council Ex p. Robinson, The Times*, January 31, 1992. The cases are discussed in Arrowsmith, "Protecting the Interests of Bidders for Public Contracts" [1994] C.L.J. 104.

[469] *R. v Birmingham City Council Ex p. Dredger*, (1993) 91 L.G.R. 532. (The decision there—to increase stall charges—may in fact have been based on the exercise of a statutory power to raise charges conferred by s.36 of the Local Government (Miscellaneous Provisions) Act 1976. If so, that would seem sufficient to attract the supervisory jurisdiction of the courts and suggestions that the decision was in substance managerial or commercial would not be sufficient to defeat the claim: see *R. v British Coal Corporation Ex p. Vardy* [1993] I.C.R. 720, discussed above at para.2–011).

[470] *R. v Brent London Borough Council Ex p. Assegai* (1987) 151 L.G. Rev. 891. See also *City and Hackney Health Authority v NUPE* [1985] I.R.L.R. 252 (whether a shop steward had a right to enter hospital premises to perform union duties was decided in terms of whether he had a contractual licence or a bare licence to enter the premise and, if so, whether the licence had been terminated). See also *Verrall v Great Yarmouth Borough Council* [1981] Q.B. 202 (whether political party able to hire a hall decided on the availability of specific performance to enforce the hire contract).

[471] *R. v East Berkshire Area Health Authority Ex p. Walsh* [1985] Q.B. 152.

[472] [1985] I.R.L.R. 258.

such unreasonableness had been established. Similarly, the Divisional Court has held that a decision not to pay wages due under a contract of employment could constitute both a breach of contract and also be so unreasonable in the public law sense that judicial review would be available to correct the error.[473] The court did grant the application for judicial review and declared that the decision to withhold the wages was unlawful. In *Walsh*[474] itself, the court indicated that had the issue involved the legality of a policy of delegation of power within the authority, then judicial review would have been available to deal with the issue.

2–152   The effect of such developments could potentially operate as a restriction of the *Walsh* doctrine. Public law remedies will not be available when a contract specifically deals with a particular issue such as the procedures to be followed on dismissal and the individual is seeking to enforce the specific provisions or rights that arise by necessary implication from those specific provisions. Apart from those situations, public law principles and remedies may still govern the actions of public authorities even in a contractual context. This is a desirable development. Public authorities are meant to act in the public interest and should not be given the same freedom of contract as would an individual. The courts should ensure the proper exercise of discretionary power by public authorities, whatever the precise source of that power.[475]

Contractual position of the Crown

2–153   The contractual position of the Crown is different from that of bodies created by statute or exercising statutory powers. Statute may vest a specific power to contract in a particular minister of the Crown. The Crown also has inherent capacity at common law to conclude contracts without statutory authority.[476] This capacity results from the fact that the Crown is a corporation sole or a corporation aggregate, that is, it has legal personality and with it the ability at common law to enter into contracts like any other person with legal personality.

2–154   The main issue is whether the exercise of the common law contractual power is subject to judicial review. In this context, the Crown (in practice, the relevant government minister or department) would not be exercising a statutory power to contract and judicial review could not be justified on the usual ground that statutory powers have to be exercised in accordance with the substantive principles of public law. Judicial review is no longer limited, however, to controlling the exercise of statutory powers but encompasses prerogative and non-statutory powers. However, in *R. v Lord Chancellor Ex p. Hibbet and Saunders*,[477] the Divisional Court held that the tendering process adopted by the Lord Chancellor's Department prior to the exercise of the common law power to enter into a contract to engage court shorthand writers was not amenable to judicial review even though the process had been procedurally unfair. The Divisional Court considered that there was no statutory underpinning to the tendering exercise, as the statutory provisions set out the framework within which

---

[473] *R. v Liverpool City Council Ex p. Ferguson and Ferguson* [1985] I.R.L.R. 501.

[474] *R. v East Berkshire Area Health Authority Ex p. Walsh* (see above, fn.471).

[475] On the availability of the tort of misfeasance in a public office for misuse of contractual powers see *Jones v Swansea City Council* [1990] 1 W.L.R. 54.

[476] *M. v Home Office* [1994] 1 A.C. 377 at 424F–G.

[477] *The Times*, March 12, 1993.

the shorthand writers were employed and did not provide the power under which they were employed. The Divisional Court concluded that there was no other public law element to the tendering process as it involved "no exceptional feature beyond the performance by a public body of normal commercial activity uncircumscribed by statute".[478] Whilst there is force in the ruling of the Divisional Court, it is submitted that its conclusion was not inevitable and there was scope for holding that the process of awarding a contract was amenable to judicial review. First, it was accepted that the Lord Chancellor who awarded the contract was a public body. Secondly, the award involved the expenditure of public money; if the making of ex gratia payments in the exercise of prerogative powers is reviewable,[479] there is no reason, in principle, why a decision to award a contract, which also involves public expenditure, should not also attract public scrutiny. Thirdly, the Lord Chancellor was a significant if not monopoly user of the services in question. Fourthly, if the Lord Chancellor's Department had been exercising a statutory power, it would probably have been subject to judicial review.[480] In those circumstances, the fact that the Department performed the same activity through common law rather than statutory means suggests that the activity is one suited to judicial review. Finally, the tendering process occurs at the pre-contractual stage; there is no contract or consensual submission to the jurisdiction such as would take the activity outside the scope of judicial review if it was otherwise public. The principle that all discretionary powers are to be exercised in the public interest in accordance with normal public law principles is sufficiently wide to bring a decision to award a contract within the scope of judicial review and the fact that the source of the power was the common law rather than statute should not prevent judicial review being available to correct a recognisable public law error.

This issue was also debated in the 1970s when the then government used its **2–155** contractual powers to enforce its anti-inflation policy. A blacklist was drawn up of companies who had not complied with the government's pay policy and the government decided not to accept tenders or enter into contracts with those companies. The legality of the policy was doubted but never tested before the courts.[481] There are particularly strong arguments in principle for arguing that the common law powers of contracting ought to be regarded as a public law matter and subject to judicial review if they are being used as instrument to achieve or bolster government policy.

Judicial review and employment relationships

The role of judicial review in employment relationships has been the source of **2–156** much litigation.[482] It is well established that the mere fact that a person is employed "by a public authority does not per se inject any element of public law"

---

[478] *R. v Lord Chancellor Ex p. Hibbert and Saunders*, *The Times*, March 12, 1993 per Rose LJ.

[479] As was accepted as long ago as 1967 in *R. v Criminal Injuries Compensation Board Ex p. Lain* [1967] 2 Q.B. 864 discussed above at para.2–018.

[480] See above, para.2–144.

[481] See Ferguson and Page, "Pay Restraint: The Legal Constraints" (1978) 128 New L.J. 515; Ganz [1978] P.L. 33.

[482] See Fredman and Morris, "Public or Private? State Employees and Judicial Review" [1991] 107 L.Q.R. 298.

into the relationship.[483] Public authorities may enter into contracts of employment with their employees and an employee may be seeking to do no more than enforce their contractual rights. That would normally involve issues of private law. Alternatively, there may be no contract of employment and the employment relationship, or at least certain aspects of it, may be directly regulated by statute or the prerogative. In such cases, issues of public law may arise. In general terms, the principles governing the exercise of powers to contract[484] apply in cases where there are contracts of employment. The courts have, in practice, adopted a different emphasis in employment cases. First, if there is a contract, the courts are less likely to superimpose on the relationship any obligation to observe the principles of public law. Secondly, there are indications that the courts may not be prepared to hold that judicial review is available even if there is no contract of employment and the relationship is one that can only be regulated by the exercise of statutory powers.[485] The courts have adopted a four-fold classification to assist in determining whether a claim raises public law issues whilst recognising that the dividing line between public and private law issues is often difficult and needs to be developed on a case-by-case basis.[486]

2–157   The first group concerns public sector employees who do have a contract of employment.[487] Disputes arising out of the employment relationship will be private law disputes. Thus claims to enforce a right derived from the contract[488] (or from statutory requirements which have been incorporated into the contract[489]) are private law claims enforceable by ordinary action for damages or a declaration or injunction. A dispute arising out of the termination of a contract of employment or service will be treated as a private law dispute, even if the claimant is seeking to have principles normally seen as public law principles (such the obligation to observe procedural fairness or natural justice) grafted onto the employment relationship.[490] The courts still view this as an essentially private law dispute and, it seems, either the claimant will only be able to claim the benefit of these principles on the grounds that there is an implied obligation in the contract to observe them (such as an implied obligation to act in accordance with

---

[483] per Sir John Donaldson M.R. in *R. v East Berkshire Area Health Authority Ex p. Walsh* [1985] Q.B. 152 at 164.

[484] See above, paras 2–126 to 2–146.

[485] See *R. v Lord Chancellor's Department Ex p. Nangle* [1991] I.C.R. 743 discussed below, para.2–157.

[486] See *McClaren v Home Office* [1990] I.C.R. 824.

[487] There are areas of uncertainty where it is not clear whether a particular group of employees such as prison officers have contracts of employment or whether their employment is solely regulated by the prerogative or statute (*McClaren v Home Office* above, fn.486). Civil servants formerly held office under the prerogative but it is now recognised that they may have contracts of employment and the likelihood is that most do (*R. v Lord Chancellor's Office Ex p. Nangle* above, fn.485) Police officers do not have contracts of employment.

[488] *R. v East Berkshire Area Health Authority Ex p. Walsh* above, fn.471; *R. v London Borough of Lambeth Ex p. Thompson* [1996] C.O.D. 217; *R. v British Broadcasting Corporation Ex p. Lavelle* [1983] 1 W.L.R. 23; *R. (Arthurworrey) v London Borough of Haringey* [2002] I.C.R. 279 and *Evans v University of Cambridge* [2003] E.L.R. 8.

[489] *Ex p. Walsh* [1985] Q.B. 152.

[490] *R. v Derby County Council Ex p. Noble* [1990] I.C.R. 808 (termination of the appointment of a police surgeon was private law only). *R. v East Berkshire Area Health Authority Ex p. Walsh* above, fn.449.

natural justice) or he will be unable to claim the benefit of these principles.[491] The fact that an employer is a public body,[492] or that there is a degree of public interest in the activities performed by the individual,[493] is not sufficient to make the matter a public law one. There may, however, be cases where there is a sufficient element of statutory underpinning to the contract of employment as to make decisions to dismiss amenable to judicial review. Thus, local authorities are required by statute to create a post of director of children's services and the functions of the post-holder are defined by statute. In those circumstances, there was a sufficient statutory underpinning to the contract of employment. The employer was obliged to observe the public law principles of procedural fairness before terminating such a contract and judicial review was available to enforce that obligation.[494] A question may also arise as to whether or not the parties have in fact entered into a contract, and if so what the terms are. These are seen as questions of private law not public law.[495]

There is a second group of situations where an employee will still be able to   **2–158**
seek judicial review. This occurs when there is some disciplinary body created by statute or the prerogative to which the employer or the employee is required to refer disputes. An example of this is the Civil Service Appeal Board. This is established under the prerogative and hears appeals by civil servants against decisions to dismiss them. Decisions of that body are subject to judicial review.[496] Other examples may include situations where there is a sufficient statutory or prerogative aspect to the dispute. These could include situations where aspects of the employment relationship are governed directly by statute, such as disciplinary matters in relation to prison officers which are regulated by a statutory code[497] or instructions given to employees which contravene specific statutory provisions[498] or situations where there is no contract of employment and the terms of service are directly regulated by statute or the prerogative.[499]

The third category of cases where judicial review may be available arises   **2–159**
where a public body takes a policy decision or a decision in relation to staff generally, even if that decision will affect individual members of staff and may involve varying their terms and conditions of employment or their dismissal. The

---

[491] See per Woolf LJ in *R. v Derby County Council Ex p. Noble* above, fn.490.

[492] *R. v East Berkshire Area Health Authority Ex p. Walsh*, fn.471 above.

[493] *R. v Derby County Council Ex p. Noble* above, fn.490.

[494] *R (Shoesmith) v Ofsted, Secretary of State for Education and the London Borough of Haringey* [2011] ICR 1195 at [76]–[91].

[495] *McClaren v Home Office* [1990] I.C.R. 824.

[496] *R. v Civil Service Appeal Board Ex p. Bruce* [1988] I.C.R. 649 (affd. by the Court of Appeal [1989] I.C.R. 171 although judicial review was not granted as there was a more appropriate alternative remedy in the form of a complaint to an industrial tribunal; see also *R. v Civil Service Appeal Board Ex p. Cunningham* [1992] I.C.R. 816 and *R. v Lord Chancellor's Department Ex p. Nangle* [1991] I.C.R. 743.

[497] *R. v Secretary of State for the Home Department Ex p. Attard* (1990) 2 Admin. L.R. 641; see also *R. v East Berkshire Area Health Authority Ex p. Walsh* [1986] Q.B. 152.

[498] *R. v City of Sunderland Ex p. Baumber* [1996] C.O.D. 211 (local authority gave instructions to educational psychologists employed by them on the preparation of reports; the lawfulness of those instructions fell to be judged by reference to the Education (Special Educational Needs) Regulations 1983 and not by reference to the contract of employment.

[499] As with the police; see *R. v Chief Constable of Devon and Cornwall Constabulary Ex p. Hay* [1996] 2 All E.R. 711.

example usually cited in this connection is the *G.C.H.Q.* case[500] where the government decided to alter the terms of all staff at a particular establishment by removing their entitlement to be a member of a trade union. Another example would be the local authority decision to terminate the contracts of all school dinner ladies and offer them new terms and conditions,[501] as that was really a policy decision of the authority as to how it was going to manage an aspect of its affairs rather than a particular employment dispute with a particular individual.

2–160   The fourth category identified in *McClaren v Home Office*[502] was disciplinary procedures which were of a purely domestic nature and, albeit that their decisions might affect the public, the process of judicial review would not be available. Woolf LJ did not explore the scope of that category. The Divisional Court has also indicated that judicial review may not be available if a civil servant had no contract of employment and he was subjected to merely internal departmental disciplinary procedures as these were purely domestic procedures which did not give rise to judicial review.[503] Such an approach is, with respect, an unsatisfactory analysis of the problem. A preferable approach to the fourth group of cases would be to recognise that there are situations where there is no contract of employment, or where aspects of the employment relationship are directly regulated by statute. Thus, the terms and conditions of employment of the police are regulated by statute[504] as they have no contract and the disciplinary code governing prison officers is statutory.[505] There is no doubt that disputes arising out of these matters are amenable to judicial review. The bodies whose actions are under challenge are public bodies and the subject-matter of the claim involves public law, usually determining the validity of action taken in the exercise of statutory powers. They can, if necessary, be seen as examples of the second group of employees referred to in *McClaren v Home Office*.[506] Alternatively, the four-fold distinction may not be an exhaustive classification of situations where employment disputes are public law matters. Regulation of employment by way of direct exercise of statutory power can be seen as another case where judicial review is available. In the context of civil servants, they will either be engaged under a contract of employment or hold office under the prerogative and their terms and conditions will be regulated by the prerogative. If there is a contract, the subject-matter of the dispute will normally involve questions of private

---

[500]   *Council of Civil Service Unions v Minister for the Civil Service* [1985] A.C. 374.

[501]   *R. v Hertfordshire County Council Ex p. NUPE* [1985] I.R.L.R. 258. See also *R. v Liverpool City Corporation Ex p. Ferguson* [1985] I.R.L.R. 501.

[502]   [1990] I.C.R. 824 at 837.

[503]   *R. v Lord Chancellor's Department Ex p. Nangle* [1991] I.C.R. 743. A similar approach was taken in respect of statutory powers in *R. v Trent Regional Health Authority Ex p. Jones, The Times,* June 19, 1986 (judicial review was not available to challenge a decision not to appoint a person to the post of consultant as there was no statutory underpinning of the appointment process and the decision was no different from a decision by any commercial or other employer not to employ a particular person). That decision also overlooks the fact that the decision to appoint involved an exercise of statutory power.

[504]   See, e.g. *R. v Chief Constable of the Devon and Cornwall Constabulary Ex p. Hay* [1996] 2 All E.R. 711; *R. v South Yorkshire Police Ex p. Middup, The Times,* May 1, 1989; *Chief Constable of North Wales Police v Evans* [1982] 1 W.L.R. 1155.

[505]   *R. v Secretary of State for the Home Department Ex p. Attard* (1990) 2 Admin. L.R. 641; *R. v Secretary of State for the Home Department Ex p. Benwell* [1985] Q.B. 554.

[506]   [1990] I.C.R. 824.

law.[507] If, however, there is no contract, the situation is that the individual will be challenging the exercise of prerogative power by a public body to enforce principles that can only be derived from public law. As such, the matter should be seen as amenable to judicial review. May LJ in the Divisional Court in *Ex p. Bruce*[508] considered that in "the absence of a contract of service between [a civil servant] and the Crown, I think that one is bound to hold that there was a sufficient public law element behind the applicant's dismissal from his appointment with the Inland Revenue and the hearing of this appeal by the board to entitle him to apply for judicial review". The only reason for not granting judicial review in that case was that a complaint to an industrial tribunal was a more appropriate forum for resolving the dispute, not that judicial review was not available.[509] Another approach is to recognise that judicial review may be available, and some at least of the principles of public law may apply to a contract of employment where there is a sufficient statutory underpinning of that contract. Thus, where statute required the creation of a particular post and defined the functions of the post-holder, decisions to terminate the contract of employment were amenable to judicial review where the employer failed to comply with the public law principles of procedural fairness.[510] The courts have not always applied this analysis however. The Court of Appeal has, for example, held that a decision to terminate the secondment of a police officer to the National Crime Squad is not amenable to judicial review.[511] The National Crime Squad is created by statute and it has statutory power to appoint officers on such terms and conditions as it considers appropriate but those terms do not form part of any contract with the officer. The Court of Appeal held that managerial or operational decisions relating to secondment of a particular officer did not have a sufficient public element to render them amenable to judicial review.

Tort

The distinction between public law rights and private law rights sounding in damages applies equally in the realm of tortious liability. The courts accept that the activities of public authorities can involve liability for damages at common law. Claims for damages may arise in the field of negligence, where a public authority may owe a common law duty of care to an individual.[512] In appropriate circumstances, a public authority may also be liable for other torts such as nuisance,[513] or trespass.[514] Such claims may raise no issue of public law, and the fact that the defendant is a public body may be irrelevant to the claim. It is,

2–161

---

[507] As the Divisional Court held was the case in *R. v Lord Chancellor's Department Ex p. Nangle* [1991] I.C.R. 743.

[508] [1988] I.C.R. 171.

[509] This, it is submitted, is the true ratio of the decision rather than analysing the decision as dependent on the fact that the Civil Service Appeal Board was sufficiently independent of the employer and employee to be judicially reviewable; see *R. v Lord Chancellor's Department Ex p. Nangle* [1991] I.C.R. 743.

[510] *R (Shoesmith) v Ofsted, the Secretary of State for Education and the London Borough of Haringey* [2011] EWCA Civ 642.

[511] *R. (Tucker) v Director-General of the National Crime Squad* [2003] I.C.R. 599.

[512] See, e.g. *Rigby v Chief Constable of Northamptonshire* [1985] 1 W.L.R. 1242.

[513] See, e.g. *Page Motors v Epsom and Ewell Borough Council* (1981) 125 S.J. 590.

[514] See, e.g. *Cooper v Wandsworth Board of Works* (1863) 14 C.B. 180.

however, particularly difficult to separate issues of public law and private law in the field of tortious liability. Questions of negligence frequently have to be assessed against the background of statutory powers and duties of the public body concerned. Public law issues concerning the extent of a public body's powers, and of the validity of its actions, may frequently be relevant in determining the existence of a common law duty of care, or whether there has been a breach.

2–162   There may also be circumstances where the same set of facts give rise to both a claim that a public body's actions violate one of the substantive principles of public law, and therefore should be set aside, and also a claim for damages for violation of a private law right. An applicant may claim that the activities of a public authority are ultra vires its statutory powers and also give rise to tortious liability at common law. Judicial review would be available in relation to the public law claim, and damages could also be claimed in the same proceedings.[515] An individual may seek judicial review for breach of a statutory duty and claim damages in the same proceedings on the grounds that the duty is one of those duties where a civil action for damages also lies for breach.[516] In the case of one tort, misfeasance in a public office, the ultra vires nature of the act is one of the central elements of the tort. A claim that an act was ultra vires could of course be brought by judicial review and this could be coupled with a claim for damages, on the grounds that the act was done maliciously or in the knowledge that it was ultra vires and would cause injury. Other torts are likely to include an issue of ultra vires at some stage. In actions for false imprisonment, for example, a public body may claim that it had power to detain a person while the person may claim that the power was invalidly exercised. Again, an application for judicial review of the legality of the act could be coupled with a claim for damages.

Statutory duties

2–163   Statutory duties raise difficulties of classification. The fact that the source of the obligation is statute, and that the body on which the duty is imposed is clearly a public body, are strong indicators that the obligation is enforceable by judicial review. Certain statutory duties may, however, give rise to a right to damages in the event of a breach: such rights are regarded as private law rights. The criteria for determining whether a statutory duty is one of those giving rise to civil liability are discussed in Chapter 15.

2–164   The following possible analyses of statutory duties arise. A statutory duty imposed on a public body could be classed as a public law duty only, which does not give rise to a right to damages in the event of breach. Such a duty could only be enforced by way of judicial review. The duty may alternatively be seen as creating both public law rights, enforceable by judicial review by a person with sufficient interest, and also giving rise to a private law right to damages for those who suffer loss. In such instances the same duty could give rise to public and

---

[515] See Senior Courts Act 1981 s.31(4); CPR r.54.3.

[516] *R. v Inner London Education Authority Ex p. Ali and Murshid* [1990] C.O.D. 317; *R. v Kensington and Chelsea Royal London Borough Council Ex p. Hammell* [1989] Q.B. 518 (interim injunction granted during course of judicial review proceedings to protect private law right).

private law claims. Thus, an individual may bring a claim for judicial review and couple that with a claim for damages.[517]

It is also possible that a statutory duty could be imposed on a public body, but be classed as giving rise to private law rights only. Even though the obligation is statutory in origin and the body performs some public functions, it may be that the subject-matter of a particular statutory duty is seen as not involving those public functions, but regulating the activities of the public body in its ordinary non-public capacity. Council tenants are given a statutory right to buy their homes: statute provides that such rights are enforceable by injunction,[518] which may be sought by ordinary claim.[519] Thus, even though the source of the obligation is statutory and local authorities are clearly public bodies, it is possible to regard the duty as regulating the capacity of the local authority as an ordinary landowner. More doubtful is the decision in *Ettridge v Morrell*.[520] Here, the Court of Appeal held that the statutory duty imposed on local education authorities, to provide a room for a public meeting for an election candidate, gave rise to private law rights enforceable by an ordinary claim. It is surprising that this particular duty was analysed as creating a private law right. The statutory source of the duty, the fact that it was imposed on a public body, and the subject-matter of the obligation, all point to it being a public law obligation. It is, of course, possible that the statute created both a public law obligation enforceable by judicial review (by a person with sufficient interest) and a private law right for those suffering special damage. This possibility was not canvassed by the Court of Appeal.

2–165

Finally, some duties are imposed on both private and public bodies, such as the health and safety duties in the employment field. Here, the only question is the private law one of whether the duties do give rise to a right of damages for breach. The fact that one employer may be a public body will be irrelevant to the obligation.

2–166

No, or no live, issue of public law raised

Judicial review may not be available where a claim that a public authority is liable in damages raises no, or no live, issue of public law. Some claims raise no substantive issues of public law, but simply involve determining whether the usual principles governing civil liability apply. Allegations of negligence may involve establishing a duty of care, breach and causation: these are matters of private law and may raise no issue of public law. Allegations of medical negligence against an area health authority, for example, will usually involve no question of public law, and will be brought by ordinary action not judicial review.[521] Allegations of nuisance may likewise raise no issue of public law.[522]

2–167

---

[517] See, e.g. *R. v Inner London Education Authority Ex p. Ali and Murshid* (see above, fn.516).

[518] Housing Act 1985 s.138.

[519] See, e.g. *Dyer v Dorset County Council* [1989] Q.B. 346; and *Dance v Welwyn Hatfield District Council* [1990] 1 W.L.R. 1097. Some ancillary issues have been brought by way of judicial review, although the jurisdictional point was not taken. See, e.g. *R. v Rushmoor Borough Council Ex p. Barrett* [1988] 2 W.L.R. 1271.

[520] (1987) 85 L.G.R. 100, CA.

[521] See, e.g. *Hotson v East Berkshire Health Authority* [1987] A.C. 750.

[522] See, e.g. *Page Motors v Epsom and Ewell Borough Council* (1981) 80 L.G.R. 337.

2–168   A claim may raise no live issue of public law as it may not seek to have the action of the public body invalidated or nullified on the grounds that one of the substantive principles of public law has been violated. Rather, the claimant may simply be seeking to establish liability in damages. A claim will raise no live issue of public law if, for practical reasons, the claimant no longer has an interest in setting aside the decision,[523] or accepts that the validity of the decision cannot be challenged,[524] or where the decision has been revoked,[525] or is invalidated in earlier proceedings,[526] and the individual is seeking compensation for the loss incurred in the period before the decision was set aside. Such claims can, and usually should, be brought by way of ordinary claim as they involve solely questions of private law. The House of Lords in *Davy v Spelthorne Borough Council* had to consider whether a claim for damages for negligence against a public body, which raised no live issue of public law (as the time for challenging the validity of the decision had passed), could be brought by way of ordinary writ, and answered that question in the affirmative.[527] Lord Wilberforce said, by way of obiter dicta, that a simple claim for damages for negligence could not be brought by way of judicial review.[528] Lord Fraser, giving the majority judgment, indicated that the judicial review procedure was " . . . entirely inappropriate . . ." in the circumstances of the case.[529]

2–169   There may be no absolute jurisdictional bar to making a claim for judicial review where the public law issues are no longer live by the time that the courts come to consider granting permission.[530] On occasions, the court has refused permission to apply for judicial review, as a matter of discretion, where the public law issues have become academic and the claim is made simply to enable the claimant to bring a claim for damages which he could have brought by an ordinary claim.[531] There may be cases where there was a live public law issue at the time that permission was granted but that issue has subsequently become academic. There, the court can order that the damages claim continue as if begun by claim.[532] This may be a more appropriate course of action in non-criminal matters rather than simply dismissing the judicial review claim and leaving the claimant to commence fresh civil proceedings to claim damages. In criminal cases, however, where there can be no appeal to the Court of Appeal from the court hearing the substantive claim for judicial review, the better course is for the Divisional Court hearing the substantive claim to refuse the claim so that the

---

[523] See, e.g. *Jones v Swansea City Council* [1990] 1 W.L.R. 54. (The House of Lords dealt with the case on other grounds: [1990] 1 W.L.R. 1453).

[524] *Davy v Spelthorne Borough Council* [1984] A.C. 262.

[525] *Bourgoin S.A. v Ministry of Agriculture, Fisheries and Food* [1986] Q.B. 716.

[526] *Calveley v Chief Constable of Merseyside Police; Norrall v Same; Park v Chief Constable of the Greater Manchester Police* [1989] A.C. 1228.

[527] *Davy v Spelthorne Borough Council* [1984] A.C. 262.

[528] *Davy v Spelthorne Borough Council* [1984] A.C. 262 at 277. The Court of Appeal indicated that if Davy had sought judicial review of the validity of enforcement notice within the relevant time-limit, he could have added a claim for damages (1983) 81 L.G.R. 580.

[529] [1984] A.C. 262 at 274.

[530] *R. v North Avon District Council Ex p. Palmer* (1994) 6 Admin. L.R. 195. That case, however, involved the housing legislation when it was thought that a damages claim could not lie unless the public law decision was first quashed in judicial review proceedings: see above at para.2–015.

[531] See, e.g. *R. v Ministry of Agriculture, Fisheries and Food Ex p. Live Sheep Traders Ltd* [1995] C.O.D. 297.

[532] Under CPR r.54.20.

claimant can issue fresh civil proceeding claiming damages. The claimant will then be able to appeal any adverse decision in the civil action to the Court of Appeal in the normal way.[533]

Family law

The courts have statutory and in some instances inherent jurisdiction[534] to determine certain matters in relation to children and those lacking mental capacity to order their own affairs. In such cases, the task of the court is to determine what is in the best interests of the child or the adult lacking mental capacity. In addition, certain courts have jurisdiction to hear care proceedings in relation to children under the Children Act 1989. Such matters are normally defined as private law or family matters. Issues arising in these contexts may, however, overlap with the public law supervisory jurisdiction of the courts over the decisions of statutory or other public bodies. Here the courts do not review the merits of a decision but simply review the lawfulness of the exercise of functions by public bodies applying the usual principles of public law. Such claims are brought by way of judicial review in the Administrative Court.

2–170

The critical question in each case is whether a particular challenge is to be determined by the courts deciding what is in the best interests of the child or the adult lacking capacity or by the courts applying the public law principles governing review of the lawfulness (but not the merits) of the decision.[535] The second question concerns the appropriate procedure for bringing a particular challenge.

2–171

The precise demarcation line between family or private law issues and public law ones is not always easy to identify. Where the court is being asked to adjudicate upon, and take for the child or adult, a decision such as whether or not to undergo particular medical treatment, or where the person should reside or with whom the person should have contact, then the issue is essentially one involving courts deciding what is in the best interests of the person concerned. Similarly, where care proceedings in relation to children are already in being, matters arising during those proceedings are usually an inappropriate method of challenging local authority decisions. Rather, such issues, including issues under the European Convention on Human Rights, should be dealt with by the court dealing with the care proceedings.[536] Where the court is reviewing the exercise of a discretionary power by a public body, then the challenge is to be determined by reference to the ordinary public law principles.[537] Thus, challenges to a public body's refusal to provide particular medical treatment on resource grounds, or challenges to a local authority's assessment of a person's needs and whether those

2–172

---

[533] *R. v Blandford Justices Ex p. Pamment* [1990] 1 W.L.R. 1490.
[534] See, e.g. the Children Act 1989 or the provisions relating to the management of a patient's affairs under the Mental Capacity 2005.
[535] See *A. v A Health Authority* [2002] Fam. 213 at [89].
[536] See *Re (A Child) (Care Proceedings: Human Rights Claims) (Practice Note)* [2004] 1 W.L.R. 1432 esp. at [95]–[100]; *In Re L* [2003] 2 F.L.R. 160; *Re M. (Care Proceedings and Judicial Review)* [2003] 2 F.L.R. 171 and see *R. (S) v London Borough of Haringey* [2004] 1 F.L.R. 50.
[537] *A. v A Health Authority* [2002] Fam. 213, [89]–[101]; and *Coventry City Council v O* [2012] 3 W.L.R. 208 at [28].

needs call for the provision of particular services,[538] or to the exercise of a statutory power to remove a child from foster carers[539] are to be determined by public law principles.

2–173 In terms of procedure, issues involving the application of the best interests test are brought in the Family Division. Challenges to the exercise of statutory or other public functions should be brought by way of a claim for judicial review. That requires permission to proceed and the judicial review claim must be brought promptly. In practical terms, it will often be appropriate, once permission has been granted, for such a claim to be dealt with by a Family Division judge, either sitting as a nominated judge in the Administrative Court,[540] or by transferring the claim to the Family Division in the exercise of powers conferred by CPR r.54.20.[541] In either case, the judge who determines the claim will apply the substantive principles of public law. Where issues of private law and public law arise out of the same set of facts, it is clearly preferable for the proceedings to be consolidated in the Family Division where one judge, applying the best-interests test or public law principles as appropriate, can deal with all the issues.[542]

F. DECLARATIONS AND INJUNCTIONS

2–174 Public law has in the past been defined in terms of the availability of the prerogative remedies. The ordinary remedies of the declaration and injunction have over the years been used as a means of exercising the supervisory jurisdiction of the courts, as well as vindicating private law rights. One of the purposes of the 1977 reforms of the judicial review procedure was to make declarations and injunctions available within the same procedure as the prerogative remedies (the remedies also continue to be available in ordinary actions outside the procedure for judicial review as before). The court has jurisdiction on a claim for judicial review to grant an injunction or a declaration instead of, or in addition to, one of the prerogative remedies, if it is just and convenient to do so having regard to:

(a) the nature of the matters in respect of which relief may be granted by mandatory orders, quashing orders and prohibiting orders;

(b) the nature of the persons and bodies against whom relief may be granted by such orders; and

(c) all the circumstances of the case.[543]

---

[538] *A. v A Health Authority* [2002] Fam. 213, [93] and [110]–[114].

[539] *Coventry City Council v O* [2012] 3 W.L.R. 208 (dealing with whether or not to grant an interim injunction: see [36]–[38].

[540] See comments of Woolf J. in *R. v Dover Magistrates' Court Ex p. Kidner* [1983] 1 All E.R. 475 suggesting that applications for permission should include a request that the claim be transferred to the Family Division if permission is granted. Munby J. considered that such claims ought, normally, to be heard in the Family Division: see *A. v A Health Authority* [2002] Fam. 213 at [89].

[541] See below, paras 2–181 to 2–182 on the powers of transfer.

[542] See comments of Woolf LJ in *Re D. (A Minor) (Wardship: Jurisdiction)* [1987] 1 W.L.R. 1400 on the desirability of ensuring that wardship applications and judicial review applications run in tandem.

[543] Senior Courts Act 1981 s.31(2).

A declaration or an injunction can be the sole relief claimed in a claim for judicial review, and does not need to be coupled with a claim for one of the prerogative remedies.[544]

2–175

It is now clear that, contrary to earlier dicta,[545] the jurisdiction of the court to award declaratory or injunctive relief is not confined to situations where the prerogative orders would be available.[546] The declaration and injunction are not merely an alternative to one of the prerogative remedies. The jurisdiction of the court is not, however, unlimited. A claim for judicial review may only be made in respect of a public law matter, as discussed in this Chapter. Only if the matter is a public law one, can the court grant declaratory or interlocutory relief in a case where a prerogative remedy is not available.[547] A declaration and injunction cannot, therefore, be sought by way of judicial review against domestic tribunals such as those who draw their jurisdiction solely from contract.[548] Although declarations and injunctions may be sought against such bodies by ordinary claim, they are still regarded as essentially private bodies and outside the ambit of judicial review. Nor can a declaration or injunction be sought by way of judicial review to enforce purely private law rights, such as those derived from contract, even though one of the parties is a public authority.[549]

2–176

The situations in which a declaration would be available, although a prerogative order would not be, would seem to be limited to situations where, for technical or historical reasons the prerogative remedies are not available but the issues are clearly ones of public law. In *R. v Bromley London Borough Council Ex p. Lambeth London Borough Council*,[550] the court considered that a prerogative order would not have been available as the respondent had not taken any decision affecting the applicant. The applicant simply wished to obtain a declaration that payments to a particular organisation would be lawful under the Local Government Act 1972. The application was made against Bromley London Borough Council because they had earlier brought judicial review proceedings against a different local authority, to stop payments to the body which then operated under a different constitution. Hodgson J. held that he had jurisdiction to grant a declaration, even though no prerogative remedy could be granted, as the dispute did lie in the field of public law, since it involved the question of the statutory powers of public bodies. Woolf J. has also held that the court has jurisdiction in an appropriate case to grant a declaration on some public law point of general importance, even if no decision has yet been taken by the public authority and so no prerogative order lay as yet. That case involved a challenge to the reasoning underlying a decision of an inspector on a planning appeal, even

2–177

---

[544] *R. v Bromley London Borough Council Ex p. Lambeth London Borough Council, The Times*, June 16, 1984.

[545] See *I.R.C. v National Federation of Self-Employed and Small Businesses* [1982] A.C. 617.

[546] *R. v Bromley London Borough Council Ex p. Lambeth London Borough Council* (see above, fn.544). See also the dicta of the Court of Appeal in *Law v National Greyhound Racing Club* [1983] 1 W.L.R. 1302, and of Pill J. in *R. v Arthur Young (a firm) Ex p. Thamesdown Borough Council* [1989] C.O.D. 392.

[547] *R. v Bromley London Borough Council Ex p. Lambeth London Borough Council, The Times*, June 16, 1984.

[548] *Law v National Greyhound Racing Club* [1983] 1 W.L.R. 1302.

[549] *R. v British Broadcasting Corp Ex p. Lavelle* [1983] 1 W.L.R. 23.

[550] *The Times*, June 16, 1984.

though the decision itself was not and could not be challenged; as a matter of discretion, Woolf J. refused the declaration.[551]

2–178   Two other examples are often given in this context. The first is judicial review of delegated legislation: it has been suggested that a quashing order is not available to quash such legislation.[552] This apparent restriction on the scope of quashing orders probably owed its origin to the now defunct doctrine that they only lay against judicial acts. This is certainly no longer true since it is now well accepted that administrative acts may be quashed by a quashing order.[553] There is now no reason in principle why legislative measures should not be similarly subject to quashing orders, and it is likely that this supposed technical restriction on the scope of the remedy no longer exists.[554] Challenges to delegated legislation would normally be a public law matter. The power to make such measures would derive from statute (or prerogative) powers, and the usual public law principles apply to such exercises of power. In addition, the justification for a separate public law procedure—such as the need for shorter time-limits and leave, to protect public authorities from undue uncertainty as to the legality of the acts that they have done – apply with especial force to legislative measures. A decision that a legislative measure is ultra vires and of no effect, and presumably that any decision taken in pursuance of the measure is also ultra vires, would have ramifications for a wide number of people making the need for speed and certainty greater. Thus, judicial review would be the appropriate means of challenge whether or not the actual remedy given is limited to a declaration, or whether a quashing order could also be granted.

2–179   The second example often quoted involves the special position of Crown. The prerogative remedies do not lie against the Crown,[555] but declarations are available.[556] The Crown is clearly a public authority, and providing a claim against the Crown raises matters of public law, then the fact that no prerogative remedy is available should not of itself prevent the grant of a declaration on a judicial review application. There are, however, more formidable obstacles to the grant of a declaration by way of judicial review. Section 21(1) of the Crown Proceedings Act 1947 provides that the courts have power to make certain orders, including declarations, against the Crown in civil proceedings. However, civil proceedings do not include judicial review proceedings.[557] The 1947 Act does not therefore provide for the grant of declarations in judicial review proceedings. The jurisdiction to award declarations in a public law matter stems from the Senior Courts Act 1981, and the rules made thereunder. There is nothing in the Senior Courts Act 1981 permitting judicial review proceedings against the Crown itself and the 1981 Act probably does not apply to the Crown, as pointed out in *R. v*

---

[551] *R. v Secretary of State for the Environment Ex p. Greater London Council, The Times,* December 30, 1985.

[552] See paras 6–008 to 6–009.

[553] See, e.g. *R. (Javed) v Secretary of State for the Home Department* [2002] Q.B. 129.

[554] In *R. v Secretary of State for Social Services Ex p. Association of Metropolitan Authorities* [1986] 1 W.L.R. 1, Webster J. refused, as a matter of discretion rather than jurisdiction, to grant certiorari to quash delegated legislation. Certiorari was granted in *R. v Secretary of State for Health Ex p. United States Tobacco International Inc.* [1991] 3 W.L.R. 529. See para.6–008.

[555] See para.6–015.

[556] Crown Proceedings Act 1947 s.21 discussed at paras 7–063 to 7–065.

[557] Crown Proceedings Act 1947 s.38.

Governor of Pentonville Prison Ex p. Herbage.[558] Thus, the 1981 Act probably does not provide jurisdiction to grant declarations against the Crown in judicial review proceedings. Declarations can therefore only be sought by ordinary action. This produces the odd result that the Crown, alone among public bodies, is denied the procedural protections granted by the judicial review procedure. In practice, the issue is unlikely to arise since decisions are rarely taken by the Crown personally and when they are, they are unlikely to be justiciable.[559] Decisions now, including decisions taken in the exercise of prerogative power, are invariably taken by ministers and their decisions may, of course, be challenged by way of judicial review and declarations granted.[560]

G. DAMAGES, RESTITUTIONARY CLAIMS AND JUDICIAL REVIEW

A claim for damages may be included in a claim for judicial review.[561] Claims for restitution, or the recovery of sums paid, may also be included in a claim for judicial review.[562] Such claims can only be made in addition to a claim for the prerogative remedies or a declaration or injunction; a claim for damages cannot be made in isolation. Damages may only be awarded if they could have been awarded in an ordinary claim; that is, only if there was a right to damages at private law or under the Human Rights Act 1998. No new remedy or right to damages is introduced by the rules. The rules simply provide, as a matter of convenience, that claims for private law damages or damages under the Human Rights Act 1998 may be included in a claim for judicial review. Interest on the amount of damages may, it seems, also be recovered.[563] The usual practice is to deal with the public law claims first, and to order the damages claim to be held over to be dealt with later.[564]

2–180

---

[558] [1987] Q.B. 872 at 885.

[559] The only such decisions are likely to be ones such as refusing a dissolution of Parliament or inviting a person to form a government in a Parliament where no party commands a majority, neither of which has yet happened.

[560] See *M. v Home Office* [1994] 1 A.C. 377 at 417C–E.

[561] Senior Courts Act 1981 s.31(4); CPR r.54.3.

[562] See Senior Courts Act 1981 s.31(4) as amended by the Civil Procedure (Modification of Supreme Court Act 1981) Order 2004. This enables restitutionary claims to be included with effect from May 1, 2004; previously such claims could not be included in a judicial review claim.

[563] *R. v Liverpool City Council Ex p. Coade, The Times,* October 10, 1986.

[564] See, e.g. *R. v Governor of Brockhill Prison Ex p. Evans (No.2)* [1998] 4 All E.R. 993 (legality of detention dealt with first, then claim for damages for false imprisonment considered); *R. v Coventry City Council Ex p. Phoenix Aviation* [1995] 3 All E.R. 37 (court first dealt with claim that the decision refusing access to an airport was ultra vires; claim for damages for breach of the contract said to have been entered into was held over to be heard later); *R. v Chief Constable of the Lancashire Constabulary Ex p. Parker* [1993] Q.B. 577 (court dealt with claim that search warrant was invalid; claim for damages for conversion held over).

H. POWER TO TRANSFER

2–181   The court has power under CPR r.54.20 to order that proceedings brought by way of a claim for judicial review are to continue as if they had not been started under CPR Pt 54 and to give directions as to the future management of the claim. The purpose of the transfer provisions is to enable judicial review claims to proceed as if they were ordinary claims brought under CPR Pt 7 or 8.[565] There is a risk that an individual will bring a claim for judicial review in the genuine but mistaken belief that his claim lies in public law but, on analysis, it may transpire that his claim is one that lies in private law. In such circumstances, the courts could order the claim to continue as if it had been brought under CPR Pt 7 or 8 rather than striking the claim out.[566] The power of transfer may also be used where a claim for judicial review has private law consequences. There may be claims, for example, that a decision to detain a person is unlawful on public law grounds and also gives rise to a private law claim for damages for false imprisonment.[567] Or a decision may be said to be unlawful and to have interfered with contractual[568] or other private law rights.[569] In such instances, the courts have frequently dealt with the issues of public law first, and considered the claim for private law damages subsequently. It may be appropriate to transfer the private law issues to another division of the High Court and to have the claim dealt with under the powers available under Pt 7 or 8 of the CPR. Similar issues arise when a claimant alleges that a particular act violates his rights under the European Convention and he also seeks damages under s.8 of the Human Rights Act 1998. Here it may be appropriate to deal with the question of the alleged violation of the Convention first on a claim for judicial review but to defer consideration of any damages claim and, if appropriate, transfer it to a district judge or master, or stay the proceedings pending mediation.[570]

2–182   CPR, Pt 30 also permits transfers between divisions of the High Court and to a specialist list. In principle, that power could permit a public law matter raised in an ordinary claim brought under CPR, Pt 7 or Pt 8 to be transferred to the Administrative Court. Permission to apply for judicial review is required whether the claim is commenced as a claim for judicial review or if a claim is transferred to the Administrative Court.[571] In principle, therefore, a claim should, generally, only be permitted to proceed after transfer to the Administrative Court if the ordinary claim had been brought within the time-limit for bringing a judicial review claim (that is promptly, or within three months at the latest from the date

---

[565] The predecessor to this rule, i.e. Ord.53 r.9(5) of the RSC, had been described as an "anti-technicality rule": see per Sir John Donaldson M.R. in *R. v East Berkshire Health Authority Ex p. Walsh* [1985] Q.B. 152 at 166.

[566] See *R. (Heather) v Leonard Cheshire* [2002] 2 All E.R. 936 at [37]–[39]. The predecessor to this rule had been held to apply only if an issue of public law arose which also gave rise to private law consequences, and the power of transfer could not be used when no issue of public law arose at all: *R. v Secretary of State for the Home Department Ex p. Dew* [1987] 1 W.L.R. 881. That restrictive approach does not reflect the scope of the transfer powers under CPR r.54.20.

[567] See, e.g. *R. v Governor of Brockhill Prison Ex p. Evans* (No.2) [1999] Q.B. 1043.

[568] See, e.g. *R. v Coventry Airport Ex p. Phoenix Aviation Ltd* [1995] 3 All E.R. 37.

[569] See, e.g. *R. v Chief Constable of the Lancashire Constabulary Ex p. Parker* [1993] Q.B. 977.

[570] See *Anufrijeva v Southwark London Borough Council* [2004] Q.B. 1124 and see chapter 16.

[571] CPR r.54.4.

when the grounds for bringing the claim first arose[572] unless there is a good reason for extending the time-limit) and if the claim was arguable.[573] To allow claims to proceed in the Administrative Court which did not comply with these requirements would appear to be inconsistent with the provisions of the Senior Courts Act 1981 and CPR r.54 itself.

---

[572] CPR r.54.5 and see para.9–016.

[573] Claims for judicial review can only proceed if permission has been granted, and the courts may only grant permission if the claim is arguable: see Senior Courts Act 1981 s.31(3) and CPR r.54.4; see paras 9-054 to 9-058.

CHAPTER 3

Choice of Forum and the Exclusivity of Judicial Review Proceedings in Public Law

A. INTRODUCTION

The judicial review procedure is a means by which public law issues, as defined **3–001** in Chapter 2, are brought before the courts for determination. One issue that arises is whether judicial review is now the sole or exclusive means by which such public law issues may be brought before the courts. Prior to the 1977 reforms of the judicial review procedure, there were two separate procedural routes by which the invalidity of a decision or action by a public authority could be established: an individual could either seek one of the prerogative remedies following the special procedure applicable to such remedies, or he could seek a declaration or injunction in an ordinary claim. The two procedures were entirely separate.

Following the 1977 reforms, declarations and injunctions in public law cases **3–002** may now be sought alongside the prerogative remedies in an application for judicial review. A claimant may also include a claim for damages or restitution. The House of Lords, in *O'Reilly v Mackman*[1] held that as a general rule, public law issues must be brought by way of judicial review and could not be brought by way of ordinary claim. The precise ambit of the rule is unclear and the rule is subject to exceptions and has been qualified by subsequent case law. This chapter considers when an issue of public law may only be raised by way of judicial review and when such an issue may be raised in other proceedings, whether in an ordinary claim, as a defence in civil or criminal proceedings, or by some other route such as an appeal by case stated.

B. THE RULE IN O'REILLY V MACKMAN

The House of Lords had to consider the exclusivity of judicial review in *O'Reilly* **3–003** *v Mackman*.[2] A number of prisoners were seeking to establish that disciplinary decisions by Boards of Visitors removing remission were ultra vires and a nullity, as the Board had acted in breach of natural justice. The prisoners sought a declaration of nullity by way of ordinary action, instituted in some cases by writ

---

[1] [1983] 2 A.C. 237.
[2] [1983] 2 A.C. 237.

and in others by originating summons.[3] The issue then arose as to whether it was an abuse of the process of the court to seek a declaration by ordinary action not judicial review. Lord Diplock, giving the unanimous judgment of the House, held that it would[4]:

> "... as a general rule be contrary to public policy, and as such an abuse of the process of the court, to permit a person seeking to establish that a decision of a public authority infringed rights to which he was entitled to protection under public law to proceed by way of ordinary action and by this means to evade the provisions of Ord.53 for the protection of such authorities."

3–004   Consequently, the claim for a declaration would be struck out under Ord.18 r.19.[5] Lord Diplock accepted that this was a general rule and that there would be exceptions. He gave two examples: namely where the invalidity of a decision arises as a collateral issue in a claim for an infringement of a right under private law, and where none of the parties objects to the use of the ordinary action. He expressly left open the possibility of other exceptions being developed by the courts on a case-by-case basis.

Rationale for the rule

3–005   There were two strands of thought underlying the exclusivity rule. First, prior to the 1977 reforms, there were certain defects inherent in the procedure for seeking the prerogative remedies, which made it necessary and reasonable to use the alternative procedure of seeking a declaration by ordinary action. In particular, there was no power to grant disclosure Evidence was provided by affidavit and cross-examination on such evidence was virtually unknown. The 1977 reforms removed these and other disadvantages. Provision is made for disclosure[6] and for cross-examination,[7] which although not automatic as in ordinary proceedings, is governed by similar principles.[8] In addition, it is now possible for a claim for a prerogative remedy to be coupled with a claim for a declaration or injunction,[9] and, if appropriate, damages or restitution,[10] in the same application. Thus, all the remedies that might prove necessary could be sought within one and the same procedure.

3–006   Secondly, there are specific protections incorporated into the judicial review procedure for the benefit of public authorities; these include the need to obtain permission which is intended to filter out unmeritorious or frivolous claims.[11] There is a short time-limit for applying for judicial review,[12] and the procedure itself is speedy. This protects the public interest in ensuring that public bodies and third parties are not kept in suspense as to the validity of a decision and the extent

---

[3] The precursor to the claim procedure introduced by the CPR, see r.8.1.

[4] [1983] 2 A.C. 237 at 285.

[5] The corresponding power now is in CPR Pt 3.4.

[6] CPR Sch.1 Ord.53 r.8. formerly, discovery. See now CPR Pt 31.

[7] CPR Sch.1 Ord.53 r.8. See now CPR Pt 31.

[8] *O'Reilly v Mackman* (see above, fn.1 at 285). But see paras 9–109 to 9–115.

[9] Senior Courts Act 1981 s.31(1) and CPR r.54.3.

[10] Senior Courts Act 1981 s.31(4) and CPR r.54.3.

[11] Senior Courts Act 1981 s.31(3) and CPR r.54.4.

[12] Senior Courts Act 1981 s.31(6) and CPR r.54.5.

to which it could be implemented or relied upon. The fact that disclosure and cross-examination is not automatic, but requires permission, also ensures greater control over the conduct of proceedings by the court to ensure that these are not used to prolong proceedings unnecessarily.[13] These protections do not exist in the ordinary claim procedure. Permission is not required. The ordinary limitation period applies and the process of establishing invalidity may be lengthy. Now that there are no procedural disadvantages for the applicant in proceedings by judicial review, it is no longer justifiable to allow an individual to bring an ordinary claim and thereby to evade the protections afforded to public bodies by the judicial review provisions. To these reasons might be added the fact that judicial review applications are heard by judges on the Crown Office List who have experience and expertise in dealing with public law issues. A specialised procedure also emphasises the uniqueness of public law, in that it is quite unlike private litigation between parties. The courts have a more limited role in judicial review and need to ensure that the wider public interest, frequently present in such cases, is not overlooked.[14]

One of the results of the rule in *O'Reilly v Mackman*, however, is that there has **3–007** been a large amount of litigation dealing solely with the question of whether proceedings are to be characterised as public law proceedings and whether the claims have been brought in the right forum rather than focussing on the legal merits of the claims. This litigation has been described as "unprofitable"[15] and has attracted judicial criticism.[16] As a consequence, the courts have recently indicated that the advantages of the judicial review procedure should not be overstated. The desire to have matters of public law determined by specialised Administrative Court judges, for example, needs to be counterbalanced by an awareness of the need not to overburden the Administrative Court and cause delays in the period before cases are heard. Furthermore, there may be instances where it is more appropriate for an issue of public law to be considered by a specialised appeal tribunal than by an application for judicial review.[17] In the past, it was considered that where questions of fact arose in public law matters, the ordinary claim procedure may be more appropriate than judicial review in dealing with these matters.[18] Now, it is recognised that while claims for judicial review do not generally involve determining questions of fact, the procedures can be adopted to deal with such questions when they arise. This consideration is,

---

[13] See, per Lord Diplock in *O'Reilly v Mackman* [1983] 2 A.C. 237 at 284.

[14] See dicta of Lord Bridge in *Cocks v Thanet DC* [1983] 2 A.C. 286 at 291. See Woolf, "Public Law and Private Law: Why the Divide?" [1986] P.L. 220 at 225–227.

[15] per Lord Woolf M.R. in *Trustees of the Denis Rye Pension Fund v Sheffield City Council* [1998] 1 W.L.R. 840 at 848A–B.

[16] See, e.g. the criticisms of Saville LJ in *British Steel plc v Commissioners of Customs and Excise* [1997] 2 All E.R. 366 and of Henry J. in *Doyle v Northumbria Probation Committee* [1991] 1 W.L.R. 1340 at 1348A–C.

[17] See, e.g. dicta of Lord Bridge in *Chief Adjudication Officer v Foster* [1993] A.C. 754 at 766H–767B.

[18] A consideration referred to in *Roy v Kensington and Chelsea Family Practitioner Committee* [1992] 1 A.C. 624 and by the Court of Appeal in *Trustees of Denis Rye Pension Fund v Sheffield City Council* [1998] 1 W.L.R. 840. The judicial review procedure can accommodate disputes of facts, particularly where this is necessary to ensure a fair hearing before an independent and impartial tribunal: see, e.g. *R. (Wilkinson) v Broadmoor Special Hospital Authority* [2002] 1 W.L.R, 419. In general, however, judicial review is generally not used as a means of determining disputed facts but rather determining whether actions of public bodies are lawful. See generally para.9–121 below.

therefore, less likely to be a significant consideration.[19] In addition, other values also have to be weighed in the balance in deciding the desirability of a rule of procedural exclusivity. In criminal matters, for example, the courts have emphasised the desirability of individuals being able to raise public law issues as a defence in magistrates' courts and Crown Courts as it may be physically easier and cheaper for them to do so than to institute separate judicial review proceedings.[20]

3–008   For these reasons, the courts are in general less willing at present to allow claims to be struck out on the purely procedural ground that they should not have been brought by an ordinary claim and should have been brought by way of judicial review. They are more prone to emphasise as a minimum that the rule in *O'Reilly v Mackman* is subject to exceptions and there is a need to retain flexibility in applying the rule[21] or to suggest that the scope of the rule still needs to be clarified.[22] Furthermore, where both public law and private law issues arise, the courts at present tend to consider whether in all the circumstances the bringing of a claim by the ordinary claim procedure involves an abuse of process, rather than assuming that the by-passing of the judicial review procedure is an abuse.[23]

Effect of the rule

3–009   It is an abuse of the process of the court to seek a declaration or injunction by ordinary claim in a public law case where the claim should proceed by judicial review. The court may therefore exercise its powers under CPR Pt 3.4, or its inherent jurisdiction, to strike out the claim.

3–010   There is power to transfer a claim to the Administrative Court instead of striking out the claim.[24] However, such a claim would still require permission to proceed as a claim for judicial review.[25] A judicial review claim must be brought promptly and within three months of the date when the grounds for bringing a claim first arose.[26] It is unlikely that permission to continue an ordinary claim transferred into the Administrative Court would be given unless the original claim, too, had been brought promptly or within three months of the date when the grounds for a claim arose. In many instances, an ordinary claim would not have been brought within that time-limit. There is power to extend the time for bringing a claim but that power is usually exercised only when there is good

---

[19] *Trim v North Dorset DC* [2011] 1 W.L.R. 1001 at [24].

[20] See, e.g. *Boddington v British Transport Police* [1999] 2 A.C. 143.

[21] See, e.g. the observations of Lord Slynn in *Mercury Communications Ltd v Director General of Telecommunications* [1996] 1 W.L.R. 48 at 57C–E.

[22] See, e.g. the observations of Lord Lowry in *Roy v Kensington and Chelsea Family Practitioner Committee* [1992] 1 A.C. 624 at 653E and in *R. v Secretary of State for Employment, Ex p. Equal Opportunities Commission* [1995] 1 A.C. 1 at 34C.

[23] See *Clark v University of Lincolnshire and Humberside* [2000] 1 W.L.R. 1988 discussed below at para.3–027. See, also, as examples of this approach, *Phonographic Performances Ltd v Department of Trade and Industry* [2004] 1 W.L.R. 2893 at [29]–[52]; *Isle of Anglesey and others v Welsh Ministers and others* [2008] EWHC 921 (the point was not taken on appeal). In cases involving public law defences, see *Rhondda Cynon Taff BC v Watkins* [2003] 1 W.L.R. 1864 at [92]–[96].

[24] See CPR Pt 30.

[25] CPR r.54.4.

[26] See CPR r.54.5 and para.9–016 et seq. below.

reason for the delay.[27] Delay resulting from the wrong choice of procedure is unlikely to be accepted as a good reason unless, possibly, the claimant was not at fault in believing that the ordinary claim procedure was available. In practice, there is a real risk that the ordinary claim will be struck out and either no transfer to the Administrative Court ordered or permission to continue the claim as a judicial review claim will be refused. There is, consequently, a real risk that the claimant will never be able to argue the merits of his case and will be denied relief solely on the grounds that he chose the wrong procedure initially and it is too late now to use the right procedure.

Given this risk, if there is any doubt as to the availability of the ordinary procedure, the wisest course of action is to bring a claim for judicial review first within the three-month time-limit.[28] If it transpires that the claim is not a public law one and cannot be brought by judicial review, the individual will normally still have time to commence his action by ordinary claim (as the usual, much longer time-limits will apply). A claimant may also apply for judicial review and pursue a parallel ordinary claim if there is any risk that the judicial review proceedings may not be determined until after the time-limit for bringing the ordinary claim has expired. The court may, in certain circumstances, direct that a claim begun by judicial review continue as if it had been begun as an ordinary claim.[29]

3–011

Scope of the rule

The precise extent of the rule in *O'Reilly v Mackman*, and the exceptions, raise difficult issues in public law. The rule is said to apply to cases involving the infringement of rights protected by public law.[30] The notion of "public law rights" is a relative newcomer to English law. The difficulty lies in indentifying what constitutes a public law matter for the purpose of the rule. The term "public law" has, in the past, been used in at least two senses. First, it may refer to the substantive principles of public law governing the exercise of public law powers, and which form the grounds for alleging that a public body is acting unlawfully. These are the familiar *Wednesbury* principles. A public law "right" in this sense could be described as a right to ensure that a public body acts lawfully in exercising its public law powers. The rights could be described in relation to the individual heads of challenge, for example, the right to ensure that natural justice is observed, or to ensure that the decision is based on relevant not irrelevant considerations, or is taken for a purpose authorised by statute, or is not *Wednesbury* unreasonable. Secondly, "public law" may refer to the remedies that an individual may obtain to negative an unlawful exercise of power. These are essentially remedies used to set aside unlawful decisions, or prevent the doing of unlawful acts, or compel the performance of public duties. These remedies now include the prerogative remedies of certiorari (now called a quashing order), mandamus (now called a mandatory order) and prohibition (now called a

3–012

---

[27] See CPR r.3.4 and para.9–034 et seq. below.
[28] As suggested by Lord Woolf M.R. in *Trustees of Dennis Rye Pension Fund v Sheffield City Council* [1998] 1 W.L.R. 840 at 848E–F.
[29] CPR r.54.20.
[30] per Lord Diplock in *O'Reilly v Mackman* [1983] 2 A.C. 237 at 285.

prohibiting order), and the ordinary remedies of declarations and injunctions when used for a public law purpose involving the supervisory jurisdiction of the courts over public bodies.

3–013   It must also be remembered that certain private law principles, such as tort and contract, apply to public bodies as well as private individuals. There may, therefore, be occasions when a public body is both subject to the special rules of public law designed to ensure that they use their public law powers lawfully and must also observe private law principles in the exercise of such powers. An individual may be claiming that action is unlawful and should be set aside, and also that the acts of the public body give rise to a private law right to damages as compensation for any loss incurred. A claim may principally involve private law principles such as negligence or breach of contract, but the application of those principles may be influenced by the statutory framework within which a public body operates or may involve questions such as the vires of acts of the public body.

3–014   There are therefore at least four possible questions that can arise in a case involving a public body:

(a)   Is the public body violating a principle of public law?
(b)   Is the individual seeking a remedy intended to set aside or nullify the unlawful actions of a public body?
(c)   Is the public body violating a principle of private law?
(d)   Is the individual seeking a private law remedy, principally damages, to compensate for the interference with his private law rights, or a declaration of those rights or an injunction to prevent further unlawful interference with those rights?

3–015   A claim by an individual may involve answering only the first two questions (which are regarded as public law questions) or the last two (which are regarded as private law questions). As there is no clear divide between private and public law, it may be that all four questions arise out of the same facts. It may be that the effect of granting a declaration or an injunction to protect a private law right will have the practical effect of nullifying a public law action.

3–016   There is also the further problem of the relationship between public law and criminal law. An individual may be charged with an offence of contravening subordinate legislation or a decision of a public body, or acting without a relevant licence. He may wish to raise as his defence in those criminal proceedings the invalidity of the measure or decision that he is charged with contravening.

3–017   There is, as yet, no absolute clarity on the basic scope of the rule in *O'Reilly v Mackman*. In one case, the House of Lords discerned two possible interpretations. On one approach, the rule applies to proceedings where only public law issues arise, and does not apply if private law rights are also at stake. On the alternative approach, the rule applies to all proceedings where some public law act or decision is challenged.[31] The general tenor of the decision in *O'Reilly v Mackman* is that the rule is to be understood in accordance with the second interpretation, namely that the rule applied whenever a public law issue arose for determination

---

[31] See per Lord Lowry in *Roy v Kensington and Chelsea Family Health Practitioner Committee* [1992] 1 A.C. 624 at 653E–H.

and that issue had to be determined by way of judicial review unless the situation fell within one of the exceptions to the rule. The issue of the precise scope of the rule did not, however, arise in *O'Reilly*. There, the claimants, who were prisoners, were challenging a decision to remove remission. The only basis of their claim and their only "rights" were public law rights; there was no possible claim in private law and no question of any private law remedy being available.[32] It was not necessary, therefore, to determine the precise ambit of the rule. The House of Lords has left open the question of the proper scope of the rule.[33] For the reasons set out below, the better approach would be to view the rule as applying where the questions that can be raised are solely public law ones, i.e. to view the rule as requiring an individual to proceed by way of judicial review when he is seeking a public law remedy because a public body has violated a principle of public law (and even then there may be exceptions justifying use of the ordinary claim procedure). An individual who therefore sought to establish that there had been a breach of a principle of public law but was also seeking to vindicate any private law right would be free either to bring a claim for judicial review (and attach a claim for damages) or to proceed by making an ordinary claim.[34] Similarly, an individual could raise the invalidity of an administrative act as a defence to an ordinary claim or a criminal charge or could, if he so wished, bring a claim for judicial review of that act.

Cases raising only public law issues

Cases where the claim is based solely on substantive principles of public law, and where the only remedy which could be sought is one to quash or set aside the consequences of the decision (and in this sense constitutes a public law remedy) are clearly within the rule. Such cases can only be brought by judicial review and not ordinary claim. *O'Reilly v Mackman*[35] is itself a clear example of such a case. The claimant prisoners were alleging breach of the rules of natural justice, which are part of the body of principles developed by the courts specifically to control the exercise of power by a public body. The remedy they sought was a declaration that the decision of the Board of Visitors to remove their remission was a nullity, and that therefore no remission had ever been removed. In other words, the only issues of law raised and the only relief sought were within the realm of public law. The decision of the Board of Visitors did not affect any private law rights of the prisoners. They had no statutory or other common law rights to remission which could have founded the basis of a claim to be entitled to a private law right. It was accepted that they had no claim in damages arising from the decision so no private law rights were affected and consequently no claim could be made for a remedy in damages (or alternatively for a declaration of such rights or an injunction to prevent interference with such rights).

    Cases where the only issues raised in the pleadings involve the substantive principles of public law, and where the remedy sought is intended to ensure that a

3–018

3–019

---

[32] As was pointed out by Lord Hoffmann in *O'Rourke v Camden LBC* [1998] A.C. 188 at 195G–H.
[33] See *Roy v Kensington and Chelsea Family Health Practitioner Committee* [1992] 1 A.C. 624.
[34] As happened in *D. v Home Office (Bail for Immigration Detainees intervening)* [2006] 1 W.L.R. 1003.
[35] [1983] 2 A.C. 237. See also, *Wessex Water Authority v Farris (V.O.)* (1990) 30 R.V.R. 78.

public body exercises its public law powers (as defined in the previous chapter) in accordance with those principles must also be brought by judicial review. This is so even if it might have been possible to have raised some issue of private law. Thus, the Court of Appeal struck out an ordinary claim that a police officer had failed to comply with his statutory obligations to allow copies of documents to be made.[36] The claim was intended to ensure the proper exercise of public law powers by a public body. As such it could only be brought by judicial review. It was uncertain whether damages were available at private law for unlawful interference with goods. However, even if such a claim could be made, it had not been made in this case. The only claim made and the only relief sought related to the supervisory jurisdiction of the court over the exercise of public law powers, and that was a matter for judicial review not ordinary claim. Similarly, a challenge to a notice alleging a breach of a condition attached to a planning permission was a challenge to a public law act on public law grounds. As such, it had to be brought by way of judicial review and an ordinary claim, brought 18 months after service of the notice, was struck out as an abuse of process.[37]

Cases involving only private law issues

3–020   Public bodies, just like individuals, can make contracts, commit torts and own land. The public nature of the body may be entirely incidental to claims arising out of such matters. Cases which raise only issues of private law and where the remedies sought are private law remedies such as damages are clearly outside the scope of judicial review. Thus, an individual cannot enforce a purely contractual right by way of judicial review.[38] Similarly, a tortious claim such as negligence, which raises no issue of public law, should be brought by ordinary claim.[39] The distinction between private law rights and public law issues is clear in principle. As Chapter 2 demonstrated, it is often very difficult in practice to determine in advance whether a particular matter will be classed as private or public.[40] Furthermore, there are numerous situations where questions of public law and private law are closely interwoven. The same set of facts may give rise to claims both in public law and private law. These cases are considered in the following sections.

Cases involving both private and public law

Decisions affecting private law rights

3–021   The same set of facts may give rise to issues of both public and private law. This may occur in a number of ways. A public body may have power to take a decision which will in some way affect or vary a private law right of an individual. Local authorities, for example, have statutory powers to vary the rents payable by their

---

[36]   *Allen v Chief Constable of Cheshire, The Times*, July 7, 1988.
[37]   *Trim v North Dorset DC* [2011] 1 W.L.R. 1901.
[38]   *R. v East Berkshire Health Authority Ex p. Walsh* [1985] Q.B. 152; *R. v British Broadcasting Corp Ex p. Lavelle* [1983] 1 W.L.R. 23.
[39]   See, e.g. *Hotson v East Berkshire Health Authority, sub nom. Hotson v Fitzgerald* [1987] A.C. 750.
[40]   See paras 2–132 to 2–133 above.

tenants or Family Practitioner Committees have power to vary the fees payable to a doctor for services provided. The source of the power is statutory and is likely to be sufficiently "public" to be susceptible to judicial review. The substance of a challenge may well be a public law issue, namely whether the power was exercised unlawfully in the public law sense, that is whether the decision or act of the public body was within the powers of the public body concerned. It is equally correct, however, that the individual's private law rights are at stake, i.e. his contractual right to a tenancy at a particular rent or a right to the payment of fees, and the *effect* of a successful challenge would be to vindicate those rights. Thus the issue inevitably arises as to whether such challenges fall within the scope of the rule in *O'Reilly v Mackman* and, if they do, whether such challenges may be brought by way of the ordinary claim procedure as well as by judicial review.

It is relatively clear that the courts are at present unlikely to strike out private law proceedings as an abuse of process where a private law right is at stake, particularly where it dominates the proceedings, whether or not the actual challenge focuses on an act or decision of a public body which is said to be ultra vires. Thus, it will be possible to raise the public law issues concerning the validity of the act in the ordinary private law claim intended to vindicate the private law right.[41] This will either be because the rule in *O'Reilly v Mackman*, properly understood, does not apply when questions of private law right as well as public law rights are in issue. Alternatively, even if the rule applies, it may be appropriate to recognise an exception to that rule where private law rights are also at issue or where they dominate the proceedings.

3–022

A number of cases demonstrate the current attitude of the courts in these cases. In *Wandsworth LBC v Winder*,[42] a local authority exercised statutory powers to increase the contractual rent payable by its tenants, including Mr Winder. Rather than challenge the decision by way of judicial review, Mr Winder refused to pay. The local authority eventually brought proceedings for possession of the property and arrears of rent. Mr Winder defended the proceedings on the ground that the rent increase was unreasonable in the public law sense of "so unreasonable that no reasonable local authority could have reached such a decision" and counter-claimed for a declaration that the decision was ultra vires. The essence of Mr Winder's claim was, then, a public law issue related to the validity of the decision to exercise the statutory power to increase the rents. The authority applied to have the defence and counter-claim struck out as an abuse of process as they raised issues of public law which should have been brought by way of judicial review. The House of Lords refused to strike out the defence and counter-claim and allowed the public law issues to be raised in the private law proceedings. Lord Fraser, giving the unanimous judgment, held that there was no abuse of process. He distinguished *O'Reilly v Mackman* on two grounds; first the decision here infringed the tenants' private law rights whereas in *O'Reilly* no private law rights were in issue and secondly the public law issues in *O'Reilly* were raised by the plaintiffs who initiated the proceedings whereas here they were raised by way of defence and counter-claim. Lord Fraser did not consider

3–023

---

[41] *D. v Home Office (Bail for Immigration Detainees Intervening)* [2006] 1 W.L.R. 1003.
[42] [1985] A.C. 461. See also *Gillick v West Norfolk and Wisbech Area Health Authority and the DHSS* [1986] A.C. 112 (parent able to proceed by way of ordinary claim when seeking to enforce a private law parental right, notwithstanding that the subject matter of the claim was in essence a public law challenge).

that any of the exceptions specifically identified in *O'Reilly* applied in the present case but, nonetheless, the proceedings were allowed to proceed. It is not clear whether he considered that the rule in *O'Reilly v Mackman* did not apply because both private and public law rights arose or whether he considered that a further exception should be made to the rule, namely that an individual should not be prevented from raising public law issues, at least by way of defence to a civil law claim. In any event, it is clear that it was not an abuse of process to raise a defence or make a counter-claim involving a challenge to a public law decision where the proceedings also involved the vindication of an existing private law right.

3–024   The House of Lords adopted a similar approach to *Winder* in *Roy v Kensington and Chelsea Family Health Practitioner Committee*.[43] There, regulations[44] provided that a doctor ought to be paid a full basic practice allowance if he provided general medical services and "he is in the opinion of the responsible committee devoting a substantial amount of time to general practice under the National Health Service . . .". The defendant committee were of the opinion that Dr Roy did not devote a substantial amount of time to general practice and reduced the allowance payable by 20 per cent. Dr Roy issued ordinary private law proceedings claiming the full basic allowance. The committee applied to have the claim struck out as it involved a public law challenge to a public law decision (the decision to reduce the basic payment) which should have been brought by way of judicial review. Their Lordships analysed the regulations as giving rise to a private law right, derived from the statute and regulations, to be paid for the work that he had done. The amount of the payment may be affected by a discretionary decision on the part of the committee but that fact did not remove the doctor's private law right nor did it mean that any challenge to such a discretionary decision had to be brought by judicial review.[45] Lord Bridge held that where a person asserts a private law right, whether by way of a claim or defence, he could proceed by an ordinary private law proceedings notwithstanding that the proceeding might also involve the examination of a public law issue. Consequently, as Dr Roy was seeking to enforce a private law right to remuneration, albeit one where the quantum was affected by a discretionary decision, he could proceed by ordinary private law proceedings.[46] Lord Lowry considered that the arguments for excluding the case from the ambit in *O'Reilly v Mackman* or for treating it as an exception to the rule were conclusive and Dr Roy could proceed by ordinary private law proceedings. Lord Lowry was influenced by eight factors which can conveniently be divided into three groups, first, the nature of the rights in issue: here, the case involved the enforcement of private law rights (derived from statute) and those private law rights dominated

---

[43] [1992] 1 A.C. 624.

[44] In practice, a statement of fees and allowances made under reg.24 of the National Health Service (General Medical and Pharmaceutical Services) Regulations 1974 (SI 1974/160).

[45] This conclusion may be right but dicta in the case suggest that an order for payment of money due could not be sought on judicial review. That is true if the right is a private law right. If, however, the duty had been a public law duty only, there is nothing to prevent the court granting an order of mandamus requiring the public body to comply with its statutory duty by paying the money (see, e.g. *R. v Liverpool City Council Ex p. Coade*, *The Times*, October 10, 1986 discussed below, para.6–051) or a declaration that the public body was under a duty to pay the money (see, e.g. *R. v Birmingham City Council Ex p. Mohammed* [1999] 1 W.L.R. 33).

[46] [1992] 1 A.C. 624 at 630D–G; in that case a writ, now by way of a claim under Pt 8 of the CPR.

the proceedings; secondly, procedural considerations such as the likelihood of factual disputes occurring which could be better dealt with in the ordinary claim procedure; and thirdly, considerations of policy or principle such as the belief that a person asserting rights should not be subjected to the need to obtain permission to institute proceedings or the special time constraints applicable in judicial review.[47]

A similar approach is evidenced by the decision of the Court of Appeal in *British Steel Plc v Commissioners of Customs & Excise*.[48] There, the plaintiffs sought to recover duty paid on the basis that the Commissioners had unlawfully refused to recognise that British Steel were entitled to relief from payment of the duty. The Court of Appeal held that British Steel had a common law or private law right to recover duty unlawfully demanded and that they were entitled to challenge the lawfulness of the refusal to grant relief (which was a matter of public law) in the context of ordinary private law proceedings for recovery of the duty. Similarly, the Court of Appeal had held that where a person is seeking to enforce a private law right, conferred by statute, to payment of a grant, he may proceed by way of an ordinary claim notwithstanding that public law issues surrounding the question of whether he has fulfilled the conditions governing entitlement to payment also arise.[49]   3–025

In *Steed v Secretary of State for the Home Department*,[50] a person complained about the delay in processing a claim for compensation under a statutory scheme whereby a person was obliged to surrender a hand gun to the authorities and then received a payment equivalent to the value of the hand gun. The claimant issued an ordinary claim for the unpaid amount, together with interest. The House of Lords held that the claimant had a right to compensation once the conditions for payment were met and that it was plainly arguable that when a person was obliged to surrender property there was an obligation to process the claim for compensation within a reasonable time. As such a claim was, in effect, a claim for money due to him and not paid when it was due and could be brought by way of ordinary claim. The claimant was not limited to challenging the reasonableness of the delay by bringing a claim for judicial review.   3–026

The issue arose again in *Clark v University of Lincolnshire and Humberside*[51] where the Court of Appeal refused to strike out a claim based on alleged breach of a contractual relationship between a student and a university notwithstanding that the issues were ones which could also have been litigated by way of judicial review. The University in that case was a statutory body created under the Education Reform Act 1988. As a body performing public functions, claims that the University had failed to act in accordance with its own regulations would be amenable to judicial review. As a fee-paying student, the claimant also had a contract with the University which was capable, in principle, of being the subject of an ordinary claim for breach of contract.[52] In the present case, the claimant   3–027

---

[47] [1992] 1 A.C. 624 at 654A–D.
[48] [1997] 2 All E.R. 366 (reversing Laws J. in [1996] 1 All E.R. 1002 at first instance on this point). See also *Hutchings v Islington LBC* [1998] 1 W.L.R. 1629.
[49] *Trustees of Denis Rye Pension Fund v Sheffield City Council* above, fn.15 and see *Doyle v Northumbria Probation Committee* [1991] 1 W.L.R. 1340.
[50] [2000] 1 W.L.R. 1169.
[51] [2000] 1 W.L.R. 1988.
[52] See above at para.2–116.

brought a claim for breach of contract, alleging, in effect, that the University was obliged to act in accordance with its own regulations but had failed to do so when awarding her a third-class degree only. The University contended that the claimant should have brought that claim by way of judicial review and that it was an abuse of process to bring the claim by contract long after the expiry of the three-month time-limit that would normally apply in judicial review challenges. The Court of Appeal declined to strike out the claim. As the claimant had a claim in contract, it would not be appropriate to strike out the claim simply because it could have been more appropriately brought by way of judicial review.[53] Rather, the court could use its powers under the CPR to ensure that such claims did not involve an abuse of process. The emphasis in such cases would not therefore be on whether the right procedure had been used but whether the use of the ordinary claim proceedings involved an improper attempt to circumvent the protections included in the judicial review procedure. This approach has been followed in subsequent cases where the courts have considered whether, in all the circumstances of the case, including questions of delay, it would be an abuse of process to allow a claim to proceed.[54]

3–028   The primary protection for public bodies is the requirement that claims for judicial review be lodged promptly and in any event within three months. The difficulty is that, if a claim raises both private and public law rights, then allowing the use of the ordinary procedure would enable the claim to be brought long after the expiry of the time-limit for judicial review. The Court of Appeal in *Clark* gave some illustrations of methods of resolving that difficulty. First, if the court were being asked to review the actions of the public body and the remedies sought were discretionary remedies, such as a declaration or an injunction, intended to have the decision of the public set aside or to prevent it giving effect to its decision, then it may be appropriate to refuse those remedies or even to grant summary judgment for the defendant on that aspect of the claim.[55] In this way, the time-limits in judicial review, and the discretion in relation to remedies in ordinary proceedings, could be used to ensure that the decisions of public bodies were not left open to challenge for unreasonable periods of time. If, however, a claimant also had a money claim, for example, breach of contract, that claim could proceed in the ordinary claim. Secondly, the court could strike out a claim, in appropriate circumstances, if it were satisfied that proceeding by way of ordinary claim, rather than judicial review, involved an abuse of process. The mere use of the ordinary proceedings, however, would not be abusive. Nor would the commencement of such proceedings within the ordinary time-limit for bringing such claims be an abuse, although delay in instituting proceedings is a

---

[53] [2000] 1 W.L.R. 1988 at [38].

[54] See, e.g. *Isle of Anglesey and others v Welsh Ministers and others* [2008] EWHC 921 (claim for a declaration that an order granting a right of sea fishery was invalid brought 45 years after the order made; in the circumstances, there was no abuse of process. The point had not become live until recently and the fishermen involved would not have been relying on the fact that the validity of the order would not be challenged. The point in relation to abuse was not taken on appeal). See also *Phonographic Performances Ltd v Department of Trade and Industry* [2004] 1 W.L.R. 2893 at paras 29–52.

[55] [2000] 1 W.L.R. 1988 at [36].

factor which can be taken into account in deciding if proceedings are abusive.[56] In practice, it is likely that the courts would only find that the institution of ordinary proceedings, rather than judicial review, was an abuse if the purpose of using the ordinary procedure was to circumvent or flout the protection given to public bodies in judicial review.

Concentration on the refusal of particular remedies is likely to be the more successful way of reconciling the interests of the public body defendant in not having its decisions left subject to challenge for an unreasonable period with the interests of the individual who wishes to vindicate his private law rights. If the real purpose of the proceedings is to seek a remedy setting aside a decision of that body, that is, in truth, an attempt to seek a public law remedy. It is in those situations that the time-limit in judicial review proceedings is regarded as important as decisions of public bodies are expected to be acted upon and, if they are to be challenged, they should be challenged relatively promptly. It is not in the wider public interest that the validity of decisions of public bodies should be left in a state of uncertainty. If ordinary proceedings are possible, either because issues of public law and private law arise out of the same facts or, as in *Clark*, both private law and public law rights arise, but if an essentially public law remedy is being sought, it may be appropriate to refuse such a remedy if there were unreasonable delay in instituting the proceedings. Any private law claim giving rise to a claim in damages, such as the contract claim in *Clark* or a claim in tort, could still be pursued. **3–029**

Public and private law claims arising

Cases raising both public law and private law issues may also arise in other, more complex ways. An individual may be claiming that certain decisions or actions are invalid and should be set aside because the public body has violated one of the substantive principles governing the exercise of public law power, and also that the public body has violated his private law rights and is liable in damages. A claim that an exercise of statutory powers is unlawful, and of no effect, may, for example, be coupled with a claim that the public body owes a common law duty of care in the exercise of those statutory powers which has been breached, and so damages are payable. An individual may be seeking to enforce a statutory duty and also claiming that it is one of those duties that gives rise to a right to compensation in damages for certain categories of persons. The tort of misfeasance in a public office, which gives rise to a right to damages classed as a private law right, requires an act by a public body which is ultra vires (a public law issue) together with malice or knowledge of the invalidity. Other torts may involve public law issues. The tort of false imprisonment, for example, may involve determining whether a public body exercising statutory powers of detention has acted lawfully or whether the detention is invalid. **3–030**

An individual may seek judicial review where the issue raised is a public law one in the sense defined in Chapter 2. The judicial review proceedings will determine whether a decision or an action involves a violation of one of the **3–031**

---

[56] [2000] 1 W.L.R. 1988 at [35]–[39]. Where a public law issue is raised as a defence, it would, however, not be appropriate to strike out the defence on the grounds of delay in raising the issue: *Rhondda Cynon Taff BC v Watkins* [2003] 1 W.L.R. 1864 at [42] and [80]–[96].

principles governing the exercise of public law power, and whether the decision should be set aside or the consequences of the action nullified. The individual may also include a claim for damages. Thus, a claim for judicial review to enforce a public law duty may include a claim for damages[57] (or an injunction in appropriate circumstances,[58]) or a request for a quashing order to quash a decision of a Board of Visitors removing remission may be coupled with a claim for damages for false imprisonment.[59]

3–032 The second question that arises is the extent to which an individual may alternatively chose to pursue such claims by the ordinary claim procedure rather than seeking judicial review and claiming damages in the course of those proceedings. The Court of Appeal has held that where claims in private law and public law arise out of the same set of facts, the individual is entitled to pursue the private law claims by ordinary claim.[60] Thus, an individual was entitled to proceed by an ordinary claim for damages in tort for breach of (a claim which is characterised in English law as akin to the private law tort of breach of statutory duty[61]), notwithstanding that other issues involving the failure to meet obligations, which were classed as public law obligations, also arose.

3–033 More difficult, is the question of whether public law claims which also arise out of the same facts can be allowed to proceed in the same ordinary action, or whether they must be struck out as an abuse of the process of the court.

3–034 In *An Bord Bainne Co-operative (Irish Dairy Board) v Milk Marketing Board*,[62] in addition to claiming damages for breach of what is now Art.102 TFEU, the plaintiff alleged that the defendant had acted in breach of an EU regulation. Breach of this regulation did not give rise to any private law right to damages, but operated in public law by giving rise to an entitlement to have action inconsistent with the regulation rights quashed or declared invalid.[63] The Court of Appeal held that the public law claims could proceed in the same ordinary action as the private law issues since they arose from the same facts and "were inextricably linked" with the private law issues.

3–035 The Court of Appeal in *Davy v Spelthorne BC*[64] took a different view. There, the substance of the case was considered to involve private law rights arising from the agreement between the parties that Davy would not challenge the enforcement notice, and the allegedly negligent advice of the authority. The Court of Appeal allowed the claim for damages to proceed since this was based on private law rights and sought private law relief in the form of damages. The plaintiff also sought an injunction to prevent the implementation of the

---

[57] *R. v Inner London Education Authority Ex p. Ali and Murshid* [1990] 2 Admin. L.R. 822.

[58] *R. v Kensington and Chelsea RBC Ex p. Hammell* [1989] Q.B. 518.

[59] *R. v Board of Visitors of Gartree Prison Ex p. Sears*, *The Times*, March 20, 1985. The claim for damages would be unlikely to suceed in the light of the decision of the House of Lords in *R. v Deputy Governor of Parkhurst Prison Ex p. Hague*: *Weldon v Home Office* [1991] 3 W.L.R. 340.

[60] *An Bord Bainne Co-operative (Irish Dairy Board) v Milk Marketing Board* [1984] 2 C.M.L.R. 584 and see *Phonographic Performances Ltd v Department of Trade and Industry* [2004] 1 W.L.R. 2893. The High Court decision in *Guevara v Hounslow LBC*, *The Times*, April 17, 1987 (which held that an individual must proceed by judicial review if substantial element of public law involved, even if claiming damages) probably no longer represents good law.

[61] *Garden Cottage Foods v Milk Marketing Board* [1984] A.C. 130. See Chapter 17.

[62] [1984] 3 C.M.L.R. 584.

[63] *An Bord Bainne Co-operative (Irish Dairy Board) v Milk Marketing Board* [1984] 2 C.M.L.R. 584.

[64] (1983) 81 L.G.R. 580.

enforcement notice and an order setting aside the notice. The Court of Appeal held that these remedies would essentially be public law remedies since they would achieve the same effect as a quashing order or a declaration in judicial review. The public authority were entitled to claim the protections granted by the judicial review procedure when relief of this nature was sought. Consequently, these claims would be struck out. This aspect of the decision was not appealed to the House of Lords.

The practical drawback of this decision is that it contemplates two sets of proceedings dealing with issues arising out of one set of facts. An individual wishing to make alternative claims would have to pursue parallel proceedings. Alternatively, Davy could have applied for judicial review in respect of the notice and attached a claim for damages, thus enabling both issues to be dealt with together. Therefore, in order to avoid two sets of proceedings, the individual is pressurised into using the judicial review procedure to protect his private law rights, even though that procedure is not primarily designed for resolving such issues and requires him to accept the considerable procedural restraints and differences of the judicial review as compared with the ordinary claim procedure.

3–036

The better view is that the approach of the Court of Appeal in *Ann Bord Bainne* is correct and that both the issues of public and private law may be considered in the ordinary claim procedure. The House of Lords has referred to *Ann Bord Bainne* with approval.[65] Furthermore, the approach in that case fits more naturally with the recent case law in this area which accepts that the fact that private law rights are raised in a particular matter is a reason for allowing related public law issues to be examined in the ordinary proceedings as well. Furthermore, if there were undue delay in instituting the proceedings, that could be a reason for refusing injunctive relief. The mere fact that the relief was sought in ordinary proceedings rather than judicial review would not, of itself, justify refusal to entertain the claim.[66]

3–037

Public law decision a precondition to creation of a private law right

One approach suggested by the courts in earlier cases to the problem of statutory duties and powers creating both public and private law rights, is to analyse the duty or decision-making powers as creating a two-tier structure. First, there is the decision as to whether a duty is owed to, or a benefit is to be conferred on, the individual. Primary responsibility for making the determination lies with the public body. The courts only exercise residual supervision to ensure that the public body observes the substantive principles of administrative law intended to prevent the abuse of power. The courts may quash unlawful decisions and require the public body to reconsider the matter according to law, but cannot substitute their view on entitlement for that of the public body. Challenges to a decision that a duty is not owed, or that a discretionary benefit should not be paid, raise issues that are classed as public law issues, and can only be raised by way of judicial review. The grounds of challenge, the role of the courts in exercising residual

3–038

---

[65] See, e.g. *Mercury Communications Ltd v Director General of Telecommunications* [1996] 1 W.L.R. 48 at 57C.

[66] See the approach in *Clark v University of Lincolnshire and Humberside* [2001] 1 W.L.R. 1988 discussed above at para.3–027.

supervision, and the nature of the remedy are all public law issues falling within the scope of the judicial review jurisdiction. Adopting this analysis, no private law right is regarded as existing at this first stage and a favourable decision by the public body is regarded as a necessary precondition to the creation of a private law right.

3–039   The second tier arises when the public body accepts that a duty is owed or a grant should be paid. At that stage, the courts may construe the statutory scheme as giving rise to a private law right, once the public body has reached a decision that the duty is owed. If the public body fails for some reason to fulfil the duty, the individual may bring an ordinary action seeking damages or an injunction to enforce the private law right.

3–040   Thus, in *Cocks v Thanet DC*,[67] the House of Lords analysed the duties imposed by the Housing (Homeless Persons) Act 1977 in this way. The decision as to whether a person qualified for permanent or temporary accommodation lay with the local authority, who thus had to determine whether the duty to accommodate was owed. That decision could only be challenged in the courts on the usual principles of administrative law and the court could only set aside the authority's decision; it could not substitute its opinion on whether the duty was owed for that of the authority. The validity of the decision of the public authority on eligibility was a public law matter to be resolved by judicial review. Once the authority accepted that a duty to house was owed to the individual, private law rights were created. These private law rights could be enforced by way of an ordinary action, seeking damages or an injunction. As the individual was seeking to challenge a decision refusing to recognise that the duty was owed, he was raising a public law matter that had to be raised by judicial review, and the ordinary action seeking an injunction to enforce the duty was struck out as an abuse of process.

3–041   That analysis has now been rejected by the House of Lords in *O'Rourke v Camden LBC*.[68] There, the House held that the duties that were created by the Housing Acts did not create any private law rights at any stage. In particular, the House were critical of the suggestion that a private law duty which had not previously existed could arise once a public body had taken a decision in favour of the applicant. The result of the ruling in *O'Rourke* is that there will be very few[69] if any situations where statute creates a private law right in this way. As no private law right arises, the situation will be one where the only rights, and the only remedies, are public law ones. As such, they may normally be claimed only by way of judicial review as this is one category of cases where the rule in *O'Reilly v Mackman* applies.[70]

3–042   There have been other attempts to analyse such situations as one where there is an antecedent public law decision which, if favourable, then gives rise to private

---

[67] [1983] 2 A.C. 286. See also *Cato v Minister of Agriculture, Fisheries and Food* [1989] 3 C.M.L.R. 286.

[68] [1989] 3 C.M.L.R. 286.

[69] They will be "a rare animal indeed" per Lord Woolf M.R. in *Rye v Sheffield City Council* [1998] 1 W.L.R. 840 at 848A.

[70] Cases striking out claims on the grounds that they involved challenges to the public law aspect of the duty to house should now be decided on the basis that no private law right arises at all: see the earlier decisions in *Mohram Ali v Tower Hamlets LBC* [1993] Q.B. 407 and *Tower Hamlets BC v Abdi* (1992) 91 L.G.R. 300.

law rights and to suggest that challenges to the antecedent decision must be brought by judicial review. The courts have, rightly, refused to encourage this kind of analysis. Rather than seeing the relationship between public and private law as a series of chronological hurdles to be dealt with in the appropriate sequence, they have largely accepted that a single factual relationship may involve interwoven elements of public and private law. Thus in *Roy*,[71] the House of Lords were not prepared to analyse the situation as one where the private law right to remuneration arose only if there was an antecedent public law decision in the doctor's favour. Similarly, the Court of Appeal has rejected the suggestion that a right to recover the payment of duty on the grounds that the payer was entitled to relief depended first on challenging the public law decision to refuse relief.[72]

There is a possibility, however, that there may be very rare situations in which   **3–043** this two-tier approach to rights will be adopted. That situation arguably might arise where a public law decision is taken which then gives rise to a right to payment of a particular sum, as is the case with home improvement grants. The Court of Appeal has accepted that an action to obtain payment of a grant where the authority had decided to pay it gave rise to a private law right.[73] The Court considered, however, that the decision as to whether or not to make the grant involved purely public law rights not private law rights.[74] If that is correct, the implication is that the rule in *O'Reilly v Mackman* would apply and a challenge to the refusal of a grant would have to be made by way of judicial review (unless one of the exceptions apply). This situation is unlikely to arise frequently and is likely to be confined to situations involving decisions to pay money.

Cases involving enforcement of a private law right where a collateral issue of public law arises

In *O'Reilly v Mackman*, Lord Diplock stated that one possible exception to the   **3–044** general rule might be: "... where the invalidity of a decision arises as a collateral issue in a claim for infringement of a right of the plaintiff arising under private law".[75] The meaning of this exception was not discussed, and it has not featured significantly in subsequent case law. The House of Lords in *Winder*[76] held that the exception did not apply where the public law issue was the central issue in the case. Other cases have been classified as raising only private law issues and so outside the scope of the rule altogether.[77] Lord Scarman in *Gillick*,[78] for example, held that Mrs Gillick's claim that a circular was unlawful interfered with her common law parental rights. As the claim involved the enforcement of private law rights it fell outside the rule in *O'Reilly v Mackman* which only dealt with the enforcement of public law rights. Alternatively, he was prepared to accept that, if

---

71 [1992] 1 A.C. 624 at 653B–C.

72 *British Steel Plc v Commissioners of Customs & Excise*]1997] 2 All E.R. 366.

73 *Rye v Sheffield City Council* [1998] 1 W.L.R. 840

74 Above fn.15. per Lord Woolf M.R. at 846B–C. See also *Cato v Minister of Agriculture Fisheries and Food* above fn.73.

75 [1983] 2 A.C. 237 at 285.

76 *Wandsworth LBC v Winder* [1985] A.C. 461 and see para.3–023.

77 See, e.g. *Davy v Spelthorne BC* [1984] A.C. 262.

78 *Gillick v West Norfolk and Wisbech Area Health Authority and the DHSS* [1986] A.C. 112.

the rule did apply, then the exception was applicable as the "... private law content of her claim was so great". A similar approach was adopted in *Roy*.[79]

Consent

3–045   The second exception suggested in *O'Reilly v Mackman* arises where neither party objects to the use of the ordinary claim procedure.[80] There has been criticism of this exception, on the ground that the courts ought not to overlook an abuse of process simply because the parties agree.[81] Yet, the rule is a judge-made rule designed to ensure that a claimant does not evade the safeguards afforded the public body: if the public body considers that those safeguards are not applicable in the instant case, or that the issue raised is so significant that it outweighs other considerations, there seems no reason for the courts to refuse to entertain the claim. The rule is not a jurisdictional limitation on the courts' power to hear public law claims by ordinary claim, and the parties are not conferring a jurisdiction on the courts that they do not have: they are simply agreeing that the reasons that normally lead to a court refusing to hear such claims by ordinary claim are not present in the instant case. The exception has not featured greatly in the case law although on one occasion it was expressly relied upon by a court.[82] In *Gillick*,[83] Lord Scarman indicated that the consent exception was an alternative reason for allowing the case to proceed. There are other cases which should have proceeded by judicial review but where ordinary claims have been allowed, and these may be explicable on the basis of implied consent by the public body as the rule in *O'Reilly v Mackman* was not invoked.[84]

C.   DEFENCES

Defences in civil proceedings

3–046   Issues of public law may be raised as a defence in civil proceedings. A public body may be seeking to enforce its rights against an individual. These may be private law rights such as contractual rights, or proprietary rights as a landowner. The individual may raise as a defence a claim that action taken by the public body, which was an integral element of the public body's claim, is ultra vires and unlawful. Substantive defences based on the invalidity of action taken by a public body do not have to be (although they may be) brought by way of separate judicial review proceedings. The public law issue of the invalidity of the public

---

[79] [1992] 1 A.C. 624.

[80] [1983] 2 A.C. 237 at 285.

[81] See Grubb, "Two Steps Towards a Unified Administrative Law Procedure" [1983] P.L. 190 and Harlow, "Gillick: A Comedy of Errors?" (1986) 49 M.L.R. 768 at 771–772. See also the dictum of Lord Scarman in *Gillick* [1986] A.C. 112 at 178, although he subsequently accepted that the exception does apply.

[82] *Securities and Investment Board v FIMBRA* [1992] Ch. 268 at 275H–276A.

[83] [1986] A.C. 112.

[84] See, e.g. *Bostock v Kay* (1989) 133 S.J. 749. The issue of bias is a public law one which has been dealt with by judicial review in other cases; see *R. v Governors of Small Heath School Ex p. Birmingham City Council* [1990] C.O.D. 23.

authority's actions may be raised as a defence in the course of the ordinary proceedings initiated by the public body.

The issue arose in *Winder*.[85] Winder had a contractual tenancy of property owned by the local authority. The authority exercised statutory powers to increase the rent. Following non-payment by Winder, the authority instituted civil proceedings for an order for possession and arrears of rent. The House of Lords held that Winder was entitled to raise as his defence a claim that the decision increasing the rent was ultra vires and *Wednesbury* unreasonable. He was not limited to raising this issue in separate judicial review proceedings. Two factors influenced the decision. First, the defendant was merely seeking to defend himself against a claim made by the authority. He had not selected the procedure to be adopted. It could not be said that Winder was abusing the process of the court by raising as a defence the illegality of the authority's decision. Secondly, Winder put forward his defence as a matter of right, whereas in judicial review proceedings the court would have to determine as a matter of discretion whether to grant him a remedy. The House considered that these considerations outweighed the need of the administration for speed and certainty and the impact on third parties, particularly ratepayers, if the basis of the authority's financial administration over the previous three years was held unlawful. It was the public interest in speed and certainty that the authority argued underlay the rule in *O'Reilly v Mackman*, and which argued strongly for applying the rule to the present case. In *Wandsworth LBC v A*,[86] the Court of Appeal held that the decision in *Winder* is one of general application and that a public law issue may be raised by way of defence to a private law claim. In *A*, a parent had an implied licence to enter onto school premises. The head teacher excluded her from the school because of her alleged abusive behaviour. The parent was not given the opportunity to make any representations before the licence to enter was terminated. The local authority subsequently brought proceedings in the county court for trespass and sought an injunction to restrain the parent from entering the school premises. The Court of Appeal held that she was entitled to raise a public law defence to the action, namely that the decision to terminate her private law right to enter the premises, arising from the implied licence, was invalid as she had not had the opportunity to make representations before the decision was taken. **3–047**

Similarly, defences may also be based on claims that a particular course of action by a public body would violate a Convention right contrary to the Human Rights Act 1998. Where, for example, a court is asked to make a possession order which will exclude a person from his home, a court will need to consider any defence based on an allegation that granting a possession order would violate the right to respect for a person's home provided for by Art.8 of the European Convention on Human Rights.[87] If the defence is made out, then it would not be reasonable for the court to make a possession order. **3–048**

---

[85] [1985] A.C. 461.

[86] [2001] 1 W.L.R. 1246. See also *Rhondda Cynon Taff BC* [2003] 1 W.L.R. 1864, esp. at [80]–[96]; *Derbyshire CC v Akrill* (2005) 8 C.C.L.R. and *Bunney v Burns Anderson Plc* [2008] Bus. L.R. 22.

[87] See *Manchester City Council v Pinnock (Secretary of State for Communities and Local Government intervening)* [2011] 2 A.C. 104; *Hounslow LBC v Powell (Secretary of State for Communities and Local Government intervening)* [2011] 2 A.C. 186.

3–049   One of the innovations in judicial review in recent years has been the willingness of the courts in purely domestic law cases to refuse a remedy to quash an administrative act on discretionary grounds, notwithstanding that the measure is technically ultra vires.[88] Where the invalidity of an act is put forward as a defence in civil proceedings, however, the clear implication is that the invalidity is raised as a matter of right and the court cannot refuse to accept the defence and ignore the invalidity on purely discretionary grounds. In *Winder*,[89] for example, the implication was that if Mr Winder had been able to establish that the resolution increasing rents was ultra vires, the courts would have had to accept his defence to a claim for arrears of rent based on the resolution. The court would not, it seems, have a discretion to reject the defence because of the impact on third parties such as council taxpayers (who may be required to make up any financial shortfall) or on the authority itself. A similar approach was adopted in *Credit Suisse v Allerdale BC*,[90] where the Court of Appeal were considering a claim for breach of contract. The local authority asserted in its defence that the contract was ultra vires its powers and so could not be enforced. The Court accepted that the defence, if made out, would render the contract unenforceable and held that it did not have any discretion (as it would have in a judicial review application) which enabled it to refuse to recognise the invalidity.[91]

3–050   An interesting situation could arise if an individual were refused judicial review on discretionary grounds and he then sought to raise the invalidity of the act as a defence in subsequent civil proceedings initiated by the public body concerned. The fact that the judicial review application would have been dismissed on discretionary grounds would not necessarily prevent him from raising the invalidity of the decision as a defence in subsequent proceedings.[92] Nor would he necessarily be mounting an attack on the judicial review decision in the other proceedings, which might be resisted on the grounds that it constituted an abuse of process to seek to challenge findings of fact made in one set of judicial proceedings in another set of judicial proceedings. In reality, he would be relying on the finding of illegality but arguing that the discretion that prevented him from obtaining a remedy in the judicial review proceedings could not be exercised to prevent him establishing a defence in the civil proceedings.

---

[88] See Chapter 12 below.

[89] [1985] A.C. 461. See also *Rhondda Cynon Taff County BC v Watkins* [2003] 1 W.L.R 1864.

[90] [1997] Q.B. 306.

[91] [1997] Q.B. 306 per Neill LJ at 343D–344C and per Hobhouse LJ at 356H–357E. The precise circumstances in which a particular public law error may give rise to a defence to a private law claim was left open for further consideration in *Charles Terence Estates Ltd. v Cornwall CC* [2013] 1 W.L.R. 466, at [27]–[37] and 45–53.

[92] Issue estoppel probably does not apply in respect of decisions given in judicial review proceedings: *R. v Secretary of State for the Environment Ex p. Hackney London Borough* [1984] 1 W.L.R. 592 (affing. [1983] 1 W.L.R. 524) and see *R. (Munjaz) v Mersey Care NHS Trust* [2003] 3 W.L.R. 1505 at [78]–[79]. The point was not considered in the House of Lords whose decision is reported at [2006] 2 A.C. 148.

Defences based on the invalidity of the decision to institute proceedings

An individual may seek to argue that the decision of the public body to institute proceedings is ultra vires and unlawful. Until recently, it was clearly established that such a matter could not be raised as a defence in the ordinary proceedings and could only be raised by way of a separate judicial review claim. The Court of Appeal held that the decision in *Winder* only applied to "true" or "substantive" defences that provided a real defence to the claim if the defence was made out. Thus, in *Winder*, the defence that the rent increases were unlawful would, if successful, have meant that the claimant had a valid tenancy, was not in arrears of rent and so was not liable to eviction. Challenges to the decision to institute proceedings were regarded, on a proper analysis, as a claim that the public body was not entitled to enforce any rights that it had and were akin to a claim that the action was commenced and was being prosecuted without authority. Where the challenge was to the decision to institute proceedings, claiming that that decision had been taken in a way which made that decision unlawful, then it could not be raised as a defence but had to be brought by way of a claim for judicial review, just as in a private law case such a claim had to be made by way of an application to strike out the claim and not as a defence to the action itself.

3–051

Thus, in *Waverley BC v Hilden*,[93] the authority sought an injunction to prevent the defendant from breaking the criminal law. Scott J. refused to allow the defendants to raise as their defence a claim that the decision to institute proceedings was *Wednesbury* unreasonable. In *Avon CC v Buscott*,[94] the Authority brought a claim for the possession of land owned by themselves but occupied by trespassers. The Court of Appeal refused to allow the defendants to raise as their defence a claim that the decision to institute proceedings was ultra vires.

3–052

If such a claim is raised in the course of civil proceedings, the proper course is for the defendants to apply for a stay of the civil proceedings in order to allow them to apply for judicial review. Such a stay will only be allowed if there is a real chance that leave to apply would be granted,[95] (bearing in mind that such applications will frequently be out of time), and the defendants have an arguable case that the decision to institute proceedings should be quashed.[96] This position in relation to the limited scope for raising challenges to the decision of bodies to institute proceedings by way of defence is now in considerable doubt following the decision in *Doherty v Birmingham City Council*.[97] That case concerned the issue of whether a defendant to possession proceedings could raise as a defence a claim that the local authority's action in seeking possession involved a violation of Art.8 of the European Convention on Human Rights. However, the clear implication of the decision is that challenges based on purely domestic or conventional public law grounds to decisions of the public authority to institute possession proceedings could also be brought by way of a defence to the claim

3–053

---

[93] [1988] 1 W.L.R. 246.
[94] [1988] Q.B. 656.
[95] [1988] Q.B. 656 per Lord Donaldson M.R. at 663.
[96] per Scott J. in *Waverly BC v Hilden* [1988] 1 W.L.R. 246 at 260.
[97] [2008] 3 W.L.R. 636. See also the earlier dicta in *Kay v Lambeth LBC* [2006] 2 A.C. 465 at [110].

for possession. That would also be consistent with the order that the House of Lords made as they remitted the matter to the first instance judge for that judge to consider the lawfulness of the decision of the authority to seek to recover possession of the site to carry out essential improvement works. Further, the House considered that any disputed issues of fact as to the basis upon which the local authority had taken its decision could also be dealt with by way of oral evidence.[98] Subsequent dicta in the Supreme Court also indicate that public law issues relating to the decision to issue or continue possession proceedings may be raised as a defence in county court proceedings and not simply by way of judicial review.[99]

Defence to criminal proceedings

3–054   Issues of public law may arise in the course of criminal proceedings. The accused is entitled to raise as a defence to the charge the invalidity of the subordinate legislation or byelaw that he is alleged to have violated,[100] or to contend that legislation creating the offence is contrary to European Union law.[101] An individual charged with failing to comply with an administrative decision or order is entitled to raise as his defence the invalidity of the order,[102] or allege that the order did not apply to the conduct in question.[103]

3–055   There were suggestions that the traditional position may have been altered by the decision in *O'Reilly v Mackman* and that challenges to the validity of an administrative act or measure might have to be brought by way of judicial review and could not be raised by way of a defence to a criminal prosecution in the magistrates' court or Crown Court. The traditional position has, however, now been largely re-affirmed by the House of Lords. As a matter of general principle, an individual can raise the invalidity of an administrative measure, such as a byelaw, or of an administrative act as a defence to a criminal charge. If he establishes that defence, he will be acquitted. Furthermore, the defendant will normally be entitled to raise all the grounds of invalidity available to him, including claims that the act or measure is substantively invalid because it is outside the powers conferred by the primary legislation as well a claim that the

---

[98]   *Doherty v Birmingham City Council* [2008] 3 W.L.R. 636 at [54] (per Lord Hope), [68] (per Lord Scott), [123] (per Lord Walker).

[99]   *Manchester City Council v Pinnock (Secretary of State for Communities and Local Government)* [2011] 2 A.C. 104 at [81]–[88]). Similarly, public law challenges to the decision to issue a notice to quit can also be brought by way of defence to possession proceedings: see *Hounslow LBC v Powell (Secretary of State for Communities and Local Government intervening)* [2011] 2 W.L.R. 287 at [120]; *Liverpool City Council v Doran (Secretary of State for Communities and Local Government intervening)* [2009] 1 W.L.R. 2365.

[100]   See, e.g. *R. v Reading Crown Court Ex p. Hutchinson; R. v Devizes Justices Ex p. Lee* [1988] Q.B. 384.

[101]   See, e.g. *Henn and Darby v DPP* [1980] 2 W.L.R. 597 and *Interfact Ltd. v Liverpool City Council* [2011] Q.B. 744 at [56] (but if the defence is not raised at the time of the proceedings the court is not necessarily obliged to re-open an appeal or allow an appeal out of time to enable the defence to be raised after the conclusion of the criminal proceedings). A defendant may contend that the domestic legislation, properly construed in the light of European Union law, does not create a criminal offence: *North Dorset Council v House* [2011] 1 W.L.R. 738.

[102]   *DPP v Head* [1959] A.C. 83.

[103]   See, e.g. *R. v Smith (Thomas George)* [1984] Crim. L.R. 630.

measure is procedurally invalid.[104] Thus, in *Boddington v British Transport Police*,[105] an individual was charged with the offence of smoking on a train in violation of a byelaw. He wished to raise in his defence a claim that the byelaw and the administrative action taken under it was invalid as they purported to prohibit all smoking on trains whereas the relevant legislation did not empower the authorities to impose a complete prohibition on smoking. The House of Lords held that he was entitled to raise the invalidity of the byelaw as a defence in the magistrates' court although, on the merits, they held that the byelaw was not ultra vires.

There is one exception to the principle that a defendant may raise the invalidity of an administrative act or measure as a defence. That arises where the particular statutory provisions, on their proper construction, make it an offence to fail to comply with an administrative act whether or not that act is liable to be quashed or set aside because there has been a violation of one of the standard principles of public law. In other words, the criminal offence (exceptionally) is *not* dependent on the act being valid, it is simply dependent on a particular act having in fact been done. Thus, in *R. v Wicks*,[106] an individual was prosecuted for failure to comply with an enforcement notice alleging a breach of planning control. He wished to raise as his defence a claim that the enforcement notice was unlawful. Lord Hoffmann identified the question as one of the proper construction of the statutory provision creating the offence of failure to comply with an enforcement notice: did that mean "an enforcement notice not liable to be quashed or set aside on appeal on any of the standard grounds of public law" or did it simply mean "an enforcement notice that complied with the formal requirements of the relevant legislation and had not in fact been set aside or quashed on appeal"? Normally, the statutory offence would be construed as meaning a valid enforcement notice and the defendant would be able to raise any alleged invalidity as a defence. Exceptionally, however, the House of Lords considered that on a proper construction of the statute, the criminal offence was made out if the individual had failed to comply with an enforcement notice which had not in fact been set aside or quashed. He was not allowed to raise any challenge to the validity of the notice in his defence; had he wished to do so, he would have had to appeal against the notice on the prescribed grounds (or seek judicial review if the challenge was based on matters other than those which could be raised on appeal). In reaching that decision, the House of Lords was influenced by the legislative history of the planning legislation which had, over time, sought to restrict the issues which a person served with an enforcement notice could raise when prosecuted for non-compliance, together with the unsuitability of many of the issues for consideration by a criminal court, the need for the validity of the enforcement notice to be conclusively determined quickly enough for planning controls to be effective and the nature of the offence.

3–056

---

[104] *Boddington v British Transport Police* [1999] 2 A.C. 143 (overruling the decision of the Divisional Court in *Bugg v DPP* [1993] Q.B. 473 which had held that an individual could raise the substantive invalidity of a byelaw but not any procedural invalidity as a defence).

[105] [1999] 2 A.C. 143.

[106] [1998] 2 A.C. 92. See also *Bracken v East Hertfordshire DC* [2000] C.O.D. 366, *Palacegate Ltd v London Borough of Camden* (2001) 82 P. & C.R. 17 and *Director of Public Prosecutions v T* [2007] 1 W.L.R. 209.

3-057 On one occasion, the Divisional Court has also held that a defendant could not raise the invalidity of a decision as a defence in criminal proceedings.[107] There, a company was prosecuted for operating a sex shop without a licence. The local authority had refused a licence and the defendant company sought to challenge the validity of that refusal. The Divisional Court held that the company could not raise that issue as a defence. Its decision was based primarily on the undesirability of magistrates' courts dealing with such issues and the risk that different magistrates' courts might reach inconsistent decisions. That reasoning would not survive the subsequent decisions of the House of Lords. In so far as the decision remains good law, therefore, it would now probably be understood as dependent on the proper construction of the precise statutory provisions in issue.

3-058 The situations in which statutes should be construed as restricting the ability of a defendant to raise public law issues by way of defence are, and should be, limited. The general position is that individuals can raise such matters by way of defence and statutes are enacted on the basis of that common law position. In construing statutory provisions creating offences there is, therefore, a "strong presumption that Parliament will not legislate to prevent individuals"[108] from raising such matters by way of defence. There should be clear and cogent indications that the statute intends to alter the general common law position that an individual may, as of right, raise the invalidity of an administrative act or measure in his defence when prosecuted. The courts appear to be proceeding on that basis. The Divisional Court, for example, has held that an individual could challenge the validity of a breach of condition notice by way of defence to a criminal charge of failing to comply with the notice.[109] Such a notice alleges that a person has acted in breach of a condition attached to a planning permission. It performs a similar, albeit more limited, function to an enforcement notice and is found in the same part of the same act with which the House of Lords was concerned in *R. v Wicks*. In the case of breach of condition notices, however, there had been no legislative history of restricting the grounds of challenge in criminal proceedings relating to breaches of condition and there was no comprehensive code providing for challenges to such notices by other means.[110] In addition, it is likely that it is only where an act is specifically directed or addressed to an individual that the individual cannot raise the invalidity of a decision as a defence to a charge of failing to comply with the act. In those circumstances, it may be more likely that the legislation intended that individual to use the alternative methods of challenging the decision specifically provided for challenging the act (rather than being able to challenge the measure at a later stage by raising its invalidity as a defence). Even here, however, the principle is

---

[107] *Plymouth City Council v Quietlynn Ltd* [1988] Q.B. 114. The decision had been distinguished and its ratio considerably narrowed by the Divisional Court in *R. v Reading Crown Court Ex p. Hutchinson* [1988] Q.B. 384 even before the decisions of the House of Lords. The Divisional Court had restricted it to individual decisions and had allowed a challenge to the validity of a byelaw.

[108] per Lord Irvine L.C. in *Boddington* [1999] 2 A.C. 143 at 160D.

[109] *Dilieto v Ealing LBC* [2000] Q.B. 381.

[110] There are dicta in *Dilieto* [2000] Q.B. 381 suggesting that defences based on bad faith, improper purpose or taking account of irrelevant considerations should not be allowed. This appears to be wrong in principle and would be an unsupportable gloss on the legislation to suggest that a breach of condition notice properly construed meant a notice where some grounds had not been established in the High Court by way of judicial review, but not a notice invalid on other grounds. The better view is that all grounds of invalidity would be available in respect of a breach of condition notice.

that the individual is entitled either to initiate proceedings *or* to await action by the authorities and to defend himself if that occurs. There would need to be a clearer statutory indication that Parliament intended to restrict the ability of the individual to defend himself than the mere fact that the individual would be likely to know of the decision and could have challenged it if he so wished. Where, however, the measure is a general one such as a byelaw or is a decision directed at another individual[111] and which the defendant may not have known about at the time, there is far less justification for construing a statute as removing the right of the individual to raise the invalidity of the administrative act as a defence.[112]

Decisions to institute criminal charges

An individual may not be challenging the particular administrative measure or act under which the offence is created. Rather, he may seek to challenge the separate decision to issue proceedings. Here, he would not be claiming that he is innocent on the grounds that the administrative measure is invalid and so he has not committed an offence. Rather he would be claiming that he should not be prosecuted for allegedly committing the offence. In the past, the alleged impropriety of decisions to initiate criminal proceedings probably could not be raised as a defence and challenges to such decisions had to be brought by way of judicial review.[113] This aspect of the matter was not considered by the House of Lords in either *R. v Wicks* or *Boddington*. The presumption that a person ought to be able to raise a defence to a charge is obviously far less strong when the person is not claiming that there is no offence of which he is guilty but rather that he ought not to be prosecuted and it might therefore be argued that the rule requiring public law matters be ventilated by way of judicial review should apply. The preferable view, however, is that, if the institution of proceedings amounts to an abuse of process or in some other way suggests that the individual should not be prosecuted, there is no reason why that issue cannot be considered by the magistrates' court or Crown Court trying the case. That view is supported by a decision of the High Court in *Postermobile Plc v Brent LBC*.[114] There, the High Court allowed an appeal by way of case stated against a conviction in circumstances where it was unfair for the local authority to have instituted criminal proceedings for displaying advertisements without the requisite planning consents. Local authority officers had told the defendant in advance that consent was not required. The High Court held that it would be an abuse of process for the criminal proceedings to continue. The defence was essentially a challenge to

3–059

---

[111] As in *DPP v Head* above, fn.102 where a person was charged with having intercourse with a person certified as a defective and the person sought to challenge the validity of the certificate relating to that other person.

[112] See dicta of Lord Irvine L.C. in *Boddington* [1999] 2 A.C. 143 at 161G–162C.

[113] See, e.g. *R. v South Somerset DC Ex p. DJB (Group)* (1989) 87 L.G.R. 624. But see also *R. v Oxford Crown Court Ex p. Smith* [1990] C.O.D. 211 which regarded the dicta in *Ex p. DJB* as irreconcilable with *Ex p. Hutchinson* [1988] Q.B. 384.

[114] *The Times*, December 8, 1997. See also the dicta *Palacegate Ltd v London Borough of Camden* [2001] A.C.D. 137 at 141 (prosecutor required to demonstrate legal authority to prosecute where that is put in issue).

the fairness of the decision to institute proceedings not a challenge to the subordinate legislation requiring consent or to any substantive decision of the local authority refusing consent.

Consequences of a successful defence in criminal cases

3–060   A person who successfully establishes a ground of invalidity will invariably be acquitted. There is no scope for the court in a criminal case to consider refusing to accept the invalidity of the administrative measure on discretionary grounds as it could do if the measure were challenged by way of judicial review. The issue of the partial invalidity of regulations or the severance of the invalid parts from the valid may, however, be considered by the lower courts or the High Court on appeal, as this goes to the substantive question of the extent of the invalidity, not the discretion of the courts in judicial review to refuse a remedy.[115]

3–061   The decision of a magistrates' court or Crown Court is only binding in the particular case. It has no power to quash or set aside the measure, nor are the decisions of these courts binding on other courts. Conflicts can, in practice, be resolved by way of an appeal by case stated from the magistrates' court to the Divisional Court. On such an appeal, the Divisional Court can only allow or dismiss the appeal and they have no jurisdiction to set aside or quash the measure itself. A decision of a Divisional Court that a measure was invalid would, however, be invariably followed by lower courts and, on one occasion, the Divisional Court even proceeded on the basis that a ruling that a measures was invalid as a matter of law would be binding on a magistrates' court or Crown Court.[116] In practice, the public body concerned would be likely to revoke the offending measure.

3–062   There has been concern over the ability of the magistrates' courts to deal with often complex issues of public law. In addition, there is concern that magistrates' court may not always have the relevant evidence before it. In planning cases and those involving local byelaws, this difficulty is unlikely to arise as the local authority which took the administrative action is likely to be the prosecutor. In other cases, if challenges are made to delegated legislation or to other general administrative measures (particularly on procedural grounds), it may be that the prosecutor would not have ready access to the evidence dealing with the way in which the decision was taken or showing what considerations were taken into account. The public body which adopted the administrative measure may not be a party to the criminal proceedings. For that reason, there is both judicial[117] and academic[118] support for the idea of creating a system whereby a magistrates' court or Crown Court could refer the issue of the validity of a particular measure to the High Court. The High Court would then be able to regulate the procedure,

---

[115] See *DPP v Hutchinson* [1990] 2 A.C. 783 and see Chapter 5 below.

[116] See *R. v Reading Crown Court Ex p. Hutchinson* above, fn.89 at 396 where Lloyd LJ appeared to proceed on the basis that this was the correct position.

[117] See per Lord Steyn in *Boddington v British Transport Police* above, fn.106 at 666C–E.

[118] See, e.g. Emery "The Vires Defence: Ultra Vires as a Defence to Criminal or Civil Proceedings" [1992] C.L.J. 300 and, in the context of claims that legislation violates European law, see Lewis, "Judicial Review and the Role of the English Court in European Community Disputes" in *European Community Law in the English Courts*, Andenas and Jacobs (eds.), (Oxford: Oxford University Press, 1998).

ensure that relevant parties were able to participate and relevant evidence obtained. The likely model for such a procedure would be a domestic variant of the procedure available in European Union law where a national court can refer questions of the interpretation or validity of European Union law to the Court of Justice of the European Union. There is a great deal to be said for such an innovation.

D. RELATOR ACTIONS

The Attorney-General has in the past been allowed to seek declarations by ordinary claim, acting either ex officio or at the relation of an individual. In the past individuals have principally sought the Attorney-General's consent to a relator action where they have lacked standing in their own right to bring an ordinary claim. The Attorney-General always has standing to enforce a public right, and ensuring that public bodies do not abuse their powers and act unlawfully is seen, in part at least, as a matter of public interest.[119] It is likely that the courts will allow the Attorney-General to proceed by ordinary claim and will not apply the rule in *O'Reilly v Mackman* to such claims even though the subject-matter of the claim is public law, in that it involves determining whether a public body has exceeded its public law powers so that its decisions should be quashed or set aside. The matter remains to be determined by the courts. They are likely to rely on the assessment of the Attorney-General as to whether the case raises an issue of sufficient public importance to justify depriving the public body concerned of the safeguards contained in the judicial review procedure. It remains to be seen whether in practice the Attorney-General will, as a general rule, authorise relator actions when an individual could have made a judicial review claim. It is very unlikely that the Attorney-General would sanction the avoidance of the judicial review safeguards without an overwhelming reason.

3–063

E. HABEAS CORPUS

Public bodies may have public law powers (as defined in the previous Chapter) to detain individuals. Examples include the detention of illegal immigrants pending deportation, the extradition or return of fugitive offenders, and detention under the mental health legislation. Challenges to the validity of the exercise of such powers may be brought either by judicial review or by means of an application for the prerogative writ of habeas corpus.[120]

3–064

---

[119] *Att-Gen, ex rel. Tilley v Wandsworth LBC* [1981] 1 W.L.R. 854. For relator actions see paras 7–084 to 7–085.

[120] The scope of review in either case has in the past been essentially similar: see *R. v Secretary of State for the Home Department Ex p. Khera*; *R. v Secretary of State for the Home Department Ex p. Khawaja* [1984] A.C. 74. The position may now be changing. See *R. v Secretary of State for the Home Department Ex p. Cheblak* [1991] 1 W.L.R. 890 and *R. v Secretary of State for the Home Department Ex p. Muboyayi* [1992] Q.B. 244, CA and see, generally, Chapter 13.

F. DECLARATIONS AGAINST THE CROWN

3–065   Declarations against the Crown or a servant of the Crown discharging a duty owned by the Crown itself probably cannot be sought by way of judicial review. Declarations will therefore have to be sought by way of ordinary claim and the rule in *O'Reilly v Mackman* will not apply.[121] This paradoxical situation is unlikely to be significant since public law powers are rarely exercisable by the Crown as opposed to ministers, and ministers are subject to judicial review.[122]

G. SPECIFIC PROVISION FOR ORDINARY CLAIMS

3–066   Statute or the CPR may specifically provide for applications in a particular matter to be made by ordinary claim. In such circumstances, it is not an abuse of the process of the court to proceed in the manner prescribed rather than proceeding by way of judicial review. Thus, it was not an abuse of process for a solicitor to challenge a decision of the Law Society exercising statutory powers to take over the funds of the practice by way of an ordinary claim (then called, an originating summons) rather than by way of judicial review, since this was specifically provided for in the Rules.[123] Nor is it an abuse of process for a district auditor to apply by a claim for a declaration that an item of local authority expenditure is contrary to law as this procedure is expressly provided by statute.[124]

H. APPEAL PROCEDURES AND ORIGINAL JURISDICTION OF TRIBUNALS

3–067   Statute may confer original jurisdiction on a tribunal to determine questions of law, or may provide an appellate machinery for challenging the validity of decisions of public bodies. The extent of the statutory jurisdiction is primarily a matter of statutory construction. The jurisdiction may sometimes be narrowly construed to enable such bodies to consider certain issues only,[125] or broadly interpreted, to enable such bodies to consider wider issues of public law, as where the social security commissioners who were empowered to hear appeals against decisions on the ground that the decisions were erroneous in law had jurisdiction to consider whether social security regulations were intra vires[126] or the appellate authorities in planning law were held competent to determine whether the

---

[121] See *R. v Governor of Pentonville Prison Ex p. Herbage* [1987] Q.B. 872, and see para.2–179.

[122] See paras 8–012 to 8–014.

[123] *Buckley v Law Society* [1983] 1 W.L.R. 985 (affd. by CA, *The Times*, December 8, 1983). See also *Chief Adjudication Officer v Foster* [1993] A.C. 654.

[124] See s.17 of the Audit Commission Act 1998.

[125] See, e.g. *R. v Secretary of State for the Home Department Ex p. Malhi* [1990] 1 Q.B. 194 (adjudicator has no jurisdiction to consider general ultra vires issues) and *T-Mobile (UK) Ltd. v Office of Communications* [2009] 1 W.L.R. 1565 (Competition Appeal Tribunal had no jurisdiction to hear appeals against decisions given effect to by way of regulations: see [44]–[51]).

[126] *Chief Adjudication Officer v Foster* [1993] A.C. 754.

principle of issue estoppel applied in the planning field.[127] Such tribunals will usually have jurisdiction to determine whether or not any rights under EU law are relevant to the issue, even though such rights may be public law rights.[128] The issues that may be raised before such tribunals frequently involve issues of public law which could also be dealt with by judicial review. It is clearly not an abuse of process to use these procedures in preference to judicial review[129]; indeed the courts will frequently require these procedures to be used rather than judicial review.[130] In addition, the rules discussed in previous sections, such as allowing defences to be raised, may also apply to original and appellate procedures before statutory bodies as they do in ordinary actions before the courts, providing that the tribunal has jurisdiction to deal with the matter.[131]

Tribunals and appellate authorities only have jurisdiction to come to a decision in the case with which they are dealing; they cannot set aside general measures that are considered ultra vires. Thus, an industrial tribunal could not set aside regulations approved by the Secretary of State, it could only give judgment in the instant case.[132] An immigration appeal tribunal cannot set aside provisions of the Immigration Rules that it considers are ultra vires, it can only hold them inapplicable in the instant case.[133] In practice, once it is clearly established that measures are as a matter of law ultra vires by the courts on appeal (if appeals to the courts are provided), or by the highest appellate authority in the decision-making structure, the public body is likely to exercise any express or implied powers it has to revoke the measures and adopt new measures.[134]

3–068

---

[127] *Thrasyvoulou v Secretary of State for the Environment* [1990] 2 A.C. 273 (see esp. the judgment of Ralph Gibson LJ in the Court of Appeal [1988] Q.B. 809 at 821). See also *R. v Oxford Crown Court Ex p. Smith* [1990] C.O.D. 211.

[128] *R. v Secretary of State for Social Services Ex p. Clarke* [1988] 1 C.M.L.R. 279; *Proll (Astrid) (alias Pattick, Anna) v Entry Clearance Officer Dusseldorf* [1988] 2 C.M.L.R. 387. (*R. v Secretary of State for the Home Department Ex p. Malhi* (see above, fn.16) accepted that the immigration law appellate authorities would have jurisdiction to consider EU issues.)

[129] See *Chief Adjudication Officer v Foster* [1993] A.C. 754.

[130] See paras 12–042 to 12–085 below.

[131] See dicta of Ralph Gibson LJ in *Thrasyvoulou v Secretary of State for the Environment* [1988] Q.B. 809 at 822.

[132] *R. v Secretary of State for Social Services Ex p. Clarke* [1988] 1 C.M.L.R. 279.

[133] *Begum* [1986] Imm.A.R. 385; *Proll (Astrid) (alias Puttick, Anna) v Entry Clearance Officer Dusseldorf* [1988] 2 C.M.L.R. 387.

[134] See dicta of Taylor J. in *R. v Secretary of State for Social Services Ex p. Clarke* [1988] 1 C.M.L.R. 279 at 291.

I.   ASSESSMENT OF THE RULE IN *O'REILLY V MACKMAN*

3–069   The rule in *O'Reilly v Mackman* has generated considerable academic[135] and judicial hostility,[136] although it also has its defenders.[137] The Law Commission which drew up the proposals for the creation of a new judicial review procedure did not recommend that the procedure be exclusive so that declarations in public law matters could only be sought by judicial review not ordinary action.[138] As Sir William Wade has pointed out, it makes little sense to have two separate procedures for seeking a declaration, one of which (judicial review), is hedged with considerable restrictions which could be easily circumvented by resort to the other procedure.[139] Consequently, it is not perhaps surprising that the courts began to hold that individuals must use the judicial review procedure.

3–070   Much criticism has been directed at the fact that many individuals have lost their case simply because they chose the wrong procedure, and never had the merits of the case considered at all. Having proceeded by ordinary claim the claim was struck out as an abuse of the process of the court, and the time-limit for applying for judicial review had passed. To a large extent this problem could be overcome in time if the boundaries of public and private law were capable of clear delineation. The real difficulty is that public law and private law have been closely interwoven in English law. Public bodies must observe private law as well as public in the discharge of their functions. In addition, public bodies frequently have power to take decisions which alter the position of private individuals. For these reasons a clear divorce between the two systems has proved impossible. In the meantime, however, claimants did raise public law issues in private law proceedings and defendants inevitably sought to argue that particular issues could not be raised except by way of judicial review, thereby preventing particular decisions, or aspects of decisions, from being challenged in private law proceedings. The courts appeared to be drawn into ever-more refined arguments as to what was and was not a public law issue and when a public law issue could be raised outside judicial review proceedings.

3–071   There is a solution which would preserve some role for the rule in *O'Reilly v Mackman*. The rule could be redefined so that it only applied to cases where the sole issues that were raised were public law issues. Only in that situation would an applicant be required to proceed by way of judicial review. If private law rights were also at stake, then the individual should be able to protect or enforce those private law rights in private law proceedings, even if the subject-matter of the dispute involves consideration of public law issues and the validity of public law decisions. That limited scope of the rule would be consistent with principle

---

[135] Wade & Forsyth, *Administrative Law*, 11th edn, pp.568–383; Fredman and Morris, "The Costs of Exclusivity: Public and Private Re-examined" [1994] P.L. 69; Tanney, "Procedural Exclusivity in Administrative Law" [1994] P.L. 39 and Emery, "Public Law or Private Law? The Limits of Procedural Reform" [1995] P.L. 450.

[136] See, e.g. the judgment of Lord Wilberforce in *Davy v Spelthorne BC*[1984] A.C. 262 at 276 and the dicta referred to in para.3–007 above.

[137] Notably Sir Harry Woolf speaking extra-judicially. See "Public Law-Private Law: Why the Divide? A Personal View" [1986] P.L. 220.

[138] See Law Com. No.73, Cmnd. 6407, reversing its earlier view that judicial review should be exclusive (Working Paper 1970 at [154]).

[139] See now Wade and Forsyth, *Administrative Law*, 11th edn, p.568.

and with the purposes behind the 1997 reforms of the judicial review procedure.[140] In terms of principle, there is inevitably a substantive divide between the principles of public law and private law. Not all statutory provisions create a private law cause of action. Not all statutory powers and duties result or manifest themselves in contractual relationships or have superadded to them any common law duty of care, a breach of which is remediable in damages. Where a private law right does arise, it has always been accepted that the individual can proceed by way of ordinary claim, with longer time-limits and full disclosure. It is perfectly consistent with principle to continue to allow proceedings which raise those issues, together with other public law issues, to proceed by ordinary claim. There is no reason to suppose that the reforms to judicial review were intended to restrict a person's ability to vindicate private law rights in the way that could have been done prior to the reforms. Rather the reforms should be understood as remedying defects in the procedure for seeking the prerogative remedies and to enable the applicant, if he so chooses, to seek prerogative remedies and couple that with a claim for relief previously obtainable only in private law proceedings. In addition, the need to obtain permission and the shorter time-limits in judicial review can be seen as ensuring that a public body is not required to be exposed to judicial review proceedings in the case of hopeless or late challenges.[141] If the proceedings raise issues of private as well as public law, there is nothing wrong in principle in allowing those issues to proceed by way of an ordinary private law claim and to leave the public body defendant to take action, for example, by way of applying to strike out the claim, if appropriate.

There are signs that the courts are already moving towards such a solution. **3–072** Lord Lowry has, for example, highlighted the possibility of interpreting the rule in *O'Reilly v Mackman* as limited to cases involving solely public law issues or, alternatively, as treating cases where private law rights are at stake as an exception to the rule.[142] As Lord Lowry has indicated,[143] this is likely in practice to solve many of the problems in this area. It is, of course, true that there might still be applications to strike out cases on the grounds that there is, in truth, no private law right raised. Such applications, however, would focus on one of the real issues in the case, namely does the claimant have the right that he claims (here a civil law cause of action) and not merely on the question of whether, irrespective of what rights he has, he has started the proceedings in the wrong forum. It is true that, if a court finds that there are no private law rights in issue (either on an application to strike out or at trial), the question then arises as to whether the courts ought then to go on to consider the public law issues. Again, provided that there is no indication of real abuse, in the sense that the individual

---

[140] This was the view supported by the Law Commission in its report on possible reforms to judicial review: see "Administrative Law: Judicial Review and Statutory Appeals" (Law Com. No.226) see pp.19–30, and [3.15] at p.25.

[141] See, by analogy, the reasoning of Simon Brown LJ in the Court of Appeal in *R. v Criminal Injuries Compensation Board Ex p. A.* [1998] Q.B. 659 at 674A–B holding that once permission has been given, the issue of whether the application was brought promptly cannot be reconsidered. The time-limit was there to protect a public body from having to meet late challenges, not as some sort of limitation period entitling the public body to defeat the substantive claim. Once permission has been given and the public body has had to face a challenge, relief should only be refused on other recognised grounds. The decision was upheld in the House of Lords: see [1999] 2 A.C. 330.

[142] In *Roy* [1992] 1 A.C. 624 at 653F–G.

[143] In *Roy* [1992] 1 A.C. 624 at 653H.

is manipulating the procedure and claiming a non-existent private law right solely to circumvent the restrictions on judicial review, there is much to be said for the courts adopting a flexible attitude and allow the proceedings to continue. The rule in *O'Reilly v Mackman* is intended to control abuses of process and if there is no real abuse, the courts ought not to be anxious to deprive the individual of the opportunity of asserting his public law rights. If there are concerns over the likely impact of any relief given, declarations and injunctions (which would be the only relief available if no private law rights in fact arise) are discretionary and the courts could approach matters on the same footing as it would if the proceedings had been brought by way of judicial review. For example, if the proceeding had been instituted long after the decision in challenge, there were no reason for the delay, and in particular if third parties or the administration would be prejudiced by granting relief now, the courts could as a matter of discretion refuse a remedy. This was a possibility canvassed in the Court of Appeal in *Clark v University of Lincolnshire and Humberside*.[144] Conversely, if the proceedings had been instituted promptly but in the mistaken belief that private law rights arose, there would seem to be no reason in principle why relief should not be granted. Such an approach would also be consistent with the emphasis on flexibility and the reminders that the rule in *O'Reilly v Mackman* was intended to stop *abuse* of process, not genuine mistakes in a complex field.

3–073   This solution would seem the most preferable solution. It would retain a degree of procedural exclusivity but only in the public law field. If no private law rights are in issue, that appears to be desirable as a matter of principle. In practice, in the vast majority of public law cases, it will be clear that there is realistically no possibility of claiming any private law rights. The need to proceed by way of judicial review will be apparent and there will be little or no excuse for circumventing the judicial review procedure by instituting an ordinary private law claim. Equally, there are cases where it is immediately apparent that both private and public law issues arise. A recognition that these are suitable for either procedure will remove the satellite litigation seeking to strike out the claims if the ordinary claim procedure is used. There are occasionally genuinely difficult cases where it is not immediately apparent from authority or principle whether private law issues arise. Provided that there is no indication of abuse, and so long as public interest concerns are protected at the remedial stage, there is no reason why the proceedings ought to be struck out on merely procedural grounds alone.

---

[144] [2001] 1 W.L.R. 1988 and see discussion above at para.3–028 to 3–029.

CHAPTER 4

Judicially Reviewable Acts and Omissions

A. INTRODUCTION

Judicial review serves a number of functions. First, it is used to determine whether decisions taken or measures adopted in the pursuance of statutory or other public law powers are lawful and valid. Secondly, it may be used to restrain public bodies from acting in an unlawful manner. Thirdly, it may be sought to compel public bodies to perform public law duties. This will usually involve compelling the body to consider exercising its powers rather than compelling the body to do a specific act, although the latter may also be appropriate if a clear duty to perform a particular act can be established.

This anatomy of judicial review is unduly simplified. The situations in which discretionary powers exist, the range of measures—legally binding and non-legally binding—that arise in public law, and the circumstances in which judicial review is sought, are numerous. No description of the acts or omissions remediable by judicial review could or should be regarded as exhaustive. In particular, the fact that a particular action has not been the subject of judicial review in the past does not guarantee that the courts will not review it in the future, as the boundaries of public law have been widening over the years. Increasingly, the courts have moved towards a position whereby, provided the issue raises questions of public law and provided that the issue is justiciable, the supervisory jurisdiction of the courts by way of judicial review will in principle be available. If the claimant can establish that the public body has acted in violation of the principles of public law, then an appropriate remedy may be made available. The courts will control the volume of judicial review by discretionary barriers such as standing and, in particular, the discretion of the court to refuse permission to bring a claim, or by refusing a remedy in particular cases. At its broadest, judicial review is designed to remedy public law wrongs; that is any unlawful exercise of public law power by a public law body. In the words of Lord Bridge[1]:

> "Just as the allegation of a wrong of a kind recognised as remediable by private law is sufficient to found the court's ordinary jurisdiction, so the allegation of a wrong of a kind recognised as remediable by public law is sufficient to found jurisdiction in judicial review."

The width of the judicial review jurisdiction is reflected in CPR, r.54.1(2)(a) which defines a claim for judicial review as a claim to review the lawfulness of

4–001

4–002

4–003

---

[1] In *Leech v Deputy Governor of Parkhurst Prison* [1988] A.C. 533 at 562.

an enactment or a decision, action or failure to act in relation to the exercise of a public function. This description is broad enough to encompass the wide range of measures or omissions that the courts have held to be amenable to judicial review.

4–004   The current approach in public law is to determine whether a particular decision or measure is subject to the judicial review procedure rather than whether one of the individual remedies is available in respect of that particular measure. If the measure is subject to judicial review, and assuming that the claimant can establish that the public authority has erred in law or abused its powers,[2] the courts will then determine which of the individual remedies or combination of remedies is appropriate in that particular case. That approach will be reflected here. This chapter will consider the range of measures that have been subject to the judicial review procedure. Subsequent chapters will consider the individual remedies—a quashing order, a prohibiting order, a mandatory order, a declaration and an injunction[3]—that are available on a successful judicial review claim to remedy the public law wrong that has occurred. Each remedy has its own traditional characteristics and has a distinct field of operation. More than one remedy may be available in respect of a particular act and certain remedies may be interchangeable. The significance of the individual remedies has declined since the introduction of a unified procedure in which all or any of the individual remedies may be sought in the course of one application for judicial review. The important issue is whether the measure is amenable to judicial review; fitting the particular remedy to the particular case is a secondary issue.

B.   ACTS AFFECTING INDIVIDUALS

Decisions and determinations

4–005   Exercises of statutory or other public law power that culminate in, or involve, a decision or determination affecting an individual[4] are subject to judicial review. Decisions affecting a wide variety of interests have been reviewed by the courts. Reviewable decisions are no longer limited to those decisions that affect rights of individuals narrowly defined.[5] The range of interests protected by the court has been expanded considerably over recent years. The position has now been reached where any exercise of power that manifests itself in a decision that has a discernible effect on an individual is subject, in principle, to judicial review.

---

[2] For the principles governing the exercise of statutory or other public law powers, see *Halsbury's Laws of England* (1989), Vol.1(1); de Smith, *Judicial Review*; and Wade and Forsyth, *Administrative Law*; Auburn, Moffatt and Sharland *Judicial Review*.

[3] See Senior Courts Act 1981, s.31 and CPR rr.54.1(2) and 54.2. Damages or restitution may be claimed in addition to one of the other remedies but may not be the sole remedy claimed: S.C.A. 1981 s.31(4) and CPR r.54.3.

[4] This includes any legal individual such as a company; see, e.g. *R. v Monopolies and Mergers Commission Ex p. Elders IXL Ltd* [1987] 1 W.L.R. 1235.

[5] A dictum of Lord Diplock, in *Council of Civil Service Unions v Minister for the Civil Service* [1985] A.C. 374, that judicial review was only available in respect of a decision affecting private rights or public law legitimate expectations does not and was probably not intended to, reflect the law. The dictum was corrected by a later decision of the House of Lords in *R. v Secretary of State for the Environment Ex p. Nottinghamshire CC* [1986] A.C. 240, where Lord Diplock's judgment was referred to as "valuable" and "already classic" but "not exhaustive": per Lord Scarman at 249.

Decisions affecting rights

Statutory or other public law powers may enable a public body to remove or vary   **4–006** existing legal rights. Decisions resulting from the exercise of such power are subject to the supervision of the courts. Thus, the courts may review a decision of a local authority to vary the contractual rent payable under a tenancy,[6] or to suspend a contractual licence to enter upon land.[7] Search warrants authorising the entry on private premises, or the confiscation or removal of private property, constitute invasions of private law rights, and if the grant of such warrants is unlawful they may be quashed or declared invalid by the courts.[8] Decisions of a public body affecting statutory rights, such as the right not to be discriminated against contrary to the provisions of the Equality Act 2010, are subject to judicial review.[9]

Decisions as to whether a person has a particular right or legal entitlement are   **4–007** also reviewable. Statutes may provide that individuals who meet stated criteria should be entitled to receive a particular benefit. Decisions as to whether a person meets the criteria are in effect determinations of questions involving legal entitlement, albeit that they are decisions establishing legal rights rather than decisions affecting existing rights. Such decisions are reviewable.[10] Decisions on whether a student meets the criteria of residence necessary for mandatory educational grants,[11] or to housing benefit[12] or a disability facilities grant[13] or establishing the right of an asylum seeker to housing[14] are all reviewable. Often, these cases will involve questions of whether or not a local authority may have regard to particular considerations (such as financial considerations) in determining whether or not a particular statutory duty is owed or what is required to satisfy the duty.[15]

Decisions affecting Convention Rights

It is unlawful for a public authority to act in a way which is incompatible with a   **4–008** Convention right, that is a right recognised by the European Convention on Human Rights and incorporated into domestic law by the Human Rights Act 1998.[16] Claims for judicial review may be brought to assert that action by a public authority is incompatible with a Convention right.[17] There are many

---

[6] In *Wandsworth BC v Winder* [1985] A.C. 461, the House of Lords accepted that such a challenge could be brought by way of judicial review or by way of defence to an action for arrears of rent.

[7] *R. v Wear Valley DC Ex p. Binks* [1985] 2 All E.R. 699.

[8] *R. v I.R.C. Ex p. Rossminster* [1980] A.C. 952. See also *R. (Energy Financing Ltd) v Bow Street Magistrates Court* [2006] 1 W.L.R. 1316.

[9] *R. v Army Board of the Defence Council Ex p. Anderson* [1991] 3 W.L.R. 42.

[10] Such decisions can only be challenged by judicial review: see paras 3–018 to 3–019.

[11] *R. v Barnet LBC Ex p. Shah* [1983] 2 A.C. 309.

[12] *R. v Ealing London Borough Housing Benefit Review Board Ex p. Saville* (1986) 84 L.G.R. 842.

[13] *R. v Birmingham City Council Ex p. Mohammed* [1999] 1 W.L.R. 33.

[14] *R. v Hammersmith and Fulham LBC Ex p. M* (1997) 30 H.L.R. 10.

[15] See, e.g. *R. v East Sussex CC Ex p. Tandy* [1998] A.C. 714 (whether a local education authority could have regard to its financial resources in determining the scope of its duty under s.298 of the Education Act 1993, now s.19 of the Education Act 1996).

[16] Human Rights Act 1998 s.6(1); see Chapter 16 below.

[17] Human Rights Act 1998 s.7(1) and (3).

examples of such claims. The courts have, for example, determined whether the refusal of support for asylum seekers contravenes their rights under Art.3 ECHR not to be subjected to inhuman or degrading treatment.[18] They have determined whether a procedure for resolving disputes conforms to the right to a fair hearing before an independent and impartial tribunal as recognised in Art.6 ECHR.[19] They have considered whether the discharge of a local authority's functions, such as those involved in community care and the provision of care and attention to those in need, has involved a violation of the right to respect for private life in Art.8 ECHR.[20] The courts have, on a number of occasions, had to consider whether the policies within schools regulating dress and the wearing of jewellery have involved a breach of Art.8 ECHR or the right to manifest religion recognised in Art.9 ECHR.[21] The courts have considered the circumstances in which the refusal of permission for persons subject to immigration control to marry violates the right to marry recognised by Art.12 ECHR.[22]

Decisions imposing legal sanctions

4–009 Decisions imposing penalties, or fines, or loss of liberty, are the frequent subject-matter of judicial review applications. Judicial review is frequently invoked to review the activities of inferior courts such as magistrates' courts and Crown Courts in matters other than those relating to trial by indictment[23] and juvenile courts, for example:

(a) convictions[24] other than those in the Crown Court;
(b) binding over orders[25];
(c) warrants of commitment for failure to pay fines[26];
(d) compensation orders other than those in the Crown Court[27];
(e) excessive sentences[28];
(f) forfeiture orders[29];
(g) decisions estreating recognisances for bail[30];
(h) orders imposing costs in criminal cases[31] imposed by magistrates' courts;

---

[18] See, e.g. *R. (Limbuela) v Secretary of State for the Home Department* [2006] 1 A.C. 396.
[19] See, e.g. *R. (Wright) v Secretary of State for the Health Department* [2009] 1 A.C. 779.
[20] See, e.g. *R. (Bernard) v London Borough of Enfield* [2003] H.L.R. 27.
[21] See, e.g. *R. (SB) v Governors of Denbigh High School* [2007] 1 A.C. 100; *R. (Watkins-Singh) v Governors of Aberdare High School* [2008] EWHC 1865 (Admin).
[22] *R. (Baiai) v Secretary of State for the Home Department* [2009] 1 A.C. 287.
[23] Senior Courts Act 1981 s.29(3) and paras 2–123 to 2–128.
[24] *R. v Knightsbridge Crown Court Ex p. Goonatilleke* [1986] Q.B. 1.
[25] *R. v Central Criminal Court Ex p. Boulding* [1984] Q.B. 813.
[26] *R. v Southampton Justices Ex p. Davies* [1981] 1 W.L.R. 374; *R. v Boston Justices Ex p. Newark* [1989] C.O.D. 311, DC.
[27] *R. v Horsham Justices Ex p. Richards* [1985] 1 W.L.R. 986.
[28] *R. v St. Albans Crown Court Ex p. Cinnamond* [1981] Q.B. 480 (sentences should usually be challenged by way of appeal not judicial review); *R. v Battle Justices Ex p. Shepherd* (1983) 5 Cr.App.R.(S.) 124.
[29] *R. v Maidstone Crown Court Ex p. Gill* [1986] 1 W.L.R. 1405; *R. v Highbury Corner Magistrates' Court Ex p. Di Mattes* [1991] 1 W.L.R. 1374.
[30] *R. v Warwick Crown Court Ex p. Smalley* [1987] 1 W.L.R. 237.
[31] *R. v Tottenham Justices Ex p. Joshi* [1982] 1 W.L.R. 631.

(i)   acquittals in the magistrates' courts.[32]

The courts have quashed search warrants[33] and arrest warrants.[34] A decision   **4–010**
by the police to caution an individual[35] or administer a warning to a young
offender may also be reviewed.[36] Although not a formal sanction, such cautions
are in practice kept on record for a number of years and a person who re-offends
within that period is more likely to be prosecuted and cannot claim good
character at his trial. Similarly, the administering of a reprimand or warning to a
child or young person is amenable to judicial review.[37]

Decisions affecting personal liberty

Personal liberty may also be affected in fields other than the criminal jurisdiction   **4–011**
of inferior courts. Decisions of mental health review tribunals refusing to
discharge an individual, and thereby authorising his further detention, have been
reviewed.[38] The Home Secretary may take decisions affecting the liberty of the
person in areas such as deportation[39] or detention of foreign nationals pending
removal from the United Kingdom[40] and parole[41] and these decisions are
amenable to judicial review.

Decisions affecting livelihood and office

Decisions affecting the ability of a person to pursue his profession or trade, or   **4–012**
removing him from an office that he holds, are reviewable. Such decisions are
often taken as a disciplinary measure, but whatever the reason for dismissal,
provided there is a sufficient public law element present, the decision will be
subject to judicial review.[42] The dismissal[43] or suspension from duty[44] of prison

---

[32] *R. v Hendon Justices Ex p. DPP* [1994] Q.B. 167; *R. v Dorking Justices Ex p. Harrington* [1984]
A.C. 743 (although a mandatory order to compel the justices to continue to hear the case rather than a
quashing order to quash the acquittal may frequently be considered a more appropriate remedy: see
para.6–007 below).

[33] See, e.g., *R. (Van der Pijl) v Crown Court at Kingston* [2013] 1 W.L.R. 2706 (search warrants
quashed) and *R. (Rawlinson and Hunter) Trustees v Central Criminal Court* [2013] 1 W.L.R. 1634
[286]–[288] (search warrants declared unlawful; claim for damages transferred to ordinary list of the
Queen's Bench Division).

[34] *R. (Necip) v City of London Magistrates' Court* [2010] 1 W.L.R. 1827.

[35] *R (Stratton) v Chief Constable of Thames Valley Police* [2013] EWHC 1561; *R. v Commissioner
for Metropolitan Police Ex p. P* (1995) 8 Admin L.Rep. 6; *R. v Commissioner of the Metropolitan
Police Ex p. Thompson* [1997] 1 W.L.R. 1519.

[36] *R. (R) v Durham Constabulary* [2005] 1 W.L.R. 1184.

[37] *R. (U) v Commissioner of Police of the Metropolis* [2003] 1 W.L.R. 897 (such reprimands and
warnings are administered under the provisions of the Crime and Disorder Act 1998 which replace the
system of informal cautions for children and young persons).

[38] *R. v Mental Health Review Tribunal Ex p. Pickering* [1986] 1 All E.R. 99.

[39] *R. v Secretary of State for the Home Department Ex p. Dannenberg* [1984] Q.B. 766.

[40] *R (WL (Congo)) v Secretary of State for the Home Department* [2012] 1 A. C. 245.

[41] *R. v Secretary of State for the Home Department Ex p. Benson* [1989] C.O.D. 329. Decisions of
the Parole Board are similarly reviewable; *R. v Parole Board Ex p. Bradley* [1990] 3 All E.R. 829
(claim dismissed on its merits).

[42] There has to be a sufficient statutory or prerogative under-pinning for the matter to be a public law
matter: see *R. (Tucker) v Director-General of the National Crime Squad* [2003] I.C.R. 599 and *R
(Shoesmith) v Ofsted and Others* [2011] I.C.R. 1195 and discussion at paras 2–011 to 2–057 above. If

officers, police officers[45] or civil servants[46] for disciplinary offences, and even the dismissal of a receptionist who refused to type a letter in connection with an abortion[47] have all been held to be reviewable. Decisions made by professional bodies exercising statutory powers to discipline members of the profession or remove their eligibility to carry on their profession are reviewable.[48] Removals from offices such as governorships of schools,[49] or a decision refusing a police officer permission to serve on a school appointments committee,[50] will be reviewed by the courts even though the offices in such cases are not linked to earning a living but are voluntary offices. Decisions imposing disciplinary sanctions short of dismissal may also give rise to judicial review.[51]

Decisions affecting legitimate expectations

4–013   In the public law field, individuals may not have strictly enforceable rights but they may have legitimate expectations. Such expectations may stem either from a promise made by a public body or from a previous practice of a public body. The promise of a hearing before a decision is taken may give rise to a legitimate expectation that a hearing will be given.[52] A past practice of consulting before a decision is taken may give rise to an expectation of consultation before any future decision is taken.[53] A promise to confer, or a past practice of conferring, a substantive benefit may give rise to an expectation that the individual will be given a hearing before a decision is taken not to confer the benefit.[54] The actual enjoyment of a benefit may create a legitimate expectation that the benefit will not be removed without the individual being given a hearing.[55] On occasions, individuals seek to enforce the promise or expectation itself, by claiming that the substantive benefit be conferred[56]or that they be treated in accordance with the expectation created.[57] Decisions affecting such legitimate expectations are subject to judicial review.

---

the issue is simply a question of enforcing rights derived from a contract then judicial review is not available; see *R. v East Berkshire Health Authority Ex p. Walsh* [1985] Q.B. 152 and para.2–135 and 2–158.

[43]   *R. v Secretary of State for Home Department Ex p. Benwell* [1985] Q.B. 554.

[44]   *R. v Secretary of State for the Home Department Ex p. Attard* [1990] C.O.D. 261.

[45]   *R. v Chief Constable of North Wales Police Ex p. Evans* [1982] 1 W.L.R. 1155.

[46]   *R. v Civil Service Appeals Board Ex p. Bruce* [1989] I.C.R. 171 (as a matter of discretion, case better dealt with by industrial tribunal rather than judicial review) but see *R. v Lord Chancellor's Department Ex p. Nangle* [1991] I.C.R. 743 discussed above, para.2–154.

[47]   *R. v Salford Health Authority Ex p. Janaway* [1989] A.C. 537.

[48]   *R. v General Medical Council Ex p. Gee* [1987] 1 W.L.R. 564.

[49]   *R. v Inner London Education Authority Ex p. Brunyate* [1989] 1 W.L.R. 542.

[50]   *Champion v Chief Constable of Gwent Constabulary* [1990] 1 W.L.R. 1.

[51]   *R. v Hampshire CC Ex p. Ellerton* [1985] 1 W.L.R. 749 (disciplinary authorities ordered a deduction of £40 from wages).

[52]   *Att-Gen of Hong Kong v Ng Yuen Shiu* [1983] 2 A.C. 629.

[53]   *Council of Civil Service Unions v Minister for the Civil Service* [1985] A.C. 374.

[54]   *R. v Secretary of State for the Home Department Ex p. Khan (Asif Mahmood)* [1984] 1 W.L.R. 1337.

[55]   *O'Reilly v Mackman* [1983] 2 A.C. 237.

[56]   On the circumstances in which such an expectation may or may not arise see, e.g. *R. v North East Devon Health Authority Ex p. Coughlan* [2001] Q.B. 213; *R. v Board of Inland Revenue Ex p. M.F.K. Underwriting Agencies Ltd* [1990] 1 All E.R. 91, *R (Patel) General Medical Council* [2013] 1 W.L.R. 2801 and see *Paponette v Attorney General of Trinidad and Tobago* [2012] 1 A.C. 1. On the

Exercises of discretionary power

Public bodies may have discretionary power to confer benefits, or permit   **4–014**
individuals to carry on certain activities. In strict terms, decisions refusing or
granting the benefit do not involve determinations of rights. In public law terms,
the potential recipient of the benefit is entitled to have his application properly
considered and determined according to law. Such decisions are therefore
reviewable to ensure that the power is validly and lawfully exercised. Decisions
of the Home Secretary[58] refusing applications for ex gratia compensation, or of
local authorities refusing discretionary educational grants have been reviewed.[59]
In the field of immigration, the decisions of the Home Secretary or an
immigration officer on whether to allow an immigrant leave to enter or remain in
the UK are reviewable although the courts will generally require the individual to
exhaust any rights of appeal before granting leave to apply for judicial review.[60]

Decisions granting or refusing licences are similarly reviewable, for example,   **4–015**
a refusal to grant an entertainments licence,[61] a licence to run a sex
establishment[62] or a licence to carry on street trading have all been judicially
reviewed.[63] In many instances, the need for a licence may affect the ability of an
individual to carry on a trade or occupation, as it may be a criminal offence to
carry on a trade without a licence. Although in strict terms such a decision may
not affect any existing rights of an individual, in practical terms it is clearly
important to the individual concerned. Judicial review will be available to ensure
that the relevant statutory provisions are properly interpreted and applied, and,
increasingly it is recognised that some degree of procedural fairness applies to
licensing functions.[64] The days when respondents might escape judicial scrutiny
by claiming that the decision affected privileges, not rights, and so was not
reviewable, are now well and truly over.[65]

Decisions having factual consequences for individuals

Judicial review has been extended to bodies performing public functions where,   **4–016**
although they have no statutory or other legal power to affect individuals, their
decisions may have de facto consequences such as leading other bodies to
exercise powers that they possess. Decisions of the Panel on Take-overs and

---

circumstances in which a past practice giving rise to a legitimate expectation may arise, see *R.
(Davies) v Her Majesty's Revenue and Customs* [2011] 1 W.L.R. 2628.

[57] *R. (Patel) v General Medical Council* [2013] 1 W.L.R. 280.

[58] See, e.g. *R. (Elias) v Secretary of State for Defence* [2006] 1 W.L.R. 3213; *R. (Christofides) v
Secretary of State for the Home Department* [2002] 1 W.L.R. 2769; *R. v Secretary of State for the
Home Department Ex p. Harrison* [1988] 3 All E.R. 86.

[59] *R. v Lancashire CC Ex p. Huddleston* [1986] 2 All E.R. 941.

[60] *R. v Secretary of State for the Home Department Ex p. Swati* [1986] 1 W.L.R. 477, and see paras
12–042 to 12–073 below.

[61] *R. v Huntingdon DC Ex p. Cowan* [1984] 1 W.L.R. 501.

[62] *R. v Birmingham City Council Ex p. Quietlynn* (1985) 83 L.G.R. 461.

[63] *R. v Bristol City Council Ex p. Pearce* (1984) 83 L.G.R. 711.

[64] (1984) 83 L.G.R. 711.

[65] Decisions such as *Nakkuda Ali v M.F. de Jayaratne* [1951] A.C. 66 and *R. v Metropolitan Police
Commissioner Ex p. Parker* [1953] 1 W.L.R. 1150 that licences were privileges not rights, and so were
unreviewable, are no longer good law: see, e.g. *Ridge v Baldwin* [1964] A.C. 40.

Mergers[66] and the Advertising Standards Authority[67] are reviewable even though they are self-regulatory and have no legal power to impose sanctions. A decision to enter a person on a register as a child abuser was reviewable, even though that decision produced no immediate legal consequences and in no way interfered with the person's private law rights[68] since the register was open to inspection by people who could exercise significant decision-making powers which could have an effect on the person. A decision of a legal aid officer determining the capital assets of an individual is reviewable as it might significantly affect the final decision on whether the individual should be granted legal aid.[69] Assessments of the age of an individual to determine whether the person is a child or an adult will influence the services to which the person is entitled and such decisions are amenable to judicial review.[70]

Procedural decisions

4–017   The decisions discussed so far have been final and binding determinations of particular questions. Decisions may be taken within the course of proceedings leading up to final decisions. Errors at an early stage within proceedings may either provide a ground for arguing that the final decision is unlawful or may themselves be the subject of a judicial review claim. A refusal of legal representation in a disciplinary hearing may either be used as a ground of challenge to the final decision on the disciplinary allegations, or may itself be the subject matter to be judicially reviewed.[71] A refusal to disclose the material upon which the Secretary of State will determine whether to exercise his statutory power to refer a criminal conviction back to the Court of Appeal may be challenged either by means of judicial review of the decision not to disclose or by challenging the substantive decision not to refer.[72] Many decisions of inferior courts provide examples of procedural decisions being reviewed. These include decisions:

(a)   refusing to hold separate trials for different defendants[73];
(b)   lifting,[74] or refusing to lift[75] reporting restrictions in hearings;
(c)   prohibiting the publication of the name and address of a defendant[76];
(d)   imposing bail conditions[77];

---

[66]   *R. v Panel on Take-overs and Mergers Ex p. Datafin* [1987] Q.B. 815.

[67]   *R. v Advertising Standards Authority Ex p. Insurance Services* (1989) 133 S.J. 1545, DC.

[68]   *R. v Norfolk CC Ex p. M* [1989] Q.B. 619.

[69]   *R. v Legal Aid Assessment Officer Ex p. Saunders* [1990] C.O.D. 193.

[70]   See, e.g. *R (Z) v Croydon LBC* [2011] PTSR 748.

[71]   See, e.g. *R. v Secretary of State for the Home Department Ex p. Tarrant* [1985] Q.B. 251 (some applications related to the final decision of the Board of Visitors and some related to decisions refusing legal representation).

[72]   *R. v Secretary of State for the Home Department Ex p. Hickey (No.2)* [1995] 1 W.L.R. 734 at 757F–758A.

[73]   *R. v Epsom Justices Ex p. Gibbons* [1984] Q.B. 574.

[74]   *R. v Leeds Justices Ex p. Sykes* [1983] 1 W.L.R. 132.

[75]   *R. v Horsham Justices Ex p. Farquharson and West Sussex County Times* [1982] Q.B. 762.

[76]   *R. v Arundel Justices Ex p. Westminster Press* [1986] 1 W.L.R. 676.

[77]   *R. v Mansfield Justices Ex p. Sharkey* [1985] Q.B. 613.

(e)   determining whether a matter was triable summarily[78];

(f)   refusing to allow a defendant to change a plea[79]; or

(g)   re-elect for trial by jury[80];

(h)   determining whether to transfer a case to another court[81];

(i)   issuing summonses[82];

(j)   committing a person for trial[83];

(k)   refusing an interim care order[84];

(l)   refusing to admit certain evidence[85];

(m)   to hold a voir dire[86];

(n)   refusing[87] or granting[88] a witness summons;

(o)   refusing to allow a witness to give evidence from behind a screen to avoid identification[89];

(p)   refusing or permitting the giving of evidence by live video link.[90]

Public bodies other than courts may have powers to take procedural decisions. **4–018** Some decisions could have legal consequences for the individual. Decisions of the Her Majesty's Revenue and Customs requiring the production of documents could, in certain circumstances, expose an individual to legal sanctions if not complied with.[91] Some procedural decisions may have important factual consequences, such as decisions of the former Monopolies and Mergers Commission to disclose sensitive commercial material to an interested party,[92] or a licensing authority to use confidential information in determining an application for a product licence.[93] Other decisions may affect the ability of individuals to defend themselves in subsequent court proceedings, such as a refusal by a local authority to disclose medical reports or to allow a second medical examination of a child whose parents were suspected of child abuse.[94] All such decisions are reviewable. A decision of a tribunal of inquiry investigating the events surrounding Bloody Sunday refusing to grant anonymity to soldiers who were to give evidence before the inquiry was quashed,[95] as was a decision refusing to

---

[78] *R. v Blyth Valley Magistrates' Court Ex p. Dobson* [1988] Crim.L.R. 381.

[79] *R. v South Tameside Magistrates' Court Ex p. Rowland* [1983] 3 All E.R. 689.

[80] *R. v Birmingham Justices Ex p. Hodgson* [1985] Q.B. 1131.

[81] *R. v Wareham Magistrates' Court Ex p. Seldon* [1988] 1 W.L.R. 825.

[82] *R. v Horseferry Road Justices Ex p. Independent Broadcasting Authority* [1987] Q.B. 54.

[83] *R. v Bedwellty Justices Ex p. Williams* [1996] 3 W.L.R. 361 *Neill v North Antrim Magistrates' Court* [1992] 1 W.L.R. 1220. *R. v Oxford City Justices Ex p. Berry* [1988] Q.B. 507.

[84] *R. v Birmingham City Juvenile Court Ex p. Birmingham City Council* [1988] 1 W.L.R. 337.

[85] *R. v Bow Street Metropolitan Stipendiary Magistrate Ex p. Noncyp Ltd* [1989] 3 W.L.R. 467.

[86] *R. v Liverpool Juvenile Court Ex p. R* [1988] Q.B. 1.

[87] *R. v Bradford Justices Ex p. Wilkinson* [1990] 2 All E.R. 833; and see also *R. v B County Council Ex p. P.* [1991] 1 W.L.R. 221.

[88] *R. v Reading Justices Ex p. Berkshire CC* [1995] C.O.D. 385.

[89] *R. v HM Coroner for Newcastle Upon Tyne Ex p. A* [1998] C.O.D. 163.

[90] *R. (Director of Public Prosecutions) v Redbridge Youth Court; R. (L) v Bicester Youth Court* [2001] 1 W.L.R. 2403.

[91] *R. v I.R.C. Ex p. Goldberg* [1989] Q.B. 267.

[92] *R. v Monopolies and Mergers Commission Ex p. Elders IXL Ltd* [1987] 1 W.L.R. 1221.

[93] *R. v Licensing Authority Ex p. Smith Kline & French Laboratories Ltd* [1989] 2 W.L.R. 397.

[94] *R. v Hampshire CC Ex p. K.* [1990] 2 All E.R. 129. See also *R. v B County Council Ex p. P.* above, [1991] 2 All E.R. 65 (decision of county council not to call material witness in child care proceedings was capable of being judicially reviewed).

[95] *R. v Lord Saville of Newdigate Ex p. A* [2000] 1 W.L.R. 1855.

allow soldiers to give evidence in London rather than in Northern Ireland.[96] Decisions that inquiries should receive evidence in private rather than public have been challenged by way of judicial review.[97]

4–019   In challenges to procedural decisions, the question will usually be whether the courts should as a matter of discretion refuse permission to apply for judicial review before a final decision is taken. There are some indications that the courts may develop a concept of prematurity whereby permission will be refused, or a remedy not granted, if the application is unduly premature.[98] The claimant would be required to await the final decision and challenge that decision, relying on the earlier illegality as a ground for impugning the later decision.[99]

Preliminary decisions

4–020   Decisions may not be conclusive binding determinations, but simply one stage in the whole decision-making process leading up to a final decision. Such a preliminary decision will still be reviewable to ensure that it is a lawful exercise of discretion and that relevant procedural requirements, if any, have been observed.[100] A decision of one body may be subject to confirmation by another body and may not take effect until confirmed, but it is still reviewable.[101] One body may submit proposals to another body for approval, as in the case of education where local authority proposals to close schools need to be approved by the Secretary of State. Judicial review may be used to challenge either the lawfulness of the proposals,[102] or the decision to approve the proposals, on the grounds that the minister could only approve proposals that were themselves lawful.[103] Judicial review may be sought of both the proposals and the subsequent approval.[104]

---

[96]   *R. (A) v Lord Saville of Newdigate* [2002] 1 W.L.R. 1249.

[97]   *R. v Secretary of State for Health Ex p. Wagstaff* [2001] 1 W.L.R. 292 (decision to hold inquiry in private quashed); *R. (Persey) v Secretary of State for the Environment, Food and Rural Affairs* [2002] 3 W.L.R. 704 (decision not to hold inquiry in public was lawful); *R. (Howard) v Secretary of State for Health* [2002] 3 W.L.R. 738 (decision to take evidence in private was lawful).

[98]   See *Ex p. Hickey (No.2)* above, fn.59.

[99]   Prematurity is discussed in detail in Chapter 12 at paras 12–013 to 12–018.

[100]   *R. v Kent Police Authority Ex p. Godden* [1971] 2 Q.B. 662.

[101]   *R. v Electricity Commissioners Ex p. London Electricity Joint Committee* (1920) Ltd [1924] 1 K.B. 171; *R. v HM Treasury Ex p. Smedley* [1985] Q.B. 657.

[102]   *R. v Brent LBC Ex p. Gunning* (1985) 84 L.G.R. 169 (court quashed the "decision" to make proposals: in substance, if not in form, this had the effect of quashing the proposals themselves).

[103]   *R. v Secretary of State for Education and Science Ex p. Birmingham DC* (1985) 83 L.G.R. 79. However, the court has a discretion to refuse relief where time and money have been spent in pursuance of the proposals: see *R. v Gateshead MBC Ex p. Nichol* (1988) 87 L.G.R. 435, and see para.12–037.

[104]   *R. v Secretary of State for Education and Science Ex p. Keating* (1985) 84 L.G.R. 469; *R. v Secretary of State for Education and Science and Bedfordshire CC Ex p. Threapleton* [1989] C.O.D. 102.

Decisions on whether or not to institute proceedings

Decisions by a public body to institute civil proceedings will be subject to judicial review. Thus, a decision by a local authority to institute proceedings to recover possession of land may be subject to judicial review.[105]   **4-021**

The decision on whether or not to prefer disciplinary charges of misconduct against a person before a professional body is reviewable although the precise grounds upon which such a decision may be reviewed may be limited in certain circumstances. In *R. v General Council of the Bar Ex p. Percival*,[106] the applicant sought judicial review of a decision not to prefer charges of professional misconduct against a barrister before a disciplinary tribunal. The Divisional Court held that prosecutorial decisions were in principle reviewable, although the precise limits of judicial review would depend upon the powers of the body subject to judicial review, the procedures which it was required to follow and the manner in which it had dealt with a particular complaint. The court rejected arguments that review of the decision not to prefer charges of serious misconduct was limited to cases where the prosecuting authority failed to perform their functions at all or had failed to consider certain types of complaint as a result of adopting an unlawful policy. The court then considered whether the particular decision in the instant case was irrational or whether there had been a procedural irregularity in reaching the decision, and concluded that the decision was not unlawful.   **4-022**

The position in relation to a decision on whether or not to prosecute in a criminal case is as follows. The courts have jurisdiction to review a decision of the police *not* to prosecute or a decision of the Crown Prosecution Service to discontinue proceedings both in cases involving juveniles[107] and cases involving adults.[108] Judicial review is, however, usually only granted in highly exceptional cases. The reasons for this judicial restraint reflect a number of factors. First, it is the prosecuting authority which is charged with making the judgments on whether or not to prosecute. Secondly, there are a wide range of relevant considerations including policy and public interest considerations which are not susceptible to judicial review as the assessment of such matters are not within the constitutional function of the courts or the courts lack the practical competence to assess the merits of such competing considerations. Thirdly, the powers are conferred in broad and unprescriptive terms.[109] Judicial review should be used sparingly and the courts will normally only intervene where the decision not to prosecute is based on an unlawful policy or if the prosecutor failed to act in accordance with a settled policy or if the decision is perverse[110] or when the   **4-023**

---

[105] *West Glamorgan CC v Rafferty* [1987] 1 W.L.R. 457. See above 3-054 to 3-058 on whether such claims must be brought by way of judicial review.

[106] [1991] Q.B. 212.

[107] See dicta in *R. v Chief Constable of Kent Ex p. L.* [1993] 1 All E.R. 756 at 767j (decision of police not to prosecute) and at 768f–g (decision of the CPS to discontinue): the decision itself involved a decision to continue proceedings.

[108] *R. v Director of Public Prosecutions Ex p. Manning* [2001] Q.B. 330.

[109] See *R. (Corner House Research) v Director of the Serious Fraud Office* [2009] 1 A.C. 756 at [30]–[31]; *R (F) v Director of Public Prosecutions* [2014] 1 W.L.R. 190 at [4]–[5].

[110] *R (F) v Director of Public Prosecutions* [2014] 2 W.L.R. 190 at [5]–[6]; *R. v DPP Ex p. C.* (1994) 7 Admin L.Rep. 385 at 389D–G; see also *R. v DPP Ex p. Treadaway, The Times*, October 31, 1997; *R. v Metropolitan Police Commission Ex p. Blackburn* [1968] 2 Q.B. 118; *R. v DPP Ex p.*

relevant authority has acted under the direction, control or pressure of another person, or acted in bad faith, or misdirected itself on the law.[111] Perversity or unreasonableness may also include circumstances where the prosecuting authority fails to have regard to a material consideration.[112] Even where the courts have jurisdiction, they may still exercise their discretion and refuse to grant judicial review. In particular, the courts are generally reluctant to allow judicial review to be used to obtain definitive rulings on whether or not particular conduct constitutes a criminal offence. They are unlikely as a matter of discretion to allow a judicial review claim to be used as a means of obtaining a declaration that particular conduct by an individual is criminal and so a refusal to prosecute is unlawful.[113] The courts are more likely to intervene where the decision not to prosecute is flawed for some reason which would not involve a ruling on the alleged criminality by the judicial review court, as where the policy underlying non-prosecution is unlawful or the prosecuting authority has failed properly to consider whether or not a prosecution is appropriate.[114] The Divisional Court has, however, warned that the "the standard of review should not be set too high, since judicial review is the only means by which the citizen can seek redress against a decision not to prosecute".[115] In that case, the Divisional Court quashed a decision not to prosecute as it was one of those rare cases where reasons for the decision should have been given as the case involved a death in custody and a finding by a jury at an inquest of unlawful killing implicating an identifiable and living person. Furthermore, the DPP had failed to have regard to a number of relevant considerations and had applied a higher standard in deciding whether to prosecute than that stipulated in the Code for Crown Prosecutors. For those reasons, the decision not to prosecute was quashed and the matter remitted for reconsideration.

4–024   A decision to prosecute is also subject, in principle, to judicial review but judicial review is likely to be available only in highly exceptional circumstances.[116] There are a number of reasons for this. First and foremost, if there is a decision to prosecute, there will be a trial and any challenges raised by the accused should, wherever possible, be resolved within the criminal trial

---

Langlands-Pearse [1991] C.O.D. 92; *R. v Crown Prosecution Service Ex p. Waterworth* [1996] C.O.D. 277 and see also *Raymond v Att-Gen* [1982] 1 Q.B. 839 (decision of DPP to intervene and discontinue proceedings is reviewable but only if the decision was manifestly one that could not honestly and reasonably be reached). A similar approach is applicable in cases involving juveniles: see dicta of Watkins LJ in *R. v Chief Constable of Kent Ex p. L* above, fn.90 at 767j and 768g.

[111] See *R (F) v Director of Public Prosecutions* [2014] 2 W.L.R. 190 at [22]–[27] (potential error in relation to the statutory definition of consent in rape cases); *R. (Corner House Research) v Director of the Serious Fraud Office* [2009] 1 A.C. 756 at [30]–[32] and the decision of the Privy Council in *Mohit v Director of Public Prosecutions of Mauritius* [2006] 1 W.L.R. 3343 at [17].

[112] See dicta of Kennedy LJ in *Ex p. C.* above, fn.106 at 393F–G.

[113] *R. v DPP Ex p. Camelot plc* (1997) 10 Admin L.Rep. 93 (challenge to a refusal to prosecute based on the ground that the DPP had wrongly decided that, on the facts, the accused was not guilty of an offence). See below, paras 7–054 to 7–062 on the discretion of the court to grant or refuse declaratory relief in criminal cases.

[114] As in *Ex p. C.* (1994) 7 Admin L.Rep. 385 where the decision not to prosecute was based on a misunderstanding of the law.

[115] *R. v Director of Public Prosecutions Ex p. Manning* [2001] Q.B. 330, [23] per Lord Bingham of Cornhill C.J.

[116] See *Sharma v Antoine-Brown* [2007] 1 W.L.R. 780 at [14](5) and [30]; *R. (Bermingham) v Director of the Serious Fraud Office* [2007] 2 W.L.R. 635 at [63].

process.[117] Secondly, the discretion to prosecute is a broad one, involving matters of policy and public interest, which may not be matters for the court or are matters which they are unsuited to resolving. Thirdly, undesirable delay could be caused to the criminal process by the pursuit of judicial review proceedings. Consequently, the courts have emphasised that it is only in highly exceptional circumstances that judicial review of a decision to prosecute would be appropriate and should be granted only very rarely.[118] The House of Lords, for example, has indicated that a decision granting consent to the bringing of a prosecution would not be amenable to judicial review unless there was something to suggest dishonesty, bad faith or some other exceptional circumstance and that such claims should normally be dealt with during the trial process or on appeal.[119] Earlier dicta indicating that decisions are not amenable to judicial review no longer represent the law.[120] The correct position is that the courts have jurisdiction to grant judicial review of a decision to prosecute but that the exercise of that jurisdiction is appropriate only in highly exceptional cases.[121]

Similar principles apply in relation to juveniles. The courts have jurisdiction to review a decision of the Crown Prosecution Service to allow proceedings against a juvenile to continue if it can be demonstrated that the decision was made regardless of, or clearly contrary to, settled policy.[122] Such applications are likely to succeed only rarely.[123] In cases where the police have instituted proceedings, those proceedings must be taken over by the Crown Prosecution Service[124] and they have the power to determine whether the proceedings should continue. For that reason, the Divisional Court considered that the proper avenue of challenge was to seek judicial review of the decision of the Crown Prosecution Service to continue the proceedings rather than challenging the initial decision of the police to prosecute.[125] It is uncertain whether this is a jurisdictional bar preventing judicial review of the initial decision by the police to prosecute or whether the courts will merely exercise their discretion to refuse permission to seek judicial review of the police decision as the more appropriate course would be to seek to

4–025

---

[117] *Sharma v Antoine-Brown* [2007] 1 W.L.R. 780 at [14](5) and esp. in the majority view at [30]–[34]; *R. v D.P.P. Ex p. Kebilene* [2000] 2 A.C. 236 esp. at 370–371.

[118] *Sharma v Antoine-Brown* [2007] 1 W.L.R. 780 at [14](5) and [30]; *R. (Bermingham) v Director of the Serious Fraud Office* [2007] 2 W.L.R. 635 at [63] (courts should avoid satellite litigation which will delay the criminal trial).

[119] *R. v D.P.P. Ex p. Kebilene* [2000] 2 A.C. 236 at 371; *R. (Pretty v Director of Public Prosecutions* [2002] 1 A.C. 800 per Lord Steyn at [67] and per Lord Hobhouse at [119]. See also *Sharma v Antoine-Brown* [2007] 1 W.L.R. 780 at [14](5) and [30]; *R. (Bermingham) v Director of the Serious Fraud Office* [2007] 2 W.L.R. 635 at [63] (discretion to review to be exercised "sparingly"; *R. (Pepushi) v Crown Prosecution Service* [2004] Imm. A.R. 549 ("very rarely"); *R. v Inland Revenue Commissioners Ex p. Mead* [1993] 1 All E.R. 772 (the circumstances where judicial review would succeed would be "rare in the extreme", per Stuart-Smith LJ at 782).

[120] See decision of Popplewell J. in *R. v Inland Revenue Commissioners Ex p. Mead* [1993] 1 All E.R. 772; dicta of Watkins LJ in *R. v Chief Constable of Kent Ex p. L* [1993] 1 All E.R. 756 at 771a; and the decision in *R. v Uxbridge Magistrate's Court Ex p. Adimi* [2003] 3 W.L.R. 434 where the Divisional Court left open the question of whether judicial review lay to quash a decision to institute or continue proceedings: see 452F.

[121] *R. (Bermingham) v Director of the Serious Fraud Office* [2007] 2 W.L.R. 635 at [63].

[122] *R. v Chief Constable of Kent Ex p. L* [1993] 1 All E.R 756 at 770d–e.

[123] *R. v Chief Constable of Kent Ex p. L* [1993] 1 All E.R 756 at 770e. See also *R. v DPP Ex p. Kebilene* [1999] 3 W.L.R. 972.

[124] See Prosecution of Offences Act 1985 s.3(2).

[125] *R. v Chief Constable of Kent Ex p. L* [1993] 1 All E.R. 756 at 767h–j.

persuade the Crown Prosecution Service to discontinue the proceedings and to review their decision if they do not. Whatever the precise mechanism of challenge, however, the position is that a juvenile does have a means whereby he can challenge the decision to subject him to criminal proceedings.

4–026   Decisions to initiate administrative decision-making processes are reviewable. Decisions of Her Majesty's Revenue and Customs to initiate the procedure for re-opening an assessment,[126] and of bodies such as the former Commission for Racial Equality to begin an investigation[127] are reviewable, for example.

Recommendations

4–027   Recommendations by one body to another may be reviewable. The phrase "recommendation" is used in a number of situations, and the status or legal effect of a recommendation will depend on the context. Recommendations may have legal significance and if so are clearly reviewable. In some instances, the existence of a recommendation may be a precondition of the exercise of a statutory power. A patient may not be detained in a hospital for medical treatment under the Mental Health Act 1983, for example, unless there are written recommendations from two doctors. The recommendations may be reviewed to ensure that the statutory criteria have been properly observed.[128] Recommendations by one body may provide a ground for another taking a particular action. A person convicted of a crime becomes liable for deportation if the court makes a recommendation to that effect. These recommendations are reviewable even though the Home Secretary is not obliged to implement them and even though other grounds for deportation may exist[129]. In the health field, statute provides for the appointment of an individual to report and make recommendations on action to be taken in relation to a hospital trust and the Secretary of State is under a duty to decide what action to take in the light of those recommendations: such recommendations are reviewable.[130] Failure to comply with a recommendation may lead to other action which does produce legal consequences. In one case, where failure by an employer to comply with a recommendation of the Advisory Conciliation and Arbitration Service entitled the union to ask the Central Arbitration Committee to make alterations to terms and conditions which would become part of the employee's contract of service, the courts considered the validity of the recommendation and declared it void.[131] Recommendations by one body may need to be taken into account by another body. Recommendations by the National Institute for Health and Clinical Excellence on the cost effectiveness of drugs must be taken into account by health professionals and primary care

---

[126]   *R. v I.R.C. Ex p. Preston* [1985] A.C. 835.

[127]   *R. v Commission for Racial Equality Ex p. Hillingdon LBC* [1982] A.C. 779.

[128]   See Mental Health Act 1983 s.3 and *R. v Hallstrom Ex p. W.* [1986] Q.B. 1090.

[129]   See Immigration Act 1971 s.3(6), and *R. v Secretary of State for the Home Department Ex p. Santillo* [1981] Q.B. 778. See also *R. v Secretary of State for the Environment Ex p. North Hertfordshire DC* (1989) 21 H.L.R. 588 ("... a proposal to acquire land" to be used as a site for gipsies was necessary before the Secretary of State had jurisdiction to consider objections; court held proposal reviewable).

[130]   *R (Lewisham LBC) v Secretary of State for Health* [2014] 1 W.L.R. 514.

[131]   *Grunwick Processing Laboratories Ltd v Advisory, Conciliation and Arbitration Services* [1978] A.C. 655.

trusts should normally make available drugs and treatment that are recommended. Such recommendations are reviewable.[132]

Recommendations may, in any event, be taken into account by the final decision-maker. If the recommendation involves some error of law it is likely that a court would, in principle, be prepared to review the error and declare the recommendation invalid, or grant a quashing order to quash it, or grant a prohibiting order or an injunction to prevent it being acted upon. In any event, a decision which took into account a flawed recommendation would itself be open to challenge on the grounds that it was based on an irrelevant consideration.[133]

4–028

Managerial decisions

The courts occasionally classify decisions as "managerial decisions". The phrase is used in at least two senses. A court may classify a decision as managerial and then hold managerial decisions to be unreviewable. As such, the phrase is a device for avoiding judicial review and tends to be used in areas where the courts consider judicial review inappropriate. This use of "managerial" runs counter to the current trend in public law which regards all public law powers to be reviewable in principle although, as a matter of discretion, the courts may decline to intervene. In one case, the Court of Appeal classified a disciplinary decision of a prison governor as managerial and so unreviewable.[134] This decision was overruled by the House of Lords, which made it clear that disciplinary decisions were not immune from review.[135] Other decisions[136] have also established that the exercise of statutory power by prison governors in non-disciplinary contexts is reviewable in principle, although the courts should, when granting permission, ensure that the claim is a proper one and that the judicial review machinery is not being misused. On one occasion, however, the Court of Appeal classified a decision to terminate a secondment of a police officer to the national crime squad as a purely managerial decision and so lacking the necessary public element to make the decision amenable to judicial review.[137]

4–029

The courts sometimes refer to a decision being within the managerial discretion of a public body which is simply another way of saying that the decision is not unlawful and reveals no error of law as it falls within the range of discretionary decisions that the public body is entitled to reach.[138]

4–030

---

[132] R. (Eisai Ltd) v National Institute for Health and Clinical Excellence [2008] EWCA Civ 438 (consultation exercise flawed).

[133] R. v Portsmouth City Council Ex p. Gregory (1990) 154 L.G.Rev. 713.

[134] R. v Deputy Governor of Camphill Prison Ex p. King [1985] Q.B. 735.

[135] Leech v Deputy Governor of Parkhurst Prison [1988] A.C. 533.

[136] See, e.g. R. v Deputy Governor of Parkhurst Prison Ex p. Hague [1992] 1 A.C. 58; R. v Secretary of State for the Home Department Ex p. Hickling [1986] 1 F.L.R. 543.

[137] R. (Tucker) v Director-General of the National Crime Squad [2003] I.C.R. 599 discussed at 2–012 to 2–013 above.

[138] R. v I.R.C. Ex p. National Federation of Self-Employed and Small Businesses [1982] A.C. 617.

Reports

4–031 Public bodies may have power to investigate and report on particular matters. Reports which impose specific legal consequences on individuals amount to a determination affecting an individual and as such are reviewable. In *Mahon v Air New Zealand*,[139] the Privy Council set aside a costs order against an individual made by a Royal Commission charged with investigating and reporting the causes of an air disaster because the rules of natural justice had been breached in the course of the investigation.

4–032 There has in the past been doubt as to the reviewability of reports which did not constitute binding determinations affecting an individual. This is largely due to the baneful influence of one frequently cited case decided in 1953, where the Divisional Court held that a quashing order only lay to quash determinations or decisions and did not lie to quash reports.[140] A report produced by visitors to a hospital and submitted to a Board of Control (which did have statutory power to release) was not therefore amenable to judicial review. This decision needs to be heavily qualified in the light of recent developments. Judicial review has moved on considerably since 1953 and in the light of the cases discussed above, it is now clear that many reports may be subject to judicial review.

4–033 Investigation and report may be a method of establishing facts even though the report may not itself lead to specific legal consequences. Where commissioners for local administration investigate allegations of maladministration against a local authority, the court has granted declaratory relief in respect of such reports where there appears to be no evidence justifying the conclusions of the ombudsman,[141] or where he has exceeded his jurisdiction.[142] The report itself does not impose any sanctions on the local authority nor provide any legal remedies. The Court of Appeal has pointed out that a report does produce some legal consequences: the local authority is obliged to publish the report and to inform the ombudsman of any action contemplated to implement the report.[143] It is clear from this case that the factor justifying judicial review is not so much the minor legal consequences of the report but the fact that the ombudsman is a public officer exercising public law powers and therefore should be amenable to supervision by the courts to ensure that those powers are not misused. Similar considerations apply in relation to the Parliamentary Commissioner for Administration and the Commissioner's reports are also amenable to judicial review.[144] The Commissioner determines whether there has been maladministration and if so whether it has caused injustice and may recommend a remedy.[145] The courts will review the findings as to maladministration or injustice on the usual public law grounds, whilst bearing in mind the wide discretion conferred

---

[139] [1984] A.C. 808.
[140] *R. v Statutory Visitors to St Lawrance's Hospital, Caterham Ex p. Pritchard* [1953] 1 W.L.R. 1158.
[141] *R. v Commissioner for Local Administration Ex p. Croydon LBC* [1989] 1 All E.R. 1033.
[142] *R. v Local Commissioner for Administration for the South, the West, the West Midlands, Leicestershire, Lincolnshire and Cambridgeshire Ex p. Eastleigh BC* [1988] Q.B. 855.
[143] [1988] Q.B. 855.
[144] *R. v Parliamentary Commissioner for Administration Ex p. Balchin (No.2)* [2000] 79 P. & C.R. 151.
[145] See Parliamentary Commissioner Act 1967 ss.5 and 10.

upon the Commissioner.[146] A decision of the government department not to accept the findings of maladministration or injustice may also be reviewed.[147] Reports of the Health Service Commissioner are also subject to judicial review.[148]

Reports may involve assessment of questions of public interest and policy as well as determination of facts. Such reports may also be reviewed in appropriate circumstances. A report prepared by the Advisory Conciliation and Arbitration Services on whether a trade union should be recognised by an employer has been declared void where the statutory procedures for preparing the report were not properly followed.[149] A report of a trust special administrator setting out recommendations for action in relation to a particular health care trust was found to be unlawful in so far as it dealt with matters that did not relate to that trust.[150] The Monopolies and Mergers Commission (now the Competition Commission) is subject to the supervisory jurisdiction of the courts in respect of their inquiries and reports as to whether proposed mergers are in the public interest.[151] Some reports, such as those of the ombudsman, constitute the final conclusion of an investigative process. Others, such as those of the Competition Commission, are a means of gathering information and assisting the final decision-maker in the exercise of his decision-making power. In either case, judicial review will in principle be available.

4–034

It is now clear that there are many instances where reports may be subjected to judicial review. This is in part due to a shift in orientation by the courts. The question now is whether a body exercising statutory powers of investigation and report has erred in law, exceeded its statutory jurisdiction, or failed to observe natural justice, if applicable,[152] or committed some other abuse of power.[153] Where such an error is established, the courts will usually be prepared to use their judicial review jurisdiction and they are unlikely to be deterred by arguments that a report is not a determination. In terms of availability of individual remedies, if a quashing order were considered an inappropriate remedy, as the report produced no legal consequences which needed to be removed, other remedies may now be claimed under the judicial review procedure. In particular, declarations that the body making the report has exceeded its jurisdiction or erred in law will be available.

4–035

---

[146] See, e.g. *R. v Parliamentary Commissioner for Administration Ex p. Balchin (No.2)* [2000] 79 P. & C.R. 151 (finding that no maladministration quashed as inadequate reasons were given for the finding); *R. v Parliamentary Commissioner for Administration Ex p. Balchin* [1998] 1. P.L.R.1 (finding that no maladministration quashed as Ombudsman failed to have regard to a material consideration).

[147] *R. (Bradley) v Secretary of State for Work and Pensions* [2009] Q.B. 1114.

[148] *R. (Cavanagh) v Health Service Commissioner for England* [2006] 1 W.L.R. 1229 (Commissioner exceeded her statutory jurisdiction in investigating complaint).

[149] *Grunwick Processing Laboratories Ltd v Advisory, Conciliation and Arbitration Service* [1978] A.C. 655.

[150] *R (Lewisham LBC) v Secretary of State for Health* [2014] 1 W.L.R. 514.

[151] *R. v Monopolies and Mergers Commission Ex p. Brown (Mathew)* [1987] 1 W.L.R. 1235. See also *R. v Monopolies and Mergers Commission Ex p. Visa International Service Association* [1991] C.O.D. 29. Now, rights of appeal exist and should generally be used: see Competition Act 1998.

[152] Reports which may have damaging factual consequences for individuals require the observance of natural justice: see *Re Pergamon Press* [1971] Ch. 388.

[153] The Privy Council in *Mahon v Air New Zealand* [1984] A.C. 808 left open the question of whether the courts have jurisdiction to rule that a finding of fact was invalid.

Advice and guidance

4–036   Public authorities may give non-binding advice or guidance. Such advice may either be directed at a particular individual or may be general advice designed to apply to a particular area of activity. Earlier authorities restricting the scope of certiorari to determinations having binding effect[154] have gradually been eroded with the evolution of judicial review. The courts have now moved to a position where such advice may, in appropriate circumstances, be reviewable.

4–037   Advice addressed to an individual which effectively amounts to a decision or determination will be subject to judicial review. In *R. v General Medical Council Ex p. Colman*,[155] the court accepted that advice given on behalf of the General Medical Council, that proposed advertising by the applicant would involve a breach of the disciplinary code, was reviewable. The advice effectively amounted to a ruling that the action was a disciplinary offence. The court considered it better to allow Colman to challenge the ruling and determine its legality rather than to act contrary to the advice and seek to challenge any disciplinary action taken as a result of a breach of the rules as interpreted.

4–038   The courts will also review advice where this advice is likely in practice to be followed by the final decision-maker. The courts have quashed an opinion of a minister that development of land was desirable, which, although not binding on a local planning authority, was likely to be followed by them.[156] Similarly, the court have granted a quashing order to quash an advisory opinion of a committee set up to advise a local housing authority on an application for accommodation for an agricultural worker as the advice was likely to be followed.[157]

4–039   The courts have also attached importance to the fact that advice is given pursuant to a specific statutory power to give advice. In *Colman*,[158] the court pointed out that the General Medical Council had specific statutory powers to give advice. The fact that statutory provision was made for the establishment of an advisory committee and that the final decision-maker was statutorily obliged to take that advice into account has also been considered important.[159] It therefore seems likely that an exercise of a specific statutory power to give advice will be reviewable as would the exercise of any other statutory power.

4–040   On one occasion,[160] a public body advised the applicant that a licence was required by statute for the operation of an incinerator. The court held that the public body's statements had to amount to a ruling or decision if they were to be

---

[154] *R. v Statutory Visitors to St Lawrence's Hospital, Caterham Ex p. Pritchard* [1953] 1 W.L.R. 1158.

[155] [1989] C.O.D. 313; affd. by the Court of Appeal: [1990] 1 All E.R. 489.

[156] *R. v Worthing BC and Secretary of State for the Environment Ex p. Burch* (G.H.) (1983) 49 P. & C.R. 53.

[157] *R. v Agricultural Dwelling-House Advisory Committee for Bedfordshire, Cambridgeshire and Northamptonshire Ex p. Brough* (1987) 19 H.L.R. 367. See also the dicta in *R. v Ethical Committee of St Mary's Hospital Ex p. Harriott* [1988] 1 F.L.R. 512 (advice by informal advisory body on whether individual should be given in vitro fertilisation treatment might, in appropriate circumstances, be reviewable).

[158] See above, fn.155.

[159] *R. v Agricultural Dwelling-House Advisory Committee for Bedfordshire, Cambridgeshire and Northamptonshire Ex p. Brough* (see above, fn.36).

[160] *R. v London Waste Regulation Authority Ex p. Specialist Waste Management Ltd* [1989] C.O.D. 288. See also *R. v Leicestershire Education Authority Ex p. Cannon* [1991] C.O.D. 120.

amenable to judicial review. The court considered that the statements were only an opinion, not a determination or ruling, based on the information currently available and so were not amenable to review. The court seemed to be influenced by the fact that the public authority did not have a statutory power to give advice. Even here, the court recognised that a declaration could have been sought by way of judicial review to determine whether, as a matter of law, a licence was required if the court had had sufficient factual information before it to decide that issue. In the light of the ease with which review of advice can be turned into questions of law, and given the readiness of courts to consider questions of law, it is possible that judicial review will be extended to advice where the courts perceive a clear need for judicial intervention.

The courts have also been prepared to review general advice or guidance **4–041** issued by a public authority.[161] It is quite common for statute to provide that a minister may issue guidance and that a local authority or other body must have regard to that guidance in the exercise of its functions. Guidance of this nature is amenable to judicial review. In one case, the courts granted a declaration that certain parts of guidance given by the Secretary of State to local authorities were incorrect in law.[162] The fact that the guidance was not binding on local authorities and they were only required to have regard to it was not a reason for refusing judicial review.[163] Similarly, the courts quashed part of the guidance given to the Local Government Commission on how they ought to exercise their functions in deciding whether to recommend changes to the structure of local government as that part of the guidance was unlawful.[164] Guidance from the National Institute for Health and Clinical Excellence on the cost effectiveness of drugs must be taken into account by health professionals and primary care trusts should normally make recommended drugs available. Such guidance is reviewable.[165] Parts of guidance issued by the Charities Commission on what activities were charitable which were legally flawed were quashed.[166]

The House of Lords has also accepted that the courts have jurisdiction to **4–042** correct errors of law contained in advice issued by governmental departments, whether the advice is statutory or non-statutory. In one case, the House considered whether advice contained in a circular letter issued by the Department of Health, that it was lawful for nurses to perform certain acts in connection with abortions, was correct in law.[167] In another, the House considered whether advice that it was lawful for doctors to prescribe contraceptives to girls under 16 years

---

[161] See, e.g. *R. (BAPIO Action Ltd) v Secretary of State for the Home Department* [2008] 2 W.L.R. 1073.

[162] *R. v Secretary of State for the Environment Ex p. London Borough of Tower Hamlets* [1993] Q.B. 632.

[163] [1993] Q.B. 632 at 664B–C.

[164] *R. v Secretary of State for the Environment Ex p. Lancashire CC* [1994] 4 All E.R. 165.

[165] *R. (Eisai Ltd) v National Institute for Health and Clinical Excellence* [2008] EWCA Civ 438 (process of consultation on cost-effectiveness of new drug was flawed).

[166] *R (Independent Schools Council) v Charity Commission* [2012] Ch. 214.

[167] *Royal College of Nursing of the United Kingdom v Department of Health and Social Security* [1981] A.C. 800. See also *R. v Secretary of State for the Environment Ex p. UK Renderers' Association* [2002] Env. L.R. 51 at [33] (statutory and non-statutory guidance issued by minister subject to judicial review).

old was correct in law.[168] Similarly, the Court of Appeal granted judicial review of a policy document issued by the Department of Health giving its views on the scope of the common law obligations of pharmacists not to disclose confidential information about patients as the views expressed in the guidance were wrong in law.[169] Advice on the interpretation of a Code of Ethics for pharmacists, issued by a body which had statutory powers of discipline over that profession, has been subject to judicial review to ensure that the advice did not conflict with EU law.[170] The High Court has considered the lawfulness of guidance on giving contraceptive advice to young persons without informing their parents.[171] The Divisional Court has also reviewed the general guidance issued by the General Medical Council prohibiting advertising by practitioners, to ensure that the advice was not irrational, based on irrelevant considerations or otherwise unlawful.[172] On one occasion, the courts considered the lawfulness of proposed guidance that the Secretary of State was about to issue.[173] In these cases clear questions of law arose for determination, and the advice, if acted upon as intended, might lead to individuals acting unlawfully. On occasions, the courts have indicated that restraint should be exercised in the granting of judicial review of non-statutory guidance in fields involving social and moral issues.[174] Such cases, however, tend to involve circumstances where the issues do not involve discrete questions of law or where it is inappropriate for other reasons to engage in judicial review because the issue is premature or there is no relevant factual context for assessing the issues of law that do arise.[175] Similarly, the courts have indicated that judicial review of guidance on the lawfulness of certain action relating to the detention and interviewing of detainees overseas would not be appropriate if the issues could not properly be determined without consideration of the particular factual context. The Court was, however, prepared to review the guidance in two respects to determine whether it was lawful.[176] In practice, the courts are prepared to undertake judicial review of non-statutory guidance even in such areas provided that a real issue of law arises and there is a genuine need for judicial intervention.

4–043   An extension of the jurisdiction arguably occurred in *R. v Secretary of State for the Environment Ex p. Greenwich LBC*.[177] There, the court accepted that a leaflet on the workings of the community charge or poll tax issued by central government could be reviewed if it mis-stated the law, even though the leaflet

---

[168]   *Gillick v West Norfolk and Wisbech Area Health Authority* [1986] A.C. 112. See also *R. v Secretary of State for Employment Ex p. Equal Opportunities Commission*, *The Times*, October 11, 1991.

[169]   *R. v Department of Health Ex p. Source Informatics Ltd* [2001] Q.B. 424 (the Court of Appeal let its judgment stand as a declaration of the correct legal position in law rather than granting the declarations sought: see [5] and [55]).

[170]   *R. v Pharmaceutical Society of Great Britain Ex p. Association of Pharmaceutical Importers* [1988] 1 F.T.L.R. 1; the question was referred to the European Court which determined that the advice was lawful: see [1989] 2 All E.R. 758.

[171]   *R. (Axon) v Secretary of State for Health* [2006] 2 W.L.R. 1130.

[172]   *R. v General Medical Council Ex p. Colman* (see above, fn.155).

[173]   *R. v Secretary of State for Environment Ex p. Shelter* [1997] C.O.D. 49.

[174]   *R. (Burke) v General Medical Council* [2006] Q.B. 1132 at [21]; *Gillick v West Norfolk and Wisbech Area Health Authority* [1986] A.C. 112 at pp.193–194.

[175]   *R. (Burke) v General Medical Council* [2006] Q.B. 1132 at [21].

[176]   *R. (Equality and Human Rights Commission) v Prime Minister* [2012] 1 W.L.R. 1380 at [51].

[177]   [1989] C.O.D. 530.

was explanatory only and was not designed as a definitive resolution of some question of law, and was not intended to be followed or acted upon by the administrators concerned. The court also confirmed that advice would be reviewable if other principles of public law had been breached, for example, where the advice was based on irrelevant considerations or issued for an improper purpose. The court expressed the view that in practice the jurisdiction to review advice would only arise in exceptional cases.

Judicial review is a useful mechanism for determining whether the law has **4–044** been properly understood by government departments or other public bodies who assume responsibility for giving advice liable to be acted upon by others. Whether judicial review should have been extended to purely explanatory material issued by government is more debatable. The main arguments in favour of such review are the significance that is likely to be attached by administrators and individuals to material emanating from government, and the fact that public funds are being used. The jurisdiction, if used sensitively, is a desirable one.

Measures may sometimes be labelled "guidance" but may in fact be binding or **4–045** produce legal consequences. Such guidance is certainly subject to judicial review. Guidance on spending targets for local authorities was held reviewable as this was the first stage in the process of determining the amount of central government grants to local authorities; the amounts would be fixed by reference to the extent to which authorities met those targets.[178]

Conduct or action other than decisions affecting an individual

The tendency of the courts in recent years has been to focus on a "decision" and **4–046** to consider remedies to quash or declare the decision invalid. Lord Diplock once expressed the view that: "The subject-matter of every judicial review is a decision made by some person (or body of persons)... the 'decision-maker' or ... a refusal by the decision-maker to make a decision."[179]

In one sense, a "decision" is a form of legal shorthand signifying a measure or **4–047** act which is capable of attracting the supervisory jurisdiction of the courts. In the majority of cases this broad use of "decision" makes no practical difference as it will usually be clear what measure the court considers unlawful and what needs to be done to rectify the situation. The use of "decision" may be misleading if it suggests that only exercises of statutory power which culminate in a final conclusive determination of a question affecting an individual's rights may be reviewable. There are cases refusing judicial review on the grounds that the public body has taken no "decision" capable of being reviewed.[180] These cases may be explicable on other grounds, for example, that no current dispute exists between the parties or that there is no ground upon which the individual can seek review as the public body has not acted unlawfully. In principle, it is undesirable to focus attention on whether there has been a "decision". There is clear authority that the courts may review actions which do not constitute a "decision".[181] As the

---

[178] *R. v Secretary of State for the Environment Ex p. Nottinghamshire CC* [1986] A.C. 240.
[179] In *Council of Civil Service Unions v Minister for the Civil Service* [1985] A.C. 374 at 408.
[180] *R. v Devon CC Ex p. L* [1991] C.O.D. 205; *R. v Leicestershire Education Authority Ex p. Cannon* [1991] C.O.D. 120.
[181] *R. v Secretary of State for the Environment Ex p. G.L.C., The Times*, December 30, 1985; *R. v Bromley LBC Ex p. Lambeth BC, The Times*, June 16, 1984.

case law in the previous sections indicates, the courts have been focusing on whether there has been an unlawful exercise of power rather than looking narrowly for a "decision" affecting "rights". There is clearly a difficulty in fixing the appropriate boundaries of judicial review. They should be fixed with reference to criteria such as whether a public body has acted unlawfully, whether a real issue arises for determination[182] or a real dispute exists and whether the act of the public body is likely to have some consequences for individuals or the public generally so that judicial review is merited. The courts can also control improper attempts to use judicial review by use of their discretion to refuse leave or a remedy rather than drawing narrow doctrinal limits on the courts' jurisdiction.

4–048   There are occasions when it is inappropriate to talk of review of a decision. The courts may be concerned with actions either taken or proposed by public bodies.[183] It may be more useful for the purpose of determining an appropriate remedy to identify specifically the particular action that is or was unlawful, and to state precisely what is necessary to remedy the situation. One such situation arises where a public body proposes to act in a particular manner but has not yet done so. To say that the body has taken a decision to act which is unlawful and to quash that decision may make it clear that the action is unlawful. However, since a quashing order is primarily concerned with removing the consequences of decisions rather than restraining someone from acting illegally, it may be more useful and accurate to declare what the law is and, if it is considered necessary, grant a prohibiting order or an injunction to restrain the public body from acting in that way. An example arose where the court declared that the refusal of police officers to await the arrival of solicitors before questioning a suspect was unlawful.[184]

4–049   A second situation where it is useful to identify the particular action which is being reviewed occurs when the courts are dealing with a past course of conduct. An example arose in *R. v Inland Revenue Commissioners Ex p. Rossminster*,[185] where the courts were considering the legality of the exercise of search and seizure powers. Lord Diplock spoke in terms of whether the decision to exercise the search and seizure powers was lawful and whether the decision should be quashed. As the powers had already been exercised, a quashing order to quash a decision that had already been implemented would not have been appropriate. There could be no question of removing the consequences of the "decision", only declaring it to have been unlawful and working out the consequences of such illegality in terms of damages for any tortious acts committed.

4–050   There may also be occasions when a decision has been implemented where, for practical reasons, it is not possible to quash it, and the appropriate remedy will be declaratory relief spelling out the consequences of the earlier illegality. Such a

---

[182] But see *R. v Secretary of State for Education and Science Ex p. Birmingham CC*, May 14, 1991, unreported (Brooke J. held court had no jurisdiction to grant a declaration as to scope of public body's powers, even though a clear issue of law arose which needed to be determined). This approach no longer reflects the current approach of the courts to the judicial review jurisdiction.

[183] CPR r.54.1 defines a claim for judicial review for the purposes of that section of the CPR as a claim to "review the lawfulness of an enactment, or a decision, action or failure to act".

[184] *R (Elosta) v Commissioner of Police of the Metropolis (Law Society intervening)* [2014] 1 W.L.R. 239.

[185] [1980] A.C. 952 at 1013.

case arose in *Chief Constable of the North Wales Police v Evans*,[186] where a decision requiring a constable to resign could not, for practical reasons, be quashed more than four years after it had been implemented, and the appropriate relief was considered to be a declaration establishing the illegality and spelling out the legal position.[187] The courts have also accepted that they have jurisdiction to allow a challenge to the reasons underlying the decision even though there is no challenge to the legality of the specific decision itself.[188] This jurisdiction is only to be used in exceptional circumstances where there is no alternative remedy available and a point of general importance is in issue.

C. ACTS BY ONE PUBLIC BODY AFFECTING ANOTHER PUBLIC BODY

One of the important functions of administrative law is to regulate relations between the individual and the State. Another important, but sometimes neglected, function of administrative law is to regulate relations between different public bodies such as relations between central and local government or between different local authorities. Power within the modern State may be given to one tier of government, or may be shared between different tiers of government. One branch of government, usually central government, may be given supervisory or controlling powers over the actions of local government or other public bodies. The possible variations are numerous. The precise relationship between different public authorities will depend on the statutory context and will differ from one area of activity to another. The relationship also changes as new statutes are enacted, altering the distribution of power and relations between the different tiers of government.

4–051

Decisions taken in the exercise of statutory power by one public authority that affect another may be challenged by way of judicial review by the public authority affected.[189] The usual principles of judicial review apply, to ensure that decisions are based upon a proper interpretation of the law, that there is no abuse of power and, increasingly, that procedural fairness is observed so that a public body which might be adversely affected by a decision of another body is given the opportunity to make representations before the final decision is taken.[190] A public body may also seek to challenge delegated legislation or a decision taken

4–052

---

[186] [1982] 1 W.L.R. 1155.

[187] The usual consequence where the holder of a public office is unlawfully dismissed is that the dismissal is void and of no legal effect and the office holder remains in post and entitled to remuneration: see the decision of the Privy Council in *McLaughlin v Governor of the Cayman Islands* [2007] 1 W.L.R. 2839. As the Privy Council recognised, there may be discretionary reasons why different remedies are appropriate as in *Chief Constable v Evans* [1982] 1 W.L.R. 1155.

[188] *R. v Secretary of State for the Environment Ex p. Greater London Council* (see above, fn.181). But see *Young v Secretary of State for the Environment* (1990) 60 P. & C.R. 560 (no statutory appeal against reasons possible).

[189] Ministers may act as appellate authorities from decisions of local authorities, particularly in the planning field, and local authorities may have statutory rights of appeal to the courts against such decisions: see Chapter 13.

[190] *R. v Secretary of State for the Environment Ex p. Brent LBC* [1982] Q.B. 593; *R. v Secretary of State for the Environment Ex p. Southwark LBC* (1987) 54 P. & C.R. 226, esp. at 231.

by another body in respect of another individual. The question then is whether the public body has standing to challenge such acts.[191]

Central-local government relations

Decisions

4–053   Statute frequently confers powers on central government ministers[192] to take decisions affecting local authorities. Actions of local authorities may, for example, only take effect when the approval of the relevant Secretary of State is given. Decisions of ministers refusing to confirm compulsory purchase orders made by local authorities,[193] refusing approval for a local development plan,[194] or determining whether to approve proposals for the closure of schools[195] may be challenged by judicial review. Ministers may have a statutory power to direct local authorities to take certain action. Directions ordering that land be sold,[196] or transferred to another local authority,[197] or ordering a local authority to make payments to another public body,[198] may be challenged by the local authority affected. Local authorities may provide services on behalf of central government and be entitled to reclaim the cost of doing so. The housing benefit system, for example, is administered by local authorities which may then reclaim costs incurred from central government. Decisions by the Secretary of State that certain items of expenditure could not be reclaimed have been quashed on judicial review.[199]

Default powers

4–054   Central government[200] may have statutory default powers to issue directions to a local authority which is failing properly to discharge certain of its statutory duties. Such directions may be challenged on the usual public law principles. Directions by the relevant Secretary of State transferring functions of one local

---

[191]   *R. v Secretary of State for Social Services Ex p. Child Poverty Action Group*, July 30, 1984, unreported (Greater London Council did not have standing). The point did not have to be decided in the Court of Appeal: see *The Times*, August 8, 1985.

[192]   In relation to Wales, the majority of such powers has now been transferred to the Welsh Ministers.

[193]   *R. v Secretary of State for the Environment Ex p. Leicester City Council* (1987) 55 P. & C.R. 364.

[194]   *R. v Secretary of State for the Environment Ex p. Southwark LBC* (see above, fn.180).

[195]   *R. v Secretary of State for Education and Science Ex p. Birmingham DC* (1985) 83 L.G.R. 79. The council sought judicial review of a decision approving their proposals, alleging that the proposals were themselves flawed; the council were refused judicial review as the error was their own, not the Secretary of State's—but the governors of the school were granted certiorari to quash the decision.

[196]   *Manchester City Council v Secretary of State for the Environment* (1987) 54 P. & C.R. 212.

[197]   *R. v Secretary of State for the Environment Ex p. Newham LBC* (1987) 85 L.G.R. 737 (successful challenge to terms on which transfer to be made: earlier unreported challenge to the direction to transfer failed on the merits).

[198]   *R. v Secretary of State for Transport Ex p. Greater London Council* [1986] Q.B. 556.

[199]   *R. v Secretary of State for Social Services Ex p. Cynon Valley BC* (1987) 86 L.G.R. 390; *R. v Secretary of State for Social Services Ex p. Waltham Forest LBC* (1987) 86 L.G.R. 383.

[200]   Again, in relation to Wales, most such default powers are exercisable by the Welsh Ministers.

authority under the National Health Service Act 1977 to another public body,[201] or assuming the functions of a local authority in the sale of public sector housing, may be challenged by the local authority concerned.[202]

Fiscal controls

Decisions taken by central government in the area of local government finance have in the past been a frequent source of judicial review. This was particularly true during the 1980s, as central government sought to control the expenditure and revenue-raising powers of local government. Decisions of central government reducing the Rate Support Grant payable to local authorities,[203] or fixing expenditure targets,[204] were challenged by the local authorities affected. The system of local authority finance was altered in the 1990s with the abolition of domestic rates and the introduction of the council tax. Central government still has statutory powers designed to enable them to control the amount of local government expenditure. The exercise of these powers has been subjected to judicial review.[205] Central government is likely to retain some control over local authority spending and the exercise of such statutory powers of control will be subject to judicial review. Central government has other statutory powers in the financial field which give rise to judicial review. One education authority, for example, sought judicial review of the refusal of the Secretary of State to change the formula determining the distribution of the cost of the provision of further education between local authorities.[206]

4-055

Determining the allocation of authority

There may be occasions when the precise allocation of powers and responsibilities between central and local governments is not clear. Judicial review may then be used to determine the extent of their respective powers. In one case, judicial review was sought by a local authority to determine the question of whether the sale of a house under the right to buy provisions of the Housing Act 1985 also required the consent of the Secretary of State under an earlier act, as the house stood in the green belt.[207] In *R. v Secretary of State for the Home Department Ex p. Northumbria Police Authority*,[208] a police authority unsuccessfully sought a declaration by way of judicial review that the Secretary of State had no power under the Police Act 1964, or the Royal Prerogative to supply plastic batons and tear gas to chief constables without their consent. Judicial review was used to

4-056

---

[201] *R. v Secretary of State for Social Services Ex p. Lewisham, Lambeth and Southwark LBC, The Times*, February 26, 1980. Such matters are now regulated by the National Health Services Act 2006 in England.

[202] *R. v Secretary of State for the Environment Ex p. Norwich CC* [1982] Q.B. 808.

[203] *R. v Secretary of State for the Environment Ex p. Brent LBC* [1982] Q.B. 593.

[204] *R. v Secretary of State for the Environment Ex p. Nottinghamshire CC* [1986] A.C. 240.

[205] *R. v Secretary of State for the Environment Ex p. Hammersmith and Fulham LBC* [1991] 1 A.C. 521 (decision to set maximum budget for 17 local authorities challenged; claim failed on its merits).

[206] *R. v Secretary of State for Education and Science Ex p. Inner London Education Authority* (1985) 84 L.G.R. 454.

[207] *R. v Secretary of State for the Environment Ex p. Enfield LBC* (1988) 86 L.G.R. 549.

[208] [1989] Q.B. 26.

determine whether the National Asylum Support Service, which was part of the Home Office, or local authorities were responsible for providing support for destitute asylum seekers.[209]

Protection of procedural rights

4–057 Local authorities may also have procedural rights derived from common law or statute to be consulted before a decision is taken or regulations made.[210] They may seek judicial review of decisions on the ground that there has been a procedural impropriety, and that the decision is therefore unlawful.[211]

Challenges by central government

4–058 Judicial review may also be sought by central government against local government. The Secretary of State for Employment successfully sought judicial review of a resolution of Liverpool City Council rejecting all use and support of a new Employment Training Scheme introduced by central government.[212] Government ministers may also invoke judicial review to enforce compliance by local authorities with directions issued by central government. In one case, the Secretary of State obtained mandamus against a local authority to compel them to comply with a direction to dispose of land.[213] The landmark case of *Secretary of State for Education and Science v Tameside MBC*,[214] was also a case where the minister sought mandamus to compel a local education authority to comply with directions issued under s.68 of the Education Act 1944. Mandamus was refused as the minister had acted unlawfully in issuing the directions.

Relations between local authorities

4–059 Local government in England (outside London) is organised in some areas on a two-tier basis, with functions being divided between county and district councils and in others by a single or unitary authority.[215] Decisions by one tier affecting the other tier are susceptible to judicial review. Challenges have largely arisen in the field of local government finance, where one authority (a precepting authority, which is usually the county council)[216] issues a precept to a charging authority requiring that authority to ensure that sufficient revenue is collected by

---

[209] *R. v National Asylum Support Service ex p. Westminster City Council* [2002] 1 W.L.R. 2956.

[210] See, e.g. *R. v Secretary of State for Transport Ex p. Gwent CC* [1988] Q.B. 429.

[211] *R. v Secretary of State for Social Services Ex p. Association of Metropolitan Authorities* [1986] 1 W.L.R. 1.

[212] *R. v Liverpool City Council Ex p. Secretary of State for Employment* [1989] C.O.D. 404.

[213] *R. v Secretary of State for the Environment Ex p. Manchester City Council* (1987) 53 P. & C.R. 369; affd. by Court of Appeal (1987) 54 P. & C.R. 212.

[214] [1977] A.C. 1014.

[215] Pursuant to orders made under the Local Government Act 1992 or the Local Government and Public Involvement in Health Act 2007. In London, following the abolition of the Greater London Council, functions are performed by one tier, the borough councils, except in the case of certain functions such as fire and civil defence which are the responsibility of a joint authority. See Local Government Act 1985. In Wales, all authorities are single tier or unitary authorities; see Local Government (Wales) Act 1994.

[216] Or the joint authorities in London.

way of the community charge (formerly the rates) to pay the precept. Local authorities have sought judicial review of such precepts, alleging that the precept is designed to fund expenditure which is ultra vires, or that the precepting authority has failed to exercise its discretion properly in determining to incur an item of expenditure. In one case,[217] a local authority successfully challenged a supplementary precept issued by the Greater London Council designed to subsidise fares on the London Underground, as the subsidy was ultra vires and an abuse of power. A local authority may challenge a decision of a precepting authority to incur certain expenditure even before a precept is actually issued. The Westminster City Council successfully challenged a decision of the Inner London Education Authority to spend money on an advertising campaign which exceeded their statutory powers.[218]

Many (but not all) of these judicial review cases arose in London in disputes **4–060** between the GLC and ILEA (the precepting authorities) and the borough. They reflected the increasing political polarisation, which resulted in an increase in judicial review cases of this sort. The reorganisation of local government with the abolition of the GLC, and the transfer of functions to the boroughs reduced the scope for disputes. The legislation providing for the abolition itself spawned judicial review cases concerning, for example: the power of the GLC to make grants before abolition in respect of the years after abolition,[219] or the powers of the London Residuary Body designed to deal with difficulties arising out of the reorganisation.[220] In addition, statutory mechanisms were put into place to provide for co-operation between London boroughs. These statutory mechanisms have given rise to disputes. One council successfully sought judicial review of an over-rigid policy of the London Borough Grants Committee to consider applications for grants only from voluntary organisations operating in three or more boroughs.[221]

Relations between other public bodies

Relations between other public bodies may also give rise to judicial review **4–061** applications. Local authorities have sought judicial review of findings of maladministration by the local ombudsman.[222] A local authority has also successfully sought judicial review of a decision by the Commission for Racial Equality to embark on an investigation of the way that the local authority was performing its housing functions.[223]

---

[217] *Bromley LBC v Greater London Council* [1983] 1 A.C. 768.

[218] *R. v Inner London Education Authority Ex p. Westminster City Council* [1986] 1 W.L.R. 28.

[219] *R. v Greater London Council Ex p. Westminster City Council* [1986] A.C. 668.

[220] *R. v London Residuary Body Ex p. Inner London Education Authority, The Times*, July 24, 1987.

[221] *R. v London Borough Grants Committee Ex p. Greenwich LBC* (1986) 84 L.G.R. 781.

[222] See, e.g. *R. v Local Commissioner for Administration for the South, the West, the West Midlands, Leicestershire, Lincolnshire and Cambridgeshire Ex p. Eastleigh BC* [1988] Q.B. 855.

[223] *R. v Commission for Racial Equality Ex p. Hillingdon London BC* [1982] A.C. 779.

D. MEASURES OF GENERAL APPLICATION

4–062   Judicial review may be sought in connection with measures of a general or legislative nature as well as decisions specifically addressed to individuals.

Acts of Parliament

4–063   The traditional constitutional position is that the Queen-in-Parliament is sovereign and there are no legal restrictions on its legislative competence. The courts cannot, therefore, quash an Act of Parliament or declare an Act to be invalid, nor can an earlier Act of Parliament lay down binding procedures which a later Parliament must follow in order for an Act of that later Parliament to be valid. Thus, in *Manuel v Att-Gen*,[224] Megarry V.-C. struck out a claim that the Canada Act 1982 was ultra vires as the consent of the Dominion of Canada had not been obtained as required by the Statute of Westminster. He re-affirmed the orthodox view that the duty of the court is to give effect to the latest expression of the legislative will. The Court of Appeal affirmed the decision on the ground that the requirements of the Statute of Westminster had, in any event, been satisfied, and left open the fundamental question of whether Parliament could bind its successor.[225] Legislation has incorporated the European Convention of Human Rights into domestic law. The legislation provides, however, that the courts may not set aside legislation which conflicts with the rights conferred by the Convention but may only grant a declaration that the legislation is incompatible with the Convention.[226] The traditional position applies to acts enacted by the Queen, Commons and Lords. It also applies to legislation enacted by the Queen and Commons alone, without the assent of the Lords, in accordance with the provisions of the Parliament Act 1911 as amended.[227] In *R. (Jackson) v Attorney General*,[228] the House of Lords rejected the suggestion that legislation enacted in accordance with the 1911 Act is a form of delegated legislation amenable to judicial review. Rather, the House held that such Acts are primary legislation and the courts cannot hold such Acts of Parliament to be invalid. Consequently, the House rejected the arguments that legislation (such as the Parliament Act 1949) enacted in accordance with the 1911 Act could not be used to amend the provisions of the 1911 Act itself (as the 1949 Act did by reducing from two years to one year the period before the Bill takes effect after being rejected by the Lords). They held that the Parliament Act 1949, amending the 1911 Act, was an Act of Parliament whose validity could not be challenged in the courts. Consequently, Acts such as the Hunting Act 2004 enacted in accordance with the Parliament Act 1911 as amended by the 1949 Act, were also Acts of Parliament of full validity and effect. The majority of the House considered, obiter, that measures enacted in accordance with the 1911 Act could not be used to amend the 1911 Act in order to repeal the provision in s.2(1) of the 1911 Act which

---

[224] [1983] Ch. 77. See also *R. (Southall) v Secretary of State for Foreign and Commonwealth Affairs* [2003] Eu.L.R. 834 at [10] (courts have not traditionally reviewed lawfulness of an act of Parliament save where it is incompatible with EU law).

[225] [1983] Ch. 77.

[226] See Human Rights Act 1998 ss.3 and 4.

[227] *R. (Jackson) v Attorney General* [2006] 1 A.C. 260.

[228] [2006] 1 A.C. 260.

expressly provided that the 1911 Act procedures did not apply to bills extending the duration of the lifetime of a Parliament beyond five years.[229] Two members of House also left open the question of whether the 1911 Act procedures could be used to bring about constitutional changes such as the abolition of the House of Lords.[230] The preferable view is that, as a matter of law, there is no limitation on the bills which may be enacted in accordance with the 1911 Act and that bills may be enacted under the 1911 Act by the Queen and Commons alone which amend the 1911 Act itself, for example, by removing the limitation on the use of the 1911 procedures for bills extending the lifetime of a Parliament or which bring about constitutional changes.[231]

Scottish courts have suggested that Acts of Parliament which violate the Act of Union between Scotland and England would be ultra vires although, even if this is the case, it is not clear whether such an issue would be justiciable in the courts.[232] There is no decided case to this effect. Although the courts can logically determine whether a measure is an authentic expression of the legislative will, the courts will not investigate the internal proceedings of Parliament to see if Standing Orders were observed or whether Parliament has been misled.[233] Once an official copy of an Act—bearing the appropriate words of enactment—is produced, the courts will invariably accept the Act as authentic and give effect to it.[234]

4-064

Acts of Parliament and EU law

The traditional doctrine of parliamentary sovereignty needs to be reconciled with the UK's membership of the EU. The Court of Justice of the European Union regards EU law as having supremacy over all national law and requires national courts to give precedence to European law and ignore conflicting national law.[235] The Court of Justice does not state that national law is invalid but that it is inapplicable in so far as it conflicts with EU law. Questions of the compatibility of national law with EU law may be dealt with by way of judicial review. The courts are under an obligation to construe national legislation in a way that is compatible with European Union law even if this involves a departure from the

4-065

---

[229] [2006] 1 A.C. 260 per Lord Nicholls at [58], Lord Hope at [122], Baroness Hale at [163], and Lord Carswell at [178] and Lord Brown at [194] both doubted such a use of the 1911 Act procedures would be lawful.

[230] [2006] 1 A.C. 260 per Lord Carswell at [178] and Lord Brown at [194] who left open the question of whether it would be possible to identify other constitutional changes which could not be brought about by legislation enacted in accordance with the 1911 Act procedures.

[231] [2006] 1 A.C. 260 per Lord Bingham at [37].

[232] *Gibson v Lord Advocate* [1975] 1 C.M.L.R. 563; McCormick v Lord Advocate 1953 S.C. 396.

[233] *Pickin v British Railways Board* [1974] A.C. 765.

[234] See *Pickin v British Railways Board* [1974] A.C. 765, *Edinburgh and Dalkeith Railway Co. v Wauchope* (1842) 8 Cl & F 710 and discussion at [78] and [203]–[204] in *R (Buckingham CC and others) v Secretary of State for Transport* [2014] 1 W.L.R. 324. See also the dicta of Megarry V.-C. in *Manuel v Att-Gen* [1983] Ch. 77 and dicta in *R. (Southall) v Secretary of State for Foreign and Commonwealth Affairs* [2003] Eu L.R. 834 at [10].

[235] *Amministrazione delle Finanze dello Stato v Simmenthal S.p.A.* [1978] E.C.R. 629.

apparently unambiguous meaning of the legislation.[236] There may be situations, however, when it is not possible to resolve a conflict between European Union law and national law in this way. In such circumstances, the House of Lords has held in *R. v Secretary of State for Transport Ex p. Factortame Ltd (No.2)* that the English courts should give precedence to EU law and, if necessary, grant relief which will override domestic legislation which is incompatible with European Union law (at least where Parliament has not expressly stated that it intends to legislate in contravention of EU law).[237]

4–066
In *Factortame*, the claimants sought judicial review alleging that the provisions of the Merchant Shipping Act 1988 conflicted with European Union law. The question of the compatibility of the English Act with European Union law was referred to the Court of Justice for a preliminary ruling.[238] The claimants also sought interim relief to suspend the operation of the 1988 Act pending the determination by the Court of Justice of the Act's compatibility with European Union law. The House of Lords held that, while as a matter of English law, the courts could not grant relief which would have the effect of suspending the operation of an Act of Parliament,[239] as a matter of EU law[240] they could not refuse to grant interim relief in appropriate circumstances where such relief was necessary to ensure the full and effective protection of rights derived from European Union law. They therefore granted an interim injunction requiring the Secretary of State not to apply certain provisions of the Merchant Shipping Act 1988 where these provisions allegedly contravened rights claimed under the EC Treaty, pending a determination by the Court of Justice as to whether such rights existed and whether the 1988 Act was incompatible with such rights.[241] In doing so, the House accepted that the courts should give precedence to EU law. The House of Lords has also held that they have jurisdiction to grant a declaration that provisions of primary legislation are incompatible with EU law.[242] The Supreme Court has, however, left open the question of what should happen as a matter of national constitutional law if there was a conflict between a fundamental principle of constitutional law, such as the principle, enshrined in Art.9 of the Bill of Rights 1689, that courts will not engage in scrutiny of the passage of domestic legislation and the internal proceedings of Parliament, with the requirements of EU law. The dispute arose in connection with the possible enactment of a Bill providing for a high speed train line in part of the United Kingdom. It had been argued that the provisions of a European Union directive required the domestic

---

[236] For the position under EU law see: Case C-106/89 *Marleasing SA v LA Commercial Internacional de Alimentacion SA* [1990] E.C.R. I-4135. For the reaction of the British courts see: *Garland v British Rail Engineering Ltd* [1983] 2 A.C. 751; *Pickstone v Freemans Plc* [1989] A.C. 66. See, generally, para.17–031.

[237] [1991] 1 A.C. 603.

[238] See judgment of Divisional Court in *R. v Secretary of State for Transport Ex p. Factortame Ltd* [1989] 2 C.M.L.R. 353. The European Court ruled that certain provisions of the 1988 Act are incompatible with European law: see [1992] Q.B. 680.

[239] *R. v Secretary of State for Transport Ex p. Factortame Ltd* [1990] 2 A.C. 85. The House referred the question of whether European law required that interim relief should be available to the Court of Justice.

[240] Following a ruling to that effect by the Court of Justice in *R. v Secretary of State for Transport Ex p. Factortame Ltd (No.2)* [1991] 1 A.C. 603.

[241] [1991] 1 A.C. 603. See, generally, para.8–018.

[242] *R. v Secretary of State for Employment Ex p. Equal Opportunities Commission* [1995] 1 A.C. 1 and see below at para.7–032 on the scope of this jurisdiction.

courts to assess the adequacy of Parliament's consideration of environmental information relating to the proposed train line. The Supreme Court held that the Directive, construed against a background where the Court of Justice would be unlikely to require national courts to exercise a supervisory jurisdiction over the internal proceedings of Parliament, did not require national courts to undertake such an exercise. The Supreme Court expressly left open the question of what the position would be in the event of a possible conflict between fundamental principles of national constitutional law, whether recognised in statute or in the common law, with the European Communities Act 1972.[243] The relationship between European Union law and national law is dealt with in detail in Chapter 17.[244]

Proposed legislation and EU law

Attempts may be made to challenge the compatibility of proposed legislation with European Union law.[245] Such attempts at judicial review may be premature as there is no certainty as to the form that the legislation will finally take, or even that legislation will be enacted at all. It is also possible that a court could construe the legislation as finally enacted in a way that does not conflict with EU law. Even if the application was not premature, the only appropriate remedy is likely to be a declaration which could, for example, set out the obligations imposed by EU law and indicate the limits on the legislative competence of Parliament. It is highly unlikely that the courts would grant a remedy which would seek to prevent Parliament even debating a Bill.[246] Once the Act has received Royal Assent there should be no reason for refusing judicial review. Permission to apply for judicial review was apparently refused, however, to challenge the Merchant Shipping Act 1988 after it had received Royal Assent, but before it came into force, on the grounds that the application was premature.[247] On one occasion, the Supreme Court has considered the requirements of EU law prior to the enactment of primary legislation. That case, however, concerned a situation where it was claimed that EU law required the domestic legislative process to ensure adequate time for the preparation and consideration of environmental information and, furthermore, that it was for the national courts to determine whether the legislative process was adequate and that the environmental information had been properly considered by the legislature prior to the enactment of domestic legislation. The Supreme Court considered that the case involved the proper construction of the EU Directive and considered that it would assist Parliament to

4–067

---

[243] *R (Buckingham CC and others) v Secretary of State for Transport* [2014] 1 W.L.R. 324 at [202]–[211]. See also the judgment of the Divisional Court in *Thoburn v Sunderland City Council* [2003] Q.B. 151 at [53]–[70]. For discussion, see Craig, "Constitutionalising constitutional law: HS2" [2014] P.L. 379.

[244] See also paras 17–031 to 17–032.

[245] Permission to apply for judicial review to quash the decision to introduce the Merchant Shipping Bill was apparently granted but the application was subsequently withdrawn: see Gravells, "Disapplying an Act of Parliament Pending a Preliminary Ruling: Constitutional Enormity or Community Law Right?" [1989] P.L. 568 at fn.25.

[246] See dicta in *R. v HM Treasury Ex p. Smedley* [1985] Q.B. 657, dealing with an analogous situation. See also, *Rediffusion (Hong Kong) v Att-Gen of Hong Kong* [1970] A.C. 1136. See, generally, para.6–009.

[247] See Gravells, p.166, (above, fn.245).

know what the requirements of EU law were before the legislative process began. As the legislative process was likely to be costly and time-consuming, it would be advantageous for those involved to have a determination as to the requirements of EU law in terms of procedure. In the event, the Supreme Court held that EU law did not require national courts to scrutinise the adequacy of internal proceedings in Parliament and there was no reason to suppose that Parliament would not have the necessary environmental available or would be unable to assess the information. Consequently, there was no basis for considering that the relevant legislative processes were incompatible with the requirements of EU law.[248]

4–068   A different issue arises where it is said that a Directive which imposes an obligation on the UK to achieve a particular result is invalid. The national courts have no jurisdiction to determine whether or not a Directive is invalid but must refer that question to the Court of Justice.[249] The courts have accepted that it may be appropriate to grant permission to apply for judicial review and refer the question of the validity of the Directive to the Court of Justice even before the UK has made or introduced draft secondary legislation to implement the Directive. Thus, the High Court granted permission to apply for judicial review and referred the question of the validity of the provisions of a Directive imposing obligation on Member States to restrict tobacco advertising even before the UK had introduced secondary legislation to give effect to the obligation.[250] On the facts, it was appropriate to grant permission and refer the matter to the Court of Justice as that would enable all concerned to know with certainty whether or not the UK was obliged to adopt measures restricting tobacco advertising. Similarly, the High Court referred the validity of provisions of a directive concerning ship-based pollution before the measure had been implemented by the United Kingdom.[251] Although these cases concern subordinate legislation, it may conceivably be appropriate to refer questions concerning the validity of an EU instrument to the Court of Justice even in cases where it was proposed to implement EU legislation by means of primary rather than subordinate legislation. The question would concern the validity of EU law, rather than any restriction on the scope of Parliament to enact legislation, and it is likely to be a practical matter as to whether there are benefits in referring questions of EU law to the Court of Justice rather than awaiting the outcome of any legislation.

Acts of the National Assembly for Wales

4–069   The National Assembly for Wales has competence to enact primary legislation, known as Assembly Acts, for Wales in the specific areas set out in Sch.7 to the Government of Wales Act 2006.[252] These include areas ranging from agriculture,

---

[248] *R (Buckingham CC and others) v Secretary of State for Transport* [2014 1 W.L.R. 324 at [93]–[97].

[249] Case C-314/85 *Firma Foto-Frost v Hauptzollamt Lubeck-Ost* [1987] E.C.R. 4199 and see below at para.18–003.

[250] *R. v Secretary of State for Health Ex p. Imperial Tobacco Ltd* [1999] C.O.D. 138.

[251] *R. (Intertanko) v Secretary of State for Transport* [2007] Env. L.R. 8

[252] See ss.107 to 115 of the Government of Wales Act 2006. The United Kingdom Parliament remains sovereign and also retains its power to legislate for Wales: see s.107(1) of the Government of Wales Act 2006. Scotland has its own Parliament and system of devolved legislation which falls outside the scope of this work.

through education, health, housing, local government to town and country planning. The legislative competence in those specific areas are subject to certain exceptions and the legislation must be compatible with the Convention rights incorporated by the Human Rights Act 1998 and EU law. The courts will determine whether or not the provision of an Assembly Act is within the scope of the Assembly's legislative competence. That is a question of law to be determined by applying the relevant provisions of the Government of Wales Act 2006. Regard may also be had to the fact that the Government of Wales Act 2006 is a statute of great constitutional significance whose purpose is to make provision for the government of Wales and to transfer legislative powers to Wales.[253] In considering whether the provisions of an Assembly Act are within the Assembly's legislative competence, the courts must first consider whether they relate to a subject listed in Sch.7 to the 2006 Act. That involves establishing more than a loose connection between the Assembly Act and the subject and will involve consideration of the purpose and effects of the Assembly Act.[254] Finally, the courts must consider whether the Assembly Act falls within one of the exceptions and also if it is compatible with Convention rights and EU law. Thus, in the decision in *Agricultural Sector (Wales) Bill*,[255] the Supreme Court had to determine whether a proposed Assembly Bill creating a scheme for the regulation of agricultural wages within Wales was within the Assembly's legislative competence. The relevant subject matter in Sch.7 to the 2006 Act was agriculture which, the Supreme Court held, meant the industry or economic activity of agriculture in all its aspects The purpose and effect of the Bill, as appeared from its provisions and the relevant consultation documents, was to regulate agricultural wages in Wales and the Bill did not fall within any of the exceptions. The Bill was, therefore, within the Assembly's legislative competence. Whilst Assembly Acts are subject to review to ensure that they are within the legislative competence of the Assembly, they are not subject to judicial review on common law grounds of judicial review such as irrationality or unreasonableness.[256] The Supreme Court has left open the question of whether there are other restrictions on the competence of a devolved legislature, such as restrictions necessary to ensure that the devolved legislature does not enact legislation which is incompatible with the rule of law or the protection of fundamental human rights.[257] The issue of the competence of the Assembly to enact a particular Assembly Act may arise in judicial review proceedings or may be referred directly by the Attorney General or the Counsel General of Wales to the Supreme Court.[258]

---

[253] See, generally, *Attorney General v National Assembly for Wales* [2013] 1 A.C. 792 at [78]–[81]; *Re Agricultural Sector (Wales) Bill* [2014] 1 W.L.R. 2622 at [6].

[254] See s.108(7) of the Government of Wales Act 2006.

[255] *Re Agricultural Sector (Wales) Bill* [2014] 1 W.L.R. 2622 at [44] and [47]–[68].

[256] *AXA General Insurance Co. Ltd. v HM Advocate* [2012] 1 A.C. 868 at [52] (per Lord Hope), [142]–[148]. The decision relates to Scotland but the same principles apply to Wales: *Attorney General v National Assembly for Wales* [2013] 1 A.C. 792 at [81].

[257] *Attorney General v National Assembly for Wales* [2013] 1 A.C. 792 at [51] (per Lord Hope); [97] (per Lord Mance) and [149]–[154] (per Lord Reed).

[258] See s.112 of the Government of Wales Act 2006.

Delegated legislation

4–070   Delegated legislation takes a wide variety of forms and there is no uniform terminology.[259] Rules, regulations, orders, schemes, Orders in Council (whether made under statute or prerogative), byelaws, directions, guidance, instructions and circulars are some of the forms used. The essence of such measures are that they are normative in nature and lay down rules for people generally. The power to enact or make such measures will usually be conferred by statute, although some may have a prerogative or even a non-statutory base. The courts will ensure that such measures are not ultra vires the parent statute[260] and that in exercising discretionary powers to make such measures there has been no abuse of power.[261] The courts may be asked to determine whether procedural requirements such as prior consultation,[262] or laying before and approval by Parliament[263] have been observed and if not, whether the failure to observe such requirements renders the delegated legislation invalid.[264] Where the parent act provided that regulations may make provision for imposing requirements on persons to participate in prescribed schemes in order to qualify for welfare benefits, regulations which did not prescribe sufficiently the schemes to which the conditions applied were ultra vires the parent act.[265] Judicial review may also be used to determine questions regarding the interpretation and the exact legal status of such rules, and the legal consequences of a breach of the rules. In relation to the Immigration Rules, for example, the Supreme Court has held that the requirements that individuals must satisfy as a condition of being given leave to enter or remain in the United Kingdom must be included in the Immigration Rules laid before Parliament in accordance with s.3(2) of the Immigration Act 1971. The Secretary of State may not rely on failure to comply with such a requirement as a reason for refusing leave if it is not included within the Immigration Rules.[266]

---

[259] See, generally, Ganz, Quasi-Legislation: Recent Developments in Secondary Legislation (1987).

[260] See, e.g. *A v HM Treasury (Justice intervening)* [2010] 2 A.C. 534 (Order in Council outside the scope of s.1 of the United Nations Act 1946 quashed).

[261] See, e.g. *Bank Mellat v HM Treasury (No.2)* [2013] 3 W.L.R. 179 (Order in Council ultra vires as it involved arbitrary and discriminatory treatment of one individual bank: see [22]–[27] and [202]). See also *R. v Secretary of State for Social Security Ex p. Joint Council for the Welfare of Immigrants* [1997] 1 W.L.R. 275; *R. v Lord Chancellor Ex p. Witham* [1998] Q.B. 575; *R. v Customs and Excise Commissioners Ex p. Hedges & Butler* [1986] 2 All E.R. 164; *R. v Worthing DC Ex p. Burch* (1949) 49 P. & C.R. 53; *R. v Secretary of State for Home Affairs Ex p. Anderson* [1984] Q.B. 778.

[262] *R. v Secretary of State for Social Services Ex p. Association of Metropolitan Authorities* [1986] 1 W.L.R. 1; *Council of Civil Service Unions v Minister for the Civil Service* [1985] A.C. 374. The common law principles of natural justice are not, however, generally applicable: see *Bates v Lord Hailsham of St Marylebone* [1972] 1 W.L.R. 1373. In individual cases, there may be a common law procedural obligation to give a person notice of, and the opportunity to make representations upon, a proposed decision involving the exercise of a draconian power in relation to that individual: see *Bank Mellat v HM Treasury (No.2)* [2013] 3 W.L.R. 179 at [46]–[49].

[263] *R. v Secretary of State for Social Services Ex p. Camden LBC* [1987] 1 W.L.R. 819.

[264] See Campbell, "Statutory Instruments – Laying and Legislation By Reference" [1987] P.L. 328.

[265] *R. (Reilly) v Secretary of State for Work and Pensions* [2013] 3 W.L.R. 1276 at [44] and [49]–[50].

[266] *R. (Alvi) v Secretary of State for the Home Department* [2012] 1 W.L.R. 228 at [57] and [94]. Provisions setting out the criteria for identifying suitable sponsors are not such requirements and do not need to be included in the Immigration Rules: see *R (New London College Ltd.) v Secretary of State for the Home Department* [2013] 1 W.L.R. 2358 at [29]. Similarly, a statement of practice setting out the conditions when the provisions of the Immigration Rules may be relaxed do not need to be included within the Immigration Rules: see *R (Munir) v Secretary of State for the Home*

Delegated legislation made by a minister frequently needs to be laid before **4–071** and sometimes approved by Parliament before it takes effect.[267] The House of Lords has held that where the exercise of power by a minister to make delegated legislation involves the formulation or implementation of national economic policy and where the delegated legislation can only take effect with the approval of the House of Commons, it is not open to the courts to challenge the exercise of power on grounds of irrationality, unless there is an element of bad faith, improper motive or manifest absurdity.[268] The courts may still review the measure on the grounds of illegality or procedural impropriety. Illegality includes misconstruction of the enabling statute. It also includes taking into account irrelevant considerations or failing to consider relevant ones or acting for an improper purpose as the question of what considerations are relevant or what purpose is authorised ultimately depends on the construction of the statute.[269] Procedural impropriety covers breach of the common law principles of natural justice and express statutory requirements. The exclusion of review on grounds of irrationality alone is unlikely to be significant in practice as the courts would be reluctant to intervene in areas of national economic policy even if that ground were available. The Court of Appeal has also held that the exercise of the power in both of those cases turned on political and economic considerations to be evaluated by ministers and Parliament and were not readily amenable to judicial review on grounds of rationality. The Court viewed the statements in the earlier cases as dealing more with the justiciability of such issues rather than seeking to lay down a rule limiting judicial review of orders approved by Parliament.[270]

It is also possible to seek judicial review of measures before they are laid **4–072** before Parliament.[271] Relief is likely to be declaratory only, and the courts are unlikely to grant a remedy such as a prohibiting order or a quashing order where this would have the effect of preventing the minister thereby submitting the measure to Parliament for consideration.[272]

Department [2012] 1 W.L.R. 2192 at [45]. The status of other rules is not always clear. For the prison rules, for example, compare *Becker v Home Office* [1972] 2 Q.B. 407 with *R. v Deputy Governor of Parkhurst Prison Ex p. Hague* [1992] 1 A.C. 58.

[267] Either because they fall within the Statutory Instruments Act 1946, which requires measures to be laid before Parliament, or because the parent Act requires a measure to be laid before, and sometimes approved by Parliament.

[268] *R. v Secretary of State for the Environment Ex p. Hammersmith and Fulham LBC* [1991] 1 A.C. 521, explaining *R. v Secretary of State for the Environment Ex p. Nottinghamshire CC* [1986] A.C. 240.

[269] *R. v Secretary of State for the Environment Ex p. Hammersmith and Fulham LBC* [1991] 1 A.C. 521 at 597C–E.

[270] *R. (Javed) v Secretary of State for the Home Department* [2002] Q.B. 129 at [49]–[51]; see also *O'Connor v Chief Adjudication Office* [2001] 3 W.L.R. 209 at 220–221. This approach was approved in *Bank Mellat v HM Treasury (No.2)* [2014] A.C. 700 at [42]–[45] and [54] of the substantive judgment.

[271] *R. v HM Treasury Ex p. Smedley* [1985] Q.B. 657; *R. v Boundary Commission for England Ex p. Foot* [1983] Q.B. 600.

[272] [1985] Q.B. 657.

Policies

4–073 Public bodies may lay down policies outlining, with a greater or lesser degree of precision, how they intend to perform their statutory functions, or they may set out general rules governing the exercise of discretionary power.[273] Judicial review may be sought to challenge the legality of the policy itself, or an individual may challenge a decision taken in implementation of the policy on the grounds that, as the policy is unlawful, a decision based on the policy is also unlawful.[274] It is also unlawful to maintain a policy which, although it appeared to be lawful when made, is shown to be unlawful when actually applied in practice.[275]

4–074 There are numerous examples of successful and unsuccessful challenges to policies. The following policies of local authorities have, for example, been declared ultra vires, namely policies:

(a) boycotting a company's products[276];

(b) rejecting all use of an Employment Scheme set up by central government[277];

(c) stating that powers to provide accommodation for children would not be used where the family was intentionally homeless[278]; and

(d) giving preference, in the allocation of school places, to children from the locality.[279]

A policy of the Felixstowe Magistrates' Bench not to disclose the identity of individual justices sitting on cases has been declared unlawful.[280] The policy of a health trust not to provide treatment for gender re-assignment was held to be unlawful as it failed to reflect the authority's acceptance of transsexualism as an illness and effectively provided a blanket policy against providing treatment in all such cases.[281] The policy of the Home Secretary of imposing a ban on visits by journalists to prisoners unless the journalist undertook not to publish any material obtained during the visit has been declared unlawful,[282] as has a policy providing that prisoners must be absent when privileged legal correspondence held by them

---

[273] Policies must not be unduly rigid and fetter statutory discretion, and there must be the possibility of making exceptions to the policy in appropriate cases: *British Oxygen Co. Ltd v Minister of Technology* [1971] A.C. 610.

[274] See, e.g. *R. v Secretary of State for Home Department Ex p. Simms* [1999] 3 W.L.R. 328 at 341D–E; *R. v North Yorkshire CC Ex p. Hargreaves* (1997) 96 L.G.R. 39. However, on one occasion, *R. v Halton BC Ex p. Poynton, The Times*, March 10, 1989, Otton J. held it was improper to seek judicial review in vacuo of a policy on granting private hire licences where the applicant had not yet made an application to the council and as he would have an alternative remedy by way of appeal from a refusal of a licence.

[275] *R. v Secretary of State for the Home Department Ex p. Handscomb* (1988) 86 Cr.App.R. 59 at 79–80. See also R. (Munjaz) v Mersey Care NHS Trust [2003] 3 W.L.R. 1505 at [93].

[276] *R. v Lewisham LBC Ex p. Shell U.K.* [1988] 1 All E.R. 938.

[277] *R. v Liverpool City Council Ex p. Secretary of State for Employment* [1990] C.O.D. 404.

[278] *Att-Gen Ex rel. Tilley v Wandsworth LBC* [1981] 1 W.L.R. 854.

[279] *R. v Greenwich LBC Ex p. Governors of John Ball Primary School, The Times*, November 16, 1987.

[280] *R. v Felixstowe Justices Ex p. Leigh* [1987] Q.B. 582.

[281] *R. v North West Lancashire Health Authority Ex p. A* [2000] 1 W.L.R. 977, esp. at 993D–995B.

[282] *R. v Secretary of State for the Home Department Ex p. Simms* [1999] 3 W.L.R. 328.

in their cells is examined by prison officers.[283] A policy document stating that the Children Act 1989 did not apply to persons aged under 18 detained in prison or a young offenders' institution has been declared wrong in law.[284] Parts of the policy adopted by the Home Secretary to deal with applications for parole by offenders serving a life sentence have been ruled unlawful.[285] The High Court quashed a policy which provided that prisoners had to wear prison clothing when leaving their cells in order to collect meals and, if they refused, they would only be provided with one meal a day in their cells as the policy conflicted with the requirement in the Prison Rules to provide adequate food for prisoners.[286]

Other measures of general application

Administrative action may manifest itself in other measures affecting the public at large or a section of the public. Such action may come under a variety of labels, but again the principle remains that an exercise of statutory or other public law power may be judicially reviewed at the application of a person with standing. Judicial review has been used to obtain a declaration that the "arrangements" adopted by a local authority for providing selective education within its area are unlawful.[287] Decisions of the Secretary of State approving the closure of a school may be viewed as a general administrative act affecting services within that area. Such decisions may be reviewed at the application of a parent of a child at the school[288] or a governor of the school.[289]

4–075

E.   FAILURE TO ACT

Failure to perform a public law duty

Judicial review may also be used to compel the performance of public duties by public authorities.[290] Statute may impose a duty upon a public body to do some specific act. Failure to act will be unlawful and may be remedied by way of judicial review, usually by the grant of mandamus, ordering the public body to carry out its duties. Mandamus has been issued, for example, to order a local authority to pay college lecturers.[291]

4–076

---

[283]   R. (Daly) v Secretary of State for the Home Department [2000] 2 W.L.R. 1622 at [21]. See also R. (Hirst) v Secretary of State for the Home Department [2002] 1 W.L.R. 2928 (declaration that policy restricting right of prisoner to contract the media by telephone on matters of legitimate public interest was unlawful: see esp. [86]–[88]).

[284]   R. (Howard League for Penal Reform) v Secretary of State for the Home Department [2003] F.L.R. 404.

[285]   R. v Secretary of State for the Home Department Ex p. Handscomb (see above, fn.254). See also R. v Secretary of State for the Home Department Ex p. T [1994] Q.B. 378.

[286]   R. v Governor of Frankland Prison Ex p. Russell [2000] 1 W.L.R. 2027.

[287]   R. v Birmingham City Council Ex p. Equal Opportunities Commission [1989] A.C. 1155.

[288]   R. v Secretary of State for Education and Science Ex p. Birmingham City Council (1985) 83 L.G.R. 79.

[289]   R. v Secretary of State for Education and Science Ex p. Keating (1985) 84 L.G.R. 469.

[290]   See, generally, Harding, Public Duties and Public Law (1989).

[291]   R. v Liverpool City Council Ex p. Coade, The Times, October 10, 1986.

4–077   Modern statutory duties frequently do not lend themselves to enforcement in the sense of enabling the courts to order public bodies to perform a specific, identified act. Some statutory provisions, on their proper interpretation, require a public body to maintain a range of services and do not impose a duty to provide a specific individual with specific services. Thus, the general duty to promote and safeguard the welfare of children in need does not impose a specific duty owed to each child to provide the services that he is assessed as needing; rather it imposes a duty on a local authority to maintain a range of services sufficient to discharge its general functions under the statute.[292] Similarly, a duty to make provision for children to be represented in family proceedings did not create a duty owed to any individual child to appoint a representative; they were "general public law powers and duties" and did not create enforceable individual rights.[293] Statutory duties frequently leave a large of amount of discretion to the public body as to the manner in which the duty is to be performed. The duty to provide sufficient primary schools for an area has been described as a "target duty", that is a duty which requires the local authority to determine the appropriate level of provision and standards to be achieved rather than an absolute duty owed to individuals where the courts determine whether or not sufficient schools have been provided.[294] Even where a court can establish that a duty to act is owed, the appropriate remedy may be to order the public body to consider what steps it should take to fulfil the duty, rather than ordering it to perform a specific act.[295]

4–078   Statutes also impose general duties on public authorities to have due regard to the need to eliminate discrimination on such grounds as, for example, race, sex and disability.[296] Such duties are seen as "an integral and important part of the mechanisms for ensuring the fulfilment of the aims of anti-discrimination legislation".[297] The courts have granted a declaration that the Secretary of State failed to comply with his duty to have due regard to this duty when setting up an ex-gratia compensation scheme for former prisoners of war.[298] Similarly the courts declared that a governing body had failed to have regard to this duty when adopting a policy on admissions criteria.[299] The courts have also found that a local authority acted unlawful in fixing eligibility criteria for community care services when it failed to have regard to this duty.[300] The Court of Appeal

---

[292] *R. (G) v London Borough of Barnet* [2003] 3 W.L.R. 1194, esp. per Lord Hope at [9]; per Lord Millet at [106] and Lord Scott at [135]–[136].

[293] *R. (R) v Children and Family Court Advisory and Support Service* [2013] 1 W.L.R. 163 at [73].

[294] *R. v Inner London Education Authority Ex p. Ali* (1990) 2 Admin.L.R. 822.

[295] *R. v Inner London Education Authority Ex p. Ali*, fn.46 above.

[296] See now the Equality Act 2010.

[297] per Arden LJ in *R. v (Elias) v Secretary of State for Defence* [2006] 1 W.L.R. 3213 at [274]. See also *R. (C) v Secretary of State for Justice* [2009] Q.B. 657 at [49]. It is, however, a duty to have regard to the need to eliminate unlawful discrimination and to promote equality, not a duty to achieve a particular result: see *R. (Baker) v Secretary of State for Communities and Local Government* [2008] 2 P. & C.R. 119 at [31].

[298] At first instance, in *R. v (Elias) v Secretary of State for Defence* [2005] I.R.L.R. 788. There was no appeal on this point to the Court of Appeal.

[299] *R. (E) v Governing Body of JFS* [2008] EWHC 1535/1538 (Admin).

[300] *R. (Chadva and others) v London Borough of Harrow* [2007] EWHC 3004 (Admin). See also the first instance decision in *R. (Eisai Ltd) v National Institute for Health and Clinical Excellence* [2007] EWHC 1941 (Admin): the point was not dealt with on appeal.

quashed an order amending the rules governing permissible physical restraints on persons in secure training centres where no race impact assessment had been carried out.[301]

Statute may impose a duty on a public body to act in certain circumstances and **4–079** may grant corresponding rights to an individual. There may still be the question of whether or not the circumstances exist or the individual has demonstrated his eligibility. That question may be a matter for the public body to determine. If the public body makes some error of law or other public law wrong in coming to its determination, the court may quash the determination. However the most a court can do in those circumstances is order the public body to reconsider the question of whether the duty is owed; the court cannot substitute its own view on eligibility, and cannot order the public body to do a specific act. A specific duty is, for example, owed to an individual if the local authority accepts that he qualifies for the provision of residential accommodation under s.21 of the National Assistance Act 1948 as he is over 18 and, for one of the specified reasons, is in need of care and attention not otherwise available.[302] If the local authority does not accept that he meets the criteria, however, that decision may be challenged on normal judicial review principles and the court will not itself determine whether the individual qualifies for residential accommodation.[303] In the case of the duty to house homeless persons, the House of Lords held that the determination of eligibility for housing was a matter for the local authority. If the authority made a reviewable error in deciding that question, the appropriate remedy would be to quash that wrongful determination and order it to reconsider the question of eligibility; the court could not substitute its own view as to whether the duty to house was owed, and could not therefore order the authority to make accommodation available.[304] Similarly, where a local education authority erred in law in determining whether an individual was entitled to a mandatory educational grant, the House of Lords held that the appropriate remedy was a quashing order to quash the erroneous determination, and referred the matter back to the authority for reconsideration.[305] The court could not order the payment of the grant or declare that the student was entitled to a grant. Often, these cases will involve the courts determining whether a public body may have regard to a particular consideration (usually financial considerations) in deciding whether a duty is owed or in determining the scope of the duty. In one case, for example, the House of Lords held that a local education authority could not take into account its own limited financial resources in determining the scope of its statutory duty to provide suitable education. The House, therefore, quashed a decision to reduce the level of home tuition provided for a child because the authority lacked the financial resources to continue providing the tuition.[306] In

---

[301] *R. (C) v Secretary of State for Justice* [2009] Q.B. 657 at [49].

[302] See, e.g. *R. v Kensington and Chelsea RLBC Ex p. Kujtim* [1999] 4 All E.R. 161 and *R. (M) v Slough BC* [2008] 1 W.L.R. 1808.

[303] See, e.g. *R. (Wahid) v The Mayor and Burgess of Tower Hamlet* (2002) 8 C.C.L.R. 239 per Pill LJ at [23] and per Hale LJ at [30].

[304] *Cocks v Thanet DC* [1983] 2 A.C. 286.

[305] *R. v Barnet LBC Ex p. Shah* [1983] 2 A.C. 309. See also *Cato v Minister of Agriculture, Fisheries and Food* [1989] 3 C.M.L.R. 513.

[306] *R. v East Sussex CC Ex p. Tandy* [1998] A.C. 714 (dealing with the duty under s.298 of the Education Act 1993, now s.19 of the Education Act 1996; if there is more than one way of providing suitable education, the authority may have regard to its resources in choosing between the various

such a case, the exercise upon which the court is engaged is, in essence, the same as determining whether a public body has taken into account an irrelevant consideration in exercising discretionary powers. There are exceptional cases when questions of fact are regarded as jurisdictional questions. In such cases, it is for the courts not the public body to determine whether the facts exist.[307]

Failure to exercise jurisdiction or discretion

4–080   Judicial review is frequently sought, not to compel a particular result, but to compel a public body to exercise their statutory powers. Courts, tribunals or other public bodies may be placed under an express duty to hear and determine any case that falls within their jurisdiction. Alternatively, a duty may be implicit in the conferment of jurisdiction or a duty may be the natural correlative of a right given to an individual to have his case determined by a particular body. Where public bodies decline to exercise jurisdiction, that refusal may be reviewed and they may be ordered to hear and determine the case. The usual remedies granted will be a mandatory order compelling the performance of a duty, or a quashing order to quash the decision declining jurisdiction either with or without a mandatory order compelling the public body to act or an order remitting the matter to the body concerned.[308] Examples of this are numerous. They include orders of mandamus issued to:

(a)   a county court judge, requiring him to hear an appeal from a registrar where he had declined jurisdiction[309];

(b)   magistrates' courts, requiring them to determine applications by parents for access to their children[310]; and

(c)   rent officers, requiring them to determine a fair rent.[311]

4–081   A decision of a magistrates' court declining jurisdiction to commit an individual for extradition has been quashed and the matter referred back to the magistrates' court.[312] Courts or tribunals may also refuse to deal with specific matters within the course of hearing which they are under a duty to consider. A mandatory order was issued, for example, to compel a juvenile court to hold a voir dire into the admissibility of a confession[313] or requiring a magistrates' court to consider a defence that a byelaw creating the offence with which the accused is charged was invalid.[314]

---

options). In *R. v Gloucestershire CC Ex p. Barry* [1997] A.C. 584 the House held that a local authority could have regard to its limited financial resources in determining whether a person was entitled to services in accordance with s.2 of the Chronically Sick and Disabled Persons Act 1970.

[307]   *R. v Secretary of State for the Home Department Ex p. Khera; R. v Secretary of State for the Home Department Ex p. Khawaja* [1984] A.C. 74.

[308]   CPR r.54.19.

[309]   *R. v Nottingham County Court Ex p. Byers* [1985] 1 W.L.R. 403.

[310]   *R. v Oxford Justices Ex p. D* [1987] Q.B. 199.

[311]   *R. v Camden London Borough Rent Officer Ex p. Ebiri* [1981] 1 W.L.R. 881.

[312]   *R. v Chief Metropolitan Stipendiary Magistrate Ex p. Secretary of State for the Home Department* [1988] 1 W.L.R. 1204.

[313]   *R. v Liverpool Juvenile Court Ex p. R* [1988] Q.B. 1.

[314]   *R. v Reading Crown Court Ex p. Hutchinson* [1988] Q.B. 384.

Public authorities may not be under a duty to act but may have a discretion as   4–082
to whether or not to exercise their statutory powers. They are still under a duty to
consider whether or not to exercise their discretion. If they refuse to exercise their
discretion unlawfully, that refusal may be reviewed, and they may be ordered to
consider, according to law, whether or not they should exercise their discretion.

E.   NON-JUSTICIABLE ACTS AND OMISSIONS

Meaning of justiciability

Certain exercises of power may not be reviewable by the courts because they do   4–083
not raise justiciable issues. Underlying the concept of justiciability is the idea that
certain issues raise questions with which the judicial process is not equipped to
deal. The concept of justiciability is not clearly defined in English public law and
issues of justiciability overlap with other reasons for judicial restraint, such as the
extent to which the courts consider judicial intervention appropriate. The
principles governing non-justiciability are, however, principles or rules of law
setting the proper limits for the courts' intervention and are not merely matters of
judicial discretion.[315]

The nature and subject-matter of a power may render disputes about a   4–084
particular exercise unsuitable for judicial review, because they raise politically
sensitive issues of national policy or national security. The procedural limitations
of judicial review may also render certain issues non-justiciable. In the words of
Lord Diplock,[316] a decision will be non-justiciable where:

> "... the reasons for the decision-maker taking one course rather than another do not
> normally involve questions to which, if disputed, the judicial process is adapted to
> provide the right answer, by which I mean that the kind of evidence that is
> admissible under judicial procedures and the way in which it has to be adduced tend
> to exclude from the attention of the court competing policy considerations which, if
> the executive discretion is to be wisely exercised, need to be weighed against one
> another, a balancing exercise which judges by their upbringing and experience are
> ill-qualified to perform."

Security issues

An exercise of power based on considerations of national security has been   4–085
described as raising "par excellence a non-justiciable issue".[317] The courts will
not review the assessment of the responsible public body as to what action is

---

[315]   R. (Campaign for Nuclear Disarmament) v Secretary of State for Foreign and Commonwealth
Affairs, unreported, December 17, 2002 per Maurice Kay J. at [50] and Richards J. at [60]. Where
judicial intervention was inappropriate as it involved reviewing the acts of a foreign state, the Court of
Appeal did not consider it necessary to decide whether the courts did not have jurisdiction or whether
the courts should refuse to entertain the claim as a matter of discretion: see R (Khan) v Secretary of
State for Foreign and Commonwealth Affairs [2014] 1 W.L.R. 872 at [29]–[31].
[316]   Council of Civil Service Unions v Minister for the Civil Service [1985] A.C. 374 at 411. See also
dicta of Simon Brown LJ in R. v Ministry of Defence Ex p. Smith [1996] Q.B. 517 (affd. by the CA).
[317]   [1985] A.C. 374 per Lord Diplock at 412. See also R. v Secretary of State for the Home
Department Ex p. Cheblak [1991] 2 All E.R. 319.

required to protect national security. The courts will, however, require evidence that the particular decision under review was in fact based on national security grounds and will require evidence that a genuine issue of national security is in issue.[318] The evidential threshold is unclear but does not seem a difficult one for the executive to cross. It is important that the courts do not allow ritual incantations of the words "national security" to bar judicial review. In the *G.C.H.Q.* case,[319] a decision was taken not to consult relevant trade unions before altering conditions of service for civil servants employed at a government security installation by removing the entitlement to join a union. The basis for this decision was alleged to be fear of disruption of the monitoring facilities at G.C.H.Q. and the consequent prejudice to national security. The House of Lords required evidence that the decision was based on national security but held, once it was shown that the decision had been based on such considerations, the substance of the decision to be non-justiciable. Similarly, in *R. v Secretary of State for the Home Department Ex p. McAvoy*,[320] Webster J. refused to review the Home Secretary's assessment of the operational and security reasons for transferring a prisoner to a more secure prison. A decision may be reviewable if it does not involve operational considerations or genuine security issues. Thus, the courts were prepared to consider the lawfulness of a policy prohibiting homosexuals from being a member of the armed forces as the issue did not raise national security considerations.[321] Similarly, the Supreme Court considered, by a majority, that action taken in relation to an individual bank, aimed at preventing nuclear proliferation by hindering the financing of such activities, was unlawful as it involved arbitrary and irrational action which was disproportionate, notwithstanding the wide discretion left to the executive in such matters.[322] The approach of the courts to questions of national security may also need to be qualified if rights under the European Convention on Human Rights arise. In *A. v Secretary of State for the Home Department*,[323] the House of Lords had to consider legislation providing for the detention of suspected international terrorists and an order derogating from Art.5 ECHR which recognises the right not to be deprived of liberty without due process. A derogation was permitted if there was a public emergency threatening the life of the nation and the measures taken were strictly required. The House of Lords held that considerable weight had to be given to the views of government and Parliament on the issue as to whether a public emergency existed was essentially a question of political judgment not a matter apt for judicial resolution. The House held that there was no basis for displacing the Secretary of State's decision, on the material before

---

[318] *G.C.H.Q.* above, fn.216 at 412. See also *Secretary of State for the Home Department v Rehman* [2003] 1 A.C. 153 at [49]–[54]; *Ex p. Cheblak* [1991] 2 All E.R. 319, esp. per Lord Donaldson M.R. at 334 and per Beldam LJ at 339; *R. v Secretary of State for the Home Department Ex p. McAvoy* [1984] 1 W.L.R. 1408 (initial affidavit considered insufficient but second affidavit permitted); and *R. v Secretary of State for Home Department Ex p. Ruddock* [1987] 1 W.L.R. 1482.

[319] *Council of Civil Service Unions v Minister for the Civil Service* [1985] A.C. 374. See also *Rehman v Secretary of State for the Home Department* [2003] 1 A.C. 153.

[320] [1984] 1 W.L.R. 1408.

[321] *R. v Ministry of Defence Ex p. Smith* [1996] Q.B. 517 (see the dicta of Simon Brown LJ at 539E–G; the Court of Appeal proceeded on the basis that the issue was justiciable).

[322] *Bank Mellat v HM Treasury (No.2)* [2014] A.C. 700 at [21]–[27] and [202] of the substantive judgment.

[323] *A. v Secretary of State for the Home Department* [2005] 2 A.C. 68.

him, that there was such an emergency. The courts were still required as a matter of law to review the proportionality of the measures adopted and, given that they affected the liberty of the subject, close scrutiny of that question was appropriate. The measures in question only applied to foreign nationals and did not apply to UK nationals even though such terrorists presented a similar threat. In the circumstances, the House held that the measures were not lawful as they did not rationally address the threat and were discriminatory.

Foreign affairs and defence

Matters relating to defence such as the decision to take military action or to deploy troops are not justiciable by the courts.[324] Similarly, matters relating to the conduct of foreign policy and relations with other states are not, generally, justiciable.[325] Thus the courts could not consider whether it would be a breach of international law for the UK to engage in military action in Iraq on the basis of existing UN resolutions as that would involve the courts dealing with matters relating to defence and would compromise the ability of the UK government to conduct international relations in this area. Similarly, the courts will not rule on the legality of actions of a foreign state or give judgment in circumstances where its rulings would, inevitably, be seen as having such an effect. Thus the courts declined to rule on the question of whether involvement by UK nationals in providing intelligence assistance to another state allegedly in connection with the use of unmanned aircraft to kill suspected terrorists was unlawful as that would, inevitably, be seen as a ruling on the lawfulness of the use by that other state of such aircraft.[326] Exceptionally, the courts may consider questions which are directed clearly at the lawfulness of the actions of the United Kingdom and would not involve any ruling on the actions of a foreign state. Thus, the courts were prepared, in an application for habeas corpus, to require the United Kingdom to show whether they had control of the custody of an individual where the United Kingdom authorities had handed him to a foreign state and had a memorandum of understanding with that state.[327]

4–086

The courts will not review operational decisions of the police. They will not give orders to the police telling them how and when to exercise their powers in specific situations as the court is not in a position to determine what action particular situations will require.[328] Nor will the courts review the disposition of forces and the allocation of resources to particular crimes or areas will not be

4–087

---

[324] *R. (Campaign for Nuclear Disarmament) v Secretary of State for Foreign and Commonwealth Affairs* at [47](ii), [50] and [59](2). See also dicta of Lord Roskill in *Council of Civil Service Unions v Minister for the Civil Service* [1985] A.C. 374 at 418 and see above at para.2–030.

[325] *R. (Campaign for Nuclear Disarmament) v Secretary of State for Foreign and Commonwealth Affairs* at [47](ii), [50] and [55]–[60] and see *R. (Abbasi) v Secretary of State for Commonwealth Affairs* [2003] U.K.H.R.R. 76 and dicta of Lord Roskill in *Council of Civil Service Unions v Minister for the Civil Service* [1985] A.C. 374 at 418. See above at para.2–030.

[326] *R (Khan) v Secretary of State for Foreign and Commonwealth Affairs* [2014] 1 W.L.R. 872 at [36]–[38].

[327] *Rahmatullah v Secretary of State for Defence (Justice intervening)* [2013] 1 A.C. 614.

[328] *R. v Chief Constable of Devon and Cornwall Ex p. Central Electricity Generating Board* [1982] Q.B. 458 (court refused mandamus ordering police to remove demonstrators from land to enable drilling to take place).

reviewed.[329] However, the court may intervene to review policy decisions which are unlawful, for example, a decision not to enforce a particular law.[330] The court may also rule on the legal extent of police powers[331] and have been prepared to determine whether the police have certain legal powers or whether action they have taken was lawful, as where the House of Lords considered whether intercepting certain coaches and sending them back to London and away from an anticipated demonstration was lawful.[332]

Matters of academic judgment

4–088   Issues of academic judgment are not justiciable as such matters are not suitable for adjudication by the courts. Such matters include whether the particular mark or class of degree awarded to a student by a university is right or wrong or outside the range of academic convention.[333] The suitability of examiners to assess a thesis[334] or the standards required for a particular degree[335] are similarly matters of purely academic judgment which the courts will not review.[336] In the past, the Court of Appeal has relied upon the non-justiciability of the task of marking examinations as a practical justification for holding that such matters should be determined by the University Visitor not the courts in the case of chartered universities. With the abolition of the jurisdiction of the University Visitor, the courts would still be unlikely to deal with such disputes as they are not suitable for adjudication by the courts. Some disputes involving students and universities do not, however, involve matters of purely academic judgment and such disputes will be amenable to judicial review.[337] The courts will ensure that a university acts in accordance with its own regulations,[338] acts in accordance with

---

[329]   *R. v Metropolitan Police Commissioner Ex p. Blackburn* [1968] 2 Q.B. 119; *R. v Chief Constable of Sussex Ex p. International Traders Ferry Ltd* [1998] 3 W.L.R. 1260.

[330]   [1968] 2 Q.B. 119.

[331]   *R. v Chief Constable of Devon and Cornwall Ex p. Central Electricity Generating Board* (see above, fn.305); also, see dicta of Glidewell LJ in *McConnell v Chief Constable of the Greater Manchester Police* [1990] 1 W.L.R. 364 at 370.

[332]   *R. (Laporte) v Chief Constable of Gloucestershire* [2007] 2 A.C. 105.

[333]   *Clark v University of Humberside and Lincolnshire* [2000] 1 W.L.R. 1988 at [12] and [29]. See also *R. (Persaud) v University of Cambridge* [2001] E.L.R. 480 at [41].

[334]   See, e.g. *R. v Cranfield University Ex p. Bashir* [1999] E.L.R. 317; *Van Mellaert v Oxford University* [2006] E.L.R. 617 and see also the dictum of Mann LJ in *R. v Her Majesty the Queen in Council Ex p. Vijayatunga* [1990] 2 Q.B. 444 at 459.

[335]   *R. v Cranfield University Ex p. Bashir* [1999] E.L.R. 322.

[336]   *Thorne v University of London* [1966] 2 Q.B. 237.

[337]   *R. (Persaud) v University of Cambridge* [2001] E.L.R. 480 (challenge to decision not to allow a graduate student to continue raised, on analysis, issues as to the fairness of the procedure by which the decision was not taken and was not a challenge to the academic judgment of the university). See generally McManus *Education and the Courts*, 2nd edn, (2004), Chapter 8. Decisions that give rise to justiciable issues should normally be referred to the Office of the Independent Adjudicator before judicial review is sought: see 2-109.

[338]   See, e.g. *R. v University of West of England Ex p. M* [2001] E.L.R. 458 (whether rules permitted expulsion of student from course); *R. v Sheffield Hallam University Ex p. R* [1995] E.L.R. 267 (whether rules required written prior notice of inadequate performance before exclusion).

the requirements of procedural fairness,[339] and has regard to relevant considerations and does not take into account irrelevant considerations.[340]

Resource allocation in the health field

The courts have recognised that the precise allocation of resources and the weighing of priorities in the field of health care call for judgments by the individual health body involved. Decisions on whether a particular treatment is appropriate in a particular case are unlikely, therefore, to be amenable to judicial review.[341] More generally, the courts accept that it is not possible, given the limited funding available, to provide all the services that may be desirable. The relevant authorities are entitled to have priorities and the precise allocation and weighting of priorities is a matter for the responsible authority. The courts will review a policy governing priorities for treatment to ensure that it is lawful and permits of exceptions in appropriate circumstances. The responsible authorities will need accurately to assess the nature and seriousness of each type of illness and determine the effectiveness of various forms of treatment and give effect to that in the formulation and application of its policy. Thus, the courts quashed a policy of not providing treatment for gender re-assignment. The authority concerned had accepted that transsexualism was an illness; a policy which failed to reflect that (as opposed to a policy which placed it low on the list of priorities) and which failed to permit of exceptional circumstances in which it should be provided was unlawful.[342] Further, while a health body may choose to limit the availability of treatments on financial grounds, if it chooses not to have regard to financial considerations but still has a policy of not providing treatment save in exceptional circumstances, the authority will need to establish a clinical basis for differentiating between those cases which do and those which do not qualify for treatment. If it cannot, its policy may be held to be unlawful.[343]

4–089

Other issues involving questions of judgment

Other areas involving questions of technical or expert judgment will not be justiciable. The court has indicated, *obiter*, that the assessment of reputation, character and temperament of individuals wishing to be accepted as foster parents is not amenable to judicial review.[344] Removal from the list of foster parents on the grounds of specific criminal or other misbehaviour without giving the individual a fair hearing would not be amenable to judicial review.[345]

4–090

---

[339] *R. v Chelsea College of Art and Design Ex p. Nash* [2000] E.L.R. 686; *R. (Persaud) v University of Cambridge* [2001] E.L.R. 480.
[340] See, e.g. *R. v Manchester Metropolitan University Ex p. Nolan* [1994] E.L.R. 380.
[341] See *R. v Cambridge Health Authority Ex p. B* [1995] 1 W.L.R. 898 at 906. See also *R. v North-west Lancashire Heath Authority Ex p. A* [2000]1 W.L.R. 977 at 991E–H. But see *R. (Ofley) v Barking and Dagenham Primary Care Trust* [2007] A.C.D. 320.
[342] See *R. v North-west Lancashire Health Authority Ex p. A* [2000] 1 W.L.R. 977 at 991H–995A.
[343] *R. (Rogers) Primary Care Trust* [2006] 1 W.L.R. 2649.
[344] *R. v Wandsworth LBC Ex p. P* (1989) 87 L.G.R. 370.
[345] (1989) 87 L.G.R. 370.

4–091   The justiciability of certain other prerogative powers has been considered in Chapter 2. Issues involving essentially political judgments, such as the grant of honours, dissolution of Parliament and the appointment of ministers, are thought to be non-justiciable.[346]

Qualifications on the concept of justiciability

4–092   There are important qualifications to the concept of non-justiciability, which go some way to minimising the extent to which non-justiciability will be a barrier to judicial review. First, in the context of prerogative powers, the courts will consider whether a claimed prerogative power does in fact exist[347] and whether it has been superseded or limited by statute.[348] Further, even though the courts have talked of certain prerogative powers being non-justiciable, it is the exercise of a power that is non-justiciable. Even in the case of powers which by their nature will usually raise non-justiciable issues, there may be occasions when a justiciable issue might arise. In the field of treaty-making, for example, which is normally unreviewable, the courts did consider whether the Anglo-Irish Agreement relating to the government of Northern Ireland violated certain provisions of statute relating to that matter.[349]

4–093   Secondly, considerations of non-justiciability may apply to exclude only some principles of judicial review. In other words, only certain aspects of a particular decision may be unreviewable. In *R. v Director of Government Communications Headquarters Ex p. Hodges*,[350] a decision to remove an individual's positive security vetting because of his sexual proclivities was based on national security considerations. The court held that the decision was not amenable to review. Those considerations did not apply to the question of whether the individual had been given a fair hearing before the decision was reached, therefore judicial review was available in that respect. The case differs from *G.C.H.Q.* in that there a decision was taken that national security considerations required disregarding the usual procedural protection enjoyed by the unions before a change of conditions of employment was imposed. In *McAvoy*,[351] the court indicated that while it could not review the assessment of the Home Secretary as to the security need for transferring a prisoner, the court would be able to intervene if other relevant considerations, such as the ability to have visits by relatives and lawyers, had not been taken into account in coming to the decision.

4–094   Thirdly, the courts are required to ensure that the rights recognised by the European Convention on Human Rights and incorporated by the Human Rights Act 1998 are respected. That may require the courts to consider whether those rights have been violated even in areas that may otherwise be regarded as

---

[346] See dicta of Lord Roskill in *Council of Civil Service Unions v Minister for the Civil Service* [1985] A.C. 374 at 418.

[347] See, e.g. *R. v Secretary of State for the Home Department Ex p. Northumbria Police Authority* [1989] Q.B. 26 (whether prerogative power to take action to maintain the peace existed).

[348] *Att-Gen v De Keyser's Royal Hotel Ltd* [1920] A.C. 508.

[349] *Re Molyneaux* [1986] 1 W.L.R. 331. See also, *Laker Airways v Department of Trade* [1977] Q.B. 643.

[350] [1988] C.O.D. 123. See also *R. v Ministry of Defence Ex p. Smith* [1996] Q.B. 517.

[351] *R. v Secretary of State for the Home Department Ex p. McAvoy* [1984] 1 W.L.R. 1408.

non-justiciable.[352] However, the fact that the issue arises in a particular context such as national security or foreign affairs and raises matters primarily for the executive not the courts to resolve may militate against the existence of such a right.

Fourthly, it is difficult to separate out considerations relating to justiciability **4–095** from other constraints on judicial review. Although the courts have indicated that it is only rarely that they will intervene in certain areas of public law they have emphasised that they will retain jurisdiction to intervene in appropriate circumstances. Issues which might be considered to raise issues of justiciability may be viewed by the courts as simply a matter of judicial caution rather than a jurisdiction barrier to intervention. In *Re Walker's Application*,[353] for example, the court was faced with an application for judicial review of a decision to postpone an operation on a baby due to lack of facilities. Such a decision, involving the allocation of resources in sensitive areas, might well have been classed as non-justiciable. The Court of Appeal preferred to hold that the exercise of powers to allocate resources was, in principle, subject to judicial review, but the jurisdiction was to be exercised very sparingly. This approach would leave judicial review available even if in practice the occasion for its use would be limited.

---

[352] See, e.g. *A. v Secretary of State for the Home Department* [2005] 2 A.C. 68 esp. at [42]. Also discussed above at 4-082. See, e.g. *R. (Gentle) v Prime Minister* [2008] A.C. 1356 at [8](2) and [60]. See above at 2–031.

[353] *The Times*, November 26, 1987. See also *R. v Secretary of State for the Home Department, Special Hospitals Service, Department of Health and Social Security Ex p. Pickering* [1990] C.O.D. 455.

CHAPTER 5

Invalidity, Partial Invalidity and Severance

A. INTRODUCTION

The previous chapters have considered the situations in which judicial review is available. This chapter deals with the legal consequences of a successful claim for judicial review. The question for the courts is what is the effect of a finding that a public authority has reached a decision unlawfully. In brief, an act which is unlawful in the public law sense is regarded by the courts as ultra vires and void. The act will be regarded as not having produced any valid legal effects since its inception and, if the courts decide to intervene and grant a remedy, the remedy will deprive the act of any legal effect. The court will either grant a quashing order to quash the act or declare it to be ultra vires and void.[1] The concept of ultra vires and voidness are deceptively simple in appearance but have given rise to theoretical and practical problems.

5–001

B. THE ULTRA VIRES PRINCIPLE

A public authority that has acted unlawfully has acted in a way that is ultra vires or beyond its powers. Or, to use another phrase, the body has acted without jurisdiction. A decision will be ultra vires where the public body has exceeded the scope of the powers vested in it by statute (or prerogative), or has breached one of the recognised principles developed by the courts to govern the exercise of discretionary power. These principles cover all the substantive grounds of judicial review, including ensuring that the public body considers relevant considerations and does not consider irrelevant ones, that the body acts for proper purposes and does not act in a way that no reasonable public body would act, that it has not unlawfully fettered or delegated its powers and that it observes common law and statutory procedural requirements.[2]

5–002

---

[1] A prohibiting order or an injunction to restrain threatened unlawful action is also available, as is a mandatory order to compel the performance of a duty.
[2] See *McLaughlin v Governor General of the Cayman Islands* [2007] 1 W.L.R. 2839 at [14]–[16]. See also *Secretary of State for the Home Department v JJ* [2008] 1 A.C. 499 at [25]–[27], [64], [85] and [109].

Basis of the ultra vires principle

5–003 The concept of ultra vires has been explained in constitutional terms by reference to parliamentary intent. The courts ensure that the powers conferred by Parliament are not exceeded. This may provide an adequate explanation for ultra vires in its narrow sense of exceeding the scope of the powers conferred by statute, but does not in itself explain the inclusion of the common law principles designed to prevent abuse of power. Judicial review is sometimes justified by regarding these principles as implied terms of the statute conferring the power; breach of those principles leading the public authority to act beyond its (implied) statutory powers.[3] This simplistic view of the basis for judicial intervention was always artificial and is now inadequate, even in theoretical terms, to explain the scope of review.[4] In addition to the review of statutory powers, the courts now engage in judicial review of the manner in which prerogative powers are exercised and, more difficult still, review the exercise of other non-statutory powers. It is not possible—nor is it necessary—to regard the courts as enforcing implied statutory limitations on the exercise of such power. The courts still regard unlawful action in these areas as rendering the exercise of power ultra vires. The reality is (and probably always was) that the courts will as a matter of law only permit public authorities to act in certain ways. If a public body acts in a way that is not permitted, or exceeds the powers that the courts recognise the body as possessing—whatever the source of the power—the courts will regard the body as acting ultra vires in the sense of going beyond its legal powers.

Exception to the ultra vires principle – errors of law within jurisdiction

5–004 There is only one recognised exception to the rule that judicial review is concerned with acts that are classified as ultra vires. The courts formerly drew a distinction between ultra vires and intra vires errors of law. An ultra vires error occurred when a public authority determined a matter of law where it had no power or jurisdiction to determine such questions. Any such determination was regarded as ultra vires since the public body lacked power to make such determinations. The courts have also accepted that public authorities may be given the power or jurisdiction to determine questions of law. If, in the exercise of that power, they were to make an erroneous determination—that is, if they answered a question of law, usually a question of statutory construction, in a way which the courts considered incorrect—the error was an intra vires error. The public authority had performed its allotted task—the determination of questions of law—and it could not be said that it had acted ultra vires. The courts,

---

[3] See Wade & Forsyth, *Administrative Law*, 11th edn.

[4] See Oliver, "Is the *Ultra Vires* Rule the Basis of Judicial Review?" [1987] P.L. 543; Craig, "Ultra Vires and the Foundations of Judicial Review" [1998] C.L.J. 63 and Sir John Laws, "Illegality: The Problem of Jurisdiction" in Supperstone, Goudie and Walker, *Judicial Review* (4th ed., 2014). Others take the contrary view: see dictum of Lord Steyn in *Boddington v British Transport Police* [1992] 2 A.C. 143 and the authors of Wade & Forsyth, *Administrative Law* above, fn.2; Elliott, "The Ultra Vires Doctrine in a Constitutional Setting: Still the Central Principle of Administrative Law" [1999] C.L.J. 129 and C. Forsyth and M. Elliott, "The Legitimacy of Judicial Review" [2003] P.L. 286. The rival arguments are contained in Forsyth (ed.), *Judicial Review and the Constitution* (Hart, 2000).

exceptionally, asserted the power to correct intra vires errors of law which appeared on the face of the record of the decision.[5]

The concept of error of law within jurisdiction is now obsolete. As a result of a series of judgments,[6] the courts now assume that Parliament does not intend to confer jurisdiction or power on inferior courts or public authorities to determine questions of law.[7] All errors of law by public authorities except superior courts, are now regarded as (or may easily be turned into) jurisdictional errors. Decisions exhibiting an error of law by an error of law will now usually be regarded as ultra vires.   **5–005**

C.   THE MEANING OF NULL AND VOID IN ADMINISTRATIVE LAW

Introduction

The primary concern here is the meaning of nullity or voidness solely in the context of the remedies granted by the courts. The concept of nullity has been used to solve other problems arising in administrative law.[8] For remedial purposes, the orthodox view is that an ultra vires act is regarded as void and a nullity. An act by a public authority which lacks legal authority is regarded as incapable of producing legal effects. Once its illegality is established, and if the courts are prepared to grant a remedy, the act will be regarded as void from its inception and retrospectively nullified in the sense that it will be regarded as incapable of ever having produced legal effects. A court will grant a quashing order to quash the decision and deprive the decision of all legal effect, or achieve the same result by granting a declaration that the decision is invalid, null and void, ultra vires or some combination of these phrases.   **5–006**

The weight of authority is to the effect that once the court decides to grant a remedy in judicial review proceedings, the effect of that remedy is to establish that the administrative act or measure is void and incapable of ever having   **5–007**

---

[5] This jurisdiction was revived in *R. v Northumberland Compensation Appeal Tribunal Ex p. Shaw* [1952] 1 K.B. 338.

[6] *Anisminic v Foreign Compensation Commission* [1969] 2 A.C. 147; *Pearlman v Keepers and Governors of Harrow School* [1979] Q.B. 56; *Re Racal Communications* [1981] A.C. 374, esp. the judgment of Lord Diplock; *R. v Greater Manchester Coroner Ex p. Tal* [1985] Q.B. 67. But see *R. v Registrar of Companies Ex p. Central Bank of India* [1986] Q.B. 1114, and the Privy Council decision in *South East Asia Firebricks Sdn. Bhd. v Non-Metallic Minerals Products Manufacturing Employees Union* [1981] A.C. 363. See judgment of Lord Browne-Wilkinson in *R. v Hull University Visitor Ex p. Page* [1993] A.C. 682 at 701.

[7] *Re Racal Communications* [1981] A.C. 374. (The High Court is a court of unlimited jurisdiction with power to determine questions of law; error of law was intra vires only.) Further, superior courts are not subject to judicial review, so errors, even if they appear on the face of the record, are not reviewable and can only be corrected if a statutory right of appeal is provided. See also *Isaacs v Robertson* [1985] A.C. 97.

[8] See, e.g. *Calvin v Carr* [1980] A.C. 574 (whether possible to appeal against ultra vires act and whether illegality could be "cured"); *London & Clydeside Estates Ltd v Aberdeen DC* [1980] 1 W.L.R. 182 (the consequence of breach of a statutory procedural requirement could not be worked out by reference to strict concepts such as "nullity").

produced legal effects.[9] That recognition is, however, tempered by the fact that the invalidity of the administrative act must first be established and secondly, in judicial review proceedings, a court has a discretion to refuse to grant a remedy even if the applicant demonstrates that there has been a breach of one of the principles of public law capable of rendering a decision void. There are also some indications that the courts may, in certain circumstances, recognise the prospective invalidity of an administrative decision or measure, that is, they may declare that a breach of one of the principles of public law has occurred and that the administrative decision or measure is incapable in future of producing valid legal effect but refuse to quash the decision or measure retrospectively and refuse to set aside the legal consequences of any action already taken on the basis of the flawed decision or measure. This is discussed in more detail below.

5–008   In private law and criminal proceedings (as opposed to judicial review proceedings), the invalidity of an administrative act has to be established but if that is done, the courts consider that the individual is entitled as of right to have the administrative act or measure treated as void and incapable of having produced legal effects. The courts do not regard themselves as able to exercise a discretion to refuse to recognise the consequences of a finding of invalidity in the way that they do in judicial review proceedings by refusing as a matter of discretion to grant a remedy. Consequently, the individual is entitled to the private law relief that he would have obtained if the administrative act purporting to alter or vary his private law rights had never been adopted[10] and, in criminal law, is entitled to an acquittal.[11]

Need to establish invalidity

5–009   Before an act can be regarded as ultra vires and a nullity, its invalidity must first be established by the courts. If an act is not the subject of an authoritative court ruling as to its validity, then the act is presumed to be valid and will be treated as binding and capable of producing legal effects. In the words of Lord Radcliffe, an act[12]:

> ". . . bears no brand of invalidity upon its forehead. Unless the necessary proceedings are taken at law to establish the cause of invalidity and to get it quashed or otherwise upset, it will remain as effective for its ostensible purpose as the most impeccable of orders."

---

[9] See, e.g. *Hoffman La Roche & Co. AG v Secretary of State for Trade and Industry* [1975] A.C. 295 discussed below and *McLaughlin v Governor of the Cayman Islands* [2007] 1 W.L.R. 2839 at [14]–[16] and *Secretary of State for the Home Department v JJ* [2008] 1 A.C. 499 at [25]–[27]. See also the dicta of the Lord Chancellor in *Boddington v British Transport Police* [1992] 2 A.C. 143; in the private law sphere, see *Credit Suisse v Allerdale BC* [1997] Q.B. 306 and *Guinness Mahon & Co. Ltd v Kensington and Chelsea Royal LBC* [1999] Q.B. 215 at 229E–H. There have been some notable occasions when the courts have left open the question of whether the effect of a successful challenge to the validity of an administrative act is that, in all circumstances, it is void from its inception and incapable of ever having produced legal effects: see, in particular, the dicta of Lord Browne-Wilkinson and Lord Slynn in *Boddington v British Transport Police* above, fn.4 at 665C–F and 656B–F respectively and of Schiemann LJ in *Percy v Hall* [1997] Q.B. 924 at 950–952.

[10] See *Credit Suisse* above, fn.9 and *Guinness Mahon* [1999] Q.B. 215.

[11] *Boddington v British Transport Police* [1992] 2 A.C. 143

[12] In *Smith v East Elloe RDC* [1956] A.C. 736 at 769.

More prosaically, judgments frequently refer to the fact that an act will be   **5–010**
binding unless and until its invalidity is established in appropriate legal
proceedings. These statements simply affirm the need to establish that an act is
unlawful. As one writer succinctly put it "it is difficult to see how, if there was no
challenge . . . it would be possible to say that the decision was ultra vires at all".[13]
The need to establish illegality says nothing about the remedy that follows once
the invalidity has been established. Nor does it necessarily say anything about the
legal status of the act in the period between the decision and the court ruling that
the act is unlawful.

Methods of establishing invalidity

A challenge to the validity of an act may be by direct action or by way of   **5–011**
collateral or indirect challenge. A direct action is one where the principal purpose
of the action is to establish the invalidity. This will usually be by way of a claim
for judicial review or by use of any statutory mechanism for appeal or review.
Collateral challenges arise when the invalidity is raised in the course of some
other proceedings, the purpose of which is not to establish invalidity but where
questions of validity become relevant. The invalidity of subordinate legislation
may be raised as a defence in criminal proceedings where an individual is
charged with an offence created by that subordinate legislation.[14] A public
authority may seek the assistance of the court to enforce a demand for payment,[15]
or to recover possession of land, and the invalidity of the acts of the public body
may be raised as a defence.[16] Or, an individual may bring a tortious action against
a public authority which may claim it is acting lawfully in the exercise of its
statutory powers. The individual may in turn allege that the public authority is
acting unlawfully as its actions are ultra vires.[17] An individual may, for example,
claim damages for the tort of false imprisonment, contending that the exercise of
statutory powers to detain him is unlawful.[18]

Situations where the courts will refuse to intervene

Even if invalidity could potentially be established there are circumstances where   **5–012**
the court will not intervene to quash the act. Rules governing standing, and the
time-limits for bringing applications for judicial review, may prevent a particular
individual from establishing the invalidity of an act. In addition, in judicial
review proceedings the courts have a wide discretion to refuse a remedy. The
courts have recognised that the consequences of retrospective nullity, with its
requirement that the invalid act be treated as if it never existed, are on occasions
too draconian. Administrative decisions may, for example, have been relied upon
by third parties. In the field of financial regulation, third parties may have relied
upon the decisions of the regulatory authorities when dealing in the shares of the

---

[13]   Craig, *Administrative Law* (1983), p.390. See also the discussion in the 7th edn.
[14]   *R. v Reading Crown Court Ex p. Hutchinson* [1988] Q.B. 384; *Boddington* [1992] 2 A.C. 143.
[15]   *Roy v Kensington and Chelsea and Westminster Family Practitioner Committee* [1992] 1 A.C.
624; *Daymond v South West Water Authority* [1976] A.C. 609.
[16]   *Wandsworth LBC v Winder* [1985] A.C. 461; *West Glamorgan CC v Rafferty* [1987] 1 W.L.R. 457.
[17]   *Cooper v Wandsworth District Board of Works* (1863) 14 C.B. (N.S.) 180.
[18]   As in *R (WL (Congo)) v Secretary of State for the Home Department* [2012] 1 A.C. 245.

company concerned. Given the need for certainty and speed in the financial markets and given the interests of third parties, retrospective nullification may be practically impossible or contrary to the wider public interest. In the education field, a decision to close a school may have been taken. Arrangements may have been made for children and staff to be transferred to other establishments. Considerable disruption and cost may occur if that decision is set aside at a late stage in the implementation of the closure plans. Challenges to measures of general application may also have a wide impact on a wide range of interest and persons. Retrospective quashing may create difficulties and unfairness for individuals and administrators who have relied upon the measure: unravelling the consequences of invalid acts may impose a heavy burden on the administration and divert resources towards re-opening decisions taken on the basis of the invalid regulations.[19]

5–013   The courts in judicial review proceedings have recognised these difficulties and have dealt with them in a variety of ways. In particular, there has been an expansion in the use of judicial discretion to refuse a remedy. The courts have, for example, refused to quash an invalid decision of the Monopolies and Mergers Commission which allowed a new bid to be made for a company because of the consequences that this would have for third parties who had relied on the decision and traded shares in the company on the financial markets.[20] The courts have, also, sometimes delayed granting a remedy in order to give the public body time to take remedial action to rectify its error. In one case, the court delayed granting prohibition to prevent a local authority from applying an unlawful test when deciding whether to license a film, in order to give the local authority time to consider whether they wished to adopt another test or discontinue film licensing altogether.[21] In another case, the court delayed issuing an order of mandamus to compel compliance with the local authority's standing orders to enable the local authority to consider suspending the orders altogether.[22] In other cases, the courts have achieved that result by a different means. They have granted a declaration that the policy governing the retention of data or photographs is unlawful but declined to quash the decision authorising the retention in order to give sufficient time for new legislation, or a new policy, to be adopted so that the retention of material could be assessed under those provisions.[23] More recently, however, the Supreme Court has declined to suspend an order quashing parts of an Order in Council designating certain persons for the purpose of imposing restrictions upon them. A suspension had been sought to enable the executive to adopt measures

---

[19] See, e.g. *R. v Secretary of State for Social Services Ex p. Child Poverty Action Group, The Times,* August 15, 1984, Woolf J. held that an administrative error had to be rectified even though this would involve checking 15 million files, using 420 staff at a cost of £4.8 million pounds in order to provide refunds of up to £25 to 16,000 people. The Court of Appeal reversed the decision on substantive grounds and held that there was no mandatory duty to review cases: see *The Times,* August 8, 1985.

[20] *R. v Monopolies and Mergers Commission Ex p. Argyll Group* [1986] 1 W.L.R. 763. See generally, Chapter 12 below.

[21] *R. v Greater London Council Ex p. Blackburn* [1976] 1 W.L.R. 550.

[22] *R. v Hereford Corporation Ex p. Harrower* [1970] 3 All E.R. 460. See also dicta in *R. v Paddington Valuation Officer Ex p. Peachey Property Corporation Ltd* [1966] Q.B. 380.

   21. See *R (GC) v Commissioner of Police of the Metropolis (Liberty intervening)* [2011] 2 W.L.R. 1230 esp. at [45]–[49]; *R. (C) v Commissioner of Police of the Metropolis* [2012] 1 W.L.R. 3007 at [56]–[58].

[23] *A v HM Treasury* [2010] 2 A.C. 534.

which would be lawful before the Order in Council was quashed. The majority considered that suspending, or staying, the order quashing the Order in Council would not alter the legal position: as the Order in Council was invalid, it could not be relied upon to justify any restrictions purportedly imposed by that order and to grant a stay or suspension of its order would not achieve anything.[24] The minority considered that suspending the quashing order would have practical effect as the quashing order would not take effect until it came into force and the Order in Council would continue to apply until that date, albeit once the quashing order did come into force it would operate retrospectively.

In the words of Professor Wade: "... the truth of the matter is that the court will invalidate an order only if the right remedy is sought by the right person in the right proceedings and circumstances."[25] Nullifying is a description of what the courts do when invalidity is properly established and the courts consider it appropriate to intervene. Nullity is not an absolute concept dictating inexorably what the courts must do when faced with a claim that an act is ultra vires. It is now clear that in practical terms if the invalidity of an act cannot be established or if the court refuses to grant a remedy, the act will be regarded as producing valid legal effects, whatever the theoretical difficulties in explaining how this can be true of an act which is beyond the powers of a public body.[26]   **5–014**

While this is true of judicial review proceedings, it is far less true of private law proceedings. There, there is little or no scope for the use of judicial discretion. The courts will treat an unlawful administrative act that appears to qualify or limit a private law right as void as a matter of course and will enforce the private law right.[27] If a contract is based on an unlawful exercise of power, the courts will treat that contract as void.[28] Similarly, in criminal law proceedings, an individual is normally entitled as of right to raise the invalidity of an administrative act or measure which is he charged with violating as a defence and is entitled to an acquittal if he establishes that the act is invalid.[29]   **5–015**

Consequences when the courts do intervene

The invalidity of an act must be established and cannot be presumed, and the court may refuse to assist an individual in establishing that invalidity. Once the courts have decided to intervene and grant a remedy, it is now clear that the act is null and void. The point is well made by Lord Diplock in *Hoffman-La Roche & Co. A.G. v Secretary of State for Trade and Industry*.[30] There, the minister sought an interim injunction to enforce a statutory instrument limiting the price for drugs. The company resisted the application on the grounds that the subordinate   **5–016**

---

[24] *A v HM Treasury* [2010] 2 A.C. 534.

[25] See Wade and Forsyth *Administrative Law* (11th edn) summarising Professor Wade's seminal articles championing the idea of nullity as a relative not an absolute concept; see "Unlawful Administrative Action: Void or Voidable?" (1967) 83 L.Q.R. 499 and (1968) 84 L.Q.R. 95.

[26] For discussion see Taggart, "Rival Theories of Invalidity in Administrative Law: Some Practical and Theoretical Consequences" in M. Taggart (ed.), *Judicial Review in the 1980s* (1986).

[27] See e.g. *Wandsworth LBC v Winder* [1985] A.C. 461 at 509E–G.

[28] *Credit Suisse* [1997] Q.B. 306 at 343A–344C (per Neill LJ) and at 354H–357E (per Hobhouse LJ).

[29] *Boddington v British Transport Police* [1992] 2 A.C. 143 (except in rare cases where statute precludes raising the invalidity of an act as a defence: see *R. v Wicks* [1998] A.C. 92).

[30] [1975] A.C. 295.

legislation was ultra vires and a nullity, and therefore could not be enforced. The House of Lords held that subordinate legislation may enjoy a presumption of validity and so may be regarded as enforceable in interim proceedings. Once the invalidity was conclusively established, however, the normal consequence would be the retrospective invalidity of the act[31];

> "... it would ... be inconsistent with the doctrine of *ultra vires* ... if the judgment of a court in proceedings properly constituted that a statutory instrument was *ultra vires* were to have any lesser consequence in law than to render the instrument incapable of ever having had any legal effect upon the rights or duties of the parties to the proceedings ..."

Similarly, the Privy Council has held that where a public body purports to dismiss the holder of a public office and acts in excess of its powers, in breach of natural justice or unlawfully in public law terms, the dismissal is null and void and without legal effect once a court of competent jurisdiction so declares. Thus the office holder remains in office and is entitled to the remuneration attaching to the office so long as he remains ready, willing and able to render the service required of him or he resigns or his tenure of office is lawfully terminated.[32] Similarly, where a decision to dismiss an individual from her post as director of children's services was unlawful, that individual was entitled to treat herself as remaining in employment and entitled to her contractual salary and other benefits.[33]

Consequences in contract and restitution

5–017   The retrospective nature of a finding that an administrative act is a nullity is clear in the private law field. In *Credit Suisse v Allerdale BC*,[34] for example, a local authority set up a company to construct a leisure development and entered into a guarantee with a bank to guarantee payment of the company's loans from the bank. The bank subsequently issued proceedings seeking to enforce the guarantee as against the local authority. The Court of Appeal held that the local authority

---

[31] [1975] A.C. 295 per Lord Diplock at 365.

[32] *McLaughlin v Governor of the Cayman Islands* [2007] 1 W.L.R. 2839 at [14]–[16]. This is subject to any exercise of discretion on the part of the court to refuse a remedy for example because of questions of standing, delay or conduct or grounds relating to the facts of a particular case. Further problems may arise if the person has resigned and the courts do not consider it practical to grant remedies resulting in reinstatement: see *Chief Constable of North Wales v Evans* [1982] 1 W.L.R. 1155.

[33] *R. (Shoesmith) v Ofsted* [2011] I.C.R. 1195 at [138]–[139] and [142]–[148]. The dismissal was based on an unlawful direction issued by the Secretary of State. The authority who dismissed the employee could have protected itself by issuing a contractual notice to terminate the employment, rather than simply dismissing her on the basis of the unlawful direction: see [139].

[34] [1997] Q.B. 306. See also *Credit Suisse v Waltham Forest BC* [1997] Q.B. 362. Dicta in *Charles Terence Estates Ltd. v Cornwall Council* [2013] 1 W.L.R 466 suggest that the ambit of this decision may be limited by a distinction between decisions which are outside the powers of a public authority (described as cases where the authority lack capacity) and cases where the authority has the power to do something but exercises the power unlawfully. That distinction, however, does not accord with the current approach of the courts which regards all material public law errors as invalidating the decision with the consequence that it cannot produce legal effect and so, cannot be a defence to a private law claim: see, e.g. *R (WL (Congo)) v Secretary of State for the Home Department* [2012] 1 A.C. 245 at [66] (dealing with a claim for false imprisonment for unlawful detention).

had no statutory power to give the guarantee and so it had acted ultra vires in purporting to do so. The guarantee was therefore void and unenforceable. Similarly, where the courts held that local authority had no power to enter into interest-rate swaps agreements, any such contract purportedly entered into by a local authority was void and unenforceable.[35] Similarly, if a local authority enters into a contract of employment which is ultra vires, the terms of that contract are unenforceable.[36] If the parties have acted in pursuance of that ultra vires contract, it may be necessary to determine what are the legal consequences of those acts. A person who, for example, has in fact provided services may be entitled to a claim for payment by quantum meruit for the value of those services or, in appropriate circumstances, it may be possible to infer the existence of some other contractual arrangement governing the provision of services.[37] Money paid pursuant to an ultra vires contract[38] or by way of an unlawful demand for tax[39] is recoverable by way of restitution subject to any available defences such as a change of position on the part of the recipient.[40]

This conclusion follows whatever the reason for the invalidity. It may be that the public body had no power to enter into the contract in the narrow sense that it had no power at all to make contracts of that type. It may be that a public body has power in principle to enter into a contract of a particular type but that the decision to enter into a particular contract was ultra vires because that decision was based on improper motives or was taken without regard to relevant considerations. **5–018**

Concern over the practical consequences of the ultra vires doctrine in the field of local authority contracts led to the adoption of the Local Government (Contracts) Act 1997. Section 1 of this Act provides that every statutory provision conferring power or imposing a function on local authorities also confers power for the authority to enter into a contract with another person for the provision or making available of assets and services. The statute also empowers a local authority, in connection with such a contract, to enter into contracts with a person providing a loan or finance. These provisions are intended to ensure that local authorities have power to enter into contracts with private sector companies to discharge their functions and to enter into associated loan agreements. Sections 2 to 4 of the Act then set out a procedure under which the contract may be certified; the effect of which is that the local authority is treated as always having had power to enter into the certified contract and as having properly exercised the power. This is intended to ensure that a private individual or company may enforce that contract against the local authority in ordinary private law **5–019**

---

[35] See, e.g. *Guinness Mahon & Co v Kensington and Chelsea RLBC* [1999] Q.B. 215.

[36] *Eastbourne BC v Foster* [2002] I.C.R. 234.

[37] *Eastbourne BC v Foster* [2002] I.C.R. 234.

[38] See, e.g. *Kleinwort Benson v Lincoln City Council* [1999] 2 A.C. 349 (money paid under a mistake of law, including a belief that a contract was intra vires when it was subsequently established by the courts to have been (and, therefore, always to have been) ultra vires and void, could be recovered by restitution); *Westdeutsche Landesbank Girozentrale v Islington LBC* [1996] A.C. 669; *Eastbourne BC v Foster* [2002] I.C.R. 234 (money paid to an employee under an invalid contract recoverable subject to a defence of change of position).

[39] *Woolwich Building Society v Inland Revenue Commissioners (No.2)* [1993] A.C. 70.

[40] See, e.g. *Eastbourne BC v Foster* [2002] I.C.R. 234 (money paid to employee under invalid contract probably not recoverable due to change of position; such an employee may, otherwise, have had a quantum meruit or other claim for the value of the services rendered).

proceedings. The Act recognises the continuing possibility that claims for judicial review may be brought to determine whether the authority had power to enter the contract, or whether any such power was properly exercised, but the courts may still determine that the contract is to be regarded as lawful even if the court is of the opinion that there was no power to contract (or the power had been exercised improperly) because of the likely consequences for the financial position of the local authority or for the provision of services.[41]

Consequences in tort

5–020   A number of cases have raised the question of the status of an administrative act prior to a finding by a court that the act is ultra vires in tortious actions, particularly those alleging false imprisonment. As a matter of general principle, false imprisonment requires simply the fact of imprisonment or restraint and the absence of a lawful justification for that imprisonment. In principle, therefore, if a person is detained pursuant to an administrative measure which subsequently transpires to be unlawful the person will have established (subject to any specific statutory provision) the necessary elements of the tort of false imprisonment. The person will in fact have been detained. Once it is established that the measure under which the person is detained is ultra vires, that measure ought, in principle, to be incapable of ever having produced legal effect and incapable ever of having justified the detention. That accords with the traditional approach in English law to the liberty of the subject. If that liberty is interfered with, and no law authorises that interference, the person will have been falsely imprisoned. Liability is not dependent upon any fault or conscious wrong doing on the part of the detaining authority; it depends upon the fact that a person has had his liberty curtailed when it should not have been curtailed.[42] That approach has now been reaffirmed by the Supreme Court.

5–021   In *R (WL) Congo)) v Secretary of State for the Home Department*,[43] the Supreme Court considered the position of foreign national criminals who had been detained in the exercise of statutory powers pending removal from the United Kingdom. The Supreme Court held that the tort of false imprisonment had two elements, the fact of imprisonment and the absence of lawful authority to justify it. Once the individual has established the fact of imprisonment, thereafter, the burden shifts to the authority to demonstrate lawful justification for the detention. Where the detention was materially influenced by a public law error, the detention was unlawful and the elements of the tort of false imprisonment were made out. Provided that the public law error had a material influence on the decision to detain, the nature of the error was not relevant to whether or not the tort had been established. In particular, it was not necessary to distinguish between a situation where the authority had no power to detain and one where it had a power but exercised that power in breach of one of the recognised principles of public law. In either case, the detention would be unlawful and the elements of the tort of false imprisonment would have been made out. In this particular case, the foreign national had been detained pursuant to an unlawful

---

[41] Local Government (Contracts) Act 1997 s.5.
[42] See *R. v Governor of Brockhill Prison Ex p. Evans (No.2)* [2001] 2 A.C. 19.
[43] [2012] 1 A.C. 245.

blanket policy of detaining all foreign national criminals, that policy being undisclosed and contrary to the published policy of the Secretary of State for the Home Department. Those errors resulted in the detention being unlawful. In terms of a private law remedy, however, the aim of tort law was to put the individual in the position he would have been in had the tort not been committed. If, on the facts, it was clear that the individuals would have been detained if the statutory power to detain had been exercised lawfully, then the individual would not have suffered loss. In those circumstances, even though the elements of the tort of false imprisonment were made out, the appropriate compensation would be nominal damages only.[44]

Another decision in keeping with the traditional approach and orthodoxy in this area is *R. v Governor of Brockhill Prison (No.2) Ex p. Evans*.[45] Here, the retrospectivity did not arise from the finding that an administrative act was ultra vires. Rather, in *Evans'* case, a Divisional Court had held that the method of calculating the time to be spent in custody following concurrent sentences for criminal offences was incorrect.[46] As a result of that ruling, Ms Evans should have been released on September 17, 1996 but was in fact released on November 15, 1996, i.e. 59 days later. She sued for false imprisonment. The House of Lords held that the decision of the Divisional Court as to how the statutory provisions governing calculation of time in custody was retrospective in the sense that the decision set out how the legislation was to be interpreted from the date that it came into force, not merely from the date of the decision. Consequently, Ms Evans' time in custody should always have been calculated in accordance with the method identified in the judgment and there was no lawful authority for the extra 59 days' detention, notwithstanding the fact that the governor was using a method that was based upon earlier decisions of the Divisional Court. The fact that the Governor acted in accordance with what was believed to be the law at the time was no defence to a claim for false imprisonment if it subsequently transpired that that view of the law was wrong and there was, in law, no basis for the detention.[47] Consequently, the claimant was entitled to damages for false imprisonment for the 59 days. The judgment of the House of Lords is, it is respectfully suggested, correct as a matter of principle and policy. The nature of judgments in English law is that they are declaratory of the law as it is and has always been. This has recently been re-affirmed by the House of Lords in a different context.[48] The policy of the common law has always been that the

5–022

---

[44] Similarly, the Court of Appeal had held that if it could be shown that the statutory powers of immigration officers to detain asylum seekers had been unlawfully exercised, the persons detained could seek damages for false imprisonment: see *D v Home Office (Bail for Immigration Detainees intervening)* [2006] 1 W.L.R. 1003.

[45] [2001] 2 A.C. 19.

[46] *R. v Governor of Brockhill Prison Ex p. Evans* [1997] Q.B. 443.

[47] The position would be different if the governor detained the individual in pursuance of an order of a superior court which had not been set aside as in *Quinland v Governor of Swaleside Prison* [2003] Q.B. 306 (order of Crown Court mistakenly said person sentenced to two years and six months in prison when sentence was two years and four months: detention pursuant to order was lawful) or which would continue to provide lawful authority until a subsequent court order, ordering release, was granted, as in *Olotu v Home Office* [1997] 1 W.L.R. 328 (person remanded in custody was entitled to be granted bail once custody limits expired but until order was made granting bail, detention pursuant to the original order was lawful).

[48] *Kleinwort Benson Ltd. v Lincoln City Council* above, fn.38.

liberty of the subject is of the highest importance. The tort of false imprisonment merely requires that there be the fact of detention and the absence of lawful justification for that detention. Both were present here. The tort of false imprisonment does not require any element of wrongfulness or blameworthiness on the part of the governor.

5–023   Statute may, of course, provide a specific defence to claims for wrongful detention. An example of this is seen in s.6 of the Mental Health Act 1983. A person may be compulsorily detained in certain circumstances in a mental hospital. Section 6(3) of the Act expressly provides that any application for the admission of a patient which "appears" to be duly made is sufficient authority for the hospital authorities to detain the individual. A hospital which relies upon an apparently valid application is immune from a claim in tort for false imprisonment if it subsequently transpires that the application was not in fact properly made.[49]

5–024   There have been cases previously where the courts have indicated a reluctance to accept that the authorities ought to be liable in tort for false imprisonment when they were acting under a byelaw or other administrative measure which was not known at the time to be invalid. They have exhibited a reluctance to apply the logic of retrospective invalidity to claims in tort. In *Percy v Hall*,[50] the Court of Appeal were faced with claims for wrongful arrest and false imprisonment against police officers who arrested certain individuals for entering a military base contrary to a byelaw. Section 17 of the Act under which the byelaw was made[51] provided that if "any person commits an offence against any byelaw under this Act" he was liable to conviction and "may be removed . . . and taken into custody". The claimants contended that the byelaws were ultra vires and, were therefore a nullity and incapable of producing legal effect and were, therefore, incapable of justifying an arrest under s.17. The Court of Appeal held that the byelaws were valid and therefore there was lawful justification for the arrest. They also considered what the position would be if the byelaws had in fact been invalid. In particular, they were concerned that treating the byelaws as a nullity and void from their inception would render the arrest unlawful. The Court of Appeal considered that there were two possible responses. First, it expressed the view, obiter, that the question of whether the constables had lawful justification for the arrest had to be considered at the time that the arrest was made. At that stage, the byelaws were apparently valid and (at least for some purposes) would be presumed to be valid. The Court indicated that although a finding by a court that the byelaw was invalid might justify setting aside a conviction it did not mean that the arrest, which appeared to be lawful at the time, subsequently became unlawful.[52] That approach would not appear to be reconcilable with the decision of the Supreme Court in *R (WL (Congo)) v Secretary of State for the Home Department*. It is contrary to the weight of

---

[49] See *R. (M) v Hackney LBC*[2011] 1 W.L.R. 2873. The detention is still unlawful; it is simply that the hospital authorities are protected from liability.

[50] *Percy v Hall* [1997] Q.B. 924.

[51] Military Lands Act 1892.

[52] [1997] Q.B. 924 per Simon Brown LJ at 947G–948C with whom Peter Gibson LJ agreed. See also the dicta in *R. v Central London County Court Ex p. London* [1999] 3 W.L.R. 1 at 11B–16A (determination by the court that a decision to admit a patient to a mental hospital was unlawful does not retrospectively render the decision invalid).

authority and the principle that an act which is found to be invalid is incapable of ever having produced legal effect. If, therefore, the lawfulness of the arrest was dependent upon there being a valid byelaw in force at the relevant time, the arrest would be unlawful. That would mean that the constables were liable for wrongful arrest (subject to any statutory defence). That would not, however, imply any moral blame or wrongdoing on the part of the police. Rather, the policy would be that people ought not to have their liberty infringed unless there is lawful justification. If it transpires subsequently that there is no lawful justification, those whose liberty has been restricted may be compensated for any loss suffered thereby.

The second basis for the approach taken by the Court of Appeal in *Percy v Hall* turns on the proper construction of the relevant statutory provision. The relevant section provided that a person could only be detained if he commits an offence against any byelaw. On the natural construction of those words, the person could not be detained if the byelaw was invalid as he would not be committing an offence against a byelaw. An alternative construction would be first to read the section as empowering a constable to remove a person if the constable *reasonably believes* that the person is committing an offence and secondly that a constable may reasonably believe that even if the byelaw is subsequently found to be invalid. In other words, the fact that the reasonable belief is based upon a mistaken view of the law (that there is a valid byelaw in force when there is not) does not deprive the constable of the statutory defence of reasonable belief.[53] In that regard, however, in an analogous situation,[54] the House of Lords had held that a power of arrest arising where a person "commits any of the following offences" meant, on a proper construction, where the officer honestly believed on reasonable grounds that an offence had been committed (even if it is subsequently established that no offence was committed). That construction was based on the view that Parliament must have intended a police officer to arrest even though he could not known at the time of the arrest that a conviction would ultimately follow from the arrest. The judgment is, therefore, based upon the assumption that the policy of the relevant act was not to expose constables to actions for damages where they acted honestly and reasonably. If that is the policy underlying statutes such as that in issue in *Percy v Hall*, it would be possible to interpret s.17 as authorising arrest whether or not the byelaw was subsequently found to be ultra vires even though it involves a construction which may be regarded as benevolent to the authority and departing from its literal words and which does not provide for the possibility of a remedy in damages for a person who has been deprived of his liberty in circumstances where there was, in fact, no lawful justification for doing so. This approach to construction of such statutes does not sit easily with the approach of the Supreme Court in *R (WL (Congo)) v Secretary of State for the Home Department* and the approach in such cases may, therefore, need to be reconsidered.

5–025

---

[53] In that regard, the Court of Appeal in *R. v Bow Street Magistrates' Court Ex p. McDonald (No.2)* (1997) 96 L.G.R. 61 held that a statutory defence based on having reasonable cause to believe that certain goods were liable to forfeiture was not prevented from relying on that defence because he mistakenly believed that the warrant under which he was acting was lawful when it was not.

[54] *Wills v Bowley* [1983] 1 A.C. 57.

Void and voidable

5–026   There was previously much confusion over whether ultra vires acts were void or voidable. Many of the situations in which it was thought necessary to use the term voidable stemmed from the belief that nullity was an absolute concept and once invalidity had been established retrospective nullity had inexorably to follow. Thus, the term voidable has been used to explain:

(a)   why it is necessary to bring court proceedings to establish that an act is ultra vires and can have no legal effect[55];

(b)   how the courts could refuse a remedy to quash an ultra vires act on grounds such as lack of standing[56]; or

(c)   a refusal of a remedy in the exercise of the court's discretion; and

(d)   to explain how a statutory provision prohibiting challenge to a decision after six weeks was effective to prevent an ultra vires decision being quashed.[57]

With the recognition of void as a relative concept it is no longer necessary to use voidable for these purposes.

5–027   The term voidable does have a generally accepted meaning in the case of intra vires errors of law. A decision which exhibited an intra vires error of law which appeared on the face of the record was not regarded as a nullity as it was not ultra vires. Such decisions were seen as truly voidable in that they remained valid until the decisions were quashed. When the court quashed such a decision, it did so only prospectively not retrospectively. Acts done in reliance on the decision before it was quashed remained valid and lawful. The category of intra vires error of law on the face of the record has become obsolete, as the courts have expanded the range of errors of law that are ultra vires to include virtually every error of law. One of the consequences of this development is that decisions vitiated by errors which might formerly have been classified as intra vires and voidable will now be classed as ultra vires and void.

D.   PROSPECTIVE DECLARATIONS

5–028   The development of judicial discretion to refuse remedies in appropriate and defined circumstances is to be welcomed. The difficulty is that the courts are generally left in a situation where they must either grant a remedy, with all the consequences that flow from retrospective nullification, or they must refuse any remedy at all. One option designed to ensure that the error of law is rectified for the future, but without invalidating decisions already taken, would be a useful addition to the judicial armoury. The courts could grant prospective relief only, declaring that an error has occurred and that any future decision exhibiting the

---

[55]   See dicta of Lord Morris of Borth-y-Gest in *Ridge v Baldwin* [1964] A.C. 40 at 125.

[56]   *Durayappah v Fernando* [1967] 2 A.C. 337 (a decision to dissolve council was not challengeable by mayor but only by council itself; decision described as voidable).

[57]   *R. v Secretary of State for the Environment Ex p. Ostler* [1977] Q.B. 122; [1976] 3 W.L.R. 288; Lord Denning M.R. subsequently recanted from his view that an ultra vires decision could be regarded as voidable: see *Firman v Ellis* [1978] Q.B. 886.

error might be quashed, but refuse to quash earlier decisions which exhibited the same legal flaw and possibly refusing to quash retrospectively the decision which triggered the judicial review application.[58] The courts could, for example, grant a declaration that regulations must henceforth be regarded as invalid, but that decisions already taken and based on the regulations were not themselves invalid. Or, the courts could declare that a particular interpretation of statutory or other legal provisions was incorrect or that certain considerations were irrelevant which would govern future exercises of the discretion so that the error would not be repeated but would not invalidate the particular decision that is the subject of challenge. A variant of this in the context of challenges to normative measures would be to grant relief that declared the regulations invalid for the future and also invalidated the decision that triggered the judicial review application, but which would leave earlier decisions based on the regulation unaffected.

There have been signs on occasions that the courts are prepared to contemplate this sort of remedial flexibility. In *R. v Panel on Take-overs and Mergers Ex p. Datafin*,[59] Sir John Donaldson M.R. indicated that, given the need for certainty in the financial markets, the courts would normally allow contemporary decisions of the panel on the interpretation of the take-over code to take their course, and would intervene only to give declaratory orders which would enable the panel not to repeat any error in the future, although in the case of disciplinary action, the courts would as usual remove the consequences of unlawful action. Although the comments of the Master of the Rolls are not free from ambiguity,[60] they seem to contemplate the court leaving intact and unaffected the particular decision that triggered the judicial review application but granting some kind of declaratory relief on the meaning of the rules which would govern future exercises of discretion by the panel.

5–029

On a number of other occasions, the courts have refused to quash the decision or measure that triggered the judicial review application but have granted declarations as to the correct legal position. In *R. v Dairy Produce Quota Tribunal for England and Wales Ex p. Caswell*,[61] the tribunal gave a decision on Caswell's claim for a quota which was based on an incorrect interpretation of the relevant regulations. The court granted a declaration stating the true meaning of the regulations, so that the tribunal would not fall into error in the future. The court refused to grant a remedy in respect of the actual decision in Caswell's case as his application was made out of time. In another case,[62] Webster J. granted a declaration that the minister had failed to comply with a mandatory statutory duty to consult before making regulations, but refused, in his discretion, to quash the regulations themselves. The Court of Appeal granted a declaration that the

5–030

---

[58] See Lewis, "Retrospective and Prospective Rulings in Administrative Law" [1988] P.L. 78.

[59] [1987] Q.B. 815. See also the decision of Woolf J. in *R. v Att-Gen Ex p. I.C.I. Plc* [1985] 1 C.M.L.R. 588 granting prospective declaratory relief; this decision was reversed in the Court of Appeal [1987] 1 C.M.L.R. 72 on the grounds that retrospective relief was necessary in the instant case; see Lewis, above fn.58.

[60] Much depends on the meaning to be given to phrases, such as the intervention should be "historic" not "contemporary," or that relief should be "declaratory" not "substantive". See also the subsequent comments of Lord Donaldson M.R. in *R. v Panel on Take-overs and Mergers Ex p. Guinness Plc* [1989] 2 W.L.R. 863 at 868.

[61] [1989] 1 W.L.R. 1089 affd. [1990] 2 A.C. 738, HL.

[62] *R. v Secretary of State for Social Services Ex p. Association of Metropolitan Authorities* [1986] 1 W.L.R. 1.

reasons given for granting planning permission did not comply with the statutory requirements but declined to quash the planning permission itself.[63]

5–031   In *Evans (No.2)*, the House of Lords left open the possibility of developing a concept of prospective overruling in appropriate circumstances for future cases.[64] There, the Divisional Court had held that, on a proper construction of the relevant statute, an incorrect method of calculating the time to be spent in custody had been used and, as a result, the claimant had spent 59 more days in custody than she would have had the statute been properly interpreted.[65] The House of Lords held that the decision as to the proper construction of the statute was declaratory in that it set out the legal position as it had always been. The House considered that it would be inappropriate, in the context of a claim for damages for false imprisonment, to give prospective effect only to the ruling as to the proper construction of the statutory formula for calculating time spent in custody. That, with respect, would appear to be correct for two reasons. First, it would, generally, be inappropriate to give prospective rulings in the context of matters concerning the liberty of the subject, or claims for damages consequent upon a detention that should not have occurred.[66] Secondly, Ms Evans herself had sought to challenge the lawfulness of her detention. Prospective declarations may be particularly appropriate when dealing with unravelling previous transactions, which perhaps took place long before,[67] or possibly, where there would be adverse affects on the administration generally but, absent such circumstances, prospective rulings should not, generally, be used to deprive a person of the benefits of the proper construction of a statute when that person instituted the proceedings which established the illegality. The courts have also canvassed the possibility of prospective declarations in the context of the Human Rights Act 1998, where a measure may become unlawful as a result of that Act but was not necessarily so prior to that Act,[68] although no such declaration appears yet to have been made. The House of Lords has also considered the issue in a different but analogous context, namely whether a decision of a court of law on the proper meaning of a statute or the common law is retrospective in the sense that the judgment declares the law as it has always been. The House of Lords accepted that the normal rule was that judgments of courts were declaratory of what the law always was but left open the possibility that, in exceptional circumstances, it may be appropriate for the courts to give prospective effect to its rulings.[69]

---

[63] *R (Macrae) v Herefordshire DC* [2012] J.P.L. 1356; see also *R (Gavin) v London Borough of Haringey* [2004] 2 P. & C.R. 13.

[64] *R. v Governor of Brookhill Prison Ex p. Evans (No.2)* [2001] A.C. 45. For a re-affirmation of the principle that a judicial decision as to the scope of the common law declares the common law as it has always been, see *Kleinwort Benson Ltd v Lincoln City Council* [1999] 2 A.C. 349, esp. per Lord Goff at 378D—379F.

[65] See *R. v Governor of Brookhill Prison Ex p. Evans* [1999] Q.B. 443.

[66] See, in *R. v Governor of Brookhill Prison Ex p. Evans (No.2)* [2001] A.C. 45, the dicta of Lord Hope at 36H–37B and see also the dicta of Lord Browne-Wilkinson at 27D–E and Lord Steyn at 29F–G.

[67] [2001] A.C. 45; see dicta of Lord Slynn at 26H-27C and Lord Hobhouse at 48G–H and 49C–D.

[68] See *R (T) v Chief Constable of Greater Manchester Police* [2014] 3 W.L.R. 96 at [156] (per Lord Reed). See, also, *Cadder v HM Advocate* [2010] 1 W.L.R. 2601 at [56]–[62] (per Lord Hope).

[69] *In Re Spectrum Plus* [2006] A.C. 680, see per Lord Nicholls at [39], Lord Steyn at [45], Lord Hope at [71]–[74], Lord Walker at [161], Baroness Hale at [162] and Lord Brown at [165].

A number of points need to be made about this type of prospective relief. First, **5–032** retrospective nullification would continue to be the normal relief granted, particularly in the case of decisions affecting an individual as opposed to a measure having widespread consequences for third parties. Prospective relief, like the denial of any relief, should be viewed as an exercise of discretion by the court at the remedial level and would be a departure from the normal pattern of relief. Secondly, it is not an attempt to resurrect the void-voidable debate. The arguments for prospective relief are based on increasing the remedial flexibility of the judicial review jurisdiction and are not dependent on theories of ultra vires or nullity. Just as the court has a power to refuse any relief, so should the courts have the power to refuse relief in respect of a particular period. In addition, the use of prospective relief in this context differs from its use in relation to the category of voidable errors of law on the face of the record. In the latter case, prospective means that the challenged decision produces valid legal effects up to and including the date that the voidable decision is quashed, but the decision is invalid thereafter. Prospective relief, as discussed here, contemplates not granting any relief in relation to a particular decision, but seeks to regulate future exercises of power. Thirdly, the conventional understanding of the nature of declaratory relief would need to be altered. The declaration is as its name implies declaratory of existing rights or legal relationships. The courts have traditionally held that declaratory relief is not constitutive in the sense that the declaration cannot be used to create new legal rights or legal relationships.[70] If the declaration were to recognise that a regulation was invalid for the future but decisions already taken were not to be quashed, it would almost certainly be creating a new legal relationship for the future and hence be constitutive.

Parliament has also expressly authorised the grant of prospective remedies in **5–033** one set of situations. The Government of Wales Act 2006 provides that a court may, when it finds that the National Assembly for Wales has made primary legislation outside its competence or subordinate legislation which it had no power to make, remove or limit the retrospective effect of the court's decision or suspend the effect of the court's decision for any period in order to allow the defect to be corrected.[71]

Attention can usefully be drawn to the case law of the Court of Justice of the **5–034** European Union in this context. The Court of Justice also engages in judicial review of legislative and administrative acts of the institutions of the EU. Here, if the challenge is made out, the Court will declare the act to be void although it has jurisdiction to limit the effects of its decision and to make a ruling that the measures is prospectively invalid only, i.e. that actions taken in reliance on the act prior to judgment remain valid and the act is only to be incapable of producing legal effects from the date of the judgment.[72] There is no general comparable

---

[70] See *Punton v Minister of Pensions and National Insurance (No.2)* [1964] 1 W.L.R. 226. For criticism, see Cane, "A Fresh Look at the Punton Case" (1980) 43 M.L.R. 266.

[71] S.153 of the Government of Wales Act 2006. See also s.102 of the Scotland Act 1998 and s.81 of the Northern Ireland Act 1998.

[72] See Art.264 of the Treaty on the Functioning of the European Union. The jurisdiction to give prospective judgments in respect of regulations is expressly recognised in relation to regulations by Art.231(2) (ex Art.174(2)) and has been assumed to exist in respect of other acts: see Case 34/86 *Council v Parliament* [1986] E.C.R. 2155 (budget declared invalid but payments already made in reliance on the budget to be regarded as valid).

power in domestic law.[73] Furthermore, the Court of Justice has also accepted that it has power to impose temporal limitations on its own judgments. Decisions of the Court are declaratory of the law as it is and always has been. Thus, if the Court declares that a particular provision of the EC Treaty is directly effective, then it has direct effect from the time that it came into force not merely from the time of the judgment in which the European Court recognised the direct effect.[74] Exceptionally, however, the Court has recognised that it may impose a temporal limitation in that the direct effect of the relevant provision may only be relied upon as from the date of the judgment.[75] There is, at present, no comparable power to impose a temporal limitation in English domestic law.

E.   PARTIAL INVALIDITY AND SEVERANCE

Measures only partially invalid

5–035   A measure or decision may be only partially invalid. An order or statutory instrument may not only deal with matters within the scope of the powers conferred upon the decision-maker but may impose conditions[76] or cover geographical areas[77] or deal with matters[78] which go beyond the powers conferred by the enabling statute. A licence[79] or court order[80] or planning

---

[73]   The courts are specifically given the power to limit or remove the retrospective effect of a determination that the Welsh Assembly did not have power to make s legislation: see the Government of Wales Act 2006 s.153. Similar provisions are to be found in the Scotland Act 1998 s.102. and in the Northern Ireland Act 1998 s.81. See above, para.5–033.

[74]   See, e.g. Case 61/79 *Amministrazione delle Finanze dello Stato v Denkavit Italiana* [1980] E.C.R. 1205 at 1223, [16]; Case 309/85 *Barra v Belgium and the City of Liege* [1988] E.C.R. 355 at 315, [11]; *R. (Bidar) v London Borough of Ealing* [2005] Q.B. 812 at [66] and see below Chapter 17 at paras 17–013 to 17–015.

[75]   See, e.g. Case 43/75 *Defrenne v SABENA* [1976] E.C.R. 455; Case 24/86 *Blaizot v University of Liege* [1988] E.C.R. 379. Usually, the effect is that the direct effect of the Treaty article cannot be relied upon in support of claims brought in respect of periods prior to the date of the judgment other than those where legal proceedings had already been started.

[76]   *R. v London Borough Transport Committee Ex p. Freight Transport Association Ltd* [1990] C.O.D. 217. The House of Lords reversed the decision on the grounds that the condition was not unlawful [1991] 1 W.L.R. 1.

[77]   *Dunkley v Evans* [1981] 1 W.L.R. 1522. See also *R. v Cornwall CC and Secretary of State for Education and Science Ex p. Nicholls* [1989] C.O.D. 507 (a decision to reorganise schools could be quashed in relation to one school only).

[78]   *DPP v Hutchinson* [1990] 2 A.C. 783 (byelaw restricting access to a military base took away rights of commoners which was not permitted by the enabling Act).

[79]   *R. v North Hertfordshire DC Ex p. Cobbold* [1985] 3 All E.R. 486; *R. v Barnet LBC Ex p. Johnson* (1991) 3 Admin.L.R. 149.

[80]   *R. v Southwark Crown Court Ex p. Customs and Excise Commissioners* [1989] 3 W.L.R. 1054. See also *R. v Inner London South Coroner Ex p. Kendall* [1989] 1 All E.R. 72 (verdict quashed as misdescribed cause of death; inquest itself not quashed as that had been properly conducted) and *R. v South Powys Coroner's Court Ex p. Jones* [1991] C.O.D. 14.

permission[81] may be granted but conditions attached which are unlawful. Demands for information may include requests for authorised and unauthorised information.[82]

The courts have accepted that in appropriate circumstances they will give effect to the intra vires parts of an act and deny validity only to those parts that are ultra vires. The courts may quash the invalid part only or may grant a declaration that the measure is not to take effect in so far as it is invalid. The difficulty comes in identifying the test and predicting the circumstances in which the courts will sever the ultra vires part of a measure or treat a measure as partially invalid. This difficulty arises in part from the wide variety of circumstances in which the question of partial invalidity arises but it also reflects differences of opinion on the proper role of the courts in this area. On the one hand, there is a desire to give effect to legal acts in so far as possible rather than striking down whole acts, much of the content of which is unobjectionable. In the words of Ormrod LJ the courts "should not strive officiously to kill to any greater extent than it is compelled to do".[83] On the other hand, there is a need to ensure that the courts do not usurp the functions of the decision-maker by quashing part of an act and leaving something in force which is different in character from the original act and which the courts cannot be sure would have been made by the decision-maker.[84] As with so much in public law, there is a balance to be struck. The third option open to the courts would be to reject any possibility of severance and always to strike down the whole act where any part of that act is shown to be ultra vires. This course has "the merit of simplicity and of encouraging the [decision-maker] to keep within his powers. The disadvantage of such a course is that much to which no objection can be taken is then unenforceable".[85] The courts have decisively rejected this option.[86] **5–036**

The test for severance or partial invalidity

The leading case on severance or partial invalidity in the context of delegated legislation which goes beyond the powers conferred by the enabling Act is the decision of the House of Lords in *DPP v Hutchinson*.[87] The Secretary of State for Defence had power to make byelaws regulating the use of land appropriated for military purposes provided that no byelaw took away the rights of commoners. The minister made byelaws declaring Greenham Common a protected area and making it a criminal offence to enter the enclosed area without authority. Greenham Common was subject to rights of common enjoyed by 62 commoners. The byelaws failed to protect these rights. Hutchinson, who was not a commoner, was convicted of contravening the byelaw. She contended that the byelaw was **5–037**

---

[81] *Hartnell v Minister of Housing and Local Government* [1965] A.C. 1134; *Mixnam's Properties Ltd v Chertsey UDC* [1965] A.C. 735; *Kingsway v Kent CC* [1971] A.C. 72.

[82] *Potato Marketing Board v Merricks* [1958] 2 Q.B. 316.

[83] In *Dunkley v Evans* [1981] 1 W.L.R. 1522 at 1525. See also *Olsen v City of Camberwell Corp.* [1926] V.R. 58.

[84] See dicta of Lord Bridge in *DPP v Hutchinson* [1990] 2 A.C. 738 at 804.

[85] per Schiemann J. in *DPP v Hutchinson* [1989] Q.B. 583 at 593 (the actual judgment was reversed by the House of Lords [1990] 2 A.C. 783).

[86] See *DPP v Hutchinson* [1990] 2 A.C. 783.

[87] [1990] 2 A.C. 783.

ultra vires as the minister had no power to make a byelaw which took away the rights of commoners. The minister contended that the byelaw was only invalid as far as commoners were concerned and could be upheld and enforced as far as others were concerned.

5–038   The House held that there were two aspects to the test of severance in public law, namely textual and substantial severability. A legislative instrument was textually severable if a clause, sentence, phrase or word could be disregarded and what remained was grammatical and coherent. The instrument was substantially severable if what remained after severance was essentially unchanged in its legislative purpose, operation and effect. The ultra vires part of a measure would be severable if it was textually and substantially severable. In addition, there would be cases where the offending part of the measure was not textually severable but where the test of substantial severability was satisfied. In such cases, the court could in certain circumstances still hold the measure to be severable or partially invalid. In the *DPP v Hutchinson* case, the byelaw was neither textually nor substantially severable and the whole byelaw was therefore invalid.

5–039   The decision deals only with delegated legislation. Similar principles can readily be applied to certain other measures such as decisions or orders which have conditions attached to them or demands for information which include authorised and unauthorised information. The test of textual and substantial severance can be applied to such measures without difficulty. It is likely that similar principles will be applied to other public law actions such as individual decisions taken by a public body. There may, however, be situations where the language of severance is not applicable. In *DPP v Hutchinson*, for example, Lord Bridge expressed the view that the principles applicable to severance of parts of a legislative instrument would not apply to a resolution of a local authority appropriating land where the resolution included land which the authority had no power to appropriate.[88] He viewed the matter as a question of construing the resolution to determine the extent of the land affected rather than as a question of severance.

Textual severability

5–040   A part of a measure will be textually severable if the offending part can be deleted or removed from the text and the text that remains is grammatical and coherent. Thus where a paragraph of a regulation imposing liability to income tax was ultra vires, the paragraph could be deleted without altering the grammatical sense of what was left.[89] It is likely that conditions attached to planning permissions or licences will be textually severable. In such cases, the courts will then go on to consider whether the offending part is also substantially severable.

5–041   There will be cases such as *DPP v Hutchinson*[90] where the measure is not textually severable. There, a single provision which prohibited entry into the protected area applied to commoners (in relation to whom the minister had no power to make such byelaws) and the public generally. In such case, it may still

---

[88] [1990] 2 A.C. 783 at 810 distinguishing *Thames Water Authority v Elmbridge BC* [1983] Q.B. 570.
[89] *R. v I.R.C. Ex p. Woolwich Equitable Building Society* [1990] 1 W.L.R. 1400.
[90] [1990] 2 A.C. 783.

be possible to uphold the measure in part, if the test of substantial severability can be satisfied. The advantage of establishing that part of a measure is textually severable would seem to lie in the fact that a court can more readily determine whether the remainder of the text is capable of operating independently of the invalid text and whether it is intended to do so.[91] It is likely to be more difficult in practice to persuade a court that a measure not textually severable can be partially upheld without changing substantially the purpose of the measure.

Substantial severability

The test of substantial severability is met in the context of delegated legislation if there is no change in the substantial purpose and effect of the measure if the offending part is excised or if the measure is declared to be only partially valid. If the measure would be substantially different, the courts cannot speculate as to whether or not the public body concerned would in any event have enacted the different and more limited measure. In such circumstances, the whole measure is ultra vires and invalid.[92]   **5–042**

The application of these principles can be seen in a number of cases. In *DPP v Hutchinson*,[93] the House of Lords considered that the purpose of the byelaw was to prohibit all access to the protected area to maintain military security. If the courts were to declare the byelaw partially invalid in so far as it sought to exclude commoners, that purpose could no longer be achieved. The byelaw that remained would not therefore be the same in purpose as that originally made. The byelaw was not therefore substantially severable and was ultra vires in its entirety. In *R. v Inland Revenue Commissioners Ex p. Woolwich Equitable Building Society*,[94] regulations were adopted in 1986 to impose liability to tax on building society interest payments made in a particular period. A sub-paragraph specified the rate of tax as being that payable during the 1985–1986 tax year. That sub-paragraph was ultra vires. The sub-paragraph was textually severable from the rest of the regulation but it was not substantially severable. The effect of excising the sub-paragraph would be to make the payments subject to a rate of tax other than that intended by the Revenue. As the regulations had been drafted on the basis that the 1985–1986 rate of tax would be the rate applicable, excising the offending sub-paragraph and leaving the regulations in place but with a different rate of tax applicable would substantially change the purpose and effect of the regulations. The entire regulations would therefore have to be quashed.   **5–043**

Conversely, there have been occasions when the courts have been satisfied that substantial severability was possible as the overall legislative purpose of a measure would not be affected by holding that the measure was partially invalid. In *Dunkley v Evans*,[95] a minister made a statutory instrument prohibiting fishing. The instrument included a small area of sea in respect of which the minister had no power to make such an order. The Divisional Court held that the order was only partially invalid, that is, it was invalid in so far as it sought to include areas   **5–044**

---

[91] [1990] 2 A.C. 783; see dicta of Lord Bridge at 811.
[92] [1990] 2 A.C. 783. See also *R. v I.R.C. Ex p. Woolwich Equitable Building Society* [1990] 1 W.L.R. 1400.
[93] [1990] 2 A.C. 783.
[94] [1990] 1 W.L.R. 1400.
[95] [1981] 1 W.L.R. 1522.

not covered by the enabling statute. This decision was considered correct in *DPP v Hutchinson*[96] since the legislative purpose was obviously not affected by the inadvertent inclusion of a small area. In *Daymond v Plymouth City Council*[97] an order imposed charges for sewerage services on householders who were connected to a sewer and those who were not. Although the issue of severance was not argued, the House of Lords held that the order was invalid so far as householders unconnected to a sewer were concerned as there was no statutory power to impose charges on such persons. This decision was analysed in *DPP v Hutchinson*[98] as one where the test of substantial severability was satisfied, as the legislative purpose and effect of charging for sewerage services was unaffected by the inclusion of people who were not eligible to pay such charges.

Measures other than delegated legislation

5–045   The decision in *DPP v Hutchinson* dealt with delegated legislation. A similar test of severability has been used in determining whether invalid conditions attached to licences or planning permission can be severed leaving the licence or permission intact or whether the whole licence or permission needs to be quashed. The courts have asked whether the condition can be struck out without altering the character of the licence or permission or whether the licence permission would be fundamentally different without the condition, in which case the whole licence or permission must be quashed.[99] Conversely, there are cases where the courts assume that a condition is severable without apparently fully considering whether the order would have been made if the condition could not have been attached.[100] In such cases, it may simply have been abundantly clear that the decision would have been taken so that no discussion of the issue was necessary.

5–046   Earlier cases have asked whether an administrative measure was a single indivisible act rather than asking whether the offending part of the measure was textually and substantially severable. In *Dyson v Att-Gen*,[101] the Court of Appeal held that a demand for information from the tax authorities was a single and indivisible form. They refused to invalidate only those questions which demanded information that the Revenue could not lawfully require and held that the inclusion of one unauthorised question invalidated the whole return. The court was influenced by the desire to encourage the authorities to frame their questions with care and not to make unauthorised requests. In addition, an individual, who would not be as well placed as the authorities in deciding whether the request for particular information was unlawful, would face heavy penalties for non-compliance with the request and be faced with onerous and time-consuming

---

[96] [1990] 2 A.C. 783 at 207, per Lord Bridge.
[97] [1976] A.C. 609.
[98] [1990] 2 A.C. 783 at 207, per Lord Bridge.
[99] *R. v North Hertfordshire DC Ex p. Cobbold* [1985] 3 All E.R. 486; *Hall v Shoreham-by-Sea UDC* [1964] 1 W.L.R. 240 and *R. v Hillingdon LBC Ex p. Royco Homes* [1974] 2 Q.B. 720. See also *Kingsway v Kent CC* [1971] A.C. 72.
[100] See, e.g. *R. v Barnet LBC Ex p. Johnson* (1991) 3 Admin. L.R. 149; *R. v Southwark Crown Court Ex p. Customs and Excise Commissioners* [1989] 3 W.L.R. 1054; *Hartnell v Minister of Housing and Local Government* [1965] A.C. 1134; *Mixnam's Properties Ltd. v Chertsey DC* [1965] A.C. 735 and *Ellis v Dubowski* [1921] 3 K.B. 621.
[101] [1912] 1 Ch. 158.

duties to provide information. Devlin J. did not allow these policy factors to influence the outcome in a subsequent case,[102] which also involved quasi-criminal penalties for non-compliance with a demand for information. As the invalid question could be struck out without affecting the character of the form, he held the rest of the form to be valid. In *R. v Secretary of State for Transport Ex p. GLC*,[103] the minister gave a direction requiring the GLC to pay £281 million to London Transport. It transpired, as the minister conceded, that this sum erroneously included a sum of £10 million. McNeill J. held that the direction was a single and indivisible direction; the relevant statute required the minister to calculate a single sum; if the court were to excise the £10 million that would amount to rewriting the direction which he was unprepared to do. These cases predate the decision in *DPP v Hutchinson* and it is now likely that they would be decided using principles reflecting the tests and the language of textual and substantial severability. In addition, some earlier cases leaned heavily in favour of severing the invalid part unless the measure without the invalid part was so substantially different that the courts could not be sure that the decision-maker would have enacted the valid part independently of the invalid part.[104] It is likely that the courts will now ask whether the purpose or effect of such measures would be the same if the measure was only partially invalidated and if not, will quash the whole measure, rather than speculating as to whether the decision-maker would have adopted this or some other decision. Some of these earlier cases would probably be decided differently today in the light of the decision in *DPP v Hutchinson*.[105]

---

[102] *Potato Marketing Board v Merricks* [1958] 2 Q.B. 316.

[103] [1986] Q.B. 556.

[104] See, e.g., *Dunkley v Evans* (above, fn.66); *Agriculture, Horticulture and Forestry Industry Training Board v Aylesbury Mushrooms* [1972] 1 W.L.R. 190 and *Hotel and Catering Industry Training Board v Automobile Proprietary Limited* [1969] 1 W.L.R. 697 (order invalid so far as it applied to members clubs as no statutory power to make order in respect of such bodies).

[105] Lord Bridge in *DPP v Hutchinson* [1990] 2 A.C. 783 at 810 doubted whether the outcome in the *Aylesbury Mushrooms* case [1972] 1 W.L.R. 190 would have been the same if severance had been discussed.

CHAPTER 6

The Prerogative Remedies: Quashing Orders, Prohibiting Orders and Mandatory Orders

A. INTRODUCTION

The prerogative remedies of certiorari, prohibition and mandamus, now called quashing orders, prohibiting orders and mandatory orders,[1] were the original public law remedies used to remedy unlawful action by public bodies. Each of the remedies has its own sphere of operation: quashing orders are issued to quash unlawful decisions; prohibiting orders are issued to restrain a public authority from acting unlawfully; mandatory orders are used to secure the performance of public law duties. These remedies may only be sought by way of judicial review application.[2] Declarations and injunctions were originally private law remedies. They were increasingly used as a means of controlling unlawful administrative action, and may now be claimed alongside or instead of a prerogative remedy in a public law case, by way of a claim for judicial review.[3]

6–001

B. QUASHING ORDERS

The control of ultra vires acts

The primary purpose of a quashing order in modern administrative law is to quash an ultra vires decision. The order is technically an order bringing a decision of a public body to the High Court so that court may determine whether the decision is valid. Where the decision is ultra vires, a quashing order will issue to quash the decision. By quashing the decision, the order confirms that the decision is a nullity and is to be deprived of all legal effect. In modern terms, quashing orders are the means of controlling unlawful exercises of power by setting aside decisions reached in excess or abuse of power. The House of Lords has said that a quashing order is the primary and most appropriate remedy for achieving the nullification of a public law decision.[4]

6–002

---

[1] See Senior Courts Act 1981 s.29(1) as amended by the Civil Procedure (Modification of the Supreme Court Act 1981) Order 2004.
[2] Senior Courts Act s.31.
[3] Senior Courts Act s.31.
[4] *Cocks v Thanet DC* [1983] 2 A.C. 286.

The scope of quashing orders

6–003   A quashing order today lies to quash any decision of a public law body exercising public law powers. The definition of public law was considered in Chapter 2, and the range of measures against which judicial review was available in Chapter 4. "Decision" is an extremely broad term used to cover virtually all actions taken in the exercise of public law powers. A quashing order, for example, will issue to quash a licence,[5] directions for the removal of an immigrant,[6] and a resolution of a local authority adopting a policy.[7] It is becoming common practice to talk of quashing the decision to grant a tenancy[8] or the decision to grant planning permission[9] or the decision to issue a circular,[10] rather than quashing the final legal instrument itself. This is in effect a form of legal shorthand. The effect of a quashing order in this instance is to make it clear that the statutory or other public law powers have been exercised unlawfully, and consequently, to deprive the public body's act of any legal basis.

6–004   A quashing order may, of course, be coupled with a declaration. This is particularly useful where the precise consequences of quashing a decision need to be articulated. It may also be coupled with one or more of the other remedies available in a judicial review claim, where appropriate.

6–005   The previous limitations on the availability of quashing orders have gradually been eroded. These restrictions were disappearing before the introduction in 1977 of the judicial review procedure. The advent of that procedure added a renewed impetus to the modernisation of judicial review. The major obstacle to the development of the prerogative remedies was the dictum of Atkin LJ in the *Electricity Commissioners* case[11] that the supervisory jurisdiction of the courts only extended to bodies having legal authority to determine questions affecting the rights of subjects and having the duty to act judicially. This dictum no longer represents the law, if indeed it ever did, and is seriously misleading. It is now clear that the judicial review jurisdiction and prerogative remedies are available against anybody exercising public law powers, whether they be derived from statute,[12] the prerogative,[13] or other non-statutory powers.[14] Any exercise of public law power having a discernible effect may be challenged by a person with sufficient interest in the matter, whether or not it affects "rights", however

[5]   *R. v North Hertfordshire DC, Ex p. Cobbold* [1985] 3 All E.R. 486.

[6]   *R. v Immigration Officer Ex p. Shah* [1982] 1 W.L.R. 544.

[7]   *R. v Liverpool City Council Ex p. Secretary of State for Employment* [1989] C.O.D. 404.

[8]   *R. v Port Talbot BC Ex p. Jones* [1988] 2 All E.R. 207.

[9]   *R. v Great Yarmouth BC Ex p. Botton Brothers Arcades Ltd* (1988) 56 P. & C.R. 99.

[10]   *R. v Secretary of State for the Home Department Ex p. Northumbria Police Authority* [1989] Q.B. 26.

[11]   *R. v Electricity Commissioners Ex p. London Electricity Joint Committee Co.* (1920) Ltd [1924] 1 K.B. 171 at 205.

[12]   See, e.g. *R. v General Medical Council Ex p. Colman* [1989] C.O.D. 313 (affd. [1990] 1 All E.R. 489), and see generally para.2–005.

[13]   *R. v Secretary of State for Foreign and Commonwealth Affairs Ex p. Everett* [1989] Q.B. 811.

[14]   *R. v Panel on Take-overs and Mergers Ex p. Datafin Plc* [1987] Q.B. 815; *R. v Norfolk CC Ex p. M.* [1989] Q.B. 619.

broadly or narrowly that concept is defined.[15] The concept of a "judicial" act is now completely discredited and has no role to play in determining the availability of the public law remedies.[16]

Non-binding acts

Another potential limitation on quashing orders has also been eroded over time. At one time it was said that certiorari only lay against determinations or decisions, and not against non-binding acts such as advisory opinions and reports.[17] It is now clear that a quashing order may, in appropriate circumstances, issue to quash a recommendation.[18] There is also no doubt that the courts may grant a declaration that a non-binding advisory circular is ultra vires,[19] and that a report is void.[20] There is no reason now why a quashing order should not be issued in similar circumstances. Indeed, on one occasion it was considered preferable to grant a quashing order to quash parts of guidance which were erroneous in law rather than simply granting a declaration.[21] A quashing order would establish that an illegality has occurred, and confirm that a non-binding act such as a report or circular or guidance should not be relied upon.

6–006

Quashing orders and nullities

It was occasionally suggested in the past that a quashing order should not be used to quash nullities on the grounds that if a decision is a nullity it cannot produce legal effects, and so does not need to be quashed.[22] This line of reasoning is misplaced. The purpose of granting a quashing order is to establish invalidity and, once established, to make it clear that the decision is devoid of legal effect. Quashing orders are constantly being granted to quash nullities. When the courts refuse to grant a quashing order to quash a decision on the ground that it is a nullity, they usually have some other reason for refusing the order. In the past, the courts have refused to grant a quashing order to quash an acquittal,[23] or a conviction.[24] Their motive has usually been to emphasise that, as the acquittal or conviction was a nullity, proceedings can begin afresh. The applicant cannot complain of double jeopardy as he was never in any danger of a valid conviction as a result of the initial proceedings. The Divisional Court has held that a

6–007

---

[15] See Chapter 4 for a discussion of the full range of interests that judicial review protects.

[16] See *R. v Hillingdon LBC Ex p. Royco Homes* [1974] 2 Q.B. 720.

[17] *R. v Statutory Visitors to St Lawrance's Hospital Caterham Ex p. Pritchard* [1953] 1 W.L.R. 1158, and see para.4–031.

[18] *R. v Agricultural Dwelling-House Advisory Committee for Bedfordshire Cambridgeshire and Northamptonshire Ex p. Brough* (1986) 19 H.L.R. 367.

[19] *Gillick v West Norfolk and Wisbech Area Health Authority* [1986] A.C. 112.

[20] *Grunwick Processing Laboratories v Advisory, Conciliation and Arbitration Service* [1978] A.C. 655.

[21] See supplementary judgment in *R (Independent Schools Council) v Charities Commission* [2012] Ch. 214.

[22] See discussion in Wade & Forsyth, *Administrative Law*, (11th edn).

[23] *R. v Dorking Justices Ex p. Harrington* [1984] A.C. 743; *R. v Sutton Justices Ex p. DPP* [1992] 2 All E.R. 129.

[24] *R. v Seisdon Justices Ex p. Dougan* [1982] 1 W.L.R. 1476.

quashing order does lie to quash a decision which is a nullity.[25] In that case, the Divisional Court was dealing with a decision by justices to dismiss an information charging two individuals with criminal offences. The Divisional Court held that an acquittal which was unlawful was a nullity and could not provide the person acquitted with the defence of autrefois acquit. In terms of remedies, the Divisional Court held that a quashing order would lie to quash a decision which was a nullity as "a convenient way of preventing the continuance of an ostensible effect".[26] The Court indicated, however, that if the prosecution wished the proceedings to continue, the more appropriate remedy would usually be a mandatory order compelling the justices to continue with the hearing. The reasoning of the Divisional Court is to be preferred to that in the earlier cases suggesting that quashing orders did not lie as it is more consistent with the modern approach to quashing orders and unlawful exercises of power by public bodies.

Quashing orders and subordinate legislation

6–008   It is sometimes said that quashing orders will not issue to quash a subordinate legislative instrument. In 1928, the Divisional Court held that certiorari did not lie against a legislative body such as the assembly of the Church of England.[27] This judgment was largely based on the now discredited view that quashing orders only lay against judicial bodies and the courts might take a different view if the question arose for discussion now.[28] The courts may review the lawfulness of subordinate legislation applying the usual principles of public law.[29] There is no doubt that the courts may grant a declaration that such an instrument is invalid.[30] There is no reason why quashing orders should not also be available. Such orders may be used to quash normative acts and are not confined to decisions affecting only a specified individual.[31] The courts have now recognised that delegated legislation which is unlawful should generally be quashed.[32] The Supreme Court has quashed parts of Orders in Council which were ultra vires the parent Act.[33] The Court of Appeal has quashed parts of a statutory instrument which were ultra vires.[34] The Divisional Court has granted a quashing order to

---

[25] *R. v Hendon Justices Ex p. DPP* [1994] Q.B. 167.

[26] [1994] Q.B. 167 per Mann LJ at 178F.

[27] *R. v Legislative Committee of the Church Assembly Ex p. Haynes-Smith* [1928] 1 K.B. 411.

[28] An ordinary claim for a declaration that a canon was ultra vires was dismissed on its merits in *Brown v Runcie*, *The Times*, February 20, 1991. The question of whether the action raised public law issues which should have been dealt with by judicial review was expressly left open by Hoffmann J. at first instance reported in *The Times*, June 26, 1990. The question of the availability of a quashing order was not considered.

[29] *R. (Javed) v Secretary of State for the Home Department* [2002] Q.B. 129 at [33]–[51].

[30] See, e.g. *R. v Customs and Excise Commissioners Ex p. Hedges & Butler* [1986] 2 All E.R. 164; *R. v Lord Chancellor Ex p. Witham* [1998] Q.B. 575.

[31] *Minister for Health v King* [1931] A.C. 494.

[32] *R (C) v Secretary of State for Justice* [2009] Q.B. 657 especially at [41] (per Buxton LJ) and [85] (per Keene LJ) (amendment to rules made pursuant to statute quashed).

[33] *A v HM Treasury (Justice intervening)* [2010] 2 A.C. 534 (one of the challenges was brought by way of judicial review, one was converted to a judicial review claim (see [2008] 3 All E.R 361) and the others were brought by way of a statutory application in accordance with the terms of the Orders themselves).

[34] *R. (ToTel Ltd) v First-tier Tribunal (Tax Chamber)* [2013] 2 W.L.R. 1136.

quash regulations made by the Secretary of State for Health.[35] A court may also choose to quash the decision adopting the normative measure, which effectively amounts to quashing the measure itself.[36]

The Court of Appeal has also held that judicial review is available to determine whether a draft order in council which was laid before Parliament for approval prior to submission to Her Majesty in Council was intra vires the powers conferred by the enabling Act.[37] The appropriate relief will usually be a declaration setting out the legal position, rather than a quashing order to quash the draft since that may be seen as an attempt to pre-empt Parliament even discussing the draft. A declaration of the legal position may appear less interventionist than quashing with its connotations of the court actively setting aside the draft.

6–009

Refusals or failure to act

A quashing order may not of itself be an adequate remedy in all circumstances. A claimant may be challenging a decision refusing to exercise a discretionary power such as a refusal by an inferior court or tribunal to grant legal representation, a decision by a public body refusing to hear a particular case on the grounds that it has no jurisdiction to do so or a refusal to confer a discretionary benefit on the applicant. A quashing order may issue to quash the decision refusing to exercise the discretionary power or refusing to act. This will establish that the public body is acting unlawfully, but will not of itself compel the public body to consider exercising its discretion or exercising its jurisdiction to act. A quashing order may need to be accompanied by a mandatory order ordering the public body to consider exercising its discretion according to law, or ordering the body to hear and determine the application according to law.[38] The court may consider that the public body can be safely relied on to act once the grant of a quashing order has established the true legal position, without the need for further coercive relief. If in doubt, the court may grant a quashing order with liberty to apply for further relief should this prove necessary.[39] More conveniently, where a court quashes the decision[40] the court has power to remit the matter to the original decision-maker, with a direction to decide the matter in accordance with the judgment. Where a public body is under a duty to act, and has refused to do so, the courts may grant certiorari to quash the refusal and a declaration setting out the scope of the public body's obligations (rather than granting mandamus). Thus, in one case where a local health authority unlawfully refused to provide psychiatric services for a patient, the court quashed the refusal and granted a

6–010

---

[35] *R. v Secretary of State for Health Ex p. United States Tobacco International Inc.* [1991] 3 W.L.R. 529.

[36] See, e.g. *R. v Secretary of State for the Home Department Ex p. Northumbria Police Authority* [1989] Q.B. 26 (judicial review sought of decision to adopt a circular, rather than of the circular itself).

[37] *R. v HM Treasury Ex p. Smedley* [1985] Q.B. 657.

[38] See, e.g. *R. v Tower Hamlets LBC Ex p. Chetnik Developments Ltd* [1987] 1 W.L.R. 593 (affd. by the House of Lords [1988] A.C. 858). Quashing order granted to quash a decision refusing discretionary refund of money and mandamus to council to hear and determine matter according to law.

[39] See, e.g. *R. v Police Complaints Board Ex p. Madden* [1987] 1 W.L.R. 447; *R. v Hillingdon LBC Ex p. Royco Homes Ltd* [1974] 2 Q.B. 720.

[40] Senior Courts Act 1981 s.31(5); CPR r.54.19(2).

declaration clarifying the scope of its obligations to provide such care and invited the authority to reconsider the case in the light of the judgment.[41]

Threatened unlawful acts

6–011   There are also occasions when public bodies threaten to exceed their jurisdiction. An inferior court may, for example, misconstrue the extent of its statutory powers, and hold that it has jurisdiction to determine a matter when it does not or a public authority may embark on an investigation it has no power to carry out. The appropriate remedy to restrain an authority from acting unlawfully is a prohibiting order (or an injunction) either alone or together with a quashing order to quash the decision to act.[42] The courts may, however, simply grant certiorari to quash the decision to hear the case, or embark on the investigation,[43] since, as a practical matter, a public body is unlikely to persist in the unlawful exercise of jurisdiction once the illegality has been established.

Restrictions on the availability of quashing orders

6–012   There are some genuine restrictions on the availability of quashing orders. The first and only significant restriction is that certiorari does not lie against superior courts.[44] Superior courts include the Supreme Court, Court of Appeal, High Court, Masters of the Senior Courts,[45] and Court-Martial Appeal Court.[46] The High Court has jurisdiction to grant a quashing order against the Crown Court, except in relation to matters relating to trial on indictment.[47]

6–013   A quashing order is not available against ecclesiastical courts.[48] A prohibiting order, however, is available to restrain an ecclesiastical court from exceeding its jurisdiction. Jurisdiction is broadly construed to cover excess of power and abuse of power, such as a failure to observe natural justice.[49] The courts are likely to be cautious in exercising their jurisdiction on questions of purely ecclesiastical law.[50] The absence of power to grant a quashing order is not, therefore, a significant restriction in practice. It used to be thought that quashing orders did not lie against university visitors who have exclusive jurisdiction over the internal affairs of universities. The House of Lords has now confirmed that quashing

---

[41]   *R. v Ealing District Local Health Authority Ex p. Fox* [1993] 1 W.L.R. 373 at 387E–H.

[42]   See, e.g. *R. v Horseferry Road Justices Ex p. Independent Broadcasting Authority* [1987] Q.B. 54.

[43]   See, e.g. *R. v Commission for Racial Equality Ex p. Hillingdon BC* [1982] A.C. 779. For criticism of this trend see Wade and Forsyth, *Administrative Law* 11th edn, pp.518–519.

[44]   *R. v Oxenden* (1691) 1 Show 217; *Suratt and others v Att-Gen of Trinidad and Tobago* [2008] 2 W.L.R. 262 at [49] and see [2]-[122].

[45]   *Murrell v British Leyland Trustees* [1989] C.O.D. 389.

[46]   S.1 of the Courts-Martial (Appeals) Act 1968. Court martials operating when martial law is declared operate outside the law altogether and are not subject to judicial review: *Re Clifford and O'Sullivan* [1921] 2 A.C. 570.

[47]   Senior Courts Act 1981 s.29(2). See above at paras 2–123 to 2–128.

[48]   *R. v Chancellor of St Edmunsbury and Ipswich Diocese Ex p. White* [1948] 1 K.B. 195; *R. v Chancellor of the Chichester Consistory Court Ex p. News Group Newspapers Ltd, The Times*, July 15, 1991.

[49]   *R. v North Ex p. Oakey* [1927] 1 K.B. 491. But not the Church in Wales following disestablishment: see *R. v The Provincial Court of the Church in Wales* [1999] C.O. 163.

[50]   See dicta of Mann LJ in *R. v Chancellor of the Chichester Consistory Court Ex p. News Group Newspapers Ltd* (above, fn.48).

orders, along with the other prerogative remedies, are available against university visitors.[51] Although quashing orders are available as against a Visitor, the House of Lords has held that the courts could not engage in review of decisions of the Visitor on the interpretation and application of internal law of the University, that is decisions relating to the University's charter, statutes and internal regulations.[52] This is a general restriction on the scope of review of the Visitor and prevents the grant of any remedy in respect of matters relating to the internal law of the University and is not a restriction that is unique to quashing orders. The jurisdiction of the Visitor at common law over complaints by students and staff has been abolished.[53] There will now remain only very limited circumstances where Visitors will take decisions in relation to universities.

There is also old authority stating that the courts cannot intervene in matters of **6–014** military conduct and purely military law affecting military rules for the guidance of officers on matters of discipline unless the actions of military authorities affected the ordinary civil rights of the soldiers.[54] That approach does not reflect the modern attitude of the courts. In general, the courts are likely to be prepared to review exercises of statutory powers or prerogative power relating to the armed forces, even in matters involving questions of discipline and conduct, providing that the issues raised are justiciable ones.[55] The courts have, for example, considered whether a decision taken under prerogative powers to discharge servicemen and women because of their sexual orientation was unlawful.[56] There is provision for the Defence Council to consider complaints with respect to any matter relating to service personnel's service.[57] The courts will judicially review the decisions of the Defence Council. The Divisional Court has, for example, granted a quashing order to quash a decision of the Army Board, acting for the Defence Council, dismissing an allegation of racial discrimination as the Board had failed to observe the requirements of natural justice in carrying out its statutory obligations to investigate complaints by soldiers.[58] In the area of military discipline, the courts have granted judicial review of a decision of the Admiralty Board of the Defence Council rejecting a petition against the severity of a sentence imposed by a court-martial which had found a sailor guilty of misconduct and ordered that he be dismissed from the navy.[59] The Divisional Court found that the sentence was grossly disproportionate to the offence. In another case, a Divisional Court held that a sentence of six months' imprisonment imposed upon a soldier was unlawful as the court-martial

---

[51] *Thomas v University of Bradford* [1987] A.C. 795; for comment see [1987] C.L.J. 384.

[52] *R. v Hull University Visitor Ex p. Page* [1993] A.C. 682.

[53] By the Higher Education Act 2004 s.20 in relation to students and by the Education Reform Act 1988 ss.203–204. See above at para.2–116.

[54] See, e.g. *R. v Secretary of State for War Ex p. Martyn* [1949] 1 All E.R. 242 (a quashing order did not lie to quash a decision of a court-martial where applicant alleged court-martial had failed to observe statutory rules of procedure); *R. v Army Council Ex p. Ravenscroft* [1917] 2 K.B. 504 (a mandatory order could not issue to order court of inquiry to investigate alleged disciplinary offences).

[55] See para.4–080 to 4–087 above.

[56] *R. v Ministry of Defence Ex p. Smith* [1996] Q.B. 517.

[57] See s.20 of the Armed Forces Act 1996, amending s.180 of the Army Act 1955, s.180 of the Air Force Act 1955 and s.130 of the Naval Discipline Act 1957 respectively.

[58] *R. v Army Board Ex p. Anderson* [1992] Q.B. 169.

[59] *R. v Admiralty Board of the Defence Council Ex p. Coupland* [1996] C.O.D. 147. See also *R. v RAF Court-Martial Ex p. Wright*, *The Times*, July 20, 1999.

had not given any reasons for the decision.[60] The right of appeal to the Court of Appeal against decisions of court-martials has been extended[61] and challenges to these decisions will now be channelled through that route.[62]

6–015   A quashing order is not available against the Crown. This limitation is more apparent than real. There is no doubt that a quashing order will lie against a Minister of the Crown exercising statutory powers. A quashing order also lies against a minister exercising power derived from the prerogative.[63] The Court of Appeal has said, obiter, that an order made by Her Majesty in Council under statutory power is subject to judicial review to determine its validity. As discussed earlier, certiorari is likely to be available in principle, although in practice a declaration is often likely to be the more appropriate remedy.[64] The limitation would seem only to apply to a situation where the Crown actually exercises the power itself, and such situations are likely to be extremely rare. It could conceivably arise, for example, if the Sovereign had to appoint a Prime Minister in a hung parliament. As such a decision is unlikely to be justiciable, the limitation is not of great significance. In any event, declaratory relief is available against the Crown.[65]

The effect of a quashing order

6–016   Decisions that are ultra vires are nullities. The effect of granting a quashing order is to establish that a decision is ultra vires and to set the decision aside. The decision is retrospectively invalidated, and deprived of legal effect since its inception.[66] Judicial review is a supervisory not an appellate jurisdiction. The court can only ensure that a decision has been reached lawfully, and if not, quash the unlawful decision. The court cannot substitute an alternative decision for that of the decision-maker. Thus, where the Secretary of State had adopted unlawful criteria for determining whether to make ex gratia payments, the appropriate remedy was to declare that the criteria adopted were unlawful. It was not, however, for the court to determine what new criteria should be adopted. That was a matter for the Secretary of State.[67] In many circumstances, the decision-maker will be free to reconsider the matter and to make a fresh decision

---

[60]   R. v Ministry of Defence Ex p. Murray, The Times, December 17, 1997.
[61]   See s.8 of the Courts Martial (Appeals) Act 1968 as amended by s.17 of the Armed Forces Act 1996. See, e.g. R. v Spear [2003] 1 A.C. 734.
[62]   The European Court of Human Rights has found that aspects of the court-martial procedure violate Art.6 of the European Convention of Human Rights: see Findlay v United Kingdom [1997] 24 E.H.R.R. 221. See also Morris v United Kingdom (2002) 34 E.H.R.R. 52.
[63]   Both where the power is expressly delegated to a minister—Council of Civil Service Unions v Minister for the Civil Service [1985] A.C. 374—and where a minister in fact exercises power R. v Secretary of State for Foreign and Commonwealth Affairs Ex p Everett [1989] Q.B. 811.
[64]   R. v HM Treasury Ex p. Smedley [1985] Q.B. 657.
[65]   See paras 7–063 to 7–065.
[66]   See McLaughlin v Governor of the Cayman Islands [2007] 1 W.L.R. 2839 at [14] and see, generally, Chapter 5.
[67]   R. (Elias) v Secretary of State for Defence [2006] 1 W.L.R. 3213 at [196]–[203]. See also, e.g. R. (Hirst) v Secretary of State for the Home Department [2002] 1 W.L.R. 2929 at [86]–[88] (court not prepared to grant an order quashing a refusal to permit a prisoner to speak to the media by telephone if certain conditions were met; that would amount to dictating to the authorities the policy it should adopt which was not the function of the court).

(which may even be the same as the original decision) providing that in doing so he does not repeat the error or make any further reviewable errors.

Thus, a minister whose decision to reduce the rate support grant payable to a local authority was quashed, due to a failure to listen to representations, was entitled to reconsider the matter. Once he had heard the representations and considered them, he could take a second decision, which could be the same in substance as the first decision.[68] An official whose decision to deport an immigrant was quashed due to a failure to give the immigrant a hearing was similarly free to reconsider the matter after giving the immigrant a hearing.[69] The decision-maker is required to consider all the relevant factors that exist at the time that he takes the second decision, and is not confined to looking at the material that existed at the time of the original invalid decision.[70]

6–017

A decision-maker will not, however, be able to retake the decision where the court has held he has no power to take the decision in question or where the decision is unlawful because it breaches a claimant's rights under the European Convention on Human Rights.[71] Nor will he able to reach an identical second decision if the initial decision was so unreasonable that no reasonable authority could have taken such a decision[72] unless, possibly, circumstances have changed since the time that the first decision was taken.

6–018

Power to remit or substitute a decision

Where the relief sought is certiorari and there are grounds for quashing the decision, the court has power to remit the matter to the original decision-maker with a direction to reconsider the matter and reach a decision in accordance with the judgment.[73] This is a useful power used in a wide variety of circumstances. If an applicant is challenging a refusal to take a decision or grant a benefit, it is often more convenient to quash the refusal and remit the matter for reconsideration rather than leaving the applicant to make a fresh application. It is often advantageous to remit where a quashing order is granted to quash a procedural decision of an inferior court or a tribunal, such as a refusal to allow

6–019

---

[68] *R. v Secretary of State for the Environment Ex p. Hackney LBC* [1984] 1 W.L.R. 592. The original decision was held invalid in *R. v Secretary of State for the Environment Ex p. Brent LBC* [1982] Q.B. 593. There may be practical difficulties in allowing the retaking of a decision if a statutory power has to be exercised by a particular time and that time has passed before the original decision is quashed. This is essentially a question of statutory construction, but the courts are likely to lean against a construction which prevents a power from ever being exercised.

[69] *Att-Gen for Hong Kong v Ng Yuen Shiu* [1983] 2 A.C. 629.

[70] Precise authority is sparse, but see the dicta in cases such as *Nadarajah v Secretary* [2005] EWCA Civ 1363; *R. v Secretary of State for the Home Department Ex p. Zeqiri* judgment, March 12, 2001 at [50], approved on appeal to the House of Lords: see [2002] UKHL 3 at [42]–[43]. *R. v Immigration Appeal Tribunal Ex p. Singh* [1987] 1 W.L.R. 1394, and *R. v Birmingham Juvenile Court Ex p. G.* [1989] 3 W.L.R. 1024. See also, *R (Perrett) v Secretary of State for Communities and Local Government* [2010] P.T.S.R. 1280 indicating that that is the position when a decision is quashed (as opposed to a remittal on appeal pursuant to s.289 of the Town and Country Planning Act 1990).

[71] See, e.g. *R. (A) v Lord Saville of Newdigate* [2002] 1 W.L.R. 1249 (decision to take evidence in a particular location would lead to breach of Art.2; matter remitted with a direction that evidence not taken in that location).

[72] See, e.g. *R. v Liverpool Crown Court Ex p. Lennon and Hongkins* [1991] C.O.D. 127.

[73] Senior Courts Act 1981 s.31(5) and CPR r.54.19(2)(b).

the individual to elect for jury trial,[74] or an order prohibiting the publication of committal evidence,[75] since the proceedings can then continue. There may also be circumstances in which it is appropriate to remit a matter rather than leaving it to the decision-maker to initiate the decision-making process afresh. In *R. v Secretary of State for the Home Department Ex p. Benwell*,[76] for example, the court quashed a decision to implement the dismissal of a prison officer for a disciplinary offence, as the Home Secretary had had regard to irrelevant material in determining the appropriate sanction. As the claimant had admitted that he had committed a disciplinary offence, some sanction (if not dismissal) might be appropriate and so the matter was remitted to the Home Secretary for reconsideration. Where a decision-maker fails to give adequate reasons for a decision, it may be more sensible to quash the decision and remit the matter for reconsideration and the provision of reasons, rather than simply quashing a decision which may in substance be unobjectionable.

6–020　　The courts have on occasion added a direction that the matter be reconsidered by a differently constituted inferior court or tribunal.[77] This is designed both to ensure that the decision-making process is seen to be impartial, and to ensure that a tribunal does approach the matter unclouded by previous impressions of the case.

6–021　　The courts have, since 2008, had power to substitute a decision for that which is subject to judicial review, but only if the decision was made by a court or tribunal and the decision was quashed on the ground that there has been an error of law and without the error there would only have been one decision which the court or tribunal could have reached.[78] The courts have not exercised this power if it could not be sure that there was only one decision that the decision-maker could reach and, instead, have quashed the decision and remitted the matter back to the primary decision-maker.[79]

6–022　　The Criminal Justice and Courts Bill 2014 proposes to amend the Senior Courts Act 1981 by adding a provision which provides that the High Court must refuse to grant a remedy if "it appears to the court to be highly likely that the outcome for the applicant would not have been substantially different if the conduct complained of had not occurred".[80] This provision will apply to all remedies including quashing orders. The precise extent of the difference between the current law where the courts must, effectively, be sure that the same decision

---

[74]　*R. v Birmingham Justices Ex p. Hodgson* [1985] Q.B. 1131.

[75]　*R. v Horsham Justices Ex p. Farquharson and West Sussex County Times* [1982] Q.B. 762.

[76]　[1985] Q.B. 554.

[77]　There is no specific power in the CPR enabling the court to give such directions. In *R. v Mental Health Review Tribunal Ex p. Clatworthy* [1985] 3 All E.R. 699 Mann J. doubted whether the court had specific power to give such a direction. Reconsideration of the issue by the same tribunal might, however, give rise to claims that the second hearing was ultra vires as the tribunal was biased because it had prior knowledge of the case. There is some suggestion of this in *R. v Hampshire CC Ex p. K.* [1990] 2 All E.R. 129 at 134–135.

[78]　See Senior Courts Act 1981 s.31(5) and (5A) as substituted by the Courts, Tribunals and Enforcement Act 2007 s.141. See also CPR r.54.19(2) which provides that the Administrative Court may substitute a decision where it is permitted to do so by statute.

[79]　See, e.g. *R (O'Connor) v Avon Coroner (Visser intervening)* [2010] 2 W.L.R. 1299 (at [15] and [31]–[33]).

[80]　See Clause 64 of the Criminal Justice and Courts Bill 2014.

would be reached[81] and the proposed "highly likely" that the outcome would not be "substantially different" will need to be worked out by the courts over time

Variation of sentences

The High Court is given extended powers by the Senior Courts Act 1981 where a magistrates' court or Crown Court (on committal for sentence or appeal from the magistrates' court) has imposed a sentence that it has no power to impose. The High Court may amend the conviction by substituting a sentence that the relevant court could have imposed, instead of granting certiorari to quash the conviction.[82] This power covers sentences imposed in a straight-forward excess of jurisdiction, and also those which are ultra vires because as they are so harsh or oppressive or so far outside the range of normal discretionary on sentence that there must have been an error of law on the part of the tribunal.[83] Similar powers have been conferred in relation to committals to prison or detention for default in paying fines.[84]

6–023

Severance or partial invalidity

Where only part of a decision is invalid and that part can be severed from the good part, the court may grant a quashing order to quash the invalid part only.[85] The principles governing severance are set out in Chapter 5.

6–024

Standing and discretion

The principles governing standing and the discretion of the court to refuse relief are largely common to all the remedies available in a claim for judicial review. They are discussed in Chapters 11 and 12.

6–025

Stay of proceedings

A court may grant directions, including ordering a stay of proceedings, where permission to apply for judicial review is given.[86] A claim for a stay should be included in the claim form. In the case of a court or tribunal, such a stay will prevent any further steps being taken in the proceedings. Stays may also be granted to prevent the implementation of a decision.[87] Even if a decision has been implemented, a stay may be granted and will have the effect of temporarily suspending the effect of the decision. Thus, a court had jurisdiction to grant a stay

6–026

---

[81] The position under s.31(5A) of the Senior Courts Act 1981 in relation to certiorari and under the general common law relating to the discretion to refuse a remedy: see *R (Smith) North East Derbyshire Primary Care Trust* [2006] 1 W.L.R. 3315 at [10] and see below at 12–026 to 12–028.

[82] Senior Courts Act 1981 s.43. See, e.g. *R. v Chelmsford Crown Court Ex p. Birchall* [1990] C.O.D. 200 and *R. v Nuneaton Justices Ex p. Bingham* [1991] C.O.D. 56.

[83] *R. v St. Albans Crown Court Ex p. Cinnamond* [1981] Q.B. 480.

[84] See Senior Courts Act 1981 s.43ZA.

[85] The same principles apply in relation to quashing orders as apply in relation to declarations; *R. v Secretary of State for Transport Ex p. Greater London Council* [1986] Q.B. 556.

[86] CPR r.54.10.

[87] See *R. (H) v Ashworth Hospital Authority* [2003] 1 W.L.R. 127 at [42].

of a decision of a mental health tribunal ordering a conditional discharge of a patient which was the subject of judicial review proceedings even after the decision had been implemented.[88] The grant of a stay in such circumstances should, however, be exercised sparingly, and only where a strong case is made out that the decision of the tribunal is unlawful.[89] Where a stay is granted, the hearing of the substantive challenge to the validity of the decision should also be determined with the greatest possible speed.

6–027   In *R. v Secretary of State for Education and Science Ex p. Avon CC*,[90] the Court of Appeal held that "proceedings" are to be construed widely to include any procedure by which a public law decision is reached or implemented. Proceedings are not limited to judicial or quasi-judicial proceedings. Thus stays may be granted against local authorities, non-judicial public bodies and Ministers of the Crown. This decision remains binding on the Court of Appeal[91] but the correctness of the decision may be re-considered by the House of Lords in the light of the decision of the Privy Council in *Minister of Foreign Affairs, Trade and Industry v Vehicle and Suppliers Ltd*.[92] In that case, the Privy Council stated, obiter, that a stay of proceedings is "an order which puts a stop to the further proceedings in court or before a tribunal" and cannot be used to prevent the implementation of a decision made by a minister in the exercise of statutory discretionary powers.[93]

6–028   The question of the scope of the jurisdiction to grant stays used to be important when it was thought that interim injunctions were not available against ministers of the Crown[94] (and when interim declarations did not exist). There was, however, no absolute bar against the grant of a stay against a minister of the Crown.[95] If stays were not limited to judicial proceedings, then they could be granted to stop the decision-making process or the implementation of a minister's decision. In those circumstances, a stay was thought to be the only means of obtaining interim relief against ministers and so holding the hearing pending the outcome of the substantive hearing. If stays were limited to proceedings of a judicial nature, it was thought that interim relief would not be available against ministers as they would not normally be engaged in judicial proceedings but the

---

[88] [2003] 1 W.L.R. 127 esp. at [35]–[38] and [92].

[89] [2003] 1 W.L.R. 127 at [47]–[48] and [93].

[90] [1991] 1 All E.R. 282.

[91] [1991] 1 All E.R. 282 at [38].

[92] [1991] 1 W.L.R. 550.

[93] *Minister of Foreign Affairs, Trade and Industry v Vehicles and Suppliers Ltd* [1991] 1 W.L.R. 550, per Lord Oliver at 556. See also dicta in *R. v Secretary of State for the Home Department Ex p. Muboyayi* [1992] Q.B. 244.

[94] As was thought to be the position by the House of Lords in *R. v Secretary of State for Transport Ex p. Factortame Ltd (No.2)* [1990] 2 A.C. 85.

[95] *R. v Secretary of State for Education Ex p. Avon CC*, n.84 above. Earlier authority had held that even stays could not be granted against a minister because of s.21(2) of the Crown Proceedings Act 1947 (which prohibits the grant of an order against a minister if it had the effect of granting an injunction): see *R. v Secretary of State for the Home Department Ex p. Kirkwood* [1984] 1 W.L.R. 913; *R. v Secretary of State for the Home Department Ex p. Yaqoob* [1984] 1 W.L.R. 920. That section, however, does not apply to judicial review proceedings and did not prohibit the grant of a stay against a minister: see s.38(2) of the Crown Proceedings Act 1947 and *R. v Secretary of State for Transport Ex p. Factortame (No.2)* fn.88 above. It is clear that a stay can be granted: see *M. v Home Office* [1994] 1 A.C. 377. The relevant question was whether the power to grant a stay was broad enough to encompass non-judicial type administrative processes.

administrative process of making or implementing a decision. The absence of a jurisdiction to grant a stay would, on that analysis, have had a very significant practical effect. Now, the House of Lords has held that interim injunctions are in principle available against a minister of the Crown on a claim for judicial review.[96] Furthermore, the CPR has created the possibility of the grant of an interim declaration which will also be available against ministers of the Crown.[97] It will, therefore, be far less important to know whether stays are limited to judicial proceedings or whether they are available in respect of any type of public law decision-making process since, if a stay is not available, an interim injunction or interim declaration can be sought against any other public body including ministers of the Crown.

The desire to give a broad interpretation of the scope of the jurisdiction was understandable when it was believed that no other form of interim relief was available. Now that understanding has been altered, there is much to be said for adopting the more limited approach to stays advocated by the Privy Council. First, as a matter of language, a stay does more naturally mean an order the purpose of which is to stop any further step in formal proceedings. As such it is not apt to describe stopping the decision-making process and is even less apt to describe the non-implementation of a decision already reached by a non-judicial body.[98] Secondly, there is much to be said for dealing with claims that individuals should be restrained from doing, or ordered to do, particular acts by way of injunction rather than a stay. In particular, this would make it clear that the normal procedures governing interim relief such as injunctions should be followed. Thus, such orders normally require notice to the other side with a hearing at which both parties are represented; orders are rarely made without the other side being given notice and then only for a limited period.[99] **6–029**

Stays will only be appropriate where it is sought to prevent a public authority from acting. They are not appropriate where it is sought to compel a public authority to act, as in *Factortame*[100] where the interim relief had the effect of forcing the Secretary of State to take positive action to suspend the registration scheme introduced by Act of Parliament. Nor will a stay be appropriate where it is not designed to stay proceedings but to control the manner in which they are performed. In *R. v Licensing Authority Ex p. Smith Kline & French Laboratories Ltd (No.2)*,[101] the applicant was seeking to prevent the licensing authority from using confidential information in processing applications for product licences and was not seeking to stay the licensing procedure. The Court of Appeal held that this was not a stay of proceedings but was really an injunction designed to stop the authority from doing certain acts. A stay has been granted to stop a minister **6–030**

---

[96] *M. v Home Office* [1994] 1 A.C. 377 and see below at para.8–012.

[97] Pt 25 of the CPR.

[98] In relation to tribunals, see *R. (H) v Ashworth Special Hospital Authority* [2003] 1 W.L.R. 127, discussed above at para.6–025.

[99] See below at para.8–039.

[100] *R. v Secretary of State for Transport Ex p. Factortame Ltd (No.2)* [1990] 2 A.C. 85. In *R. v HM Treasury Ex p. British Telecommunications Plc* [1994] 1 C.M.L.R. 621 the applicant originally applied for an interlocutory mandatory injunction requiring the minister to introduce amending legislation to correct what was alleged to be an incorrect implementation of a European Community directive. The applicant then sought to amend the application to seek a stay of the application of the subordinate legislation. The Court refused the application.

[101] [1989] 2 W.L.R. 378.

implementing a decision or taking physical action. In *R. v Secretary of State for the Environment Ex p. Greenwich LBC*,[102] for example, the applicant sought an order of prohibition to prevent the minister distributing an allegedly inaccurate leaflet. When granting leave to apply for judicial review, McCowan J. granted a stay prohibiting the distribution of the leaflet.

Principles governing the grant of a stay

6–031 The principles governing the discretion to grant a stay have yet to be worked out by the courts. The courts have given some guidance on the principles governing the grant of interim injunctions and this is discussed in Chapter 8. Similar principles are likely to be applied to applications for a stay. The Court of Appeal has specifically held that where the grant of a stay against a public body will detrimentally affect the operations of a third party, the proper approach is to treat the matter as an application for an injunction against the third party.[103] In particular, the applicant will normally be expected to give a cross-undertaking in damages to the third party and the courts will be reluctant to grant a stay in the absence of such a cross-undertaking.[104] Thus, in that case, the claimant, Greenpeace, sought judicial review of a decision varying the licence conditions governing the discharge of radioactive waste from a nuclear reprocessing plant. The claimant also sought a stay of the decision. This would have delayed various tests that the owner of the plant wished to carry out and there was a risk that the owner would suffer loss as a result. The Court held that they would apply the same principles to the application for a stay against the government department as they would if the application had been for an interim injunction against the third party. Given the risk of loss to the third party, and the absence of any offer of a cross-undertaking in damages, the court refused a stay.[105] Even where the application for a stay involves only the applicant and the respondent, the courts will, it seems, treat the application for a stay as an application for an interim injunction if, in substance, the order that is sought is one to restrain the respondent from doing a particular act.[106] The courts have also indicated that a stay may not be granted if there can be an early hearing of the substantive application.[107] The general implications are that the grant of interim relief against ministers, whether by stay or interim injunction, is likely to be rare in practice.[108]

---

[102] *The Times*, May 17, 1989. See also *R. v Secretary of State for the Home Department Ex p. Ganeshanathan*, July 27, 1988, unrep. (stay granted to prevent deportation of immigrant pending judicial review hearing). But see *Minister of Foreign Affairs, Trade and Industry v Vehicles and Suppliers* [1991] 1 W.L.R. 550.

[103] *R. v Inspectorate of Pollution Ex p. Greenpeace* [1994] 1 W.L.R. 570.

[104] See, e.g. *R. v Secretary of State for the Environment Ex p. Royal Society for the Protection of Birds* (1995) 7 Admin. L.Rep. 434.

[105] *Ex p. Greenpeace* [1994] 1 W.L.R. 570.

[106] *R. v Advertising Standards Authority Ex p. Vernons* [1992] 1 W.L.R. 1289 (application for a stay of the publication of a decision upholding a complaint that an advertisement breached the code of advertising practice).

[107] *R. v Secretary of State for Education and Science Ex p. Avon CC* [1991] 1 All E.R. 282.

[108] See dicta of Lord Woolf in *M v Home Office* [1994] 1 A.C. 377 at 422H–423B; and dicta in *R. v Licensing Authority Ex p. Smith Kline & French Laboratories Ltd (No.2)* [1989] 2 W.L.R. 378.

Consequences of breach of a stay

A stay is an order of the court. The Privy Council has held that an order granting **6–032** a stay is not enforceable by proceedings for contempt. It did so on the basis that a stay is an order putting a stop to further proceedings in a court or tribunal and so is not capable of being breached by a party to the proceedings.[109] Anything done in breach of the stay will, it seems be ineffective.[110] If, however, a stay under the CPR is of a different and wider nature than the stay granted under the provisions of the Jamaican code of civil procedure considered by the Privy Council, the question arises as to whether, in theory, an order staying a decision-making process or the implementation of a decision could be punishable by contempt. The preferable view is that breach of such a stay is still not of itself punishable by contempt.[111] If a party seeking an interim order wishes to preserve the possibility of instituting contempt proceedings for breach of an interlocutory order, the better course of action is for that party to invite the court to grant an interim injunction. It is clear that a breach of an interim injunction (even one made against a minister of the Crown) is enforceable by proceedings for contempt.[112] If the claimant wishes to have available the possibility of committing a minister or other person for contempt for breach of an order, the more appropriate course of action is to apply for an interim injunction which will, if granted, specify what the particular individual respondent is to do or refrain from doing and which will make it clear to that individual that a breach of the order is punishable by contempt. Such an interim injunction will normally only be granted where the party to be made the subject of the injunction is given notice of the application and only after a hearing at which both parties are present.[113] Even then, the courts are likely to prove extremely reluctant to grant interim injunctions against ministers of the Crown and are more likely to grant an interim declaration or a stay.[114]

Errors of law on the face of the record

A secondary purpose of a quashing order is to quash a decision exhibiting an intra **6–033** vires error of law, which appears on the face of the record of the decision. The doctrine of error on the face of the record was resurrected in 1951 after languishing in obscurity for almost a century.[115] This aspect of judicial review is unique as it is not based on the concept of control of ultra vires action. Rather, the doctrine rests on the courts' inherent willingness to correct patent errors of law where these are readily detectable from the record of the administrative body

---

[109] *Minister of Foreign Affairs v Vehicles and Suppliers Ltd* [1991] 1 W.L.R. 550 at 556E–F.

[110] *Minister of Foreign Affairs v Vehicles and Suppliers Ltd* [1991] 1 W.L.R. 550 at 556F–G.

[111] It is possible that there may be cases of criminal contempt if a party knowingly does acts that are inconsistent with the stay and interferes with the administration of justice: see *Att-Gen v Times Newspapers Ltd* [1992] A.C. 191 and *Att-Gen v Newspaper Publishing* [1997] 1 W.L.R. 926 although it is difficult to imagine circumstances where contempt proceedings could realistically be pursued in such circumstances.

[112] See *M. v Home Office* [1994] 1 A.C. 377. See also *R (JM) Croydon LBC (Practice Notice)* [2010] 1 W.L.R. 1658 at [12].

[113] *R. v Kensington and Chelsea RBC Ex p. Hammell* [1989] QB 518 at 538–539 and see paras 8–039 to 8–040.

[114] See dicta in *M v Home Office* [1994] 1 A.C. 377 at 422–423.

[115] *R. v Northumberland Compensation Appeal Tribunal Ex p. Shaw* [1952] 1 K.B. 338.

concerned. This function of a quashing order has declined to near obsolescence with the virtual abolition of intra vires errors of law. Almost all errors of law by public authorities, tribunals and inferior courts are now classified as jurisdictional errors.[116] There is consequently no need to demonstrate that the error of law is apparent on the face of the record. The error may be established by way of written evidence, as with any other reviewable error. There may also be a statutory right of appeal on a question of law against a decision. As a practical matter, this further reduces the number of situations in which it will be necessary to rely on the doctrine of errors on the face of the record.[117]

Definition of the record

6–034   If an error is classified as an intra vires error of law, the error must appear on the face of the record for the courts to be able to intervene. The courts have enlarged the range of material that constitutes the record. The record includes the document initiating the proceedings, the pleadings and the adjudication.[118] Documents referred to in the adjudication are incorporated, by reference, into the record.[119] Evidence given in the proceedings does not constitute part of the record unless it is actually incorporated into the record.[120] Errors of law will frequently be detected from the reasons given for a decision. At common law, decision-makers are not normally required to give reasons. If a decision-maker chooses to supply written reasons, these will be treated as part of the record.[121] The oral judgment of an inferior court or tribunal setting out the reasons for the judgment will also be treated as part of the record.[122] The Tribunals and Inquiries Act 1992 imposes a statutory duty on a range of administrative tribunals and ministers to give reasons for their decisions and further provides that these reasons are to be incorporated into the record.[123]

---

[116] As a result of a series of cases, including *Anisminic v Foreign Compensation Commission* [1969] 2 A.C. 147; *Re Racal Communications* [1981] A.C. 374 and *R. v Greater Manchester Coroner Ex p. Tal* [1985] Q.B. 67 the effect of which is summarised most recently in *R. v Bedwellty Justices Ex p. Williams* [1996] 3 W.L.R. 361. See paras 5–004 to 5–005 and Wade and Forsyth, above, fn.22. There may be occasional cases where the presumption that an error of law goes to jurisdiction may be rebutted: see *R. v Registrar of Companies Ex p. Central Bank of India* [1986] Q.B. 1114.

[117] S.11 of the Tribunal and Inquiries Act 1992 confers a right of appeal on a point of law in relation to the tribunals specified by the Act. Various statutes also provide for rights of appeal.

[118] *R. v Northumberland Compensation Appeal Tribunal Ex p. Shaw* [1952] 1 K.B. 338.

[119] *R. v Medical Appeal Tribunal Ex p. Gilmore* [1957] 1 Q.B. 574; *Baldwin & Francis Ltd v Patents Appeal Tribunal* [1959] A.C. 663 (majority of their Lordships assumed but did not decide that decisions of superintending examiners, notice of appeal and patent specifications of appellants formed part of the record).

[120] per Denning LJ in *R. v Northumberland Compensation Appeal Tribunal Ex p. Shaw* (see above, fn.118). But see now *R. v Knightsbridge Crown Court Ex p. The Aspinall Curzon Ltd, The Times,* December 16, 1982.

[121] *R. v Supplementary Benefits Commission Ex p. Singer* [1973] 1 W.L.R. 713 (letter from DHSS explaining earlier decision was part of the record).

[122] *R. v Knightsbridge Crown Court Ex p. International Sporting Club (London) Ltd* [1982] Q.B. 304.

[123] Tribunals and Inquiries Act 1992 s.10.

Definition of error of law

The concept of an error of law is an important one both for errors on the face of the record, and jurisdictional errors. In the former it determines the availability of review, and in the latter the courts are far more disposed to intervene if the error can be characterised as one of law rather than fact. The courts generally accord a greater degree of autonomy to the public authority in the fact-finding area. The concept of error of law is not susceptible to easy definition.[124] At one end of the spectrum there is misinterpretation of statutory provisions or legal rules. A decision-maker who incorrectly understands the meaning of the law governing his decision makes an error of law. At the other end, there are questions of primary fact such as whether an event did or did not occur. Difficulties arise in classifying the process of drawing inferences from these primary facts in order to determine whether a particular factual situation comes within a particular legal rule. The classification of an error as one of law or fact may vary from one area to another and depends on whether the courts consider the situation to be an appropriate one for judicial intervention. The courts may hold that the application of law to facts is a matter of law which they consider is an appropriate one for judicial intervention. The courts may classify the matter as one of fact and unreviewable if they consider the matter unsuitable for judicial intervention. One approach frequently utilised by the courts is to regard the application of law to facts as primarily a matter of fact or degree, unless the decision-maker reaches a conclusion that is so unreasonable that no reasonable body properly directing itself on the law could reach it.[125]

6–035

Effect of a quashing order in relation to intra vires of law on the fact of the record

Decisions exhibiting an intra vires error of law are not nullities. They are valid since they are decisions that the decision-makers are empowered to reach. A quashing order, therefore, only quashes such decisions prospectively not retrospectively. They remain valid until they are quashed and all acts done in reliance on the decision up to that time remain valid. The courts will not necessarily quash a decision because it exhibits an error of law. A quashing order is a discretionary remedy[126] and may be refused where the error is not fundamental[127] or has not caused the applicant any prejudice.[128]

6–036

---

[124] See, generally, Beatson, "The Scope of Judicial Review for Error of Law" [1984] O.J.L.S. 22.
[125] *Edwards v Bairstow* [1956] A.C. 14.
[126] *R. v Knightsbridge Crown Court Ex p. Marcrest Properties Ltd* [1983] 1 W.L.R. 300.
[127] *R. v Chief Registrar of Building Societies Ex p. New Cross Building Society* [1984] 1 Q.B. 227 at 260.
[128] *R. v Crown Court at Knightsbridge Ex p. Marcrest Properties Ltd* [1983] 1 W.L.R. 300.

C. PROHIBITING ORDERS

Purpose of a prohibiting order

6–037   A prohibiting order is used to restrain a public body from acting unlawfully. The remedy was initially used to ensure that inferior courts and tribunals did not exceed their jurisdiction. In modern times, it will issue to prevent any public body from exceeding its statutory or other public law powers, or from abusing those powers. A prohibiting order, like a quashing order, is a means of supervising the exercise of public law power. The scope of a prohibiting order is virtually identical to that of a quashing order, and the same definition of public law power applies.

Prevention of unlawful action

6–038   A quashing order issues to quash a decision that has already been reached and is unlawful. A prohibiting order may operate at an earlier stage to prevent the body acting unlawfully and reaching flawed decisions.[129] Thus, a prohibiting order will issue to prevent an inferior court or tribunal dealing with matters over which it has no jurisdiction.[130] The courts have, for example, prohibited an inferior court from committing an individual for trial where the offence could only be tried summarily,[131] or prohibited a court proceeding with a case where to do so would involve an abuse of power.[132]

6–039   Public bodies may also be prohibited from exercising powers in a way that would give rise to a reviewable error. The courts have prohibited public bodies from exercising powers in breach of natural justice. In one case, the courts prohibited a named doctor determining whether a chief inspector was permanently disabled, as the doctor had been involved in the case previously and might not be seen to be impartial.[133] In another, the courts prohibited a local authority from licensing additional taxi-cabs unless they first granted a hearing to existing taxi-drivers or their representatives.[134] Public bodies may be prohibited from exercising powers on the basis of a misunderstanding of the relevant law as where a local authority applied an incorrect test in licensing films.[135] The remedy may be appropriate to prevent a body submitting ultra vires proposals to another body for approval, or preventing a body from approving ultra vires proposals. As a matter of judicial discretion, a prohibiting order will not normally be granted to

---

[129] It is becoming common practice to talk of granting a quashing order to quash the "decision" to initiate proceedings or to accept jurisdiction, rather than prohibition to restrain unlawful exercises of power. See above at para.4–046.

[130] See, e.g. *R. v Board of Visitors of Dartmoor Prison Ex p. Smith* [1987] Q.B. 106; *R. v Horseferry Road Justices Ex p. Independent Broadcasting Authority* [1987] Q.B. 54 (prohibition to prevent court dealing with summons disclosing no offence known to law).

[131] See, e.g. *R. v Dudley Justices Ex p. Gillard* [1986] A.C. 442; *R. v Hatfield Justices Ex p. Castle* [1981] 1 W.L.R. 217.

[132] *R. v Newcastle-upon-Tyne Justices Ex p. Hindle* [1984] 1 All E.R. 770.

[133] *R. v Kent Police Authority Ex p. Godden* [1971] 2 Q.B. 662.

[134] *R. v Liverpool Corp. Ex p. Liverpool Taxi Fleet Operators' Association* [1972] 2 Q.B. 299.

[135] *R. v Greater London Council Ex p. Blackburn* [1976] 1 W.L.R. 550.

prevent a minister's submission of invalid draft orders to Parliament for approval: the appropriate remedy is a declaration.[136]

A prohibiting order may also be used to prevent the implementation of a decision which is unlawful. Thus, the courts have prohibited a statutory corporation from implementing an invalid decision to demolish a house[137] and the execution of a court order imposing a fine which was vitiated by a breach of natural justice.[138] A quashing order (or now, a declaration of invalidity) may be coupled with a prohibiting order to prevent the implementation of that decision.[139]

6–040

Conditional prohibiting orders

Where the error is one that may be corrected, the courts may grant a prohibiting order which will only restrain the public body from exercising its powers until it has corrected the error. Thus, the courts prohibited a local authority from exercising its licensing powers until it had consulted interested parties.[140] The Privy Council has, however, indicated that where a decision has been taken in breach of natural justice, the appropriate remedy is a quashing order to quash the decision—leaving the decision-maker free to retake it after giving the individual a hearing—rather than a prohibiting order to restrain the implementation of the decision until a hearing had been granted.[141]

6–041

Restrictions on prohibiting orders

Technicalities surrounding the prerogative remedies have largely been cleared away. In particular, a prohibiting order is no longer limited to judicial tribunals taking decisions affecting rights.[142] Like quashing orders, a prohibiting order is in principle available to control any exercise of public law power by a public body. Technical arguments as to whether a quashing rather than a prohibiting order should have been claimed (as the decision has been taken and there is no act left to prohibit) are no longer of importance.[143] Both remedies may be claimed in the same claim for judicial review, or the claim may be amended at a relatively late stage to include additional relief to that originally sought.

6–042

Occasional technicalities which have long outlived their rationale survive. For historical reasons, which no longer seem justified, a prohibiting but not a quashing order will issue to ecclesiastical courts.[144] The courts may not have jurisdiction to intervene in matters of purely military law.[145] A prohibiting order

6–043

---

[136] *R. v Boundary Commission for England Ex p. Foot* [1983] Q.B. 600.

[137] *Estates and Trust Agencies (1927) Ltd v Singapore Improvement Trust* [1937] A.C. 898.

[138] *R. v North Ex p. Oakey* [1927] 1 K.B. 491.

[139] See, e.g. *R. v Horseferry Road Justices Ex p. Independent Broadcasting Authority* [1987] Q.B. 54.

[140] *R. v Liverpool Corp. Ex p. Liverpool Taxi Fleet Operators' Association* (see above, fn.128).

[141] *Att-Gen of Hong Kong v Ng Yuen Shiu* [1983] 2 A.C. 629.

[142] *R. v Greater London Council Ex p. Blackburn* [1976] 1 W.L.R. 550.

[143] See, e.g. *Estates and Trust Agencies (1927) Ltd v Singapore Improvement Trust* (above, fn.131) (prohibiting order would issue to prevent implementation so long as an act other than a ministerial act was left to be performed).

[144] *R. v Chancellor of St. Edmundsbury and Ipswich Diocese Ex p. White* [1948] 1 K.B. 195.

[145] See above para.6–014.

also probably only applies to restrain ultra vires action and does not apply to the implementation of decisions exhibiting an intra vires error of law.[146] This is of very little significance, as virtually all reviewable errors of law render a decision ultra vires. A prohibiting order does not apply to the Crown where the Crown acts personally; again, this is a restriction of little significance.[147] More importantly, a prohibiting order does not lie against superior courts of record; this is discussed above in relation to quashing orders where the same principles apply.[148]

Premature applications for prohibiting orders

6–044   Questions may arise as to whether a prohibiting order is being sought prematurely and whether it would be more appropriate to allow the decision-maker to reach a decision which could, if appropriate, be the subject of a quashing order. This is now only one aspect of the broader issue of premature claims for judicial review where the court may, in its discretion, refuse permission or refuse remedial relief. There is no hard and fast rule dictating when it is premature to seek prohibiting orders.[149] It will be appropriate to apply for such orders where a reviewable error can easily be identified and dealt with quite separately, or where there are advantages in having the matter dealt with before the statutory power is exercised, so the court can consider whether the public body has any jurisdiction or power to act at all in relation to a particular matter[150] or whether the proposed decision-maker is disqualified from acting by the rules of bias.[151] Judicial review by way of a prohibiting order (or a declaration) will also be useful where a public body has adopted a policy governing how it will exercise powers in the future.[152]

Interim relief, standing and the discretionary refusal of prohibiting orders

6–045   The position on interim relief is the same as for quashing orders, and is discussed above. The principles governing standing, and the discretion of the courts to refuse relief are largely similar for all the remedies available on a judicial review claim, and are discussed in Chapters 11 and 12 respectively.

---

[146] See the dicta in *R. v Comptroller-General of Patents and Designs Ex p. Parke, Davis & Co.* [1953] 2 Q.B. 48 (the case turned on other points and was subsequently affirmed on those points by the House of Lords [1954] A.C. 321).

[147] See para.6–015.

[148] See para.6–012.

[149] *R. v Tottenham and District Rent Tribunal Ex p. Northfield (Highgate) Ltd* [1957] 1 Q.B. 103, and see paras 12–013 to 12–018.

[150] [1957] 1 Q.B. 103.

[151] *R. v Kent Police Authority Ex p. Godden* [1971] 2 Q.B. 662.

[152] *R. v Greater London Council Ex p. Blackburn* [1976] 1 W.L.R. 550. Alternatively and more usually, the courts may grant a declaration that the policy is unlawful: *R. v Liverpool City Council Ex p. Secretary of State for Employment* [1989] C.O.D. 404.

Failure to comply with a prohibiting order

Breach of a prohibiting order will be punishable as a contempt of court. The **6–046** principles governing contempt proceedings are the same as those applicable where there is a failure to comply with a mandatory order and are discussed below.[153]

D. MANDATORY ORDERS

The purpose of a mandatory order is to compel the performance of a public **6–047** duty.[154] A public duty is one derived from public law as defined in Chapter 2. A mandatory order will not now be granted to enforce a private law duty, such as a duty to make restitution of money owing.[155] Historically, mandatory orders were used in a wide variety of situations, not all of which would necessarily be treated as public law situations today, such as the restoration of freemen and burgesses to their offices. Such cases are of only historical interest today.

Duty to exercise jurisdiction or discretion

The most common use of mandatory orders in modern times is to compel a public **6–048** body to exercise a jurisdiction to hear and determine a case, or to consider exercising a discretionary power. Courts, tribunals or public bodies may be under a specific duty to hear and determine certain cases, or such a duty may be implicit in the statute setting out their powers. A public body may decline to exercise a jurisdiction altogether, usually as a result of a misconstruction of its statutory remit.[156] In such cases, the courts will usually order the body concerned to hear and determine the matter according to law. A public body may decide a case adversely to the applicant in a way that involves a reviewable error. A court may grant a mandatory order requiring the public authority to reconsider the case according to law. Frequently the courts will grant a quashing order to set aside the unlawful decision together with either a mandatory order, requiring the public authority to redetermine the matter, or an order remitting the matter to the decision-maker for reconsideration.[157]

Public bodies may not be under a duty to act, but may be given a discretion as **6–049** to whether or not to act. Such bodies are under a common law duty to consider whether or not to exercise their discretion. Where a public body fails to consider exercising its discretion or makes a reviewable error in deciding not to exercise it, a mandatory order can issue to order the body to consider according to law whether or not to exercise the discretion.[158]

Mandatory orders may be sought when an individual claims that there has **6–050** been delay in determining an application. In one case, the court held that there

---

[153] See para.6–069.
[154] See Harding, *Public Duties and Public Law*.
[155] *R. v Barnet Magistrates' Court Ex p. Cantor* [1998] 2 All E.R. 333 at 341–344.
[156] See, e.g. *R. v Nottingham County Court Ex p. Byers* [1985] 1 W.L.R. 403.
[157] CPR r.54.19(2).
[158] See, e.g. *R. v Tower Hamlets LBC Ex p. Chetnik Developments* [1988] A.C. 858.

was an implied duty on the Home Secretary to determine applications for certificates proving a right of abode in a reasonable time, and to set up the necessary machinery for this.[159] Similarly, the House of Lords has held that the powers to detain immigrants pending examination by immigration officials must be exercised reasonably and that immigration officials must act reasonably in fixing a time for examination and for arriving at a decision.[160] Other cases have qualified this approach, however, indicating that an applicant could only obtain relief where the delay was *Wednesbury* unreasonable.[161] They have emphasised the dangers of dictating how functions should be performed and how resources are to be deployed in particular areas.[162]

Duty to perform a specific act

6–051   A mandatory order can issue to order a public body to perform a specific act, where statute imposes a clear and qualified duty to do that act. This may take the form of a duty to act imposed on a public body or the conferment of a specific public law right on an individual which he may enforce by way of a mandatory order. In practice, the situations where the courts are willing and able to order a public authority to do a specific act are limited. The courts have granted mandatory orders to compel a local authority to pay sums of money specified by statutory instrument.[163] Even here, the courts may prefer to grant appropriate declarations rather than issue a coercive remedy such as a mandatory order, relying on the public authorities concerned to comply with the duty once it is clearly established.[164] In one case, the court declared that individuals concerned were entitled to be paid specified sums, with liberty to apply for further relief if necessary.[165] In addition, statutory duties which appear absolute in their terms may be held to be subject to implied exceptions for public policy reasons. A statutory duty will not be enforced if this would facilitate the commission of a crime in future. Thus, the Court of Appeal refused a claim for judicial review of a refusal by the Registrar-General to give the claimant a copy of his birth certificate as there was a significant risk that the applicant might attack his biological mother.[166] Nor will the courts enforce a statutory entitlement where to do so

---

[159] *R. v Secretary of State for the Home Department Ex p. Phansopkar* [1976] Q.B. 606.

[160] *R. (Saadi) v Secretary of State for the Home Department* [2002] 1 W.L.R. 3131 at paras 25–26; see also *Tan Te Lam v Superintendent of Tai A Chau Detention Centre* [1997] A.C. 97.

[161] *R. v I.R.C. Ex p. Opman International U.K.* [1986] 1 W.L.R. 568; *R. v Secretary of State for the Home Department Ex p. Rofathullah* [1989] Q.B. 219 (distinguishing *Ex p. Phansopkar* on the grounds that it involved a right to enter and not an individual requiring leave to enter). But see also *R. v Thamesdown BC Ex p. Pritchard* [1989] C.O.D. 377. Much will depend on the statutory context and possibly the view the court takes of the reason for the delay.

[162] See dicta of Purchas LJ in *R. v Secretary of State for Home Department Ex p. Rofathullah* [1989] Q.B. 219.

[163] *R. v Liverpool City Council Ex p. Coade, The Times*, October 10, 1986.

[164] See, e.g. *R. v Secretary of State for the Home Department Ex p. Anderson* [1984] Q.B. 778. See also *R. (van Hoogstraten) v Governor of Belmarsh Prison* [2003] 1 W.L.R. 263 at [47].

[165] *R. v Liverpool City Corp. Ex p. Ferguson* [1985] I.R.L.R. 501.

[166] *R. v Registrar-General Ex p. Smith* [1990] 2 W.L.R. 782.

would involve enabling a person to profit from criminal activities. Thus, a widow who had murdered her husband could not enforce her entitlement to a widow's allowance.[167]

More problematically, the courts sometimes hold that an individual's entitlement is dependent firstly on a public law decision by the public body on whether as a matter of fact or law the individual is entitled to the benefit that he claims. If an individual is challenging a decision that he has no entitlement, the appropriate remedy will be a quashing order to quash the decision, and a mandatory order ordering the body to reconsider the matter according to law (not an order compelling the authority to provide the benefit sought).[168]

6–052

To complicate matters further, a duty imposed by statute may give rise to a private law right, not a public law duty enforceable by a mandatory order.[169] In such circumstances, the private law right is enforceable by ordinary claim for an injunction or damages and not judicial review. It has also been suggested in the past that it was possible to have a situation where the decision as to whether or not a duty was owed was a public law decision, but once a decision had been taken that the duty was owed, that gave rise to a private law right.[170] Challenge to a decision that a duty was not owed would be by way of judicial review; enforcement of a decision that a duty was owed would be by way of injunction and damages. Consequently, a decision that there was no duty to house a person was subject only to judicial review; once a decision had been taken that a person was eligible for housing so that a duty to house was owed, failure to comply with that duty created a private law cause of action.[171] This approach has, however, been disavowed by the House of Lords. The House has rejected the argument that a private law duty could arise when a decision has been taken acknowledging the existence of the duty even though no such duty was owed previously.[172] Thus, no private law cause of action for breach of statutory duty arose either in respect of the initial refusal to accept that a person was entitled to be housed or in respect of a failure to house after the local authority had decided that the person did qualify for housing. In both cases, the appropriate remedy was a public law remedy available in judicial review. This reasoning is likely to be applied generally and is unlikely to be limited to the statutory provisions in the housing field.

6–053

One area where the courts are more prepared to grant a mandatory order to compel a public body to do a specific act involves procedural obligations owed to individuals. A mandatory order will issue to order an inferior court to state a case in appropriate circumstances.[173] Also, common law duties to give an individual a

6–054

---

[167] *R. v Chief National Commissioner Ex p. Connor* [1981] Q.B. 758. See also *R. v Secretary of State for the Home Department Ex p. Puttick* [1981] Q.B. 767 (immigrant who married British citizen not entitled to naturalisation as marriage obtained by fraud and perjury).

[168] *R. v Barnet LBC Ex p. Shah* [1983] 2 A.C. 309.

[169] *Ettridge v Morrell* (1987) 85 L.G.R. 100 (duty to provide schoolroom for election meeting; it is difficult to justify treating this duty as creating a private law right).

[170] *Cocks v Thanet DC* [1983] 2 A.C. 286 at 292–293; *Cato v Ministry of Agriculture Fisheries and Food* [1989] 3 C.M.L.R. 513.

[171] [1989] 3 C.M.L.R. 513.

[172] *O'Rourke v London Borough of Camden* [1998] A.C. 188.

[173] *R. v Bromley Magistrates' Court Ex p. Waitrose* [1980] 3 All E.R. 464; *R. v Croydon Justices Ex p. Lefore Holdings Ltd* [1981] 1 W.L.R. 1465. For a case where mandamus was inappropriate, see *R. v North West Suffolk (Mildenhall) Magistrates' Court Ex p. Forest Health DC* [1997] C.O.D. 352.

fair hearing or disclose information for that purpose[174] may be enforced by way of mandatory orders. The courts have also ordered an inferior court to determine the validity of a byelaw where it is raised as a defence to a criminal charge[175] or to hold a voir dire to determine the admissibility of a confession.[176] On one occasion, a minister was held to be under a duty to enact subordinate legislation, although a declaration, instead of a mandatory order, was granted.[177]

6–055   There are rare occasions when if all the circumstances point to a discretionary power being exercised in a particular way the courts may regard the body as being under a duty to exercise the discretion. The highwater mark of this reasoning was reached in *Padfield*,[178] where the courts indicated in clear terms that a power to refer a complaint to a committee of investigation should be exercised. Even here, a mandatory order only issued requiring the minister to consider according to law whether to refer the complaint and did not order the minister actually to make a reference. Subsequently, in *R. v Secretary of State for Trade and Industry Ex p. Lonrho*,[179] the Divisional Court specifically required a minister to refer a merger to the Monopolies and Mergers Commission even though the minister had a discretion (as opposed to a duty) to refer. This decision was reversed on appeal: the House of Lords refused to accept a form of reasoning which, as they pointed out, would convert a discretion into a duty. *Lonrho* marks a return to the position whereby the courts will not normally grant mandatory orders to compel a public body to exercise a discretion in a particular way,[180] although they will of course quash an unlawful exercise of the discretion and require the public body to reconsider the decision. There are good practical and constitutional reasons for this; it is the public body in whom the power is vested and which will have access to the full range of material relevant to the decision.

Duties derived from EU Law

6–056   One area where rights may become more relevant is in the sphere of European law. Provisions of EU law may confer enforceable rights on individuals which national courts must protect. Decisions interfering with those rights will be quashed. Public bodies may also be required by the courts to do the specific acts necessary to enable European Union law rights to be enjoyed.[181] The courts will frequently be the arbiter of what must be done to ensure the rights are

---

[174] *R. v Kent Police Authority Ex p. Godden* [1972] 2 Q.B. 662 (mandamus to disclose medical reports to applicant's adviser).

[175] *R. v Reading Crown Court Ex p. Hutchinson* [1988] Q.B. 384.

[176] *R. v Liverpool Juvenile Court Ex p. R* [1988] Q.B. 1.

[177] *R. v Secretary of State for the Environment Ex p. Greater London Council, The Times*, December 2, 1983.

[178] *Padfield v Minister for Agriculture, Fisheries and Food* [1968] A.C. 997. See also the alternative reasoning for concluding that there was a duty to make regulations in *R. v Secretary of State for the Environment Ex p. Greater London Council* (see above, fn.171).

[179] The decision of the Divisional Court is reported in *The Times*, January 18, 1989. The decision was reversed by the Court of Appeal (1989) New LJ 150 whose decision was upheld by the House of Lords [1989] 1 W.L.R. 525.

[180] But see subsequently *R. v I.R.C. Ex p. T.C. Coombs & Co.* [1991] 2 W.L.R. 682.

[181] See, e.g. *R. v Minister of Agriculture, Fisheries and Food Ex p. Bell Lines Ltd* [1984] 2 C.M.L.R. 502 (declaration that minister required to designate certain ports as authorised ports of entry for Irish milk).

exercisable, and will not be confined to their more limited role of supervising public bodies to ensure that they do not act unreasonably in the public law sense.[182] This is discussed in detail in Chapter 17.

Duties derived from the European Convention on Human Rights

Certain of the rights guaranteed by the European Convention on Human Rights have been incorporated into domestic law by the Human Rights Act 1998. Certain of these rights also generate positive obligations in certain circumstances. Such obligations may be capable of enforcement by way of a claim for judicial review.   **6–057**

Duties to provide services

Statutes may impose general obligations on public bodies to provide services in the general public interest. It is here that the courts need to be acutely conscious that they do not usurp the role of the administrator by assuming the task of deciding how resources are to be allocated as between competing claims. In practical terms, the situations in which the courts will be able and willing to order a public body to perform its duty, by ordering it to do a specific act, will be infrequent.   **6–058**

Many modern statutory provisions do not lend themselves to enforcement by way of a mandatory order. Provisions which appear to cast duties on public authorities may in fact leave a discretion to the authority as how it should fulfil its duties. A duty to assert and protect legal rights of way, for example, was held to confer a discretion as to how this duty should be performed and in particular, whether it was appropriate to take legal proceedings.[183] The duty on local authorities to provide sufficient primary schooling has been described as a "target duty"[184]: it is for local authorities to determine what is "sufficient" and to decide what steps they should reasonably take to comply with the duty. In such cases, the courts would be unlikely to grant a mandatory order requiring the authority to do specific acts.   **6–059**

Duties that appear to be unqualified may be interpreted by the court as duties to make reasonable efforts or best endeavours. In one case, the court held that a duty to secure accommodation for an individual was a duty to do the best that the public body could do to secure accommodation, as soon as practicable.[185] The court also held that the public body was entitled to consider the needs of the individual against the needs of others on the waiting list, and was not obliged to give automatic priority to the individual. A gloss may sometimes be added to the statute so that a public body which fails to act, but has just cause or excuse for not acting, will not be held in breach.[186] A variant of this is for the courts to hold that   **6–060**

---

[182] [1984] 2 C.M.L.R. 502; *R. v Minister of Agriculture, Fisheries and Food Ex p. Roberts* [1991] 1 C.M.L.R. 555.

[183] *R. v Lancashire CC Ex p. Guyer* [1980] 1 W.L.R. 1024.

[184] *R. v Inner London Education Authority Ex p. Ali* (1990) 2 Admin. L.R. 822.

[185] *R. v Bristol Corp. Ex p. Hendy* [1974] 1 W.L.R. 498. But see also *R. v Newham LBC Ex p. Begum* [2000] 2 All E.R. 72 on the limits to the ability of the courts to read statutory provisions in this way.

[186] *R. v Inner London Education Authority Ex p. Ali*, (1990) 2 Admin. L.R. 822; Meade v Haringey LBC [1979] 1 W.L.R. 637.

a breach has occurred, but to decline to make a mandatory order as a matter of discretion.[187] Some duties may be so vague or general as to be incapable of judicial enforcement.

Duty to comply with orders or directions

6-061   Statutes may confer power on one authority to issue instructions or directions to a subordinate authority requiring it to act. Statute may provide that a mandatory order is available to ensure compliance with any instructions. Thus, the Secretary of State was able to obtain a mandatory order compelling a local authority to comply with instructions to dispose of land.[188] Default powers are frequently enforceable by way of a mandatory order in this way. In the field of education, for example, duties to provide education facilities are imposed on local authorities: the Secretary of State may issue instructions if the authority fails to perform its duties,[189] or acts unreasonably,[190] and may enforce such instructions by a mandatory order. Similar default powers may be found in other fields. An application for a mandatory order may be successfully resisted if the instructions are shown to be unlawful.[191]

Restrictions on the availability of mandatory orders

Superior court

6-062   A mandatory order does not lie against superior courts. The principles applicable to quashing orders apply to mandatory orders, and are discussed above.[192] This is the most significant restriction on mandatory orders.

The Crown

6-063   A mandatory order does not lie against the Crown or a Minister of the Crown, when acting purely as a servant of the Crown for the purpose of performing a duty owed by the Crown.[193] This doctrine was invoked on a number of occasions during the nineteenth century to justify the refusal of a mandatory order against ministers. The courts held that a mandatory order was not available to compel the Secretary of State to pay a pension due under royal warrant issued under the prerogative.[194] The courts also held in the last century that duties imposed on ministers could be owed to the Crown, and not to the public, and therefore be unenforceable. A mandatory order was not therefore available to compel the Inland Revenue to pay out money provided by Parliament, as the money was granted to the Crown and the duties of the Revenue were owed exclusively to the

---

[187]   *R. v Secretary of State for the Environment Ex p. Lee* (1987) 54 P. & C.R. 311; *R. v Newham LBC Ex p. Begum* [2000] 2 All E.R. 72 at 79g–j.
[188]   *R. v Secretary of State for the Environment Ex p. Manchester City Council* (1987) 85 L.G.R. 832.
[189]   Education Act 1996 s.497.
[190]   Education Act 1996 s.496.
[191]   *Secretary of State for Education and Science v Tameside MBC* [1977] A.C. 1014.
[192]   See para.6–012.
[193]   *R. v Powell* (1841) 1 Q.B. 352.
[194]   *R. v Secretary of State for War* [1891] 2 Q.B. 326.

Crown.[195] This approach has not been followed in modern case law. Where statute imposes a duty on ministers of the Crown or other Crown servants, as is the usual practice in modern times, the duties will be construed as duties owed to the public, not the Crown, and mandatory orders will be available at the suit of a person with standing to enforce that duty.[196] Difficulties could arise if legislative practice altered, and a statute imposed a duty specifically on the Crown as opposed to a named minister.

Difficulties could also arise in relation to prerogative powers exercised by the sovereign. One option would be for the courts to recognise that in modern constitutional terms, powers are in reality exercised by the Crown on the advice of ministers. There may be situations where a minister refuses unlawfully to consider whether or not to advise the Sovereign to do a particular act, such as refusing to consider whether a pardon should be granted. The relief could focus on the minister's unlawful refusal to consider exercising the discretion to advise the Sovereign. The courts could grant a quashing order to quash the refusal, and a mandatory order to compel the minister to consider according to law whether or not to advise the Sovereign. There are signs that the courts may reach this conclusion. The Privy Council has suggested obiter that as the Malaysian Head of State had to exercise his functions on the advice of the responsible minister, a mandatory order would lie against the minister to order him to advise the Head of State to perform his duty.[197] It should also be noted that the courts have indicated that quashing orders are now available to quash a decision actually taken by a minister in the exercise of the prerogative. This suggests that the courts are prepared to look at the reality of the exercise of power and will not be deterred, by constitutional fictions, from granting relief where appropriate.[198] Even if the courts could not separate out the minister from the Crown for remedial purposes, a declaration would be available against the Crown,[199] which although not coercive, is unlikely to be disobeyed.

6–064

These developments would restrict the immunity of the Crown only to those powers personally exercised by the Sovereign: a result which would be more in accordance with modern constitutional theory. There are few powers which are exercisable personally by the Sovereign and even fewer which are justiciable. One of the few that could conceivably arise is the appointment of a Prime Minister where no party commands a parliamentary majority. In such circumstances it is inconceivable that the courts would grant a mandatory order requiring a particular appointment or requiring the crown to make an appointment. The usual reasons given are that, as the remedies emanate from the Crown, it is incongruous for the Crown to command itself and, far more importantly, disobedience of the order would amount to contempt of court. It is

6–065

---

[195] *R. v Lords Commissioners of the Treasury* (1872) L.R. 7 Q.B. 387.

[196] *R. v Commissioners of Customs and Excise Ex p. Cook* [1970] 1 W.L.R. 450; *R. v I.R.C. Ex p. National Federation of Self-Employed and Small Businesses Ltd* [1982] A.C. 617 and see dicta of Lord Woolf in *M v Home Office* [1994] 1 A.C. 377 at 425.

[197] *Teh Cheng Poh v Public Prosecutor, Malaysia* [1980] A.C. 458.

[198] *R. v Secretary of State for Foreign and Commonwealth Affairs Ex p. Everett* [1989] Q.B. 811; *R. v Secretary of State for the Home Department Ex p. Bentley* [1994] Q.B. 349.

[199] Such a declaration would, perversely, probably have to be sought by way of ordinary action since it is unlikely that the Senior Courts Act 1981 s.31 binds the Crown. See *R. v Secretary of State for the Home Department Ex p. Herbage* [1987] Q.B. 872 at 885 and para.2–179.

possible that a declaration could issue but it is equally likely that the courts would decline to intervene on the grounds that the issue was not justiciable.

Matters of military law

6–066   There is authority that the courts cannot intervene in matters of military conduct and purely military law affecting discipline. Thus, a mandatory order would not lie to compel a court of inquiry to complete its investigation of alleged disciplinary offences.[200] The relevance of these authorities for the modern day is considered above in connection with quashing orders where the same limitations apply.[201]

Technical restrictions

6–067   There is old authority requiring the claimant to have made an express demand for the authority to act and for the authority to have refused.[202] In modern terms this formalistic approach is unlikely to be required. The public body is likely to be aware of the need to act, from the conduct of the parties, and the circumstances of the case, rather than a formal demand and refusal. In the case of an individual seeking to compel performance of a duty owed specifically to him, it is extremely unlikely that the individual would not have made an application first. In the case of duties owed to the public generally, the courts are unlikely to be deterred from granting mandatory orders because of the absence of a formal demand, provided that it is clear from the evidence that the authority is unwilling to perform the duty in question.[203] A mandatory order can issue to prevent an apprehended breach of duty.[204]

6–068   There is also old authority that mandatory orders will not lie to undo acts already done.[205] Providing the factual situation is suitable for the grant of a mandatory order, there is no longer any reason to regard this as a restriction. As the other remedies would be available in the context of judicial review, there would seem no valid reason for resurrecting ancient technicalities where mandatory orders are otherwise appropriate. Similarly, ancient case law suggesting that mandatory orders will not lie to minor officials can be consigned to history.

---

[200]   *R. v Army Council Ex p. Ravenscroft* [1917] 2 K.B. 504.

[201]   See above para.6–014.

[202]   *The State (Modern Homes (Ireland)) Ltd v Dublin Corp.* [1953] I.R. 202; *R. v Brecknock & Abergavenny Canal Co.* (1835) 3 Ad. & E. 217.

[203]   But see *R. v Kent CC Ex p. Bruce, The Times*, February 8, 1986 (mandatory injunction, not a mandatory order, sought to enforce duties under Chronically Sick and Disabled Person Act 1970—before an individual could establish breach must identify precise needs, make express request and for local authority clearly to have failed to satisfy request).

[204]   *Fleming v Lees* [1991] C.O.D. 50.

[205]   *R. v Hanley Revising Barrister* [1912] 3 K.B. 518.

Effect of a mandatory order

A public body is obliged to comply with a mandatory order. Where the order is **6–069** addressed to a corporate body, it is addressed to each member of that body.[206] Failure to comply is a contempt of court which may be punished by a fine or imprisonment. In the case of corporate bodies, the individuals who have control of the corporate body should be named in the writ of attachment.[207] Findings of contempt may also be made against a government department or a minister acting in his official capacity[208]. In these situations, the contempt jurisdiction is not personal or punitive. It would, therefore, not be appropriate to impose a fine or sequestrate the assets of the department nor would imprisonment be imposed. Rather, the very fact of a finding of contempt against a minister or department is considered sufficient vindication of the rule of law and sufficient to ensure that orders of the courts are obeyed. The finding of contempt will be normally made against the minister acting in his official capacity as the order granted in judicial review will normally have been made against the minister.[209] In exceptional circumstances, a minister may be personally liable for contempt if he has himself engaged in action which amounts to a default. Normally, however, the appropriate action will be to make a finding of contempt against the minister acting in his official capacity rather than his personal capacity. Where, therefore, the Home Office failed to comply with an interim injunction, the appropriate finding was one of contempt by the Secretary of State for the Home Department (that is, the minister acting in his official capacity) rather than against the Home Secretary personally.[210]

Interim relief

There is no provision in the CPR for the grant of interim relief where the claimant **6–070** seeks a mandatory order (that is, the prerogative order formerly called mandamus). In practice, this is not a problem as injunctions, including a mandatory interim injunction, may now be granted against public bodies in a claim for judicial review.[211]

Standing and discretion to refuse a remedy

Standing and discretionary grounds for refusing relief are common to all **6–071** remedies available on a judicial review application, and are considered in Chapters 11 and 12 respectively. Mention may be made here of one ground for refusing relief which has figured particularly in cases involving mandatory orders, namely the existence of alternative remedies. A statute may impose a duty and provide a remedy for non-compliance, such as complaint to a minister who is empowered to order a public body to perform its duty. In such circumstances, the

---

[206] *R. v Poplar BC Ex p. London CC (No.2)* [1922] 1 K.B. 95.
[207] [1922] 1 K.B. 95.
[208] *M. v Home Office* [1994] 1 A.C. 377. Or, it seems, public authorities: see *R (JM) v Croydon LBC Practice Note* [2010] 1 W.L.R. 1658 at [10]–[12].
[209] [1994] 1 A.C. 377 at 425E–F.
[210] [1994] 1 A.C. 377 at 425F–427F.
[211] *R. v Kensington and Chelsea RLBC Ex p. Hammell* [1989] Q.B. 518.

courts have in the past held that the remedy is intended to be an exclusive remedy and the courts may not grant a mandatory order to compel the performance of the duty.[212] The courts have tended to regard the existence of an alternative remedy as a factor relevant to the courts discretion to refuse a remedy, rather than a jurisdictional barrier to the grant of a mandatory order.[213] This would bring the position into line with the general principles governing all public law remedies. The existence of such default powers may also be influential in persuading a court to grant a declaration that a public body is in breach of its duty rather than granting a mandatory order leaving it to the minister to exercise his powers to issue directions specifying precisely what the public body is required to do.[214]

---

[212] *Pasmore v Oswaldtwistle UDC* [1898] A.C. 387; *R. v Kensington and Chelsea RLBC Ex p. Birdwood* (1976) 74 L.G.R. 424. For a fuller discussion see below at paras 12–078 to 12–085.

[213] See, e.g. *R. v Secretary of State for the Environment Ex p. Lee* (1985) 54 P. & C.R. 311 and *R. v Secretary of State for the Environment Ex p. Ward* [1984] 1 W.L.R. 834.

[214] *R. v Secretary of State for the Environment Ex p. Lee* [1984] 1 W.L.R. 834. But see *R. v Inner London Education Authority Ex p. Ali* (1990) 2 Admin. L.R. 822.

CHAPTER 7

Declarations

A. INTRODUCTION

Declaratory relief plays a significant role in both private and public law disputes. Such relief declares what the legal position is or what the rights of the parties are. In public law cases declarations may, and now usually must, be sought by way of a claim for judicial review. Here the declaration is primarily used to declare that a particular decision or action of a public body is ultra vires and a nullity, or to determine the existence and scope of public law powers and public law duties or to declare actions of a public body unlawful as they are incompatible with rights derived from the European Convention on Human Rights.[1] In addition, courts may in appropriate circumstances grant a declaration that provisions of primary legislation are incompatible with Convention rights.[2]

7–001

B. HISTORICAL OUTLINE

The history of the declaration has been fully traced by Zamir[3] and de Smith.[4] In brief, the courts were traditionally hostile to granting purely declaratory relief as a general remedy.[5] The Court of Chancery had a settled practice of not granting declaratory relief where other consequential relief was not or could not be sought. Legislative action was required to overcome this judicial antagonism. In 1852, an Act was passed providing that the courts could grant binding declarations of right without granting consequential relief.[6] The courts narrowly construed this as permitting the grant of declaratory relief only in cases where the courts could have granted consequential relief (but did not do so). The Act was not interpreted as encouraging the use of pure declarations in cases where consequential relief was not available in any event. Rules of the Supreme Court were first enacted to

7–002

---

[1] Human Rights Act 1998 s.6.
[2] Human Rights Act 1998 s.4.
[3] Zamir and Woolf, *The Declaratory Judgment*, 3rd edn (2002), Ch.2.
[4] De Smith, *Judicial Review*, 7th edn. (2013) 15-060–15-073.
[5] The special position of declaratory relief in relation to the Crown is discussed below at paras 7–063 to 7–064.
[6] Court of Chancery Procedure Act 1852 s.50.

deal with this problem in 1883.[7] The relevant provision today is contained in CPR r.40.20 which provides that the "court may make binding declarations whether or not any other remedy is claimed".

7–003   The rule confirms the general availability of the grant of declaratory relief and makes it clear that the fact that consequential relief could not be claimed is no bar to the granting of pure declarations of right. The courts may therefore grant declarations of right even where the claimant has no cause of action entitling him to relief other than the claim for the declaration itself.

7–004   The change in judicial attitudes to the declaration came in the case of *Dyson v Att-Gen.*[8] The Inland Revenue Commissioners required Dyson to provide a statement of the annual value of his land or face a penalty for non-compliance with the request. Dyson brought an action for a declaration that the demand was ultra vires the Commissioners' statutory powers. The Court of Appeal held that the action for a declaration was a proper method of proceeding, and rejected arguments that the proper course was for Dyson to wait until a penalty for non-compliance was imposed and challenge that either directly or by setting up the invalidity of the demand as a defence. The judgments were fulsome in their praise of the action for a declaration as a convenient and suitable procedure for determining whether statutory powers had been lawfully exercised. Since then the courts have abandoned their historic distrust of declaratory judgments, and the declaration has become a useful and widely used remedy in both private and public law.[9]

Pre-1978 position

7–005   Until 1978, declarations in either a public law or private law matter were sought by action instituted either by writ or originating summons. Individuals were faced with a choice of either seeking the prerogative remedies or bringing an action for a declaration. The declaration possessed certain advantages in that:

(a)   there was no need to seek permission to institute proceedings;
(b)   disclosure was automatic;
(c)   time limits were longer;
(d)   the declaration did not suffer from the technicalities which then surrounded the prerogative remedies;
(e)   there was no need to consider whether a body was under a duty to act judicially; and
(f)   there was no need to distinguish between public and private bodies since the declaration, unlike the prerogative remedies, applied to both.

---

[7]   Originally in Ord.25 r.5; made pursuant to powers conferred by the Judicature Acts 1873 and 1875. The Court of Appeal in *Guaranty Trust Co. of New York v Hannay & Co.* [1915] 2 K.B. 536 held that the court had always had jurisdiction to grant pure declarations but had adopted a settled practice of not granting them; the rule merely altered this practice and so was intra vires the power conferred by the Judicature Act 1875 s.17 to make rules for the practice and procedure.

[8]   [1911] 1 K.B. 410 (deciding that the courts did have jurisdiction to grant a declaration). Also [1912] 1 Ch. 158 (deciding that the demand was ultra vires and a declaration to that effect should be granted).

[9]   See Zamir and Woolf (above, fn.3), Chs 2 and 3.

On the other hand, the test for standing was stricter, as the individual had to show that the action complained of affected a specific legal right or caused him special damage over and above that suffered by the public generally.[10]

7–006

Position from 1978 onwards

The procedural position has now changed considerably. The 1977 reforms to the judicial review procedure, which came into force in 1978, made declarations and injunctions available alongside the prerogative remedies in an application for judicial review.[11] The declaration was clearly seen as performing a public law role in controlling public power, and not only a private law role in vindicating private law rights. The division between public law and private law matters was further emphasised by *O'Reilly v Mackman*.[12] The House of Lords held that declarations in public law matters should normally be brought by way of judicial review and could not be brought by way of the ordinary claim procedure (declarations in private law matters continue to be available by ordinary claim). The exceptions to this rule are discussed in Chapter 3.

7–007

The result of this development is that in public law cases the prerogative remedies, and the declaration and injunction are obtained by the same procedure with the same rules on time limits, discovery and cross-examinations, and a uniform test for standing. The discretionary principles governing the grant of relief will apply equally to all the remedies obtainable by way of judicial review. There has been a division of private and public law and a harmonisation of the principles governing remedial relief in the public law sphere. The price to be paid for this harmonisation lies in the fact that it is not always easy to determine whether a case is properly classified as public law or private law. Individuals who seek a declaration by ordinary claim may lose their action because they have used the wrong procedure, not because their case lacks merit, and it may then be too late to bring a claim for judicial review. The implications of this are considered in Chapter 3.

7–008

C.   USES OF THE DECLARATION IN PUBLIC LAW

The extent of the jurisdiction to grant declaratory relief is extremely broad. Over the years it has become clear that the courts will grant declaratory relief wherever a real issue arises between parties who have a genuine interest in contesting the issue, and where there is a need for some relief to be granted.[13] On occasions the

7–009

---

[10]   *Gregory v Camden LBC* [1966] 1 W.L.R. 899; *Gouriet v Union of Post Office Workers* [1978] A.C. 435.

[11]   And these were placed on a statutory footing by s.31 of the Senior Courts Act 1981.

[12]   [1983] 2 A.C. 237.

[13]   See dicta of Woolf LJ in *R. v Secretary of State for Social Services Ex p. Child Poverty Action Group* [1989] 3 W.L.R. 1116 at 1127–1128. See also dicta of Lord Dunedin in *Russian Commercial and Industrial Bank v British Bank for Foreign Trade Ltd* [1921] 2 A.C. 438 at 448, approved by Viscount Kilmuir in *Vine v National Dock Labour Board* [1957] A.C. 488 at 500, and *Re F* [1989] 2 W.L.R. 1025. For a restrictive approach in the private law area, see *Meadows Indemnity Co. Ltd v Insurance Corp. of Ireland Plc* [1989] 2 Lloyd's Rep. 298.

simple desire to vindicate the law by establishing that a public body has acted unlawfully has been the reason for granting a declaration in public law cases.[14]

7–010   Declaratory relief has the advantage of being uniquely flexible, in that the courts may in their own words identify and particularise what is objectionable in legal terms. This has enabled the declaration to be used not only for the primary purpose of establishing whether or not particular administrative action or inaction is unlawful, but also to perform an ancillary role in clarifying the consequences of a finding of invalidity, or settling other questions of public law that need to be resolved.

7–011   The classification adopted here is used simply for descriptive purposes; it is not exhaustive. The situations in which declaratory relief may be granted are not closed. Given the flexibility of the remedy and the variety of situations in which public law powers and duties are exercised, new examples of the use of declaratory relief are likely to arise.

To establish whether a decision, order, conduct or other act is ultra vires

7–012   Declarations may be granted declaring a particular decision or action by a public body to be unlawful and ultra vires. Declarations may be used to establish the invalidity of all the types of administrative actions discussed in Chapter 4. Decisions or orders of inferior courts and tribunals may be declared invalid.[15] The courts have declared invalid a wide range of actions including, for example:

(a)   a decision of the Home Secretary to revoke a television licence[16];

(b)   a resolution of a local education authority to appoint an advertising agency[17];

(c)   a supplementary precept issued by a local authority[18];

(d)   a policy adopted by magistrates not to disclose the names of magistrates sitting on individual cases[19]; and

(e)   a policy of a local authority not to provide housing to families with children where the family was found to be intentionally homeless.[20]

Reports and recommendations may also be declared void and of no effect.[21] The non-statutory decisions of public bodies may be quashed by a quashing order or declared invalid.[22] Non-statutory circulars giving incorrect legal advice may also be declared ultra vires or unlawful, in that the advice is erroneous and cannot

---

[14]   *R. v Avon CC Ex p. Rexworthy* (1989) 58 P. & C.R. 356.

[15]   *Anisminic v Foreign Compensation Commission* [1969] 2 A.C. 147.

[16]   *Congreve v Home Office* [1976] Q.B. 629.

[17]   *R. v Inner London Education Authority Ex p. Westminster City Council* [1986] 1 W.L.R. 28.

[18]   *Bromley LBC v Greater London Council* [1983] 1 A.C. 768.

[19]   *R. v Felixstowe Justices Ex p. Leigh* [1987] Q.B. 582.

[20]   *Att-Gen, ex rel. Tilley v Wandsworth LBC* [1981] 1 W.L.R. 854.

[21]   *Grunwick Processing Laboratories v Advisory, Conciliation and Arbitration Service* [1978] A.C. 655; *R. v Hallstrom Ex p. W (No.2)* [1986] Q.B. 1090; *R. v Local Commissioner for Administration Ex p. Croydon LBC* [1989] 1 All E.R. 1033.

[22]   For quashing orders see, *R. v Norfolk CC Social Services Department Ex p. M* [1989] Q.B. 619. For declarations see, *R. v Panel on Take-overs and Mergers Ex p. Datafin* [1987] Q.B. 815.

be relied upon.[23] The courts may grant declarations as to whether particular conduct is or would be lawful. In one case, the court granted a declaration that a local education authority's proposed arrangements for selective education for boys and girls were unlawful as the arrangements would violate the provisions of the Sex Discrimination Act 1975.[24] Declarations have been granted that a chief constable acted unlawfully in preventing demonstrators travelling to a demonstration and requiring them to return to London[25] and that immigration officers operating at Prague airport discriminated against Roma seeking to travel to the United Kingdom by treating them less favourably contrary to the Race Relations Act 1976.[26] The court declared that the refusal of a police officer who had detained a person at an airport to wait for the arrival of the detainee's solicitor before questioning him was unlawful.[27]

The House of Lords has expressed the view that a quashing order remains the primary and most appropriate remedy where all that is sought is the quashing of a decision, even though the same result could be achieved by a declaration.[28] There is, however, no perceivable rule governing which remedy to use and no particular pattern emerges from the case law. It is ultimately a matter for the discretion of the court. Declarations have certain advantages in terms of flexibility. The courts may wish to avoid granting coercive relief, particularly where the public body may need time to respond to the judgment and more than one means of remedying the unlawful conduct needs to be considered. In one case, for example, the court refused to grant an order quashing a refusal to permit a prisoner access to the media. The court did grant a declaration that a policy restricting a prisoner from speaking to the media by telephone unless prior details were provided in advance and the interview was pre-recorded was unlawful but declined to grant further orders as the precise policy to be adopted, and the safeguards to be incorporated, were matters for the public authorities to determine.[29] Similarly, the courts have granted declarations that a policy governing the retention of data or photographs is unlawful but declined to quash the decision authorising the retention in order to give sufficient time for new legislation, or a new policy, to be adopted so that the retention of material could be assessed under those provisions.[30] Courts have on occasions granted both a

7–013

---

[23] *Gillick v West Norfolk and Wisbech Area Health Authority* [1986] A.C. 112.

[24] *R. v Birmingham City Council Ex p. Equal Opportunities Commission* [1989] A.C. 1155.

[25] *R. (Laporte) v Chief Constable of Gloucestershire* [2007] A.C. 105.

[26] *R. (European Roma Rights Centre) v Immigration Officer at Prague Airport* [2005] 2 A.C. 1 at [194].

[27] *R. (Elosta) v Commissioner of Police of the Metropolis* [2014] 1 W.L.R. 239 at [54].

[28] *Cocks v Thanet DC* [1983] A.C. 286. The courts have also considered it preferable to quash parts of unlawful guidance rather than simply declaring which parts were unlawful: see supplementary judgment in *R (Independent Schools Council) v Charities Commission* [2012] Ch.214.

[29] *R. (Hirst) v Secretary of State for the Home Department* [2002] 1 W.L.R. 2929 at [86]–[88]; *R. v Birmingham City Council Ex p. Equal Opportunities Commission* (see above, fn.24) where the court refused to grant a mandatory order.

[30] See *R. (GC) v Commissioner of Police of the Metropolis (Liberty intervening)* [2011] 2 W.L.R. 1230 esp. at [45]–[49]; *R. (C) v Commissioner of Police of the Metropolis* [2012] 1 W.L.R. 3007 at [56]–[58].

quashing order and a declaration that an act is ultra vires and void.[31] This is usually done where there is a need to confirm the consequences of finding that a measure is invalid.

To establish the invalidity of subordinate legislation

7–014 Statutory instruments have been declared invalid in whole or in part.[32] Rules of procedure made pursuant to statute have been declared unlawful.[33] Standing orders governing prisoners have also been declared invalid.[34] There was in the past some doubt as to whether a quashing order was available to challenge subordinate legislation,[35] and declarations tended to be the favoured remedy.

7–015 Declarations are the appropriate remedy when an applicant is challenging the validity of delegated legislation which is to be laid before Parliament for approval. The courts will not normally grant a quashing order to set aside a draft Order in Council submitted to Parliament for approval,[36] or a prohibiting order where this would have the effect of preventing Parliament considering draft subordinate legislation.[37] Declarations may be granted before a draft instrument is laid before Parliament and even while it is actually before Parliament. A declaration in such circumstances is not regarded by the courts as undue interference with the process of Parliament at least so long as the courts confine themselves to determining whether the instrument is ultra vires the parent statute.[38]

To specify the consequences of a finding of invalidity

7–016 The consequences of a finding of invalidity may normally be deduced from the fact that the act is retrospectively a nullity and incapable of producing legal effects. This is explained in Chapter 5. The courts may, where appropriate, grant a declaration specifying precisely what consequences flow from a finding that an act is ultra vires. In one case, the court granted a quashing order to quash a decision to grant a tenancy and a declaration that the purported tenancy was void, thereby making it clear that the public law consequences of nullity affected the private law agreement.[39] On another occasion, the courts declared that regulations permitting the issuing of a certificate terminating judicial review proceedings were ultra vires and declared that existing judicial review

---

[31] See, e.g. *A v HM Treasury* [2012] 1 A.C. 245; Bromley LBC v Greater London Council (see above, fn.18).
[32] See, e.g. *R. v Lord Chancellor Ex p. Witham* [1998] Q.B. 575 at 586H; *R. v Secretary of State for the Home Department Ex p. Leech* [1994] Q.B. 198; *R. v Secretary of State for Social Security Ex p. Joint Council for the Welfare of Immigrants* [1997] 1 W.L.R. 275; *R. v Customs and Excise Commissioners Ex p. Hedges & Butler* [1986] 2 All E.R. 164; *R. v I.R.C. Ex p. Woolwich Equitable Building Society* [1990] 1 W.L.R. 1400.
[33] *R v Secretary of State for the Home Department Ex p. Saleem* [2001] 1 W.L.R. 443.
[34] *R. v Secretary of State for the Home Department Ex p. Anderson* [1984] Q.B. 778.
[35] See para.6–008.
[36] *R. v HM Treasury Ex p. Smedley* [1985] Q.B. 657.
[37] *R. v Boundary Commission for England Ex p. Foot* [1983] Q.B. 600.
[38] *R. v H.M. Treasury Ex p. Smedley* [1985] Q.B. 657.
[39] *R. v Port Talbot BC Ex p. Jones* [1988] 2 All E.R. 207.

proceedings remained in existence.[40] A more unusual case is *R. v Chief Constable of North Wales Police Ex p. Evans*.[41] Following a disciplinary inquiry conducted in breach of natural justice, the Chief Constable threatened to dismiss Evans from the police force unless he resigned his post as a probationary police constable. Evans resigned. The House of Lords refused as a matter of discretion to grant a mandatory order requiring the Chief Constable to re-appoint Evans. Their Lordships did, however, grant a declaration that the Chief Constable had acted unlawfully and that Evans was entitled to all the remedies, short of re-instatement, that he would have had if in fact he had been unlawfully dismissed.[42] In another case,[43] the Divisional Court declared that the Home Secretary's policy of treating prisoners transferred to a mental hospital as if they were not serving part of their sentence was unlawful and granted further declarations as to the status of the prisoners whilst in hospital.

To determine the extent of the powers of a public body

Doubts may arise as to the scope of powers conferred on a public body. Declarations are a convenient method of determining the extent of powers. There are a number of examples of such declarations being granted. Where questions arose as to the extent of the statutory powers of the Lord Chancellor concerning property transfer schemes relating to magistrates' courts, the court granted declarations that he had no power to effect a grant of a new lease or a transfer of existing leases or freeholds of certain buildings.[44] The Divisional Court has granted a declaration that statutory powers to disperse persons aged under 16 from particular areas did not include a power to use force in doing so.[45] In one case,[46] doubt arose as to the extent to which the Greater London Council was empowered to make grants to London Transport, following a House of Lords ruling that earlier proposals were unlawful.[47] Before implementing new proposals, the GLC obtained a declaration that the new proposals were within their statutory powers and that it was lawful for London Transport to comply with them.   **7–017**

A declaration has been sought by the Home Office to determine the extent to which the Commission for Racial Equality was empowered to investigate alleged   **7–018**

---

[40] *R (Ignaoua) v Secretary of State for the Home Department* [2014] 1 W.L.R. 651.

[41] [1982] 1 W.L.R. 1155. Where a person is unlawfully dismissed, the usual remedy is a remedy quashing the dismissal or declaring it unlawful: see *McLaughlin v Governor of the Cayman Islands* [2007] 1 W.L.R. 2839 at [14]–[16] and see para.5–016 above.

[42] Lord Brightman suggested that Evans might be able to bring an action for damages. However, Evans had no contract of employment, and no action for breach of statutory duty lies in relation to the relevant regulations (see *Calveley v Chief Constable of Merseyside Police* [1989] A.C. 1228). Wade suggests the tort of intimidation, see (1983) 99 L.Q.R. 171.

[43] *R. v Secretary of State for the Home Department Ex p. T.* [1994] Q.B. 378. See also *R. v Secretary of State for the Home Department Ex p. Simms* [1999] 3 W.L.R. 328 (declarations granted that policy of the Home Secretary and decisions of certain prison governors pursuant to that policy were unlawful).

[44] *R. (Lord Chancellor) v Chief Land Register* [2006] Q.B. 795.

[45] *R. (W) v Commissioner of the Metropolitan Police* [2005] 1 W.L.R. 3706.

[46] *R. v London Transport Executive Ex p. Greater London Council* [1983] Q.B. 484.

[47] *Bromley LBC v Greater London Council* (see above, fn.18).

discrimination in the performance of immigration functions.[48] The courts have granted a declaration that the Broadcasting Complaints Commission had jurisdiction to investigate a complaint that the policy of the broadcasting organisations on overall coverage of political events was unfair as to a particular political party, and was not restricted to investigating personal complaints of unfair treatment in a specific broadcast.[49] The courts have considered whether public bodies have power to dispose of land without first hearing objections[50]; whether the consent of the Secretary of State was necessary before a tenant could buy a council house situated in the green belt,[51] and; whether a public body intending to sell land had first to offer the land to previous owners.[52] A declaration was granted that a police authority had power to provide financial assistance to existing and former police officers in respect of expenses incurred in relation to private prosecutions brought against them and judicial review proceedings in which they were involved.[53]

7–019   The jurisdiction to grant declarations in appropriate cases as to the scope of a body's statutory powers is a useful one. While declarations originated in the field of private law, they have been extended into the public law field. Public bodies possess rights but more often and just as importantly they have a wide range of powers. Restricting the jurisdiction to grant declarations to questions of rights is therefore unsound and unhelpful.[54] It is often as necessary to determine the powers of a public body as it is to determine the extent of their rights. Provided a real question of law arises, and an appropriate defendant can be found,[55] the current practice of the courts in granting declarations as to the extent of a public body's powers is a salutary one.

To determine the existence and extent of public duties

7–020   Declarations may be granted to determine that a public duty exists, to clarify the scope of a duty or to determine whether there has been a breach of the duty. The courts have, for example, declared that a local authority was in breach of its statutory duty to provide adequate accommodation for gypsies[56]; that a minister was in breach of a statutory duty to consult interested parties before making subordinate legislation[57]; and that a local authority was under a statutory duty to

---

[48] *Home Office v Commission for Racial Equality* [1982] Q.B. 385. Such declarations should now be sought by judicial review not ordinary claim: *O'Reilly v Mackman* [1983] 2 A.C. 237.

[49] *R. v Broadcasting Complaints Commission Ex p. Owen* [1985] Q.B. 1153.

[50] *R. v Doncaster MBC Ex p. Braim* (1986) 57 P. & C.R. 1.

[51] *R. v Secretary of State for the Environment Ex p. Enfield LBC* (1988) 86 L.G.R. 549.

[52] *R. v Commission for the New Towns Ex p. Tomkins and Leach* (1988) 58 P. & C.R. 57.

[53] *R. v Director of Public Prosecutions Ex p. Duckenfield* [2000] 1 W.L.R. 55.

[54] The decision in *R. v Secretary of State for Education Ex p. Birmingham City Council* judgment May 14, 1991, that courts could only grant declarations as to the rights of a public body and the courts could not grant a declaration in respect of the responsibilities of a local education authority to ensure that its arrangements for education did not violate the Sex Discrimination Act 1975, no longer reflects the scope of the law on this issue.

[55] It may be difficult to find an appropriate defendant, i.e. someone with an interest in ensuring all relevant arguments on the point of law are put before the court.

[56] *R. v Secretary of State for the Environment Ex p. Lee* (1987) 54 P. & C.R. 311; *R. v Avon CC Ex p. Rexworthy* (see above, fn.14).

[57] *R. v Secretary of State for Social Services Ex p. Association of Metropolitan Authorities* [1986] 1 W.L.R. 1.

pay lecturers their wages.[58] The courts have also declared that the government was under a duty imposed by EU law not to implement a state aid until approved by the European Commission,[59] and that a minister was obliged to designate certain ports as authorised ports of entry for milk imports.[60] Statutes also impose general duties on public authorities to have due regard in the exercise of their functions to the need to eliminate discrimination on such grounds as, for example, race, sex and disability.[61] The courts have granted a declaration that the Secretary of State failed to comply with his duty to have due regard to this duty when setting up an ex-gratia compensation scheme for former prisoners of war.[62] Similarly the courts declared that a governing body had failed to have regard to this duty when adopting a policy on admissions criteria.[63]

Declarations may be considered more appropriate than mandatory orders, particularly when the duty is a duty to provide general services. A court may prefer to declare that a duty exists or that a public body is in breach, on the assumption that a responsible authority will remedy the consequences of a breach.[64] This may be preferable, at least in the first instance, to granting coercive remedies, which could result in a public body being in contempt of court if they failed adequately to remedy the breach. The courts may grant liberty to apply for further relief to ensure that the claimant can return to the court if that should prove necessary.[65] Ministers may have power to direct a local authority to take specified actions if it is in breach of its statutory duties. In such circumstances, a court may prefer simply to declare that the local authority is breach leaving the appropriate minister to issue directions as to how the breach should be remedied, thus avoiding a conflict between the courts and the minister as to what action is necessary to remedy the breach.[66]

7–021

To determine rights

Courts do sometimes exercise an original jurisdiction to declare rights as opposed to a supervisory jurisdiction to determine whether an exercise of public law power is ultra vires. This usually occurs in the sphere of private law where the

7–022

---

[58] *R. v Liverpool City Corp. Ex p. Ferguson* [1985] I.R.L.R. 501.

[59] *R. v Att-Gen Ex p. I.C.I. Plc* [1987] 1 C.M.L.R. 72.

[60] *R. v Minister for Agriculture, Fisheries and Food Ex p. Bell Lines & An Bord Bainne Co-operative (Irish Dairy Board)* [1984] 2 C.M.L.R. 502.

[61] Equality Act 2010 s.149.

[62] At first instance, in *R. v (Elias) v Secretary of State for Defence* [2005] IRLR 788. There was no appeal on this point to the Court of Appeal [2006] 1 W.L.R. 3213 at [274].

[63] *R. (E) v Governing Body of JFS and others* [2008] EWHC 1535/1538 (Admin). See also *R. (Chadva and others) v London Borough of Harrow* [2007] EWHC 3004 (Admin) (local authority acted unlawfully in failing to have regard to its duties under the Disability Discrimination Act 1995 when determining eligibility for community care services; the first instance decision in *R. (Eisai Ltd) v National Institute for Health and Clinical Excellence* [2007] EWHC 1941 (Admin): the point was not dealt with on appeal and *R. (C) v Secretary of State for Justice* [2008] EWCA Civ 882.

[64] The matter is essentially one for the discretion of the court. In *R. v Liverpool City Corp. Ex p. Ferguson* (see above, fn.58), Mann J. granted a declaration; in *R. v Liverpool City Council Ex p. Coade, The Times*, October 10, 1986, Simon Brown J. granted mandamus on similar facts.

[65] *R. v Secretary of State for the Environment Ex p. Lee* (see above, fn.56). *R. (Cali) v Waltham Trust* [2006] A.C.D. 344.

[66] *R. v Secretary of State for the Environment Ex p. Lee* (see above, fn.56). See also *R. v Secretary of State for the Environment Ex p. Ward* [1984] 1 W.L.R. 834.

courts may, for example, declare the rights of parties to a contract or under a will. Public bodies enter into contracts and own land. The courts may on occasion declare what the private law rights of a public body are.[67] This will usually be done by way of ordinary claim not judicial review, since the issues raised are ones of private not public law.[68]

7–023   There are situations when an individual might have public law rights. These public law rights are usually the counterpart of the public law duties discussed above. Statute might impose a duty on a public body, and such duty might be classified as giving an individual a right to sue for damages for breach, or a declaration, or injunction. These rights are private law rights which can be protected by ordinary action not be way of judicial review. However, a duty might be classified as a public law duty remediable by way of judicial review only. The appropriate remedy would then be a mandatory order to order the public body to perform the duty or a declaration that a duty is owed to an individual. Thus, an individual may have a public law right which is to be protected by way of judicial review. The procedural duties conferred on police officers may be enforceable by judicial review,[69] but not give rise to a right to sue for damages in the event of a violation of those rights.[70] The duty to accommodate gypsies did not give rise to an individual right to sue for damages for breach, but did entitle an individual gypsy to bring judicial review proceedings to enforce the duty.[71] There is a need to distinguish more clearly than in the past between those duties where a breach gives rise to a tortious action for damages, and those where breach gives rise to a right to seek judicial review on the part of an individual with sufficient interest. There does occasionally appear to be a tendency on the part of the courts to assume that if a sufficiently precise duty is imposed for the benefit of an individual then it must be a private law right remediable in damages. This is not necessarily the case, and the courts should not overlook the possibility that a duty is remediable in public not private law.[72]

7–024   In *O'Rourke v Camden LBC*,[73] for example, the House of Lords held that the duties owed to the homeless were remediable in public law only, not private law, and so could not be the subject of a claim for damages. In addition, Lord Hoffmann criticised the suggestion made in earlier cases that a statute might create a two-tier process whereby there was first a public law decision as to

---

[67] See, e.g. *Coin Street Community Builders Ltd v Barking and Dagenham LBC, The Times*, July 20, 1988; *Sainsbury (J) Plc v Enfield LBC* [1989] 1 W.L.R. 590; such matters can be reformulated so that the issue becomes the question of whether the authority has statutory power to sell, or as a challenge to a decision to sell, without being bound by a covenant; it may then be dealt with by way of judicial review: see *R. v Westminster City Council Ex p. Leicester Square Coventry Street Association* (1989) 59 P. & C.R. 51.

[68] Questions of public and private law may arise on the same facts. In *R. v Kensington and Chelsea RLBC Ex p. Hammell* [1989] Q.B. 518, the Court of Appeal held that they could grant an interim mandatory injunction to protect the applicant's private law right to be provided with temporary accommodation pending the local authority's public law decision on whether the applicant was entitled to permanent accommodation.

[69] *R. v Chief Constable of the Merseyside Police Ex p. Calveley* [1986] Q.B. 424.

[70] *Calveley v Chief Constable of the Merseyside Police* [1989] A.C. 1228.

[71] *R. v Secretary of State for the Environment Ex p. Ward* [1984] 1 W.L.R. 834.

[72] In *Ettridge v Morrell* (1987) 85 L.G.R. 100 for example, a statutory duty to provide a schoolroom during an election campaign was held to create a private law rights; possibility of a public law right arising not considered.

[73] [1998] A.C. 188.

whether a duty was owed, and, if a favourable decision was reached and the public body decided a statutory duty was owed, then a private law right arose. In the light of the decision in *O'Rourke*, it is unlikely that many duties will be seen as creating a mixture of public law and private law rights. If a duty exists, it will exist in public law and be remediable by way of judicial review with an order for mandamus, or, more usually, a declaration that the duty is owed. The Court of Appeal has, however, indicated that the position may be different in relation to duties to pay money, such as housing improvement grants.[74] Here, the decision as to whether a person qualifies for a grant may be a public law decision, but once that had been decided, the right to payment may be a private law right. An alternative, and in many ways, preferable analysis is that the duty to pay a certain sum in certain circumstances remains a public law duty throughout. If the public body is satisfied that a person qualifies for receipt of a sum, there is a duty to pay which is a public law duty. The courts can grant a declaration that the duty is owed or that a person is entitled to the money.[75]

Statute may not only create the right but may also create an exclusive statutory mechanism to determine whether the right exists. In these circumstances, an individual may only use that exclusive statutory machinery to enforce the right.[76] The modern trend, however, is not to treat the statutory mechanism as an exhaustive right ousting the normal jurisdiction of the courts but as a factor relevant to the discretion of the court in deciding whether to grant a remedy in judicial review (as an alternative remedy is available) and as an indicator that the statutory right was not intended to create a private law right to damages.[77]

7–025

In addition to statutory rights, the courts may declare an individual's common law rights. A public body is obliged as a matter of common law, for example, to observe the principles of natural justice or procedural fairness. This could equally well be expressed as a public law right on the part of the individual to be treated fairly although, traditionally, the issue is seen as an obligation of the public body not a right of the individual. The courts are prepared to grant a declaration that common law rights have been breached. In *R. v Department of Health Ex p. Gandhi*[78] the Divisional Court granted a declaration that the failure to disclose all relevant documents prior to a hearing amounted to a procedural impropriety. In *R. v Chief Constable of South Wales Ex p. Merrick*,[79] the Divisional Court ruled that a person held in custody in a magistrates' court had a common law right of access to a solicitor as soon as reasonably practicable after making a request to see a solicitor and granted a declaration that the failure to allow such access in the particular case constituted a breach of that right.

7–026

---

[74] *Trustees of Denis Rye Pension Fund v Sheffield City Council* [1998] 1 W.L.R. 840 and see above at para.3–043.

[75] See, e.g. *R. v Birmingham City Council Ex p. Mohammed* [1999] 1 W.L.R. 33 (one difficulty is that if the right is solely a public law right, the appropriate procedure is by way of judicial review and, where a person has proceeded by ordinary proceedings, concern not to prevent a person establishing a right may lead the courts to characterise the right as a private law right).

[76] *Barraclough v Brown* [1897] A.C. 615; *R. v Trinity House London Pilotage Committee Ex p. Jensen* [1985] 2. C.M.L.R. 413.

[77] *R. v Secretary of State for the Environment Ex p. Ward* [1984] 1 W.L.R. 834.

[78] [1991] 1 W.L.R. 1053.

[79] [1994] 1 W.L.R. 663.

To determine questions arising out of legitimate expectations

7–027   In the realm of public law, individuals may have legitimate expectations that public authorities will act in particular ways. Such legitimate expectations may arise where a public authority has made a clear, unqualified and unambiguous representation to a particular individual that it will act in a particular way[80] or where it has a policy or a consistent practice[81] of acting in a particular way. Such expectations may be procedural in nature such as a practice or promise that the public authority will consult a person before deciding on whether to confer or remove a particular benefit.[82] In general, the courts will enforce procedural legitimate expectations, for example by quashing or declaring invalid a decision reached in breach of that expectation.[83]

7–028   In other cases, the promise may be that the individual will be able to enjoy, or continue enjoying, a particular substantive benefit. The public authority may subsequently decide in an individual case not to honour the promise. In such circumstances the burden is on the individual to demonstrate that an unqualified, unambiguous and unqualified representation was made. Thereafter, if the authority wishes to depart from that representation, it will need to demonstrate that there is an overriding public interest in doing so. The courts will then need to determine whether or not it would be so unfair as to amount to an abuse of power on the part of the authority to resile from the expectation that it has created.[84] Individuals may seek to rely on representations contained in polices. In general terms, an individual only has a legitimate expectation of being treated in accordance with the current policy of the authority.[85] There may be more difficult cases where a previous policy initially applied to an individual but the authority now wishes to apply the current policy to the individual. The fact that the individual had a legitimate expectation under the former policy may simply be a material consideration to be borne in mind by the decision-maker in making his decision so that a failure to have regard to that consideration may make a particular decision unlawful but providing that the decision-maker does take the legitimate expectation into account the precise weight to be attributed to it will be a matter for the decision-maker.[86] There may, however, be cases where it would

---

[80] *R. v Inland Revenue Commissioners Ex p. MFK Underwriters Agents Ltd* [1990] 1 W.L.R. 1545 at 1569G; *R (Patel) v General Medical Council* [2013] 1 W.L.R. 2801. Those cases establish that the individual must also have made full disclosure of relevant matters if he seeks to enforce a representation made to him.

[81] See, e.g. *Council of Civil Service Unions v Minister of the Civil Service* [1985] A.C. 374. See *R (Davies) v HM Revenue and Customs Commissioners* [2011] 1 W.L.R. 2625.

[82] See *R. v North and East Devon Health Authority Ex p. Coughlan* [2001] Q.B. 213 at [57] and *Att-Gen of Hong Kong v Ng Yuen Shiu* [1983] 2 A.C. 639.

[83] *R. (Bhatt Murphy) v Independent Assessor* [2008] EWCA Civ 755 at [42]; *R. (Patel) v General Medical Council* [2013] 1 W.L.R. 2081 at [40].

[84] *Paponette v Attorney-General of Trinidad and Tobago* [2011] 3 W.L.R. 219 at [28]–[44]; *R. (Bancoult) v Secretary of State for Foreign and Commonwealth Affairs (No.2)* [2009] A.C. 453 at [60]; *R. (Patel) v General Medical Council* [2013] 1 W.L.R. 2801 at [56]–[62].

[85] *In Re Findlay* [1984] A.C. 318 (only expectation that prisoners had was that any application for parole would be considered in the light of the policy prevailing at the time, not any earlier policy) and see also *R. v Secretary of State for the Home Department ex p. Hargreaves* [1997] 1 W.L.R. 906.

[86] *R. v North and East Devon Health Authority Ex p. Coughlan* [2001] Q.B. 213 at [57]; *R. (Patel) v General Medical Council* [2013] 1 W.L.R. 2081 at [81] and *R. (Bibi) v Newham LBC* [2002] 1 W.L.R. 237 at [49]–[51].

be so unfair as to amount to an abuse of power to depart from the previous policy, at least without making some transitional arrangements.[87] The precise circumstances in which such unfairness arises have not yet been exhaustively settled by the courts. Factors that indicate that the circumstances do not amount to an abuse of power include the extent to which the change involves question of policy properly left to the executive[88] or involves balancing the interests of third parties against the person claiming the legitimate expectation[89] or whether enforcing the expectation would have a wide-ranging effect on a large number of individuals.[90] Conversely, where the expectation arises out of a promise made to one, or a small number of individuals, it is more likely to be capable of generating unfairness amounting to an abuse of power for the public authority to resile from the promise, particularly if the individual has relied upon it to his detriment or it involves a matter of real importance to the individual involved.[91] Where the failure to honour the promise or act in accordance with the policy amounts to an abuse of power, the courts may quash, or declare invalid, a decision which breaches that expectation[92] or declare that the authority is not entitled to resile from the promise it made.[93]

To determine questions of law

Declarations are granted to determine questions of law that arise in the course of a judicial review application. Declarations have been granted, for example: 7–029

(a)   on the standard of proof in a Coroner's Court[94];

(b)   stating that a particular factor could not be taken into account when deciding whether to exercise a statutory discretion[95];

---

[87] *R. v North and East Devon Health Authority Ex p. Coughlan* [2001] 1 Q.B. 613 at [78]–[82]; *R (Patel) v General Medical Council* [2013] 1 W.L.R. 2801; *R. v Inland Revenue Commissioners Ex p. Unilever Plc* [1996] S.T.C. 681; *R. v Secretary of State for Education Ex p. Begbie* [2000] 1 W.L.R. 1115 at 1129H (per Laws LJ). For an alternative analysis based on whether the authority is pursuing a legitimate aim and has acted proportionally in departing from a promise, see dicta of Laws C.J. in *Nadarajah v Secretary of State for the Home Department* [2005] EWCA Civ 1363.

[88] *R. v Secretary of State for Education Ex p. Begbie* [2000] 1 W.L.R. 1115 at 1130F–1131F; *R. (Bibi) v Newham LBC* [2002] 1 W.L.R. 237 at [40].

[89] *R. (Bibi) v Newham LBC* [2002] 1 W.L.R. 237 at [57]–[59] (legitimate expectation of person that he would be provided with a secure tenancy of accommodation had to be weighed against the interests of others on the housing waiting list).

[90] *R. v Secretary of State for Education Ex p. Begbie* [2000] 1 W.L.R. 1115 at 1124C–D and 1131F–H; *R (Bibi) v Newham LBC* [2002] 1 W.L.R. 237 at [28]–[31].

[91] *R. v North and East Devon Health Authority Ex p. Coughlan* [2001] 1 Q.B. 613 at [60] and [86]; *R. v Secretary of State for Education Ex p. Begbie* [2000] 1 W.L.R. 1115 at 1131A–B; *R. (Patel) v General Medical Council* [2013] 1 W.L.R. 2018 at [84] (trainee doctor undertook a course over four years, involving considerable expense, on the basis of a representation that the course would be recognised by the General Medical Council which then changed its criteria after the individual had begun the course).

[92] *R. v North and East Devon Health Authority Ex p. Coughlan* [2001] 1 Q.B. 613 at [60].

[93] *R. (Patel) v General Medical Council* [2013] 1 W.L.R. 2018 at [93].

[94] *R. v West London Coroners' Court Ex p. Gray* [1988] Q.B. 467.

[95] See, e.g., *R. v Secretary of State for Education and Science Ex p. Inner London Education Authority* (1985) 84 L.G.R. 454 and *R. (Sainsbury's Supermarkets Ltd.) v Wolverhampton City Counci* [2010] 2 W.L.R.1173 at [79] (opportunity of redeveloping one site not a material consideration in deciding whether to make a compulsory purchase order for another site)

(c)   setting out the true meaning of legislative provisions[96]; and

(d)   declaring that documents are privileged and do not need to be produced to the Inland Revenue[97]; and

(e)   determining which statutory provisions governed the duration of the licence of a prisoner released following an earlier recall to prison.[98]

7–030   Procedural questions have been dealt with by way of declarations. The courts have, for example, declared that the police have a right to be heard before a detained child is released,[99] that it was unlawful to refuse to allow an asylum-seeker not to tape record his interview when unaccompanied by a legal adviser or an interpreter,[100] and that justices could not determine an application for an interim care order without evidence and without giving the parties an opportunity to cross-examine and call witnesses.[101]

7–031   Declarations on questions of law are usually sought alongside relief designed to establish that a particular decision is ultra vires. Otherwise a court may refuse a declaration on the grounds that no issue arises and the matter is hypothetical. The courts are, however, prepared to grant declarations to give general guidance on matters of public law where there is a real need to do so. They will not be deterred from granting relief where this would be of assistance to future exercises of statutory power, even where there is no need for a remedy for the particular applicant who began the judicial review proceedings.

To determine questions of EU law

7–032   Directly effective rights which are derived from European Union law and are enforceable against public bodies will in most instances raise issues of public law.[102] Questions of European Union law arise in a variety of ways. For example, exercises of statutory power which violate European Union law may be declared invalid[103] or the courts may declare that a public body misdirected itself in law when it acted in a way that contravened an individual's directly effective EU law rights.[104] The courts may grant a declaration that domestic subordinate legislation does not fully and properly implement the requirements of a directive.[105] Where the Court of Justice of the European Union rules that a European Union regulation or directive is invalid, a decision[106] or subordinate legislation[107] adopted to implement that regulation or directive may be declared invalid. The courts may declare that a claimant has an enforceable European Union law

---

[96] *R. v Dairy Produce Quota Tribunal for England and Wales Ex p. Caswell* [1989] 1 W.L.R. 1089.

[97] *R. v I.R.C. Ex p. Goldberg* [1989] Q.B. 267.

[98] *R. (Stellato) v Secretary of State for the Home Department* [2007] 1 W.L.R. 60; affd. by the House of Lords [2007] 2 W.L.R. 531.

[99] *R. v Bristol Justices Ex p. Broome* [1987] 1 W.L.R. 352.

[100] *R. (Dirshe) v Secretary of State for the Home Department* [2005] 1 W.L.R. 2685.

[101] *R. v Birmingham City Juvenile Court Ex p. Birmingham City Council* [1988] 1 W.L.R. 337.

[102] *Bourgoin S.A. v Minister for Agriculture, Fisheries and Food* [1986] Q.B. 716.

[103] *R. v Secretary of State for Social Services Ex p. Bomore Medical Supplies* [1986] 1 C.M.L.R. 228.

[104] *R. (Barker) v London Borough of Bromley* [2007] 1 A.C. 470 at [26].

[105] *R. (Barker) v London Borough of Bromley* [2007] 1 A.C. 470 at [26].

[106] *R. v Intervention Board for Agricultural Produce Ex p. E.D. & F. Man* [1986] 2 All E.R. 115.

[107] *R. v Minister of Agriculture Fisheries and Food Ex p. Fèdèration Europèene de la Santè Animale* [1988] 3 C.M.L.R. 661.

right[108] or that a public body is under a duty imposed by European Union law.[109] Although the prerogative remedies or an injunction could be granted, the courts have tended to use the declaration in such cases. Remedies for breach of European Union law are considered in detail in Chapter 17.

In *R. v Secretary of State for Employment Ex p. Equal Opportunities Commission*,[110] the House of Lords also held that the courts may grant a declaration that primary legislation is incompatible with EU law. The House held that certain provisions of domestic legislation were incompatible with Art.119[111] of the EC Treaty guaranteeing equal pay to men and women for equal work and the individuals could rely upon those rights in national courts and tribunals and those courts or tribunals would have to give precedence to the directly effective European law right and disapply or ignore any inconsistent provisions of domestic law.

7–033

It is not yet settled whether the courts have jurisdiction to grant a declaration where the provisions of EU law are not capable of having direct effect. This may arise in one of two situations. First, the rights in question may be derived from a directive and, unlike rights conferred by the Treaty on the Functioning of the European Union or a regulation, are only directly effective against an emanation of the state. The individual applicant may, however, be concerned ultimately to enforce rights against another private individual not an emanation of the state. In the employment field for example, an individual may wish to enforce rights to equal treatment conferred by the Council Directive on equal treatment but he may be employed by a private individual or company. The rights conferred would not be enforceable as against the individual employer.[112] On one occasion,[113] for example, an employee sought judicial review of legislation, which restricted the ability of the individual to claim that she had been unfairly dismissed by her employer, claiming that the legislation was indirectly discriminatory and contrary to the equal treatment directive.

7–034

Two issues arise in these circumstances: first, whether the court can grant a declaration of incompatibility where the individual concerned has no directly effective rights and secondly, what would be the effect of such a declaration. On the second question, it is clear that the declaration would not assist the individuals to enforce any rights in the national courts as they have no directly effective rights as against the employer in question. On the first question, in the light of the *EOC* case, the better view is that the courts do have jurisdiction to grant a declaration of incompatibility in such circumstances. The EOC itself had no directly effective rights and yet the House of Lords held it was able to grant a declaration that domestic law was incompatible with EU law and the EOC had sufficient interest to give it standing to bring a claim for judicial review. In *Seymour-Smith*, Lord Hoffmann appeared to take the view that, in principle, the courts did have jurisdiction to grant a declaration of incompatibility to an

7–035

---

[108] *R. v Inner London Education Authority Ex p. Hinde* (1984) 83 L.G.R. 695.

[109] *R. v Att-Gen Ex p. I.C.I. Plc* [1987] 1 C.M.L.R. 72.

[110] [1995] 1 A.C. 1.

[111] Now Art.157 of the Treaty on the Functioning of the European Union.

[112] See below at 17–018.

[113] *R. v Secretary of State for Employment Ex p. Seymour-Smith* [1997] 1 W.L.R. 473. In fact, the House considered that the domestic legislation fell to be measured against Art.119 (now Art.141 EC) of the EC Treaty not the Equal Treatment Directive and so could be enforced against the employer.

individual in such circumstances, primarily it seems, as such a declaration would inform the government of its failure to comply with European law and fulfil the function of supervising the implementation of European Union law.[114] The difficulty in *Seymour-Smith*, however, was that the declaration actually granted by the Court of Appeal was not that the domestic legislation was incompatible with European law in 1995 but that it was incompatible on evidence relating to 1991. As such, that declaration did not perform any function in telling the government whether or not there was currently a failure to comply with European law and for that reason it was discharged.

7–036   The second situation in which a provision of the TFEU may be incapable of direct effect is where it is not sufficiently precise and unconditional to be enforced in the courts or the provision may not be intended to govern relations between individuals and the Member State. Again, the question is whether the courts have jurisdiction to grant a declaration that primary legislation or other action taken by the executive is incompatible with provisions of European Union law which are not directly effective. In the light of the *EOC* decision, it is difficult to see why the courts do not have jurisdiction to grant a declaration of incompatibility merely because the provision is not directly effective. The real difficulty may be that if a provision is not sufficiently precise and unconditional to be directly effective it may not be possible for the courts to identify whether there has in fact been a breach of European Union law or to frame an appropriate declaration.[115] There may, however, be rare cases where it can be established that a particular act is incompatible with a non-directly effective provision of European Union law and the issue of granting a declaration of incompatibility may arise. The issue arose in *R v HM Treasury ex p. Shepherd Neame Ltd.*,[116] where it was contended that legislation increasing the duty on beer was incompatible with what is now Art.4 of the Treaty on European Union read with the provisions in what is now Art.120 of the Treaty on the Functioning of the European Union on the co-ordination of economic policies. The Court of Appeal found that there had been no breach of the relevant Treaty articles and left the issue undecided.

To determine questions concerning Convention Rights

7–037   It is unlawful for a public authority to act in a way that is incompatible with a Convention right, that is one of the rights derived from the European Convention on Human Rights incorporated into domestic law by the Human Rights Act

---

[114] Lord Hoffmann did not consider that the declaration could properly be sought for the purposes of laying the foundation for a claim for damages for breach of European Union law by failing to implement the Directive: see [1997] 1 W.L.R. 473 at 480D–F.

[115] If the provision is not directly effective because it is intended to regulate relations between Member States and the EU (e.g. obligations to consult or inform the Commission), the question may be whether it is appropriate to grant a remedy to an individual and, possibly, even whether an individual has standing, that is sufficient interest, to seek a remedy.

[116] (1999) 11 Admin. L.Rep. 517 (and see the decision of the Divisional Court in [1998] 1 C.M.L.R. 1139). The Court of Appeal has expressed the view that Art.4 of the Treaty on European Union, read with other provisions of the Treaty on the Functioning of the European Union which were not themselves directly effective, is not directly effective: see *R. (Bancoult) v Secretary of State for Foreign and Commonwealth Affairs (No.3)* [2014] 1 W.L.R. 2921 at [134]–[148]. See Chapter 17 below.

1998.[117] Such claims are frequently brought by way of judicial review. Declarations may be granted that a particular action, or omission, by a public authority is a breach of a Convention right. Thus, where the system of prison governors adjudicating on disciplinary accusations against prisoners was found to be incompatible with the right to a fair hearing before an independent tribunal recognised by Art.6 ECHR, the House of Lords declared that the Secretary of State had acted unlawfully by failing to provide the prisoner with a hearing before an independent tribunal and in refusing to allow him to be legally represented.[118] The courts have also declared, for example, that consideration of a person's application for parole did not comply with the requirements of Art.5(4) of the Convention.[119] The courts have declared that guidance is incompatible with a Convention right.[120] The courts may grant a declaration setting out the interpretation to be given to a particular statutory provision to avoid the statute being interpreted in a way which will breach a person's Convention right.[121]

Declarations of incompatibility under the Human Rights Act 1998

The incompatibility may, however, arise out of a conflict between the provisions of primary or delegated legislation and the Convention. Here, there is a special procedure dealing with such a conflict. The courts are required to construe any legislation in conformity with the Convention if it is possible to do so.[122] The courts should first ascertain whether the legislation (without consideration of s.3 of the Human Rights Act 1998) would be a breach of the Convention.[123] If so, the courts are then under an obligation to construe the legislation "so far as it is possible to do so" in a way that is consistent with the Convention. That is a strong obligation and does not first require the court to detect any ambiguity in the legislation.[124] However, the task of the court is to interpret the legislation so far as it is possible to do so and not to amend the legislation or legislate itself.[125] To give particular statutory provisions a meaning which departs substantially from a fundamental feature of the legislative scheme is likely to involve crossing the boundary between interpretation and amendment.[126] If that is not possible, the Act gives the High Court jurisdiction to grant a declaration of incompatibility, i.e. a declaration that a provision of primary or subordinate legislation is incompatible with a particular Convention right.[127] A declaration of incompatibility does not affect the validity, continuing operation or enforcement of the legislative provision declared incompatible and is not binding on the parties to

7–038

---

[117] Human Rights Act 1998 s.6. See chapter 16.
[118] *R. (Greenfield) v Secretary of State for the Home Department* [2003] 1 W.L.R. 673.
[119] *R. (Noorkoiv) v Secretary of State for the Home Department* [2002] 1 W.L.R. 3284 esp. at [48].
[120] *R. (GC) v Commissioner of Police of the Metropolis* [2011] 1 W.L.R. 1230.
[121] See, e.g. *R. (Baiai) v Secretary of State for the Home Department* [2008] 3 W.L.R. 549 at [32].
[122] Human Rights Act 1998 s.3. See 16–020.
[123] *Poplar Housing and Regeneration Community Association Ltd v Donoguhe* [2002] Q.B. 48 at [75]; *Re S (Minors) (Care Order: Implementation of Care Plan)* [2002] A.C. 291 at [41].
[124] *Re S (Minors) (Care Order: Implementation of Care Plan)* [2002] A.C. 291 at [37] and see also *R. v A (No.2)* [2002] 1 A.C. 45.
[125] *Re S (Minors) (Care Order: Implementation of Care Plan)* [2002] A.C. 291 at [38]–[41]; *Poplar Housing and Regeneration Community Association Ltd v Donoguhe* [2002] Q.B. 48 at [75].
[126] *Re S (Minors) (Care Order: Implementation of Care Plan)*, fn.7 above.
[127] Human Rights Act 1998 s.4 and see *Wilson v First County Trust Ltd (No.2)* [2003] 3 W.L.R. 568.

the proceedings.[128] A minister may, if he has compelling reasons, amend the domestic legislation.[129] Otherwise, it will be a matter for Parliament to consider any appropriate amendment to incompatible domestic legislation. Declarations of incompatibility have been granted. The House of Lords has, for example, granted declarations that statutory provisions authorising the detention of foreign nationals suspected international terrorism were incompatible with Arts 5 and 14 ECHR as they were disproportionate and discriminated on grounds of nationality.[130] The courts have declared provisions requiring categories of immigrants to obtain permission to marry, and which applied to all marriages except those contracted in accordance with the rites of the Church of England, to be incompatible with Arts 12 and 14 ECHR.[131] Such declarations may also be granted in ordinary proceedings in appropriate circumstances. The House of Lords has granted a declaration that provisions of the Matrimonial Causes Act 1973 were incompatible with Arts 8 and 12 of the Convention as it did not provide for recognition of the marriage of a transsexual.[132] Declarations are discretionary. The courts may refuse to grant such a remedy where the litigation was unnecessary, as where the claimants sought a declaration that provisions governing treason were incompatible with Art.10 ECHR, as there was no prospect of prosecution under the relevant provisions.[133] The House of Lords did not consider a declaration of incompatibility necessary where the legislation had been amended by the time that the matter came before them[134] or where the matter was under consideration by Parliament.[135] The courts will not, as a matter of discretion, normally grant a declaration of incompatibility to a person who is not affected by the breach of the Convention rights in question.[136] The operation of the Human Rights Act 1998 and the procedure governing declarations of incompatibility is discussed in Chapter 16.

D.   RESTRICTIONS ON THE GRANT OF DECLARATORY RELIEF

Non-legal claims

7–040   The courts will only grant relief in respect of legal claims which are enforceable in law, and not moral or political claims. The court has no power to grant a declaration that the Crown has a duty to protect citizens from unlawful detention,

---

[128]   Human Rights Act 1998 s.4(6).

[129]   Human Rights Act 1998 s.10(2).

[130]   *A v Secretary of State for the Home Department* [2005] 2 A.C. 68.

[131]   *R (Baiai) v Secretary of State for the Home Department* [2009] 1 A.C. 287 (declaration of incompatibility granted in relation to discriminatory effect of provisions; other declarations set aside: see [32]).

[132]   *Bellinger v Bellinger* [2003] 2 W.L.R. 1174.

[133]   *R. (Rusbridger) v Attorney General* [2004] 1 A.C. 357.

[134]   See, e.g. dicta in *Doherty v Birmingham City Council* [2009] 1 A.C. 367 per Lord Walker at [105] and Lord Mance at [164].

[135]   *R. (Chester) v Secretary of State for Justice* [2013] 3 W.L.R. 1076 (compatibility of legislation prohibiting prisoners from voting).

[136]   *Lancashire CC v Taylor* [2005] 1 W.L.R. 2688 at [37]–[44]; *R. (Chester) v Secretary of State for Justice* [2013] 3 W.L.R. 1076 at [102] and [111].

since that duty is not enforceable in a court of law.[137] The courts will not, therefore, grant relief in respect of obligations arising under international treaties, since these do not create obligations enforceable in English law unless incorporated by statute[138] or unless it is necessary to interpret the treaty in order to adjudicate on a claim arising under domestic law[139] (including these arising under the ECHR[140]). In one case, however, the courts did consider whether treaty obligations undertaken by the Crown in respect of Canadian Indians had devolved on the Government of Canada or were still the responsibility of the UK Government, even though such obligations were not enforceable and no breach had been alleged.[141] The courts will not grant a remedy preventing the Crown from entering into a treaty, nor traditionally have they considered whether a proposed or actual treaty conflicts with a statute or the common law, since the treaty has no effect in English law until incorporated by an Act of Parliament.[142] However, in *Re Molyneaux*,[143] Taylor J. did consider whether the Anglo-Irish Treaty was in breach of statute or the common law. While this opens up the possibility of the courts looking at such questions in the future, it must be considered unlikely. Even if the issues could be considered legal issues they are so heavily overlaid with political considerations that they are likely to be regarded as non-justiciable. The Court of Appeal dismissed an appeal against a refusal of permission to argue that there was a constitutional convention that no Act of Parliament would be enacted which altered the constitution in a fundamental way without there first being a referendum (in that case, an act seeking to give effect to a new draft constitution for the EU). The Court of Appeal was not persuaded that it was arguable that such a convention existed but, even if it were arguable, declaratory relief would have been refused as a matter of discretion as no draft treaty had yet been adopted by the Member States.[144] The Divisional Court has been asked to consider whether a claimant had a legitimate expectation that a referendum would be held before the ratification of the Treaty of Lisbon amending the treaties establishing the European Union. The claimant contended that a previous representation given in relation to an earlier treaty impliedly applied to the Treaty of Lisbon as there were no material differences

---

[137] *Mutasa v Att-Gen* [1980] Q.B. 114. But an individual may have a limited, domestic public law legitimate expectation that the UK authorities will consider making representations to a foreign state: see *R. (Abbasi) v Secretary of State for the Foreign and Commonwealth Office and the Secretary of State for the Home Department* [2003] U.K.H.R.R. 76 discussed below.

[138] See *J.H. Rayner (Mincing Lane) Ltd v Department of Trade and Industry* [1990] 2 A.C. 418 (House of Lords refused to enforce obligations contained in an international treaty); *R. v Lyon* [2002] 3 W.L.R. 1652; *R. (Campaign for Nuclear Disarmament) v The Prime Minister of the United Kingdom*, unreported, December 17, 2002 and see above paras 2–030 to 2–033.

[139] See, e.g. *R. v Secretary of State for the Home Department Ex p. Adan* [2001] 2 A.C. 477 (necessary to interpret Geneva Convention to determine whether Secretary of State could remove an asylum-seeker to third countries taking a different view of the meaning of the Convention). See generally, Sales and Clement: "International Law in Domestic Courts: The Developing Framework" (2008) 124 L.Q.R. 388.

[140] See, e.g. *R. (Al-Jedda) v Secretary of State for Defence (Justice intervening)* [2008] 2 W.L.R. 31 (necessary to consider international law to resolve arising under Art.5 ECHR).

[141] *R. v Secretary of State for Foreign and Commonwealth Office Ex p. Indian Association of Alberta* [1982] Q.B. 892 (Kerr LJ expressed doubts as to whether they had jurisdiction).

[142] *Blackburn v Att-Gen* [1971] 1 W.L.R. 1037; *McWhirter v Att-Gen* [1972] C.M.L.R. 882.

[143] [1986] 1 W.L.R. 331. See paras 2–030 to 2–033.

[144] *R. (Southall) v Secretary of State for Foreign and Commonwealth Affairs* [2003] Eu.L.R. 833.

between the two treaties. The Divisional Court doubted that the issue of the materiality of the differences between the two treaties raised a justiciable issue as it involved questions of political judgment. The Divisional Court found that no legitimate expectation had been made out.[145]

Matters outside the jurisdiction of municipal courts

7–041 Declarations cannot be granted in respect of matters that lie outside the jurisdiction of municipal courts. The English courts will not, therefore, as a general rule grant declarations in respect of the validity of foreign legislation or the executive acts of foreign governments; such claims are a matter for the courts of the country concerned[146] although the courts may, in appropriate circumstances, be able to take cognisance of a clear and admitted breach of an established principle of international law.[147] Similarly, the courts will not generally adjudicate on decisions taken by the executive in its dealings with foreign states. Thus the court would not grant a remedy requiring the UK to make representations to the US in relation to detainees held in Guantanamo Bay although the court recognised that individuals might, as a matter of domestic public law, have a limited legitimate expectation that the UK authorities would consider whether to make representations which could be the subject, in appropriate circumstances, of declaratory relief.[148] Nor will the courts adjudicate on claims raising the validity or meaning of the constitution of a Commonwealth country, even though it may owe its origin to an Act of the British Parliament or delegated legislation made thereunder.[149] Obligations owed by the Crown in respect of another Commonwealth country are enforceable in the courts of the

---

[145] *R. (Wheeler) v Office of the Prime Minister and the Secretary of State for Foreign and Commonwealth Affairs* [2008] EWHC 1409 (Admin) at [37].

[146] See, e.g. *Buttes Gas and Oil Co. v Hammer (No.3)* [1982] A.C. 888; *R (Khan) v Secretary of State for Foreign and Commonwealth Affairs* [2014]1 1 W.L.R. 872 at [25]–[36] (courts would not grant a declaration which in substance involved ruling on the legality of acts of a foreign state in using unmanned aircraft to kill suspected terrorists).

[147] See, e.g. *Kuwait Airways Corporation v Iraqi Airways (Nos 4 and 5)* [2002] 2 A.C. 883 (claim by Kuwait for return of aircraft seized by Iraq following its invasion of Kuwait; court able to take account of fact that the Iraqi invasion was a breach of international law); and see discussion in *R. (Abbasi) v Secretary of State for Foreign and Commonwealth Affairs and Secretary of State for the Home Department* [2003] U.K.H.R.R. 76 at [51]–[57].

[148] *R. (Abbasi) v Secretary of State for Foreign and Commonwealth Affairs and Secretary of State for the Home Department* [2003] U.K.H.R.R. 76 and see *R. (Al Rawi) v Secretary of State for Foreign and Commonwealth Affairs* [2007] 2 W.L.R. 1219 and *R. (Campaign for Nuclear Disarmament) v Prime Minister of the United Kingdom*, unreported, December 17, 2002 (courts would not rule on lawfulness of military action abroad as that would involve the courts in matters of national security and foreign policy).

[149] *Buck v Att-Gen* [1965] Ch. 745. See also *R. v Secretary of State for Foreign and Commonwealth Affairs Ex p. British Council of Turkish Cypriots* [1998] C.O.D. 336 (courts could not consider a claim that UK support for the accession of Cyprus to the EU was unlawful; no issue of domestic law arose concerning s.1 of the Cyprus Act 1960 which granted independence to Cyprus; once cut free, Cyprus became an independent state with a constitution that belonged to it and that constitution was not justiciable in the UK). See also the judgment of Megarry V.-C. in *Manuel v Att-Gen* [1983] Ch. 77 (affd. on another ground). But the court will consider the constitutionality of a foreign law if that issue is relevant to some issue within the court's jurisdiction: *Dubai Bank Ltd v Galadari (No.5), The Times*, June 26, 1990 (whether foreign entity had legal capacity to sue for moneys owed involved questions of constitutionality of a foreign law).

other country and cannot be enforced by way of declaration in the English courts. Thus, once it was decided that any treaty obligations owed by the Crown to Canadian Indians were the responsibility of the Canadian government, not the UK government, the English courts had no jurisdiction to grant any declarations as to the continued existence or extent of the obligations: those were matters for the Canadian courts.[150]

Validity of Acts of Parliament

The traditional constitutional position is that the courts cannot question the validity of an Act of Parliament. As Parliament is sovereign, there is no restriction on its legislative competence; therefore the courts cannot declare an Act to be ultra vires or beyond the powers of Parliament.[151]   **7–042**

The traditional doctrine of parliamentary sovereignty needs to be reconciled with the UK's membership of the EU. The European Court regards EU law as having supremacy over all national law, and requires the courts of Member States to give preference to European law and to ignore conflicting national law.[152]   **7–043**

The House of Lords has held that the English courts should give preference to EU law and should disregard conflicting English legislation (at least where Parliament has not expressly stated that it intends to legislate in contravention of EU law).[153] The courts could declare an Act of Parliament to be inapplicable or incapable of taking legal effect as it contravenes EU law. It is also possible that declarations may be sought as to the compatibility of proposed legislation with EU law. This topic is discussed fully elsewhere.[154]   **7–044**

The courts may also grant a declaration under s.4 of the Human Rights Act 1998 that provisions of primary legislation are incompatible with rights derived from the European Convention on Human Rights. Such a declaration does not, however, affect the validity or operation of the Act of Parliament.[155]   **7–045**

Internal proceedings of Parliament

Declarations will not be granted in respect of purely internal proceedings of either House of Parliament. In *Bradlaugh v Gossett*,[156] the court held that they had no power to declare invalid a resolution preventing Bradlaugh from taking   **7–046**

---

[150] *R. v Secretary of State for Foreign and Commonwealth Office Ex p. Indian Association of Alberta* [1982] 2 W.L.R. 670 (dicta of Lord Diplock when refusing leave to appeal); *Mutasa v Att-Gen* (see above, fn.16); *Tito v Waddell (No.2)* [1977] Ch. 196 at 259 (no jurisdiction to grant declaration in respect of acts of colonial government). Liability for acts done by the British Army abroad may be attributed to the Crown in respect of the government of the UK, and the Att-Gen of England could be an appropriate defendant; but other obstacles may exist to a successful action: *Trawnik v Lennox* [1985] 1 W.L.R. 532.

[151] See *R. (Jackson) v Att.-Gen.* [2006] 1 A.C. 260 discussed above at para.4–063. Judgment of Megarry V.-C. in *Manuel v Att-Gen* (above, fn.149) (affd. on another ground) and see also *R. (Southall) v Secretary of State for Foreign and Commonwealth Affairs* [2003] Eu. L.R. 832 at [10].

[152] Case 106/77 *Amministrazione delle Finanze dello Stato v Simmenthal S.p.A.* [1978] E.C.R. 629.

[153] *R. v Secretary of State for Transport Ex p. Factortame Ltd (No.2)* [1991] 1 A.C. 603.

[154] See Chapter 17.

[155] See above at para.7–038. Parliament may amend the Act or a minister may take remedial action to amend the legislation under the Human Rights Act 1998 s.10.

[156] (1884) 12 Q.B.D. 271.

the oath, as the effect of such a declaration would be to allow him to take his seat. The courts will not look into the internal procedures of Parliament to see if legislation has been properly enacted.[157] In one case, a claimant asserted that he had a legitimate expectation that a referendum would be held before ratification of a treaty reforming the European Union. Such an expectation could only be fulfilled if a Bill providing for a referendum was introduced into Parliament. The courts held that the introduction of a Bill before parliament was part of the proceedings in Parliament. The courts would not order that a particular Bill be brought before Parliament as that would be to "trespass impermissibly into the province of Parliament".[158] Nor would the court grant a declaration as the practical effect would be the same. The Supreme Court considered a claim that a particular European Union Directive required the courts to review whether the legislature had given adequate consideration to environmental information relevant to a proposed bill authorising the creation of a high speed train line. The Supreme Court held that, properly construed, the Directive did not require national courts to scrutinise the adequacy of the internal proceedings in Parliament and left open the question of whether or not such an exercise would be compatible with national constitutional law.[159] Different considerations apply to subordinate legislation. The courts may grant a declaration that proposed subordinate legislation that is before Parliament for approval, or about to be submitted to Parliament, is not within the powers conferred by the parent statute and would be ultra vires if adopted.[160] Statute may require certain procedures to be followed for subordinate legislation to be enacted: the courts may consider whether such procedures are mandatory and whether they have been observed, and if not declare the subordinate legislation ultra vires.[161] It is unclear whether the courts would rule on such questions before Parliament has considered the subordinate legislation.

Intra vires errors of law

7–047   In the past the courts have not granted a declaration where a decision was vitiated by an intra vires error of law appearing on the face of the record.[162] The reason for this is bound up with the nature of the declaratory remedy. As its name implies, the remedy is purely declaratory in that it declares what the legal position is: it is not constitutive and cannot create new legal rights or relationships. A declaration is therefore appropriate where a decision is ultra vires since it will establish that the decision is a nullity and so incapable of producing legal effects and can be ignored. In the case of an intra vires error of law, the decision remains valid until it is actually set aside by the courts. A declaration is said to be inappropriate as it would achieve nothing; it would simply say that there is an intra vires decision in existence which is flawed and capable of being quashed,

---

[157]   *British Railways Board v Pickin* [1974] A.C. 765.
[158]   *R. (Wheeler) v Office of the Prime Minister and the Secretary of State for Foreign and Commonwealth Affairs* [2008] EWHC 1409 (Admin).
[159]   *R. (Buckinghamshire CC and others) v Secretary of State for Transport* [2014] 1 W.L.R. 325.
[160]   *R. v H.M. Treasury Ex p. Smedley* [1985] Q.B. 657.
[161]   *R. v Secretary of State for Social Services Ex p. Camden LBC* [1987] 1 W.L.R. 819. *R. (Javed) v Secretary of State for the Home Department* [2002] Q.B. 129.
[162]   *Punton v Minister of Pensions and National Insurance (No.2)* [1964] 1 W.L.R. 226.

but could not actually quash the decision itself. A quashing order is needed to quash the decision in the sense of setting it aside and depriving it of legal effects. This limitation is not important in practice as far as errors of law are concerned. First, virtually all errors of law now render a decision ultra vires.[163] Secondly, declarations and quashing orders can both be claimed in judicial review proceedings. If an error were held to be intra vires, the courts could grant a quashing order to quash the decision.[164]

Hypothetical and academic disputes

Other restrictions flow from the general principle that declarations will only be granted where a genuine justiciable issue arises for determination, and relief will not be granted if the matter is hypothetical or academic.[165] These restrictions are increasingly seen as discretionary barriers rather than absolute jurisdictional bars.

7–048

A matter might be hypothetical because the issue is raised prematurely either because the facts have not yet arisen or a declaration is sought at an early stage of the administrative decision-making process. In one case, the High Court refused to grant a declaration as to whether a particular transaction, if carried out, would be subject to a particular form of taxation. The transaction had not yet been carried out and the claim was based to a significant extent on hypothetical facts. The court noted that the "greater the extent to which the dispute between the parties is based on hypothetical facts, the more likely it is that, as a matter of discretion, the court will refuse to grant relief".[166] In another case,[167] the House of Lords dismissed an appeal dealing with the question of whether the Secretary of State had power to charge a prisoner the travel and escort costs of producing him in court to enable him to make an application for judicial review. The House held that they were being asked to decide a hypothetical dispute as the prisoner had never formally applied to be produced in court (he had in fact torn up the application form when he was told that he would have to pay the costs). The

7–049

---

[163] *Anisminic v Foreign Compensation Commission* [1969] 2 A.C. 147; *R. v Hull University Visitor Ex p. Page* [1993] 2 A.C. 682; *Re Racal Communications* [1981] A.C. 374; and *R. v Greater Manchester Coroner Ex p. Tal* [1985] Q.B. 67. There are occasional cases where the presumption that an error of law goes to jurisdiction is rebutted: *R. v Registrar of Companies Ex p. Central Bank of India* [1986] Q.B. 811.

[164] Although declarations were made available in judicial review proceedings as an alternative to a quashing order there is nothing to suggest that reform was intended to alter the nature of the declaration. However, Wade and Forsyth suggest at p.569, that declarations are now available in respect of decisions which exhibit an intra vires error of law which appears on the face of the record.

[165] See, e.g. *R. v Secretary of State for the Home Department Ex p. Wynne* [1993] 1 W.L.R. 115. See generally Zamir and Woolf above, fn.3 at pp.136–163 and see Beatson "Prematurity and Ripeness for Review" in Forsyth and Hare "The Golden Metwand and the Crooked Cord" (O.U.P. 1998) 221 at pp.243–251.

[166] *R. v Inland Revenue Commissioners Ex p. Bishopp; R. v Inland Revenue Commssioners Ex p. Allan* [1999] S.T.C. 531 at 545.

[167] *R. v Secretary of State for the Home Department Ex p. Wynne* [1993] 1 W.L.R. 115. See also *R. v Secretary of State for Education and Science Ex p. Birmingham City Council* above, fn.47. In cases dealing with an existing set of facts and the issue is whether a particular proposed course of action would be involve a breach of the criminal law, the courts may be prepared to grant declaratory relief: see, e.g. *Airedale NHS Trust v Bland* [1993] A.C. 789 (whether surgeons could withdraw certain medical treatment from a person incapable of consenting); *Re F (mental patient sterilisation)* [1990] 2 A.C. 1 (see below at para.7–057).

House held that, in those circumstances, the dispute was hypothetical as it was not based upon any decision or concrete set of facts. On another occasion, the court refused to grant a declaration relating to the way in which a child should be treated in future. The particular medical emergency which had triggered the claim had passed and a different hospital would treat the child in future. As the circumstances which might arise were infinite, it was inappropriate to act in anticipation of an emergency but rather to wait and deal with particular problems, involving specific facts, as they arose.[168] The courts have emphasised the undesirability of seeking declarations on hypothetical facts divorced from a specific factual context.[169] The courts have also declined to grant a declaration on certain questions of law in advance of a statutory appeal to the Secretary of State as that would inappropriately anticipate that appeal.[170] Judicial intervention may be appropriate in cases involving existing facts and where the issue is whether a particular proposed course of action would involve a breach of the law[171] or would be in the best interests of a person[172] or involve questions of the compatibility of certain actions with the European Convention on Human Rights.[173]

7–050   An issue might be academic because the claimant no longer actually needs a remedy as a practical matter. In one case,[174] the Divisional Court refused to grant relief where the applicant challenged the compatibility of legislation with EU law. The legislation had been repealed before the claimant applied for judicial review and the court refused to grant relief which would have served no practical utility. In particular, the court would not grant a remedy merely to show that the public body had behaved improperly.[175] The House of Lords refused to entertain proceedings intended to demonstrate that provisions of the Treason Act 1848 which, on one reading, prohibited a campaign for the replacement of a monarchy with a republic, was incompatible with the ECHR. The House considered that no

---

[168] *R. v Portsmouth Hospital NHS Trust Ex p. Glass* [1999] 2 F.L.R. 905.

[169] *R. (Burke) v General Medical Council* [2006] Q.B. 1132 at [21] and see *R. (Anti-Waste Ltd) v Environment Agency* [2008] 1 W.L.R. 923 at [47].

[170] *R. (Anti-Waste Ltd) v Environment Agency* [2008] 1 W.L.R. 923 at [47].

[171] See, e.g. *R (Clue) v Birmingham City Council* [2011] 1 W.L.R. 99 at [81] (court declined to rule on what the law would be in relation to six hypothetical factual situations agreed by the parties); *Airedale NHS Trust v Bland* [1993] A.C. 789 (whether surgeons could withdraw certain medical treatment from a person incapable of consenting); *Re F (mental patient sterilisation)* [1990] 2 A.C. 1. See below at para.7–057. Such claims are usually brought by way of an ordinary claim in the Family Division rather than judicial review. See *Practice Direction (Declaratory Proceedings: Incapacitated Adults)* [2002] 1 W.L.R. 325 on the practice relating to claims for the grant of declarations in the exercise of the inherent jurisdiction of the court.

[172] *Re F (Adult: Court's Jurisdiction)* [2000] 3 W.L.R. 1740 (court had inherent jurisdiction to determine disputes relating to the welfare of an adult lacking mental capacity to determine his or her own best interests).

[173] Although in *R. (Burke) v General Medical Council* [2006] Q.B. 1132, the Court of Appeal did not consider it necessary to determine if the refusal of food and water delivered by artificial means would contravene Arts 2, 3 or 8 of the European Convention on Human Rights.

[174] *R. v Ministry of Agriculture, Fisheries and Food Ex p. Live Sheep Traders Ltd* [1995] C.O.D. 297.

[175] See also *R. v British Broadcasting Corporation Ex p. Quintavelle* (1997) 10 Admin. L.R. 428 (permission to apply for judicial review refused in relation to refusal to allow a party political broadcast prior to a general election as the date for transmission had passed and relief would be unlikely to be granted: but the Court left open the possibility that, in certain exceptional circumstances, it might be appropriate to grant permission if there was a need for clarification of the law).

practical purpose would be served by the litigation as there was no prospect of any proceedings being brought and the issue raised was not a live, practical issue.[176] The Privy Council has also indicated that it would not normally grant declarations in the abstract or when they would serve no practical purpose. In that case, the claim concerned an individual who contended that he had been unlawfully passed over for promotion some years previously. By the time of the appeal he had been appointed to the relevant post. The Privy Council dismissed the appeal but indicated that, as the proceedings served no practical purpose, it should not be assumed that it would have been prepared to grant a declaration or costs.[177]

The courts have jurisdiction to grant a declaration if there is a need for clarification of the law on an issue of general importance even if the need for a remedy in the particular case has now passed and there is no live issue between the parties. The discretion to hear such disputes, even in public law matters, is to be exercised with caution and the courts ought to not entertain such cases unless there is a good reason in the public interest in doing so. One such case is where the claim raises a discrete point of law not dependent on the facts of the case and where a large number of similar claims are likely to need to be resolved in the near future.[178] The Court of Appeal, for example, entertained a claim for judicial review relating to the lawfulness of the import of endangered species, in that case mahogany from Brazil, notwithstanding no issue in relation to the particular shipment was in issue at the time of the appeal, as the matter raised matters of general importance and further similar shipments were then anticipated.[179]

7–051

There is a strong argument that the courts ought to have jurisdiction in limited circumstances at least to grant advisory declarations in appropriate circumstances.[180] As appears from the above discussion, there are occasions when the courts are prepared to grant declaratory relief in relation to public law issues of general public importance, but there are equally cases indicating that this not appropriate or even possible if there is no concrete, live dispute in existence. The Law Commission considered that the jurisdiction of the courts to grant advisory declarations should be placed on a clear footing and that the courts ought to be specifically empowered to grant such a declaration if the point is one of general public importance.[181]

7–052

---

[176] *R. (Rusbridger) v Att-Gen* [2004] 1 A.C. 357.

[177] *Singh v Public Services Commission, The Times,* August 21, 2014.

[178] *R. v Secretary of State for the Home Department Ex p. Salem* [1999] A.C. 450 (although it was not appropriate to exercise the discretion in that case as the determination would depend on the facts of each particular case).

[179] *R. (Greenpeace Ltd) v Secretary of State for the Environment* [2002] 1 W.L.R. 3304 (permission had been refused at first instance but was granted by the Court of Appeal which reserved the hearing of the substantive claim to the Court of Appeal).

[180] *R. (Campaign for Nuclear Disarmament) v Prime Minister of the United Kingdom* unreported, December 17, 2002 (per Simon Brown LJ at [46]).

[181] "Administrative Law: Judicial Review and Statutory Appeals" 1994 Law Com. No.226 at p.76 [8.14].

Other grounds for refusing a declaration

7–053   The courts may refuse a declaration if the declaration is framed at too high a level of abstraction or too vague as to be of any practical utility.[182] Declaratory relief may be refused if the judgment in the case is adequate for the purpose of clarifying the law.[183]

E.   DECLARATIONS AND THE CRIMINAL LAW

7–054   The courts have had to consider the appropriateness of granting declarations in civil proceedings[184] as to whether particular conduct would or would not be a criminal offence. The courts have jurisdiction to grant a declaration that certain conduct is or is not lawful and the question is whether it is appropriate for them to exercise that jurisdiction. In general terms, the courts are reluctant to grant such declarations in civil proceedings, including claims for judicial review, except in exceptional circumstances. No clear pattern of what constitutes exceptional circumstances, or what criteria are relevant in determining that question emerges from the case law.[185]

7–055   The House of Lords held in *Imperial Tobacco Ltd v Att-Gen*[186] that it was inappropriate for the courts to grant a declaration that certain conduct did not constitute a criminal offence after a prosecution had been started in respect of that conduct. In the words of Lord Lane, where "criminal proceedings have been properly instituted and are not vexatious or an abuse of the process of the court, it is not a proper exercise of the court's discretion to grant a declaration to the defendant in those proceedings that the facts alleged by the prosecution do not in law prove the offence charged".[187]

7–056   The *Imperial Tobacco* case concerned a situation where criminal proceedings had already been instituted and where the reluctance to grant declaratory relief in civil proceedings is greatest.[188] Subject to that consideration, the discretion to grant declaratory relief, whilst exceptional, is essentially flexible. The courts have normally had regard to the following considerations although they are not exhaustive and the weight to be given to particular factors will differ depending on the case. First, the courts are unlikely to be prepared to grant a declaration where the case is fact sensitive in that the outcome may depend on the view taken of the particular facts in a case.[189] This factor is "of great importance" and it has always been recognised that a question of pure law may be more readily made the

---

[182]   *R. (Southall) v Secretary of State for Foreign and Commonwealth Affairs* [2003] Eu. L.R. 832.

[183]   *R. v Secretary of State for Social Services Ex p. Child Poverty Action Group* [1989] 3 W.L.R. 1116; *R. v Barnet LBC Ex p. Johnson* [1989] C.O.D. 538; *R. (Purja) v Ministry of Defence* [2004] U.K.H.R.R. 309 at [73].

[184]   In this context, that means proceedings which are not criminal proceedings before a magistrates' court or Crown Court.

[185]   *R. (Rusbridger) v Att.-Gen.* [2003] 2 W.L.R. 232 at [20].

[186]   [1981] A.C. 718. See also Zamir and Woolf, *The Declaratory Judgment*, 3rd edn (2001), pp.201–216.

[187]   [1981] A.C. 718 at 752. See also *R. v DPP Ex p. Kebilene* [1999] 3 W.L.R. 972.

[188]   See dicta of Simon Brown LJ in *R. v DPP Ex p. Camelot Plc* (1997) 10 Admin. L.Rep. 93 at 104.

[189]   *R. (Rusbridger) v Att-Gen* [2004] 1 A.C. 357, per Lord Steyn at [23]; *R v DPP Ex p. Camelot* (1997) 10 Admin. L.Rep. 93 at p.104.

subject matter of a declaration.[190] Secondly, even where pure questions of law arise, and there is no dispute on the facts, the courts have indicated that, generally, they will not grant declaratory relief in civil proceedings where criminal proceedings have not yet been instituted on the grounds that, all other matters being equal, criminal disputes are best decided in criminal courts between the parties most affected by the outcome.[191] Thirdly, the existence of a cogent public or individual interest in granting a declaration is relevant.[192] Fourthly, the availability of alternative remedies, including a private prosecution, is relevant and may be decisive. Thus, in one case, the Divisional Court refused to quash a decision of the Director of Public Prosecutions not to prosecute a particular company for running the lottery as she did not consider that the lottery was unlawful. The challenge was based on the claim that the Director had erred in law as running the lottery did involve the commission of an offence. The Divisional Court refused to grant a remedy as it considered that a private prosecution brought by the claimant against the rival company for the offence of running an unlawful lottery was a preferable course of action.[193] Fifthly, the courts should be particularly cautious of granting declaratory relief in relation to existing, rather than future conduct, and should be warier of granting a declaration that particular conduct is criminal rather than that particular conduct would not involve the commission of a criminal offence.[194] If the courts granted a declaration in respect of existing conduct, it would be performing the task of the jury. If it declared that certain conduct was not criminal as a matter of law, it would be performing the function of a judge in deciding there was no case to answer. Further, the courts are reluctant to stigmatise the conduct of particular individuals as criminal and are more likely to be prepared to grant a declaration if it involves a declaration as to the interpretation of a particular statutory provision without the need for consideration of the actions of particular individuals.[195] Conversely, in *Ex p. Camelot*, the Divisional Court were influenced in their refusal to grant a remedy in respect of the decision of the Director not to prosecute a company for running an unlawful lottery as to do so would involve stigmatising the conduct of third parties.[196] Sixthly, the fact that there is no genuine dispute or any real risk of criminal proceedings is relevant and influenced the House of Lords in dismissing a claim that the Treason Act 1848 was incompatible with the European Convention on Human Rights as it prohibited campaigning for a republic system of government in place of the monarchy.[197] In practice there was no risk of such a prosecution being brought and no evidence that the statute had had a chilling effect on freedom of expression. Other factors are also relevant to the exercise of

---

[190] See, e.g. *R. v DPP Ex p. Camelot Group Plc* (1998) 10 Admin. L.Rep. 93.

[191] *R. v DPP Ex p. Camelot* (1997) 10 Admin. L.Rep. 93 at 104.

[192] *R. (Rusbridger) v Att-Gen* [2004] 1 A.C. 357 per Lord Steyn at [24]; *R. (Haynes) v SBC* [2007] 1 W.L.R. 1365 at [16].

[193] *R. v DPP Ex p. Camelot* (1997) 10 Admin. L.Rep. 93 at p.104.

[194] *Att-Gen v Able* [1984] Q.B. 795 at 807–808; *R. (Haynes) v Stafford BC* [2007] 1 W.L.R. 1365 at [18]; *R. v D.P.P. Ex p. Camelot* (1997) 10 Admin. L.Rep. 93 at 104.

[195] *R. (Haynes) v Stafford BC* [2007] 1 W.L.R. 1365 at [32] (court prepared to grant a declaration on the true construction of a particular act as to whether a particular activity required to be licensed but was not prepared to grant declarations involving particular individuals who may have engaged in particular conduct and where the issues were fact-sensitive).

[196] *R. v D.P.P. Ex p. Camelot* (1997) 10 Admin. L.Rep. 93.

[197] *R. (Rusbridger) v Att-Gen* [2004] 1 A.C. 357.

the discretion of the courts. These include the fact that the bodies responsible for enforcing the law are not represented before the court and their views are not known.[198] Conversely, the courts may be more prepared to grant declarations where they are sought by the Attorney General.[199]

7–057   There have been occasions when the courts have exceptionally been prepared to entertain civil proceedings not withstanding that the proceedings involve determining whether conduct is or would be unlawful. In general, these cases involve a recognition that a real or cogent public interest is served by dealing with matters in ordinary civil proceedings. In one group of cases, the courts have been prepared to grant declarations on questions of law or statutory construction where there was a real need to do so and this could be done without granting declarations that particular conduct by individuals would contravene the criminal law. The court was prepared to grant a declaration as to the proper construction of statutory provisions governing the sale of birds at a fair. There was a cogent public interest in resolving the issue as different views were being taken by different local authorities in different parts of the country. There was no realistic prospect of a private prosecution being brought. The court was not prepared to grant declarations that particular conduct by particular persons, not party to the proceedings, involved the commission of an offence.[200] Similarly, the court was prepared to consider whether the public authority incorrectly relied on legal advice that it may commit a criminal offence under the Health and Safety Act at Work Act 1974 if it allowed unsupervised swimming in its ponds. There was no other means of testing the lawfulness of the legal advice upon which its decision rested.[201] In another group of cases in the medical field, the courts have recognised that the courts do have jurisdiction to grant a declaration that proposed treatment of a person who has no capacity to consent is lawful and that it is appropriate for the courts to grant declaratory relief. In *Re F*[202] the House of Lords accepted that it was appropriate for the courts to consider whether to grant a declaration that the proposed sterilisation of a mentally incapacitated woman would be lawful. Similarly, in *Airedale National Health Trust v Bland*,[203] the House of Lords accepted that it was appropriate for the courts to rule on whether the withholding of certain medical treatment would be lawful. The House recognised in that case that it would not be desirable to leave doctors in a state of uncertainty as to whether or not proposed action, which they considered appropriate on clinical or ethical grounds, was criminal. In such cases, there was a need for authoritative guidance.[204] The Court of Appeal has emphasised that such declarations should not be granted on an interim basis or at a hearing held without notice having been given to the other parties but should, in accordance

---

[198] *R. (Hampstead Heath Winter Swimming Club) v Corporation of London* [2005] 1 W.L.R. 2930 at [23].

[199] *R. v D.P.P. Ex p. Camelot* (1997) 10 Admin. L.Rep. 93; *R. (Haynes) v Stafford BC* [2007] 1 W.L.R. 1365 at [19].

[200] *R. (Haynes) v Stafford BC* [2007] 1 W.L.R. 1365 esp. at [32]–[33].

[201] *R. (Hampstead Heath Winter Swimming Club) v Corporation of London* [2005] 1 W.L.R. 2930 at [21]–[25].

[202] [1990] 2 A.C. 1.

[203] [1993] A.C. 789. See also *St George's NHS Trust v S* [1998] 3 All E.R. 673.

[204] [1993] A.C. 789.

with normal principle, be dealt with at a hearing where all parties may be represented. Any order made in the absence of a patient would, in any event, not be binding on such a patient.[205]

In a third group of cases, the courts have considered whether advice given by government departments that certain conduct, if carried out, would be lawful and granted appropriate declaratory relief. Here, there is an obvious public interest in individuals generally knowing what the correct legal position is and not having to determine for themselves whether the guidance is correct and whether they would be acting lawfully if they engaged in such conduct.[206]

7–058

The courts considered whether the advice contained in departmental circulars in the area of abortion,[207] and the provision of contraceptive advice to girls under 16 years of age[208] would, if followed, lead to the commission of criminal offences. In a third case, the court considered whether the distribution of a booklet on suicide would constitute an offence.[209] In each case the criminality of conduct was in issue, but actions for declaratory relief were considered appropriate. Where questions of law arise and where there is a genuine need to obtain authoritative judicial guidance, there is much to be said for using declaratory relief to clarify the law. In the sphere of criminal law it is particularly appropriate that individuals should know in advance what the law is.[210] The courts have adequate means to prevent the process of the court being abused, such as their discretion to refuse relief. Another potential group of cases may involve those where the claim is that provisions of primary legislation creating criminal offences are incompatible with provisions of the European Convention on Human Rights. Such claims may, of course, be raised by way of defence to a prosecution.[211] There may be instances where the courts will consider a pure question of law as to compatibility with the Convention in civil proceedings, including judicial review. In *R. (Pretty) v Director of Public Prosecutions*,[212] for example, the House of Lords considered whether the law providing that it was a

7–059

---

[205] *St George's NHS Trust v S* above, fn.203 at 700d–f. The Court of Appeal set out guidelines governing the appropriate procedure at 703c–704j.

[206] See, particularly, the dicta of Lord Goff in the *Bland* case, above, fn.198 at 862B–863D. See also, the dicta in *R (Hilali) v City of Westminster Magistrates' Court* [2010] 1 W.L.R. 241 at [42] (declaration could only be granted against a party to proceedings).

[207] *Royal College of Nursing v Department of Health and Social Security* [1981] A.C. 800.

[208] *Gillick v West Norfolk and Wisbech Area Health Authority* [1986] A.C. 112.

[209] *Att-Gen v Able* [1984] Q.B. 795. Woolf J. gave a judgment setting out his view of what needed to be proved to establish that the distribution of the booklet involved a criminal offence. As the facts would vary from case to case and would have to be proved in each individual instance, he declined to grant a declaration.

[210] See Smith, "Clarifying the Criminal Law: Declarations in Criminal Proceedings" in *Criminal Law: Essays in Honour of J.C. Smith* (1987).

[211] See, e.g. *Barnfather v London Borough of Islington* [2003] 1 W.L.R. 2318 (prosecution for the strict liability offence of failing to secure regular attendance of a child at school; parent claimed, unsuccessfully, that a strict liability offence was incompatible with the right to a fair trial under Art.6 ECHR).

[212] The claim was brought by way of judicial review of a refusal by the Director of Public Prosecutions to give an undertaking not to prosecute, but the Director had no power to give such an undertaking. The claim could have been brought by way of an ordinary claim for a declaration that the conduct they proposed was lawful: see the observations of the Divisional Court in *R. (Pretty) v DPP* [2002] U.K.H.R.R. 97 at 111. See also *R (Nicklinson) v Ministry of Justice* [2014] 3 W.L.R. 200.

criminal offence to assist suicide was compatible with Convention rights, notwithstanding that the procedural mechanism by which the challenge was raised was inappropriate.

7–060   There has been discussion over the effect of a declaration granted in such proceedings. The declaration probably binds only the parties to the proceedings.[213] It would not bar subsequent criminal proceedings nor would it constitute a defence of autrefois acquit.[214] In practice, however, it is unlikely that the carrying out of an operation that a court had declared to be lawful would (absent some change in circumstances) be the subject of a criminal prosecution or if, there were such a prosecution, the criminal courts would inevitably be influenced by the declaration in deciding whether the conduct complained of did, in law, amount to an offence.

7–061   It is also relevant to note that the courts do exercise a supervisory jurisdiction over criminal proceedings started in the magistrates' courts. The Divisional Courts have quashed summonses and prohibited further proceedings where the summonses have disclosed no offence known to the law[215] or where the proceedings constituted an abuse of process.[216] The latter group of cases pose no difficulties as the issue there is whether there has been an abuse and that will not normally involve determining whether conduct is criminal. The former group of cases may be seen as raising the question of whether judicial review proceedings are, as a matter of discretion, appropriate given the fact that questions of criminality also arise. The Divisional Court has, however, refused relief in a claim for judicial review to challenge the lawfulness of a decision not to prosecute where the claim was that the decision-maker had erred in law in concluding that no criminal offence had been made. The Divisional Court concluded that it was inappropriate in such circumstances to grant judicial review and indicated that the appropriate method of proceeding would be a private prosecution.[217]

7–062   Challenges to the legality of advice issued by public bodies, or to decisions by public bodies to initiate criminal proceedings, should be brought by judicial review.[218] Individuals seeking to establish whether their own conduct, actual or proposed, would involve an infringement have sought declarations in ordinary claims brought against the Attorney-General. Where the criminal offence is created by regulations made by a government minister, it will usually be appropriate to seek judicial review of the regulations, naming the responsible minister as the defendant.[219] Declarations sought by the Attorney-General to establish whether conduct engaged in by individuals gives rise to a criminal offence can only be brought by ordinary claim, as judicial review is not available

---

[213] See dicta of Lord Brandon in *Re F* [1990] 2 A.C. 1 at 644G–H and dicta of Judge LJ in *St George's NHS Trust v S* above, fn.203 at 669a–700h.

[214] per Viscount Dilhorne in *Imperial Tobacco Ltd v Att-Gen* above, fn.187 at 741 and see dicta of Lord Goff and Lord Mustill in the *Bland* case above, fn.203 at 862F–G and 888H–889A respectively.

[215] *R. v Horseferry Road Justices Ex p. Independent Broadcasting Authority* [1987] Q.B. 54.

[216] See, e.g. *R. v Horseferry Road Magistrates' Court Ex p. Stephenson* [1989] C.O.D. 470.

[217] *R. v DPP Ex p. Camelot Plc* (1997) 10 Admin.L.Rep. 93.

[218] Although both the *Royal College of Nursing* and the *Gillick* cases were brought by the ordinary claim procedure, it is clear from the judgments that both could be, and the first now should be, brought by way of judicial review (the second, *Gillick*, involved the common law private rights of a parent and so could be brought by ordinary claim proceedings). See Chapter 3 above.

[219] See, e.g. *R. v Secretary of State for Health Ex p. United States Tobacco Inc.* [1992] Q.B. 353.

against private individuals. The Attorney-General always has standing to act in the public interest. Individuals wishing to challenge the legality of conduct of other individuals could not invoke the judicial review procedure against those other individuals, as judicial review is only available as against public bodies, not private individuals.[220] They would either need to seek judicial review of a decision by a public body not to prosecute[221] or bring judicial review proceedings naming the Attorney-General as the respondent. They would be unlikely to have standing to bring an ordinary claim for a declaration as they would need to establish that they had a specific legal right or had suffered some special damage over and above that suffered by the general public.[222] They could, therefore, only bring an ordinary claim if they were able to obtain the consent of the Attorney-General to bring a relator action.

F.   DECLARATIONS AGAINST THE CROWN

Declarations can be granted against the Crown. Historically, the courts had jurisdiction to entertain petitions of right where the Attorney-General (on behalf of the Crown) consented to the bringing of such a claim. The courts also had jurisdiction to grant declaratory relief, and this jurisdiction was revived in *Dyson v Att.-Gen.* in 1911.[223] Proceedings against the Crown in respect of the government of the UK are now governed by the Crown Proceedings Act 1947.[224] This Act abolishes the petition of right. Declaratory relief is now sought in an ordinary action against the authorised department or, if none is appropriate, the Attorney-General.[225]   **7–063**

Declarations against the Crown in public law cases probably cannot be brought by way of judicial review and must be brought by ordinary claim. First, the Crown Proceedings Act 1947 only authorises the bringing of civil proceedings excluding judicial review, and thus provides no jurisdiction to grant declarations by way of the judicial review procedure.[226] The jurisdiction to grant declarations in judicial review is conferred by the Senior Courts Act 1981, but this Act probably does not bind the Crown.[227] Secondly, it could be argued that the availability of the declaration in judicial review cases is tied to the availability of the prerogative remedies,[228] and as these are not available against the Crown   **7–064**

---

[220] See above Chapter 2.

[221] As happened, e.g. in *R. v DPP Ex p. Camelot* above, fn.191.

[222] See *Gouriet v Union of Post Office Workers* [1978] A.C. 435 and see below at para.11–040.

[223] [1911] 1 K.B. 410. For doubts about the correctness of the decision see de Smith, Woolf and Jowell at pp.645–646.

[224] See s.40(2)(b). A certificate to that effect issued by the Secretary of State under s.40(3) is conclusive so far as proceedings under the Act are concerned. The certificate is not necessarily conclusive so far as proceedings brought under the inherent jurisdiction revived in *Dyson v Att-Gen* are concerned, and the Court of Appeal has left open the possibility of allowing proceedings where the court considers that the interest of the Crown in right of the government of the UK is concerned: see *Trawnik v Lennox* [1985] 1 W.L.R. 532.

[225] See Crown Proceedings Act 1947 s.17.

[226] See s.38(2).

[227] See dicta in *R. v Secretary of State for the Home Department Ex p. Herbage* [1987] Q.B. 872 at 885.

[228] Senior Courts Act 1981 s.31(2) and para.2–176.

neither is the declaration available—this argument is unconvincing. That said, the first reason probably precludes the grant of declaratory relief against the Crown by way of judicial review. It is remarkable that the Crown is the only public body not amenable to judicial review, particularly when the review procedure is meant to incorporate safeguards to protect public bodies.

7–065   The matter is not of great practical importance. Statutory powers are normally vested in ministers. The judicial review jurisdiction lies against ministers exercising statutory powers, and a declaration may be granted together with, or as an alternative to, the prerogative remedies. The courts also allow the exercise of prerogative powers by ministers to be challenged by way of judicial review. Even a statutory power vested in Her Majesty in Council may be the subject of a judicial review claim.[229] The situations in which relief would need to be sought against the Crown would seem to be few, and limited to the exercise of prerogative powers by the Sovereign personally. In so far as these raise justiciable issues, the appropriate procedure would be to seek a declaration by an ordinary claim.

G.   STANDING

7–066   An applicant seeking a declaration in a claim for judicial review will have standing if he has sufficient interest in the matter to which the application relates.[230] The test for sufficient interest is now essentially the same for all the remedies sought by way of judicial review, and is discussed in Chapter 11.

7–067   In those cases where a declaration in a public law matter may still be sought by way of ordinary claim, the test for standing is different and stricter. The individual must demonstrate that he has a specific legal right which is affected by the challenged act, or that he has suffered special damage over and above that suffered by the public generally.[231] This, too is considered in Chapter 11.

H.   DISCRETION

7–068   The declaration is a discretionary remedy. Many of the principles governing the discretion of the court to refuse relief in public law cases apply to all the remedies that may be claimed by way of judicial review. These principles are discussed later in Chapter 12. Specific restrictions connected with the nature of the declaratory remedy have been discussed above.

---

[229]   *R. v H.M. Treasury Ex p. Smedley* [1985] 1 Q.B. 657.
[230]   Senior Courts Act 1981 s.31(3).
[231]   *Barrs v Bethell* [1982] Ch. 294.

I. SEVERANCE OR PARTIAL INVALIDITY

The courts may grant a declaration that only part of an order, decision, subordinate legislative instrument or other measure is invalid, if the invalid part can be separated out from the valid part.[232] The principles governing severance, which apply to all the remedies available in a judicial review claim, are discussed in Chapter 5.

7–069

J. INTERIM RELIEF

Interim declarations have not, until recently, existed in English law.[233] The courts insisted that only final declarations of right could be granted under the rules of the Supreme Court. The Crown Proceedings Act 1947 expressly authorises the use of declaratory relief against the Crown but the courts held that this provision only authorised final declarations of right not interim declarations.[234] Now, r.25.1(b) of the CPR creates an interim declaration.

7–070

The precise scope of the interim declaration and the conditions in which the courts will be prepared to grant such a remedy remain to be worked out by the courts. The most likely use of the interim declaration is to spell out the basis upon which a particular law should be understood and applied by public bodies pending the final hearing of a judicial review claim. This may be of particular use in cases involving central government ministers. The courts have jurisdiction to grant interim injunctions against such ministers but appear reluctant in practice to make such orders.[235] Part of the concern may be that interim injunctions have penal consequences if there is a breach and there may be a reluctance to place public bodies, particularly ministers, in a position where they may find themselves facing allegations that they are in contempt. Interim declarations, however, would not be punishable by contempt and would not in fact constitute an order to a person to do or refrain from doing a particular act. They are more likely to be framed as a declaration that a particular law is to be construed in a particular way or that a public body should approach an exercise of discretion on a particular basis (for example, on the basis that certain considerations are or are not relevant to the exercise of that discretion). Public bodies are likely to comply with any such declaration. There may, therefore, be a greater willingness on the part of the courts to grant interim declarations.[236] There may also be a greater flexibility with interim declarations.

7–071

---

[232] See, e.g. *Dunkley v Evans* [1981] 1 W.L.R. 1522.

[233] *International General Electric Co. of New York v Customs and Excise Commissioners* [1962] Ch. 784; *Riverside Mental Health NHS Trust v Fox* [1994] 1 F.L.R. 614; *St George's NHS Trust v S* above, fn.198 at 700c–d.

[234] *International General Electric Co. of New York v Customs and Excise Commissioners*, above, fn.228; *Underhill v Ministry of Food* [1950] 1 All E.R. 591; *R. v I.R.C. Ex p. Rossminster* [1980] A.C. 952.

[235] *M. v Home Office* [1994] 1 A.C. 377 and see below at para.8–024. The courts also have power to grant stays although the applicability of a stay to decisions of ministers is uncertain: see above at paras 6–026 to 6–030.

[236] *M. v Home Office* above, fn.230 per Lord Woolf at 423A–B. In *R. v I.R.C. Ex p. Rossminster* [1980] A.C. 952 Lords Wilberforce and Scarman and Viscount Dilhorne doubted the advisability of creating an interim declaration and only Lord Diplock favoured the proposal. In *R. v Secretary of*

7–072   There is the possibility of granting a final declaration in interlocutory proceedings.[237] There is no reason why such a final declaration should not, in appropriate circumstances, be available against a minister. It is sometimes suggested that *Underhill v Ministry of Food*[238] is authority that no final declaration of rights can be granted against the Crown on an interlocutory application. In a subsequent case,[239] Upjohn LJ in the Court of Appeal expressly left open the possibility of final declarations being granted in interlocutory applications. The Court of Appeal in *R. v Inland Revenue Commissioners Ex p. Rossminster*,[240] granted a final declaration at an interlocutory stage in proceedings. However, the House of Lords reversed the decision on the grounds that a final declaration was inappropriate as questions of fact had not been resolved, not because the jurisdiction did not exist.[241] The Crown Proceedings Act 1947 authorises the granting of any relief that could be granted in proceedings, except for injunctions (and certain other coercive remedies). The courts have a power in exceptional circumstances to grant a final declaration in interlocutory proceedings between subjects, so there is no reason why the courts cannot do so against Crown officers.

7–073   The real difficulty is not the absence of jurisdiction, but the fact that the power is an exceptional one and its use will be "infrequent and only sparingly exercised".[242] The jurisdiction could only be exercised where there was no dispute of fact,[243] and the court was in a position to determine conclusively the relevant questions of law. There are likely to be few occasions when this will be possible if any.[244]

K.   EFFECT OF GRANTING DECLARATORY RELIEF

7–074   A declaration merely declares the rights of the parties or the true legal position in a dispute. It is not a coercive order, and does not require the parties to do any act. Failure to respect a declaratory order is not contempt. The court may grant liberty to apply for coercive relief to ensure that the declaration is in fact respected.[245] In *Webster v Southwark London BC*,[246] Forbes J. exceptionally approved the issuing of a writ of sequestration, where the defendant disregarded a declaration that the plaintiff was entitled to be given the use of a hall for an election meeting. The

---

State for the Environment Ex p. Royal Society for the Protection of Birds (1995) 7 Admin. L.Rep. 434, the House of Lords was prepared to proceed on the basis that interim declarations were available considered that the case was not suitable for such a type of remedy in any event. See also Zamir and Woolf above, fn.3 at p.299 and see Law Commission above, fn.53 at pp.61–64.

[237] *International General Electric Co. of New York v Customs and Excise Commissioners* [1962] Ch. 784; *Clarke v Chadburn* [1985] 1 W.L.R. 78.

[238] [1950] 1 All E.R. 591.

[239] In *International General Electric Co. of New York v Customs and Excise Commissioners* see above, fn.237.

[240] [1980] A.C. 952.

[241] [1980] A.C. 952.

[242] per Upjohn LJ in *International General Electric Co. of New York v Customs and Excise Commissioners* [1962] Ch. 784 at 789.

[243] *R. v I.R.C. Ex p. Rossminster* (see above, fn.236).

[244] See dicta in *St George's NHS Trust v S* above, fn.203 at 700d, 701c and 702h–704gj.

[245] See, e.g. *Wheeler v Leicester City Council* [1985] A.C. 1054.

[246] [1983] Q.B. 698 cited with approval in *St George's NHS Trust v S.* above, fn.198 at 700f–h.

circumstances were exceptional, as the court had been misled by the defendants into believing that a declaratory order would be respected.

L. PROSPECTIVE DECLARATIONS

A declaration is usually granted to establish that a decision or other measure is ultra vires. The practical effect of this is that the decision or measure is retrospectively invalidated. There are clear signs of further developments in the use of the declaration. The courts may refuse relief in respect of the particular decision that triggers off the judicial review application, but go on to deal with the general question of law or statutory interpretation that the case raises. They may then grant a declaration setting out the true meaning of the statutory provision, which will prevent the decision-maker making the same error of law in the future, but which does not grant relief in the individual decision. Such declarations are described here as prospective declarations as they guide decision-makers as to their future actions, but do not retrospectively upset past actions.[247]   **7–075**

The reasons for refusing relief in the individual case are usually connected with the impact of judicial review on third parties or on the administration. Administrators may have been relying on a particular interpretation of a statute or delegated legislation and made numerous decisions on the basis of that interpretation. A decision may have consequences for third parties: decisions of regulatory bodies such as the Monopolies and Mergers Commission or the Panel on Take-overs and Mergers as to whether a take-over bid was or was not permissible may be relied on by numerous third parties trading in good faith in the financial markets.   **7–076**

For the above reasons the courts have, in their discretion, refused to grant any relief in respect of invalid decisions.[248] The next development would be to consider refusing relief in the instant case, but to take the opportunity to clarify the law for the future by granting a declaration on the true meaning of the relevant rules. This would leave the particular decision untouched but offer guidance for future cases. This possibility was first canvassed by the Master of the Rolls in *R. v Panel on Takeovers and Mergers Ex p. Datafin*,[249] when dealing with a decision of the Panel based on an alleged misinterpretation of its own rules. Given the fact that thousands of individuals would have traded in good faith in reliance on the decision and given the time scales inherent in such a market, it would not necessarily be desirable to invalidate the decision. The Master of the Rolls indicated that in such circumstances an appropriate course of action would be for the court to declare the true meaning of the rule, to avoid the Panel repeating the error in future, but not to upset the actual decision in question.[250]   **7–077**

---

[247] See, generally, Lewis, "Retrospective and Prospective Rulings In Administrative Law" [1988] P.L. 78. See the discussion on prospective overruling in Chapter 5 above.

[248] *R. v Monopolies and Mergers Commission Ex p. Argyll Group Plc* [1986] 1 W.L.R. 763.

[249] [1987] Q.B. 815. See also *R. v Panel on Take-overs and Mergers Ex p. Guinness Plc* [1989] 2 W.L.R. 863 at 868.

[250] Any disciplinary sanctions imposed would also be set aside.

7-078 The courts have on occasions refused relief in the specific case but have granted declarations on the correct legal position.[251] In *R. v Dairy Produce Quota Tribunal for England and Wales Ex p. Caswell*,[252] the tribunal gave a decision on Caswell's claim for a quota which was based on an incorrect interpretation of the relevant regulations. The courts granted a declaration stating the true meaning of the regulations. They refused, however, to grant relief in respect of the actual decision on Caswell's claim as the judicial review application had been made with undue delay, and it would be detrimental to good administration to grant relief. In *R. v Secretary of State Ex p. Association of Metropolitan Authorities*,[253] Webster J. granted a declaration that the minister was in breach of a mandatory duty to consult before making regulations restricting eligibility for housing benefit. He refused, however, to quash the regulations for a number of reasons, including the fact that to do so would remove the restrictions on housing benefit and leave local authorities having to meet fresh claims for which they would not have made financial provision.[254] On other occasions, the Court have granted a declaration that a local planning authority had failed to comply with the relevant procedure for considering an application for planning permission but declined to quash the planning permission itself as this would cause substantial hardship or prejudice.[255]

7-079 There are clear advantages in this use of the declaration. Such declarations would allow the court to tread a middle-path which enables them to deliver authoritative guidance on the law to ensure it is properly applied in future, whilst recognising limitations on the use of judicial review to quash decisions with the automatic consequences that flow from the rather blunt instrument of retrospective nullity. The invalidation of individual decisions would continue to be the norm in administrative law. The use of prospective declarations should normally only apply to decisions or measures having ramifications for third parties or the administrative process itself.

7-080 There are, of course, objections to the use of declarations in this fashion. Some may find it repugnant that the courts should, in effect, say to an individual that although the administration has acted unlawfully the courts are unwilling to grant him any relief. It might be argued that the function of the courts is to determine what the law is and that they should not carry out the delicate balancing operation of weighing the interests of the administration against the interests of ensuring that the law is properly interpreted and applied. Such balancing exercises cannot be avoided in modern administrative law. It is generally recognised that the courts

---

[251] This could be said to be contrary to the normal position that a decision of the courts is declaratory of the law. However, the House of Lords had left open the possibility that in certain circumstances, the courts may grant a remedy having a prospective effect only. See *In Re Spectrum Plus* [2006] A.C. 680, per Lord Nicholls at [39], Lord Steyn at [45], Lord Hope at paras [71]–[74], Lord Walker at [161], Baroness Hale at [162] and Lord Brown at [165]. The topic is discussed fully in Chapter 5 above.

[252] [1989] 1 W.L.R. 1089 (affd. decision of Popplewell J.).

[253] [1986] 1 W.L.R. 1. See also *R. v Att-Gen Ex p. I.C.I. Plc* [1987] 1 C.M.L.R. 72.

[254] The dicta suggesting that delegated legislation should not normally be quashed go too far and do not represent the proper approach: see *R. (C) v Secretary of State for Justice* [2008] EWCA Civ 882 at [40]–[41].

[255] See, e.g. *R. (Macrae) v Herefordshire DC* [2012] J.P.L.1356 (CA) (declaration that reasons given failed to comply with the statutory requirements; planning for permission for house not quashed; that was not itself unlawful and the house had already been built); *R v (Gavin) v Haringey LBC* [2004] 2 P. & C.R. 13.

must have the ability to refuse relief for reasons of delay, and the Senior Courts Act 1981 actually expresses this in terms of balancing the interests of the administration against the claims of the applicant. Once it is accepted that the courts can refuse relief, even though the decision-making process is flawed, it is but a short and beneficial step to saying that the courts will refuse relief to the individual but take steps to ensure that the error is not repeated again by granting a prospective declaration. It is interesting to note that the Court of Justice of the European Union has accepted that it has power to limit the effect of its declaratory judgments interpreting European law, so that the interpretation only applies to future situations not past situations.[256] Accepting the concept of prospective declarations also involves a change in the nature of declaratory relief. As their name implies, declarations are currently regarded as declaratory in nature, setting out what the law is. Prospective declarations arguably involve creating or establishing rights and may be seen as constitutive. This in itself should not prevent the development of such declarations, if they are considered desirable.

The discussion so far has concentrated on decisions based on a misinterpreta-   **7–081** tion of the legal rules. Problems may arise if the legal rules are invalid not simply misinterpreted by decision-makers. The question then arises as to whether the courts would grant a declaration that the rules were henceforth invalid, but refuse to upset decisions already taken on the basis of the flawed regulations. The position is in fact the same as misinterpretation of the rules. In both cases decisions are taken without appropriate legal authority existing for those decisions. There may, however, be more resistance to allowing decisions to stand when the instrument authorising the decisions is itself declared invalid than when there is a regulation pursuant to which decisions could be taken but the regulation has been wrongly interpreted. However, in the *Association of Metropolitan Authorities* case,[257] Webster J. granted a declaration that there had been a breach of a mandatory procedural requirement of consultation, but refused to quash the regulations even though (in law) that is the normal consequence of a breach of mandatory requirements. The Treaty on the Functioning of the European Union expressly permits the Court of Justice of the European Union to limit the normal consequences of retrospective nullity when it invalidates regulations.[258]

The legislation creating devolved administrations in Wales, Scotland and   **7–082** Northern Ireland also confers powers on courts to limit the retrospective effect of certain of their decisions. A court which finds that the National Assembly for Wales did not have the power to make subordinate legislation, for example, may make an order removing or limiting the retrospective effect of its decision.[259] These provisions suggest a degree of Parliamentary acceptance or recognition of the appropriateness of prospective remedies.

---

[256] See, e.g. Case 24/86 *Blaizot v University of Liege* [1988] E.C.R. 379; Case 43/75 *Defrenne (Gabrielle) v SABENA* [1976] E.C.R. 471.

[257] [1986] 1 W.L.R. 1.

[258] Art.264 of the Treaty on the Function of the European Union. See, e.g. Case 34/86 *Re 1986 Budget: EC Council v European Parliament* [1986] E.C.R. 2155. See below at para.15–012.

[259] See Government of Wales Act 2006 s.153(2). See also Government of Scotland Act 1998 s.102(2) and the Northern Ireland Act 1998 s.81(2).

M. DECLARATORY RELIEF OUTSIDE CPR PART 54

7–083 Declarations continue to be available in ordinary actions brought by way of writ or originating summons. In such proceedings they will usually be concerned with private law rights not public law rights. Claims for a declaration in a public law matter must normally be brought by way of judicial review.[260] The exceptions to this rule are discussed in Chapter 3.

N. RELATOR ACTIONS

7–084 Declarations may be sought by ordinary claim where the Attorney-General brings an action to enforce a public right,[261] but not a purely private right.[262] The Attorney-General may either bring an action himself acting ex officio, or he may act on the relation of an individual. Relator actions have been used to obtain declarations that action by a public body was ultra vires.[263] The use of relator actions was useful as declarations could only be brought by ordinary action, and the standing requirements for individuals were restrictively applied. Declarations may now be sought by judicial review, where the individual needs only a sufficient interest in the matter to qualify for standing, and the court's interpretation of this requirement is relatively liberal. There is therefore likely to be far less need for relator actions as a means of controlling ultra vires action. It is generally assumed that relator actions are unaffected by the rule in *O'Reilly v Mackman*,[264] and declarations may be sought in ordinary proceedings.[265] This opens up the theoretical possibility that relator actions could be used to circumvent other restrictions, such as the short time-limit and the need to apply for leave. In practical terms, it would seem unlikely that the Attorney-General would accede to relator actions, which were designed solely to avoid the restrictions in the judicial review procedure (which is designed to protect the public interest). Relator actions might possibly be used to circumvent statutory provisions seeking to oust the jurisdiction of the courts, as such provisions may not bind the Crown acting through the Attorney-General.[266]

7–085 In relator actions, the Attorney-General will require the following documentation:

(a) a copy of the claim form;
(b) a certificate of counsel that the claim is a proper one for the Attorney-General to allow; and

---

[260] [1983] 2 A.C. 237.

[261] See, e.g. *Att-Gen, ex rel. Yorkshire Derwent Trust v Brotherton* [1992] 1 All E.R. 230 (claim failed on its merits).

[262] *Att-Gen, ex rel. Scotland v Barratt (Manchester) Ltd, The Times*, July 11, 1991.

[263] *Att-Gen, ex rel. Tilley v Wandsworth LBC* [1981] 1 W.L.R. 854. But see dicta of Scott J. at first instance in *Att-Gen, ex rel. Scotland v Barratt (Manchester) Ltd, The Times*, January 25, 1990, suggesting that review of unlawful decision might not amount to enforcing a public right.

[264] [1983] 2 A.C. 237.

[265] See Grubb, "Two Steps Towards a United Administrative Law Procedure" [1983] P.L. 190 at p.200.

[266] See dicta in *R. v Registrar of Companies Ex p. Central Bank of India* [1986] Q.B. 1114.

(c)   a certificate of the solicitor that the relator is a proper person to be relator and can meet the costs of the proceedings.

Once the Attorney-General has accepted that the claim is a proper one, he will usually leave the actual conduct of proceedings in the hands of the relator.[267] The Attorney-General has a discretion as to whether to consent or not. So far the courts have refused to review the exercise of that discretion.[268]

---

[267] See comments of Lord Denning M.R. in *Att-Gen, ex rel. McWhirter v Independent Broadcasting Authority* [1973] Q.B. 629 at 647.
[268] *Gouriet v Union of Post Office Workers* [1978] A.C. 435. See also *R. v Solicitor-General Ex p. Taylor* (1995) 8 Admin. L.Rep. 206 and see above at para.2–043.

CHAPTER 8

Injunctions

A. INTRODUCTION

An injunction is an order by a court to a party directing him to do or to refrain **8–001** from doing a specified act.[1] Thus, injunctions may be mandatory or prohibitory in form. They may be permanent in that they are granted after a full trial of the issues, and constitute a final settlement of the rights of the parties involved. They may be interim or interlocutory: interim injunctions are temporary remedies which preserve the status quo until a specified date; interlocutory injunctions are temporary remedies which preserve the status quo until the final hearing and disposition of the dispute.

The injunction is an equitable remedy which is used in private law to prohibit **8–002** a person from committing an unlawful act, such as a tort or a breach of contract. The injunction can be used in public law to restrain a public body from acting in a way that is unlawful or ultra vires, or to compel the performance of a duty.

Position prior to 1978

Prior to the reforms in 1977 of the judicial procedure, the injunction was applied **8–003** for by way of ordinary action. The injunction could not be applied for in the same proceedings as the prerogative remedies. Injunctions offered some advantages over the prerogative remedies: the claimant did not need permission to apply; disclosure and cross-examination were available; interlocutory relief designed to preserve the status quo could be claimed. The disadvantage lay in the restrictive rules on standing to sue. Injunctions were primarily a private law remedy designed to vindicate private law rights. An individual could only seek an injunction if he could demonstrate that the actions of the public body affected a specific right of his, or caused him special damage over and above that caused to the public generally.[2]

These restrictions limited the usefulness of injunctions in public law cases as **8–004** an individual seeking to prevent a public authority from acting unlawfully frequently could not demonstrate that he had any private right at stake. He was asserting a public law claim that a public body should not be allowed to act in an unlawful manner.

---

[1] The source of the jurisdiction to grant injunctions is the Senior Courts Act 1981 s.37.
[2] *Boyce v Paddington BC* [1903] 1 Ch. 109; *Gouriet v Union of Post Office Workers* [1978] A.C. 435.

The position at the present time

8–005   Since the introduction of the new judicial review procedure in 1977 which came into force in 1978, injunctions in public law cases may,[3] and usually must,[4] be sought by way of an application for judicial review either alongside or instead of the prerogative remedies. A uniform test of sufficient interest applies to all the remedies, including injunctions, which are available in judicial review proceedings. This test is considerably less restrictive than the former test of specific right or special damage. The earlier cases have been distinguished on the grounds that they dealt with injunctions in the context of private law rights not public law claims. In addition, the principles governing matters such as time-limits, permission to apply, disclosure and cross-examination apply to all the remedies sought by way of judicial review.

B.   USES OF THE INJUNCTION IN PUBLIC LAW

Restraining public bodies from acting unlawfully

8–006   Injunctions may be used to stop a public body from acting unlawfully by exceeding or abusing its statutory, prerogative or other public law powers, or by acting in breach of statutory or common law procedural requirements. The courts have, for example, granted an injunction ordering a local authority not to implement proposals for altering a school where those proposed changes were unlawful,[5] or where there had been a failure to observe a mandatory procedural requirement to give public notice and allow the Secretary of State to consider objections.[6] In another case,[7] Roch J. granted injunctions restraining a local authority from withdrawing its consent to gypsies remaining on a site without first informing the gypsies of the reasons and allowing them 21 days to make objections, and restraining the council from taking a decision to seek possession of the site without first hearing representations. Injunctions could be granted restraining tribunals and inferior courts from hearing cases which are outside their jurisdiction, although the more usual remedy would be prohibition.

Restraining implementation of unlawful decisions

8–007   A court may restrain a public body from taking action to implement an unlawful decision. In *R. v North Yorkshire CC Ex p. M*,[8] Ewbank J. granted a quashing order to quash a decision to place a child for adoption, as the local authority had failed to consult the guardian *ad litem*. He also granted an injunction restraining the local authority from taking any action to implement the decision without first consulting the guardian *ad litem*.

---

[3]   Senior Courts Act 1981 s.31(2), and see paras 2–174 to 2–179.
[4]   *O'Reilly v Mackman* [1983] 2 A.C. 237, and see Chapter 3.
[5]   *Lee v Enfield LBC* (1967) 11 S.J. 772.
[6]   *Bradbury v Enfield LBC* [1967] 1 W.L.R. 1311.
[7]   *R. v Brent LBC Ex p. MacDonagh* [1990] C.O.D. 3.
[8]   [1989] Q.B. 411.

Enforcing public duties

The third potential public law use of injunctions is to compel a public authority to comply with its statutory duty. Public law duties would normally be enforced by way of the prerogative remedy of a mandatory order, but it is possible for a mandatory injunction to be granted ordering the public body to take the necessary action to comply with its statutory duty.[9] An interim mandatory injunction could be granted.[10] This adds a useful weapon to the judicial review armoury, as no interim relief can be granted in respect of a claim for the prerogative remedy of a mandatory order, and an interim injunction is the only means by which a duty could be enforced on an interim basis pending the hearing of the judicial review claim.

8–008

Mandatory injunctions will not be granted unless the courts can specify precisely what the public body needs to do in order to perform its duties[11]; nor will they be granted if they require close supervision by the courts to ensure that they are being observed.[12] There is also authority that the courts should be reluctant to intervene in industrial disputes by the grant of mandatory injunctions. Thus, if a public body is prevented from performing its duties by industrial action by others, the courts are unlikely to grant a permanent or interlocutory mandatory injunction.[13]

8–009

Duties need to be separated out into those which are enforceable in public law and those which give rise to a private law right on the part of an individual. Public law duties are enforceable by a mandatory order or mandatory injunction sought by way of judicial review. Duties imposed on public law bodies but which create a private law right may be enforced by a claim for damages or an injunction (as a private law remedy) sought by way of an ordinary claim.

8–010

Injunctions in the nature of quo warranto

Injunctions may be granted to restrain persons from acting in offices to which they are not entitled to act. Prior to 1938, any information in the nature of *quo warranto* could be laid by the Attorney-General or private prosecutor to determine whether a person was entitled to a particular office. The procedure was abolished in 1938, and since then injunctions are available for this purpose. Section 30 of the Supreme Court Act 1981 empowers the courts to grant an injunction to restrain a person acting in an office of a public nature and of a permanent character which is held under the Crown or created by statute or Royal Charter. Applications for such an injunction can only be made by way of judicial review.[14] There is no modern example of the use of such injunctions.

8–011

---

[9] Mandatory injunctions rather than mandatory orders were sought in *R. v Kent CC Ex p. Bruce, The Times*, February 8, 1986.
[10] *R. v Kensington and Chelsea RLBC Ex p. Hammell* [1989] Q.B. 518.
[11] See dicta of Sir Stanley Rees in *Meade v Haringey LBC* [1979] 1 W.L.R. 637.
[12] [1979] 1 W.L.R. 637.
[13] *Stephen (Harold) & Co. v The Post Office* [1977] 1 W.L.R. 1172, per Geoffrey Lane LJ at 1180. See *Meade v Haringey LBC* (above, fn.11), per Sir Stanley Rees; but see dicta to the contrary of Lord Denning M.R.
[14] Senior Courts Act 1981 s.31(1)(c).

C. INJUNCTIONS AGAINST THE CROWN

8-012 The House of Lords has held that final and interim injunctions can be granted in judicial review proceedings against officers of the Crown, such as central government ministers, exercising statutory powers conferred upon them. It was previously thought that injunctions did not lie against ministers of the Crown acting in their official capacity except to enforce rights derived from European law.[15] The House of Lords in *M. v Home Office*[16] held that injunctions could be granted against officers of the Crown in judicial review proceedings. The House reasoned as follows. Statutory duties now are normally conferred upon ministers rather than upon the Crown. The courts have always drawn a distinction for the purposes of the prerogative remedies, such as mandatory and prohibiting orders, between a minister exercising statutory powers vested in the minister himself and a minister exercising powers vested in the Crown. The prerogative remedies were available in respect of the former but not the latter.[17] Injunctions, including interlocutory injunctions, could be granted against ministers personally in respect of a tort committed by them personally in private law proceedings. Now that injunctions could be obtained in judicial review proceedings, there was no reason to interpret s.31 of the Senior Courts Act 1981 as not empowering the courts to grant injunctions against ministers in judicial review proceedings. Consequently the courts were empowered to grant injunctions in addition to, or instead of, prerogative remedies in judicial review proceedings where a minister was exercising statutory powers conferred upon him.[18] The power to grant injunctions in judicial review proceedings included the power to grant interim injunctions.

8-013 The real difficulty in this area had been the perceived absence of interim rather than final injunctions. There was concern that the courts could not grant an interim injunction requiring ministers to maintain the status quo pending the disposition of the judicial review application. Until recently, no interim declarations were available. Stays may have been available if the final order sought was a quashing or prohibiting order, although the question of whether stays are available to prevent a minister taking or implementing a decision or are limited by their nature to being an order stopping proceedings in a court or tribunal awaits definitive resolution by the House of Lords.[19] In any event, a stay could not positively order the minister to take a particular action and no interim

---

[15] See *R. v Secretary of State for Transport Ex p. Factortame* [1990] A.C. 85 (holding that injunctions were not available as a matter of domestic law) and *R. v Secretary of State for Transport Ex p. Factortame (No.2)* [1991] 1 A.C. 603 (accepting that the courts had to have jurisdiction to grant an injunction against ministers to enforce a right derived from EU law where appropriate, in order to ensure the effective protection of European law rights): see generally para.17–078.

[16] [1994] 1 A.C. 377.

[17] See, e.g. *Padfield v Minister of Agriculture Fisheries and Food* [1968] A.C. 997 (mandatory order issued against a minister).

[18] In relation to ordinary civil proceedings (i.e. proceedings other than judicial review), the House held that injunctions were available against an officer who personally committed a tortious act, such as breach of a statutory duty which gave rise to a private law claim for damages, but only where the individual wrongdoer could be identified and did not lie against an officer of the Crown in his official capacity. That position had not been altered by s.21 of the Crown Proceedings Act 1947.

[19] The Court of Appeal has held that stays may be granted in such circumstances: *R. (H) v Ashworth Hospital Authority* [2003] 1 W.L.R. 127 at [42] but the Privy Council has doubted the availability of a stay in such circumstances: *Ministry of Foreign Affairs, Trade and Industry v Vehicles and Suppliers Ltd* [1991] 1 W.L.R. 550. See above at para.6–027.

relief could be granted if the applicant were seeking mandamus. It was therefore important to determine whether the courts had power to grant interim injunctions against ministers of the Crown.

Since the decision in *M v Home Office*, the CPR have provided for the grant of interim declarations.[20] That empowers the court to grant an interim declaration, setting out the legal basis upon which a minister should proceed pending final resolution of the judicial review application, rather than to grant an interim injunction. The House of Lords has indicated that the jurisdiction to grant final injunctions would only be exercised in limited circumstances and the declaration would continue to be the appropriate remedy as ministers of the Crown could be relied upon to co-operate fully with such declarations.[21] The courts are likely to take a similar attitude to interim relief and it is only in limited circumstances that interim injunctions (rather than interim declarations) will be granted against the central government.[22]

8–014

D. INJUNCTIONS AND LEGISLATION

The courts cannot as a matter of English law grant an injunction which will have the effect of suspending the operation of an Act of Parliament. Thus, as a matter of English law, the courts could not grant an interim injunction which would have the effect of preventing the provisions of the Merchant Shipping Act 1988 from coming into operation.[23] (The position under European Union law is considered below).

8–015

Injunctions will not lie to prevent the enactment of a Bill. The most fundamental reason for this rule is that the Queen-in-Parliament is sovereign and can enact any law it wishes. The courts cannot therefore have jurisdiction to prevent the enactment of legislation as that would deny the sovereignty of Parliament. There would also be difficulties in respect of the grant of injunctions at the different legislative stages. Injunctions will not lie to prevent either House of Parliament debating or even approving a Bill. Such an injunction would violate Art.9 of the Bill of Rights which prohibits the courts questioning proceedings in Parliament. Injunctions are still not available against the Crown when she is acting personally. It would not be possible to obtain an injunction restraining the Queen personally from giving her assent to a bill.

8–016

The courts accept in principle that they have jurisdiction to enforce a contractual obligation not to support a Bill before Parliament or to promote a private Bill.[24] They have also made it clear that they will not in practice grant such an injunction.[25]

8–017

---

[20] See CPR Pt 25 and paras 7–070 to 7–073 above.
[21] *M v Home Office* [1994] 1 A.C. 377 at 422H–423B.
[22] See above at para.7–073.
[23] *R. v Secretary of State for Transport Ex p. Factortame Ltd* [1990] 2 A.C. 85.
[24] *Bilston Corp. v Wolverhampton Corp.* [1942] Ch. 391.
[25] [1942] Ch. 391.

EU law and legislation

8–018   The traditional position now has to be reconciled with the UK's membership of the EU. The Court of Justice of the European Union regards European Union law as having supremacy over all national law. The courts of Member States are required by European Union law to give precedence to European law and disapply conflicting national legislation.[26] The House of Lords, in one of its most significant judgments, has accepted that if there is a conflict between the provisions of domestic legislation and EU law, the English courts are required to give precedence to EU law (at least where Parliament has not expressly stated that it intends to legislate in contravention of EU law). The House accepted that interim injunctions could be granted by virtue of the jurisdiction granted in s.37 of the Senior Courts Act 1981 interpreted in the light of the requirements of European Union law. The House of Lords, therefore, granted an interim injunction requiring the Secretary of State not to apply provisions of the Merchant Shipping Act 1988 where these allegedly contravened rights and claims under the EC Treaty pending a final determination by the Court of Justice as to whether such rights did exist.[27]

8–019   The question also arises as to whether the courts have jurisdiction to grant an injunction to restrain the enactment of legislation which would be incompatible with European Union law or to grant an interim injunction to restrain the enactment of legislation pending a ruling from the Court of Justice of the European Union on the competence of the UK to enact such legislation. Member States of the European Union are under an obligation not to pass legislation which conflicts with European law and not to legislate in areas where the EU has exclusive competence.[28] As a matter of English law, it is unlikely that the domestic courts would accept that they have jurisdiction to prevent the enactment of legislation as opposed to disapplying legislation when enacted to the extent that is incompatible with European Union law. The domestic courts are likely to require an express ruling by the Court of Justice that national courts are under an obligation to prevent the enactment of incompatible legislation before accepting that they had such a jurisdiction. Even if such a ruling were made, the national courts would then need to consider whether there was a conflict between a fundamental principle of national constitutional law, which precludes courts from considering the internal processes of Parliament, with the obligation in the European Communities Act 1972, recognised by the House of Lords in *Factortame (No.2)*, to accept the ruling of the Court of Justice and to give effect to European Union law and act accordingly. If there is such a conflict, the courts would then need to determine how to resolve that conflict as a matter of national constitutional law.[29] If the courts accepted that they were required to prevent the enactment of legislation which was incompatible with European Union law, there would be a number of possibilities so far as final relief were concerned. The courts might grant a prohibiting order restraining the minister presenting the Bill

---

[26] Case 106/77 *Amministrazione delle Finanze dello Stato v Simmenthal S.p.A.* [1978] E.C.R. 629; *R. v Secretary of State for Transport Ex p. Factortame (No.2)* [1991] 1 A.C. 603 and see Chapter 17.
[27] [1991] 1 A.C. 603.
[28] *Amministrazione delle Finanze dello Stato v Simmenthal S.p.A.* [1978] E.C.R. 629.
[29] *R. (Buckinghamshire CC and others) v Secretary of State for Transport* [2014] 1 W.L.R. 324 at [98]–[116] and [203]–[204].

to Parliament or presenting it for Royal Assent. They may grant a prohibiting order restraining Parliament from considering the Bill (on the grounds that European Union law overrode national constitutional law, including Art.9 of the Bill of Rights) although this is extremely unlikely.[30]

Such matters are not mere constitutional speculation, particularly in the light of *Factortame (No.2)*. Permission was granted to apply for judicial review of the decision to introduce the Merchant Shipping Bill 1987 but the application was withdrawn and not proceeded with. On a recent occasion, the Supreme Court had to consider whether a European Union Directive would require the courts to scrutinise the adequacy of Parliamentary consideration of environmental information when enacting a bill providing for the construction of a high speed train line. The Supreme Court considered that, properly construed, the Directive did not require national courts to undertake a scrutiny of the adequacy of the legislative process so that a possible constitutional conflict did not arise.[31]

8–020

Injunctions and subordinate legislation

The courts may be able to restrain the making of subordinate legislation which is ultra vires the powers conferred by the parent Act. The courts could, in principle, grant a prohibiting order or an injunction in judicial review proceedings restraining a minister from making subordinate legislation or even to restrain the minister from laying draft subordinate legislation before Parliament for approval or requiring the minister to withdraw draft subordinate legislation which has been placed before Parliament for approval.[32] In practice, the courts are extremely unlikely to grant such orders or injunctions as they would prevent Parliament even debating subordinate legislation. It is more likely that the courts will grant a declaration, indicating that the proposed subordinate legislation would be ultra vires so that Parliament is aware of the legal position when it considers the subordinate legislation.[33] So far as interim relief is concerned, the courts could grant an interim injunction restraining the minister from preventing draft subordinate legislation to Parliament for approval or requiring the withdrawal of the draft. Again, it is extremely unlikely in practice that the courts would grant interim relief particularly if the effect would be to prevent Parliament having the draft subordinate legislation placed before them and so preventing Parliament from discussing it. It is more likely that the courts will simply grant permission to apply for judicial review and indicate that serious issues as to the validity of the proposed draft need to be considered or grant an interim declaration expressing the court's provisional view as to the lawfulness of the draft subordinate legislation.

8–021

---

[30] The Privy Council in *Rediffusion (Hong Kong) Ltd v Att-Gen for Hong Kong* [1970] A.C. 1136 held that it would not be unlawful for the Hong Kong subordinate legislature to debate a Bill as the restrictions on its legislative competence might be removed by Act of Parliament. Quaere whether the same reasoning would apply to consideration of Bills conflicting with European law.

[31] *R. (Buckinghamshire CC) v Secretary of State for Transport* [2014] 1 W.L.R. 324 at [203]–[204].

[32] See dicta in *M v Home Office* [1994] 1 A.C. 377 confirming the existence of the jurisdiction but indicating that it would be unlikely to be exercised in practice.

[33] See, by analogy, *R. v Boundary Commissioners for England and Wales Ex p. Foot* [1983] Q.B. 600; *R. v HM Treasury Ex p. Smedley* [1985] Q.B. 657 (dealing with a prohibiting order; similar considerations apply to injunctions).

8–022   Particular difficulties may again arise in relation to EU law. The courts have jurisdiction to grant final and interim injunctions suspending the operation of subordinate legislation which is alleged to be incompatible with EU law. The question which arises is whether the courts have jurisdiction to grant injunctions, including interim injunctions, restraining the making of subordinate legislation which conflicts or may conflict with EU law. The Court of Justice has held that Member States are under an obligation not to adopt legislation which conflicts with EU law or to adopt legislation in areas where the EU has sole competence. This obligation would apply to subordinate legislation. It is likely that the English courts would require a clear ruling from the Court of Justice that the courts ought to consider granting an interim injunction preventing the making of potentially incompatible subordinate legislation (as opposed simply to allowing the subordinate legislation to be made and then considering whether to grant an injunction effectively suspending its operation).

Injunctions and Parliament

8–023   The courts will not intervene in the internal proceedings of Parliament. In *Bradlaugh v Gossett*,[34] the courts held that Parliament had exclusive jurisdiction over the internal proceedings of the House, including the interpretation of the law relevant to its internal procedures. They therefore refused an injunction to restrain the Sergeant at Arms from enforcing a resolution of the House of Commons requiring him to exclude Bradlaugh from Parliament, and refused to consider whether the order was void as the House of Commons had misconstrued the relevant legislation. An attempt was made on January 22, 1987 to obtain an injunction restraining named Members of Parliament from showing a film in a committee room of the House of Commons about a Ministry of Defence spy satellite project: Kennedy J. dismissed the application in less than one minute.[35]

E.   INTERIM RELIEF

8–024   Interim injunctions are available in judicial review proceedings. This includes granting interim prohibiting and mandatory injunctions in judicial review against all public authorities[36] including central government ministers.[37] The interim injunction plays a useful role in public law particularly in restraining the implementation of decisions or proposals which are potentially ultra vires pending the hearing of the judicial review application to determine their validity.

8–025   The principles governing interim relief in ordinary private law disputes are set out in the *American Cyanamid* case.[38] They are intended to avoid courts determining disputes of fact or difficult questions of law at the interlocutory stage of an action. Broadly, a plaintiff no longer needs to establish a prima facie case.

---

[34] (1884) 12 Q.B.D. 271.

[35] See, "Parliamentary Privilege, Zircon and National Security" [1987] P.L. 1.

[36] *R. v Kensington and Chelsea RLBC Ex p. Hammell* (see above, fn.10). See also *R. (JM) v Croydon LBC (Practice Note)* [2010] 1 W.L.R. 1658.

[37] *M v Home Office* [1994] 1 A.C. 377 (confirming that injunctions were available against officers of the Crown acting as such).

[38] *American Cyanamid Co. v Ethicon Ltd* [1975] A.C. 396.

He need only establish that a serious issue arises, or that the claim is not frivolous or vexatious or that the application discloses a reasonable prospect of success. Thereafter, the governing consideration is the balance of convenience: this involves assessing whether the plaintiff could be adequately compensated by damages if refused an injunction, or whether the defendant could be adequately compensated in damages if an injunction were granted.

In public law disputes, the adequacy of damages as a remedy will rarely determine whether or not it is appropriate to grant or refuse an interim injunction.[39] For that reason, the courts will normally need to consider the wider balance of convenience and in doing so, the courts must take into account the wider public interest.[40]   **8–026**

Serious issue to be determined

There is still doubt as to whether the claimant in judicial review needs only to prove that there is a serious issue that the proposed act is ultra vires, or whether he needs to establish a prima facie case that the measure is invalid. There are dicta indicating that the serious issue test applies, and that the reasons for not inquiring into the merits of cases at the interlocutory stage apply as much to cases involving public bodies as they do to private individuals.[41] The courts have approached the question by considering whether the claimant can demonstrate a real prospect of success at trial not a merely fanciful prospect.[42] Equally, there are dicta suggesting that public bodies should not be prevented from exercising public law powers unless the plaintiff can establish a prima facie case that the public authority is acting unlawfully.[43]. The courts are certainly reluctant to grant an interim mandatory injunction to compel the performance of public law duties unless the applicant can establish a prima facie case that the public body is acting unlawfully.[44]   **8–027**

A claimant can only be granted permission to apply for judicial review if he can establish an arguable case that the measure under challenge is unlawful. If a claimant cannot establish an arguable case and permission to apply for judicial review is refused, the claim for an interim injunction will also inevitably fail.[45] Conversely, it has been argued that once permission has been granted,[46] there   **8–028**

---

[39] *R. v Secretary of State for Transport Ex p. Factortame Ltd (No.2)* [1991] 1 A.C. 603 at 672G–673B and see below at paras 8–036 to 8–038.

[40] [1991] 1 A.C. 603 at 673B–C. See also *Belize Alliance of Conservation Non-Governmental Organisations v Department of the Environment of Belize* [2003] 1 W.L.R. 2839 at [35] and see also *R v Ministry of Agriculture Fisheries and Food ex p. Monsanto Ltd.* [1999] Q.B. 1161 at pp.1172–1173.

[41] See dicta of Browne LJ in *Smith v Inner London Education Authority* [1978] 1 All E.R. 411, and Sir Stanley Rees in *Meade v Haringey LBC* [1978] 1 All E.R. 411.

[42] *R (Medical Justice) v Secretary of State for the Home Department* [2010] EWCH 1425 (Admin) at [6].

[43] See dicta of Lord Denning M.R. and Geoffrey Lane LJ in *Smith v Inner London Education Authority* [1978] 1 All E.R. 411. See also *Sierbein v Westminster City Council* (1987) 86 L.G.R. 431.

[44] *R. v Kensington and Chelsea RBC Ex p. Hammell* [1989] Q.B. 518; *De Falco v Crawley BC* [1980] Q.B. 460. But see *Meade v Haringey London BC* [1978] 1 All E.R. 411.

[45] See, e.g. *R (Press Standards Board of Finance Ltd.) v Secretary of State for Culture, Media and Sport* [2013] EWHC 3814 (Admin) at [29] (challenge to decision to present a draft Royal Charter to the Privy Council for consideration: no arguable case that decision unlawful so permission refused and claim for interim injunction necessarily failed).

[46] The point was left open in *Sierbein v Westminster City Council* (1987) 86 L.G.R. 431.

must necessarily be a serious issue to be decided and the first stage of the *American Cyanamid* test has been satisfied. This, however, is unlikely to be the case. The threshold for obtaining permission is relatively low,[47] and the courts have refused an injunction where they considered the applicant's case to be speculative and unpromising, notwithstanding the fact that permission had been granted.[48]

8–029   An alternative approach is to take account of the strength of the applicant's case when weighing the balance of convenience. This was the course preferred by Lord Goff in *R. v Secretary of State for Transport Ex p. Factortame Ltd (No.2)*.[49] He considered that the wider public interest which needed to be taken into account included the interest in enforcing apparently valid subordinate legislation or apparently authentic legislation which allegedly contravened EU law. Although not laying down a rule that a prima facie case needs to be made out, he considered that a court should not normally restrain[50]:

> "... a public authority by interim injunction from enforcing an apparently authentic law unless it is satisfied that the challenge to the validity of the law is, prima facie, so firmly based as to justify so exceptional a course being taken."

Balance of convenience: relevance of damages

8–030   The balance of convenience in public law cases must take account of the wider public interest and cannot be measured simply in terms of the financial consequences to the parties.[51] In private law disputes, the balance of convenience is primarily measured in terms of whether the parties could be compensated in damages if interlocutory relief were or were not granted.[52] These considerations are unlikely to play a significant role in public law cases.[53] So far as the claimant is concerned, damages will not usually be available. Damages are not awarded simply because a public body has acted ultra vires its powers[54]; the claimant will need to establish misfeasance or a recognised tort which will often not be possible in many public law contexts or that an award of damages is necessary to vindicate a Convention right. In the relatively rare situations where damages are available, the courts should consider whether they would be adequate to compensate the individual.[55]

---

[47] See Chapter 9.

[48] *R. v London Borough Transport Committee Ex p. Freight Transport Association* [1989] C.O.D. 572. The applicant did succeed in the Divisional Court: see *The Times*, November 17, 1989 and the Court of Appeal: *The Times*, October 4, 1990 but this decision was reversed in the House of Lords [1991] 1 W.L.R. 1.

[49] [1991] 1 A.C. at 603.

[50] [1991] 1 A.C. 674D–E.

[51] *Sierbein v Westminster City Council* (see above, fn.40); *Smith v Inner London Education Authority* [1978] 1 All E.R. 411 and see *Belize Alliance of Conservation Non-Governmental Organisations v Department of the Environment of Belize* [2003] 1 W.L.R. 2839 at [35].

[52] *American Cyanamid Co. v Ethicon Ltd* (see above, fn.36).

[53] *R. v Secretary of State for Transport Ex p. Factortame Ltd (No.2)* [1991] 1 A.C. 603 at 674.

[54] See *Financial Services Authority v Sinaloa Gold Plc* [[2013] 2 A.C. 28 at [31]; and *X v Bedfordshire CC* [1995] A.C. 633 at 70G. There may also be occasions when a claim for damages is possible under EU law and then the question of adequacy of damages may need to be considered: see, e.g. *R v Ministry of Agriculture, Fisheries and Food Ex p. Monsanto Plc* [1999] Q.B. 1161.

[55] See, e.g. *R v Ministry of Agriculture, Fisheries and Food Ex p. Monsanto Plc* [1999] Q.B. 1161.

Damages are not likely to be relevant so far as the public body is concerned. **8–031** An applicant may not be in a position to be able to give a worthwhile undertaking. Where the result of an interim injunction would be to prevent a public body enforcing a decision or other measure, and stopping the applicant from doing a particular act, it may be difficult to identify the individuals who would suffer damage if the applicant was able to ignore the measure.[56]

Balance of convenience: the wider public interest

More significantly, the public interest frequently cannot be measured in terms of **8–032** financial consequences. The public body will have taken the decision or adopted the measure in the exercise of powers which it is meant to use for the public good. The courts must take into account that wider public interest in deciding whether to grant interim relief.[57] The courts will be placed in the difficult position of trying to place a value on the public interest, and balancing that against the financial or other consequences suffered by the individual. In *Sierbein v Westminster City Council*,[58] for example, the applicant sought an interim injunction to suspend a decision refusing him a licence for a sex shop so that he could re-open the sex shop. The court had to weigh the public interest in controlling the number of sex shops in the area against the financial loss suffered by the individual having to close his business, given the fact that damages would not be available if it transpired that the refusal of a licence was ultra vires and he could lawfully have kept his business open. The court came down in favour of refusing an injunction.[59] In another case, the courts refused to grant an interim injunction to prevent the Secretary of State from taking steps to implement a decision banning the transmission of a particular foreign satellite service carrying pornographic material. The Secretary of State's decision was based, in part, upon the need to protect children who might gain access to the programmes. The Divisional Court, whose decision was upheld by the Court of Appeal, considered that the need to protect the welfare of children far outweighed any commercial damage to the broadcaster in not being able to broadcast the programme and refused an interim injunction.[60] Conversely, the court granted interim relief to prevent the Secretary of State implementing a policy permitting removal of persons from the United Kingdom without first giving 72 hours notice. The court accepted that there was a public interest in the executive being able to implement its policy. That had to be weighed against other factors, including the risk of persons being removed without having the opportunity to make a case that removal was not justified, the fact that the impact on the Secretary of State's overall policy was likely to be minimal as this aspect of the policy affected a

---

[56] See, e.g. *R. v Secretary of State for Transport Ex p. Factortame Ltd (No.2)* (above, fn.53).

[57] See *Smith v Inner London Education Authority* [1981] 1 All E.R. 411, esp. at 422 and *Factortame (No.2)* (above, fn.53), esp. at 870.

[58] (1987) 86 L.G.R. 431.

[59] See also, *R. v Knight Ex p. Khan* [1989] C.O.D. 434; *R. v London Borough Transport Committee Ex p. Freight Transport Association* [1989] C.O.D. 572.

[60] *R. v Secretary of State for the National Heritage Ex p. Continental Television BV* [1993] 1 C.M.L.R. 387 at 398.

relatively small number of individuals and the fact that this was a policy and was not contained in subordinate legislation and had not been laid before Parliament.[61]

8–033   One area where different views of the public interest have been taken by the courts concerns publication of reports. It is now common for statute to set up an inspectorate to investigate and report on standards in such areas as schools and further and higher education. Regulatory bodies may also have jurisdiction to investigate individual complaints and publish their findings. The standing or reputation of individuals or bodies may be materially affected by such reports. They may seek judicial review alleging that they have not been given a fair opportunity to comment on the allegations or proposed findings. The question will then arise as to whether the courts ought to grant interim relief preventing the publication of the report pending the outcome of the judicial review claim. The courts are generally reluctant to grant injunctions restraining the publication of information. The High Court refused to grant an interim injunction restraining the publication by the Advertising Standards Authority of a report on a complaint.[62] The court took the view that, as a matter of general principle, the courts would not normally prevent the publication of opinion or the dissemination of information save on pressing grounds. The court considered that any damage to the reputation of the individual would not be irreparable and the individual would have other means of correcting any adverse impression left by the report if it were found to be unlawful. On another occasion, however, the High Court did grant an interim injunction restraining disclosure of a report by the Advertising Standards Authority upholding a complaint. The court considered that the damage to the individual's reputation outweighed the cost to the authority of not publishing its report (and that cost could, in any event, be calculated) and so granted an interim injunction.[63]

8–034   The preferable view is that the courts ought not, in general, to restrain the publication of reports and there needs to be a convincing reason as to why such an order should be made. There is unlikely to be sufficient reason to restrain the publication of reports of bodies investigating standards in schools or other institutions. Their educational reputation may be affected by an adverse report but there are means of correcting such impressions and, if the report ultimately were found to be unlawful, the report could not be used as a means of disadvantaging the institution. Reports which make damaging findings of misconduct in relation to individuals may possibly fall within another category, particularly if the report will influence the person's livelihood and is unlikely to be easily remedied. In such circumstances, there may be a case for granting an interim injunction. Even here, there will generally be a countervailing public interest in the ability to inform the public immediately of the views that the appropriate public body have formed of the individual's conduct and also in ensuring freedom of expression.

---

[61] *R (Medical Justice) v Secretary of State for the Home Department* [2010] EWHC 1425 (Admin).

[62] *R. v Advertising Standards Authority Ex p. Vernon's Organisation Ltd* [1992] 1 W.L.R. 1289. That approach has been followed in subsequent cases: see e.g., *R (Mathias Rath BV) v Advertising Standards Authority Ltd.* [2001] H.R.L.R. 22 at [30] and *R (City College Birmingham) v Ofsted* [2009] E.L.R. 500 and cases cited therein.

[63] *R. v Advertising Standards Authority Ex p. Direct Line Financial Services Ltd* [1998] C.O.D. 20. See also *R. v National Health Service Executive Ex p. Ingoldby* [1999] C.O.D. 167 and *R. (Debt Free Direct Ltd) v Advertising Standards Authority Ltd* [2007] EWHC 1337 (Admin).

Cases affecting third parties

Claims for interim relief in judicial review are generally made against the public body which is the defendant to such a claim. Such claims may, however, affect third party individuals. They may have relied upon the decision or measure that is said to be unlawful or they may intend themselves to take action based upon the measure that is under challenge. First, the claimant may, in appropriate circumstances, seek interim relief against an individual who is an interested party to prevent them from acting in reliance on a measure that is under challenge. The claimant will not have to establish a private law cause of action against the interested third party. In judicial review proceedings, it is sufficient if the claimant is challenging a public law measure and it is appropriate, in all the circumstances, to grant interim relief preventing a third party from acting in reliance on the challenged measure.[64] Secondly, if interim relief is sought against the public body, but it could have serious financial consequences for an interested third party, the court may be reluctant to grant interim relief unless the claimant provides an undertaking in damages to compensate the third party for any loss suffered.[65]

8–035

Cases involving EU law

Particular difficulties arise in cases where it is alleged that national law or administrative measures are contrary to EU law and questions as to the proper interpretation are referred to the Court of Justice for a preliminary ruling under Art.267 of the Treaty on the Functioning of the European Union. It may be 18 months or so before the preliminary ruling is received.[66] In such cases, the approach to determining whether interim relief should be granted is a matter of national law applying the existing national law principles governing the discretion to grant interim relief.[67] Normally, this involves the court considering the adequacy of damages and the balance of convenience, including the wider public interest.[68] A very wide range of matters may be relevant to the consideration of the balance of convenience and the public interest and no

8–036

---

[64] See *R. v The Licensing Authority Established by The Medicines Act 1968 (acting by The Medicines Control Agency) Ex p. (1) Rhone Poulenc Rorer Ltd and (2) May & Baker Ltd* [1998] Eu. L.R. 127 at 142; and *R. (Prokopp) v London Underground Ltd, The Times,* May 2, 2003 (decision of High Court granting injunction to prevent development pending decision by local planning authority on whether to take enforcement action alleging breach of planning control; Court of Appeal allowed the appeal on the grounds that the court would not intervene by way of injunctive relief unless there were reason to believe that the local planning authority might have acted unlawfully in not taking enforcement action which was not so in the present case; the Court of Appeal did not cast doubt on the ability of the courts to grant interim injunctive relief in principle in an appropriate case: see [2004] Env. L.R. 170 esp. at [48]–[50]).

[65] See, e.g. *R. v Secretary of State for the Environment Ex p. Royal Society for the Protection of Birds* [1997] Env.L.R. 431; *Belize Alliance of Conservation Non-Governmental Organsiations v Department of Environment of Belize* [2003] 1 W.L.R. 2839 at [38]–[39]; *R. v Inspectorate for Pollution Ex p. Greenpeace Ltd* [1994] 1 W.L.R. 50 (dealing with a stay, rather than interim relief but similar principles apply).

[66] See *R. v Minister of Agriculture Fisheries and Food Ex p. Monsanto Plc* [1999] Q.B. 1161.

[67] *R. v Secretary of State for Transport Ex p. Factortame Ltd (No.2)* [1991] 1 A.C. 603.

[68] [1991] 1 A.C. 603 at 672–673.See also *R. v Minister of Agriculture Fisheries and Food Ex p. Monsanto Plc* [1999] Q.B. 1161.

particular consideration is to be regarded as necessarily decisive.[69] In cases involving challenges to national legislation, a court will, however, need to have regard to the strength of the claim that the legislation is incompatible with European Union law and a court will not normally grant an interim injunction disapplying national legislation unless it is satisfied that the challenge is so firmly based as to justify such a course of action.[70] In cases which do not involve disapplying national legislation but involve a claim that administrative action contravenes European Union law, the courts may have regard to the likelihood of the claim succeeding or failing.[71] There may be existing European Union case law which indicates that a question, although referable, is likely to be answered in a particular way.[72] In general, however, the courts do not encourage detailed consideration of the likelihood of success or failure in deciding whether to grant interim relief.[73] Further, in many case, the chances of success are equally balanced and the courts are not in a position to determine the likelihood of one or other party succeeding. In those circumstances, the court necessarily will have regard to the adequacy of damages and the wider public interest.[74]

8–037   Different considerations arise where the national measure is one intended to implement or give effect to EU legislation, such as a regulation, and it is claimed that the EU measure is invalid. The national courts have no jurisdiction to rule on the validity of an EU act and, if they entertain doubts as to its validity, they must refer that question to the Court of Justice of the European Union.[75] The Court of Justice has also given guidance on the appropriate test to be adopted by the national courts in considering whether to grant interim relief restraining the national authorities from implementing the EU act until the preliminary ruling is made.[76] The Court of Justice has held that national courts should only grant interim relief if they are satisfied that there are serious doubts as to the validity of the measure; and there is an urgent need for interim relief in order to avoid serious and irreparable damage to the party seeking interim measures. Purely financial damage will not be sufficient to justify the grant of interim relief as it will not be irreparable. The national court is also required to have regard to the

---

[69] *R. v HM Treasury Ex p. British Telecommunications Plc* [1994] 1 C.M.L.R. 621 at 647; *Factortame (No.2)* above, fn.60 at 674A–D.

[70] *Factortame (No.2)* [1991] 1 A.C. 603 at 674C–D; *Kirklees BC v Wickes Building Supplies Ltd* [1993] A.C. 227 at 280F–G.

[71] *R. v Secretary of State for the National Heritage Ex p. Continental Television BV* [1994] 1 C.M.L.R. 387 at 398; *R. v HM Treasury Ex p. British Telecommunications Ltd* [1994] 1 C.M.L.R. 621 at 648.

[72] *R. v HM Treasury Ex p. British Telecommunications Plc* [1994] 1 C.M.L.R. 387 at 647.

[73] *R. v HM Treasury Ex p. British Telecommunications Plc* [1994] 1 C.M.L.R. 387 at 648.

[74] *R. v Secretary of State for the National Heritage Ex p. Continental Television*, above, fn.63 at 398; *R. v Secretary of State for Health Ex p. Generics (U.K.) (E.R. Squibb and Sons Ltd intervening)* [1997] C.O.D. 294.

[75] Case 314/85 *Foto-frost v Hauptzollamt Lubeck-Ost* [1987] E.C.R. 4199 at [20]; Case C-344/4 *R. (IATA) v Secretary of State for Transport* [2006] E.C.R. I-403 and see below at para.18–003. For an application of the test in domestic courts, see *R. (Intertanko) v Secretary of State for Transport* [2007] Env. L.R. 8 at [46].

[76] Joined Cases C-143/88 and C-92/89 *Zuckerfabrik Suderdithmarschen AG v Hauptzollamt Itzehoe* [1991] E.C.R. I-451 and Case C-465/93 *Atlanta Fruchthandelsgesellschaft mbH v Bundesamt fur Ernahrung und Forstwirtschaft* [1995] E.C.R. I-3761 at [31]–[51] at 3790–3795 and see also *R. v Secretary of State for Health Ex p. Macrae Seafoods Ltd* [1995] C.O.D. 369 (reference to Court of Justice but no interim relief granted).

obligation to ensure that full effect is given to European Union law and, where doubts as to its validity arise, that the EU interest is taken into account. This requires the national court to consider whether the EU measure would be deprived of all effectiveness if interim relief were granted or, if there were to be a financial risk to the EU from the grant of interim relief, that adequate financial guarantees such as the deposit of money or security (or presumably in the UK, cross-undertakings in damages) are in place. The national courts are also required to have regard to the decisions of the Court of Justice and national courts cannot grant interim relief if the Court of Justice has already dismissed a materially similar claim that an EU instrument is invalid. The High Court has, on one occasion, found that the restrictive criteria for granting interim relief were satisfied. The case involved the implementation of a Directive requiring manufacturers of compound feeding stuffs to state the percentage by weight of the various ingredients used. The producers contended that the Directive was unlawful as the EU had no legal power to adopt the Directive and that it was disproportionate and involved a breach of their industrial property rights. The question of the validity of the Directive was referred to the Court of Justice. The High Court granted interim relief to suspend the operation of the implementing domestic legislation as, while accepting that interim relief would deprive the Directive of effectiveness, it also accepted that the measure would cause serious and irreparable harm to the businesses involved.[77]

The position is less clear in relation to interim relief to suspend national measures which are intended to implement a Directive alleged to be invalid but which are adopted before the date by which the Directive must be implemented. In *R. v Secretary of State for Health Ex p. Imperial Tobacco Ltd*[78] the Court of Appeal held by a majority that an application for interim relief to prevent the UK government acting to implement a Directive in such circumstances was to be determined in accordance with the principles developed by the Court of Justice in the *Zuckerfabrik*[79] case and not on the basis of the domestic law principles governing interim relief. By the time that the case reached the House of Lords, the matter had become academic as the government had undertaken not to make any national regulations implementing the Directive in question given the opinion of the Advocate General in proceedings before the Court of Justice that the Directive was invalid. Three members of the House of Lords held that it was at least arguable that the appropriate test was that laid down in EU law, not the domestic law test, and would have referred the matter to the Court of Justice under Art.267 TFEU for a preliminary ruling on what was the proper test to apply in considering the grant of interim relief.[80] Two of their Lordships considered that the appropriate test was the domestic law test and, further, that the matter was

8–038

---

[77] *R. (ABNA) v Food Standards Agency and The Secretary of State for Health* [2004] Eu. L.R. 88. Responsibility for implementing the Directive had been transferred to the devolved administrations. This case concerned the implementing regulations made for England. Subsequently, similar orders were made in respect of the implementing regulations made by the respective devolved administrations for Wales, Scotland and Northern Ireland.
[78] [2000] 2 W.L.R. 834.
[79] Joined Cases C-143/88 and C-92/89 *Zuckerfabrick Suderdithmarshcen AG v Hauptzolllamt Itzehoe* [1991] E.C.R. I-415 and *Atlanta Fruchthandelsgesellschaft mbH v Bundesamt fur Ernahrung und Forstwirschaft* [1995] E.C.R. I-3761.
[80] [2001] 1 W.L.R. 127.

acte clair and no reference was required. The Court of Justice has subsequently held that where it is alleged that national legislation is incompatible with provisions of Community law, it is a matter for national law to determine the criteria for deciding on the grant of interim relief to suspend the national law.[81]

Procedure for applying for interim relief in judicial review claims

8–039   Claims for interim relief must be included in the claim form.[82] Claims for judicial review may only be commenced if the claimant is given permission.[83] The usual procedure for dealing with claims for judicial review is for the claim form to be served on the public body which is the defendant and any interested party.[84] They have 21 days in which to put in an acknowledgment of service.[85] The judge will then consider the claim on the papers, and without a hearing to determine whether to grant permission to proceed.[86] A judge may grant interim relief on the papers but, except in cases of urgency, the better practice is for any application for interim relief to be put over to an oral hearing, with notice being given to the other parties who are able to file evidence in advance if appropriate and attend and make representations at the hearing.[87]

8–040   Frequently, there is an urgent need to consider a claim for permission to apply for judicial review or interim relief or both. The Administrative Court has introduced a procedure for urgent cases[88] and the Divisional Court has given guidance on that procedure.[89] Claimants should complete a form requesting urgent consideration of the claim,[90] setting out why there is a need for urgency, the time within which consideration of the application for permission should take place and the date by which any substantive hearing should take place and, importantly, the date and time when it was first appreciated that an immediate application might be necessary and the reasons for any delay.[91] If the claimant is also seeking interim relief in addition to an urgent consideration of the application for permission, he should provide a draft order and the grounds for seeking interim relief. The claim form, the application for urgent consideration, the draft order and grounds for seeking interim relief, should be served on the defendant and any interested party. The claimant is under an obligation to make full and frank disclosure of relevant matters, including matters adverse to his case.[92] The matter will then be considered by a judge who will make appropriate

---

[81]   Case C-432/05 *Unibet (London) Ltd v Justitiekanslern* [2007] E.C.R. I-2271 at [79]–[81].

[82]   CPR r.54.6. See generally Chapter 9 below.

[83]   CPR r.54.4.

[84]   CPR r.54.7.

[85]   CPR r.54.8.

[86]   Practice Direction – Judicial Review, para.8.4. The claim may be renewed at an oral hearing if permission is refused on the papers: see CPR r.54.12.

[87]   See dicta of Parker LJ in *R. v Kensington and Chelsea RBC Ex p. Hammell* [1989] Q.B. 538–539.

[88]   See Practice Statement (Administrative Courts: Listing and Urgent Cases) [2002] 1 W.L.R. 810.

[89]   In *R (Hamid) v Secretary of State for the Home Department* [2012] EWHC 3070 (Admin).

[90]   The appropriate form is N463.

[91]   Failure to provide this information alone might justify a court refusing to consider the application: see *R (Hamid) v Secretary of* State *for the Home Department* [2012] EWHC 3070 (Admin) at [8].

[92]   See *R. (Lawler) v Restormel BC* [2007] EWHC 2299; [2007] A.C.D. 2. Specific guidance has been given by the Court of Appeal on applications for interim relief in cases where the claimant is about to be removed from the United Kingdom: see *R. (Madan) v Secretary of State for the Home Department*

directions.[93] These could include abridging the time for service of an acknowledgment of service, ordering expedition or giving directions relating to the filing and service of written evidence. Where a claim for interim relief is made, the judge may direct that there be an oral hearing to consider the application for interim relief and that, usually, will be an appropriate method of proceeding. If necessary, for example because of urgency, the court can grant interim relief on the papers only, pending an oral hearing of the application, and will also give liberty to the defendant to apply to discharge the interim injunction if appropriate.[94] Interim relief can, in urgent cases, be granted before permission to proceed with the claim is given.[95] If an application for interim relief is refused on the papers, the appropriate course is for the claimant to seek an oral hearing before a judge, either in court or, if time does not permit that, to the out of hours duty High Court judge rather than applying to the Court of Appeal for permission to appeal the refusal of interim relief.[96]

F. INJUNCTIONS OUTSIDE THE JUDICIAL REVIEW PROCEDURE

Injunctions in aid of the criminal law

One use of the injunction is to restrain an individual from breaking the criminal law.[97] Such injunctions are sought in ordinary civil proceedings against individuals or companies, not by judicial review. They will be dealt with here partly for reasons of convenience and partly as the enforcement of the criminal law can legitimately be viewed as a public law function.

8–041

[2007] 1 W.L.R. 2891. See also *R. (Hamid) v Secretary of State for the Home Department* [2012] EWHC 3070 (Admin). Specific problems have also occurred in relation to asylum seekers who have been refused support because they did not make their claim as soon as reasonably practicable, in accordance with s.55 of the Nationality, Immigration and Asylum Act 2002. Specific guidance has been issued by the Administrative Court and any claim for interim relief in such cases should follow that guidance: see *R. (Q, D, KH, OK, JK H, T and S) v Secretary of State for the Home Department* [2004] J.R. 5 and subsequently see *Practice Statement (Judicial Review: Asylum Support)* [2004] 1 W.L.R. 644.

[93] See *Practice Statement (Administrative Courts: Listing and Urgent Cases)* [2002] 1 W.L.R 810 at 811C–812B.

[94] *R. (Lawler) v Restormel BC* [2007] EWHC 2299 (Admin); [2007] A.C.D. 2. In urgent cases where the courts grant an interim order prohibiting removal of a foreign national from the United Kingdom, the courts do not normally fix an oral hearing but simply give the defendant liberty to apply to discharge the order. The courts will consider the application for permission to apply for judicial review on the papers at a later date and, if that is refused, the interim order will usually be discharged. If permission is granted, the order is usually continued subject to the defendant having liberty to apply.

[95] *M v Home Office* [1994] 1 A.C. 377 at 423C.

[96] *R. (MD (Afghanistan)) v Secretary of State for the Home Department (Practice Note)* [2012] 1 W.L.R. 2422 at [21]–[24].

[97] The court may also grant a mandatory order requiring the defendant to take positive steps to undo the act in question: see *Kensington & Chelsea RBC v Harvey Nichols & Co. Ltd* [2001] 1 P. & C.R. 378 at [38] (defendant ordered to remove unlawful advertising).

Criteria for determining whether to grant an injunction

8–042   The use of the jurisdiction to grant an injunction to aid the criminal law needs to be carefully exercised, as the penalties for contempt for disregarding the injunction may far exceed the criminal penalties provided by Parliament for the offence in question.[98] It is an exceptional jurisdiction to be used with great caution.[99] There must be more than a mere infringement of the criminal law before the civil jurisdiction can be invoked in aid.[100] The question is whether: " ... criminal proceedings are likely to prove ineffective to achieve the public interest purposes for which the legislation in question has been enacted."[101] Before the court will exercise the jurisdiction, they must be able[102]:

> " ... to draw the inference that the defendant's unlawful operations will continue unless and until effectively restrained by law and that nothing short of an injunction will be effective to restrain them."

8–043   Earlier formulations of the test which focused on whether the conduct was "deliberate and flagrant",[103] or whether the criminal sanctions were inadequate are now to be viewed as illustrative of the situations in which the basic test is likely to be satisfied.[104] They are not to be read as limitations on the jurisdiction to grant injunctions, but as examples of where it is appropriate to grant them. A number of factors emerge from the case law as relevant in determining whether injunctions are necessary to restrain unlawful conduct.

Conduct of the defendant

8–044   The conduct and attitude of the defendant is clearly significant. The fact that there has been a "deliberate and flagrant" disregard of the law is clearly highly relevant in determining whether to grant an injunction, even though it is not now an essential precondition. Such conduct may be evidenced by the fact that previous convictions have not deterred the individual from committing an offence on subsequent occasions. It is not, however, necessary to attempt criminal prosecutions first if there is other clear evidence that the defendant is not going to

---

[98]   *Stoke-on-Trent City Council v B & Q (Retail) Ltd* [1984] A.C. 754.

[99]   *City of London Corp. v Bovis Construction Ltd* (1988) 86 L.G.R. 660, CA; *Gouriet v Union of Post Office Workers* [1978] A.C. 435.

[100]   *Stoke-on-Trent City Council v B & Q (Retail) Ltd* [1984] A.C. 754.

[101]   per Kerr LJ in *Portsmouth City Council v Richards* [1989] 1 C.M.L.R. 673 at 681–683.

[102]   per Millett J. in *Wychavon DC v Midland Enterprises (Special Event) Ltd* [1988] 1 C.M.L.R. 397 at 402: the test was approved by the Court of Appeal in *City of London Corp. v Bovis Construction Ltd* (1988) 86 L.G.R. 660; and see *Kirklees BC v Wickes Building Supplies Ltd* [1993] 2 A.C. 227 at 270A–B.

[103]   per Bridge LJ in *Stafford BC v Elkenford Ltd* [1977] 1 W.L.R. 324 at 330, and see *Stoke-on-Trent City Council v B & Q (Retail) Ltd* [1984] A.C. 754. The Court of Appeal in *Runnymede BC v Ball* [1986] 1 W.L.R. 353, held that the jurisdiction was not confined to such cases.

[104]   *Portsmouth City Council v Richards* [1989] 1 C.M.L.R. 673 at 683.

observe the law.[105] Persistent or repeated contraventions,[106] particularly following warnings or notices that the conduct is unlawful, are relevant even if no criminal proceedings have been brought.[107] The courts are more likely to grant an injunction where it is clear that the defendant intends to continue the illegal conduct if no injunction is granted,[108] or is unprepared to give assurances that he will observe the law if no injunction is granted.[109]

Adequacy of the criminal penalties

The inadequacies of the criminal sanctions will be considered.[110] The penalties may be inadequate to deter the defendant from continuing to engage in the illegal conduct. Fines may be small compared with the profits that can be obtained from the illegal conduct[111]: this may be particularly true if the illegal operations are being carried on on a large scale by big organisations.[112] If heavy penalties could in theory be imposed, the courts may assess how realistic it is to expect the appropriate proceedings to be brought. A trading company could, for example, have been fined for aiding and abetting each individual trader at a Sunday market and could have been fined up to £1,000 in respect of each offence. The difficulties of bringing a mass of individual prosecutions against hundreds of traders and prosecuting the trading company for aiding and abetting each one made it an unrealistic prospect. The only effective way of ensuring observance of the law was to grant an injunction.[113] There may also be delays in the prosecution process which may result in widespread disregard of the law, or enable individuals to continue breaking the law pending the resolution of the criminal proceedings.[114]

8-045

Other considerations

The extent of the harm to the public interest may be relevant. The fact that the defendant is engaged in conduct which breaches planning controls in the green belt and which will, in practical terms, be irreversible has influenced the courts in favour of granting an injunction.[115] Conversely, the fact that the conduct has taken place over a long period of time without any action being taken to restrain

8-046

---

[105] See, e.g. *Mayor of London v Hall* [2011] 1 W.L.R. 504 at [55]–[56] (evidence that defendants would not be deterred by penalties from continuing to breach the byelaws).
[106] *Wychavon DC v Midland Enterprises (Special Event) Ltd* (above, fn.91); *City of London Corp. v Bovis Construction Ltd* [1988] 1 C.M.L.R. 397.
[107] *Runnymede BC v Ball* [1986] 1 W.L.R. 353.
[108] *Stoke-on-Trent City Council v B & Q (Retail) Ltd* [1984] A.C. 754.
[109] *Wychavon DC v Midland Enterprises (Special Event) Ltd* [1988] 1 CMLR 397.
[110] *Gouriet v Union of Post Office Workers* [1978] A.C. 435.
[111] In cases involving breach of the Shops Act 1950, the profit from trading on a Sunday may well far exceed the available fines: see *Stoke-on-Trent City Council v B & Q (Retail) Ltd* [1984] A.C. 754.
[112] See dicta of Millett J. in *Wychavon District Council v Midland Enterprises (Special Event) Ltd* [1988] 1 C.M.L.R. 397 at 402.
[113] [1988] 1 C.M.L.R. 397.
[114] See dicta of Fox LJ in *Runnymede BC v Ball* [1986] 1 W.L.R. 353) at 359, and of Lord Templeman in *Stoke-on-Trent City Council v B & Q (Retail) Ltd* [1984] A.C. 754 at 776.
[115] *Runnymede BC v Ball* [1986] 1 W.L.R. 353; *Kent CC v Batchelor (No.2)* [1979] 1 W.L.R. 213 (injunction to prevent disregard of tree preservation order in order to ensure protection of public interest in areas of natural beauty).

it may suggest that there is no urgency or no real harm to the public interest warranting the grant of an injunction.[116] Where Parliament has legislated to create a detailed statutory scheme in relation to a particular area of activity, the matters should generally be dealt with under those legislative provisions rather than by resort to injunctions in aid of the criminal law save in exceptional circumstances.[117]

8–047   Urgency may also be relevant. The courts granted an injunction prohibiting the occupation of a building where there was a serious risk of fire, notwithstanding the fact that the magistrates could fine and prohibit the occupation. There would be a delay of several weeks before the magistrates' court could act, and there was an immediate need to act to prevent possible loss of life.[118]

Interlocutory injunctions

8–048   The courts may grant interlocutory injunctions requiring the defendant to restrain from engaging in the conduct complained of, pending trial. The claimant will not be granted an injunction unless, on the facts, the defendant is acting in breach of the law. It is not enough for the claimant to show that a serious question arises as to whether the law has been broken. Precisely what test the claimant must meet is not yet decided: in the one case where the issue arose, the court was satisfied that a perfectly clear breach of the criminal law had been established.[119] The language used in that case points to the claimant having to show a clear and obvious breach of the criminal law. In the majority of the cases there has been no question of whether the defendant was committing an offence; the only question was whether an injunction should be granted to restrain admittedly unlawful conduct. The courts would be unlikely to grant interim relief if the witness statements or affidavits disclosed a genuine dispute of fact.[120]

8–049   An interlocutory injunction will not be granted unless the criteria discussed in the previous section applies, so that interim relief is necessary to ensure that the criminal law is observed.[121] The *American Cyanamid* test of the balance of convenience used in ordinary civil litigation does not apply to claims for interlocutory injunctions to aid the criminal law.[122]

Defences to the action

8–050   A defendant may claim that he has a defence to the law. He may claim that subordinate legislation creating an offence is ultra vires. If the criminal offence involves failing to comply with an administrative decision, such as trading

---

[116] *London Borough of Walthamstow v Scott Markets Ltd* [1988] 3 C.M.L.R. 773.

[117] *Mayor of London v Hall* [2011] 1 W.L.R. 504 at [52]. Thus, where Parliament provided for a system for seeking anti-social behaviour order, it was not appropriate to deal with such matters by seeking an injunction in aid of the criminal law: see *Birmingham City Council v Shafi* [2009] 1 W.L.R. 1961. Legislation subsequently provided for the possibility of injunctions in such cases: see *Birmingham City Council v Jones* [2014] 1 W.L.R. 23.

[118] *Att-Gen v Chaudry* [1971] 1 W.L.R. 1614.

[119] [1971] 1 W.L.R. 1614.

[120] *London Borough of Walthamstow v Scott Markets Ltd* (see above, fn.104). (Dispute of fact to be determined at final hearing, not interlocutory hearing.)

[121] *Portsmouth City Council v Richards* [1989] 1 C.M.L.R. 673.

[122] [1989] 1 C.M.L.R. 673.

without a licence or failing to comply with a stop notice in planning law, the defendant may contend that the decision is ultra vires and that he has not therefore committed an offence. At the final hearing the courts would simply decide the issue. The difficulty arises in a claim for interlocutory relief.

The courts have yet to consider fully the relevance of a possible defence to a claim for interlocutory relief. The fact that a measure is alleged to be ultra vires does not of itself prevent the grant of an injunction. The subordinate legislation or administrative measure will enjoy a presumption of validity, with the courts presuming that the measure is within the powers conferred by the parent Act. Thus, in *Hoffman-La Roche (F.) & Co. A.G. v Secretary of State for Trade and Industry*,[123] the House of Lords held that the Minister could obtain an interim injunction to enforce a statutory instrument fixing drug prices. Breach of the order did not render the plaintiff subject to criminal sanctions, but the parent Act did specifically permit civil proceedings for an injunction. There is no reason to doubt that the presumption of validity applies also to subordinate legislation creating criminal offences or administrative decisions, breach of which involve a criminal offence. The presumption of validity can be rebutted at the interlocutory stage, and the court may decline to enforce the contested measure. The test for determining whether the presumption is rebutted has not been finally determined. The point did not arise for decision in *Hoffman-La Roche*, but dicta of Lord Diplock suggest that the defendant would have to establish a strong prima facie case of invalidity.[124]

8–051

Defences under EU law

A defendant may claim that the legislation creating the offence is contrary to EU law, and that the EU law therefore provides a defence to the offence. He may claim that no injunction should be granted to enforce an English criminal law which conflicts with his European Union law rights. If the matter is dealt with at the final hearing, then the national courts must assess the claims under EU law, and must come to a conclusion as to whether or not the English law conflicts with European law, or the court must stay proceedings and refer to the Court of Justice.[125] The difficulty arises again if the claim is one for interlocutory relief, either pending the final hearing in the English court or pending the outcome of a reference to the Court of Justice on the issue of European Union law.

8–052

Neither the fact that such a claim is made, nor the fact that the matter has been referred to the Court of Justice for a preliminary ruling prevents the court granting an interlocutory injunction to enforce the domestic law.[126] There is a presumption that domestic legislation is compatible with European Union law: this plays an analogous role to the presumption of validity.[127] However, the presumption is rebuttable, and in appropriate circumstances the courts may

8–053

---

[123] [1975] A.C. 295.

[124] [1975] A.C. 295 at 367.

[125] European Communities Act 1972 s.3(1).

[126] *Kirklees BC v Wickes Building Supplies Ltd* [1993] 2 A.C. 227 at 270B-271C; *Portsmouth City Council v Richards* [1989] 1 C.M.L.R. 673.

[127] *Kirklees BC v Wickes Building Supplies Ltd* [1993] 2 A.C. 227 at 270B-271C; *R. v Secretary of State for Transport Ex p. Factortame Ltd* [1990] 2 A.C. 85 and see also *R. v Secretary of State for Transport Ex p. Factortame Ltd (No.2)* [1991] 1 A.C. 603.

decline to grant an injunction to enforce the domestic law.[128] The test for determining when a court might refuse an injunction is by no means clear. The courts will not grant an injunction where they have formed a very clear view that the domestic law is incompatible with European Union law.[129] Apart from that, it is as yet uncertain when the courts would refuse to enforce a provision of domestic law. The indications are that the courts would rely heavily on the presumption of compatibility.[130]

Procedure

8–054   Injunctions may be sought by the Attorney-General either ex officio or at the relation of an individual.[131] An individual has no standing to sue unless a private right is affected by the conduct complained of, or he has suffered special damage over and above that suffered by the public generally.[132] The courts have so far declined to hold that the decision of the Attorney-General to refuse or consent to a relator action is reviewable.[133]

8–055   Local authorities are also empowered by s.222 of the Local Government Act 1972 to institute civil proceedings in their own name where they consider " . . . it expedient for the promotion or protection of the inhabitants of their area". This power enables local authorities to seek injunctions to enforce the criminal law without needing to obtain the consent of the Attorney-General.[134] Local authorities are now the main source of applications for such injunctions. A decision to institute or not to institute proceedings is, like any other exercise of statutory power, subject to judicial review.[135] Challenges to the validity of such a decision must be brought by direct action in separate judicial review proceedings. The invalidity of the decision cannot be raised as a defence in the proceedings for the injunction.[136] The action for an injunction does not have to be stayed pending the outcome of the judicial review claim[137]: it is possible for both sets of proceedings to be heard together.[138]

---

[128] *Kirklees BC v Wickes Building Supplies Ltd* [1993] 2 A.C. 227 at 270B–271C.

[129] *Polydor and R.S.O. Records Inc. v Harlequin Record Shops and Simons Records* [1980] 2 C.M.L.R. 413, CA (Court referred question to European Court, but refused to grant interim injunction since they considered the European law defence to the action for breach of copyright was made out).

[130] *Portsmouth City Council v Richards* (see above fn.12). But this case was decided before *Factortame* (see above, fn.3), made it clear that the presumption was rebuttable not absolute. The courts may place less weight upon the presumption now.

[131] Relator actions are discussed in Chapter 7.

[132] *Gouriet v Union of Post Office Workers* [1978] A.C. 435.

[133] [1978] A.C. 435 and see paras 2–043 to 2–044.

[134] *Stoke-on-Trent Council v B & Q (Retail) Ltd* [1984] A.C. 754. The provision is a procedural provision, enabling a local authority to bring proceedings in cases where an injunction is available: it does not confer additional substantive powers on the authority to claim an injunction: see *Birmingham City Council v Shafi* [2009] 1 W.L.R. 1961 at [22]–[24]. Thus, an injunction could not go further than restraining a breach of the criminal law: see *Worcestershire County Council v Tongue* [2004] 2 W.L.R. 1193 at [31]–[32] (no power to grant injunction to permit entry onto land to remove cattle).

[135] *Stoke-on-Trent Council v B&Q Retail Ltd* [1984] A.C. 754.

[136] *Avon County Council v Buscott* [1988] Q.B. 656.

[137] *R. v South Somerset DC Ex p. DJB (Group) Ltd* (1989) 153 L.G. Rev. 813, DC.

[138] (1989) 153 L.G. Rev. 813, DC.

The House of Lords in *Hoffman-La Roche*[139] held that cross-undertakings in damages would not usually be required from the Crown as a condition of granting the interim injunction where the Crown is seeking to enforce the law of the land as opposed to enforcing the Crown's proprietary rights. In that case, the government department in question was seeking to enforce a provision of subordinate legislation prohibiting a drugs company from charging prices in excess of prescribed maximum prices. The House of Lords has also held that the courts have a discretion not to require a local authority to give a cross-undertaking in damages when it is under a statutory duty to enforce the law and takes steps to do so.[140] In such circumstances, it is relevant in deciding whether to require an undertaking in damages to consider whether the respondent will continue to act in breach of the law unless restrained and whether, in practical terms, proceedings by injunction are the only means open to the local authority to perform its duty to ensure that the law is enforced.[141] As those circumstances will prevail in most, if not all, cases where it is appropriate for such an injunction to be sought, it is unlikely in practice that a local authority would in normal circumstances be required to give an undertaking in damages where an interlocutory injunction in aid of the criminal law is granted. The position of public bodies seeking injunctions in the discharge of their public functions has been reviewed by the Supreme Court in *Financial Services Authority v Sinaloa Gold Plc*.[142] There the Financial Services Authority was seeking an interim injunction, freezing the assets of the defendants, who were allegedly trading in breach of certain regulatory requirements. The Supreme Court considered that there was a difference between private parties seeking interim injunctions, where a cross-undertaking is generally required, and public bodies performing law enforcement functions. In the latter type of case, the public authority is seeking to enforce the law in the general public interest, often in pursuance of a duty to do so, and has only the resources assigned to it for its functions. It would not be liable in damages for unlawful administrative action (absent misfeasance or a breach of a Convention right where an award of damages might be necessary). As a result, different considerations applied in relation to such cases. The courts would not generally require a public body seeking an interim injunction in the performance of its public law functions of enforcing the law to give a cross-undertaking in damages unless, on the particular facts, it was appropriate to do so.[143] The Financial Services Authority was seeking an injunction to enforce the law by the means provided by statute and was performing its statutory functions in doing so by seeking, in the general public interest, to stop allegedly unlawful activity on the part of the defendants. In those circumstances, the starting point was that the authority should not have been required to give any cross-undertaking in damages in order to obtain the injunction and there was no reason to depart from that position.[144]

---

[139] [1975] A.C. 295.
[140] *Kirklees B.C. v Wickes Building Supplies* [1993] A.C. 227 at 275C–D.
[141] *Kirklees B.C. v Wickes Building Supplies* [1989] 1 C.M.L.R. 227 at 283B–D.
[142] [2013] A.C. 28.
[143] [2013] A.C. 28 at [27] and [31]–[33].
[144] [2013] A.C. 28 at [36]–[38] and [41].

Injunctions in public law cases

8–057   Injunctions continue to be available in ordinary private law proceedings. In such proceedings they will usually be concerned with enforcing private law not public rights.[145] Claims for injunctions in public law cases must be brought by way of judicial review and cannot be brought by ordinary action.[146] There are exceptions to this rule and they are discussed in Chapter 3.

Injunctions to enforce a public right

8–058   The Attorney-General may bring an action either ex officio or at the relation of an individual, to restrain a public body from acting unlawfully in the public law sense.[147] Such actions can probably be brought by ordinary action as an exception to the rule in *O'Reilly v Mackman*. The Attorney-General acting himself or through a relator may also take action to enforce rights owed by individuals to the public at large.[148] The essence of such claims involves unlawful action by an individual, such as creating a public nuisance, or interfering with public rights of way.[149] The Attorney-General cannot enforce purely private rights, such as those derived from contract.[150] An individual will not have standing to enforce a public right unless he can show that the conduct complained of also affects a specific legal right of his, or has caused him special damage over and above that suffered by the general public.[151]

Local authorities

8–059   Local authorities have power under s.222 of the Local Government Act 1972 to institute civil proceedings where they consider it expedient for the promotion or protection of the inhabitants of their area. It is this power which enables them to seek injunctions in aid of the criminal law.[152] The power also enables them to take action to restrain a public nuisance in their area[153] or to seek an injunction under s.187B of the Town and Country Planning Act 1990 to restrain a breach of planning control.[154]

---

[145] See, e.g. *Parker v Camden LBC* [1986] 2 Ch. 162 (mandatory injunction to compel compliance with terms of tenancy.)

[146] *O'Reilly v Mackman* [1983] 2 A.C. 237.

[147] Relator actions are discussed in Chapter 7.

[148] See, generally, de Smith Woolf and Jowell, *Judicial Review of Administrative Action* (7th edn).

[149] See, e.g. *Att-Gen, ex rel. Yorkshire Derwent Trust v Brotherton* [1992] 1 All E.R. 230 (action for a declaration as to whether a public right of navigation existed over a river).

[150] *Att-Gen, ex rel. Scotland v Barratt (Manchester) Ltd, The Times*, July 11, 1991, CA.

[151] *Gouriet v Union of Post Office Workers* [1978] A.C. 435.

[152] See above at para.8–055.

[153] *Nottingham City Council v Zain* [2002] 1 W.L.R. 607 (interim injunction to restrain persons suspected of dealing in drugs from entering a housing estate).

[154] It is for the court to determine whether it is just, having regard to all the circumstances (including any Convention rights that may be in issue): see generally *South Buckinghamshire DC v Porter* [2003] 2 W.L.R. 1547.

Statutory provision for injunctions

Statute may impose a duty on an individual and provide that a Minister,[155] or **8–060** other named public body,[156] may bring civil proceedings to restrain breaches. The injunctions are sought by ordinary claim not judicial review. They are mentioned here partly for convenience and partly because the enforcement of the civil law, like the criminal law, can be seen as a public law function. Decisions of public bodies exercising statutory powers to institute proceedings for injunctions will be subject to judicial review on normal principles.

In *Broadmoor Special Hospital Authority v Robinson*,[157] the Court of Appeal **8–061** held that where a public body is given a statutory responsibility which it is required to perform in the public interest, then, in the absence of an implication to the contrary in the statute, it has standing to apply to the court for an injunction to prevent interference with the performance of its public responsibilities and the courts have jurisdiction to grant the application where it is just and convenient to do so. There, the hospital authority sought an injunction to restrain publication of a book by an inmate. Lord Woolf M.R. and Waller LJ accepted that the courts had a jurisdiction to grant injunctions to assist a public body to perform its statutory functions. Lord Woolf M.R. considered that this jurisdiction was wide enough to encompass the grant of an injunction in the present case but decided as a matter of discretion that it was not appropriate to grant an injunction. Waller LJ took a narrower view of the scope of the authority's statutory responsibilities which were essentially concerned with the treatment of the defendant and of others. He considered that the defendant's conduct in the present case could not be said to frustrate his treatment or that of others and the injunction sought could not be said to be necessary to prevent interference with the performance of the authority's public responsibilities. Morritt LJ considered that the real issue was whether or not there was a right or power for the hospital authorities to control publications liable to frustrate the treatment of patients could be implied from its statutory duties. He held that such a power could not be implied.

The extension of the jurisdiction to grant injunctions is unobjectionable **8–062** provided that the jurisdiction is limited to supporting a public body's specific express or implied statutory responsibilities in the sense that injunctions are granted which restrain conduct which prevents an authority exercising a specific statutory power. The jurisdiction to grant injunctions would then be performing an equivalent function in the field of public law (enabling a public body to exercise specific statutory powers or carry out specific duties) to that which it

---

[155] See, e.g. *Hoffman-La Roche (F.) & Co. A.G. v Secretary of State for Trade and Industry* [1975] A.C. 295.

[156] See, e.g. *Financial Services Authority v Sinaloa Gold Plc* [2013] A.C. 28 (Financial Services Authority could seek an order restraining a person from disposing of assets if not complying with regulatory requirements relating to financial trading) and *Director General of Fair Trading v Tobyward Ltd* [1989] 1 W.L.R. 517 (Director General entitled to seek injunction on regulations prohibiting misleading advertisements). If there is no specific statutory provision for seeking an injunction, and if no established legal right exists, the courts will not have jurisdiction to grant an injunction: see *Chief Constable of Leicestershire v M* [1989] 1 W.L.R. 20, and *Securities and Investments Board v Pantell* [1989] 3 W.L.R. 698.

[157] [2000] 1 W.L.R. 1590. See also *In re L (Vulnerable Adults: Court's Jurisdiction)* [2013] 2 W.L.R. 445 (injunction granted to prevent an individual from hampering a local authority's discharge of its statutory obligations to provide community care services to a vulnerable adult).

performs in private law (enabling a person with standing to enforce his private law rights). Similarly, once it is recognised that the basis of the jurisdiction is that the courts may grant an injunction to assist the public body to exercise its statutory powers or duties, the public body possessed of the power or duty would obviously have standing to bring a claim for such an injunction.

Injunctions and chartered bodies

8–063   A member of a chartered body may obtain an injunction to prevent the body doing acts that are not permitted by charter.[158] It is not clear whether such cases are to be classed as private or public law, and consequently, whether such injunctions continue to be available only in ordinary actions or may (and possibly must) be brought by judicial review.[159]

---

[158]   *Rendall v Pharmaceutical Society of Great Britain* [1921] 1 Ch. 392.
[159]   Dicta in the Court of Appeal in *Hazell v Hammersmith and Fulham LBC* [1990] 2 W.L.R. 1038 at 1053–1054 suggest that such injunctions should be sought by judicial review. The matter was not mentioned in the House of Lords: [1992] 2 A.C. 1.

CHAPTER 9

Machinery of Judicial Review

A. INTRODUCTION

The procedures for bringing a claim for judicial review are now governed by Pt 8 as modified by Pt 54 of the CPR, together with the Practice Direction on Judicial Review.[1] In addition, the statutory basis for judicial review remains s.31 of the Senior Courts Act 1981 and that section directly regulates certain parts of the procedure.

9-001

There are a number of distinct stages in the bringing of a claim for judicial review. The claimant should first normally comply with the pre-action protocol for judicial review. That requires the claimant to send a letter to the defendant identifying the matter being challenged and the issues that arise and giving the defendant sufficient time to respond. If that process does not resolve matters, the claimant may bring a claim for judicial review.

9-002

Judicial review involves a two-stage procedure. In summary, the claimant must first obtain permission to apply for judicial review. To do that, the claimant must file a claim form in the Administrative Court[2] and then serve it on the defendant and any interested party within seven days.[3] They have 21 days in which to file an acknowledgment setting out a summary of the grounds for resisting the claim.[4] The court will normally deal with the application for permission on the papers without an oral hearing; if permission is refused, the application for permission can be renewed at an oral hearing.[5] If permission is granted, the defendant and interested party then have 35 days in which to put in detailed grounds of resistance and any written evidence[6] and there will then be a hearing of the claim for judicial review. There is also a Planning Court. This is a specialist list within the Administrative Court[7] dealing with planning claims, that is judicial reviews or statutory challenges involving planning permission or environmental matters.[8] CPR Part 54 and Part 8 as modified apply to planning

9-003

---

[1] They replace the former Ord.53 of the Rules of the Supreme Court which governed claims made before October 2, 2002.

[2] CPR r.54.5.

[3] CPR r.54.7.

[4] CPR r.54.8.

[5] CPR r.54.12.

[6] CPR r.54.14.

[7] CPR r.54.22.

[8] CPR r.54.21.

claims save where specific provision is made by the rules or a practice direction.[9] Judicial review claims in certain categories of cases, notably immigration decisions, must now be started in the Upper Tribunal not the Administrative Court. This is dealt with in Chapter 10.

B. THE PRE-ACTION PROTOCOL

9–004 The pre-action protocol requires individuals to send a letter to the claimant before making a claim for judicial review. The purpose of the letter is to establish the issues in dispute and whether litigation can be avoided. There is a standard form letter at Annex A to the pre-action protocol. In addition to formalities such as the name and contact details of the defendant, the letter should identify the matters being challenged and should set out a brief summary of the facts and why it is contended that the act or omission of the public body is unlawful. The letter should set out the action that the defendant is asked to take. The defendant should be given adequate time, usually 14 days, to reply. There is a standard form response at Annex B to the pre-action protocol. The reply should set out the public body's response to the contention that it has acted unlawfully and should state whether the claim will be conceded in whole or in part. The pre-action protocol does not suspend the time-limits for making a claim for judicial review.[10] Where a claim may be out of time if the pre-action protocol were to be followed, the better course of action is to file the claim and to explain in the claim form why the pre-action protocol was not used.

C. APPLICATIONS FOR PERMISSION

Procedure for applying for permission

9–005 Applications for permission are now made by filing a claim form in the Administrative Court Office which will then issue the claim form[11]. The claim form must be accompanied by the written evidence (usually witness statements) relied on by the claimant, together with a copy of the decision that the claimant seeks to have quashed, and, if the decision is that of a court or tribunal, an approved copy of the reasons for reaching that decision. The claim must also be accompanied by copies of the documents (usually exhibited to a witness statement) that the claimant relies upon and copies of any relevant statutory material[12] and a list of essential documents for advance reading.[13] This will usually include the claim form, the witness statement, the decision letter and any other documents which need to be read to understand the claim. The claim form,

---

[9] CPR r.54.23. See in particular Practice Direction 54E – Planning Court Claims which makes specific provision for time scales for dealing with permission applications and substantive hearings in planning claims.

[10] See *Finn-Kelcey v Milton Keynes BC* [2009] Env. L.R. 17 at [27].

[11] CPR r.54.6 and para.2.1 of Practice Direction 54A – Judicial Review.

[12] If the case involves EU law, it is desirable to include the relevant provisions of the relevant Treaty and the relevant European Union legislation such as any Regulation or Directive.

[13] Para.5.6 of Practice Direction 54A – Judicial Review.

written evidence and documents must be contained in a paginated indexed bundle and two copies of the bundle must be filed with the Administrative Court Office.[14] The claim is brought in the name of the Crown on the application of the claimant against the public body[15] whose actions or omissions are challenged and which is the defendant to the claim. The involvement of the Crown is, however, purely nominal, reflecting the history of the prerogative remedies. Judicial review proceedings are in substance a contest between the claimant and the defendant public authority.[16]

The claim form must be served on the defendant and any interested parties within seven days after the claim form has been issued by the Administrative Court Office.[17] The defendant is the person whose actions or failure to act is under challenge. An interested party is a person who will be directly affected by the grant of a remedy.[18] **9–006**

Form N461

The appropriate claim form for bringing a claim for judicial review is form N461.[19] The claim form will include the claimant's name and the name and address of the claimant's solicitors. The claim form should identify the enactment, decision, action or omission in respect of which the claim for judicial review is made. In addition, the claim form will contain or have attached to it[20]: **9–007**

(1) a statement that the claimant is requesting permission to apply for judicial review;
(2) the name and address of any person considered to be an interested party;
(3) the remedies, including interim remedies, that are claimed;
(4) a detailed statement of the grounds for seeking judicial review;
(5) a statement of the facts relied upon;
(6) any application to extend the time for filing the claim form; and
(7) any directions sought and the time estimate for the hearing if permission is granted.

The claim form will also need to be accompanied by a statement of truth. Additional requirements need to be fulfilled where the claim raises issues under the Human Rights Act 1998, for example a claim that a public authority has acted in breach of a Convention right or a claim for a declaration that legislation is incompatible with a Convention right. The claimant must specify that fact in the claim form, give precise details of the Convention right relied upon and details of the alleged infringement and specify the remedies sought.[21] Similarly, where a

---

[14] Para.5.9 of the Practice Direction 54A – Judicial Review.
[15] And should be styled accordingly: see Practice Direction: Administrative Court [2000] 1 W.L.R. 1654.
[16] *R. (Ben-Abdelaziz) v Haringey LBC* [2001] 1 W.L.R. 1485 at [29].
[17] CPR r.54.7.
[18] CPR, r.54.1(1)(f) for the definition of interested party. See below at para.9–052.
[19] Or N461PC in planning claims.
[20] CPR rr.8.2 and 54.6 and para.5.6 of Practice Direction 54A – Judicial Review.
[21] Para.5.3 of Practice Direction 54A – Judicial Review and [15] of Practice Direction 16 – Statements of Case.

claim raises a devolution issue, the claim form must specify that fact, and give a summary of the facts, circumstances and points of law on the basis of which it is alleged a devolution issue arises.[22] The Criminal Justice and Courts Bill 2014, if enacted, will also require the claimant to provide any information about the financing of the claim that rules of court specify must be provided.

Need to specify the measure challenged and the remedies sought

9–008   The claim form should also identify the enactment or decision or other measure that is being challenged, or the action or failure to act that is the subject of complaint.[23] The claim form must set out the remedies claimed.[24] The remedies sought should be related to the measure that is challenged and should reflect the aim that the judicial review claim is designed to fulfil. The individual remedies that may be claimed, together with their particular uses and characteristics, are considered in Chapters 6 to 8. If a decision is being challenged, for example, then a quashing order to quash or set aside the decision, or a declaration that the decision is invalid, would be appropriate remedies. If the claimant is seeking to compel a public body to perform a public law duty, then a mandatory order, or a declaration that a duty is owed, would be appropriate remedies. The claimant may claim more than one remedy and this will frequently be necessary or convenient. Damages or restitution or the recovery of money may also be claimed provided that they could have been claimed in ordinary private law proceedings.[25] Claims for any interim remedy should be included in the claim.[26] The court can give directions which can include a stay.[27] A claimant who wishes to apply for a stay should therefore include in the claim form a request for a stay as one of the directions sought.

Need to specify grounds and facts in respect of which a remedy is claimed

9–009   The claim form must set out a detailed statement of the grounds for bringing the claim and the facts relied upon.[28] In order for a claim for judicial review to succeed, the claimant must establish that the public body has acted in a way that breaches one or more of the substantive principles governing the exercise of public law powers, such as making an error of law or failing to comply with relevant procedural requirements or otherwise committing an abuse of power.[29] The claimant must identify the error in sufficient detail to enable the court and

---

[22] [5.4] and [5.5] of the Practice Direction 54A – Judicial Review.

[23] *R. (Brookes) v Secretary of State for Work and Pensions* [2010] 1 W.L.R. 2448 at [4].

[24] CPR r.54.6.

[25] CPR r.54.3(2).

[26] CPR r.54.6.

[27] CPR r.54.10(2) and see above at para.6–026.

[28] Para.5.6 of Practice Direction 54A – Judicial Review and see *R. (Gjini) v London Borough of Islington*, judgment of April 15, 2003, stressing the obligation on the claimant to set out clearly what their case is in the statement of facts and grounds.

[29] Reference should be made to the one of the standard works on judicial review, such as De Smith, Woolf and Jowell, *Judicial Review of Administrative Action*, 7th edn, Auburn, Moffett and Sharland *Judicial Review* or Wade and Forsyth, *Administrative Law*, 11th edn for a detailed description of the substantive grounds for judicial review.

other parties to identify the essential issues of law which the claimant alleges demonstrate that the public body has acted unlawfully in some way. General, unfocussed complaints of illegality are insufficient.[30] If the claimant is alleging that the defendant is in breach of a public law duty, the nature of the duty and the alleged breach should be identified in the claim form.[31]

The claimant must also identify all the relevant facts. A claimant is under a duty to disclose all material facts.[32] These include all material facts known to the applicant and those that he would have known had he made the proper and necessary inquiries before applying for leave.[33] The extent of the inquiries that should be made depend on all the circumstances of the case, including the nature of the case, the order for which the applicant is applying, the degree of legitimate urgency and the time available for making inquiries.[34] Non-disclosure is a sufficient ground for refusing the remedy sought,[35] or for setting aside the grant of permission[36] or refusing permission, and the claimant may be penalised in costs. In addition, any delay in making the claim should be explained. The claimant should also disclose any outstanding appeal against the decision,[37] or any rights of appeal that exist but have not been used and explain why, in the circumstances, judicial review is appropriate. The claim should also identify any relevant statutory provision that appears to oust the jurisdiction of the courts and to explain why the provision is said not to bar judicial review proceedings.[38]

9–010

In drafting a claim form, it is useful to remember that the application for permission will be considered by a judge on the basis of the papers alone, that is the claim form and the written evidence, together with the defendant's acknowledgment of service. The claim form should ensure that a judge is in a position to see what the issues are and why a remedy is being claimed. Failure to achieve this may result in the refusal of permission, with the consequent necessity and expense of seeking reconsideration of the refusal at an oral hearing.

9–011

Practice differs in drafting and each case is different. Form N461 currently provides for the grounds to be set out in section 5 and the statement of facts in section 9. In practice, it is often best to combine the description of the facts and

9–012

---

[30] R. (Brookes) v Secretary of State for Work and Pensions [2010] 1 W.L.R. 2448 at [4].

[31] R (Kaiyam) v Secretary of State for Justice [2014] 1 W.L.R. 1208 at [40].

[32] See, e.g. R. v Lloyds Corporation Ex p. Briggs [1993] 1 Lloyd's L.Rep. 176; R. v Secretary of State for the Home Department Ex p. Ketowoglo, The Times, April 6, 1992; R. v British Rail Board Ex p. Great Yarmouth BC, The Times, March 15, 1983; R. v Jockey Club Licensing Committee Ex p. Wright (Barrie John) [1991] C.O.D. 306 and R. (Burkett) v Hammersmith and Fulham LBC [2002] 1 W.L.R. 1593 at [50].

[33] R. v Jockey Club Licensing Committee Ex p. Wright (Barrie John) [1991] C.O.D. 306.

[34] R. v Jockey Club Licensing Committee Ex p. Wright (Barrie John) [1991] C.O.D. 306.

[35] R. v Kensington General Commissioners Ex p. Polignac (Princess) [1917] 1 K.B. 486; R. v North East Thames Regional Health Authority Ex p. de Groot [1988] C.O.D. 25 (inadvertent misstatement of fact was a ground for refusing a remedy).

[36] R. v Secretary of State for the Home Department Ex p. Sholola [1992] Imm.A.R. 135; R. v Wealden District Council Ex p. Pinnegar [1996] C.O.D 64; R. v District Auditor No.10 Audit District Ex p. Judge [1989] C.O.D. 390. Applications to set aside may now only be made rarely (see para.9–080 below) and as the claim form is now served on the defendant any misstatements are likely to be identified before the application for permission is considered.

[37] R. v Humberside CC Ex p. Bogdal (1992) 5 Admin. L.R. 405 at 411c–e; R. v Greenwich Justices Ex p. Aikens, The Times, July 3, 1982; R. v Mid-Worcestershire Justices Ex p. Hart [1989] C.O.D. 397.

[38] R. v Cornwall CC Ex p. Huntington [1992] 3 All E.R. 566 at 576e–h (the substantive decision was affirmed by the Court of Appeal [1994] 1 All E.R. 694).

the grounds. A useful general approach is to start with a brief introductory paragraph or paragraphs summarising the claim by identifying the measure challenged and the reasons why it is said to be unlawful. Then it is often useful to set out a brief description of the basic legislative framework followed by a summary of the essential facts in the case. The specific grounds of challenge can be set out, explaining what statutory provision has been misconstrued or misapplied, or which common law principle has been breached and why (for example, a breach of natural justice has occurred because of a failure to disclose the case against the claimant). Any issue relating to delay and the reasons for extending time can then be dealt with. In addition, any issues relating to standing or alternative remedies can be dealt with. Where a claim for interim relief is made, a summary of the reasons why interim relief is appropriate can then be set out.

Written evidence in support of claim

9–013   A claim will usually be supported by written evidence, usually a witness statement. The witness statement usually expands on the statements of facts in the claim form, providing additional information and exhibiting and identifying any relevant documentation. The witness statement and claim form will contain the evidential basis of the claimant's case and so should record all the relevant facts.

Procedure in urgent cases and cases involving interim relief

9–014   The usual procedure for dealing with applications for permission is for the claimant to serve the claim form on the defendant who then has 21 days to file an acknowledgment of service setting out a summary of the grounds of resistance. A period of time will normally elapse before the judge considers the papers. Frequently, there is an urgent need to consider a claim for permission to apply for judicial review and interim relief and the usual timetable may be inappropriate. The Administrative Court has introduced a procedure for urgent cases.[39] Claimants should complete a form requesting urgent consideration of the claim[40] setting out why there is a need for urgency and the time within which consideration of the application for permission should take place and the date by which any substantive hearing should take place and should give the date upon which it was first realised that an immediate application would be necessary and the reasons for any delay in making it. The importance of compliance with these requirements has been emphasised by the Divisional Court and failure to provide this information may of itself justify a court in refusing to consider the urgent application.[41] If the claimant is also seeking interim relief he should provide a draft order and the grounds for seeking interim relief. The claim form, the application for urgent consideration, and the draft order and grounds for seeking interim relief, should be served on the defendant and any interested party. The

---

[39]   See Practice Statement (Administrative Courts: Listing and Urgent Cases) [2002] 1 W.L.R. 810.
[40]   The appropriate form is N463 or N463PC in planning claims.
[41]   *R. (Hamid) v Secretary of State for the Home Department* [2012] EWHC 3070 (Admin).

matter will then be considered by a judge who will make appropriate directions.[42] These could include abridging the time for filing an acknowledgment of service to enable any decision on permission to be taken quickly. The judge might—in cases of exceptional urgency where the claim for judicial review would be academic unless matters were dealt with within a very short time frame—order that the application for permission be heard orally, with the substantive hearing to follow immediately afterwards if permission is granted. The judge may order expedition and give directions relating to the provision of written evidence. Where there is an application for interim relief, the judge may direct that there be an oral hearing to consider both the application for permission and interim relief and that, often, will be an appropriate method of proceeding. If necessary, the court can grant interim relief pending that oral hearing (or for a fixed period) and give liberty to the defendant to apply to discharge the interim injunction if appropriate.[43] Interim relief can, in urgent cases, be granted before permission to proceed with the claim is given.[44] If an application for interim relief is refused on the papers, the appropriate course is for the claimant to seek reconsideration at an oral hearing before a High Court judge, either in court or, if time does not permit that, to the out of hours duty High Court judge rather than applying to the Court of Appeal for permission to appeal against the refusal of interim relief.[45]

Applications to be made in London, Cardiff or one of the regional centres

Applications must be commenced at the Administrative Court Office of the High Court in London or the district registry of the High Court at Cardiff or Birmingham, Leeds or Manchester save for certain limited classes of cases which may only be issued in London.[46] These include certain claims relating to orders in terrorist matters, confiscation proceedings, extradition matters, cases where a Divisional Court is required or matters involving the disciplining of solicitors. The claim will be administered in the Administrative Office in which it is issued unless the case is transferred to another venue.[47]

9–015

---

[42] See Practice Statement (Administrative Courts: Listing and Urgent Cases) [2002] 1 W.L.R. 810 at 811C–812B. Specific guidance has been given by the Court of Appeal on applications for interim relief in cases where the claimant is about to be deported: see *R. (Madan) v Secretary of State for the Home Department* [2007] 1 W.L.R. 2891. Specific problems have also occurred in relation to asylum seekers who have been refused support because they did not make their claim as soon as reasonably practicable, in accordance with s.55 of the Nationality, Immigration and Asylum Act 2002. Specific guidance has been issued by the Administrative Court and any claim for interim relief in such cases should follow that guidance: see *R. (Q, D, KH, OK, JK H, T and S) v Secretary of State for the Home Department* [2004] J.R. 5 and see Practice Statement (Judicial Review: Asylum Support) [2004] 1 W.L.R. 644.

[43] *R. (Lawler) v Restormel BC* [2008] A.C.D. 2.

[44] *M v Home Office* [1994] 1 A.C. 377 at 423C.

[45] *R. (MD (Afghanistan)) v Secretary of State for the Home Department (Practice Note)* [2012] 1 W.L.R. 2422 at [21]–[24].

[46] Para.2.1 of the Practice Direction 54D – Administrative Court (Venue)

[47] See the discussion on venue below at 9-068.

Time-limits for bringing the claim and delay

9–016   The basic provision is that a claim form must be filed promptly and in any event within three months of the date when the grounds for making the claim first arose.[48] The court has jurisdiction to grant an extension of time[49] but the time-limit cannot be extended by agreement between the parties.[50] The time-limit runs from the date when the grounds of challenge arose and not from the date when the claimant first learned of the decision or action under challenge nor from the date when the claimant considered that he had sufficient information or evidence to apply for judicial review, although those matters, together with all the other facts, will be relevant to the question of whether there is good reason for extending the time-limit. They do not stop the time-limit from beginning to run.[51] Different considerations apply in relation to claims involving European Union law and these are discussed below.

9–017   Claims must be brought "promptly" and the courts have emphasised that a claim will not necessarily be made promptly simply because it is made within the three-month period. Permission may be therefore be refused on grounds of delay even where the claimant has lodged the claim within three months of the decision if on the facts the court considers that the claim was not made promptly.[52] The need to act promptly reflects the fact that the decision may affect others, not simply the claimant and the decision-maker, and it is important that those affected, and the public generally, know that they can proceed on the basis that the decision is no longer open to challenge.[53] The House of Lords left open the question of whether the use of the concept of promptness as the test for delay is compatible with the European Convention on Human Rights.[54] The time-limit for judicial review is likely to be compatible with the requirements of the Convention. The European Court of Human Rights has rejected a challenge to the former provisions dealing with time-limits which are materially identical to the current provisions of the CPR as it considered that the requirements were a

---

[48] CPR r.54.5.

[49] Under CPR r.3.2(a). Where a shorter time-limit is provided by any statute or subordinate legislation for a bringing a claim, that shorter time-limit applies: see CPR 54.5(3). Section 38(1) of the Inquiries Act 2005, for example, prescribes a period of 14 days for challenging certain decisions in relation to inquiries held under that Act.

[50] CPR r.54.2. The fact that a defendant does not object to the claim being brought out of time may be a relevant factor in deciding whether to grant an extension of time.

[51] *R. v Secretary of State for Transport Ex p. Presvac Engineering Ltd* (1991) 4 Admin. L.Rep. 121 at 133–134.

[52] See, e.g. *R. v Independent Television Commissioners Ex p. TV NI Ltd, The Times,* December 20, 1991; *Finn-Kelcey v Milton Keynes BC* [2009] Env. L.R. 17 at [21]; *R. (Hardy) v Pembrokeshire CC* [2006] Env. L.R. 28 at [10]; *R. v Cotswold District Council Ex p. Barrington Parish Council* (1997) 75 P. & C.R. 515 at 522–523; *R. v Bath City Council Ex p. Crombie* [1995] C.O.D. 283; *R. v Greenwich London Borough Council Ex p. Governors of John Ball Primary School* [1990] C.O.D. 103; *R. v Exeter City Council Ex p. J.L. Thomas & Co.* [1991] 1 Q.B. 471; *R. v Greenwich BC Ex p. Cedar Transport Group Ltd* [1983] R.A. 173. See also *R. (Candlish) v Hastings B.C.* [2006] 1 P. & C.R. 337 at [19]–[29].

[53] See observations in *Finn-Kelcey v Milton Keynes BC* [2009] Env. L.R. 17 at [21].

[54] See *R. (Burkett) v Hammersmith and Fulham LBC* [2002] 1 W.L.R. 1593. No detailed reasoning was given and claimants should operate on the basis that the rule is compatible until it is declared incompatible: see *R. (Young) v Oxford City Council* [2002] EWCA Civ 990, judgment on June 27, 2001.

proportionate measure taken in pursuit of a legitimate aim which did not deny the claimants access to the courts but ensured they acted quickly in the public interest of avoiding prejudicing the rights of others.[55]

Time limits and EU law

The Court of Justice has consistently held that it is for national law to determine procedural rules governing claims, providing that those rules do not prevent the effective enforcement of EU law rights and do not treat EU law rights less favourably than similar domestic law rights.[56] The Court of Justice has accepted that national law may lay down reasonable time-limits for bringing claims.[57] In the context of public procurement challenges, however, the Court of Justice considered that a rule which provided that claims must be brought promptly and in any event within three months of the date when the grounds for bringing the proceedings first arose did not satisfy the requirements of EU law. The Court first held that the date from which the time limit should begin to run was the date when the claimant knew, or ought to have known of the infringement. Secondly, the Court held that the requirement that claims be brought "promptly" was precluded by EU law as such a provision would make the time limit dependent upon an exercise of judicial discretion and would not be predictable.[58] The High Court subsequently held that the discretion to extend time conferred by the rules should be exercised in a manner that rendered the operation of the time limit compatible with EU law, that is, time should be extended so that it ran for a three month period from the date when the claimant knew, or ought to have known, of the infringement.[59]

9–018

The time limit for judicial review claims is expressed in the same way as the former time limit in procurement cases. It is recognised, therefore, that the time-limit for seeking judicial review to enforce rights derived from EU law must also be operated in accordance with the case law of the Court of Justice. In practice this means that the time limit for bringing a judicial review claim challenging a decision or other measure on the basis that it contravenes rights derived from EU law will be seen as three-months from the date when the claimant knew, or ought to have known, that the grounds for a challenge had arisen. Claims for judicial review may be brought both on EU law grounds and domestic law grounds. In *R (Berky) v Newport City Council*,[60] a majority of the

9–019

---

[55] Application no.4167/98 *Lam v United Kingdom* decision of July 5, 2001 ruling that the claim was inadmissible. The decision was not referred to in *R. (Burkett) v Hammersmith and Fulham LBC* [2002] 1 W.L.R. 1593. See also *R. (Hardy) v Pembrokeshire CC* [2006] Env. L.R. 28 at [13]–[18] ("no realistic prospect of establishing that CPR 54.5(1) in so far as it requires a claim to be filed 'promptly' is contrary to European law" per Keene LJ). There were subsequent proceedings in *Hardy* and also an application in the European Court of Human Rights (2012) 55 E.H.R.R. 55 but those proceedings did not deal with this issue.
[56] See, e.g., Case C-261/95 *Palmisani v INPS* [1997] E.C.R. 4025 at [27]. See Chapter 17 below.
[57] Case C-188/95 *Fantask* [1997] E.C.R. I-6873 at [50]–[51].
[58] Case C-406/08 *Uniplex (UK) Ltd v NHS Business Services Authority* [2010] P.T.S.R. 1377. The domestic rules governing time-limits were subsequently amended to reflect the decision of the Court of Justice: see Public Contracts Regulations 2006, reg.47D.
[59] *SITA UK Ltd v Greater Manchester Waste Disposal Authority* [2010] 2 C.M.L.R. 47.
[60] [2012] L.G.R. 592, per Carnwath LJ at [35] and per Moore-Bick LJ at [53]. Buxton LJ took a different view on this point: see [64]–[68].

Court of Appeal considered, obiter, that the provisions of the CPR requiring promptness, operating in the usual way, applied to the domestic law grounds of challenge and it was only in respect of challenges derived from EU law that a different approach to time-limits needed to be adopted.

Specific time-limits for procurement and planning claims

9–020   Specific provision is made in the CPR in relation to procurement claims and planning claims. The time limit for bringing a claim for judicial review in relation to decisions governed by the Public Contracts Regulations 2006 (that is, decisions in the field of procurement by public bodies) is 30 days from the date when the claimant knew or ought to have known that grounds for commencing proceedings had arisen.[61] A claim for judicial review of a decision made by a local authority or the Secretary of State under the planning legislation must be filed not later than six weeks after the grounds for making the claim first arose.[62] There are targets for dealing with planning claims. Applications for permission to apply for judicial review should be considered within three weeks of the filing of an acknowledgement of service and oral hearings requesting reconsideration of a refusal of permission should occur within one month of receipt of the request. If permission is granted, the substantive hearing should be heard within ten weeks after the expiry of the time for the defendant to file detailed grounds.[63]

Date from which time begins to run in cases of decisions and other acts

9–021   Where the claim is for a quashing order in relation to a judgment, order or conviction of an inferior court or tribunal, the date when the grounds of claim first arose, and when time begins to run,[64] is the date of that judgment, order or conviction.[65] Where a claimant is challenging a decision, the date when the grounds first arose, and when the time-limit begins to run, will usually be the date on which the relevant decision was taken. The claimant should challenge the decision which brings about the legal situation of which complaint is made. There are occasions when a claimant does not challenge that decision but waits until some consequential or ancillary decision is taken and then challenges that later decision on the ground that the earlier decision is unlawful. If the substance of the dispute relates to the lawfulness of that earlier decision and if it is that earlier decision which is, in reality, determinative of the legal position and the later decision does not, in fact, produce any change in the legal position, then the

---

[61] CPR r.54.5(6) (as inserted by the Civil Procedure (Amendment No. 4) Rules 2013.

[62] CPR r.54.5 (as inserted by the Civil Procedure (Amendment No. 4) Rules 2013. The "planning acts" are defined as meaning the same as in s.336 of the Town and Country Planning Act 1990: see CPR r.54.5(A1). This includes matters such as decisions granting planning permission.

[63] Practice Direction 54E – Planning Court Claims.

[64] Save where a challenge relates to a procurement decision (see para.9–020 above) or is based on a ground of EU law, in which case, in relation to that ground, the likelihood is that EU law requires the national courts to treat the time-limit as running from the date when the claimant knew, or ought to have known that that ground had arisen: see, by analogy, Case C-406/08 *Uniplex (UK) Ltd v NHS Business Services Authority* [2010] P.T.S.R. 1377 discussed above.

[65] Para.4.1 of Practice Direction 54A – Judicial Review.

courts may well rule that the time-limit runs from that earlier decision.[66] Similarly, where a decision has been taken, a claimant cannot avoid the application of the time-limits in relation to a challenge to that decision by writing a fresh letter to the decision-maker and obtaining a reply and then characterising that reply as a fresh decision.[67] The position may be different if the decision-maker actually does reconsider the decision and reaches a fresh decision. The position may also be different where a public body has an express or implied power to reconsider decisions and an individual asks the public body to reconsider an earlier decision on the grounds that it is now clear that it is invalid (where, for example, a subsequent judicial decision makes it clear that the decision was incorrect in law). On one occasion, the Court of Appeal allowed a claimant to seek review of a decision refusing to reconsider an earlier flawed decision, even though they had refused permission to apply for judicial review out of time of the earlier decision.[68]

Staged decision-making processes

Administrative decision-making processes vary widely. The process may take place over a period of time or in a number of stages and do not necessarily involve a single stage with a hearing and decision. A preliminary decision may, for example, need to be confirmed or approved by another body before it takes effect. A local planning authority may resolve to grant planning permission subject to conditions; planning permission will only be granted once the conditions are satisfied. If the preliminary or conditional decision is flawed, the question arises as to whether a claimant must challenge that preliminary or conditional decision promptly or within three months or whether he may wait to see if confirmation is given or the conditions satisfied and then bring a claim for judicial review of that later decision, raising as a ground of challenge, the earlier flaw in the decision-making process. If that latter course is acceptable, then the time-limit would run from the date of the second or confirming decision. The practical arguments in favour of this course are that it is sensible to wait to see if the confirming authority deals with the claimant's complaint, thereby avoiding the need and expense of a claim for judicial review.[69] Furthermore, focussing on

9–022

---

[66] *R. v Cardiff City Council Ex p. Gooding Investments Ltd* [1996] C.O.D. 129 and *R. v Avon CC Ex p. Adams* [1994] Env. L.R. 442. Those cases still appear to be compatible with the principles laid down by the House of Lords in *R. (Burkett) v Hammersmith and Fulham LBC* [2002] 1 W.L.R. 1593 that the time-limit runs from the decision or act which creates legal rights or obligations. Earlier decisions suggesting that the claimant must move against the substantive act or decision which is the real basis of the complaint are no longer correct in so far as they indicate that a claimant must bring a claim before the decision that is constitutive of legal effects comes into being; see *R. (Burkett) v Hammersmith and Fulham LBC* [2002] 1 W.L.R. 1593 at paras [40]–[51] disapproving *R. v Secretary of State for Trade and Industry Ex p. Greenpeace Ltd* [1998] Env. L.R. 415.
[67] *R. v Commissioner for Local Administration Ex p. Field* [2000] C.O.D. 58 (the case involved an application to set aside the grant of permission whereas now the issue would need to be raised in the defendant's acknowledgment of service as applications to set aside are not generally permitted: see CPR r.54.13 and see below at para.9–080).
[68] *R. v Hertfordshire CC Ex p. Cheung*, The Times, April 14, 1984. See Lewis "Judicial Review, Time Limits and Retrospectivity" [1987] P.L. 21.
[69] See dicta of Lord Steyn in *R. (Burkett) v Hammersmith and Fulham LBC* [2002] 1 W.L.R. 1593 at [50] and of Woolf LJ in *R. v Secretary of State for Education and Science Ex p. Threapleton* [1988] C.O.D. 102.

the measure that has actual legal consequences, rather than some earlier point, may have advantages in terms of certainty and simplicity in that claimants, defendants and third parties know when the time-limit begins to run and can arrange their affairs accordingly.[70] On the other hand, the courts are reluctant to countenance delay of any kind, particularly if time and money might be wasted in furtherance of proposals which are flawed[71] or if the delay creates uncertainty for third parties or the administration.[72]

9–023   The issue has arisen primarily in the planning and education fields. In planning matters, the question is whether the time runs from the date when the local planning authority resolve to grant planning permission for a development or the date when planning permission is actually granted. In *R. (Burkett) v Hammersmith and Fulham LBC*,[73] the House of Lords held that the date when the grounds first arose was the date when planning permission was actually granted, that being the date on which rights and obligations were created, and not the earlier resolution of the local planning authority. The time-limit, therefore, only began to run from the date of the actual grant of planning permission. The claimant could, if he wished, seek judicial review of the earlier resolution but did not have to do so; the claimant could wait to see if the conditional resolution did ultimately result in the grant of planning permission and challenge that grant.[74] Similarly, the Court of Appeal has held that where the planning authority issued a screening opinion, which is an opinion that a development did not require an environmental impact assessment, the time ran from the grant of planning permission not from the date of the screening opinion.[75] The House in *Burkett* recognised that there may be cases where granting a remedy could prejudice the interests of third parties or be harmful to good administration. In such cases, the courts would have power either under their inherent jurisdiction to refuse a remedy as a matter of discretion[76] or, if applicable, under s.31(6) of the Senior Courts Act 1981.[77]

9–024   In the education field, the question arises where a local education authority makes proposals for changes to schools and those proposals are subsequently submitted to another body for approval, such as the schools organisation committee and, if they cannot reach agreement, the schools adjudicator.[78] The courts have in the past held that a claimant may either bring a claim for judicial review of the initial decision proposing the changes or closure of a school, or wait until confirmation or approval of that decision is given and challenge that

---

[70]   *R. (Burkett) v Hammersmith and Fulham LBC* [2002] 1 W.L.R. 1593 at [45]–[46].

[71]   See dicta in *R. v Gateshead MBC Ex p. Nichol* (1988) 87 L.G.R. 435. See also *Lovelock v Minister of Transport* [1980] J.P.L. 817.

[72]   See dicta in *R. v Leeds City Council Ex p. N* [1999] E.L.R. 324 at 334C–D.

[73]   [2002] 1 W.L.R. 1593.

[74]   [2002] 1 W.L.R. 1593 at [42] and [51].

[75]   *R. (Catt) v Brighton and Hove City Council* [2007] 2 P. & C.R. 225 at [49] and [52].

[76]   When the matter came back before the High Court, the court held that the public body had not acted unlawfully but if there had been an error, the court would not, as a matter of discretion, have granted a remedy in any event: *R. (Burkett) v Hammersmith and Fulham LBC* [2004] 1 P. & C.R. 74 at [45].

[77]   If the claim although made within three months of the final decision, was not made promptly, there is still undue delay in those circumstances and the discretion in the Senior Courts Act 1981 s.31(6) arises: see *R. v Dairy Produce Quota Tribunal for England and Wales Ex p. Caswell* [1990] 2 A.C. 738.

[78]   See ss.24 and 25 of the School Standards and Framework Act 1998.

decision promptly.[79] In later cases, however, the courts indicated that they might refuse permission if the error giving rise to the claim occurred at the initial stage and they would not necessarily accept that the time-limit did not run from, or that there was good reason to wait until, the decision approving the proposals.[80] In the light of the decision in *Burkett*, the likelihood is that the fact that the error occurred at an early stage in the process will not of itself be sufficient to justify refusing permission. The likelihood is that the courts will accept that, in principle, the time for bringing a claim will run from the decision to close the school and not from earlier steps in the process such as the publication of a notice of proposals for closure.[81] However, different considerations will arise if there are distinct and separate processes being undertaken, rather than a single process divided into stages. Thus, where a local authority decide to contract out certain services, and then subsequently conducted a procurement exercise to identify a suitable contractor, the two exercises were distinct. The duty to consult arose in relation to the first exercise, the decision to contract out, and the time limit ran when that duty first arose, and the claimant could not choose to wait until the second, different process of awarding a contract was complete.[82] Furthermore, even if there is a single decision, if there is evidence of real prejudice to third parties or detriment to good administration, the courts will be unlikely to grant a remedy either relying on their inherent discretion to refuse a remedy even if the claim is technically made within the time-limit[83] or, where applicable, s.31(6) of the Senior Courts Act 1981.[84] The longer the period between the error and the actual challenge, and the further advanced the process, the greater the likelihood that there will be such prejudice or detriment particularly given the recognised importance of certainty from the point of view of children, parents, and the local education authority.[85] However, such matters are properly to be regarded as

---

[79] *R. v Secretary of State for Education Ex p. Birmingham City Council* (1985) 83 L.G.R. 168 (proposals flawed and then approved; judicial review sought within three months of approval but 14 months of the error); *R. v Brent LBC Ex p. Gunning* (1985) 84 L.G.R. 168 (both initial flawed proposals and later approval challenged); *R. v Secretary of State for Education and Science Ex p. Threapleton* [1988] C.O.D. 102; *R. v Northamptonshire CC Ex p. Tebutt*, unreported, June 26, 1988; and *R. v Secretary of State for Wales Ex p. Williams* [1997] E.L.R. 100.

[80] See, e.g. *R. v Secretary of State for Education Ex p. Bandtock* [2001] E.L.R. 333. See the discussion in McManus, *Education and the Courts*, 3rd edn (Bristol: Jordans).

[81] See dicta in *R. (Elphinstone) v Westminster City Council and others* [2008] EWHC 1287 (Admin). The issue did not strictly arise as the court dismissed the challenge on its merits. An appeal to the Court of Appeal also failed.

[82] *R (Nash) v Barnet LBC* [2013] P.T.S.R. 1457.

[83] The Court of Appeal recognised that this residual discretion existed in *R. v Gateshead MBC Ex p. Nichol* (1988) 87 L.G.R. 435.

[84] Where an application, although made within three months of the relevant decision, is not made promptly, there is still undue delay for the purposes of Senior Courts Act 1981, s.31(6) and the discretion to refuse a remedy under that discretion still arises. *R. v Dairy Produce Quota Tribunal for England and Wales Ex p. Caswell* [1990] 2 A.C. 738. The position in relation to claims based on EU law is different. There, the claim will not be out of time unless brought more than three months after the date when the claimant knew, or ought to have known, of the infringement and a majority of the Court of Appeal has indicated that the discretion to refuse a remedy under s. 31 does not arise in those circumstances: see *R (Berky) v Newport City Council* [2012] L.G.R. 592 per Moore-Bick LJ at [50]–[52] and Buxton LJ at [71]–[77].

[85] See, e.g. *R. v Leeds City Council Ex p. N* [1999] E.L.R. 324 at 334; *R. v Rochdale MBC Ex p. B, C, and K* [2000] Ed.C.R. 117 approved in *R. (Burkett) v Hammersmith and Fulham LBC* [2002] 1 W.L.R. 1593 at [18].

matters going to the discretion of the courts to refuse a remedy, rather than a matter of delay and a failure to comply with time-limits[86] and this is more likely to be dealt with at the substantive hearing than at the permission stage.[87] This approach is also consistent with the decision of the House of Lords in *Burkett*.[88]

9–025　　The possibility cannot be ruled out that the courts may take a different view of the applicability of *Burkett* in the education field. In one case, a local education authority had made proposals for closing a school and these were approved by the school's organisation committee. The claimant sought to challenge that decision on the grounds that the local education authority had erred in law as the wrong committee had made the proposals and, consequently, the school's organisation committee erred in law by approving invalid proposals. No challenge had been made to the decision of the local education authority and they were not party to the judicial review proceedings. The High Court refused to permit the challenge based on the alleged error by the local education authority as they were interested parties yet had not been joined and, more fundamentally, if the decision of the local education authority was immune from challenge because of delay in instituting proceedings against it, then the decision of the school's organisation committee was similarly immune from challenge on the grounds of any alleged illegality on the part of the local education authority earlier in the process.[89] That decision is more consistent with an approach which requires distinct errors made by distinct bodies in the administrative process to be challenged promptly and within three months of the error occurring, rather than accepting that the claimant may wait and challenge the final decision in the process.

9–026　　Another administrative technique is to have an investigation, followed by a decision or report, as in the case of the local ombudsman. A decision to embark on an investigation which is beyond the powers of the body concerned may be challenged immediately.[90] The courts have also held that the claimant may await the outcome of the investigation, and if it is unfavourable may be allowed to challenge the final outcome.[91]

Alternative administrative remedies

9–027　　Analogous difficulties arise in relation to the exhaustion of alternative administrative remedies. The courts as a general rule require, and certainly encourage, the use of such remedies before resorting to judicial review.[92] In

---

[86] [2002] 1 W.L.R. 1593 at [19].

[87] The courts can, however, take the view that if no remedy would be granted because of the prejudice to third parties or detriment to good administration, then no purpose would be served by granting permission. The court would, however, need to have evidence of such prejudice or detriment and this is unlikely to occur at the permission stage unless an oral hearing has been ordered and unless both the permission application and the substantive hearing are to be heard together so that evidence will have been filed. See *R. (Watford Boys' Grammar School) v Schools Adjudicator*, unreported, judgment March 29, 2004 where such a course was followed.

[88] *R. (Burkett) v Hammersmith and Fulham LBC* [2002]1 W.L.R. 1593 at [18] and [53].

[89] *R. (Louden) v Bury School Organisation Committee* [2002] EWHC 2749 (Admin) judgment December 19, 2002.

[90] *R. v Commissioner for Racial Equality Ex p. Hillingdon LBC* [1982] A.C. 779.

[91] *R. v Commissioner for Local Administration Ex p. Croydon LBC* [1989] 1 All E.R. 1033; *Re Prestige Group Plc* [1984] 1 W.L.R. 335.

[92] See, e.g. *R. v Secretary of State for the Home Department Ex p. Swati* [1986] 1 W.L.R. 477.

relation to claims of procedural unfairness in the early stages of the process, it is possible to discern various categories of cases. There are some situations where, having regard to the statutory or other framework governing appeals, there is intended to be an initial decision and then a subsequent rehearing which are properly to be treated as parts of one overall process and where the later decision supersedes the earlier decision.[93] In such cases, the claimant would not be granted permission to challenge the initial decision. There is also an intermediate category of cases where the statutory or other provisions governing the appeal contemplate that if there has been a fair result reached by fair procedures, an initial defect would not normally render the process invalid.[94] In such cases, the courts will not normally grant permission to challenge the initial decision unless there was some flagrant defect at the earlier stage or authoritative guidance from the courts on a real point of principle is required.[95] Furthermore, unless any unfairness at an earlier stage tainted the fairness of the appeal hearing, the courts would not normally grant permission to challenge an otherwise fair hearing by the appeal body.[96] Thus, the courts will not normally review a decision of a governing body confirming a decision of a head teacher to exclude a pupil from school but will require the claimant to exercise the statutory right to appeal to an independent appeal panel. Nor will the courts grant permission to challenge an otherwise fair hearing of the independent appeal panel because of some defect in the earlier stages of the process.[97] Finally, there is a category of cases, notably where criminal penalties are in issue, where, on a proper construction of the statutory framework, the individual is intended to have both a fair hearing before the initial body and before the appeal body. In such instances, the individual may either bring a claim for judicial review in respect of an unfair hearing of the initial body or may appeal.[98] Thus, an individual who received an unfair hearing before the magistrates' court may either seek judicial review to quash its decision or appeal to the Crown Court.[99]

Similar principles are likely to be followed where it is alleged that the public body acted unreasonably or failed to have regard to relevant considerations or made an error of law. There is much to be said for encouraging claimants to seek to correct such errors through any appeal process provided rather than resorting to judicial unless there is a real need to so. A claimant who delayed challenging a flaw in the initial decision in order to pursue an appeal should not therefore be penalised and should be allowed to seek judicial review if the appeal body fails to correct some error by the initial decision-maker. One possibility is to allow a challenge to the appeal decision on the grounds that it was flawed, as it failed to correct the error in the initial decision. Another possibility is to allow a challenge to the initial decision (and also the appeal decision) with time beginning to run

9–028

---

[93] *R. v Secretary of State for Home Department Ex p. Swati* [1986] 1 W.L.R. 477; *R. v Birmingham City Council Ex p. Ferrero Ltd* [1993] 1 All E.R. 530.

[94] *Calvin v Carr* [1980] A.C. 574; *R. (DR) v Headteacher of S School* [2003] E.L.R. 104.

[95] *R. (DR) v Head Teacher of S School* [2003] E.L.R. 104 at [45] and [54].

[96] *R. (DR) v Head Teacher of S School* [2003] E.L.R. 104 at [43] and [55].

[97] *R. (DR) v Head Teacher of S School* [2003] E.L.R. 104.

[98] *R. v Hereford Magistrates' Court Ex p. Rowlands; R. v Hereford Magistrates' Court Ex p Ingram; R. v Harrow Youth Court Ex p. Prussia* [1998] Q.B. 110; *Calvin v Carr* [1980] A.C. 574.

[99] *R. v Hereford Magistrates' Court Ex p. Rowlands; R. v Hereford Magistrates' Court Ex p Ingram; R. v Harrow Youth Court Ex p. Prussia* [1998] Q.B. 110.

from the date of the appellate decision. Alternatively, time could be regarded as running from the date of the initial decision, but the use of the appeal process could be treated as a good reason for extending that period.[100] The disadvantage of this course of action is that the courts might still consider that objectively there was undue delay arising from the use of the appeal process, and that they could still exercise their discretion under s.31(6) of the Senior Courts Act 1981 to refuse the application on grounds of substantial hardship. This disadvantage may be more apparent than real. The courts have a wide inherent remedial discretion, and they would be unlikely to grant a remedy if this would cause unacceptable prejudice to the administration or third parties, whether or not the claim is treated as technically within the time-limit.[101]

Subordinate legislation

9–029   The time-limit for challenges to subordinate legislation normally runs from the date when the subordinate legislation is made, although it has been suggested that the time only begins to run from the date when it comes into force.[102] Attempts to challenge the "continuing practices" based upon earlier subordinate legislation are unlikely to succeed since the real measure under challenge will be the earlier legislation. Thus, in one case,[103] a company sought to challenge the continuing practices of the Commissioners of Customs and Excise in not levying indirect taxes on duty-free goods, in reliance on statutory instruments implementing European Directives. The challenge was made more than three months after the date when the statutory instruments were made. The Divisional Court held that the challenge to the Commissioner's continuing practice was a disingenuous attempt to disguise the fact that the real challenge was to the validity of the statutory instruments and Directives. In those circumstances, they found that the claim had not been brought promptly and there was no good reason for extending the time for making the claim.

9–030   In most cases, subordinate legislation immediately affects the legal rights and obligations of persons and there is good reason to require that any challenge be made immediately. There may, however, be cases where the subordinate legislation sets out the framework for future action. In those circumstances, it may be inappropriate for the courts to refuse the claimant permission solely because he did not move promptly after the subordinate legislation was made. Rather, the time-limit may run from the date when a decision is taken applying or implementing the provisions of the subordinate legislation.[104]

---

[100]   *R. v Rochdale BC Ex p. Cromer Ring Mill Ltd* [1982] 3 All E.R. 761.

[101]   *R. v Gateshead MBC Ex p. Nichol* (1988) 87 L.G.R. 435.

[102]   *R. v HM Treasury Ex p. Smedley* [1985] Q.B. 657; *R. v Commissioners of Customs & Excise Ex p. Eurotunnel* [1995] C.L.C. 392.

[103]   *R. v Commissioners of Customs & Excise Ex p. Eurotunnel* [1995] C.L.C. 392.

[104]   This appears consistent with the decision in *R. (Burkett) v Hammersmith and Fulham LBC* [2002] 1 W.L.R. 1593 which regarded the time-limit as running from the date of the act which gives rise to legal rights and obligations.

Primary legislation and EU law

It is not yet clear how the time limit applies to a challenge to the compatibility of   **9–031**
domestic primary legislation with EU law. Much will depend upon the
circumstances in which the challenge is made. As a minimum, in cases where a
person is asserting a directly effective right, there is a strong case that the earliest
date upon which it could be said that the grounds for making the claim first arose,
so far as that claimant is concerned, is the date when the claimant became eligible
to claim the directly effective right. It would be at that stage that the claimant
would know, or ought to know, that the legislation was incompatible with his
directly effective right. That approach would also be consistent with the approach
of the Court of Justice to time limits generally: in the procurement field the Court
considered that the need to ensure that an individual was able effectively to
enforce a right derived from EU law meant that the time limit for bringing a claim
should run from the date when the claimant knew, or ought to have known, of the
infringement.[105] In any event, the courts are likely to treat a person who brought
a claim for judicial review within a reasonable period of time from the date when
he first acquired a directly effective right and first had a real interest in
challenging the legislation having good reason for not making the claim before
that date and for extending the time for bringing the claim if necessary. There is
also an argument that claims may be brought at any time when the allegedly
incompatible legislation remains in force or, alternatively, that the importance of
ensuring that legislation complies with EU law is sufficiently important to grant
an extension of time.[106] In *R. v Secretary of State for Employment Ex p. Equal
Opportunities Commission*,[107] a public body brought a challenge to the
compatibility of domestic legislation with EU law many years after the legislation
was adopted and came into force. No point about delay was taken.

Primary legislation and declarations of incompatibility

Similar problems could arise in the context of a claim brought by way of judicial   **9–032**
review for a declaration under s.4 of the Human Rights Act 1998 that provisions
of primary legislation are incompatible with a Convention right.[108] The preferable
view is that a claim may be made at any time when the allegedly incompatible
legislation remains in force. Alternatively, even if the time-limit in an individual
case ran from the date when the legislation was first applied to him, the question
of the compatibility of legislation with the Convention may well be of sufficient
importance to grant an extension of time. The courts would be unlikely to refuse
to address a real issue of substance on the compatibility of primary legislation
with the Convention on grounds of delay.[109]

---

[105] Case C-406/08 *Uniplex (UK) Ltd v NHS Business Services Authority* [2010] P.T.S.R. 1377 and see above at para.9–018.

[106] See below at para.9–040 on extensions of time on this basis.

[107] [1995] 1 A.C. 1.

[108] Such claims may arise in ordinary civil proceedings: see, e.g. *Bellinger v Bellinger* [2003] 2 W.L.R. 1174 claim for a declaration that legislation preventing transsexuals from marrying was incompatible with Convention rights was brought by way of an ordinary claim in the Family Division.

[109] See by analogy *R. (Robertson) v Wakefield MDC* [2002] 2 W.L.R. 889 at [12].

Date from which time runs in cases of failure to act

9–033 A claimant may be seeking to enforce a duty owed to him either by claiming a mandatory order or a declaration that a duty is owed. One question that arises is whether the time-limit begins to run from the date when the duty is first owed, or whether a duty creates a continuing obligation, so that a claim can be brought at any time when the duty is still owed. The issue is in part a question of statutory construction of the provision creating the duty. Where the statute contemplates a single, specific determination as to whether or not an act should be done, the courts may find that the time-limit runs from the date that the duty is first owed. Otherwise, the public authority may find itself facing claims demanding that an outstanding duty be performed, perhaps years after the duty to act first arose. Thus, the Court of Appeal has rejected the argument that the duty to pay a grant under the Education Act 1962 was a continuing duty so that the claim could seek a mandatory order in 1983 even though the grant had been refused in 1978.[110] Similarly, where statute imposed a duty to consult before making arrangements for the improvement of the exercise of its functions, the time for bringing a claim began to run from the date when the duty to consult first arose, i.e. in that case, before the making of arrangements to contract out the provision of certain services.[111] Conversely, if the statute imposes a duty to provide a service over a particular period of time, it is more likely that such a duty is a continuing duty owed in respect of the whole period when the service should be provided. The time-limit would not then run from the date that the duty first arose and a claim could be made at any time when the duty was still owed.[112]

Extension of time for bringing claims for judicial review

9–034 The courts insist on strict observance of the time-limits.[113] The courts have power to extend the time. This power was formerly specifically provided for in the rules governing judicial review which provided that there had to be good reason for extending the time for bringing a judicial review claim. Now the power is contained in the general powers of the court to extend time.[114] The previous case law applicable in judicial review cases, however, is likely to be applied in cases involving claims for judicial review as that case law simply reflects the need, in a public law case, for the claimant to act with speed.[115] A court is likely to require good reason for extending the time-limit for bringing a judicial review claim and

---

[110] *R. v Herefordshire CC Ex p.Cheung, The Times*, April 14, 1984. See also *R. v Dairy Produce Quota Tribunal for England and Wales Ex p. Hood* [1990] C.O.D. 184 (duty to give reasons not a continuing duty).

[111] *R. (Nash) v Barnet LBC* [2013] P.T.S.R. 1457.

[112] Such as the duty to provide suitable education to a child or to provide free school transport where this is necessary to enable a child to attend school: see Education Act 1996, ss.19 and 509 respectively.

[113] See, e.g. *R. v Newbury District Council Ex p. Chieveley Parish Council* (1998) 10 Admin.L.Rep. 676; *R. v Hammersmith and Fulham LBC Ex p. CPR, E* (1999) 81 P & C.R. 73 at [78]–[79] and see *M. (A Child) v School Organisation Committee* [2001] EWHC Admin 245, judgment March 23, 2001 (confirming that a strict approach should be adopted to delay under the provisions of CPR, Pt 54).

[114] Under CPR r.3.1(2)(a).

[115] *R. (Hardy) v Pembrokeshire CC* [2006] Env. 28 at [24]. See also *R. v Institute of Chartered Accountants in England and Wales Ex p. Andreou* (1996) 8 Admin. L.Rep. 557; *Re S* [1998] 1 F.L.R.

will scrutinise with care the reasons for any delay before finding that there is good reason for extending the time-limit. No comprehensive definition of good reason can be offered, since much depends on the facts of the case and the extent to which the courts regard the actions taken by the applicant as reasonable in the circumstances.

Delay caused by the claimant's lawyers[116] in making the application will not generally be a good reason for extending the time-limit, unless the reasons for the delay are satisfactorily explained. The delay may be excusable if it results from factors outside the applicant's or his advisors' control, and provided that they have acted reasonably throughout. The courts have accepted that the delay that occurs in obtaining legal aid may be a good reason.[117] They have also accepted that the time taken in obtaining permission to use copies of a planning application and drawings as exhibits was a good reason for delay.[118]

9–035

A claimant who has behaved reasonably and sensibly in pursuing a course of action should not be prejudiced by the refusal of permission on the grounds of delay provided that no prejudice is caused to others by the delay.[119] A claimant who is not informed that a decision has been taken has good reason for the delay, so long as he moves expeditiously once he is aware of the decision.[120] The time-limit still runs from the date of the decision, not the date when the claimant learned of the decision,[121] and the claimant will need to demonstrate that he acted as quickly as was reasonable once he learned of the decision.[122] The pursuit of internal inquiries by a local authority to determine the true facts surrounding a decision has been regarded as good reason,[123] as has the inevitable delay in calling a committee meeting to consider whether to seek judicial review.[124] Reasonable attempts to obtain information as to the procedure followed by the public body justified delay in bringing the claim.[125]

9–036

---

970 and see *R. (Melton) v School Organisation Committee* [2001] EWHC Admin 245, judgment on March 23, 2001 confirming that a similar approach applies to public law cases under the CPR.

[116] See, e.g. *R. v Institute of Chartered Accountants in England and Wales Ex p. Andreou* (1996) 8 Admin. L.Rep. 557 (delay in service of notice of motion due to error by the claimant's lawyers; court refused to extend time); *R. v Council for Licensed Conveyancers Ex p. Bradford and Bingley Building Society* [1999] C.O.D. 5; *R. v Isle of Wight CC Ex p. O'Keefe* (1990) 59 P. & C.R. 283 (claim not brought promptly due in part to conduct of solicitors; time extended for other reasons). See also *R. v Secretary of State for Health Ex p. Furneaux* [1994] 2 All E.R. 652 (unexplained delay by solicitors in lodging claim a factor justifying refusal of remedy).

[117] *R. v Stratford-on-Avon District Council Ex p. Jackson* [1985] 1 W.L.R. 1319; *R. v Wareham Magistrates' Court Ex p. Seldon* [1988] 1 W.L.R. 825.

[118] *R. v Stratford-upon-Avon District Council Ex p. Jackson* [1985] 1 W.L.R. 1319.

[119] See dicta of Woolf LJ in *R. v Commissioner for Local Administration Ex p. Croydon LBC* [1989] 1 All E.R. 1033 at 1046.

[120] *R. v Secretary of State for the Home Department Ex p. Ruddock* [1987] 1 W.L.R. 1482; *R. v Secretary of State for Foreign and Commonwealth Affairs Ex p. World Development Ltd* [1995] 1 W.L.R. 386 at 402H; *R. v Secretary of State for Transport Ex p. Presvac Engineering Ltd* (1991) 4 Admin. L.Rep. 121 at 133–134; *R. v Greenwich LBC Ex p. Governors of John Ball Primary School* [1990] C.O.D. 103; *R. v London Borough of Redbridge Ex p. G* [1991] C.O.D. 398.

[121] *R. v Secretary of State for Transport Ex p. Presvac Engineering Ltd* (1991) 4 Admin. L.Rep. 121 at 133–134; and see also *R. (Macrae) v Herefordshire DC* [2012] J.P.L. 457 at [22].

[122] *R. (Rayner) v Secretary of State for the Home Department* [2007] 1 W.L.R. 2239 at [9].

[123] *R. v Port Talbot BC Ex p. Jones* [1988] 2 All E.R. 207.

[124] *R. v Port Talbot BC Ex p. Jones* [1988] 2 All E.R. 207.

[125] *R. (Young) v Oxford City Council* [2002] EWCA Civ. 990.

9-037 An issue that has not yet fully been resolved by courts is the extent to which it is reasonable for a claimant to make attempts to resolve the matter by means other than judicial review. The exhaustion of alternative administrative appeal procedures has been regarded as good reason for extending the time-limit.[126] This follows naturally from the fact that the courts generally require the exhaustion of alternative remedies before claiming judicial reviews.

9-038 Difficulties arise when there is no clear appeal structure and the claimant wishes to make informal attempts to persuade the public authority to reconsider its decision or to involve another public body in attempts to settle the matter informally. There are occasions when the courts have extended the time-limit because the claimant was making other attempts to resolve the dispute. Reasonable attempts to persuade a court to reconsider its decision may in some,[127] but not all circumstances,[128] be good reason. There are, however, contrary examples where attempts at informal settlement were not considered a good reason. The High Court held that an immigrant who wishes to challenge an immigration officer's decision should do so immediately, and should not delay bringing the claim for judicial review simply in order to ask the Home Secretary to exercise his residual discretion to depart from the Immigration Rules.[129] Applications to the Home Secretary should be made contemporaneously with, not instead of judicial review. In that case, the court was much influenced by the fact that the Home Secretary was not obliged under the Immigration Act or Rules to act as an appeal tribunal in the case in question. Attempts to persuade a Crown Court to revoke a binding-over order will not necessarily be a good reason for not applying for judicial review immediately.[130] Nor would attempts to obtain the assistance of Members of Parliament.[131]

9-039 Much depends on the extent to which it is reasonable and realistic to pursue such alternative avenues. If the possibility of some other public body intervening is in practical terms remote, or where no power to intervene exists, it will not be reasonable to pursue that course of action. Given the importance of compliance with time-limits, the safest course of action is to bring the claim for judicial review and pursue alternative dispute resolution methods contemporaneously. This will avoid the risk that the courts may not regard the pursuit of the alternative remedy as a good reason for deferring the judicial review claim. It does, of course, mean increased costs. Furthermore, in terms of attempts to persuade the decision-maker to reconsider, the claimant should now use the pre-action protocol which requires the claimant to send a letter to the public body concerned, setting out why the claimant considers the public body has acted unlawfully and what remedy the claimant seeks.[132] If the public body makes it clear in its response that it does not believe that it has acted unlawfully or has no

---

[126] *R. v Rochdale BC Ex p. Cromer Ring Mill Ltd* [1982] 3 All E.R. 207.
[127] *R. v Wareham Magistrates' Court Ex p. Seldon* [1988] 1 W.L.R. 825.
[128] *R. v Lincoln Crown Court Ex p. Jones* [1990] C.O.D. 15.
[129] *R. v Secretary of State for the Home Department Ex p. Hindjou* [1989] Imm. A.R. 24. See also dicta in *R. v Secretary of State for the Home Department Ex p. Oladehinde* [1990] 2 W.L.R. 1195 (pursuit of appeal where no such right existed might be characterised as unreasonable delay).
[130] *R. v Lincoln Crown Court Ex p. Jones* [1990] C.O.D. 15.
[131] *R. v London Borough of Redbridge Ex p. G* [1991] C.O.D. 398.
[132] See above at para.9-004.

power to reconsider the matter, it is unlikely that further attempts to persuade that public body to reconsider the matter would justify delay.

Public importance

The fact that a claim raises issues of general public importance may also provide good reason for extending the time-limit and allowing the claim to proceed.[133] This may be because the claim raises an issue of law which is of general importance, and not simply of interest to the claimant. Thus the courts have been prepared to extend time where important questions of the compatibility of domestic legislation with the European Convention on Human Rights[134] or of EU law arise.[135] The courts extended time when an important issue concerning the circumstances in which a pregnant woman who refused admission to a hospital could be detained under the Mental Health Act 1983.[136] This ground for extending the time-limit may also arise where the subject-matter of the claim is of general public interest, such as a claim alleging unlawful telephone-tapping[137] or a claim alleging that the use of aid from the development budget to assist in the construction of a dam in a third country was unlawful.[138] The grant of an extension of time on this ground is likely to be appropriate only in exceptional cases.[139] The courts will not generally grant an extension on these grounds if the claim, although important to the parties, does not involve an important point of law which needs to be resolved or which is of no wider significance.[140]

9–040

Parties cannot extend time by agreement

An additional problem arises from the fact that the rules provide that the time-limit for filing a claim form cannot be extended by agreement.[141] This creates difficulties in a number of ways. First, the proposed defendant may ask the claimant for additional time to consider the matter before proceedings are

9–041

---

[133] *R. v Secretary of State for the Home Department Ex p. Ruddock* [1987] 1 W.L.R. 1482; *Re S* [1998] 1 F.L.R. 790; *R. (Robertson) v Wakefield MDC* [2002] 2 W.L.R. 889 at [12]; *R. v Secretary of State for Trade and Industry Ex p. Greenpeace Ltd (No.2)* [2000] Env. L.R. 221 at 263 and see *R. v Secretary of State for Foreign and Commonwealth Affairs Ex p. World Development Movement Ltd* [1995] 1 W.L.R. 386 at 402H.

[134] *R. (Robertson) v Wakefield MDC* [2002] 2 W.L.R. 889 at [12] (compatibility of arrangements for sale of electoral register with Convention and EU law).

[135] *R. v Secretary of State for Trade and Industry Ex p. Greenpeace Ltd (No.2)* [2000] Env.L.R. 221 (whether the obligations of the UK under the Habitats Directive extended beyond the 12-mile territorial limit of the continental shelf).

[136] *Re S* [1998] 1 F.L.R. 790.

[137] *R. v Secretary of State for the Home Department Ex p. Ruddock* [1987] 1 W.L.R. 1482.

[138] *R. v Secretary of State for Foreign and Commonwealth Affairs Ex p. World Development Movement Ltd* [1995] 1 W.L.R. 386 and see *B.T. v Gloucester City Council* [2002] 2 P. & C.R. 512 at 554 (matter of public significance as it involved development in a conservation area of historical and archaeological interest).

[139] See *Re S* [1998] 1 F.L.R. 790 at 795.

[140] *R. v Secretary of State for Transport Ex p. Presvac Engineering Ltd* (1991) 4 Admin. L.Rep. 121 at 137–138 (technical breach in form of a failure to check valves at sea not shown to be a threat to public safety and no issue of public importance arose); *M (A Child) v School Organisation Committee* [2001] EWHC Admin 245, judgment March 23, 2001 (closure of school important to parties but not of wider public significance).

[141] CPR 54.5(2).

issued. The likelihood is that, although the parties cannot agree to extend time, a court would regard the fact that the defendant requested additional time as a good reason for extending the time-limit. The courts are unlikely to want to encourage the unnecessary issuing of proceedings. Given the provisions of the CPR, a claimant may be reluctant to agree to such a course of action if there is a risk that the time-limit for issuing a claim would expire and may not wish to be dependent upon the possible exercise of discretion by the courts to extend time. One solution would be to issue the claim and ask for it to be stayed. Secondly, problems arise where a number of cases are affected by a decision based on a particular interpretation of a point of law. The sensible course of action is for the public authority and the representatives of the various claimants to seek to identify an appropriate test case and to agree that the decisions in other cases will be reviewed in the light of the decision. There will then either be a fresh decision in the other cases, so the time-limit starts afresh (and judicial review proceedings can be issued if it is arguable that the fresh decision is unlawful) or the courts would be likely to view the fact that the parties were awaiting the outcome of the test case as a good reason for extending the time limit.[142] A claimant can also issue proceedings and request a stay pending the outcome of the test case. There would be merit, however, in amending the provision governing extension of time so that the parties can, in appropriate circumstances, agree an extension. Whilst there is a public interest in ensuring that public law matters are litigated promptly, if the public body is content to extend time for issuing a claim there would seem to be little reason for refusing to allow a claim to proceed simply on the basis of delay. The court will retain its inherent jurisdiction to refuse a remedy if there is prejudice to third parties.

Effect of a grant of an extension of time

9–042   A finding that good reason exists to allow the claim to be brought out of time is final and cannot be re-opened at the substantive hearing of the claim.[143] The defendant will not, therefore, be able to resist the claim merely because there has been delay. However, there is still undue delay for the purposes of s.31(6) of the Senior Courts Act 1981 where the application is not made promptly or within three months even where there is good reason for extending the time-limit. A court may, therefore, still refuse permission or a remedy at the substantive hearing if granting a remedy would cause substantial hardship or substantial prejudice to the rights of any person, or would be detrimental to good administration.[144] Furthermore, as the remedies available in judicial review are discretionary, the courts also have an inherent jurisdiction to refuse a remedy on grounds that granting a remedy would cause undue prejudice to third parties or be detrimental to good administration.[145] In practice, once good reason for extending

---

[142] See dicta of the Court of Appeal in *R. v Secretary of State for the Home Department Ex p. Zeqiri* judgment, March 12, 2001 at [42]–[43] and *R. v Hertfordshire CC v Cheung* judgment, April 4, 1986.

[143] *R. v Criminal Injuries Compensation Board Ex p. A* [1999] 1 A.C. 330 (decision of the House of Lords overruling *R. v Tavistock General Commissioners Ex p. Worth* [1985] S.T.C. 564).

[144] *R. v Dairy Produce Quota Tribunal for England and Wales Ex p. Caswell* [1990] 2 A.C. 738.

[145] See, e.g. *R. v Brent LBC Ex p. O'Malley* (1997) 10 Admin. L.Rep. 265 at 293–294; *R. v Gateshead MBC Ex p. Nichol* (1988) 87 L.G.R. 435; and see the dicta of Lord Steyn in *R. (Burkett) v Hammersmith and Fulham LBC* [2002] 1 W.L.R. 1593 at [18]–[19] and at 1611C (in regard to truly

the time-limit is shown, the court is likely to grant permission and to let the question of substantial hardship or prejudice be determined at the full hearing rather than the permission hearing.[146] These issues are accordingly dealt with in the discussion of the remedial discretion of the courts.[147]

Effect of a finding that a claim was brought promptly

The House of Lords in *Ex p. A* only dealt with the question of whether there was good reason for extending the time-limit, as the claim was brought more than three months after the decision and an extension of time was clearly needed. There may be instances where the claim was not brought promptly even though it was brought within three months of the decision. Logically, the same reasoning applies to a finding that a claim was made promptly as applies to findings that there was good reason for any delay. Such a finding (with the implication that no extension of time for filing the claim is necessary) should also be final and not open to reconsideration at the substantive hearing. The Court of Appeal has held, however, that where a court grants permission on the basis that the claim was brought promptly, the court dealing with the substantive hearing may still consider the question of whether the claim was made without undue delay for the purpose of deciding whether the discretionary grounds for refusing a remedy set out in s.31(6) of the Senior Courts Act 1981 applied.[148] The Court of Appeal held that the defendant should only be able to recanvass the question of undue delay (1) where the judge hearing the initial application had expressly so indicated, (2) if new and relevant material is produced at the hearing, (3) if, exceptionally, the issues as they have developed at the substantive hearing put a different aspect on the question of promptness, or (4) the judge has plainly overlooked a relevant matter or reached a decision *per incuriam*. The issue was seen as important for the following reason. Section 31(6) of the Senior Courts Act 1981 only provides for the refusal of a remedy where there has been undue delay: if the finding of the court considering the application for permission was that the application was made promptly, then, strictly, the discretion to refuse a remedy under s.31(6) does not arise as there is no delay. The problem is, however, more theoretical than real as the remedies are discretionary. The courts possess an inherent jurisdiction to refuse a remedy (irrespective of the discretion conferred by s.31(6) of the Senior Courts Act 1981) where they are satisfied that granting a remedy would cause unacceptable prejudice to third parties or the administration of justice even if the application was made promptly.[149]

9–043

---

urgent cases the court would in any event have its ultimate discretion or under section 31(6) of the 1981 Act be able to refuse relief where it is appropriate to do so").

[146] *R. v Dairy Produce Quota Tribunal for England and Wales Ex p. Caswell* [1990] 2 A.C. 738 at 746–747. The courts may order that both the application for permission and the substantive hearing should be heard together; this enables the court to deal with the question of delay at the full hearing, or to refuse to grant permission because, as a matter of discretion, no remedy would be granted in any event: see, e.g. *R. v Secretary of State for Trade and Industry Ex p. Greenpeace Ltd (No.2)* [2000] Env. L.R. 221; *R. (Watford Grammar School for Boys) v Schools Adjudicator*, unreported, March 29, 2004.

[147] See Chapter 12.

[148] *R. v Lichfield BC Ex p. Lichfield Securities Ltd* [2001] 3 P.L.R. 33.

[149] See *R. v Brent LBC Ex p. O'Malley* (1999) 10 Admin. L.Rep. 265 at 293–294 and *R. v Gateshead MBC Ex p. Nichol* (1988) 87 L.G.R. 435 (neither of which were cited in *R. v Lichfield BC Ex p.*

Applications for protective costs orders

9–044   The unsuccessful party to legal proceedings is, generally, ordered to pay the costs of the successful party.[150] Thus, a claimant who brings a claim for judicial review and is unsuccessful will normally be ordered to pay the defendant's costs in resisting the claim.[151] This may deter a claimant from bringing a claim that might otherwise be in the public interest. The courts have jurisdiction to make a protective costs order[152] and a claimant seeking such an order should include an application for such an order in the claim form, supported by evidence and a schedule of the claimant's likely costs.[153] Protective costs orders can take a number of forms. Thus, where the claimant is not seeking an order that it will be able to recover costs if he is successful (as where his lawyers are acting pro bono for example), the claimant may seek an order that the claimant[154] will not have to pay the defendant's costs, or that the claimant's liability for those costs will be capped, in the event that the claimant is unsuccessful.[155] More usually, a claimant may seek an order that enables him to recover his costs if he is successful but limits his liability in costs or provides that there will be no order for costs in favour of the defendant if the defendant is successful. The amount of costs that a claimant will be allowed to recover under such orders are likely to be limited to a reasonable amount sufficient to enable the claimant to obtain appropriate legal representation.[156] Furthermore, if the courts do exercise their discretion to make

---

Lichfield Securities Ltd [2001] EWCA Civ 304, judgment March 8, 2000) and dicta of Lord Steyn in *R. (Burkett) v Hammersmith and Fulham LBC* [2002] 1 W.L.R. 1593 at [53] that in urgent cases "the court in any event in its ultimate discretion or under section 31(6) of the 1981 Act be able to refuse relief where it is appropriate to do so".

[150]   CPR r.44.2 and see *R. (M) v Croydon LBC* [2012] 1 W.L.R. 2607 at [29], [44] to [46] and [52] to [58].

[151]   See *R. (Davey) v Aylesbury Vale DC*[2008] 1 W.L.R. 878 at [29]. and *R. (M) v Croydon LBC* [2012] 1 W.L.R. 2607 at [58]. In exceptional circumstances, the courts may, in their discretion, determine not to order an unsuccessful claimant in judicial review cases to pay the defendant's costs: see, e.g. *R. v Secretary of Environment Ex p. Shelter* [1997] C.O.D. 49 and see discussion at 9-122 below.

[152]   The jurisdiction, and the principles governing the grant of such orders, are described in *R. (Corner House Research) v Secretary of State for Trade and Industry* [2005] 1 W.L.R. 2006 at [78]–[81].These are orders made by the court to protect a party from liability to costs in the event that the party is unsuccessful. They are to be distinguished from cost capping orders made under CPR r.44.18 which are intended to control a party from incurring disproportionate incurring future costs and which seek to prevent him from recovering such costs in the future. The rules on costs capping orders do not apply to protective costs orders: CPR r.44.18(3).

[153]   *R. (Corner House Research) v Secretary of State for Trade and Industry* [2005] 1 W.L.R. 2006 at [78]–[81].

[154]   Or even, in exceptional circumstances, in favour of a defendant: see *R. (Ministry of Defence) v Wiltshire and Swindon Coroner* [2006] 1 W.L.R. 134 (although the court recognised that the conditions for making such an order would be unlikely to be satisfied although it could arise where a defendant was an individual performing public functions, had no protection in relation to costs and where, presumably, no other person would defend the decision if the defendant did not: see per Collins J. at [34]).

[155]   *R. (Corner House Research) v Secretary of State for Trade and Industry* [2005] 1 W.L.R. 2600 at [75].

[156]   *R. (Corner House Research) v Secretary of State for Trade and Industry* [2005] 1 W.L.R. 2600 at [75]; *R. (Medical Justice) v Secretary of State for the Home Department* [2011] 1 W.L.R. 2852 at [30] (costs to be restricted to a "reasonably modest amount" and claimant's counsel should not expect to be able to charge commercial rates). There is now no rule that the claimant is limited to junior counsel

an order limiting the claimant's liability in costs if the claimant is unsuccessful, they are also likely to impose a limit on the amount of costs that the defendant will be liable to pay if the defendant is unsuccessful.[157] The court will not re-open the question of the amount of costs that can be recovered if, in fact, the claimant is successful and its costs are higher than anticipated.[158]

The existence of the jurisdiction reflects the fact that there may be a public interest in resolving issues of public law but there may be difficulties in that occurring unless a protective costs order is made. Consequently, the Court of Appeal has held that the courts should only exercise their jurisdiction to make a prospective costs order where the courts are satisfied that: **9–045**

(1)   the issues raised are of general public importance;
(2)   the public interest requires that those issues be resolved;
(3)   the applicant has no private interest in the outcome of the case;
(4)   having regard to the financial resources of the applicant and the defendant, and to the amount of costs involved, it is fair and just to make the order; and
(5)   if the order is not made, the applicant will probably discontinue the proceedings and would be acting reasonably in doing so.[159]

The prospects of obtaining such an order will also be enhanced if those acting for the applicant are acting pro bono. It is for the court, in the exercise of its discretion, to decide whether it is fair and just to make the order in the light of those considerations.[160] The Court of Appeal consequently granted a protective costs order in the *Corner House* case as it considered that the issues raised were ones of general public importance, involving as they did the lawfulness of certain changes made to the information required from British companies backed by export guarantee guarantees funded by the taxpayer, which changes were said to weaken the ability of the authorities to combat bribery and corruption, and the consultation policy of the public body. They were issues that should be resolved. The applicant had no private interest in the claim, as it was a non-profit making company limited by guarantee which had a particular interest and expertise in examining the incidence of bribery and corruption in international trade. The Court of Appeal was satisfied that the other requirements for making a protective costs order were met.[161]

---

only; rather the question depends on whether, in the circumstances, such a restriction would be just: see *R. (Buglife Invertebrate Trust) v Thurrock Thames Gateway Development Corporation* [2009] EWCA Civ 1209 at [25].

[157] *R. (Corner House Research) v Secretary of State for Trade and Industry* [2005] 1 W.L.R. 2600 at [76](ii) and *R. (Buglife Invertebrate Trust) v Thurrock Thames Gateway Development Corporation* [2009] EWCA Civ 1209 at [21]–[23].

[158] *R (Badger Trust) v Welsh Ministers* [2010] 6 Costs L.R. 896.

[159] *R. (Corner House Research) v Secretary of State for Trade and Industry* [2005] 1 W.L.R. 2600 at [74](1).

[160] *R. (Corner House Research) v Secretary of State for Trade and Industry* [2005] 1 W.L.R. 2600 at [74](2) and (3). The five listed considerations determine if the case is sufficiently exceptional: it is not the case that these considerations must be satisfied and, in addition, the case must be exceptional: see *R. (British Union for the Abolition of Vivisection) v Secretary of State for the Home Department* [2007] A.C.D. 14.

[161] *R. (Corner House Research) v Secretary of State for Trade and Industry* [2005] 1 W.L.R. 2600.

9–046   The Court of Appeal has subsequently indicated that the guidelines as to what constitutes an issue of general public importance should not be interpreted too restrictively. Thus, a court was entitled to conclude that the closure of a local hospital raised an issue of general public importance and there was a public interest in resolving the issue even though it did not affect the national interest generally and affected only a section of the population.[162] The courts have indicated that the third criterion, namely that the individual has no private interest in the matter, is a difficult one to apply in the context of litigation intended to enable issues of general public importance to be litigated when they would not be unless a protective costs order were granted.[163] On one occasion, the Court of Appeal considered that the requirement that a claimant has no private interest generally means that an individual claimant who has a financial or other interest in the outcome of the judicial review claim will not be able to benefit from a protective costs order. Thus a woman seeking judicial review of a coroner's verdict following an inquest into the death of her father had a private interest in the outcome of the claim and the courts declined to make a protective costs order.[164] The courts have more recently indicated that they will take a flexible approach to this requirement, at least where the claimant shares an interest with others in the matter and there is a public interest in the resolution of a matter.[165] A person who has no private interest in the claim, and is merely acting as a public spirited citizen[166] or simply as a member of a public interest group,[167] may be granted a protective costs order if they satisfy the other criteria. Public interest groups are unlikely to have any private interest in the outcome of a dispute and may be granted a protective costs order if they satisfy the other criteria.

9–047   The courts have granted protective costs orders in a number of cases in addition to the order in the *Corner House* case. By way of example, in two cases, the courts have granted a reciprocal costs order limiting the amount that both the claimant and the defendant could be ordered to pay to £10,000 at first instance and in the Court of Appeal. In one case, the challenge was to the lawfulness of an order providing for a cull of badgers in Wales,[168] in the other, the challenge was to the grant of planning permission for a development which was said to threaten a nationally important site hosting invertebrate habitats.[169] In another case, the court granted an order limiting the liability of the claimant to meet the costs of the defendant, if it were unsuccessful, to £25,000. The court was satisfied that the issues raised were ones of general importance as they concerned the lawfulness of

---

[162] *R. (Compton) v Wiltshire Primary Care Trust (Practice Note)* [2009] 1 W.L.R. 1436 at [23]–[24] (per Waller LJ) and 75–77 (per Smith LJ).

[163] *Morgan v Hinton Organics* [2010] 1 Costs L.R. 1 at [38]–[39].

[164] *R. (Goodson) v HM Coroner for Bedfordshire and Luton* [2005] EWCA Civ. 1172 esp. at [28].

[165] *Morgan v Hinton Organics* [2010] 1 Costs L.R. 1 at [39]; *R. (Compton) v Wiltshire Primary Care Trust (Practice Note)* [2009] 1 W.L.R. 1436 at [23].

[166] *R. (Goodson) v HM Coroner for Bedfordshire and Luton* [2005] EWCA Civ 1172 esp. at [28].

[167] *R. (England) v London Borough of Tower Hamlets* [2006] EWCA Civ 1742 at [15]. It appears that a limited company formed of parents opposed to a scheme of school re-organisation was granted a protective costs order capping liability for the defendant's cost to a sum of £13,000. Whilst such bodies may have standing to claim judicial review, it is less clear that they should be able to obtain a protective costs order if, in fact, the persons who formed the company have a personal interest in the outcome.

[168] *R. (Badger Trust) v Welsh Ministers* [2010] 6 Costs L.R. 896.

[169] *R. (Buglife Invertebrate Trust) v Thurrock Thames Gateway Development Corporation* [2009] EWCA Civ 1209.

military action in Iraq and the pressure group in question would not have time to raise further money to fund the challenge and the sum of £25,000 would be likely, in any event, to meet the defendant's costs of a two-day hearing.[170] On another occasion, the court granted a protective costs order limiting the liability of an anti-vivisection charity to the sum of £40,000 when it brought a claim for judicial review of the Secretary of State's decision to grant licences for animal research.[171]

The Court of Appeal has also outlined a procedure for applying for protective costs orders. The application for such an order should be included in the claim form seeking judicial review, supported by evidence and containing a schedule of the claimant's likely costs. If the defendant wishes to resist the application, it should set out its reasons for doing so in the acknowledgement of service. The judge will then decide the application on the papers. If the defendant successfully resists the application, it should normally be entitled to recover the costs of doing so, although the costs awarded will be limited to £1,000 as that will be a proportionate amount of costs and will be unlikely to deter the applicant from making the application. A further single set of costs, limited to £1,000, may also be available to an interested party or parties who resist such an application. If the applicant renews the application at an oral hearing, and is unsuccessful, the defendant will generally be entitled to recover its costs for doing so but that amount is likely to be limited to £2,500. An interested party may also seek costs if it successfully resists an application for a protective costs order although the courts are likely to make only one order for costs in respect of the interested parties and that will generally be limited to £2,500.[172]

9–048

Proposed legislative changes

The Criminal Justice and Courts Bill 2014, if enacted, will place protective costs orders (which the Bill refers to as cost capping orders) on a statutory basis. Such orders could only be made if the proceedings are public interest proceedings and the claimant would be likely to withdraw the claim, and would be acting reasonably in doing so, if a costs capping order is not made. Public interest proceedings are defined as proceedings raising an issue of general public importance which the public interest requires to be resolved and the proceedings are likely to provide an appropriate means of resolving it. The matters to which the courts are to have regard to when determining if proceedings are public interest proceedings include the number of people likely to be affected if a remedy is granted and how significant the effect on those people is likely to be and whether the proceedings involve a point of law of general public importance. The provisions also provide for the making of rules of court to specify information to be included in an application for a costs capping order, including the source, nature and extent of the financial resources likely to be available to

9–049

---

[170] R. (Campaign for Nuclear Disarmament) v Prime Minister of the United Kingdom, unreported, December 17, 2002.
[171] R. (British Union for the Abolition of Vivisection) v Secretary of State for the Home Department [2007] A.C.D. 14.
[172] R. (Corner House Research) v Secretary of State for Trade and Industry [2005] 1 W.L.R. 2600 at [78]–[81]. See also R. (Compton) v Wiltshire Primary Care Trust (Practice Note) [2009] 1 W.L.R. 1419 at [42]–[46].

the claimant to meet any liabilities arising in connection with the claim or, if the claimant is a corporate body unable to demonstrate that it is likely to have the financial resources to meet such liabilities, information about its members and their ability to provide financial support. When deciding whether to make a costs capping order, or the terms of such an order, the court will be required to consider the financial resources of the parties, including the resources of those who may provide financial support to the parties, the likely benefit to the claimant or anyone providing financial support if a remedy is granted, whether the legal representatives are acting free of charge and whether the claimant is an appropriate person to represent the interests of other persons or the public interest generally.

Protective costs orders and environmental challenges falling within the Aarhus Convention

9–050   Specific provisions now apply in relation to claims concerning matters falling with the Aarhus Convention on access to information, public participation and access to justice in environmental matters. Article 9 of that Convention provides that states who are party to the Convention must ensure that individuals claiming a right of access to information or the right to public participation for the purposes of the Convention have access to review procedures before a court and that those procedures are not prohibitively expensive. The provisions of the Aarhus Convention have been implemented in various EU legislative instruments including those dealing with the need to carry out environmental impact assessments on certain proposed developments and those governing integrated pollution control. The Court of Justice has set out the factors relevant in assessing whether a costs order would render the proceedings prohibitively expensive.[173] The Court of Justice has held that the assessment of the costs payable by a claimant should not exceed the financial resources of the claimant nor be objectively unreasonable. The analysis cannot be based on the estimated resources of an average claimant as the financial resources of the actual claimant may not reflect the position of the average person. Furthermore the court may take into account whether a claimant has a reasonable prospect of success, what is at stake for the claimant, the complexity of the issues, whether the claim is frivolous (all factors which might indicate that a higher award of costs against an unsuccessful claimant might be justified[174]) and the importance of the protection of the environment (which might indicate a lower award of costs against an unsuccessful claimant[175]). The Court of Justice subsequently indicated that the absence of clear and unequivocal rules, and reliance on a body of case law which, at the time, appeared not to ensure adequate protection in environmental cases, failed properly to implement the obligations in the relevant EU Directive to ensure that proceedings were not prohibitively expensive.

---

[173] Case C-260/11 *R. (Edwards) v Environment Agency (No.2)* [2013] 1 W.L.R. 2914; Case C-530/11 *Commission v United Kingdom* judgment of 13 February 2014.

[174] See the decision of the Supreme Court, following the preliminary ruling of the Court of Justice, in *R. (Edwards) v Environment Agency (No.2)* [2014] 1 W.L.R. 55 at [28].

[175] *R. (Edwards) v Environment Agency (No.2)* [2014] 1 W.L.R. 55 at [28].

CPR Part 45[176] now makes specific provision for protective costs orders in   **9–051**
judicial review claims[177] concerning decisions, actions or omissions falling
within the scope of the Aarhus Convention. A claimant in an Aarhus Convention
case will not be ordered to pay costs exceeding the sum £5,000 (or £10,000 if the
claimant is an organisation) in the event that it is unsuccessful.[178] If there is more
than one claimant, it appears from the provisions in CPR Part 45 that each
claimant may be ordered to pay up to £5,000. The claimant needs to specify in the
claim form that the Aarhus Convention applies. If the defendant does not contest
that issue, the provisions in CPR Part 45 will apply. If the defendant contests the
applicability of the Aarhus Convention, it must say so in its acknowledgement of
service. The matter will then need to be determined by the court. If the court
determines that the claim is not an Aarhus Convention claim, no order for costs in
relation to the determination of that issue will normally be made; if it is such a
claim, the defendant will normally be ordered to pay the costs, on an indemnity
basis, and the amount is added to the amount that the defendant can be ordered to
pay if unsuccessful in the substantive claim.[179]

Service of the claim form on the defendant and interested parties

The claim form must be served on the defendant and any interested party within   **9–052**
seven days of it being issued by the Administrative Court Office.[180] The
defendant will be the public body whose decision, action or failure to act is under
challenge. An interested party is a person who is directly affected by the claim.[181]
A person will be directly affected if he would be affected simply by the grant of a
remedy. In *R. v Liverpool City Council Ex p. Muldoon*,[182] dealing with the
interpretation of the phrase "directly affected" in the former Ord.53, the House of
Lords held that the Secretary of State was not affected by a challenge to a
decision of the housing authority to pay the claimant housing benefit. He was
indirectly affected by the claim for judicial review in that he would be liable to
pay 95 per cent of the amount of the benefit if the refusal to pay was quashed, but
he was not directly affected by the grant of a remedy. On occasions, claim forms
are served on persons, particularly other public bodies or pressure groups, who
are not directly affected themselves but are likely to want to ask the court for
permission to file evidence or make representations at the hearing.[183] A non-party
may obtain a copy of the claim form from the court.[184]

---

[176] CPR r.45.41–45.44 and Practice Direction 45.
[177] Other proceedings, such as statutory applications to quash under the Town and Country Planning
Acts 1990, are not claims for judicial review and do not fall within CPR r.45.41: see *Venn v Secretary
of State for Communities and Local Government* [2014] J.P.L. 447 (on appeal to the Court of Appeal).
A protective costs order may be made in appropriate cases, applying the *Corner House* criteria.
[178] Presumably a court could the claimant to pay less if that were necessary to ensure that the costs
did not exceed the claimant's own financial resources.
[179] CPR r.45.44.
[180] CPR r.54.7.
[181] CPR r.54.1(1)(f).
[182] [1996] 1 W.L.R. 1103.
[183] Under CPR r.54.17.
[184] Pursuant to CPR r.5.4C and see *R. (Corner House Research Campaign against the Arms Trade) v
the Director of the Serious Fraud Office* [2008] EWHC 246 (Admin); [2008] A.C.D. 246.

Acknowledgment of service

9–053   Any person served with a claim form who wishes to take part in the judicial review proceedings must serve file an acknowledgment of service within 21 days after service and must then serve it on the claimant and any other party within seven days of filing.[185] The acknowledgment of service must set out a summary of the grounds for contesting the claim and state the name of any person considered to be an interested party.[186] The acknowledgment of service gives the defendant the opportunity of setting out reasons why permission should not be granted. In particular, the defendant will wish to raise issues such as delay, the availability of alternative remedies, or the lack of an arguable case. The purpose of the summary of grounds for resisting the claim is to assist the judge to determine whether to grant permission and if so on what terms.[187] Applications for permission should not normally be determined before the claimant has had the opportunity to put in an acknowledgment of service.[188] Where the matter is urgent, the claimant may use the urgent application procedure and the court may give directions abridging the time for filing an acknowledgment of service.[189] Where a person fails to file an acknowledgment of service, he is not entitled to take part in any oral hearing of an application for permission unless the court permits him to do so. He may take part in the subsequent substantive hearing, if permission is granted, provided he serves detailed grounds of resistance and any written evidence.[190] A non-party may obtain a copy of a public authority's acknowledgement of service containing the summary grounds from the court.[191]

Consideration of the initial application for permission

9–054   Claims for judicial review may only be brought where the court has first granted permission to apply for judicial review.[192] The application for permission will initially be dealt with by a judge on the basis of the papers alone without an oral hearing, that is on the basis of the claim form, written evidence and acknowledgment of service.[193] There is no specific provision in the CPR for the claimant to respond in writing to the acknowledgement of service. If a claimant does file a written response that is usually considered by the judge provided that it is received before the decision on the application for permission is taken. While decisions on permission are usually dealt with on the paper, the court has a discretion to order that the application be dealt with at an oral hearing. The rules

---

[185]   CPR r.54.8. The time-limit may not be extended by agreement between the parties (see CPR r.54.8(3)) but may be extended by the court under CPR r.3.2(1)(a). Requests are usually made by letter setting out the reasons why additional time is required.

[186]   CPR r.54.8(4).

[187]   *R. (Ewing) v Office of the Deputy Prime Minister* [2006] 1 W.L.R. 1260 at [43].

[188]   *R. (Webb) v Bristol City Council* [2001] EWCA Admin 696, judgment July 25, 2001; *R. (BG) v Medway Council* [2006] 1 F.L.R. 663 at [40].

[189]   See *R. (BG) v Medway BC* [2006] 1 F.L.R. 663 at [40] and above at para.9–014.

[190]   CPR r.54.9.

[191]   Pursuant to CPR 5.4C as interpreted by Collins J. in *R. (Corner House Research, Campaign against the Arms Trade) v the Director of the Serious Fraud Office* [2008] EWHC 246 (Admin) [2008] A.C.D. 246.

[192]   CPR r.54.4.

[193]   See para.8.4 of the Practice Direction 54A – Judicial Review.

no longer provide for there to be an oral hearing of the application at the request of the claimant. If permission is refused, the claimant may then request that the refusal be reconsidered at an oral hearing.[194]

Exceptionally, and usually in cases of urgency, the courts may order a "rolled-up" hearing where the application for permission and the substantive hearing will be dealt with at the same hearing, with the substantive hearing following immediately if permission is granted. In such circumstances, the claimant, defendant and interested parties will need to ensure that all the relevant evidence is filed before that hearing. There may also be exceptional cases where the claimant may need, as a matter of urgency, to seek permission and interim relief before the usual time for filing an acknowledgment of service has passed. In such cases, the claimant may use the urgent application procedure.[195] In cases where interim relief is sought, the court will usually direct that there be an oral hearing of the application for interim relief and often of the application for permission, unless the matter is particularly urgent.[196] The court can grant directions abridging the time for service of the acknowledgment of service and directing that written evidence and skeleton arguments be filed. In cases of real urgency, the court may grant an interim remedy immediately and without giving notice to the defendant. The courts have jurisdiction to grant interim remedies at any time and may grant a remedy before permission is granted.[197] As a matter of principle, it is preferable for such orders to be granted for a specific, usually relatively short, period of time enabling the matter to be brought back to an oral hearing on notice to the defendant or alternatively the defendant is given liberty to apply to discharge the interim remedy.[198]

9–055

Once permission is granted, the court may also direct that there be a stay of the proceedings to which the claim relates.[199] Again the implication is that stays will be granted on the basis of the consideration of the papers, rather than at an oral hearing. In the past, however, the practice was for the question of a stay, particularly if it had the same effect as the grant of an interim injunction, to be considered at an oral hearing on notice to the defendant so that he may attend and be heard.[200]

9–056

---

[194] CPR r.54.12.

[195] See Practice Statement (Administrative Court: Listing and Urgent Cases) [2002] 1 W.L.R. 810 discussed above at para.9-014.

[196] See *R. v Kensington and Chelsea RLBC Ex p. Hammell* [1989] Q.B. 518 at 539B–C (dealing with the practice under the former rules but the same principles should apply under the CPR).

[197] See CPR, r.25.2 and *M v Home Office* [1994] 1 A.C. 377 at 423C (interim relief may be granted in urgent cases even before permission to apply for judicial review is granted).

[198] See dicta in *R. (Lawler) v Restormel B.C.* [2000] A.C.D. 2. Specific guidance has been given by the Administrative Court in relation to claims for interim remedies by asylum-seekers who are refused support by virtue of s.55 of the Nationality, Immigration and Asylum Act 2002 and that guidance should be followed for such claims: see *R. (Q, D, KH, OK, JK, H, T and S) v Secretary of State for the Home Department* [2003] EWHC 2507 (Admin); [2004] J.R. 5.

[199] CPR r.54.10.

[200] *R. v London Boroughs Transport Committee Ex p. Freight Transport Association* [1989] C.O.D. 572.

Test for granting permission

9–057 The requirement of permission is designed to filter out claims which are groundless or hopeless at an early stage. The purpose is:

> "... to prevent the time of the court being wasted by busybodies with misguided or trivial complaints of administrative error and to remove the uncertainty in which public ... authorities might be left ...".[201]

As such, the aim is to prevent a wasteful use of judicial time and to protect public bodies from the harassment (intentional or otherwise) that might arise from the need to delay implementing decisions where the legality of such decisions has been challenged. The requirement for permission also enables an individual to obtain a quick and relatively cheap judicial consideration of whether his case has any prospect of success. In essence, the courts will normally refuse permission "unless satisfied that there is an arguable ground for judicial review having a realistic prospect of success and not subject to a discretionary bar such as delay or an alternative remedy".[202] The following factors will, or may, be considered in determining whether to grant permission.

Arguable case

9–058 The claimant must demonstrate that there is an arguable case that a ground for seeking judicial review exists.[203] The Court of Appeal has indicated that permission should be granted where a point exists which merits investigation on a full hearing, with both parties represented and with all the relevant evidence and arguments on the law.[204] Conversely, if the claimant cannot demonstrate an arguable case that a ground for review exists, permission will be refused. Initially, permission was regarded as a means of filtering out hopeless cases and it was thought that permission would be granted if on a quick perusal of the papers there appeared to be a point which might on further consideration turn out to be an arguable case.[205] The courts have indicated, however, that permission should be granted only where the court is satisfied that the papers actually disclose that there is an arguable point (not merely that the court is satisfied that an arguable point might emerge on further consideration of the papers) and that was not necessarily to be determined on a quick perusal of the material although any in-depth examination was inappropriate.[206] Furthermore, the court will now

---

[201] per Lord Diplock in *R. v I.R.C. Ex p. National Federation of Self-Employed and Small Businesses Ltd* [1982] A.C. 617 at 643.

[202] per Lord Bingham in the Privy Council in *Sharma v Brown-Antoine* [2007] 1 W.L.R. 780 at [14](4).

[203] "Arguable case" is the formulation most frequently used: see, e.g. *R. v Secretary of State for the Home Department Ex p. Swati* [1986] 1 W.L.R. 477; *R. v Commissioners for Special Purposes of the Income Tax Acts Ex p. Stipplechoice* [1985] 2 All E.R. 465.

[204] *R. v Secretary of State for the Home Department Ex p. Rukshanda Begum and Angur Begum* [1990] C.O.D. 107.

[205] See dictum of Lord Diplock in *R. v I.R.C. Ex p. National Federation of Self-Employed and Small Businesses Ltd* [1982] A.C. 617 at 644a.

[206] *R. v Legal Aid Board Ex p. Hughes* (1992) 5 Admin. L.Rep. 623 at 628; and see *Sharma v Brown-Antoine* [2007] 1 W.L.R. 780 at [14](4) (point must be arguable, not "potentially arguable").

generally have an acknowledgment of service from the defendant setting out the summary grounds for resisting the claim when it considers an application for permission; this may indicate that the claim is unarguable and provide reasons why that is said to be so.

Cases totally without merit

A case may not only be unarguable but may be totally without merit. That means **9–059** that the case is hopeless and bound to fail.[207] A claim that is certified as totally without merit cannot be renewed at an oral hearing.[208] The only option for renewal is to seek permission to appeal, on the papers, to the Court of Appeal.[209] The introduction of this certification is intended to deal with the growth in claims which were bound to fail but which created difficulties for public authorities and imposed unjustified burdens on the Administrative Court. There is no requirement that the claimant has acted abusively or vexatiously in bringing the claim, simply that the claim itself is so hopeless that it is bound to fail. The safeguards are twofold. First, the judge considering the papers will bear in mind the seriousness of the issue and the consequences for the claimant not simply of refusing permission but also of certifying the claim as totally without merit and so depriving the individual of renewing the application at an oral hearing. Secondly, there is the possibility of applying to the Court of Appeal, on the papers, for permission to appeal against the refusal of permission.

Procedure

As indicated, the court will generally consider whether to grant permission on the **9–060** papers only and there will not normally be an oral hearing of the application for permission.[210] However, it is still open to the court in the exercise of its discretion to direct that there be an oral hearing of the application for permission and a claimant can ask to have any refusal of permission reconsidered at an oral hearing.[211] In most instances, at a contested oral hearing of permission, the courts are still concerned to ensure if there is an arguable case and will still discourage lengthy and fully argued oral hearings.[212] In the exceptional case where the court has all the relevant material before it and there has been full argument from both the claimant and the defendant at the hearing of an application for permission,[213] the court is unlikely to grant permission unless the claimant can demonstrate a reasonably good chance of success at the substantive hearing.[214]

See also *R. (Davey) v Aylesbury Vale* DC[2008] 1 W.L.R. 878 at [12] (not usual, save in exceptional circumstances, to explore issue in depth at the permission stage).

[207] CPR 54 r.12(7).

[208] *R. (Grace) v Secretary of State for the Home Department* [2014] 1 W.L.R. 3432.

[209] CPR r.52.15(2).

[210] Para.8.4 of Practice Direction 54A – Judicial Review.

[211] CPR r.54.12 and see below at para.9–071.

[212] See dictum of Auld LJ at [73] in *R. (Mount Cook Land Ltd and Mount Eden Land Ltd) v Westminster City Council, The Times*, October 16, 2003.

[213] Usually in cases of urgency, where the court has directed that there be an oral hearing or directed that evidence and skeleton arguments be filed.

[214] *Mass Energy Ltd v Birmingham City Council* [1994] Env. L.R. 298; *R. v Cotswold District Council Ex p. Barrington* Parish Council (1997) 75 P. & C.R. 515.

Delay

9–061 As discussed above,[215] the claimant must apply for permission promptly, and in any event, within three months of the date on which grounds for the claim first arose.[216] Where the claim is made outside these limits, the claimant must apply for an extension of time and provide adequate reasons for the delay. Failure to bring the claim promptly will result in the refusal of permission unless an extension of time is granted.

Alternative remedies

9–062 One factor which has grown noticeably more important is the existence of alternative remedies to judicial review. Such remedies may be alternative judicial remedies, such as a right of appeal to the courts or an appeal to a tribunal or inferior court, or there may be an alternative administrative appeal process or an internal complaints procedure. Judicial review is generally regarded as a remedy of last resort. The courts will generally refuse permission if an adequate alternative remedy exists[217] or existed and should have been used.[218] The Court of Appeal has emphasised the importance of using alternative administrative means, such as an internal complaints procedure and, if appropriate mediation, as an alternative to litigation in appropriate cases.[219] The courts may also refuse to grant a remedy at the substantive hearing if an adequate alternative remedy exists or existed and should have been used.[220] A claim form should state whether any alternative remedy exists and whether or not the claimant is pursuing such a remedy.[221] The claimant should also provide adequate reasons as to why judicial

---

[215] See para.9–016.

[216] Save in cases where the challenge is based on EU law where the time limit will be applied so that the claim must be brought within three months of the date when the claimant knew, or ought to have known, of the breach of EU law, and in challenges to procurement decisions when the time-limit starts is 30 days from the date when the claimant knew, or ought to have known, of the existence of a ground for bringing the claim: see above at 9-018 and 9-020 respectively.

[217] *R. v Secretary of State for the Home Department Ex p. Swati* [1986] 1 W.L.R. 477; *R. (Davies) v Financial Services Authority* [2004] 1 W.L.R. 185. See Chapter 12 below.

[218] *R. (Carnell) v Regents Park College and Conference of Colleges Appeal Tribunal* [2008] E.L.R. 798 at [31]–[33].

[219] *R. (Cowl) v Plymouth City Council* [2002] 1 W.L.R. 803. Mediation may be useful in cases such as those involving decisions on appropriate community care services for individuals or in education cases, as a means of resolving differences of view between the public authority and the individual. They are not likely to be useful in the majority of judicial review cases involving questions of public law.

[220] *R. v Brentford General Commissioners Ex p. Chan* [1986] S.T.C. 64; *R. v Birmingham City Council Ex p. Ferrero Ltd* [1993] 1 All E.R. 539. But on one occasion, the courts indicated that it would not be compatible with the overriding objective of dealing with cases justly to refuse a remedy after a substantive hearing with full argument and after costs have been incurred: *R. v Chief Constable of Merseyside Police Ex p. Bennion* [2001] A.C.D. 114. The existence of an alternative remedy is likely, in any event, to weigh more heavily at the permission stage, particularly as the claimant is under a duty to draw attention to any such remedy and the defendant will have the opportunity to draw the court's attention to any such remedy in the summary grounds of resistance in his acknowledgment of service.

[221] *R. v Humberside CC Ex p. Bogdal* [1992] C.O.D. 467; *R. v Greenwich Justices Ex p. Aitkens, The Times*, July, 3, 1982.

review is appropriate notwithstanding the alternative remedies.[222] The relationship between judicial review and alternative remedies is discussed in Chapter 12.

Discretion to refuse a remedy

The question of the discretion of the courts to refuse a remedy, even if grounds for judicial review are made out, may arise at the permission stage as the defendant may argue that there is no point in granting permission as the court would not ultimately grant any remedy in any event.[223] The Courts and Criminal Justice Bill 2014, if enacted, would provide that permission must be refused if it appeared to the court to be highly likely that the outcome for the applicant would not have been substantially different if the allegedly unlawful conduct had not occurred.

9–063

Standing

In addition to establishing an arguable case on the merits, other questions need to be addressed. The claimant is required to show sufficient interest in the matter to which the application relates.[224] The House of Lords has held that there is a two-tier test of standing.[225] At the permission stage, standing is to be regarded as a threshold issue, designed to exclude frivolous or vexatious applications. A full consideration of whether the claimant does have sufficient interest to claim the particular remedy sought will be undertaken at the full hearing of the claim. Standing is considered in more detail in Chapter 11.

9–064

Permission limited to certain grounds or decisions only

A claimant may specify a number of grounds of challenge in his claim form. The court may grant the claimant permission to argue particular grounds only and refuse permission to argue the other grounds. That was the position under the former rules governing the judicial review procedure.[226] That is also implicit in Part 54 of the CPR which permits the claimant to request that a decision granting permission to apply for judicial review on certain grounds only be reconsidered. It is frequently done in practice.[227] It is desirable that the courts should have power to restrict the grant of permission so that only certain grounds may be

9–065

---

[222] *R. v Secretary of State for the Home Department Ex p. Swati* [1986] 1 W.L.R. 477. Failure to disclose may consist of material non-disclosure justifying refusal of permission: see *R. v District Auditor No.10 District Ex p. Judge* [1989] C.O.D. 390. In practice, the defendant will draw attention to the existence of alternative remedies in his acknowledgment of service so the court will be aware of them and is likely to refuse permission for that reason rather than non-disclosure.

[223] See, e.g. *Lambeth BC v Secretary of State for the Environment* (1989) 59 P. & C.R. 299; *R. (Watford Grammar School for Boys) v Schools Adjudicator*, unreported, March 29, 2004.

[224] Senior Courts Act 1981 s.31(3).

[225] *R. v I.R.C. Ex p. National Federation of Self-Employed and Small Businesses Ltd* [1982] A.C. 617.

[226] *R. v Staffordshire CC Ex p. Ashworth* (1996) 4 Admin. L.Rep. 373; *R. v Advertising Standards Authority Ex p. City Trading* [1997] C.O.D. 202.

[227] For cases where this was done, see e.g. *R. (Smith) v Parole Board* [2003] 1 W.L.R. 2548; *R. (Opoku) v Principal of Southwark* [2003] 1 W.L.R. 234; and *R. (Hunt) v Criminal Cases Review Commission* [2001] Q.B. 1108 at [14].

argued. This will save the defendant having to file evidence to deal with points that a court considers unarguable and prevents the time of the court at the substantive hearing being used to deal with arguments that a judge has already indicated are hopeless.

9–066 A claimant who wishes to challenge a decision on a ground where he has expressly been refused permission should, therefore, ask for that decision to be re-considered at an oral hearing.[228] Where permission to advance a particular ground has been refused at an oral hearing, the court still has a discretion to allow the ground to be argued at the substantive hearing if it is in the interests of justice to do so.[229]

9–067 The court may also grant permission in respect of one decision that is challenged but refuse permission in respect of other decisions.[230] A court granting permission may also impose conditions as to costs and the giving of security[231] and, as indicated above, may make a protective costs order.

Directions, venue and ancillary orders

9–068 The court may, and usually will, give directions relevant to the conduct of the substantive hearing[232] and any application for specific directions should be included in the claim form. Such directions may include a direction that a hearing be expedited and, if appropriate, may abridge the time for the defendant and interested parties to serve their detailed grounds and written evidence.[233] The court may also give directions as to the court by which the claim is to be administered and heard.[234] The general expectation is that the claim will be administered and determined in the region with which the claimant has the closest connection although this expectation is subject to a number of specific considerations such as any reason expressed by a party for preferring a particular venue, where the defendant is located, where the claimant's legal representatives are based, considerations relation to travel, media interest, timing, resources and other matters.[235] Where the claim raises a devolution issue, consideration should be given as to whether that issue should be tried in Cardiff or London.[236] There is

---

[228] That is the clear implication of CPR, r.54.12.

[229] *R. (Smith) v Parole Board* [2003] 1 W.L.R. 2548 at [12]–[16]; *R. (Opoku) v Principal of Southwark College* [2003] 1 W.L.R. 234 at [14]. For discussion of when the courts will exercise this discretion, see below at paras 9–104 to 9–106.

[230] See, e.g. *R. v London Borough of Hammersmith and Fulham Ex p. CPRE (London Branch)* [2000] Env. L.R. 532 (Richards J. refused permission to apply for judicial review of the decision to grant outline planning permission and the decision approving reserved matters; he granted judicial review of a refusal to revoke planning permission. That decision was affirmed by the Court of Appeal (1999) 81 P. & C.R. 73. The court subsequently dismissed the substantive claim for judicial review of the refusal to revoke: see (1999) 81 P. & C.R. 61).

[231] See, e.g. *R. v Westminster City Council Ex p. Residents' Association of Mayfair* [1991] C.O.D. 182.

[232] CPR r.54.10.

[233] Normally, these must be served within 35 days of the notification of the grant of permission: see CPR r.54.14.

[234] See para.5.6 of Practice Direction 54D – Administrative Court (Venue).

[235] Paragraph 5.2 of Practice Direction 54D – Administrative Court (Venue).

[236] Paragraph 5.2(1) of Practice Direction 54D – Administrative Court (Venue). Devolution issues, so far as Wales is concerned, are defined in para.1 of Sch.9 to the Government of Wales Act 2006: see para.5.4 of Practice Direction 54A – Judicial Review.

an expectation that challenges to decisions made in a devolved area by the Welsh Ministers should ordinarily be heard in Wales unless there is a good reason for the hearing to be elsewhere.[237]

It is desirable for claims in family matters to be dealt with by a Family Division judge sitting as an additional judge of the Queen's Bench Division and suitable directions may be given for this.[238] Persons may be detained in the exercise of statutory powers in certain areas such as immigration. The High Court has jurisdiction to grant bail providing that the application for bail is incidental to some other proceedings.[239] The High Court may grant bail so long as it is seized of an application for permission to apply for judicial review even if that application has been adjourned. If permission is granted the High Court may grant bail as it seized of the substantive claim for judicial review. Bail may be granted subject to conditions including the provisions of sureties. If the High Court refuses the permission to apply for judicial review, it is then functus and has no jurisdiction to grant bail.[240] The Court of Appeal has jurisdiction to hear an appeal against the grant or refusal of bail.[241] It may also grant bail when seized of an application for permission to appeal against a refusal of permission to apply for judicial review.[242]

9–069

Notification

The court will serve the order giving or refusing permission, together with its reasons for making the order, and any directions on the claimant, the defendant and any other person who has filed an acknowledgment of service.[243]

9–070

Renewal of application if permission is refused

Where permission is refused without a hearing, the claimant may not appeal that decision but may request that the decision be reconsidered by the High Court at an oral hearing provided that the application was not certified as being totally without merit.[244] A request must be filed within seven days after service of the notification of refusal of permission[245] and the claimant, defendant and any person who has filed an acknowledgment of service must be given two days'

9–071

---

[237] R. (Deepdock Ltd) v The Welsh Ministers [2007] EWHC 3347 (Admin). See also R. (Condron) v National Assembly for Wales [2007] 2 P. & C.R. 4 at [10].

[238] See R. v Dover Magistrates' Court Ex p. Kidner [1983] 1 All E.R. 475; In Re D (A Minor) (Wardship: Jurisdiction) [1987 1 W.L.R. 1400 (desirable that wardship applications and judicial review claims run in tandem); A. v A Health Authority [2002] 3 W.L.R. 24 at [71]–[73] (decisions relating to children and adults lacking mental capacity); R. (P) v Secretary of State for the Home Department [2001] 1 W.L.R. 2002 at [120].

[239] R. v Secretary of State for the Home Department Ex p. Turkoglu [1988] Q.B. 398; R. (Sezek) v Secretary of State for the Home Department [2002] 1 W.L.R. 348 at [16].

[240] See, generally, R. v Secretary of State for the Home Department Ex p. Turkoglu [1988] Q.B. 398.

[241] R. (Sezek) v Secretary of State for the Home Department [2002] 1 W.L.R. 348 at 16].

[242] See dictum in R. (Sezek) v Secretary of State for the Home Department [2002] 1 W.L.R. 348 at [8]. Bail in criminal cases is dealt with by magistrates' courts and Crown Courts in accordance with the Bail Act 1976.

[243] CPR rr.54.11 and 54.12(2).

[244] CPR r.54.12(3).

[245] CPR r.54.12(4).

notice of the date of the hearing.[246] If the defendant or a person served with the claim form did not serve an acknowledgment of service they will not be permitted to take part in the oral hearing to determine whether permission should be granted unless the court allows them to do so.[247] The implication is that if a defendant or interested party has filed an acknowledgment he is entitled, but not obliged, to attend and make representations. Any contested oral permission hearing is intended only to determine whether the claimant has an arguable case and the courts will not allow lengthy and fully argued oral submissions of the sort that is more appropriate for the substantive hearing.[248] The Court of Appeal in *R. (MD) v (Afghanistan) v Secretary of State for the Home Department (Practice Note)*,[249] considered that it may have jurisdiction to hear an appeal against a refusal of permission to apply for judicial review even where that refusal had been made on the papers and there had been no oral hearing of a request for re-consideration. The Court of Appeal was prepared to proceed on the assumption that CPR 54 r.12(3), in so far as it prevented such an appeal, was inconsistent with s.16 of the Senior Courts Act 1981 and the rule, to that extent, would be ultra vires. However, even if the Court of Appeal had jurisdiction to hear an appeal against a refusal of permission made on the papers only, it would not normally exercise that jurisdiction. Rather the claimant should seek reconsideration of the refusal at an oral hearing before a High Court judge before seeking permission to appeal to the Court of Appeal.

9–072   If permission has been refused by the High Court, and the claim has been certified as being totally without merit, the claimant cannot request that the matter be considered at an oral hearing.[250] Cases are certified as being totally without merit if they are bound to fail.[251] The only option available to a claimant is to seek permission from the Court of Appeal to appeal against the refusal. The application will be considered by the Court of Appeal on the papers and not at an oral hearing.[252]

Appeals against refusal of permission: the distinction between criminal and non-criminal or civil matters

9–073   The procedure for the initial consideration of application for permission in the High Court is the same in both criminal and non-criminal matters. Thereafter the procedure in relation to appeals diverges.[253] Appeals can be made to the Court of Appeal against the refusal of permission to apply for judicial review in civil

---

[246] CPR r.54.12(5).

[247] CPR r.54.9(1)(a).

[248] *R. (Mount Cook Land Ltd and Mount Eden Land Ltd) v Westminster City Council*, *The Times*, [2004] 2 P.V.C.R. 405 at [73]. Occasionally, usually because the matter is urgent, the court will have directed an oral hearing and filing of evidence and skeleton arguments. In such cases, exceptionally, the permission hearing is likely to involve full argument..

[249] [2012] 1 W.L.R. 2422.

[250] CPR r.54.12(7). See above at para.9–059.

[251] *R. (Grace) v Secretary of State for the Home Department* [2014] 1 W.L.R. 3432.

[252] CPR r.52.15(2).

[253] See below at paras.9–077 to 9–0078.

matters in the way described below. Appeals cannot be made to the Court of Appeal against the refusal of permission to apply for judicial review in criminal matters.[254]

Matters are "criminal" if they arise in the context of criminal proceedings, that is, if they arise in proceedings which if carried to their ultimate conclusion might result in conviction and punishment of a person.[255] This includes matters occurring in the course of a criminal trial. Thus challenges to convictions or sentence are obviously criminal matters. A challenge to a refusal by the Home Secretary to refer a conviction to the Court of Appeal under s.17 of the Criminal Appeal Act 1968 is also a criminal matter since it involves an extension of a convicted person's right to appeal against conviction or sentence.[256] A recommendation for deportation by a magistrates' court or Crown Court following conviction is an order made in a criminal matter.[257] Other orders made in the course of criminal proceedings with a view to a criminal prosecution such as witness summonses[258] and orders in extradition or fugitive offender cases[259] are all criminal matters. Orders made which dispose of a criminal matter otherwise than by a conviction, such as the administering of a caution[260] or the making of an order requiring an accused person who is unfit to plead to be admitted to hospital, remain a criminal matter.[261] The fact that the underlying proceedings in which an order is made are criminal does not, however, mean that any order in those proceedings must be criminal.[262] Rather, matters which arise in the course of criminal proceedings but are really collateral to the proceedings, such as an order restraining the disposal of assets in order that they might subsequently be made the subject of a confiscation order[263] or a decision to forfeit a surety provided for an accused who failed to answer bail,[264] will not be criminal matters. Similarly, an order refusing an application by a representative of the media for access to documents referred to, but not read, in open court was not an order in a criminal matter. While the underlying proceedings were criminal (as they involved extradition), the application for disclosure of the material was collateral to the extradition proceedings. It was made by a person who was not a party to those proceedings, and the order refusing access did not involve the court invoking its criminal jurisdiction or making an order which would have any bearing on the extradition proceedings.[265]

9-074

---

[254] See below at para.9–079.
[255] *Amand v Home Secretary* [1943] A.C. 147.
[256] *R. v Secretary of State for the Home Department Ex p. Garner* [1990] C.O.D. 457.
[257] *R. v Secretary of State for the Home Department Ex p. Dannenberg* [1984] Q.B. 766 (but the decision of the Home Secretary to accept the recommendation and make a deportation order is not an order made in a criminal matter and refusal of permission against that decision can be appealed).
[258] *Day v Grant* [1987] Q.B. 972.
[259] *R. v Governor of Brixton Prison Ex p. Savakar* [1910] 2 K.B. 1056.
[260] *R. (Aru) v Chief Constable of Merseyside Police* [2004] 1 W.L.R. 1697.
[261] *R. (South Yorkshire Mental Health NHS Trust) v Bradford Crown Court* [2004] 1 W.L.R. 1664.
[262] *Government of the United States of America v Montgomery* [2001] 1 W.L.R. 196 at [19].
[263] *Government of the United States of America v Montgomery* [2001] 1 W.L.R. 196 (approving *Re O* [1991] 2 Q.B. 520).
[264] This is now regarded as the correct basis for the decision in *R. v Southampton Justices Ex p. Green* [1976] Q.B. 963.
[265] *R. (Guardian News & Media Ltd.) v Westminster Magistrates' Court* [2011] 1 W.L.R. 3253 esp. at [36].

9–075 Criminal matters also include matters arising in the course of a criminal investigation, even though no criminal proceedings have actually been started at that stage.[266] Thus, an order made by a circuit judge requiring the production of certain material under the Police and Criminal Evidence Act 1984 is a criminal matter, as it is designed to assist a criminal investigation.[267]

9–076 A matter may still be criminal even if the claim for judicial review is heard after the conclusion of the criminal proceedings. Thus a challenge to a decision to refuse bail except on certain conditions was still a challenge in a criminal cause or matter notwithstanding the fact that the main criminal proceedings had been concluded before the judicial review claim was heard by the Divisional Court.[268]

Appeals against refusals of permission in civil cases

9–077 Where a claimant is refused permission in a civil case after an oral hearing, he may apply to the Court of Appeal for permission to appeal against that refusal.[269] The application must be made within seven days of the decision of the High Court.[270] The claimant must lodge an appellant's notice (and three copies), the order of the High Court refusing permission, the claim form, a copy of the original decision under challenge, any written evidence in support of any application included in the appellant's notice, a copy of the bundle used in the High Court, the skeleton arguments relied on below and the approved transcript of the judgment.[271] Where the Court of Appeal intends to allow the application, it may (and usually will) grant permission to apply for judicial review, rather than granting permission to appeal.[272] The claim for judicial review will then continue in the normal way in the High Court, unless the Court of Appeal orders otherwise.[273] The Court of Appeal may, exceptionally, decide to deal with the substantive claim itself rather than return the claim to the High Court. This may be appropriate where, for example, the High Court would be bound by authority or the matter is likely to come before the Court of Appeal in any event[274] or where there has been full hearing below with all parties represented[275] or where the matter raises an issue of public importance which should be deal with urgently.[276]

---

[266] *Carr v Atkins* [1987] Q.B. 963 (holding that the earlier cases of *R. v Southampton Justices Ex p. Green* [1976] Q.B. 11; *R. v Crown Court at Sheffield Ex p. Brownlow* [1980] Q.B. 530 and *R. v Lambeth Stipendiary Magistrate Ex p. McComb* [1983] Q.B. 551 which sought to restrict criminal matters to those decisions which might directly lead to prosecution and punishment were no longer good law in the light of the dicta of the House of Lords in *Re Smalley* [1985] A.C. 622).

[267] *Carr v Atkins* [1987] Q.B. 963. See also *R. v Central Criminal Court Ex p. Francis & Francis* [1988] 3 W.L.R. 989 (order made under s.27 of the Drug Trafficking Offences Act 1986 requiring a claimant to give police access to material was a criminal matter). See also *Re O'C* [1991] C.O.D. 251.

[268] *R. v Blandford Magistrates' Court Ex p. Pamment* [1990] 1 W.L.R. 1490.

[269] CPR r.52.15.

[270] CPR r.52.15(2).

[271] See para.3 of Practice Direction 52C – Appeals to the Court of Appeal.

[272] CPR r.52.15(3).

[273] CPR r.52.14.

[274] See, e.g. *R. (Smith) v Parole Board* [2003] 1 W.L.R. 2548 at [20].

[275] *R. (Greenpeace Ltd) v Secretary of State for the Environment, Food and Rural Affairs* [2002] 1 W.L.R. 3304 at [1].

[276] See, e.g. *R. v Panel on Take-overs and Mergers Ex p. Datafin Plc* [1987] Q.B. 815 where the Court granted an appeal in the form of a renewed application for permission under the former rules

Where the Court of Appeal refuses permission to appeal against the refusal, then there is no further avenue of appeal. The Supreme Court has no jurisdiction to entertain any petition against the refusal of permission to appeal.[277] Where the Court of Appeal, however, grants permission to appeal, then hears the appeal but refuses permission to apply for judicial review (for example, on grounds of delay), the Supreme Court does have jurisdiction to entertain a petition for leave to appeal and, if permission is granted, the appeal itself.[278] Another way in which the Court of Appeal may preserve the possibility of the matter going before the Supreme Court, is to grant permission to appeal and, on the appeal, grant permission to apply for judicial review and then immediately dismiss the substantive claim for judicial review.[279] In those circumstances, the Supreme Court has jurisdiction to entertain a petition for leave to appeal against the decision dismissing the substantive application for judicial review. **9–078**

Refusal of permission in a criminal cause or matter

A claimant who is refused permission after an oral hearing in a criminal cause or matter has no avenue for challenging that refusal. There can be no appeal to the Court of Appeal if permission is refused as s.18(1)(a) of the Senior Courts Act 1981 prohibits appeals in a criminal cause or matter.[280] No appeal may be made against the refusal of permission by the High Court to the Supreme Court. The High Court may consider that the claim raises an important point of law but that the claim would fail. In those circumstances, the court may grant permission to apply for judicial review, dismiss the substantive claim and certify that the claim raises a point of law of general public importance.[281] In that way, the claimant may still petition the Supreme Court for leave to appeal against the dismissal of the substantive claim whereas he could not petition against a refusal of permission to apply for judicial review. **9–079**

Challenging the grant of permission

Application to set aside the grant of permission

The court has inherent jurisdiction to set aside orders, including orders granting permission to apply for judicial review, which have been made without notice **9–080**

(RSC Ord.59 r.14.3) and then heard the substantive claim for judicial review itself as the question of whether the court had jurisdiction to review the Panel's decision was a matter of public importance and hearing the substantive claim would save time in a situation of considerable urgency. See also *R. (Abbasi) v Secretary of State for Foreign and Commonwealth Affairs* [2003] U.K.H.R.R. 76.

[277] *R. v Secretary of State for Trade and Industry Ex p. Eastaway* [2000] 1 W.L.R. 2222 (as explained in *R. (Burkett) v Hammersmith and Fulham LBC* [2002] 1 W.L.R. 1593 at [12]).

[278] *R. (Burkett) v Hammersmith and Fulham LBC* [2002] 1 W.L.R. 1593 at [10]–[13] (distinguishing *Re Poh* [1983] 1 W.L.R. 2).

[279] See, e.g. *R. v HM Treasury Ex p. Shepherd Neame Ltd* (1999) 12 Admin. L.Rep. 51; *R. v Parliamentary Commissioners for Standards Ex p. Fayed* (1997) 10 Admin. L.Rep. 69.

[280] Formerly, an application for permission in a criminal cause or matter could only be refused by a Divisional Court but that requirement has been removed. A claimant may therefore be refused permission by a single judge at an oral hearing in a criminal cause or matter and there is at present no means of challenging that decision.

[281] *R. v DPP Ex p. Camelot Plc* (1997) 10 Admin. L.Rep. 93 at 105D–G.

being given to the defendant or other interested party.[282] Now, however, the claim form has to be served on the defendant and any interested party and they will have the opportunity to put in a summary of the grounds for resisting the claim. Consequently, the CPR provides that neither the defendant nor any other person served with the claim form may apply to set aside an order giving permission to apply for judicial review.[283] Once permission has been granted, the claim will therefore be determined at an oral hearing (unless the parties agree to dispense with the hearing) and the defendant cannot apply to set aside the grant permission even if the claim has become academic.[284] An application to set aside the grant of permission will now only be entertained in the rare cases where permission has, for some reason, been granted before the defendant has had the opportunity to put in an acknowledgment of service.[285] Even then, the jurisdiction will be exercised sparingly and the courts are likely only to set aside permission in a very plain case.[286] Applications to set aside should be made promptly after the person concerned has discovered the grant of permission.[287] Permission may be set aside where there was delay because the claimant did not bring the claim promptly,[288] should have used an alternative remedy[289] or failed to disclose material facts[290]; or where the judicial review proceedings could serve no further purpose[291]; or where there is a statutory provision ousting the jurisdiction of the courts[292] or where the claimant has no arguable case (although only rarely and in a very clear case is it appropriate to set aside permission on this ground).[293] The fact that the claim form has to be served on the defendant means that these matters should now normally come to light before permission is granted. It is unlikely, therefore, that applications to set aside the grant of permission will have much role to play in judicial review.

---

[282] R. v Secretary of State for the Home Department Ex p. Chinnoy (1992) 5 Admin. L.Rep. 457.

[283] CPR r.54.13.

[284] R. (Parsipoor) v Secretary of State for the Home Department [2011] 1 W.L.R. 3187 (claim academic as claimant obtained what he sought; application by the defendant to set aside the grant of permission was, however, misconceived and the claim had to proceed to a hearing unless the parties agreed otherwise: see [12] and [38]). See CPR r.54.18 and para.9–125 below for termination of proceedings by agreement.

[285] i.e. the 21 days for serving an acknowledgment of service (or any abridged period) has not expired. The court's inherent jurisdiction to set aside permission has not been removed in such cases: see R. (Webb) v Bristol City Council [2001] EWHC 696 (Admin). Generally, applications for permission should not be determined before the period for filing an acknowledgement of service has expired: R. (Webb) v Bristol City Council [2001] EWHC 696 (Admin) and R. (BG) Medway Council [2006] 1 F.L.R. 663 at [40].

[286] See the former practice in relation to applications to set aside: R. v Secretary of State for the Home Department Ex p. Chinnoy (1992) 5 Admin. L.Rep. 457 at 462. See also, in the Privy Council, Sharma v Brown-Antoine [2007] 1 W.L.R. 780 at [14](6).

[287] R. v Eurotunnel Developments Ex p. Stephens (1995) 73 P. & C.R. 1 at 5.

[288] R. v Criminal Injuries Compensation Board Ex p. A [1999] 1 A.C. 330; R. v Commissioners of Customs and Excise Ex p. Eurotunnel Ltd [1995] C.L.R. 392.

[289] R. v Secretary of State for the Home Department Ex p. Doorga [1990] C.O.D. 109; R. v Law Society Ex p. Kingsley [1996] C.O.D. 153; R. v Secretary of State for the Environment Ex p. Watts [1997] C.O.D. 153.

[290] R. v Secretary of State for the Home Department Ex p. Sholola [1997] Imm.A.R. 135 at 138; R. v Lloyd's of London Ex p. Briggs [1993] 1 Lloyd's L.R. 176.

[291] R. v General Medical Council and the Review Board for Overseas Qualified Practitioners Ex p. Popat [1991] C.O.D. 245 (decision-maker voluntarily reconsidered the decision under challenge).

[292] R. v Cornwall CC Ex p. Huntington [1994] 1 All E.R. 694.

[293] R. v Social Security Commissioners Ex p. Pattini (1992) 5 Admin. L.Rep. 219.

Appeal

In theory, a defendant or an interested party who is directly affected by the decision could appeal against the grant of permission although the matter is not free from doubt.[294] In practice, the existence of an appeal has not been important and is unlikely to become so. Permission to appeal is unlikely to be granted and a defendant is likely to be required to contest the claim at the substantive judicial review hearing rather than challenging the grant of permission.

9–081

Striking out

The defendant and an interested party who is directly affected could in theory apply to strike out the claim form if it discloses no reasonable grounds for bringing the claim or is an abuse of process or is otherwise likely to obstruct the just disposal of proceedings or there has been a failure to comply with a rule, practice direction or court order.[295] It is highly unlikely that the courts would use this power simply because it considered that the grant of permission should not have been made. It is possible that the court may, in rare cases, order the trial of a preliminary issue, such as whether the defendant is a public body,[296] or possibly give summary judgment. In most instances, however, once permission is granted, the likelihood is that the defendant will need to resist the claim at a substantive hearing.

9–082

Challenging a decision to set aside permission

A claimant may wish to challenge a decision of the judge setting aside a grant of permission. In the past, it has been suggested that there are two possible avenues by which such a challenge could reach the Court of Appeal. Either the claimant could be regarded as having failed to obtain permission and so could appeal that refusal to the Court of Appeal, or the claimant could be regarded as appealing against the order of the judge setting aside the grant of permission. The Court of Appeal has not yet decided whether both of these avenues are available, and if so which avenue is more appropriate.[297] The better view is that the latter course of action is the appropriate course.

9–083

---

[294] See, e.g. dicta of Sir John Donaldson M.R. in *R. v Monopolies and Mergers Commission Ex p. Argyll Group Plc* [1986] 1 W.L.R. 763 at 774 (". . . there can be no appeal from the grant of leave to apply for judicial review").

[295] Under CPR r.3.5. or the inherent jurisdiction of the court (see, e.g. *R. v Secretary of State for the Home Department Ex p. Dew* [1987] 1 W.L.R. 881.

[296] See, e.g. *R. v Association of British Travel Agents Ex p. Sunspell Ltd (t/a as Superlative Travel)* [2001] A.C.D. 88 (preliminary issue determined as to whether the defendant was a public body). Previously such an issue could have been dealt with on an application to set aside permission (see *R. v Eurotunnel Developments Ltd Ex p. Stephens*) (1995) 73 P. & C.R. 1.

[297] *R. v Secretary of State for the Home Department Ex p. Begum (R) and Begum (A)* [1990] C.O.D. 109 and *R. v Secretary of State of the Home Department Ex p. Al-Nafeesi* [1990] C.O.D. 106.

Costs at the permission stage

Costs where permission is granted

9–084 The courts have jurisdiction to award costs where an application for permission to apply for judicial review has been made.[298] If permission is granted, whether on the papers or after an oral hearing, the claimant's costs of bringing the claim are deemed to be costs in the case and will be the subject of the outcome of the substantive hearing.[299] Consequently, if the claimant succeeds in his claim and the court at the final hearing orders an unsuccessful defendant to pay the claimant's costs,[300] those costs will include the claimant's costs of obtaining permission.

9–085 Similarly, if permission is granted, the defendant's costs of the acknowledgement of service and any costs reasonably incurred prior to the grant of permission (save for an oral permission hearing which is dealt with separately[301]) will be deemed to be costs in the case unless the court makes a different order. If the defendant ultimately succeeds in resisting the claim, and the court orders the claimant to pay the defendant's costs, they will include the costs of preparing the acknowledgement of service and other reasonably incurred preparation costs unless the court makes a different order.[302]

Costs where permission refused on the papers

9–086 A claimant who is refused permission by the court after consideration of the papers only will normally bear his own costs of bringing a claim. Exceptionally, a claimant may be able to recover the costs of bringing a claim from a defendant in appropriate cases as where the claimant sent a clear pre-action protocol letter to which the defendant failed to respond adequately so that the claimant had to issue proceedings but then discontinued when the defendant subsequently took action to meet the claimant's concerns.[303]

9–087 Where the defendant has complied with the pre-action protocol, filed an acknowledgement of service and permission has been refused, the defendant can,

---

[298] Pursuant to the Senior Courts Act 1981. The courts have jurisdiction to award the costs of the preparation of an acknowledgement of service and also the costs of attending at an oral hearing to consider an application for permission: see *R. (Mount Cook Ltd) v Westminster City Council* [2004] 2 P. & C.R. 405 at paras [67]–[76], *Re Leach,* [2001] 4 P.L.R. 28 and *R. v Camden LBC Ex p. Martin* [1997] 1 W.L.R. 359 at p.356. See below for the circumstances in which the jurisdiction to order the payments of costs will be exercised.

[299] Practice Statement (Judicial Review: Costs) [2004] 1 W.L.R. 1760. An order that costs be in the case is an order which means that the party in whose favour the court makes an order for costs at the end of the proceedings is entitled to his costs of the part of the proceedings to which the order providing for costs in the case relates (see The Costs Practice Directions relating to Pt 44 para.8.5).

[300] At the substantive hearing costs usually follow the event and the courts usually order the unsuccessful party to pay the costs of the successful party: see below at 9-140.

[301] Practice Statement (Judicial Review: Costs) [2004] 1 W.L.R. 1760 and see *R. (Davey) v Aylesbury Vale*DC[2008] 1 W.L.R. 878 at [5] and [21].

[302] See *R. (Davey) v Aylesbury Vale*DC[2008] 1 W.L.R. 878 at [21] and [29]–[30].

[303] *R. v Royal London Borough of Kensington and Chelsea Ex p. Ghebregiogis* (1994) 27 H.L.R. 602 (the defendant was ordered, exceptionally, to pay the claimant's costs of bringing proceedings where the letter before action was clear, the point at issue was a simple one and the defendant failed to give proper attention to the letter before action). See below on costs and discontinuance generally.

generally, recover the costs incurred in filing the acknowledgement of service from the claimant.[304] The fact the defendant is required by the CPR to file an acknowledgement of service when a claim is served on him if he wishes to take part in the proceedings is regarded as a sufficient reason for ordering the claimant to pay the costs of doing so.[305] There is no specific provision in the CPR at present dealing with the mechanism for applying to recover such costs. The Court of Appeal has suggested the following procedure. A defendant or interested party seeking costs at the permission stage should include an application for costs in the acknowledgement of service and attach a schedule setting out the amount claimed. The judge refusing permission should include in that refusal a decision in principle on whether to award costs and an indication of the amount which he proposes to award. The claimant should be given 14 days to respond in writing and should serve a copy on the defendant or interested party who will have seven days to respond in writing. The judge will then make a decision.[306] The courts have indicated that it is only the costs of preparing the acknowledgement of service that may be recovered at this stage and not the costs of responding to the pre-action protocol letter or other preparation costs. The courts have emphasised that the amount of such costs that may be ordered should reflect the fact that it is only summary grounds, not detailed grounds, of resistance that need to be prepared and, if the pre-action protocol has been complied with, the defendant is likely to have undertaken the bulk of the necessary work and it should be possible to prepare an acknowledgement of service without incurring substantial expense.[307]

The Court of Appeal has also held that the claimant may, generally, be ordered **9–088** to pay the costs of filing an acknowledgment of service incurred by an interested party who complied with the pre-action protocol procedure although the liability of an interested party to pay such costs did not arise for decision in that case.[308] Generally, the courts are reluctant to order an unsuccessful claimant to pay the costs of an interested party in addition to those of a defendant.[309] As, however, the interested party will have been served with the claim form by the claimant and as he must file an acknowledgment of service if he wishes to take part in the judicial review and he will not normally know what the defendant's grounds for resisting the claim are before acknowledgments of service are filed, it may be reasonable to order an unsuccessful claimant to pay the costs incurred by an interested party in preparing an acknowledgment of service.

---

[304] *R. (Mount Cook Ltd.) v Westminster City Council* [2004] 2 P. & C.R. 405 at [76](1); *Re Leach* [2001] 4 P.L.R. 28.

[305] See CPR r.54.14 and *R. (Mount Cook Ltd) v Westminster City Council* [2004] 2 P. & C.R. 405 at [74]; *Re Leach* [2001] 4 P.L.R. 28.

[306] *R. (Ewing) v Office of the Deputy Prime Minister* [2006] 1 W.L.R. 1260 at [47].

[307] *R. (Ewing) v Office of the Deputy Prime Minister* [2006] 1 W.L.R. 1260 at [43] and [51]–[54]; *R. (Davey) v Aylesbury Vale DC* [2008] 1 W.L.R. 878 at [13] and [32]–[33].

[308] *R. (Ewing) v Office of Deputy Prime Minister* [2006] 1 W.L.R. 1260 and see also *R. (Mount Cook Land Ltd) v Westminster City Council* [2004] 2 P. & C.R. 405 at [76](1).

[309] *Bolton Metropolitan District Council v Secretary of State for the Environment* [1995] 1 W.L.R. 1176.

Costs where permission refused at an oral hearing

9–089   A claimant who is refused permission at an oral hearing[310] will bear his own costs of bringing the claim and the oral hearing. A defendant or interested party is not obliged to attend an oral hearing. If they choose to do so, and successfully argue that permission should not be granted, they will not generally be able to recover the costs of attending the oral hearing.[311] The question of costs at the permission stage has been reviewed by the Court of Appeal which has confirmed that a court should only order an unsuccessful claimant to pay a defendant's costs of attending an oral permission hearing in exceptional circumstances. The court's discretion as to whether circumstances are exceptional is a broad one. Exceptional circumstances may include, but are not limited to, the presence of one or more of the following features: (a) the hopelessness of the claim; (b) the persistence by the claimant in the claim after having been alerted to facts or the law demonstrating its hopelessness; (c) the extent to which the court considers that the claimant has sought to abuse the process of judicial review for collateral purposes; (d) whether, as a result of full argument and the deployment of documentary evidence, the claimant has, in effect, had the advantage of an early substantive hearing of the claim. The court may also consider the extent to which the unsuccessful claimant has substantial resources which he has used to pursue an unfounded claim and which are available to meet an order for courts.[312] An unsuccessful claimant will also generally be ordered to pay the costs of the defendant where a rolled-up hearing is ordered, that is an oral hearing of the application for permission with the substantive hearing to follow immediately if permission is granted. The parties will have to prepare for and attend the permission hearing on the basis that they may have to argue the full case. If permission is refused, a successful claimant will generally have to pay the defendant's costs.[313] Similar principles will apply to an interested party but in addition, the courts are likely to follow the general rule that they should not order a claimant to pay two sets of costs and will not order him to pay the interested party's costs unless there was some separate issue or some separate interest requiring the interested party to appear.[314]

Wasted costs

9–090   The courts have no jurisdiction under s.51(6) of the Senior Courts Act 1981 to make a wasted costs order requiring the claimant's legal representatives to pay the proposed defendant the costs incurred as a result of the representatives, improper, unreasonable or negligent act or omission.[315] The court does, however,

---

[310] Usually following a request by the claimant for a reconsideration of the refusal of permission on the papers: see CPR, r.54.12.

[311] Para.8.6 of Practice Direction 54A – Judicial Review; and *R. (Mount Cook Land Ltd) v Westminster City Council* [2004] P. & C.R. 405 at [76]. See, e.g. *R. (Islamic Human Rights Commission) v Civil Aviation Authority* [2007] A.C.D. 12 at [19]–[20].

[312] *R. (Mount Cook Land Ltd) v Westminster City Council* [2004] P. & C.R. 405.

[313] *R. (Bancroft) v Secretary of State for Culture, Media and Sport* [2004] EWHC 1822 (Admin.).

[314] *Bolton Metropolitan District Council v Secretary of State for the Environment* [1995] 1 W.L.R. 1176 and see below at para.9–142.

[315] *R. v Camden LBC Ex p. Martin* [1997] 1 W.L.R. 359.

retain a common law jurisdiction to make wasted costs orders and this jurisdiction will be exercised in a similar way and according to the same procedures as the statutory jurisdiction.[316] Such orders are likely to be rare.

Costs where proceedings are discontinued or settled

There may be situations where the proceedings are discontinued after permission has been granted. There may be a variety of reasons for this. The claimant may, for example, take the view, after seeing the defendant's evidence, that the claim is unlikely to succeed or there may be other reasons why the claimant decides not to pursue the proceedings. The general rule is that a party who discontinues proceedings will be liable for the costs of the defendant prior to the date of discontinuance.[317]

9–091

There will be occasions when the parties settle the claim. A claimant may, in those circumstances, seek to recover his costs of bringing the proceedings. The court has power to make a costs order in such cases and it will ordinarily be irrelevant that the claimant is legally aided. The overriding objective will be to do justice between the parties without unnecessarily using court time or incurring additional cost.[318] A number of different situations have been identified in the case law. The first is where the defendant effectively concedes the claimant's case and accepts that he is entitled to the remedy he seeks. Here, assuming that the claimant properly set out his case in a pre-claim protocol letter, the general rule is that the defendant must pay the claimant's costs unless there are good reasons for not making such an order.[319] Good reasons may include a failure by the claimant to set out his case clearly in the pre-action protocol letter or the introduction of substantial additional evidence in the claim not previously drawn to the attention of the defendant[320] or, possibly, the fact that the case was complex and the defendant needed time to consider it.[321] In such cases, a claimant may only be awarded part of his costs or there may be no order for costs. That may also be the case if the actions of a third party render outcome of the challenge academic.[322] The fact that the defendant takes a decision to settle the proceedings and reconsider the matter rather than risk litigation is unlikely now to justify refusing to order the claimant's costs. The Court of Appeal has emphasised that the time for taking that decision is when the defendant receives the pre-action protocol letter, not after the proceedings have been issued because of the refusal of the defendant to concede the claim.[323]

9–092

There may be situations where the claimant has only been partially successful following a contested hearing or a settlement. In considering a claim for costs after there has been a contested hearing, the courts will generally consider how

9–093

---

[316] R. v Immigration Appeal Tribunal Ex p. Gulson [1997] C.O.D. 430.

[317] CPR r.38.6 and Practice Direction (Administrative Court: Uncontested Proceedings) [2008] 1 W.L.R. 1377 at [3](c).

[318] R. (Boxall) v Waltham Forest LBC (2001) 4 CCLR 258 at [22], approved by the Court of Appeal in R. (Scott) v Hackney LBC [2009] EWCA Civ. 217.

[319] R. (M) v Croydon LBC [2012] 1 W.L.R. 2607 at [61]-[62]; R. (Bahta) v Secretary of State for the Home Department [2011] 5 Costs. L.R. 857 at [59]-[60].

[320] R. (M) v Croydon LBC [2012] 1 W.L.R. 2607 at [57].

[321] R. (M) v Croydon LBC [2012] 1 W.L.R. 2607 at [54].

[322] R. v Liverpool City Council Ex p. Newman (1993) 5 Admin. L.R. 699 at 671G.

[323] R. (M) v Croydon LBC [2012] 1 W.L.R. 2607 at [54].

reasonable the claimant was in pursuing the unsuccessful part of claim, how important it was compared with the successful claim and how much the costs were increased as a result of pursuing the unsuccessful claim. The courts will normally be in a good position to determine such matters after a contested hearing. The court will be much less able to do so where there has been a settlement, rather than a contested hearing. If the courts are able to determine such issues, they may make an order, including an order that the claimant recover a proportion of his costs.[324] The courts may, however, make no order for costs if they are not able to determine such matters without disproportionate expenditure of judicial time.[325] Similarly, if the claim is settled on terms which do not reflect the claimant's case, it may not be possible to identify whether or not the claimant is truly the successful party and so should be awarded his costs. Again, in such cases, the appropriate order may be to make no order for costs. If it is reasonably clear who is the successful party, it may be appropriate to award costs to that party.[326]

9–094   The courts have indicated that they may need to consider the unresolved substantive issues for the purposes of determining the issue of costs, but will do so only to the extent that it is appropriate to do so having regard to the amount of the costs at stake and the conduct of the parties.[327] It will often be sensible to deal with such matters by written submissions on the papers rather than an oral hearing which would, invariably, lead to higher costs.[328] Exceptionally, a claimant may decide to continue the proceedings solely for the purpose of determining liability for costs up to the date when the claim became academic and may ask the courts to determine the substantive issue solely to decide whether the claimant would have been successful. In one case, a claimant insisted on seeking a costs order from the court at first instance in order to determine liability to costs. The claimant was unsuccessful on the merits at first instance and then appealed against the order refusing costs. The Court of Appeal held that they had jurisdiction to hear the appeal, as there was a live issue as to costs.[329] This can rarely be a sensible course of action, not least because of the extra costs that will be incurred in arguing about the liability for costs.

---

[324] *R. (M) v Croydon LBC* [2012] 1 W.L.R. 2607 at [61]; *R. (Bahta) v Secretary of State for the Home Department* [2011] 5 Costs. L.R. 857 at [59].

[325] *R. (M) v Croydon LBC* [2012] 1 W.L.R. 2607 at [62], [64] and [77].

[326] *R. (M) v Croydon LBC* [2012] 1 W.L.R. 2607 at [63].

[327] *R. (Boxall) v Mayor and Burgess of Waltham Forest LBC* (2001) 4 CCLR 258 at [22](iv). The principles established in *Boxall* were approved by the Court of Appeal in *R. (Kuzeva) v London Borough of Southwark* [2002] EWCA Civ. 781. See also *DB v Worcestershire CC* [2006] EWHC 2613 (Admin) at [7]–[10].

[328] A claimant may, it seems, insist on an oral hearing. But if a claimant insists on an oral hearing, rather than written submissions, the court may in its discretion decide not to award the claimant the costs of the oral hearing; *R. (Kemp) v Denbighshire Health Board* [2007] 1 W.L.R. 639 at [76]–[79] and [126].

[329] *R. v Holderness BC Ex p. James Roberts Developments Ltd* (1992) 66 P. & C.R. 46.

D. THE CLAIM FOR JUDICIAL REVIEW

Once permission to apply for judicial review has been granted, the second stage of the judicial review is the processing and hearing of the claim for judicial review itself. This involves the defendant and interested parties serving their written evidence and then the substantive hearing of the claim.

9–095

Defendant and interested parties' detailed grounds and written evidence

The court serves any order granting permission on the claimant, the defendant and any person who filed an acknowledgment of service (that is, a person who is an interested party as he is a person directly affected by the grant of permission).[330] A defendant and any person served with the claim form have 35 days after the date of service on them of the order granting permission to file detailed grounds for contesting (or supporting on additional grounds[331]) the claim and any written evidence in the Administrative Court Office and to serve them on the claimant (and each other).[332] The evidence will also usually exhibit the documents that the defendant intends to rely upon in addition to those already lodged by the claimant.[333] The previous time-limit for filing written evidence was intended to be strictly adhered to and extensions were only to be granted in exceptional circumstances and for compelling reasons. The courts are likely to take a similar attitude to the filing of evidence by the defendant and interested parties under the CPR. Although the time limit is shorter (35 days instead of 56), defendants and interested parties will have been served with the claim form and will have had 21 days to set out their summary grounds of resistance together with any time taken before permission is granted and the 35 days from service of the notice of the grant of permission. The defendant will not therefore have less time than previously to consider the matter (and in practice, may have more). To ensure that the 35-day time-limit is met, however, does mean, that defendants and interested parties are likely to have to do work and incur costs in the preparation of written evidence before it is known whether permission has been granted. The detailed grounds should identify the issues that the defendant wishes to argue. The written evidence should set out any facts on which the defendant intends to rely. It should also address the issues raised by the claimant. The written evidence should also specify any matters that the defendant or the interested party wishes the court to consider when deciding whether to exercise its discretion to grant or refuse a remedy. On one occasion, for example, written evidence alleging that there had been undue delay in bringing the claim for judicial review (which had

9–096

---

[330] CPR r.54.11.

[331] An interested party may wish to support the claim that the decision, act or omission is unlawful.

[332] CPR r.54.14. A non-party may obtain access to the detailed grounds from the court pursuant to CPR r.5.4(C). See also *R. (Corner House Research, Campaign against the Arms Trade) v the Director of the Serious Fraud Office* [2008] EWHC 246 (Admin) [2008] A.C.D. 246.

[333] See Practice Direction 54A – Judicial Review, para.10.1.

caused substantial detriment) was excluded as it had been filed outside the time-limit. As a result, the court granted relief and did not consider the issues raised by the defendant.[334]

Duty of candour

9–097 The courts generally recognise that there is an obligation on a public authority to make candid disclosure to the court of its decision making process, laying before it the relevant facts and the reasoning for the decision challenged.[335] The Court of Appeal has indicated that judicial review is unlike civil litigation and once permission has been granted the defendant should provide sufficient information to enable the court to determine whether the actions complained of were lawful.[336] Sir John Donaldson M.R. expressed the view that the defendant was under " ... a duty to make full and fair disclosure" once permission was granted.[337] Purchas LJ expressed his views more circumspectly, stating that the defendant " ... should set out fully what they did and why so far as is necessary fully and fairly to meet the challenge" made by the claimant.[338]

9–098 A number of separate issues arises in relation to the defendant's duty of candour. These include the extent of the duty, the extent to which it encompasses an obligation to provide copies of relevant documents and the consequences if a defendant fails to act in accordance with the duty of candour. Modern authorities recognise that there is an obligation on a defendant to give a candid explanation of "its decision-making process, laying before the courts the relevant facts and the reasoning behind the decision challenged"[339] and the "very high duty on public authority defendants, not least central government, to assist the court with full and accurate explanations of all the facts relevant to the issues that the court must decide".[340] The obligation, therefore, extends to ensuring that a defendant explains, either by a witness statement or by the voluntary provision of material documents, or both, the reasoning process underlying the decision under challenge. The position in relation to an obligation to provide documents is more complex. The obligation to give disclosure does not, generally, apply in relation to judicial review claims.[341] The following considerations are, however, relevant to the disclosure of documents. First, the defendant may well choose to exhibit documents to witness statements or to provide disclosure of significant and relevant documents and that may be the means by which it ensures that its duty of

---

[334] *R. v Dairy Produce Quota Tribunal for England and Wales Ex p. Vevers, The Times,* December 7, 1988 (a decision based on the 21-day time-limit which was the time-limit which applied prior to the 56-day time-limit).

[335] See *Tweed v Parades Commission for Northern Ireland* [2007] 1 A.C. 650 per Lord Carswell at [31] and Lord Brown at [54].

[336] *R. v Lancashire CC Ex p. Huddleston* [1986] 2 All E.R. 941.

[337] [1986] 2 All E.R. 941 at 945. The Master of the Rolls reiterated his view in *R. v Civil Service Appeal Board Ex p. Cunningham* [1991] I.R.L.R. 297 at 300.

[338] *R. v Lancashire CC Ex p. Huddleston* [1986] 2 All E.R. 941 at 945.

[339] *Tweed v Parades Commission of Northern Ireland* [2007] 1 A.C. 650 at [31] (per Lord Carswell) and at [54] (per Lord Brown).

[340] *R. (Quark) v Secretary of State for Foreign and Commonwealth Affairs* [2002] EWCA Civ. 1409 at [50].

[341] See para.12.1 of Practice Direction 541 – Judicial Review and below at paras 9–109.

candour is discharged.[342] Secondly, there are also cases indicating that the duty of candour may require the provision of material documents. The Administrative Court has referred to the duty on the defendant authority to explain the full facts and reasoning underlying the decision challenged and to disclose the relevant documents.[343] There may well be situations where the courts are dealing with disputes of fact, particularly but not only, in relation to claims alleging breach of Convention rights, where disclosure of primary, relevant documents will be necessary to enable the courts to resolve those factual disputes or, if there is to be cross-examination, to enable that to be effective. In these cases, it may well be appropriate to refer to a duty to disclose documents as part of the duty of candour, not least because failure to do so will be likely, in any event, to lead to an order for specific disclosure.[344] Thirdly, however, it would not be correct, given the present state of the authorities, to treat the duty of candour as imposing an obligation on a defendant public body to provide disclosure of all documents that might conceivably be relevant to a claim or which a claimant might request. The obligations of the defendant arise in the context of judicial review. Disclosure of documents is not, generally, applicable as the majority of judicial review claims will involve questions of law rather than disputed facts and where disclosure of documents is not necessary to deal fairly with the claim.[345] The duty of candour ought, in principle, to be similarly focussed on ensuring that the defendant has explained the particular decision-making process under challenge and, where appropriate, provided the material documents specifically relevant to that decision-making process unless there is some specific reason for declining to do so. There may well be instances where the defendant has material available which is significant to the decision-making process and which may well demonstrate some public law legality on its part. There, the duty to disclose does apply and the courts will expect the defendant to disclose significant material even if it is adverse to its case.[346]

Failure by a public body to explain its actions may lead to the court ordering **9–099** disclosure of documents or cross-examination of witnesses, or the courts may in the absence of adequate explanation infer that no valid reason for the defendant's action exists (although the courts are in practice reluctant to make such inferences).[347] Further, if there is a credible explanation for the failure of the defendant to put forward evidence, the courts are unlikely to draw adverse inferences from the defendant's silence. Thus, where a claimant challenged the validity of a notice served by the Inland Revenue inspector requiring disclosure of certain documents, the House of Lords upheld the notice and refused to draw any adverse inferences from the failure of the Revenue to adduce any evidence since this failure could be credibly explained by their general duty of

---

[342] *Tweed v Parades Commission of Northern Ireland* [2007] 1 A.C. 650 at [4] (per Lord Bingham).
[343] *R. (AHK) v Secretary of State for the Home Department (No.2)* [2012] EWHC 1117 (Admin) at [22] (per Ouseley J.). See also the Privy Council in *Graham v Police Services Commission* [2011] UKPC 46 at [18].
[344] *R. (Al Sweady) v Secretary of State for Defence* [2012] H.R.L.R. 12.
[345] See, e.g. *Tweed v Parades Commission of Northern Ireland* [2007] 1 A.C. 650 at [31] (per Lord Carswell) and at [56] (per Lord Brown).
[346] See, e.g. the comments in *R. (Bancoult) v Secretary of State for Foreign and Commonwealth Affairs* [2001] Q.B. 1067 at 1106.
[347] The House of Lords has warned against drawing such inferences too readily: *R. v Secretary of State for Trade and Industry Ex p. Lonrho Plc* [1989] 1 W.L.R. 525.

confidentiality.[348] Failure to produce materially significant documents may lead to an order for specific disclosure if that is necessary to enable the courts to dispose of a claim fairly and justly.

Written evidence and reasons

9–100   The courts have considered the circumstances in which a defendant may rely upon written evidence for the reasons for a decision. Where there is a statutory duty to give reasons and the decision was originally accompanied by reasons, the courts will be reluctant to receive written evidence to supplement or add to the reasons given.[349] The courts will not permit a defendant to rely upon written evidence which seeks to assert that the real reasons for the decision were wholly different from the reasons given at the time[350] or to show that the decision-maker meant something different from what was unambiguously said in a reasoned decision letter.[351] Where, therefore, an authority sent a decision letter stating that a person was intentionally homeless and that there was no evidence to confirm his story that he had left his original home because of intimidation, they could not thereafter rely upon written evidence giving entirely different reasons, namely that the authority had accepted his story but still considered he was intentionally homeless.[352] The courts may permit evidence to elucidate or confirm the reasons given, but not to alter or contradict them, for example where an error has been made in transcribing the decision or where the language is lacking in clarity,[353] or to deal with other matters such as what happened at a particular hearing.[354]

9–101   Where there is no statutory duty to give reasons but reasons were in fact given, the courts will also be cautious about accepting written evidence giving reasons for the decision.[355] In particular, the courts will be alert to ensure that any written evidence does indeed reflect the reasons existing at the time of the decision and are not an ex post facto rationalisation of the decision. Thus, in one case, a child was permanently excluded from school and the reason given was simply that that was a reasonable course of action in the circumstances. Although that statement of reasons was inadequate, the courts allowed the defendant to rely upon written evidence setting out the reasons as there was no suggestion that the written evidence did not in fact record the contemporaneous reasons and there had been no change of position and the affidavit evidence was not offering an ex post facto

---

[348] *R. v I.R.C. Ex p. T.C. Coombs & Co.* [1991] 2 W.L.R. 682 (a significant factor was that a commissioner, acting as an independent check on the exercise of power to serve such notices, had to approve the notice before it was issued and this strengthened the presumption that the actions of a public body are valid unless shown to be invalid).

[349] *R. v Westminster City Council Ex p. Ermakov* [1996] 2 All E.R, 303 at 315g–316h; *Ali v Kirklees MBC* [2001] L.G.R. 448 (generally inappropriate for the chairman of a tribunal to supplement reasons for a decision).

[350] *R. v Westminster City Council Ex p. Ermakov* [1996] 2 All E.R. 303.

[351] *Re C and P* [1992] C.O.D. 29. There are a small number of tribunals such as arbitration tribunals and immigration tribunals and a small category of decision where the mere failure to give reasons renders the decision invalid, where, it seems, no evidence can be adduced to expand upon the reasons given.

[352] *R. v Westminster City Council Ex p. Ermakov* [1996] 2 All E.R. 303.

[353] *R. v Westminster City Council Ex p.Ermakov* [1996] 2 All E.R. 303 at 515 h–j.

[354] *Ali v Kirklees MBC* [2001] L.G.R. 448.

[355] *R. (Leung) v Imperial College of Science, Technology and Medicine* [2002] E.L.R. 653 at [28], approving the decision in *Nash v Chelsea College of Art and Design*, [2001] EWHC Admin 538.

rationalisation.[356] Among the considerations that are relevant in deciding whether to permit such evidence are whether the new reasons are consistent with the original reasons, whether they reflect the reasons of the whole committee or panel whose decision is under challenge, whether there is a real risk that the later reasons have been composed subsequently in order to support the decision or are a retrospective justification of the decision, the delay before the later reasons were put forward, the circumstances in which they were put forward, the nature of the case (as the courts may be less prepared to accept subsequent reasons where the matter raises issues of human rights or other fundamental rights) and the qualifications and experience of the persons involved.[357] In relation to this latter point, the courts may be more prepared to accept that lawyers and those who regularly sit on tribunals should ensure that the original reasons given are full and adequate and consequently there is less justification for permitting subsequent reasons; the same standards may not be demanded of other persons. Two further matters are first the extent to which the decision-maker would have been expected to state in the decision letter the reasons that are adduced later, and secondly, and fundamentally, whether it would be just in the circumstances to refuse to admit the subsequent reasons of the decision-maker. Where no reasons at all have been given for the original decision, written evidence explaining the decision is generally to be encouraged[358] and it would be strange if a decision-maker were not allowed to produce evidence to respond to the claim.[359]

Duty on claimant to reconsider claim

The claimant and his legal advisers have a duty once the defendant's evidence is provided to reconsider whether there is sufficient merit to continue the claim.[360] The court may penalise the claimant in costs if the claim continues once it becomes clear that the claim is unfounded.[361]   9–102

Further written evidence

The rules for judicial review provide that no written evidence may be relied upon unless it has been served in accordance with a rule under CPR, Part 54[362] or a direction of the court or with the court's permission.[363] It is common practice for further written evidence to be served to deal with new matters that have occurred   9–103

---

[356] R. v Northamptonshire CC Ex p. W [1998] E.L.R. 291.
[357] See R. (Leung) v Imperial College of Science, Technology and Medicine [2002] E.L.R. 653 at [28], approving the decision in Nash v Chelsea College of Art and Design, [2001] EWHC Admin 538.
[358] Re C and P [1992] C.O.D. 29. This is in accordance with the duty on the public body to make full and frank disclosure as discussed above. See also R. v Secretary of State for the Home Department Ex p. Peries [1998] C.O.D. 110.
[359] R. (Leung) v Imperial College of Science, Technology and Medicine [2002] E.L.R. 653 at [30].
[360] R. v Liverpool Justices Ex p. Price [1998] C.O.D. 453; R. v Commissioners of Inland Revenue Ex p. Continental Shipping Ltd [1996] C.O.D. 335.
[361] R. v Liverpool Justices Ex p. Price [1998] C.O.D. 453; R. v Commissioners of Inland Revenue Ex p. Continental Shipping Ltd [1996] C.O.D. 335.. See also R. v Secretary of State for the Home Department Ex p. Panther (1996) 8 Admin. L.R. 154 at 164.
[362] i.e. CPR r.54.14 permitting the defendant's and interested party to serve written evidence within 35 days of the notification of the grant of permission.
[363] CPR r.54.16(2).

since the filing of earlier evidence or for one party to respond to earlier written evidence or for the defendant to serve evidence dealing with new grounds that the claimant wishes to advance. A claimant or defendant proposing to ask for permission to submit further evidence should normally inform the other parties and provide copies of the written evidence in sufficient time to enable them to respond before the hearing.

Amendments

Additional grounds

9–104   A claimant may only rely upon the grounds set out in the claim form issued when seeking permission to apply for judicial review (i.e. Form N461) and for which permission has been granted. The court's permission is required to rely upon additional grounds of challenge other than those for which permission has been given.[364] The claimant must give notice to the court and to any other person served with the claim form no later than seven clear days before the hearing (or the warned date) that he intends to rely on additional grounds.[365] The claimant should provide a properly drafted amendment setting out the amended grounds of challenge, the relevant facts and any evidence in support.[366]

9–105   The general principles governing amendments in private law cases is that they should only be allowed if no injustice is caused, and there will be no injustice if the defendant can be adequately compensated in costs.[367] In the specific case of judicial review, amendments raising new grounds of challenge are also allowed relatively freely where the new grounds do not call for any further evidence but involve questions of law. There may be difficulty in allowing new grounds to be raised which would require evidence. The court may be reluctant to permit amendments, particularly if they are made late and the claimant has not provided the relevant evidence.[368] If the claimant seeks to amend, the defendant may also need time to prepare new evidence dealing with the allegations. Often, the defendant will have produced evidence in response to the notification of the proposed additional new grounds and amendments may cause no prejudice. In other cases, the courts have power to ensure that potential prejudice resulting from having to deal with the additional grounds at the hearing can be dealt with by an adjournment and can order the claimant to pay the costs of such an adjournment.

9–106   Different considerations arise where a claimant seeks to rely upon a ground of challenge which he has expressly been refused permission to argue.[369] In such circumstances, the courts retain a discretion to permit the refused ground to be argued but will require significant justification before allowing a claimant to

---

[364]   CPR r.54.15.

[365]   Para.11 of the Practice Direction54A – Judicial Review.

[366]   *R. (P) v Essex CC* [2004] EWHC 2027 (Admin) at [35]; endorsed by the Court of Appeal in *R. (O) v Hammersmith and Fulham LBC* [2012] 1057 at [18].

[367]   *Clarapede v Commercial Union Association* (1883) 32 W.R. 263.

[368]   See, e.g. *R. (Glenn & Co.) v Revenue and Customs Commissioners* [2011] 1 W.L.R. 1964 at [10].

[369]   If permission to argue a ground was refused on the papers, the claimant would be entitled to seek reconsideration of that refusal at an oral hearing: see CPR r.54.12.

argue a ground where permission has expressly been refused.[370] Situations in which it may be appropriate to exercise that discretion include, but are not limited to, situations in which there has been a significant change of circumstances, or the claimant has become aware of new facts which he could not reasonably have known at the time of the permission hearing, or that a proposition of law is now open to him to argue.[371] The discretion to grant permission to allow the refused ground to be argued is not, however, limited to new situations but extends to any situation in which it would be in the interests of justice, bearing in mind the interests of the defendant, to permit the additional ground to be argued.[372] The courts will need to ensure that this discretion does not result in unfairness to the defendant. It would not seem right, for example, for a defendant routinely to have to produce evidence in advance of a substantive hearing to deal with grounds which have been rejected but which the claimant has notified him he intends to seek permission to raise. Nor would it appear fair to expect a defendant routinely to deal in skeleton arguments prepared for the hearing, or to appear at the hearing ready to deal with, grounds of challenge where the court has expressly refused permission to argue those grounds.

Additional remedies or challenges to new decisions

The court also has inherent jurisdiction to allow the claimant to amend and seek a different remedy from that claimed in the claim form. One of the advantages of the judicial review procedure is that the remedies available are interchangeable. The remedy granted should obviously fit the facts of the case, and if the particular remedy claimed is not appropriate the court will allow an alternative appropriate remedy to be substituted. The courts may also permit a claimant to amend and challenge a decision taken after the issue of the claim form.[373]   **9–107**

Interlocutory applications

The court has power in judicial review proceedings to make interlocutory orders—including orders for disclosure, further information, cross-examination and orders disposing of the proceedings with the consent of the parties either in their inherent jurisdiction or pursuant to specific provisions of the CPR or practice directions. The usual method of applying for one of these orders is by means of an application under CPR Part 23 made using form NF244, accompanied by any necessary written evidence in support. The application can be dealt with by a master or by a judge.   **9–108**

---

[370] *R. (Smith) v Parole Board* [2003] 1 W.L.R. 2548 at [12]; *R. (Opoku) v Principal of Southwark College* [2003] 1 W.L.R. 234 at [14].
[371] *R. (Opoku) v Principal of Southwark College* [2003] 1 W.L.R. 234 at [16], as qualified by the Court of Appeal in *R. (Smith) v Parole Board* [2003] 1 W.L.R. 2549 at [16].
[372] *R. (Smith) v Parole Board* [2003] 1 W.L.R. 2549 at [16].
[373] *R. (Burkett) v Hammersmith and Fulham LBC* [2002] 1 W.L.R. 1593 at [31]; *E v Secretary of State for the Home Department* [2004] 1 Q.B. 1004.

Disclosure

9–109　In private law proceedings, parties are usually ordered to make standard disclosure of certain categories of documents.[374] Parties may also be ordered to make specific disclosure of particular documents or classes of documents.[375] Disclosure of documents is not required in claims for judicial review, however, unless the court otherwise orders.[376] Applications in judicial review proceedings are usually for specific disclosure and inspection of particular documents rather than standard disclosure. A party to proceedings is also entitled to inspect any document referred to in an affidavit or witness statement.[377] In practice, the written evidence of a defendant will usually exhibit any relevant document.

Circumstances when disclosure may be ordered

9–110　The test for determining whether disclosure of a document should be ordered is whether, in a given case, disclosure is necessary in order to resolve the matter fairly and justly. In practice, the nature of judicial review is in most cases unlikely to require disclosure. The courts have emphasised that the nature of judicial review proceedings is different from ordinary private law litigation.[378] The court in judicial review proceedings is not usually concerned with making findings of fact. The court is performing a supervisory role. Facts will often be agreed or will appear in documentary form. Furthermore, defendants are under a duty of candour to explain in their evidence to the court the relevant facts and reasoning underlying the decision under challenge.[379] It will usually be the legal consequences attaching to those facts which will be in issue. Disclosure is therefore likely in practice to be ordered in far fewer cases and will be more circumscribed in its extent that would be the case in judicial review proceedings.[380]

9–111　There are occasions when a court dealing with a judicial review claim may need to resolve disputed factual issues which are crucial to the outcome of a claim. Disclosure may be necessary to resolve those matters. Questions of fact may arise in cases involving claims that public authorities have acted incompatibly with rights arising under the European Convention on Human Rights. In one case, the court had to resolve questions of fact as whether detainees had been tortured or killed at a British base or been subject to unlawful detention. The court considered that disclosure of the documents would be necessary to resolve those issues, and to enable cross-examination of witnesses, and noted that courts should not be reluctant to order disclosure in those

---

[374]　CPR r.31.16. Disclosure is by way of list (r.31.10) and each party has the right to inspect disclosed documents.

[375]　CPR r.31.12.

[376]　Para.12.1 Practice Direction 54A – Judicial Review.

[377]　CPR rr.31.14–15.

[378]　See, e.g. *Tweed v Parades Commission for Northern Ireland* [2007] 1 A.C. 650 at [2], [32] and [56]. See also, *R. (Elias) v Secretary of State for Defence* [2006] 1 W.L.R. 3213 at paras [45]–[49]; *R. v Secretary of State for the Home Department Ex p. Harrison* unreported December 10, 1987 and *R v Secretary of State for the Environment Ex p. Doncaster BC* [1990] C.O.D. 441.

[379]　*R. v Lancashire CC Ex p. Huddleston* [1986] 2 All E.R. 941; and see *Tweed v Parades Commission for Northern Ireland* [2007] 1 A.C. 650 at paras [31] and [54]. See above at para.9–097.

[380]　See *Tweed v Parades Commission for Northern Ireland* [2007] 1 A.C. 650 at [2], [32] and [56].

circumstances if disclosure was not provided voluntarily.[381]. Questions of fact may occasionally arise in cases involving purely domestic law issues, such as cases of jurisdictional fact[382] or disputes as to the procedure followed during a decision-making process.[383] Again, disclosure may be relevant there if disclosure of documents is necessary for the courts to resolve those particular factual issues. Furthermore, questions as to whether action is compatible with a Convention right may involve consideration of the proportionality of the action taken. Here the courts will need to adopt a more intensive scrutiny of the decision. This may involve a close factual analysis of the justification for the action taken. That in turn may require consideration of the principal documentation underlying the decision in order to assess the merits of such a claim. The courts are likely to show "a somewhat greater readiness than hitherto"[384] to order disclosure of documents in such cases if they are not already exhibited. However, even in proportionality challenges, judicial review still remains a different process, concerned usually with the legality of what has occurred rather than fact-finding and the occasions when disclosure will be necessary are likely to remain infrequent.

Public authorities frequently give voluntary disclosure of documents that are material to the decision-making process.[385] Where a public authority summarises relevant documentation, it will ordinarily be good practice to exhibit the document to a witness statement and not merely to summarise its contents in the witness statement.[386] If the public authority does not exhibit the document, and an application is made for disclosure, the court will need to consider whether disclosure of that document is necessary in order to deal fairly and justly with the case. The former practice whereby disclosure was not ordered unless there was material outside the written evidence which suggested that the written evidence was inaccurate, misleading or incomplete in some material respect, no longer reflects an appropriate approach to disclosure. Rather, the courts should adopt a more flexible and less prescriptive principle, depending on whether on the facts and circumstances of a particular case, disclosure is required to deal fairly and justly with the claim.[387] Where objections are made to disclosure on the grounds, for example, of confidentiality or the volume of the material concerned, it may be necessary for the court to consider the material first to determine whether disclosure is necessary. In *Tweed*, for example, the claimant challenged the lawfulness of conditions attached to a public procession contending that they

9–112

---

[381] *R. (Al Sweady) v Secretary of State for Defence* [2012] H.R.L.R.12 at [15]–[29].

[382] For, example, whether an individual is a child or over 18 years as the services to which the individual is entitled depends upon the resolution of that factual issue: see *R (A) v Croydon LBC* [2009] 1 W.L.R. 2557 at [26]–[33]. See also *R. (Kadri) v Birmingham City Council* [2013] 1 W.L.R. 1755 at [50]–[54].

[383] *Tweed v Parades Commission for Northern Ireland* [2007] 1 A.C. 650 at [54].

[384] per Lord Simon Brown in *Tweed v Parades Commission for Northern Ireland* [2007] 1 A.C. 650 at [57].

[385] See the discussion on the defendant's duty of candour at paras.9-097 to 9-099 above.

[386] *Tweed v Parades Commission for Northern Ireland* [2007] 1 A.C. 650 at [4]. Defendants do generally exhibit such documents and it is not normally in their interests to refuse to do so, not least because they would then run the risk of adverse inferences being drawn or disclosure being ordered. Usually, there is a specific reason, such as confidentiality, which results in documents being summarised in the witness statement rather than being exhibited.

[387] *Tweed v Parades Commission for Northern Ireland* [2007] 1 A.C. 650 at [32].

infringed certain Convention rights. The defendant had summarised in its written evidence advice and reports from the police. The claimant sought disclosure of those documents. The House of Lords accepted that, given the nature of the challenge, which raised issues of proportionality and Convention rights, disclosure of the underlying documents may be needed. Given that the documents was based on information provided in confidence, the House of Lords ordered that the judge consider the material himself to determine whether the underlying documentation provided sufficient extra assistance to the claimant in his proportionality challenge over and above the summary already provided in the written evidence so as to justify the disclosure of the documents in the interests of fairly dealing with the case. If so, the judge could decide whether any parts of the documents should be redacted.[388]

9–113 The courts will not allow "fishing expeditions" where a claimant seeks disclosure of documents in the hope that something will emerge which might form the basis of a claim for review.[389] The courts will not, for example, order disclosure where the claimant claims that a decision is so unreasonable that it must be flawed and seeks disclosure in the hope that it might turn up evidence to support that or another allegation.

9–114 There are, therefore, relatively limited circumstances when disclosure will be ordered. The courts will only order disclosure where it is necessary to deal fairly and justly with an issue raised in the judicial review proceedings. Disclosure will normally be limited to ordering disclosure of those particular documents that the court considers are necessary to enable it to deal with the judicial review claim. Clearly, if documents are relevant and central to the claim, there is a greater likelihood that the courts will order disclosure.[390] The courts have, for example, ordered disclosure of medical reports that allegedly supported the claim that a prisoner was being kept in unlawful conditions.[391] Disclosure is also likely to be more relevant in areas such as claims that public authorities have acted incompatibly with a Convention right where the courts may have to undertake a more rigorous scrutiny of the lawfulness of the decision.[392]

9–115 Disclosure will only be ordered where it is necessary for the purposes of dealing with the judicial review claim. The court cannot order disclosure of documents for use in other proceedings. A court which quashes a decision and remits the matter to the decision-maker for reconsideration cannot, for example, order disclosure of documents where these would be used in proceedings before that decision-maker.[393]

---

[388] *Tweed v Parades Commission for Northern Ireland* [2007] 1 A.C. 650 at [41] and [57]–[58].

[389] *R. v Secretary of State for the Environment Ex p. Islington LBC and the London Lesbian and Gay Centre* [1992] C.O.D. 67; *R. v Secretary of State for the Environment Ex p. Doncaster BC* [1990] C.O.D. 441. See also dicta of Lord Simon Brown in *Tweed v Parades Commission for Northern Ireland* [2007] 1 A.C. 650 at [56].

[390] *R. v Secretary of State for the Home Department Ex p. Benson* [1989] C.O.D. 329.

[391] *R. v Secretary of State for the Home Department Ex p. Herbage (No.2)* [1987] Q.B. 1077.

[392] See *Tweed v Parades Commission for Northern Ireland* [2006] 1 A.C. 650. Even here, orders for disclosure are likely to be infrequent, at least if public authorities continue their existing practice of disclosing the main documents underlying the decision under challenge: see [2007] 1 A.C. 650 at [57].

[393] *R. v Secretary of State for Education and Science Ex p. G, The Times*, July 1, 1989.

Public interest immunity and legal professional privilege

Disclosure will not be ordered where a party successfully claims public interest   **9–116**
immunity for the documents. The courts will not order disclosure where the
public interest in the proper functioning of a body performing public functions
requires non-disclosure and that public interest outweighs the public interest in
full disclosure to ensure the proper administration of justice.[394] The consequences
of the court finding that documents should not be disclosed for reasons of public
interest immunity is that the documents are not disclosed to the claimant and may
not be relied upon by the public authority as part of its case.[395] As judicial review
proceedings involve claims against public bodies acting in the public interest,
claims of public interest immunity are bound to arise from time to time.
Reference should be made to the standard works on evidence for a discussion of
the scope of public interest immunity.

The courts will not order disclosure where the documents in question are   **9–117**
legally privileged. For example, the court refused to order disclosure of a report
prepared by the Inland Revenue in connection with anticipated litigation as it
enjoyed legal professional privilege.[396] Reference should be made to the standard
works on evidence for a full discussion of the circumstances in which privilege
may be claimed.

Closed material procedures

The question has arisen as to whether particular types of evidence, usually   **9–118**
evidence damaging to national security, may be relied upon by a public authority
and disclosed to the court but not disclosed to the claimant (although it may be
disclosed to a special advocate appointed by the court to represent a claimant's
interests: the special advocate could make submissions on the material but could
not disclose it to the claimant or take instruction from the claimant on the
evidence). The Supreme Court held that the common law did not permit the use
of such a closed material procedure in civil claims including claims for judicial
review. That would run contrary to two principles underlying the common law,
namely open justice and natural justice or procedural fairness. Open justice
requires that hearings are held in public and the evidence and arguments are heard
in public, subject to certain limited exceptions. The principles of natural justice
require that the party to proceedings has the right to know the case advanced
against him. Disclosure of evidence only to the court (and a special advocate)
would run counter to those fundamental common law principles and could not be

---

[394] See, generally, *Conway v Rimmer* [1968] A.C. 910; *Burmah Oil Ltd v Governor and Co. of the Bank of England* [1980] A.C. 1090 and *Air Canada v Secretary of State for Trade and Industry (No.2)* [1983] 2 A.C. 394. The importance of accuracy on the part of a public authority seeking an order that documents do not need to be disclosed because they attract public interest immunity was emphasised in *R. (Al Sweady) v Secretary of State for Defence* [2009] EWHC 1687 (Admin). Disclosure is available against the Crown: see Crown Proceedings Act 1947 s.28.
[395] See *Al Rawi v Security Service (Justice intervening)* [2011] 3 W.L.R. 388 at [41].
[396] *R. v I.R.C. Ex p. Taylor* [1989] 1 All E.R. 906. See also *R. v Secretary of State for Transport Ex p. Factortame Ltd* [1997] C.O.D. 433.

ordered absent legislation enacted by Parliament for that purpose.[397] Parliament has subsequently enacted the Justice and Security Act 2013. That permits the court to declare that civil proceedings, including judicial review claims, are ones in which closed material applications may be made.[398] The court must be satisfied that the proceedings would involve the disclosure of sensitive material, that is material damaging to national security, and that it is in the interests of the fair and effective administration of justice to make such a declaration. Rules of court may make provision for sensitive material to be disclosed to the court and to a special advocate appointed for the claimant but not to the claimant himself.[399]

Further information

9–119 The courts may order any party to clarify any matter which is in dispute or to give additional information in such matters.[400] In practice, such orders are rarely made in judicial review proceedings.

Cross-examination

9–120 Cross-examination of a person making an affidavit or witness statement may be allowed in judicial review proceedings[401] but is ordered extremely rarely. In principle " ... the grant of leave to cross-examine ... is governed by the same principles as it is in actions begun by originating summons; it should be allowed whenever the justice of the particular case so requires".[402]

9–121 In practice, the view that the courts take of the nature of judicial review means that cross-examination will be rare. The courts act as supervisory bodies only and leave the findings of fact to the decision-maker. The courts will usually only determine whether, given the facts as found, the decision-maker has made a reviewable error, such as taking into account irrelevant factors or erring in law.[403] The courts may have to adopt a heightened degree of scrutiny in cases where a claimant alleges that actions by a public body conflicts with his rights under the European Convention on Human Rights.[404] Even here the role of the court is usually a reviewing one and it is not often that the courts will consider that oral

---

[397] See *Al Rawi v Security Service (Justice and others intervening)* [2012] 1 A.C. 531 at [10]-[12], [47]-[50], [74], [86], [88] and [192]. Specific statutory exceptions existed in relation to procedures relating to suspected terrorists and in relation to employment disputes: see *Tariq v Home Office* [2012] 1 A.C. 452.

[398] See s.6 of the Justice and Security Act 2013. For a case where such a declaration was given, see *F v Security Service and others; Mohammed v Foreign and Commonwealth Office* [2014] 1 W.L.R. 1699.

[399] See s.8 of the Justice and Security Act 2013. The rules are in CPR Part 82.

[400] CPR Pt 18.

[401] Under CPR r.32.1 or its inherent jurisdiction: see *R. (G) v Ealing LBC*, *The Times*, March 18, 2002.

[402] per Lord Diplock in *O'Reilly v Mackman* [1983] 2 A.C. 237 at 282–283.

[403] *O'Reilly v Mackman* [1983] 2 A.C. 237 at 282–283 and see *George v Secretary of State for the Environment* (1979) 77 L.G.R. 689 and *R. v London Residuary Body Ex p. Inner London Education Authority*, *The Times*, July 24, 1987.

[404] See, e.g. *R. (Daly) v Secretary of State for the Home Department* [2001] 2 A.C. 532 at [27].

evidence and cross-examination will be necessary to resolve the dispute.[405] In exceptional circumstances, oral evidence and cross-examination may be allowed if there is a dispute on a critical factual issue and it is necessary to resolve that issue by cross-examination.[406] Thus, cross-examination was necessary where there were crucial issues of fact as to whether detainees were tortured or killed at a British base and cross-examination was necessary to resolve those issues.[407] If a clear conflict of fact arises on the written evidence of the claimant and the defendant, as to what procedure was followed at a hearing, or what factors were actually taken into account, or what the real purpose of the decision-maker was, then cross-examination to resolve that conflict may be appropriate.[408] Even in those cases, the courts may refuse cross-examination and may rely on the contemporaneous documents which should be exhibited to affidavits or witness statements.[409] The Divisional Court has also indicated that there are virtually no circumstances in which it would be appropriate to allow cross-examination to determine what procedure was followed before an inferior court.[410] Questions of jurisdictional fact may also arise. Even these may be decided on the basis of the written evidence alone, although if there were clear conflicts of evidence, then cross-examination may be necessary to resolve these.[411] Allegations of bad faith on the part of a decision-maker may also have to be investigated by cross-examination.[412] If there is a dispute of fact and no cross-examination is allowed, the courts will proceed on the basis of the written evidence presented by the person who does not have the onus of proof. As the onus is on the claimant to make out his case for judicial review, this means that in cases of conflict on a critical matter which are not resolved by oral evidence and cross-examination, the courts will proceed on the basis of the defendant's written evidence.[413]

Interim relief and stays

The need for interim relief may be apparent at the time that the claim is made in which case a claim for interim relief should be included in the claim form and, if necessary, the claimant can use the procedure for urgent applications.[414] The

9–122

---

[405] *R. (N) v M* [2003] 1 W.L.R. 562 at [39].

[406] *R. (Wilkinson) v Broadmoor Special Hospital Authority* [2002] 1 W.L.R. 419 (whether proposed medical treatment of a detained mental patient would be a breach of Convention rights) as explained in *R. (N) v M* [2003] 1 W.L.R. 562 at [39]; *R. (Al Sweady) v Secretary of State for Defence* [2012] H.R.L.R. 2 at [15]–[29].

[407] *R. (Al Sweady) v Secretary of State for Defence* [2012] H.R.L.R. 12 at [15]–[29].

[408] *R. v Waltham Forest LBC Ex p. Baxter* [1989] Q.B. 419 (cross-examination to determine real reasons for councillors voting for particular resolution). See also *Jones v Secretary of State for Wales* (1995) 70 P. & C.R. 211.

[409] *R. v Chief Constable of Thames Valley Police Ex p. Cotton* [1990] I.R.L.R. 64.

[410] *R. v Reigate Justices Ex p. Curl* [1991] C.O.D. 66.

[411] *R. v Secretary of State for the Home Department Ex p. Khawaja* [1984] A.C. 74 per Lord Bridge at 124–125 (although it would be rare when the interests of justice require a deponent to return from overseas. Now, it may be possible for cross-examination to be conducted by video link).

[412] See, e.g. *R. v Derbyshire CC Ex p. The Times Supplements Ltd* [1991] C.O.D. 129 and see *Kent v University College, The Times*, February 18, 1992.

[413] *R. v Reigate Justices Ex p. Curl* [1991] C.O.D. 66; *R. (Al Sweady) v Secretary of State for Defence* [2012] H.R.L.R. 2 at [17] and *R. v Board of Visitors at Hull Prison* [1979] 1 W.L.R. 1401 at 1410H.

[414] See above at para.9–014.

better course of action is for the application for interim relief to be referred to an oral hearing, although in cases of urgency, a court may grant interim relief for a limited period or give the defendant liberty to apply to discharge the interim order.[415] A court which grants permission may also grant a stay.[416] Occasionally, the question of interim relief may arise after permission has been granted. The claimant may apply for interim relief using the procedure set out in CPR, Parts 23 and 25.

Protective costs orders

9–123   An unsuccessful claimant will normally be ordered to pay the defendant's costs. The court have also on occasions been asked to make a pre-emptive costs order that the claimant would not be liable to pay the defendant's costs, or that the claimant's liability to restricted to a particular amount, even if the claimant proved to be unsuccessful at the hearing.

9–124   An application for a protective costs should be included in the claim form but they can be made at any stage in the proceedings. The principles and procedure for dealing with such applications is discussed above.[417]

Orders disposing of proceedings

9–125   Once permission to apply for judicial review is granted, the claim must be dealt with at an oral hearing unless the parties agree otherwise.[418] There is specific provision for enabling the parties to agree to the termination of proceedings without the necessity for appearing at a hearing. Where the parties are agreed as to the terms on which a final order should be made in a claim for judicial review, they may lodge in the Administrative Court Office a document signed by the parties, together with one copy, setting out the terms of the proposed agreed order and a short statement of the matters relied upon as justifying the order and any authorities and statutory provisions relied upon.[419] Termination will usually occur when the defendant accepts that it has acted unlawfully and agrees to the granting of an appropriate remedy (such as a quashing order to quash an unlawful decision). Costs are also usually dealt with in the order if they are agreed.[420] The document is then submitted to the court which, if satisfied with the proposed order, may make the order without the need for the parties to attend for a hearing.

9–126   There is also provision for withdrawal of proceedings. Where the parties are agreed that the proceedings should be withdrawn but require the leave of the court to do so, they should lodge a document signed by the parties, together with one copy, setting out the terms of the proposed withdrawal. If the court is satisfied that the order should be made, it will make the order without the need

---

[415]   See above at para.9–014. See also *R. (Lawler) v Restormel BC* [2008] A.C.D. 2.

[416]   CPR r.54.10.

[417]   See paras 9–044 to 9–051.

[418]   *R. (Parsipool) v Secretary of State for the Home Department* [2011] 1 W.L.R. 3187.

[419]   See para.17.1 of Practice Direction 54A – Judicial Review.

[420]   The position on costs if the parties are not agreed will be determined by the principles set out at para.9–091. If the parties cannot agree on the appropriate costs order, there may need to be an oral hearing on costs or the parties may agree to deal with this issue by way of written submissions so that the court can determine the matter on the papers.

for the attendance of the parties.[421] One issue may be whether any order for costs should be made. The position on costs where proceedings are discontinued is set out above.[422] If the parties are not agreed on costs, there may need to be an oral hearing on costs or the parties may invite the court to deal with costs on the basis of written submissions. If leave of the court is not required to withdraw,[423] and no order for costs is sought, a claimant may withdraw by informing the Administrative Court Office in writing of the withdrawal, confirming that all other parties have been notified.[424]

Listing of cases

Judicial review claims are included in the Administrative Court List.[425] Where a case is ready to be heard, it enters a warned list and all parties are informed of this by letter.[426] Expedited cases take priority over other cases and these enter the expedited warned list. The Administrative Court Office will usually contact counsel for the parties to agree a fixed date for the hearing. Once fixed, a date will only be vacated if both parties consent. Failing that, an application for an adjournment must be made. The same procedure is followed when the claimant is a litigant in person. There are cases which enter a short warned list. These are cases that are ready to be heard but are not allocated a fixed date. The parties will be notified that their case is likely to be listed from a specified date and will be brought into the list at short notice, which may be less than a day.

9–127

Bundles of documents

The claimant is responsible for providing a paginated index bundle for the use of the court when he lodges his skeleton, i.e. not less than 21 working days before the date of the hearing (or the warned date).[427] The bundle will usually contain the claim form, the written evidence and exhibits and documents relied upon by the claimant, the defendant and the interested party, and the order granting permission.[428] The order or decision under challenge will usually be exhibited to a witness statement but if not it should be included in the paginated bundle. The bundle must be lodged in the Administrative Court Office. The claimant should provide one bundle if the case is to be heard by a single judge and two if it is to

9–128

---

[421] Practice Direction (Administrative Court: Uncontested Proceedings) [2008] 1 W.L.R. 1377 at [3](a).

[422] See above at para.9–091.

[423] The circumstances when permission of the court is required to discontinue proceedings are set out in CPR r.38.2.

[424] Practice Direction (Administrative Court: Uncontested Proceedings) [2008] 1 W.L.R. 1377 at [3](b).

[425] Practice Direction (Crown Office List) [1987] 1 W.L.R. 232. The Crown Office List has been renamed the Administrative Court List: Practice Direction: The Administrative Court [2000] 1 W.L.R. 1654.

[426] The listing arrangements are described in the Practice Statement (Administrative Court: Listing and Urgent Cases) [2002] 1 W.L.R. 810 at 813–814.

[427] Para.16.1 of Practice Direction 54A – Judicial Review.

[428] The bundle must contain the documents relied upon by the claimant and the defendant and any other party who is to make representations at the hearing: see paras 16.1–2 of Practice Direction 54 – Judicial Review.

be heard by a Divisional Court. In practice, the claimant will also liaise with the defendant and interested parties and either provide them with a bundle or an index to ensure that the parties and the court are working from the same bundle.

Skeleton arguments

9–129 The claimant is required to lodge a skeleton argument in the Administrative Court Office and to serve a copy on the defendant and other party wishing to make representations at the hearing no later than 21 working days before the warned date or the fixed date for the hearing.[429] The defendant (or any other person wishing to be heard) is required to lodge and serve a skeleton not less than 14 working days before the hearing date or the warned date.[430] Failure to comply with the time-limits may result in an adjournment and the party may be penalised in costs. The skeleton argument must include the time estimate for the hearing, a list of issues, a list of the legal points to be taken, together with the relevant authorities, with page references, to be relied upon and a chronology.[431] The skeleton should also include a list of essential documents for advance reading by the court and a time estimate for the reading.[432] A list of persons referred to may also need to be included.[433]

E.   THE HEARING

Parties

9–130 The parties at the hearing will be the claimant and the defendant or defendants (that is, those persons whose decisions, actions or failure to act are challenged). All interested parties (that is, persons directly affected by the claim) should also have been served with the claim form and will therefore be parties.[434] There may be instances where the court considers that a person should have been served with the claim form or a person may wish to intervene. The court has inherent jurisdiction to adjourn and direct that the claim form be served on another party. Any other party, usually referred to as an intervener, given permission by the court to make representations may also appear.[435] Such interveners may be

---

[429] Para.15.1 of Practice Direction 54A – Judicial Review.

[430] Para.15.2 of Practice Direction 54A – Judicial Review.

[431] Para.15.3 of Practice Direction 54A – Judicial Review.

[432] Para.15.3 of Practice Direction 54A – Judicial Review.

[433] Formerly, this was only required where the number of persons referred to warranted the inclusion of a list. It was usually unnecessary to provide one in judicial review cases. The Practice Direction now draws no distinction between cases where a list is and is not needed. In practice, such lists are rarely used.

[434] CPR rr.54.7 and 54.1(2)(f) and Senior Courts Act 1981 s.151 and see above para.9–052.

[435] CPR.54.17. Applications may be made by letter and do not require a formal application under CPR Part 32: see para.15.1 Practice Direction 54A – Judicial Review. If necessary, case management directions should be given dealing with evidence and skeleton arguments to ensure the substantive judicial review hearing is not adversely affected: see dicta in *R. (Unison) v Lord Chancellor (Equality and Human Rights Commission intervening)* [2014] I.C.R. at [10]–[11].

individuals or pressure groups or statutory bodies with particular knowledge or interest in the subject matter of the judicial review.[436]

There is an established practice in relation to inferior courts such as magistrates' courts and Crown Courts: they are not usually represented by counsel but file written evidence with the Administrative Court Office or indicate that they do not intend to appear.[437] The clerk to the justices should send the written evidence directly to the Administrative Court Office.

9–131

Forum

The substantive claim for judicial review will usually be heard by a single judge sitting in open court[438] unless the court directs otherwise.[439] A court may, however, hear all or part of the case in private if there are adequate reasons to do so, such as the need for secrecy to safeguard national security,[440] or to protect commercially sensitive material.[441] The court may decide the claim for judicial review without a hearing if all parties agree.[442] That power is rarely, if ever, invoked in practice.

9–132

Burden of proof

The burden is on the claimant to establish that a ground for review exists.[443] The standard of proof is the civil standard of the balance of probability.[444] Even if the claimant establishes one of the grounds of the claim, the court may still, in its discretion, refuse a remedy. The better view is that, once the claimant has established a ground for review, the burden is on the defendant to show some adequate reason why the court should exercise its discretion and refuse a remedy. In practice, judicial review claims rarely, if ever, depend upon who bears the burden of proof on a particular issue.

9–133

---

[436] See *E v Chief Constable of the Royal Ulster Constabulary* [2008] 3 W.L.R. 1211 at [2].

[437] See *R. v Newcastle-Under-Lyme Justices Ex p. Massey* [1994] 1 W.L.R. 1684 at 1692; *R. v Gloucester Crown Court Ex p. Chester* [1998] C.O.D. 365; *R. v Feltham Justices Ex p. Haid* [1998] C.O.D. 440. See para.9–141 below on costs in such cases.

[438] The importance of open justice has frequently been stressed by the courts: see, for example, the decision of the Supreme Court in *Al Rawi v Security Service (Justice intervening)* [2011] 3 W.L.R. 388 at [10] (the case concerned a damages claim but similar principles apply to judicial review claims: see [62]).

[439] For example, the court may direct that the matter be heard by a Divisional Court if it is a matter of public importance or if it is a criminal matter (criminal matters formerly had to be dealt with by a Divisional Court but that is no longer required).

[440] *R. v Secretary of State for the Home Department Ex p. Ruddock* [1987] 1 W.L.R. 1482.

[441] *R. v Monopolies and Mergers Commission Ex p. Argyll Group plc* [1986] 1 W.L.R. 763; *R. v Monopolies and Mergers Commission Ex p. Elders IXL Ltd* [1987] 1 W.L.R. 1221. In so far as the court is determining a civil right within the meaning of Art.6 of the European Convention on Human Rights, the courts must sit in public unless any of the exceptions in Art.6 applies or the parties consent as the court itself is a public authority and is obliged to act in accordance with the Convention: see Human Rights Act 1998 s.6.

[442] CPR r.54.18. If they do not agree there must be a hearing: see *R. (Parsipool) v Secretary of State for the Home Department* [2011] 1 W.L.R. 3187.

[443] *R. v Reigate Justices Ex p. Curl* [1991] C.O.D. 66.

[444] *R. v Secretary of State for the Home Department Ex p. Khawaja* [1984] A.C. 74.

Fresh evidence

9–134   In a claim for judicial review, a court is concerned with reviewing the decision of a public body to ensure that the decision is not ultra vires. The courts will usually only look at the material before the decision-maker at the time that he took the decision in order to determine whether he has made a reviewable error. The courts do not consider fresh evidence, that is evidence which, if it had been put before the decision-maker, might have influenced his decision.[445] The court cannot, therefore, admit in evidence material that became available after the decision in order to determine whether the decision-maker erred in coming to his decision.[446] Nor can the courts have regard to material which existed before the decision was taken and which, if it had been drawn to the decision-maker's attention and been considered by him, might have influenced his decision. Thus, the courts could not consider fresh evidence as to the existence of a right of way in order to undermine a decision of a public body that no such right of way existed.[447] The courts will not admit evidence of experts expressing the view that decisions of a public authority on technical or other matters is irrational: such material was not material before the decision maker at the material time and it is for the court, not a witness, to determine if a decision is irrational.[448]

9–135   At present, the only categories of fresh evidence admissible on judicial review are as follows.[449] The court may receive evidence showing what material was before a decision-maker when he took the decision. The court may also receive evidence where the issue is one of jurisdictional fact for the court[450] to decide or where the evidence is intended to support an allegation of bad faith or of procedural error by the public body in reaching its decision.[451] The courts may also need to have regard to later material where the court is itself assessing

---

[445] *R. v Secretary of State for the Environment Ex p. Powis* [1984] 1 W.L.R. 584; *R. (Dwr Cymru Cyfyngedig) v Environment Agency of Wales, The Times,* February 28, 2003; *R. v London Residuary Body Ex p. Inner London Education Authority, The Times,* July 24, 1987 (affd. by the Court of Appeal, November 25, 1987, unreported); *R. v Wycombe District Council Ex p. Mahsood* [1989] C.O.D. 200; *R (L) v Chief Constable of Cumbria Constabulary* [2014] 1 W.L.R. 601 at [32](i). For an analogous principle in relation to statutory applications to quash, see *Kingswood v Secretary of State for the Environment* (1987) 57 P. & C.R. 153; *Sharif v Secretary of State for the Environment* (1999) 80 P. & C.R. 382; *Ashbridge Investments Ltd v Ministry of Housing and Local Government* [1965] 1 W.L.R. 1320.

[446] *R. v Immigration Tribunal Ex p. Jaifor Ali* [1991] C.O.D. 37.

[447] *R. v West Sussex Quarter Session Ex p. Johnson Trust* [1974] Q.B. 24.

[448] *R. (Harlow) v South Cambridgeshire DC*[2005] EWHC 173 (Admin) at [32]; *Lynch v General Medical Council* [2003] EWHC 2987 (Admin) at [18]–[25].

[449] *R. v Secretary of State for the Environment Ex p. Powis* [1984] 1 W.L.R. 584; *R. (Dwr Cymru Cyfyngedig) v Environment Agency of Wales, The Times,* February 28, 2003.

[450] *R. v Secretary of State for the Environment Ex p. Powis* [1984] 1 W.L.R. 584 but see dicta of Neil LJ in *R. v Secretary of State for the Environment Ex p. Davies* (1990) 61 P. & C.R. 487 (court entitled to consider the matter afresh and make up its own mind as to the existence of a jurisdictional fact but is limited to looking at the matter on the basis of the evidence before the decision-maker).

[451] There are suggestions that the courts might develop a new ground of judicial review, namely material error of fact, which may affect the extent to which evidence of matters existing at the time of the decision is admissible: see *R. v Criminal Injuries Compensation Board Ex p. A* [1999] 1 A.C. 330 and *E v Secretary of State for the Home Department* [2004] Q.B. 1044 at [68]–[88] and [91]. There may also be instances where it is said that the deciding-body failed to acquaint itself with relevant information before taking a decision. In such cases, however, the courts are still reluctant to allow

whether a particular course of action involves a breach of a claimant's rights under the European Convention on Human Rights.[452]

Remedies

A court may grant one or more of the remedies available on a judicial review claim if a claimant successfully establishes that the public body has acted unlawfully in that it has breached one of the public law principles governing the exercise of its functions. The remedies of a quashing order, a prohibiting order, a mandatory order, declaration and injunction have been considered in detail in previous chapters. The court will select the remedy (or remedies) that are appropriate bearing in mind the nature of the measure challenged and the factual circumstances of the case. Where the court makes a quashing order, it may also remit a matter to the decision-maker to be reconsidered in accordance with the findings of the court.[453] Courts also have power to substitute a decision for that which is subject to judicial review but only if the decision was made by a court or tribunal, the decision was quashed on the ground that there has been an error of law and without the error there would only have been one decision which the court or tribunal could have reached.[454] Statute may give the courts wider powers to substitute its decision and, in a criminal case, the court does have statutory power to vary the sentence imposed rather than quash the conviction.[455]

9–136

The remedies are discretionary. Even if the claimant has established a ground for review, the court may decline to grant a remedy. The principles governing the remedial discretion are discussed in Chapter 12. If the claim fails to establish a ground for review, the claim will be dismissed.

9–137

Damages, restitution and recovery of money

The court may also award damages, providing that a claim for damages was included in the claim and that, if the matter had been brought by an ordinary claim and not judicial review, damages would have been available.[456] This provision does not create any new substantive right to damages, but is a procedural provision only.[457] If a private law cause of action for damages is made out, then damages may be awarded even though they have been sought in a claim for judicial review not an ordinary claim. Claims for restitution or the recovery of

9–138

---

such a claim to become a vehicle by which a claimant may adduce fresh evidence which might have affected the decision: see *R. (Dwr Cymru Cyfyngedig) v Environment Agency of Wales, The Times,* February 28, 2003.

[452] *R. (L) v Chief Constable of Cumbria Constabulary* [2014] 1 W.L.R. 601 at [23].

[453] CPR r.54.19(2).

[454] See Senior Courts Act 1981 s.31(5) and (5A) as substituted by the Courts, Tribunals and Enforcement Act 2007 s.141. See also CPR r.54.19(2) which provides that the Administrative Court may substitute a decision where it is permitted to do so by statute.

[455] Senior Courts Act 1981 s.43. See also the power to vary orders made on committal for default in paying a fine in Senior Courts Act 1981 s.43ZA.

[456] Senior Courts Act 1981 s.31(7) and CPR r.54.3(2).

[457] Interest may be payable on damages or debts. If the claimant is seeking a mandatory order to compel payment of a statutory grant, that is not a debt or damages within the meaning of the Supreme Court Act 1981 s.35A, and no interest is payable *R. v Secretary of State for Transport Ex p. Sherriff and Sons Ltd (No.2), Independent,* January 12, 1988 and see [1988] P.L.R. 197.

money may also now be included in a claim for judicial review.[458] A claim for judicial review may also include a claim for damages where a public body has committed a sufficiently serious breach of EU law which causes loss.[459] In addition, the court may order a public body to pay damages under s.8 of the Human Rights Act 1998 if it has acted in a way that is incompatible with a right derived from the European Convention on Human Rights. A court may only grant damages if it is necessary to ensure just satisfaction for the person concerned, having regard to the other remedies granted and the consequences of the unlawful act.[460] The usual practice is to deal with the public law issues first and then, if necessary, deal with any outstanding claims for damages subsequently.[461]

Conversion to a Part 7 claim

9–139   The court may also order the matter to be treated as if it had been commenced by a claim for judicial review, but rather as a claim under Pt 7 of the CPR and may give directions as to its management.[462] The purpose underlying the CPR is to provide "a framework which is sufficiently flexible to enable all the issues between the parties to be determined".[463] Thus a transfer may be ordered where the claimant mistakenly brings a claim for judicial review alleging that he has public law rights but, in fact, only has private law rights.[464] More usually, a public law claim may also raise ancillary claims to damages in private law as indicated above.[465] In such instances, the courts have frequently dealt with the issue of public law first, and considered the claim for private law damages subsequently. Where appropriate, the courts have transferred the damages part of the proceedings to another division of the High Court to have the claim dealt with under the powers available under Pt 7 of the CPR rather than dealing with the matter in the Administrative Court by way of judicial review.[466] A flexible

---

[458] CPR r.54.3 as amended by Civil Procedure (Amendment No.5) Rules 2003 with effect from May 1, 2004.

[459] See Joined Cases C-46/93 and C-48/93 *Brasserie du Pecheur SA v Federal Republic of Germany; R. v Secretary of State for Transport Ex p. Factortame Ltd* [1996] E.C.R. I-1029 and see below paras.17–063 to 17–073.

[460] Human Rights Act 1998, s.8(3) and see on the general principles *R. (Greenfield) v Secretary of State for the Home Department* [2005] 1 W.L.R. 673 and see below at para.15–115.

[461] See, e.g. *R. v Chief Constable of the Lancashire Police Ex p. Parker* [1993] Q.B. 577 (lawfulness of search warrants determined first, damages claim to be stood over for subsequent consideration); *R. v Coventry City Council Ex p. Phoenix Aviation Ltd* [1995] 3 All E.R. 37 (lawfulness of ban on use of airport determined first; claim for damages for breach of contract stood over); *R. v Governor of Brockhill Prison Ex p. Evans (No.2)* [2000] 3 W.L.R. 843 (lawfulness of detention determined first; damages for false imprisonment considered subsequently).

[462] CPR r.54.20.

[463] per Lord Woolf in *R. (Heather) v Leonard Cheshire* [2002] 2 All E.R. 936 at [39].

[464] *R. v Leonard Cheshire Foundation* [2002] 2 All E.R. 936 at [38]–[39]. The predecessor to this rule had been held to apply only if an issue of public law arose which also give rise to private law consequences, and the power of transfer could not be used when no issue of public law arose at all: *R. v Secretary of State for the Home Department Ex p. Dew* [1987] 1 W.L.R. 881. That restrictive approach does not reflect the scope of the transfer powers under CPR r.54.20.

[465] See above para.9–138.

[466] *R. (Rawlinson & Hunter Trustees) v Central Criminal Court* [2013] 1 W.L.R. 1634 at [288]; *R. (Bhatti) v Croydon Magistrates' Court* [2011] 1 W.L.R. 948 at [32].

approach to transfer is clearly preferable to requiring the claimant to start an ordinary claim afresh and is more consistent with the overriding objective underlying the CPR.

Costs

The general rule

Costs usually follow the event in judicial review proceedings.[467] An unsuccessful defendant will normally be ordered to pay the successful claimant the costs of the substantive hearing and the costs of bringing the claim and obtaining permission.[468] A claimant who is unsuccessful will usually be ordered to pay the costs of the successful defendant. These costs will include the costs of the substantive hearing, the costs of the acknowledgement of service and costs reasonably incurred prior to the grant of permission (but not normally the costs of attending any oral permission hearing) unless the court otherwise orders.[469] In exceptional circumstances, the courts have very occasionally departed from the practice of ordering that an unsuccessful claimant, who is not legally aided, should pay the successful defendant's costs. These rare cases have tended to involve situations where the challenge raised issues of public importance.[470] It is for the claimant to demonstrate that there should be a departure from the ordinary rule that the unsuccessful party pays the costs of the successful party.[471] A claimant may establish that the defendant has acted unlawfully but may be refused a remedy on discretionary grounds such as failure to use an alternative remedy. Costs may still be awarded against the claimant in such circumstances.[472]

9–140

Different principles apply in relation to inferior courts or tribunals such as a magistrates' court or a Crown Court whose decisions are challenged by way of judicial review. Such courts are not normally represented at any hearing. The courts will not order an inferior court which has not appeared to pay the costs of a successful claimant unless the inferior court has acted in a way that calls for

9–141

---

[467] Following the general rule in relation to costs: CPR r.44.4.(2): see *R. (M) v Croydon LBC* [2012] 1 W.L.R. 2607 at [52]–[58].

[468] *R. v Lord Chancellor Ex p. Child Poverty Action Group* [1998] 2 All E.R. 755 at 754b–h; *R. v East Sussex Valuation Tribunal, Ex p. Silverstone* [1996] C.O.D. 402. *R. (Davey) v Aylesbury Vale* DC[2008] 1 W.L.R. 878.

[469] *R. (Davey) v Aylesbury Vale* DC[2008] 1 W.L.R. 878 at [29]–[30].

[470] See, e.g. *R. v Secretary of State for the Environment Ex p. Shelter* [1997] C.O.D. 49 (series of cases before the court raising a question of general public importance; the claimant charity had assisted in resolving that issue and if the matter had been dealt with in separate proceedings the claimant would have been likely to have been legally aided and so the defendant would not have been able to recover his costs in any event). See also *R. v East Sussex Valuation Tribunal Ex p. Silverstone* [1997] C.O.D. 402. A claimant can now apply for a protective costs order in advance of the hearing: see above at 9–044 to 9–051.

[471] *R. (Davey) v Aylesbury Vale* DC[2008] 1 W.L.R. 878.

[472] *R. v Trafford Justices Ex p. Colonel Foods Ltd* [1990] C.O.D. 351 (remedy refused as alternative remedy available; claimant had to pay costs even though it had established a procedural irregularity on the part of the defendant); *R. v Swale BC Ex p. Royal Society for the Protection of Birds* (1990) 2 Admin. L.Rep. 790 (claimant established a breach of a legitimate expectation but was refused a remedy on grounds of delay; claimant ordered to pay one set of costs to the interested party). See *R. (Hunt) v North Somerset Council* (2013) 16 C.C.L. Rep 530 (now on appeal to the Supreme Court).

strong disapproval.[473] Similar principles apply to coroner's courts; if they appear at a hearing as an active party resisting the claim and lose, they are likely to be ordered to pay the costs of the successful claimant's costs.[474] If they do not appear, and if their decision is found to be unlawful, they will not normally be ordered to pay the successful claimant's costs unless they have done something calling for the strong disapproval of the court.[475] If a court or tribunal appear to assist the court neutrally on questions of law, the practice is not to award costs against, or in favour, of it.[476]

Two or more parties opposing the claim

9–142   There may on occasions be more than one party opposing the claim. There may be the defendant whose decision is under challenge and one or more interested parties, that is a person or persons directly affected by the proceedings and entitled to be served with the claim form. The courts will not usually order an unsuccessful claimant to pay two sets of costs, one to the defendant and one to an interested party.[477] The claimant will normally only be ordered to pay one set of costs, usually to the defendant whose decision is under challenge.[478] The courts do have a discretion in relation to costs and may in appropriate cases depart from this practice. They may award two sets of costs where an interested party deals with a separate issue not dealt with by the defendant[479] or where the interests of the two parties are separate and distinct and require separate representation.[480] A second set of costs may be awarded, for example, if a person wishes to meet allegations of bad faith or dishonesty made against him.[481] The fact that issues are complex[482] or the case raises a matter of exceptional importance to an interested party may justify the conclusion that it was reasonable for him to attend to resist the claim for judicial review and so justify the award of a second set of costs.[483]

Intervener's costs

9–143   The usual practice when a person intervenes pursuant to CPR r.54.17 is that he bears his own costs. Where a claimant is successful, the intervener may also be

---

[473] *R. v Newcastle-under-Lyme Justices Ex p. Massey* [1994] 1 W.L.R. 1684.

[474] *R. (Davies) v HM Coroner for Birmingham (No.2)* [2004] 1 W.L.R. 2739.

[475] *R. v Inner London North Coroner Ex p. Touche* [2001] Q.B. 1206.

[476] *R. (Davies) v HM Coroner for Birmingham (No.2)* [2004] 1 W.L.R. 2739.

[477] See *Bolton MBC v Secretary of State for the Environment* [1995] 1 W.L.R. 1176 (dealing with statutory appeals in the planning context but the same principles apply in judicial review); *R. v Secretary of State for the Environment Ex p. Kirkstall Valley Campaign Ltd* [1996] 3 All E.R. 304 at 342–343; *R. v Ogwr BC Ex p. Carter Commercial Developments Ltd* [1989] 2 P.L.R. 54.

[478] *Bolton MBC v Secretary of State for the Environment* [1995] 1 W.L.R. 1176.

[479] *Bolton MBC v Secretary of State for the Environment* [1995] 1 W.L.R. 1176.

[480] See, e.g. *R. v Registrar of Companies Ex p. Central Bank of India* [1986] Q.B. 1114 at 1162; *R. v Director General of Telecommunications Ex p. Cellcom Ltd* [1999] C.O.D. 105; *R. (William Hill) v Horserace Betting Levy Board* [2013] 1 W.L.R. 3656 at [45]–[46]. The fact that a person has a separate interest may not sufficient to justify a second of costs if that interest did not require separate representation, *Bolton MBC v Secretary of State for the Environment* [1995] 1 W.L.R. 1176 (separate interest of developer in upholding planning permission did not justify ordering a second set of costs).

[481] *R. v Ogwr BC Ex p. Carter Commercial Developments Ltd* [1989] 2 P.L.R. 54.

[482] *R. v Registrar of Companies Ex p. Central Bank of India* [1986] Q.B. 1114.

[483] *Bolton MBC v Secretary of State for the Environment* [1995] 1 W.L.R. 1176.

ordered to pay any costs that are attributable to the intervention.[484] Exceptionally, where the intervener has, in effect, become a party to proceedings, the intervener may be ordered to pay part of the successful claimant's costs.[485] The Criminal Justice and Courts Bill 2014, if enacted, will provide that an intervener will not be able to recover in judicial review proceedings save in exceptional circumstances.

Appeals to the Court of Appeal in non-criminal matters

A claimant may wish to appeal against a decision dismissing a claim for judicial review. A defendant or interested party[486] may wish to apply for permission to appeal against a decision of the court granting the claim for judicial review. An intervener, that is a person who was not served with the claim form and is not directly affected by proceedings, but was given permission to intervene[487] and make representations, may also seek permission to appeal.[488]

9–144

A person may seek to challenge a finding by the court that a ground for judicial review had (or had not) been made out or may challenge a refusal of a remedy on discretionary grounds.[489]

9–145

Applications for permission to appeal

Appeals against a decision of the court granting or refusing the claim may only be appealed to the Court of Appeal with permission.[490] Permission will only be given where there is a real prospect of an appeal succeeding or where there is some other compelling reason why the appeal should be heard,[491] for example because it raises an issue of general public importance where it is appropriate to have a definitive ruling from the Court of Appeal.

9–146

Permission may and usually should be sought in the first instance from the court giving the decision.[492] If permission to appeal is refused by the first instance court, an application for permission may be made to the Court of Appeal by filing an appellant's notice (form N161) setting out the grounds for appeal and including the application for permission to appeal within 21 days after the date of the decision of the lower court that the appellant wishes to appeal or within such

9–147

---

[484] *R. (Barker) v Bromley LBC* [2006] 3 W.L.R. 1209 at [31]–[32].

[485] *R. (Barker) v Bromley LBC* [2006] 3 W.L.R. 1209 at [33]; *R (E) v Governing Body of JFS and another (United Synagogue intervening)* [2010] 2 W.L.R. 153 at [216]–[217].

[486] Both will have been served with the claim form and are parties within the meaning of Supreme Court Act 1981 s.151. An interested party appealed against a coroner's decision: see *R. (Hurst) v London Northern District Coroner* [2005] 1 W.L.R. 3892.

[487] Under CPR r.54.17. Indeed, non-parties affected by a decision may be given permission to appeal: see *George Wimpey UK Ltd v Tewkesbury BC* [2008] 1 W.L.R. 1649.

[488] Such persons are also parties within the meaning of Supreme Court Act 1981 s.151 and see *R. v Licensing Authority Ex p. Smith Kline & French Laboratories (Generics) (U.K.) Ltd and Harris Pharmaceutical Ltd Intervening* [1988] C.O.D. 62 (intervener was served with notice of the appeal but the notice was withdrawn and the intervener was given permission to appeal at the discretion of the court).

[489] See, e.g. *R. v I.R.C. Ex p. National Association of Self-Employed and Small Businesses Ltd* [1982] A.C. 617.

[490] CPR r.52.3.

[491] CPR r.52.3(6).

[492] CPR r.53.2.

time as directed by the lower court.[493] The applicant must also pay the appropriate fee.[494] The applicant for permission must serve the appellant's notice on each respondent as soon as practicable and in any event within seven days of it being filed but the respondent is not required to take any action until permission is granted unless directed to do so by the court.[495] The applicant for permission must file the following documents in the Court of Appeal office: an appellant's notice together with one additional copy for the Court of Appeal and one copy for each respondent, a skeleton argument, a sealed copy of the order being appealed against, the order of the court below refusing permission to appeal and the reasons, any written evidence in support of the application for permission, and those parts of the bundle of documents that were used in the judicial review hearing below which are reasonably necessary to deal with the appeal (that will include the claim form, written evidence, any decision letter and key documents).[496] A respondent seeking to appeal part of the order to or vary the order below must file and serve a respondent's notice and obtain permission to appeal.[497] A respondent seeking to uphold the judgment below on different or additional grounds may also file a respondent's notice.[498] A respondent's notice must lodge a skeleton argument and serve it on other parties within 14 days of filing a respondent's notice.[499]

9–148   An application for permission to appeal will usually be dealt with on paper by a single Lord or Lady Justice of Appeal although the court may direct that it be heard at an oral hearing either with or without notice to the respondent. Where permission is refused, the applicant for permission may, within seven days after service of the notice of refusal, request that that decision be reconsidered at oral hearing unless the judge refusing permission on the papers has certified that the application is totally without merit.[500] Respondents will be notified of the hearing but will not be expected to attend unless the court so directs and if they attend voluntarily will not normally be able to recover their costs of doing so.[501]

Processing the appeal

9–149   If permission is granted by the court below or the Court of Appeal, there is a timetable prescribed for the lodging of an agreed appeal which must include certain specified documents and may include others if they are relevant to the appeal, and skeleton arguments.[502]

---

[493]   CPR rr.52.3(3) and 52.4.
[494]   Para.3(1) of Practice Direction 52C – Appeals to the Court of Appeal.
[495]   CPR r.52.4(3) and para.19 of Practice Direction 52C – Appeals to the Court of Appeal.
[496]   Para.3(2) of Practice Direction 52C – Appeals to the Court of Appeal.
[497]   CPR 52 r.4 and para.8 of Practice Direction 52C – Appeals to the Court of Appeal.
[498]   CPR 52 r.4 and para.8 of Practice Direction 52C – Appeals to the Court of Appeal.
[499]   Para.9 of Practice Direction 52C – Appeals to the Court of Appeal.
[500]   CPR r.52.3(4) and (5) and (4A).
[501]   Paras 16(2) and 19 of Practice Direction 52C – Appeals to the Court of Appeal.
[502]   See timetable and paras 27–32 of Practice Direction 52C – Appeals to the Court of Appeal.

The appeal

If permission is granted, an appeal is by way of a review of the decision of the court below and the appeal will be allowed where the court below was wrong or the decision is unjust because of some procedural irregularity.[503] A party may not rely on any matter not contained in an appeal notice unless the appeal court gives permission.[504] Nor will the Court of Appeal usually allow grounds of appeal to be argued where they were not raised before the court below.[505] Fresh evidence will not usually be admitted where the evidence could have been obtained with reasonable diligence for use at the substantive hearing in the court below, or if it would not have an important influence on the case, or if the new evidence is not credible.[506] The court has a discretion to depart from these principles where the justice of the case so requires.[507] **9–150**

There is a further appeal to the Supreme Court if permission to appeal is given either by the Court of Appeal or by the Supreme Court. **9–151**

Appeals in criminal cases

There is no appeal in a criminal matter to the Court of Appeal.[508] Appeals do lie to the Supreme Court, provided that the court below certifies that the cases raises a point of law of general public importance, and if either that court or the Supreme Court gives permission to appeal.[509] **9–152**

---

[503] CPR rr.52.11(1) and (2).

[504] CPR r.52.11(5).

[505] Particularly if they raise issues where other parties would have been served or sought to intervene: *R. (H) v Secretary of State for the Home Department* [2002] 3 W.L.R. 967 at [47].

[506] CPR r.52.11(2). The principles set out in *Ladd v Marshall* [1954] 1 W.L.R. 1489 remain relevant to the exercise of discretion under this rule: see *Aylwen v Taylor Joynson Garret* [2002] 1 P.N.L.R. 1 and *Hertfordshire Investments Ltd v Bubb* [2000] 1 W.L.R. 2318. The principles do not strictly apply to appeals in judicial review cases but similar principles will generally be followed: see *R. v Secretary of State for the Home Department Ex p. Ali (Momin)* [1984] 1 W.L.R. 663, and the Court of Appeal has held that that remains the position: *R. v Secretary of State for Education and Employment Ex p. Amraf Training Plc, The Times*, June 28, 2001 (reported only briefly on this point) and see dicta in *E. v Secretary of State for the Home Department* [2004] Q.B. 1044 at [81]–[82].

[507] See *R. v Chief Constable of Sussex Ex p. International Traders' Ferry Ltd* [1998] 3 W.L.R. 1260; *E v Secretary of State for the Home Department* [2004] 1 Q.B. 1044 at 91.

[508] Senior Court Acts 1981 s.18(1)(a).

[509] Administration of Justice Act 1960 s.1.

CHAPTER 10

Judicial Review and the Upper Tribunal

A. INTRODUCTION

Judicial review by the Upper Tribunal

While the overwhelming majority of judicial review cases are brought and heard in the Administrative Court, the creation under the Tribunals, Courts and Enforcement Act 2007[1] of the Upper Tribunal has, for the first time, permitted judicial reviews to be determined outside the High Court. Although a creature of statute, the Upper Tribunal has the power to grant the prerogative remedies, as well as injunctions, declarations and awards of damages. In doing so, it must apply the principles which the High Court would apply.

10–001

The judicial review jurisdiction of the Upper Tribunal is limited. There are certain types of cases which must be heard by the Upper Tribunal, and other types of case may be heard by Upper Tribunal. The Administrative Court may transfer some types of case into the Upper Tribunal. The majority of immigration and asylum judicial reviews are now heard in the Immigration and Asylum Chamber of the Upper Tribunal.

10–002

For the most part, where a judicial review claim proceeds in the Upper Tribunal the procedure is substantively the same as that found, in much greater detail, in Part 54 of the CPR and discussed in Chapter 9. However, the CPR does not apply to the Upper Tribunal, and the governing procedural rules are the Upper Tribunal Rules 2008.[2] Although there are minor differences of terminology, and some of detail, the basic two-stage procedure which requires permission to apply for judicial review before the claim is heard is the same. The same time limits and rules of standing apply. The Upper Tribunal has a statutory power to grant all the remedies available on judicial review, including interim relief. The Upper Tribunal does, however, take a more restrictive approach to the award of costs and where the review is of a decision of the First-tier Tribunal will not award costs unless they would have been awarded below. Where there is no express discussion of an issue in this chapter, it may be assumed that the principles set out in Chapter 9 apply.

10–003

---

[1] Referred to in this chapter as the TCEA.
[2] The Tribunal Procedure (Upper Tribunal) Rules 2008 (SI 2008/2698), referred to in this chapter as the UT Rules.

Judicial review of the Upper Tribunal

10–004   In relation to decisions of the Upper Tribunal which are not the subject of a right of appeal (predominantly refusals of permission to appeal), the Upper Tribunal is itself subject to judicial review. However, that right of judicial review is narrowly confined. An application for permission must be made in the High Court no later than 16 days after notice of the decision was sent,[3] and there is no right to renew the application for permission at an oral hearing.[4] The judge determining the application on the papers may give permission only where there is an arguable case with a real prospect of success that both the refusal of permission to appeal and the underlying first instance decision were wrong in law, and that there is either an important point of principle or practice, or that there is some other compelling reason.[5]

B.   JUDICIAL REVIEW IN THE UPPER TRIBUNAL

The Upper Tribunal

10–005   The Upper Tribunal was created by s.3(2) of the TCEA, and by s.3(5) was designated a superior court of record. As a superior court of record, decisions of the Upper Tribunal will be binding on inferior courts and lower tier tribunals. Decisions of the Upper Tribunal will be persuasive for courts of equal jurisdiction and will not be departed from unless "plainly wrong".[6] It is certainly to be expected that the Upper Tribunal will follow its own consistent line of authority, particularly where the decision on a point of law was handed down by a panel of more than a single judge.[7] However, it is not absolutely bound to do so.

10–006   The Upper Tribunal is comprised of Upper Tribunal judges but may also include judges drawn from the High Court, the Court of Appeal, and the Court of Session and may also include a circuit or district judge.[8]

10–007   The Upper Tribunal is currently divided into four Chambers. The Administrative Appeals Chamber hears appeals from all the First–tier Tribunals (except the Tax Chamber, the Immigration and Asylum Chamber and charities cases from the General Regulatory Chamber), as well as various miscellaneous other matters. The Tax and Chancery Chamber hears appeals from the First-tier Tax Chamber and the charities cases from the General Regulatory Chamber as well as appeals from the Financial Services Authority and appeals from the Pensions Regulator. The Lands Chamber deals with certain disputes concerning land and appeals from the First-tier Property Chamber. The Immigration and Asylum Chamber hears appeals from the Immigration and Asylum Chamber of the First-tier Tribunal in immigration and asylum matters.

---

[3] CPR r.54.7A(3).
[4] CPR r.54.7A(8).
[5] CPR r.54.7A(7).
[6] *R. v Greater Manchester Coroner Ex p. Tal* [1985] Q.B. 67.
[7] *Dorset Healthcare NHS Trust v MH* [2009] P.T.S.R. 1112 at [38].
[8] TCEA s.6.

Allocation of judicial review within the Upper Tribunal

Secondary legislation makes provision for the allocation of particular types of judicial review case to the Chambers of the Upper Tribunal.[9] **10–008**

The Immigration and Asylum Chamber is allocated judicial review of cases which relate to claims made by a person that they are a minor from outside the United Kingdom challenging a defendant's assessment of that person's age; categories of cases which are directed to be heard in the Immigration and Asylum Chamber; and cases which are transferred to the Immigration and Asylum Chamber by the Administrative Court.[10] **10–009**

The Lands Chamber is allocated judicial review cases which relate to a decision of the Property Chamber of the First-tier Tribunal, the Valuation Tribunal in England, or various Welsh leasehold valuation, residential property, Agricultural Land and Valuation tribunals.[11] **10–010**

The Tax and Chancery Chamber is allocated judicial review cases which relate to a decision of: the Tax Chamber of the First-tier Tribunal or a charities case in the General Regulatory Chamber; a function of HMRC (with the exception of any function in respect of which an appeal would be allocated to the Social Entitlement Chamber); the exercise by the National Crime Agency of Revenue functions (with the exception of any function in relation to which an appeal would be allocated to the Social Entitlement Chamber); and a function of the Charity Commission, the Financial Compensation Authority, the Bank of England, a person assessing compensation or consideration under the Banking (Special Provisions) Act 2008, or the Pensions Regulator.[12] **10–011**

The Administrative Appeals Chamber is allocated all other judicial review cases which are not otherwise allocated to the other Chambers of the Upper Tribunal.[13] The Administrative Appeals Chamber is therefore the primary home of the Upper Tribunal's judicial review jurisdiction, but with certain exceptions for cases in which the subject matter will be most obviously within the expertise of the judges of another Chamber. **10–012**

The powers and remedies of the Upper Tribunal

The Upper Tribunal's judicial review jurisdiction is governed by s.15 of the TCEA. This provides that the Upper Tribunal may grant: a mandatory order; a prohibiting order; a quashing order; a declaration; or an injunction. These are the same orders as the Administrative Court is empowered to make in judicial review cases before it. Such orders have the same effect as they would have if granted by the High Court and are enforceable in the same way as they would be if made by the High Court.[14] In deciding whether to make such orders, the Upper Tribunal is required, by s.15(4)–(5), to apply the same principles as the High Court would apply on an application for judicial review. **10–013**

---

[9] The First-tier Tribunal and Upper Tribunal (Chambers) Order 2010 (SI 2010/2655).
[10] Art.11(c)–(e).
[11] Art.12(c).
[12] Art.13(g).
[13] Art.10(b).
[14] TCEA s.15(3).

10–014　Where a quashing order is made, the Upper Tribunal may in addition remit the matter concerned to the court, tribunal or authority that made the decision which is the subject of the order, or it may substitute its own decision for the decision in question.[15] However, a substituted decision may only be made where the decision in question was made by a court or tribunal on the basis of error of law and without such error there would only have been one decision that the court or tribunal could have reached.[16]

10–015　The Upper Tribunal has no power to make a declaration of incompatibility under s.4 of the Human Rights Act 1998.

10–016　Although the TCEA makes no express provision for interim remedies, it has been accepted by the Administrative Appeals Chamber of the Upper Tribunal in a special educational needs case, where an appeal was pending before the Health, Education and Social Care Chamber of the First-tier Tribunal, that the Upper Tribunal has the power to order an interim injunction when exercising its judicial review jurisdiction.[17] The statutory requirement in s.15(4)–(5) to apply the same principles as the High Court is just as applicable in interim relief cases. However, the Upper Tribunal indicated that in the context of that case the jurisdiction to order interim relief should be exercised with considerable restraint and only in exceptional circumstances.[18] It seems likely that the jurisdiction to order interim relief would be accepted in respect of any relief mentioned in s.15, which will exclude other forms of relief, such as habeas corpus.

10–017　The Upper Tribunal may also award an applicant damages, restitution, or the recovery of a sum if a claim for such relief has been made, and such an award would have been made by the High Court in the same circumstances.[19]

Circumstances in which judicial review claims must be determined by the Upper Tribunal

10–018　The mandatory judicial review jurisdiction of the Upper Tribunal only arises where certain conditions are satisfied under s.18 of the TCEA or the case has been transferred to the Upper Tribunal from the High Court under s.19 of the TCEA. Cases dealt with under s.18 will arise where the application for permission is made directly to the Upper Tribunal, whereas s.19 applies to claims commenced in the Administrative Court.

10–019　Four conditions are imposed by s.18, each of which must be satisfied. First, the application must be seeking a form of relief listed in s.15; permission to apply for judicial review; an award of damages or restitution under s.16(6); or costs or interest.[20] Secondly, the application must not call into question anything done by the Crown Court.[21] Thirdly, the application must fall within a category of case specified in a direction made by the Lord Chief Justice under Part 1 of Sch.2 to

---

[15] TCEA s.17(1).
[16] TCEA s.17(2).
[17] *R. (JW) v The Learning Trust* [2010] E.L.R. 115 at [26].
[18] *R. (JW) v The Learning Trust* [2010] E.L.R. 115 at [29]. The Upper Tribunal confirmed that the First-tier Tribunal has no power to order interim relief: at [23].
[19] TCEA s.16(6).
[20] TCEA s.18(4).
[21] TCEA s.18(5).

the Constitutional Reform Act 2005.[22] Those directions are described below. Fourthly, the judge hearing the case must be a High Court or Court of Appeal judge in England, Wales or Northern Ireland or such other person as has been agreed by the Lord Chief Justice and the Senior President of Tribunals.[23]

For cases commenced in the High Court, the transfer mechanism has been achieved by s.19 of the TCEA, introducing a new s.31A into the Senior Courts Act 1981. Where the first three conditions as those set out above under s.18 apply, the transfer is mandatory.[24] Following the enactment of s.22 of the Crime and Courts Act 2013, there is no longer any restriction on the type of immigration decision which may be transferred to the Upper Tribunal, providing it is the subject of a direction of the Lord Chief Justice.

10–020

Relevant judicial review directions

There are now a number of relevant directions affecting judicial review in the Upper Tribunal in England and Wales, which together have brought a number of different types of case within the jurisdiction of the Upper Tribunal. The judicial review categories for these purposes are as follows:

10–021

(1) Any decision of the First-tier Tribunal on an appeal made in the exercise of a right conferred by the Criminal Injuries Compensation Scheme in compliance with s.5(1) of the Criminal Injuries Compensation Act 1995[25];

(2) Any decision of the First-tier Tribunal (other than of the Immigration and Asylum Chamber) made under the Tribunal Procedure Rules or s.9 of the TCEA where there is no right of appeal to the Upper Tribunal and that decision is not an excluded decision within TCEA s.11(5)(b), (c) or (f)[26];

(3) Any decision under the Immigration Acts, under any instrument made under the Immigration Acts, or otherwise relating to leave to enter or remain in the UK[27];

(4) Any decision of the Immigration and Asylum Chamber of the First-tier Tribunal from which no appeal lies.[28]

In relation to categories (3) and (4), the direction sets out a number of exceptions, which include challenges to the validity of primary or secondary legislation, the lawfulness of detention, a decision concerning UKBA licensed sponsors, any decision as to citizenship, a decision on asylum support, and a decision of the Upper Tribunal or of the Special Immigration Appeals Commission.[29] The effect remains that the vast majority of immigration judicial review cases must now take place in the Upper Tribunal and are routinely heard in the Immigration and Asylum Chamber.

10–022

---

[22] TCEA s.18(6).

[23] TCEA s.18(8).

[24] Senior Courts Act 1981 s.31A(4)–(6).

[25] Practice Direction (Upper Tribunal: Judicial Review Jurisdiction) [2009] 1 WLR 327 at para.2.

[26] Practice Direction (Upper Tribunal: Judicial Review Jurisdiction) [2009] 1 WLR 327 at para.2.

[27] Practice Direction (Upper Tribunal: Judicial Review Jurisdiction), 21 August 2013, para.1(i).

[28] Practice Direction (Upper Tribunal: Judicial Review Jurisdiction), 21 August 2013, para.1(ii).

[29] Practice Direction (Upper Tribunal: Judicial Review Jurisdiction), 21 August 2013, para.3.

10–023   Pursuant to the power conferred by TCEA s.11(5)(f), secondary legislation has prescribed a series of types of decision against which there is no appeal to the Upper Tribunal.[30] Challenges to these decisions now also fall within the scope of the judicial review jurisdiction.

10–024   The directions do not have effect where an application seeks (whether or not alone) a declaration of incompatibility under s.4 of the Human Rights Act 1998.

10–025   Where an appeal is lodged against a decision which is excluded it will be treated as an application for judicial review instead.[31] However, any decision which is not expressly defined as excluded by s.11(5) can and should be appealed rather than judicially reviewed.[32]

Circumstances in which judicial review claims may be determined by the Upper Tribunal

10–026   In circumstances where the third condition set out in s.18(6) is not met (i.e. that there is no specification under a relevant direction) but the other conditions are met, the High Court has a discretion to transfer a judicial review application to the Upper Tribunal where it is just and convenient to do so.[33] There has been limited guidance on the scope of this discretion.

10–027   Relevant considerations may be whether the case calls for a factual determination more suited to the fact-finding experience of the Upper Tribunal—such as age assessment cases[34]—or where there is an existing case in the Upper Tribunal with which the judicial review could be joined.[35]

Effect of transfer of cases as between the High Court and the Upper Tribunal

10–028   Where a judicial review claim for permission has been transferred to the Upper Tribunal the effect of such transfer is that the Upper Tribunal has the function of deciding all subsequent applications and the substantive claim.[36] The claim is treated for all purposes as if it had been brought in the Upper Tribunal.[37] The transfer may occur before or after the grant of permission. Following transfer into the Upper Tribunal, the Upper Tribunal must give directions as to the future conduct of the hearing and notify the parties that the proceedings have been transferred.[38]

---

[30] Appeals (Excluded Decisions) Order 2009 (SI 2009/275).
[31] *Dorset Healthcare NHS Foundation Trust v MH* [2009] P.T.S.R. 1112.
[32] *LS v London Borough of Southwark (HB)* [2010] UKUT 461 (AAC).
[33] Senior Courts Act 1981 s.31A(3).
[34] Following *R. (FZ) v London Borough of Croydon* [2011] P.T.S.R. 748 age assessment cases are usually transferred to the Immigration and Asylum Chamber.
[35] *R. (Reed Personnel Services) v HM Revenue & Customs* [2009] EWHC 2250 (Admin); *R. (Independent Schools Council) v Charity Commission for England and Wales* [2010] EWHC 2604 (Admin).
[36] TCEA s.19(4).
[37] TCEA s.19(3).
[38] UT Rules r.27(1).

Where the Upper Tribunal lacks judicial review jurisdiction it is required to transfer the case to the High Court.[39] Where it does so, the application is treated for all purposes as if it had been made to the High Court.[40]   **10–029**

Grounds for seeking judicial review

The grounds for seeking judicial review in the Upper Tribunal are the same as for any judicial review claim in the Administrative Court. The Upper Tribunal must apply the same principles when considering the grant of relief.[41] It applies the judicial review principles with the same intensity that the Administrative Court would. By analogy, in *British Sky Broadcasting Group Plc v The Competition Commission*[42] the Competition Appeal Tribunal was reviewing a decision of the Competition Commission, in which circumstances it applied the same principles of judicial review as the High Court would.[43] It was argued that the CAT should apply those principles with a greater intensity than an ordinary court would because of the specialist nature of the CAT. The Court of Appeal rejected that argument. It was contrary to the clear wording of the statute; it was contrary to authority;[44] and it sought to engage the CAT in reassessing the weight accorded to the evidence and substituting its own judgment, contrary to the purpose of judicial review. There is no basis for applying any different approach in the Upper Tribunal given the very similar statutory wording.   **10–030**

Judicial review procedure in the Upper Tribunal

Procedure in judicial review cases in the Upper Tribunal is governed by Part 4 of the UT Rules. The procedure very closely matches that in the Administrative Court under CPR Part 54. However, the UT Rules use slightly different terminology to the CPR. They refer to an "application" rather than a "claim" and to "applicant" rather than "claimant". The public body is referred to as the "respondent" rather than the "defendant".   **10–031**

Pre-action protocol

As with all other judicial reviews, those taking place in the Upper Tribunal fall within the scope of the judicial review pre-action protocol set out in the CPR.[45] Parties should accordingly comply with it. However, where the judicial review is of the decision of the First-tier Tribunal it will not be necessary to comply as the First-tier Tribunal would not ordinarily be expected to participate in the proceedings.   **10–032**

---

[39] TCEA s.18(3).
[40] TCEA s.18(9).
[41] TCEA s.15(4)-(5).
[42] [2010] 2 All E.R. 907.
[43] By virtue of s.120 of the Enterprise Act 2002.
[44] *Office of Fair Trading v IBA Health Ltd* [2004] 4 All E.R. 1103 at [90]–[100].
[45] See para.9–004.

Application for permission

10–033   An application for judicial review of a decision must be given permission by the Upper Tribunal before it can proceed to a substantive hearing.[46]

Time limits

10–034   An application for permission must be made in writing to the Upper Tribunal and must be made promptly and in any event received by the Upper Tribunal within three months of the decision, act or omission to which the application relates.[47] This replicates the time limit for bringing a judicial review claim in the Administrative Court and is to be construed in the same way.

10–035   Where the challenge is to a decision of the First-tier Tribunal, the relevant time limit is one month from the date on which the lower Tribunal sent written reasons for its decision, or a notification that an application to set aside the decision was unsuccessful, even if that time is later than the three month limit.[48]

Form of application

10–036   The application must provide the name and address of the applicant, the respondent and any other person whom the applicant considers to be an interested party; the name and address of the applicant's representative (if any); an address where documents for the applicant may be sent or delivered; details of the decision challenged (including the date, the full reference and the identity of the decision maker); that the application is for permission to bring judicial review proceedings; the outcome that the applicant is seeking; the facts and grounds on which the applicant relies; a copy of any written record of the decision in the applicant's possession or control; and copies of any other documents in the applicant's possession or control on which the applicant intends to rely.[49] Any party to challenged proceedings not an applicant or respondent must be named as an interested party.[50] Documents may be filed with the Upper Tribunal by post, document exchange or fax.[51]

10–037   Where an application is made out of time it must include a request for an extension of time and the reason why the time limit has not been complied with. Unless the Upper Tribunal extends the time period in the exercise of its case management powers it must not admit the application.[52]

10–038   Except in immigration judicial reviews (i.e. judicial reviews allocated to the Immigration and Asylum Chamber), when the Upper Tribunal receives the application it must send a copy of the application and accompanying documents

---

[46] TCEA s.16(2); UT Rules r.28(1).

[47] UT Rules r.28(2).

[48] UT Rules r.28(3).

[49] UT Rules r.28(4), (6).

[50] UT Rules r.28(5).

[51] UT Rules r.13(1).

[52] UT Rules r.28(7). The Upper Tribunal has held that it will generally apply a less strict approach to time limits (particularly in the context of Tribunal orders or directions) than would apply under the CPR: *Leeds City Council v Revenue and Customs Commissioners* [2014] UKUT 350 (TCC).

to any other party.[53] This is a distinction from the Administrative Court, in which the claimant is required to serve the other parties himself. In immigration cases, it is for the applicant to serve the application and accompanying documents on each named respondent and interested party within nine days of making an accepted application, and he must provide the Upper Tribunal with a written statement of when and how this was done.[54] The application in immigration cases must not be accepted by the Upper Tribunal until the required fee is paid or an undertaking to pay the fee is accepted.[55]

The Upper Tribunal has a "Request for Urgent Consideration" form which may be used for judicial review applications which are urgent.

10–039

Acknowledgement of service

Any party wishing to take part in the permission proceedings must, on receipt of the documents sent by the Upper Tribunal, ensure that the Tribunal receives an acknowledgement of service within 21 days.[56] The acknowledgement of service must state whether permission is opposed or supported, the grounds for support or opposition, any other information which may assist the Tribunal, and the name and address of any person not named which the party considers may be an interested party to the proceedings.[57] An acknowledgement of service in immigration cases must also be provided to the applicant and to any other person named in the application or the acknowledgment of service within the same 21 days.[58]

10–040

If a party decides not to take part in the permission proceedings it need not supply an acknowledgement of service and this does not bar it from taking part in the substantive hearing if permission is granted.[59] A failure to serve the acknowledgement of service within the time limit is a failure which can be waived or time can be extended.[60]

10–041

The permission decision

Standing

The Upper Tribunal may not grant permission unless the applicant has a "sufficient interest" in the matter.[61] This is the same test of standing as in judicial review claims in the Administrative Court: see Chapter 11 below.

10–042

---

[53] UT Rules r.28(8).
[54] UT Rules r.28A(2).
[55] UT Rules r.28A(1).
[56] UT Rules r.29(1).
[57] UT Rules r.29(2).
[58] UT Rules r.29(2A).
[59] UT Rules r.29(3).
[60] UT Rules rr.7(2)(a) and 5(3)(a).
[61] TCEA s.16(3).

Test

10–043   Section 16(4)–(5) of the TCEA provides that permission may be refused where the Tribunal considers that there has been undue delay in making the application; or that granting the relief sought on the application would be likely to cause substantial hardship to, or substantially prejudice the rights of, any person or would be detrimental to good administration. The former essentially replicates the promptness requirement. The latter is essentially the same as s.31(6) of the Senior Courts Act 1981.

10–044   Applicants in the Upper Tribunal will also need to show that their claim is arguable. Although TCEA s.16 does not refer to that matter, the fact that arguability is part of the process of determining whether permission should be granted is reflected in r.8(3)(c) of the UT Rules which gives the Upper Tribunal power to strike out judicial review proceedings where the Tribunal considers that "there is no reasonable prospect" of the applicant's case, or part of it, succeeding. This mirrors the test set out in *Sharma v Brown-Antoine*,[62] although the terminology of striking out is not normally used in judicial review proceedings.

Procedure on permission decisions

10–045   The Upper Tribunal must send to all parties a written notice of its decision on permission, and the reasons for any refusal of permission or conditions applied to the grant of permission.[63] As in the Administrative Court, the decision is usually likely to have been taken on the papers only.

Renewal hearing

10–046   If the decision on the papers is to refuse permission, or to grant permission only on conditions, the applicant may apply to have that decision reconsidered at an oral hearing. Such an application must be made in writing and received by the Tribunal within 14 days of the date on which its written reasons were sent to the applicant.[64] In an immigration case, the application for an oral renewal hearing must be made within 9 days of the same date.[65]

10–047   In any immigration case, or in an application for which the Upper Tribunal has refused to extend time, the Upper Tribunal may certify the application as totally without merit. Where it does so, there is no right to request an oral renewal hearing.[66]

Procedure following the grant of permission

10–048   As in all proceedings in the courts and tribunals system, the UT Rules contain an overriding objective that cases be dealt with fairly and justly.[67]

---

[62] [2007] 1 WLR 780. See above 9-057.

[63] UT Rules r.30(1).

[64] UT Rules r.30(3)–(5).

[65] UT Rules r.30(5).

[66] UT Rules r.30(4A).

[67] UT Rules r.2(1).

The response

Where permission has been granted, any party notified of the grant of permission may provide detailed grounds in writing to the Upper Tribunal for supporting or contesting the substantive application, and may raise additional grounds not considered at the permission stage.[68] That response must be received by the Upper Tribunal within 35 days of date on which the notice of permission was sent.[69]

10–049

The hearing

The successful applicant may not rely at the substantive hearing on grounds other than those put forward in support of permission unless the Upper Tribunal has consented.[70]

10–050

Each party (and any other person with the Upper Tribunal's permission) may submit evidence, make representations at a hearing and make written representations where the case will be decided without a hearing.[71]

10–051

Where any hearing is held (either on permission or substantively) the Upper Tribunal must provide a minimum of 2 working days' notice.[72]

10–052

There is no requirement in relation to bundles of documents, and the UT Rules provide no equivalent to CPR PD54. Procedural requirements in the Immigration and Asylum Chamber have been set out in Immigration Judicial Review Practice Directions, as amended by the Senior President on 1 November 2013.

10–053

It is not uncommon for the Upper Tribunal, in the exercise of its appellate jurisdiction, to hear oral evidence. It is an experienced fact-finding body. As a result, it is far more likely than the Administrative Court to be willing to hear oral evidence in the course of a judicial review hearing. Indeed, the deliberate informality of the Tribunal structure means that it is not uncommon for the Upper Tribunal to ask to hear evidence from a person present without having seen witness statements or a formal application to do so.

10–054

The Upper Tribunal hearing the judicial review will usually be comprised of one judge, but cases of greater significance will be heard by a panel of three judges. A case which falls under TCEA s.18 must be heard by a High Court or Court of Appeal Judge.[73]

10–055

Remedies

The forms of remedy available and the principles applicable have been discussed above.[74]

10–056

---

[68] UT Rules r.31(1).
[69] UT Rules r.31(2).
[70] UT Rules r.32.
[71] UT Rules r.33.
[72] UT Rules r.36(2)(a).
[73] TCEA s.18(8).
[74] See para.10–013 above.

Costs

10–057 One significant potential area of difference between judicial review proceedings in the Upper Tribunal and in the Administrative Court is in relation to the award of costs. Ordinarily, the Upper Tribunal is a no-costs jurisdiction, with awards being made only where a party has acted unreasonably.[75] However, in addition to unreasonable conduct of the proceedings, a further express exception to the bar on making a costs order is in judicial review proceedings.[76] This provision might be thought to be an indication that costs in judicial review proceedings are likely to follow the event, and match the approach of the Administrative Court. The potential justification of principle for this is to avoid costs-led forum shopping, particularly where a party has had a case transferred into the Upper Tribunal, perhaps against their preference.

10–058 The award of costs in judicial review proceedings was the subject of detailed consideration in *R. (LR) v First-tier Tribunal (HESCC) & Hertfordshire CC*.[77] In that case, the Upper Tribunal was considering a judicial review of a decision of the First-tier Tribunal against which there was no right of appeal and which had been mandatorily transferred by the High Court. The Upper Tribunal held that there was no general principle in r.10 that costs should follow the event in judicial review proceedings in the Upper Tribunal. Instead, they held that where the judicial review was linked to the jurisdiction of the lower tribunal, it would not be appropriate to make an award of costs unless the First-tier Tribunal could have done so.[78] The Upper Tribunal should be generally wary of reading in principles from the CPR.[79] The Upper Tribunal expressly stated that it was not deciding that this approach was also appropriate for discretionary transfer cases, or categories of judicial review (principally in the Immigration and Asylum Chamber) which were not reviews of First-tier Tribunal decisions.[80] There are some indications that in those cases the Immigration and Asylum Chamber will take the conventional approach whereby the losing party pays the costs of the successful party.[81]

10–059 Any application for costs must be made in writing, although a simple sentence to that effect in the pleadings or skeleton should suffice, and the application must include a schedule of the costs claimed so that summary assessment can be made.[82] Detailed assessment is, however, available.[83] A costs application may not be made later than one month after the Upper Tribunal sends its decision or the withdrawal notice.[84] A paying person must have the opportunity to make

---

[75] UT Rules r.10(3)(d).

[76] UT Rules r.10(3)(a).

[77] [2013] UKUT 294 (AAC). The Upper Tribunal consisted of Sullivan LJ (the Senior President of Tribunals), UT Judge Ockleton and UT Judge Ward.

[78] *R. (LR) v First-tier Tribunal (HESCC) & Hertfordshire CC* [2013] UKUT 294 (AAC) at [25]–[26], [31]–[35].

[79] *R. (LR) v First-tier Tribunal (HESCC) & Hertfordshire CC* [2013] UKUT 294 (AAC) at [30].

[80] *R. (LR) v First-tier Tribunal (HESCC) & Hertfordshire CC* [2013] UKUT 294 (AAC) at [26], [34] and [36].

[81] *R. (ES) v London Borough of Hounslow* [2012] UKUT 138 (IAC).

[82] UT Rules r.10(5).

[83] UT Rules r.10(8)–(10).

[84] UT Rules r.10(6).

representations if costs are to be ordered, and any individual must have their financial circumstances considered by the Tribunal.[85]

Appeals

The refusal of permission to apply for judicial review may be appealed to the Court of Appeal.[86] Permission to appeal must be sought from the Upper Tribunal first,[87] following the provision of its written reasons,[88] and if refused may be sought from the Court of Appeal. In immigration cases, where a decision which disposes of proceedings is given at an oral hearing, permission to appeal must be determined at that oral hearing.[89] The time limit for making a written application for permission is one month from the date the reasons were sent,[90] or seven days where an immigration claim has been certified as totally without merit.[91]

10–060

When the Court of Appeal grants an application for permission to appeal against the Upper Tribunal's refusal of permission to apply, it has no jurisdiction at that stage to grant permission to apply but is required to proceed to hear the appeal against the refusal of such permission.[92] It has an inherent jurisdiction to stay the effects of decision being appealed pending the resolution of permission to appeal.[93]

10–061

An appeal against a substantive judicial review decision of the Upper Tribunal also lies to the Court of Appeal upon the grant of permission by either the Upper Tribunal or the Court of Appeal. The same procedure applies as set out in the preceding paragraph.

10–062

Permission to appeal to the Court of Appeal in England and Wales shall not be granted unless the Upper Tribunal or, where the Upper Tribunal refuses permission, the Court of Appeal, considers that (a) the proposed appeal would raise some important point of principle or practice; or (b) there is some other compelling reason for the relevant appellate court to hear the appeal.[94] The procedure applicable in the Court of Appeal has been discussed in Chapter 9.[95]

10–063

---

[85] UT Rules r.10(7).

[86] TCEA s.16(8).

[87] TCEA s.13(5).

[88] UT Rules r.44(4).

[89] UT Rules r.44(4A).

[90] UT Rules r.44(4). Where permission is refused by the Upper Tribunal, permission must be sought from the Court of Appeal within 28 days of the date on which the notice refusing permission was sent by the Upper Tribunal: CPR PD52D, para.3.3.

[91] UT Rules r.44(4C).

[92] R. (NB (Algeria)) v Secretary of State for the Home Department [2013] 1 W.L.R. 31. See CPR r.52.15(3).

[93] R. (NB (Algeria)) v Secretary of State for the Home Department [2013] 1 W.L.R. 31. This means that an application to the Court of Appeal for permission to appeal in an immigration deportation case may include an application for a stay of the removal directions as soon as the Upper Tribunal refuses permission to appeal.

[94] TCEA s.13(6) and the Appeals from the Upper Tribunal to the Court of Appeal Order 2008 (SI 2008/2834) art.2.

[95] See paras 9–146 to 9–151.

C. JUDICIAL REVIEW OF THE UPPER TRIBUNAL

The decision in *Cart* and amenability to judicial review

10–064 Following the establishment of the Upper Tribunal (and its designation in TCEA s.13(5) as a superior court of record) there was room for doubt as to whether or not a decision of the Upper Tribunal was amenable to judicial review at all. The Upper Tribunal was clearly intended to occupy a significant place in the legal hierarchy. However, it is the creation of statute, and importantly there is a statutorily defined category of decisions of the Upper Tribunal against which there is no right of appeal.[96] The most commonly encountered of these is where the Upper Tribunal refuses permission to appeal from the First-tier Tribunal.[97]

10–065 In *R. (Cart) v The Upper Tribunal* judicial review was sought of a refusal of permission to appeal against a social security decision of the (now) First-tier Tribunal. The Divisional Court rejected the argument that the designation of the Upper Tribunal as a superior court of record rendered it immune from judicial review and the absolutist position was not resurrected on appeal.[98] The Court of Appeal agreed with the Divisional Court that judicial review should be available only in circumscribed cases.[99] The Supreme Court unanimously dismissed the appeal, but for different reasons.[100] The leading judgment of the Supreme Court was given by Lady Hale, with whom the rest of their Lordships agreed. Rejecting the application of an unrestricted judicial review jurisdiction over all decisions in the Tribunal structure, and the application of an exceptional circumstances test limited to an excess of jurisdiction and denial of fundamental justice, the Supreme Court settled on the following approach. Where an application is made for judicial review of an Upper Tribunal decision the High Court should apply the criteria applicable to cases involving second appeals, namely that (a) the proposed case would raise some important point of principle or practice, or (b) there is some other compelling reason for the court to hear the case.[101] It was considered by the Court that this test was a proportionate and rational restriction on the availability of judicial review which nonetheless recognised the importance of correcting errors in the Tribunal's case load.[102] The exceptionality test would have been too narrow, and permitting judicial review without limitation would have led to the courts being swamped with applications in respect of a system designed to make the process easier, quicker and cheaper (especially in the light of its application to immigration and asylum cases). The suggestion was made by a number of their Lordships that the situation would be made clearer by an amendment to the CPR to remove the potential four stages of judicial review permission applications in these quasi-second appeal cases. As discussed below, those amendments have been enacted.

---

[96] TCEA s.13(8).
[97] TCEA s.13(8)(c).
[98] [2010] 2 W.L.R. 1012.
[99] [2011] Q.B. 120.
[100] [2012] 1 A.C. 663. The same analysis was adopted in the Scottish appeal dealing with the same issues: *Eba v Advocate General for Scotland* [2012] 1 A.C. 710.
[101] *R. (Cart) v The Upper Tribunal* [2012] 1 A.C. 663 at [57], [94], [104]–[105] and [129]–[133].
[102] *R. (Cart) v The Upper Tribunal* [2012] 1 A.C. 663 at [57].

The procedure for judicially reviewing the Upper Tribunal

A judicial review of a decision of the Upper Tribunal is governed by CPR Part 54 **10–066** in the ordinary way and is subject to the rules and principles discussed in Chapter 9. However, there is one important exception. Special provision for a judicial review of a refusal by the Upper Tribunal of permission to appeal has been introduced in CPR r.54.7A.[103] There are three differences of particular practical importance. First, the claim for judicial review must be filed no later than 16 days after the date on which notice of the Upper Tribunal's decision was sent.[104] Secondly, there is no right to request an oral renewal hearing where permission is refused on the papers.[105] This does not, of course, prevent the court holding an oral hearing to determine permission providing there has not already been a paper determination. Thirdly, the court will only give permission if it considers that there is an arguable case with a real prospect of success that both the refusal of permission to appeal and the underlying first instance decision were wrong in law, and that there is either an important point of principle or practice, or that there is some other compelling reason.[106] The grounds served by the claimant should expressly address how the test in r.54.7A(7) is met, by reference to the necessary documentation.[107]

A further difference from the ordinary procedure is that if permission to apply **10–067** for judicial review is granted the Court will quash the Upper Tribunal's refusal of permission to appeal without a further hearing, unless the Upper Tribunal or any interested party makes a request for a hearing of the substantive application within 14 days after service of the order granting permission.[108] This time limit can be extended, but this will not be permitted readily.[109]

The claimant must provide with the claim form the decision of the Upper **10–068** Tribunal which is under review, the grounds of appeal and accompanying documents before the Upper Tribunal, the decision of the First-tier Tribunal (including the application for permission to appeal and that Tribunal's reasons for refusal), and any other documents essential to the claim.[110] The claim form and the supporting documents must be served on the Upper Tribunal and any other interested party—which will always be the other party to the Tribunal proceedings—within seven days of issue.[111]

---

[103] Oddly, r.54.7A does not apply to any other excluded decision provided for in TCEA s.13(8). There can be no doubt that judicial review continues to lie in such cases, and it is probably the case that the procedural categories of excluded decision (such as a decision to set aside) will fall within the principle established in *Cart*, even if r.54.7A does not itself apply. It will be more open to argument whether the national security certificate cases in s.13(8)(a)–(b) should be dealt with differently.

[104] CPR r.54.7A(3). This time limit will be quite strictly applied: *R. (Sharma) v Upper Tribunal* [2012] EWHC 3930 (Admin).

[105] CPR r.54.7A(8).

[106] CPR r.54.7A(7).

[107] *R. (Khan) v Secretary of State for the Home Department* [2011] EWHC 2763 (Admin).

[108] CPR r.54.7A(9).

[109] *R. (Osayende) v Secretary of State for the Home Department* [2013] EWHC 3603 (Admin).

[110] CPR r.54.7A(4).

[111] CPR r.54.7A(5).

10–069 Any person, including the Upper Tribunal, who wishes to take part in the proceedings must file and serve on the applicant and any other party within 21 days of service of the claim form, an acknowledgement of service in the usual form.[112]

The permission test

10–070 The very restricted test for permission in these cases has been the subject of judicial consideration in *PR (Sri Lanka) v Secretary of State for the Home Department*.[113] The aspect of the rule which incorporates the second appeals criteria must be satisfied for permission to be granted; it is not sufficient for it to be arguably satisfied.[114] The second appeals criteria expressly sets a high threshold; it has been put as needing to "cry out" for consideration, or that the prospects of success are "very high".[115] A "compelling" reason must be legally compelling which justifies a third judicial consideration of the issue.[116] It is not sufficient that not granting permission will have dire consequences for the individual.[117] The exception might apply where the first decision was "perverse or otherwise plainly wrong", for example because inconsistent with authority of a higher court. Alternatively a procedural failure in the Upper Tribunal might make it "plainly unjust" to refuse a party a further appeal.[118] A difference of view as between the First-tier and Upper Tribunals is likely to be relevant, but not necessarily sufficient.[119]

10–071 Where the second appeals criteria was satisfied so that permission was granted, it need not be satisfied again at the substantive hearing in order to be granted relief.[120]

Appeals

10–072 Where permission is refused under r.54.7A, the claimant may apply to the Court of Appeal for permission to appeal the refusal, but that application will be determined on paper without an oral hearing.[121] Any such application must be made within seven days of the service of the order of the High Court refusing permission to apply for judicial review.[122] By virtue of CPR r.52.15(4), where the Court of Appeal gives permission to apply for judicial review, the case will proceed in the High Court unless otherwise ordered.

---

[112] CPR r.54.7A(6).

[113] [2012] 1 W.L.R. 73.

[114] *R. (HS) v Upper Tribunal (Immigration and Asylum Chamber)* [2013] Imm. A.R. 579; *R. (Nicholas) v Upper Tribunal (Administrative Appeals Chamber)* [2013] EWCA Civ 799.

[115] *PR (Sri Lanka) v Secretary of State for the Home Department* [2012] 1 W.L.R. 73 at [35].

[116] *PR (Sri Lanka) v Secretary of State for the Home Department* [2012] 1 W.L.R. 73 at [36].

[117] *JD (Congo) v Secretary of State for the Home Department* [2012] 1 W.L.R. 3273 at [27].

[118] *PR (Sri Lanka) v Secretary of State for the Home Department* [2012] 1 W.L.R. 73 at [35].

[119] *JD (Congo) v Secretary of State for the Home Department* [2012] 1 W.L.R. 3273 at [23].

[120] *R. (Essa) v Upper Tribunal* [2012] EWHC 1533 (Admin); [2012] 3 C.M.L.R. 26 at [3].

[121] CPR r.52.15(1A).

[122] CPR r.52.15(2).

CHAPTER 11

Standing

A. INTRODUCTION

An applicant for judicial review must demonstrate that he has standing to apply for judicial review. An applicant will have standing if he has a sufficient interest in the matter to which the claim for judicial review relates.[1] Section 31(3) of the Senior Courts Act 1981 provides that the court should not grant permission to make the application unless the applicant has a sufficient interest. This suggests that standing is a preliminary threshold question to be determined at the permission stage. The House of Lords has, however, held that the question of permission involves a two-stage process.[2] **11–001**

At the permission stage, the court is primarily concerned to exclude hopeless cases where the applicant has no private interest and is not bringing the claim in the public interest and is acting out of ill-will or for some improper purpose[3] or is no more than a "meddlesome busybody".[4] At the full hearing, the sufficiency of the applicant's interest will be assessed against the full legal and factual background to the application. Consideration of standing at this stage frequently merges into the question of the discretion to grant or refuse a remedy.[5] The court will be asking whether the claimant ought to be granted a particular remedy having regard to a number of factors including those relevant to the particular claimant, the merits of the challenge and the importance of the issue raised.[6] **11–002**

There has been "an increasingly liberal approach to standing on the part of the courts" over recent years.[7] This has manifested itself in recognising that individuals ought to be able to bring a genuine and serious issue of public law[8] **11–003**

---

[1] Senior Courts Act 1981, s.31(3). The CPR uses the term claimant and permission whereas the Senior Courts Act 1981 refers to applicants and leave. In this chapter, as elsewhere, the term claimants and permission are generally used as those terms are now in common usage.

[2] *R. v I.R.C. Ex p. National Federation of Self-Employed and Small Businesses Ltd* [1982] A.C. 617.

[3] *R. (Feakins) v Secretary of State for the Environment* [2014] 1 W.L.R. 1761 at [23]–[24]; Land Securities Plc v Fladgate Fielder [2010] Ch. 467 at [70].

[4] per Lord Donaldson M.R. in *R. v Monopolies and Mergers Commission Ex p. Argyll Group Plc* [1986] 1 W.L.R. 763 at 773.

[5] *R. v Secretary of State Ex p. Presvac Engineering Ltd* (1992) 4 Admin.L.Rep. 121.

[6] *R. v Secretary of State for Foreign and Commonwealth Affairs Ex p. World Development Movement Ltd* [1995] 1 W.L.R. 386 at 395G–H.

[7] [1995] 1 W.L.R. 763 per Rose LJ at 395E–F. Early cases, notably *R. v Secretary of State for the Environment Ex p. Rose Theatre Ltd* [1990] Q.B. 505, indicating a more restrictive attitude, no longer represent the modern approach and some at least of the propositions in the case do not represent the law.

[8] See, e.g. *R. v Secretary of State for Foreign and Commonwealth Affairs Ex p. Rees-Mogg* [1994] Q.B. 552 (applicant with a "sincere concern for constitutional issues") and see below at para.11–018.

before the courts and a recognition that representative bodies or pressure groups acting on behalf of their members or the wider public interest should also be recognised as having standing to seek judicial review in appropriate cases.[9]

11–004   The court will only have jurisdiction to grant relief at the substantive hearing if the claimant does have standing.[10] The parties concerned cannot waive the question of standing, and cannot confer jurisdiction on the court by agreeing to treat the claimant as having a sufficient interest. The court may require full argument if there is any doubt as to whether the claimant has standing.

B.   A UNIFORM TEST OF SUFFICIENT INTEREST

11–005   Prior to the introduction of the new procedure for judicial review in 1978, the individual remedies each had their own test for standing, and the tests were by no means clear.[11] The prerogative remedies of a quashing order and a prohibiting order were regarded as having the most liberal test for standing.[12] A mandatory order was regarded as having a stricter test. One line of authority restricted standing to those having a specific legal right which they wished to enforce,[13] although there were signs of a relaxation even before 1978.[14] Standing to seek a declaration or injunction was restricted to those who had a specific legal right or had suffered special damage over and above that suffered by the public in general.[15]

11–006   One of the main purposes of the reform of the judicial review procedure was to make all the individual remedies available in a single procedure. One consequence of this has been to introduce a single uniform test for standing for all the remedies. The speeches of the majority of the House of Lords in *R. v Inland Revenue Commissioners Ex p. National Federation of Self-Employed and Small Businesses Ltd*[16] favour the view that there is now a uniform test for standing to make a judicial review application. Since this decision, the courts have proceeded on the basis that the test for standing is the same whichever remedy is being sought. There has been some suggestion that a stricter test for mandatory orders may prevail.[17] The better view is that the test is in principle the same, but that the nature of the relief sought is one factor that is relevant to assessing whether the applicant has a sufficient interest.[18]

---

[9] *R. v Secretary of State for Foreign and Commonwealth Affairs Ex p. World Development Movement Ltd* [1995] 1 W.L.R. 386 and see below at para.11–024.

[10] *R. v Secretary of State for Social Services Ex p. Child Poverty Action Group* [1989] 3 W.L.R. 1116 and see *R. v Secretary of State for Foreign and Commonwealth Affairs Ex p. World Development Movement Ltd* [1995] 1 W.L.R. 385 at 395E.

[11] See, generally, Wade and Forsyth *Administrative Law* 11th edn.

[12] *R. v Thames Magistrates' Court Ex p. Greenbaum* (1957) 55 L.G.R. 129.

[13] Beginning with *R. v The Guardians of the Lewisham Union* [1897] 1 Q.B. 498.

[14] *R. v Commissioner of Police of the Metropolis Ex p. Blackburn* [1968] 2 Q.B. 118.

[15] *Boyce v Paddington BC* [1903] 1 Ch. 109, reaffd. in *Gouriet v Union of Post Office Workers* [1978] A.C. 435.

[16] [1982] A.C. 617.

[17] [1982] A.C. 617 at 631 per Lord Wilberforce.

[18] *R. v Felixstowe Justices Ex p. Leigh* [1987] Q.B. 582, at 597.

Test for standing at the permission stage

The purpose of the permission requirement is to filter out hopeless cases where **11–007** there is no realistic prospect of success. The test for standing at this stage reflects this purpose. Only where the applicant is a busybody, or a crank, or a mischief-maker,[19] or motivated by ill-will or some improper purpose[20] will it be appropriate to refuse permission to apply on the grounds of lack of standing. On one rare occasion a priest in the Church of England was held to be a busybody when he sought judicial review of the decision of the Church of Wales to ordain women priests.[21] He was not a member of that Church and had no connection with it. The claim was, however, unarguable for other reasons. A claimant who has a genuine interest in obtaining a remedy will not be a busybody even though he has no personal interest in the particular ground of challenge advanced. Thus in one case, a claimant who was a parish councillor with an active interest in local affairs, particularly planning, contended that a grant of planning permission was unlawful because the local planning authority had failed properly to consider the question of the provision of affordable housing. The Court of Appeal held that the fact that the claimant had no personal interest in the particular ground of challenge concerning the provision of affordable housing did not make her a busybody and did not debar her from advancing that ground of challenge to the planning permission.[22]

Test at the hearing – meaning of sufficient interest

Sufficient interest has to be assessed against the whole legal and factual context **11–008** of the claim. The issue is a mixed question of law and fact and is not purely a matter of discretion for the court.[23] In considering standing in any particular case[24]:

---

[19] *R. v I.R.C. Ex p. National Federation of Self-Employed and Small Businesses Ltd* (see above, fn.2). The Court of Appeal has suggested that the question of standing only deals with the threshold exercise and the issue at the substantive hearing is better seen as a question of the remedial discretion of the courts: *R. v Department of Transport Ex p. Presvac Engineering Ltd* (1991) 4 Admin. L.Rep. 121.

[20] *R. (Feakins) v Secretary of State for the Environment, Food and Rural Affairs* [2004] 1 W.L.R. 1761 at [23].

[21] *R. v Dean and Chapter of St Paul's Cathedral and The Church in Wales* [1996] C.O.D. 130. The claimant was in fact a vexatious litigant seeking permission to be allowed to make an application. The court considered that the test for granting permission there was the same as the test for granting permission to apply for judicial review.

[22] *R. (Kides) v South Cambridgeshire DC* [2003] 1 P. & C.R. 298 at [132]–[136] (reversing the decision of the High Court on this point at [2003] 1 P. & C.R. 41 at [109]).

[23] *R. v I.R.C. Ex p. National Federation of Self-Employed and Small Businesses Ltd.* [1982] A.C. 617. In Scotland, the courts consider the particular context to determine what is required for standing. In some contexts, it is appropriate to require a claimant to have a particular interest in the matter; in others, where the alleged abuse of power affects the public generally, a broad approach may be required: see *Axa General Insurance Ltd. v HM Advocate* [2012] 1 A.C. 868 at [169]–[172].

[24] per Lord Wilberforce in *R. v I.R.C. Ex p. National Federation of Self-Employed and Small Businesses Ltd* ([1982] A.C. at 630).

"... it will be necessary to consider the powers or duties in law of those against whom the relief is asked, the position of the applicant in relation to those powers or duties, and to the breach of those said to have been committed."

11–009 In addition, a number of other relevant factors can be identified from the case law. These include the merits of the challenge, the importance of vindicating the rule of law, the importance of the issue raised, the likely absence of any other challenger and the expertise of any representative body seeking judicial review.[25] The assessment of sufficient interest may be complicated further by the fact that more than one factor may be present in any case, and the court may not give any indication to the weight to be attached to a particular factor. Furthermore, standing is also sometimes assumed to exist without any discussion of the relevant factors. Assessing standing is not an entirely mechanical process. As well as the variables inherent in the wide variety of factual and legal matters that occur in public law, judicial attitudes and value judgments influence the issue of standing.

Scope of the statutory power or duty

11–010 The court must consider the scope of the statutory powers or duties to assess whether there are any express or implied indications as to whether the applicant is within the range of people entitled to challenge the exercise of the statutory power or to insist upon the performance of a duty.[26] In part, this entails looking at the legislative framework in order to determine the type of decision-making process that the court is dealing with. A description of the type of decision-making process will give some indication of the range of people affected. The decision-making mechanism may be primarily concerned with the taking of a decision in respect of a particular individual, based on the facts of that individual's case. In such circumstances, the recipient of the decision will invariably have standing. The issue is whether standing is limited to the recipient or whether other third parties have a sufficient interest in challenging the decision.

11–011 Other decisions may be directed at a particular individual but also affect a wider section of the public; the issue then is the range of other individuals or groups who may challenge the decision. The grant of planning permission, for example, is of concern not only to the grantee but also to owners of adjacent land, residents of the area, or others whose rival applications for planning permission for a particular site have been refused. Some decisions, such as a decision to close a school or a hospital, may affect a sector of the public rather than being aimed at an individual. A court is likely to accept that a responsible member of the public is entitled to seek judicial review for the benefit of the section of the public of which they are members.[27] At the other end of the spectrum there are normative

---

[25] *R. v Secretary of State for Foreign and Commonwealth Affairs Ex p. World Development Movement Ltd* [1995] 1 W.L.R. 386 at 395G–396 and *R. v Inspectorate of Pollution Ex p. Greenpeace Ltd (No.2)* [1994] 4 All E.R. 329 at 349–350.

[26] *R. v I.R.C. Ex p. National Federation of Self-Employed and Small Businesses Ltd* (see above, fn.2); *R. v Tower Hamlets LBC Ex p. Thrasyvalou* [1991] C.O.D. 123 (owners of hotels no standing to challenge the way in which local authorities performed their duties in relation to homeless persons).

[27] See dictum of Nolan LJ in *R. v Legal Aid Board Ex p. Bateman* [1992] 1 W.L.R. 711 at 718B.

or legislative measures which affect all citizens equally, rather than affecting any particular section. A decision to approve a supplementary budget for the EU is of interest to all taxpayers, and arguably all electors, and the Court of Appeal has held that any taxpayer may bring a challenge.[28]

There may be indications in the statute of the range of people who have an interest in ensuring that the statutory powers are properly exercised. The House of Lords has, for example, held that normally one taxpayer cannot challenge the tax assessment of another taxpayer.[29] In reaching this decision, the House was strongly influenced by the fact that tax assessments were confidential, and the facts were known only to the taxpayer concerned and the Inland Revenue. No other taxpayer had any right to inspect information on another taxpayer. All these factors suggested that a tax assessment was in normal circumstances a matter of concern to the Inland Revenue and the taxpayer only, and third parties were not intended to interfere in such matters. In another context, the Divisional Court has suggested (without deciding) that an order of a circuit judge requiring an individual to disclose information in connection with a crime is challengeable by that individual and not by the person actually suspected of the crime.[30] The statutory safeguards were primarily designed to protect the holder of the information, and he therefore had standing to ensure that the safeguards were observed by the court. The suspect could not seek a declaration simply in the hope that it might form the basis of an argument at any trial that the evidence had been improperly obtained. A person being deported may, however, challenge the directions given by the Home Secretary to an airline, since the directions were an integral part of the overall deportation machinery, and were not only of concern to the airline but were of concern to the person being deported.[31]

11–012

Nature of the claimant's interest

The nature of the claimant's interest in the matter is of great relevance to the question of standing. Individuals will invariably have standing to challenge decisions that are taken specifically in respect of them, and based on facts personal to them. Individuals will have standing to challenge the exercise of power directed at them whatever the nature of their interest. Individuals can therefore challenge decisions affecting their legal rights, legitimate expectations, or a refusal to confer some discretionary benefit upon them.

11–013

The difficulties arise in determining when one individual may challenge a decision taken in respect of another individual, or who may challenge a decision that affects the public generally or a sector of the public. Claimants no longer need to have a direct financial or legal interest, although the possession of such an interest will strengthen the claim for standing. Claimants who will be financially affected by the outcome of a case will usually have standing[32]:

11–014

---

[28] *R. v HM Treasury Ex p. Smedley* [1985] Q.B. 657 (Sir John Donaldson M.R. left the point open but was of the opinion that the applicant had standing).

[29] *R. v I.R.C. Ex p. National Federation of Self-Employed and Small Businesses Ltd* [1982] A.C. 617).

[30] *R. v Manchester Crown Court Ex p. Taylor* [1988] 1 W.L.R. 705.

[31] *R. v Immigration Officer Ex p. Shah* [1982] 1 W.L.R. 544.

[32] See, e.g. *R. v Secretary of State for Transport Ex p. Presvac Engineering Ltd* (1992) 4 Admin. L.R. 121 at 145E–F; *R. v Canterbury City Council Ex p. Springimage Ltd* (1993) 68 P. & C.R. 171 at 174.

(a) individuals have been allowed to challenge the grant of a licence[33] or a permit[34] to a commercial rival;

(b) an unsuccessful applicant for planning permission to develop a site has been allowed to challenge the decision to permit a rival applicant to develop the site[35] and the fact that grant of planning permission might affect the prospects of some other person obtaining permission or the prospects of the development being successful may generate standing[36];

(c) one taxpayer was allowed to challenge the decision of the Inland Revenue on the method of valuation of a rival company's profits, despite the rule that one taxpayer is not normally able to challenge another taxpayer's assessment[37]; the taxpayer was suing as a competitor whose particular interests would be affected by the valuation, as this would confer a competitive advantage on the other companies;

(d) in the context of contested take-over bids, one bidder has been allowed to challenge decisions of regulatory bodies in respect of rival bids by other companies[38];

(e) an unsecured creditor has standing to challenge a decision of the Companies' Registrar to register a charge at any time after the presentation of a winding-up petition[39];

(f) potential contractors with local authorities have been allowed to seek review to ensure statutory restrictions on clauses in the contract are observed[40];

(g) potential tenderers have been able to seek review of decisions removing them from the approved list of tenderers,[41] or decisions to sell land without giving them the opportunity to submit a bid.[42] A 1960s authority[43] holding that contractors did not have standing in this capacity, to seek mandamus to enforce local authority standing orders, probably no longer represents the law, and has been distinguished in subsequent cases.[44]

However, there are rare occasions when a financial interest will not be enough to grant standing. In one case, a claimant retained by a firm of solicitors to conduct a defence to a criminal charge was held not to have standing to apply for review of a decision of a taxing master on costs, even though they were obviously

---

[33] *R. v Thames Magistrates' Court Ex p. Greenbaum* (1957) 55 L.G.R. 129. See also *R. v Department of Transport Ex p. Presvac Engineering Ltd* (1992) 4 Admin. L.R. 121.

[34] *R. (Rockware Glass Ltd) v Chester City Council* [2007] Env. L.R. 3 (the court at first instance held that the claimant had standing: see [2006] A.C.D. 41. If the court has concerns that judicial review is being used to frustrate a competitor's approved development, then it may wish to subject the application to rigorous examination before granting permission to determine whether there is really an arguable case: see *R. (the Noble Organisation Ltd) v Thanet DC* [2006] 1 P & C.R. 197 at [68]).

[35] *R. v St Edmundsbury BC Ex p. Investors in Industry Commercial Properties* [1985] 1 W.L.R. 1157.

[36] *R. v Canterbury City Council Ex p. Springimage Ltd* (1993) 68 P & C.R. 171 at 175.

[37] *R. v Att-Gen Ex p. I.C.I. Plc* [1987] 1 C.M.L.R. 72.

[38] *R. v Monopolies and Mergers Commission Ex p. Argyll Group* [1986] 1 W.L.R. 763.

[39] *R. v Registrar of Companies Ex p. Central Bank of India* [1986] Q.B. 1114.

[40] *R. v Islington LBC Ex p. Building Employers Confederation* [1989] C.O.D. 432.

[41] *R. v Enfield LBC Ex p. T.F. Unwin (Roydon) Ltd* [1989] C.O.D. 466.

[42] *R. v Barnet LBC Ex p. Pardes House School Ltd* [1989] C.O.D. 512.

[43] *R. v Hereford Corp. Ex p. Harrower* [1970] 1 W.L.R. 1424.

[44] See, particularly, comments of Lord Diplock in *R. v I.R.C. Ex p. National Federation of Self-Employed and Small Business Ltd* (above, fn.2) at 640–641.

financially interested in the decision.[45] The court took the narrow view that, as the claimant had not been a party to the taxation proceedings, he did not have standing. Such decisions are rare, and a financial interest will usually generate standing.

Claimants who will be factually affected by a decision may have standing: **11–015**

(a)   parents and governors may challenge decisions to reorganise schools[46];

(b)   residents in a particular area,[47] or owners of adjacent land,[48] may challenge the grant of planning permission;

(c)   gypsies had standing to enforce a duty to provide adequate accommodation for gypsies[49];

(d)   the Divisional Court has held that a licence holder had standing to enforce the statutory duties owed by the Independent Broadcasting Authority.[50]

Non-material interests may also generate standing: spouses,[51] parents,[52] and   **11–016** siblings[53] of a deceased person have been allowed to seek review of decisions of a coroner's court. A person who had lived in an area for more than 30 years had a real and genuine interest in seeking to prevent development and had standing to challenge the grant of the planning permission authorising the development.[54] A person who refers a complaint to a disciplinary body has standing to challenge a decision of that body not to investigate or proceed with the complaint.[55]

Procedural entitlement as an indication of sufficient interest

Individuals who have a statutory or common law entitlement to make   **11–017** representations or objections during the course of a decision-making process will usually have standing. They must at the very least be allowed to seek judicial review to protect these procedural rights. In addition, the existence of such rights may indicate more generally that they have an interest in the decision. Those who have a legitimate expectation of consultation before a decision is taken will have standing to sue if that expectation is not fulfilled.[56] Parents, governors and probably teachers have a legitimate expectation of consultation before a decision is taken to reorganise schools, and will have standing on this basis to ensure that

---

[45] *R. v Shemilt (A Taxing Officer) Ex p. Buckley* [1988] C.O.D. 40.

[46] See, e.g. *R. v Kirklees Metropolitan BC Ex p. Molloy* (1987) 86 L.G.R. 115; *R. v Secretary of State for Education and Science and Bedfordshire CC Ex p. Threapleton* [1988] C.O.D. 102.

[47] *Covent Garden Community Association v Greater London Council* [1981] J.P.L. 183 and *R. (Kides) v South Cambridgeshire DC* [2003] 1 P. & C.R. 298 at [136].

[48] *R. v Monmouth DC Ex p. Jones* (1985) 53 P. & C.R. 108.

[49] *R. v Avon CC Ex p. Rexworthy* (1989) 21 H.L.R. 544; *R. v Secretary of State for the Environment Ex p. Ward* [1984] 1 W.L.R. 834.

[50] *R. v Independent Broadcasting Authority Ex p. Whitehouse, The Times,* April 14, 1984. The Court of Appeal did not find it necessary to decide the issue of standing; *The Times,* April 4, 1985.

[51] *R. v Greater Manchester North District Coroner Ex p. Worch and Brunner* [1988] Q.B. 513.

[52] *R. v East Sussex Coroner Ex p. Healy* [1989] 1 All E.R. 30.

[53] *R. v HM Coroner, sitting at Hammersmith Ex p. Peach* [1980] Q.B. 211.

[54] *R. (Kides) v South Cambridgeshire DC* [2003] 1 P. & C.R. 298 at [136].

[55] *R. v General Council of the Bar Ex p. Percival* [1990] 3 W.L.R. 323.

[56] *Council of Civil Service Unions v Minister for the Civil Service* [1985] A.C. 374. See also *Re Findlay* [1985] A.C. 318 at 338.

their objections are properly taken into account.[57] Claims may also be brought in the name of children who will be affected by the re-organisation provided that this is not done for the purpose of obtaining public funding or protection against a possible costs order.[58] Individuals or groups who are entitled or allowed to give evidence at a local inquiry may have standing to challenge the final decision.[59] Involvement in negotiations leading up to a decision may generate standing to challenge the legality of the final decision.[60] An individual cannot, however, acquire standing simply by making representations to a decision-maker where there is no entitlement or expectation to make representations, even if the decision-maker sends a considered reply.[61]

Public interest in challenge

11–018   A public spirited citizen may be allowed to seek judicial review where there is a serious issue of public importance which the court considers should be examined. The press have been described as the guardians and watch-dogs of the public interest in the proper administration of justice, and allowed to seek review of decisions of magistrates' courts and examining justices.[62] A journalist, therefore, had sufficient interest to seek a declaration that a policy of non-disclosure of the names of magistrates was unlawful although he had no standing to seek mandamus.[63] Journalists involved in broadcasting were allowed to challenge, albeit unsuccessfully, the ban imposed by the Home Secretary on broadcasting interviews with members or supporters of proscribed organisations.[64] A public-spirited taxpayer who raised a serious issue as to the powers to make an order in council, that would automatically lead to substantial expenditure by the government, was held to have standing.[65] Similarly, a citizen who had a "sincere concern for constitutional issues" was allowed to challenge the lawfulness of the ratification of the Treaty of EU.[66] No objection was taken to the standing of an activist opposed to the use of troops in Afghanistan in a challenge to the policy and practice governing the transfer of suspected insurgents to the Afghan

---

[57]   See, e.g. *R. v Gwent CC and the Secretary of State for Wales Ex p. Bryant* [1988] C.O.D. 19.

[58]   *R. (Boulton) v Leeds School Organisation Committee* [2003] E.L.R. 67 (clear evidence of abuse would be required). The position is in relation to challenges on appeals against decisions on school admissions is different as the right of appeal is conferred on parents not the child and it would be an abuse to bring proceedings in the name of the child: *R. v Richmond LBC* [2001] E.L.R. 21.

[59]   *R. v Hammersmith and Fulham LBCs Ex p. People before Profit* (1983) 45 P. & C.R. 364; *R. v Secretary of State for Transport Ex p. Gwent CC* [1988] Q.B. 429.

[60]   *R. v Att-Gen Ex p. I.C.I. Plc* [1987] 1 C.M.L.R. 72.

[61]   *R. v Secretary of State for the Environment Ex p. Rose Theatre Trust Co.* [1995] 1 W.L.R. 763.

[62]   *R. v Felixstowe Justices Ex p. Leigh* [1987] Q.B. 582, per Watkin LJ at 598.

[63]   [1987] Q.B. 582, per Watkin LJ at 598 (no sufficient interest for mandamus to order disclosure of name in a specific case, as the journalist had no interest or connection with that case). See also *R. v Horsham Justices Ex p. Farquharson and West Sussex County Times* [1982] Q.B. 762; *R. v Malvern Justices Ex p. Evans* [1988] Q.B. 540.

[64]   *R. v Secretary of State for the Home Department Ex p. Brind* [1991] 2 W.L.R. 588.

[65]   *R. v HM Treasury Ex p. Smedley* [1985] Q.B. 657.

[66]   *R. v Secretary of State for Foreign and Commonwealth Affairs Ex p. Rees Mogg* [1995] 1 W.L.R. 386. [1995] 1 W.L.R. 386. See also *R. v Somerset CC Ex p. ARC Southern Ltd, ex p. Dixon* [1997] C.O.D. 323 at 326–331.

authorities.[67] The courts have also allowed a wide range of representative and campaigning groups to bring challenges.[68]

There has been a generally liberal attitude towards standing. Providing a good case on the merits could be made out, the courts are unlikely to deny relief solely on the ground of standing. Woolf J. once said that: "... it would be regrettable if a court had to come to the conclusion that in a situation where the need for the intervention of the Court has been established this intervention was prevented by rules as to standing."[69]

11–019

Representative bodies

Some groups act in a representative capacity, taking action on behalf of their members, or to protect their members' interests. They will have standing to seek judicial review if an individual member would have had sufficient interest to make a challenge to a decision. They will also have standing where a decision or measure affects the general interests of their members.

11–020

There are numerous examples of such cases. The Royal College of Nursing, which represented the interest of nurses, had standing to challenge the legality of a circular advising that it was lawful for nurses to do certain acts in connection with abortion.[70] Two of the largest trade unions sought judicial review to challenge the regulations dealing with consultation on redundancies and transfers of undertakings on the grounds that they failed to comply with the relevant EU directives.[71] A trade union brought judicial review proceedings to challenge the lawfulness of the introduction of fees for bringing certain claims in employment tribunals.[72] Representative associations of road haulage contractors were allowed to challenge an order requiring the fitting of silencers to lorries.[73] The Building Employers Federation have been allowed to challenge the inclusion of certain clauses in draft contracts prepared by a local authority.[74] A representative of a street traders association has been allowed to challenge a decision to charge fees for street traders' licences.[75] The Association of British Civilian Internees Far East Region, which represented a substantial number of individuals and their spouses who were interned during the war, challenged a refusal of the Secretary of State to make compensation payments to certain classes of internees.[76]

11–021

The representative groups do not need to be representing a commercial interest. The British Parachute Association has been allowed to seek review of a recommendation made by a jury in a coroner's court about the sport of

11–022

---

[67] R. (Evans) v Secretary of State for Defence [2010] EWHC 1445 (Admin).
[68] See below paras 11–020 to 11–026.
[69] In R. v Att-Gen Ex p. I.C.I. Plc [1985] 1 C.M.L.R. 588 at 618.
[70] Royal College of Nursing of the United Kingdom v Department of Health and Social Security [1981] A.C. 800; standing was discussed in detail by Woolf J. in [1981] All E.R. 545.
[71] R. v Secretary of State for Trade and Industry Ex p. Unison [1996] I.C.R. 1003 (the claimants lost on the merits).
[72] R. (Unison) v Lord Chancellor (Equality and Human Rights Commission intervening) [2014] I.C.R. 498.
[73] R. v London Boroughs Transport Committee Ex p. Freight Transport Association, The Times, July 25, 1991 (the claimants finally lost on the merits in the House of Lords).
[74] R. v Islington LBC Ex p. Building Employers Confederation (see above, fn.36).
[75] R. v Manchester City Council Ex p King [1991] C.O.D. 422.
[76] R. v (ACBIFER) v Secretary of State for Defence [2003] 3 W.L.R. 81 at [1].

parachuting.[77] The president of a Jewish Burial Society challenged a decision of a coroner's court which had implications for the way in which Jewish burials would be carried out.[78]

11–023   There must be a sufficiently close nexus between the body seeking judicial review, the people whom it represents, and the subject matter of the dispute. The National Union of Mineworkers had standing to challenge instructions to reduce supplementary benefits to striking miners during an industrial dispute.[79] The Trade Union Congress, however, did not have standing, as it had no sufficiently close nexus with striking miners.[80]

Public interest groups

11–024   Public interest groups may be set up to represent particular interest groups in society, or to campaign on a particular issue. The courts have traditionally adopted a liberal attitude to standing on the part of such groups. They have held that a responsible public interest group may have standing to seek an appropriate remedy in relation to measures affecting the activities or the interests that they represent. The courts have had regard to a number of factors in deciding that a public interest group ought to be recognised as having standing. The issue came to the fore when the World Development Movement Ltd challenged the lawfulness of a decision to grant overseas aid to fund the building of a dam. The applicant was a company limited by guarantee; it was a non-partisan pressure group which had existed for 20 years and received financial support from a wide variety of development charities, churches and other bodies. It had a UK membership of 13,000. It was particularly concerned with issues of development aid. The Divisional Court held that it did have standing.[81] They identified a number of factors relevant to standing in this context. These included the merits of the challenge as the real issue was whether the applicant could demonstrate a real abuse of power which required judicial intervention to vindicate the rule of law rather than the need to demonstrate that the applicant's personal rights or interests were involved.[82] In addition, the importance of vindicating the rule of law, the importance of the issue raised, the likely absence of any other responsible challenger, the nature of the breach and the prominent role paid by the body in respect of the issue in question were all factors relevant to standing.[83]

11–025   There is little doubt that a nationally or internationally recognised body with accepted expertise in an area will have standing to challenge decisions taken in that area. The courts have accepted, for example, that the environmental group, Greenpeace, has standing in respect of environmental issues, commenting on its international reputation, large membership, and the fact that it was a responsible body with a genuine concern for the environment.[84] The court considered it

---

[77] *R. v Shrewsbury Coroners Court Ex p. British Parachute Association* (1988) 152 J.P. 123.

[78] *R. v Greater Manchester North District Coroner Ex p. Worch and Brunner* (see above, fn.49).

[79] *R. v Chief Adjudication Officer Ex p. Bland, The Times,* February 6, 1985, D.C.

[80] *Ex p. Bland, The Times,* February 6, 1985, D.C.

[81] *R. v Secretary of State for Foreign and Commonwealth Affairs Ex p. World Development Movement Ltd* above, fn.9.

[82] See above, fn.9 at 395F–H.

[83] See above, fn.9 at 395G–H.

[84] *R. v Inspectorate of Pollution Ex p. Greenpeace Ltd (No.2)* [1994] 4 All E.R. 329 at 349–350e.

would be assisted if a challenge were brought by Greenpeace rather than an individual simply because Greenpeace would be likely to have greater resources and expertise available.[85] The court have accepted that the World Development Movement Ltd should have standing to challenge the lawfulness of the grant of overseas aid because of its national and international expertise and interest in overseas aid.[86] Well-known and established public interest groups have brought challenges in respect of measures taken in their particular areas, including Shelter[87] in relation to housing and the Child Poverty Action Group and National Association of Citizen's Advice Bureaux[88] in relation to social security, the Howard League for Penal Reform in relation to prisons[89] and Corner House Research in relation to bribery and corruption in international trade.[90] The Court of Appeal pointed out that those bodies played a prominent role in the field of social welfare in giving advice, guidance and assistance. Other interest groups may be less well-known or operate in a localised area rather than on a national scale. Again, the courts are likely to accept that they have standing. A non-governmental organisation based abroad and concerned with the protection of the rights of Roma[91] was able to bring a claim for judicial review. The League of Friends of a local hospital, for example, has been allowed to challenge a decision to close a hospital.[92]

There may be situations where a pressure group is formed to campaign on one particular issue. The likelihood is that the courts will accept that such a body has standing, both to bring proceedings and obtain an appropriate remedy if it is able to establish that some action is unlawful. The courts have allowed single interest pressure groups to proceed, at least where the body is incorporated or the proceedings are brought in the name of a member or officer.[93] Examples have occurred in the planning field, where pressure groups have been formed to oppose a particular development[94] or where a local action group opposed the

11–026

---

[85] [1994] 4 All E.R. 329 at 350e–j.

[86] *R. v Secretary of State for Foreign and Commonwealth Affairs Ex p. World Development Movement Ltd* [1995] 1 W.L.R. 386 at 396B–C.

[87] See, e.g. *R. v Secretary of State for the Environment Ex p. Shelter* [1997] C.O.D. 49.

[88] *R. v Secretary of State for Social Services Ex p. Child Poverty Action Group* [1989] 3 W.L.R. 1116.

[89] *R. (Howard League for Prison Reform) v Secretary of State for the Home Department* [2003] 1 F.L.R. 484.

[90] See, e.g. *R. (Corner House Research) v Director of the Serious Fraud Office* [2008] 3 W.L.R. 568. The interest and expertise of Corner House Research is described in *R. (Corner House Research) v Secretary of State for Trade and Industry* [2005] 1 W.L.R. 2600 at [90] and [91].

[91] *R. (European Roma Rights Centre) v Prague Immigration Officers* [2005] 2 A.C. 1.

[92] *R. v Shropshire Health Authority Ex p. Duffus* [1990] C.O.D. 131.

[93] *R. (Quintavalle) v Human Fertilisation and Embryology Authority* [2005] 2 A.C. 561 at [8]; *R. (Quintavalle) v Human Fertilisation and Embryology Authority* [2003] 3 W.L.R. 878 at [1] (claim brought on behalf of a group whose purpose was to focus and facilitate debate on ethical issues arising from human reproduction); *R. (Quintavalle) v Secretary of State for Health* [2003] 2 W.L.R. 692 (claim brought on behalf of pro-life alliance). See below at para.11–039 as to whether an unincorporated association has capacity to bring proceedings.

[94] *R. v Hammersmith and Fulham LBC Ex p. People before Profit* (1983) 45 P. & C.R. 364 (unincorporated association formed to oppose a particular development and which gave evidence at a local inquiry had standing).

demolition of listed buildings[95]. At one stage, the decision in the *Rose Theatre* case[96] indicated that the courts might be about to take a more restrictive view of standing. There, a company formed to protect the remains of the Rose Theatre, and representing archaeologists, artists and politicians, applied for judicial review of a decision not to schedule the remains as a national monument. The court found that a pressure group could have no greater interest than its individual members and no individual citizen had standing to seek review of the decision. The courts have not followed this restrictive approach.[97] They recognise both that individual citizens acting out of a genuine public concern may have standing and have also held that pressure groups, even groups formed for one single purpose, may have standing in appropriate circumstances.[98] A company formed by residents concerned about environmental matters in their area[99] has been held to have standing, as has a company formed by parents concerned about proposed school reorganisations[100] and a company created to challenge proposed changes to national health services and funded by public contibutions.[101] If there is concern that the use of a company may be a means of limiting or avoiding liability to costs, the appropriate course of action is to require security for costs.[102]

Standing under the Human Rights Act 1998

11–027   The one area where a restrictive test of standing now exists is in relation to the Human Rights Act 1998. It is unlawful for a public authority to act in a way that is incompatible with certain rights derived from the European Convention of Human Rights.[103] Section 7(3) of the Human Rights Act 1998 specifically provides, however, that a person is only to be taken to have sufficient interest for the purposes of seeking judicial review of an unlawful act if he is, or would be, a victim of the unlawful act applying the test set out in the case law of the European Court of Human Rights.[104] A victim for Convention purposes will be a natural or legal person directly affected by the act or omission which is said to

---

[95] *R. v Stroud DC Ex p. Goodenough* (1982) 43 P. & C.R. 59; see also *Covent Garden Community Association v Greater London Council* [1981] J.P.L. 183. In *R. v Westminster City Council Ex p. Monahan* [1989] 3 W.L.R. 408 an application was brought by two members on behalf of the association.

[96] *R. v Secretary of State for the Environment Ex p. Rose Theatre Trust Co.* [1990] 1 Q.B. 504; and see Lewis, "Standing and Judicial Review" [1990] C.L.J. 189 and see Schiemann J., writing extra-judicially on his decision, in "Locus Standi" [1990] P.L. 42.

[97] See *Ex p. World Development Movement Ltd* above, fn.9 and cases discussed there. The courts expressly declined to follow the Rose Theatre case in *R. v HM Inspectorate of Pollution Ex p. Greenpeace (No.2)* above fn.84 at 351g–h; *R. v Somerset CC Ex p. Dixon* [1997] C.O.D. 323 at 327.

[98] See, e.g. *R. v Secretary of State for the Environment Ex p. Kirkstall Valley Campaign Ltd* [1996] 3 All E.R. 304 at 308–309 (court satisfied that company incorporated to raise and hold funds and not for the purpose of escaping the impact of a costs order).

[99] See, e.g. *R. (Residents Against Waste Limited) v Lancashire CC* [2008] Env. L.R. 27; *R. v Leicestershire CC ex p. Blackfordby and Boothorpe Action Group Ltd* [2001] Env. L.R. 35.

[100] *R. (Parents for Legal Action Ltd.) v Northumberland CC* [2006] E.L.R. 397.

[101] *R. (Save our Surgeries Ltd.) v Joint Committee of Primary Care Trusts* [2013] EWHC 439 (Admin) (company created for purposes of bringing a challenge and funded by public contributions).

[102] *R. (Residents Against Waste Limited) v Lancashire CC* [2008] Env. L.R. 27 at [19]–[22].

[103] Human Rights Act 1998 s.6(1).

[104] See *R. (Hooper) v Secretary of State for Work and Pensions* [2003] 1 W.L.R. 2623 at [29].

give rise to a breach of a Convention right.[105] This requirement prevents public spirited citizens or representative groups from challenging the compatibility of actions of public authorities with the rights derived from the European Convention of Human Rights and seeking to obtain declarations that legislation is incompatible with the Convention. The likelihood is, however, that public interest groups will support individuals who are victims in making claims. Public interest groups are likely to have greater expertise and greater resources than most individuals and their support for a claimant may be necessary and beneficial. A claimant for a declaration under s.4 of the Human Rights Act 1998 that provisions of primary legislation are incompatible does not have to establish that he is a victim,[106] although the court may well refuse a declaration as a matter of discretion if he is not adversely affected by the provisions in question.[107]

Challenges to local authority decisions

Courts have in the past regarded ratepayers (now council taxpayers) as having standing to challenge local authority decisions. Ratepayers have been allowed to challenge their own rating assessment and the rating assessment of others,[108] and also the level of the rates.[109] The justification for this is that ratepayers, unlike taxpayers, have access to information on the assessment of others, and that the income from rates goes into a common fund applicable for the benefit of the ratepayers.[110] Local authorities also owe ratepayers a fiduciary duty in respect of income from rates.[111] **11–028**

Ratepayers have also had standing to challenge decisions of local authorities which have financial implications for local authority expenditure, such as a decision to offer subsidised transport for certain groups.[112] The courts have also allowed ratepayers to challenge the exercise of statutory power by a local authority, even where there is no direct financial implication for the authority concerned. Thus, the court has referred to the fact that the applicant is a ratepayer when allowing a challenge to an authority's approach to licensing films[113] or proposals to reorganise schools[114] and even on one occasion to a decision to grant planning permission.[115] **11–029**

It is not only ratepayers who seek to challenge local authority decisions. On two occasions, the leader of a local authority was held to have standing to challenge a decision of the authority to allocate housing to a particular **11–030**

---

[105] See *Corigliano v Italy* (1983) 5 E.H.R.R. 334 at [31].
[106] *R. (Rusbridger) v Att.-Gen.* [2004] 1 A.C. 357.
[107] *Lancashire CC v Taylor* [2005] 1 W.L.R. 2668 at [37]–[44]; *R (Chester) v Secretary of State for Justice* [2014] 2 A.C. 271 at [102] and [111].
[108] *R. v Paddington Valuation Officer Ex p. Peachey Property Corp. (No.2)* [1966] 1 Q.B. 380.
[109] *R. v Waltham Forest LBC Ex p. Baxter* [1988] Q.B. 419.
[110] See *Arsenal Football Club v Ende* [1979] A.C. 1, and discussion in *R. v I.R.C. Ex p. National Federation of Self-Employed and Small Business Ltd* (see above, fn.2).
[111] *Bromley LBC v Greater London Council* [1983] 1 A.C. 768.
[112] *Prescott v Birmingham Corp.* [1955] Ch. 210.
[113] *R. v Greater London Council Ex p. Blackburn* [1976] 1 W.L.R. 550.
[114] *Lee v Enfield LBC* (1967) 66 L.G.R. 195 (applicant also a parent).
[115] *Steeples v Derbyshire CC* [1985] 1 W.L.R. 256 (applicant also owned adjacent land); *R. v Sevenoaks DC Ex p. Terry (W.J.)* [1985] 3 All E.R. 226 (applicant also traded from property that was encompassed by the planning permission).

individual.[116] Individual councillors have challenged decisions refusing them access to council documents.[117] It is likely that a councillor would have sufficient interest to challenge any decision of his authority that he considered to be unlawful, although the issue has not yet been decided by the courts.

11–031   Individuals may be affected by specific decisions of the local authority. They may have sufficient interest to challenge a specific decision as a result of the impact of that decision on their interests. A resident of an old people's home[118] and of a housing estate[119] had standing to challenge a decision to sell the property. Tenants have standing to challenge decisions to raise council rents.[120] The position of contractors has been discussed above.

Challenges by public bodies

11–032   There are occasions when the applicant is a public body seeking to challenge the decision of another public body. A public body will usually have a sufficient interest, where the decision under attack affects the way in which they perform their functions. The police have used judicial review to establish their rights to give evidence at a hearing to determine whether to release a detained child.[121] The Director of Public Prosecutions has sought judicial review to establish the appropriate procedure in magistrates' courts[122] or to challenge the refusal of courts to grant orders which the police seek to assist them in their investigations.[123] The Home Secretary has sought review of court decisions in connection with extradition[124] or the production of evidence to assist foreign investigating authorities.[125] The House of Lords has held that the former Equal Opportunities Commission had standing to seek judicial review of the compatibility of provisions of domestic law with the EU law on equal pay and sex discrimination.[126] The Equal Opportunities Commission had a statutory duty to work towards the elimination of discrimination and to promote equality of opportunity. As such, it had standing to bring judicial review proceedings related to sex discrimination. Similarly, the Secretary of State for the Environment had standing to challenge a decision of a local authority to set the community charge at a particular level. Although not directly affected by the decision, the Secretary

---

[116] *R. v Port Talbot BC Ex p. Jones* [1988] 2 All E.R. 207; *R. v Bassetlaw DC Ex p. Oxby*, *The Times*, December 11, 1997.

[117] *R. v Birmingham City DC Ex p. O.* [1983] 1 A.C. 578.

[118] *R. v Bradford Metropolitan City Council Ex p. Wilson* [1989] 3 All E.R. 140.

[119] *R. v Hammersmith and Fulham LBC Ex p. Beddowes* [1987] Q.B. 1050.

[120] *R. v Bradford Metropolitan City Council Ex p. Corris* [1989] 3 All E.R. 156 (standing to challenge resolutions other than that relating to rent not decided).

[121] *R. v Bristol Justice Ex p. Broome* [1987] 1 W.L.R. 352.

[122] *R. v Watford Magistrates' Court Ex p. DPP* [1989] C.O.D. 477.

[123] *R. v Snaresbrook Crown Court Ex p. DPP* [1988] Q.B. 532.

[124] *R. v Chief Metropolitan Stipendiary Magistrate Ex p. Secretary of State for the Home Department* [1988] 1 W.L.R. 1204.

[125] *R. (Secretary of State for the Home Department) v Crown Court at Southwark* [2014] 1 W.L.R. 2529.

[126] *R. v Secretary of State for Employment Ex p. Equal Opportunities Commission* [1995] 1 A.C. 1 at 26A–E. See also *R. v Birmingham City Council Ex p. Equal Opportunities Commission* [1989] A.C. 1155 (standing to challenge policy of council in relation to the provision of grammar school places for boys and girls).

of State had many specific statutory duties under the relevant legislation and had a legitimate interest in ensuring that the local authority was acting lawfully.[127]

Challenges by local authorities

Local authorities have statutory power to initiate proceedings, including judicial review, where they " . . . consider it expedient for the promotion or protection of the interests of the inhabitants of their area".[128] Applications for judicial review by local authorities are subject to two hurdles. First, the exercise of this power is itself subject to judicial review and a decision to apply for judicial review may be quashed if, for example, the local authority takes irrelevant considerations into account or acts unreasonably.[129] Secondly, a local authority also has to demonstrate that it has sufficient interest to bring the proceedings.[130]   **11–033**

Local authorities may have a direct financial or other interest in the decision, and would have a sufficient interest on normal principles. One local authority could challenge a precept issued to it by another local authority,[131] or could challenge an expenditure decision of a precepting authority which they might be called upon to finance in part.[132] A local authority has standing to challenge decisions of other authorities where these decisions may have financial consequences for the local authority. For example, local authorities had standing to challenge decisions of central government affecting their income.[133]   **11–034**

Local authorities have also acted to protect local interests and the interests of their inhabitants. Local authorities have, for example, sought judicial review of recommendations that local hospital services be reconfigured[134] and of the decision of the Director General of Water Services, challenging the lawfulness of his decision not to prohibit the use of pre-payment devices for water, which automatically cut off the supply to domestic premises if charges had not been paid.[135] Local authorities in the vicinity of the Severn Bridge sought judicial review of a decision to increase the tolls payable, since this might affect the local economy.[136] On one occasion Woolf J. held that the Greater London Council did not have sufficient interest to challenge social security regulations, as it owed no special responsibility to such claimants and would not be affected by the outcome of the judicial review.[137] The Court of Appeal left the question open and held that the claim failed on its merits.[138] On a later occasion, the Court of Appeal did hold   **11–035**

---

[127] *R. v London Borough of Haringey Ex p. Secretary of State for the Environment* [1991] C.O.D. 135.

[128] Local Government Act 1972 s.222.

[129] Such a challenge must be made by way of judicial review and cannot be raised as a defence to the proceedings: *Avon CC v Buscott* [1988] Q.B. 656.

[130] *R. v Secretary of State for Social Services Ex p. Child Poverty Action Group*, July 30, 1984, unreported. The point was not decided in the Court of Appeal, *The Times*, August 8, 1985.

[131] *Bromley LBC v Greater London Council* (see above, fn.91).

[132] *R. v Inner London Education Authority Ex p. Westminster City Council* [1986] 1 W.L.R. 28.

[133] See, e.g. *R. v Secretary of State for the Environment Ex p. Nottinghamshire CC* [1986] A.C. 240.

[134] *R. (Lewisham LBC) v Secretary of State for Health* [2014] 1 W.L.R. 514.

[135] *R. v Director General of Water Services Ex p. Oldham Metropolitan BC* (1998) 96 L.G.R. 396.

[136] *R. v Secretary of State for Transport Ex p. Gwent CC* [1988] Q.B. 429.

[137] *R. v Secretary of State for Social Services Ex p. Child Poverty Action Group* (see above, fn.10).

[138] *R. v Secretary of State for Social Services Ex p. Child Poverty Action Group and G.L.C.*, *The Times*, August 8, 1985.

that two London Borough councils had standing to challenge social security regulations since they had claimants living in their area.[139]

Nature of the breach

11–036   Even if a claimant would not have standing on normal principles, there is the possibility that the courts may still grant the applicant standing if the breach or violation of public law principles is sufficiently grave to merit judicial intervention. This possibility was expressly left open by three of their Lordships in *R. v Inland Revenue Commissioners Ex p. National Federation of Self-Employed and Small Business Ltd*[140] who, having ruled that one taxpayer would not normally have standing to seek review of another taxpayer's assessment, left open the possibility that a challenge might be allowed in a case of sufficient gravity. The precise degree of illegality needed to attract judicial intervention was variously expressed. Lord Fraser talked of " ... some exceptionally grave or widespread illegality ..."[141] Lord Roskill of " ... a most extreme case ... " where there had been a failure to act due to " ... some grossly improper pressure or motive ... "[142] and Lord Wilberforce of a case of " ... sufficient gravity ... ".[143]

11–037   Arguments addressed to the seriousness of the breach have not featured in subsequent cases. The intention of the House of Lords seemed to have been to leave open the possibility of intervention in extreme cases,[144] where the individual would not normally have standing but the abuse of power was so unacceptable as to merit judicial intervention. It is difficult in principle to justify a distinction between different levels of legality, and difficult in practice to predict when the courts might utilise this reasoning.

C.   EFFECT OF A FINDING OF NO SUFFICIENT INTEREST

11–038   The implication of s.31(3) Senior Court Acts 1981 is that standing is to be decided at the permission stage. The House of Lords has decided that standing involved a two-stage test, with standing primarily being decided at the substantive hearing alongside the merits of the claim. The question arises as to the effect of a finding at the hearing that the claimant has no sufficient interest. The ruling might operate as a refusal of permission so that the proper method of challenging the refusal would be by seeking permission to appeal against the refusal of permission to the Court of Appeal within seven days of the decision.[145] Alternatively, the finding of no sufficient interest at the hearing might operate as a refusal to grant a remedy as a matter of the courts' discretion in relation to

---

[139] *R. v Secretary of State for Social Services Ex p. Child Poverty Action Group* [1989] 3 W.L.R. 1116.
[140] [1982] A.C. 617.
[141] [1982] A.C. 617 at 647.
[142] [1982] A.C. 617 at 662.
[143] [1982] A.C. 617 at 633.
[144] [1982] A.C. 617 generally.
[145] CPR r.52.15 and see para.9–077.

remedies,[146] so that the proper method of challenge would be by seeking permission to appeal to the Court of Appeal within 21 days.[147] This last option is, in practical terms, the more attractive. In the *Rose Theatre* case,[148] Schiemann J. allowed a challenge to his finding at the hearing that the claimant had no sufficient interest to be appealed against directly to the Court of Appeal, although he expressed doubts as to the correctness of that procedure.

D. CAPACITY

The question of whether the claimant has legal capacity to institute proceedings has arisen before the courts. Capacity and standing are different issues. Capacity concerns the question of whether the applicant has the ability to institute proceedings at all. Standing concerns the question of whether the particular applicant has a sufficient interest in a particular matter to bring judicial review proceedings. Individuals and corporate bodies have capacity to institute proceedings. The issue is whether unincorporated associations have capacity as they have no legal personality. In *R. v Darlington BC Ex p. Association of Darlington Taxi Owners and Darlington Owner Drivers Association*,[149] Auld J. held that an unincorporated association cannot sue or be sued and did not, therefore, have the capacity to make a claim for judicial review. Subsequent cases have taken a different view and held that judicial review proceedings could be brought by an unincorporated association (which had a sufficient interest in the matter).[150] In reality, the real issue is likely to be costs. If the unincorporated association has no assets, there may be no way of enforcing a costs order against it. That problem can be overcome by directing that a costs order be enforceable against an individual officer or member of the association. Alternatively, the court could grant permission on condition that a legal person be joined as a party to the proceedings for the purposes of enforcing any costs order in favour of the defendant.[151] Similar problems could arise if an interest group was incorporated as a company purely for the purposes of making an application.[152] That company would have capacity but may not have any assets to meet a costs order. The incorporated body could be required to give security for costs.[153] Alternatively,

11–039

---

[146] See *R. v Secretary of State for Transport Ex p. Presvac Engineering Ltd* (1992) Admin. L.R. 121.

[147] CPR r.52.4 and see para.9–146.

[148] *R. v Secretary of State for the Environment Ex p. Rose Theatre Trust Co.* [1990] 1 Q.B. 504.

[149] [1994] C.O.D. 424.

[150] See, e.g. *R. v Traffic Commissioner for the North Western Traffic Area Ex p. "Brake"* [1996] C.O.D. 248; *R. v Leeds City Council Ex p. Allwoody* [1995] New Property Cases 149; *R. v London Borough of Tower Hamlets Ex p. Tower Hamlets Combined Traders Association* [1994] C.O.D. 325. But see *R. v Director of Passenger Rail Franchising Ex p. Save our Railways*, unreported, December 15, 1995 (doubt about capacity of certain applicants; as other applicants had standing application could proceed in any event).

[151] *R. v Ministry of Agriculture, Fisheries and Food Ex p. British Pig Industry Support Group* [2000] Eu. L.R. 725.

[152] See, e.g. *R. v Secretary of State for the Environment Ex p. Kirkstall Valley Campaign Ltd* [1996] 3 All E.R. 307 at 309 where Sedley J. satisfied himself that the company had not been incorporated for the purpose of escaping the impact of a costs order and see also *R. (Residents Against Waste Limited) v Lancashire CC* [2008] Env. L.R. 27.

[153] See, e.g. *R. v Leicestershire CC Ex p. Blackfordby and Boothorpe Action Group Ltd* [2000] J.P.L. 1266.

the courts could, as a matter of discretion, refuse permission if it appeared that a body was incorporated solely to avoid possible costs orders. The preferable view, therefore, is that unincorporated associations should be able to bring judicial review claims in appropriate circumstances.[154] The question of costs should be addressed by imposing conditions on the grant of permission such as providing security or by allowing costs orders to be enforced against individual members or officers or refusing permission as a matter of discretion, rather than through a finding that the claimant has no capacity to institute judicial review proceedings.[155]

E. STANDING OUTSIDE CPR, PART 54

11–040 Public law cases will usually be brought by way of judicial review.[156] There are exceptions to this rule when a matter with a public law element may still be raised by way of an ordinary action for a declaration or injunction. These are discussed in Chapter 3. An individual will not have standing to bring an ordinary claim unless he has a specific legal right, or has suffered damage over and above that suffered by the public generally.[157] The relaxation in the standing requirements for declarations and injunctions sought by way of judicial review do not apply when those same remedies are sought by ordinary claim. Earlier cases[158] allowing ratepayers to bring ordinary claims have been distinguished on the grounds that standing was assumed and not considered.[159] There is one authority supporting the view a person with standing to bring a judicial review claim also has standing to seek an injunction or declaration by the ordinary claim procedure, although it was not necessary to decide the point.[160] The case was decided before the House of Lords decision in *O'Reilly v Mackman*,[161] and before the difference between public law and private law was clearly established, and has been distinguished on those grounds.[162]

11–041 The Attorney-General always has standing to enforce a public right,[163] although he has no standing to enforce a purely private right.[164] The

---

[154] The safest course of action is for the application to be made both by the association and by an officer or member (so that there can be no doubt about the capacity of at least one of the applicants and costs can be ordered against the association if it has assets).

[155] In *R. v Secretary of State for Foreign and Commonwealth Affairs Ex p. British Council of Turkish Cypriot Associations* [1998] C.O.D. 336, the court indicated that when dealing with questions of costs it was inappropriate to direct that the costs order be enforceable against individual members until it was known that the unincorporated association as a whole was not going to meet the costs order.

[156] *O'Reilly v Mackman* [1983] 2 A.C. 237. See Chapter 3.

[157] *Barrs v Bethell* [1982] Ch. 294; *Ashby v Ebdon* [1985] Ch. 394; *Holmes v Checkland, The Times,* April 15, 1987, CA.

[158] See, *Prescott v Birmingham Corp.* [1955] Ch. 210; *Bradbury v Enfield LBC* [1967] 1 W.L.R. 1311, and *Lee v Enfield LBC* (1967) 66 L.G.R. 195. All these were decided when injunctions and declarations were only available in ordinary action.

[159] *Barrs v Bethell* (see above, fn.157).

[160] *Steeples v Derbyshire CC* [1985] 1 W.L.R. 256 (decided in February, 1981 but not reported until 1985).

[161] [1983] 1 A.C. 237.

[162] *Barrs v Bethell* [1982] Ch. 294.

[163] See Chapter 7.

[164] *Att-Gen Ex rel. Scotland v Barratt (Manchester) Ltd, The Times,* July 11, 1991.

Attorney-General has standing to seek a declaration as to whether a public body is acting ultra vires.[165] An individual who does not have standing may also seek the consent of the Attorney-General to a relator action. Actions by the Attorney-General or relator actions are probably an exception to the rule that all public law cases must be brought by way of judicial review and they may be brought by way of ordinary claim.[166]

---

[165] See, e.g. *Att-Gen Ex rel. Tilley v Wandsworth LBC* [1981] 1 W.L.R. 854.
[166] *Barrs v Bethell* (see above, fn.157); *Holmes v Checkland* (see above, fn.151). See Chapter 3.

CHAPTER 12

The Discretion of the Court to Refuse a Remedy and the Exclusion of Judicial Review

A. INTRODUCTION

Judicial review is a discretionary jurisdiction. The prerogative remedies, the declaration and the injunction are all discretionary remedies. A court may in its discretion refuse to grant a remedy, even if the claimant can demonstrate that a public authority has acted unlawfully.[1] If the courts refuse to grant a remedy recognising that an act is unlawful and ultra vires, the act is effectively treated as if it were valid.[2]

12–001

There are a variety of considerations discernible in the case law which are relevant to the exercise of the judicial discretion to refuse a remedy. Some are related to the conduct of the claimant, such as delay or waiver; others are related to the circumstances of the particular case, such as the fact that a remedy would be of no practical effect. Other considerations relate to the particular nature of public law where the court may need to have regard to the wider public interest as well as the interest of the claimant in obtaining an effective remedy. This point was made by the Master of the Rolls in refusing to quash a decision of the Monopolies and Mergers Commission, even though the decision was legally flawed.[3] The interests of the claimant had to be measured against the needs of good administration, which included: the need for speed, finality in decision-making, the public interest, the purpose of the administrative process and the need to consider substance not form.

12–002

The factors listed below are relevant to the exercise of the court's remedial discretion. The grounds for refusing a remedy may overlap. More than one ground may be present in a particular case. Discretionary grounds for refusing a remedy may also overlap with the substantive principles governing judicial review. Ultimately, the question of whether or not a remedy should be refused is a matter for the discretion of the reviewing court in the light of all the

12–003

---

[1] See *R. (Edwards) v Environment Agency* [2008] Env. L.R. 34 at [63] and see generally, Bingham, "Should Public Law Remedies Be Discretionary?" [1991] P.L. 64.

[2] Although in certain circumstances the invalidity could be raised by way of collateral challenge in other proceedings. See, generally, Chapters 3 and 5.

[3] *R. v Monopolies and Mergers Commission Ex p. Argyll Group* [1986] 1 W.L.R. 763. See also *R. v Brent LBC Ex p. O'Malley* (1997) 10 Admin. L.Rep. 265 at [295A]–[296F].

circumstances existing at the time of the hearing (not the original decision).[4] The court will need to consider the nature of the flaw in the decision and the ground for exercising the discretion.[5] This discretion, like all discretions, should be exercised on the basis of clear, consistent and defensible principles, otherwise there is a risk that this judicial discretion may become arbitrary making it impossible to predict the attitude of the courts.

12–004   It is important to note that costs may be awarded against a claimant who is refused a remedy at the discretion of the court, even if he was successful in establishing that the defendant had acted unlawfully.[6]

B.   CONDUCT OF THE CLAIMANT

12–005   The court may take the conduct of the claimant into account in determining whether he should now be entitled to complain about the decision and be granted a remedy. A ratepayer was refused a remedy to quash a refusal to make a refund of rates because of his previous deliberate and unjustifiable withholding of rates owed, and because there would be no unjust enrichment as far as the council was concerned, since the money not refunded represented fair compensation for the loss of interest on sums that ought to have been paid previously.[7] A local authority which pursued pointless litigation was refused any remedy.[8] Another authority which sought to challenge ministerial confirmation of its own proposals for re-organising schools, relying on their own procedural error, was refused relief: a remedy would not necessarily have been refused if some other claimant, such as a school governor, had sought a remedy.[9] If a claimant were motivated by some improper purpose or ill-will in bringing the claim, the courts might decline to grant a remedy.[10]

12–006   A claimant who knows that a decision is potentially flawed and fails to object may find the courts refusing him a remedy if he subsequently seeks to challenge the decision. Failure to object to certain members voting at a meeting has

---

[4] *R. v Secretary of State for Foreign and Commonwealth Affairs Ex p. Everett* [1989] Q.B. 811. See also *R. v Brent LBC Ex p. O'Malley* (1997) 10 Admin. L.R. 265 at [296A]–[296B].

[5] *R. (Edwards) v Environment Agency* [2008] Env. L.R. 34 at [63].

[6] *R (Hunt) North Somerset Council* [2013] EWCA Civ. 1483 (remedy refused as a matter of discretion; wrong in principle to award claimant his costs as the defendant was the successful party and would be entitled to its costs); *R. v Trafford BC Ex p. Colonel Foods* [1990] C.O.D. 357 (alternative remedy available); *R. v Swale BC Ex p. Royal Society for the Protection of Birds* (1991) 2 Admin. L.Rep. 790 (delay). The matter is ultimately one for the discretion of the courts which may choose to award costs against the claimant, make no order for costs or award the claimant part or all of the costs depending on the extent to which the claimant has been successful on the substantive law and the reason for refusing a remedy. Where, for example, a claimant was granted a declaration but refused an order quashing a planning permission, the claimant was awarded 75 per cent of his costs: see *R. (Guiney) v London Borough of Greenwich* [2008] EWHC 2012 (Admin).

[7] *Dorot Properties Ltd v London Borough of Brent* [1990] C.O.D. 378.

[8] *Windsor and Maidenhead Royal BC v Brandrose Investments Ltd* [1983] 1 W.L.R. 509.

[9] *R. v Secretary of State for Education and Science Ex p. Birmingham City Council* (1985) 83 L.G.R. 79.

[10] See dicta in *R. (Mount Cook Land Limited and Mount Eden Land Ltd) v Westminster City Council* [2004] 2 P. & C.R. 405 at [45]. See also *R. (Feakins) v Secretary of State for the Environment, Food and Rural Affairs* [2004] 1 W.L.R. 1761 at [23]–[24] (dealing with standing but similar principles would apply to the discretion to grant a remedy).

influenced the court against granting a remedy.[11] Waiver of an objection has been significant in natural justice cases, where it has been woven into the substantive rules governing bias. An individual who fails to object to the presence of a member of a tribunal, once he knows the facts entitling him to object, may be taken to have waived his objection.[12]

An individual who has acquiesced in a decision may not be granted a remedy if he subsequently seeks to challenge it. Where a local councillor allegedly acquiesced in a decision to allocate a house to a particular tenant, he was not prevented from challenging it in his capacity as leader of the council, however, as he was acting on behalf of the general community interest. He might have been refused a remedy, if the claim of acquiescence had been made out if he had been challenging the decision in his own interests.[13]

12–007

Misconduct in the course of judicial review proceedings, such as failing to make material disclosure of all the facts in an affidavit or witness statement, may well lead to the court refusing to grant that claimant any remedy.[14] Even inadvertent mis-statement of fact is a reason for refusing a remedy, as a claimant is required to show great care (as well as candour) in a judicial review claim.[15]

12–008

Delay

Delay in bringing a claim is a recognised ground for refusing a remedy. The courts will not assist a claimant who sleeps on his rights.[16] Delay is now primarily governed by the Senior Courts Act 1981 and the provisions of CPR, r.54.5. Delay is particularly important at the permission stage: a claimant must in general bring his claim promptly, and in any event within three months of the date when grounds for review arise.[17] Shorter time-limits apply in relation to procurement decisions[18] and planning claims.[19] A finding at the permission stage that a claim was not made promptly is conclusive and cannot be reconsidered at the full hearing.[20] The courts may allow a claim to proceed even if it was not

12–009

---

[11] *R. v Governors of Small Heath School Ex p. Birmingham City Council* [1990] C.O.D. 23.

[12] *R. v Nailsworth Licensing Justices Ex p. Bird* [1953] 1 W.L.R. 1046; *Locabail (UK) Ltd. v Bayfield Properties Ltd.* [2000] Q.B. 451 at [26]. In *R. v Essex Justices Ex p. Perkins* [1927] 2 K.B. 475, a court quashed a decision where the facts were known to the applicant but he did not appreciate that he was entitled to object. Agreement to a particular procedure may mean that the procedure is not unfair: see *R (Hill) v Institute of Chartered Accountants in England and Wales* [2014] 1 W.L.R. 86 at [44] (per Beatson LJ) and [54] (per Underhill LJ).

[13] *R. v Port Talbot BC Ex p. Jones* [1988] 2 All E.R. 207.

[14] *R. v Kensington Income Tax Commissioners Ex p. Princess Edmond de Polignac* [1917] 1 K.B. 486 and see para.9–010.

[15] *R. v North East Thames Regional Health Authority Ex p. De Groot* [1988] C.O.D. 25.

[16] *R. v Aston University Senate Ex p. Roffey* [1969] 2 Q.B. 538.

[17] CPR 54 r.5. In relation to claims derived from EU law, the claim must, in effect, be brought within three months of the date when the claimant knew, or ought to have known, of the alleged breach: see Case C-406/08 *Uniplex (UK) Ltd. v NHS Business Services Authority* [2010] E.C.R. I-817, discussed above at para.9-018.

[18] CPR 54 r.5(6): the time limit is 30 days from when the claimant knew or ought to have known of the alleged breach.

[19] CPR r.54(5); the time limit is six weeks after the grounds of claim first arose.

[20] *R. v Criminal Injuries Compensation Board Ex p. A* [1999] 2 W.L.R. 974 and see above para.9–043.

made promptly if the claimant can show good reason.[21] Even if the court extends the time-limit, there remains undue delay for the purposes of s.31(6) of the Senior Courts Act 1981.[22] Thus, a court may still refuse a remedy if it considers that granting a remedy would be likely to cause substantial hardship to, or substantially prejudice the rights of, any person, or would be detrimental to good administration.[23]

12–010   This provision was considered in *R. v Dairy Produce Quota Tribunal for England and Wales Ex p. Caswell*.[24] There the claimant was refused a quashing order to quash a decision fixing his dairy quota, as he had applied out of time and granting relief would be detrimental to good administration. Lord Goff, giving the sole judgment, stated that a precise definition of what constitutes detriment to good administration could not be formulated as the need for finality would differ from one context to another. In *Caswell*, the detriment to good administration stemmed from the fact that if Caswell were to succeed in having his quota quashed notwithstanding the delay, a substantial number of claimants could be encouraged to seek review of their quotas. If a substantial number of those claimants were successful, it would involve re-opening all allocations over the previous four years, since increased quotas could only be given to successful claimants if the quotas of other producers were correspondingly reduced. This would undermine the interests of good administration in a regular flow of consistent decisions reached with reasonable speed, which enabled the citizen to order his affairs in the light of those decisions. Relevant factors in assessing the detriment would be the length of the delay, the extent and effect of the decision under challenge, and the impact if it were to be re-opened. The judge had been correct in concluding that the detriment to good administration outweighed the financial hardship suffered by the claimant as a result of the decision, and in refusing to quash the decision.[25] Similarly, the Court of Appeal refused to quash an outline planning permission where the challenge was brought more than three years after the grant. The Court noted that there was an interest in good administration in not invalidating planning permissions in such circumstances given that the planning permission was intended to benefit the land and public and private bodies and individuals may have taken decisions on the basis of the planning permission.[26] Similarly, the Court of Appeal has held that it would be detrimental to good administration to quash a budget of a local authority in relation to a financial year that had already ended three months before the judicial

---

[21] CPR r.3.1(2)(a).

[22] *R. v Dairy Produce Quota Tribunal for England and Wales Ex p. Caswell* [1990] 2 A.C. 738. See also *R. v Chichester Justices Ex p. Chichester DC* [1990] C.O.D. 248 (detriment occurs when granting leave might lead to a flood of claims based on past events or where one person in a class would, by being allowed to challenge, gain an unfair advantage over others in the class).

[23] Unless the claim seeks to enforce a right derived from EU law, in which case the discretion in s.31(6) of the Senior Courts Act 1981 does not apply: see *R (Berky) v Newport City Council* [2012] BLGR 592 at [50]–[52] (per Moore-Bick LJ) and [71] (per Buxton LJ).

[24] [1990] A.C. 738.

[25] Popplewell J. did, however, grant a declaration as to the proper construction of the regulations to guide tribunals in the future: see [1989] 2 C.M.L.R. 502. The uncertainty generated by quashing a planning permission, on which third parties would have relied, was also held to be contrary to good administration: see *R. (Gavin) v London Borough of Haringey* [2004] 2 P. & C.R. 13.

[26] *R. v Newbury DC Ex p. Chieveley Parish Council* [1999] P.L.C.R. 51 at [66]–[67].

review hearing.[27] Other judgments recognise the conflict between the interest of legal certainty in preserving decisions and the interest in ensuring that unlawful decisions should, in general, not be allowed to stand.[28] The precise balance between the interests of good administration in legal certainty and the principle of ensuring public bodies do not misuse their powers will depend on the context and all the factors involved in the particular case. In particular, if the dispute is in fact between competing private interests, such as that of a developer and a council over compensation[29] or the rights of owners of a village green and the local inhabitants, questions of good administration may not arise or may not have much significance.[30]

A remedy may also be refused where it would cause substantial hardship or substantial prejudice to the rights of others. Examples of such prejudice have arisen in the context of planning permission where the recipient has relied on the planning permission and entered into contracts with third parties to carry out the development contemplated by the planning permission. Where the benefit of such contracts would be lost, or where the quashing of the planning permission would lead to further costs being incurred, the court may refuse a remedy. In one case,[31] a conservation body brought a challenge out of time to the granting of planning permission to reclaim mudflats near the mouth of the Medway river. In reliance on the permission, the port authority had entered into a dredging contract with another company. The benefit of that contract would be lost and the spoil dredged from the channel would either have to be disposed of at sea (not on the mudflats) or stored, both of which would lead to substantially higher costs. The overall development, of which the land reclamation scheme formed a part, would be delayed resulting in further substantial losses. A remedy was therefore refused, because of the substantial prejudice that would be caused. Similarly, the court refused to quash a planning permission where there had been a substantial delay in bringing a claim for judicial review and there would be adverse financial consequences to the developer. The developer was committed to a substantial programme of works and would have incurred significant financial liability in respect of work carried out and materials ordered. The court held that the substantial hardship to the developer justified refusing an order quashing the planning permission but granted a declaration that there had been a failure to comply with the relevant statutory procedural requirements.[32]

12–011

The courts have a discretion to refuse relief even if the claim was made promptly.[33] The courts have a broad discretion in relation to remedies and may still need to balance the interests of the claimant and the requirements of good administration and the effects of the grant of relief on third parties even where the

12–012

---

[27] *R. (Hunt) v North Somerset DC* [2104] B.L.G.R. 1.

[28] See dicta in *R. v Restormel BC ex p. Corbett* [2001] P.L.R. 108 at [16] and the dicta of Lady Hale in *Betterment Properties Ltd. v Dorset CC* [2014] 2 W.L.R. 300 at [21]–[36].

[29] *R. v Bassetlaw DC ex p. Oxby* [1998] P.L.C.R. 283.

[30] *Betterment Properties Ltd. v Dorset CC* [2014] 2 W.L.R. 300 at [41]–[43] (dealing with the issue in the context of a statutory application to rectify the register of village greens, rather than judicial review, but the Supreme Court recognised that there was a public law element to such claims).

[31] *R. v Swale BC Ex p. Royal Society for the Protection of Birds* (1991) 2 Admin. L.Rep. 790. See also *R. v Exeter City Council Ex p. J.L. Thomas & Co. Ltd* [1990] 3 W.L.R. 100.

[32] *R. (Gavin) v London Borough of Haringey* [2004] 2 P. & C.R. 13.

[33] *R. v Brent LBC Ex p. O'Malley* (1997) 10 Admin. L.Rep. 265 at [293D–F] and [295F]–[296B]; *R. v Gateshead Metropolitan BC Ex p. Nichol* (1988) 87 L.G.R. 435.

claimant has made the judicial review claim within time.[34] In one case a claimant challenged a decision of a local authority to dispose of housing stock on a housing estate as there had been a failure to comply with the relevant statutory requirements on consultation. The courts refused to grant relief notwithstanding the illegality. The implementation of the scheme had already begun and there was a substantial risk that the scheme would collapse if judicial review were granted. The costs already incurred were in excess of £3 million and those costs and years of work would be wasted.[35] The majority of tenants on the housing estate were in favour of the scheme and the grant of relief would mean that their interests would be adversely affected even though they were blameless.[36] In the circumstances, the courts held that the interests of third parties and the effect on the administration were factors justifying the refusal of a remedy.

Prematurity

12–013   Claims may be made unduly early as well as unduly late. A claimant may seek to review an error in the decision-making process before that process is completed and a final decision reached, or he may seek to review a preliminary decision such as a decision refusing an adjournment or allowing certain evidence to be admitted. Decisions of this nature are subject, in principle, to judicial review. The issue is whether the court will refuse to grant permission to apply for judicial review, or refuse a remedy and require the individual to wait until the final decision has been reached before mounting a challenge, relying on the error at the preliminary stage as a ground for invalidating the final decision.

12–014   English law is beginning to develop a concept of prematurity.[37] There are numerous dicta indicating that premature challenges should not normally be allowed, although the courts have often found "exceptional" reasons why an otherwise premature application should be allowed. The courts have primarily dealt with the concept of premature challenges in the context of attempts to seek judicial review of interlocutory decisions, particularly ones concerning the disclosure or use of evidence or other procedural matters, made during a decision-making process. The courts have indicated that "it is only in exceptional circumstances that the court will grant judicial review of a decision taken during the course of a hearing ... before that hearing has been concluded".[38] The courts have indicated that it is usually inappropriate to seek review of a preliminary ruling on a point of law by a magistrates' court.[39] Questions of law and the admissibility of evidence in committal proceedings are best left to be dealt with at the trial rather than by judicial review.[40] The courts should be slow to intervene

---

[34] See also para.9–026.

[35] *R. v Brent LBC Ex p. O'Malley* (1997) 10 Admin. L.R. 265 at [291G]–[292B].

[36] *Ex p. O'Malley* (1997) 10 Admin. L.R. 265 at [295A–G].

[37] See Beatson, "Prematurity and Ripeness For Review" in Forsyth and Hare, *The Golden Metwand and the Crooked Cord* (Oxford University Press, 1998).

[38] *R. v Association of Futures Brokers and Dealers Ltd Ex p. Mordens Ltd* (1991) 3 Admin.L.Rep. 254 at [263D–F]. See also *R. (Surat Singh) v Stratford Magistrates' Court* [2007] 1 W.L.R. 3119 at [6].

[39] See dicta of Woolf LJ at first instance in *R. v Bow Street Magistrates' Court Ex p. Noncyp Ltd* [1988] 3 C.M.L.R. 84 at [94]. (decision affd. by Court of Appeal [1989] 1 C.M.L.R. 634).

[40] *R. v Oxford City Justices Ex p. Berry* [1988] Q.B. 507.

where it is claimed that there is insufficient evidence to justify a committal[41] and should only intervene in cases where inadmissible evidence had in fact been admitted where there is a really substantial error leading to demonstrable injustice.[42] The Court of Appeal has also indicated that normally an individual should await the final outcome of a disciplinary hearing and not seek judicial review of a preliminary decision, such as a finding that notice of the disciplinary charges had been given as soon as possible.[43] A decision of a planning inspector not to admit certain evidence at an inquiry would not normally be reviewed, but may be if the effect of the decision is to block the main argument put forward by the objector and so render the inquiry a barren exercise.[44] Similarly, the Divisional Court has indicated that it is not normally appropriate to seek review of a decision by a tribunal that certain evidence need not be disclosed.[45] If the non-disclosure affected the decision, that matter could be raised on appeal (if available) or by way of judicial review of the final decision. However, in exceptional circumstances, it might be appropriate to avoid the waste of time and expense of holding a hearing, if it is clear that the hearing process would be tainted.[46] There may also be cases where the challenge is directed towards the fairness of the procedures adopted to deal with a particular type of case. The central issue may be whether the principles of natural justice and procedural fairness require the disclosure of certain information. In such instances, it may be appropriate to deal with the matter by way of judicial review of the decision to refuse to disclose the information rather than waiting until a substantive decision is taken and challenging that on the grounds of breach of natural justice. In one case, the Secretary of State had a policy of not disclosing the evidence obtained by him in the course of deciding whether to refer a conviction back to the Court of Appeal. The court granted judicial review of decisions applying that policy and refusing to disclose information on the grounds that, exceptionally, it was appropriate to do so.[47] Similarly, if the hearing is to proceed on the basis that there can be no cross-examination of witnesses and no legal representation under the relevant regulations, it may be appropriate to determine whether, as a matter of law, that is correct.[48]

Questions of prematurity may arise outside the context of challenges to **12–015** interlocutory or procedural decisions. A question may arise as to whether a body has jurisdiction or power to undertake a particular act. The courts have jurisdiction to intervene and could, for example, grant prohibition in an appropriate case prohibiting the body from acting. In general, however, the courts have indicated that it is generally inappropriate for the courts to intervene before

---

[41] *R. v Bedwellty Justices Ex p. Williams* [1997] 2 A.C. 225.
[42] *Neill v North Antrim Magistrates' Court* [1992] 1 W.L.R. 1220.
[43] *R. v Chief Constable of Merseyside Police Ex p. Merrill* [1989] 1 W.L.R. 1077.
[44] *R. v Secretary of State for the Environment Ex p. Kensington and Chelsea Royal BC* (1987) 19 H.L.R. 161.
[45] *R. v Attendance Allowance Board Ex p. Moran* [1990] C.O.D. 381. See also *R. v Association of Futures Brokers and & Dealers Ltd Ex p. Mordens Ltd.* (1991) 3 Admin. L.Rep. 254.
[46] *R. v Attendance Allowance Board Ex p. Moran* [1990] C.O.D. 381.
[47] *R. v Secretary of State for the Home Department Ex p. Hickey (No.2)* [1995] 1 W.L.R. 734. See also *R. v Kent Police Authority Ex p. Godden* [1971] 2 Q.B. 662 (prohibition appropriate to restrain holding of a hearing until information disclosed to other party).
[48] See, e.g. *R. (S) v Knowsley NHS Primary Care Trust* [2006] A.C.D. 280.

the final decision of the body on the substantive issue is known. In one case,[49] Laws J. had to consider whether the Broadcasting Complaints Commission had jurisdiction to entertain a particular complaint. He accepted that, in general, a public body would normally be allowed to carry out their functions without interference by the courts at an interim stage, and that it would not normally be appropriate for a court to intervene until all the facts were known. However, he considered that the courts could intervene if a clear issue of law arose as to whether the body had jurisdiction. In a subsequent case,[50] the Court of Appeal considered that it was premature to review a provisional decision by an ombudsman that he had jurisdiction to entertain a complaint. The Court of Appeal doubted whether the fact that a clear issue of law arose was sufficient reason to justify engaging in judicial review before a final decision had been reached. A body may have a discretion to act but may not have decided whether to exercise that discretion or what factors to take account in deciding whether to do so. It would clearly be premature to seek judicial review until the decision-maker had decided to act and all the relevant facts were known. There may be other instances where the facts are not known or whether the whole statutory procedure has not been completed and where judicial intervention at an early stage in the proceedings would be inappropriate.[51]

12–016   There are strong arguments against allowing premature challenges. The error might be corrected during the decision-making process or the error might not affect the final decision or the individual might not be dissatisfied with the final decision. It could be a waste of judicial time to review preliminary decisions rather than awaiting the final decision. Challenges to preliminary decisions may provide a way to circumvent an appeals process. An appeal may only be available against a final decision, not a preliminary or interlocutory decision, and it may be preferable to insist upon the individual appealing against the final decision relying on the preliminary error as a ground for overturning the decision rather than challenging the preliminary decision itself. Other factors may be relevant to this question such as the significance of the alleged error,[52] and the extent to which the decision-making body or appellate authorities are equipped to deal with the point in issue.

12–017   Conversely, there are factors suggesting that a challenge to a preliminary decision may, on occasions, be appropriate. There may be savings in terms of cost in not exposing the applicant to the full decision-making process, if the matter is dealt with immediately.[53] The courts have tended to allow judicial review of

---

[49] *R. v Broadcasting Complaints Commission Ex p. BBC* (1994) 6 Admin. L.Rep. 714.

[50] *R. v Personal Investment Authority and PIA Ombudsman Ex p. Burns-Anderson Network Plc* (1997) 10 Admin. L.Rep. 57.

[51] See, e.g. *R. v IRC Ex p. Bishopp* (1999) 11 Admin. L.Rep. 575 (court declined to engage in judicial review of a refusal by the Inland Revenue to give pre-transaction clearance to a proposed transaction, inter alia, as the facts were hypothetical at that stage and the transaction might not proceed in any event). See also *R. v IRC Ex p. Ulster Bank* [1997] S.T.C. 636.

[52] *R. v Secretary of State for the Environment Ex p. Kensington and Chelsea Royal BC* (1987) 19 H.L.R. 161.

[53] *R. v Horseferry Road Magistrates' Court Ex p. Independent Broadcasting Authority* [1987] Q.B. 54.

decisions initiating a process or commencing criminal proceedings, at least where a clear question of law arises,[54] or if it would be unfair to allow the process even to begin.[55]

The nature of the administrative process is also relevant. Prematurity has its place primarily in the context of decisions which only affect the individual concerned. Administrative decision-making may affect the public generally and may involve a number of stages. Expenditure and effort may be incurred at various stages in the process. A challenge should be made as early as possible and failure to do so, or failure to inform the authorities of the possibility of a challenge may count against the claimant when the court considers how to exercise its remedial discretion. Even if the individual is technically only required to make his challenge within three months of the final decision, the court may refuse relief in view of the administrative inconvenience, delay and expenditure that would be caused by allowing a late challenge.[56]

12–018

C. REMEDY OF NO PRACTICAL USE

The courts may refuse a remedy where it is no longer necessary in the circumstances, or where the issues have become academic or of no practical significance. The courts have refused to grant a declaration that a decision to establish a special prison unit was unlawful, where the unit had been closed and there was no prospect of it being reopened,[57] or to quash a decision to disclose a report to the guardian *ad litem* when the report had been disclosed by the date of the hearing.[58] The court also refused a declaration that the Inner London Education Authority was in breach of its statutory duty, when the authority was due to be abolished a few weeks after the date of the judgment.[59] Where the effects of a decision are likely to be of a short duration, the courts may require compelling evidence of a significant breach of the duty owed to the claimant before the court will grant a remedy.[60]

The court has refused to hear a claim for judicial review of a decision by a headteacher to take no disciplinary action against a pupil as the matter came before the court on the last day of the school year and the two pupils involved

12–019

12–020

---

[54] [1987] Q.B. 54 (Question was whether the offence was known to law.)

[55] See, e.g. *R. v I.R.C. Ex p. Preston* [1985] A.C. 835; *R. v Commissioners for the Special Purposes of the Income Tax Acts Ex p. Stipplechoice* [1985] 2 All E.R. 465; *R. v Telford Justices Ex p. Badhan* [1991] 2 All E.R. 854 (decision to commit for trial could be challenged by judicial review where it is alleged that it would be an abuse of process to commit as the applicant would not be able to have a fair trial).

[56] *R. v Brent LBC Ex p. O'Malley* (1997) 10 Admin. L.Rep. 265; *R. v Gateshead Metropolitan BC Ex p. Nichol* (1988) 87 L.G.R. 435 and *R. v Cornwall CC Ex p. Nicholls* [1989] C.O.D. 507. See also *R. v HM Treasury Ex p. Smedley* [1985] Q.B. 657 at [666]–[667]. See dicta in *BBC v Sugar* [2007] 1 W.L.R. 2583 at [70] affd. by Court of Appeal [2008] EWCA Civ 191 at [13] and see *R. (Edwards) v Environment Agency* [2008] Env.L.R. 34 at [62]–[65].

[57] *Williams v Home Office (No.2)* [1981] 1 All E.R. 1211, (affd. [1982] 2 All E.R. 564). See also *R. v Secretary of State for the Home Department Ex p. Handscomb* (1987) 86 Cr.App.R. 59.

[58] *R. v Sunderland Juvenile Court Ex p. G. (A Minor)* [1988] 1 W.L.R. 398.

[59] *R. v Inner London Education Authority Ex p. Ali and Murshid* [1990] C.O.D. 317.

[60] *R. (Sacupima) v Newham LBC* [2001] 1 W.L.R. 563 at [572C–F].

were due to leave the primary school and go to different secondary schools.[61] A court may still choose formally to quash a decision even if that would have no practical effect. The House of Lords has once held that a quashing order should be granted to quash an order requiring deportation on specified dates which were long past by the time judgment was given.[62]

12–021   Even if there is no point in granting remedies such as quashing orders, so far as the particular claimant is concerned, there may still be a need to clarify the law or give guidance for decision-makers in the future. A court may grant a declaration setting out the true legal position,[63] or may give judgment clarifying the law but without making a formal declaration.[64]

No injustice or prejudice suffered

12–022   The fact that the applicant has suffered no prejudice as a result of the error complained of may be a reason for refusing him a remedy. It is necessary to keep in mind the purpose of the public law principle that has technically been violated, and ask whether that underlying purpose has in any event been achieved in the circumstances of the case. If so, the courts may decide that the breach has caused no injustice or prejudice and there is no need to grant a remedy.

12–023   The courts may, for example, refuse relief if there has been a breach of natural justice but where the breach has in fact not prevented the individual from having a fair hearing. Failure by an investigatory body, for example, to disclose material may not entitle an applicant to relief, where the material was in fact known to him and he has had the opportunity to deal with it.[65] Where a claimant was not told of all relevant material initially but had been told and made representations before the final decision was taken, the court may refuse relief as he has not suffered injustice.[66]

12–024   Similar principles apply in the case of statutory procedural requirements. The courts may refuse a remedy where there is technically a breach of a mandatory requirement but where the breach does not prejudice the claimants.[67] One method of assessing prejudice is to ask whether the purpose underlying the statutory requirements have been fulfilled in the circumstances of the case. Failure to comply with a requirement that an education authority have access to a report

---

[61] *R. v Headteacher and Governors of Fairfield Primary School and Hampshire CC Ex p. W* [1998] C.O.D. 106.

[62] *R. v Secretary of State for the Home Department Ex p. Bugdaycay* [1987] A.C. 514. See also *R. v Clerkenwell Metropolitan Stipendiary Magistrate Ex p. Hooper* [1998] 4 All E.R. 193 (applicant already served a term of imprisonment pursuant to a binding over order; too late to quash the order but declaratory relief appropriate instead).

[63] *R. v Birmingham City Juvenile Court Ex p. Birmingham City Council* [1988] 1 W.L.R. 337 (conflicting first instance decisions on proper procedure in interim care proceedings). See also *R. v Leicester Crown Court Ex p. DPP* [1987] 1 W.L.R. 1371 and *R. v Nottingham Justices Ex p. Davies* [1981] Q.B. 38 (both cases where general guidance as to procedure was sought rather than specific relief in the instant case).

[64] *R. v Bromley Licensing Justices Ex p. Bromley Licensed Victuallers* [1984] 1 W.L.R. 585. See also *R. v Bromley Magistrates' Court Ex p. Smith* [1995] 1 W.L.R. 944 and *R. (Sacupima) v Newham LBC* [2001] 1 W.L.R. 563 at [565G–H].

[65] *R. v Monopolies and Mergers Commission Ex p. Brown (Matthew)* [1987] 1 W.L.R. 1235.

[66] *R. v Secretary of State for Foreign and Commonwealth Affairs Ex p. Everett* [1989] Q.B. 811.

[67] *R. v Secretary of State for Education and Science & Bedfordshire CC Ex p. Threapleton* [1988] C.O.D. 103; *R. v Cornwall CC Ex p. Nicholls* (see above, fn.56).

may not lead to the court quashing a decision if the authority in fact had access to all the relevant material before reaching its decision.[68] Failure to conform exactly with statutory requirements for publicising planning proposals may not justify quashing a decision, if in fact the public was adequately informed of the proposals and objectors were able to make their objections.[69]

These principles are increasingly being incorporated into the substantive rules rather than classified as a matter on which the courts have discretion to refuse a remedy.[70] The courts may hold that there is no breach of natural justice or no unfairness if no prejudice has been caused, rather than accepting that an error has been made but refusing relief as the error did not prejudice the applicant.[71] The courts may hold that there need only be substantial compliance with a mandatory statutory requirement rather than absolute compliance,[72] or may abandon the mandatory-directory classification altogether and focus on the consequences of non-compliance and asking what Parliament would have intended the consequences of non-compliance with the particular procedural requirement to be.[73]   **12–025**

Decision would be the same irrespective of the error

A court may be influenced by the fact that a public body would have exercised its powers in the same way or reached the same decision, even if it had not fallen into error. Thus, a court may not quash a decision where there was an error of law,[74] or a failure to take account of a relevant consideration,[75] if the decision-maker would have reached the same decision even if he had correctly interpreted the law or taken account of all relevant material. A decision reached in breach of natural justice may not be quashed if the courts are satisfied that the decision-maker would have come to the same decision if natural justice had been observed.[76]   **12–026**

---

[68] *Ex p. Threapleton* [1988] C.O.D. 103.

[69] *R. v Lambeth LBC Ex p. Sharp* (1988) 55 P. & C.R. 232.

[70] *R. v Immigration Appeal Tribunal Ex p. Jeyeanthan* [1999] 3 All E.R. 231.

[71] *George v Secretary of State for the Environment* (1979) 38 P. & C.R. 609 at [617]; *R. v Secretary of State for the Environment Ex p. Fielder Estates (Canvey) Ltd* (1989) 57 P. & C.R. 424 at [429]; *R. v Deputy Chief Constable of Thames Valley Police Ex p. Cotton* [1990] 1 R.L.R. 344.

[72] *Coney v Choyce* [1975] 1 W.L.R. 422.

[73] *R. v Soneji* [2006] 1 A.C. 340 at [15]–[23]; *R v Clarke* [2008] 1 W.L.R. 338 at [14]; *London & Clydeside Estates v Aberdeen DC* [1980] 1 W.L.R. 182; and *R. v Immigration Appeal Tribunal Ex p. Jeyeanthan* [1999] 3 All E.R. 231. On some occasions, the courts have held failure to comply with particular statutory requirements, in particular those governing the institution of proceedings, did render the subsequent proceedings invalid: see *R. v Clarke* [2008] 1 W.L.R. 338 (failure to comply with requirement that indictment be signed by proper officer resulted in the quashing of a subsequent conviction) and *Seal v Chief Constable of South Wales Police* [2007] 1 W.L.R. 1910 (failure to obtain leave of the High Court to bring proceedings in respect of acts done under the Mental Health Act 1983 invalidated subsequent civil proceedings).

[74] *R. v Deputy Governor of Parkhurst Prison Ex p. Hague* [1992] 1 A.C. 58 (the House of Lords reversed the Court of Appeal decision on the separate issue of damages for false imprisonment: [1991] 3 W.L.R. 340); *R. v Knightsbridge Crown Court Ex p. Marcrest Properties* [1983] 1 W.L.R. 300.

[75] *R. v Mansfield Justices Ex p. Sharkey* [1985] Q.B. 613 at [630]; *R. v Lincolnshire CC and Wealden DC Ex p. Atkinson* (1996) 8 Admin. L.Rep. 529 at [549G]–[551] (court refused to quash a decision to issue a removal direction under the Criminal Justice and Public Order Act 1994 as all material had subsequently been considered by a local authority and it would have reached the same decision; court still granted a declaration that local authority had acted unlawfully).

[76] See, e.g. *Glynn v Keele University* [1971] 1 W.L.R. 487.

12–027   This line of reasoning carries with it the danger that the courts might substitute its own view of the merits of the case for that of the decision-maker.[77] The usual position at common law is that the courts determine whether the decision has been lawfully reached and if not quash it, leaving the decision-maker to reconsider the matter.[78] The courts themselves recognise this, and will not normally refuse a remedy if there can be any doubt as to whether the decision-maker would reach the same decision if he had not made the error in question.[79] Thus, in the natural justice area where the claimant has been refused a hearing or the proper procedures were not followed, there are numerous cases warning of the danger of assuming that the decision-maker would have reached the same decision even if a hearing had been held or the proper procedures followed.[80]

12–028   The courts have also recognised the public interest in ensuring that public bodies do observe the relevant public law principles in exercising their discretionary power. For that reason: " . . . it would not be right routinely to refuse relief in cases . . . merely because the decision would probably be unaffected."[81] Sanctions, in the form of quashing unlawful decisions, may therefore be necessary to ensure that public bodies do take care to ensure that they are acting lawfully.

12–029   For these reasons, the courts have taken the view that they should not refuse relief unless the same decision would undoubtedly be reached irrespective of the error, and there is a clear countervailing public interest in not quashing the decision.[82] The Criminal Justice and Courts Bill 2014 will, if enacted, alter the test. The Bill provides that a court must refuse a remedy if it appears to the court to be "highly likely that the outcome for the applicant would not been substantially different" if the conduct complained of had not occurred.[83]

12–030   Two specific situations also arise in this regard. First, there is a problem where a decision is taken by a collective body and one or more of its members acts for an improper reason or is disqualified from participating, due to a pecuniary or other interest in the matter. There may be a majority for the decision even without the vote of the person acting unlawfully. On the other hand, it is difficult to assess

---

[77] See D. H. Clark, "Natural Justice: Substance and Shadow" [1975] P.L. 27.

[78] See, e.g. *R. (Smith) v North East Derbyshire Primary Care Trust* [2006] 1 W.L.R. 3315 at [10]; *R. v General Medical Council Ex p. Toth* [2000] 1 W.L.R. 2209 at [6]; *R. v Wealden DC Ex p. Atkinson* (1995) 8 Admin. L.Rep. 529.

[79] See, e.g. *Organon Laboratories Limited v Department of Health and Social Security* [1990] 2 C.M.L.R. 49 at [79]–[80]. *R. (Amin) v Secretary of State for the Home Department* [2003] 3 W.L.R. 1169 at [39] and [52]; *Raji v General Medical Council* [2003] 1 W.L.R. 1052 at [17] and *Berkeley v Secretary of State for the Environment* [2001] 2 A.C. 603 at [8].

[80] See, e.g. *John v Rees* [1970] Ch. 345, at [402]; *R. v Secretary of State for the Environment Ex p. Brent LBC* [1982] Q.B. 593 at [734]. And see *R. (Al-Hasan) v Secretary of State for the Home Department* [2005] 1 W.L.R. 688 esp. at [43] (once proceedings impugned for lack of independence and impartiality, decision should be quashed).

[81] *R. v Governors of John Bacon School Ex p. Inner London Education Authority* [1990] C.O.D. 414. See also *R. v Governors of Small Heath School Ex p. Birmingham City Council* (1989) 2 Admin. L.Rep. 154 and *R. v Lincolnshire CC and Wealden DC Ex p. Atkinson* above, fn.69 (in normal circumstances, a remedy will follow if illegality is established) and see *Raji v General Medical Council* [2003] 1 W.L.R. 1052 at [17].

[82] *Ex p. Inner London Education Authority* [1990] C.O.D. 414.

[83] The Bill proposes that a court must also refuse to grant permission to apply for judicial review on this basis if the point is raised either by the defendant or by the court of its own motion.

the significance of that person's participation, or even silent presence, on the deliberations of the collective body. There is also the important consideration that justice must not only be done but be seen to be done. The presence of one or more persons tainted with bias may leave a reasonable person in doubt as to the impartiality of the collective decision-making body.

In the past, the courts have quashed a decision where only some members of the body were tainted by bias.[84] On one occasion, the courts quashed a decision of a committee where one person had a pecuniary interest even though he had not participated in the deliberations.[85] More recently, the Divisional Court considered that where two members of a local authority committee with a pecuniary interest voted for a decision, that only affected the size of the majority for the final decision. This was a factor which could legitimately influence the court to refuse a remedy.[86] The Court of Appeal affirmed the decision on other grounds, but Glidewell LJ indicated, obiter, that such a consideration was relevant.[87] The Court of Appeal in another case left open the issue.[88] The issue remains to be fully considered by the courts.

12–031

The second difficulty occurs where a public body may have more than one reason for taking a decision. One reason may be lawful whilst the other may not be. The decision will be invalid if the unlawful reason materially influenced the decision-maker[89]and the decision will be quashed unless the factor played no material or significant part in the decision-making process.[90] There are circumstances where it is possible to separate out the valid and the invalid reasons. The court will not quash a decision where the reasons for the decision can clearly be disentangled and the court is satisfied that, even though one reason is bad in law, the public body would have reached the same decision on the valid ground alone.[91] The courts will intervene to quash a decision if the valid and invalid reasons cannot be disentangled or where the reasons can be separated out, but the invalid reason materially or substantially influenced the decision-maker.[92] These principles can either be seen as part of the substantive law so that the decision is not treated as invalid, or as an aspect of the remedial discretion of the court.[93]

12–032

---

[84] See, e.g. *Hannam v Bradford Corp.* [1970] 1 W.L.R. 937 (three members of committee of ten not eligible to participate—decision invalid).

[85] *R. v Hendon Rural DC Ex p. Chorley* [1933] 2 K.B. 696.

[86] *R. v Governors of Small Heath School Ex p. Birmingham City Council, The Times*, May 31, 1989, DC.

[87] *R. v Governors of Small Heath School Ex p. Birmingham City Council* (1989) 2 Admin. L.Rep. 154.

[88] *R. v Waltham Forest LBC Ex p. Baxter* [1988] Q.B. 419, esp., per Lord Donaldson M.R. at [426].

[89] *R. v Inner London Education Authority Ex p. Westminster City Council* [1986] 1 W.L.R. 28; *Hanks v Minister of Housing and Local Government* [1963] 1 Q.B. 999. This formulation of the test is now preferred to asking what was the true or dominant purpose of the decision-maker.

[90] *Simplex GE (Holdings) Ltd. v Secretary of State for the Environment* (1988) 57 P.& C.R. 306 at [325]–[326]; *R. (First Division Association) v Secretary of State for Work and Pensions* [2014] 1 W.L.R. 444 at [67].

[91] *R. v Broadcasting Complaints Commission Ex p. Owen* [1985] Q.B. 1153, at [1177]; *R (First Division Association) v Secretary of State for Work and Pensions* [2014] 1 W.L.R. 444 at [67]–[69].

[92] *R. v Lewisham BC Ex p. Shell U.K.* [1988] 1 All E.R. 938.

[93] *R. v Broadcasting Complaints Commission Ex p. Owen* [1985] Q.B. 1153.

D. IMPACT ON THIRD PARTIES

12–033 Decisions of public bodies may affect not only the claimant, but third parties who may have acted in the belief that the decision was valid. The court may have regard to the interests of such third parties, whether or not they are before the court, in deciding whether to exercise their remedial discretion to refuse relief. In the financial field, decisions of regulatory bodies, such as the Monopolies and Mergers Commission,[94] or the Panel on Take-overs and Mergers,[95] may be relied upon in good faith by dealers in the market. The court will take into account their interests in determining whether to grant a remedy. In the education field, where a local authority challenges a decision of the Minister on the status of a particular school, the interests of that school and of other schools affected by the proposals need to be considered in deciding whether to grant a remedy.[96] Similarly, the court will have regard to the impact on parents and child of quashing decisions in relation to school closures or school re-organisations.[97]

12–034 A claimant may be seeking to challenge a normative act such as delegated legislation. Again, the court may take into account the consequences on third parties of invalidating the measure. On one occasion Webster J. went so far as to say that it would not necessarily be the "normal practice" to quash delegated legislation unless there were special reasons for doing so.[98] This approach, however, goes too far and the Court of Appeal has declined to approve it. The Court accepted that, if there were pressing reasons, it may be appropriate not to quash delegated legislation but such legislation did not have any specially protected position in that respect.[99]

E. IMPACT ON ADMINISTRATION

12–035 The courts now recognise that the impact on the administration is relevant in the exercise of their remedial jurisdiction. Quashing decisions may impose heavy administrative burdens on the administration, divert resources towards re-opening decisions, and lead to increased and unbudgeted expenditure. Earlier cases took the robust line that the law had to be observed, and the decision invalidated

---

[94] *R. v Monopolies and Mergers Commission Ex p. Argyll Group* [1986] 1 W.L.R. 763. See also *R. v Swale DC Ex p. Royal Society for the Protection of Birds* (1990) 2 Admin. L.Rep. 790 and *R. v Brent LBC Ex p. O'Malley* (1997) 10 Admin. L.Rep. 265.

[95] *R. v Panel on Take-overs and Mergers Ex p. Datafin* [1987] Q.B. 815; *R. v Panel on Take-overs and Mergers Ex p. Guinness Plc* [1990] 1 Q.B. 146.

[96] See, e.g. *R. v Secretary of State for Education and Science Ex p. Avon CC* [1990] C.O.D. 237.

[97] See, e.g. *R. v Leeds City Council Ex p. N* [1999] E.L.R. 324 at [333]–[334]; *R. v Rochdale Metropolitan BC Ex p. B, C and K* [2000] Ed. C.R. 117 (cited with approval in *R. (Burkett) v Hammersmith and Fulham LBC* [2002] 1 W.L.R. 1593 at [18]); *R. v Governors of Bacon School Ex p. I.L.E.A.* [1990] C.O.D. 414.

[98] *R. v Secretary of State for Social Services Ex p. Association of Metropolitan Authorities* [1986] 1 W.L.R. 1 at [15].

[99] *R. (C) v Secretary of State for Justice* [2009] Q.B. 657 at [41]. The courts will scrutinise claims of administrative inconvenience and financial embarrassment carefully: *R. v Secretary of State for Health Ex p. Natural Medicines Group* [1991] C.O.D. 60.

whatever the administrative inconvenience caused.[100] The courts nowadays recognise that such an approach is not always appropriate and may not be in the wider public interest. The effect on the administrative process is relevant to the courts' remedial discretion and may prove decisive. This is particularly the case when the challenge is procedural[101] rather than substantive, or if the courts can be certain that the administrator would not reach a different decision even if the original decision were quashed.[102] Judges may differ in the importance they attach to the disruption that quashing a decision will cause. They may also be influenced by the extent to which the illegality arises from the conduct of the administrative body itself, and their view of that conduct.

This approach is best exemplified by *R. v Monopolies and Mergers Commission Ex p. Argyll Group.*[103] Sir John Donaldson M.R. emphasised the need to take into consideration the principles of good public administration in deciding whether to grant a remedy. There, a decision that a take-over bid had been abandoned, leaving the bidder free to make a fresh bid, was taken by the Chairman of the Commission. Under the statute, the decision should have been taken by the Commission and there was no power to delegate the decision to the Chairman. The Court of Appeal refused a remedy, referring to the need for speedy decision-making, finality and decisiveness once a decision has been reached, particularly in the financial markets. Compelling reasons would be needed to quash a decision in such circumstances. The public interest had been protected as the Secretary of State had approved the decision. Against that the interest of the applicant, who was simply a commercial rival seeking to prevent the bidder from making a fresh bid, was insufficient to merit granting certiorari to quash the decision. — 12–036

Similar concern for the administrative burdens imposed by quashing measures can be seen in other areas. The Court of Appeal stated that it would not quash a scheme for re-organising schools, as much effort and money had been spent on implementing the scheme.[104] The Court of Appeal also declined to quash a decision relating to the budget available for youth services where there had been a failure to have due regard to the impact of the decision pursuant to the public sector equality duty imposed by s.149 of the Equality Act 2010. The decision related to a financial year that had ended three months before the hearing and it would not be feasible, and would be detrimental to good administration, to — 12–037

---

[100] See, e.g. dicta of Lord Denning M.R. in *Bradbury v Enfield LBC* [1967] 3 All E.R. 434 at [441], and of Salmon LJ in *R. v Paddington Valuation Officer Ex p. Peachey Property Corp. (No.2)* [1966] 1 Q.B. 380 at [419]. See also *R. v Governors of Small Heath School Ex p. Birmingham City Council* [1990] C.O.D. 23 (doubting whether administrative inconvenience was a sound and relevant reason for refusing relief).

[101] *R. v Secretary of State for Social Services Ex p. Association of Metropolitan Authorities* ([1983] 1 W.L.R. 1. See also *R. v Brent LBC Ex p. O'Malley* (1997) 10 Admin. L.Rep. 265.

[102] *R. v Monopolies and Mergers Commission Ex p. Argyll Group* (see above, fn.3); see also *R. v Governors of Bacon's School Ex p. I.L.E.A.* [1990] C.O.D. 414 (courts do have such a discretion but should not routinely refuse relief; there is a public interest in providing a sanction for breach which also has to be considered) and see also *R. v Secretary of State for Health Ex p. Natural Medicines Group* [1991] C.O.D. 60.

[103] [1986] 1 W.L.R. 763.

[104] *R. v Gateshead Metropolitan BC Ex p. Nichol; R. v Cornwall CC Ex p. Nicholls* (see above, fn.44) and *R. v Dorset CC Ex p. Greenwood* [1990] C.O.D. 235. See also *R. v Governors of Bacon School Ex p. I.L.E.A.* [1990] C.O.D. 414. See also *R. v Brent LBC Ex p. O'Malley* (1997) 10 Admin. L.Rep.. 265.

re-open the budget for the previous financial year.[105] The Court of Appeal refused to quash a local authority's decision to dispose of housing stock on a housing estate where there had been a failure to consult as the implementation of the scheme had already begun and there was a substantial risk that the scheme would collapse if judicial review were granted. The costs already incurred were in excess of £3 million and those costs and years of work would be wasted if relief were granted.[106] Webster J. refused to quash regulations restricting housing benefit, as this would impose an undue burden on all local authorities who had acted upon the regulations and who would be faced with fresh claims for benefits if the regulations were quashed.[107] The challenges were principally concerned with the lack of consultation not the substance of the regulations, and in the circumstances it would be inappropriate to quash the regulations. Similar considerations are relevant in the planning area.[108]

12–038   The courts have on occasions delayed the granting of a remedy rather than refusing it altogether, in order to give a local authority time to determine how it would react to a judgment.[109]

12–039   The courts may take account of the potential effect on the administration in determining the substantive principles of judicial review. It may influence a court in classing a procedural requirement as mandatory or directory[110]; or whether a duty is absolute or qualified by notions of reasonableness[111]; or whether, on a true construction, a statutory duty arises.[112] Criticism could be made of the courts having regard to such factors, on the grounds that they should be concerned with legality not administrative policy, and may not be well versed in matters of public administration. It would, however, be unrealistic and probably unsatisfactory for the courts to ignore administrative realities. The discretion to refuse relief is unobjectionable so long as it is exercised sensibly, with due regard for both the interests of the applicant and the administration. Parliament has sanctioned judicial involvement in such areas: the provisions on delay in the Senior Courts Act 1981 expressly require the court to consider the impact on administration.[113]

---

[105] *R. (Hunt) v North Somerset Council* (2013) 16 CCL. Rep. 530 now on appeal to the Supreme Court).

[106] *R. v Brent LBC Ex p. O'Malley* (1997) 10 Admin. L.Rep 265. at [291G]–[292B].

[107] *R. v Secretary of State for Social Services Ex p. Association of Metropolitan Authorities* (see above, fn.87).

[108] *Lovelock v Minister of Transport* (1980) 40 P. & C.R. 336 (the concern with the effect of quashing a scheme years after its implementation is a safer ground for upholding the decision today than its novel use of presumptions of validity); *R. v Swale DC Ex p. Royal Society for the Protection of Birds*, above fn.5.

[109] *R. v Greater London Council Ex p. Blackburn* [1976] 1 W.L.R. 550; *R. v Hereford Corp. Ex p. Harrower* [1970] 1 W.L.R. 1424. See also *R. (Cali) v Waltham Forest L.B.* [2006] A.C.D. 344 (declaration granted that housing policy was unlawful; no mandatory order granted, thereby allowing the authority time to review its policy). In *A v HM Treasury* [2010] 2 A.C. 534 the Supreme Court declined to suspend an order quashing parts of an Order in Council: see decision at paras 5–012 to 5–013 above.

[110] *Main v Swansea City Council* (1985) 49 P. & C.R. 26.

[111] *Meade v Haringey LBC* [1979] 1 W.L.R. 637.

[112] See, e.g. *R. v Secretary of State for Social Services Ex p. Child Poverty Action Group*, *The Times*, August 8, 1985 (Court of Appeal rejected a construction of a statute which would have required re-opening cases which would have cost £4.8 million).

[113] s.31(6) and see para.12–010.

F. NATURE OF DECISION

The nature of the decision-making process in question may influence the **12–040** willingness of the courts to intervene. Some matters are not justiciable, in that they are unsuitable for resolution by the courts.[114] Other matters are not strictly speaking non-justiciable and the courts maintain the possibility of review in appropriate circumstances. In practice, judicial review is likely to be rare in certain areas. The courts have indicated, for example, that they will not normally interfere in decisions involving the allocation of resources, particularly in a field involving difficult expert judgments such as the health service.[115] The House of Lords has emphasised the undesirability of the courts intervening too readily to review decisions involving the allocation of limited resources.[116] It is also unlikely that a court would state that they were exercising their discretion to refuse a remedy where a clear reviewable error had been committed. The nature of the dispute may, however, influence the court, and they may exercise a less stringent degree of supervision in certain areas or take a broader view of the range of reasonable actions that a public body could take in the area.

Nature of the error committed

The nature of the error may affect the willingness of the courts to grant or refuse **12–041** a remedy. Some decisions are ones that the public body is capable in law of taking, but for some reason there has been an error in the decision-making process. If the decision were quashed, the public body could reconsider the matter and would be entitled to reach the same decision. In such cases, the courts may be more prepared to accept that other considerations, such as the financial impact on third parties or the administration, should outweigh the need to correct illegalities in the decision-making process. Thus, the courts have, when refusing a remedy, referred to the fact that the error that has occurred is a procedural error such as a failure to consult, and that fact is outweighed by other considerations.[117] If, however, the decision is one that the body has no power at all to make, there is some suggestion that the courts may be less prepared to refuse a remedy, since this would amount to allowing the body to do things that it has not been authorised to do.[118]

---

[114] See para.4–083.

[115] *Re Walker's Application, The Times*, November 26, 1987.

[116] *R. v Chief Constable of Sussex Ex p. International Trader's Ferry Ltd* [1999] 2 A.C. 418. See also *R. v Cambridge Health Authority Ex p. B.* [1995] 1 W.L.R. 898 at [906].

[117] *R. v Swale BC Ex p. Royal Society for the Protection of Birds* (see above fn.6); *R. v Secretary of State for Social Services Ex p. Association of Metropolitan Authorities* (see above, fn.87).

[118] *R. v Exeter City Council Ex p. J.L. Thomas & Co. Ltd* [1990] 3 W.L.R. 100 at [111]–[112].

G. ALTERNATIVE REMEDIES

Existence of alternative remedies

12–042　Judicial review may not be the only available avenue of challenging a particular decision. Statute may create an appellate machinery to deal with appeals against decisions of public bodies. There is wide variety in the pattern of such schemes. There may be an appeal from a decision to a tribunal or other appellate body, with a further right of appeal on a point of law or by way of case stated to the High Court or the Court of Appeal.[119] Such mechanisms exist in a number of fields, most importantly in the field of revenue law[120]; enforcement notices in planning law[121]; and decisions of inferior courts in the criminal sphere, such as magistrates' courts.[122] There may be an appeal from a decision to an administrative tribunal or inferior court, but with no right of appeal direct to the High Court. There may be appeal from decisions to an administrative body such as a Secretary of State, either with provision for appeal to the courts—as with appeals against enforcement notices issued by planning authorities alleging a breach of planning control[123]—or without any further right of appeal. Furthermore, there has now been a rationalisation of the process of appeals to tribunals. The Tribunals, Courts and Enforcement Act 2007 establishes a system of First-tier tribunals, with appeals to the Upper Tribunal. The jurisdiction of many tribunals to hear appeals has now been transferred to the First-tier Tribunals with an appeal to the Upper Tribunal.[124] Many appeals against decisions of public authorities are, therefore, now heard by the First-tier Tribunal with a right of appeal, if permission is granted, to the Upper Tribunal. A public authority may have a statutory or non-statutory internal procedure to consider complaints.[125]

Exhaustion of alternative remedies

12–043　A court may, in its discretion, refuse to grant permission to apply for judicial review[126] or refuse a remedy at the substantive hearing[127] if an adequate alternative remedy exists, or if such a remedy existed but the claimant had failed

---

[119] See, generally, Chapter 14.

[120] See, e.g. Part V of the Taxes Management Act 1970.

[121] Town and Country Planning Act 1990 s.289.

[122] Magistrates' Courts Act 1980 s.111.

[123] Town and Country Planning Act 1990 s.289.

[124] For a description of the new system, see *R. (Cart) v Upper Tribunal* [2012] 1 A.C. 663 at [22]. See also Chapter 10.

[125] Local authorities, e.g., have to maintain a complaints procedure in relation to its social services functions: see Local Authorities Social Services Act 1970 s.7B.

[126] *R. v Secretary of State for the Home Department Ex p. Swati* [1986] 1 W.L.R. 477; *R. v Secretary of State for the Home Department Ex p. Capti-Mehmet* [1997] C.O.D. 61. Permission has been set aside where there was an alternative remedy available: see, e.g. *R. v Secretary of State for the Home Department Ex p. Doorga* [1990] C.O.D. 109; *R. v Secretary of State for the Environment Ex p. Watts* [1997] C.O.D. 152. The point is now likely to arise before permission is granted, as the defendant now has the opportunity to raise the point in the acknowledgment of service. A defendant served with a claim form cannot now apply to set aside permission: CPR, r.54.13.

[127] In *R. v Birmingham City Council Ex p. Ferrero Ltd* [1993] 1 All E.R. 530 the Court of Appeal allowed an appeal from a successful judicial review application on the ground that the applicant

to use it. The courts have evolved a general principle that an individual should normally use alternative remedies where these are available rather than judicial review.[128] The courts take the view that: "... save in the most exceptional circumstances, that [judicial review] jurisdiction will not be exercised where other remedies were available and have not been used."[129] In the case where there is an appeal from a decision to an administrative tribunal or inferior court, this means that individuals should only resort to judicial review after exhausting their rights of appeal. At that stage, the decision of the appellate body will be subject to judicial review if the individual is still dissatisfied with the outcome and there is no further right of appeal. In cases where there is an ultimate appeal against the decision of the tribunal to the High Court or Court of Appeal, that will be the appropriate route to follow rather than seeking judicial review of the decision of the tribunal. An individual who fails to appeal within the appropriate time-limit (which may be shorter than the three month time-limit for judicial review) may be unable to seek judicial review and unable to challenge the decision.[130] There are also a group of cases involving inferior courts and tribunals where permission is needed to appeal. In cases involving decisions of the Upper Tribunal refusing leave to appeal against decisions of the First-tier Tribunal, permission to apply for judicial review may only be granted if there is an arguable case that the decisions of both the Upper Tribunal and the First-tier Tribunal were wrong in law and the claim raises an important point of principle or practice.[131] In other cases, involving county court or other inferior courts or tribunals, judicial review of a decision refusing permission has been refused save in exceptional circumstances.[132] In cases where there is an alternative administrative procedure, such as a complaints procedure, the courts will require the claimant to use that procedure before resorting to judicial review.[133]

The position is not as straightforward as the dicta suggest. The exhaustion of **12–044** remedies "rule" is only a general principle governing the exercise of judicial discretion. There are qualifications on that principle, and different formulations

---

should have used the statutory appeals procedure. See also *R. v Commissioners for Customs and Excise Ex p. Mortimer* [1998] 3 All E.R. 229 at [235f–j] (Customs acted unlawfully in failing to give individual opportunity to rebut presumption that importing goods illegally; remedy refused as the claimant had right of appeal to the magistrates' court).

[128] See, particularly, *R. v Chief Constable of Merseyside Police Ex p. Calveley* [1986] Q.B. 424; *R. v Secretary of State for the Home Department Ex p. Swati* [1986] 1 W.L.R. 477; *R. v Birmingham City Council Ex p. Ferrero Ltd* [1993] 1 All E.R. 530; *R. (Sivasubramaniam) v Wandsworth County Court* [2003] 1 W.L.R. 475 at [47]; *R. v Falmouth and Truro Port Health Authority* [2000] 3 W.L.R. 1464 at [1490H]–[1491A] and [1494B]–[1495C]; *R. (Davies) v Financial Service Authority* [2004] 1 W.L.R 185 at [29]–[32]; *R. (G) Immigration Appeal Tribunal* [2005] 1 W.L.R. 1445. For a more circumspect approach, see *R. v Hereford Magistrates' Court Ex p. Rowlands* [1998] Q.B. 110.

[129] per Sir John Donaldson M.R. in *R. v Epping and Harlow General Commissioners Ex p. Goldstraw* [1983] 3 All E.R 257 at [262].

[130] As happened in *Ex p. Goldstraw* ([1983] 3 All E.R. 257 at [262]). The court may exceptionally allow judicial review even if the individual should have appealed and the time-limit for appealing has passed, where it considers that on the merits the case should be heard: see *R. v Secretary of State for the Environment Ex p. Davidson* (1990) 59 P. & C.R. 480 and *R. v Tower Hamlets LBC Ex p. Ahern (London) Ltd.* (1990) 59 P. & C.R. 133.

[131] CPR r.54.7A and *R. (Cart) the Upper Tribunal* [2012] 1 A.C. 663.

[132] *R. (Sivasubramaniam) v Wandsworth County Court* [2003] 1 W.L.R. 475.

[133] *R. (Cowl) v Plymouth City Council* [2002] 1 W.L.R. 803 at [10]–[14]; *R. v Barking and Dagenham LBC Ex p. Lloyd* [2001] L.G.R. 421; *R. (Carnell) v Regents Park College and Conference of Colleges Appeal Tribunal* [2008] E.L.R. 739.

and understandings of the rule can be seen in the case law. Judges have also exhibited "... varying emphasis on the reluctance to grant judicial review".[134] One recurrent theme is the extent to which errors which could be corrected by way of judicial review should be left to the appellate system. Another important issue is the adequacy of the alternative remedy as a means of resolving the complaint. These issues can be seen as defining the scope of the "exhaustion of remedies" principle, or as exceptions to the general rule. In addition, an alternative remedy which may normally be adequate may not on the particular facts of a case be appropriate, and that may justify allowing recourse to judicial review. In exceptional circumstances, which, "... by definition... defy definition",[135] judicial review may be used notwithstanding the availability of alternative remedies.

Rationale for the principle

12–045   The rationale for the exhaustion of alternative remedies principle is relevant to the scope of that principle.[136] A two-fold justification has been put forward. First, that where Parliament has provided for a statutory appeals procedure, it is not for the courts to usurp the functions of the appellate body.[137] The principle applies equally to bodies not created by statute which have their own appellate system.[138] Secondly, the public interest dictates that judicial review should be exercised speedily, and to that end it is necessary to limit the number of cases in which judicial review is used.[139] More generally, the courts now encourage parties to resolve disputes without resorting to the expense of litigation.[140] To these reasons can be added the additional expertise that the appellate bodies possess. In employment cases, for example, the system of employment and Employment Appeal Tribunals may be better equipped to deal with industrial issues than the High Court.[141] In the financial services field, specialist procedures and a specialist tribunal have been established to deal with certain matters.[142] Similarly, where there is a further appeal to the courts, this may be to a division of the High Court particularly familiar with the area in question, as in tax cases, where the appeal is heard in the Chancery Division not the Queen's Bench Division. A third related reason exists in relation to cases where a challenge to a decision of an

---

[134] per Sir John Donaldson M.R. in *R. v Chief Constable of Merseyside Police Ex p. Calveley* [1986] Q.B. 424 at [433].

[135] per Sir John Donaldson M.R. in *R. v Secretary of State for the Home Department Ex p. Swati* [1986] 1 W.L.R. 477 at [485].

[136] See Lewis, "The Exhaustion of Alternative Remedies in Administrative Law" [1992] C.L.J. 138.

[137] *R. v Panel on Take-overs and Mergers Ex p. Guinness Plc* [1990] Q.B. 146 at [176G]–[178] and see *R. (Sivasubramaniam) v Wandsworth County Court* [2003] 1 W.L.R. 475 at [48] and *R. (Davies) v Financial Services Authority* [2004] 1 W.L.R. 185 at [30]–[31]. See also in a different context, *Autologic Holdings Plc v Inland Revenue Commissioners* [2006] 1 A.C. 118 at [11]–[15].

[138] The Panel on Take-overs and Mergers is itself such a body and the Court of Appeal considered that the principle applied.

[139] *R. v Panel on Take-overs and Mergers Ex p. Guinness Plc* [1990] Q.B. 146.

[140] See dicta in *R. (Cowl) v Plymouth City Council* [2002] 1 W.L.R. 803 at [14] and [25]–[27].

[141] See, e.g. *R. v Civil Service Appeals Board Ex p. Bruce* [1989] I.C.R. 171. The courts have, also, emphasised the expertise of tribunals in considering whether to grant permission for a second appeal to the Court of Appeal: see, e.g. *Cooke v Secretary of State for Social Security* [2002] 2 All E.R 279 (at [15]–[17]); *AH (Sudan) v Secretary of State for the Home Department* [2008] A.C. 678 at [30].

[142] See *R. (Davies) v Financial Services Authority* [2004] 1 W.L.R. 185 at [31].

inferior court or tribunal may be brought only with leave. If permission to appeal is refused, judicial review will only be granted exceptionally and, in normal circumstances, the claimant has no means of challenging the initial decision or the refusal of permission to appeal. Here the justification for refusing judicial review lies in the fact that the scheme as a whole provides a fair, adequate and proportionate protection for claimants. Where Parliament has put in place an adequate system for challenging and reviewing decisions of inferior courts and tribunals, it is not appropriate to provide an additional means of challenge by way of judicial review save in exceptional circumstances.[143]

Scope of the principle

The courts have developed guidelines for determining when a matter should be brought by way of the appellate procedure, and not by way of judicial review. The following factors have been identified as relevant to that question.   **12–046**

Type of error

A distinction can be drawn between cases raising the sort of issues which the statutory procedure is specifically set up to deal with, and cases involving generalised principles of public law developed by the courts to control the exercise of power. The former includes the construction and the application of the relevant legislation.[144] The latter would include reviewable errors, such as abuse of power. There are considerable areas of overlap. An error in construing the legislation would be an error of law which would also be susceptible to judicial review now that the courts have decided that any error of law is reviewable. In principle, if the error arises out of the application of the specialised legislative code that the appellate system is set up to deal with, the matter should normally go on appeal not review. In the words of the Master of the Rolls[145]:   **12–047**

> "...where Parliament provides an appeal procedure, judicial review will have no place unless the applicant can distinguish his case from the type of case for which the appeal procedure was provided."

In some cases, the issue is one that is particularly suited to the appellate system. In one case, for example, a company sought judicial review of a suspension notice issued under the relevant consumer protection legislation prohibiting the sale of a product which was believed to be dangerous to children. There was a statutory right of appeal to the magistrates' court which could set   **12–048**

---

[143] *R. (Sivasubramaniam) v Wandsworth County Court* [2003] 1 W.L.R. 475 at [49]–[57]; *R. (G) v Immigration Appeal Tribunal* [2005] 1 W.L.R. 1445 at [26]–[27]. See also dicta in *R (Cart) v Upper Tribunal* [2012] 1 A.C. 63 recognising that proportionality and appropriate use of judicial resources is relevant in assessing when judicial review should be available in respect of decisions refusing permission to appeal (see [41]–[42], [89] and [124]).

[144] See, e.g. *R. v Chief Adjudication Officer Ex p. Bland, The Times*, February 6, 1985 and *R. v Commissioner for the Special Purposes of the Income Tax Acts Ex p. Napier* [1988] 3 All E.R. 166 at [171] for discussion of this distinction.

[145] per Sir John Donaldson M.R. in *R. v Secretary of State for the Home Department Ex p. Swati* [1986] 1 W.L.R. 477 at [485]. See also *R. v Birmingham City Council Ex p. Ferrero Ltd* [1993] 1 All E.R. 530.

aside the notice only if they were satisfied that the product met the safety requirements imposed by the legislation. Under the legislation, the real issue to be determined, therefore, was whether the product was safe. The appeal process was geared exactly to deciding that issue. The courts therefore held that, as a matter of discretion, judicial review should be refused.[146]

12-049   One issue that has arisen is the extent to which questions of procedural error or breach of natural justice are suitable for resolution by an appellate mechanism. This area straddles the border between general public law and the specialised statutory scheme, since the issue of what procedure is appropriate depends on what is fair in the circumstances of a particular case. Breaches of the procedural rules will normally be dealt with on appeal, where the statutory scheme itself sets out the relevant procedural rules.[147] Breach of the common law principles of natural justice may be dealt with on appeal, providing that the appellate body can deal adequately with such complaints. In the tax field, for example, the courts have held that issues of natural justice may be dealt with by the appeal system.[148] Appeals on points of law to the county court in the housing field encompass all the grounds of judicial review, including procedural irregularity.[149] Where challenges to the fairness of the initial decision may be raised on appeal, it would not generally be appropriate to grant judicial review of the initial decision.[150] In some instances, notably where criminal penalties are in issue, the individual is intended to have both a fair hearing before the initial body and before the appeal body. In such instances, individuals may be permitted either to appeal or to seek judicial review of the first decision on the grounds of procedural unfairness. The Divisional Court has, for example, held that a person complaining of procedural unfairness in the magistrates' court could proceed by way of judicial review.[151] He was not required to exercise his right of appeal to the Crown Court nor was he required to appeal by way of case stated, even though the question of whether there had been a breach of procedural fairness could be dealt with on an appeal by case stated. The decision in relation to the right of appeal to the Crown Court is readily understandable as the legislation is intended to ensure that there is a fair trial in the magistrates' court and a fair re-hearing in the Crown Court. The Crown Court is not intended to act as a supervisory body controlling the procedure in the magistrates' court. A claimant would be prejudiced if he had to be content with an unfair hearing in the magistrates' court but a fair hearing on appeal.[152] The decision is less readily explicable in respect of the appeal by way of case stated. The Divisional Court did not give reasons why this remedy was not adequate. It may have been influenced by the long-standing practice of using judicial review to ventilate complaints about procedural unfairness in magistrates' courts. The Divisional Court considered that challenges other than those

---

[146] *R. v Birmingham City Council Ex p. Ferrero Ltd* [1993] 1 All E.R. 530 at [538h]–[539h].

[147] *R. v Secretary of State for the Home Department Ex p. Swati* [1986] 1 W.L.R. 477.

[148] *R. v Brentford General Commissioners Ex p. Chan* [1986] S.T.C. 65; *R. v Commissioner for the Special Purposes of the Income Tax Acts Ex p. Napier* [1988] 3 All E.R. 166 and see *Banin v Mackinlay (Inspector of Taxes)* [1985] 1 All E.R. 842.

[149] *Begum v Tower Hamlets LBC* [2000] 3 W.L.R. 306 and see *Rung Begum v Tower Hamlets LBC* [2003] 2 A.C. 430 at [7] and [17].

[150] *R. (DR) v Head Teacher of S School* [2003] E.L.R. 104 at [45] and [54].

[151] *R. v Hereford Magistrates' Court Ex p. Rowlands* [1998] Q.B. 110.

[152] [1998] Q.B. 110 at [864]–[866].

complaining of procedural unfairness, such as a complaint that the magistrates had erred in law or that there was no evidence upon which the justices were entitled to convict, would normally be pursued by appeal by way of case stated.[153] In other fields, the courts have also left open the possibility of allowing complaints of natural justice to be dealt with by judicial review rather than appeal.[154]

Challenges based on distinct principles of public law or general issues of law unconnected with the specific statutory code may be dealt with by judicial review. The courts have allowed the use of the judicial review procedure where an applicant raises an arguable case that a public body has acted for an improper purpose, or has acted unfairly,[155] or has unlawfully fettered its discretion[156] or raises the general question of the extent to which representations can bind public bodies.[157] This is particularly the case where the issue is one of law in a developing field and there is a need for authoritative guidance from the courts.[158] The House of Lords considered the compatibility of employment legislation with EU law on a judicial review claim. The true defendant was the Secretary of State, not the individual employer, and the issues of fact that arose were widely different from those which an industrial tribunal usually dealt with.[159] It may also be the case that a challenge to the lawfulness of a particular system, rather than its application to the facts of, and the decision in, a particular case will be more readily allowed to proceed by way of judicial review.[160] The distinction between an error suitable for correction on appeal and an error suitable for judicial review is not always easy to draw.[161]

12–050

It should also be noted that statutory appeal procedures may limit the grounds on which, or the decisions against which an appeal may be brought. The Court of Appeal has, for example, held that an appeal to an immigration adjudicator against a decision to make a deportation order may only be made on the ground that a power to deport the person does not exist. The appeal body could not consider whether the power was improperly exercised or whether there was a procedural irregularity. Such questions could only be raised by judicial review, as the appeal body has no jurisdiction to determine such issues.[162]

12–051

---

[153] [1998] Q.B. 110 at [859].

[154] See, e.g. the dicta of Taylor LJ in *R. v Civil Service Appeals Board Ex p. Bruce* [1989] I.C.R. 171.

[155] *R. v I.R.C. Ex p. Preston* [1985] A.C. 835.

[156] *R. v Nottingham City Council Ex p. Howitt*, unreported, May 25, 1999.

[157] *R. v I.R.C. Ex p. M.F.K. Underwriting Agencies* [1990] 1 All E.R. 91. *R. v Devon CC Ex p. Baker* [1995] 1 All E.R. 73.

[158] *R. v Devon CC Ex p. Baker* [1995] 1 All E.R. 75 at [87b–d] per Dillon LJ and at [92f–h] per Simon Brown LJ See below at para.12–064.

[159] *R. v Secretary of State for Employment Ex p. E.O.C.* [1995] 1 A.C. 1.

[160] See dicta in *R. (T) v Commissioner of the Police of the Metropolis* [2012] 1 W.L.R. 2978 at [104].

[161] See, e.g. *R. v Secretary of State for the Home Department Ex p. Hindjou* [1989] Imm.A.R. 24 distinguishing *Ex p. Swati* [1986] 1 W.L.R. 477 on the grounds that misapplication of the criteria by the immigration officer was a reviewable error and distinguishing the case from the normal run of cases where appeal was appropriate. See also *R. v Birmingham City Council Ex p. Ferrero Ltd* (above, fn.116).

[162] *R. v Secretary of State for the Home Department Ex p. Malhi* [1990] 2 W.L.R. 932, approved by the House of Lords in *R. v Secretary of State for the Home Department Ex p. Oladehinde* [1991] 1 A.C. 254.

Distinction between appeal and review

12–052   A more traditional distinction is that between appeal and review. Appeal deals
with the merits of the case whereas review deals with the legality of the exercise
of power. Appeal may frequently be wider than review and the appellate body
may be able to look at facts, opinion and policy where a reviewing court would
not. Appeal will be more appropriate where such questions are interwoven with
issues of law, since all such issues may be dealt with by the appeal body whereas
a reviewing court would be limited to correcting errors of law.[163] Some
complaints raise questions of law. Here, the area of overlap between appeal and
review is now great, as potentially all errors of law are reviewable. Such errors
may now be corrected either by way of appeal or judicial review. As the scope of
judicial review has expanded, the theoretical distinction between appeal and
review has narrowed considerably in practice. The distinction is therefore not of
much assistance in determining the scope of the exhaustion of remedies rule.[164]
The question of whether appeal or review is a more appropriate method for
dealing with such errors must be settled by other considerations.

Situations in which alternative remedy inadequate

12–053   The courts will not insist that claimants pursue an alternative remedy which is
inadequate. The principle can be defined as one that requires the use of adequate
alternative remedies, or the fact that an alternative remedy is inadequate may be
seen as an exceptional reason why judicial review may be used.[165]

12–054   Inadequacy may arise in a number of ways: the lack of a power to remedy a
complaint fully and appropriately is one example. In *R. v Deputy Governor of
Parkhurst Prison Ex p. Leech*,[166] the Home Secretary had power on appeal to
remit a disciplinary punishment but at that time lacked power to quash the
decision. As a result, a finding of guilty remained on a prisoner's record and
might influence other decisions such as parole decisions. The House of Lords
held that such an appeal was inadequate.[167] The lack of a power to quash
decisions on appeal by way of case stated from Mental Health Tribunals has been
cited as a reason for preferring judicial review.[168]

12–055   An individual may be seeking to challenge the validity of a regulation rather
than appealing against a decision applying or construing that regulation. The
tribunal may not have power to quash the regulation. In such circumstances, the
proper method of challenge is by way of judicial review.[169] Similarly an

---

[163] *R. v Hillingdon LBC Ex p. Royco Homes* [1974] Q.B. 720.

[164] For a contrary view see Wade and Forsyth, 8th edn, pp.691–696.

[165] See the formulation of the Master of the Rolls in *R. (Sivasubramaniam) v Wandsworth County Court* [2002] 1 W.L.R. 475 at [4].

[166] [1988] A.C. 533.

[167] The Home Secretary was subsequently given power to quash: see Prison (Amendment) Rules 1989 (SI 1989/330).

[168] *Bone v Mental Health Review Tribunal* [1985] 3 All E.R. 330.

[169] *Moss (Henry) of London v Customs and Excise Commissioners* [1981] 2 All E.R. 86. See also *T-Mobile (UK) Ltd. v Office of Communication* [2009] 1 W.L.R. 1565; *Chief Adjudication Officer v Foster* [1991] 3 All E.R. 846; *R. v Secretary of State for Social Services Ex p. Clarke* [1988] 1 C.M.L.R. 279, and see also *Proll (Astrid) (alias Puttick, Anna) v Entry Clearance Officer, Dusseldorf* [1988] 2 C.M.L.R. 387.

individual in a particular profession may challenge the validity of new disciplinary rules by judicial review. He is not limited to waiting until he is found guilty of a breach and then appealing against that decision on the grounds that the rules are invalid.[170] A complaint may involve a claim for damages for breach of EU law or of a right derived from the European Convention on Human Rights. An appeal procedure may not be able to deal with such claims and it may be appropriate to seek judicial review, challenging the lawfulness of the act in question and including a claim for damages.[171]

Certain remedies are generally considered an inadequate alternative to judicial review. The opportunity to complain about a local authority decision to the local ombudsman does not affect the ability of an individual to seek judicial review of the decision, if grounds for doing so exist.[172] The role of the local ombudsman is to supplement judicial review remedies, not replace them. The same is presumably true in relation to central government decisions and the ombudsman. A claimant will not normally be refused judicial review against a decision of the police not to enforce certain criminal offences, simply because the opportunity exists to bring private prosecutions against alleged offenders; private prosecutions are not generally an adequate remedy.[173] An anomaly exists in relation to appeals by way of case stated from a magistrates' court in a civil matter where the individual is in custody and the court refuses bail. An individual cannot apply to the High Court for bail until the case stated is lodged. He must therefore apply for judicial review of the decision so that there is an immediate substantive High Court procedure to which an application for bail can be attached.[174]

12–056

Appellate machinery inadequate to resolve dispute

An appellate tribunal may lack the machinery to enable it fully to resolve an issue. An appeal may involve disputed factual issues which, if the appeal is not by way of rehearing or if the appellate body lacks the power to order disclosure,[175] may mean that the appellate body cannot adequately resolve the dispute. In *R. v*

12–057

---

[170] *Pharmaceutical Society of Great Britain v Dickson* [1970] A.C. 403; *R. v General Medical Council Ex p. Colman* [1990] 1 All E.R. 489.

[171] See, e.g. *R. (Hoverspeed Ltd) v Commissioners for Customs and Excise* [2003] 2 W.L.R. 950 at [57]–[58].

[172] *R. v Monmouth DC Ex p. Jones* (1987) 53 P. & C.R. 108. Local Government Act 1974 s.26(1) provides that the local ombudsman should not investigate a complaint which may be dealt with by way of judicial review unless the ombudsman is satisfied that it is not reasonable to expect the person to resort to judicial review: see *R. v Commissioner for Local Administration Ex p. Croydon LBC* [1989] 1 All E.R. 1033. See also *R. v Lambeth LBC Ex p. Crookes* [1996] C.O.D. 398.

[173] *R. v Metropolitan Commissioner of Police of the Metropolis Ex p. Blackburn* [1968] 2 Q.B. 118 and see *R. v Bristol City Council Ex p. Everett* [1998] 3 All E.R. 603 at [617b–f]. In *R. v DPP Ex p. Camelot Plc* (1997) 10 Admin. L.Rep. 93 the Divisional Court indicated that a private prosecution was an appropriate alternative remedy, but, as the Court indicated there, judicial review was inappropriate for other reasons in any event and the reality was that a private prosecution was the only remedy available to the claimant: see above at para.7–056.

[174] *Benham v Poole BC, The Times*, October 10, 1991.

[175] Appellate bodies have no inherent power to order disclosure and need express statutory authority: see *R. v Immigration Adjudicator Ex p. Secretary of State for the Home Office, The Times*, March 29, 1989. Appellate bodies have not normally been given such express powers.

Deputy Governor of Parkhurst Prison Ex p. Leech,[176] appeals against disciplinary awards were conducted by civil servants on the basis of the papers alone. This was considered inadequate where alleged breach of natural justice was in issue, as the appellate authority lacked the power to order discovery and could not resolve disputes of fact. The lack of a power to order disclosure does not render an alternative remedy inadequate, where an issue of statutory construction rather than disputed fact arises for decision.[177]

12–058   Appeal or alternative complaints procedures will frequently be adequate and will often be better equipped to deal with questions of fact than a court considering a judicial review claim. On an appeal to a magistrates' court, for example, the justices will be able to try contested facts on oral evidence.[178] Complaints procedures will frequently provide for there to be an oral hearing before a panel.[179] An appeal by way of case stated against a decision of a Crown Court as to the appropriate sentence was considered more appropriate than judicial review as the case "... bristles with factual difficulties ...".[180] The facts could be set out fully in the case stated, which was more convenient than setting out the facts in a witness statement as would normally happen in judicial review. In addition, the occasions when a reviewing court would determine questions of fact are relatively limited. The issue in judicial review usually concerns the legal significance of established facts rather than resolving a dispute of fact. The appellate machinery may be equally or even more appropriate than judicial review where disputes of fact need to be resolved.

Urgency and speed

12–059   Judicial review is capable of providing a swift means of resolving disputes. There is a procedure for urgent cases whereby applications for permission and also interim relief can be considered within a matter of days. In cases where there is a genuine and urgent need to resolve an issue quickly, judicial review may, exceptionally, be more appropriate than an appeal.

12–060   More generally there are dicta to the effect that if a complaint raises questions of law which could be dealt with either by appeal or by judicial review, the latter

---

[176] [1988] A.C. 533. See also *R. v Paddington Valuation Officer Ex p. Peachey Property Corp. (No.2)* [1966] 1 Q.B. 380.

[177] [1988] A.C. 533 and see *R. v Chief Adjudication Officer Ex p. Bland, The Times*, February 6, 1985 (no problems with discovery as issue raised was solely a question of construction of relevant regulations).

[178] See, e.g. dicta in *R. v Birmingham City Council Ex p. Ferrero Ltd* [1993] 1 All E.R. 530 at [537j].

[179] See, e.g. *R. (Cowl) v Plymouth City Council* [2002] 1 W.L.R. 804 at [9]. In the case of complaints to ministers, the minister may have the means to conduct an appropriate factual inquiry: see dicta in *R. v Devon CC Ex p. Baker* [1995] 1 All E.R. 73 at [92g].

[180] *R. v Ipswich Crown Court Justices Ex p. Baldwin (Note)* [1981] 1 All E.R. 596 at [597]. See also *R. v Battle Justices Ex p. Shepherd* (1983) 5 Cr.App.R.(S) 124 (challenge to imposition of compensation orders better dealt with by appeal against sentence to Crown Court, as full information available to Crown Court). See also *R. v Secretary of State for the Home Department Ex p. Botta (Jacqueline)* [1987] 2 C.M.L.R. 189 (conflict of fact best determined by appeal procedures not judicial review); *R. v Birmingham City Council Ex p. Ferrero Ltd* [1993] 1 All E.R. 530 (justices able to determine contested issues of fact on oral evidence); *R. v Dover Magistrates' Court Ex p. Webb* [1998] C.O.D. 274 (issue of fact in magistrates' court better dealt with by appeal to the Crown Court).

may be preferable as it may be quicker than the appeal procedure.[181] Such dicta probably no longer accurately reflect the current approach of the courts to determining whether the exhaustion of remedies principle applies. The greater speed of judicial review is unlikely of itself to justify circumventing an appeals procedure.[182] Delay in the appellate procedure may be a factor to take into account, and may tip the balance in favour of allowing judicial review.[183] In one case, the Court of Appeal considered the extent to which a challenge to a notice requiring the abatement of a public nuisance and requiring certain steps be taken (namely ceasing to discharge sewage into a particular body of water) within three months could be dealt with by judicial review rather than the statutory appeal procedure. As it was thought that the statutory appeal would not be heard within the three-month period by which the works were to be carried out, the claimant challenged the notice by way of judicial review alleging failure to consult, claiming that the relevant body of water was not a watercourse to which the statutory provision applied and claiming that the notice did not adequately specify the works to be carried out. Permission was granted and a stay of the abatement notice ordered. The judicial review claim was not heard for a further nine months. The Court of Appeal considered that judicial review was not generally appropriate given the statutory right of appeal.[184] Pill LJ considered that it would only be in rare cases that judicial review would be appropriate. He did not consider that questions of convenience and speed justified the use of judicial review rather than the statutory machinery provided.[185] Simon Brown LJ considered that permission should only exceptionally be given where a statutory right of appeal existed but in considering that question, the courts ought to have regard to all relevant considerations, including any public health considerations, the comparative speed, expense and finality of the alternative administrative process, the need for fact-finding, the need for an authoritative ruling on any point of law arising and (possibly) the strength of the claimant's case. He would not have granted permission to argue that there had been a failure to consult but considered that, exceptionally, it was appropriate to consider the other two issues.[186] Much depends on the view that judges take of the need to encourage the use of alternative remedies in order to limit the number of judicial review claims, to ensure that those that are allowed are dealt with speedily, and how that principle is weighed against the need speedily to resolve individual cases suitable for review.

---

[181] See, especially, per Lord Widgery C.J. in *R. v Hillingdon LBC Ex p. Royco Homes* (above, fn.163) at [729].

[182] See, particularly, the dicta of May LJ in *R. v Chief Constable of Merseyside Police Ex p. Calveley* [1986] Q.B. 424 at [436] and *Hilditch v Westminster City Council* [1990] C.O.D. 434. But see Woolf LJ in *R. v Panel on Take-overs and Mergers Ex p. Guinness Plc* [1989] 2 W.L.R. 863 at [908] where he referred to Royco Homes as authority for exceptions to the exhaustion of remedies principle but without addressing precisely the role of delay in appellate procedures.

[183] As happened in *Ex p. Calveley* [1986] Q.B. 424 at [436] itself.

[184] *R. v Falmouth and Truro Port Health Authority Ex p. South West Water Ltd* [2000] 3 W.L.R. 1464.

[185] [2000] 3 W.L.R. 1464 at [1494G–H].

[186] [2000] 3 W.L.R. 1464 at [1490A]–[1491B]. And see dicta of Simon Brown LJ in *R. v Devon CC Ex p. Baker* [1995] 1 All E.R. 73 at [92f–h].

Need for an interim remedy

12–061 There may be cases where there is a genuine need for an interim remedy which would not be available under the alternative appeals or complaints system. In such cases, it may be appropriate to seek judicial review, using the urgent applications procedure if necessary, and seek interim relief. Conversely, where interim relief can be claimed in the alternative procedure, that procedure, not judicial review, should generally be used.[187]

Costs

12–062 Costs are often not available in appellate proceedings, and even where a power to award costs exists it is rarely exercised. The fact that costs are not recoverable in the alternative remedy procedure is unlikely now to justify the use of judicial review. The current approach is to encourage the use of alternatives to litigation, including alternative remedies in public law cases, precisely to avoid the costs of litigation.[188] It is unlikely, therefore, that it would be appropriate for a claimant to use judicial review rather than an alternative remedy because costs were available in the judicial review procedure. There have been cases in the past where the courts have been influenced by the fact that the individual could not recover the costs incurred in using an appeal procedure and therefore allowed the complaint to brought by way of judicial review where costs could be recovered. In *R. v Commissioner for the Special Purposes of the Income Tax Acts Ex p. Stipplechoice*,[189] the Court of Appeal allowed an individual to seek judicial review of a decision by the commissioners to grant leave to raise an assessment of tax after the normal six-year period for assessing tax had expired, as there were reasonable grounds for suspecting neglect, fraud or default on the part of the taxpayer. The facts of this case are, however, exceptional. There was no right of appeal against the grant of leave, so the only means of challenging the decision to grant leave was by judicial review. A taxpayer could appeal against the final assessment and could raise the issues of neglect, fraud and default that were relevant to the grant of leave. He would, however, be unable to recover the expense of such an appeal. As the levying of an assessment out of time was an exceptional procedure and as the individual would be unable to recover the costs of an appeal against the final assessment, the Court of Appeal allowed judicial review.

12–063 In *R. v Inspector of Taxes Ex p. Kissane*,[190] Nolan J. allowed an individual to seek judicial review of an ordinary tax assessment, rather than requiring him to use the appeal procedure. Nolan J. was much influenced by the fact that costs would not be available if the individual was successful in his appeal. These cases are likely to be seen as turning on their particular facts. As a general rule, the

---

[187] *BX v Secretary of State for the Home Department* [2010] 1 W.L.R. 2463 at [34].
[188] *R. (Cowl) v Plymouth City Council* [2002] 1 W.L.R. 803.
[189] [1985] 2 All E.R. 465.
[190] [1986] 2 All E.R. 37.

courts do require the exhaustion of alternative remedies notwithstanding the absence of a power to award costs, or, if the power exists, a practice of not exercising it.[191]

Need for authoritative judicial guidance

Judicial review may be allowed where the applicant raises an issue of general importance going beyond the significance of the particular case involved. In *R. v Huntingdon DC Ex p. Cowan*,[192] Glidewell J. allowed the applicant to seek judicial review of a licensing decision rather than use the appeal procedure. The case raised for the first time the question of how local authorities were required to exercise their licensing functions under a particular statute. It was in the public interest that the court should give a ruling which would provide authoritative guidance for all local authorities. The Court of Appeal considered that judicial review was appropriate to determine whether a local authority was under an obligation to consult the residents of a residential home prior to closing the home. The scope of the duty of procedural fairness raised issues of law in a developing field which required authoritative resolution and was so the matter was better suited to judicial review rather than the use of the complaints procedure.[193]   **12–064**

Test cases may, in appropriate circumstances, be prosecuted through the statutory appeal procedure. This may be particularly appropriate if there is no urgency in determining the point, and providing that there is no difficulty in finding an appropriate test case.[194] An appeal procedure may also provide an opportunity to appeal to the High Court or Court of Appeal, which could provide a ruling binding on all administrative bodies and tribunals.[195]   **12–065**

Relevance of an ultimate right of appeal to a court

It is sometimes said that the fact that the statutory appeals procedure provides ultimately for an appeal to the courts makes it less likely that the courts will allow judicial review to be used instead of the appeals procedure. There are occasions when this factor could be relevant. Appeals in tax cases used to be heard in the Chancery Division, which has specialised expertise in the revenue field, and that was an additional reason for preferring appeal to judicial review. In relation to test cases on points of general importance, it may be relevant that a ruling will ultimately be available from a court which will provide a clear reference point for inferior courts and tribunals, and settle any conflicts between inferior courts or tribunals.   **12–066**

As a general rule, the courts do not draw a distinction between the exhaustion of appeals to an administrative tribunal with judicial review of the ultimate appellate decision, and an appeals procedure which provides for appeal to the   **12–067**

---

[191] As normally happened in ordinary appeals against tax assessments: see *R. v Epping and Harlow General Commissioners Ex p. Goldstraw* [1983] 3 All E.R. 257.
[192] [1984] 1 All E.R. 58.
[193] *R. v Devon CC Ex p. Baker* [1995] 1 All E.R. 73 per Dillon LJ at [87a–d] and per Simon Brown LJ at [92e–h].
[194] *R. v Chief Adjudication Officer Ex p. Bland, The Times*, February 6, 1985.
[195] *R. v Chief Adjudication Officer Ex p. Bland, The Times*, February 6, 1985.

courts. In both cases the exhaustion of remedies principle applies.[196] The rationale underlying the principle—the desire not to circumvent the statutory appeals procedure and to limit the number of judicial review applications—applies equally to both types of appeal.

12–068   A different problem arises where a decision of the High Court on appeal or appeal by case stated is made final so that no further appeal may be made to the Court of Appeal.[197] By challenging the decision by way of judicial review (rather than appeal), a claimant would be able to obtain a decision of the High Court which would be subject to appeal. The Divisional Court has confirmed that judicial review should not be used in such circumstances. An appeal by way of case stated was the appropriate remedy and, furthermore, to allow a claimant to seek judicial review rather than use the statutory procedure for challenge would run counter to the clear purpose of the statutory provisions.[198]

Preliminary decisions

12–069   There are preliminary decisions against which no appeal is available. No appeal, for example, lies against:

(a)   a decision refusing to adjourn an inquiry into a planning appeal[199]; or
(b)   a decision determining a preliminary point of law in a criminal case in the magistrates' court,[200] or Crown Court[201]; or
(c)   granting leave to levy a tax assessment.[202]

12–070   In appropriate circumstances it may be possible to use an error at the preliminary stage as a ground for appealing against the final decision. The courts may also allow an individual to apply for judicial review of the preliminary decision itself,[203] so long as this is not premature.[204]

Other exceptional circumstances

12–071   Even where there is an alternative remedy which is usually adequate, there may be exceptional circumstances which take a particular case outside the exhaustion of remedies principle. In the immigration field, for example, the Court of Appeal has held that challenges to refusal of leave to enter should be made by way of appeal not judicial review, notwithstanding the fact that the individual has to

---

[196] See, e.g. *R. v Secretary of State for the Home Department Ex p. Swati* [1986] 1 W.L.R. 477 where the Court of Appeal applied the principle to an appeals procedure which did not provide for a further appeal to a court.

[197] As is the case, e.g. with appeals by way of case stated from the magistrates' court in non-criminal cases: see Senior Courts Act 1981 s.28A and para.14–034 below.

[198] *Sheffield City Council v Kenya Aid Programme* [2013] 3 W.L.R. 422 at [53]–[58].

[199] *Co-operative Retail Services Ltd v Secretary of State for the Environment* [1980] 1 All E.R. 449.

[200] *Streames v Copping* [1985] Q.B. 920.

[201] *Loade v DPP* [1990] C.O.D. 58.

[202] *R. v Commissioner for the Special Purposes of the Income Tax Acts Ex p. Stipplechoice* [1985] 2 All E.R. 465.

[203] See, e.g. *Legal and General Assurance Society Ltd v Pensions Ombudsman* [2000] 1 W.L.R. 1525 at [14].

[204] On prematurity see paras 12–013 to 12–012.

leave the country before the appeal could be heard. Yet, an Iranian child was allowed to seek judicial review of a decision refusing him leave to enter since, if he were sent back to Iran, he would not be allowed out even if his appeal in the UK was successful.[205] Excessive delay in bringing disciplinary proceedings against a policeman, even though remediable on appeal, justified judicial review as the policeman ought not to be placed in peril of disciplinary action unless there was substantial compliance with the procedural regulations.[206]

No appeal available

Appellate systems are not always comprehensive and there may be certain decisions which are not appealable. Judicial review will therefore be the only method of seeking redress. In the tax field, for example, an appeal lies against an assessment but not a decision requiring the payment of interest. The latter must be challenged by judicial review.[207] In the planning field, a decision to refuse planning permission is appealable. However, a decision granting planning permission is not, and third parties seeking to challenge the decision must seek judicial review.[208] Individuals who do not have standing to bring an appeal may be able to seek judicial review. One taxpayer has no standing to appeal against another taxpayer's assessment: he normally has no sufficient interest to seek judicial review either, but in exceptional circumstances he may be allowed to seek judicial review.[209]   **12–072**

The courts generally allow questions of ultra vires to be raised in the course of a statutory right of appeal.[210] Statute may, however, limit the grounds of appeal so that only certain questions may be raised. In *R. v Secretary of State for the Home Department Ex p. Malhi*,[211] the Court of Appeal held that an overstayer could only appeal against a deportation decision on the ground that no power to deport existed. Challenges to the manner in which the power was exercised, or claims of procedural irregularity could not be raised on appeal, and could only be raised by way of judicial review. Similarly, regulations made by a regulatory body were not intended to be the subject of an appeal to the Competition Appeal Tribunal; the court noted that it was not the function of a statutory tribunal to impugn legislative powers and such challenges were classically matters for judicial review.[212]   **12–073**

---

[205] *R. v Chief Immigration Officer, Gatwick Airport Ex p. Kharrazi* [1980] 1 W.L.R. 1396.
[206] *R. v Chief Constable of Merseyside Police Ex p. Calveley* [1986] Q.B. 424.
[207] *Thorne v General Commissioners of Income Tax for Sevenoaks; R. v General Commissioners of Income Tax for Sevenoaks Ex p. Thorne* [1989] S.T.C. 560. (Appeal against assessment and judicial review application against certificate of interest heard together.)
[208] *R. v Monmouth DC Ex p. Jones* (1987) 53 P. & C.R. 108.
[209] *R. v Att-Gen Ex p. I.C.I. Plc* [1987] 1 C.M.L.R. 72.
[210] See, e.g. *Chief Adjudication Officer v Foster* [1993] A.C. 754. *Nolan v Leeds City Council* (1990) 89 L.G.R. 385; *R. v Oxford Crown Court Ex p. Smith* [1990] C.O.D. 211.
[211] [1990] 2 W.L.R. 932, approved by the House of Lords in *R. v Secretary of State for the Home Department Ex p. Oladehinde* [1991] 1 A.C. 254.
[212] *T-Mobile (UK) Ltd v Office of Communications* [2009] 1 W.L.R. 1565 at [51].

Decisions of inferior courts and tribunals where permission required to appeal

12–074   Specific considerations apply in relation to inferior courts and tribunals. Parliament may provide for a specific right of appeal but only if permission to appeal is granted. If permission is not granted, then there is no further right of appeal against a decision. As a matter of principle, the courts have jurisdiction judicially to review decisions of inferior courts and tribunals including decisions refusing permission to appeal.[213] As a matter of discretion, however, the courts may conclude that Parliament has created a system of appeals which is fair, adequate and proportionate to the issues and gives sufficient protection to a claimant against the risk of an erroneous decision being taken by the inferior court or tribunal. Thus, the courts may decline to grant judicial review as a matter of discretion, save in exceptional circumstances, even where permission to appeal has been refused and the claimant has no other means of challenging the decision.[214] In deciding whether a particular scheme is considered adequate and proportionate to deal with particular types of cases, regard will be had to the generic nature of the issues involved in such cases, the effect of the statutory procedures, the nature and constitution of the tribunals or courts involved, and the legislative intention underlying the creation of the statutory system. These considerations need to be weighed against other fundamental considerations such as the desirability of finality in litigation, minimising delay and cost, the desirability of achieving a correct legal answer and the practicalities.[215] The question, ultimately, is what level of judicial review of the tribunal structure in question is required by the rule of law.[216]

12–075   In the context of challenges to decisions of the Upper Tribunal refusing permission to appeal against a decision of the First-tier Tribunal, the Supreme Court considered that judicial review should only be available if the claim raised an important issue of principle or practice or there was some other compelling reason for allowing the judicial review claim to proceed.[217]. The courts had, earlier, indicated in the context of tribunals and the county court that permission to apply for judicial review should only be granted in exceptional circumstances which, at that stage was understood as involving a situation where the court had embarked on an enquiry which it lacked all power to undertake, or declined to adjudicate upon a matter which it was obliged to adjudicate or had made procedural errors amounting to a denial of the right to a fair hearing before the lower court or tribunal.[218] That approach was disapproved by the Supreme Court in *Cart*.[219]

---

[213] *R. (Sivasubramaniam) v Wandsworth County Court* [2003] 1 W.L.R. 475 at [33]–[44].

[214] *R. (Sivasubramaniam) v Wandsworth County Court* [2003] 1 W.L.R. 475 at [45]–[57]; *R. (G) v Immigration Appeal Tribunal* [2005] 1 W.L.R. 1445 at [26]–[27]; *R. (F (Mongolia)) v Asylum and Immigration Tribunal* [2007] 1 W.L.R. 2523.

[215] See the discussion in *R. (Cart) v Upper Tribunal* [2012] 1 A.C. 663 at paras [57], [62]–[74], [115]–[127].

[216] *R. (Cart) v Upper Tribunal* [2012] 1 A.C. 663 at [51] and [89].

[217] *R. (Cart) v Upper Tribunal* [2012] 1 A.C. 663 and see now CPR r.54.7A(7) and Chapter 10.

[218] *R. (Sivasubramaniam) v Wandsworth County Court* [2003] 1 W.L.R. 475 at [56]; *R (Sinclair Gardens Investment (Kengsington) Ltd. v Lands Tribunal* [2006] 3 All E.R. 650.

[219] *R. (Cart) v Upper Tribunal* [2012] 1 A.C. 663.

Stage at which existence of alternative remedies should be considered

The existence of alternative remedies is a reason for refusing permission to apply **12–076** for judicial review.[220] Alternative remedies are also relevant at the substantive hearing, even if permission has been granted, and the court may refuse a remedy if an adequate alternative remedy existed which should have been used.[221] The court may consider the existence of an alternative remedy as a preliminary issue before dealing with the substantive grounds of challenge.[222] It is obviously desirable that the question of alternative remedies be raised as soon as possible, and preferably at the permission stage, particularly given the present emphasis on seeking means of avoiding litigation.[223] The claimant should state in the claim form whether any alternative remedy existed and, if so, why it is appropriate to seek judicial review.[224] The claim form will be served on the defendant and the defendant can raise the existence of an alternative remedy as a reason why permission should not be granted in the summary grounds for resisting the claim included in its acknowledgment of service. If necessary, the court can arrange for an oral hearing of the permission application, with both sides represented, and ask why an alternative remedy has not been used to resolve the issue.[225]

---

[220] See, e.g. *R. v Secretary of State for the Home Department, Ex p. Swati* [1986] 1 W.L.R. 477; *R (Davies) v Financial Services Authority* [2004] 1 W.L.R. 184. Permission has been set aside where there was an alternative remedy available: see, e.g. *R. v Secretary of State for the Home Department Ex p. Doorga* [1990] C.O.D. 109; *R. v Secretary of State for the Environment, Ex p. Watts* [1997] C.O.D. 152. The point is now likely to arise before permission is granted, as the defendant now has the opportunity to raise the point in the acknowledgment of service. A defendant served with a claim form cannot now apply to set aside permission: CPR, r.54.13.

[221] *R. v Birmingham City Council Ex p. Ferrero Ltd* [1993] 1 All E.R. 530 (Court of Appeal allowed an appeal on the grounds that the claimant should have used the statutory appeals procedure); *R. v Epping and Harlow General Commissioners Ex p. Goldstraw* [1983] 3 All E.R. 257; *R. v Brentford General Commissioners Ex p. Chan* [1986] S.T.C. 65 (Taylor J. expressed the view that the courts should resist the temptation to give judgment simply before the case was before them as that would undermine the policy underlying the exhaustion of remedies rule); see also the dicta in *R. v Rochester City Council Ex p. Hobday* (1989) 58 P. & C.R. 424 at [433] and *R. v Commissioners of Customs and Excise Ex p. Mortimer* [1998] 3 All E.R. 229. But see *R. v Chief Constable of Merseyside Police Ex p. Bennion* [2001] A.C.D. 113 (the overriding objective of dealing justly with cases pointed overwhelmingly in favour of the court dealing with the case rather than refusing a hearing with the consequence that the time and financial resources used in preparing for the judicial review hearing would be wasted).

[222] *R. v Chief Adjudication Officer Ex p. Bland, The Times*, February 6, 1985.

[223] See *R. (Cowl) v Plymouth CC* [2002] 1 W.L.R. 803 and see *R. (BG) v Medway BC* (2005) 8 C.C.L.R. 448.

[224] *R. v Humberside CC, ex p Bogdal* (1992) 5 Admin. L.Rep. 405 at [411c]–[412]; *R. v Greenwich Justices Ex p. Aikens, The Times*, July 3, 1982; *R. v Mid-Worcestershire Justices Ex p. Hart* [1989] C.O.D. 397.

[225] *R. (Cowl) v Plymouth City Council* [2001] 1 W.L.R. 803 at [1]–[3].

H.   IMPLIED EXCLUSION OF JUDICIAL REVIEW

General position

12–077   The courts have in the past held that the existence of an alternative statutory remedy impliedly excluded the inherent supervisory jurisdiction of the court. An individual could not, therefore, seek the prerogative remedies to control an abuse of power, but was restricted to using the statutory remedy.[226] This approach no longer represents the current approach of the courts to alternative remedies: the existence of an alternative remedy does not oust the jurisdiction of the court to grant judicial review, although it is relevant to the discretion of the court to grant permission or a remedy.[227] The existence of alternative remedies will not impliedly exclude the possibility of review: only clear express statutory provisions of the sort discussed below can exclude the supervisory jurisdiction of the High Court. In the words of Lord Bridge[228]:

> "...the allegation of a wrong of a kind recognised as remediable by public law is sufficient to found jurisdiction in judicial review. ... [The] jurisdiction is only ousted by clear express statutory provision. The existence of an alternative remedy has never been sufficient to oust jurisdiction in judicial review ..."

The Court of Appeal has re-iterated that "the weight of authority makes it impossible to accept that the jurisdiction to subject a decision to judicial review can be removed by statutory implication".[229] The Supreme Court has held that statutory provisions designating a tribunal as a superior court of record did not have the effect of rendering the tribunal immune from judicial review. The Supreme Court emphasised that the exclusion of judicial review could only be achieved by "the most clear and explicit language and not by implication".[230]

---

[226] *Pasmore v Oswaldtwistle UDC* [1898] A.C. 387.
[227] *Leech v Deputy Governor of Parkhurst Prison* [1988] A.C. 533.
[228] *Leech v Deputy Governor of Parkhurst Prison* [1988] A.C. 533 at [562].
[229] See *R. (Sivasubramaniam) v Wandsworth County Court* [2003] 1 W.L.R. 475 at [44]; *R. (G) v Immigration Appeal Tribunal* [2005] 1 W.L.R. 1445. A similar approach is taken in relation to the powers of the courts in appeals in public law cases; the jurisdiction to deal with matters of vires will only be ousted by clear, express language: see, e.g. *Earthline Ltd v Secretary of State for Transport, Local Government and the Regions* [2003] 1 P. & C.R. 393. There is be less objection to a court not having power to deal with a matter if an alternative appeal structure is put in place which can deal with the matter: see, e.g. *R (Hilali) v Governor of Whitemoor Prison* [2008] A.C. 805 at [20]–[21] (remedies by way of judicial review and habeas corpus excluded in respect of certain extradition decisions where a right of appeal provided, *Farley v Secretary of State for Work and Pensions (No.2)* [2006] 1 W.L.R. 817 esp. at [16]–[25] (magistrates' court did not have power to determine whether a person was liable to pay child maintenance when making a liability order; that issue was be dealt with through the appellate structure).
[230] Per Lady Hale in *R. (Cart) v Upper Tribunal* [2012] 1 A.C. 664 at [30].

Duties and default powers

In *Pasmore v Oswaldtwistle UDC*,[231] the House of Lords held that where a duty   **12–078**
is imposed by statute and a specific statutory remedy is created for the
enforcement of that remedy, the statutory remedy is the only remedy available
and other remedies are excluded. This principle has been particularly relied upon
in cases involving default powers, where a central government department may
order a local authority to perform a statutory duty if it is in default. The question
here is whether the existence of an alternative remedy, particularly a default
power, excludes the possibility of seeking judicial review usually by way of
mandamus to compel the performance of a duty, or a declaration that the duty has
been breached.

Early exceptions to Pasmore

Earlier cases held that the *Pasmore* principle might exclude the possibility of   **12–079**
mandamus,[232] or injunction, or declaration,[233] (sought by ordinary action in the
days before the 1977 reform made them available in a judicial review
application). The principle has gradually been eroded and exceptions made.
Alternative remedies were held not to exclude application to the courts in cases of
"mis-feasance", as opposed to "non-feasance",[234] although there were "inescap-
able practical difficulties"[235] in drawing a distinction between the two. Recourse
could be had to the courts in cases where the body subject to the duty had acted
ultra vires.[236] The precise meaning of ultra vires in this context was not clear: it
covered acting or not acting for an improper purpose, such as failing to perform a
duty as a result of undue pressure, or an unlawful wish to aid industrial action.[237]
It was uncertain whether it applied to a simple failure to act. In *Meade v Haringey
LBC*,[238] Lord Denning M.R. took the view that all the usual common law
remedies were available where a public authority failed to perform a statutory
duty by commission or omission, in such a way as would hinder the policy of the
act. The judgments of the rest of the Court of Appeal are consistent with Lord
Denning's approach.

---

[231] [1898] A.C. 387, and the discussion in Chapter 6 at para.6–071. See also Harding, *Public Duties and Public Law*.

[232] *R. v Kensington and Chelsea Royal LBC Ex p. Birdwood* (1976) 74 L.G.R. 424. (Public Health Act 1936 s.322; although Lord Widgery C.J. did say that mandamus "would not normally go", not "could never go".)

[233] *Bradbury v Enfield LBC* [1967] 1 W.L.R. 1311.

[234] [1967] 1 W.L.R. 1311 per Diplock LJ See also the exceptions outlined by Sir Stanley Rees in *Meade v Haringey LBC* [1979] 1 W.L.R. 637.

[235] per Sir Stanley Rees in *Meade v Haringey LBC* [1967] 1 W.L.R. 1311.

[236] per Sir Stanley Rees in *Meade v Haringey LBC* 1[967] 1 W.L.R. 1311.

[237] per Sir Stanley Rees in *Meade v Haringey LBC* [1967] 1 W.L.R. 1311 and see also *R. v Ealing LBC Ex p. Times Newspapers* [1987] I.R.L.R. 129.

[238] [1979] 1 W.L.R. 637.

Current approach to alternative remedies and statutory duties

12–080 The position has now been reached that the existence of an alternative remedy, such as a default power, does not exclude recourse to judicial review.[239] A mandatory order or a declaration sought by judicial review, or other remedies if appropriate, are available notwithstanding the existence of an alternative remedy. The existence of default powers is relevant to the discretion of the court in deciding whether to grant permission or a remedy.[240] Many duties are so broad that they may not be readily susceptible to enforcement by a mandatory order or injunction in the absence of specific directions given by a minister in the exercise of a default power. A court may, therefore, choose in the exercise of its discretion to refuse a remedy altogether,[241] or to grant a declaration that a breach of duty has occurred and leave the minister in the exercise of any default power to give precise directions as to what a public body should do to remedy the breach.[242]

12–081 The existence of default powers, whilst they do not exclude the possibility of a public law remedy, is still relevant to the separate issue of whether an individual has a private law right to bring an ordinary civil action for damages, for breach of a statutory duty.[243]

Enforcement of a statutory right

12–082 The courts have in the past held that where statute imposes a duty or creates a right, and also provides a remedy for enforcement, the statutory remedy may impliedly exclude recourse to the ordinary courts. In *Barraclough v Brown*,[244] the House of Lords held that where statute created a right to recover expenses and provided for that right to be enforced in a court of summary jurisdiction, the statutory right could not be enforced by action in the High Court. This principle applies only where statute both grants a right and provides a means of enforcement. It does not apply to common law rights which may be enforced by way of action in the courts, rather than through the statutory enforcement method.[245]

12–083 The issue here is concerned with a specific duty owed to an individual rather than a general public law statutory duty which an individual has sufficient interest to enforce by seeking judicial review by way of a mandatory order (such as those discussed in the preceding sections). It is useful for these purposes to distinguish between a private law right and a public law right. A private law right is a right derived from statute which enables an individual to bring an ordinary civil action

---

[239] *R. v Inner London Education Authority Ex p. Ali and Murshid* [1990] 2 Admin. L.R. 822 (default powers under the Education Act 1944); *R. v Secretary of State for the Environment Ex p. Ward* [1984] 1 W.L.R. 834; *R. v Secretary of State for the Environment Ex p. Lee* (1987) 54 P. & C.R. 311 (both dealing with default powers under the Caravan Sites Act 1968). See also *R. v Ealing LBC Ex p. Times Newspapers* [1987] I.R.L.R. 129 (default power in relation to failure to provide comprehensive library services dealt with on basis of discretion to grant judicial review; remedies granted).

[240] *Ex p. Ali and Murshid* (1990) 2 Admin L.R. 822.

[241] *R. v Inner London Education Authority Ex p. Ali and Murshid* (1990) 2 Admin. L.Rep. 822.

[242] *R. v Secretary of State for the Environment Ex p. Lee* (1987) 54 P. & C.R. 311.

[243] *R. v Secretary of State for the Environment Ex p. Ward* [1984] 1 W.L.R. 834 (distinguishing *Wells v Kensington and Chelsea LBC* (1973) 72 L.G.R. 289); *Watt v Kesteven CC* [1955] 1 Q.B. 408.

[244] [1897] A.C. 615.

[245] *Pyx Granite Co. v Ministry of Housing and Local Government* [1960] A.C. 260.

for damages. A public law right is a right derived from a public law source which does not entitle the individual to damages, but entitles him to enforce the right by judicial review. The courts have not always clearly recognised this distinction, partly because the separation of public law and private law is relatively recent. One area where such a distinction is important is in relation to rights derived from EU law. Directly enforceable rights operating in the public field and enforceable against public bodies are frequently classified as public law rights.[246]

The question then arises as to whether a specific statutory right classified as a public law right must be pursued through any statutory remedy provided or whether judicial review is available. In *Jensen v The Corporation of the Trinity House of Deptford*,[247] the Court of Appeal held that a statutory right of appeal against a refusal of a pilotage licence was an exclusive remedy, and an ordinary action could not be maintained even though the plaintiff was alleging a breach of a right derived from what is now Art.18 of the Treaty on the Functioning of the European Union. The Court analysed the position as one where the statute granted a right to an examination for a licence, with an expectation of the licence being granted if the individual passed, and a statutory mechanism for enforcing that right by way of an appeal. The Court of Appeal did, however, confirm that judicial review of the decision of the appellate authority would be available if they misdirected themselves in law.[248] It is not clear whether this decision would be followed in other cases involving rights derived from European Union law.[249] The Supreme Court also adopted this approach in relation to the powers of the Investigatory Powers Tribunal in connection with claims against the security services. The Supreme Court considered that the statutory provisions incorporating certain of the rights guaranteed by the European Convention on Human Rights and the provisions providing for the exclusive jurisdiction of the Tribunal to hear claims relating to such rights in respect of the security services fell within this principle. Both the statutory rights, and the statutory provisions governing the remedy by means of which the right was to be enforced in claims against the security services, were to be read together and the Tribunal had exclusive jurisdiction to enforce such rights.[250]

12–084

It is likely that, absent special circumstances or clear statutory provisions linking a particular right with a particular remedy, the courts would now follow the policy of regarding statutory remedies as relevant to the discretion of the courts to refuse judicial review, rather than excluding the judicial review jurisdiction altogether.

12–085

---

[246] See Chapter 15.

[247] [1982] 2 Lloyd's Rep. 14.

[248] *R. v Trinity House London Pilotage Committee Ex p. Jensen* [1985] 2 C.M.L.R. 413.

[249] European Union law requires national courts to give immediate protection to European law rights and not to wait for a particular court to set aside inconsistent national law; see the *Simmenthal* case Case 106/77 [1978] 1 E.C.R. 629. (But European Union law does allow national law to determine the forum and remedy for enforcing rights: see *Salgoil S.p.A. v Italian Ministry for Foreign Trade* [1968] E.C.R. 453. See, generally, Chapter 17.)

[250] *R. (A) v Director of Establishments of the Security Service* [2012] 2 W.L.R. 1 at [21]–[24].

I. STATUTORY EXCLUSION AND RESTRICTION OF JUDICIAL REVIEW

Introduction

12–086   Statutory provisions are found from time to time which seek to oust or restrict the supervisory jurisdiction of the courts to determine the lawfulness of particular decisions or exercises of power. Such provisions are variously referred to as ouster, privative, protective or preclusive clauses. Such clauses tend to fall into one of two groups. There are those clauses which seek to oust the jurisdiction of the courts completely, and render a decision immune from any challenge in the courts. A variety of formulae have been used to achieve this result and they are considered below. Then there are those clauses which exclude judicial review but provide some other remedy which allows challenges to be made, but may restrict the scope of such challenge. Such remedies may, for example, impose a very short time period for seeking the remedy, or limit the grounds of challenge, or the range of people who may challenge.

12–087   The courts have traditionally been hostile to complete ouster clauses. They have adopted restrictive interpretations of such clauses, which has largely deprived them of any meaningful effect. The courts have therefore maintained their supervisory jurisdiction largely intact. Statutory reforms have also assisted the courts in ensuring that they are not precluded from determining whether statutory decision-makers are acting lawfully. Section 12 of the Tribunals and Inquiries Act 1992 provides that certain types of exemption clause contained in an Act passed before August 1, 1958 are not to prevent the courts from granting certiorari or mandamus.

12–088   The courts have taken a more lenient view of clauses which restrict the scope of challenge but which leave open the possibility of judicial supervision. Such partial ouster clauses are seen as akin to limitation clauses, not exclusion clauses.

Final and conclusive and similar clauses

12–089   Statute may provide that a decision is to be "final" or "final and conclusive". Such clauses do not exclude judicial review. The fact that the decision is final means that it cannot be appealed. The fact that it is conclusive means that the decision is binding on the parties.[251] It is " . . . well settled that the remedy by certiorari is never to be taken away by any statute except by the most clear and explicit words".[252] Judicial review by way of quashing orders (formerly an order of certiorari[253]) and the other prerogative remedies, together with declarations and injunctions in their public law role, remain available.[254] Decisions may still

---

[251] *R. (Revenue and Customs Commissioners) v Machell* [2006] 1 W.L.R. 609 at [24].
[252] per Denning LJ in *R. v Medical Appeal Tribunal Ex p. Gilmore* [1957] 1 Q.B. 574 at [583]. See also *R. v Hallstrom Ex p. Waldron* [1986] Q.B. 1090.
[253] *R. v Medical Appeal Tribunal Ex p. Gilmore* [1957] 1 Q.B. 574 at [583]; *South East Asia Fire Bricks Sdn. Bhd. v Non Metallic Mineral Products Manufacturing Employees Union* [1981] A.C. 363.
[254] See, e.g. *Pollway Nominees v Croydon LBC* [1987] A.C. 79.

be reviewed either where they are ultra vires or where they exhibit an intra vires error of law which appears on the face of the record.[255]

Finality clauses will exclude an appeal both on facts and law. There are dicta in the Court of Appeal suggesting that such clauses only exclude appeal on facts, and do not exclude an appeal on a point of law.[256] However, there are contrary dicta in the House of Lords.[257] In one sense, the point is not of importance since an error of law can as easily be corrected by judicial review as by appeal.   **12–090**

Such clauses may also exclude civil actions for damages. An action for damages for negligence, in respect of a decision of an adjudication officer, could not be maintained where statute provided that such a decision was final.[258] It would seem irrelevant whether the action was brought by ordinary claim, or if a claim for damages was attached to an application for judicial review. In both cases, the courts would be prevented from considering the damages claim. The tort of misfeasance in a public office may raise special problems. The essence of the tort is ultra vires action coupled with malice or knowledge of the illegality. A finality clause clearly would not prevent judicial review to establish the illegality. It is doubtful that such a clause would prevent the court from considering whether the additional element of malice or knowledge was present.[259]   **12–091**

Shall not be questioned and similar clauses

Statute may provide that a particular decision " . . . shall not be questioned in any court of law", or words to that effect. The House of Lords held in *Anisminic* that such clauses do not prevent the courts reviewing a decision which is ultra vires.[260] Such clauses do prevent the courts from reviewing decisions on the ground that the decision-maker has made an intra vires error of law which appears on the face of the record.[261] Similarly, a provision precluding "review" will not prevent the court quashing the decision or declaring it to be a nullity if the decision is ultra vires, although it would prevent the courts reviewing it for an intra vires error of law.[262] The significance of this distinction has been eroded almost completely by the parallel developments which have led to most, if not all, errors of law being classed as jurisdictional errors which render a decision ultra vires.[263] Few errors of law would therefore be classified as intra vires errors. Such ouster clauses, therefore, have little meaning.   **12–092**

This interpretation has been justified on the grounds that review for jurisdictional error does not involve questioning a decision, rather it involves determining whether in law any decision exists. In the case of intra vires errors, however, a valid decision does exist but it is patently flawed. To quash such a   **12–093**

---

[255] *Ex p. Gilmore* (see above, fn.22); *South East Asia Fire Bricks* (see above, fn.235).

[256] In *Pearlman v Keepers and Governors of Harrow School* [1979] Q.B. 56, per Lord Denning M.R. at [71], Eveleigh LJ at [79].

[257] In *Re Racal Communications* [1981] A.C. 374, per Lord Diplock (Lord Keith agreeing) at [382].

[258] *Jones v Department of Employment* [1989] Q.B. 1.

[259] On the tort of misfeasance in a public office, see below at paras 15–097 to 15–106.

[260] *Anisminic Ltd v Foreign Compensation Commission* [1969] 2 A.C. 147, *Re.* the Foreign Compensation Act 1950 s.4(4).

[261] [1969] 2 A.C. 147.

[262] *South East Asia Fire Bricks Sdn Bhd. v Non Metallic Mineral Products Manufacturing Employees Union* [1981] A.C. 363.

[263] See Chapter 5.

decision would involve questioning the decision, not merely determining its validity. In truth, the explanation lies in the extreme reluctance of the courts to allow their role in ensuring that power is exercised lawfully to be circumscribed by such provisions. The development of the presumption that all errors of law by a body of limited jurisdiction are ultra vires errors reflects the courts' view that they should be the ultimate arbiters of questions of law.

12–094   There may be rare instances when a clause might have effect. The Interception of Communications Act 1985 sets up a tribunal to hear applications that there has been an unlawful interception of mail or telephone calls. Section 7 provides that a decision of "The Tribunal" ("including any decisions as to their jurisdiction") shall not be questioned. It remains to be seen whether the courts will accept that this provision effectively insulates the tribunal from judicial review, even for jurisdictional errors.

Designation of a court or tribunal as a superior court of record

12–095   Judicial review is not available against certain of the superior courts such as the High Court or Court of Appeal.[264] The designation of a court or tribunal as a superior court of record is not, however, sufficient of itself to render such a body immune from judicial review.[265]

No certiorari and similar clauses

12–096   Statute may specifically provide that the remedy of certiorari (now a quashing order) is not to be available in respect of a particular decision. A clause providing that a decision " . . . should not be 'quashed' " has a similar effect.[266] Such clauses do not exclude the jurisdiction of the courts to grant a quashing order to quash a decision which is ultra vires. However, they will preclude the court quashing a decision which exhibits an intra vires error of law on the face of the record.[267]

Conclusive evidence and similar clauses

12–097   Statute may provide that a certificate or other legal instrument is "conclusive evidence" of certain matters. Such a certificate may be conclusive that certain procedural requirements have been observed, or that a particular state of affairs exists, or that a particular decision or measure is within the powers of the decision-maker. The Court of Appeal has held that such clauses prevent the admission of evidence which contradicts the matters certified in the certificate. This may prevent an applicant from adducing evidence that a decision is invalid, where this evidence contradicts a certificate. It would preclude the admission of evidence to support an application for judicial review of the certificate itself, where this involves contradicting the terms of the certificate. Although such

---

[264] See above at para.2–122.

[265] *R. (Cart) v Upper Tribunal* [2012] 1 A.C. 663 at [30].

[266] *South East Asia Fire Bricks Sdn. Bhd. v Non Metallic Mineral Products Manufacturing Employees Union* [1981] A.C. 363.

[267] *South East Asia Fire Bricks Sdn. Bhd. v Non Metallic Mineral Products Manufacturing Employees Union* [1981] A.C. 363.

conclusive certificates do not preclude applications for judicial review in theory, such applications are doomed to failure as no evidence to support the application can be adduced.

There are two leading cases on the interpretation of such evidential ouster clauses. In *R. v Registrar of Companies Ex p. Central Bank of India*,[268] the companies registrar registered a charge. The registrar also issued a certificate which statute provided was conclusive evidence that the requirements of the statute had been met. The Court of Appeal held that that provision prevented the admission of evidence to show that the registrar had not in fact complied with the statutory requirements, and that the decision of the registrar was therefore invalid.

12–098

In *R. v Secretary of State for Foreign and Commonwealth Affairs Ex p. Trawnik*,[269] the minister issued a certificate pursuant to s.40(3)(a) of the Crown Proceedings Act 1947, stating that liability arising in respect of the British army based in Berlin arose otherwise than in respect of the government in the UK. Such a certificate was conclusive evidence of that matter. The Court held that the clause precluded the admission of evidence for the purpose of contradicting the facts stated in the certificate. Although the statutory provision did not preclude an application for judicial review of the certificate, such an application was bound to fail if it relied on adducing evidence which contradicted the facts in the certificate. Thus, a claim that the certificate was so clearly wrong as to be perverse or to lead to the inference that the Minister must have misdirected himself in law was bound to fail. The applicant would be unable to adduce any evidence to show that the certificate was so clearly wrong.

12–099

The approach of the courts is based on what is seen as a generally applicable rule of construction in relation to such statutory provisions. Such an approach would therefore probably be followed in other statutory contexts where a similar provision existed. In the *Central Bank of India* case, the Court of Appeal considered that there were good commercial reasons for encouraging certainty so that once a charge is registered the chargee, and all dealing with the chargee and the company, would deal on the basis that the charge was valid. For that reason, it might have been possible to limit the decision to those cases where there were overwhelming reasons for not engaging in judicial review. These could include the need for commercial certainty, or cases where the matter certified lay within the particular knowledge of the public body concerned or involved sensitive issues, such as national security or international affairs. In other cases, such a clause would not have rendered a certificate immune from challenge. It is clear from *Trawnik*, however, that the Court of Appeal does not accept such a limited view of the decision in *Central Bank of India*. They clearly regarded the decision as reflecting a general approach to the question of construing such clauses, irrespective of context.[270] The fact that the certificate there dealt with difficult

12–100

---

[268] [1986] Q.B. 1114. See also *Ex p. Ringer* (1909) 73 J.P. 436 and dicta in *Minister of Health v R. Ex p. Yaffe* [1931] A.C. 494.

[269] *The Times*, February 21, 1986. Such provisions may contravene European Union law: see below at para.12–122. Such provisions may also contravene Art.6 of the European Convention of Human Rights: see *Tinnelly & Sons Ltd v United Kingdom* (1999) 27 E.H.R.R. 249. See below at para.12–123.

[270] But see dicta in *R. v HM Treasury Ex p. Smedley* [1985] Q.B. 657 where the Court of Appeal apparently considered that judicial review might be available notwithstanding such a clause.

issues in the field of international relations was an additional reason, quite unconnected with the proper construction of the evidential ouster clause, for declining to review the certificate.

12–101   There may be situations in which the courts will still quash a certificate or a decision protected by a certificate. First, the statutory provisions precluding the admission of evidence will not bind the Crown unless they expressly or impliedly state that they are to have that effect. The Attorney-General (acting either ex officio or at the relation of an individual) will be able to challenge a certificate in any cases where the statute does not bind the Crown.[271] Secondly, it may be possible to quash a certificate where the error appears on the face of the certificate itself.[272] Thirdly, the courts may exceptionally hold that the clause was not intended to exclude evidence that the certificate was obtained by fraud.[273] Fourthly, the statutory provision may only render the certificate conclusive of certain matters. It will still be possible to adduce evidence that the certificate or a decision to which a certificate relates is invalid for other reasons. A certificate that is conclusive evidence that the statutory requirements have been observed does not preclude evidence that it is invalid for some other reason.[274] Similarly, a certificate that is conclusive evidence on one matter may be challenged if it demonstrates a reviewable error in respect of some other matter.[275]

Partial ouster clauses

12–102   Statute may provide a right of appeal against a decision, and couple that with an ouster clause providing that the decision cannot be questioned except by use of that machinery.

12–103   The Supreme Court has held that where statute provided a statutory right of appeal to the courts to challenge certain decisions in relation to extradition, those decisions could not be challenged by way of judicial review or habeas corpus.[276] If the decision is not one against which there was a right of appeal, judicial review is available.[277] In relation to planning, s.174 of the Town and Country Planning Act 1990[278] provides for an appeal on certain grounds to the minister against an enforcement notice issued by a local planning authority. Section 285 of that Act provides that the validity of an enforcement notice issued by a local authority may not be questioned in any proceedings on any of the grounds on which an appeal may be brought. The Court of Appeal held that this clause was effective to oust the court's jurisdiction, both in a direct action,[279] and by way of a defence in criminal proceedings alleging failure to comply with the notice.[280]

---

[271] *R. v Registrar of Companies Ex p. Central Bank of India* [1986] Q.B. 1114.
[272] [1986] Q.B. 1114 per Slade LJ at [1117].
[273] *R. v Registrar of Companies Ex p. Central Bank of India* (above, fn.255).
[274] *R. v Registrar of Companies Ex p. Central Bank of India* (above, fn.255).
[275] *R. v Secretary of State for Foreign and Commonwealth Affairs Ex p. Trawnik, The Times,* February 21, 1986.
[276] *R. (Hillaili) v Governor of Whitemoor Prison* [2008] A.C. 805 at [20]–[21].
[277] See, e.g. *R. (Asilturk) v City of Westminster Magistrates' Court* [2011] 1 W.L.R. 1139 at [23]–[31]; *R. (Nikonovs) v Governor of Brixton Prison* [2006] 1 W.L.R. 1518.
[278] Formerly Town and Country Planning Act 1971 s.88.
[279] *Square Meals Frozen Foods v Dunstable Corp.* [1974] 1 W.L.R. 59.
[280] *R. v Smith (Thomas George)* (1984) 48 P. & C.R. 392.

Yet, in one case,[281] the Court of Appeal proceeded on the basis that judicial review would have been available if a defect rendered a notice a nullity, even though the defect could have been appealed. Challenges by way of judicial review (rather than appeal) on grounds other than those which could be the subject of an appeal are not prohibited by s.285.[282]

An appeal against the minister's decision on the initial appeal to him under s.174 could be made to the High Court, under s.289 of the 1990 Act. Perversely, this right of appeal is not coupled with an ouster clause. Thus, there is no express exclusion of the judicial review jurisdiction. The existence of an appeal may impliedly exclude the judicial review jurisdiction, but again the modern approach is to see this as a matter of discretion not jurisdiction. The courts could as a matter of discretion refuse to allow a judicial review claim and insist that the appeal mechanism be used.[283]   **12–104**

"As if" enacted clauses

Statute may provide that subordinate legislation or ministerial orders should have effect "as if enacted", or "as if contained" in the parent Act. This formula has been the subject of two rulings in the House of Lords which are difficult to reconcile. In 1894, the House of Lords held that the validity of rules made under an Act and covered by the formula could not be considered by the courts.[284] Yet in 1931, the House held that certiorari could issue to quash a ministerial order, again covered by such a formula, where there had been a failure to observe the relevant procedural requirements for making such an order.[285] The House also indicated that certiorari could issue to quash an order that conflicted with the parent Act or went beyond the scope of the discretionary power conferred by the Act.[286] The general tenor of the judgments is that an ultra vires order could be reviewed and quashed, and that the "as if enacted", formula would not oust the supervisory jurisdiction of the court. The House took the view that the statutory formula only applied to intra vires orders, and was not intended to protect ultra vires orders from challenge. Although purporting to apply the earlier decision, the House seems in effect to be contradicting it. The later decision is more in keeping with the current approach to statutory interpretation, which seeks to limit the effect of ouster clauses. The issue is unlikely to be of practical importance as this form of exclusion clause is no longer used, although it can still be found in certain older statutes still in force.[287]   **12–105**

---

[281] *R. v Greenwich LBC Ex p. Patel* (1985) 51 P. & C.R. 282.
[282] *Gazelle Properties Ltd. and Sustainable Environmental Services Ltd. v Bath and North East Somerset Council* [2011] J.P.L. 702. The same position applied in relation to the predecessor of s.285: see *Davy v Spelthorne BC* [1984] A.C. 262.
[283] See above, para.12–042.
[284] *Institute of Patent Agents v Joseph Lockwood* [1894] A.C. 347.
[285] *Minister of Health v R. Ex p. Yaffe* [1931] A.C. 494.
[286] *Minister of Health v R. Ex p. Yaffe* [1931] A.C. 494.
[287] See, e.g. Emergency Powers Act 1920 s.2(4).

Statutory reform of ouster clauses

12–106 The legislature has also removed the immunity from judicial review conferred by certain types of ouster clauses. The statutory reform provides an additional method of rendering such clauses ineffective. In fact, the restrictive approach to interpretation adopted by the courts has already rendered most such clauses nugatory. The statutory reform is therefore less necessary as a means of undermining immunity from review, than as legislative confirmation of the general policy of the courts towards preserving their supervisory jurisdiction.

12–107 Section 12 of the Tribunal and Inquiries Act 1992 provides that any provisions in an Act passed before August 1, 1958 which provides that any order or determination shall not be called into question in any court, or which by similar words excludes any of the powers of the High Court, are not to have effect as to prevent the proceedings being removed into the High Court by a quashing order or preventing the grant of a mandatory order.

Scope of section 12

Measures within section 12

12–108 The section removes the statutory restriction on the grant of quashing and mandatory orders in certain types of cases. However, this reform is limited in a number of ways. First, the precise range of public bodies to which the section applies has not yet been determined. The section applies to any "order or determination", and it might be thought to apply to any exercise of any public law power by any public body (subject to the exceptions discussed in the next paragraph). Yet, in *Central Bank of India*,[288] the Court of Appeal held that the provision had to be read in the context of an Act which dealt primarily with tribunals and decisions of ministers made pursuant to an inquiry. The provision did not apply to any order or determination of any administrative body or official. The provision did not apply to a decision of the companies registrar exercising powers under the 1948 Companies Act.

12–109 Section 12 does not apply to any order or determination of a court of law.[289] Nor does the section apply to time-limited ouster clauses of the sort discussed below.[290]

Types of ouster clauses within section 12

12–110 The section applies to statutory provisions which provide that an order shall not be called into question or which, by similar words, exclude any powers of the High Court. This provision clearly covers the "shall not be questioned" clauses discussed above. This would enable decisions to be reviewed if they were ultra vires (applying the *Anisminic* doctrine or s.12) and also if they exhibited an intra

---

[288] *R. v Registrar of Companies Ex p. Central Bank of India* [1986] Q.B. 1114.
[289] Tribunals and Inquiries Act 1992 s.12(3).
[290] Tribunals and Inquiries Act 1992 s.12(3).

vires error of law (applying s.12). In practice, reviewable errors of law would be regarded as making the decision ultra vires and subject to judicial review, without the need for reliance on s.12.

There is dicta to the effect that s.12 applies to "final and conclusive clauses," although such decisions are in any event reviewable for ultra vires and intra vires errors.[291] Such clauses would seem to be "similar words" within s.12. The section only applies if the words exclude any powers of the High Court. The clauses do not exclude any of the supervisory powers of the High Court but do remove other powers, such as the jurisdiction to hear appeals (if such a right exists) or, more significantly, jurisdiction to entertain an ordinary civil action. This would probably be sufficient to satisfy the requirements of s.12. The section almost certainly applies to "no certiorari clauses", and will make them reviewable for intra vires errors of law as well as ultra vires errors.
12–111

There appears to be no reported case on whether the section applies to partial ouster clauses, in particular s.285 of the Town and Country Planning Act 1990. It may be that as these sections were enacted post-1958, the section does not apply. There is, however, an argument that as the 1990 Act only re-enacts pre-1958 provisions, s.12 does apply. It may be that enforcement notices are not "orders or determinations" within s.12,[292] although that would seem doubtful. Section 12(3), which excludes time-limited ouster clauses, would not seem to save the partial ouster clauses in s.285 of the 1990 Act,[293] since it concerns appeals not applications, and the Act does not specify a time-limit for bringing the appeal (although it authorises the making of rules which lay down a time-limit which may be sufficient to satisfy the section).
12–112

There is no authority on the applicability of the section to "as if enacted" clauses. It is submitted that such clauses do constitute similar words. Section 12 would provide the means of circumventing such clauses in so far as they restrict the scope for review, provided that the order or determination was one within the opening words of s.12.
12–113

Conclusive evidence clauses are not within s.12. A statement in a certificate which is conclusive is not seen as an order or determination for the purposes of s.12.[294] It is difficult to see why the certificate cannot be regarded as a determination of the question to which it relates. Even if this hurdle were overcome, a provision that a certificate is conclusive may not constitute "similar words" for the purpose of s.12.[295]
12–114

Acts within section 12

Section 12 only applies to provisions contained in Acts passed before August 1, 1958. Statutory provisions included in Acts passed after that date are not deprived of effect by s.12. Professor Wade has suggested that a post-1958 clause which
12–115

---

[291] *R. v Preston Supplementary Benefits Appeal Tribunal Ex p. Moore* [1975] 1 W.L.R. 624 at [628].
[292] See *Ex p. Central Bank of India* [1986] Q.B. 1114 on the meaning of this phrase.
[293] Formerly, Town and Country Planning Act 1971 s.243.
[294] *R. v Secretary of State for Foreign Affairs Ex p. Trawnik, The Times*, February 12, 1986.
[295] per Lawton LJ in *R. v Registrar of Companies Ex p. Central Bank of India* [1986] Q.B. 1114 at [1170] accepting counsel's argument to this effect.

substantially re-enacts a pre-1958 clause may be treated as falling within s.12.[296] An alternative argument would be that the fact that the legislature deliberately chose to include such clauses in subsequent legislation must indicate that they intended them to have effect. Otherwise the legislature would be enacting words which had no meaning or purpose.

Remedies restored by section 12

12–116   The section only restores the remedies of a quashing order and a mandatory order. The section cannot therefore be relied on in relation to a prohibiting order, declaration or injunction. These remedies are, however, available in relation to ultra vires determinations, applying *Anisminic*. So far as intra vires errors are concerned, a quashing order is generally considered the only appropriate remedy and prohibiting orders, declarations and injunctions are not available in any event. In practice, a reviewable error of law now renders a decision ultra vires and all the remedies will be available applying *Anisminic*.

Statutory applications to quash and time-limited ouster clauses

12–117   Statute may provide an alternative statutory procedure for challenging the validity of a decision, and provide that a decision cannot be questioned in any other legal proceedings. Section 288 of the Town and Country Planning Act 1990,[297] for example, provides that a person aggrieved may apply in respect of specified decisions to the High Court within six weeks of the decision, alleging that the decision or order was not one within the powers of the Act or that any requirement of the Act has not been complied with and that as a result the applicant has suffered substantial prejudice. Section 286 of the 1990 Act[298] provides that the validity of such decisions may not be questioned in any legal proceedings except by use of the statutory procedure. This will prohibit direct challenge by way of judicial review, and raising the invalidity of the decision as a defence in criminal proceedings. Decisions other than those to which the ouster clause applies will still be subject to judicial review.[299] The courts may take a narrow approach to the range of decisions falling within such provisions.[300]

---

[296] Wade and Forsyth, 11th edn interpreting *R. v Preston Supplementary Benefits Appeal Tribunal Ex p. Moore* [1975] 1 W.L.R. 624 which referred to s.12 in connection with a 1966 Act which re-enacted a pre-1958 Act.

[297] Formerly, Town and Country Planning Act 1971 s.245.

[298] Town and Country Planning Act 1990 s.243.

[299] In *R. v Cornwall CC Ex p. Huntington* [1994] 1 All E.R. 694, the Court of Appeal held that the fact that a statute specifically provided for an application to quash a modification order, when confirmed, under the Wildlife and Countryside Act 1981, meant that it was only the confirmed modification order that could be challenged. The court could not grant judicial review of a decision to make the order or the order itself prior to confirmation. In *R. v Wiltshire CC Ex p. Lazard Brothers and Co. Ltd, The Times*, December 31, 1997 the High Court held that the existence of remedy in relation to the confirmed modification order went to the discretion (rather than the jurisdiction) of the courts to grant judicial review at an earlier stage. The court held that it was inappropriate on the facts of that that case for the applicant to have to go through the process of the public inquiry and waiting for the modification order to be confirmed and the applicant could seek judicial review of the decision of the County Council to make an order.

[300] See, e.g. *R. v Camden LBC Ex p. Comyn Ching & Co. (London) Ltd.* (1984) 47 P. & C.R. 417. Acquisition of Land Act 1981 s.25 did not exclude review of resolution to make a compulsory

The courts have accepted that such clauses are effective to preclude challenges **12–118** by way of judicial review and that the only avenue of challenge is the statutory procedure. The House of Lords, in *Smith v East Elloe RDC*,[301] held that a similar clause excluded the possibility of challenge after the six-week period, on the grounds that a decision was vitiated by bad faith. Despite suggestions that the reasoning in *Anisminic* undermined the decision in *Smith*, the Court of Appeal has on a number of occasions—in at least three different statutory contexts—given effect to such partial ouster clauses.[302] Challenges can only be made using the statutory machinery during the six-week period, and judicial review is not available at all either during the six-week period or after that period.

Anisminic has been distinguished, principally on the grounds that the ouster **12–119** clause there sought to oust the jurisdiction of the courts completely. Partial ouster clauses regulate the method of judicial supervision by providing an exclusive statutory remedy, and do not oust the jurisdiction of the court.[303] They are often regarded as more akin to limitation clauses since they allow challenge, albeit within a short period. This is particularly true now that the grounds for a statutory application are regarded as virtually replicating the traditional common law grounds of judicial review.[304] It should be noted, however, that standing under the statutory procedure may be more limited than the sufficient interest test for applying judicial review. In one case,[305] only the person to whom the decision related could make an application. This excluded others who would probably have sufficient interest to bring judicial review proceedings. Nevertheless, the ouster clause was effective to exclude judicial review.

Possible exceptions

There have been largely unsuccessful attempts to argue that the general words in **12–120** the time-limited ouster clause do not prevent judicial review for certain errors. The House of Lords has rejected an argument that general words do not exclude the jurisdiction to hear claims based on fraud or bad faith.[306] In *R. v Carmarthen DC Ex p. Blewin Trust Ltd and Felinfoel Brewery Co. Ltd*,[307] however, Nolan J. considered that there was an exception where the public body was proposing to

---

purchase order although it prevented the review of the order itself). See also *Islington London Borough v Secretary of State for the Environment* (1982) 43 P. & C.R. 300 (under predecessor statute, judicial review not precluded in relation to an order that minister refused to confirm).

[301] [1956] A.C. 736.

[302] *R. v Secretary of State for the Environment Ex p. Kent* (1990) 154 L.G.Rev. 53, affd. Pill J. (1989) 57 P. & C.R. 431 (Town and Country Planning Act 1971, ss.242 and 245); *R. v Medicines Commission Ex p. Organon Laboratories Ltd* [1989] C.O.D. 479, affd. by the Court of Appeal [1990] 2 C.M.L.R. 49 (Medicines Act 1968 s.107(1)); *R. v Secretary of State for the Environment Ex p. Ostler* [1977] Q.B. 122 (Sch.2 para.2 to the Highways Act 1959, now Sch.2 para.2 to the Highways Act 1980). See also *Khan v Newport BC* [1991] C.O.D. 157; *R. v Test Valley BC Ex p. Peel Estates Ltd* [1990] C.O.D. 215.

[303] See, *Ex p. Kent* (1990) 154 L.G. Rev 53 and *Ex p. Ostler* [1977] Q.B. 122. The other distinctions suggested in *Ostler*, namely that the decision was administrative not judicial or was voidable not void, are now recognised as not soundly based.

[304] See Chapter 14.

[305] *R. v Medicines Commission Ex p. Organon Laboratories Ltd* [1989] C.O.D. 479, affd. by the Court of Appeal, [1990] 2 C.M.L.R. 49.

[306] *Smith v East Elloe RDC* [1956] A.C. 736.

[307] [1990] C.O.D. 5.

act contrary to good conscience. Here, the applicant alleged that there had been a material change of circumstances between the making of a compulsory purchase order (which could only be challenged within six weeks) and the implementation of the order. On the facts, Nolan J. found that the public body was not acting unconscionably, and relief was refused.

Significance of the Tribunals and Inquiries Act 1992

12–121   Section 12(3) of the Tribunal and Inquiries Act 1992 specifically provides that s.12 of the 1992 Act does not apply where an Act makes special provisions for an application to the High Court within a time limited by the Act. The 1992 Act does not, therefore, prevent time-limited ouster clauses from precluding judicial review.

Ouster clauses and EU law

12–122   Directly effective rights conferred by EU law must be recognised and given effect to in the national courts. Judicial remedies must be available to ensure that those rights can be effectively protected.[308] National law cannot make it difficult or impossible in practice to enforce rights derived from European Union law.[309] A provision which sought to oust the jurisdiction of the courts in respect of those rights would conflict with European Union law, and be unenforceable to that extent. Statutory provisions restricting the range of evidence that might be adduced to support claims[310] or "conclusive evidence" clauses which seek to prevent courts from considering whether a European Union law right was being violated, are unenforceable. In *Johnston v Chief Constable of the Royal Ulster Constabulary*,[311] a statutory provision provided that a certificate issued by a minister was conclusive evidence that a particular act was done for reasons of national security, public safety or public order. The Court of Justice of the European Union held that the provision was contrary to European Union law as it excluded any possibility of review by the courts, and so prevented the courts from ensuring that an effective judicial remedy was available to enforce a European Union law right.

Ouster clauses and the European Convention on Human Rights

12–123   Article 6 of the European Convention on Human Rights embodies a right of access to a court in cases involving the determination of civil rights. Ouster clauses restricting or excluding the jurisdiction of a court in such cases may conflict with Art.6. The European Court of Human Rights has accepted that the right of access to a court is not absolute and may be subject to limitations, but the

---

[308] *Union Nationale des Entraineurs et Cadres Techniques Professionnels du Football (UNECTEF) v Georges Heylens* (Case 222/86) [1987] E.C.R. 4097.
[309] *ReweHandelsgesellschaft Nord mbH and Rewe-Markt Steffen v Hauptzollamt Kiel* (Case 158/80) [1981] 1 E.C.R. 1805.
[310] *Amministrazione delle Finanze v San Giorgio* (Case 199/82) [1983] E.C.R. 3595.
[311] (Case 222/84) [1987] Q.B. 129. See generally Chapter 17 below.

limitation must pursue a legitimate aim and be proportionate.[312] A provision providing that a certificate issued by a minister was conclusive evidence that an act was done on grounds of national security breached Art.6, however, as it was a disproportionate restriction on the right of access to a court as it prevented the court from considering all relevant facts and the concern to ensure protection of national security could be met by the introduction of other procedures which would allow full consideration of the evidence and issues in a case without compromising national security.[313]

---

[312] *Tinnelly v United Kingdom* (1998) 27 E.H.R.R. 249 at [72].
[313] (1998) 27 E.H.R.R. 249 at [74]–[78].

CHAPTER 13

Habeas Corpus

A. INTRODUCTION

The prerogative writ of habeas corpus *ad subjiciendum* is a means of securing the release of a person unlawfully detained.[1] The writ requires the person responsible for the detention to produce the prisoner in court, and make a return stating the grounds for the detention. The court will then inquire into the legality of the detention and, if it is unlawful, order the release of the prisoner. The modern practice is for the application for the writ to be made on behalf of the applicant without notice to the defendant. If the court considers there is an arguable case that the detention is unlawful, it will adjourn the application to a hearing on notice to the defendant. At the hearing of the application for the issue of the writ, a court may determine whether the detention was unlawful, and if so order the release of the prisoner without formally issuing the writ of habeas corpus.[2] The writ is a prerogative one obtainable by its own procedure.[3] The jurisdiction to grant the writ existed at common law but has been recognised and extended by statute.[4]

13–001

B. SCOPE OF THE JURISDICTION

The writ of habeas corpus is available to determine the legality of any detention of a person by another person, whether that other person is a public body or private individual. It has, for example, been used to determine the legality of detention:

13–002

(a) pending deportation[5];
(b) pending the removal of immigrants[6];

---

[1] Sharpe, *The Law of Habeas Corpus* (3rd edn, 2011).
[2] See CPR Sch.1; RSC Ord.54 r.4. The modern practice is described in the decision of Lord Phillips in *Rahmatullah v Secretary of State for Defence* [2012] 3 W.L.R. 1087 at [89].
[3] See CPR Sch.1; RSC Ord.54 and Practice Direction – Sch.1 Ord.54 (application for Writ of Habeas Corpus).
[4] Habeas Corpus Act 1679 (criminal cases) and Habeas Corpus Act 1816 (non-criminal cases).
[5] See, e.g. *R. v Governor of Brixton Prison Ex p. Soblen* [1963] 2 Q.B. 243.
[6] See, e.g. *R. v Governor of Durham Prison Ex p. Singh (Hardial)* [1984] 1 W.L.R. 704; *Azam v Secretary of State for the Home Department* [1974] A.C. 18; *Tan Le Lam v Superintendent of Tai A Chau Detention Centre* [1997] A.C. 97.

(c)   pending extradition[7]; or

(d)   pending the return of fugitive offenders[8];

(e)   under the mental health legislation[9];

(f)   by the police[10]; and

(g)   on remand in custody.[11]

13–003   The purpose of the writ is to facilitate the release of those detained in unlawful custody. The writ is only available where the respondent has custody or physical control of the applicant or where there are reasonable grounds for considering that the respondent is be able to exercise such control. Thus, where the United Kingdom authorities had detained an individual in Iraq and transferred him to the custody of the United States, and where there was a memorandum of understanding between the two countries indicating that the United States would return the detainee upon request, the Supreme Court held that the writ would issue.[12] The authorities subsequently informed the court that the American authorities had indicated that they considered they were entitled to detain the individual concerned and were not proposing to discuss his release with the British authorities. The courts accepted that the British authorities would not therefore be able to assert control over the individual and discharged the writ.[13] The writ will not be granted after the person has been released nor will it be directed against someone who no longer has custody of the person[14] or the possibility of obtaining control of the individual although the courts may take the opportunity to give judgment to provide general guidance on points of law.[15]

Nature of review on habeas corpus application

Questions of fact

13–004   The position in relation to determination of facts is complex. In some cases, the determination of questions of fact will be a matter for the public body, subject only to the supervisory jurisdiction of the courts. The courts will only ensure that there is sufficient evidence on which a reasonable court or public body could properly reach the decision that it has reached. In extradition cases, for example,

---

[7] See, e.g. *Oskar v Government of Australia* [1988] A.C. 366. Certain decisions in extradition cases are now subject to appeal and cannot be the subject of applications for habeas corpus: see Extradition Act 2003 s.34 and *R. (Hilali) v Governor of Whitemoor Prison* [2008] A.C. 805. Not all decisions under the Extradition Act 2003 are subject to a right of appeal and habeas corpus remains available in respect of such decisions: *R. (Nikonovs) v Governor of Brixton Prison* [2006] 1 W.L.R. 1518; *R (Asliturk) v City of Westminster Magistrates' Court* [2011] 1 W.L.R. 1139.

[8] See, e.g. *R. v Governor of Pentonville Prison Ex p. Osman* [1990] 1 W.L.R. 277.

[9] *R. v Board of Control Ex p. Rutty* [1956] 2 Q.B. 109.

[10] *R. v Holmes Ex p. Sherman* [1981] 2 All E.R. 612 (whether period of detention in police custody reasonable: this particular matter is now regulated by the Police and Criminal Evidence Act 1984); *R. (Littlejohn) v South Wales Police* [2008] EWHC 301 (Admin).

[11] *R. v Governor of Armley Prison Ex p. Ward*, *The Times*, November 23, 1990.

[12] *Rahmatullah v Secretary of State for Defence* [2012] 3 W.L.R. 1087 at [64].

[13] *Rahmatullah v Secretary of State for Defence* [2012] 3 W.L.R. 1087 at [77]–[85]. See also the decision of the Court of Appeal [2012] 1 W.L.R. 1462 at 1490–1494.

[14] *Barnardo (Thomas John) v. Ford (Mary)* [1892] A.C. 326.

[15] *R. v Governor of Brixton Prison Ex p. Walsh* [1985] A.C. 154; *R. v Governor of Canterbury Prison Ex p. Craig* [1990] 3 W.L.R. 126.

the courts will consider whether there was sufficient evidence on which a reasonable magistrate properly directing himself in law could commit.[16]

There are cases, however, where the existence of a particular fact is a necessary pre-condition to the exercise of a statutory power: these are referred to as jurisdictional facts. It is for the courts to determine whether such jurisdictional facts exist. In *R. v Secretary of State for the Home Department Ex p. Khawaja*,[17] if a person was an illegal immigrant, the authorities had power to detain and remove him from the UK. The question of whether the person was in fact an illegal immigrant was a jurisdictional or precedent fact which had to be established to the satisfaction of the courts before the power to detain and remove arose. The courts were not limited to ensuring that there was sufficient evidence upon which a reasonable immigration officer could conclude that the person was an illegal immigrant. Similarly, the Privy Council has held that a power to detain an immigrant "pending removal" could only be exercised during the period necessary to effect the removal and if it becomes clear that the removal will not be possible within a reasonable time continued detention is unlawful. The Privy Council held that the facts relevant to whether the applicant was being detained pending removal were jurisdictional or precedent facts and their existence had to be proved to the satisfaction of the court. The courts were not limited to determining whether the detaining authority's assessment of those facts was *Wednesbury* unreasonable.[18] The Supreme Court left open the question of whether the courts should determine if an applicant was a child where that may be relevant to the lawfulness of detention.[19]

It is difficult to predict when a court will classify a fact as jurisdictional. Dicta in *Khawaja*[20] suggest that the presumption should be that facts are jurisdictional in cases involving interference with liberty, unless Parliament has made it clear that review should be supervisory and residual only. In practice, however, the courts are reluctant to classify facts as jurisdictional and prefer to leave such determinations to the public body concerned, subject to residual supervision by way of judicial review or habeas corpus. This is certainly the case where decisions of lower courts are concerned. The courts prefer to leave the initial factual determination to the lower courts, not least because they are better equipped to investigate facts than is the High Court in applications for habeas corpus which tends to proceed on witness statements or affidavit evidence only and rarely allows cross-examination or oral evidence.[21] The courts are often

13–005

13–006

---

[16] [1985] A.C. 154. See also *R. (Al-Fawwaz) v Governor of Brixton Prison* [2001] 1 W.L.R. 1235 at [44] and [54] (and confirming that the position is not altered by the European Convention on Human Rights); *R. v Governor of Brixton Prison Ex p. Kahan* [1989] Q.B. 716 at [726]–[727].

[17] *R. v Secretary of State for the Home Department Ex p. Khawaja* [1984] A.C. 74.

[18] *Tan Le Lam v Superintendent of the Tai A Chau Detention Centre* [1996] 2 W.L.R. 863.

[19] *R. (AA (Afghanistan)) v Secretary of State for the Home Department* [2013] 1 W..L.R. 2224 at [52]–[53] (but see also [56]–[58] for the view of Lord Carnwarth).

[20] [1984] A.C. 74 and of the Privy Council in *Tan Le Lam v Superintendent of the Tai A Chau Detention Centre* [1996] 2 W.L.R. 863.

[21] See, e.g. *R. v Governor of Pentonville Prison Ex p. Osman* (above, fn.6); *R. v Governor of Brixton Prison Ex p. Kahan* [1989] Q.B. 716.

reluctant to classify a fact as jurisdictional even where the power to decide to detain a person is placed in the hands of an administrative rather than a judicial authority.[22]

13-007   The court may also use the writ where there is doubt as to whether the person is as a matter of fact being restrained against his will. So habeas corpus was issued by the Northern Irish courts where there was doubt as to whether a person was being detained by the police against her will or whether she had voluntarily placed herself under police protection.[23] It is not usually the fact of restraint that is in issue, but the legality of the restraint.

13-008   The courts are entitled to look at all the available material in determining whether they are satisfied that any relevant facts exist.[24] They are not limited only to considering evidence that would be admissible under the common law rules of evidence. They are, therefore, entitled to have regard to hearsay evidence such as reports of interviews conducted by immigration officers.

Questions of legal validity

13-009   A public body may detain a person in the exercise of statutory powers. The public body may seek to justify the detention by stating that the detention is done pursuant to the exercise of those statutory powers. The applicant may seek to challenge the validity of the exercise of those statutory powers. Such challenges may be brought either by way of a claim for judicial review or by way of an application for habeas corpus. The approach of the courts on a habeas corpus application should be essentially similar to that adopted by the courts when reviewing the exercise of statutory power by way of judicial review.[25] In *Khawaja*, Lord Scarman considered that the substance of the law of judicial review and habeas corpus were the same and the differences related to procedure[26] and Lord Wilberforce did not consider it appropriate to make a distinction between judicial review and habeas corpus unless it was unavoidable.[27] On a habeas corpus application, the court will act as a supervisory body. They will not interfere with a discretion properly exercised. Rather, the courts will apply the normal substantive principles of administrative law to determine whether the decision to detain was valid.[28] The Privy Council has also consistently held that the validity of a detention may also be reviewed on an application for habeas corpus.[29]

---

[22] See, e.g. *R. v Secretary of State for the Home Department Ex p. Bugdaycay* [1987] A.C. 514 (whether a person is a "refugee" is a question of fact left to the authorities not a jurisdictional fact).

[23] *Quigley v Chief Constable of Northern Ireland* [1983] N.I. 238. See also *Barnardo (Thomas John) v Ford (Mary)* [1892] (above, fn.14). As to what constitutes detention, see *R. v Bournewood and Community Mental Health NHS Trust Ex p. L* [1998] 3 All E.R. 289.

[24] *R. v Secretary of State for the Home Department Ex p. Rahman* [1997] 3 W.L.R. 990.

[25] See, e.g. dicta in *R. v Secretary of State for the Home Department Ex p. Khawaja* [1984] A.C. 74 and see dicta of the Privy Council in *Cartwright v Superintendent of Her Majesty's Prisons* [2004] 1 W.L.R. 894 at [16].

[26] [1984] A.C. 74 at [111B]–[C].

[27] [1984] A.C. 74 at [99].

[28] *R. v Governor of Pentonville Prison Ex p. Osman* [1990] 1 W.L.R. 277.

[29] See, e.g. *Gibson v Government of the United States of America* [2007] 1 W.L.R. 2367 at [18]–[21]; *Knowles v Government of the United States* [2007] 1 W.L.R. 47 at [12]–[14]; *Cartwright v Superintendent of Her Majesty's Prison* [2004] 1 W.L.R. 902.

Certain decisions of the Court of Appeal and the Divisional Court have **13–010** suggested that the scope of habeas corpus is different from and narrower than judicial review and that the extent to which the court will review the legality of exercises of power leading to detention may be limited. In *R. v Secretary of State for the Home Department Ex p. Muboyayi*,[30] an immigrant had been refused leave to enter the UK. As he had been refused leave to enter, a power to detain him arose under para.16(2) of Sch.2 to the Immigration Act 1971. The immigrant applied for habeas corpus alleging that the decision to refuse him leave to enter was unlawful and therefore no power to detain arose. He contended that, just as the courts would consider whether any precedent facts necessary to justify detention existed, so the courts could review the legality of any underlying administrative decision to detain him. The Court of Appeal held that habeas corpus could not be used to determine whether the underlying administrative decision to refuse leave to enter was invalid on the normal grounds of administrative law such as a procedural error or misappreciation of the law or a failure to take account of relevant matters or taking into account irrelevant matters or acting unreasonably. Such a challenge could only be made by way of judicial review. Habeas corpus would be available if the power to detain was dependent upon the existence of certain precedent facts and the existence of those facts was in dispute.

The process of limiting the scope of judicial review appears to have been **13–011** carried further by the Divisional Court in *R. v Oldham Justices Ex p. Cawley*.[31] In that case, three applicants applied for habeas corpus to challenge their detention following committal to prison by magistrates for non-payment of fines. A person under 21 could only be committed to prison if the magistrates were satisfied that no other method of dealing with the offender was appropriate. Furthermore, statute required the magistrates to state the grounds for so concluding in the warrant for committal. The magistrates failed to set out the grounds in the warrant. The relevant rules provided, however, that the warrant was not to be void simply because of the failure to set out the grounds. The question arose, however, as to whether the magistrates had simply failed to complete the warrant properly or whether they had failed to have regard to the relevant statutory provisions and so had erred in law in issuing the warrant for committal. The Divisional Court held that habeas corpus was not available to challenge the detention on the grounds that the magistrates had erred in law. The decision, in part at least appears, to be influenced by the view that judicial review was a "more flexible and responsive jurisdiction" and that the need for a "parallel, blunter remedy by way of habeas corpus has diminished."[32] Furthermore, the Divisional Court considered that there was in reality no practical advantage in using habeas corpus. Although habeas corpus took precedence over other all other business in the courts and issued as of right, in practice judicial review claims dealing with the

---

[30] [1992] Q.B. 244. See also the judgment of Lord Donaldson M.R. in *R. v Secretary of State for the Home Department Ex p. Cheblak* [1991] W.L.R. 890 at [894].
[31] [1996] 1 All E.R. 464.
[32] See *R. v Oldham Justices Ex p. Cawley* [1996] 1 All E.R. 464 at 467g–h; *R. v Barking and Havering Community Healthcare NHS Trust* [1999] 1 F.L.R. 106 at 104–107; *R. v Manchester Crown Court Ex p. McDonald* [1999] 1 W.L.R. 841 at 855D.

liberty of the citizen were given the same priority[33] and the court would be unlikely to refuse judicial review in such cases as a matter of discretion. The Divisional Court also considered that judicial review had other advantages such as greater flexibility and the fact that it was directed at the real respondent, i.e. the person whose decision was under challenge not the person who happened to be detaining the applicant pursuant to that decision. The difficulty with this series of decisions, however, does not lie with the assessment of whether judicial review is in practical terms equally or more capable of resolving a challenge to the lawfulness of decisions leading to detention. Rather, the question is whether the restrictions now being placed on the availability of habeas accord with principle and are logical and defensible restrictions.

13–012   This restrictive approach to the habeas corpus jurisdiction has been subjected to powerful criticism by the Law Commission.[34] The decision in *Ex p. Muboyayi* appears to be premised in part on the basis that habeas corpus is only available to deal with issues of precedent fact. There is no reason in principle why it should be confined in such a way and to do so appears inconsistent with the approach adopted by the House of Lords[35] and the Privy Council.[36] Secondly, the restrictive approach advocated by Lord Donaldson M.R. in *R. v Secretary of State for the Home Department Ex p. Cheblak*[37] appears to draw a distinction between a situation where detention is outside the powers of the administrative authority (where habeas corpus was said to be available) and one where the administrative authority has a power to detain but has made some reviewable error, such as an error of law or a procedural error (where only judicial review is available). The modern approach, certainly since the decision of the House of Lords in *Anisminic*,[38] is to regard all reviewable errors as going to jurisdiction. There is no reason for having separate categories of error for the sole purpose of deciding whether habeas corpus is available. The practical consequences are also undesirable. If habeas corpus is capable of being used as a means of determining the validity of administrative action, it is difficult to see why, as in *Ex p. Cawley*,[39] a court should refuse relief because the application was made by an application for one particular prerogative remedy, habeas corpus, rather than for another, for example a quashing order sought by way of a claim for judicial review. That appears to be drawing a rigid procedural dichotomy between the different prerogative orders which appears to be unjustifiable.[40]

---

[33] Strictly, claims for judicial review must be served and the defendant given 21 days to file an acknowledgment of service. There is, however, a procedure for urgent applications (see para.9–014 above), and if a real issue of liberty arose, the courts would, in practice, ensure it was dealt with speedily, irrespective of the procedure chosen.

[34] "Administrative Law: Judicial Review and Statutory Appeals" Law Com. No.226 at paras 11.4—11.6.

[35] For example, in *Khawaja* [1984] A.C. 74 and see para.13–009. See also *Armah v Government of Ghana* [1968] A.C. 192.

[36] See, e.g. *Gibson v Government of the United States of America* [2007] 1 W.L.R. 2367 at [18]–[21]; *Knowles v Government of the United States* [2007] 1 W.L.R. 47 at [12]–[14]; and the dicta in *Cartwright v Superintendent of Her Majesty's Prison* [2004] 1 W.L.R. 90 at [16].

[37] [1991] 1 W.L.R. 890 at [894].

[38] *Anisminic v Foreign Compensation Commission* [1969] 2 A.C. 147 and see, in a different context, *Boddington v British Transport Police* [1999] 2 A.C. 143.

[39] Above, fn.31.

[40] It is reminiscent of the decision in *O'Reilly v Mackman* [1983] 2 A.C. 237: see above Chapter 3.

In one subsequent case,[41] the Court of Appeal distinguished *Ex p. Muboyayi*. **13–013** That case involved an application to admit a person to hospital under the Mental Health Act 1983. The application could be made by a social worker, provided that the person's nearest relative had not objected. The social worker purported to make an application, notwithstanding that she knew that the person's nearest relative had objected. The Court of Appeal held that an application for habeas corpus was an appropriate course to pursue to challenge the validity of the detention. The Court distinguished, without giving reasons, the earlier decision of *Ex p. Muboyayi*. This decision is to be welcomed but it is unfortunate that the case law in an area involving the liberty of the citizen is contradictory and the circumstances in which habeas corpus is available are not clear.[42]

Burden and standard of proof

The writ of habeas corpus is a writ of right but not of course. This means that the **13–014** applicant has to show a prima facie case that he is being unlawfully detained. Thereafter the burden of justifying the legality of the detention passes to the respondent. The respondent may assert that the detention is pursuant to the exercise of a statutory or other public law power. If so, and providing that the assertion is not bad on its face, it will be for the applicant to establish that the statutory power has been invalidly exercised and the detention is illegal. The standard of proof is the civil standard of the balance of probabilities. Fresh evidence, in addition to that placed before the authorities taking the initial decision, will not normally be admitted before the Divisional Court.[43]

The exercise of a statutory power may be dependent on the existence of a **13–015** jurisdictional fact. Here, the applicant has to establish a prima facie case that the detention is unlawful. Thereafter, the burden of proving the existence of the jurisdictional fact is transferred to the respondent.[44] He must establish the existence of that fact to the satisfaction of the court. The standard of proof is the civil standard of the balance of probability, bearing in mind that a higher degree of probability will be required where liberty is at stake.[45] Fresh evidence relevant to a jurisdictional fact will be admitted.[46]

---

[41] In *re S-C (Mental Patient: Habeas Corpus)* [1996] Q.B. 599. See also the dicta in *R. v Central London County Court Ex p. London* [1999] 3 W.L.R. 1 at 13A–C.

[42] The Privy Council, in a very different context, has also recognised that habeas corpus and judicial review are based on common principles and that there is considerable overlap between them: see *Cartwright v Superintendent of Her Majesty's Prisons* [2004] 1 W.L.R. 894 at [16] and see *Gibson v Government of the United States of America* [2007] 1 W.L.R. 2367 at [18]–[21]; *Knowles v Government of the United States* [2007] 1 W.L.R. 47 at [12]–[14].

[43] See, e.g. *Schtraks v Government of Israel* [1964] A.C. 556.

[44] *R. v Secretary of State for the Home Department Ex p. Khawaja* [1984] A.C. 74.

[45] [1984] A.C. 74.

[46] [1984] A.C. 74.

Discretion to refuse habeas corpus

13–016 The writ of habeas corpus is frequently referred to as a writ of right. Once it is established that the detention is unlawful, the applicant is entitled to the writ and the court has no discretion to refuse it.[47] There is no doubt that where the circumstances necessary to justify detention do not exist, the courts will invariably grant a remedy. The detention may be unlawful because it is based on an invalid exercise of a statutory power to detain. In judicial review applications, the court has a wide discretion to refuse relief.[48] In habeas corpus cases, it is frequently thought that the discretion is non-existent. The true position would seem to be that the courts could in principle refuse relief on a habeas application but, given the importance of the liberty of the subject, it is extremely unlikely that the courts would refuse relief. The court might be similarly reluctant to refuse relief in a judicial review claim involving liberty of the subject.[49] The Divisional Court has said, obiter, that the court could refuse the writ of habeas corpus where there was a purely technical flaw in the process leading to detention.[50] The court may also refuse an application for habeas corpus where a previous claim for judicial review has been refused as an abuse of process if there is no explanation for the further application to the courts.[51]

13–017 One area where the discretion of the courts might be relevant is in relation to alternative remedies. First, there may be cases where statute provides a right of appeal to a court in respect of certain decisions, and provides that those decisions cannot be challenged in other proceedings. In such circumstances, the courts may require the individual to use the statutory appeal mechanism and may regard the remedy of habeas corpus as being excluded[52]. Secondly, the existence of alternative remedies such as a statutory right of appeal will not in other circumstances oust the jurisdiction of the court to grant habeas corpus[53] but it may be relevant to whether the court in its discretion ought to grant a remedy. The courts have allowed habeas corpus applications in the past notwithstanding the

---

[47] See dicta of Lord Kerr in *Rahmatullah v Secretary of State for Defence* [2012] 2 W.L.R. 1087 at [41] and Lord Wright in *Greene v Secretary of State for Home Affairs* [1942] A.C. 284 at [302]. See also the decision of the Privy Council in *Phillip v DPP* [1992] 1 All E.R. 665 at [676b]–[d].

[48] See Chapter 12.

[49] See, e.g. *R. v Secretary of State for the Home Department Ex p. Khawaja* [1984] A.C. 74 which involved a judicial review application but similar concern for the liberty of the subject was expressed.

[50] *R. v Governor of Pentonville Prison Ex p. Osman (No.3)* [1990] 1 W.L.R. 878. But see the decision of the Privy Council in *Phillip v DPP* above, fn.47.

[51] *Sheikh v Secretary of State for the Home Department* [2001] A.C.D. 193.

[52] *R. (Hilali) v Governor of Whitemoor Prison* [2008] A.C. 805 at [20] Not all decisions under the Extradition Act 2003 are subject to a right of appeal and habeas corpus remains available in respect of such decisions: *R. (Nikonovs) v Governor of Brixton Prison* [2006] 1 W.L.R. 1518; *R (Asliturk) v Westminster City Magistrates' Court* [2011] 1 W.L.R. 1139. Where child care proceedings are in process, those proceedings not habeas corpus should be used to challenge a decision allegedly involving a detention of a child: *R. (S) v London Borough of Haringey* judgment, November 13, 2003. See Chapter 12 above on the exhaustion of remedies principle in judicial review.

[53] *R. v Secretary of State for the Home Department Ex p. Mughal* [1973] 1 W.L.R. 1113 at 1116, and see dictum of Lord Denning M.R. in the Court of Appeal in *Azam v Secretary of State for the Home Department* (above, fn.6) at 32. But see the decision of the Privy Council in *Phillip v DPP* above, fn.47 at 676c–d.

existence of a statutory appeal mechanism.[54] The courts have, however, traditionally refused to allow habeas corpus applications to challenge convictions or sentences by courts of record or inferior courts,[55] or for committals for contempt of court,[56] but have left the applicant to his statutory rights of appeal. The Divisional Court has also stated that habeas corpus is not normally an appropriate means of challenging an extension of the time, by the magistrates' court, within which the person can be held in custody pending committal proceedings. The Divisional Court considered that the applicant should use the statutory appeals mechanism specifically provided.[57]

There are arguments against allowing the use of habeas corpus to circumvent the appeals procedure, particularly where there are greater powers available to the court on appeal to correct, rather than simply quash an invalid order.[58] Habeas corpus could continue to be available where the matter was urgent and there was a need for speed or where the appeal mechanism could not correct the particular illegality complained of. Habeas corpus may also be appropriate where the application raises questions of law of general application on which authoritative judicial guidance is required.[59] On the other hand, the liberty of the subject has been seen as a paramount concern of the courts. The desire to ensure liberty may itself be a good reason for allowing habeas corpus to be available to challenge any allegedly unlawful detention, irrespective of any other avenue of challenge. **13–018**

Habeas corpus and superior courts of record

Habeas corpus is in principle available against orders of superior courts of record, but will rarely if ever be issued in practice. It has been suggested that habeas corpus cannot issue against a superior court of record which is a court of unlimited jurisdiction as any error by such a court does not take such a court outside its jurisdiction.[60] Yet, such courts can make errors of law which render their decision irregular, and liable to be set aside on appeal or by way of application to the court that made the order.[61] There is no reason why habeas corpus should be restricted to jurisdictional errors (as that term is now understood), but should encompass all errors liable to vitiate a decision of a superior court. Modern authority supports the view that habeas corpus is available against superior courts.[62] In practice, however, habeas corpus will rarely issue against a superior court. Review will be made more difficult as the courts will accept a bald statement that the committal is done pursuant to an order of a **13–019**

---

[54] See, e.g. *R. v Governor of Durham Prison Ex p. Singh Hardial* (above, fn.6); *Azam* (above, fn.6); *Ex p. Mughal* (above, fn.53).

[55] *Re Corke* [1954] 1 W.L.R. 899; *Re Wring and Cook* [1960] 1 W.L.R. 138; *Re Featherstone* (1953) 37 Cr.App.R. 146.

[56] *Linnett v Coles* [1987] Q.B. 555.

[57] *R. v Governor of Canterbury Prison Ex p. Craig* [1990] 3 W.L.R. 126; *Re C* [1990] C.O.D. 119.

[58] A point made in *Linnett v Coles* 1987] Q.B. 555.

[59] *R. v Governor of Canterbury Prison Ex p. Craig* [1990] 3 W.L.R. 126.

[60] *Re Racal Communications* [1981] A.C. 374. See Chapter 5.

[61] *Isaacs v Robertson* [1985] A.C. 97.

[62] See *Linnett v Coles* [1987] Q.B. 555 (committals by High Court for contempt reviewable in exceptional cases by habeas corpus); *R. v Governor of Spring Hill Prison Ex p. Sohi* [1988] 1 W.L.R. 596 (habeas corpus to determine validity of conviction in Crown Court; application dismissed on its merits).

superior court and will not inquire into the reasons for the order of committal to see if there has been an error of law,[63] although the court may order release if the return to the writ itself showed the committal was unlawful.[64]

Habeas corpus and criminal appeals

13–020 The courts are extremely reluctant to allow habeas corpus to be used as a means of appeal against conviction or sentence, thereby circumventing the usual appeals procedure with the wider discretionary powers available in such appeals.[65] This is true both of superior courts of unlimited jurisdiction and inferior courts of limited jurisdiction.[66] The Divisional Court has, however, considered the legality of a conviction and sentence by the Crown Court where it was alleged that breach of the rules governing the time within which the trial must occur rendered the sentence invalid.[67] The courts may use habeas corpus if it is alleged that the person is detained beyond the proper length of the sentence.[68] The Court of Appeal has also stated, obiter, that habeas corpus could be used in exceptional cases to quash a High Court order committing a person for contempt of court, but that such committals should normally be challenged by way of the statutory right of appeal provided.[69]

Habeas corpus and the Crown

13–021 Habeas corpus may be issued against Crown servants such as ministers.[70]

Committals by Parliament

13–022 The courts will not inquire into the legality of committals by the House of Commons or the House of Lords for contempt or breach of privilege.[71] This is not a problem in practice as no such committals have occurred since the last century.

---

[63] *Ex p. Fernandez* (1861) 10 C.B. (N.S.) 3.

[64] *Hamond v Howell* (1674) 1 Mod.Rep. 184.

[65] *Re Corke (Practice Note)* [1954] 1 W.L.R. 899; *Re Wring and Cook (Practice Note)* [1960] 1 W.L.R. 138; *Linnett v Coles* [1987] Q.B. 555. But see *R. v Governor of Spring Hill Prison Ex p. Sohi* [2988] 1 W.L.R. 596.

[66] *Re Featherstone* (1953) 37 Cr.App.R. 146.

[67] *R. v Governor of Spring Hill Prison Ex p. Sohi* [1988] 1 W.L.R. 596.

[68] *R. v Governor of Blundeston Prison Ex p. Gaffney* [1982] 1 W.L.R. 696 (whether days spent in custody to be counted towards sentence). See also dicta in *Re Featherstone* (1953) 37 Cr.App.R. 146.

[69] *Linnett v Coles* [1987] Q.B. 555.

[70] *R. v Secretary of State for the Department Ex p. Muboyayi* [1992] Q.B. 244.

[71] *Burdett v Abbott* (1811) 14 East 1, per Lord Ellenborough at 150 and *Middlesex Sheriff's Case* (1840) 11 A. & E. 273. The court will accept as adequate a return that states that committal is for contempt of Parliament. The courts might review the committal if the return itself showed that the order for committal was bad.

Territorial scope of habeas corpus

The High Court of England and Wales may issue the writ of habeas corpus to any part of England and Wales, Berwick-upon-Tweed, the Isle of Man and the Channel Islands.[72] The English writ does not run to Scotland,[73] nor to Northern Ireland.[74] The English courts could formerly issue the writ to any part of the Crown's dominions including the colonies. Statute now provides that no writ of habeas corpus shall issue out of England by authority of any English judge or court to any colony or foreign dominion.[75] The writ may issue to a protectorate.[76] The writ cannot be issued to foreign countries.[77] British subjects and aliens within the jurisdiction may apply for habeas corpus.[78]

13–023

C. PROCEDURE

Application for the writ

An application may be, and often is, made without notice being served on the other party and must be made to a judge in court unless:

13–024

(a) the court directs that it is to be made to a Divisional Court; or
(b) if no judge is sitting in court, it may be made to a judge otherwise than in court; or
(c) the application is made on behalf of a minor, in which case it must in the first instance be made otherwise than in court.[79]

An application may be made by the person restrained and must be supported by a witness statement or affidavit by him, showing that the application is made at his instance and setting out the nature of the restraint.[80] Where a person under restraint cannot make an affidavit or witness statement, a relative or friend may make an application on his behalf, stating that the person restrained is unable to make the affidavit or witness statement himself and explaining the reasons why this is so.[81]

By established practice, applications for habeas corpus take precedence over all other court business.

13–025

---

[72] Both at common law and pursuant to Habeas Corpus Act 1679 s.10 and Habeas Corpus Act 1816 s.5.
[73] *R. v Cowle* (1759) 2 Burr. 834.
[74] *Re Keenan* [1972] 1 Q.B. 533.
[75] Habeas Corpus Act 1862 s.1.
[76] *Ex p. Mwenya* [1960] 1 Q.B. 241.
[77] *R. v Pinckney* [1904] 2 K.B. 84.
[78] *R. v Secretary of State for the Home Department Ex p. Khawaja* [1984] A.C. 74.
[79] CPR Sch.1; Ord.54 r.1. Applications for custody or care of a minor must be made in the Family Division: CPR Sch.1; Ord.54 r.11.
[80] CPR Sch.1; Ord.54 r.1(2).
[81] CPR Sch.1; Ord.54 r.1(3).

Powers of court on an application without notice

13–026 The court or judge before whom the without notice application is made may make an order for the writ to issue.[82] This will usually only be done in exceptional circumstances where the facts and law are clear, or where delay could defeat the purpose of the application. If no writ is issued, the court or judge may make one of the following orders[83]:

(a) where the application is made otherwise than to a judge in court, direct that a claim form seeking the writ be issued, or that an application be made by claim form[84] to a Divisional Court or to a judge in court;

(b) where the application is made to a judge in court, adjourn the application so that notice may be given to the respondent, or direct that the application be made by claim form to the Divisional Court;

(c) where the application is made to a Divisional Court, adjourn the application so that notice[85] may be given to the respondent.

13–027 The notice of adjournment, or the claim form, should be served upon the person having control of the person restrained. The claim form must be entered for hearing by filing a copy of the form in the Crown Office.[86] Every witness statement or affidavit used in proceedings must also be filed in the Crown Office. There must be eight clear days between service and the date of the hearing, unless the court otherwise directs.[87] The person detained will remain in detention pending the hearing unless the court grants bail.

Procedure at the hearing

13–028 Evidence will usually be by way of witness statement or affidavit evidence only.[88] Every party to an application must supply to every other party on demand, and on payment of the proper charges, copies of the witness statements and affidavits that are to be used at the hearing of the application.[89] Cross-examination is possible,[90] but is not normally ordered. The courts will rarely order the attendance for cross-examination where the deponent of an affidavit or witness statement is overseas.[91] The person detained will not be brought to the court at the hearing of the application unless the court has so directed.

---

[82] CPR Sch.1; Ord.54 r.2(1).

[83] CPR Sch.1; Ord.54 r.2(1).

[84] Using Form 87: see para.3.1 of the Practice Direction – Sch.1 Ord.54 (application for Writ of Habeas Corpus).

[85] Using Form 88: see para.3.1 of the Practice Direction – Sch.1 Ord.54 (application for Writ of Habeas Corpus).

[86] See para.6.1 of the Practice Direction – Sch.1 Ord.54 (application for Writ of Habeas Corpus).

[87] CPR r.32.7.

[88] *R. v Secretary of State for Home Department Ex p. Khawaja* [1984] A.C. 74.

[89] CPR Sch.1; Ord.54 r.3.

[90] CPR Sch.1; Ord.38 r.2(3).

[91] *R. v Secretary of State for Home Department Ex p. Khawaja* [1984] A.C. 74 at [125].

Power of the court at a hearing

The judge may order the release of the person detained at the hearing of the application, and such an order is a sufficient authorisation for the person to be released.[92] The modern practice is for the court to make such an order, rather than formally issuing the writ requiring the prisoner to be brought to court and the detention justified. Alternatively, a judge (or Divisional Court) may dismiss the application and decline to make an order for the release of a person detained.[93]

13–029

A person whose application has been dismissed cannot make a second application unless there is fresh evidence to support such an application.[94] An applicant is required to put forward the whole of his case fairly available to him on his initial application.[95] Fresh evidence means not merely evidence which is additional to or different from that put forward at the initial application, but also evidence which could not reasonably have been put forward at the initial application.[96] The position in relation to appeals against the grant or refusal of the writ is discussed below.

13–030

Issue of the writ

The writ of habeas corpus formally directs the person having custody of the prisoner to produce the body of the prisoner and make a return, stating the day and cause of the detention. The court or judge issuing the writ must give directions as to the court or judge before whom, and the date at which, the return to the writ is to be made.[97] The writ must be in the prescribed form.[98] The writ must be served personally or if it is directed to a prison governor or public official, by leaving it with the servant or agent of that person, at the place where the prisoner is detained.[99] A notice in the prescribed form setting out the time and place where the prisoner is to be brought and the return made, and stating that, in default of obedience, committal proceedings will be taken must be served with the writ.[100]

13–031

Return of the writ and procedure at the hearing

The return to the writ must be indorsed with all the causes of the detention.[101] The return may be amended or another return substituted with leave of the court or judge before whom the writ is returnable.[102] At the hearing, the return will be

13–032

---

[92] CPR Sch.1; Ord.54 r.4(1).
[93] Formerly, a single judge could not refuse order an order for release in a criminal case and had to refer the matter to a Divisional Court: see s.14(1)(a) of the Administration of Justice Act 1960. That provision has been removed by the Access to Justice Act 1999 s.65(1)(a).
[94] Administration of Justice Act 1960 s.14(2). The same section prohibits applications to the Lord Chancellor.
[95] *R. v Governor of Pentonville Prison Ex p. Tarling* [1979] 1 W.L.R. 1417.
[96] [1979] 1 W.L.R. 1417.
[97] CPR Sch.1; Ord.54 r.5.
[98] CPR Sch.1; Ord.54 r.10.
[99] CPR Sch.1; Ord.54 r.6(1).
[100] CPR Sch.1; Ord.54 r.4.
[101] CPR Sch.1; Ord.54 r.7(1).
[102] CPR Sch.1; Ord.54 r.7(2).

read and a motion made for discharging or remanding the person detained, or for quashing or amending the return.[103] Counsel for the prisoner will be heard first, then counsel for the respondent, then counsel for the prisoner in reply.[104] Failure to produce the prisoner make a return or a sufficient return is punishable by committal for contempt of court. The court or judge will order discharge of the prisoner if the reasons given for detention in the return are insufficient in law to justify the detention. In practice, this stage is never reached as the application is dismissed or an order for discharge is made at the hearing of the application.

Costs

13–033   The court has a discretion to award costs against either the applicant or the respondent on a habeas corpus application.[105] The discretion exists in relation to applications in criminal and non-criminal cases.[106] It is not in every case that costs will be awarded, and the Divisional Court has suggested that it may be exceptional to award costs in habeas corpus cases.[107]

Appeals

13–034   An appeal against the refusal of an order for release on an application for habeas corpus in a non-criminal cause or matter may be made as of right to the Court of Appeal.[108] An appeal may also be made against the grant of an order for the release but that would need the permission of the court which heard the application or the Court of Appeal.[109] An appeal may be made from the Court of Appeal to the House of Lords in either case, provided the permission of the Court of Appeal or the House of Lords is obtained.

13–035   An appeal against the grant or refusal of an order by the High Court in a criminal case may be made to the House of Lords,[110] provided that leave of the High Court or the House of Lords is obtained.[111] There is no requirement that the High Court must first grant a certificate that the case raises a point of law of

---

[103]   CPR Sch.1; Ord.54 r.8.

[104]   CPR Sch.1; Ord.54 r.8.

[105]   Supreme Court Act 1981 s.51. Costs were awarded against the respondent in *R. v Jones* [1894] 2 Q.B. 382 and *Union of India v Narang* [1978] A.C. 247 and against the respondent in *R. v Chief Metropolitan Stipendiary Magistrate Ex p. Osman* [1988] 3 All E.R. 173 and *Government of Denmark v Nielsen* [1984] A.C. 606 and *Tan Le Lam v Superintendent of the Tai A Chau Detention Centre* [1996] 2 W.L.R. 863.

[106]   *R. v Chief Metropolitan Stipendiary Magistrate Ex p. Osman* [1988] 3 All E.R. 173.

[107]   [1988] 3 All E.R. 173 at 175.

[108]   Administration of Justice Act 1960 s.15(1) and CPR r.52.3(1)(a)(ii). The Court of Appeal confirmed that the respondent can appeal against the issue of a writ in *Muboyayi v Chief Immigration Officer Gatwick Airport*, May 24, 1991, unreported.

[109]   See Administration of Justice Act 1960 s.15 and CPR r.52.3.

[110]   In *R. v Secretary of State for the Home Department Ex p. Muboyayi* [1992] Q.B. 244, at [453] the applicant contended that he did not need permission: the matter was left undecided.

[111]   Administration of Justice Act 1960 s.1(2). Formerly, there could be no appeal against an order of a single judge releasing the detained person: see Administration of Justice Act 1960 s.15(2). That section has been repealed by the Access to Justice Act 1999 s.65(1)(b).

general importance.[112] An appeal against an order of release will not affect the right of the person to be released, and if released the person will remain "at large" irrespective of the outcome of the appeal, unless the High Court orders the person to be detained pending the appeal or released on bail only.[113] A criminal cause or matter is one where the proceedings might ultimately lead to the conviction and punishment of a person,[114] or matters that arise in a criminal investigation even though no criminal proceedings have been started at that stage.[115] Cases involving extradition or the return of fugitive offenders, which provide the bulk of habeas corpus cases, are criminal cases.[116] Detention under the mental health legislation is specifically made a criminal cause by statute.[117]

Other writs of habeas corpus

There are two writs available for bringing up a prisoner to give evidence. The writ of habeas corpus *ad testificandum* requires a prisoner to be brought before a court to give evidence.[118] The writ of habeas corpus *ad respondendum* issues to bring up a prisoner for trial or examination. An application must be made on affidavit to a judge in chambers.[119] The proper form of the writ must be used.[120] The reasonable expenses of the prisoner and his escort must be tendered.[121] Another method of bringing up a prisoner is by way of warrant or order of a judge directing that a prisoner who is serving a sentence or committed for trial be brought to court.[122] An application must be made on witness statement or affidavit to a judge in chambers.[123] The Home Secretary also has statutory powers to direct that a person in custody be taken to any place.[124]

13–036

---

[112] Administration of Justice Act 1960 s.15(3). Nor is a certificate required when the court on a habeas corpus application is exercising powers conferred by statute, such as, formerly, the Fugitive Offenders Act 1967 s.8 or the Extradition Act 1989 s.11; see *Zacharia v Republic of Cyprus* [1963] A.C. 634.

[113] Administration of Justice Act 1960 s.15(4) and see *Government of the United States of America v McCaffery* [1984] 1 W.L.R. 867.

[114] *Amand v Home Secretary and Minister of Defence of Royal Netherlands Government* [1943] A.C. 147.

[115] *Carr v Atkins* [1987] Q.B. 963. See also *Day v Grant* [1987] Q.B. 972.

[116] *Ex p. Woodhall* (1888) 20 Q.B.D. 832; *R. v Governor of Her Majesty's Prison, Brixton Ex p. Savakar* [1910] 2 K.B. 1056.

[117] Mental Health Act 1983 ss.35–55 (but orders under s.73(2)(e) or (f) are not criminal matters).

[118] See, e.g. *Re Quigley* [1983] N.I. 245.

[119] CPR Sch.1; Ord.54 r.9(1).

[120] CPR Sch.1; Ord.54 r.10. 1991, Vol.2, App.

[121] Criminal Procedure Act 1853 s.9.

[122] *Becker v Home Office* [1972] 2 Q.B. 407.

[123] CPR Sch.1; Ord.54 r.9(2).

[124] Criminal Justice Act 1961 s.29.

CHAPTER 14

Appeals and Statutory Applications

A. INTRODUCTION

Statute may specifically provide a means by which a decision of an inferior court, tribunal or administrative body may be challenged in the courts. The statutory mechanisms for challenging decisions may be divided into three main categories. First, statute may provide for an appeal by way of case stated, secondly, statute may provide a right of appeal from a minister, government department, tribunal or other public body and thirdly, statute may provide for an application to be made to quash a decision of a public body. These statutory rights of challenge exist quite separately from the general inherent common law supervisory jurisdiction of the courts over all public law bodies, which the courts exercise by way of judicial review. The general rules governing statutory appeals and appeals by way of case stated are now contained in CPR Part 52 and the various Practice Directions relating to that Part. In addition, any further appeals from the High Court to the Court of Appeal are second appeals which require permission from the Court of Appeal which may only be granted where there is some important point of principle or practice or some other compelling reason for the Court of Appeal to hear the appeal.[1]

There has been a radical transformation of the system of tribunals and appeals. The Tribunals, Courts and Enforcement Act 2007 sets out provisions intended to enable the creation of a unified tribunal system. The Act creates a First-tier Tribunal and an Upper Tribunal.[2] The functions of most pre-existing tribunals have been transferred to those tribunals.[3] Appeals lie from the First-tier Tribunal to the Upper Tribunal with further appeals if permission is granted to the Court of Appeal.[4] Appeals to the Upper Tribunal have replaced appeals to the Administrative Court in these areas. Appeals to the First-tier Tribunal and Upper Tribunal are outside the scope of this work. Judicial review of and by the tribunals is dealt with in Chapter 10. This chapter deals with appeals by way of case stated, those appeals that lie direct to the High Court and statutory applications to quash.

14–001

14–002

---

[1] Access to Justice Act 1999 s.55 and CPR r.52.13 and see *Clark v Perks* [2001] 1 W.L.R. 17.
[2] Tribunals, Courts and Enforcement Act 2007 s.3. See Chapter 10.
[3] Tribunals, Courts and Enforcement Act 2007 s.30 and Sch.6.
[4] Tribunals, Courts and Enforcement Act 2007 ss.11 and 13.

B.   APPEAL BY WAY OF CASE STATED

General

14–003 Statute may provide for a right of appeal by way of case stated against a decision of courts, tribunals or other public bodies. Specific provisions exist in relation to decisions of magistrates' courts[5] and of the Crown Court, other than those relating to trial on indictment.[6] Statute also provides a right of appeal by case stated against decisions of certain tribunals. Section 11 of the Tribunals and Inquiries Act 1992 provides a right, in accordance with the procedure prescribed by the relevant rules of court, to appeal from a range of specified tribunals to the High Court on a point of law or to require the tribunal to state and sign a case.

14–004 Appeals are generally expressed to be on a point of law, although statute may provide that an appeal lies where a decision is wrong in law or constitutes an excess of jurisdiction. In practice, either formulation is wide enough to cover misconstruction of the relevant statutory provisions, and also other reviewable errors similar in scope to those that might be corrected on an application of judicial review.[7] Appeals on a point of law may therefore be based on the ground that there is no evidence to support the decision,[8] or that no reasonable decision-maker could have come to the decision.[9] Other public law principles, such as a claim that natural justice was not observed in the course of the initial hearing, may be raised as a ground of appeal.[10] The decision-maker remains responsible for findings of fact, and such findings may not be questioned where the appeal lies on a point of law.

C.   APPEALS BY CASE STATED FROM THE CROWN COURT

Jurisdiction to state a case

14–005 Section 28 of the Senior Courts Act 1981 provides that any party to proceedings may challenge any order, judgment or other decision of the Crown Court (other than a decision relating to trial on indictment or certain stipulated decisions[11]), on the ground that the decision is wrong in law or is in excess of jurisdiction, by applying to the Crown Court for that court to state a case for the opinion of the High Court.

---

[5] Magistrates' Court Act 1980 s.111 and see below.

[6] Senior Courts Act 1981 s.28 and see paras 2–123 to 2–128

[7] For circumstances when judicial review rather than an appeal by case stated will be appropriate, see paras 12–042 to 12–074.

[8] *Bracegirdle v Oxley* [1947] K.B. 349; *Lodge v DPP* [1989] C.O.D. 179.

[9] [1947] K.B. 349.

[10] *R. v Brentford Commissioner Ex p. Chan* [1985] 57 S.T.C. 651; *Banin v Mackinlay (Inspector of Taxes)* [1985] 1 All E.R. 842. In *R. v Hereford Magistrates' Court Ex p. Rowlands* [1997] 3 W.L.R. 854, the Divisional Court accepted that complaints of procedural fairness could be, but did not need to be, brought by way of an appeal by case stated.

[11] Decisions under the Betting Gaming and Lotteries Act 1963, the Licensing Act 1964, the Gaming Act 1968 or the Local Government (Miscellaneous Provisions) Act 1982.

The main source of appeals in criminal cases stems from the appellate **14–006** jurisdiction of the Crown Court over decisions in the magistrates' court. A decision by the Crown Court to allow or dismiss an appeal by the prosecutor or defendant against a decision of a magistrates' court may be further appealed to the High Court by way of case stated. There are other decisions of the Crown Court which may be appealed against, such as a decision to refuse bail pending sentencing by the magistrates' court.[12] Decisions relating to trial on indictment are not subject to appeal by way of case stated to the High Court.[13] The scope of this exception has been considered previously.[14]

Rights of appeal to the Crown Court also exist in non-criminal or civil matters. **14–007** Statutory rights of appeal to the Crown Court have been conferred in a haphazard manner. Statute may provide a right of appeal from a decision of a licensing authority or other public body to a magistrates' court. There may be a further right of appeal to the Crown Court. Certain decisions of the Crown Court are made final by statute and there can be no further appeal by case stated to the High Court.[15] Other decisions of the Crown Court will be subject to appeal to the High Court by case stated by virtue of s.28 of the Senior Courts Act 1981. Thus a decision of a local authority to revoke a taxi driver's licence[16] may be appealed first to a magistrates' court, then by any person aggrieved[17] to the Crown Court, then to the High Court. Statute may provide directly for an appeal from a public body to the Crown Court, as is the case with appeal from a decision of a chief constable refusing,[18] or revoking[19] a firearms certificate. There is no universal pattern by which matters come before the Crown Court, or which may be appealed to the High Court: it is simply a question of considering the statutory framework in the relevant area.

Interlocutory decisions by the Crown Court

In criminal matters, "decision" in s.28(1) of the Senior Courts Act 1981 means a **14–008** final decision. The Crown Court may only state a case in a criminal matter after it has reached a final determination in the matter before it.[20] There can be no appeal against an interlocutory decision, such as a preliminary ruling on a point of law or a decision to refuse or admit certain evidence.[21] If the Crown Court purports to state a case in such a matter, the High Court has no jurisdiction to hear the

---

[12] *Eastwood and Crockford v DPP* [1989] C.O.D. 167.
[13] There may be a right of appeal to the Court of Appeal (Criminal Division): see Criminal Appeal Act 1968.
[14] See paras 2–123 to 2–127.
[15] Those decisions made under the statutes listed in fn.11 above may not be appealed.
[16] *Cook v Southend BC* [1990] 2 Q.B. 1.
[17] See *Cook v Southend BC* [1990] 2 Q.B. 1 on the meaning of "person aggrieved".
[18] Firearms Act 1968 s.26(4); see, e.g. *Kavanagh v Chief Constable of Devon and Cornwall* [1974] Q.B. 624.
[19] Firearms Act 1968 s.30(3); see, e.g. *Chief Constable of Kent v Spencer-Stewart* [1989] C.O.D. 372.
[20] *Loade v DPP* [1990] Q.B. 1052; for appeals against decisions of magistrates' courts see *Streames v Copping* [1985] Q.B. 920 discussed below at para.14–019.
[21] [1990] Q.B. 1052.

appeal.[22] A claim for judicial review of the interlocutory decision may be made, but the court has a discretion to dismiss such a claim on the grounds that it is premature.[23]

14–009   The position in relation to non-criminal matters is different. Here, the High Court does have jurisdiction to hear an appeal by way of case stated against an interlocutory decision of the Crown Court, such as a decision as to the admissibility of certain evidence.[24] The jurisdiction should be exercised sparingly and in exceptional circumstances.[25]

Procedure for stating a case

14–010   An application to the Crown Court to state a case must be made in writing to the appropriate officer (usually the chief clerk) of the Crown Court within 21 days of the decision being appealed.[26] Any party to the proceedings in the Crown Court may appeal.[27] Thus, in criminal cases, either the defendant or the prosecution may appeal against an unfavourable decision of the Crown Court. The application must state the ground on which the application is based.[28] The applicant must send a copy of the application to the other parties to the proceedings.[29] On receipt of the application, the appropriate officer must send it to the judge who presided over the proceedings. The judge must inform the appropriate officer if he decides to state a case, and the officer must notify the applicant in writing.[30] The judge may refuse to state a case if he considers that the application is frivolous.[31] Frivolous in this context means that the application is futile, misconceived, hopeless or academic.[32] The applicant may obtain a certificate from the judge stating the reasons for refusal,[33] and may apply for a mandatory order to require the judge to state a case.[34]

14–011   The following procedure applies if the judge decides to state a case (or is ordered to do so). The applicant must, within 21 days of being informed of the

---

[22] The court can give directions enabling the matter to proceed by way of judicial review: see *Gillan v D.P.P.* [2007] 1 W.L.R. 2214.

[23] See paras 12–013 to 12–018.

[24] *Kavanagh v Chief Constable of Devon and Cornwall* (see above, fn.23).

[25] *Loade v DPP* (see above, fn.25); see *R. v Chesterfield Justices Ex p. Kovacs* [1990] C.O.D. 367 discussed below at para.14–019 for the position in relation to appeals against interlocutory decisions of magistrates' courts.

[26] Crown Court Rules 1982 (SI 1982/1109) r.26(1).

[27] Senior Courts Act 1981 s.28.

[28] Crown Court Rules 1982 r.26(2).

[29] Crown Court Rules 1982 r.26(3).

[30] Crown Court Rules 1982 r.26(5).

[31] Crown Court Rules 1982 r.26(6).

[32] *R. v North West Suffolk (Mildenhall) Magistrates' Court Ex p. Forest Heath DC* [1997] C.O.D. 352 (dealing with identical provision in relation to magistrates' court).

[33] Crown Court Rules 1982 r.26(6). (The Divisional Court in *R. v Carlisle Crown Court Ex p. Jackson, Watson and McDonagh* [1991] C.O.D. 273 doubted whether the judge had to give his underlying reasons for a refusal and indicated that a statement that an application was frivolous might be sufficient.)

[34] The court may deal with the substantive matter by way of the judicial review application rather than requiring the Crown Court to state a case: see *Sunworld Ltd v Hammersmith and Fulham LBC* [2000] 1 W.L.R. 2102. See also, in the context of a magistrates' court, *R. (Griffin) v Richmond Magistrates' Court* [2008] 1 W.L.R. 1525 at [36].

judge's decision to state a case (or of the granting of the order of mandamus[35]), draft a case and send a copy to the appropriate Crown Court officer and the other parties to the proceedings.[36] Each party must, within 21 days of receiving the draft case, state that they do not intend to take part in the appeal, or indicate in writing (on the draft) that they agree with the case and return it to the appropriate officer, or draft an alternative case and send that and the applicant's draft to the appropriate officer.[37] The judge then considers the draft and any alternatives. The judge will then state and sign a case within 14 days of the receipt of all the documents, or of the expiry of the 21-day period within which the documents should be returned.[38] All these time-limits may be extended by the Crown Court.[39] The case stated must state the facts found by the Crown Court, the submissions of the parties, any authorities relied upon, the decision in respect of which the application is made, and the question on which the opinion of the High Court is sought.[40] In an unreported *Practice Direction* on December 4, 1978, Lord Widgery C.J. stated that appeals by case stated from the Crown Court should adopt the same form and content as appeals from magistrates' courts.[41] Ideally, after the introductory paragraphs, the case should set out the facts found by the court, then the submissions of each side arising from those facts, followed by the court's opinion on those submissions and the basis upon which it reached its conclusions. Then the case should set out the questions of law upon which the opinion of the High Court is sought. If, but only if, the question arises as to whether the court could reach any of the conclusions which it did on the evidence before it should the case include a summary or statement of the evidence.[42] The Crown Court may require a recognisance from the applicant before the case is stated, having regard to his means, to ensure that the appeal is prosecuted without delay.[43]

Lodging the appeal

The case is sent to the appellant (the person who applied to have a case stated). **14–012** The appellant must lodge an appellant's notice[44] together with the case and a copy of the judgment, order or decision of the Crown Court (and of the decision of the inferior court or body, if the matter came to the Crown Court on appeal) in the Administrative Court Office within 10 days of the receipt of the case.[45] Applications to extend time may be made.[46] The appellant's notice and accompanying documents must be served on all respondents within four days.[47]

---

[35] Crown Court Rules 1982 r.26(15).
[36] Crown Court Rules 1982 r.26(8).
[37] Crown Court Rules 1982 r.26(9).
[38] Crown Court Rules 1982 r.26(12) for the appropriate procedure, see *DPP v Coleman* [1998] All E.R. 912.
[39] Crown Court Rules 1982 r.26(14).
[40] Crown Court Rules 1982 r.26(13).
[41] See at para.14–026.
[42] *DPP v Sutton* [1996] C.O.D. 11.
[43] Crown Court Rules 1982 r.26(11).
[44] In form N161.
[45] See paras 2.2 and 2.3 of Practice Direction 52E – Appeals by way of Case Stated.
[46] Under CPR r.3.1(2)(a).
[47] Para.2.4 of Practice 52E – Direction Appeals by way of Case Stated.

Listing of cases

14–013   Appeals fall within the ambit of the Administrative Court List. The procedure for listing cases is discussed in Chapter 9.[48]

Procedure on appeal

14–014   Appeals in a criminal cause or matter[49] may be heard by a single judge or may be heard by a Divisional Court comprising a Lord Justice of Appeal and a High Court judge or, in exceptional circumstances, two High Court judges.[50] Appeals in other cases are heard by a single judge sitting in court, unless a court directs that it be heard by a Divisional Court. Bail may be granted by the Crown Court pending the hearing of the appeal.[51] The powers of the High Court on appeal are generally considered to be similar to those on appeal from the magistrates' court.[52] Section 28A of the Senior Courts Act 1981[53] provides specific powers for the High Court to remit the case back to the Crown Court for amendment. The High Court is also given specific power to reverse, affirm or amend the determination of the Crown Court or to remit the matter back.[54] Costs may be awarded in civil cases and the unsuccessful party is usually ordered to pay the costs of the successful party.[55] In criminal cases, the Divisional Court may order the costs of the accused to be paid out of central funds.[56]

Appeals

14–015   A decision of the High Court on an appeal by way of case stated from the Crown Court in a civil case is final.[57] There can be no further appeal in a civil case to the Court of Appeal.[58]

---

[48]   See para. 9–102.

[49]   See paras 9–056 to 9–059 above for the definition of "criminal cause or matter".

[50]   As occurred in *Barnfather v Islington Education Authority* [2003] 1 W.L.R. 2318 at [33]. The former requirement that appeals in a criminal cause or matter be heard by a Divisional Court has been repealed.

[51]   Senior Courts Act 1981 s.81.

[52]   Identical powers have existed for some time in relation to appeals by way of case stated from the magistrates' court: see below at paras 13–030 to 13–031.

[53]   As amended by the Access to Justice Act 1999 s.61. Earlier legislation dealing with the powers of the High Court dealing with an appeal by case stated had been repealed but without any re-enactment of the section conferring powers on the High Court. This appears to have occurred by oversight: see the Law Commission Report "Administrative Law: Judicial Review and Statutory Appeal" Law Com. No.226 at para.12.9, p.105. The Access to Justice Act 1999 remedies the situation.

[54]   Senior Courts Act 1981 s.28A(3) as amended.

[55]   Senior Courts Act 1981 s.51 and CPR Pt 44. These provisions deal with the costs of the appeal to the High Court. Where there is an initial appeal from an administrative authority to the Crown Court, there is no general rule that the Crown Court will order the unsuccessful party to pay the costs of the appeal to the Crown Court: see *R. v Crown Court at Stafford Ex p. Wilf Gilbert (Staffs) Ltd* [1999] 2 All E.R. 955.

[56]   Prosecution of Offences Act 1985 s.16(5). No interest on costs is payable: see *Westminster City Council v Wingrove* [1991] C.O.D. 85.

[57]   Senior Courts Act 1981 s.28A.

[58]   See *Westminster City Council v O'Reilly* [2004] 1 W.L.R. 195 (dealing with the effect of Senior Courts Act 1981 s.28A in the context of appeals by way of case stated from magistrates' courts).

There can be no appeal from the High Court to the Court of Appeal in a criminal cause or matter.[59] An appeal from the High Court to the Supreme Court may be made, provided that the High Court certifies that the case raises a point of law of general importance, and either the High Court or the Supreme Court grants permission to appeal.[60]

14–016

D. APPEALS BY CASE STATED FROM A MAGISTRATES' COURT

Jurisdiction to state a case

Section 111 of the Magistrates' Court Act 1980 provides that any person who is a party to proceedings before a magistrates' court or is aggrieved by a conviction, order, determination or other proceeding, may question that proceeding on the ground that it is wrong in law or in excess of jurisdiction, by applying to the justices to state a case for the opinion of the High Court.[61]

14–017

This provision confers jurisdiction to state a case in a wide range of criminal and civil cases. Appeals by case stated may be made against decisions of magistrates exercising their summary jurisdiction to try criminal offences. A defendant may appeal against a conviction or a prosecutor may appeal against an acquittal or the dismissal of the case on the grounds that there is no case to answer, or a decision that the magistrates' court lacks jurisdiction to hear the case.[62] In civil cases, magistrates' courts have statutory powers to make orders in a wide range of matters. They act as licensing justices under the Licensing Act 1964 and their decisions may either be appealed to the Crown Court (whose decision is final and unappealable[63]), or by case stated to the High Court.[64] Magistrates' courts also have statutory jurisdiction to make orders in a wide variety of other matters, such as orders stopping up a highway,[65] or issuing notices about levels of pollution.[66] Magistrates' courts may also have jurisdiction to hear appeals from decisions of local authorities and other public bodies. They hear appeals in such disparate matters as decisions of licensing authorities,[67] or

14–018

---

[59] Senior Courts Act 1981 s.18(1)(a).

[60] Administration of Justice Act 1960 s.1(1).

[61] But no case may be stated if there is a right of appeal to the High Court against the decision or if the decision is final by virtue of any enactment passed after December 31, 1879: see Magistrates' Court Act 1980 s.111(1).

[62] *R. v Clerkenwell Metropolitan Stipendiary Magistrate Ex p. DPP* [1984] Q.B. 821.

[63] See fn.11 above.

[64] *Jeffrey v Evans* [1964] 1 W.L.R. 505 and see *R. v East Riding of Yorkshire Quarter Sessions Ex p. Newton* [1968] 1 Q.B. 32.

[65] Highways Act 1980 s.116 and see, e.g. *Ramblers Association v Kent CC* [1990] C.O.D. 327.

[66] Control of Pollution Act 1974 and see, e.g. *Johnson News of London (a company) v. Ealing LBC* [1990] C.O.D. 135.

[67] Local Government (Miscellaneous Provisions) Act 1982. Such appeals are by way of a rehearing and the justices may have regard to all the material available at the time when they hear the appeal: *Rushmoor BC v Richards* [1996] C.O.D. 313.

against decisions imposing conditions on the use of caravan sites.[68] The determination of such appeals may themselves be appealed by way of case stated to the High Court.[69]

Interlocutory decisions of magistrates' courts

14–019 Magistrates' courts have no power to state a case in a criminal matter until they have reached a final determination on the matter before them. They cannot state a case on an interlocutory decision made in the course of proceedings such as a decision as to whether they have jurisdiction, a ruling on a preliminary point of law, or a decision on the admissibility of evidence.[70] If a magistrates' court does purport to state a case on an interlocutory matter, the High Court has no jurisdiction to hear the appeal. An application for judicial review of an interlocutory decision may be made, but the court has a discretion to dismiss such an application on the grounds that it is premature.[71]

14–020 It has been held that magistrates sitting as examining justices, deciding to commit for trial, cannot state a case as they do not reach a final determination of the matter.[72] However, it is uncertain whether that ruling is still good law in view of the wording of ss.111 and 148 (which defines a magistrates' court) of the Magistrates' Court Act 1980.[73] Even if an appeal were possible, it would rarely be appropriate given that any issue of law could be dealt with at the trial.[74] A person challenging committal could do so by habeas corpus or judicial review. The public authorities wishing to challenge a refusal to commit could do so by judicial review.[75]

14–021 A magistrates' court does have a discretion to state a case on an interlocutory matter in a non-criminal case, and the High Court has jurisdiction to hear such an appeal.[76] The discretion to state a case should, however, be used sparingly, and only in exceptional circumstances.[77]

---

[68] Caravan Sites and Control of Development Act 1960 s.7.

[69] See, e.g. *Babbage v North Norfolk DC* (1989) 59 P. & C.R. 249.

[70] *Streames v Copping* (see above, fn.25). But see dicta in *R. (Donnachie) v Cardiff Magistrates' Court* [2007] 1 W.L.R. 3085 at [6]. The case involved a claim for judicial review not case stated.

[71] See paras 12–123 to 12–127. The Divisional Court has accepted that a decision to adjourn may be challenged by way of judicial review but such claims should be brought urgently, within a matter of days rather than weeks so as not to affect the continued progress of the criminal proceedings *Balogun v Director of Public Prosecution* [2010] 1 W.L.R. 1915 at [31]–[32].

[72] *Card v Salmon* [1953] 1 Q.B. 392. See also *Wilkinson v Crown Prosecution Service* [1998] C.O.D. 367. See also *Atkinson v United States Government* [1971] A.C. 197 (decision of magistrates to commit for extradition under the Extradition Act 1870 was not subject to appeal by way of case stated). The system of extradition now provides for appeals: see Extradition Act 2003.

[73] It was assumed that magistrates' court do not come to a final decision when committing for trial in *R. (Donnachie) v Cardiff Magistrates' Court* [2007] 1 W.L.R. 3085 at [6].

[74] See the approach adopted in judicial review cases involving committal proceedings in *R. v Oxford City Justices Ex p. Berry* [1988] Q.B. 507. See also *Neill v North Antrim Magistrates' Court* [1992] 1 W.L.R. 1220 and *R. v Bedwellty Justices Ex p. Williams* [1997] 2 A.C. 225 discussed above at para.12–014.

[75] *R. v Chief Metropolitan Stipendary Magistrate Ex p. Secretary of State for the Home Department* [1988] 1 W.L.R. 1204.

[76] *R. v Chesterfield Justices Ex p. Kovacs* [1990] C.O.D. 352.

[77] *R. v Chesterfield Justices Ex p. Kovacs* [1997] C.O.D. 352.

Procedure for stating a case

An application to state a case must be made within 21 days of the decision of the justices.[78] This time-limit is mandatory and cannot be extended by the High Court.[79] The justices may refuse to state a case if they consider that the application is frivolous but, if the applicant so requests, must give a certificate to that effect.[80] An applicant may apply for a mandatory order requiring the justices to state a case.[81]

14–022

The procedure governing the application to state a case is contained in the Magistrates' Court Rules.[82] These rules are directory, not mandatory, and failure to comply does not render the appeal invalid. Providing the application to state a case is made within 21 days of the decision, any failure to comply with the rules may be corrected outside that time-limit.[83]

14–023

Applications must be made in writing to the clerk of the magistrates' court and must identify the question upon which the opinion of the High Court is sought.[84] The clerk must prepare a draft case and send it to the applicant and the respondent within 21 days of the receipt of the application[85] (or of the mandatory order requiring the justices to state a case[86]). If the clerk cannot do this within 21 days, he must do so as soon as practicable and ensure that a statement of the reasons for the delay is included in the draft and the final case.[87] Each party then has 21 days to make representations in writing to the clerk.[88] The clerk may extend the time-limit for making representations, and must record extension of time and the reasons in the final case.[89] The justices must state and sign a case, making any adjustments to the draft that they consider necessary, within 21 days after the expiry of the period for receiving representations.[90] If the justices are unable to do so within 21 days, they must do so as soon as practicable and record the delay and the reasons for it in the final case.[91] A case may be stated by two or more justices, and they may authorise the clerk to sign on their behalf.[92]

14–024

---

[78] Magistrates' Court Act 1980 s.111(2). The time-limit runs from the date of sentence if the justices adjourn after conviction: s.111(3).
[79] *Michael v Gowland* [1977] 1 W.L.R. 296.
[80] Magistrates' Court Act 1980 s.111(5).
[81] Magistrates' Court Act 1980 s.111(6).
[82] SI 1981/552 as amended.
[83] *Robinson v Whittle* [1980] 1 W.L.R. 1476 and see also *R. v Bideford Justices Ex p. South West Water Authority* [1990] C.O.D. 369. *R. v Bromley Magistrates' Court Ex p. Waitrose* [1980] 3 All E.R. 464 and *R. v Croydon Justices Ex p. Lefore Holdings* [1980] 1 W.L.R. 1465 suggest that there must be substantial compliance with the rules. See also *The Vehicle Inspectorate v T.D. and C. Kelly Ltd* [1997] C.O.D. 225.
[84] Magistrates' Court Rules 1981 (SI 1981/552) r.76(1) and (3).
[85] Magistrates' Court Rules 1981 r.77(1). The applicant should seeks to ensure that the case contains the facts necessary to make good the grounds of appeal: see *Revitt v D.P.P.* [2006] 1 W.L.R. 3172 at [20].
[86] Magistrates' Court Rules 1981 r.77(3).
[87] Magistrates' Court Rules 1981 r.79(1).
[88] Magistrates' Court Rules 1981 r.77(2).
[89] Magistrates' Court Rules 1981 r.79(2).
[90] Magistrates' Court Rules 1981 r.78(1).
[91] Magistrates' Court Rules 1981 r.79(3).
[92] Magistrates' Court Rules 1981 r.78(2).

14–025   The justices may decline to state a case if they consider that the application is frivolous.[93] Frivolous in this context means futile, misconceived, hopeless or academic.[94] It is helpful if the justices indicate the reasons, however briefly, for declining to state a case.[95] An applicant may ask for a certificate that the application has been refused.[96] He may apply to the court for an order of mandamus requiring the justices to state a case.[97] Where permission is granted by the High Court to make such an application, the justices ought to consider carefully whether to state a case. If they decline to do so after permission has been granted, and if there is no reason for maintaining that stance after the grant of permission, they may be ordered to pay the costs of the hearing of the application for a mandatory order.[98] The justices may also decline to state a case until the applicant has given a recognisance with or without sureties to ensure that the appeal is prosecuted without delay.[99] Where the justices state a case, they may grant bail to the appellant pending the disposition of the appeal if he is custody.[100]

Form of the case

14–026   The case stated should state the facts found by the magistrates' court, a summary of the arguments on the law put by each party, the conclusions of the magistrates and the question of law or jurisdiction on which the opinion of the High Court is sought.[101] The questions raised by the case should be stated as simply as possible and should be directed to the crucial issue on which the case turns and the summary of competing submissions should be reasonably succinct.[102] The case should not contain a statement of the evidence heard in the case, unless one of the questions is whether there was sufficient evidence on which a magistrates' court could reasonably find a particular fact.[103] In that case, the case should identify the particular finding of fact which it is claimed cannot be supported,[104] and should contain a summary of the evidence relevant to that finding of fact.[105] The

---

[93]   Magistrates' Court Act 1980 s.111(5). The justices may not, however, refuse to state a case if the application is made by the Att-Gen.
[94]   *R. v North West Suffolk (Mildenhall) Magistrates' Court Ex p. Forest Heath DC* [1997] C.O.D. 352.
[95]   *Ex p. Forest Heath DC* [1997] C.O.D. 352.
[96]   Magistrates' Court Act 1980 s.111(5).
[97]   Magistrates' Court Act 1980 s.111(6). The court may deal with the substantive matter by way of the judicial review application rather than requiring the magistrates to state a case in order to save costs: see *Sunworld Ltd v Hammersmith and Fulham LBC* [2000] 1 W.L.R. 2102; *R. (Griffin) v Richmond Magistrates' Court* [2008] 1 W.L.R. 1525 at [36].
[98]   *R. v Huntingdon Magistrates' Court Ex p. Percy* [1994] C.O.D. 323; *R. v Aldershot Justices Ex p. Rushmoor BC* [1996] C.O.D. 21 (and see the sequel in *R. v Aldershot Justices Ex p. Rushmoor BC (No.2)* [1996] C.O.D. 280).
[99]   Magistrates' Court Act 1980 s.114 and see *R. v Croydon Magistrates' Court Ex p. Morgan* [1997] C.O.D. 177 and *R. v Warrington Magistrates' Court Ex p. Worsley* [1996] C.O.D. 347.
[100]   Magistrates' Court Act 1980 s.113(1). For difficulties where magistrates refuse bail in a civil case, *Benham v Poole BC, The Times,* October 10, 1991.
[101]   Magistrates' Court Rules 1980 r.81(1). See also *Crompton and Crompton v North Tyneside MBC* [1991] C.O.D. 52 and *DPP v Kirk* [1993] C.O.D. 99.
[102]   *Nottingham City Council v Amin* [2000] 1 W.L.R. 1071 at 1081C–D.
[103]   Magistrates' Court Rules 1981 r.81(3).
[104]   Magistrates' Court Rules 1981 r.81(2).
[105]   *Horner v Sherwoods of Darlington Ltd* [1989] C.O.D. 542 and see *A.G. Stanley Ltd v Surrey CC Trading Standards Officer* [1995] C.O.D. 308.

Divisional Court has encouraged magistrates' courts to state their findings in one, preferably an early, paragraph of the case.[106] They should not let the case become burdened by over-elaborate discussion of the law, even when repeatedly pressed to do so by one of the parties.[107] They should state their reasons for dismissing a submission of no case to answer succinctly.[108]

Lodging the appeal

Once the case has been stated and signed, it is sent to the appellant,[109] (that is the person who made the application to have a case stated). The appellant must lodge an appellant's notice[110] within ten days of receipt of the stated case together with the case stated, a copy of the judgment, order or decision of the magistrates' court (and, if the matter was dealt with on appeal, a copy of the judgment, order or decision appealed from).[111] The appellant's notice and accompanying documents must be served on all respondents within four days.[112] Applications to extend time may be made.[113]

14–027

Listing of cases

Appeals fall within the ambit of the Administrative Court Office List. The procedure for listing cases is discussed in Chapter 9.

14–028

Procedure on appeal

The appeal may be heard by a single judge in a criminal cause or matter, but may be heard by a Divisional Court. The appeal in a civil case is usually assigned to a single judge but the court may direct that it be heard by a Divisional Court.

14–029

Amendment

The court hearing the appeal may send the case to be sent back to the magistrates' court for amendment.[114] The court should only remit if it is satisfied that the justices did, or must have, found facts which they omitted from the stated case.[115] The justices may oppose an application for amendment. They may be represented by counsel, or they may provide statements in the form of an affidavit or witness statement explaining why a case is settled in a particular form.[116]

14–030

---

[106] *Riley v DPP* [1990] C.O.D. 152.
[107] [1990] C.O.D. 152.
[108] [1990] C.O.D. 152.
[109] Magistrates' Court Rules 1981 (SI 1981/552) r.78(3).
[110] In form N161.
[111] Paras 2.2 and 2.3 of Practice Direction 52E – Appeals by way of Case Stated.
[112] Para.2.4 of Practice Direction 52E – Appeals by way of Case Stated.
[113] Under CPR r.3.1(2)(a).
[114] Senior Courts Act 1981 s.28A(2). On the proper approach to an application to remit for amendment, see *Consolidated Goldfields Plc v Inland Revenue Commissioners* [1990] 2 All E.R. 398 (dealing with a materially similar power in s.56(7) of the Taxes Management Act 1970).
[115] *Practice Note* [1953] 1 W.L.R. 334. See *DPP v Clarke* [1991] C.O.D. 235.
[116] *Horner v Sherwoods of Darlington Ltd* [1989] C.O.D. 542.

Powers of the court

14–031   The High Court may reverse, affirm or amend the determination in respect of which the case was stated, or may remit the matter to the justices with the opinion of the High Court, or may make such other order as it considers fit.[117] In criminal cases, for example, the court may set aside a conviction or an acquittal, and remit the matter to the justices, with a direction to acquit or convict as the case may be.[118] If the justices have accepted a submission of no case to answer, the court may allow the appeal and remit the matter to the justices, with a direction to continue and complete the hearing in the normal way.[119] The power to "make such other order" includes the power to order a re-hearing.[120] The Court cannot, however, vary a sentence.[121]

14–032   The court is not obliged to remit a matter, and may exceptionally refuse to do so in its discretion. Where the appeal court has allowed an appeal against the acceptance of a submission of no case to answer or an acquittal, the court may refuse to remit the matter if there has been delay which might prejudice the defendant.[122] If the primary purpose of the appeal was to clarify a point of law for future prosecutions, the court may not remit the matter.[123]

Costs

14–033   The court has jurisdiction to award costs in an appeal by case stated.[124] Costs are at the discretion of the court. In civil cases, the costs will usually follow the event and the unsuccessful party will pay the costs of the successful party.[125] In criminal cases, the High Court or the House of Lords on appeal[126] may order the costs of the accused to be paid out of central funds.[127]

---

[117]   Senior Courts Act 1981 s.28A(3).
[118]   See, e.g. *K. v DPP* [1990] 1 All E.R. 331.
[119]   See, e.g. *DPP v Quinn* [1989] C.O.D. 303.
[120]   *Griffiths v Jenkins* [1992] A.C. 76 dealing with the Summary Jurisdiction At 1857 s.6 but the material words are identical to the Supreme Court Act 1981 s.28A.
[121]   But the court may substitute the only available penalty: *Coote v Winfield* [1980] R.T.R. 42.
[122]   *R. v Clerkenwell Metropolitan Stipendiary Magistrates Ex p. DPP* [1984] 1 Q.B. 821; *Pascoe v Nicholson* [1981] 1 W.L.R. 1061.
[123]   *DPP v Hynde* [1998] 1 All E.R. 649 at 656d–f; *Forestry Commission v Frost* [1990] C.O.D. 1; *Pascoe v Nicholson* (see above, fn.23).
[124]   Senior Courts Act 1981 s.28A(3).
[125]   Senior Courts Act 1981 s.51; CPR Part 44.
[126]   See, e.g. Griffiths v Jenkins [1992] A.C. 76.
[127]   Prosecution of Offences Act 1985 s.16(5). Interest on such costs cannot be awarded: *Westminster City Council v Wingrove* [1991] C.O.D. 85.

Appeal

There can be no appeal from the High Court to the Court of Appeal in a criminal cause or matter.[128] There may be an appeal to the Supreme Court, provided that the High Court certifies that the case raises a point of law of general public importance, and either the High Court or the Supreme Court grants leave to appeal.[129]

14–034

In civil cases, s.28A(4) of the Senior Courts Act 1981 provides that all orders of the High Court are to be final. Section 18(1)(c) of the Senior Courts Act 1981 provides that there is to be no appeal to the Court of Appeal from any order of the High Court which is expressed by statute to be final. The Court of Appeal therefore does not have jurisdiction to entertain any appeal from a decision on an appeal by case stated from the magistrates' court.[130]

14–035

Relationship between appeal by case stated and other remedies

An individual may have a statutory right of appeal from the magistrates' court to the Crown Court, as well as a right to appeal to the High Court by case stated. Appeals to the Crown Court are by way of re-hearing. Section 111(4) of the Magistrates' Court Act 1980 provides that if a person applies[131] to have a case stated, he loses any right of appeal to the Crown Court.

14–036

In criminal cases, if the individual appealed to the Crown Court, he would also have a further right to appeal to the High Court by case stated from the decision of the Crown Court.[132] If the individual wishes to appeal both against the findings of fact and determinations of law by the magistrates' court, he must appeal to the Crown Court first as only the Crown Court can investigate the findings of fact. If the Crown Court upholds the determination of law, that determination can be challenged by way of case stated.

14–037

In certain civil cases, notably those to do with licensing,[133] the decision of the Crown Court is final and cannot be appealed by way of case stated. Thus, the individual seeking to challenge a decision of the magistrates' court may either go to the Crown Court on appeal or to the High Court by way of case stated. If he chooses to appeal to the Crown Court he cannot make a further appeal to the High Court, but judicial review remains available to correct errors of law by the Crown Court.[134] The better course for an individual who wishes to challenge both the findings of fact and law is to appeal to the Crown Court. Thereafter, if the Crown Court upholds the determination of law, that determination may be challenged by judicial review. In other civil cases, the individual may appeal to the Crown Court and then appeal from that determination to the High Court or go straight to the

14–038

---

[128] Senior Courts Act 1981 s.18(1)(a).

[129] Administration of Justice Act 1960 s.1. See, e.g. *D.P.P. v Collins* [2006] 1 W.L.R. 2223.

[130] *Westminster City Council v O'Reilly* [2004] 1 W.L.R. 195; *Maile v Manchester City Council* [1998] C.O.D. 19.

[131] The application must be a valid one, i.e. one that is made within 21 days: *P. & M. Supplies (Essex) Ltd v Hackney LBC* [1990] Crim.L.R. 569.

[132] See above paras 14–005 to 14–007.

[133] Decisions under the Betting Gaming and Lotteries Act 1963, the Licensing Act 1964, the Gaming Act 1968 or the Local Government (Miscellaneous Provisions) Act 1982.

[134] See para.12–049.

High Court. If he wishes to challenge findings of fact, he is well advised to appeal to the Crown Court first rather than appeal to the High Court.

14–039   Judicial review is also available to correct errors of law by magistrates' courts. The circumstances in which it will be appropriate to seek judicial review, rather than appeal by case stated, have been considered in Chapter 12.

E.   APPEALS BY CASE STATED BY OTHER PUBLIC BODIES TO THE HIGH COURT

Jurisdiction to hear appeals by case stated

14–040   Statute may provide a right of appeal by way of case stated from a specific decision of minister, or tribunal, or other public body to the High Court (although, increasingly, provision is being made for transferring existing rights of an appeal to either the First-tier Tribunal or the Upper Tribunal and new statutes tend to provide for rights of appeal within the tribunal structure rather than by way of case stated to the High Court). The statute conferring the right of appeal against specific public bodies may set out provisions governing the exercise of the right. A general code of procedure for appeals is set out in Practice Direction 52E – Appeals by Way of Case Stated. That procedure has to be read subject to the specific statutory enactment conferring the right of appeal. The precise scope of the right of appeal, and the range of people entitled to appeal, will depend on the terms of the particular statute conferring the right.

Application

14–041   Statute may provide for a public body to state a case at the request of one of the parties, or may enable a party to proceedings to apply to the High Court for an order directing the public body to state a case. If the public body declines to state a case, an application may be made to the court asking for an order requiring the public body to state a case.[135] The notice must contain the grounds of the application, the question of law on which it is sought to have the case stated and any reasons given for the refusal to state a case.[136] The application must be served on the minister, department or secretary of the tribunal concerned and every other party to the proceedings within 14 days of receipt of the notice of refusal to state a case.[137] The application for an order to state a case will be determined by a single judge. Statute may also provide for a public body to state a case of its own motion.

---

[135]   Para.3.11 of Practice Direction 52E – Appeals by Way of Case Stated. The application must be made in accordance with CPR Part 23.
[136]   Para.3.13 of Practice Direction 52E – Appeals by Way of Case Stated.
[137]   Para.3.14 of Practice Direction 52E – Appeals by Way of Case Stated.

Interlocutory decisions

The availability of appeals against a preliminary or interlocutory decision of a tribunal depends in part on the statute itself. If an appeal lies against a decision, this is likely to be construed as a final decision only.[138] Some statutes contemplate stating a case during proceedings and so would appear to allow appeals on interlocutory orders.[139]

14–042

Procedure for stating a case

A case stated by a tribunal must be signed by the chairman or president of the tribunal.[140] A case stated by any other person must be signed by that person, or by a person authorised to sign on his behalf.[141] The case must be served on the person who requested it, or who applied to the court for an order to have a case stated.[142] If the public body has stated a case of its own motion, the case must be served on those parties to the proceedings that the public body considers appropriate.[143]

14–043

The case should ideally set out the findings of fact, the determination in respect of which the case is stated, the question of law to be determined and the submissions on the law of the parties. The evidence should not be included unless the applicant contends that there is no evidence on which a finding of fact could have been, or that no decision-maker could reasonably have made a finding of fact on the evidence adduced.

14–044

Proceedings for determination of a case

The person served with the stated case must file an appellant's notice and the stated case in the appeal court and serve copies of the appellant's notice and stated case on the minister or tribunal who stated the case and every party to the proceedings to which the stated case relates within four days after the case was served.[144] If the person served with the case does not do so within four days, any other party may file an appellant's notice and serve the notice and case stated within a further 14 days.[145] The minister has a specific right to appear and be heard in proceedings where he has stated a case.[146] Appeals fall within the ambit of the Administrative Court List. The procedure for listing case is discussed in Chapter 9.[147] The appeal by case stated will be heard and determined by a single judge.

14–045

---

[138] See for an analogous provision, *Loade v DPP* [1990] 1 Q.B. 1052.

[139] See, e.g. Tribunals and Inquiries Act 1992 s.11(3) which authorises rules allowing appeal in the form of a special case stated in the course of proceedings.

[140] Para.3.2 of Practice Direction 52E – Appeals by Way of Case Stated.

[141] Para.3.2. of Practice Direction 52E – Appeals by Way of Case Stated.

[142] Para.3.3 of Practice Direction 52E – Appeals by Way of Case Stated.

[143] Para.3.4 of Practice Direction 52E – Appeals by Way of Case Stated

[144] Para.3.5 of Practice Direction 52E – Appeals by Way of Case Stated.

[145] Paras 3.7 and 3.8 of Practice Direction 52E – Appeals by Way of Case Stated.

[146] Para.3.10 of Practice Direction 52E – Appeals by Way of Case Stated.

[147] See para.9–109.

Amendment

14–046   The court hearing the case stated may amend the case or order that it be returned to the person who stated it for amendment.[148]

F.   APPEAL BY CASE STATED TO THE COURT OF APPEAL

14–047   A statutory right of appeal by way of case stated to the Court of Appeal lies from a small number of tribunals such as the Foreign Compensation Commission.[149] The procedure governing applications for a case to be stated will normally be governed by the statute creating the right of appeal and, subject to any specific statutory provision, the procedure laid down in the relevant Practice Direction 52E – Appeals by Way of Cases Stated described above apply and regulate the stating of the case, lodging and serving the appellant's notice and provision for amendment.[150]

G.   APPEAL TO THE HIGH COURT

Jurisdiction to hear appeals

14–048   Statute may provide a right of appeal for a particular person from the decision of a public body, such as a tribunal or minister, to the High Court. A general code of procedure governing such appeals is laid down in CPR Part 52 and the various Practice Directions on Appeals. This code has to be read subject to the statute conferring the right of appeal, and to any other relevant provision of Civil Procedure Rules. CPR Part 52 deals with a wide range of appeals. Appeals may be limited to points of law or may be unlimited as to the grounds. In any event, an appeal is limited to a review of the decision below unless a practice direction makes different provision or the interests of justice call for a re-hearing.[151]

14–049   Appeals from tribunals and ministers are usually confined to points of law. Section 11 of the Tribunals and Inquiries Act 1992, for example, confers a right of appeal to the High Court on a person dissatisfied on point of law with a decision of certain specified tribunals. In the planning field, there is an appeal on a point of law from certain decisions of the Secretary of State[152] and from decisions of the Pensions Ombudsman.[153]

14–050   Statute will prescribe which persons entitled to appeal. Any party to proceedings before a tribunal to which s.11(1) of the Tribunals and Inquiries Act 1992 applies has a right of appeal in respect of decisions of that tribunal. A party to the proceedings means a litigant, not a person who might benefit from the

---

[148]   Para.3.9 of Practice Direction 52E – Appeals by Way of Case Stated.
[149]   See the Foreign Compensation Act 1969 s.3.
[150]   Practice Direction 52E – Appeals by way of Case Stated.
[151]   CPR r.52.11.
[152]   See, e.g. Town and Country Planning Act 1990 ss.289 and 290. Orders for costs at an inquiry may also be appealed against: *R. v Secretary of State for the Environment Ex p. Botton, The Times*, March 26, 1991.
[153]   Pensions Schemes Act 1993 s.151.

litigation.[154] In appeals against the decision of the minister in the planning field, the local planning authority, the person who appealed to the minister against the decision of the minister and any other person who has an interest in the land has a right to appeal to the High Court.[155]

A person may not appeal against a decision which was in his favour.[156] Thus, if the party obtains a favourable decision but the decision also includes adverse findings of fact or is based on a number of grounds, one of which is considered unfavourable, those individual elements of the otherwise favourable decision may not be appealed against by the person who has obtained a favourable decision on the case as a whole. On occasions, a statutory provision will be interpreted as providing for an appeal on decisions by a tribunal as to whether it has jurisdiction as well as decisions on the merits. This enables a party who has succeeded on the merits to challenge a decision of the tribunal that it had jurisdiction.[157] Even in these instances, it may well be that the statute does not provide for an appeal against a decision as to whether a tribunal has jurisdiction and that decision may have to be challenged by way of judicial review.[158] **14–051**

The scope for appeals on points of law to the Administrative Court has been reduced as the functions of a number of tribunals have been transferred to the First-tier Tribunal established by the Tribunals, Courts and Enforcement Act 2007.[159] There will be a right of appeal to the Upper Tribunal rather than an appeal to the Administrative Court with a further appeal, with permission, to the Court of Appeal.[160] There remain, however, a number of statutory rights of appeal to the High Court including in the field of planning and appeals against disciplinary decisions of regulatory bodies discussed below. **14–052**

Procedure for appealing

Appeals must be made by filing an appellant's notice using Form N161.[161] The appellant's notice must state the grounds of the appeal and whether the appeal is against the whole of the decision, and if not, must specify the part against which appeal is made. The bringing of the appeal will not operate as a stay of proceedings unless the court which is to hear the appeal orders otherwise,[162] or unless statute provides for the appeal to have suspensive effect. **14–053**

The appellant's notice must be filed within the time prescribed by statute or the CPR or the relevant provisions of Practice 52D – Statutory Appeals. The notice must be served on the respondent and on the decision-maker, for example, **14–054**

---

[154] S. v Special Educational Needs Tribunal [1996] 1 W.L.R. 382. That means a person who was properly a party to proceedings before the initial tribunal, i.e. a person who was entitled to appeal under the terms of the legislation providing the right of appeal: see Fairpo v Humberside CC [1997] 1 All E.R. 183 at 186e–j.
[155] Town and Country Planning Act 1990 s.289.
[156] Young v Secretary of State for the Environment (1990) 60 P. & C.R. 560.
[157] See, e.g. Secretary of State for Work and Pensions v Morina [2007] 1 W.L.R. 3033.
[158] See, e.g. R. (Secretary of State for Defence) v Pension Appeals Tribunal judgment July 15, 2008.
[159] Pursuant to orders made under s.30 of the Courts, Tribunals and Enforcement Act 2007.
[160] Tribunals, Courts and Enforcement Act 2007 ss.11 and 33.
[161] CPR r.52.4 and para.4.1 of the Practice Direction 52B – Appeals in the County Court and High Court.
[162] CPR r.52.7.

the minister or chairman of the tribunal which took the decision.[163] Permission to appeal is not required by the CPR or by the relevant Practice Directions on Appeals[164] but may be required by the particular statutory provision creating the right of appeal.[165]

14–055   The period for filing may be extended unless statute prescribes a period within which the appeal must be filed.[166] The courts are, however, reluctant to extend the time-limits in public law matters.[167] In particular, the usual practice in inter partes civil disputes – that an extension will be granted if it does not prejudice the other party in a way that cannot be compensated in costs – does not apply. There is a public interest in prompt challenges to decisions by public bodies. There will need to be an explanation for the delay.[168] The fact that the appellant's legal advisers or representatives was unaware of the time-limit or unable to comply because of pressure of work will not normally, of itself, justify extending time.[169] Even if there is an acceptable explanation for the delay, the courts might decline to extend time if the delay was substantial or caused prejudice to the respondent.[170]

Amendment

14–056   The notice of appeal may not be amended by the appellant without permission.[171] No grounds of appeal other than those set out in the notice may be argued, unless the court grants permission.[172]

Listing of cases

14–057   Statutory appeals fall within the ambit of the Administrative Court List. The procedure for listing cases is discussed in Chapter 9.[173]

---

[163]   CPR r.52.4 and para.3.4 of Practice Direction 52D – Statutory Appeals and Appeals Subject to Special Provision.

[164]   See *Colley v Council for Licensed Conveyancers* [2002] 1 W.L.R. 160.

[165]   See, e.g. Town and Country Planning Act 1990 s.289(6).

[166]   CPR r.3.1(2)(a) and para.3.5 of Practice Direction 52D – Statutory Appeals and Appeals Subject to Special Provision.

[167]   *Regalbourne Ltd v East Lindsey DC* (1994) 6 Admin. L.Rep. 102; *Cartwright v McMahon* [1989] C.O.D. 184. See, by analogy, the approach that the courts take to applications to extend time to enter an application for judicial review: *R. v Institute of Chartered Accountants in England and Wales Ex p. Andreou* (1996) 8 Admin. L.Rep. 557. But see *R. (Wandsworth LBC) v Secretary of State for Transport, Local Government and the Regions* [2004] 1 P. & C.R. 507 where an extension was granted where the delay was of short duration and no prejudice had been caused.

[168]   *Regalbourne Ltd v East Lindsey DC* (1994) 6 Admin. L. Rep. 102; *Phillips v Derbyshire CC* [1997] C.O.D. 1997 131. See, generally, *Savill v Southend Health Authority* [1995] 1 W.L.R. 1254 on the need to provide some material for the court to exercise its discretion.

[169]   *Regalbourne Ltd v East Lindsey DC* (1994) 6 Admin. L.Rep. 102; *Van de Velde v Special Educational Needs Tribunal* [1996] C.O.D. 121; *Phillips v Derbyshire CC* [1997] C.O.D. 131 (delay by special adviser and failure by solicitor to ascertain time-limit).

[170]   *Regalbourne Ltd v East Lindsey DC* (1994) 6 Admin. L.Rep. 102.

[171]   CPR r.52.8.

[172]   CPR r.52.11(5).

[173]   See para.9–127.

Procedure at the hearing

The appeal is heard by a single judge unless the court otherwise orders. The **14–058** appeal will be limited to a review of the decision of the lower court or tribunal unless a practice direction provides for there to be a re-hearing or the interests of the justice require a re-hearing.[174] The court will not receive oral evidence or evidence which was not before the court below unless it orders otherwise. The appeal court will allow an appeal where the decision of the lower court was wrong or unjust because of a procedural or other irregularity.

Powers of the High Court

Statute may specifically deal with the power of the High Court in allowing an **14–059** appeal. Statute may empower the court to make such an order or give such directions as it thinks fit. In the absence of specific provisions in the statute or a rule or practice direction, the court has all the powers of the body appealed from and, in particular, the court may affirm, set aside or vary any order or judgment of the body appealed from and may refer any issue for determination back to the body appealed from.[175]

Costs

The court has power to award costs.[176] The usual rule is that the unsuccessful **14–060** party pays the costs of the successful party. The parties to the appeal will be the original parties to the decision by the tribunal or other decision-maker. A tribunal that is not represented at, and does not participate in, the appeal hearing will not normally be ordered to pay the costs of the appeal even if it transpires that its decision was wrong.[177] If the tribunal or decision-maker is represented at the hearing as an active party seeking to uphold its decision, then the courts may order the tribunal to pay the costs of a successful appeal.[178] If the tribunal appears in a neutral capacity to assist the court, the normal practice is not to award costs in favour of or against the tribunal.[179]

Planning appeals

One of the more frequent sources of appeals involves planning. The principal **14–061** source of such appeals is s.289 of the Town and Country Planning Act 1990. This concerns appeals against a decision of the Secretary of State on an appeal against an enforcement notice issued by a local authority and alleging a breach of

---

[174] CPR r.52.11.

[175] CPR r.52.10.

[176] Senior Courts Act 1981 s.51 and CPR r.52.10(2)(e).

[177] *Moore's (Wallisdown) Ltd v Pensions Ombudsman* [2002] 1 W.L.R. 1649. See, by analogy, the position in relation to inferior courts in judicial: *R. (Touche) v Inner London Coroner's Court* [2001] Q.B. 1206; *R. v Newcastle-under-Lyme Justices Ex p. Massey* [1994] 1 W.L.R. 594 and see above at para.9–141.

[178] *R. (Davies) v HM Coroner for Birmingham (No.2)* [2004] 1 W.L.R. 2739.

[179] [2004] EWCA Civ 207.

planning control. These claims are now dealt with by the Planning Court.[180] The procedure for appealing is regulated by CPR Part 52 and para.26 of Practice Direction 52D – Statutory Appeals and Appeals Subject to Special Provision.

14–062   The appellant in the enforcement notice proceedings, the local planning authority or any other person with an interest in the land may seek to appeal.[181] A person must first obtain permission to appeal from the High Court.[182] An application for permission must be made in writing and must set out the reasons why permission should be granted. The application and a draft appellant's notice, together with any witness statement verifying any facts relied upon and a statement giving details of the persons served must be filed at the Administrative Court Office within 28 days.[183] If the time for appealing has expired, an applicant may include an application for an extension of time in his application for permission.[184] The application and draft appellant's notice must be served on the minister and the respondent to the appeal (either the local planning authority or the person who appealed against the enforcement notice).[185] Permission may be granted by a judge on consideration of the papers or, if permission is refused on the papers, the applicant for permission may request that the matter be reconsidered at an oral hearing.[186] If permission is granted, the provisions of CPR Part 52 apply. The hearing will usually be before a single judge in the Planning Court. Any person served (or whom the court considers should have been served) has the right to appear at the hearing and made representations: this includes the Secretary of State, the local planning authority and any person with an interest in the land.[187]

14–063   The court may either dismiss the appeal or if it considers that the decision was erroneous in law it must remit the matter to the Secretary of State for a re-hearing

---

[180] See CPR r.54.21. Such appeals are to be seen as a statutory challenge relating to the enforcement of planning control. Practice Direction 54E – Planning Court Claims envisages that such claims are planning claims and provides specific timescales within which permission to appeal, and the substantive hearing if permission is given, will be considered. Para.26(6) of Practice Direction 52D – Statutory Appeals and Appeals Subject to Special Provision confirm that the Practice Direction 54D applies to such appeals. The target set by para.3.4(c) of Practice 54D – Planning Court Claims for considering permission applications is that they should be heard within one month of issue although para.26(5) of Practice Direction 52D – Statutory Appeals and Appeals Subject to Special Provision provide for applications for permission to be dealt with within 21 days.

[181] See Town and Country Planning Act 1990 s.289(1) and CPR r.52.20.

[182] Town and Country Planning Act 1990 (as amended) s.289(6).

[183] Para.26(1) and (2) of Practice Direction 52D – Statutory Appeals and Appeals Subject to Special Provision.

[184] CPR rr.3.1(2) and 52.6 and para.5.2 of Practice Direction 52D – Statutory Appeals and Appeals Subject to Special Provision. The courts are likely to adopt the same approach to applications for extension of time as they apply in relation to applications to extend the time for appealing under CPR r.3.1(2)(a); see above at para.14–055. In particular, each period of delay will need to be explained by good reasons. Delay due to the applicant's legal advisers is unlikely of itself to be sufficient to justify an extension of time: *Mayflower Glass Ltd v Secretary of State for the Environment and South Tyneside MBC* [1992] C.O.D. 225.

[185] Para.26(3) of Practice Direction 52D – Statutory Appeals and Appeals Subject to Special Provision.

[186] CPR r.52.3(4).

[187] See paras 26(7) and (10) read with paras 26(3) and (12) of Practice Direction 52E – Statutory Appeals and Appeals Subject to Special Provision.

and determination: the court cannot set aside the decision.[188] The Secretary of State has a discretion as to the process of re-hearing and may simply re-consider those matters where the court has found an error rather than hearing the entire appeal again.[189] The court has jurisdiction to award costs and the normal rule is that the unsuccessful party pays the costs of the successful respondent. If an appellant fails in his appeal and there are two respondents, such as the Secretary of State and the developer (or local planning authority), the normal practice is for the court only to order the appellant to pay one set of costs.[190] There may be a further appeal to the Court of Appeal but only with permission of that Court.[191]

An appeal is a second appeal for the purposes of s.55 of the Access to Justice   **14–064**
Act 1999. An appeal may only be made with the permission of the Court of Appeal and permission may only be granted where the appeal would raise an important point of principle or practice or there is some other compelling reason for the Court of Appeal to hear the appeal.[192]

Appeals from professional disciplinary bodies

A certain number of statutes have also established disciplinary machinery to   **14–065**
regulate standards in certain professions. These statutes may confer a right of appeal to the High Court against the decisions of these statutory disciplinary bodies, as is the case, for example, with disciplinary tribunals dealing with the conduct of and solicitors,[193] licensed conveyancers,[194] and nurses and mid-wives.[195] The High Court has also acquired jurisdiction in relation to appeals from other professional regulatory bodies which were formerly dealt with by the Privy Council including certain appeals by doctors[196] and dentists.[197] The precise scope of the right to appeal will depend upon the particular statutory provision conferring a right of appeal.

The statute concerned will generally describe the decisions that may be   **14–066**
appealed and the time-limit for appealing.[198] Appeals may usually be brought as of right and neither CPR r.52.3 nor the Practice Direction on Appeals imposes any requirement to obtain permission to appeal in relation to such statutory

---

[188]   See para.26(15) of Practice Direction 52D – Statutory Appeals and Appeals Subject to Special Provision.

[189]   *R. (Perrett) v Secretary of State for Communities and Local Government* [2010] P.T.S.R. 1280 (contrasting the position with the situation where the Court quashes a decision where the decision will need to be retaken).

[190]   See, by analogy, the position in relation to statutory applications to quash and *Bolton MDC v Secretary of State for the Environment (No.2)* [1995] 1 W.L.R. 1176 discussed below at paras 14–084 to 14–085 and the position in relation to claims for judicial review discussed above at para.9–142.

[191]   Town and Country Planning Act 1990 s.289(6).

[192]   See fourth proposition of Brooke LJ in *Clark v Perks* [2001] 1 W.L.R. 17 at [13].

[193]   Solicitors Act 1974.

[194]   Administration of Justice Act 1985 s.26(7) and see, e.g. *Colley v Council for Licensed Conveyancers* [2002] 1 W.L.R. 160.

[195]   Nurses, Midwives and Health Visitors Act 1997 s.12.

[196]   See Medical Act 1983 s.40 as amended by the National Health Service Reform and Health Care Professions Act 2002 s.30.

[197]   See Dentists Act 1984 s.29 as amended by the National Health Service Reform and Health Care Professions Act 2002 s.30.

[198]   See, e.g. Medical Act 1983 s.40(1) setting out the appealable decisions and s.40(4) providing for an appeal within 28 days.

appeals.[199] An appellant's notice will need to be filed and served.[200] The jurisdiction of the High Court, whether expressed as a review or a rehearing,[201] is appellate but the appeals are conducted on the basis of the transcript of what occurred below and will not normally involve the hearing of oral evidence.[202] The High Court will intervene where the decision of the professional regulatory body is erroneous in law or is reached in breach of natural justice or is plainly wrong[203] or inadequate reasons are given.[204] In relation to matters of fact and witness credibility, the High Court will not have had the advantage of hearing the witnesses and will be reluctant to substitute their own view for that of the professional regulatory body and setting aside its decisions on fact.[205] The High Court has jurisdiction to consider whether the sanctions imposed were appropriate and necessary in the public interest or disproportionate and excessive.[206] The High Court will accord an appropriate measure of respect to the decisions of the professional regulatory body on the appropriate sanction but will not defer more than is warranted by the circumstances.[207] In addition, a decision of a professional tribunal affecting the right to practise a profession involves a determination of civil rights for the purposes of Art.6 of the European Convention on Human Rights.[208] As such, the proceedings before the disciplinary body and the High Court must, taken as a whole, ensure a fair hearing before an independent and impartial tribunal. That may influence the course of a particular appeal, as the extent to which the procedures before the disciplinary tribunal, and its degree of independence, ensure a fair hearing may affect the way in which the High Court exercises its jurisdiction to hear the appeal. Where, for example, the general disciplinary structures in place fail to ensure a fair hearing before an independent tribunal, and where there had been breaches of procedure, the court's reluctance to interfere with the decision of the professional body and its findings of fact may diminish.[209] The precise powers of the High Court on appeal will depend upon the particular statutory provision but, typically, the High Court is

---

[199] See *Colley v Council for Licensed Conveyancers* [2002] 1 W.L.R. 160.

[200] See CPR r.52.4.

[201] Para.19.1(3) of Practice Direction 52D – Statutory Appeals and Appeals Subject to Special Provision provides that appeals by architects and the health care professional listed are to be way of re-hearing.

[202] See *Gupta v General Medical Council* [2002] 1 W.L.R. 1691 at [10] and *Ghosh v General Medical Council* [2001] 1 W.L.R. 1915 at [33] (appeals to the Privy Council but similar principles will be followed before the High Court).

[203] *Raschid v General Medical Council* [2007] 1 W.L.R. 1460 at [20]. See also e.g. *Holwell v Council for Licensed Conveyancers* [1988] C.O.D. 95; *Reza v General Medical Council* [1990] C.O.D. 408.

[204] See, e.g. *Stefan v General Medical Council* [1999] 1 W.L.R. 1293; *Threlfall v General Optical Council* [2005] A.C.D. 287.

[205] *Gupta v General Medical Council* [2002] 1 W.L.R. 1691 at [10] and [18] (dealing with an appeal to the Privy Council but similar principles apply to the High Court).

[206] *Ghosh v General Medical Council* [2001] 1 W.L.R. 1915 at [34].

[207] *Raschid v General Medical Council* [2007] 1 W.L.R. 1460 at [18]–[20]. *Ghosh v General Medical Council* [2001] 1 W.L.R. 1915 at [31]; *Gupta v General Medical Council* [2002] 1 W.L.R. 1691 at [19]–[22] and *Bolton v Law Society* [1994] 1 W.L.R. 512.

[208] *Albert and Le Compte v Belgium* (1983) 5 E.H.R.R. 1; *Preiss v General Dental Council* [2001] 1 W.L.R. 1926 at [9].

[209] *Preiss v General Dental Council* [2001] 1 W.L.R. 1926 at [27].

given power to dismiss an appeal, allow the appeal and quash the decision, substitute a different decision or remit the matter to the body concerned.[210]

Appeals to the Court of Appeal

Where statute provides that the decision of the High Court is to be final, there is no possibility of a further appeal to the Court of Appeal.[211] Where a decision of the High Court is not expressed to be final, an appeal to the Court of Appeal is possible if either the High Court or the Court of Appeal grants permission.[212]   **14–067**

H.   APPEAL TO THE COURT OF APPEAL

Statute may provide for an appeal on a point of law direct to the Court of Appeal rather than to the High Court. An appeal lies, for example, from the Competition Commission Appeals Tribunal,[213] and Employment Appeal Tribunal[214] to the Court of Appeal.[215] Leave of the tribunal or of the Court of Appeal is necessary. In the case of appeals from Social Security Commissioners, there is no appeal against a decision of the Commissioner refusing leave for an appeal to be made to the Commissioner from an adjudication officer or social security appeals tribunal,[216] or refusing to extend the time-limit within which appeals to the Commissioner must be made.[217]   **14–068**

I.   STATUTORY APPLICATIONS TO QUASH

Jurisdiction to hear applications

Statute may specifically provide for a particular order or decision of a public body to be challenged by way of an application to the High Court to quash the decision. This is in effect a form of statutory judicial review. Examples include applications to quash decisions of the licensing authority granting or refusing   **14–069**

---

[210]   See, e.g. Dentists Act 1984 s.29(3); Medical Act 1983 s.40(7).

[211]   Senior Courts Act 1981 s.18(1)(c) and see *Westminster v City Council v O'Reilly* [2004] 1 W.L.R. 195. Where the Court of Appeal had, erroneously, heard an appeal and held that the decision of the court below was wrong, they held that they could entertain an application for judicial review, grant it, dismiss it, allow an appeal and give a substantive decision to enable that to be appealed to the House of Lords. The Court recognised that ordinarily that would be an abuse of process but considered it necessary in the unusual circumstances of that case to enable justice to be done. See *Farley v Secretary of State for Work and Pensions* [2005] 2 F.L.R. 1075, and in the House of Lords at [2007] 1 W.L.R. 1817. Absent such special circumstances, a court should not generally grant judicial review where there is provision for an appeal to the High Court and statute provides that the decision of that court is final: see *Sheffield City Council v Kenya Aid Programme* [2014] Q.B. 62.

[212]   CPR r.52.3.

[213]   Competition Act 1998 s.49.

[214]   Employment Protection (Consolidation) Act 1978 s.136(4).

[215]   See paras 7–17 of Practice Direction 52D – Statutory Appeals and Appeals Subject to Special Provision.

[216]   *Bland v Chief Supplementary Benefit Office* [1983] 1 W.L.R. 262.

[217]   *White v Chief Adjudication Officer* [1986] 2 All E.R. 905.

licences to sell, manufacture or import a medicinal product,[218] or allowing a challenge to an order providing a definitive map of an area or modifying such a map.[219] One of the most frequently used procedures is that for applying to quash a compulsory purchase order,[220] or to challenge a wide range of decisions in the planning field.[221] Such matters are now designated as planning claims and are dealt with by the Planning Court.[222] The procedural steps, the scope of review, and the powers of the court on statutory applications to quash depend in part upon the precise wording of the particular statute. In addition, a generalised code of procedure, applicable when statute does not regulate the matter, is set out in CPR Part 8 and Practice Direction 8A – Alternative Procedures for claims.

14–070   The statutory provisions for challenge usually provide for an application to be made where the order or decision is not one within the powers of the Act, or where the applicant has suffered substantial prejudice as a result of a failure to comply with any relevant requirements. Despite earlier judicial disagreement over the meaning of these words,[223] it is now generally accepted that a decision will be outside the powers of the Act if it is flawed by any of the errors rendering a decision ultra vires in judicial review terms. Thus error of law,[224] failure to take account of relevant considerations or ignoring relevant ones,[225] reaching a decision no reasonable decision-maker could reach,[226] or acting on no evidence or for an improper purpose or in bad faith,[227] will mean that the decision is outside the powers of the Act. A breach of natural justice will render a decision outside the powers of the Act, and will also be a breach of a relevant requirement.[228] This creates a problem, in that substantial prejudice must exist for a decision to be quashed on the latter ground but not the former. The problem has been solved by some judges by regarding any breach of natural justice as automatically involving substantial prejudice,[229] and conversely by others by insisting that there must be substantial prejudice before any breach of natural justice can be found.[230]

14–071   The question of whether an application may be made in respect of some preliminary decision or ruling, or may only be made against a final decision, depends on the precise wording of each statute. The Court of Appeal has held that an application to quash a decision of the Secretary of State, on an appeal against the refusal of planning permission, only lies against the final decision of the

---

[218] Medicines Act 1968 s.107.

[219] Wildlife and Countryside Act 1981 Sch.15 para.12.

[220] Acquisition of Land Act 1981 s.23.

[221] Town and Country Planning Act 1990 s.288.

[222] CPR 54 rr.21 to 23 and Practice Direction 54E – Planning Court Claims.

[223] See, in particular, the three different interpretations contained in the five separate judgments in the House of Lords in *Smith v East Elloe RDC* [1956] A.C. 736.

[224] *Peak Park Joint Planning Board v Secretary of State for the Environment* (1979) 39 P. & C.R. 361.

[225] *Ashbridge Investments Ltd v Minister of Housing and Local Government* [1965] 1 W.L.R. 1320.

[226] [1965] 1 W.L.R. 1320.

[227] *Webb v Minister of Housing and Local Government* [1965] 1 W.L.R. 755 at 770.

[228] *Fairmount Investments Ltd v Secretary of State for the Environment* [1976] 1 W.L.R. 1255; *Hibernian Property Co. Ltd v Secretary of State for the Environment* (1973) 27 P. & C.R. 197; *Errington v Minister of Health* [1935] 1 K.B. 249.

[229] per Browne J. in *Hibernian Property Co. Ltd v Secretary of State for the Environment* (1973) 72 L.G.R. 350.

[230] per Lord Denning M.R. in *George v Secretary of State for the Environment* (1979) 77 L.G.R. 689.

minister after the appeal proceedings have been concluded.[231] There could not, therefore, be an application against a decision of the minister to refuse an adjournment of a local inquiry during the course of appeal proceedings (although failure to do so might lead to a breach of natural justice, which might be a ground for challenging the final decision). It is likely that the courts will construe decisions as meaning final decisions, and clear words will be necessary to allow applications to be made against interlocutory or preliminary decisions.

Standing

Questions governing standing are governed by the precise wording of the statute. **14–072**
Statute usually, but not invariably, provides that any person aggrieved may apply to quash the order.[232] The courts have in the past given this phrase a restricted meaning. In *Buxton v Minister of Housing and Local Government*,[233] the court held that an adjoining landowner was not a person aggrieved, and could not challenge a planning decision relating to neighbouring land. A person aggrieved meant someone with a legal grievance, and as a neighbouring landowner had no legal rights affected by the development he had no right to challenge the decision. This restrictive approach has been relaxed. In the context of applications to quash a decision of the Secretary of State dismissing an appeal against the refusal of planning permission, the court has held that the appellant, any person who took a sufficiently active role in the planning process or who has a relevant interest in the land is a person aggrieved for the purposes of s.288 of the Town and Country Planning Act 1990.[234] The courts have accepted that anyone who makes objections at a local inquiry is a person aggrieved, and may challenge the validity of the final decision.[235] A successor in title to the original landowner is entitled to appeal against a decision of a minister in planning matters even though he was not a party to the proceedings before the minister.[236] The Court of Appeal has ruled in the context of appeals to the Crown Court that a person does not have to have a legal grievance or be subjected to a legal burden before he can be regarded as a person aggrieved.[237] A similar relaxation is likely to occur in the analogous areas of statutory applications to quash. The standing rules in judicial review have similarly been relaxed since 1977,[238] and as Woolf LJ has pointed out,[239] statutory rights of challenge do little more than confer a statutory right of judicial review. It would be absurd to insist on a stricter test of standing for statutory challenges.

---

[231] *Co-operative Retail Services Ltd v Secretary of State for the Environment* [1980] 1 All E.R. 449.
[232] See, e.g. Town and Country Planning Act 1990 s.288(1); Acquisition of Land Act 1981. For a different test see, e.g. Medicines Act 1968 s.107.
[233] [1961] 1 Q.B. 278.
[234] *Eco-energy (GB) Ltd. v First Secretary of State* [2005] 2 P. & C.R. 5 at [7].
[235] *Turner v Secretary of State for the Environment* (1973) 28 P. & C.R. 123. Although the Court of Appeal in *Eco-energy (GB) Ltd. v First Secretary of State* [2005] 2 P. & C.R. 5 indicated that a person who objected and played a role in the planning process in support of that objection would be a person aggrieved but not a person who objected and then did nothing in relation to his objection.
[236] *Times Investment Ltd v Secretary of State for the Environment and London Borough of Tower Hamlets* [1991] 61 P. & C.R. 98.
[237] *Cook v Southend BC* [1990] 2 Q.B. 1.
[238] See Chapter 11.
[239] *Cook v Southend BC* [1990] 2 Q.B. 1.

14–073   Local planning authorities in planning cases are expressly recognised as a body entitled to apply to challenge the validity of a decision of the Secretary of State.[240] As a matter of general principle, public bodies whose decisions are overturned on appeal are now likely to be persons aggrieved for the purpose of any statutory right of challenge.[241]

Time-limits

14–074   The time-limits for bringing a claim will be set out in the statute providing the right of appeal. Statute frequently provides for applications to be made within six weeks,[242] although individual statutes may allow a longer period.[243] The period from which time begins to run will be determined by the statutory wording. In applications in planning cases, statute provides that the six weeks runs from the date that the disputed order is confirmed or the disputed action taken.[244] The House of Lords has held that action is taken when the date-stamp is placed on the decision letter, not from the date that notification is given to the individual concerned.[245] Other statutes provide for time to run from the date of publication or notification of the decision. There are occasions when the appeal involves the determination of a civil right within the meaning of Art.6 of the European Convention. Here, the provision governing time-limits will need to be interpreted as conferring a power to extend time but only where that is necessary to ensure compliance with Art.6 of the Convention. There will need to be exceptional circumstances and the applicant must have done all that he can to bring the appeal within time.[246]

Procedure for applying

14–075   Applications must be made by claim form.[247] The claim form must be entered in the Administrative Court Office.[248] An application will normally only be validly made within the meaning of an Act when it is entered in the Administrative Court Office. An application entered in another office within the High Court is not validly made.[249] The Practice Direction also provides that the claim form must be served on the relevant minister or government department within the time-limit

---

[240] Town and Country Planning Act 1990 s.288(2).

[241] *Cook v Southend BC* (see [1990] 2 Q.B. 1).

[242] See, e.g. Town and Country Planning Act 1990 s.288; Wildlife and Countryside Act 1981 Sch.15 para.12 (period expressed as 42 days). This is compatible with Art.6 of the European Convention on Human Rights: see *Matthews v Secretary of State for the Environment, Transport and the Regions* [2002] 2 P. & C.R. 558.

[243] Medicines Act 1968 s.107 (three months).

[244] Town and Country Planning Act 1990 s.288(3).

[245] *Griffiths v Secretary of State for the Environment* [1983] 2 A.C. 51.

[246] *Adesina v Nursing and Midwifery Council* [2013] 1 W.L.R. 3156. See also *Parkin v Nursing and Midwifery Council* [2014] EWCH 519 (Admin).

[247] CPR Part 8 and para.9 of Practice Direction 8A – Alternative Claims Procedure.

[248] Para.22.3 of Practice Direction 8A – Alternative Claims Procedure

[249] *Low v Secretary of State for Wales* [1992] C.O.D. 253. If it is not validly made within time, the court does not have jurisdiction to deal with the matter and cannot extend the time and accept filing at the Crown Office outside the statutory time-limit.

set down by the statute for making the application.[250] This is a rule of procedure, not a precondition of the making of a valid application under the relevant Act, and the court has discretion to extend time for service of the claim form.[251] Notice must be served on the relevant minister or government department and on the public authority concerned.[252]

If a judicial review claim form is used but the claim is brought within the statutory time-limit for bringing a statutory application to quash, the courts may grant permission for the judicial review claim form to stand as a claim form.[253]   **14–076**

Witness statements

Evidence at the hearing of the application will be by witness statement[254] although the court may allow cross-examination on such written evidence. Witness statements in support must be filed in the Administrative Court Office within 14 days of service of the claim form and copies must be served on the respondent.[255] Witness statements in opposition must be filed in the Administrative Court Office within 21 days after the service of written evidence in support, and copies must be served on the applicant.[256]   **14–077**

Interim relief

Statute may provide for the court to grant interim relief, by way of suspending an order pending the hearing of the application.[257]   **14–078**

Amendments

Provided that an application is made within the time-limit prescribed by statute, the court has jurisdiction to allow amendments, including amendments substituting new grounds, after the expiry of the time-limit.[258] In deciding whether to exercise that jurisdiction, the court will bear in mind the fact that those affected would not have been able to rely upon the validity of the decision as a challenge within time had been made. The court will, therefore, consider whether or not the amendment would cause further substantial delay or prejudice. Where the additional delay was comparatively small, the court exercised its discretion to   **14–079**

---

[250]   Para.22 of the Practice Direction 8A – Alternative Claims Procedure.
[251]   *Mendip DC v Secretary of State for the Environment and Castle Housing Society Ltd* [1993] C.O.D. 274. Similarly, provided an application has been made within the meaning of the relevant Act and within the statutory time-limit, so that the court has jurisdiction to entertain the application, the court has power to correct other matters where there has been an error of procedure: see CPR r.3.10.
[252]   Para.22.4 of Practice Direction 8A – Alternative Claims Procedure.
[253]   *Cala Homes v Chichester DC* (2000) 79 P. & C.R. 430.
[254]   Para.22.7 of Practice Direction 8A – Alternative Claims Procedure.
[255]   Para.22.8 of Practice Direction 8A – Alternative Claims Procedure.
[256]   Para.22.9 of Practice Direction 8A – Alternative Claims Procedure.
[257]   See, e.g. Town and Country Planning Act 1990 s.288(5).
[258]   *San Vicente v Secretary of State for Communities and Local Government* [2014] 1 W.L.R. 966 holding that the basis for this jurisdiction is CPR r.17.2.

allow an otherwise proper claim to be advanced.[259] Similarly, where a claim has been brought within time, the court has power to substitute a party for an existing party. Thus the court permitted the vice-chairman of a local society to be substituted as a claimant when the society itself decided not to pursue the claim on its own behalf.[260]

Hearing of the application

14–080 The application involving planning claims will be heard by a single judge of the Planning Court and other applications will be heard by a single judge of the Queen's Bench Division. The hearing will not take place earlier than 14 days after the time for the filing of written evidence by the respondent has expired, unless the court otherwise orders.[261]

Powers

14–081 The precise powers of the court on hearing an application will depend on the wording of the statute. A statute usually confers the right to apply to challenge the validity of a decision or order. It will usually provide for the order to be quashed if the court considers that it is not within the power of the Act, or fails to meet a relevant requirement. The effect is similar to that in ordinary judicial review cases. The decision is set aside and is a nullity. The decision-maker must then proceed to reconsider the matter de novo and must have regard to any relevant considerations arising since the date of the original decision.[262] Statute usually provides that the High Court *may* quash a decision if it is flawed. The use of the word "may" supports the view that there is a discretion as to whether to quash the decision, and the court is not obliged to quash once an error has been discovered. The courts have proceeded on the basis that the jurisdiction to quash is discretionary.[263] Although the issue has not been fully argued, it is likely that the same principles governing the discretionary refusal of judicial review will be applied to the statutory application to quash.

14–082 Statute may specifically provide for part of an order to be quashed, or for the order to be set aside only in so far as it affects the interests of the applicant.[264] It

---

[259] *San Vicente v Secretary of State for Communities and Local Government* [2014] 1 W.L.R. 966 at [60]–[64]. See also *Cheshire East v Secretary of State for Communities and Local Government* [2014] EWHC 3536 (Admin) at [42]–[44].

[260] *River Thames Society v First Secretary of State* [2007] J.P.L. 782. The basis of this jurisdiction was held to be the inherent jurisdiction of the court as CPR Part 19 did not apply to public law claims.

[261] Para.22.11 of Practice Direction 8A – Alternative Claims Procedure.

[262] *Kingswood DC v Secretary of State for the Environment* (1987) 57 P. & C.R. 153; and see *R. (Perrett) v Secretary of State for Communities and Local Government* [2010] P.T.S.R. 1280 at [18a] and [22] confirming that this is the position where statute provides for quashing a decision (as compared with a power only to remit a matter).

[263] See, e.g. *R. v Warwickshire City Council Ex p. Boyden* [1991] C.O.D. 31; the judgment of Pill Q.C. in *Robbins v Secretary of State for the Environment* (1987) 56 P. & C.R. 416 (decision invalid but refused in his discretion to quash; decision affd. on different ground that the decision not invalid [1989] 1 W.L.R. 166).

[264] See, e.g. Wildlife and Countryside Act 1981 Sch.15 para.12.

remains to be seen whether the general common law principles governing severance in judicial review proceedings[265] also apply to statutory applications to quash.

Costs

Costs are in the discretion of the court. They usually follow the event, although the court has a discretion to depart from this practice. A court has, for example, refused to order costs against the applicant even where it dismissed an application on the ground that the error of law identified did not affect the decision. It was in the public interest that a manifestly wrong test should be corrected publicly and quickly, even though it had not affected the applicant.[266]

14–083

An application may be made to challenge an order involving two public bodies, such as a planning authority and the Secretary of State. As a general rule, an individual will not have to pay the costs of both respondents.[267] The courts do have a discretion in relation to costs and may in appropriate cases depart from this practice. They may award two sets of costs where a respondent deals with a separate issue not dealt with by the other respondent[268] or where the interests of the two parties are separate and distinct and require separate representation.[269] A second set of costs may be awarded, for example, if a person wishes to meet allegations of bad faith or dishonesty made against him.[270] The fact that issues are complex[271] or the case raises a matter of exceptional importance to a second respondent may justify the conclusion that it was reasonable for him to attend to resist the application and so justify the award of a second set of costs.[272]

14–084

Relationship with other remedies

Statute may provide that the statutory remedy is to be the sole remedy for challenging the validity of a particular category of decisions.[273] This provision may oust the common law judicial review jurisdiction leaving the statutory application, with its shorter time-limits and possibly more restrictive rules on standing,[274] as the exclusive remedy.[275] If there is no ouster clause, the existence

14–085

---

[265] See Chapter 5.

[266] *South Western Regional Health Authority v Secretary of State for the Environment and Bristol City Council* [1990] C.O.D. 301.

[267] *Bolton MBC v Secretary of State for the Environment (No.2)* [1995] 1 W.L.R. 1176.

[268] *Bolton MBC v Secretary of State for the Environment (No.2).* [1995] 1 W.L.R. 1176. See para.9–142 above.

[269] See, e.g. *R. v Registrar of Companies Ex p. Central Bank of India* [1986] Q.B. 1114 at 1162. The fact that a person has a separate interest may not be sufficient if that separate interest does not require separate representation *Bolton*, above fn.267 (interest of developer in upholding a planning permission did not of itself justify a second set of costs).

[270] *R. v Ogwr BC Ex p. Carter Commercial Development Ltd* (1989) 2 P.L.R. 54.

[271] *R. v Registrar of Companies Ex p. Central Bank of India* [1986] Q.B. 1114 at 1162.

[272] *Bolton MBC v Secretary of State for the Environment (No.2)* [1995] 1 W.L.R. 1176.

[273] See, e.g. Town and Country Planning Act 1990 s.284.

[274] See, e.g. *Organon Laboratories v Department of Health* [1990] 1 C.M.L.R. 49.

[275] This topic is discussed in detail at paras 12–117 to 12–119.

of a statutory mechanism for challenge is relevant to the discretion of the court in deciding whether to grant judicial review, but does not oust the jurisdiction of the court.[276]

Miscellaneous

14–086 Various miscellaneous statutory procedures exist for challenging the validity or establishing the unlawfulness of action or decisions of a public body. Two of the more significant such procedures are those dealing with coroners and local government finance. Statute provides that an applicant may apply with the authority of the Attorney-General to quash the inquisition of an inquest, and order a new inquest to be held if certain grounds are made out.[277] The appropriate procedure is to apply by following the procedure in CPR, and Practice Direction 8A – Alternative Claims Procedure. Where these statutory powers are inadequate, such an application should be combined with an application for judicial review.[278]

14–087 Statute also provides for an auditor to apply for a declaration that certain items of local authority spending are contrary to law.[279]

---

[276] See para.12–043.

[277] Coroners Act 1988 s.13.

[278] per Woolf LJ in *Re Rapier* [1988] Q.B. 26 at 29.

[279] Audit Commission Act 1998 s. 17.

CHAPTER 15

Damages and the Principles Governing Public Authority Liability

A. INTRODUCTION

An individual may seek compensation against public bodies for harm caused by the wrongful acts of such bodies. Such claims may arise out of the exercise of statutory or other public powers by public bodies. Decisions or measures which are ultra vires their powers may be set aside by means of judicial review. The fact that an administrative act is ultra vires and so unlawful does not of itself entitle the individual to damages for any loss suffered. An individual must establish that the unlawful action also constitutes a recognised tort or involves a breach of contract.[1] The general principles governing tortious and contractual liability apply to public bodies exercising public powers, although their application may have to be adapted or modified to reflect the special factors relevant in such cases. In addition, there is the one tort which is unique to public bodies, namely the tort of misfeasance in a public office. Public bodies may also be exercising powers derived from contract or ownership of property, rather than public law powers. The general principles governing tortious and contractual liability will apply to these activities. Finally, restitutionary claims may be made by or against public bodies where money has been collected or paid out pursuant to a measure or a contract which is subsequently found to be ultra vires.   **15–001**

Damages may also be awarded under s.8 of the Human Rights Act 1998 where this is necessary to afford just satisfaction to a person who has suffered loss as a result of a public authority acting in breach of the person's rights under the European Convention on Human Rights.[2] In certain circumstances, breach of a right derived from European Union law may also give rise to a right to compensation.[3]   **15–002**

---

[1] See *X v Bedfordshire CC* [1995] 2 A.C. 633 at [730G]; *R. v Knowsley MBC Ex p. Maguire* (1992) 90 L.G.R. 653; and *Financial Services Authority v Sinaloa Gold Plc* [2013] A.C. 28 at [31].
[2] See Chapter 16.
[3] See Chapter 17.

B.   TORTIOUS LIABILITY

Negligence

Introduction

15–003   Public bodies may be liable in negligence just like private individuals. To establish liability, a claimant must demonstrate that a duty of care was owed by the defendant to the claimant; that there was a breach of that duty; and that the breach caused recoverable loss. Reference should be made to the standard works on tort for a detailed discussion of these principles.[4]

15–004   Some situations involving public bodies raise considerations that are no different from those that apply in assessing tort claims against private individuals. The identity of the defendant is not material. The tortious liability of drivers who cause accidents whilst engaged in public sector activities is usually governed by the same considerations as liability for any ordinary motorist. Doctors owe a duty of care to their patients; public health authorities may be vicariously liable but their identity is not relevant to the issues of tortious liability.[5] The occupiers of property owe a duty of care to ensure that the property under their control does not become a source of danger to neighbouring properties: this may include a duty to prevent third parties, such as vandals, entering and causing damage to adjacent properties.[6] The same duty applies to private occupiers and public bodies occupying land.[7]

15–005   Liability in tort may, however, be imposed in respect of the way that a public body carries out its statutory powers or duties.[8] The ordinary principles apply, but there are additional factors to be taken into account in deciding how the law of negligence applies in a particular case. The question of whether a common law duty of care exists in respect of action taken pursuant to the exercise of statutory functions, and if so, its ambit, is likely to be "profoundly influenced" by the statutory framework within which the acts complained of were done.[9] The influence of the statutory framework may manifest itself in a number of ways. The courts will not, for example, impose a duty of care at common law if to do so would be inconsistent with the statutory framework.[10] The purpose for which the statutory functions are conferred, and the persons intended to benefit from the exercise of those functions may influence the question of whether the common law recognises particular duties of care to take reasonable steps to protect particular categories of persons from certain types of harm.[11] Furthermore, the exercise of certain statutory functions gives rise to issues that are not justiciable as they involve the weighing of competing policy considerations which the courts

---

[4]   Clerk and Lindsell, *Tort*; Winfield & Jolowicz, *Tort*; Markesinis and Deakin, *Tort Law*.
[5]   See, e.g. *Roe v Minister of Health* [1954] 2 Q.B. 66.
[6]   *Smith v Littlewoods Organisation Ltd* [1987] A.C. 241.
[7]   *King v Liverpool City Council* [1986] 1 W.L.R. 890.
[8]   *Merseyside Docks and Harbour Board Trustees v Gibbs* (1866) L.R. 1 H.L. 93.
[9]   See per Lord Browne-Wilkinson in *X v Bedfordshire CC* [1995] 2 A.C. 633 at [739B].
[10]   See, e.g. *Stovin v Wise* [1996] A.C. 923 at 935; *A. v Essex CC* [2004] 1 W.L.R. 1881 at [37].
[11]   See below at paras 15–011 to 15–013.

are ill-suited to judge and where Parliament could not have intended the courts to substitute their views for that of the public bodies concerned by imposing common law duties of care.[12]

Duty of care

A duty of care must be owed before liability for negligence can arise. A duty of care arises where the law recognises in principle that liability may be imposed in respect of the situation that has occurred. This depends on whether the law recognises an obligation on a defendant not to cause certain types of harm to certain categories of claimant by negligently doing the act complained of. Assuming that the law recognises that a duty of care exists, there will be a question of whether on the facts this duty was owed by this particular defendant to this particular claimant; or in other words, whether the parties concerned fall within the recognised duty-situation.   **15–006**

In the past, the courts have sought some single universal test applicable in all situations for determining whether a potential duty of care exists. The "neighbour principle" enunciated by Lord Atkin in *Donoghue v Stevenson*[13] was one such example. In *Anns v Merton LBC*,[14] Lord Wilberforce framed a two-tier test. First, the court had to determine whether a sufficient relationship of proximity existed, so that a defendant may reasonably foresee that a failure to take care on his part may cause damage to the plaintiff. If so, the second question asked whether there were any policy factors which suggested that the duty should be limited or negatived. This, somewhat vague, two-tier test is not now seen by the courts as a useful determinant of the existence of a duty of care.[15]   **15–007**

The current approach to determining the existence of a duty of care is as follows. First, there must be foreseeability of harm to the claimant. Foreseeability of harm is a necessary but not sufficient ingredient in establishing duty of care.[16] Secondly, there must be proximity between the claimant and defendant, in the sense of a direct and close relationship which on all the circumstances of the case justifies imposing liability on the defendant.[17] Thirdly, it must be fair, just and reasonable to impose a duty of care.[18] Even where a duty of care can be established in the light of these principles, public policy may require that no liability should be imposed.[19] The factors likely to lead to such a conclusion are   **15–008**

---

[12] See, e.g. *Barrett v Enfield LBC* [2001] 2 A.C. 550 at [583D]; *Phelps v Hillingdon LBC* [2001] 2 A.C. 619; *Carty v Croydon LBC* [2005] 1 W.L.R. 2312 at [21] and *A. v Essex CC* [2004] 1 W.L.R. 1881 at [36].

[13] [1932] A.C. 562.

[14] [1978] A.C. 728.

[15] *Yuen Kun-Yeu v Att-Gen of Hong Kong* [1988] A.C. 175 and see dicta of Lord Hoffmann in *Stovin v Wise* [1996] A.C. 923 at [949A–C].

[16] *Caparo Industries Plc v Dickman* [1990] 2 W.L.R. 358; *Hill v Chief Constable of West Yorkshire* [1989] A.C. 53.

[17] *Caparo Industries Plc v Dickman* [1990] 2 W.L.R. 358; *Yuen Kun-Yeu v Att-Gen of Hong Kong* [1989] A.C. 53.

[18] *Caparo* [1990] 2 W.L.R. 358; *Governors of the Peabody Donation Fund v Sir Lindsay Parkinson* [1985] A.C. 210.

[19] *Hill v Chief Constable of West Yorkshire* [1989] A.C. 53.

now more likely to be considered in determining the existence and scope of the duty of care, and it will rarely be necessary to rely on public policy to refute liability.[20]

15–009 The "tests" of proximity or fairness are not susceptible to any precise definition and are:

> "... little more than convenient labels to attach to features of different specific situations which, on a detailed examination of all the circumstances, the law recognises pragmatically as giving rise to a duty of care of a given scope."[21]

The courts have moved away from establishing a single or general test for establishing liability. The closer the facts of the case in issue to a case in which a duty of care has been held to exist, the readier a court will be to find that the fair, just and reasonable test is satisfied.[22] In the particular context of the exercise of statutory powers, the courts will consider carefully whether the imposition of liability would be inconsistent with the statutory framework and whether underlying policy considerations do, on analysis, justify a conclusion that it would not be fair, just or reasonable to impose a duty of care in negligence in respect of the exercise of a particular statutory power.[23] The area of negligence in relation to the exercise of statutory powers and duties is also seen as a complex and evolving area of the law.[24] There is a degree of reluctance to strike out claims as disclosing no reasonable cause of action and to leave the individual facts of the case to be determined at trial so that the evolution of the law can be based on actual factual findings[25] although, it should be noted that the courts are still prepared to deal with the existence of a duty of care in a strike-out application where it is unlikely that further facts would be found at trial[26] or where the courts are satisfied that, assuming all the facts alleged by the claimant are true, the claim must necessarily fail for other reasons.[27]

---

[20] *Brooks v Commissioners of Police of the Metropolis* [2005] 1 W.L.R. 1495 at [27]; *Yuen Kun-Yeu v Att-Gen of Hong Kong* [1988] A.C. 175. See also *An Informer v A Chief Constable* [2013] 2 W.L.R. 694 (Toulson LJ considered that a duty to take reasonable care to avoid harm to the financial well-being of an informer did not arise; Pill LJ held a duty did exist but there had been no breach; only Arden LJ held that there was a duty of care but the public policy considerations protecting the police from immunity in investigations displaced that duty).

[21] per Lord Bridge in *Caparo Industries Plc v Dickman* [1990] 2 W.L.R. 358 at [365].

[22] *Davis v Radcliffe* [1990] 1 W.L.R. 821; *Caparo v Industries Plc v Dickman* [1990] 2 W.L.R. 358 per Lord Bridge at 365 (approving the approach adopted by Brennan J. in *Sutherland Shire Council v Heyman* (1985) 60 A.L.R. 1 at 43–44).

[23] See, e.g. *D v East Berkshire Community NHS Trust* [2004] Q.B. 558 esp. at [81]–[83] (policy reasons for holding that no duty of care owed to a child in respect of decisions to take a child into care discredited and a duty was owed). This finding was not appealed to the House of Lords: see [2005] 2 A.C. 373.

[24] See, e.g. dicta of Lord Steyn in *Gorringe v Calderdale MBC* [2004] 1 W.L.R. 1057 at [2].

[25] See, e.g. *Barrett v Enfield LBC* [2001] 2 A.C. 550; *W v Essex CC* [2001] 2 A.C. 592; *Waters v Commissioner of Police of the Metropolis* [2001] 1 W.L.R. 1607.

[26] *Brooks v Commissioner of Police of the Metropolis* [2005] 1 W.L.R. 1495 at [4].

[27] *Rowley v Secretary of State for Work and Pensions* [2007] 1 W.L.R. 2861 at [21]–[25]. See also, e.g. *Chief Constable of the Hertfordshire Police v Van Colle, Smith v Chief Constable of Sussex Police* [2009] 1 A.C. 225 (House of Lords considered whether the policy considerations recognised as militating against the imposition of a common law duty of care in respect of policing functions remained valid).

Given the infinite variety of factual circumstances that can arise, it is not **15–010** possible to give a comprehensive or exhaustive list of factors relevant to determining whether a duty of care exists. The following are some of the factors that arise, particularly in relation to public authorities when it is sought to impose a duty of care in the exercise of their statutory functions. The division of these factors into categories is not water-tight, as categories tend to overlap and a number of factors will usually be relevant in any one case. In any event, the basic question is whether in all the circumstances of the case, liability should be imposed. The following factors are only guides to the sorts of issues that may be raised in determining this question.

Purpose for which a statutory power is conferred

The courts will look at the purpose for which statutory powers have been **15–011** conferred in deciding whether any common law duty of care ought to be imposed on those carrying out their functions under the statute. The House of Lords has emphasised that the question of whether a common law duty is to be imposed must be "profoundly influenced by the statutory framework"[28] within which the act is done. Moreover, a common law duty of care will not be imposed if the observance of such a duty would be inconsistent with and have a tendency to discourage the due performance of a public body's statutory duties.[29] While the policy of the law is to recognise that wrongs should be remedied,[30] the law also accepts that there may be other policy considerations inherent in the statutory system which are sufficiently strong to outweigh that policy and indicate that liability in negligence ought not to be imposed. One relevant question is whether the statutory power was conferred for the purposes of protecting the interests of the claimant. A second question is whether the nature of the function militates against the imposition of liability. A third issue is whether there would be adverse practical consequences if liability were imposed.

The courts do consider whether the purpose or the scheme of the statute is to **15–012** protect the claimant and to compensate him in the event that he suffers loss as a result of the exercise of the statutory power. In *Philcox v the Civil Aviation Authority*,[31] for example, the Court of Appeal held that statutory powers of supervision and inspection over aircraft were intended to ensure that the owner had properly carried out maintenance on the aircraft. The powers were there to protect the public against an owner's failure to maintain; they were not conferred to protect the owner against his own failure to maintain. The Civil Aviation Authority therefore owed the owner no duty of care to inform him that he had not

---

[28] *X v Bedfordshire CC* [1995] 2 A. C. 633 per Lord Browne-Wilkinson at [739B–C].

[29] *X v Bedfordshire CC* [1995] 2 A.C. 633 per Lord Browne-Wilkinson at [739C–D]. The court will not hold a public authority vicariously liable for the acts of its employees, who may owe common law duties of care in their own right, if that would interfere with the performance of the public authorities duties; such cases are likely to be exceptional, however: see per Lord Slynn in *Phelps v Hillingdon LBC* [2001] 2 A.C. 619 at [653].

[30] See *X v Bedfordshire CC* [1995] 2 A.C. 633 at [749]. See also *Gorringe v Calderdale MBC* [2004] 1 W.L.R. 1057 at [2].

[31] *The Times*. June 5, 1995. See also *Reeman v Department of Transport* [1997] 2 Lloyd's Rep. 648 (Department did not owe a duty of care to the purchasers of a fishing boat who relied on an inaccurate safety certificate; the object of the statutory scheme was to promote safety at sea not protect the economic interests of the purchasers of vessels).

properly maintained his aircraft and the owner could not recover damages for the loss of the aircraft. Conversely, a passenger in an aircraft could claim damages for personal injuries against an inspector of the aircraft who negligently approved the aircraft as fit to fly. The regulatory framework was designed, at least in substantial part, for the protection of those who may be injured if an aircraft was certified as fit to fly when it was not.[32] In another context, in *Curran v Northern Ireland Housing Association*,[33] the court held that a statute empowered a public body to pay a grant to the owners of property to enable them to improve the property. The body had no powers to control the manner in which the work was carried out. The body did have a power to withhold payment of the grant if the work was not carried out satisfactorily. The House of Lords held that the purpose of these statutory powers was to protect the public revenue not to protect the recipients of grants or successors in title. Consequently, no duty of care was owed by the public body to grant recipients or subsequent owners to ensure that the work was not carried out in a defective manner. The statutory scheme enabling urgent ex parte applications to be made for the closure of registered care homes was intended to protect a particular group of vulnerable persons, namely the infirm residents of a nursing home. The statutory scheme was not intended to protect the economic interests of the owners and no duty of care was owed to the owners when the health authority exercised its statutory powers to apply for such an order.[34]

15–013   The statutory purpose is also relevant in determining the scope of any duty that does exist, the people to whom a duty is owed and the kind of damage for which the plaintiff may recover loss. No duty of care to guard against financial loss resulting from depositing with an uncreditworthy company could be imposed in relation to parent companies making deposits with subsidiaries, for example, as the statutory powers excluded such deposits from the supervision of the Bank of England. Therefore, the legislature could not have contemplated the Bank being liable in respect of such deposits.[35] Local planning authorities are not, generally, liable for any financial loss arising from the exercise of their statutory planning functions[36] but may be liable in negligence if they exercise their powers in a way that results in the creation of a danger to the public.[37]

Nature of the function

15–014   A public body may be performing functions requiring it to act in the interests of particular groups of vulnerable persons such as children or the infirm. The courts will not impose duties of care on professionals in respect of other groups of individuals if this would be inconsistent with or be likely to undermine the performance of the statutory duties and powers. The courts have held in the field

---

[32] *Perrett v Collins* [1998] 2 Lloyd's Law Reports 255 esp. at [270].

[33] [1987] A.C. 718.

[34] *Jain v Trent Strategic Health Authority* [2009] A.C. 853 at [28] and [36].

[35] *Minories Finance Ltd v Arthur Young* [1989] 2 All E.R. 105.

[36] *Strable v Dartford BC* [1984] J.P.L. 329; *Kane v New Forest DC* [2001] 1 W.L.R. 312 at [22] and [33].

[37] *Kane v New Forest DC* [2001] 1 W.L.R. 312 (planning authority required construction of a dangerous footpath). See also dicta in *Gorringe v Calderdale MBC* [2004] 1 W.L.R. 1057 at [42]–[44] (per Lord Hoffman), [76] (per Lord Scott) and [85]–[87] (per Lord Rodger).

of protection of children from abuse that there is a potential conflict of interests between the child and the person suspected of carrying out the abuse. The courts have held that health professionals and social workers do not owe a common law duty of care to parents or others suspected of carrying out the abuse. The risk of harm, and the gravity of the harm, to children was such that the relevant professionals should not be subjected to duties of care owed to the parent when discharging their statutory functions in relation to children.[38] To impose such a duty, and to create the possibility that the relevant professionals could be liable in damages to the parents in the exercise of their statutory functions, could inhibit the relevant professionals in the investigation and prevention of abuse to children. Similarly, in the context of adoption, the Court of Appeal has held that the primary duty of care is towards the child. Thus there was no duty owed by the adoption agency to the prospective adopters in respect of the preparation of forms and reports containing information about the child.[39] The House of Lords has also recognised that there is a conflict of interests between the infirm residents in a nursing home and the proprietor. The purpose of the statutory scheme providing powers to apply for closure of the home was to protect the interests of the residents. To impose on the authorities a common law duty of care owed to the proprietor could inhibit the registration authorities in the exercise of their statutory powers which would be potentially adverse to the interests of the persons that the statute was intended to protect [40]

The application of these considerations to particular factual areas may be **15–015** difficult as appears from the differences of view that emerged over time in relation to the exercise of statutory functions concerning whether children should be taken into care. The House of Lords held that it would not be appropriate to impose a duty of care of care on local authorities in respect of the exercise of their statutory powers under the child protection legislation.[41] The claimants were children who alleged that, in one case, the local authority had negligently taken a child into care, believing erroneously that the mother's boyfriend had abused the child and, in the second case, that the local authority had been negligent in not taking them into care, despite warnings over several years that the children might be at risk. The House of Lords considered that the imposition of a common law duty of care would cut across the whole statutory system set up for the protection of children at risk. The system depended upon an interdisciplinary approach involving a wide array of professionals. The tasks involved in that exercise were extremely delicate ones. Imposing liability on all participants would also lead to impossible problems of disentangling the respective liabilities of the different participants whilst imposing liability on one participant, the local authority, would be unfair. Imposing liability might also encourage a more cautious and defensive approach on the part of social workers to their duties than would be

---

[38] *D. v East Berkshire Community Health NHS Trust* [2005] 2 A.C. 373 esp. at [85]–[91]; *Lawrence v Pembrokeshire CC* [2007] 1 W.L.R. 2991 at [43]–[55] and *D. v Bury MBC* [2006] 1 W.L.R. 917.

[39] *A. v Essex CC* [2004] 1 W.L.R. 1881 at [49]–[56] (there was a duty of care owed in relation to the communication of information. If therefore, the adoption agency decided to disclose information to the prospective parents, there would be a duty of care owed to the prospective parents and if the adoption agency failed to take reasonable steps to communicate that information and the prospective parents suffered loss, the agency would be liable).

[40] *Jain v Trent Strategic Health Authority* [2009] A.C. 853 at [28] and [36].

[41] i.e. the Children and Young Persons Act 1969, the Child Care Act 1980 and the Children Act 1989.

appropriate and which might be prejudicial for the child. Further, the relationship between social workers and parents in this situation was frequently one of conflict and the recognition of a duty of care might be expected to lead to costly and often hopeless litigation.[42] The Court of Appeal, however, subsequently held that a duty of care was owed to a child who alleged that there had been negligence in the investigation of allegations of child abuse. The Court of Appeal considered that the policy reasons underlying the earlier decision of the House of Lords had been discredited and could not survive the incorporation of the European Convention on Human Rights where similar factual issues would need to be investigated in relation to alleged breaches of Arts 3 and 8 as would arise if a common law duty of care were imposed.[43] The Court of Appeal accepted that policy considerations dictated that no duty was owed to the parent as the interests of the child may be in conflict with those of the parents and the primary concern of the professionals involved was to ensure the best interests of the child.[44] Even where the courts accept that policy considerations mean that it is not generally fair, just or reasonable to impose a duty of care in one particular situation, the courts may find that those considerations do not apply in other, apparently similar situations. The courts did not, for example, strike out claims for negligence in respect of actions taken once a child has been placed in care as the policy considerations relating to such considerations may be different from those that prevailed in respect of the initial decision on whether to place the child in care. Thus, decisions taken after a child was taken into care, such as placement with unsuitable foster parents or in children's homes might give rise to a duty of care.[45]

15–016   The House of Lords initially held that local education authorities owed no common law duty of care in respect of their statutory powers under the relevant education Acts in identifying and providing for children with special educational needs. The aim of the relevant statute was to provide an administrative machinery to help one disadvantaged section of society. That statute had its own machinery for securing that the statutory purpose was performed. The parents were involved in the decision-making process and could appeal; the number of cases that could be successfully brought would be very small yet if a duty of care were recognised there would be very many hopeless cases requiring expenditure of time and money to defend. It was not therefore appropriate to impose a common law duty of care in respect of the exercise of these statutory powers. The House of Lords,

---

[42]   *X v Bedfordshire CC* [1995] 2 A. C. 633 at [749H]–[751A]. See summary of May LJ in *S. v Gloucestershire CC* [2001] Fam. 313 at [329]–[330].

[43]   *D. v East Berkshire Community Health NHS Trust* [2004] Q.B. 558 at [79]–[85]. This point was not appealed: see *D. v East Berkshire Community Health NHS Trust* [2005] 2 A.C. 373 esp. at [85]–[91]. The Court of Appeal ought not normally to depart from an earlier decision of the House of Lords in reliance on considerations arising out of the Human Rights Act 1998 but that case was exceptionally for a number of reasons: see *Kay v Lambeth LBC* [2006] 2 A.C. 465 at [43]–[45].

[44]   *D. v East Berkshire Community NHS Trust* [2004] 2 W.L.R. 58 at [86]–[87]. The decision was upheld by the House of Lords on appeal: see *D. v East Berkshire Community Health NHS Trust* [2005] 2 A.C. 373.

[45]   *Barrett v Enfield LBC* [2001] 2 A.C. 550 (House of Lords refused to strike out such a claim); *S. v Gloucestershire CC* [2001] Fam. 313 (placement with a foster parent alleged to have abused the child). See also *W. v Essex CC* [2001] 2 A.C. 592 (court refused to strike out claim of negligence by foster parents and their child in respect of a placement with them of a 15-year-old boy being investigated for sexual offences).

however, subsequently took a different view of the policy considerations and left open the question of whether a local education authority could be directly liable in negligence in respect of the exercise of its statutory functions in relation to children with special educational needs.[46] The House noted that teachers and psychologists, as persons exercising a particular skill or profession, would owe common law duties of care for which the authority would be vicariously liable; it would rarely be necessary to invoke a direct claim against a local education authority.

The need to act in the wider public interest may also mean that a decision has to be taken which will be of general public benefit notwithstanding that it involves a risk of foreseeable harm to others. This is true of the modern financial regulatory system operated by governments and others, designed to ensure that financial institutions are creditworthy and are conducting their affairs properly. The Privy Council has refused to impose liability on such financial regulatory bodies. The licensing system is intended to operate in the public interest as a whole. Decisions to register a company or not to revoke a registration may foreseeably cause loss to members of the public who might deposit money with the company. This has to be weighed against the consequences to existing investors if a registration is revoked. The Privy Council considered that[47]: **15–017**

> "... the very nature of the task, with its emphasis on the broader public interest, is one which militates strongly against the imposition of a duty of care being imposed upon such an agency in favour of any particular section of the public."

These cases clearly reflect a reluctance on the part of the courts to impose liability in this area. They must be read against their statutory background. It cannot be concluded that such a public body can never be liable, although liability is likely to be extremely rare. In one case, Saville J. considered that it was not possible to argue that the Bank of England could never owe a duty of care to depositors in banks which it regulated.[48] However, the Bank did not owe a duty to a parent company making a deposit in a subsidiary, since such deposits were expressly excluded from the statutory supervision of the bank. It could not be argued that a common law duty of care was owed to investors whom the Bank were not required to protect. **15–018**

Similar factors have been taken into account by the Official Referee in holding that a local planning authority deciding whether to grant planning permission did not owe a duty of care to the owners of adjacent land.[49] It was foreseeable that a failure to exercise reasonable care might cause loss to adjacent owners. However, the authority was performing a regulatory function and was required to act in the public interest as a whole, and some of its decisions might inevitably have an adverse effect on adjacent owners. These factors militated against imposing liability. **15–019**

---

[46] *Phelps v Hillingdon LBC* [2001] 2 A.C. 550. See also *Carty v Croydon LBC* [2005] 1 W.L.R. 2312 at [36].

[47] *Davis v Radcliffe* [1990] 1 W.L.R. 821 at [827]. See also *Yuen Kun-Yeu v Att-Gen of Hong Kong* [1988] A.C. 175.

[48] *Minories Finances Ltd v Arthur Young* [1989] 2 All E.R. 105.

[49] *Ryeford Homes Ltd v Sevenoaks District Council* [1990] J.P.L. 36.

15–020   The nature of the function being carried out by a public body may also lead the court to the conclusion that there is no sufficient proximity between the public body and the person claiming to have suffered loss and consequently no duty of care. There is, generally, no sufficiently special relationship giving rise to proximity between the emergency services and the public such as to lead to the imposition of a duty of care on the emergency services. The courts have held that there is no duty of care on the fire brigade,[50] the police[51] or the coastguard[52] to respond to emergency calls. There will not, generally, be sufficient proximity even where they attend the scene of an emergency and assume control for dealing with the emergency but fail to do so adequately.[53] There may, however, be sufficient proximity if the emergency services do a positive act which causes a new or additional danger.[54] Different considerations apply to the ambulance service. The nature of those services is more akin to the provision of health services provided to an individual rather than emergency services such as the fire or police services which are intended for the benefit of the public at large. Consequently, where an ambulance was called and the operators accepted the call and indicated that an ambulance was on its way, it was foreseeable that a person would suffer injuries if there were a delay and there was sufficient proximity. The ambulance service did, therefore, owe a duty of care which was breached when there was a 34-minute unexplained delay in the arrival of the ambulance and that delay caused further injuries.[55] Provided that there are no policy reasons making it unfair and unreasonable to impose a duty of care, liability might arise. Generally, there are policy considerations making it inappropriate to impose a duty of care on the police for acts done in the course of the investigation and suppression of crime[56] but not in relation to the fire[57] or ambulance services.[58]

15–021   Even where the courts have indicated that policy considerations mean that it would not, generally, be just and reasonable to impose a duty of care or that there is no proximity, there may still be special circumstances outweighing these considerations.

15–022   In the police and prosecution context, where policy considerations generally negative the imposition of liability, the courts have occasionally recognised that there may circumstances where there is proximity and it is fair and reasonable to impose liability. The precise basis upon which a duty of care arises in these cases is not always clear. In some instances, the court have said that there are other policy considerations which indicate that it may be just and reasonable to impose

---

[50] *Capital and Counties Plc v Hampshire CC* [1997] Q.B. 1004 at [1030A].

[51] *Alexandrou v Oxford* [1993] 4 All E.R. 328. Nor do the police owe a duty to take reasonable steps to protect persons from harm caused by others; the police were not therefore liable for failing to warn road users of hazards created by others: see *Ancell v McDermott* [1993] 4 All E.R. 355.

[52] *OLL v Secretary of State for Transport* [1997] 3 All E.R. 897.

[53] *Capital and Counties Plc v Hampshire CC* [1997] Q.B. 1004 (fire brigade not liable when failed to inspect adjacent premises or when failed to secure adequate water supply).

[54] *Capital and Counties Plc v Hampshire CC* [1997] Q.B. 1004 (fire brigade were liable when they turned off a sprinkler system); *Rigby v Chief Constable of Northamptonshire* [1985] 1 W.L.R. 1242 (police fired CS gas canister without checking if fire engine still present); *Knightley v Johns* [1982] 1 W.L.R. 349 (police at the scene of an action instructed two motorcyclists to drive against the flow of traffic down a tunnel).

[55] *Kent v Griffiths* [2001] Q.B 36.

[56] *Hill v Chief Constable of West Yorkshire Police* [1989] A.C. 53 and see below at para.15–024.

[57] *Capital Counties Plc v Hampshire CC* [1997] Q.B. 1004.

[58] *Kent v Griffiths* [2001] Q.B. 36.

liability.[59] In other cases, it is said that there has been a voluntary assumption of responsibility such as to lead to the imposition of a duty of care.[60]

Practical consequences of imposing liability

The courts may have regard to the consequences of imposing liability in determining whether a duty of care should be imposed. The imposition of liability is intended to lead to a higher standard of care in carrying out certain activities.[61] There may, however, be situations where the imposition of liability on public authorities produces adverse consequences. The House of Lords was concerned, for example, that the imposition of a duty of care on local authorities in respect of the exercise of statutory powers under the child care legislation might lead to local authorities taking an unduly defensive and cautious approach in determining whether or not to place children in care. Furthermore, the relationship between social worker and parent frequently involved conflict and this could breed litigation which would be expensive but hopeless.[62] The Court of Appeal subsequently has held that these considerations were not sufficient to justify excluding a duty of care to the child, although they accepted that there was generally no duty owed to a parent.[63] The Privy Council has observed that the imposition of a duty of care on public bodies to take legal advice before taking a decision might lead to officials being unduly cautious and going to unnecessary lengths to obtain advice: this might cause unnecessary delay. As the number of instances in which liability would be made out would be likely to be small, it might be against the public interest to impose liability, given that that might lead to delay in decision-making in a very great number of cases.[64] The Privy Council did not decide whether such a duty could ever exist as the case could be dealt with on other grounds. The recognition of potential liability might also lead to public bodies refusing to act at the margin of their powers or in cases of any doubt, lest liability be subsequently imposed. It may be in the public interest that decisions be taken in these areas, and any doubts about legality of any individual decision can be resolved by judicial review. More recently, the House of Lords

15–023

---

[59] See, e.g. *Swinney v Chief Constable of Northumbria Police* [1997] Q.B. 464 (arguable that the police owed a duty to take reasonable care to secure information provided in confidence; the need to preserve the sources of information, to protect informants and encourage them to come forward may outweigh the other policy considerations suggesting that no duty of care ought to be imposed). See also *Swinney v Chief Constable of Northumbria Police (No.2), The Times*, May 25, 1999.

[60] *Welsh v Chief Constable of Merseyside* [1993] 1 All E.R. 692 (Crown Prosecution Service voluntarily assumed responsibility for informing the magistrates' court that offences had been taken into consideration by the Crown Court; they failed to do so and the claimant was arrested and imprisoned; duty of care was owed). See also *L v Reading BC* [2001] 1 W.L.R. 1575.

[61] See, e.g. dicta of Lord Clyde in *Phelps v Hillingdon LBC* [2001] 2 A.C. 619 and dicta of Lord Slynn in *Barrett v Enfield London Borough* [2001] 2 A.C. 550.

[62] *X v Bedfordshire CC* [1995] 2 A. C. 633 and see *Phelps v Hillingdon LBC* [2001] A.C. 619 (per Lord Slynn) and see the decision in the House of Lords: *D. v East Berkshire Community Health NHS Trust* [2005] 2 A.C. 373 esp. at [85]–[91].

[63] *D v East Berkshire Community NHS Trust* [2004] Q.B. 558 and see above at para.15–014. The House of Lords affirmed the decision and held there was no duty of care owed to the parents in *D. v East Berkshire Community Health NHS Trust* [2005] 2 A.C. 373 esp. at [85]–[91]. There was no appeal against the finding that a duty of care was owed to the child.

[64] *Rowling v Takaro Properties Ltd* [1988] A.C. 473.

did not accept that such considerations justified refusing to recognise that teachers and other educational professionals owed a duty of care.[65]

15–024   The practical consequences of imposing a duty of care are relevant to the existence and scope of the duty. The House of Lords refused to recognise a duty on the police to take reasonable care in the conduct of criminal investigations into a series of murders to apprehend the perpetrator of the crimes.[66] Such liability could lead to functions being performed in a " ... detrimentally defensive frame of mind." Further, the need to defend such actions might well involve police time, trouble and expense, with a consequent diversion of resources away from the suppression of crime. More recently, the House of Lords has held that there is no duty of care owed by the police to take reasonable steps to prevent threats made by one person against another from being carried out. The House of Lords again considered that imposing such a duty would be likely to have a detrimental effect in that the police might act defensively out of a desire to minimise the risk of legal proceedings and that time and resources would be devoted to meeting claims which would be better directed to their primary duties.[67] For similar reasons, the House of Lords has held the police do not owe a duty of care to take reasonable steps to assess whether a person was a victim of crime and then to afford him protection, support, assistance and treatment or afford protection and assistance and support to a key-witness or to give reasonable weight to the account of a person and act upon it accordingly. Those functions were all inextricably linked with the police function of investigating crime.[68] The Court of Appeal has also taken a similar approach in holding that the Crown Prosecution Service did not owe a duty of care to those it prosecuted.[69] The Court considered that such a duty would have an inhibiting effect on the function of prosecuting crimes and might lead to a defensive approach in some cases with the prosecuting authority acting so as to protect themselves from a negligence claim rather than acting in the best interests of the community as a whole. Further, a great deal of time and resources would need to be expended in order to guard against the risk of negligence actions and this would involve diverting the time and energy of prosecutors away from their function of prosecuting.[70]

Relevance of alternative remedies

15–025   Decisions taken in the exercise of statutory power will be subject to judicial review, and sometimes a statutory right of appeal. Unlawful decisions can be nullified and the individual relieved of the consequences of such a decision. The existence of these remedies is sometimes regarded by the courts as an indicator that no additional remedy in negligence need be provided, particularly where the

---

[65] *Phelps v Hillingdon LBC* [2001] 2 A.C. 619.
[66] *Hill v Chief Constable of West Yorkshire Police* [1989] A.C. 53. See also *Alexandrou v Oxford* [1993] 4 All E.R. 328; *Osman v Ferguson* [1993] 3 All E.R. 344. See also *Ancell v McDermott* [1993] 4 All E.R. 355.
[67] *Chief Constable of the Hertfordshire Police v Van Colle, Smith v Chief Constable of Sussex Police* [2009] 1 A.C. 225 (and for proceedings in the European Court of Human Rights see (2013) 56 EHRR 23).
[68] *Brooks v Commissioner of Police for the Metropolis* [2005] 1 W.L.R. 1495.
[69] *Elgouzouli-Daf v Commissioner of Police of the Metropolis* [1995] Q.B. 355.
[70] [1995] Q.B. 355.

judicial review or appeal is adequate to rectify matters, and the only real damage suffered by the individual is the delay and possibly the expense involved in establishing that a decision is invalid. Where the statutory scheme provides for means of challenging decisions, it may be inconsistent with the statutory scheme to recognise additional common law duties of care.[71]

The existence of alternative remedies has been referred to in a number of **15–026** cases.[72] In *Jones v Department of Employment*,[73] for example, the Court of Appeal considered that the existence of a statutory right of appeal against decisions of an adjudication officer determining eligibility for employment benefit was a factor to be considered in holding that an adjudicator owed no duty of care to a claimant in processing a claim. The Court of Appeal even suggested that, as a general principle and subject to the specific statutory provisions, a public body charged with making payments out of public funds, where there is a statutory right of appeal, owes no common law duty of care to potential recipients of payments. The statutory remedies available, together with judicial review, in cases where the Child Support Agency failed to collect or enforce arrears provided a sufficiently comprehensive system of remedies and lead to the conclusion that no common law duty of care was owed in respect of the assessment and collection of such payments.[74] Similarly, the remedies for the unlawful exercise of statutory duties and powers of the Secretary of State for the Home Department in the immigration field lay in the field of public law and the exercise of those statutory functions did not give rise to a concurrent duty of care giving rise to private law rights to damages.[75] One consideration is the extent to which the system of remedies is comprehensive and caters adequately for the kinds of losses that might arise.[76] In *X v Bedfordshire CC* the House of Lords considered that the statutory complaints procedure and the local government ombudsman were more appropriate remedies for the investigation of maladministration in dealing with children at risk or children with special educational needs than a negligence action.[77] Such remedies may not provide sufficient redress for the loss suffered and may not justify refusing to recognise that a duty of care is owed.[78]

Kind of harm

As a matter of general tort law, the courts will almost always recognise that a **15–027** duty of care is owed in relation to conduct causing physical injury to a person. The courts will also usually find there is potential liability for damage to property. These considerations apply equally to acts done by public bodies exercising

---

[71] *Rowley v Secretary of State for Work and Pensions* [2007] 1 W.L.R. 2861 at [71]–[74].
[72] See, e.g. *Rowling v Takaro Properties Ltd* [1988] A.C. 473; *Calveley v Chief Constable of Merseyside* [1989] A.C. 1228; *Ryeford Homes Ltd v SevenoaksDC* [1990] J.P.L. 30.
[73] [1989] Q.B. 1. But see *R. v HM Treasury Ex p. Petch* [1990] C.O.D. 19.
[74] *Rowley v Secretary of State for Work and Pensions* [2007] 1 W.L.R. 2861 at [73]–[77].
[75] *Mohammed v Home Office* [2011] 1 W.L.R. 2862 at [12] and [18].
[76] *Rowley v Secretary of State for Work and Pensions* [2007] 1 W.L.R. 2861 at [73]–[77].
[77] [1995] A.C. 633 at [751A–B] and [762F–G].
[78] See dicta of Lord Slynn in *Barrett v Enfield LBC* [2001] 2 A.C. 550 doubting that such remedies were as efficacious as imposing a duty of care and providing for damages for breach. See also *Phelps v Hillingdon LBC* [2001] 2 A.C. 619.

statutory powers, where the courts are more inclined to superimpose a common law duty of care if damage to the person or to property is caused.[79]

15–028   Certain types of damage are excluded from the ambit of the duty of care. Economic loss is not generally recoverable in negligence.[80] The courts will rarely impose a duty of care on a public body exercising statutory powers to avoid causing purely economic loss. The House of Lords in *Murphy v Brentwood DC*,[81] held that there was no duty of care on a local authority, exercising statutory powers to ensure compliance with building regulations, to prevent purely economic loss arising. The authority was not therefore liable for any loss incurred in remedying a defect in a building which resulted from the failure to ensure that the building complied with building regulations, since that loss was pure economic loss.

15–029   In the context of statutory powers, judicial review is available to set aside an unlawful decision. Thus, in many instances, the only damage suffered will be the delay and expense in challenging an unlawful decision. This may be classed by the courts as economic loss, and hence be unrecoverable.[82]

Omissions and failure to exercise a power

15–030   The general principle is that a person is not liable for omitting to take an action. There are exceptions where a person is under a duty to act by virtue of his relationship with the claimant, and these are discussed in the next section. There was formerly a distinction between statutory duties and statutory powers. A public body could be liable for failure to perform a duty, but could not be liable for failure to exercise a power.[83] A public body could only be held liable in negligence if it chose to exercise the power and did so negligently. The House of Lords in *Anns v Merton LBC*[84] appeared to change that rule. The House contemplated liability for failure to exercise a power of inspection, not merely for inspecting but doing so negligently. Lord Wilberforce, giving the majority judgment, held that there was no absolute distinction between powers and duties. *Anns* has now been overruled on the grounds that there was no duty of care on the local authority to prevent pure economic loss occurring.[85] The precise implication of the *Anns* judgment for liability for non-feasance or failure to exercise a power

---

[79] See, e.g. *Furber v Krater*, *The Times*, July 21, 1988. (Henry J. refused to strike out a claim in negligence by a mental patient seeking damages for suffering, discomfort and loss of amenity arising from allegedly unnecessarily harsh treatment). On property damage, see, *e.g. Fellowes v Rother DC* [1983] 1 All E.R. 513 (liability for erosion of land in exercise of statutory powers to remove coastal sea defence.)

[80] See *Muirhead v Industrial Tank Specialities Ltd* [1986] Q.B. 507; *Leigh and Sullivan v Aliakmon Shipping Co. Ltd* [1986] A.C. 785; *Simaan General Contracting Co. v Pilkington Glass Ltd (No.2)* [1986] Q.B. 528.

[81] [1990] 3 W.L.R. 414, where the House of Lords formally overruled *Anns v Merton LBC* [1978] A.C. 728.

[82] See dicta in *Calveley v Chief Constable of Merseyside* [1989] A.C. 1228 and *Ryeford Homes Ltd v Sevenoaks DC* [1990] J.P.L. 36.

[83] *Sheppard v Glossop Corp.* [1921] 3 K.B. 132; *East Suffolk Rivers Catchment Board v Kent* [1941] A.C. 74.

[84] [1978] A.C. 728.

[85] *Murphy v Brentwood DC* [1990] 3 W.L.R. 414.

is still uncertain. This aspect of the *Anns* judgment has also been criticised.[86] Lord Bridge said, obiter, in *Curran v Northern Ireland Co-ownership Housing Association* that the judgment obscured the "... important distinction between misfeasance and non-feasance".[87] The decision in *Anns* has also been the subject of further criticism by the House of Lords in *Stovin v Wise*.[88] There, the issue concerned the failure of a local authority to exercise statutory powers[89] which would have enabled them to remove a bank of earth which obscured the view at a road junction. An accident occurred and the issue arose as to whether the authority were liable in negligence for failing to take action to remove the bank. The majority of the House of Lords held that the mere existence of a public power could not of itself justify a conclusion that it was fair, just and reasonable to impose a common law duty of care.[90] The majority of the House of Lords appeared to leave open the question of whether there could ever be liability in negligence for damage sustained by an individual as a result of a failure to exercise power, although they considered that it would only be in very exceptional circumstances, if at all, that the policy of the Act would contemplate compensation being paid for the non-exercise of a power. Liability, if it could arise at all, would only arise if two pre-conditions were satisfied: first that it was irrational (in the public law sense of that word) in the circumstances for the public body not to have exercised the power, so that a public law duty to act had in effect arisen, and secondly, that there were exceptional grounds for holding that the policy of the statute required compensation to be paid to persons who suffered loss because of the failure to exercise the power. The local authority in the present case would not in any event be liable for the loss caused by its failure to exercise its statutory powers. It would not have been acting irrationally if it had decided not to remove the bank. Even assuming that it should have carried out the work, there was nothing to indicate that, exceptionally, the intention underlying the statute was to compensate individuals if they suffered loss because the work was not carried out. The House of Lords has subsequently emphasised that the basis of the ruling in *Stovin v Wise* was that the mere existence of statutory powers could not justify the imposition of a common law duty of care and so no duty was owed in that case rather than any finding that there had been no irrational failure to exercise the duty.[91] The implication is that rarely, if ever,

---

[86] See Smith and Burns, "Donoghue v Stevenson – The Not So Golden Anniversary" (1983) 46 M.L.R. 147; Bowman and Bailey, "Negligence in the Realm of Public Law – A Positive Obligation to Rescue" [1984] P.L. 277, and Craig, "Negligence in the Exercise of a Statutory Power" (1978) 94 L.Q.R. 428.

[87] [1987] A.C. 718 at [724].

[88] [1996] A.C. 923. The position is different if the public authority itself creates the danger, rather than failing to exercise powers to remove it: see *Kane v New Forest DC* [2002] 1 W.L.R. 312 (local planning authority required the construction of a footpath which was dangerous).

[89] Under the Highways Act 1959 s.79.

[90] See *Gorringe v Calderdale MBC* [2004] 1 W.L.R. 1057 explaining the basis of the decision in *Stovin v Wise* [1996] A.C. 923. See also *Sandhar v Department of Transport* [2005] 1 W.L.R. 1632 at [36]–[38].

[91] *Gorringe v Calderdale MBC* [2004] 1 W.L.R. 1057. See also the dicta in *Carty v Croydon LBC* [2005] 1 W.L.R. 2312 at [21] ("a claim in negligence will rarely, if ever, lie where the carelessness relied upon is *merely* the failure to perform the statutory duty").

would the mere omission to exercise a statutory power give rise to liability in negligence as rarely, if ever, would the mere existence of such powers give rise to a duty of care.[92]

15–031   There are, however, circumstances when a duty to act will arise. There may be something in the nature of an assumption of responsibility towards a person, so that failure to do an act which would prevent harm being caused may give rise to actionable negligence. Liability might arise whether the assumption is voluntary, or because statute imposes a duty on public authorities to take responsibility for third parties. The courts have accepted that there is a duty on the police to take reasonable care to prevent a person in custody who was known to be a suicide risk from committing suicide[93] and to pass on information relating to his suicidal tendencies to the prison authorities.[94] Failure to do so constituted actionable negligence on the part of police, and they were held liable when the man subsequently committed suicide. There may also be a duty to take reasonable steps to identify whether or not a prisoner represents a suicide risk.[95]

15–032   The distinction between misfeasance and non-feasance is also difficult to draw on occasions. Some "omissions" are better characterised as a bad way of performing an activity. A motorist who negligently "fails" to stop at a red traffic light is in reality driving badly, not omitting to do an act.

Liability for acts of third parties

15–033   A defendant is not, in general, liable for damage caused by the acts of a third party. There are, however, exceptions to this rule, both in relation to private individuals,[96] and public bodies. There must exist a special relationship between the public body and the person who has caused the harm, such as to make the public body responsible for the acts of that person.

15–034   One situation where such a duty arises is where the public authority exercises control over the acts of the third party. Examples of such a relationship can be found in the criminal justice system, where prison and police officers exercise physical control over those in their custody. In *Dorset Yacht Co. v Home Office*,[97] for example, young offenders escaped from borstal and caused damage to property in the vicinity. The House of Lords held that the prison officers did owe a duty to take reasonable care to prevent the escape, and were negligent in the circumstances in allowing the young offenders to do so. There is also a duty to take reasonable care to ensure the personal safety of those within the prison,

---

[92] See dicta in *Sandhar v Department of Transport* [2005] 1 W.L.R. 1632 at [36]–[38].

[93] *Reeve v Commissioner of Police of the Metropolis* [2000] 1 A.C. 360.

[94] *Kirkham v Chief Constable of the Greater Manchester Police* [1990] 2 Q.B. 283. See also *Clarke v Chief Constable of Northamptonshire Police; The Times*, June 14, 1999 (police owed duty of care to prisoner to inform prison authorities of time spent in police cells and were liable when prisoner detained longer than permitted).

[95] *Orange v Chief Constable of Yorkshire* [2001] 3 W.L.R. 736.

[96] See, e.g. *Smith v Littlewoods Organisation* [1987] A.C. 241.

[97] [1970] A.C. 1004. See also *Writtle (Vicar) v Essex CC* (1979) 77 L.G.R. 656. And see also *Reeve v Commissioner of Police of the Metropolis* [2000] 1 A.C. 360 (duty of police to take reasonable care to stop a prisoner from committing suicide arose from the complete control exercised by the police and the special danger of prisoners taking their own lives).

including inmates.[98] An infant school exercised a sufficient degree of control over its pupils to make them responsible when a child ran out of school and caused a traffic accident.[99]

Liability will not normally be imposed in the absence of control. Thus, the **15–035** police were not liable for the acts of a criminal who had not yet been apprehended.[100] Regulatory bodies may exercise powers of supervision over third parties in a number of areas. The courts have not imposed liability on regulatory bodies in the financial field for the acts of third parties, where the regulatory body did not have control over the day-to-day activities of those third parties, but simply exercised general powers to refuse or revoke authorisation to carry on the activity in question.[101]

Relevance of the European Convention on Human Rights

Article 6 of the European Convention on Human Rights, which guarantees access **15–036** to the courts in cases involving the determination of civil rights, does not guarantee any particular content for those rights. The question of whether a duty of care arises and, in particular, whether it is fair, just and reasonable to recognise such a duty of care in a particular context, are matters for domestic law. The fact that domestic law does not recognise such a duty in a particular context does not involve a breach of Art.6 of the Convention.[102] An individual may, however, be alleging that action taken by a public authority is incompatible with other Convention rights, such as Art.8 and the right to respect for private life. The fact that such issues may need to be canvassed in the courts may lead the courts to conclude that any policy considerations which might otherwise mitigate against recognition of a duty of care may carry less weight[103] particularly as the courts may have to investigate particular matters to determine if there has been a violation of a Convention right. However, the fact the possibility of a claim under the Human Rights Act 1998 might be said to weaken to some extent the reasoning of the decision that the police did not owe a duty of care in respect of their investigation functions, was not a reason for abrogating the common law rule[104] or for developing the common law in a way that reflected the law relating to claims of a breach of a Convention right.[105]

---

[98] *Ellis v Home Office* [1953] 2 Q.B. 135.
[99] *Carmarthenshire CC v Lewis* [1955] A.C. 549.
[100] *Hill v Chief Constable of West Yorkshire* [1989] A.C. 53.
[101] *Yuen Kun-Yeu v Att-Gen of Hong Kong* ([1988] A.C. 175; *Davis v Radcliffe* [1990] 1 W.L.R. 821.
[102] See *TP and KM v United Kingdom* (2002) 34 E.H.R.R. 2 at [92]–[103]; *Z v United Kingdom* (2002) 34 E.H.R.R. 97 at [87]–[103] (effectively, reversing its earlier decision in *Osman v United Kingdom* (2000) 29 E.H.R.R. 245); *Matthews v Ministry of Defence* [2003] 1 A.C. 1163.
[103] See the Court of Appeal decision in *D. v East Berkshire Community NHS Trust* [2004] Q.B. 558 at [79]–[85].
[104] *Chief Constable of the Hertfordshire Police v Van Colle, Smith v Chief Constable of Sussex Police* [2009] 1 A.C. 225 at [137].
[105] *Chief Constable of the Hertfordshire Police v Van Colle, Smith v Chief Constable of Sussex Police* [2009] 1 A.C. 225 esp. at [136]–[139].

Negligent misstatement

15–037   In *Hedley Byrne & Co. Ltd v Heller & Partners Ltd*,[106] the House of Lords recognised that in certain circumstances, a person could be liable for negligent misstatements causing economic loss. Liability exists where there is a special relationship of proximity between the maker of the statement and the plaintiff, which justifies the imposition of liability. The precise circumstances giving rise to the special relationship are still being worked out by the courts. Liability may be imposed where a defendant makes a statement intending the recipient to act upon it. Liability may also be imposed where the defendant knows that the recipient will rely upon it, or knows that it is highly probable that the statement will be shown to some other ascertainable class of persons who will rely on it, and the plaintiff does so rely.[107] Thus, in one case,[108] a local authority acting as mortgagee of property instructed a valuer to prepare a valuation of a house, and the valuer knew that it was highly probable that the purchaser of the house would rely on the valuation report in deciding to proceed with the purchase. The House of Lords held that the valuer owed a duty of care to the purchaser as well as to the local authority mortgagee. This case also makes it clear that a voluntary assumption of responsibility by the defendant is not a prerequisite for liability. The essential question is whether on the facts, there is a special relationship between the parties sufficient to justify the imposition of liability.

15–038   The maker of a statement may make a disclaimer of responsibility. Section 2(2) of the Unfair Contract Terms Act 1977, however, provides that liability cannot be excluded at all in cases of death or personal injury, and in other cases can only be excluded in so far as the disclaimer is reasonable.[109]

15–039   Public bodies may be held liable for negligent misstatements, provided that the necessary elements of this form of the tort of negligence are made out. A government department has been held liable for a negligent statement that an exporter was covered by export credit insurance in the event of default by a foreign company,[110] and a local authority was held liable where it stated that there were no proposals for a subway.[111] Depositors in a deposit-taking company sought to argue that registration of the company by the regulatory authorities amounted to a statement that the company was credit-worthy. The Privy Council held that in the circumstances, the system of financial regulation was not so stringent that a potential depositor could reasonably and justifiably regard registration as a guarantee of the financial soundness of the company. Accordingly, no duty of care was owed in this respect.[112]

15–040   This tort was also used in the Court of Appeal in *Ministry of Housing v Sharp*.[113] The Ministry had registered a planning charge in the local land charges

---

[106] [1964] A.C. 465.

[107] *Caparo Industries Plc v Dickman* [1990] 2 W.L.R. 358.

[108] *Smith v Eric S. Bush* [1990] 1 A.C. 831.

[109] [1990] 1 A.C. 831.

[110] *Culford Metal Industries Ltd v Export Credits Guarantee Department*, *The Times*, March 25, 1981.

[111] *Coats Patons (Retail) Ltd v Birmingham* (1971) 69 L.G.R. 356. See also *Shaddock & Associates Ltd Paramatta City Council* (1980) 150 C.L.R. 225 (public body making a practice of issuing information could be liable).

[112] *Yuen Kun-Yeu v Att-Gen of Hong Kong* [1989] A.C. 175.

[113] [1970] 2 Q.B. 223.

register against particular land. A local authority clerk searched the register and negligently overlooked the charge. The clerk issued a clear certificate to the purchaser of the land. As a result the Ministry were unable to recover the money secured by the charge from the purchaser. The clerk was held liable, applying *Hedley Byrne*, even though the certificate was not relied on by the Ministry. A duty of care was owed to the purchaser who relied on the certificate, and to a person who had registered a charge whom the clerk knew or ought to have known would be injuriously affected by the misstatement. The case has been described as "difficult",[114] and possibly rests on its unique facts relating to the land charges registration system.

Breach, causation and loss

Even assuming a duty of care can be established, a plaintiff must establish that   **15–041**
the defendant was negligent, and so in breach of the duty. The plaintiff must establish that the breach caused the loss. The loss must be of the kind that the law generally recognises as recoverable, and further that it must have been foreseeable in the present case. These requirements are essential ingredients of any successful claim. The same underlying principles apply to all claims in negligence, whether the defendant is a private individual or a public body. Discussion of these principles properly belongs in textbooks on tort and reference should be made to the standard texts on the subject.

Non-justiciable decisions, discretion and the operational-policy distinction

Particular problems occur in seeking to apply the concepts of common law   **15–042**
negligence to the exercise of statutory discretionary power. When the courts are engaged in judicial review, they must take care not to substitute their views for that of the public body responsible for exercising that statutory power. They may consider the legality of a decision and may quash the decision if it is unlawful (in the public law sense of that word). The courts cannot retake the decision instead of the public authority. Constitutional theory and considerations of practicality require that when statute confers power on a body that body is responsible for deciding how it should be exercised. Similarly, the courts must avoid substituting their views for that of the public body by imposing a duty of care on the public body and then concluding that there has been a breach of that duty because they consider that the manner in which the power has been exercised has been negligent.

The courts deal with claims of negligence in the making of decisions in the   **15–043**
exercise of a statutory discretion in the following way. First, it may be clear that the issues concerned are not justiciable and that the courts have no role to play.[115] The courts are unsuited to determining whether liability in negligence should arise in respect of the exercise of statutory discretionary power involving matters of social policy[116] or the making of policy decisions involving the balancing of

---

[114] per Lord Oliver in *Caparo Industries Plc v Dickman* [1990] 2 W.L.R. 358 at [382].

[115] See *A. v Essex CC* [2004] 1 W.L.R. 1881 at [33]; *Carty v Croydon LBC* [2005] 1 W.L.R. 2312 at [20].

[116] *X v Bedfordshire CC* [1995] 2 A.C. 633 at [731F–G].

different public interests[117] or the allocation of resources or the distribution of risks within society.[118] The wider the discretion involved and the greater the policy element, the more likely it is that the claim involves non-justiciable issues unsuitable for judicial resolution in the context of a negligence claim.[119]

15–044 The second issue has been how to apply the law of negligence to the exercise of statutory powers and discretions in a way which does not impinge upon or prevent the lawful exercise of statutory discretions by public authorities. No entirely satisfactory method has been found for accommodating this factor into the framework of the law of negligence. One approach has been to hold that, providing that the actions taken fall within the scope of the discretionary power, no liability can arise as the action taken will then be authorised by statute.[120] Liability arising out the exercise of discretion can only arise if the exercise of discretion is so unreasonable as to be not a real exercise of discretion at all.[121] "Unreasonable" in this sense is not be equated with the act being ultra vires. There will be many instances where the exercise of the power will subsequently transpire to be ultra vires but that does not mean that the exercise of discretion is unreasonable in the sense necessary to attract a potential liability in negligence. A public body may, for example, misconstrue the scope of its statutory powers or take into account an irrelevant consideration or make a procedural error. This does not mean that the public body was at fault or negligent in making this mistake. Public law ultra vires cannot be equated with common law negligence. A local authority decision to restrict the height of proposed buildings, for example, was unlawful because it was based on a misconstruction of the relevant regulations.[122] It was not, however, a negligent decision as the true construction of the regulations involved a difficult question of law on which views could differ and the local authority had taken legal advice before reaching its decision. The concept of an unreasonable exercise of discretion such as might attract potential liability, therefore, involves a decision which is so unreasonable that it is difficult to regard it as a real exercise of the statutory discretion at all.

15–045 The fact that an act falls outside the scope of the statutory discretion and is unreasonable means that it can, but not necessarily will, give rise to common law liability.[123] In addition, a claimant still needs to establish the other elements of a duty of care, namely foreseeability of harm, proximity and it must be fair and reasonable to impose a duty of care in respect of the exercise of the discretion. There may be no proximity or there may be policy considerations which make it unreasonable or unfair to impose a duty of care even where a statutory discretion has been exercised in a wholly unreasonable fashion.

15–046 Consideration has been given as to whether the concern to ensure that authorities are not made subject to liability in negligence for lawful exercises of statutory duties or powers could be dealt with when considering whether the

---

[117] *Barrett v Enfield LBC* [2001] 2 A.C. 550.

[118] *Rowling v Takaro Properties Ltd* [1988] A.C. 473; *X v Bedfordshire CC* [1995] 2 A.C. 663 at [747C] and see *S v Gloucestershire CC* [2001] Fam. 313.

[119] *Carty v Croydon LBC* [2005] 1 W.L.R. 2312 at [21].

[120] *X v Bedfordshire CC* [1995] 2 A.C. 633 1 at [737E–F]; *Barrett v Enfield LBC* [2001] 2 A.C. 550. See also the discussion in *Connors v Surrey CC* [2010] 3 W.L.R. 1302 at [76]–[85] and [103].

[121] *Barrett v Enfield LBC* [2001] 2 A.C. 550. See *A v Essex CC* [2004] 1 W.L.R. 1881 at [36]–[38].

[122] *Dunlop v Wollahara Municipal Council* [1982] A.C. 158.

[123] *X v Bedfordshire CC* [1995] 2 A.C. 633 at [738G–H].

authority had breached any duty of care. The implication is that if the authority had acted in a way that was lawful in public law terms, it would not have acted negligently in private law. Whilst recognising the attraction of such an approach, the courts have not yet held that this approach would be appropriate in the context of the application of the common law of negligence to the exercise of statutory duties and powers.[124] If, however, a duty of care is found to be owed, then the fact that the public authority were involved in making discretionary choices may well be relevant in assessing if the authorities failed to take reasonable care.[125]

The courts have in the past also drawn a distinction between the policy and operational aspects of the exercise of discretion.[126] A decision as to whether or how a particular discretion was to be exercised was a policy decision. The implementation of that decision was seen as an operational decision. The policy-operational distinction has not proved easy to apply in practice and the distinction is increasingly seen "not as a touchstone of liability, but rather is expressive of the need to exclude altogether those cases ... in which the decision ... is of such a kind that the question of whether it has been made negligently is unsuitable for judicial resolution".[127] The policy-operation distinction is therefore simply a guide in deciding whether an issue is justiciable. The greater the policy element, the greater the likelihood that the matter is non-justiciable.[128] Conversely, even if the matter were to be characterised as an operational decision, there is still a need to establish that a duty of care was owed.   **15–047**

The current trend is that, provided the matter is justiciable, public law concepts of ultra vires should not, generally, be imported as a precondition to establishing liability in negligence.[129] It is recognised that the mere fact that a public body has statutory powers or is subject to statutory duties will not of itself be sufficient to justify the imposition of a duty of a care or to lead to a successful claim in negligence.[130] Where, however, a public body acts in the exercise of that statutory function, the mere fact that the act was done in the exercise of a statutory function will not mean that a duty in negligence will not be owed unless the act is unlawful in public law terms. The question will be whether a duty of care is owed in respect of the acts done having regard to policy considerations and factors such as the purpose of the statute, the practical consequences of imposing liability, the kind of harm, the existence of adequate alternative remedies and other relevant circumstances. Consequently, the importance of considering the lawfulness, in public law terms, of the action would be less important than the assessment of the private law issues of whether or not a duty of care is owed.[131]   **15–048**

---

[124] See dicta of Lord Nicholls in *D v East Berkshire Community Health NHS Trust* [2005] 2 A.C.373 at [92]–[94]; *Lawrence v Pembrokeshire CC* [2007] 1 W.L.R. 2991 at [48]–[50].

[125] See dicta of Lord Steyn in *Gorringe v Calderdale MBC* [2004] 1 W.L.R. 1056 at [5] and see *Carty v Croydon LBC* [2005] 1 W.L.R. 2312 at [26]–[28].

[126] *Anns v Merton LBC* [1978] A.C. 728; *Dorset Yacht Co. v Home Office* [1970] 2 A.C. 1004.

[127] per Lord Keith in *Rowling v Takaro Properties Ltd* [1988] A.C. 473 at [501]; see also *Barrett v Enfield LBC*, [2001] 2 A.C. 550.

[128] *Barrett v Enfield LBC* [2001] 2 A.C. 550.

[129] See, e.g. *Barrett v Enfield London Borough* [2001] 2 A.C. 550 per Lord Hutton at [573]; *Phelps v Hillingdon LBC* [2001] 2 A.C. 619; and *Carty v Croydon LBC* [2005] 1 W.L.R. 2312 at [25].

[130] *Gorringe v Calderdale BC* [2004] 1 W.L.R. 1057 at [21]–[26] (explaining the decision in *Stovin v Wise* [1996] A.C. 923); and *Carty v Croydon LBC* [2005] 1 W.L.R. 2312 at [21].

[131] See, e.g. *Carty v Croydon LBC* [2005] 1 W.L.R. 2312 at [28].

Striking out

15–049 A number of the cases dealing with negligence claims against public authorities have arisen in the context of applications to strike out a claim on the grounds that it discloses no reasonable cause of action. In such cases, the court assumes that the facts pleaded are true and hears no evidence. It simply determines whether, as a matter of law, it is arguable that a duty of care arises. That matter is then finally determined at trial after full evidence. Applications to strike out can only succeed where it is clear and obvious that the claim cannot succeed. In developing areas of the law, it is normally inappropriate to proceed on the basis of hypothetical facts and best to await the full hearing and evidence.[132]

15–050 A previous difficulty in the use of the striking out procedure was thought to be the decision of the European Court of Human Rights in *Osman v United Kingdom*.[133] The Court considered that the striking out of a claim amounted to a breach of Art.6 as the court failed to have regard to other public interest considerations indicating that liability in negligence might be appropriate. The Court considered that the rule operated as a blanket immunity preventing the authority being sued which was incompatible with the right of access to a court to determine disputes about civil rights. The practical consequence would have been that cases would not be struck out but the courts would have needed to consider in each individual case, after hearing the evidence, whether the recognition of liability because of policy considerations was justified. The Court has subsequently recognised that its ruling was based on an understanding of the domestic law of negligence which needed to be reviewed.[134] In particular, the question of whether or not it is fair, just and reasonable to recognise a duty of care is an intrinsic element in determining whether any substantive common law right exists and is not a procedural bar or immunity on enforcing a right. As Art.6 does not determine any specific content of the substantive right, it would be open to domestic law to strike out claims if no right existed because no common law duty of care was owed because, having regard to all the competing policy considerations, it was not fair, just or reasonable to recognise such a duty.[135] As a matter of domestic law, the court may be reluctant to strike out claims as disclosing no reasonable cause of action in complex and evolving areas of law. Here is may be preferable to leave the individual facts of the case to be determined at trial so that the development of the law can be based on actual

---

[132] See, e.g. *W v Essex CC* [2001] 2 A.C. 592; *Barrett v Enfield LBC* [2001] 2 A.C. 550; *Waters v Commissioner of Police of the Metropolis* [2000] 1 W.L.R. 1607 and *X v Bedfordshire CC* [1995] A.C. 633 at [740H]–[741D]. See also *Lonrho v Tebbit* [1992] 4 All E.R. 280 (the Secretary of State for Trade and Industry, exercising statutory powers, had required Lonrho to give an undertaking not to acquire more than 30% of Harrods; the court considered that the claimant faced "considerable difficulties" in its claim that the Secretary of State owed a private law duty to take reasonable care in deciding whether to release Lonrho from that undertaking and had been negligent in continuing the undertaking longer than was required but it was inappropriate to strike out the claim).
[133] (2000) 29 E.H.R.R. 245 at [147]–[152].
[134] See *TP and KM v United Kingdom* (2002) 34 E.H.R.R. 2 at [92]–[103]; *Z v United Kingdom* (2002) 34 E.H.R.R. 97 at [87]–[103].
[135] See *D v East Berkshire Community NHS Trust* [2004] Q.B. 558 at [9]–[23].

factual findings[136] although the courts are still prepared to deal with the existence of a duty of care in a strike-out application where it is unlikely that further facts would be found at trial[137] or where the courts are satisfied that, assuming all the facts alleged by the claimant are true, the claim must necessarily fail for other reasons.[138]

Summary judgment

The courts may also entertain an application for summary judgment dismissing the claim in addition to, or instead of, an application to strike out the claim.[139] Such applications will only succeed in cases where a strike out application would not succeed if the court were satisfied that all substantial facts relevant to the allegations were before the court and the facts were undisputed or where there were no realistic prospects of disputing them or of oral evidence affecting the court's assessment of the facts. There may be cases where there are gaps in the evidence but the court may conclude that there is no prospect of the gaps being filled (this may be particularly true in cases involving the treatment of children in the social services or education field as such claims may be brought years after the event as the time-limit for bringing claims does not expire until the claimant is 21 years old). Secondly, the court would need to be satisfied that there was no real prospect of the negligence claim succeeding and no reason why it should go to trial rather than being dealt with summarily.[140] There have been instances of summary judgment being given but in general, the circumstances in which such a course will be appropriate are likely to be rare.

15–051

Nuisance

A public body, like a private individual, may be liable for damages if its acts constitute actionable nuisance.[141] If, however, an act is expressly or implied authorised by statute, there is no liability for any loss that is caused as the inevitable result of doing the authorised act.[142] This principle was reaffirmed by the House of Lords in *Allen v Gulf Oil Refining Ltd.*[143] A private Act of Parliament expressly authorised the construction of an oil refinery. The House of Lords held that the Act also authorised the operation of the refinery. No action lay

15–052

---

[136] See, e.g. *Barrett v Enfield LBC* [2001] 2 A.C. 550; *W v Essex CC* [2001] 2 A.C. 592; *Waters v Commissioner of Police of the Metropolis* [2001] 1 W.L.R. 1607; *Brooks v Commissioner of Police of the Metropolis* [2005] 1 W.L.R. 1495 at [4].

[137] *Rowley v Secretary of State for Work and Pensions* [2007] 1 W.L.R. 2861 at [21]–[25].

[138] [2007] 1 W.L.R. 2861 at [21]–[25]. See also, e.g. *Chief Constable of the Hertfordshire Police v Van Colle, Smith v Chief Constable of Sussex Police* [2009] 1. A.C. 225 (House of Lords considered whether the policy considerations recognised as militating against the imposition of a common law duty of care in respect of policing functions remained valid).

[139] *S v Gloucestershire CC* [2001] Fam. 313. See e.g. *D v East Berkshire Community Health NHS Trust* [2005] 2 A.C. 373.

[140] In *S v Gloucestershire CC* [2001] Fam. 313, summary judgment was given dismissing the appeal in one case but the Court of Appeal declined to strike out or give summary judgment on the other claim.

[141] [1995] 2 A.C. 633 and see, e.g. *L.E. Jones (Insurance Brokers) Ltd v Portsmouth City Council* [2003] 1 W.L.R. 427.

[142] See, e.g. *Hammersmith and City Railway Co. v Brand* (1869) L.R. 4 H.L. 171.

[143] [1981] A.C. 1001.

for any nuisance such as smell, noise or vibration, which was the inevitable result of constructing or operating the refinery.

15–053 Much depends on the interpretation given to "inevitable". This is ultimately a question of construing the statute in question to see precisely what was authorised. The courts have distinguished between statutes which authorise a specific undertaking and those which confer permissive powers to do an act, but leave the choice of site and method to the body concerned. In the latter cases, the presumption is that parliament intends the powers to be exercised in a way that does not interfere with private rights.[144] The donee of the power must therefore choose a site or a method of operating which does not create a nuisance. In one leading case,[145] statute conferred power to build hospitals in London but did not specify any particular sites. The hospital authority was therefore liable in nuisance when it decided to site a smallpox hospital in Hampstead, as the creation of the nuisance was not specifically authorised. This approach has been criticised as imposing liability on a fortuitous basis and as inappropriate to modern legislation, which is frequently framed in permissive terms.[146] The courts have shown no inclination to alter the established legal position.

15–054 A public body whose actions constitute a nuisance will not be able to rely upon the defence of statutory authority if it fails to exercise due diligence or is negligent in the sense of carelessness or failing to act with all reasonable care and regard for the rights of others (not its special common law sense of breach of a duty of care).[147] Statutory provisions may also deal specifically with the question of liability. In the case of acts done in the performance of a duty, a body will not be liable in the absence of negligence (in the sense described above) even if the statute expressly makes the body liable for nuisance or states it is not exempt from liability.[148] In the case of acts done in the exercise of statutory powers, a body will be liable in nuisance, even if it is not negligent, if statute expressly makes it liable or states it is not exempt from liability.[149] In other words, the courts will not construe statutes as imposing liability for acts done in the performance of duties, but will normally do so in the case of powers where the body has a choice as to whether to act, and knows that it may incur liability in nuisance if it does.[150]

15–055 If the act is not authorised by statute, then the public body may be liable for nuisance in the ordinary way. Public bodies have, for example, been held liable for discharging effluent into a stream (even though this was the only reasonable course of action open to them in the circumstances)[151]; allowing trees to cause subsidence to a neighbouring house,[152] and even for failing to remove gypsies from its land.[153] In all these cases, there was no statutory authority for doing the act that gave rise to nuisance.

---

[144] [1981] A.C. 1001.

[145] *Metropolitan Asylum District Managers v Hill* (1881) 6 App.Cas. 193.

[146] Craig, *Administrative Law*, 7th edn.

[147] *X v Bedfordshire CC* [1995] 2 A.C. 633 at [732D]–[733F] and *Allen v Gulf Oil Refining Ltd*, above, fn.14.

[148] *Department of Transport v North West Water Authority* [1984] A.C. 336.

[149] [1984] A.C. 336.

[150] But see *Dunne v North Western Gas Board* [1964] 2 Q.B. 806.

[151] *Pride of Derby and Derbyshire Angling Association v British Celanese Ltd* [1953] Ch. 149.

[152] *Russell v Barnet LBC* (1984) 93 L.G.R. 152.

[153] *Page Motors Ltd v Epsom BC* (1981) 80 L.G.R. 337.

The courts will not, however, recognise a cause of action in nuisance if that would be inconsistent with a statutory scheme.[154] Thus, the House of Lords held that a statutory sewerage undertaker was not liable in nuisance for flooding caused by overloaded sewers. A statutory scheme had been created imposing duties on the sewerage undertakers to provide an adequate system of sewers with an independent regulator who had powers to enforce those duties. It would run counter to that statutory scheme to recognise a parallel cause of action in nuisance.[155]

15–056

The rule in Rylands v Fletcher

The rule in *Rylands v Fletcher* provides that where a "person who for his own purpose brings on his lands and collects and keeps there anything likely to do mischief if it escapes, must keep it in at his peril . . . and is prima facie answerable for all the damage which is the natural consequence of its escape".[156] The rule only applies to a non-natural use of land. The rule imposes strict liability on the defendant or a person who creates situations of special danger. There is no need to prove negligence (in the sense of carelessness) on the part of the defendant.

15–057

There is doubt as to whether the rule applies to public bodies. The Court of Appeal has pointed out that public bodies act for the general public benefit not for their own purposes, and for that reason the rule may be inapplicable.[157] The courts have left open the question of whether local authorities (and presumably other public bodies) were in principle subject to the rule. The point could have been argued in a first instance decision of Taylor J.[158] The police fired a gas canister into a shop where a criminal had taken refuge. Taylor J. did not consider the issue of whether the activities of a public body such as the police were outside the rule altogether. He doubted whether the rule applied to an intentional release of a thing (he considered trespass, rather than the rule in *Rylands v Fletcher*, was the appropriate basis of liability). In the event, he held that a defence of necessity existed, and that the defence had been made out. The modern trend is, however, clearly against the imposition of strict liability in common law, particular in relation to public bodies exercising public powers.

15–058

A public body performing a statutory duty or exercising statutory powers may also be able to plead statutory authority for its acts. Thus, there was no liability under *Rylands v Fletcher* for the discharge of gas or water, where statute expressly authorised the provision of supply of gas and water and clearly

15–059

---

[154] *Marcic v Thames Water Utilities Ltd* [2004] 2 A.C. 42; *Barratt Homes Ltd. v Dwr Cymru Cyfyngedig (No.2)* [2013] 1 W.L.R. 3486.
[155] [2004] 2 A.C. 4 at [35] and [82]–[85].
[156] per Blackburn J. (1866) 1 Ex. 265 at [279]; affd. by the House of Lords (1868) L.R. 3 H.L. 330.
[157] *Dunne v North Western Gas Board* [1964] 2 Q.B. 806. But see *Smeaton v Ilford Corp.* [1954] Ch. 450 (no justification for treating local authorities differently although point left open), and *Pearson v North Western Gas Board* [1968] 2 All E.R. 669 where Rees J. considered the House of Lords might take a different view. The House of Lords has, however, held that the rule in *Rylands v Fletcher* does not form part of Scottish law: *RHM Bakeries (Scotland) Ltd v Strathclyde Regional Council* [1985] S.L.T. 214, suggesting, perhaps, a reluctance to accept strict liability. See also *Charing Cross Electricity Supply Co. v Hydraulic Power Co.* [1914] 3 K.B. 772.
[158] *Rigby v Chief Constable of Northamptonshire* [1985] 1 W.L.R. 1242.

contemplated the risk of escape.[159] In such circumstances, it is necessary to establish negligence. Statute may deal specifically with the question of liability as it has, for example, in relation to water,[160] and nuclear installations.[161]

Breach of statutory duty

Introduction

15–060   A breach of a statutory duty may give rise to a civil action for damages by a person who has suffered harm as the result of that breach. Not all statutory duties give rise to a right to damages. One of the more difficult and unsatisfactory areas of tort law is that concerned with determining whether a particular statutory duty is remediable in damages.[162] In principle, the question is whether, as a matter of statutory construction, Parliament intended to confer a right to sue for damages in the event of a breach of the duty imposed by the statute.[163] The central question is whether, from the provisions and structure of the statute, an intention can be discerned to create a private law remedy in damages.[164] In considering that question, relevant considerations include "the object and scope of the provisions, the class (if any) intended to be protected by them, and the means of redress open to a member of such a class if the statutory duty is not performed".[165]

15–061   Modern statutes frequently deal specifically with the question of civil liability. The statutes privatising various state-owned entities have, for example, dealt specifically with liability for breach of the duties imposed on the privatised companies.[166] Great difficulties can arise when statute is silent on the question of liability. Statute may provide little or no indication as to whether an action for damages should be available. The courts have in the past sought to deal with this problem by developing various presumptions to assist in determining whether a civil action exists. However, these presumptions are not conclusive, and they often give way to other conflicting considerations.[167] For these reasons,

---

[159] *Dunne v North Western Gas Board* [1964] 2 Q.B. 806. Although the gas industry has now been privatised, public gas suppliers operate under statutory duties very similar in terms to those under which this case was decided: see the Gas Act 1986 ss.9 and 10. See also *Green v Chelsea Waterworks Co.* (1894) 70 L.T. 547; *Dunn v Birmingham Canal Co.* (1872) L.R. 8 Q.B. 42.

[160] See, formerly, Water Act 1981 s.6 imposing strict liability for escapes.

[161] Nuclear Installations Act 1965 s.12 (as amended).

[162] See, generally, Clerk and Lindsell, *Torts*; Stanton, *Breach of Statutory Duty*; Harding, *Public Duties and Public Law* (1989) Ch.7; Winfield and Jolowicz, *Tort*; Harlow, *Compensation and Government Torts* (1982); Buckley, "Liability for Breach of Statutory Duty in Tort" (1984) 100 L.Q.R. 204.

[163] *R. v Deputy Governor of Parkhurst Prison Ex p. Hague* [1992] 1 A.C. 58; *X v Bedfordshire CC* [1995] 2 A.C. 633 at [731]; *Cullen v Chief Constable* [2003] 1 W.L.R. 1763.

[164] See per Lord Steyn in *Gorringe v Calderdale MBC* [2004] 1 W.L.R. 1056 at [3]; *Carty v Croydon LBC* [2005] 1 W.L.R. 2312 at [21].

[165] per Bingham L.C.J. in *Olotu v Home Office* [1997] 1 W.L.R. 328 at [336F–H].

[166] See, e.g. Gas Act 1986 s.22; Electricity Act 1989 s.27.

[167] See, generally, Williams, "The Effect of Penal Legislation in the Law of Tort" (1960) 23 M.L.R. 233.

commentators,[168] and some judges[169] doubt the utility of seeking any parliamentary intent, and regard the question as ultimately a matter of judicial discretion.

Nevertheless, the courts continue to justify their conclusion as to whether or not liability should be imposed, by reference to the presumed intent of Parliament. The presumptions are still referred to in the judgments. It is unclear as to what extent these presumptions are used as a prescriptive guide in deciding whether liability should be imposed or as an ex post facto rationalisation for a conclusion, reached on other unarticulated grounds, that liability should or should not be imposed. The task of the courts might therefore be described as deciding whether liability should be imposed, bearing in mind the need to give effect so far as possible to the overall policy of the statute and bearing in mind the considerations (or presumptions) articulated in previous case law, together with any further specific or general considerations that may be relevant.

15–062

Liability for breach of statutory duty may be imposed on public bodies in two types of cases. First, statute may be seeking to regulate an activity carried on by both private individuals and public bodies. In this area, the general principles governing breach of statutory duty apply, and the identity of the defendant is irrelevant to the question of liability. Industrial safety legislation, for example, may apply to both private individuals and statutory corporations. The fact that a body is a statutory corporation is not relevant to the question of liability for breach, and the ordinary principles of liability apply. Statute may also impose duties on public bodies alone. These may be essentially public law duties enforceable by way of judicial review, in particular by a mandatory order, by a person with sufficient interest. However, it may be that certain statutory duties also impose private law liability in damages for breach. The principles governing liability may need modification or additional considerations may need to be taken into account in determining whether a remedy in damages should be available for breach of a public law duty. Public law duties vary in nature. Statute may impose general duties to provide services or benefits. General duties in the field of social welfare[170] or education[171] have been held to be public law duties, enforceable by way of judicial review. Other duties may regulate in detail specific administrative functions which again may be enforceable by way of judicial review or other remedies and do not give rise to a private law action in damages. The current trend appears to be against the imposition of civil liability for breach of a duty imposed solely on a public body, although there are notable exceptions to this modern trend. The following factors are relevant in determining whether damages are available for breach of a statutory duty.

15–063

---

[168] (1960) 23 M.L.R. 233.

[169] Notably, Lord Denning M.R. See, e.g. *Ex p. Island Records Ltd* [1978] Ch. 122 at [135] ("... the dividing line ... is so blurred and ill-defined that you might as well toss a coin to decide it").

[170] *O'Rourke v Camden LBC* [1988] A.C. 188 (duties to provide housing for the homeless did not give rise to a private law action in damages); *X v Bedfordshire CC* [1995] 2 A.C. 633.

[171] *Phelps v Hillingdon London Borough* [2001] 2 A.C. 619 (duties to make special educational provision for children with special educational needs did not give rise to a private law action in damages).

Relevance of alternative remedies

15–064   Statute may create a duty and specifically provide a means of enforcing the duty, whether by way of criminal penalty or administrative remedy. The existence of an alternative remedy points against the imposition of ordinary civil liability in damages, although there are exceptions to this principle where is it clear that Parliament intends to confer protection on a particular class of persons and to make the duty enforceable by an action for damages, as is the case with duties imposed upon employers to ensure safe working premises for their employees.[172] In the words of Lord Tenterden C.J.[173]:

> "... where an Act creates an obligation, and enforces the performance in a specified manner, we take it to be a general rule that performance cannot be enforced in any other manner. If an obligation is created, but no mode of enforcing its performance is ordained, the common law may in general find a mode suited to the particular nature of the case."

Default powers and administrative remedies

15–065   Default powers and other administrative remedies are of particular relevance to public law duties. Statute may impose duties on local authorities or other public bodies to provide services or benefits. In the event of a failure to perform these duties, another body, usually central government ministers or in Wales, the National Assembly[174] may be given powers to declare the body in default. The minister may be empowered to take over the functions himself or to give directions instructing the authority to do certain acts, and such directions may be enforceable by mandamus. Statute may sometimes specifically provide that mandamus shall be available to enforce a particular duty.[175] Statute may create individual rights of appeal against decisions, as in the education field where parents have a right to appeal to a statutory tribunal against local education authority decisions on the provision of education for children with special educational needs.[176]

15–066   The courts have generally regarded the presence of such remedies as excluding the possibility of an action for damages for breach of statutory duty.[177] Early authorities went so far as to hold that the existence of alternative

---

[172] *Groves v Wimbourne* [1898] 2 Q.B. 402.

[173] *Doe d. Murray v Bridges* (1831) 1 B. & Ad. 847 at [849] and see *Cutler v Wandsworth Stadium Ltd* [1949] A.C. 398 and *X v Bedfordshire CC* above, fn.1 at [731F–G].

[174] The functions of the Secretary of State for Wales, including the exercise of default powers, have been transferred to the Welsh Ministers.

[175] See above at para.6–061.

[176] As discussed in *X v Bedfordshire CC* [1995] 2 A.C. 633 at [769G–H] (the existence of such rights was seen as an indicator that Parliament did not additionally intend to confer a right to sue for damages for breach of the statutory duties governing the assessment of children with special educational needs).

[177] See, e.g. *X v Bedfordshire CC* [1995] 2 A.C. 663 at [769F–G]; *R. v Inner London Education Authority Ex p. Ali and Murshid* [1990] C.O.D. 317: *Watt v Kesteven CC* [1955] 1 Q.B. 408 and *Wood v Ealing LBC* [1966] 3 All E.R. 514 (duty in Education Act 1944 s.8 to provide schools remediable by complaint to minister under s.99); *Wyatt v Hillingdon LBC* (1978) 76 L.G.R. 727 (duty in Chronically Sick and Disabled Act 1970 s.2(1) remediable by complaint under National Assistance Act 1948 s.36). See also *Williams v Southwark LBC* [1971] 1 Ch. 734 and cases in fn.179 below.

administrative remedies excluded both private law actions for damages for breach and also the public law remedies, notably a mandatory order, available on an application for judicial review to compel performance of the public law duty.[178] The modern case law tends to adopt the view that such administrative remedies do not exclude the judicial review jurisdiction (although it is a factor relevant to the discretion to refuse a remedy), but that they do exclude an ordinary civil action for damages.[179]

The courts have sometimes allowed actions in damages even where alternative administrative remedies exist. These are largely cases where the administrative remedy would be inadequate. In *Reffell v Surrey CC*,[180] the court held that the duty to ensure that school premises conformed to certain standards gave rise to an action for damages, where a child was injured as a result of putting her hand through a glass plate which was not of the required thickness. A complaint to a minister would not be an adequate remedy in the circumstances.

15–067

Alternative means of enforcement and the availability of judicial review

Another issue concerns the relevance of public law remedies to compel performance of a public duty in determining the availability of a civil action. Authority establishes that where statute provides a specific remedy, civil liability generally does not lie, and conversely that where statute does not provide a specific remedy liability should be presumed.[181]

15–068

Statutory duties imposed upon public bodies are enforceable by way of judicial review even though no specific statutory remedy is provided. The presumption that civil liability is necessary in the absence of a specific statutory remedy is intended to ensure that the statute does not become a "pious aspiration".[182] In cases of public law duties, there is often little risk of this occurring, given the common law supervisory jurisdiction of the courts exercised by way of judicial review. There is the possibility of an appropriate public law remedy to enforce the duty. The general trend of the modern case law is to regard the fact that a breach of a duty imposed upon a public body can be adequately remedied by judicial review as a pointer that Parliament did not intend the duty to be enforceable by way of a civil action in damages. Thus, the duty to bring a prisoner to court[183] or to allow access to a solicitor[184] was enforceable by way of judicial review and did not give rise to private law remedies. Many statutory duties, for example, involve the provision of services or the conferment of benefits on sections of the public as part of a scheme of social welfare. In addition, such statutes tend to make the existence of a duty dependent upon the exercise of discretion or the judgment, often in difficult areas, of public

15–069

---

[178] *Pasmore v Ostwaldtwistle UDC* [1898] A.C. 387.

[179] *R. v Secretary of State for the Environment Ex p. Ward* [1984] 1 W.L.R. 834 and *R. v Secretary of State for the Environment Ex p. Lee* (1987) 54 P. & C.R. 311 (distinguishing *Kensington and Chelsea LBC v Wells* (1973) 72 L.G.R. 289 on this point—dealing with duty to provide accommodation for gipsies in Caravan Sites and Control of Development Act 1960 s.6.)

[180] [1964] 1 W.L.R. 358.

[181] *Doe d. Murray v Bridges* (1831) 1 B. & Ad. 847; *Cutler v Wandsworth Stadium Ltd* [1949] A.C. 398.

[182] per Lord Simmonds in *Cutler v Wandsworth Stadium Ltd* [1949] A.C. 398 at [407].

[183] *Olotu v Home Office* [1997] 1 W.L.R. 328.

[184] *Cullen v Chief Constable of Royal Ulster Constabulary* [2003] 1 W.L.R. 1763.

authorities. In such cases, it is unlikely that Parliament intended to give rise to an obligation to pay damages in the event of errors of judgment. The statutory functions of local education authorities in respect of children with special educational needs conferred discretionary powers or imposed administrative duties in an area of social welfare; although intended to benefit particular groups of children, the duties imposed were part of the general structure governing the education of children and were intended to be enforced by way of appeals to the specialist tribunals and judicial review not claims for damages.[185] The duties owed in relation to homeless persons were part of a scheme of welfare policy intended to confer benefits at public expense on grounds of public policy. Control by the public law remedies is generally regarded as more appropriate.[186]

15–070   Even in the case of public law duties owed to individuals, the fact that judicial review would be an adequate remedy to ensure compliance with the duty may indicate that the duty does not give rise to a private law action for damages. In *Calveley v Chief Constable of Merseyside*,[187] a constable sued for damages, for breach of a duty to give him adequate notice of disciplinary charges. The disciplinary decision had previously been quashed in judicial review proceedings. The House of Lords rejected the claim. Their Lordships accepted that the obligation was imposed for the benefit of a particular individual. Nevertheless, the purpose of the obligation was to ensure that disciplinary proceedings were properly conducted, not to provide damages in the event of a failure to comply with the duty. That aim could be achieved by judicial review to set aside the decision and nullify its consequence. It was not necessary to provide a civil remedy to achieve the purposes of the statute.

15–071   There are situations where judicial review will not be adequate. A breach of a statutory duty causing physical harm to the individual cannot be rectified by judicial review. It is not then a question of nullifying decisions taken in contravention of statute, or compelling performance of a duty. If the purpose of the statute was to prevent such harm, the courts are more likely to lean in favour of imposing liability.[188]

Obligations imposed for a defined class of persons

15–072   Statutory obligations may be imposed for the benefit of the public generally. If so, they will not normally give rise to a civil action on the part of any individual. Conversely, a statutory obligation may be imposed for the benefit or protection of a defined and limited class of people. This factor, particularly if there is no other adequate remedy for enforcing the duty, may be an indication that Parliament intended the duty to be enforceable by way of an action for damages.[189]

15–073   This consideration is relevant to public law duties, particularly those statutes imposing wide general duties to provide services or benefit. Even though specific groups of individuals may benefit from the duty, the duty may be seen as enacted

---

[185]   *Phelps v Hillingdon LBC* [2001] 2 A.C. 619.
[186]   *O'Rourke v Camden LBC* [1998] A.C. 188 at [194B–E].
[187]   [1989] A.C. 1228.
[188]   *Reffell v Surrey CC* [1964] 1 W.L.R. 358.
[189]   See, e.g. *Ministry of Housing and Local Government v Sharp* [1970] 2 Q.B. 223; *Garden Cottage Foods v Milk Marketing Board* [1984] A.C. 130 and *X (Minors) v Bedfordshire CC* [1995] 2 A.C. 633 at [731]–[732].

for the public generally, and so not giving rise to a civil action on the part of any individual affected by a breach of the duty.[190] The House of Lords has held that the duty to provide adequate schools was intended to benefit the public generally not individual litigants[191] and similarly duties owed to children with special educational needs were part of the overall structure of educational provision and did not give rise to a claim for damages on the part of the individual children concerned.[192] The Divisional Court similarly considered that a statute designed to confer welfare benefits was not by its nature such as to give rise to individual rights of action for damages. A plaintiff could not, therefore, recover damages for an alleged breach of statutory duties to provide home help imposed by s.2 of the Chronically Sick and Disabled Persons Act 1970.[193] The House of Lords has held that the duties owed to provide housing to the homeless are imposed not merely for the benefit of the homeless but for the general public interest.[194] Such duties are not enforceable by way of an action for damages.[195]

Underlying the reluctance of the courts to impose civil liability in such cases is   **15–074** concern to prevent potentially widespread liability on the part of public authorities. Given the availability of adequate alternative remedies, there is much to be said for not imposing civil liability. In cases involving personal injury where judicial review or administrative remedies would not be adequate, the courts have indicated their willingness to impose civil liability.[196] The courts are also sensitive to the fact that such duties may involve large elements of discretion, particular in relation to the allocation of resources or determination of priorities.[197] If the courts were to impose civil liability for breach, they might be unduly drawn into substituting their views on such questions for those of the authorities. A similar attitude can be seen in relation to the superimposition of common law duties of care in negligence on the exercises of statutory powers. The courts accept that liability may have to be excluded in respect of certain types of administrative decision for this reason.[198]

Even if a duty is imposed for the benefit of a particular individual, that does   **15–075** not mean that it was intended that liability for damages should be imposed for breach. In each case, the question is whether the legislature intended a breach of duty to give rise to a private law right to damages.[199] That will depend on the nature and purpose of the statute.[200] Other factors, such as the availability of judicial review or other specific statutory remedies, may lead the courts to

---

[190] See, generally, *O'Rourke v Camden LBC* [1988] A.C. 188 [1988] A.C. 188 at [193C]–[194B].

[191] See, *X v Bedfordshire CC* [1995] 2 A. C. 633 at [768A]–[769H]; *R. v Inner London Education Authority Ex p. Ali and Murshid* [1990] C.O.D. 317.

[192] *Phelps v Hillingdon LBC* [2001] 2 A.C. 619.

[193] *Waytt v Hillingdon LBC* (1978) 76 L.G.R. 727.

[194] *O'Rourke v Camden* [1988] A.C. 188 (overruling *Thornton v Kirklees Borough Metropolitan Council* [1979] Q.B. 626).

[195] *O'Rourke v Camden* [1988] A.C. 188 (overruling *Thornton v Kirklees Borough Metropolitan Council* [1979] Q.B. 626).

[196] *Reffell v Surrey CC* [1964] 1 W.L.R. 358.

[197] See, e.g. *X v Bedfordshire CC* [1995] 2 A.C. 633 at 769D–H; *O'Rourke v Camden LBC* [1988] A.C. 188.

[198] *Rowling v Takaro Properties Ltd* [1988] A.C. 473 and see paras 15–042 to 15–048.

[199] See *R. v Deputy Governor of Parkhurst Prison Ex p. Hague* [1992] 1 A.C. 58.

[200] [1992] 1 A.C. 58 (duties in field of health and safety at work different from duties under the Prison Act 1952).

conclude that no civil liability need be imposed.[201] In the context of public law duties, it may be more appropriate to regard the fact that the duty is imposed for the public generally as a reason for excluding liability, rather than regarding the fact that a duty is imposed for the benefit of individuals as a reason for concluding that liability should be imposed. The fact that the performance of the statutory duty involves the exercise of a substantial amount of discretion is often treated as an indication that the act was not intended to give rise to liability in damages. The duties under the child care legislation were, for example, primarily intended to protect children but the duties required the exercise of a large amount of judgment by the social services authorities in a difficult field; that was not consistent with any intention by Parliament to make the authorities liable in damages if the decisions taken subsequently proved to be inconsistent with the relevant statutory duty.[202] The purpose of a statute may not be to protect individuals against loss. The duties under the Prison Act 1952 and the regulations made under that act, for example, were intended to provide a framework within which the prison regime was intended to operate but were not intended to protect prisoners against loss or injury. Segregation of an individual prisoner, even if done in breach of the relevant regulations, was not therefore intended to give rise to a right to compensation.[203]

15–076   The approach based on the class of people affected by a statutory duty has been criticised, not least because it is difficult to predict what precisely constitutes a defined class, and because it can lead to arbitrary results.[204] In *Read v Croydon Corporation*,[205] for example, Stable J. held that a duty to provide a wholesome water supply was owed to ratepayers only, since they were the class of people entitled to demand the supply. Thus, the daughter of a ratepayer had no cause of action when the water supply became affected with typhoid and she contracted the disease and died. Her father who did not contract the disease did, as a ratepayer, have a cause of action and could recover for the loss caused by the death of his daughter.

Non-feasance and highways

15–077   In the context of duties to repair the highway, the common law drew a distinction between misfeasance and non-feasance. Liability in damages could exist in the former case but not the latter.[206] The immunity from liability for non-feasance has been abolished by statute.[207] The highway authority is now under a statutory duty

---

[201] See, e.g. *Cullen v Chief Constable of the Royal Ulster Constabulary* [2003] 1 W.L.R. 1763 (judicial review adequate to enforce right of access to a lawyer); *Olotu v Home Office* [1997] 1 W.L.R. 328 (judicial review and opportunity to apply for bail were appropriate methods of ensuring compliance with the provision imposing a maximum limit on the time spent in custody); *Calveley v Chief Constable of Merseyside* [1989] A.C. 1228 discussed above at para.15–070.

[202] *X v Bedfordshire CC* [1995] 2 A.C. 633 at 747C–748B. See also *O'Rourke v Camden LBC* [1988] A.C. 188.

[203] *R. v Deputy Governor of Parkhurst Prison Ex p. Hague* [1992] 1 A.C. 58.

[204] See Harding, *Public Duties and Public Law* (1989), pp.236–238.

[205] [1938] 4 All E.R. 631.

[206] Harding, *Public Duties and Public Law* (1989), pp.239–245.

[207] By the Highways (Miscellaneous Provisions) Act 1961 s.1.

to maintain the highway[208] and breach of this duty gives rise to a civil action in damages for personal injury or damage to property resulting from an accident but not for purely economic loss.[209] Highway authorities have a statutory defence if they can demonstrate that they took reasonable care in the circumstances.[210] Other duties in the Highways Act 1981, such as the duty to prevent obstructions of the highway do not give rise to a right to damages in the event of a breach.[211] The distinction between misfeasance and non-feasance has not been applied in other areas.[212]

Conditions of liability

Even if a statutory duty is capable of giving rise to liability, the other conditions of liability need to be established. Damages are intended to compensate a person for the loss or damage suffered as a result of a breach. Thus, where a breach of a particular duty, such as the obligation to allow an individual access to a lawyer, would cause an individual no personal injury, injury to property or economic loss, it is unlikely that a private law right to claim damages was intended.[213] Furthermore, the injury suffered must be the kind of injury which the statute was intended to guard against. In *Gorris v Scott*,[214] for example, there was a duty to provide pens for animals aboard a ship. The ship owner failed to do so, and animals were swept overboard. The plaintiff was unable to recover as the statute was intended to reduce the risk of disease, not to guard against animals being lost at sea. The statutory duty to repair the highway is intended to provide a remedy for personal injury and damage to property; it is not intended to compensate for economic loss consisting of the loss of profit to a farmer who was not able to have his milk collected as the tanker taking the milk away could not use the road due to non-repair.[215]   **15–078**

The defendant must be in breach of the statutory obligation. This involves determining precisely what duty was owed. In particular, it may be necessary to decide whether the duty was an absolute duty, so that a failure to achieve the state of affairs prescribed by the statute constitutes a breach. In other cases, the duty may be a duty to exercise due diligence or take reasonable steps to bring about the specified state of affairs.[216] The breach of duty must have caused the damage. In addition, a defence based on consent (except in cases involving duties placed   **15–079**

---

[208] See s.41 of the Highways Act 1980. The duty to maintain did not originally extend to the removal of ice and snow: *Goodes v East Sussex CC* [2000] 1 W.L.R. 1356. The position has been altered by an amendment to add a specific duty: see s.41(1A) of the Highways Act 1980.

[209] *Wentworth v Wiltshire CC* [1993] Q.B. 694.

[210] Highways Act 1980 s.58.

[211] See *Ali v Bradford MDC* [2012] 1 W.L.R. 161 (dealing with s.130 of the Highways Act 1980).

[212] *Pride of Derby and Derbyshire Angling Association v British Celanese Ltd* [1953] Ch. 149; *Smeaton v Ilford Corp.* [1954] Ch. 450.

[213] *Cullen v Chief Constable of the Royal Ulster Constabulary* [2003] 1 W.L.R. 1763 esp. at [41]–[44].

[214] (1874) L.R. 9 Ex. 125.

[215] *Wentworth v Wiltshire CC* [1993] Q.B. 694.

[216] See, e.g. *Ministry of Housing v Sharp* [1970] 2 Q.B. 223.

on employers), or contributory negligence may be available. These matters are primarily questions of ordinary tort law, and reference should be made to the standard texts on such subjects.[217]

Trespass

15–080   Trespass to land involves an unlawful intrusion or entry by a person onto the land of another person. It is no defence that the trespasser was operating under a mistake of law or of fact. Public bodies frequently have express statutory authority to enter premises. The police and other law enforcement agencies have specific statutory power to enter premises in certain circumstances, or may apply for a warrant to enter. Other public bodies, such as central government departments or local authorities, may similarly be given statutory powers to enter premises in certain circumstances. Any person who enters premises in pursuance of a valid exercise of statutory power will not be a trespasser. If, however, it transpires that the decision to enter was ultra vires for any reason, then there is no lawful authority for the entry and the person will be liable for damages. The classic example of such a situation arose in *Cooper v Wandsworth Board of Works*.[218] The defendant public body, exercising statutory powers, entered on the claimant's land and demolished his house. The actions of the defendant were subsequently found to be ultra vires, as it had acted in breach of natural justice by failing to give notice of its proposed action to the defendant and enabling him to make representations. As the action was ultra vires, the defendant was liable in trespass for damages.

15–081   Various torts have evolved to deal with unlawful interference with property. Trespass to goods and conversion are two of the most relevant torts here. Public bodies, particularly law enforcement agencies, may have statutory or other powers to seize goods. A public body will not be liable so long as it is acting pursuant to a valid exercise of power. If, however, a public body is acting ultra vires, then the seizure of goods is unlawful and may give rise to an action for trespass or conversion. Section 3(2) of the Torts (Interference with Goods) Act 1977 provides three remedies:

(a)   the court may make an order for delivery of the goods and for payment of consequential damage. This remedy is in the discretion of the courts;
(b)   the court may make an order for the delivery of the goods, but giving the defendant the alternative of paying damages;
(c)   the court may award damages.

A claimant may choose between the second and third remedies. Courts may also have specific powers to order forfeiture or otherwise deal with property. If, for example, the police come into the possession of goods during a criminal

---

[217] See, generally, Clerk and Lindsell, *Torts*; Markesinis and Deakin, *Tort Law*; Stanton, *Breach of Statutory Duty*; Harding, *Public Duties and Public Law*; Winfold and Jolowicz, *Tort*; Harlow, *Compensation and Government Torts*; Buckley, "Liability for Breach of Statutory Duty in Tort" (1984) 100 L.Q.R. 204.
[218] (1863) 14 C.B.(N.S.) 180.

investigation, the Police (Property) Act 1897 provides for a police officer or a claimant of the property to apply to the magistrates' court for an order in respect of the property.[219]

False imprisonment

False imprisonment occurs when a person suffers a complete deprivation of liberty for any period of time without lawful cause. The two ingredients of the claim are the fact of imprisonment and the absence of lawful authority to justify it.[220] The claimant does not have to prove fault on the part of defendant; it is a tort of strict liability.[221] It is not necessary that the person is aware that he has been falsely imprisoned.[222] The tort of false imprisonment is actionable per se and proof of special damage is not necessary.[223] The purpose of tort law is, however, to compensate the individual for loss and damage caused by the wrongdoing. If, therefore, the court is satisfied that the claimant would have been detained in any event in the lawful exercise of a power to detain, he would not have suffered any loss and will only receive nominal damages.[224]

15–082

This tort has obvious relevance to the various public bodies involved in the criminal justice system, and also to those engaged in detaining and looking after the mentally ill, removing children at risk[225] or detaining immigrants.[226]. The police have statutory[227] and common law powers to arrest and detain individuals. So long as an arrest is done in the exercise of lawful authority, no liability arises.[228] If an arrest or detention is unlawful or becomes unlawful, then there is no longer any lawful cause for the detention and liability for false imprisonment will arise. An arrest may be unlawful because the statutory conditions permitting an arrest may not exist, as where a police constable does not have reasonable cause to suspect that a person is committing an offence.[229] The House of Lords has also held that the exercise of the power to arrest is subject to review on the usual public law principles to ensure, for example, that the power is not being used for improper purposes or on the basis of irrelevant considerations.[230] If an exercise of the power is ultra vires, the arrest is unlawful and an action for false imprisonment may be maintained. An arrest may also be unlawful if the police fail to inform the person that he is under arrest and of the grounds for arrest.[231] If

15–083

---

[219] See *R. v Uxbridge Justices Ex p. Commissioner for Metropolitan Police* [1981] Q.B. 829 for the appropriate procedure.

[220] *R. (WL (Congo)) v Secretary of State for the Home Department* [2012] 1 A.C. 245 at [65]; *R. v Deputy Governor of Parkhurst Prison ex p. Hague* [1992] 1 A.C. 58, at 162C-6.

[221] *R. v Governor of Brockhill Prison Ex p. Evans (No.2)* [2001] 2 A.C. 19. See also *D. v Home Office (Bail for Immigration Detainees Intervening)* [2006] 1 W.L.R. 1003 esp. at [54]–[59] and [113]–[123].

[222] *Murray v Ministry of Defence* [1988] 1 W.L.R. 692, HL (NI).

[223] Ibid. [1988] 1 W.L.R. 692, HL(NI).

[224] *R. (WL (Congo)) v Secretary of State for the Home Department* [2012] A.C. 245 at [95]–[96].

[225] See, e.g. *Langley v Liverpool City Council* [2007] 1 W.L.R. 375.

[226] See, e.g. *D v Home Office (Bail for Immigration Detainees Intervening)* [2006] 1 W.L.R. 1003.

[227] See general powers of arrest in Police and Criminal Evidence Act 1984, ss.24–25. Individual statutes may also confer specific powers of arrest.

[228] See, e.g. *McGrath v Chief Constable of the Royal Ulster Constabulary* [2001] 3 W.L.R. 312.

[229] Police and Criminal Evidence Act 1984 s.24(b).

[230] *Mohammed-Holgate v Duke* [1984] A.C. 437.

[231] See Police and Criminal Evidence Act 1984 s.28.

reasons are subsequently given, the arrest is lawful from that time and the continued deprivation of liberty is lawful.[232] Detention may become unlawful if the statutory provisions in the Police and Criminal Evidence Act 1984 governing detention are not complied with.

15–084 The tort of false imprisonment depends upon the fact of imprisonment and the absence of lawful authority. In principle, and subject to any statutory provisions to the contrary, once it is demonstrated that there was no lawful authority for the detention, the individual ought to be able to claim damages for false imprisonment. The usual consequence of a finding that a measure is unlawful is that it is not and has never been capable of producing valid legal effects. Therefore, it cannot have provided lawful authority for the detention. The fact that the public body quite legitimately and reasonably believed that they had authority is irrelevant; the tort is not dependent on negligence or fault on the part of the public authority but solely on proof of the fact of imprisonment and the absence of lawful authority. Similarly, if the exercise of a power to detain has been materially influenced by an error of law, then the detention is unlawful. The fact that the public body could and would lawfully have detained the individual in any event does not alter the fact that the actual exercise of the power to detain, and hence the detention itself, is unlawful.

15–085 That position has been reaffirmed by the Supreme Court in *R (WL (Congo)) v Secretary of State for the Home Department*.[233] There, the claimants were foreign nationals who had committed criminal offences in the United Kingdom and who were to be deported in consequence. The Secretary of State detained them pending deportation. In doing so, however, the Secretary of State failed to act in accordance with her published policies and acted in accordance with unpublished policies. The Supreme Court held that the two requirements for establishing the tort of false imprisonment were the fact of imprisonment and the absence of lawful justification. If the decision to detain were influenced by a material error of public law, the detention would be unlawful. The detention in the present case was unlawful as the defendant applied an unpublished blanket policy of detaining all foreign national prisoners and did not consider whether any exception should be made. Further, that unpublished policy was inconsistent with the published policy. The decision should have been made in accordance with the published policy unless there were good reasons from departing from it. Therefore, the detentions in the present case had been materially influenced by public law errors. The fact that the claimants would have been detained, in any event, even if the correct policy had been applied, did not render the detention lawful. However, the purpose of tort law was to compensate an individual for loss and damage suffered as a consequence of wrongdoing. If the claimant would have been detained, in any event, pursuant to the lawful exercise of authority, the claimant would have suffered no damage as a result of the wrong and should only receive nominal damages.[234]

---

[232] *Lewis v Chief Constable of South Wales Constabulary* [1991] 1 All E.R. 206.

[233] [2012] 1 A.C. 245.

[234] *R. (WL (Congo)) v Secretary of State for the Home Department* [2012] A.C. 245 at [95]–[96], [170], [236]–[237] and [252]–[256].

The orthodox position is also is reflected in the decision of the House of Lords **15–086** in *R. v Governor of Brockhill Prison Ex p. Evans (No.2)*.[235] There the governor of the prison had calculated a prisoner's release date in accordance with certain decisions of the Divisional Court which were believed to be applicable. It subsequently transpired that that method of calculating the release date was wrong in law and the claimant ought to have been released from prison 59 days earlier than she was. The House held that the claimant was entitled to damages for false imprisonment. The fact that the governor had acted reasonably, on the basis of the law as he believed it to be, was not a defence to the strict liability tort of false imprisonment.

The courts have, however, proved reluctant on occasions in the past to accept **15–087** the orthodox position in cases where the claimant was arrested and detained on the basis of a bye-law believed to be valid at the time but which, it subsequently transpired, was invalid. In *Percy v Hall*,[236] an individual was detained pursuant to a byelaw. The Court of Appeal held that the byelaw was valid. If, however, they had come to a contrary conclusion, they indicated that they would not have found the detaining authority liable for false imprisonment for two reasons. First, they indicated that the question of whether the constables had lawful justification for the arrest had to be considered by reference to the time that the arrest was made. At that stage, the byelaws were apparently valid and (at least for some purposes) would be presumed to be valid. The Court indicated that although a finding by a court that the byelaw was invalid might justify setting aside a conviction it did not mean that the arrest, which appeared to be lawful at the time, subsequently became unlawful.[237] That reasoning is not compatible with the decision of the Supreme Court in *R (WL (Congo) v Secretary of State for the Home Department*.[238] The second reason turned on the proper construction of the relevant statutory provision. The relevant section provided that a person could only be detained if he commits an offence against any byelaw. On the natural construction of those words, the person could not be detained if the byelaw was invalid as he would not be committing an offence against a byelaw. An alternative construction, however, would be first to read the section as empowering a constable to remove a person if the constable *reasonably believes* that the person is committing an offence and secondly that a constable may reasonably believe that even if the byelaw is subsequently found to be invalid. In other words, the fact that the reasonable belief is based upon a mistaken view of the law (that there is a valid byelaw in force when there is not) does not deprive the constable of the statutory defence of reasonable belief.[239] That reasoning does less violence to the traditional principles of administrative law. It does appear, however, to involve an

---

[235] [2001] 2 A.C. 19. The position might be different under domestic law if a valid, but mistaken, order authorising detention for a particular period: see *Quinland v Governor of Swaleside Prison* [2003] Q.B. 306.

[236] [1996] Q.B. 924.

[237] [1996] Q.B. 924 per Simon Brown LJ at [947G]–[948C] with whom Peter Gibson LJ agreed. See also the dicta in *R. v Central London County Court Ex p. London* [1999] 3 W.L.R. 1 at [11B]–[16A] (determination by the court that a decision to admit a patient to a mental hospital was unlawful does not retrospectively render the decision invalid).

[238] [2001] 2 A.C. 19. See also *D v Home Office (Bail for Immigration Detainees Intervening)* [2006] 1 W.L.R. 1003.

[239] In that regard, the Court of Appeal in *R. v Bow Street Magistrates' Court Ex p. McDonald (No.2)* (1997) 96 L.G.R. 61 held that a police constable relying on a statutory defence based on having

unnaturally restrictive interpretation of statutes and not to give sufficient weight to the liberty of the subject which requires that he should not be detained without lawful authority. If in truth there was no lawful authority, he ought to be compensated for damage suffered as a result of the detention.[240]

15–088   One issue that has arisen is whether a detention which is otherwise lawful may become unlawful because of the conditions under which a person is detained. In general, the conditions surrounding detention will not affect the legality of the detention itself, and will not give rise to an action for false imprisonment. In the case of prisoners, for example, s.12(1) of the Prison Act 1952 provides that a convicted prisoner may be lawfully confined to any prison. The section acts as a defence to claims for false imprisonment, irrespective of the conditions of detention.[241] Detention in breach of the prison rules, whilst remedial in public law, does not constitute false imprisonment.[242] Detention in breach of the rules which deprive a prisoner of residual rights, such as rights of movement and association which he would normally retain, does not give rise to the tort of false imprisonment. Thus, holding a prisoner in a special unit,[243] or unlawfully segregating the prisoner from other prisoners[244] is not actionable.

15–089   The House of Lords has held that a claim of false imprisonment cannot be maintained against a prison governor or a person acting with the governor's authority where the conditions in which a prisoner is confined are intolerable.[245] The lawfulness of the detention is not affected by the conditions of detention. If the conditions pose a threat to health or physical well-being, that may give rise to a claim in negligence against the governor.[246] There is also the possibility of a claim of misfeasance in a public office if the governor or prison officer acted ultra vires the rules and did so maliciously or knowing that they were acting in breach of the rules.[247] Similarly, there may be liability for breach of Art.3 (right not to be subjected to degrading treatment) or Art.8 (right to respect for private life) of the European Convention, but not for breach of Art.5 (the right not to be unlawfully detained).[248] The question has arisen as to whether a prison officer, who was not acting in accordance with the governor's order, failed to unlock a prisoner's cell could be liable for false imprisonment. The issue arose in the context of industrial action by prison officers who failed to unlock prisoners' cells in accordance with the normal prison regime. The Court of Appeal held that an individual would not normally be liable for false imprisonment as a result of an omission or failure to act at least in the absence of any specific duty to act. In the present case,

---

reasonable cause to believe that certain goods were liable to forfeiture was not prevented from relying on that defence because he mistakenly believed that the warrant under which he was acting was lawful when it was not.

[240] The topic is discussed in greater detail at paras 5–020 to 5–025 above.
[241] *R. v Deputy Governor of Parkhurst Prison Ex p. Hague* [1992] 1 A.C. 58, H.L.; *Williams v Home Office (No.2)* [1981] 1 All E.R. 1211.
[242] *Ex p. Hague* [1992] 1 A.C. 58, HL.
[243] *Williams v Home Office (No.2)* [1981] 1 All E.R. 1211.
[244] *R. v Deputy Governor of Parkhurst Prison Ex p. Hague* [1992] 1 A.C. 58. See also *R. v Board of Visitors of Gartree Prison Ex p. Sears, The Times*, March 20, 1985.
[245] *R. v Deputy Governor of Parkhurst Prison Ex p. Hague* [1992] 1 A.C. 58.
[246] *Ex p. Hague* [1992] 1 A.C. 58.
[247] See *Karagozlu v Commissioner of Police of the Metropolis* [2007] 1 W.L.R. 1881. See below at paras 15–097 to 15–106.
[248] *R. (Munjaz) v Mersey Care NHS Trust* [2003] 3 W.L.R. 1505 at [66]–[70].

therefore, the prison officers were not liable for false imprisonment in the present case as a result of their failure to let the prisoners out of their cells.[249] The Master of the Rolls observed that principle and practicality indicated that it was appropriate to limit claims to prisoners left locked in their cells by the inaction of prison officers to cases where misfeasance in a public office could be established.[250]

Liability for false imprisonment may be regulated by statute. In the context of compulsory detention under the Mental Health Act 1983, a person may be detained on an application made by an approved mental health professional (who must comply with specific procedural obligations) and on the recommendation of two registered mental health practitioners. The detaining hospital will not be liable for false imprisonment if it acts on the basis of the opinions of two registered practitioners notwithstanding the fact that the application by the approved mental health practitioners is invalid due to failure to comply with the relevant statutory requirements. Section 6(3) of the Mental Health Act 1983 removes liability from the hospital for the false imprisonment in such circumstances. That section, however, does not render the detention lawful; it simply means that the detaining hospital is protected from liability. The approved mental health practitioner (and the local authority which is vicariously liable for that professional's actions) may be liable for false imprisonment provided that the act involves an element of bad faith as s.139 of the Mental Health Act 1983 gives limited protection to such professionals. There also remains an unlawful deprivation of liberty for the purposes of Art.5 of the European Convention on Human Rights and s.139 of the domestic statute must be interpreted as not precluding liability under that provision.[251]

15–090

Other torts relevant to the criminal justice system

Malicious prosecution is a recognised tort. Liability will arise where a person institutes a criminal prosecution[252] which is terminated in favour of the person claiming damages, and the prosecution was instituted maliciously and without reasonable or probable cause.[253] The tort does not extend to the malicious institution of disciplinary proceedings.[254] Maliciously procuring a search warrant

15–091

---

[249] Iqbal v Prison Officers Association [2010] Q.B. 732.

[250] Iqbal v Prison Officers Association [2010] Q.B. 732 at [41]. The Court left open the question of whether a prison officer who deliberately locked a prisoner in a cell contrary to the governor's clear instruction would be liable for false imprisonment. In principle, however, the detention within the prison is lawful by reason of s.12 of the Prison Act 1952. The better approach, therefore, is to consider whether the action by the prison officer amounts to misfeasance in a public office which has caused loss to the prisoner.

[251] R. (M) v Hackney LBC [2011] 1 W.L.R. 2873 at [56]–[69].

[252] The tort also extends to the institution of civil proceedings for insolvency but probably not to other civil proceedings: see Metall und Rohstoff AG v Donaldson Lufkin & Jenrette Inc. [1990] 1 Q.B. 391 at [471]. There is a tort of abuse of civil proceedings, the ambit of which is uncertain, but it does not extend to claims for economic loss allegedly caused by the bringing of judicial review proceedings for collateral purpose: see Land Securities Plc v Fladgate Fielder [2010] 2 W.L.R. 1265.

[253] McDonagh v Commissioner of Police for the Metropolis, The Times, December 28, 1989.

[254] Gregory v Portsmouth City Council [2000] 1 A.C. 419 (although statements made during the course of such proceedings may constitute defamation or malicious falsehood or misfeasance in a public office).

is also a recognised tort.[255] This involves the making of an application for a search warrant without reasonable and probable cause for doing so where the person concerned is motivated by malice and damage results from the issue or execution of the warrant.[256] Other ordinary torts may arise in the context of law enforcement. Assault and battery may be relevant as, for example, where a police constable searches a person and the search is unlawful,[257] or if unreasonable force is used in the course of arresting an individual[258] or where a person is shot during a police operation.[259]

Mode of trial

15–092 Under s.69 of the Senior Courts Act 1981, where the court is satisfied that there is in issue a claim for false imprisonment or malicious prosecution,[260] then any party to the action may have the action tried by jury unless the court is of the opinion that the trial involves prolonged examination of documents or local investigation which cannot conveniently be made with a jury. Similar provisions exist in relation to claims in the county court.[261] Applications must be made with 28 days of service of the defence.[262]

General considerations governing tortious liability in the criminal justice field

Liability of the police

15–093 A police constable will be personally liable for any torts committed by him. By virtue of s.88 of the Police Act 1996, a chief constable will be vicariously liable in respect of constables acting in the performance or purported performance of their duties. A chief constable will not be liable if the act in question is unconnected with the performance of his duties as a police officer so that it could not be regarded as a mode, albeit an improper one, of carrying out those duties. So a chief constable was not liable for the acts of a police constable who blackmailed a suspect into having sexual intercourse with him and committed the torts of trespass to the person, assault and battery.[263] The Privy Council held that a chief constable was not liable when a probationary police constable took a gun, left his post and travelled to another location and shot in anger at individuals in a bar. The use of the firearm had nothing to do with the constable's police duties. Rather he deliberately and consciously abandoned his post and duties and armed

---

[255] *Reynolds v Commissioner for the Metropolitan Police* [1985] Q.B. 881. See also *Gibbs v Rea*, *The Times*, February 4, 1998.

[256] *Keegan v Chief Constable of Merseyside* [2003] 1 W.L.R. 2187.

[257] See, e.g. *Lindley v Rutter* [1981] Q.B. 128.

[258] See, e.g. *Allen v Commissioner of Metropolitan Police* [1980] Crim.L.R. 441.

[259] See, e.g. *Ashley v Chief Constable of Sussex Police* [2008] 2 W.L.R. 975.

[260] Once such a claim is raised the courts have no discretion to refuse trial by jury: see *Hill v Chief Constable of South Yorkshire Police* [1990] 1 W.L.R. 946 (interpreting the similar section cited in fn.308 below).

[261] County Court Act 1984 s.66.

[262] CPR r.26.11.

[263] *Makanjuola v Commissioner of Police of the Metropolis* (1990) 154 L.G. Rev. 248.

with the police revolver set out on a personal vendetta.[264] Any damages awarded and any costs incurred may be paid out of police funds.

Exemplary damages

The House of Lords has held that exemplary damages may be awarded where there has been a tort involving "oppressive, arbitrary or unconstitutional action by the servants of government".[265] "Servants of the government" is to be interpreted broadly to cover all those acting in the service of the state, including the police and local authorities,[266] and is not confined simply to those employed by central government.

15–094

The precise range of acts falling within this category is not clear. The categories are disjunctive, so exemplary damages may be awarded for unconstitutional action that is not arbitrary or oppressive.[267] The examples given by the House of Lords were the eighteenth century cases involving unlawful searches.[268] The fact that a police constable acts without authority or acts ultra vires does not of itself render the act unconstitutional even, it seems, if the effect is to deprive the individual of his civil rights.[269] Precisely what conduct by the wrongdoer or what surrounding circumstances are necessary before exemplary damages are given is unclear. The Privy Council were prepared to award exemplary damages for unlawful detention in humiliating and unsanitary conditions.[270] The Court of Appeal considered that physically restraining an individual without legitimate reason, handcuffing her, placing her in a police van, causing unnecessary pain by tugging at the handcuffs and procuring her continued detention in custody by giving false information and providing false evidence at trial were capable of being sufficiently serious to justify an award of exemplary damages.[271] There is no rule of law that exemplary damages are only available in respect of torts for which such awards were made before 1964.[272] The availability of exemplary damages depends upon whether the facts fall within the categories for which exemplary damages may be awarded, not the precise cause of action. The Court of Appeal has also given guidance on the appropriate amount to be paid by way of exemplary damages.[273]

15–095

---

[264] *Att-Gen of the British Virgin Islands v Hartwell* [2004] 1 W.L.R. 1273 (the police authorities were negligent for their own acts in permitting access to the revolver).

[265] *Rookes v Barnard* [1964] A.C. 1129; *Broome v Cassell & Co. Ltd* [1972] A.C. 1027.

[266] *Arora v Bradford Metropolitan Council* [1991] 2 W.L.R. 1377.

[267] *Holden v Chief Constable of Lancashire* [1987] Q.B. 380.

[268] *Wilkes v Wood* (1763) Lofft 1; *Benson v Frederick* (1766) 3 Burr. 1845; *Huckle v Money* (1763) 2 Wils 205.

[269] *Holden v Chief Constable of Lancashire* [1987] Q.B. 380.

[270] *Att-Gen of St Christopher, Nevis and Anguilla v Reynolds* [1980] A.C. 637.

[271] *Rowlands v Chief Constable of Merseyside Police* [2007] 1 W.L.R. 1065 at [34].

[272] *Kuddus v Chief Constable of Leicestershire Constabulary* [2001] 2 W.L.R. 1789 (overruling *AB v South West Water Services Ltd* [1993] Q.B. 507). The House of Lords left open the question of whether such awards were available against a person vicariously liable for the acts of the wrongdoer.

[273] See *Thompson v Commissioner of Police of the Metropolis* [1997] 3 W.L.R. 403.

Miscellaneous torts

15–096   A variety of other common law torts including defamation or the economic torts, such as inducing breach of contract, could (given the right combination of circumstances) apply to a public body as much as any other individual.[274] There are also statutorily created torts providing for compensation for discrimination on grounds such as race, gender, sexual orientation, or general disability.[275] These torts are of only peripheral relevance to public bodies, they are omitted here and reference should be made to the standard works on tort.

Misfeasance in a public office

15–097   Misfeasance in a public office is a tort that is unique to public bodies. The essence of the tort is a deliberate and dishonest abuse of power by a public officer or a public body.[276] Such abuse may arise where the act is done maliciously, that is, either with the intention of injuring the claimant or knowing or being reckless as to whether the act is ultra vires the powers of the public body and knowing that the claimant will probably suffer loss.[277] The tort has been described as "well-established".[278] Its origins are frequently traced to *Ashby v White*,[279] decided in 1703, where the plaintiff obtained damages as he had been unlawfully prevented from casting his vote at an election. Despite these assertions, there has until recently been a dearth of English authority on the elements of tort. The tort has begun to enjoy a renaissance and the courts are in the process of working out the precise elements of the tort.

Meaning of public office

15–098   The tort is referred to as misfeasance in a public office.[280] It may be committed by an individual or by a corporate body, such as a local authority created by statute.[281] A public authority may also be vicariously liable for the acts of its employees if their unauthorised actions are a misguided and unauthorised method of performing their authorised duties. The authority will not be liable if the actions giving rise to liability for misfeasance are so unconnected with the

---

[274] For an illustration of a potential defamation action, see *Calveley v Chief Constable of Merseyside* [1989] A.C. 1228; for an (unsuccessful) claim of inducing breach of contract, see *R. v Powys CC Ex p. Horner* [1989] C.O.D. 223.

[275] See the Equality Act 2010. For an example, see *Alexander v Home Office* [1988] 1 W.L.R. 968 (racially discriminatory report prepared by prison authorities).

[276] See *Three Rivers DC v Governors of the Bank of England* [2003] 1 A.C. 1. See Andenas and Fairgrieve, "Misfeasance in a Public Office" (2002) 51 I.C.L.Q. 757.

[277] [2003] 1 A.C. 1.

[278] per Lord Diplock in *Dunlop v Woollahara Municipal Council* [1982] A.C. 158 at [172].

[279] (1703) 2 Ld. Raymond 938, 3 Ld. Raymond 320 or even earlier: see *Three Rivers DC v Bank of England (No.3)* [2003] 1 A.C. 1.

[280] There is also, separately, a criminal offence of misconduct in a public office: see *R. v Mitchell* [2014] 2 Cr. App. R. 2; *R. v Cosford* [2014] Q.B. 81. The criminal law performs a different purpose from the civil law and the definition of what constitutes a public office for the purposes of imposing criminal sanctions does not indicate what is the proper scope of the definition of public officer for the different purpose of determining civil liability.

[281] *Dunlop v Woollahara Municipal Council* [1982] A.C. 158; *Jones v Swansea City Council* [1990] 3 W.L.R. 1453.

employees' authorised duties as to be independent of and outside those duties.[282] The tort may be committed in respect of the purported exercise by a public officer of a statutory power. There is no reason why the tort should not be available in respect of the purported exercise by a public officer of a prerogative or other public law, as defined in Chapter 2. In principle, any exercise of power by a public officer amenable to judicial review should also be remediable in damages if the necessary elements of malice or knowledge, together with foreseeability and causation, can be established.

The ambit of the tort may, however, go wider than the exercise by a public officer of public powers amenable to judicial review. Public bodies, that is, bodies set up by statute or the prerogative, may also exercise private law powers derived from contract or land ownership. Although the exercise of such powers may not be the subject of a judicial review claim,[283] the malicious exercise of private law functions could give rise to the tort. In *Jones v Swansea City Council*, the local authority had power under a lease to refuse consent to a change of use of the premises by the tenant. The plaintiff alleged that the local authority had refused to grant consent because it was motivated by malice towards her husband. The Court of Appeal held[284] that the basis of the tort was not the nature of particular power that had been exercised but the nature of the officer or body exercising the power. Public bodies such as local authorities were under a duty to exercise their powers, whatever their origin, for the general public good. The exercise of power maliciously for the purpose of injuring the plaintiff, or knowing that the exercise of power was ultra vires was sufficient to found the tort whether the power was public or private. The fact that judicial review might not be available in respect of the exercise of private power did not prevent the public body being liable in tort, as the boundaries of judicial review and misfeasance in a public office were not co-terminous. On appeal, the House of Lords did not decide whether an action would lie in respect of a malicious exercise of a power derived from a lease.[285] They were able to allow the appeal on other grounds. Lord Lowry, giving the only reasoned judgment, did state that he was inclined to agree with the view of the Court of Appeal, and considered that the tort would be established if a plaintiff who could prove that a majority of local councillors voted for a resolution with the object of damaging the plaintiff.[286] A dictum of Lord Bridge,[287] however, refers to the "... purported exercise by the public officer of some power or authority with which he is clothed by virtue of the office he holds". Lord Bridge did state that he was not seeking to explore the precise limits of the tort of misfeasance in a public office. The House of Lords has subsequently indicated that the exercise of private-law functions by a public body is capable of satisfying this element of the tort.[288] Conversely, where a body does not exercise governmental powers conferred upon it by statute or other public law source and where it is a commercial organisation or body, then it is not a public officer for the purposes of the tort of misfeasance. Thus the Society of Lloyds,

15–099

---

[282] *Racz v Home Office* [1994] 2 A.C. 45.

[283] See paras 2–131 to 2–160.

[284] [1990] 1 W.L.R. 54.

[285] [1990] 1 W.L.R. 1453.

[286] [1990] 1 W.L.R. 1453 at [1458]–[1459].

[287] In *Calveley v Chief Constable of Merseyside* (see above, fn.274) at [1240].

[288] *Three Rivers DC v Bank of England (No.3)* [2003] 2 A.C. 1.

which was a commercial organisation established to deal with the commercial interests of its own members, was not a public officer for the purposes of the tort of misfeasance in a public office.[289]

Malice or knowledge of unlawfulness

15–100   The fact that a public body has acted in an ultra vires manner, and that the plaintiff has suffered loss as a result, will not of itself give rise to liability. The Privy Council[290] and the House of Lords[291] have made it clear that ultra vires action of itself does not give rise to civil liability. The public officer must either (a) have acted maliciously, that is with the specific intention of injuring a person or persons, or (b) acted knowing that he had no power to do the act complained of and that the act would probably injure the claimant or a class of which the claimant is a member. These are alternative, not cumulative, conditions of liability. For the purposes of the second form of the tort the public officer must either have known that his actions were unlawful, or have acted with reckless indifference as to whether or not he had the power to do the act in question and whether it would harm the claimant.[292]

15–101   The leading decision now is the House of Lords decision in *Three Rivers DC v Governors and Company of the Bank of England*.[293] The claim arose out of the Bank of England's supervisory powers over the Bank of Credit and Commerce International. It was claimed, inter alia, that the Bank of England had knowingly acted contrary to the statutory scheme for licensing banks and had granted a licence to BCCI to act as a bank knowing that it did not satisfy the relevant statutory criteria and that persons who had deposited money with BCCI lost that money when BCCI subsequently collapsed. The House of Lords held that the basis underlying the tort was a deliberate and dishonest abuse of power. Such an abuse could arise either whether there was malice in that the public officer purported to exercise power with the intention of injuring the claimant. Alternatively, liability could arise where the public officer acted, or omitted to act, in a way that was ultra vires, knowing of the illegality and knowing that the act or omission would probably injure the claimant or a person of a class of which he is a member. In this context, the requisite degree of knowledge reflects the fact that the tort is based on dishonesty. Knowledge will be established where a public officer has actual knowledge or displays reckless indifference as to the lawfulness of his actions which is inconsistent with acting honestly, for example by shutting one's eyes to the obvious. In deciding whether he was acting honestly, regard must be had to all the circumstances known to the public officer at the time and also his attributes such as his experience and intelligence. Furthermore, knowledge is necessary both as to the illegality and the probability of harm. The public officer must have known that the acts would probably harm the claimant or have been recklessly indifferent as to the consequences of his action. It may be

---

[289]   *Society of Lloyd's v Henderson* [2008] 1 W.L.R. 2555 at [21]–[25].

[290]   *Dunlop v Woollahara Municipal Council* (see above, fn.278) at [170]–[171].

[291]   *Lonrho Ltd v Shell Petroleum Co. Ltd (No.2)* [1982] A.C. 173 at 187–188 and see dicta of Lord Browne-Wilkinson in *X v Bedfordshire CC* above, fn.1 at [730F]–[731B].

[292]   *Three Rivers DC v Bank of England (No.3)* [2003] 2 A.C. 1; *Society of Lloyd's v Henderson* [2008] 1 W.L.R. 2555 at [21].

[293]   [2003] 2 A.C. 1.

possible for a public officer to know that he is acting unlawfully without appreciating that the actions will probably harm the claimant.

Malice implies an intent to injure a person. A local authority would have been liable if a claimant could have proved that a majority of its members refused consent to a change of use of premises, due to a desire to cause financial harm on the claimant's husband. The alleged cause of the malice was personal and political antipathy towards the claimant's husband, and a desire to exact revenge for the political defeat that he had previously inflicted on the ruling party on the local authority. In the event, the plaintiff was unable to prove that such malice existed.[294] In the case of a corporate body, it is sufficient to demonstrate that a majority of its members participating in the decision was actuated by malice.[295]

15–102

Causation and damages

The act or omissions must also have caused the loss. That is a question of fact.[296] There should be no difficulty where a decision affects rights or revokes an existing permission. If it had not been for the decision the claimant would have continued to exercise his rights or engage in the permitted activity. Although in theory the revocation is a nullity and of no legal effect, that ought not to prevent recovery of loss on the ground that the claimant could have ignored the illegal revocation. The claimant will not know that the revocation is unlawful until that is established in appropriate proceedings. If, in practice, the decision has prevented the claimant from doing an act and that has caused him loss, he ought to be able to recover for loss suffered (at least for the period until a valid decision is taken).

15–103

Difficulties in relation to causation might arise if the claimant is claiming that he has unlawfully been refused a licence or permission to do an act. The claimant might have been refused a licence for valid reasons even if malice or deliberate ultra vires action were not present.[297] In one case, the plaintiff sought to overcome this difficulty by pleading that he had done everything necessary to qualify for a licence and that he ought to be granted one.[298] Unless there was a duty to grant a licence in certain specified circumstances, or unless it would be *Wednesbury* unreasonable to refuse a licence, it might be difficult to establish causation.

15–104

A claimant must prove that he has suffered special damage, that is some financial loss or physical or mental injury. Thus, a prisoner whose correspondence had been removed and inspected in bad faith by prison officers could not establish the tort of misfeasance as he had not suffered any damage.[299] Loss of liberty is sufficient, however, to constitute special damage for these purposes and a prisoner who alleged that he had been moved from an open prison to a closed prison, and so was subject to greater practical restraints on his freedom, would be able to establish that he had suffered damage.[300] Subject to that, the courts have

15–105

---

[294] *Jones v Swansea City Council* [1990] 3 W.L.R. 1453.
[295] Ibid. [1990] 3 W.L.R. 1453.
[296] *Three Rivers DC v Bank of England (No.3)* [2003] 1 A.C. 1.
[297] See Beatson and Matthews, *Administrative Law: Cases and Materials*, 2nd edn (1989), p.597.
[298] *David (Asoka Kumar) v Abdul Cader* [1963] 1 W.L.R. 834.
[299] *Watkins v Home Office* [2006] 2 A.C. 395.
[300] *Karagozlu v Commissioner of Police for the Metropolis* [2007] 1 W.L.R. 1881.

not yet worked out the principles governing the heads of damage that are recoverable. There have as yet been few claimants who have succeeded in establishing misfeasance.[301] Exemplary damages are, in principle, available if the claimant establishes that the facts fall within the category of cases where such damages are available.[302]

Proximity

15–106 Proximity is not an ingredient of the tort of misfeasance.[303] The fact that the public officer must know that his actions will probably harm the claimant or a class of persons of which the claimant is a member, or be recklessly indifferent as to that fact, is considered to be sufficient to keep the scope of liability for the tort within reasonable bounds.[304] Neither the individual nor the potential members of the class need to be identifiable; thus where allegations of misfeasance arose in circumstances where an individual was released and subsequently murdered a person, the fact that the victim, or potential group of victims, were not identifiable was not a reason for striking out the claim.[305]

Relationship with other torts

15–107 Certain acts by public bodies may be dealt with by torts other than misfeasance in a public office. The act complained of may not be an exercise of power by a public officer for the purpose of misfeasance. Thus, the preparation of a report which is defamatory had to be dealt with by way of an action in defamation not misfeasance.[306] Some torts require not only malice but also other ingredients before liability can be established. The courts are unlikely to allow a claim to be framed for misfeasance relying on invalidity and malice alone, and thereby circumventing the need to establish the elements required by the other relevant tort. Thus, the tort of malicious prosecution requires the claimant to establish that he was prosecuted, and, that the authority acted maliciously, and also that there was no reasonable or probable cause for the prosecution. Popplewell J. refused to allow a claim in misfeasance based on malice alone, and held that the claimant was restricted to claiming for malicious prosecution, with its additional element of proving the absence of any reasonable or probable cause for the prosecution.[307]

---

[301] The plaintiff did succeed in *Roncarelli v Duplessis* [1959] S.C.R. 121. In *Bourgoin SA v Minister of Agriculture, Fisheries and Food* [1986] Q.B. 716, the Government eventually settled out of court following the determination of the preliminary issue: see [1987] 1 C.M.L.R. 169.

[302] *Kuddus v Chief Constable of Leicestershire Constabulary* [2001] 2 W.L.R. 1789.

[303] *Three Rivers DC v Bank of England (No.3)* [2003] 1 A.C. 1.

[304] [2003] 1 A.C. 1.

[305] *Akenzua v Secretary of State for the Home Department* [2003] 1 W.L.R. 741.

[306] *Calveley v Chief Constable of Merseyside* (see above, fn.274).

[307] *McDonagh v Metropolitan Police Commissioner, The Times,* December 28, 1989.

Immunities

Judicial immunity

Judges of a superior court of record will not be liable for judicial acts done in the exercise of their jurisdiction, even where it is alleged that they are acting maliciously.[308] Judges will be personally liable if they exceed their jurisdiction and do an act which gives rise to a recognised tort.[309] The use of the word "jurisdiction" here may be misleading. Superior courts are courts of unlimited jurisdiction, whose responsibility includes determining the extent of their jurisdiction and resolving questions of law.[310] Their decisions cannot be quashed by judicial review. They may be set aside on appeal if rights of appeal are provided but the appeal will be correcting an erroneous exercise of their inherent jurisdiction not quashing an act done without jurisdiction. References to a superior court judge acting without jurisdiction probably refers to a situation where a judge of a superior court acts without any colour or show of legal authority whatsoever. The example usually given is that of the judge who imposes a sentence following an acquittal by a jury because he considers the verdict perverse.[311] Apart from such extreme cases, superior court judges are likely to have absolute immunity for judicial acts done in the exercise of their jurisdiction.[312]

15–108

The position in relation to inferior courts of limited jurisdiction is different. So far as errors within jurisdiction are concerned, an action lay at common law against justices for actionable wrongs resulting from a wrong and malicious decision of justices made within jurisdiction. In *Re McC*,[313] Lord Bridge and Lord Templeman expressed the view, obiter, that such actions were now obsolete and no longer available. The matter awaits definitive resolution. The position in relation to justices is now regulated by ss.31 and 32 of the Courts Act 2003. Section 31 provides that no action shall lie against a justice or a justice's clerk in respect of any act or omission occurring in the course of his duty. Section 32 provides that an action shall lie in respect of any act or omission done in the *purported* exercise of jurisdiction only if there is bad faith.

15–109

Judges of inferior courts were personally liable at common law for actionable wrongs suffered as a result of acts done without jurisdiction.[314] This rule has been altered so far as justices and justices' clerks are concerned, who are only be liable for acts done outside their jurisdiction if they acted in bad faith.[315] The common

15–110

---

[308] *Fray v Blackburn* (1863) 3 B. & S. 576.

[309] *Re McC* [1985] A.C. 528 at [540] (Lord Bridge referred to a judge acting in bad faith doing what he knew he had no power to do). In *Sirros v Moore* [1975] Q.B. 118 at 137, Buckley LJ considered that a judge would be liable if he acted without jurisdiction even if acting in good faith and in the mistaken belief that he had jurisdiction.

[310] *Re Racal Communications* [1981] A.C. 374; *Isaacs v Robertson* [1985] A.C. 97. On the relevance of this approach to the issue of civil liability of judges, see the judgment of Buckley LJ in *Sirros v Moore* [1975] Q.B. 118, [139]–[140].

[311] *Re McC* [1985] A.C. 528 at [540].

[312] See Buckley LJ in *Sirros v Moore* (above, fn.310) at [140].

[313] [1985] A.C. 528.

[314] *Sirros v Moore* (see above, fn.310). See also *R. v Board of Visitors of Gartree Prison Ex p. Sears*, *The Times*, March 20, 1985.

[315] Section 32 of the Courts Act 2003.

law rule probably still exists in relation to other courts of limited jurisdiction. The majority judgment of the Court of Appeal in *Sirros v Moore*,[316] stating that the position of inferior court judges should be equated with that of superior court judges, cannot stand with the dicta of the House of Lords in *Re McC*, even though the decision was not formally overruled.

15–111   Jurisdiction for the purposes of this area of the law has a special meaning. In particular, jurisdiction does not have the meaning given to it by *Anisminic*,[317] where in effect the House of Lords held that any reviewable error by an inferior court takes it outside its jurisdiction, so that the decision may be quashed in judicial review proceedings. Not all such errors render a decision outside jurisdiction for the different purposes of the rules governing civil liability of judges.[318] The cases in which an inferior court may act without jurisdiction, or in excess of jurisdiction, can be conveniently grouped in three categories.[319] First, there are those cases where the inferior court lacks jurisdiction at the outset as they have "no jurisdiction of the cause".[320] The courts may lack jurisdiction over the subject-matter,[321] the persons[322] or the geographical area[323] in question. Secondly, a court may properly begin a trial but may exceed jurisdiction during the course of the trial. Not every error constitutes an excess of jurisdiction. There must be something exceptional or some "gross or obvious irregularity".[324] Finally, the justices may have jurisdiction of the cause and have conducted the trial impeccably, but the conviction of the defendant or other determination does not provide a proper foundation for the sentence imposed. Failure to observe a statutory condition precedent to the imposition of a sentence will take an inferior court outside its jurisdiction. Thus, failure to inform a person of the right to apply for legal aid,[325] or failure to consider whether non-payment of the rates was caused by the defaulter's wilful refusal or culpable neglect will take a court outside its jurisdiction.[326]

15–112   A justice may be indemnified out of local funds in respect of damages awarded against him or costs reasonably incurred. He is entitled to be indemnified if he acted reasonably and in good faith.[327]

Specific statutory immunities

15–113   Statute may confer immunity on specific public bodies in respect of their statutory functions. The Mental Health Act 1983, for example, provides that a person is not to be civilly liable for acts done in the pursuance of the statute unless the act was done in bad faith or without reasonable care.[328] Further, an

---

[316] [1975] Q.B. 118.
[317] *Anisminic v Foreign Compensation Commission* [1969] 2 A.C. 147 and see paras 5–004 to 5–005.
[318] *Re McC* [1985] A.C. 528.
[319] See, per Neill LJ in *R. v Manchester City Magistrates' Court Ex p. Davies* [1989] Q.B. 631.
[320] per Coke C.J. in *Marshalsea Case* (1612) 10 Co.Rep. 68b at [76a].
[321] See *Polley v Fordham (No.2)* (1904) 91 L.T. 525; *Wills v Maclaghlan* (1876) 1 Ex. D. 376.
[322] *Marshalsea Case* (see above, fn.315).
[323] *Houlden v Smith* (1850) 14 Q.B. 841.
[324] per Lord Bridge in *Re McC* [1985] A.C. 528 at [546].
[325] *Re McC* (see above, fn.305).
[326] *R. v Manchester City Justices Ex p. Davies* [1989] Q.B. 631.
[327] Courts Act 2003 s.35.
[328] Mental Health Act 1983 s.139(1).

action against an individual (but not the Secretary of State or health authority[329]) cannot be brought without the leave of the court.[330] Constables are not liable for acts done in the execution of a warrant issued by a justice.[331] Persons appointed to conduct certain investigations into complaints are not liable for acts done in pursuance of certain of their functions under the Financial Services Act 2012, unless they act in bad faith.[332] More generally, the Court of Appeal has held that a provision providing that the decision of an administrative body should be final precluded an action for negligence against that body where it would involve challenging the decision.[333] Immigration officers exercising statutory powers to detain immigrants do not, however, have any immunity from claims.[334]

C. BREACH OF EU LAW

Public authorities may act in violation of directly effective rights derived from EU law or may fail to implement the provisions of a directive. A Member State may be required to compensate an individual who suffers loss as a result of a sufficiently serious breach by the Member State of a rule or provision of EU law which is intended to confer rights on the individual.[335] This topic is considered in detail in Chapter 17. In procedural terms, the English courts are required to ensure that the rights derived from EU law are effectively enforced and treated no less favourably than similar rights derived from domestic law. This topic is also considered in Chapter 17.

15–114

D. DAMAGES UNDER THE HUMAN RIGHTS ACT 1998

The courts have jurisdiction under s.8 of the Human Rights Act 1998 to award damages, where the court considers it just and appropriate to do so, to a claimant where a public authority acts in a way that is incompatible with that claimant's rights under the European Convention on Human Rights. Damages may only be awarded if it is necessary to do so to afford just satisfaction to the claimant and the court must take account of all the relevant circumstances including any other

15–115

---

[329] Mental Health Act 1983 s.139(4).

[330] Mental Health Act 1983 s.139(2). See *Winch v Jones* [1986] Q.B. 296 and *Seal v Chief Constable of South Wales* [2007] 1 W.L.R. 1910 (and see the decision of the European Court of Human Rights which considered that there was no violation in the present case of any Convention right: (2012) 54 EHRR 6). There may, in certain circumstances, be liability for unlawful detention contrary to Art.5 of the Convention on the part of local authority for unlawful detention if an individual is detained pursuant to an invalid application made by an approved mental health professional for whom the authority is vicariously liable: see *R. (M) v Hackney LBC* [2011] 1 W.L.R. 2873 discussed above at para.15–090.

[331] Constables Protection Act 1750 s.6.

[332] Financial Services Act 2012 s.88.

[333] *Jones v Department of Employment* [1989] Q.B. 1 (interpreting Social Security Act 1975 s.117(1)).

[334] *D v Home Office (Bail for Immigration Detainees Intervening)* [2006] 1 W.L.R. 1003 esp. at [113]–[123].

[335] See, e.g. Joined Cases C-6/90 and C-9/90 *Francovich v Italian Republic* [1991] E.C.R. 5357 and Joined Cases C-46/93 and C-48/93 *Brasserie du Pecheur S.A. v Federal Republic of Germany; R. v Secretary of State for Transport Ex p. Factortame Ltd* [1996] E.C.R. I-1029 at [1142]–[1143].

remedy granted in respect of the violation.[336] The courts must also take into account the principles applied by the European Court of Human Rights in determining whether to award damages or the amount of damages to be awarded.[337] In many cases, an award of damages will not be necessary to afford just satisfaction to a claimant. The finding of a violation of a Convention right, and the fact that remedies are available on judicial review which will bring about an end to the violation, may constitute just satisfaction.[338] This topic is considered in detail in Chapter 16.

E.   CONTRACT

15–116 Public bodies may have power to enter into contracts. Statute may expressly or implied confer power on a public body to enter into contracts in order to enable it to discharge its functions.[339] Disputes arising out of the terms of such contracts or alleged breaches will be settled by the ordinary principles of contract law. The fact that one of the parties to the agreement is a public body will not of itself affect the principles to be applied. Thus, disputes about the meaning of a covenant in a lease[340] or the enforceability of a restrictive covenant in a conveyance of land[341] will be determined according to the usual principles of land law. Contracts of employment between public bodies and their staff may not raise any public law issue, and the enforcement of specific contractual rights and the question of the remedies available will be dealt with in accordance with the usual principles applicable to such disputes.[342]

Whether contract exists

15–117 One issue that may arise is whether any contract actually exists between a public body and an individual. A public body may choose simply to rely on using its statutory powers to achieve its objectives rather than entering into a contract with an individual. The exercise of public powers may be controlled by way of judicial review, but abuse of power will not normally give rise to damages. An individual may, however, wish to establish that there is a contract and claim damages for breach. In one sense, this is simply the ordinary contract law question of whether the requisite elements for a contract exist. However, the availability of public law powers to achieve a particular goal may well influence the court in determining the intentions of the parties. In one case, for example, the carrying out of the statutory functions of licensing hackney carriages was found to lie within the field of public law and could not reasonably be placed within the framework of contract. Policy documents adumbrated by a local authority in the field of local

---

[336] Human Rights Act 1998 s.8(3) and see *Anufrijeva v Southwark LBC* [2004] 2 W.L.R. 603 at [55].

[337] Human Rights Act 1998 s.8(4).

[338] *Anufrijeva v Southwark LBC* [2004] 2 W.L.R. 603 at [53]; *R. (Bernard) v Enfield LBC* [2003] L.G.R. 423 at [39].

[339] See, e.g. Local Government Act 1972 s.111.

[340] *Stent v Monmouth DC* (1987) 54 P. & C.R. 193.

[341] *J. Sainsbury Plc v Enfield LBC* [1989] 1 W.L.R. 590.

[342] See, e.g. *R. v British Broadcasting Corp. Ex p. Lavelle* [1983] 1 W.L.R. 23; *R. v East Berkshire Health Authority Ex. p. Walsh* [1985] Q.B. 152.

government administration could not sensibly be construed as contractual offers to the world at large. Nor were letters to individuals setting out the current policy of a local authority capable of being construed as a contractual offer to each person to issue a licence provided that the recipient fulfilled the conditions set out and notified the authority of that fact.[343] In two cases, the courts have considered the exercise of statutory powers to pay grants to individuals. The courts considered that where a public authority is administering such a scheme, the conditions are inappropriate to the existence of an intention to enter a contractual relationship. Thus, in one case, the individual could not circumvent the judicial review machinery by bringing an ordinary claim for breach of contract.[344] In the other, the individual was prevented from seeking interest for late payment of a grant. Interest was not payable since the enforcement of a right to payment of a grant in judicial review proceedings was not an action for debt, and, as no contract existed, the claim could not be characterised as damages on which interest would be payable. There was therefore no jurisdiction to pay interest under s.35A of the Senior Courts Act 1981, and no common law jurisdiction to pay interest existed.[345] Conversely, the Court of Appeal has held that the invitation for tenders to carry out work did impliedly create a contractual obligation to open and consider all valid tenders received.[346] The court was heavily influenced by the fact that the tendering process was heavily weighted in favour of the local authority who could invite as many tenders as it wished, was not obliged to accept the highest tender, and did not have to give reasons for accepting or refusing a tender. Since the preparation of a tender could involve considerable expense, the court was concerned to ensure that at the very least the formal procedure for considering the tender should be followed, and the authority forced to pay compensation if it were not.[347]

Contract and public sector employment

Employment in the public service may be by appointment to an office in the exercise of statutory or prerogative powers, as in the case of the police,[348] or some civil servants.[349] However, public bodies may choose (or even be required by statute) to employ staff under a contract of employment.[350] Prison officers have in the past been regarded as office holders without contracts of employment,[351] and their employment relationship regulated by statutory powers amenable to judicial review.[352] The Court of Appeal has held that it is possible for prison officers to be employed under a contract of employment; whether they have in fact been so employed depends on whether the elements of a contract

15–118

---

[343] *R. v Knowsley MBC Ex p. Maguire* (1992) 90 L.G.R. 653 at [661]–[664].

[344] *Cato v Minister of Agriculture, Fisheries and Food* [1989] 3 C.M.L.R. 513.

[345] *R. v Secretary of State for Transport Ex p. Sherriff & Sons Ltd, The Times*, December 18, 1986.

[346] *Blackpool and Fylde Aero Club Ltd v Blackpool BC* [1990] 1 W.L.R. 1195.

[347] [1990] 1 W.L.R. 1195.

[348] *R. v Chief Constable of North Wales Police Ex p. Evans* [1982] 1 W.L.R. 1155.

[349] *R. v Civil Service Appeal Board Ex p. Bruce* [1989] I.C.R. 171.

[350] *R. v East Berkshire Health Authority Ex p. Walsh* [1985] Q.B. 152; *R. v British Broadcasting Corp. Ex p. Lavelle* [1983] 1 W.L.R. 23.

[351] *R. v Secretary of State for Home Department Ex p. Benwell* [1985] Q.B. 554.

[352] [1985] Q.B. 554. *R. v Secretary of State for the Home Department Ex p. Attard* [1990] C.O.D. 261.

have been made out, namely offer and acceptance, consideration and, most crucially, the intention to create legal relations.[353] In the past, it was thought that bringing the employment relationship within the sphere of public law, rather than contract, had advantages for the individual. The principles of natural justice applied to public office holders and the prerogative remedies, were available to quash a decision to dismiss and effectively to restore the individual to office.[354] This may still be important as the claimant will be able to claim unpaid wages and that sum exceeds any damages available for wrongful dismissal (or the compensation for unfair dismissal in employment tribunals).[355] Now, many public sector employees have specific procedural rights included in their terms of appointment,[356] and in addition there may be implied into any contract of service an obligation to observe natural justice.[357] Injunctions may be available to prevent dismissal in breach of those terms, thus achieving in practical terms the same result as the prerogative remedies.[358] In addition, if the courts consider it undesirable to grant an injunction, or where dismissal has occurred and it is not practical to order restoration to the employment relationship,[359] damages for wrongful dismissal will be available. Thus, as a tactical matter, the balance of advantage between contract and public office holder is more even than previously.[360] There is one risk in bringing a contractual action: if the courts decide that no contract exists, and the relationship is regulated by public law, it will usually be too late to apply for judicial review. An individual may also wish to rely on other principles of public law, such as *Wednesbury* unreasonableness. There are cases where the courts have allowed such claims to be brought by way of judicial review, even where a contractual relationship exists.[361] The precise relationship between contract and public law principles awaits authoritative clarification.[362]

---

[353] *McClaren v Home Office* [1990] C.O.D. 257.

[354] *Ridge v Baldwin* [1964] A.C. 40. See also *McLaughlin v Governor of the Cayman Islands* [2007] 1 W.L.R. 2839.

[355] As in *R. (Shoesmith) v Ofsted* [2011] I.C.R. 1195: see Chapter 5 above.

[356] See, e.g. *R. v British Broadcasting Corp. Ex p. Lavelle* [1983] 1 W.L.R. 23.

[357] *Stevenson v United Road Transport Union* [1977] I.C.R. 893.

[358] *R. v British Broadcasting Corp. Ex p. Lavelle* (see above, fn.346). See also Ewing and Grubb, "The Emergence of a New Labour Law Injunction?" (1987) 16 I.L.J. 145.

[359] Even in a public law case, the courts would be likely to refuse to grant a quashing order or a mandatory order in such circumstances: see *R. v Chief Constable of North Wales Police Ex p. Evans* [1982] W.L.R. 1155 but see *McLaughlin v Governor of the Cayman Islands* [2007] 1 W.L.R. 2839 and *R. (Shoesmith) v Ofsted* [2011] ICR 1195: statutory office not lawfully terminated and officer holder continued in office and entitled to receive payment.

[360] See, generally, Fredman and Lee, "Natural Justice and Employees: the Unacceptable Face of Proceduralism" (1986) 15 I.L.J. 15; Walsh, "Judicial Review of Dismissal from Employment: Coherence or Confusion" [1989] P.L. 131.

[361] See, e.g. *R. v Hertfordshire CC Ex p. National Union of Public Employees* [1985] I.R.L.R. 258.

[362] See paras 2–131 to 2–160.

Public law principles and contract

There are situations when questions of contract may become intermingled with **15–119** public law. A statutory corporation or a body exercising statutory powers can only do those acts which are expressly or impliedly authorised by statute.[363] Statute may not empower a public body to enter into certain types of transaction at all.[364] Statute may allow a public body to enter into a contract for certain purposes but not for other purposes. Statute may specifically prohibit certain clauses being included in certain contracts.[365] The power to contract may be unlawfully delegated by a public body, so that a person not authorised by statute may seek to enter into contracts on behalf of the public body.[366] In these cases, the contract (or particular clauses thereof) will be ultra vires the powers of the board. This will normally render the contract (or only the particular clauses which are unlawful if these are severable[367]) itself unenforceable. Thus in one case, the court made a quashing order to quash a decision to enter into a tenancy agreement, and granted a declaration that the agreement itself was void.[368] On another occasion, the court quashed a decision of a local authority to award a catering contract as parent governors had unlawfully been prevented from voting at the relevant meeting, and declared the contract between the local authority and the third-party contract should be treated as void and of no effect.[369]

There are restrictions on the extent to which a public body may fetter the **15–120** exercise of statutory powers by entering into a contract. A public body cannot bind itself to exercise or not to exercise its discretionary powers in the future. Thus, a statutory body could not give a binding contractual undertaking that they would not build on a piece of land, as such a promise would be incompatible with their specific statutory power to build.[370] Nor could a local authority agree in advance not to grant planning permission, since they had to be free to consider exercising their discretionary power.[371] A term cannot be implied into a contract that the public body will not exercise its discretionary powers in a way that materially affects the profitability of the contract.[372] Yet, a public body may have express or implied power to enter into contracts, and such contracts may be a valid way of performing its public functions. In such cases, the contract is a valid method of exercising power, not an improper fetter. Thus, a statutory corporation providing electricity was entitled to enter into binding agreements governing its

---

[363] *Att-Gen v Great Eastern Railway Co.* (1880) 5 App.Cas. 473; *Hazell v Hammersmith and Fulham LBC* [1992] 2 A.C. 1.
[364] *R. v Wirral MBC Ex p. Milstead, The Times*, March 27, 1989.
[365] See Local Government Act 1988 s.17 and see *R. v Islington LBC Ex p. Building Employers Confederation* [1989] C.O.D. 432.
[366] *R. v Port Talbot BC Ex p. Jones* [1988] 2 All E.R. 207.
[367] See, e.g. *R. v Islington LBC Ex p. Building Employers Confederation* (above, fn.368).
[368] *R. v Port Talbot BC Ex p. Jones* (see above, fn.366). In *Hazell v Hammersmith and Fulham LBC* (see above, fn.363) the House of Lords, having ruled certain contracts to be ultra vires, declined to rule on the enforceability of the contracts and that is now the subject of separate litigation.
[369] *R. (Transport and General Workers Union) v Walsall MBC* [2002] E.L.R. 341.
[370] *Ayr Harbour Trustees v Oswald* (1883) 8 App.Cas. 623. But see also *Stourcliffe Estates Co. Ltd v Bournemouth Corp.* [1910] 2 Ch. 12.
[371] *Stringer v Minister of Housing and Local Government* [1970] 1 W.L.R. 1281.
[372] *Cory (William) & Sons Ltd v London Corp.* [1951] 2 K.B. 476.

charges.[373] The essential question is whether the entry into a binding agreement is compatible with the purpose for which the discretionary power has been conferred. Further difficulties occur when a public body has a number of different powers exercisable for different purposes. Here the exercise of one power by way of a binding contract may affect the ability of the public body to exercise other overlapping or conflicting powers. Here it is necessary to ascertain what the primary purpose or object of the statute is. The other powers are subordinate to the primary purpose.[374] If a statutory power is honestly and reasonably exercised for the furtherance of the statutory purpose, then it cannot be regarded as a fetter on the exercise of another power.[375] This principle was applied where a local authority had power to enter into restrictive covenants and had power to use the land for housing purposes. The object of these overlapping powers was to provide housing accommodation. The council entered a series of restrictive covenants regarding the redevelopment and eventual sale of flats owned by the council. The power was exercised to achieve the object of providing accommodation, albeit owner-occupied rather than owned by the council and let to council tenants. Consequently, the contract was not an improper fetter on the power of the council to retain the land and use it for housing.[376]

15–121   Public law principles may also be superimposed on the exercise of contractual powers, where the courts consider that some public element is involved in the use of the power.[377] Thus, the courts have engaged in judicial review of powers to grant or revoke licences where these have been used in breach of natural justice,[378] or for improper purposes.[379]

F.   RESTITUTION

15–122   Individuals may make payments of money in response to a demand by a public body. The demand may turn out to be ultra vires the statutory powers to levy money exercisable by public bodies. The question then arises as to whether the individual is entitled to recover the money unlawfully paid. Similarly, money may be paid under an agreement with a public body and that agreement may subsequently transpire to be ultra vires and outside the powers of the public body. The question then is whether either party to the agreement can recover money paid pursuant to the ultra vires agreement.

15–123   In relation to the first category of cases, the House of Lords has held that money paid by a citizen to a public authority in the form of taxes or other levies pursuant to an ultra vires demand by the authority is recoverable as of right by the citizen.[380] Recovery is not dependent on any mistake, compulsion or agreement. Thus, a building society contended that regulations authorising the levying of certain taxes were ultra vires the parent legislation. The society paid the taxes and

---

[373]   *Birkdale District Electricity Supply Company v Southport Corp.* [1926] A.C. 355.

[374]   *Blake v Hendon Corp.* [1962] Q.B. 283.

[375]   *R. v Hammersmith and Fulham LBC Ex p. Beddowes* [1987] Q.B. 1050.

[376]   [1987] Q.B. 1050.

[377]   See paras 2–146 to 2–148.

[378]   *R. v Wear Valley DC* [1985] 2 All E.R. 699.

[379]   *Wheeler v Leicester City Council* [1985] A.C. 1054.

[380]   *Woolwich Building Society v Inland Revenue Commissioners (No.2)* [1993] A.C. 70.

challenged the legality of the regulations by way of judicial review. The regulations were found to be ultra vires. The Revenue repaid the amount of the tax paid with interest from the date of the judgment but refused to pay interest from the date of the payment to the date of the judgment. The building society then sought to establish that it was entitled to recover the money paid and so was entitled to interest. The majority of the House of Lords decided that the building society were entitled as of right to recover money paid pursuant to an ultra vires demand and were entitled to interest on that money. The case concerned a demand for tax which was ultra vires in the narrow sense that there was no authority at all for the demand once the subordinate regulations were quashed. Two of the three members of the House of Lords forming the majority also expressed the view that the same principle applied in the event that the tax was not lawfully due for other reasons such as a misconstruction of the relevant statute or regulation.[381] In principle, that is correct. Money paid by way of tax or levy where there is no lawful authority requiring such payment ought, as a matter of principle, to be recoverable by the citizen.[382]

The House of Lords has also radically reformulated the law governing restitution in relation to the second category of cases, namely cases where money was paid under an agreement but where the parties were unaware at the time that the payment was made that the agreement was ultra vires. Previously, the law was considered to be that money paid under a mistake of law was not recoverable.[383] In *Kleinwort Benson Ltd v Lincoln City Council*,[384] the House of Lords held that this rule does not form part of English law. A person who pays money under a mistake of law is, prima facie, entitled to recover the money on the ground of unjust enrichment (the recipient having received money to which he is not entitled and being unjustly enriched thereby). Money is paid under a mistake of law even if, at the time of the payment, the parties were unaware that the agreement was ultra vires or where the settled view of the law, whether as a result of earlier judicial decisions or otherwise, was that agreements of the type in issue were lawful. There is no principle that money paid under a settled understanding of the law which is subsequently departed from by judicial decision cannot be recovered.[385] Consequently, a party who paid money under an interest rate swap agreement was entitled to recover that money when it subsequently transpired that such contracts were ultra vires the powers of local authorities. Interest, including compound interest, may be awarded.[386]

15–124

---

[381] [1993] A.C. 70 per Lord Goff at 177F–G and per Lord Slynn at 205A–D. Lord Browne-Wilkinson, the third member in the majority, did not deal with the point. See also the dicta of Scott V.C. in *British Steel Plc v Commissioners of Customs and Excise* [1997] 2 All E.R. 366 at [375j]–[376e].

[382] The money may be recoverable if paid pursuant to a mistake as to whether or not the money was lawfully due: see para.15–122 on the recovery of money paid under a mistake of law.

[383] See *Bilbie v Lumley* (1802) 2 East 469.

[384] [1999] 2 A.C. 349 overruling *Bilbie v Lumley* (1802) 2 East 469.

[385] *Kleinwort Benson Ltd v Lincoln City Council* [1999] 2 A.C. 349 (Lord Browne-Wilkinson and Lloyd dissenting on this point).

[386] *Sempra Metals Ltd (formerly Metallgesellschaft Ltd) v Inland Revenue Commissioners* [2008] 1 A.C. 561.

Possible defences and time limits

15–125   The courts have begun to recognise a number of possible defences to a claim for recovery of money paid under a mistake of law. These include situations where the recipient in good faith has changed his position in reliance on the payment such that it would be inequitable to order restitution.[387] Other defences are likely to be that the money was paid under a compromise agreement or in honest settlement of a legal claim.[388] The full scope of these defences remains to be worked out. It is not, however, a defence that the defendant honestly believed that he was entitled to retain the money nor that the money is paid under a void contract which has been fully performed.[389] In relation to claims based upon the right to recover tax paid pursuant to an ultra vires demand, the courts have left open the possibility of a defence arising whether the taxpayer has in fact been able to pass on the tax to his customers.[390]

15–126   One of the particular concerns in relation to claims for the recovery of taxes paid pursuant to an ultra vires demand is the need for certainty. This is particularly important in relation to public bodies who need to know whether they might be subjected to claims, especially where an error of law has been made which affects a large number of people. Claims for recovery could cause severe budgetary problems for a public body which had already spent income received, and was then faced with unanticipated calls on funds. That concern seems to underlie in part the statutory proviso applied in certain areas, that money will not be repaid where the error was based on a general practice. This allows for correction of individual errors, but prevents recovery in cases of an error affecting a large number of people. The courts may develop a defence based on public policy grounds in such circumstances.[391] Statute has itself addressed the problem by reference to the period within which claims must be brought. Such claims could formerly be brought either on the basis of restitution of monies unlawfully levied where the time limit for bringing the claim was within six years of the date on which the cause of action was paid (usually, when the tax was paid) or on the basis of money paid under a mistake of law where the time limit for bringing the claim was six years from the date when the mistake was discovered.[392]The latter, extended, period no longer applies in relation to mistakes of law in relation to taxation matters by the Commissioners of Inland Revenue.[393]

---

[387] See *Lipkin Gorman (a firm) v Karpnale Ltd* [1991] 2 A.C. 548.

[388] See *Kleinwort Benson Ltd v Lincoln City Council* [1999] 2 A.C. 349 at [1112F–G].

[389] See *Kleinwort Benson Ltd v Lincoln City Council* [1999] 2 A.C. 349 at [1112F–G].

[390]   *Woolwich Building Society (No.2) v Inland Revenue Commissioners* [1993] A.C. 70.

[391] See dicta of Lord Goff in *Kleinwort Benson Ltd v Lincoln City Council*]1999] 2 A.C. 349 at [1122B–D]; see dicta in another context of Lord Goff in *R. v Tower Hamlets LBC Ex p. Chetnik Developments Ltd* [1988] A.C. 858 at [882]. In this case normal restitutionary principles were overriden by the statutory framework.

[392]   *Deutsche Morgan Grenfell plc v Inland Revenue Commissioners* [2007] 1 A.C. 558.

[393]   Finance Act 2004 s.320 and Finance Act 2007 s.107. See Chapter 17 below on the compatibility of these provisions with EU law.

Recovery of money paid by a public body

Money paid out of the consolidated fund (that is, the exchequer into which public **15–127** revenue is paid) without statutory authorisation is ultra vires expenditure.[394] The government may recover such money providing it can be traced.[395]

Procedure

A claim for restitution involves two separate aspects. First, the individual will **15–128** need to establish that the demand for tax is ultra vires or otherwise unlawful or that the contract under which payment has been made is ultra vires. Secondly, the individual will need to assert his private law right to restitution of the money paid.

The issue of ultra vires raises a question of public law. This can be dealt with **15–129** by way of judicial review. The second issue, the claim for recovery, may be included in a claim for judicial review.[396] That enables the courts to deal both with the public law issue and any consequential private law issues relating to restitution in one set of proceedings.

An alternative is to institute one set of civil proceedings by way of an ordinary **15–130** claim for recovery of the money paid and have both the issues of ultra vires and of recovery dealt with in the ordinary claim proceedings. The rule in *O'Reilly v Mackman*[397] would not now appear to prevent the public law aspects of the matter from being raised in ordinary claim proceedings and would not require the ultra vires question to be dealt with first by way of judicial review. The right to recover money by way of restitution is clearly an ordinary private law right. Where an individual is asserting such a right, the rule in *O'Reilly v Mackman* would not preclude the individual from raising issues of public law in the ordinary claim proceedings intended to vindicate that right.[398] The Court of Appeal has also held that a company may challenge the lawfulness of a decision of the Customs and Excise Commissioners levying fuel duties in the course of an ordinary claim for the recovery of the duty paid and the company was not required first to challenge that decision by way of judicial review.[399]

---

[394] See *R. (Hooper) v Secretary of State for Work and Pensions* [2003] 1 W.L.R. 2623 at [131]–[135] on when payments are unauthorised.

[395] *Auckland Harbour v The King* [1924] A.C. 318 at [326]–[327]. *Quaere* whether the same principle applies to other public bodies, such as local authorities, who pay out money unlawfully. A local authority may now be able to recover the money on the grounds that it was paid under a mistake of law.

[396] See Senior Courts Act 1981 s.31(4) as amended by the Civil Procedure (Modification of Supreme Court Act 1981) Order 2004 (previously only claims for damages could be claimed in judicial review and this did not include claims for restitution: see dicta of Lord Woolf M.R. in *Rye Pension Fund v Sheffield City Council* [1988] 1 W.L.R. 840 at [849G–H]).

[397] [1983] 2 A.C. 237 and see Chapter 3 above.

[398] See, e.g. *Roy v Kensington and Chelsea and Westminster Family Practitioner Committee* [1992] 1 A.C. 624 and see above at paras 3–024 to 3–029.

[399] *British Steel Plc v Commissioners of Customs and Excise* [1997] 2 All E.R. 366.

Statutory provision for recovery and set-off

15–131 Statute may specifically provide a mechanism for repayment of charges unlawfully levied. Where a statutory code is intended to provide an exhaustive code for the recovery of particular types of payment, that statutory code should normally be used as a means of seeking the recovery of monies paid at least in the first instance.[400] The statutory regime may not, however, apply to a particular payment of tax mistakenly made by a taxpayer or the statutory procedure may not be available for particular reasons. In those circumstances, the taxpayer remains free to bring a restitutionary claim for the recovery of tax levied unlawfully or paid under a mistake of law.[401]

15–132 Statute may also provide for money unlawfully paid to be set-off against any subsequent liability. Thus, the House of Lords has held that regulations permitted overpaid value added tax to be set-off against value added tax due in the next quarter.[402]

Charges levied contrary to EU law

15–133 EU law prohibits the levying of certain charges. Member States cannot, for example, levy customs duties or charges having equivalent effect.[403] Taxes levied in a way which is incompatible with the freedom of establishment are prohibited.[404] Nor can Member States charge nationals of other EU countries fees for services falling within the scope of the EC Treaty that are higher than the fees they charge their own nationals.[405]

15–134 The Court of Justice of the European Union has held that an individual has a right to recover taxes or charges that are levied contrary to a directly effective provision of Community law.[406] This, in effect, requires national courts to provide a restitutionary remedy. The illegality of a charge is also a defence to enforcement proceedings to recover the charge.[407] Such claims may be brought in the domestic courts on the grounds that the money was not lawfully due, or that it was paid under a mistake of law[408] or using the relevant statutory procedure for seeking recovery of money.[409] This topic is dealt with in Chapter 17.

---

[400] *Autologic Plc v Inland Revenue Commissioners* [2006] 1 A.C. 118.

[401] *Deutsche Morgan Grenfell Group Plc v Inland Revenue Commissioners* [2007] 1 A.C. 558 (s.33 did not apply and did not permit recover of the payments in that case: see [135])

[402] *Customs and Excise Commissioners v Fine Art Developments Plc* [1989] A.C. 914.

[403] See Art.25 of the Treaty on the Functioning of the European Union.

[404] See, e.g. Case C-362/12 *Test Claimants in Franked Income Group Litigation* [2014] 2 C.M.L.R. 33.

[405] See, e.g. Case 24/86 *Blaizot v University of Liège* [1988] E.C.R. 379 (discriminatory fees for higher education unlawful).

[406] See, e.g. Case C-362/12 *Test Claimants in Franked Income Group Litigation* [2014] 2 C.M.L.R. 33; *Administrazione delle Finanze v San Giorgio* [1983] E.C.R. 3595; and Case 222/82 *Apple and Pear Development Council v Lewis (K.J.)* [1983] E.C.R. 4083.

[407] *Apple and Pear Development Council v Lewis (K.J.)* (see above, fn.406).

[408] See, e.g. *Deutsche Morgan Grenfell Group plc v Inland Revenue Commissioners* [2007] 1 A.C. 558. The claimant may seek to recover the ground on the basis of whichever rule is more favourable to him. In this case, the taxpayer sought to recover money on the basis of mistake as that provided, at that stage, for a longer time limit for bringing claims before they became statute barred: see Limitation Act 1980 s.32. The law in relation to claims for recovery of tax has now been amended by

G. RELEVANCE OF REMEDIAL DISCRETION OF THE COURTS TO PRIVATE LAW CLAIMS

A finding that a decision is ultra vires is a necessary element in a number of the private law actions discussed in the previous sections. A claim for false imprisonment, for example, may involve establishing that a decision to exercise statutory powers of detention was unlawful. Restitutionary claims involve establishing that the money was not lawfully due. In judicial review claims, the courts have a wide remedial discretion to refuse a public law remedy.[410] Where the claim involves private as well as public law issues, however, the claim may be brought by way of ordinary claim or the public law invalidity of a contract or other measure may be raised as a defence to the private law claim. The courts have taken the view that they cannot exercise the remedial discretion available to them in a judicial review claim in a private law action. In such cases, they are concerned with establishing whether or not a person has the private law right that is claimed. Where, therefore, a local authority facing a claim for breach of contract, raises the fact that the contract was ultra vires their powers, the courts in a private law action will simply determine whether or not that defence is made out. They will not exercise any remedial discretion and will not refuse to recognise the invalidity of a contract or measure on discretionary grounds.[411] Similarly, in *Wandsworth LBC v Winder*, Lord Fraser drew a distinction between judicial review proceedings where discretion might be relevant and civil actions, where a defence of ultra vires was put forward as of right.[412] This topic is dealt with in detail in Chapter 5.

15–135

H. STATUTORY COMPENSATION

Statute may make provision for compensation for loss resulting from the acts of public bodies in certain circumstances. This is so in the field of planning where, for example, compensation may be payable in cases of compulsory purchase.[413] Compensation for nuisance resulting from certain types of public works may also be payable.[414] Consideration of the provisions governing statutory compensation is outside the scope of this work and reference should be made to specialist planning works.[415]

15–136

---

the Finance Act 2004 s.320 which provides that the extended time limit for bringing claims on the grounds of mistake does not apply to claims relating to taxation.

[409] See, e.g. *Autologic Plc v Inland Revenue Commissioners* [2006] 1 A.C. 118.

[410] See Chapter 12.

[411] See *Crèdit Suisse v Allerdale BC* [1997] Q.B. 306; *Stretch v West Dorset DC* (1998) 10 Admin. L.Rep. 129.

[412] [1985] A.C. 461 at [509].

[413] Land Compensation Act 1973.

[414] Land Compensation Act 1973.

[415] See, e.g. Telling, *Planning Law and Procedure*; Heap, *An Outline of Planning Law*.

I. CROWN PROCEEDINGS

Introduction

15–137 The Crown historically enjoyed certain advantages in relation to civil liability. First, the Crown was immune from liability in tort: no action lay against the Sovereign personally, nor could the Crown be made liable for torts committed by its servants, including ministers and civil servants. Secondly, the actions against the Crown for breach of contract and restitution of property could only be brought by petition of right. A petitioner required the consent of the Crown to bring such a petition. The Crown Proceedings Act 1947 was principally intended to remove these advantages and make the Crown liable in tort, in the same way as any individual citizen is liable. The 1947 Act abolished the petition of right,[416] and reformed the procedure for bringing civil actions against the Crown so that, with certain exceptions, the Crown is in a similar position as any ordinary defendant to a civil action.

Liability in tort

15–138 Section 2(1) of the 1947 Act provides that the Crown will be liable in tort as if it were a private person in respect of:

(a) torts committed by its servants or agents;

(b) any breach of those duties which a person owes to his servants or agents at common law by reason of being their employer; and

(c) any breach of the duties attaching at common law to the ownership, occupation, possession or control of property.

The Crown will only be liable under (a) if there would be a cause of action against the servant.

15–139 The Crown will be civilly liable in damages for any breach of a statutory duty where a statute binds the Crown as well as other persons, and if the duty is such that a breach is remediable in damages.[417] The Crown, whilst able to take the benefit of statutes, is not bound by statutes unless the statute expressly or impliedly states that it binds the Crown.[418] The benefit of this rule is preserved by s.40(2)(f) of the 1947 Act.

Immunities

Judicial functions

15–140 The Crown is not liable for any act done by a person in the discharge of responsibilities of a judicial nature, or in connection with the execution of the

---

[416] Crown Proceedings Act 1947 s.1 and Sch.1.

[417] Crown Proceedings Act 1947 s.2(2).

[418] *Lord Advocate v Dumbarton DC* [1990] 2 A.C. 580. See also *R. (Cherwell DC) v First Secretary of State* [2005] 1 W.L.R. 1128.

judicial process.[419] That immunity extends to acts connected with the implementation of the judicial process.[420] The Crown is not, therefore, liable for the acts of judges, magistrates or constables or court officers. Thus, the Lord Chancellor's Department could not be sued in respect of a failure by the Criminal Appeals Office to implement a court order and process an appeal expeditiously.[421] Administrative officials performing adjudicative functions are not exercising judicial functions for the purposes of the 1947 Act. Thus, an adjudication officer determining eligibility for unemployment benefit was not discharging a judicial function.[422] The Crown was not, therefore, immune from suit on that ground alone.[423]

Armed forces

Section 10 of the 1947 Act conferred extensive immunity on the Crown from liability in respect of members of the armed forces who suffer death or personal injury whilst on duty.[424] The House of Lords has held that s.10 defined the scope of the substantive civil law right to claim damages against the Crown and, as such, did not operate as an immunity or procedural bar and was not incompatible with Art.6 of the European Convention on Human Rights.[425] That section has now been repealed, and the Crown has no exemption in respect of acts or omissions occurring after May 15, 1987.[426] The exemption conferred by s.10 of the 1947 Act may be resurrected by the Secretary of State where it appears to him to be necessary or expedient by reason of "imminent national danger" or any "great emergency," or for the "purposes of warlike operations ... outside the United Kingdom".[427]

15–141

Personal liability of the Sovereign

The immunity in tort of the Sovereign for acts done in his or her personal capacity is preserved.[428]

15–142

Acts not done in respect of the government of the UK

The 1947 Act only authorises actions in tort against the Crown in respect of the government of the UK.[429] The Secretary of State may grant a certificate that any alleged liability of the Crown arises otherwise than in respect of the government

15–143

---

[419] Crown Proceedings Act 1947 s.2(5).
[420] *Quinland v Governor of Swaleside Prison* [2003] Q.B. 306.
[421] *Quinland v Governor of Swaleside Prison* [2003] Q.B. 306.
[422] *Jones v Department of Employment* [1989] Q.B. 1.
[423] The claim was struck out on other grounds.
[424] See *Pearce v Secretary of State for Defence* [1988] A.C. 755 on the meaning of s.10.
[425] *Matthews v Ministry of Defence* [2003] 1 A.C. 1163. The matter is likely to be the subject of an application to the European Court of Human Rights.
[426] Crown Proceedings (Armed Forces) Act 1987 s.1.
[427] Crown Proceedings (Armed Forces) Act 1987 s.2.
[428] Crown Proceedings Act 1947 s.40(1) or in the right of the Duchy of Lancaster or as Duke of Cornwall: s.(38)(3).
[429] Crown Proceedings Act 1947 s.40(2)(b).

of the UK, and such a certificate is conclusive of that matter.[430] The Crown continues to be immune from liability in tort in respect of acts arising other than in respect of the government of the UK. Thus, the Crown could not be sued in tort for nuisance allegedly arising out of the use of a military base in West Germany, as the matter was certified to arise otherwise than in respect of the government of the UK.[431]

Definition of the Crown

15–144 The Crown is liable for the acts of its servants and agents. "Servants" is statutorily defined as officers appointed directly or indirectly by the Crown and paid out of money provided by Parliament or out of certain funds, or would normally be so paid.[432] This includes ministers, central government departments and civil servants. Agents includes independent contractors.[433]

15–145 Agencies carrying out functions on behalf of the central government, such as health boards set up under statute, are not the Crown.[434] Nor would they fall within the definition of servants of the Crown for the purpose of the Crown Proceedings Act 1947.[435] Thus, the Crown is not liable for the actions of such bodies. The bodies are of course liable in tort for their own actions and those of their employees. Actions against such bodies are therefore governed by the ordinary principles governing civil litigation and not by the Crown Proceedings Act 1947.

Liability in contract

15–146 The Crown was recognised as being liable for a debt or for a breach of contract. Claims could only be enforced by a petition of right which needed the consent of the Crown. Section 1 of the 1947 Act provided that where a claim could previously have been the subject of a petition, such a claim could now be brought against the Crown as of right. The claimant no longer needed the fiat of the Crown to bring an action. The petition of right was abolished.[436]

15–147 The Crown has inherent capacity to enter into contracts. A Crown servant who enters into a contract acting in his official capacity will not be personally liable for any breach of the contract.[437] This is a natural result of the law of agency; the principal, not the agent, is liable for a breach. There is also a rule of public law that provides that where a government minister or department acting as such enters into a contract, the contract is made on behalf of the Crown. Thus, where a government minister took a lease of land, the tenant was the Crown not the minister.[438] These rules are subject to any statutory provisions to the contrary.[439]

---

[430] Crown Proceedings Act 1947 s.40(3).
[431] *Trawnik v Lennox* [1985] 1 W.L.R. 532. Nor can this rule be circumvented by seeking a declaration rather than damages.
[432] Crown Proceedings Act 1947 s.2(6).
[433] Crown Proceedings Act 1947 s.38(2).
[434] *British Medical Association v Greater Glasgow Health Board* [1989] A.C. 1211.
[435] [1989] A.C. 1211.
[436] Crown Proceedings Act 1947 s.1 and Sch.1.
[437] *Macbeath v Holdimand* (1786) 1 T.R. 172.
[438] *Town Investments v Department of the Environment* [1978] A.C. 359.

The normal rules governing contractual liability apply to the Crown. There **15–148** are, however, at least two areas where special principles apply to Crown contracts. The first occurs in relation to the employment of civil servants. At common law, a civil servant is dismissible at pleasure and cannot sue for breach of contract for wrongful dismissal, even where he was engaged for a specified period of time which has not expired.[440] This was initially said to be based on an implied term in the conditions of appointment and a rule of public policy preventing the engagement of civil servants except on that basis. More recently, the rule has been viewed either as a rule of constitutional law or as an aspect of the prerogative power.[441] The fact that civil servants may be dismissed at will was thought at one stage to be incompatible with the existence of a binding contract of employment, so that a dismissed civil servant was not even able to sue for arrears of salary.[442] It is now recognised that this is an erroneous view and that the possibility of dismissal at will does not of itself prevent the existence of a contract until the contract is actually determined. The Divisional Court has held that the employment of civil servants may be regulated directly by the prerogative, or may be regulated by a contract of employment if all the elements of a binding contract exist, including the intention to create contractual relations.[443] It would seem that such contracts are still subject to the rule providing for dismissal at will.[444] A civil servant certainly cannot seek specific performance or an injunction to restrain dismissal until, for example, the requisite notice period has expired or any procedural requirements observed.[445] Nor would it seem possible to seek damages for wrongful dismissal as that may be seen as incompatible with, or a fetter on, the freedom to dismiss. Contractual actions alleging breaches whilst the contract was still in existence, and for arrears of salary would be possible.[446]

There is authority that the government cannot enter into a contract which will **15–149** restrict its future executive action, where it is necessary for the welfare of the state that the government retain its freedom of manoeuvre. Thus, there could be no action for breach of contract where, during war time, the government allegedly promised that a Swedish ship would be free to leave the UK and then it was prevented from doing so.[447] Ordinary commercial contracts were said to be unaffected by this rule. The exact scope of the principle remains uncertain.

---

[439] See, e.g. *Linden v Department of Health and Social Security* [1986] 1 W.L.R. 164.

[440] *Dunn v The Queen* [1896] Q.B. 116; *Denning v Secretary of State for India* (1920) 37 T.L.R. 589.

[441] See judgment of Lord Diplock in *Council of Civil Service Unions v Minister for the Civil Service* [1985] A.C. 374 at [409].

[442] *Mulvenna v The Admiralty* 1926 S.C. 842; *Lucas v Lucas* [1943] 2 All E.R. 110.

[443] *R. v Civil Service Appeals Board Ex p. Bruce* [1988] I.C.R. 649 (decision affd. by Court of Appeal on other grounds and position in relation to contract left open: [1989] I.C.R. 171); *R. v Lord Chancellor's Department Ex p. Nangle* [1991] I.R.L.R. 343.

[444] Roch J. expressly referred to this in *R. v Civil Service Appeals Board Ex p. Bruce* [1988] I.C.R. 649 but May LJ did not mention the point.

[445] Crown Proceedings Act 1947 s.21.

[446] See the decision of the Privy Council in *Kodeeswaran v Att-Gen of Ceylon* [1970] A.C. 1111.

[447] *Rederiaktiebolaget Amphitrite v The King* [1921] 3 K.B. 500.

Personal liability of the Sovereign

15–150 Prior to the 1947 Act, a petition of right against the Sovereign personally could lie for breach of contract. The 1947 Act abolishes the petition of right. However the 1947 Act also provides that nothing in the Act applies to the Sovereign in his or her personal capacity. Thus, it would not be possible to use an ordinary civil action against the Sovereign for breach of contract. It might be that there is now no method of taking action against the Sovereign personally (a matter likely to be of more theoretical and symbolic, rather than practical importance). It may be that the 1947 Act will be interpreted as abolishing the petition of right only where alternative methods of proceeding are provided by the Act itself. This would leave available the petition of right for claims against the Sovereign personally.[448]

Procedure

15–151 Detailed provisions governing procedure are contained in the Crown Proceedings Act 1947, and rules made thereunder. The principal rules are contained in CPR Pt 66.

15–152 Civil proceedings are to be instituted against the authorised government department.[449] They may be issued against the Attorney-General if none of the authorised departments are appropriate, or there is reasonable doubt as to which is appropriate.[450] The Treasury is required to publish a list of authorised departments, and the name and address of the person for service who will be the solicitor acting for the department.[451] The claimant must include the names of the government departments of the officers of the Crown concerned and brief details of the circumstances in which liability of the Crown is alleged to arise.[452]

15–153 Civil proceedings may be instituted either the High Court or the county court.[453] The Crown can apply for the transfer of the proceedings to another court and the location of the relevant government department or officers of the Crown is one factor to which the court must have regard when considering whether to order a transfer.[454]

---

[448] See Wade and Forsyth, *Administrative Law* 11th edn.
[449] Crown Proceedings Act 1947 s.17(3). The private law claim is not made against the minister although this does happen on occasion and no point is usually taken on the misnaming of the defendant: see, e.g. *Akenzua v Secretary of State for the Home Department* [2003] 1 W.L.R. 741 at [1]. CPR r.6.4 and see r.6.5(8) for rules on service.
[450] Crown Proceedings Act 1947 s.17(3).
[451] Crown Proceedings Act 1947 s.17(1). The list is annexed to CPR 66.
[452] CPR r.16.2(1A).
[453] Crown Proceedings Act 1947 s.15.
[454] Crown Proceedings Act 1947 s.20 and CPR r.30.3(2)(h).

Disclosure, further information and evidence

Disclosure and further information may be sought from the Crown.[455] They are **15–154** not automatically available and require an order of the court. The rules permitting non-disclosure, where a document is privileged or enjoys public interest immunity from disclosure, apply.[456] The ordinary rules of evidence apply.[457]

Remedies and execution

The court may make any order that it has power to make in proceedings between **15–155** ordinary citizens, subject to certain important exceptions. The court cannot order specific performance or grant an injunction against the Crown, or make an order for the recovery of land, but it may make a declaration of right in lieu.[458] Nor can an injunction be granted against an officer of the Crown.[459] Where the individual owes money to the Crown, no set-off may be made against any money alleged to be owed by the Crown to the individual. The ordinary law providing for payment of interest on debts, damages and costs applies.[460]

Where an order is made, the proper officer of the court must, on application by **15–156** a person in whose favour the order is made, provide a certificate containing particulars of the order.[461] If the order provides for the payment of damages or costs, the certificate shall specify the amounts. The appropriate government department is required to pay the damages or costs so certified.[462] The machinery for execution of the judgment or attachment cannot be invoked to enforce compliance with the court order.[463] No person is individually liable under any such order for payment.[464] As the duty is imposed on the government department by statute, it has been suggested that, in the highly unlikely event that the government department did not honour the order, a mandatory order might issue to compel the minister to comply with his duty to pay the damages.[465]

---

[455] Crown Proceedings Act 1947 s.28.
[456] Crown Proceedings Act 1947 s.28.
[457] CPR Pt 66.
[458] Crown Proceedings Act 1947, s.21(1).
[459] Crown Proceedings Act 1947 s.21(2).
[460] Crown Proceedings Act 1947 s.24.
[461] Crown Proceedings Act 1947 s.25(1).
[462] Crown Proceedings Act 1947 s.25(3).
[463] Crown Proceedings Act 1947 s.25(4).
[464] Crown Proceedings Act 1947 s.25(4).
[465] See Wade and Forsyth, *Administrative Law* (11th edn).

CHAPTER 16

Remedies under the Human Rights Act 1998

A. INTRODUCTION

The Human Rights Act 1998[1] has had a very significant impact on public law litigation in England and Wales, both in terms of substantive law and remedies and procedure. The considerable proportion of public law cases which involve some use of the HRA, as well as the distinct remedies it provides, renders specific treatment of the HRA important. Discussion of the substantive rights provided under the HRA is outside the scope of this book, and reference should be made to specialist works on human rights for more detailed consideration of the provisions of the HRA itself.[2]   **16–001**

This chapter outlines the structure of the HRA and its principal provisions. Section 6(1) provides that it is unlawful for a public authority to act in a way which is incompatible with a Convention right, that is, one of a number of rights guaranteed by the European Convention on Human Rights and specified as a Convention right for the purposes of the HRA. Most cases in which s.6 arises involve readily identifiable public authorities, often referred to as core public authorities, all of whose functions are treated as public for the purposes of the HRA. In addition, certain bodies perform functions some of which are public and some of which are private. The determination of whether a body is a public authority for the purposes of s.6 where it has both public and private functions is vexed. There is no single test and the courts will conduct an analysis of the relevant functions, rather than focussing on the nature of the body.   **16–002**

Incompatibility with a Convention right may arise because of a provision of primary legislation which, applying usual principles of construction, would conflict with the Convention rights. In such circumstances, s.3 requires the courts to construe that legislation, so far as it is possible to do so, in a way that is compatible with Convention rights. If the courts are unable to do so, because the interpretation would be irreconcilable with the language adopted by Parliament, it may make a declaration of incompatibility under s.4.   **16–003**

By virtue of s.8, damages may be awarded for breach of s.6 where that is necessary to afford just satisfaction. The approach of the courts has been to tie the conditions for, and the measure of, damages to what the European Court of   **16–004**

---

[1] In this chapter, the Human Rights Act 1998 will be referred to as the HRA.
[2] See especially: Clayton and Tomlinson, *The Law of Human Rights* (2nd edn, 2009); Lester, Pannick and Herberg, *Human Rights Law and Practice* (3rd edn, 2009); Beatson, Grosz, Hickman and Singh, *Human Rights: Judicial Protection in the United Kingdom* (2008).

Human Rights would award. In considering whether damages should be awarded in such cases, the courts may have regard to the gravity or severity of the violation, the manner or way in which the violation occurred and the impact on the individual. Each case revolves closely around its own facts, but the usual understanding is that the European Court of Human Rights does not generally award large sums for non-pecuniary losses, and the courts of England and Wales have adopted the same approach.

16–005   Section 7 is the principal source of the machinery for bringing a claim for breach of Convention rights and contains a number of procedural aspects which differ from a claim for judicial review under CPR Part 54. Only a victim of the breach of Convention rights has standing to bring the claim. Where a judicial review claim is the vehicle by which the claim is brought the three-month time limit will apply, but in other cases there is a limitation period of one year. In particular types of case, legislation has allocated the adjudication of human rights cases to particular courts or tribunals. Human rights may be relied upon both as a defence to a claim.

B. THE STRUCTURE OF THE HUMAN RIGHTS ACT

Convention rights

16–006   The HRA gives domestic effect to rights contained in the Convention for the Protection of Human Rights and Fundamental Freedoms 1950, otherwise known as the European Convention on Human Rights, or ECHR. The Convention is an international treaty, to which the United Kingdom is a State party, and the rights it provides are interpreted and considered by the European Court of Human Rights, which sits in Strasbourg. Since 1966, the United Kingdom has accepted the jurisdiction of the European Court of Human Rights over individual petitions, in which a person may allege that the United Kingdom has violated a Convention right.

16–007   Unlike many other State parties to the Convention, the United Kingdom has not implemented the Convention through its own set of domestic rights intended to cover broadly the same ground. Instead, the HRA incorporates certain of the rights guaranteed by Convention by defining those rights as Convention rights for the purposes of the HRA. The rights that are Convention rights for the purposes of the HRA are those contained in Arts 2 to 12, 14, Arts 1 to 3 of the First Protocol and Art.1 of the Thirteenth Protocol.[3] Some Convention rights have been interpreted by the European Court of Human Rights as imposing implicit obligations on States to take positive steps. Positive obligations under the Convention are an aspect of Convention rights and are enforceable in the same way.[4] The most commonly referred to Articles of the Convention which are not incorporated are Arts 1 (territorial extent of the Convention) and 13 (right to an effective remedy). Unincorporated Convention rights continue to bind the United

---

[3] HRA s.1(1), Sch.1.

[4] Examples of the domestic courts providing remedies for breach of positive obligations include *Rabone v Pennine Care NHS Trust* [2012] 2 A.C. 72 (award of damages) and *R. (Limbuela) v Secretary of State for the Home Department* [2006] 1 A.C. 396 (mandatory orders).

Kingdom in international law and may be relevant to domestic legal proceedings under ordinary principles of statutory interpretation.[5] The incorporated Convention rights are subject to any derogation or reservation on the part of the United Kingdom.[6] Derogations are provided for under s.14 and must be set out in Sch.3 to the HRA.[7] Reservations are provided for under s.15 and must also be set out in Sch.3 to the HRA.[8] Whenever a Bill is introduced in Parliament, the sponsoring Minister is obliged to make a statement to the effect that in his view the provisions of the Bill are compatible with the Convention rights, or that they are not but that the Government nonetheless wishes to proceed.[9]

Decisions of the European Court of Human Rights

Section 2(1) of the HRA imposes an obligation on any court or tribunal determining a question in connection with Conventions rights to "take into account" any relevant case law of the European Court of Human Rights (or the European Commission and Committee of Ministers, the former of which is now defunct). The HRA does not oblige a domestic court to follow the case law of the European Court of Human Rights.[10] Although the scope of this obligation has been the subject of differing judicial and academic views, the domestic courts should, in principle, follow the "clear and constant" jurisprudence of the European Court of Human Rights,[11] unless there are particular special circumstances which would justify not doing so. Those circumstances might be a misunderstanding on the part of the European Court as to nature or content of domestic law[12] or where it is inconsistent with some fundamental substantive or procedural aspect of domestic law.[13] Although it has been suggested that it is not for the domestic courts to go beyond the case law of the European Court in the protection of human rights under the Convention,[14] it is clear that the domestic courts have, on occasion, done so.[15] In any event, the absence of express authority on an issue does not absolve the domestic court from deciding the

16–008

---

[5] See, for example: *Assange v Swedish Prosecution Authority* [2012] 2 A.C. 471 at [10], [98], [112] and [122] but c.f. *R. v Secretary of State for the Home Department, ex p Brind* [1991] A.C. 696.

[6] HRA s.1(2).

[7] HRA s.14(5), Sch.3, Part I. There are currently no derogations.

[8] HRA s.15(5), Sch.3, Part II. The only current reservation is to the second sentence of Article 2 of the First Protocol: s.15(1)(a), Sch.3, Part II.

[9] HRA s.19. A Ministerial statement of non-compatibility is rare, but was in issue in *R. (Animal Defenders International) v Secretary of State for Culture, Media and Sport* [2008] 1 A.C. 1312.

[10] Citation should be of an authoritative and complete report, and copies taken from the European Court's database (known as HUDOC) may be used: see para.8.1 of CPR Practice Direction 39A.

[11] The wording is taken from *R. (Alconbury Developments Ltd) v Secretary of State for Environment, Transport and the Regions* [2003] 2 A.C. 295 at [26] but the case most often cited for the principle is *R. (Ullah) v Special Adjudicator* [2004] 2 A.C. 323 at [20]. See also *R. (Chester) v Secretary of State for Justice* [2014] A.C. 271.

[12] *R. v Horncastle* [2010] 2 A.C. 373; *R. v Lyons* [2003] 1 A.C. 976.

[13] *Manchester City Council v Pinnock* [2011] 2 A.C. 104 at [48].

[14] *R. (Al-Skeini) v Secretary of State for the Home Department* [2008] 1 A.C. 153 at [106]; *Ambrose v Harris* [2011] 1 W.L.R. 2435.

[15] *Re G (Adoption: Unmarried Couple)* [2009] 1 A.C. 173; *R. (Limbuela) v Secretary of State for the Home Department* [2006] 1 A.C. 396; *EM (Lebanon) v Secretary of State for the Home Department* [2009] 1 A.C. 1198; and arguably *R. (Ullah) v Special Adjudicator* [2004] 2 A.C. 323 itself.

point.[16] Where there is binding House of Lords or Supreme Court authority on an issue, that remains binding even if subsequent European Court case law suggests that it is incompatible with Convention rights; however, the Court of Appeal may depart from one of its own previous decisions if to do so would resolve an incompatibility.[17]

Primary and subordinate legislation

16–009   Section 3 of the HRA provides that legislation must be read and given effect in a way which is compatible with the Convention rights, so far as is possible to do so. Where it is not possible to do so in respect of primary legislation, the High Court, Court of Appeal or the Supreme Court may issue a declaration of incompatibility under s.4. These provisions are discussed below. Where a declaration of incompatibility is made under s.4, the power to take remedial action provided by s.10 arises and a Minister may by order amend the incompatible provisions of primary legislation.

Challenges to administrative action

16–010   Section 6 of the HRA provides that it is unlawful for a public authority—which includes courts and tribunals by virtue of s.6(3)(a) and s.9—to act in a way which is incompatible with Convention rights. This is discussed below. Section 7 of the HRA provides the procedural mechanism for bringing claims alleging a breach of the s.6(1) duty and is discussed below. The remedies available to the courts include, where necessary to afford just satisfaction, damages for breach of a Convention right under s.8: this is discussed below.

Other provisions

16–011   Where a court is considering whether to grant relief which may affect the exercise of the Art.10 Convention right to freedom of expression the court is required to "have particular regard to the importance of" the Art.10 right.[18] This may limit the willingness of the courts to grant, for example, interim relief to prevent publication: interim relief is not to be granted unless the court is satisfied that the applicant is likely to establish that publication should not be allowed.[19] Courts are also instructed to have particular regard to the importance of the Art.9 right to freedom of thought, conscience and belief where that right is exercised by a religious organisation.[20] Nothing in the HRA restricts any other right or freedom conferred under English law.[21]

16–012   For the purposes of the HRA, there are specific definitions of primary and subordinate legislation. The former includes any Act of Parliament; a Measure of the Church Assembly or the General Synod; certain types of Order in Council

---

[16] *Rabone v Pennine Care NHS Trust* [2012] 2 A.C. 72 at [112].

[17] *R. (RJM) v Secretary of State for Work and Pensions* [2009] 1 A.C. 311.

[18] HRA s.12(4).

[19] HRA s.12(3); *Cream Holdings Ltd v Bannerjee* [2005] 1 A.C. 253.

[20] HRA s.13. It has had no practical effect: *R. (Amicus) v Secretary of State for Trade and Industry* [2007] I.C.R. 1176; *R. (Core Issues Trust) v Transport for London* [2014] P.T.S.R. 785.

[21] HRA s.11.

(made under the prerogative and amending Acts of Parliament); and any other secondary legislation which brings into force or amends primary legislation.[22] Subordinate legislation is defined to include any Order in Council which is not primary legislation; Acts or Measures of the devolved Assemblies and Parliaments in Scotland, Wales and Northern Ireland; and any secondary legislation which is not defined as primary legislation.[23] The HRA came into force on October 2, 2000, does not generally have retrospective effect and does not render unlawful acts done before that date.[24]

C.   ACTS INCOMPATIBLE WITH CONVENTION RIGHTS

Acts of a public authority which are incompatible with Convention rights are a breach of s.6(1) of the HRA. An incompatible act is one which is inconsistent with, i.e. is a violation of, the Convention right.[25] Section 6(6) provides that "act" includes a failure to act. "Act" is interpreted as including a process leading to a decision,[26] but does not encompass failures to lay before Parliament a proposal for legislation or a failure to make primary legislation.[27]   **16–013**

The only exceptions are where, as a result of one or more provisions of primary legislation, the public authority could not have acted differently[28] or where a provision of, or made under, primary legislation cannot be read and given effect in a way which is compatible with Convention rights.[29] Distinguishing between the two situations is not always straightforward.[30] The treatment of primary legislation is dealt with below. Public law remedies sought by claims for judicial review are available in relation to acts which are incompatible with a Convention right. A decision of a public body may be quashed or declared invalid. Declarations may be granted that a particular act or omission is a breach of a Convention right.   **16–014**

Meaning of public authority

One of the most vexed questions under the HRA has been the extent of the meaning of "public authority" in s.6. Section 6(3) defines the term as including any court or tribunal and "any person certain of whose functions are functions of a public nature". It does not include Parliament, or a person exercising functions in connection with proceedings in Parliament.[31] The case law and commentary   **16–015**

---

[22] HRA s.21(1).

[23] HRA s.21(1).

[24] HRA s.22(3). Compare *Re McKerr* [2004] 1 W.L.R. 807 with *Re McCaughey* [2012] 1 A.C. 725.

[25] *Attorney General's Reference (No.2 of 2001)* [2004] 2 A.C. 72 at [7].

[26] *R. v Lambert* [2002] 2 A.C. 545 at [114].

[27] HRA s.6(6). This may prevent there being a breach of Convention rights in respect of subordinate legislation, made before the HRA, which has not been amended: *R. (T) v Chief Constable of Greater Manchester Police* [2014] 3 W.L.R. 96 per Lord Reed at [148]-[149].

[28] For examples see: *Wilson v First County Trust* [2004] 1 A.C. 816; *R. (Wilkinson) v Inland Revenue Commissioners* [2005] 1 W.L.R. 1718.

[29] HRA s.6(2).

[30] *R. (Hooper) v Secretary of State for Work and Pensions* [2005] UKHL 29; [2005] 1 W.L.R. 1681.

[31] HRA s.6(3)(b).

has generally distinguished for s.6 purposes between two types of public authority, referred to as core public authorities and hybrid public authorities.

Core public authorities

16–016   The category of core public authorities is generally easy to recognise. It includes central government departments, governmental executive agencies, local authorities, police forces and the armed forces.[32] Maintained schools, NHS bodies and publicly run prisons are also generally accepted as core public authorities. Where there is doubt, an appropriate analysis will consider whether the body has "special powers, democratic accountability, public funding in whole or in part, an obligation to act only in the public interest and a statutory constitution".[33] All the acts of a core public authority are subject to the obligation in s.6 and it must ensure that it acts in way that is compatible with Convention rights.[34]

Hybrid public authorities

16–017   A hybrid public authority is a body performing both public and private functions. By virtue of s.6(3)(b) they are subject to the s.6(1) duty only when they exercise a function of a public nature, and if a particular act is private in nature then the body will not be a public authority in respect of the doing of that act and the obligation in s.6 will not apply to that act.[35] The House of Lords has twice considered the test for hybrid public authorities. In *Aston Cantlow and Wilmcote with Billesley Parochial Church Council v Wallbank* the House of Lords reviewed the nature of a public authority under the HRA generally, and held that a parochial church council might be a hybrid public authority, but that the particular act of enforcing a lay rector's obligation to repair the church chancel was an act of a private nature.[36] *YL v Birmingham City Council* concerned an individual in a private care home which was paid for a local authority.[37] The majority held that a private care home did not carry out functions of a public nature because it carried on business for a profit, entered into contracts with residents, had no special statutory powers and made no distinction between residents paid for by the local authority and those who were privately funded. The outcome was reversed by subsequent legislation.[38] When assessing a hybrid public authority the courts will conduct an analysis of the relevant functions, rather than focussing on the nature of the body.[39] There is no single test of universal application for determining whether functions are public ones.[40] Among

---

[32] *Aston Cantlow and Wilmcote with Billesley Parochial Church Council v Wallbank* [2004] 1 AC 546 at [7].
[33] *Aston Cantlow and Wilmcote with Billesley Parochial Church Council v Wallbank*; [2004] 1 AC 546 at [6]–[8].
[34] *YL v Birmingham City Council* [2008] 1 A.C. 95.
[35] HRA s.6(5).
[36] [2004] 1 AC 546
[37] [2008] 1 A.C. 95.
[38] Health and Social Care Act 2008 s.145.
[39] *Aston Cantlow and Wilmcote with Billesley Parochial Church Council v Wallbank* [2004] 1 AC 546 at [63]–[64]; *YL v Birmingham City Council* [2008] 1 A.C. 95 at [148].
[40] *Aston Cantlow and Wilmcote with Billesley Parochial Church Council v Wallbank* [2004] 1 A.C. 546 at [10].

the factors that may indicate that the function is a public one is whether it involves the exercise of statutory powers, whether the body exercising the function is publicly funded or is performing functions that would otherwise be performed by central or local government.[41] The fact that the body concerned has a range of coercive statutory powers that it exercises points towards the function it performs being a public one[42] although the fact that the activity is regulated by statute is unlikely to be sufficient to render it a public function for the purposes of s.6(3)(b).[43] The fact that a function is performed by a private company, under contract to a local authority, is an indication that the function is not public at least in the absence of strong countervailing factors.[44] The reference to a body performing public functions is reminiscent of the test used in deciding whether a body is performing functions which have a sufficiently public element to make them subject to judicial review.[45] The fact that a function is, or is regarded as, a public function amenable to judicial review may therefore be an indication as to whether or not the function is a public function for the different purpose of s.6(3)(b) but is unlikely to be determinative.[46] It will be important to bear in mind the case law of the European Court of Human Rights in deciding whether a body is a public authority for the purposes of the HRA.[47]

When considering the public nature of a particular act under s.6(5) the analysis must not slide back into a functional one; there a difference between an act and a function.[48] It may be a function of a hybrid public authority to issue particular types of licence, but the act of purchasing paper or the employment of staff are individual acts in furtherance of that function and are not public in nature. By contrast, the termination of a tenancy by a registered social landlord, even though pursuant to a contractual basis, was a public act,[49] as were decisions as to the arrangement of wards and staffing in a private psychiatric hospital.[50]   **16–018**

Given that the purpose of s.6 is to determine which bodies, exercising which functions, are obliged to comply with the European Convention on Human Rights, it is possible that the range of bodies that are public authorities for the purposes of the HRA might be different from, and arguably narrower than, the range of bodies whose activities are sufficiently public to make them subject to judicial review and obliged to observe domestic public law principles in the   **16–019**

---

[41] *Aston Cantlow and Wilmcote with Billesley Parochial Church Council v Wallbank* [2004] 1 A.C. 546 at [10].

[42] See, e.g. *YL v Birmingham City Council* [2008] 1 A.C. 95 at [69] and 167.

[43] *YL v Birmingham City Council* [2008] 1 A.C. 95 at [116] and [134]. A contrary view was taken by Lord Bingham, dissenting, who considered that a high degree of statutory regulation of a function may indicate that it was public in nature: see [17].

[44] *YL v Birmingham City Council* [2008] 1 A.C. 95.

[45] See *Poplar Housing Association v Donoghue* [2002] Q.B. 48 at [65]; *R. (Beer) v Hampshire Farmers' Market Ltd* [2004] 1 W.L.R. 233 at [25].

[46] *YL v Birmingham City Council* [2008] 1 A.C. 95 at [156]. The fact that the activities of a private company in providing care to elderly persons under a contract was not a public function amenable to judicial review was a factor taken into account by the majority: see per Lord Mance at [120] and Lord Neuberger at [160].

[47] *Aston Cantlow and Wilmcote with Billesley Parochial Church Council v Wallbank* [2004] 1 A.C. 546.

[48] *Aston Cantlow and Wilmcote with Billesley Parochial Church Council v Wallbank* [2004] 1 AC 546 at [88]; *YL v Birmingham City Council* [2008] 1 A.C. 95 at [25], [34].

[49] *R. (Weaver) v London & Quadrant Housing Trust* [2010] 1 W.L.R. 363.

[50] *R. (A) v Partnerships in Care Ltd* [2002] 1 W.L.R. 2610.

exercise of those functions. In any event, if a body is exercising a public function for the purposes of the HRA, judicial review would be available against those bodies in respect of that function to ensure that they complied with their Convention rights and they will also normally be a public body for the purposes of judicial review and will have to observe the usual principles of domestic public law.[51]

D.   PRIMARY LEGISLATION INCOMPATIBLE WITH CONVENTION RIGHTS

Section 3

16–020   Where there is a conflict between the provisions of primary or subordinate legislation and the Convention there is a special procedure. The courts are required, by s.3 of the HRA, to construe any legislation in conformity with the Convention if it is possible to do so. The courts should first ascertain whether the legislation (without consideration of s.3) would be a breach of the Convention.[52] If so, the courts are then under an obligation to construe the legislation so "far as it is possible to do so" in a way that is consistent with the Convention rights. That is a strong obligation and does not first require the court to detect any ambiguity in the legislation.[53] It also does not matter whether the legislation was enacted before or after the HRA.[54] However, the task of the court is to interpret the legislation so far as it is possible to do so and not to amend the legislation or legislate itself.[55] Interpretation of legislation in a way that is "plainly impossible" is not consistent with the s.3 duty.[56] The House of Lords in *Ghaidan v Godin-Mendoza* suggested various forms of words to indicate when the courts would be going beyond the legitimate scope of s.3—such as whether the proposed interpretation would go against the grain of the legislation, or would remove its pith and substance, or would be incompatible with the underlying thrust of the legislation.[57] To give particular statutory provisions a meaning which departs substantially from a fundamental feature of the legislative scheme is likely to involve crossing the boundary between interpretation and amendment, as is an interpretation which leads to practical consequences which the court is not equipped to consider.[58] In *Ghaidan* itself, the Lords were prepared to read the Rent Act 1977 as though the survivor of a homosexual couple who had lived together was the surviving spouse of the original tenant, so that the right of survivorship was not restricted to heterosexual couples. By contrast, the House of

---

[51]   *R. (A) v Partnerships in Care Ltd* [2002] 1 W.L.R. 2610 at [9].

[52]   *Poplar Housing and Regeneration Community Association Ltd v Donoghue* [2002] Q.B. 48 at [75]; *Re S (Minors) (Care Order: Implementation of Care Plan)* [2002] 2 A.C. 291 at [41].

[53]   *Re S (Minors) (Care Order: Implementation of Care Plan)* [2002] 2 A.C. 291 at [37] and see also *R. v A (No.2)* [2002] 1 A.C. 45.

[54]   HRA s.3(2)(a).

[55]   *Re S (Minors) (Care Order: Implementation of Care Plan)* [2002] 2 A.C. 291 at [38]–[41]; *Poplar Housing and Regeneration Community Association Ltd v Donoghue* [2002] Q.B. 48 at [75].

[56]   *R. v A (No.2)* [2002] 1 A.C. 45 at [45].

[57]   [2004] 2 A.C. 557.

[58]   *Re S (Minors) (Care Order: Implementation of Care Plan)* [2002] 2 A.C. 291.

Lords did not consider that it was possible to interpret the provisions conferring power on the Secretary of State to set a minimum tariff for a prisoner serving a mandatory life sentence as a matter only for a judge, because there was a clear legislative intent that the decision would be for the Secretary of State.[59]

Section 4

Where it is not possible to rely upon s.3, the HRA gives the High Court and other appellate courts jurisdiction to grant a declaration of incompatibility, i.e. a declaration that a provision of primary legislation is incompatible with a particular Convention right.[60] A declaration of incompatibility may also be made in respect of subordinate legislation where that subordinate legislation is made under primary legislation which effectively requires the subordinate legislation to be in the form it is.[61] Where a court is considering such a declaration, the Crown is entitled to notice of that fact.[62] A notice given under s.5 should always be served by the court. However, once a party seeks a declaration of incompatibility, or acknowledges that such a declaration may be made, it should give as much informal notice to the Crown and to the court as practical.[63] The Crown shall be joined as a party.[64] A declaration of incompatibility does not affect the validity, continuing operation or enforcement of the legislative provision declared incompatible and is not binding on the parties to the proceedings.[65] A number of declarations of incompatibility have been granted. The House of Lords has, for example, granted a declaration that statutory provisions authorising the detention of foreign nationals suspected of international terrorism were incompatible with Arts 5 and 14 of the Convention as they were disproportionate and discriminated on grounds of nationality.[66] The Supreme Court granted a declaration that statutory provisions imposing lifetime notification and monitoring requirements on sex offenders was a disproportionate interference with Art.8 of the Convention.[67] Declarations may be granted in ordinary proceedings in appropriate circumstances, such as where the House of Lords has granted a declaration that provisions of the Matrimonial Causes Act 1973 were incompatible with Arts 8 and 12 of the Convention as they did not provide for recognition of the marriage of a transsexual.[68] However, declarations are discretionary. The courts may refuse to grant such a remedy where the litigation was unnecessary, as where a

16–021

---

[59] R. (Anderson) v Secretary of State for the Home Department [2003] 1 A.C. 837.

[60] HRA s.4 and see Wilson v First County Trust Ltd (No.2) [2004] 1 A.C. 816.

[61] HRA s.4(3)–(4). Where incompatible primary legislation does not in and of itself require the incompatible provisions of the subordinate legislation no s.4 declaration can be made in respect of that subordinate legislation: R. (T) v Chief Constable of Greater Manchester Police [2014] 3 W.L.R. 96 per Lord Reed at [151].

[62] HRA s.5 and CPR r.19.4A.

[63] Poplar Housing and Regeneration Community Association Ltd v Donoghue [2002] Q.B. 48 at [20].

[64] CPR r.19.4A(2). Frequently, the Crown, in the form of the appropriate minister will already be the defendant in judicial review proceedings and the claim form should include any claim for a declaration of incompatibility under s.4 HRA.

[65] HRA s.4(6).

[66] A v Secretary of State for the Home Department [2005] 2 A.C. 68.

[67] R. (F) v Secretary of State for the Home Department [2011] 1 A.C. 331.

[68] Bellinger v Bellinger [2003] 2 A.C. 467.

declaration was sought that provisions governing treason were incompatible with Art.10, where there was no prospect of prosecution under the relevant provisions.[69] The House of Lords did not consider a declaration of incompatibility necessary where the legislation had been amended by the time that the matter came before them[70] or where the matter was under consideration by Parliament.[71] The courts will not, as a matter of discretion, normally grant a declaration of incompatibility to a person who is not affected by the breach of the Convention rights in question.[72]

E. DAMAGES FOR BREACH OF CONVENTION RIGHTS

16–022 The courts have jurisdiction under s.8 of the HRA to award damages, where the court considers it just and appropriate to do so, to a claimant where a public authority acts in a way that is incompatible with that claimant's rights under the European Convention on Human Rights. Damages may only be awarded by a court with jurisdiction to do so in civil proceedings; damages under s.8 are not available from the criminal courts.[73] Damages may only be awarded if it is necessary to do so to afford just satisfaction to the claimant and the court must take account of all the relevant circumstances including any other remedy granted in respect of the violation.[74] The courts must also take into account the principles applied by the European Court of Human Rights in determining whether to award damages or the amount of damages to be awarded.[75] When citing European Court decisions, cases involving the UK or from other countries with a comparable cost of living will be of greatest assistance.[76] The approach of the English courts has been authoritatively set out by the House of Lords in *R. (Greenfield) v Secretary of State for the Home Department*[77] and the Supreme Court in *R. (Faulkner) v Secretary of State for Justice.*[78]

16–023 In many cases, an award of damages will not be necessary to afford just satisfaction to a claimant. The finding of a violation of a Convention right, and the fact that remedies are available on judicial review which will bring about an end to the violation, may constitute just satisfaction.[79] The fundamental principle underlying the European Court of Human Rights jurisprudence is that the courts should seek to achieve restitutio in integrum, that is to restore the claimant to the

---

[69] *R. (Rusbridger) v Attorney General* [2004] 1 A.C. 357.

[70] See, e.g. dicta in *Doherty v Birmingham City Council* [2009] 1 A.C. 367 per Lord Walker at [105] and Lord Mance at [164].

[71] *R. (Chester) v Secretary of State for Justice* [2014] A.C. 271 (compatibility of legislation prohibiting prisoners from voting). A declaration had already been made in *Smith v Scott* 2007 S.C. 345.

[72] *Lancashire CC v Taylor* [2005] 1 W.L.R. 2668 at [37]–[44]; *R. (Chester) v Secretary of State for Justice* [2014] A.C. 271 at [102] and [111].

[73] HRA s.8(2); *R. v Plinio Galfetti* [2002] EWCA Crim 1916.

[74] HRA s.8(3). On damages under s.8 generally see *McGregor on Damages* (19th edn, 2014), Ch.48.

[75] HRA s.8(4).

[76] *R. (Faulkner) v Secretary of State for Justice* [2013] 2 A.C. 254 at [38].

[77] [2005] 1 W.L.R. 673.

[78] [2013] 2 A.C. 254.

[79] *Anufrijeva v Southwark LBC* [2004] Q.B. 1124 at [53]; *R. (Bernard) v Enfield LBC* [2003] L.G.R. 423 at [39].

position that he would have been in if there had been no breach of his Convention rights.[80] Many of the Convention rights are not such that a breach will give rise to financial or pecuniary loss and the range of factual situations that may result in a finding of a breach of a Convention right is wide. In considering whether damages are necessary to ensure just satisfaction and in particular, in calculating the amount of damages, it is also appropriate to bear in mind first that the HRA is not a tort statute and its objects are different and broader from those of an act intended to provide compensation.[81] The finding of a violation will of itself be an important part of the remedy and a vindication of the person's Convention right. Awards of damages would not ordinarily be needed to encourage high standards of compliance with the Convention. In any event, an award of damages is discretionary, even where pecuniary loss can be proved, although the European Court of Human Rights does not articulate the principles upon which it decides whether damages should be awarded.[82] Secondly, the purpose of incorporating the Convention into domestic law was intended to give victims the same remedies in the domestic courts that they could have in the European Court of Human Rights, not to provide better remedies. Thirdly, the HRA requires domestic courts to look at the principles established by the European Court of Human Rights. Its awards are those it considers equitable, that is, fair to the individual in the particular case but without being precisely calculated. That is an indication that the domestic courts should apply a similar approach and not be significantly more or less generous than the European Courts of Human Rights rather than having regard to the levels of damages that might be payable for comparable domestic torts.[83] In considering whether damages should be awarded in such cases, the courts may have regard to the gravity or severity of the violation, the manner or way in which the violation occurred and the impact on the individual.[84] A procedural breach may be less likely to result in a damages award than a substantive breach.[85]

Following the European Court's approach, a claimant who wishes to claim **16–024** pecuniary loss must prove causation. Awards representing the loss of a chance will not normally be made.[86] However, where the breach of the relevant Convention right can be shown to have caused pecuniary loss that will ordinarily be recoverable. In principle, damages are also available for non-pecuniary loss in respect of matters such as distress, psychiatric trauma, injury or loss of liberty. Exemplary damages are not awarded.[87] Every award of damages must turn on the facts of the particular case. The following examples from the English case law

---

[80] *Anufrijeva v Southwark LBC* [2004] Q.B. 1124 at [59]; *R. (KB) v Mental Health Review Tribunal* [2004] Q.B. 936 at [22].

[81] *R. (Greenfield) v Secretary of State for the Home Department* [2005] 1 W.L.R. 673 at [19].

[82] Although terrorists unlawfully killed in the act of planting a bomb were thought not to require an award of damages: *McCann v United Kingdom* (1996) 21 E.H.R.R. 97.

[83] *R. (Greenfield) v Secretary of State for the Home Department* [2005] 1 W.L.R. 673 at [18]–[19].

[84] *Anufrijeva v Southwark LBC* [2004] Q.B. 1124 at [66]–[70].

[85] *R. (Greenfield) v Secretary of State for the Home Department* [2005] 1 W.L.R. 673 at [16]; *Re P* [2007] H.R.L.R. 14; although the Supreme Court declined to apply such an approach as a general rule in *R. (Faulkner) v Secretary of State for Justice* [2013] 2 A.C. 254.

[86] *R. (Greenfield) v Secretary of State for the Home Department* [2005] 1 W.L.R. 673 at [11].

[87] *Watkins v Secretary of State for the Home Department* [2006] 2 A.C. 395 at [64].

under s.8 provide some assistance as to the circumstances in which damages have been awarded, and the quantum of those awards.[88]

Article 2

16–025   A number of cases have now been decided in relation to the positive obligation on the State under Art.2 ECHR to act to prevent death where there is a real and immediate risk of it. The estate of a patient on an open psychiatric ward who left the hospital and committed suicide was awarded £10,000.[89] In a similar case where a psychiatric patient committed suicide whilst on a home visit the Supreme Court suggested that an award of £5,000 to each of the victim's parents was arguably too low, but did not alter the award as it had not been the subject of an appeal.[90] Where a prosecution witness had been threatened and then killed by the accused, the Court of Appeal awarded the deceased's parents £15,000 for the police's breach of Art.2, along with £10,000 to the deceased's estate in respect of his distress prior to his death.[91]

Article 3

16–026   A breach of the positive obligation under Art.3 on the police to investigate allegations of inhuman and degrading treatment which caused anxiety and distress for a period of some 15 to 18 months merited an award of £5,000.[92] The dropping of a prosecution of a crime committed against the claimant on the basis of the claimant's mental illness was held to be a breach of Art.3 and damages were awarded in the sum of £8,000.[93] In *DSD v Commissioner of Police for the Metropolis*, breaches of Art.3 had been found in respect of repeated failures on the part of the police to apprehend a rapist who attacked women in his taxi.[94] Although both victims had already received civil awards, it was held that an award under Art.3 was appropriate. Both victims had suffered prolonged depression, at least some of which was attributable to the police failings rather than the rape itself. They were awarded £22,500 and £19,000 respectively.

Article 5

16–027   Claims under Art.5 have been the most frequent uses of s.8 because of the range of situations in which individuals may be unlawfully detained by the State. Often the breaches are procedural defects, and the detention is not for long periods. In many cases the claimant will have already received compensation under the tort of false imprisonment. The case which determined the widest range of facts

---

[88] For more detailed treatment and discussion of the European Court's case law, see: *McGregor on Damages* (19th edn, 2014), Ch.48; Scorey and Eicke, *Human Rights Damages: Principles and Practice* (2001).

[89] *Savage v South Essex Partnership NHS Foundation Trust* [2010] U.K.H.R.R. 838.

[90] *Rabone v Pennine Care NHS Trust* [2012] 2 A.C. 72.

[91] *Van Colle v Chief Constable of Hertfordshire Police* [2007] 1 W.L.R. 1821. Although the House of Lords overturned the finding of liability, it made no comment on damages: [2009] 1 A.C. 225.

[92] *O v Commissioner of Police for the Metropolis* [2011] H.R.L.R. 29.

[93] *R. (B) v DPP* [2009] 1 W.L.R. 2072.

[94] [2014] EWHC 2493 (QB).

remains *R. (KB) v Mental Health Review Tribunal*, in which Stanley Burnton J made decisions on a number of unlawful detentions in mental health facilities, with findings which ranged from no damages to cases in which there was evidence of real distress and the loss of an opportunity to be discharged so that a sum of £4,000 was appropriate.[95] The Supreme Court held that in cases of a breach of Art.5(4) where a prisoner cannot prove that but for the delay he would have been released, a modest award for frustration or anxiety should still be made where the delay has been for three months or more. This led to an award of £300 for one claimant whose Parole Board hearing was delayed for six months, but £6,500 for a claimant whose approved conditional release from custody was delayed for the same period.[96] A breach of Art.5(4) which delayed release by three months was remedied by an award of £1,750.[97]

Article 6

No award of damages was necessary to afford just satisfaction in cases where the relevant body was not an independent and impartial tribunal contrary to the requirements of Art.6(1) because of the way in which the body was structured.[98]   **16–028**

Article 8

Damages of £10,000 were awarded in *R. (Bernard) v Enfield LBC* for breaches of Art.8 which led to a severely disabled woman being left in accommodation under deplorable conditions for 20 months.[99] Where a local authority had abandoned a care plan in relation to the claimant's son the Court of Appeal held that the removal of the child was lawful, and the violation of Art.8 was purely procedural and not significant and that a damages award was unnecessary to provide just satisfaction.[100] Where a decision was wrongly taken not to prosecute an individual for harassment, the victim of the repeated course of harassment could show that the CPS was in breach of its duty to take proper measures to protect her and was entitled to damages of £3,500.[101] An award of £500 was made where the claimant had been unlawfully cautioned and placed on the sex offenders register for taking a picture of his girlfriend's child (who was subsequently taken into care) playing naked in the park.[102] A water company which failed to bring to an end the continuing nuisance which was flooding the claimant's home was in principle liable under Art.8 for the pecuniary loss in value of the property.[103]   **16–029**

[95] [2004] Q.B. 936.

[96] *R. (Faulkner) v Secretary of State for Justice* [2013] 2 A.C. 254.

[97] *R. (Pennington) v The Parole Board* [2010] EWHC 78 (QB).

[98] *R. (Greenfield) v Secretary of State for the Home Department* [2005] 1 W.L.R. 673 at [16].

[99] [2003] L.G.R. 423.

[100] *Re P* [2007] H.R.L.R. 14.

[101] *R. (Waxman) v Crown Prosecution Service* [2012] EWHC 133 (Admin).

[102] *R (Mohammed) v Chief Constable of the West Midlands* [2010] EWHC 1228 (Admin).

[103] *Marcic v Thames Water Utilities Ltd* [2002] Q.B. 1003. On appeal, the Court of Appeal held that the damages in nuisance would be sufficient remedy: [2002] Q.B. 929. The House of Lords held that there had been no breach of Art.8: [2004] 2 A.C. 42.

Article 8 may justify a remedy for the intentional invasion of privacy by a public authority even if no damage was suffered other than distress.[104]

Article 12

16–030   A successful challenge to the procedure requiring certificates of approval in order to marry in the UK did not merit the award of damages.[105]

Article 14

16–031   It has been suggested, obiter, that an award of damages would not be required to provide just satisfaction where men had been denied a widow's bereavement allowance, because had the State complied with its Convention obligations the bereavement allowance would have been abolished for both men and women.[106] Lord Brown recognised that in other types of discrimination, such as equal pay cases, damages would need to recognise the value an employer had placed upon the work.[107]

Article 1 of the First Protocol

16–032   Claims under Art.1 of the First Protocol are the most likely to involve clear, and potentially substantial, pecuniary losses. The highest award of damages by the European Court of Human Rights is believed to be €1.9 billion to the shareholders of the Russian oil company Yukos, for breaches of Art.1 of the First Protocol by the retrospective application of penalties and various unlawful fees and charges.[108] The leading domestic authority is *R. (Infinis Plc) v Gas and Electricity Markets Authority*, in which the authority had unlawfully refused to grant the claimant a renewables obligations certificate in respect of their electricity generating stations.[109] That refusal was a breach of Art.1 of the First Protocol, and the claimant was entitled to the pecuniary value of the certificates: £94,393.62. It was not necessary to establish a legitimate expectation that there should be both a legal provision giving the applicant entitlement to some pecuniary benefit and a legal act such as a judicial decision confirming that entitlement.

---

[104]   *Wainwright v Secretary of State for the Home Department* [2004] 2 AC 406 at [51] (obiter because the HRA was not in force at the relevant time).

[105]   *R. (Baiai) v Secretary of State for the Home Department* [2006] EWHC 1035 (Admin).

[106]   *R. (Wilkinson) v Inland Revenue Commissioners* [2005] 1 W.L.R. 1718.

[107]   *R. (Wilkinson) v Inland Revenue Commissioners* [2005] 1 W.L.R. 1718 at [48]–[52].

[108]   *Oao Neftyanaya Kompaniya Yukos v Russia* (2014) 59 E.H.R.R. SE12. No award was made for non-pecuniary loss. The applicant had sought damages of some €38 bllion.

[109]   [2013] J.P.L. 1037. See too: *Breyer Group Plc v Department of Energy and Climate Change* [2014] EWHC 2257 (QB).

Article 3 of the First Protocol

Although the United Kingdom has repeatedly been found in violation of the right   **16–033**
to vote in Art.3 of the First Protocol, the European Court of Human Rights has
held that the finding of a violation was just satisfaction, and no damages should
be awarded for non-pecuniary loss.[110]

Judicial acts

Damages may not be awarded in respect of a judicial act which breached   **16–034**
Convention rights where it was done in good faith, except to the extent required
by Art.5(5) of the Convention.[111] Article 5(5) does not require an award of
damages in all cases.[112]

Procedure

Claims for damages against a public authority will often be attached to a claim   **16–035**
for judicial review alleging that the public authority has acted incompatibly with
a Convention right. The courts may deal with the substantive claim first and
adjourn consideration of the damages claim until later.[113] In the absence of any
order to that effect, however, the claimant will be required to advance his case
and adduce the evidence as part of his claim.[114] Where the claim for damages is
based on maladministration resulting in a breach, the amount of the award of
damages, if any is appropriate at all, is likely to be small and the courts are
concerned to ensure the procedure used reflects the likely amount of damages.
The claim should be brought in the Administrative Court either by way of a claim
for judicial review (if other public law remedies are sought) or an ordinary claim
under Part 7 of the CPR if damages only are sought. The court will consider
whether an internal complaints procedure or use of the ombudsman would be a
more appropriate means of dealing with such claims. Where a legitimate claim
for other, public law, remedies is brought, the court may still consider adjourning
or deferring the damages claim until alternative dispute resolution methods have
been tried or may remit the matter to a district judge or master. Hearings of such
claims should generally be limited to half a day unless there are exceptional
circumstances.[115]

---

[110] *Firth v United Kingdom*, App. No. 47784/09, (judgment of 12 August 2014) at [18].
[111] HRA s.9(3).
[112] *R. (KB) v Mental Health Review Tribunal* [2004] Q.B. 936.
[113] As happened in *Anufrijeva v Southwark LBC* [2004] Q.B. 1124 and *R. (KB) v South London and
South and West Region Mental Health Review Tribunal* [2004] Q.B. 936 and as happens, generally, in
cases where judicial review and damages are claimed: see above at para.9–138 above.
[114] *R. (Greenfield) v Secretary of State for the Home Department* [2005] 1 W.L.R. 673 at [30].
[115] *Anufrijeva v Southwark LBC* [2004] Q.B. 1124 at [81].

F. MACHINERY UNDER THE HUMAN RIGHTS ACT 1998

16–036 The procedural machinery for dealing with claims of a violation of a Convention right by a public authority is found in ss.6–8 of the HRA. As discussed above, s.6 generally makes it unlawful for a public authority to act incompatibly with Convention rights.[116] The power to award damages, or other remedies, is found in s.8. Section 7 provides the principal mechanism for bringing a claim for breach of Convention rights.

16–037 Section 7(1) generally provides that a claim that a public authority has acted (or proposes to act) in a way which is made unlawful by s.6(1) may be brought in the appropriate court or tribunal under the HRA, and that person may rely upon his Convention rights in any legal proceedings. Reliance on Convention rights can be used as a defence. The HRA defines "legal proceedings" as including proceedings brought by or at the instigation of a public authority, and it includes an appeal against a judicial decision.[117]

16–038 As a matter of practice, the majority of claims under s.7 are brought in judicial review proceedings, and the judicial review procedure discussed in Chapter 9 above will apply. A claim for judicial review will be appropriate where it is alleged that a public body has acted incompatibly with a Convention right. A claim for judicial review will also be appropriate if it is alleged that primary or secondary legislation should be interpreted to avoid incompatibility or to obtain a declaration of incompatibility if that is not possible. A claim for damages only under the HRA can, and ordinarily should, be brought in ordinary private law proceedings under Part 7 of the CPR. It is unlikely that the choice of procedure will cause a court to feel obstructed in reaching what it considers the correct outcome.[118]

Standing

16–039 The right to bring proceedings is limited by s.7(1) to a person who is, or would be, a "victim" of the unlawful act. A person is a victim of an unlawful act only if he would be a victim for the purposes of Art.34 of the Convention if proceedings were brought in the European Court of Human Rights in respect of that act.[119] A victim for Convention purposes will be a natural or legal person directly affected by the act or omission which is alleged to give rise to the breach of Convention rights,[120] although this does not necessarily require specific application of a general measure to the individual.[121] The test usually prevents public spirited citizens or representative groups from challenging the abstract compatibility of actions of public authorities with the rights derived from the Convention, but would not prevent a representative group supporting an individual victim who can benefit from the greater resources and expertise of the group. A person may also be a victim where the breach has directly affected a third party, most

---

[116] Section C above.
[117] HRA s.7(6).
[118] *R. (Wilkinson) v Responsible Medical Officer of Broadmoor Hospital* [2002] 1 W.L.R. 419.
[119] HRA s.7(7).
[120] *Corigliano v Italy* (1983) 5 E.H.R.R. 334 at [31].
[121] *Klass v Germany* (1978) 2 E.H.R.R. 214 at [34].

commonly a close relative.[122] The Supreme Court has confirmed that a close family member of a deceased victim may bring a claim for breach of Art.2 of the Convention.[123] The Supreme Court also held that a person's status as a victim was not lost where the deceased's estate settled a claim with the public authority, but the family members continued to seek non-pecuniary damages for their bereavement.[124] Where the claim is brought by way of judicial review, the applicant is to be taken to have a sufficient interest for judicial review purposes in relation to the unlawful act only if he is, or would be, a victim of that act for Convention purposes.[125]

A claimant for a declaration of incompatibility under s.4 does not have to establish that he is a victim, because such relief does not fall within the scope of s.7(1),[126] although the court may well refuse a declaration as a matter of discretion if he is not adversely affected by the provisions in question.[127]

16–040

Appropriate court or tribunal

There has been limited consideration of the "appropriate court or tribunal" in which to bring a claim under s.7(1) of the HRA. Any claim which is not in respect of a judicial act may be brought in any court. A claim which is in respect of a judicial act may only be brought in the High Court.[128] Proceedings which seek a declaration of incompatibility under s.4 must also be brought in the High Court (or on appeal from the High Court), as no other court or tribunal may grant such a declaration.[129]

16–041

Section 7(2) provides that rules may be made by the Secretary of State under s.7 which designate a particular court or tribunal as the appropriate venue to hear certain proceedings, or that rules of court may do so.[130] Few such rules have been made. The Proscribed Organisations Appeal Commission has been designated as the appropriate s.7 tribunal for certain types of case concerning proscribed organisations.[131] The Supreme Court has held that the Investigatory Powers Tribunal has exclusive jurisdiction over s.7 claims brought against the security services by virtue of s.65(2)(a) of the Regulation of Investigatory Powers Act 2000, including a challenge to a refusal of consent to the publication of the memoirs of a former Security Service employee.[132]

16–042

---

[122] *Kilic v Turkey* (2001) 33 E.H.R.R. 58 (applicant was the brother of a murdered journalist alleging a breach of Art.2 ECHR).

[123] *Rabone v Pennine Care NHS Trust* [2012] 2 A.C. 72.

[124] *Rabone v Pennine Care NHS Trust* [2012] 2 A.C. 72 at [49]–[63].

[125] HRA s.7(3); and see Chapter 11.

[126] *R. (Rusbridger) v Attorney General* [2004] 1 A.C. 357.

[127] *Lancashire CC v Taylor* [2005] 1 W.L.R. 2668 at [37]–[44].

[128] CPR r.7.11.

[129] HRA s.4(5).

[130] HRA s.7(9)(a).

[131] Proscribed Organisations Appeal Commission (Human Rights Act 1998 Proceedings) Rules 2006 (SI 2006/2290).

[132] *R. (A) v B* [2010] 2 A.C. 1.

Judicial acts

16–043   A judicial act of a court or tribunal alleged to be a breach of Convention rights contrary to s.6(1) of the HRA can only challenged by way of appeal, judicial review, or in such other forum as may be prescribed.[133] A court or tribunal which would not otherwise be amenable to judicial review is not rendered amenable by virtue of the HRA.[134] A judicial act for these purposes means a judicial act of a court and includes an act done on the instructions of, or on behalf of, a judge.[135]

Time limits

16–044   Section 7(5)(a) imposes a time limit for bringing proceedings under s.7(1) of one year beginning with the date on which the act complained of took place. This is subject to two qualifications. First, the court has the power to extend time to such longer period as is considered "equitable in all the circumstances".[136] Secondly, s.7(5) makes the time limit of one year subject to "any rule imposing a stricter time limit in relation to the procedure in question". This has the effect that where the claim is brought by way of judicial review the three month time limit, and the requirement of promptitude, will apply.

16–045   The highest court has considered the power to extend time under s.7(5) three times. In *Somerville v Scottish Ministers*[137] the House of Lords applied the concept of a continuing act familiar from discrimination law, to be distinguished from a one-off act with continuing consequences,[138] to breaches of the HRA and held that time only began to run when the breach ended. In *A v Essex CC* the Supreme Court upheld and approved the trial judge's refusal to extend time because the claim was brought some time after the breach had ended, and even if an award of damages was made it was likely to be modest and disproportionate to the costs of the proceedings.[139] In *Rabone v Pennine Care NHS Trust* Lord Dyson held that the court has a wide discretion and that the principles contained in s.33 of the Limitation Act 1980 may be helpful where the claim concerns, as in that case, personal injury or death, but that s.7 should not be read as if it included the s.33 factors.[140] Lord Dyson held that time should be extended because the required extension was short (four months); the defendant had suffered no prejudice; the claimants had acted reasonably in holding off proceedings in waiting for a particular report; and, most importantly, there was a good claim for breach of Art.2 of the Convention.[141]

---

[133] HRA s.9(1).

[134] HRA s.9(2).

[135] HRA s.9(5).

[136] HRA s.7(5)(b).

[137] [2007] 1 W.L.R. 2734.

[138] Contrast: *R. (Cockburn) v Secretary of State for Health* [2011] Eq.L.R. 1139 with *Mohammed v Home Office* [2011] 1 W.L.R. 2862.

[139] [2011] 1 A.C. 280 at [167]–[169].

[140] [2012] 2 A.C. 72 at [75].

[141] *Rabone v Pennine Care NHS Trust* [2012] 2 A.C. 72 at [79].

CHAPTER 17

Remedies for the Enforcement of European Union Law in National Courts

A. THE SIGNIFICANCE OF THE LAW OF THE EUROPEAN UNION

The importance and impact of EU law has grown immeasurably since the accession of the UK in 1973 to the three Treaties creating the European Community, the European Atomic Energy Community and the European Steel and Coal Community. These three Treaties, and in particular the Treaty of Rome creating the European Community, created a Community with its own institutions and legal capacity and endowed those institutions with legislative, executive and judicial powers within the field of competences covered by the Treaties. The Treaties and the secondary legislation enacted thereunder constitute an important and ever growing source of law. The major legislative and other measures constituting a source of rights and obligations are regulations, directives and decisions. The Member States have now created a European Union with legislative competence in a wide variety of areas and an institutional framework comprising the Council, the Parliament, the Commission and the Court of Justice of the European Union based on two treaties, the Treaty on European Union and the Treaty on the Functioning of the European Union. The treaties are referred to in this work as the TEU and the TFEU respectively.   **17–001**

The principal source of specific rights and obligations, however, is the TFEU and the legislation made under that treaty. In addition, Art.6 TFEU provides that the European Union recognises the rights set out in the Charter of Fundamental Rights of the European Union. That Charter guarantees a series of rights which apply to the institutions of the European Union and also to the Member States, but only when they are implementing European Union law.[1]   **17–002**

The case law of the Court of Justice[2] has ensured that the rights and obligations created by European Union law,[3] although originating in treaties   **17–003**

---

[1] See Art.51(1) of the Charter of Fundamental Rights of the European Union (referred to in this work as the Charter).

[2] The name given to the judicial body by the TEU and the TFEU is the Court of Justice of the European Union. The European Communities Act 1972 refers to it as the European Court. The name used in this work is the Court of Justice (to distinguish between the Court dealing with the law of the European Union which sits in Luxembourg and the different court, the European Court of Human Rights, dealing with the interpretation of the European Convention on Human Rights which sits in Strasbourg).

[3] The term "EU law" is used in this book to describe the law derived from the TEU and the TFEU and the secondary legislation made under it, together with the jurisprudence of the Court of Justice. In the

between states, have effect not just on relations between Member States on the international plane but also penetrate the national legal systems of the Member States, and are enforceable in national courts. The two main principles originally developed by the Court of Justice to achieve this were the concept of direct effect and the supremacy of EU law over national law. Direct effect means that provisions of EU law may confer rights on individuals. Such rights may be enforced in the national courts of Member States. The supremacy of European Union law means that EU law takes precedence over conflicting national law. National courts are also under a duty to construe national law in accordance with EU law. The Court of Justice has added a third fundamental principle, namely the obligation on national courts to ensure the full and effective protection of rights derived from EU law.[4] The courts within the United Kingdom are working out which remedies are appropriate for dealing with a breach of EU law. In addition, the TFEU provides that national courts and tribunals may, and in certain circumstances must, refer questions of EU law to the European Court for determination. This system of making references to the European Court for a preliminary ruling on a question of European law is discussed in Chapter 18.

17–004   This work deals only with remedies available in national courts, where national authorities or individuals violate EU law. The Court of Justice has jurisdiction to hear actions against Member States accused of violating EU law, as well as to review of acts of the institutions of the EU, to award damages against such institutions. These matters are outside the scope of this work.[5]

B.   DIRECT EFFECT—THE POSITION UNDER EU LAW

Treaty provisions

17–005   The European Court has consistently held that provisions of the TFEU may have direct effect. By direct effect, the European Court means that such a provision gives rise to rights and obligations which an individual can enforce in legal proceedings before national courts.[6] Directly effective provisions of the TEU or the TFEU are enforceable against a public authority or against another individual, as is the case, for example, with Art.157 TFEU which guarantees the principle of equal pay for equal work and which is enforceable against private employers[7] or

---

case law, the term "Community law" is frequently used to describe the law derived from the former Treaty creating the European Community (and, sometimes, to embrace the law derived from the Treaties creating the Coal and Steel Community and the European Atomic Energy Community). Given the creation of an EU, the terminology of "European Union law" and "European Union" or "EU" is generally used in this work rather than "Community law" and "Community".

[4] See, e.g. Joined Cases C-6/90 and C-9/90 *Francovich v Italian Republic* [1990] E.C.R. I-5357, at [31] to [33] of the judgment; Case C-213/89 *R. v Secretary of State for Transport Ex p. Factortame (No.2)* [1991] 1 A.C. 603 at 643-644, [18] and [19].

[5] See Arts 256 to 266 TFEU. For a discussion, see Hartley, *Foundations of European Union Law* (8th edn, 2014).

[6] *Van Gend en Loos v Nederlandse Administratie der Belastingen* Case 26/62 [1963] E.C.R. 1.

[7] Formerly, Art.119 and then 141 of the EC Treaty: see *Defrenne (Gabrielle) v SABENA* Case 43/75 [1976] E.C.R. 547 and see case C-256/01 *Allonby v Accrington and Rossendale College* [2004] I.C.R. 1328.

Art.101 TFEU prohibiting anti-competitive agreements.[8] Rights derived from the Charter are similarly capable of being directly effective and relied upon by individuals in areas of national law falling within the scope of EU law.[9] Article 6 of the TFEU recognises the rights guaranteed by the Charter and gives them the same legal value as TFEU.

Test for direct effect

A provision of the TEU or TFEU will be directly effective if the obligation it imposes is sufficiently precise, clear and unconditional.[10] The precise phrasing used by the Court of Justice in different judgments and by academic commentators[11] to describe the requirements varies, and to an extent the requirements are overlapping, but in essence they reflect the idea that the provision is capable as it stands of judicial enforcement. The case law gives an indication on the types of factors that are relevant.

17–006

Provisions which lay down general objectives will not be sufficiently precise to be directly effective. Provisions setting out the objectives of the European Union expressed with a very high degree of generality, for example, ensuring the progressive approximation of economic policies and promoting balanced development, will not be directly effective.[12] The predecessor of Art.4(3) of the TEU, which imposes a general duty on Member States to facilitate the achievement of the tasks of the European Union and to refrain from jeopardising the attainment of its objectives, has in the past been held to be too imprecise to be directly effective.[13] However, there may be situations where Art.4(3) of the TEU,

17–007

---

[8] Case C-453/99 *Courage Ltd v Crehan* [2001] 3 W.L.R. 1646.

[9] Case C-617/10 *Aklagaren v Fransson* [2013] 2 C.M.L.R. 46; *R. (NS) v Secretary of State for the Home Department* [2013] Q.B. 102 (Art.4 of the Charter, prohibiting torture and inhuman or degrading treatment, in terms similar to Art.3 of the European Convention on Human Rights, could be relied upon to prevent the return of an asylum seeker to another Member State). See also *R. (NS (Afghanistan)) v Secretary of State for the Home Department* [2013] Q.B. 102 at [116]–[122] (provisions of the Charter capable of direct effect in areas where national law implementing EU law; Protocol 30 to the TFEU providing that the Charter does not extend the ability of the Court of Justice or the UK courts does not preclude this conclusion as the Charter gives effect to general principles of EU law already recognised by EU law and does not create new rights or extend the jurisdiction of the courts). The Supreme Court in the United Kingdom has held that provisions of the Charter can be directly effective: see *Rugby Football Union v Consolidated Information Services Ltd. (formerly Viagogo Ltd.)* [2012] 1 W.L.R. 3333 at [26]–[28]: see below at para.17–038.

[10] See, e.g. *Hurd v Jones (Inspector of Taxes)* Case 44/84 [1986] Q.B. 892 at 947, [47] and for a similar formulation in relation to the provisions of directives, see case C-62/00 *Marks & Spencer Plc v Customs and Excise Commissioners* [2003] Q.B. 866 at [25].

[11] Hartley, *Foundations of European Union Law* (8th edn, 2014).

[12] See Arts 2 and 3 of the former Treaty of Rome (containing obligations now contained in part in Art.3 TEU): see Case C-339/89 *Alsthom Atlantique SA v Compagnie de Construction mecanique Sulzer SA* [1991] E.C.R. I-107; Joined Cases C-78/90 and C-83/90 *Compagnie commerciale de l'Ouest v Receveur principal des douanes de la Pallice-Port* [1992] E.C.R. I-1847 and see Case C-9/99 *Echirolles* [2003] 2 C.M.L.R. 506 at [25]. The Court of Appeal considered that Arts 198 and 199 TFEU, setting out the objective of promoting the economic and social development of overseas territories and countries, were not directly effective: *R. (Bancoult) v Secretary of State for Foreign and Commonwealth Affairs (No.3)* [2014] 1 W.L.R. 2921 at [142]–[143].

[13] *Hurd v Jones (Inspector of Taxes)* Case 44/84 [1986] Q.B. 892. For a similar conclusion by a domestic court, the Court of Appeal, see *R. (Bancoult) v Secretary of State for Foreign and Commonwealth Affairs (No.3)* [2014] 1 W.L.R. 2921 at [142]–[143].

read with other specific provisions of the TFEU or secondary legislation, may be capable of producing direct effects.[14] Furthermore, the Court of Justice has recognised that Art.4(3) of the TEU may require the national authorities to exercise any powers they may have to remedy a breach of EU law and that obligation may be enforceable in the national courts[15]; and may prevent a Member State from adopting legislation to restrict the effect of a judgment of the Court of Justice.[16] A provision that is conditional, particularly on legislative action by the Member State to implement the provision, will not be directly effective. An obligation that is conditional may, however, become unconditional. In particular where the provision imposes an obligation on the Member State to implement the provision within a particular time, the obligation, if sufficiently precise, will become unconditional on the expiry of the time-limit.[17]

17–008   A provision which does not specify how an objective is to be achieved, but leaves the Member State a discretion as to the appropriate means for achieving an objective, will not be directly effective.[18] The application of a provision may involve the evaluation of economic or other factors by institutions of the EU, such as the prohibition on state aids that are incompatible with the Common Market. Such provisions may be unsuitable for judicial enforcement and may not therefore be directly effective.[19]

17–009   A provision may confer a right on an individual but permit a Member State to derogate from that right in certain circumstances—such as the provision permitting limitation of the right to free movement on grounds of public policy and security.[20] Such a provision can be directly effective. The creation of the right is not dependent on the implementation of the measure by the Member State, and the exercise of discretion to derogate can be controlled by the national courts to ensure that no irrelevant factors are taken into account.[21] Similarly, where EU law provided for certain exemptions to be applied in relation to liability to tax under conditions laid down by the Member State, an individual who could demonstrate that his case fell within the scope of the exemption was entitled to rely on the

---

[14] See, e.g. Case C66/86 *Ahmed Saeed Flugreisen v Zentrale zur Bekampfung unlauteren Wettberwebs* [1989] E.C.R. 803; the question was considered and left unanswered in *R. v HM Treasury Ex p. Shepherd Neame Ltd* (1999) 11 Admin. L.Rep. 517. See also Lewis, *Remedies and the Enforcement of European Community Law* (1996) at 28–29.

[15] Case C-201/02 *R. (Wells) v Secretary of State for Transport, Local Government and the Regions* [2004] 1 C.M.L.R. 1027 (failure by planning authority to carry out environmental impact assessment under Dir.85/337; authorities obliged to take all general or particular measures within their powers to remedy the failure and for national court to determine if planning consent can be revoked or suspended).

[16] See, e.g., Case C-147/01 *Weber's Wine World Handels-GmbH v Abgabenberufungskommission Wien* [2003] E.C.R. I-11365.

[17] *Defrenne v SABENA* [1976] E.C.R. 547.

[18] Case 14/83 *Von Colson and Kamann v Land Nordrhein-Westfahlen* [1984] E.C.R. 1891.

[19] See Case 77/72 *Capolongo v Maya* [1973] E.C.R. 611 holding that what is now Art.101 TFEU is not directly effective in the absence of a decision by the Commission. The final sentence of what is now Art.108(3) TFEU which prohibits Member States from putting a measure granting State aid into effect until the Commission has been informed of the measures and ruled on their legality, is directly effective.

[20] Art.48(3) and Dir.64/221.

[21] Case 41/74 *Van Duyn v Home Office* [1975] Ch 358 and Case C-374/97 *Feyrer v Landkreis Rottal-Inn* [1999] E.C.R. I-5153 and see, e.g. Joined Cases C-397/01 and C-403/01 *Pfeiffer* [2004] ECR I-8835 at [103].

provisions of the Directive and the Member State could not rely on its own failure to lay down the conditions in order to avoid the provisions having direct effect.[22]

Other provisions of EU law may be intended to govern relations between Member States or between EU institutions and Member States and may not be intended to confer rights or obligations on individuals and may not, therefore, be directly effective. Procedural obligations imposed on Member States, such as obligations to consult[23] or to provide information to the European Commission, may be imposed to enable the relevant European institutions to monitor or co-operate with the Member States. If so, they are unlikely to confer rights on individuals enforceable in the national courts. It is uncertain whether the provisions governing responsibility for processing asylum claims as between different Member States is intended to regulate relations between Member States and, so are not directly effective,[24] or are intended to give rise to rights enforceable by individuals. The Court of Justice considered that a provision conferring a discretion on Member States to assess an asylum claim, rather than returning the asylum seeker to the Member State responsible for dealing with his claim, did not give rise to any obligation to do so.[25]

17–010

There are, however, a very large number of articles of the TFEU and provisions of secondary legislation which are sufficiently precise and are intended to give individuals rights which they can rely upon in national courts. These include rights in the area of free movement of workers, freedom of establishment and freedom to provide services, competition law, employment equal rights for men and women, agriculture, and many other areas.

17–011

Partial direct effect

The Court of Justice has, on occasions, held provisions to be partially directly effective. The Court has done this where some part of the provision is capable of application in certain areas by national courts, but where further implementing measures are necessary for the provision to be enforceable over the whole range of its contemplated application. In *Defrenne*[26] the Court of Justice accepted that what is now Art.157 TFEU guaranteeing equal pay for equal work was directly

17–012

---

[22] See, e.g. Case C-141/00 *Kugler Gmbh v Finanz for Korperschaften I in Berlin* [2002] ECR I-6833; Case C-45/01 *Christoph-Dornier-Stiftung fur Klinische Psychologie v Finanzamt Giessen* [2003] ECR I-12911.

[23] See, e.g. Case 6/64 *Costa v ENEL* [1964] E.C.R. 585 at 595 (obligation on Member States imposed by Art.97 (ex Art.102) to consult with the Commission before taking action which might distort competition was relevant to relations between the Member States and the Commission and did not create individual rights).

[24] That is how the domestic courts in England and Wales understand the position: see, e.g., *R. (MK (Iran)) v Secretary of State for the Home Department* [2010] EWCA Civ 116.

[25] Case C-4/11 *Germany v Puid* [2014] 2 W.L.R. 98. It is less clear whether this conclusion was based on the view that the particular provision in question, on its proper interpretation, conferred a discretion on the Member State not a right on the individual, or whether the Court of Justice saw the provisions of the Regulation as regulating relations between Member States.

[26] *Defrenne v SABENA* [1976] E.C.R. 547. The Court of Justice has subsequently accepted that Art.157 TFEU (ex Art.119 EC) is directly effective in relation to indirect discrimination, that is in relation to measures which appear to affect both men and women but in practice have a disproportionate adverse impact on women which cannot be objectively justified on grounds unconnected with sex: see Case 96/82 *Jenkins v Kingsgate (Clothing Productions) (UK) Ltd* [1981] E.C.R. 911. It seems that Art.141 (ex Art.119) will only fail to produce direct effect in relation to

effective in so far as direct discrimination was concerned. That Article was not directly effective in so far as indirect or disguised discrimination was concerned, as further implementing measures would be necessary to set out criteria for identifying such discrimination.

Temporal limitations and prospective direct effect

17–013 A provision is usually directly effective from the date on which the obligation came into force, not merely from the date on which the Court of Justice holds that the provision is directly effective.[27] A ruling of the Court of Justice is declaratory of the law and does not create new rights. The interpretation given by the Court of Justice to a provision of EU law clarifies and defines its meaning and scope as it should have been understood from the time of its entry into force.[28] The Court of Justice may in exceptional circumstances limit the temporal effect of a provision of European law, by holding that it is only directly effective from the date of the judgment.[29] The provisions will then be given prospective effect only. The Court of Justice may hold that the provision only applies to the instant case (and others already pending before national courts) and future cases; the provision will not be directly effective so far as factual situations arising before the date of the judgment are concerned.[30]

17–014 The Court of Justice will only impose a temporal limitation where two conditions are satisfied.[31] First, the national authorities concerned must have acted in good faith so that, in essence, that they have been led into adopting national rules which did not comply with EU law because, for example, there was, objectively, significant uncertainty as to the proper meaning or application of EU law. Secondly, the application of the ruling of the Court of Justice without any temporal limitation would be likely to lead to severe harm to the interests of those who relied in good faith upon the previous understanding of EU law. Both conditions must be satisfied. The financial implications of a ruling will not in itself justify imposing temporal limitations on a ruling of the Court of Justice.[32] Furthermore, in the absence of sufficient, detailed information as the financial consequences of a ruling, the Court of Justice may not accept that the second condition is satisfied.[33] In *Barber*,[34] for example, the Court of Justice ruled for

---

"disguised discrimination", that is discrimination which requires the adoption of further national measures to identify the discrimination and cannot be identified simply from a consideration of the facts and relevant legal provisions.

[27] Case 309/85 *Barra v Belgian State and The City of Liège* [1988] E.C.R. 355. See also Case C-262/88 *Barber v Guardian Royal Exchange Assurance Group* [1991] Q.B. 344.

[28] See, e.g. Case C-481/99 *Heininger v Bayerische Hypo-und-Veriensbank AG* [2003] 2 C.M.L.R. 1291 at [51] of the judgment.

[29] [2003] 2 C.M.L.R. 1291 at [51].

[30] See, e.g. Case 24/86 *Blaizot v University of Liège* [1988] E.C.R. 379. See also Case 112/83 *Sociètè des Produits de Mais SA v Administration des Douanes et Droits Indirects* [1985] E.C.R. 719 (in declaring regulation invalid, the Court of Justice even held it could limit the effect of its judgment to future cases only and need not apply the judgment to the case in which it declares the regulation invalid).

[31] See, e.g. Case C-209/03 *R. (Bidar) v Ealing London Borough* [2005] Q.B. 812; Case C-73/08 *Bressol v Gouvernement de la Communaute francaise* [2010] 3 C.M.L.R. 20 at [89]–[95].

[32] See, e.g. Case C-423/04 *Richards v Secretary of State for Work and Pensions* [2006] E.C.R. I-3585.

[33] See, e.g. Case C-313/05 *Brezinski* [2007] E.C.R. I-513 at [59]–[61]; Case C-209/03 *R. (Bidar) v Ealing London Borough* [2005] Q.B. 812 at [69]–[70].

the first time that the definition of pay in what is now Art.157 TFEU included contracted-out occupational pensions and required the elimination of different pension ages for men and women. Member States and employers and pension funds had reasonably believed that that provision of EU law did not apply to this situation, not least because secondary European legislation (wrongly) expressly authorised the deferment of equal treatment with regard to pension ages in occupational pensions. Further, applying the ruling retrospectively would upset the financial balance of many occupational pension schemes. The ruling would therefore only apply to pensions payable in respect of years of service after the date of the judgment.[35] In another case, the Court of Justice extended the principle of non-discrimination against EU nationals to fees charged for university education. They limited the effect of that judgment by holding that higher fees paid by EU nationals before the date of the judgment were not recoverable. There, the European Commission had written to the Belgian government indicating that the imposition of different university fees for non-nationals did not contravene European law. The Belgian authorities were therefore justified in considering that the relevant Belgian legislation was compatible with European law. Further, the Court of Justice was concerned about the financial effects on universities of allowing retrospective claims.[36] In another case, the Court of Justice limited the principle of equal pay for equal work to claims arising after the judgment because of the potentially devastating effect on employers of allowing retrospective claims.[37]

The Court of Justice alone can determine that the temporal effect of its judgment is to be limited. National courts cannot limit the effects of a judgment in this way and must regard a judgment as being declaratory and applicable retrospectively to claims arising during the period before the judgment, unless the Court of Justice expressly rules otherwise.[38] Even if a temporal limitation is not imposed, national law will generally have procedural rules prescribing the time limits within which a claim, including a claim for breach of EU law, must be made. National time-limits are compatible with EU law provided that they meet certain conditions.[39] Temporal limitations need to be distinguished from national time limits. A temporal limitation is imposed by the Court of Justice and provides that a right derived from EU law may only be relied upon and, therefore, only creates rights, from the date of the judgment of the Court of Justice. A time-limit in national law applies when a right derived from EU law exists but national law requires that a claim to enforce that right be brought within a prescribed period.[40]

17–015

---

[34] [1991] Q.B. 344.

[35] As clarified in Case C-200/91 *Coloroll Pension Trustees v Russell* [1995] I.C.R. 179; Case C-152/91 *Neath v Hugh Steeper Ltd* [1995] I.C.R. 158; see also Case C-128/93 *Fisscher v Voorhuis Hengelo BV* and Case C-57/93 *Vroege v N.C.I.V. Insituut voor Volkshuivesting B.V.* [1995] I.C.R. 635.

[36] *Blaizot v University of Liège* [1988] E.CR. 379.

[37] *Defrenne v SABENA* [1976] E.C.R. 547

[38] *Barra v Belgian State and The City of Liège* [1988] E.C.R. 355.

[39] See below on need for such rules to comply with the principle of effectiveness and equivalence.

[40] See Case C-231/96 *Edis v Ministero delle Finanze* [1998] E.C.R. I-4951.

Regulations

17–016 Article 288 TFEU provides that the institutions of the European Union may make regulations, issue directives and take decisions. The TFEU itself contains specific provisions authorising the institutions to take legislative or executive action in the various areas of economic activity covered by the TFEU and will usually specify which of the various measures may be used. Article288 TFEU also sets out the legal effect of each measure.

17–017 Article 288 TFEU provides that regulations are binding in their entirety and are directly applicable in all Member States. One of the consequences of direct applicability is generally taken to be that the provisions of regulations enter national law without any need for implementing measures by the Member State. Regulations are capable of being directly effective in the same way as provisions of TFEU, that is, they may confer rights and obligations on individuals which they may enforce in legal proceedings before national courts.[41] The same test for direct effect applies, that is the, provision of the Regulation must be sufficiently precise, clear and unconditional to be capable of judicial enforcement as it stands.[42]

Directives

17–018 Article 288 TFEU provides that a directive " . . . shall be binding as to the result to be achieved, upon each Member State to which it is addressed but shall leave to the national authorities the choice of form of methods". In other words, directives set out the objectives that are to be achieved, but leave the precise method of implementation to the individual Member States. They constitute a direction to the Member States to bring about the changes in national law or administrative practice necessary to achieve the stated objectives. As such, directives expressly contemplate further implementing measures by national authorities. They invariably set a time-limit within which Member States are to implement the directive. Although directives contemplate further implementing action by a Member State, the Court of Justice has held that the provisions of a directive may have direct effect if they are sufficiently precise and unconditional and the time-limit for implementing the directive has passed.[43] Furthermore, even if the directive has been implemented into national law, the provisions of a directive may still be relied in the national courts if, in fact, the full and effective

---

[41] Case 106/77 *Amministrazione delle Finanze dello Stato v Simmenthal S.p.A.* [1978] E.C.R. 629 and see, e.g. Case C-253/00 *Munoz y Cia SA v Frumar Ltd* [2003] 3 W.L.R. 58 (provisions of EU Regulation enforceable in civil proceedings in national courts).

[42] See, e.g. in a domestic court, *R. (Jaspers (Treburley) Ltd. v Food Standards Agency* [2013] P.T.S.R. 1271 at [29]–[45] (EU Regulation part of domestic law but did not create an enforceable obligation on individuals to pay charges for meat inspections).

[43] See, e.g. case C-9/81 *Becker v Finanzamt Munster-Innenstadt* [1982] E.C.R. 53 at [25] of the judgment; Case C-62/00 *Marks & Spencer Plc v Customs and Excise Commissioners* [2003] Q.B. 866 at [25] of the judgment.

application of the directive is not ensured by the implementing measures or if the implementing measures are not understood or applied in a way which achieves the results required by the directive.[44]

The Court of Justice clarified the position in relation to directives in the *Marshall* case.[45] The provisions of a directive may be relied on by an individual in legal proceedings before national courts, but only against the State or an emanation or organ of the State. Directives cannot impose obligations on individuals and, therefore, neither an individual nor the State can rely on the provisions of a directive as against another individual. The fact that enforcing the provisions of a Directive against the organs of the state may have an adverse effect on third parties does not, however, prevent the directive being directly effective and capable of being relied upon in the national courts. Thus, obligations in the planning field, such as the obligation not to grant planning consent without consideration of an environmental impact assessment, are obligations imposed on the organs of the state in respect of the exercise of their planning functions. The obligations are capable of being directly effective and enforced in the national courts notwithstanding the fact that enforcing that obligation against the authorities may have adverse implications for individuals.[46] Directives are therefore regarded as having "vertical" direct effect but not "horizontal" direct effect. The reasoning underlying this limitation is akin to English law notions of equity and estoppel. Directives impose obligations on Member States to achieve certain objectives and grant certain rights to their individual citizens. It would be inequitable for Member States which had failed to take action to confer rights in national law to take advantage of that failure by claiming that no rights in national law existed, and that provisions of directives were not directly effective and could not grant individual rights enforceable in national courts. Member States would be profiting from their own failure to implement the directive in national law.

17–019

The position has been complicated by recent decisions of the Court of Justice. The Court has held that provisions of a Directive may in fact reflect a specific implementation of a general principle of EU law. That general principle may be enforceable in a national court to preclude the application of a national law which contravenes the general principle even in a case involving only individuals and even where the provisions of the Directive itself could not be enforced by one individual against another. Thus, in one case, an individual brought a claim against a private employer contending that, under domestic law, she should have been given a certain number of months' notice of dismissal based on years of service. The national law, however, excluded years of service prior to the age of 25 from the calculation. The individual could not enforce the provisions of the

17–020

---

[44] See Case C-62/00 *Marks & Spencer Plc v Customs and Excise Commissioners* [2003] Q.B. 866 at [27] of the judgment.

[45] Case 152/84 *Marshall v Southampton and South-West Hampshire Area Health Authority* (*Teaching*) [1986] Q.B. 401. The Court of Justice reaffirmed that position in Case C-91/92 *Paola Faccini Dori v Recreb Srl* [1994] E.C.R. I-3325 at 3355–3358, [19]–[30]. National courts are, however, under a duty to interpret national law so far as possible in a way that achieves the result required by a directive: see below at 17-033.

[46] See Case C-201/02 *R. (Wells) v Secretary of State for Transport, Local Government and the Regions* [2004] 1 C.M.L.R. 1027 at [54]–[58] and to like effect in the Court of Appeal *R. v Durham CC Ex p. Huddleston* [2000] 1 W.L.R. 1484.

Directive prohibiting discrimination on grounds of age against the employer. She could, however, rely on the general principle of non-discrimination, which was part of the general principles of EU law, to preclude the application of the provision in the national legislation excluding years of service prior to the age of 25 in calculating the amount of notice to which she was entitled.[47]

Definition of emanation of the State

17–021 Directives are only enforceable against organs or emanations of the State or public authorities. The Court of Justice has held that a body is an emanation of the State for these purposes if " . . .the body was subject to the authority or control of the State or had special powers beyond those which result from the normal rules applicable to relations between individuals".[48] Thus, the Court of Justice has ruled that national tax authorities,[49] local or regional authorities,[50] public authorities providing health services[51] and constitutionally independent authorities responsible for maintaining public order such as the police,[52] are organs of the State. The Court of Justice has referred to a number of factors in reaching these conclusions, including the fact that a body's functions and composition were governed by legislation,[53] its members were appointed by the State[54]; it performed functions not normally performed by ordinary individuals[55] and it was funded by the State.[56]

17–022 In the context of publicly owned corporations, the Court of Justice has ruled that such a body will be an organ of the State if, whatever its legal form, it has been made responsible pursuant to a measure adopted by the State for providing a public service under the control of the State and has special powers over and above those powers enjoyed by ordinary individuals.[57] In applying that ruling, the House of Lords had held that British Gas was an emanation of the State in the period prior to privatisation when it was still a publicly owned corporation.[58] The House attached significance to the fact that it had a statutory duty to provide gas supplies and did so under the control of the State. Its members were appointed by the minister, it was responsible to the minister who could issue directions as to how it performed its functions and could require the payment of surplus revenue to the minister. Statute also provided that no other person could supply gas. British Gas therefore enjoyed powers over and above those enjoyed by ordinary individuals.

17–023 Two questions still remain to be determined. First, are all other publicly owned industries also emanations of the State? The Court of Appeal has held that Rolls

---

[47] See Case C-557/07 *Kucukdeveci v Swedex GmbH & Co.* [2011] 2 C.M.L.R. 27 at [48]–[56].

[48] Case C-188/89 *Foster v British Gas Corp.* [1991] 2 A.C. 306 at [18] of the judgment.

[49] Case 8/81 *Becker v Finanzamt Munster-Innenstadt* [1982] E.C.R. 53.

[50] Case 103/88 *Fratelli Constanza S.p.A. v Commune di Milano* [1989] E.C.R. 1839.

[51] *Marshall v Southampton and South-West Hampshire Area Health Authority (Teaching)* [1986] QB. 401.

[52] Case 222/84 *Johnston v Chief Constable of the Royal Ulster Constabulary* [1987] Q.B. 129.

[53] See Case 31/87 *Beentjes BV v Holland* [1988] E.C.R. 4635.

[54] [1988] E.C.R. 4635 and see *Marshall* [1986] QB. 401

[55] *Johnston v Chief Constable of the RUC* [1987] Q.B. 129.

[56] *Beentjes BV v Holland* [1988] E.C.R. 4635.

[57] *Foster v British Gas Corp.* [1991] 2 A.C. 306.

[58] *Foster v British Gas Corp.* [1991] 2 A.C. 306.

Royce prior to privatisation was not an emanation of the State.[59] The ruling is surprising as publicly owned utilities would, in the light of the ruling of the Court of Justice in *Foster*, appear to fall within the definition of organs of the State. Secondly, what is the position of the newly privatised utilities? Many of the features referred to by the House of Lords in *Foster* are absent, such as the power of ministers to give directions, to require payment of surplus and the enjoyment by the company of a statutory monopoly over the provision of services. The public utility companies are still regulated by the State and need to be authorised by the State to provide service. Once licensed, they are subject to certain duties and have certain powers in respect of providing the service. On one occasion,[60] the High Court has held that a newly privatised water company was an emanation of the State, applying the tripartite test set out in *Foster v British Gas*,[61] namely, whether the body has been made responsible for providing a public service, has special powers over and above those enjoyed by an individual and is subject to State control. The first was satisfied as the relevant statute imposed a duty on every water undertaker to develop an efficient system of water supply. The second was met as the privatised company had special powers including powers to enter land and lay pipes. The third was satisfied as the Secretary of State had sufficient control over the company; he appointed them as a water undertaker and could terminate the appointment and he and the regulator had wide regulatory control.

17–024 The Court of Appeal has emphasised that the courts ought not to adopt the rigid, three-fold classification applied in cases involving commercial undertakings to other types of bodies. Rather there are a number of indicia which point to the appropriateness of treating a body as an emanation of the State none of which is conclusive.[62] In that case, the Court of Appeal was dealing with a voluntary-aided school, that is a body which was originally a purely private school established by the church, but which was now "voluntary aided" in that a large amount of its funding was provided by the State and the school had, to a large measure, been integrated into the state education sector. The Court held that the three-fold test applied in cases of commercial undertakings was not appropriate in considering the status of governing bodies of such schools and concluded that the governing body was an emanation of the State.

17–025 Directives may be invoked against a body which is an organ of the State, regardless of the particular capacity in which it is acting in the particular case. It is not necessary for an organ of the State to be acting in a public capacity for a directive to be enforceable against it. Public authorities acting as employer rather than as public bodies have had directives relating to equality in employment matters enforced against them.[63] This raises an anomaly in that employees of public bodies may be entitled to enforce rights derived from EU law but employees of private employers are not so entitled. As the Court of Justice has

---

[59] *Doughty v Rolls Royce* [1992] I.C.R. 358.
[60] *Griffin v South West Water Services Ltd* [1994] I.R.L.R. 15.
[61] [1991] 2 A.C. 306.
[62] *National Union of Teachers v Governing Body of St Mary's Church of England (Aided) Junior School* [1997] I.C.R. 334.
[63] *Marshall v Southampton and South-West Hampshire Area Health Authority (Teaching)* [1986] Q.B. 401; *Johnston v Chief Constable of the Royal Ulster Constabulary* [19897] Q.B. 129.

pointed out,[64] the anomaly can be easily rectified by the Member State implementing the directive in national law as it is required to do.

Test for direct effect

17–026   Directives must also satisfy the same test as Treaty provisions in order to be directly effective. Directives will usually provide a time-limit within which Member States are required to implement the directive. Provisions of a directive will only be directly effective once that time-limit has expired.[65]

Decisions

17–027   Article 288 TFEU provides that decisions are to be binding in their entirety on those to whom they are addressed. Decisions are used for a variety of purposes. They may be addressed to Member States and require the Member State to take action such as abolishing an unlawful state aid, or they may authorise the Member State to take particular action such as imposing import restrictions.

17–028   Decisions addressed to Member States are directly effective providing they are sufficiently clear and precise to enable judicial enforcement.[66] In principle, a decision addressed to an individual would also seem to be directly effective and enforceable against the individual addressee.

Agreements between the EU and non-Member States

17–029   The TFEU expressly provides that the European Union has treaty-making powers in certain fields.[67] More importantly, the Court of Justice has held that where the TFEU confers power on the institutions of the EU to take action within the European Union in a particular area, the institutions have an implied power to conclude international agreements with non-EU countries in respect of such matters.[68] The internal powers or jurisdiction of the EU carry with them implied jurisdiction on the external plane.

17–030   The provisions of agreements with non-Member States can have direct effect.[69] It is irrelevant that the provisions may not be directly effective within the non-Member State. The test for determining whether Treaty provisions and regulations are directly effective applies.[70] The Court of Justice has emphasised that the approach to interpretation of provisions in an agreement with

---

[64] In *Marshall v Southampton and South-West Hampshire Area Health Authority (Teaching)* [1986] Q.B. 401 at 422, [51].

[65] Case 148/78 *Pubblico Ministero v Ratti* [1979] E.C.R. 1629; Case 62/00 *Marks & Spencer Plc v Customs and Excise Commissioners* [2003] Q.B. 866. A Member State must also refrain from taking measures during the period for implementation which would seriously compromise the result intended to be achieved by a directive: see Case C-129/96 *Inter-Environnement Wallonie ASBl* [1997] E.C.R. 7411 and Case C-144/04 *Mangold v Helm* [2005] E.C.R. I-9981.

[66] Case 9/70 *Grad (Franz) v Finanzamt Traunstein* [1970] E.C.R. 825.

[67] See Arts 216 to 218 TFEU.

[68] Opinion 1/76 on the *Laying-up Fund for Inland Waterways* [1977] E.C.R. 741.

[69] *Hauptzollamt Mainz v Kupferberg (CA) & Cie KGaA* Case 104/81 [1982] E.C.R. 3641.

[70] See, e.g. Case C-37/98 *R. v Secretary of State for the Home Department Ex p. Savas* [2000] 1 W.L.R. 1828 at [41]–[44]; Case C-268/99 *Jany v Staatssecretaris van Justitie* [2003] 1 C.M.L.R. 1 at [26]–[28].

non-Member States differs from that used in interpreting the TFEU and even where the same words are used in both they may mean different things.[71] The reason for this is that provisions of the TFEU have to be interpreted against the general objectives set out in the TEU and the TFEU which aim at uniting the different national markets into one common market. Agreements with non-Member States will not necessarily have similar aims and will be interpreted accordingly.

C. SUPREMACY OF EUROPEAN LAW—THE POSITION UNDER EU LAW

The Court of Justice has consistently and unequivocally held that, as a matter of EU law, directly effective European Union law is supreme and takes precedence over any conflicting provisions of national law. The supremacy of European Union law requires that national courts apply EU law in preference to national law, whether that national law was enacted before or after the relevant provision of EU law.[72] Every national court is required to give immediate precedence to EU law, and may not wait for the inconsistent national law to be repealed,[73] or set aside by a higher court or a constitutional court. The position is conveniently summarised in *Simmenthal*,[74] where the Court of Justice held that the Italian court had to give precedence to European Union law, which prohibited import charges, over subsequent Italian legislation authorising the levying of such charges. The Court said[75]:

> "[E]very national court must, in a case within its jurisdiction, apply Community law in its entirety and protect rights which the latter confers on individuals and must accordingly set aside any provision of national law which may conflict with it, whether prior or subsequent to the Community rule."

17–031

This principle was re-affirmed by the Court of Justice in *R. v Secretary of State for Transport Ex p. Factortame Ltd (No.2)*.[76] In that case, the European Court ruled that the English courts were required to set aside the rules of English law prohibiting the grant of interlocutory injunctions against the Crown and the grant of interim relief which would have the effect of suspending the operation of an Act of Parliament. The Court of Justice held that these rules impaired the full effectiveness of EU law and prevented the protection, albeit on a temporary basis, of rights claimed under EU law. The House of Lords accepted that English Courts must give precedence to EU law, even over Acts of Parliament.[77]

17–032

---

[71] *Polydor and R.S.O. Records Inc. v Harlequin Record Shops and Simons Records* Case 270/80 [1982] E.C.R. 329 at 349–350.
[72] See Joined Cases 10-22/97 *Ministere delle Finanze v In. Co.GE. '90 Srl* [2001] 1 C.M.L.R. 800.
[73] There is, however, also an obligation on Member States to repeal the legislation to avoid confusion: see Case 167/73 *Commission v France* [1974] E.C.R. 359.
[74] Case 106/77 *Amministrazione delle Finanze dello Stato v Simmenthal S.p.A.* [1978] E.C.R. 629.
[75] *Amministrazione delle Finanze dello Stato v Simmenthal S.p.A.* [1978] E.C.R. 629 at 644. See, in the context of the Charter, Case C-617/70 *Aklargen v Fransson* [2013] 2 C.M.L.R. 46 at [45].
[76] Case C-213/89 [1991] 1 A.C. 603.
[77] See below at para.17–045.

D. DUTY OF CONSISTENT INTERPRETATION

17–033 Some provisions of EU law are not directly effective either because they are insufficiently precise or, in the case of directives, an individual wishes to enforce the provisions against an individual and not against an organ of the State. In these circumstances, the provision of EU law does not confer rights enforceable in national courts. The individual must wait until the provision of EU law is implemented by national law. In the context of directives, the Court of Justice has held[78] that national courts applying national law in the relevant field are under a duty to interpret national law in the light of the wording and purpose of EU law so far as possible to achieve the result that the directive has in view once the implementing the directive has passed.[79] This duty applies in respect of all national legislation whether it pre-dates or post-dates the relevant directive.[80] It is therefore irrelevant whether the national legislation was adopted for the purposes of implementing the directive or whether it existed before the directive was adopted.[81] There is an exception in relation to criminal law: criminal liability cannot be imposed or the penalties aggravated solely on the basis of provisions of EU law.[82] Thus, for example, the obligation of consistent interpretation did not require national legislation to be interpreted in accordance with the provisions of a Directive for the purpose of imposing more severe penalties than would otherwise be imposed under the national law.[83]

E. THE OBLIGATION TO ACHIEVE FULL AND EFFECTIVE PROTECTION

17–034 The Court of Justice has emphasised that national courts are under an obligation to achieve the full and effective protection of rights derived from EU law.[84] The implications for the remedies necessary to give effect to EU law are discussed below.

---

[78] *Von Colson and Kamann v Land Nordrhein-Westfahlen* (see above, fn.19); *Faccini Dori v Recreb Srl* above, fn.43; Case C-185/97 *Coote v Granada Hospitality Ltd* [1998] E.C.R. I-5199. A similar obligation applies in relation to Framework Decisions adopted under Art.34 of the Treaty on European Union which are similar to directives in that they bind the Member State as to the result to be achieved but leave the choice of form and methods to Member States: see Case C-105/03 *Criminal Proceedings Against Pupino* [2006] Q.B. 83.

[79] Case C-212/04 *Adeneler v Ellinikos Organismos Galataktos* [2006] E.C.R. I-6057 at [115]. See also Case C-241/11 *Criminal Proceedings against Lopes da Silva Jorge* [2013] 2 W.L.R. 264 at [56]–[57].

[80] Case 106/89 *Marleasing SA v La Commercial Internacional di Alimentacion* [1990] E.C.R. I-4135.

[81] See Joined Cases C-397/02 and C-403/01 *Pfeiffer* [2004] E.C.R. I-8835 at [113]–[120].

[82] See Case 80/86 *Officer van Justitie v Kolpinghuis Nijmegen BV* [1987] E.C.R. 3969; Joined Cases C-74 and 129/95 *Criminal Proceedings against X* [1996] E.C.R. I-6609.

[83] Joined Cases C-387, 391 and 403/02 *Criminal Proceedings against Berlusconi* [2005] E.C.R. I-3565; Case C-105/03 *Criminal Proceedings against Pupino* [2006] Q.B. 83 at [45].

[84] Case C-213/89 *R. v Secretary of State for Transport Ex p. Factortame Ltd (No.2)* [1991] 1 A.C. 603 at 643–645, [18]–[19]; Joined Cases C-6/90 and C-9/90 *Francovich v Italian Republic* [1991] E.C.R. I-5357 [32]–[33] at 5414; (these cases build on the judgment in Case 106/77 *Amministrazione delle Finanze dello Stato v Simmenthal SpA* [1978] E.C.R. 629 at 643–644, [14]–[17]).

F. STATE LIABILITY IN DAMAGES FOR VIOLATION OF EU LAW

In *Francovich v Italian Republic*,[85] the Court of Justice had to consider whether a   **17–035**
Member State could be liable in damages for loss caused to an individual as the
result of a breach of EU law, in that case a failure to implement a directive. The
Court of Justice held that it was inherent in the system of EU law that, as a matter
of general principle, a Member State must be liable for loss caused to individuals
as a result of a breach of EU law for which the State can be held responsible. The
precise conditions under which state liability in damages arises depended on the
nature of the breach of EU law. This topic is considered in detail below.[86]

G. EU LAW IN THE UK

Direct effect

The European Communities Act 1972 was enacted to give effect to European   **17–036**
Union law within the UK. As a matter of English constitutional law, treaties
(including those creating the European Communities) have no effect within the
domestic legal system until Parliament enacts legislation giving effect to the
treaties.[87]

Direct effect is provided for by s.2(1) of the 1972 Act which provides that: **17–037**

> "All such rights, powers, liabilities, obligations and restrictions from time to time
> created or arising by or under the Treaties, and all such remedies and procedures
> from time to time provided for by or under the Treaties, as in accordance with the
> Treaties are without further enactment to be given legal effect or used in the UK
> shall be recognised and available in law, and be enforced, allowed and followed
> accordingly; and the expression "enforceable EU right" and similar expressions
> shall be read as referring to one to which this subsection applies."

This section ensures that all existing and future directly effective rights   **17–038**
derived from the Treaties and legislation made under the Treaties[88]are
enforceable in UK courts.

---

[85] [1991] E.C.R. I-5357.

[86] See 17–063 to 17–073.

[87] *McWhirter v Att-Gen* [1972] C.M.L.R. 882.

[88] The Treaties to which s.2(1) applies are defined in European Communities Act 1972, s.1(2). The
rights derived from the Charter are also capable of direct effect in national law and are enforceable
when national legislation implements EU law: Art. 6 of the TEU (listed in s.2(1)) recognises that the
Charter is to have the same legal value as the Treaties: see *Rugby Football Union v Consolidated
Information Ltd. (formerly Viagogo Ltd.)* [2012] 1 W.L.R. 333 at [27] and see the decision of the
Employment Appeal Tribunal in *Benkharbouche v Embassy of the Republic of Sudan* [2014] I.C.R.
169 (provisions of Art.47 of Charter relied upon to disapply provisions of legislation preventing
claims being brought against a foreign state to enforce rights derived from EU law).

Implementation of EU obligations

17–039 Section 2(2) of the 1972 Act provides for the making of subordinate legislation for the purpose of implementing any Community obligation[89] or of enabling any rights arising under the treaties to be exercised or for dealing with matters related to such rights.[90] The power conferred by s.2(2) applies to directly effective and non-directly effective EU law obligations. The provision authorises, for example, the making of subordinate legislation to implement a directive or an obligation contained in the TFEU, such as Art.157 guaranteeing equal pay, which requires further implementing measures in order to be fully effective.[91] Section 2(2)(a) also enables ministers to make regulations for transitional provisions, including provisions retaining in force existing domestic legislation relating to matters occurring before a harmonising directive was adopted.[92] The power conferred by s.2(2) may be exercised by Order in Council or by a designated minister or department making regulations. Other statutory powers may also provide for the making of regulations which will enable EU obligations to be implemented. There is no presumption that implementing domestic regulations only apply to the provisions of the EU Regulations or Directives in force at the time that the implementing regulations were made; rather the regulations may be drafted in a way that gives effect to the existing EU provisions and to any future amendments to those provisions.[93] If, however, provisions of a domestic regulation are drafted in a way that only imposes criminal penalties for a breach of provisions of a specific EU Regulation, and if they do not make provision for the offences to apply to that Regulation and any future amendments to it, then the domestic regulations may, as a matter of construction, cease to impose any criminal sanction once the specific EU Regulation is repealed.[94]

17–040 The power to make subordinate legislation does not include a power to impose or increase taxation; to enact retroactive legislation; to sub-delegate legislative power (except for making rules of procedure for a court or tribunal) or to create a new criminal offence punishable by more than two years imprisonment or

---

[89] European Communities Act 1972 s.2(2)(a). A community obligation is defined as any obligation arising under the Treaties creating each of the three separate Communities and the amending Treaties: see Sch.1 Pt II and s.1(2) of the European Communities Act 1972.

[90] European Communities Act s.2(2)(b). The powers conferred by s.2(2) of the European Communities Act 1972 are wide, general powers: see *R. v Secretary of State for Trade and Industry Ex p. Unison* [1996] I.C.R. 1003 and the words "relating to" in s.2(2)(b) should be given their natural meaning. The precise width of the powers conferred by s.2(2)(b) was considered in *Oakley Inc v Animal Inc* [2006] Ch. 337 but left undetermined as the relevant legislation fell within s.2(2)(a): Waller LJ indicated that the subsection empowered the making of measures which "naturally arise from or closely relate to" the Community obligation: see [2006] Ch. 337 at [39]. Jacob LJ provisionally considered that s.2(2)(a) covered all forms of implementation, that s.2(2)(b) was intended to go further but how much further depended on what the particular statutory instrument purported to do and the overall context and that s.2(2)(b) would not empower the making of regulations which had had only a tenuous relationship with a Community obligation: see [2006] Ch. 337 at [68]–[81]. May LJ left the matter open: see [47].

[91] e.g. regulations were made under this power amending the Equal Pay Act 1970 in order to implement Directive 75/117 following a decision by the European Court that the 1970 Act did not fully implement the Directive: see *Pickstone v Freemans* [1989] A.C. 66.

[92] *Oakley Inc v Animal Ltd* [2006] Ch. 373.

[93] *Department for the Environment, Food and Rural Affairs v Asda Ltd* [2004] 1 W.L.R. 105.

[94] *Dorset CC v House* [2011] 1 W.L.R. 727.

punishable on summary conviction by a fine above a prescribed level or imprisonment for three months. In these four cases, primary legislation will be necessary to implement European Union obligations.

The power is conferred by s.2(2) for the purpose of implementing an EU **17–041** obligation. In the event that a directive or other EU measure imposing an obligation on Member States were to be declared invalid, no EU obligation would exist and any order or regulations made under s.2(2) to implement that obligation would be void.[95] An order or regulation made pursuant to s.2(2) which went further than was necessary to implement the Community obligation may be void to that extent.[96]

Supremacy of EU law before UK courts

There is both a need to ensure that rights derived from European Union law are **17–042** available in domestic law within the United Kingdom (which is catered for by s.2(1) of the 1972 Act) and a need to ensure that those rights take precedence over any provisions of domestic law, and in particular any Act of Parliament. Legislation enacted prior to the European Communities Act 1972 presents no problems, as this can be regarded as impliedly repealed in so far as the legislation is inconsistent with European Union law as incorporated by the 1972 Act. Thus legislation enacted before the 1972 Act which confers powers to seize imported goods[97] or creates criminal offences[98] can be regarded as impliedly repealed by the 1972 Act in so far as that earlier legislation is inconsistent with European law. Subordinate legislation made after the 1972 Act but in reliance upon powers conferred by pre-1972 legislation can be regarded as invalid to the extent that the subordinate legislation conflicts with European law, on the grounds that the earlier legislation has been repealed in so far as it conflicts with European law and the effect of subordinate legislation can be no greater than the parent act.

The issue of the supremacy of EU law arises in its most acute form where **17–043** there exists both an Act of Parliament enacted after the 1972 Act and provisions of EU law which seek to regulate the same field of activity.

Prior to the accession of the UK to the European Union, the basic **17–044** constitutional position was that Parliament[99] was sovereign. There could be no enforceable restrictions on the legislative competence of Parliament. The domestic courts of the United Kingdom were therefore required to give effect to the most recent Act of Parliament as the latest expression of the will of the legislature. Despite the previous constitutional understanding, the House of Lords

---

[95] *R. v Minister of Agriculture, Fisheries and Food Ex p. FEDESA* [1988] 3 C.M.L.R. 661.

[96] per MacKay L.C. in *Hayward v Cammell Laird Shipbuilders (No.2)* [1988] A.C. 894 at 903. If the subordinate legislation is made under some other Act, then that other Act may confer power to create greater rights than those required by European law providing that the subordinate legislation is intra vires the parent act and that there is no prohibition in Community law on national authorities enacting legislation in the relevant area.

[97] See Case 121/85 *Conegate v HM Customs and Excise* [1987] Q.B. 254.

[98] In *Henn and Darby v DPP* [1981] A.C. 850, it was accepted that s.42 of the Customs Consolidation Act 1876 would have been impliedly repealed if it had been contrary to Art.28EC (ex Art.30); in the event the European Court held that the legislation was justified under Art.30EC (ex Art.36).

[99] Meaning, in this context, the Queen-in-Parliament (i.e. legislation which has passed the House of Commons and the House of Lords and received Royal Assent or enacted in accordance with the Parliament Act 1911).

had no difficulty in accepting that EU law was supreme and took precedence over Acts of Parliament, including acts passed after the UK acceded to the EU. In *Factortame (No.2)*,[100] a group of applicants alleged that the Merchant Shipping Act 1988, which imposed restrictions on the ability of EU nationals (other than British nationals) and companies where less than 25 per cent of their directors and shareholders were British nationals to register their ships as British fishing vessels, contravened European law. This issue was referred to the Court of Justice.[101] The applicants also sought an interim injunction to "disapply" the provisions of the legislation in the period before the judgment of the Court of Justice. The House of Lords held that as a matter of English law no interim injunction could be granted which had the effect of suspending the operation of an act of Parliament.[102] However, the House of Lords referred to the Court of Justice the question of whether European law required the granting of interim relief. The Court of Justice held that rules of national law which impaired the full and effective protection of European law should be set aside.[103]

17–045   When the matter came back before the House of Lords, the House held that the effect of the ruling of the Court of Justice was that they did have jurisdiction to grant interim relief. Their Lordships then went on to grant an interim injunction restraining the Secretary of State effectively from withdrawing or preventing certain vessels from entering the register of British fishing vessels.[104] In doing so, the House recognised that the courts were obliged to give supremacy to the rules of EU law even where this involved suspending or disapplying the provisions of a later UK statute. Lord Bridge simply stated that the notion of the supremacy of European law was clearly established in the jurisprudence of the Court of Justice long before the UK became a member of the European Union.[105] Thus, any limitation of the supremacy of Parliament had been voluntarily accepted by Parliament when it enacted the European Communities Act 1972. The Divisional Court has held that, as a matter of domestic constitutional law, the European Communities Act 1972 is a constitutional statute which incorporates EU law into domestic law. Any domestic law provisions, including provisions in primary legislation, take effect subject to EU obligations. In so far as they are inconsistent with rights derived from EU law, they must be disapplied or modified. The European Communities Act 1972 cannot be impliedly repealed by any later Act of Parliament which is inconsistent with EU law. Rather, there would need to be specific provision repealing the provisions of the European Communities Act 1972 if the later Act were to be given primacy.[106]

17–046   In the Merchant Shipping Act 1988, Parliament did not expressly state that it was intending to legislate in conflict with European law. It was simply that the Act was incompatible with European law. In the unlikely event that Parliament did expressly state that it intended to derogate from a provision of the EC Treaty,

---

[100] Above, fn.84.

[101] *R. v Secretary of State for Transport Ex p. Factortame Ltd* [1989] 2 C.M.L.R. 353. For the decision of the European Court see [1992] Q.B. 680.

[102] *R. v Secretary of State for Transport Ex p. Factortame Ltd* [1990] 2 A.C. 85.

[103] Case C-213/89 *R. v Secretary of State for Transport Ex p. Factortame Ltd (No.2)* [1991] 1 A.C. 603.

[104] *R. v Secretary of State for Transport Ex p. Factortame Ltd (No.2)* (above, fn.84).

[105] *R. v Secretary of State for Transport Ex p. Factortame Ltd (No.2)* (above, fn.84) at 857.

[106] *Thoburn v Sunderland City Council* [2002] 3 W.L.R. 247 at [61] and [68]–[70].

the question might then arise as to whether the British courts would recognise the supremacy of EU law or whether at that stage their loyalties would revert to upholding the supremacy of Parliament.[107]

More recently, the Supreme Court has left open the question of what should happen as a matter of national constitutional law if there were a conflict between a fundamental principle of constitutional law, such as the principle, enshrined in Art.9 of the Bill of Rights 1689 that courts will not engage in scrutiny of the passage of domestic legislation and the internal proceedings of Parliament and the requirements of EU law. The dispute arose in connection with the possible enactment of a Bill providing for a high speed train line in part of the United Kingdom. It had been argued that the provisions of a European Union directive required the domestic courts to assess the adequacy of Parliament's consideration of environmental information relating to the proposed train line. The Supreme Court held that the Directive, construed against a background where the Court of Justice would be unlikely to require national courts to exercise a supervisory jurisdiction over the internal proceedings of Parliament, did not require national courts to undertake such an exercise. The Supreme Court expressly left open the question of what should happen in the event of a possible conflict between fundamental principles of national constitutional law, whether recognised in statute or in the common law, with the European Communities Act 1972.[108]

17–047

Duty of uniform interpretation

The UK courts are also under an obligation to construe domestic law in a way that is compatible with EU law. This is particularly important in the context of directives as these are not directly effective against an individual. A person seeking to enforce a right derived from a directive against a private individual will therefore not succeed unless any relevant national law can be construed in a way that achieves the aim set out in the directive.[109]

17–048

The domestic courts and tribunals have accepted the scope of this duty of uniform interpretation. Acts of Parliament which are specifically enacted or amended to give effect to an obligation imposed by provision of the TFEU[110] or a directive[111] will be construed in a way that is consistent with the requirements of European Union law. Similarly, subordinate legislation made under s.2(2) of the European Communities Act 1972 to implement an EU obligation will also be construed to give effect to that obligation.[112] These principles apply whether the

17–049

---

[107] The implication of the decision of the Divisional Court in *Thoburn v Sunderland City Council* [2002] 3 W.L.R. 247 is that there would need to be specific provision amending s.2(4) of the European Communities Act 1972 which provides that provisions of domestic law take effect subject to any EU obligations.

[108] *R. (Buckinghamshire CC) v Secretary of State for Transport* [2014] 1 W.L.R. 324 at [206]–[214].

[109] If it cannot, the individual may have a *Francovich* claim against the UK government for failing to implement the directive. See below at paras 17–063 to 17–073.

[110] *Garland v British Rail Engineering Ltd* [1983] 2 A.C. 751.

[111] See, e.g. *Webb v Emo Air Cargo (U.K.) Ltd (No.2)* [1995] 1 W.L.R. 1454.

[112] *Pickstone v Freemans* [1989] A.C. 66.

EU provision is directly effective or non-directly effective.[113] Nor is it necessary for the Act or regulations to be ambiguous before the courts can turn to the European instrument.[114]

17–050   This approach to obligations derived from EU law has been adopted by the courts in a number of decisions. The courts have departed from the natural meaning of apparently unambiguous provisions of UK regulations[115] and primary legislation[116] and have read in words[117] in order to ensure that UK law conforms with European Union law. They have also had regard to Hansard where the implementation of an obligation derived from EU law was brought about by regulations which were not subject to Parliamentary amendment.[118]

17–051   The duty is to construe national law so far as possible in a manner that gives effect to and is consistent with EU law. On occasions, the domestic courts have considered that it was not possible to construe national law in a way that was compatible with EU law as that would involve distorting national law and giving it a meaning that it could not reasonably bear.[119] This can create difficulties for English courts as the nature of UK legislation is such that it frequently sets out in detail the circumstances in which rights arise and the groups who can claim such rights. Courts may therefore be reluctant to construe legislation in a way that conforms with EU law as that may involve ignoring or changing the wording of the legislation, a process which the English courts may see as distorting the legislation. They are, however, prepared to set aside or disapply provisions of national law which contravene directly effective provisions of European Union law. The obligation of uniform interpretation is, however, important in cases involving directives as these cannot be enforced against another individual; for a right to arise, national law must be construed in a way that gives effect to the directive. Notwithstanding the difficulties faced by domestic courts, the current approach is for courts to go to great lengths in seeking to ensure that national law

---

[113] See *Webb v Emo Air Cargo (U.K.) Ltd* [1995] 1 W.L.R. 1454 (not following *Duke v GEC Reliance Ltd* [1988] A.C. 618 on this point).

[114] *Pickstone v Freemans* above, fn.107; *Litster v Forth Dry Dock Engineering Co.* [1990] 1 A.C. 546. Earlier cases such as *Haughton v Olau Lines (U.K.)* [1986] 1 W.L.R. 504 and *National Smokeless Fuels v Inland Revenue Commissioners* [1986] 3 C.M.L.R. 227, which hold that an Act of Parliament must be ambiguous before the courts can have regard to the European instrument, are no longer good law.

[115] *Pickstone v Freemans* [1989] A.C. 66.

[116] *Webb v Emo Air Cargo (U.K.) Ltd (No.2)* [1995] 1W.L.R. 1454.

[117] *Litster v Forth Dry Dock and Engineering Co.* [1990] 1 A.C. 546; *Vodafone 2 v Revenue and Customs Commissioners* [2010] 2 W.L.R. 288 at [39]–[60] and [71] (Court of Appeal read in exception to a scheme of taxation to ensure that companies established in a Member State and carrying on genuine economic activities there were not subject to a tax, contrary to the right of freedom of establishment contained in what is now Art.49 TFEU.

[118] *Pickstone v Freemans* [1989] A.C. 66. Quaere whether the courts would have regard to Hansard in other situations, given the restrictions on the use of Hansard: see *Pepper v Hart* [1993] A.C. 593. In one sense, the use of Hansard is not of great significance as the courts will in any event have to have regard to the European instrument whether or not Hansard indicates that it was introduced to give effect to an obligation derived from European law.

[119] *Duke v GEC Reliance Ltd* [1988] 1 A.C. 618; *Finnegan v Clowney Youth Training Ltd* [1990] 2 A.C. 407; *Re Hartlebury Printers Ltd* [1994] 2 C.M.L.R. 705 at 712–713, (High Court); *Bhudi v IMI Refiners Ltd* [1994] 2 C.M.L.R. 296.

gives effect to directives[120]and other provisions of EU law.[121] In addition, it is important to bear in mind that in many instances, EU law requires domestic legislation to be interpreted so that it prohibits discrimination as between UK and other EU nationals; it does not require the legislation to be interpreted in a way that would also extend the more favourable treatment accorded to UK nationals to non-EU nationals from third countries.[122]

H.   REMEDIES FOR BREACHES OF EU LAW

Principles laid down by the Court of Justice on remedies

The concept of direct effect simply means that individuals can derive rights from EU law which they can invoke in legal proceedings before national courts. Direct effect does not state which remedies a national court should use to vindicate those rights in an individual case. The question that arises is which remedies are available when a public authority or an individual acts in a way that is contrary to European law, and violates the rights enjoyed by an individual under European law.   17–052

The TEU and the TFEU, and their predecessors, do not provide any guidance on the issue of remedies although Art.47 of the Charter now provides that everyone whose rights and freedoms guaranteed by law are violated has the right to an effective remedy. The Court of Justice traditionally took the view that, while EU law determined the rights that the individual enjoyed, it was for the national law of the Member State where the action was brought to determine all matters relating to remedies and procedure. In particular, national law determined which national courts and tribunals had jurisdiction to hear the claim and determined the substantive and procedural rules governing the enforcement of the claim provided that national law did not treat rights derived from EU law less favourably than similar domestic law rights and did not make it impossible in practice to exercise a right EU law.[123]   17–053

The need to ensure full and effective protection

The traditional approach has been radically altered over the years. Whilst continuing to recognise that it is for national law to designate the appropriate courts and tribunals having jurisdiction to deal with claims and to lay down detailed procedural rules for enforcing claims, the Court of Justice now emphasises that national courts are under an obligation to ensure the full and   17–054

---

[120] See, e.g. *Webb v Emo Air Cargo (U.K.) Ltd (No2)* [1995] 1 W.L.R. 1454, where the House of Lords gave an interpretation to domestic law which clearly did not accord with their view of what the domestic law intended (see the earlier judgment at [1993] 1 W.L.R. 49).

[121] *Vodafone 2 v Revenue and Customs Commissioners* [2010] 2 W.L.R. 288.

[122] See *Gingi v Secretary of State for Work and Pensions* [2002] Eu. L.R. 37 at [12]–[20]; and see Case C-246/96 *ICI v Colmer (Inspector of Taxes)* [1998] E.C.R. I-4695 at [32]–[34].

[123] Case 45/76 *Comet BV v Produktschap voor Siegerwassen* [1976] E.C.R. 2043; Case 33/76 *Rewe-Zentralfinanz eG and Rewe-Zentral A.G. v Landwirtschafstkammer fur das Saarland* [1976] E.C.R. 1989.

effective protection of rights derived from EU law.[124] EU law itself (as interpreted by the Court of Justice) may determine what is necessary at the remedial level to guarantee effective protection. Thus, European Union law may determine that, as a matter of general principle, a Member State may be required to pay compensation for damage caused by a breach of EU law if certain conditions are satisfied.[125] The Court of Justice may decide that a particular remedy, available to particular individuals, must be available in domestic law to ensure the full and effective application of EU law.[126] The Court of Justice may also rule that substantive or procedural rules of national law limiting the availability of a remedy undermine the effective protection of a right derived from European Union law and so must be set aside. Thus, in *Factortame*,[127] the Court of Justice considered that the English common law rules prohibiting the grant of interim relief against the Crown and the grant of relief which had the effect of suspending the operation of an Act of Parliament undermined the effective protection of EU law rights and impaired the full effectiveness of EU law. National courts had to have the power to grant interim relief and national rules denying the courts the jurisdiction to grant such relief in appropriate circumstances had to be set aside.

The principles of effectiveness and equivalence

17–055 In practical terms, a national court dealing with a claim that a person has a European Union law right which is being violated will need to consider both the need to ensure the effective protection of that EU law right and the need to ensure that the right is not treated less favourably than similar domestic law rights.[128] The need to ensure effective protection will involve considering whether the rights conferred by EU law require that particular types of remedies be made available such as an action for damages to compensate for loss suffered as a result of a breach of EU law or restitution to enable the recovery of money paid by way of taxes or charges levied contrary to EU law. National courts will also need to consider whether any provisions of national law governing the remedy, for example, a requirement that damages is not to be available in certain circumstances[129] or that interim relief cannot be granted,[130] undermines the effective protection of EU law rights. If they do, those provisions must be set

---

[124] Case C-213/89 *R. v Secretary of State for Transport Ex p. Factortame Ltd (No.2)* [1991] 1 A.C. 603 at 643–645, [18]–[19]; Joined Cases C-6/90 and C-9/90 *Francovich v Italian Republic* [1991] E.C.R. I-5357 at 5414, [32]–[33]; (these cases build on the judgment in Case 106/77 *Amministrazione delle Finanze dello Stato v Simmenthal SpA*) [1978] E.C.R. 629 at 643–644, [14]–[17]).

[125] See *Francovich* [1991] E.C.R. I-5357. State liability in damages is discussed below at 17–063 to 17–0073.

[126] See, e.g. case C-253/00 *Munoz y Cia SA v Furmar Ltd* [2003] Ch. 328 (domestic law must provide that a trader or competitor could bring civil proceedings to prevent breach of EU regulations on quality standards).

[127] *R. v Secretary of State for Transport Ex p. Factortame (No.2)* above, fn.84. See also case C-432/05 *Unibet (London) Ltd v Justitiekanslern* [2007] E.C.R. I-2271.

[128] Referred to in the jurisprudence of the Court of Justice as the principle of effectiveness and the principle of equivalence, respectively: see, e.g. Case C-261/95 *Palmisani v INPS* [1997] E.C.R. 4025 at 4046, [27]; Case C-78/98 *Preston v Wolverhampton NHS Trust* [2001] A.C. 415 at [31] of the judgment. For a modern statement of the current position, see, e.g. Case C-446/04 *Test Claimants in FII Group Litigation v Inland Revenue Commissioners* [2006] E.C.R. I-11753 at [203].

[129] See also case C-173/03 *Treghetti v Italy* [2006] E.C.R. I-5117.

aside. Subject to that, it is for national law to designate which courts have jurisdiction to hear the claim and to determine the substantive and procedural rules applicable to the claim. The national courts must, however, ensure that European law rights are not treated less favourably than similar domestic law rights. This will first involve determining what the equivalent or similar domestic law rights are, and secondly, ensuring that any procedural rules applied to the right derived from EU law are not, in fact, less favourable than those applied to the similar domestic law right.[131] In addition, the courts will need to ensure that any rules of national law do not make it impossible in practice to enforce the European Union law right.[132]

The criteria of effective protection and equivalence are cumulative.[133] National courts must ensure that the remedies available for breaches of European Union law rights ensure full and effective protection and do not make it impossible to exercise the European Union law right whether or not such remedies would be available, on the same basis, to protect a purely domestic right. Further, if the remedies available to enforce a domestic law right go further than is necessary to ensure the effective enforcement of the right, those remedies must also be available on the same terms to enforce a similar European law claim.

17–056

Meaning of equivalence

A national legal system may have more than one set of procedural rules governing different claims. The national legal system cannot apply less favourable procedural rules to the claim derived from EU law than it applies to a similar domestic law claim. The question of what is a similar domestic law right for these purposes is a matter for the national court to determine having regard to the guidance given by the Court of Justice.[134] The Court has offered some guidance on how a national court should assess questions of similarity or equivalence although its guidance is not easy to apply in practice. National courts are not required to extend the most favourable set of procedural rules to the EU law right.[135] Rather they are required to consider which domestic law right is similar to the right derived from EU law having regard to the "purpose, cause of

17–057

---

[130] See, e.g. case C-213/89 *R. v Secretary of State for Transport Ex p. Factortame Ltd (No.2)* [1991] 1 A.C. 603.

[131] See, e.g. *Preston v Wolverhampton NHS Trust* [2001] A.C. 415 (question of what was the comparable domestic law claim for the purpose of determining the appropriate time-limits to a claim alleging discriminatory refusal of access to a pension scheme contrary to Art.141EC (ex Art.119). See also *Levez* [1999] I.C.R. 521 (what was the comparable domestic law claim for a breach of the principle of equal pay).

[132] To a large extent, this principle may overlap with (or be subsumed within) the principle of effectiveness. It is still referred to by the Court of Justice, particularly in relation to matters where this principle was applied before the principle of effectiveness was recognised).

[133] Case C-199/82 *Amministrazione delle finanze dello Stato v San Giorgio* [1983] E.C.R. 3595.

[134] Case C-78/98 *Preston v Wolverhampton NHS Trust* [2001] A.C. 415 at [59] of the judgment.

[135] Case C-2651/95 *Palmisani v Istituto Nazionale della Previdenza Sociale* [1997] E.C.R. I-4025.

action and essential characteristics" of the allegedly similar domestic right.[136] Furthermore, when considering whether a particular provision was less favourable than that applied to the claim derived from EU law, the national court should not consider that procedural rule in isolation but should assess the procedures as a whole, and should do so by reference to an abstract, objective comparison of the procedures not merely considering whether, on the particular facts of the case, the particular rule operates less favourably in that instance. In essence, the Court of Justice appears to require national law to have regard to the nature of the right and the nature of the remedies being sought, together with a consideration of the procedural advantages and disadvantages of the different procedural rules (such as whether a particular procedure would require a claimant to incur additional costs and delay) in comparing the two sets of procedures. There may, in fact, be cases where there is simply no comparable domestic law claim and the application of the particular procedural rules to the EU law claim cannot violate the principle of equivalence (although the national procedural rules will have to be assessed to determine whether they violate the principle of effective protection).[137] There may be cases where there are similar domestic claims but the procedural rules applicable to the EU law claim although different are not, in fact, less favourable than the rules applied to the similar domestic law claim so that, again, there would be no breach of the principles of equivalence.

17–058   The difficulties of applying the principle of equivalence can be seen from the case law. In *Preston*, for example, the claim concerned the rules applicable to claims for access to a pension scheme. Under domestic law, the rules required claims to be brought in an employment tribunal within six months of the end of the employment to which the claim related. The claimants contended that that breached the principle of equivalence as a claim in contract could be brought within six years. When the matter returned to the House of Lords following the Court of Justice ruling, the first question was whether the right derived from what is now Art.157 of the TFEU to equal treatment for men and women in terms of pay, including access to a pension scheme, was equivalent to a claim for breach of contract. Two members of the House of Lords considered that it was. A claim was intended to obtain retroactive membership of the pension scheme so that the necessary contributions to obtain future pension benefits would be paid. A claim in contract would be for damages for the failure to pay the sums necessary to obtain those pension rights. The majority of the House of Lords considered that a claim under the formerArt.141 EC was one in essence which required a clause to be added to the employees' contracts entitling them to equal treatment. The purpose of that action would be to recognise in domestic law the right derived from EU law which should be included among the terms of the contract of employment. An action for breach of contract, however, would be based on a claim that the employer had breached an obligation included in a contract. The

---

[136] Case C-78/98 *Preston v Wolverhampton NHS Trust* [2001] 2 W.L.R. 408 at [57] of the judgment; Case C-326/96 *Levez v T.H. Jennings (Harlow Pools) Ltd* [1999] I.C.R. 521 at [43] of the judgment and Case C-2651/95 *Palmisani v Istituto Nazionale della Previdenzia Sociale* [1997] E.C.R. I-4025 at [38]–[40] of the judgment.

[137] *Palmisani v Istituto Nazionale della Previdenzia Sociale* [1997] E.C.R. I-4025 at [38]–[40] of the judgment.

majority of the House of Lords doubted that those two actions were comparable, although recognised the possibility that approaching the matter in that way may involve too strict a test of similarity.

On the second issue, however, all five members of the House agreed that if the proper comparison was a claim for contract, the procedural rules governing a claim in the employment tribunal for breach of the Equal Pay Act 1970 were not, in fact, less favourable than those governing a claim for breach of contract. A claim for breach of contract would have to be brought within six years of each breach of the contract, i.e. within six years of each failure by the employer to admit the employee to the pension scheme and pay the contributions to the trustees necessary to secure future benefits; the claim for each individual breach would be statute barred after six years. In contrast, the time-limit of six months under the Equal Pay 1970 ran from the end of the employment, whenever the failure to admit the employee to the scheme occurred. Further, the lower costs and the informality of the tribunal hearing, coupled with the short time within which those proceedings were likely to be concluded, were also factors indicating that the procedural rules governing equal pay claims in the employment tribunal were not less favourable than the rules governing breach of contract in the ordinary courts.[138]

17–059

The difficulties of applying the concept of equivalence can also be seen from the case law dealing with the rights derived from the directive governing public procurement in the field of services. There is a distinct statutory code governing remedies for such claims, requiring, amongst other things, notifying the contracting authority of the alleged breach before instituting proceedings and a strict time-limit which requires claims to be brought within three months of the breach.[139] In considering the question of equivalence, the Court of Appeal considered whether the "juristic structure" of the allegedly similar domestic law right (with different and allegedly more favourable procedural rules) was the same as the right derived from the directive.[140] The Court of Appeal therefore rejected a claim that a breach of the directive governing public procurement was equivalent to the English tort of breach of statutory duty as that was simply too broad a category to satisfy the test of equivalence. The Court also rejected a claim that the equivalent domestic law right was a claim for judicial review. That remedy was a public law remedy whereas the rights conferred by the Directive contemplated a remedy in damages which in English law is characterised as a private law remedy. Judicial review and a right under the Directive did not, therefore, have the same nature and were not equivalent. Eventually, the Court of Appeal concluded that there was no comparable domestic law action and the strict time limits laid down for the bringing of a claim alleging breach of the Directive could not, therefore, violate the principle of equivalence.[141] The Court of Appeal subsequently rejected a claim that the tort of misfeasance was a similar

17–060

---

[138] *Preston v Wolverhampton NHS Trust (No.2)* [2001] A.C. 455.

[139] See Public Services Contracts Regulations 2006 r.47.

[140] *Matra Communications SA v Home Office* [1999] 1 W.L.R. 1646 at 1658 applying the language used in Case C-326/96 *Levez v T.H. Jennings (Harlow Pools) Ltd* [1999] I.C.R. 521 and Case C-2651/95 *Palmisani v Istituto Nazionale della Previdenzia Sociale* [1997] E.C.R. I-4025 at [38]–[40] of the judgment which was subsequently endorsed by the European Court in Case C-78/98 *Preston v Wolverhampton NHS Trust* [2001] 2 W.L.R. 408.

[141] [1999] 1 W.L.R. 1646.

domestic right to a claim based on a right derived from the directive.[142] In other areas, where the Court of Justice considered that a directive conferred a right for victims of loss caused by uninsured vehicles equivalent to that enjoyed by victims of loss caused by insured vehicles, the essence of the right was akin to a claim in damages for tort. The time-limit for bringing a tort claim was six years and there was, therefore, less favourable treatment when a three-year time limit was applied to bringing claims to enforce rights derived from the directive.[143]

The principle of full and effective protection: specific requirements

Breach of European Union law: appropriate remedies

17–061 One common situation that arises is a breach of EU law by the public authorities in a Member State. Primary or secondary legislation may contravene European Union law. Public bodies may exercise discretionary power in a way that conflicts with EU law. EU law requires national courts to disapply legislative measures or set aside decisions which conflict with European law. Any court or tribunal dealing with a dispute will therefore have to disapply any incompatible national legislation. Alternatively, the compatibility of the national legislation with EU law may, in appropriate circumstances, be the subject of a claim for judicial review.[144] The public authorities may also exercise discretionary powers in a way that involves a violation of an individual's directly effective rights. In England, challenges to decisions by public bodies will usually be brought by way of judicial review to have the decision set aside or quashed[145] on the grounds that the decision is invalid as it breaches a EU law right.

17–062 The question also arises as to whether EU law requires national courts to go further and grant a remedy in damages to compensate individuals for loss suffered as a result of a breach of EU law. The traditional approach of the European Court appeared to allow national courts to determine which remedies should be available to enforce a EU law right. Thus, it had been thought that where an individual asserted that a Member State had acted in violation of EU law, it was for the national court applying national law to determine whether the appropriate remedy was a public law remedy available in the administrative courts annulling the administrative action or whether the Member State was liable under national law for damages.[146]

State liability in damages

The decision in Francovich

17–063 The traditional approach to the question of state liability in damages was, however, fundamentally altered by the judgment of the Court of Justice in

---

[142] *Luck (t/a Luck Arboricultural & Horticultural) v London Borough of Tower Hamlets* [2003] Eu. L.R. 143.

[143] *Byrne v Motor Insurers' Bureau* [2008] 3 W.L.R. 1421 at [28]–[31].

[144] See below at 17-090.

[145] See below at para.17-087.

[146] See, e.g. Case 13/68 *Salgoil v Italian Ministry of Foreign Trade* [1968] E.C.R. 453; Case 179/84 *Bozzetti v Invernizzi SPA* [1985] E.C.R. 2301.

Francovich v Italian Republic.[147] There, Italy had failed to implement a directive[148] intended to guarantee the payment of unpaid salaries to employees whose employer became insolvent. Italian workers who were owed arrears of salary by an insolvent employer were, therefore, unable to rely on any domestic implementing legislation to recover the sums. They brought an action in the Italian courts alleging that the directive was directly effective or alternatively that they were entitled to sue the Italian State for damages for non-implementation. The matter was referred to the Court of Justice. The Court held that the directive was not directly effective. Although the provisions were sufficiently precise so far as the identity of the beneficiaries of the guarantee and the content of the guarantee was concerned, the identity of the institution which had to meet the claims was not defined with sufficient precision to enable the national courts to know against whom the directive should be enforced. The Court of Justice, therefore, went on to consider whether under EU law the Member State could be made responsible in the national courts for the loss caused by the non-implementation of the directive.

The Court of Justice held that, in principle, a State could be liable to compensate an individual for damage caused by an infringement of EU law for which that State was responsible. The full effectiveness of EU law would be impaired and the protection of the rights conferred by EU law would be weakened if individuals were unable to obtain compensation where their rights were infringed by a breach of EU law for which a Member State was responsible. The principle of liability was, therefore, inherent in the scheme of the EC Treaty. In addition, what is now Art.4(3) of TEU also required Member States to take all appropriate measures to ensure the fulfilment of obligations arising from EU law. This included eliminating the consequences of an infringement of EU law and making good any damage caused by an infringement for which the State was responsible.   **17–064**

The precise conditions under which liability in damages would arise depended upon the nature of the infringement. Where, as in *Francovich* itself, a Member State had failed to take any steps to implement a directive, a Member State would be liable in damages if three conditions were satisfied. First, the result that the directive was intended to achieve must be the creation of rights for individuals. Secondly, the content of those rights had to be identifiable from the provisions of the directive. Thirdly, there had to be a causal link between the breach and the damage suffered by the individual claimant. Those conditions were satisfied in the *Francovich* case. The directive was intended to give individuals the right to a guarantee of payment for unpaid wages. The content of that right could be identified from the provisions of the directive. The non-availability of that right resulted from the Member State's failure to implement the directive and to specify which institution should be liable to pay the unpaid wages.   **17–065**

---

[147] Joined Cases C-6/90 and C-9/90 [1991] E.C.R. I-5357. The academic commentary on the decision is voluminous: see, e.g. Lewis and Moore, "Duties, Directives and Damages in Community Law" [1993] P.L. 151; Craig, "Francovich, Remedies and the Scope of Damages Liability" [1993] 109 L.Q.R. 595; Steiner, "From Direct Effects to Francovich: Shifting Means of Enforcement of Community Law" (1993) 18 E.L.Rev. 3; Caranta, "Governmental Liability after Francovich" [1993] C.L.J. 272; Curtin, "State Liability under Private Law: a New Remedy for Private Parties" [1992] I.L.J. 94.
[148] Directive 80/987.

Conditions for State liability

17–066   The principle of State liability in damages for loss caused as a result of breaches of EU law is a general principle capable of arising in all situations where a Member State has violated Community law. The principle is not limited to situations where a Member State has failed to implement a directive.[149] A Member State may also be liable in damages where it adopts legislation or takes a decision which violates a person's directly effective right. The Court of Justice has even held that the principle of state liability was capable of applying to all branches of the state including a court of last resort which failed to apply Community law properly.[150] Since the decision in *Francovich*, a series of cases before the European Court has established that there are three conditions which must be satisfied before liability in damages may arise. First, the rule of law which has been infringed must have been intended to confer rights on individuals; secondly the breach must be sufficiently serious and thirdly, there must be a direct causal link between the breach and the damage suffered.[151]

17–067   The first condition will be met when a Member State violates a person's directly effective EU law rights or, in the case of a failure to implement a directive, if the directive was intended to confer rights on individuals and the content of those rights can be identified.[152] Conversely, where a directive imposed obligations on national authorities relating to the supervision of banks, the directive was not intended to confer any rights on individual depositors if their money was lost due to defective banking supervision. The national authorities were not therefore liable in damages.[153]

17–068   The second condition depends on nature of the breach. One situation which may arise is where a Member State adopts legislation in an area where it has a degree of discretion as to what actions it can take, but it subsequently transpires that the legislation adopted exceeds the discretion left to it by European law. The breach will be sufficiently serious if Member State has manifestly and gravely disregarded the limits on its discretion.[154] The Court of Justice has identified a number of factors that a national court may take into account in deciding whether a breach is sufficiently serious. These include the clarity and precision of the rule

---

[149] See Joined Cases C-46/93 and C-48/93 *Brasserie du Pecheur SA v Federal Republic of Germany; R. v Secretary of State for Transport Ex p. Factortame Ltd* [1996] E.C.R. I-1029 at 1142–1143, [18]–[22].

[150] See case C-224 *Kobler v Austria* [2004] Q.B. 848. See also Case C-173/03 *Treghetti v Italy* [2006] E.C.R. I-5117. A claim for damages for failure to identify and act in accordance with the requirements of EU law, or to refer the matter to the Court of Justice failed in the Court of Appeal: see *Cooper v Attorney-General* [2011] Q.B. 976.

[151] Case C-127/95 *Norbrook Laboratories Ltd v Ministry of Agriculture Fisheries and Food* [1998] E.C.R. I-1531 at 1599, [107]; Joined Cases C-46/93 and C-48/93 *Brasserie du Pecheur v Federal Republic of Germany and R. v Secretary of State for Transport Ex p. Factortame* [1996] E.C.R. I-1029 at 1149, [531]; Case C-5/94 *R. v Ministry of Agriculture Fisheries and Food Ex p. Hedley Lomas* [1996] E.C.R. I-2553 at 2613, [25]–[26] and Joined Cases C-178/94, C-179/94, C-188/94 and C-190/94 *Dillenkofer v Germany* [1996] E.C.R. I-4845 [20]; Case C-224 *Kobler v Austria* [2004] Q.B. 848.

[152] As in *Francovich* [19900] E.C.R. I-5357.

[153] See Case C-222/02 *Peter Paul v German Republic* [2004] E.C.R. I-9425.

[154] *Brasserie du Pecheur* [1996] E.C.R. I-1029, [55] (adapting the test for liability for the institutions of the EU under Art.288 (ex Art.215)); and see *Norbrook* above, fn.34 at 1599, [109]; Case C-392/93 *R. v HM Treasury Ex p. British Telecommunications Plc* [1996] E.C.R. I-1631 at 1668–1669.

of EU law that has been breached, the extent of the discretion left to the Member States, whether the damage caused was intentional or voluntary, whether any error of law was excusable and whether the position adopted by one of the institutions of the EU contributed to the adoption or retention of the national measures that violated EU law.[155] As the Court of Appeal has recognised, the application of these factors essentially "requires a value judgment by the national court, taking account of the various factors".[156]

There are situations where a breach will inevitably be sufficiently serious. **17–069** These include maintaining legislation in force after the Court of Justice has ruled that it is incompatible with European Union law.[157] Failure to take any steps to implement a Directive will also be a sufficiently serious breach justifying the imposition of liability in damages.[158] The Member State is under a clear obligation under Art.288 TFEU to implement the Directive within the period specified and has no discretion as to whether to implement the directive. It is also clear that the Court of Justice will not accept any excuse or defence for non-implementation. Consequently, it is self-evident that a total failure to implement a directive involves a manifest and grave disregard of a Member State's obligations under Art.288 TFEU.[159] Different considerations will apply where a Member State takes action to implement the directive but implements it incorrectly. Here, the national court will again have to determine whether or not the failure correctly to transpose the directive involved a manifest and grave disregard of its obligations under European Union law. In one case, the UK incorrectly implemented a directive. The Court of Justice held that there was no sufficiently serious breach. The provisions of the directive itself were imprecise, and were reasonably capable of the interpretation placed upon it in good faith by the UK. Furthermore other Member States also interpreted the directive in the same way and the interpretation was not manifestly contrary to the wording or the objective of the directive. The case law of the Court of Justice did not offer the UK any guidance on the proper construction of the directive. The European Commission had not indicated that it believed the UK had wrongly interpreted the directive when it adopted the national legislation. In those circumstances, the

---

[155] *Brasserie du Pecheur* [1996] E.C.R. I-1029 at 1150, [56]. See below, para.17–108 for the House of Lords decision on whether the breach in that case was sufficiently serious to justify the imposition of liability in damages. See also Case C-63/01 *Evans v Secretary of State for the Environment, Transport and the Region and the Motor Insurers' Bureau* [2003] E.C.R. I-1447 at [82]–[88] and Case C-224 *Kobler v Austria* [2004] Q.B. 848 and Case C-446/04 *Test Claimants in FII Group Litigation v Inland Revenue Commissioners* [2006] E.C.R. I-11753 at [213].

[156] per Carnwarth LJ in *Byrne v Motor Insurers' Bureau* [2008] 3 W.L.R. 1421 at [45] in finding that the United Kingdom authorities were liable in damages for failure properly to implement a directive dealing with compensation for damage caused by uninsured drivers.

[157] *Brasserie du Pecheur* [1996] E.C.R. I-1029 at 1150, [57] or failing to adopt the measures necessary to comply with an interim order of the Court of Justice at 1152, [64].

[158] *Dillenkofer* [1996] E.C.R. I-4845 at 4880, [26]. Similarly, the failure to review the compatibility of UK arrangements governing claims in relation to uninsured drivers following a judgment of the Court of Justice setting out the requirements of EU law was particularly important in determining whether there was a sufficiently serious breach of EU law by the UK: see *Byrne v Motor Insurers' Bureau* [2008] 3 W.L.R. 1421 at [44].

[159] *Dillenkofer* [1996] E.C.R. I-4845 at 4878–4880, [20]–[27].

European Court was satisfied there was not a sufficiently serious breach of European law to justify the imposition of liability in damages.[160]

17–070   There will be situations where EU law gives a Member State little or no discretion as to how it should act and the Member State may not be called upon to make any legislative choices. In such instances, the mere infringement of EU law itself may be enough to establish that there has been a sufficiently serious breach.[161] In one case,[162] the UK refused to grant an export licence to individuals seeking to export animals to Spain for slaughter. There was in place a directive setting out common standards for slaughter. The UK was, however, concerned that certain Spanish slaughterhouses did not comply with the standards set by the directive. It believed that there was a significant risk that animals exported to Spain would therefore undergo slaughter in a manner contrary to that set out in European law, although it had no evidence that the slaughter houses for which the export licence was sought failed to meet the standards set by the directive. The refusal of an export licence constituted a breach of Art.29 EC which prohibited export bans. The Court of Justice considered that the mere infringement of that provision was a sufficiently serious breach to attract liability in damages. There, of course, it was well-established that Member States could not take unilateral action to prohibit exports when the EU had itself adopted common standards to regulate a particular trade. Furthermore, it was also well-established that the fact that one Member State may not have complied with the directive did not justify another Member State from taking unilateral action to stop exports; the proper course of action in such circumstances is for the European Commission to take action against the Member State under Art.258 TFEU. In addition, the UK did not even have proof of any non-compliance by the slaughter-houses in question. In those circumstances, it is not surprising that the Court of Justice considered that the breach of what is now Art.35 TFEU itself amounted to a sufficiently serious breach.

17–071   In all cases, there must be a direct causal link between the breach and the damage sustained by the individual claimant in order for liability to arise in respect of that loss or damage.

Substantive and procedural conditions governing State liability in damages

17–072   Where liability is established, Member States must make good the loss or damage caused by its breach, in accordance with the national laws on liability, provided that national laws do not treat the EU law claim less favourably than a similar domestic claim and do not make it impossible or excessively difficult in practice to obtain compensation.[163] In other words, EU law determines the test for liability

---

[160] Case C-392/93 *R. v HM Treasury Ex p. British Telecommunications Plc* [1996] E.C.R. I-1631 at 1668–1669, [42]–[45]. See also Case C-446/04 *Test Claimants in FII Group Litigation v Inland Revenue Commissioners* [2006] E.C.R. I-11753 at [215] (national court entitled to take into account the state of Community law and the extent to which it was clear or was evolving).

[161] See, e.g. case C-127/95 *Norbrook Laboratories Ltd v Ministry of Agriculture Fisheries and Food* [1998] E.C.R. I-1531 at [10]; Case C-446/04 *Test Claimants in FII Group Litigation v Inland Revenue Commissioners* [2006] E.C.R. I-11753 at [212]; Case C-470/03 *AGM-Cos-Met Srl v Suomen valtio and Tarmo Lehtinen* [2007] E.C.R. I-27449 at [81].

[162] Case C-5/94 *R. v MAFF Ex p. Hedley Lomas* [1996] E.C.R. I-2553

[163] *Factortame* [1996] E.C.R. I-1029 at 1153–1155, [67]–[74].

but national law determines matters such as time-limits and procedural rules for bringing claims subject to the usual tests of equivalence and not making it impossible in practice to enforce the EU law right. In that regard, the Court of Justice has ruled that English law rules which restrict liability to cases where the elements of the tort of misfeasance in a public office are established makes it impossible in practice to enforce liability where the national legislature is responsible for the breach. Misfeasance requires proof that the public body acted maliciously or knowing that it was acting unlawfully.[164] The Court of Justice considered it inconceivable to prove such matters in the case of a legislature.[165] The Court of Justice did not deal with administrative action by a public body but, again, the addition of a requirement of misfeasance on top of the need to establish a sufficiently serious breach by the public body would appear to make it excessively difficult for an individual to obtain compensation. Similarly, national law may not make liability in damages depend on proof of fault (whether intentional or negligence) in so far as that requirement differs from or is more restrictive than the concept of a sufficiently serious breach.[166]

The Court of Justice has also held that national legal systems cannot totally 17–073 exclude loss of profit as a head of damages since, in the context of economic or commercial litigation, such a total exclusion of loss of profit would be such as to make it practically impossible to obtain compensation for the harm done.[167] Subject to that, the Court of Justice has ruled that it is for national law to determine the heads of recoverable damage. The appropriate starting-point would seem to be to consider the nature of the rights that the individual was intended to enjoy under the relevant provisions of EU law. As damages are awarded to compensate for the violation of those rights, damages should be related to the nature of the rights and should compensate for the loss occurred as a result of being deprived of those rights. It is also for national law to determine whether or not exemplary damages should be available (although if they are available for comparable domestic law claims, then the need to ensure no less favourable treatment for the EU law rights requires that exemplary damages be available on the same conditions in cases involving breaches of EU law[168]). National law may also apply its normal rules requiring the individual to mitigate his loss[169] and, it seems, apply normal national rules on time limits for bringing claims.[170]

Restitutionary claims

There are other situations in which the Court of Justice has defined the content of 17–074 a European Union law right in such a way that national courts must make available a particular remedy. In the context of the recovery of charges and taxes levied contrary to European Union law, the Court of Justice has held that it is an adjunct of the right not to be subjected to the charges or taxes that the individual

---

[164] See below at para.17–106.
[165] *Factortame* [1996] E.C.R. I-1029 at 1154, [73].
[166] *Factortame* [1996] E.C.R. I-1029 at 1155–1156, paras [75]–[80].
[167] *Factortame* [1996] E.C.R. I-1029 at 1157–1158, [87]–[88].
[168] *Factortame* [1996] E.C.R. I-1029 at 1158, [89]–[90].
[169] *Factortame* [1996] E.C.R. I-1029 at 1157, [84]–[85].
[170] *Factortame* [1996] E.C.R. I-1029 at 1160–1161, [97]–[100].

may seek repayment of the monies unlawfully levied.[171] The Court of Justice leaves the legal classification of the nature of the claim to national law. However, in practice, the need to enable the individual to recover the money claimed means, effectively, that a restitutionary remedy must be made available.[172] The national courts can still apply the substantive rules of national law such as the principle against allowing unjust enrichment in determining whether restitutionary remedies are available in a particular case.[173]

Other specific remedies

17–075 Other EU law rights also call for certain types of remedy or particular remedies will be necessary to ensure the full and effective protection of the EU rights. Article 157 TFEU guarantees equal pay for equal work. The essence of this right points to a monetary remedy calculated by reference to the wage paid to the man with whom comparison is being made. In addition certain articles, notably Arts 101 and 102 TFEU on anti-competitive behaviour and Art.157 TFEU on equal pay apply to individuals as well as public authorities. The fact that the provisions apply to individuals suggest that the appropriate remedies are likely to be found in private law not public law. The Court of Justice has held that the need to ensure the full effectiveness of such rules requires that an individual may claim damages for loss caused to him by an anti-competitive contract or conduct liable to distort competition.[174] The Court also held that national law cannot prevent a party to such an unlawful contract bringing a claim solely on the grounds that he is a party to the contract and is, therefore, seeking to rely on his own wrongful acts, although national law may prohibit this where the party bears significant responsibility for the distortion of competition.[175] Not all situations which impact on individuals give rise to a right to claim damages. The provision by a Member State of unlawful state aid to an undertaking does not give a competitor a right to bring a claim for damages against the recipient of the unlawful state aid.[176]

---

[171] Case 199/82 *Amministrazione delle Finanze dello Stato v San Giorgio* [1983] E.C.R. 3595; Case 309/85 *Barra v Belgium* [1988] E.C.R. 355 and Joined Cases C-397 and 410/98 *Metallgesellschaft Ltd v Inland Revenue Commissioners* [2001] 1 Ch. 620 at [84] of the judgment. See also case C-446/04 *Test Claimants in FII Group Litigation v Inland Revenue Commissioners* [2006] E.C.R. I-11753; Case C-524/04 *Thin Cap Group Litigation v Inland Revenue Commissioners* [2007] E.C.R. I-2107 and Case C-201/05 *Test Claimants in CFC Dividend Group Litigation v Inland Revenue Commissioners* [2008] 2 C.M.L.R. 53; Case C-362/12 *Test Claimants in Franked Investments Group v Commissioners of Inland Revenue* [2014] 2 C.M.L.R. 33 at [30].

[172] In theory, a remedy in damages which enabled the recovery of the amount would be permissible. In the United Kingdom, claims have been brought by way of a claim for restitution although the courts have recognised that a claim could be brought for breach of statutory duty: see *Deutsche Morgan Grenfell Group Plc v Inland Revenue Commissioners*[2007] 1 A.C. 518 at [7].

[173] Case 68/79 *Just v Danish Ministry of Fiscal Affairs* [1980] E.C.R. 501 and Case C-147/01 *Weber's Wine World Handels-GmbH v Abgabenberufungskommission Wien* [2004] 1 C.M.L.R. 147 and see Case C-309/06 *Marks & Spencer Plc v Commissioners of Customs and Excise* [2008] 2 C.M.L.R. 42. Money collected on behalf of the European Union as opposed to that collected by national authorities acting under national law is dealt with by Council Reg.1430/79 (the repayment or remission to individuals of import or export duties improperly levied) and Council Reg.1697/79 (recovery by national authorities of import or export duties that should have been paid by individuals): see, generally, Oliver, "Enforcing Community Rights in the English Courts" (1987) 50 M.L.R. 881.

[174] Case C-453/99 *Courage Ltd v Crehan* [2002] Q.B. 507.

[175] [2002] Q.B. 507.

[176] See *Betws Anthracite Ltd v DSK Anthrazit Ibben buren GmbH* [2004] Eu. L.R. 241.

Right to a judicial remedy

National law must ensure that an individual has an effective remedy available   **17–076**
from a court or tribunal to vindicate a directly effective right derived from
European law. The individual must have a means of challenging a measure
alleged to be contrary to EU law in a national court or tribunal. An individual
must, for example, be able to challenge a decision of a public body refusing to
recognise a EU law right. A decision of a national body that a person does not
have equivalent qualifications to those required under national law must, for
example, be capable of challenge in the courts as otherwise the person may not be
able to enforce his right to freedom of movement or freedom of establishment
under Arts 45 and 49 TFEU.[177] The Court of Justice has gone further and ruled
that national authorities must provide reasons for their decision refusing to
recognise a EU law right so that the national courts can review the legality of that
decision, making the right to a judicial remedy effective in practical terms.[178] The
Court has also ruled that national courts must disapply an ouster clause excluding
the jurisdiction of the courts to determine if there has been a breach of EU law or
making a decision of a government minister or public body conclusive evidence
of certain matters.[179]

Courts having jurisdiction

The Court of Justice has consistently ruled that it is for national law to determine   **17–077**
which courts have jurisdiction to deal with a claim that there has been a breach of
EU law.[180] By this, the Court of Justice appears to mean that the system that
prevails in many national legal systems whereby certain claims are allocated to
certain types of courts or tribunals does not offend against EU law. Thus, it would
not be contrary to EU law for national law to allocate jurisdiction over claims for
enforcement of Art.157 TFEU on equal pay or the Directive on equal treatment to
a system of employment tribunals. Nor would it be objectionable per se for
matters classified as public law matters to be dealt with in specialised
administrative courts rather than through the ordinary civil courts.[181] If a national
court or tribunal has jurisdiction in a particular case, however, then it must be
able to give immediate and full protection to European Union law rights. It must
be able to disapply any conflicting rule of national law. It cannot be required, for
example, to wait for a ruling from some other court, such as a constitutional
court.[182]

---

[177] Case C-222/86 *UNCTEF v Heylens* [1987] E.C.R. 4097 at 4116, [14].

[178] Case C-340/89 *Vlassopoulou v Ministerium for Justiz Bundes-und Europaangelegenheiten Baden-Wurttemberg* [1991] E.C.R. I-2357 at 2385, [22]. That too is required by Art.47 of the Charter and requires the person to be given reasons for the decision (or where a court is satisfied that the requirements of national security prevents disclosure of the full grounds for the decision, at least of the essence of the grounds for the decision): see Case C-300/11 *ZZ (France) v Secretary of State for the Home Department* [2013] Q.B. 1136 and applied by the Court of Appeal [2014] 2 W.L.R. 791.

[179] Case C-222/84 *Johnston v Chief Constable of the Royal Ulster Constabulary* [1986] E.C.R. 1651 at 1651, [13]–[21].

[180] *Comet* [1976] E.C.R. 2043 at 2053, [13]; *Rewe* [1976] E.C.R. 2043 at 1997, [5].

[181] See, e.g. Case C-13/68 *SpS Salgoil v Italian Ministry for Foreign Trade* [1968] E.C.R. 453.

[182] Case 106/77 *Amministrazione delle Finanze dello Stato v Simmenthal SpA* [1978] E.C.R. 629 at [644]–[645], [644]–[645] and see above at para.17–031.

Availability of interim relief

17–078   In the second *Factortame*[183] case, the Court of Justice recognised that the need to ensure effective protection for EU law rights extends to requiring national courts to set aside rules of national law which prevented the grant of interim relief to protect European rights pending the full hearing of the case. Thus, where the English courts considered that as a matter of domestic law it could not grant relief to suspend the operation of an Act of Parliament or grant relief against a minister, the Court of Justice held that that rule of national law had to be set aside. This ruling has been understood as meaning that national courts must have jurisdiction to grant interim relief in an appropriate case but leaving national law to determine the criteria for determining whether to grant interim relief in a particular case.[184]

Time-limits

17–079   Time-limits for bringing claims alleging a breach of European Union law are a matter of practical importance. The Court of Justice has consistently held that national law may lay down reasonable time-limits for bringing claims provided that the rules do not treat EU law rights less favourably than similar domestic rights and do not make it impossible in practice to enforce EU law rights.[185] That remains the position today and the setting of a national time-limit does not make it impossible in practice to enforce a right even if the fact that the claim is brought outside that period necessarily entails the dismissal of the whole or part of a claim.[186] Similarly, rules limiting claims for arrears of benefits to a particular period before the institution of a claim are also compatible with EU law.[187] Exceptionally, however, the European Court has held that the rule that, in claims under Art.157 TFEU for equal access to a pension scheme, the successful claimant's pensionable service was to be calculated only by reference to the two years of service before the claim was instituted (together with any subsequent service) was incompatible with the principle of effectiveness.[188] EU law does not require national courts to re-open judicial decisions which have become final after all rights of appeal have been exhausted.[189]

---

[183] *R. v Secretary of State for Transport Ex p. Factortame (No.2)* [1991] 1 A.C. 603 and also at [1990] E.C.R. I-2433.

[184] See judgment of the House of Lords, [1991] 1 A.C. 603. See also Case C-432/05 *Unibet (London) Ltd v Justitiekanslern* [2007] E.C.R. I-2271 at [79]–[81].

[185] See *Comet* [1976] E.C.R. 2043; *Rewe* [1976] E.C.R. 2043; *Levez* [1999] I.C.R. 521.

[186] Case C-188/95 *Fantask A/S v Industriministeriet* [1997] E.C.R. I-6783. Exceptionally, particular time-limits may make it impossible in practice to enforce a right. In *Levez* [1999] I.C.R. 521, e.g. the employer told a female employee that she was being paid the same as a male employee which was not true. Exceptionally, the employer could not rely on the two year limit for bringing an action as that would make it impossible in practice in the circumstances of that case for the employee to have enforced her right within time.

[187] Case C-338/91 *Steenhorst-Neerings v Bestuur van de Bedrijfsvereniging* [1993] E.C.R. I 5475; Case C-410/92 *Johnson v Chief Adjudication Officer* [1994] E.C.R. I-5383.

[188] Case C-78/98 *Preston v Wolverhampton NHS Trust* [2001] 2 W.L.R. 408 and Case C-246/96 *Magorrian v Eastern Health & Social Services Board* [1998] I.C.R. 979.

[189] Case C-234/04 *Kapferer v Schland & Schick GmbH* [2006] E.C.R. I-2585 (discussed by the Court of Appeal in *Interfact Ltd. v Liverpool City Council (Secretary of State for Culture, Media and Sport Intervening)* [2011] 2 W.L.R. 396. EU law may, however, preclude national laws preventing the

The period of the limitation, is in principle, a matter for national law to determine. However, the principle of effectiveness requires that the period be sufficiently precise, clear and foreseeable to enable individuals to ascertain their rights and obligations and, further, that the period begins when the claimant knows, or ought to know, that his rights have been infringed. Thus, in the *Uniplex* case[190], the Court of Justice was dealing with the rules in England and Wales for bringing a challenge to a procurement decision. The rules provided that the claim had to be brought promptly and in any event within three months of the date when the grounds for a challenge first arose (which could be before the claimant became aware of the infringement). The Court held that the time limit had to begin from the time when the claimant knew, or ought to have known, of the alleged breach. Further, the requirement that the claim be brought promptly gave rise to uncertainty and also contravened the requirements of effectiveness. EU law therefore precluded the application of such a provision.[191]   **17–080**

It is open to Member States to alter their limitation periods and to introduce different limitation periods for particular types of claims, such as claims for recovery of money, alongside the general limitation periods applicable in domestic law.[192] In principle, such special limitation periods will be compatible with EU law, even if they apply to claims based on EU law, providing that the limitation periods are not intended to limit the consequences of a ruling by the Court of Justice that a specific national tax is incompatible with EU law, but apply to all such claims,[193] and provided that there are transitional arrangements made for persons who would have been entitled to submit claims for repayment under the original limitation periods.[194]   **17–081**

Interest

The current position is that interest must be available on money paid as compensation or damages for breach of EU law at least where that is essential to ensure that the damage caused by the breach is repaired.[195] Thus, in *Marshall*   **17–082**

---

re-opening of administrative decisions (as opposed to judicial decisions) in certain circumstances: see Case C-249/11 *Byankov v Glaven sekretar na Ministerstvo na vatreshnite raboti* [2013] 2 W.L.R. 293.

[190] Case C-406/08 *Uniplex (UK) Ltd. v NHS Business Authority* [2010] P.T.S.R. 1377.

[191] Case C-406/08 *Uniplex (UK) Ltd. v NHS Business Authority* [2010] P.T.S.R. 1377. An earlier case, C-208/90 *Emmott v Minister for Social Welfare and the Att-Gen* [1991] E.C.R. 4269, appeared to indicate that, in relation to directives, the time-limit began to run from the date of eventual implementation of the directive, has now been confined to its particular facts: see *Fantask* [1997] E.C.R. I-6783 at 6839, [50]–[52].

[192] Case C-228/96 *Aprile Srl v Amministrazione delle Finanze dello Stato (No.2)* [2000] 1 W.L.R. 126.

[193] Case C-147/01 *Weber's Wine World Handels-GmbH v Abgabenberufungskommission Wien* [2004] 1 C.M.L.R. 147 at [86]–[92] of the judgment; Case 240/87 *Deville v Administration des impots* [1988] E.C.R. 3513.

[194] Case C-62/00 *Marks & Spencer Plc v Customs and Excise Commissioners* [2003] Q.B. 866 at [36]–[42] of the judgment; Case C-362/12 *Test Claimants in Franked Investments Group v Commissioners of Inland Revenue* [2014] 2 C.M.L.R. 33 at [37] (there the time limits could not be relied upon as they were introduced retrospectively and without transitional arrangements).

[195] Joined Cases C-397 and 410/98 *Metallgesellschaft Ltd v Inland Revenue Commissioners* [2001] Ch. 620 at [95] of the judgment.

(*No.2*),[196] where national law provided that compensation was available as a remedy for a breach of the Equal Treatment Directive, interest had to be payable on the award of compensation to ensure the full and effective protection of the EU law right. The Court of Justice has also impliedly ruled that interest is payable in respect of damages paid under the principle of state liability for a sufficiently serious breach of EU law.[197] Similarly, where advance corporation tax was required to be paid in breach of EU law, the claimant was entitled to interest which represented, in effect, an amount equal to the loss of the use of the sums paid in advance.[198] At the same time, the Court of Justice has held that interest is not payable on arrears of social security benefit as such benefits are not compensation for loss and damages for breach of European Union law.[199] The right to equal treatment for men and women in respect of social security benefits only entitled a person to claim the benefits that he or she had been unlawfully refused and did not automatically carry with it the right to interest on those benefits. If, however, the failure to implement the Directive on equal treatment in social security matters also constituted a sufficiently serious breach of EU law, the Court of Justice took the view that damages would be payable and interest, it seems, would be payable on that amount.[200] In the past, the Court of Justice has ruled that whether or not interest is payable in actions brought by the Member State to recover money or taxes levied contrary to European Union law is a matter of national law.[201] That principle needs to be reformulated in the light of subsequent case law. Interest will need to be awarded where the recovery of interest is an essential component of the claim for breach of the EU law right or where it is essential to award interest to ensure full compensation for breach of EU law. Where the claim is not one for damages and interest is merely an ancillary matter to the recovery of benefits or charges, questions relating to entitlement of interest may be a matter for national law.[202] The rationale for this distinction is unsatisfactory and the criteria for identifying when interest is an ancillary matter are unclear.

Ancillary procedural conditions

17–083   National law determines the other procedural conditions governing actions in the national courts. Thus national law determines such procedural questions as the availability of set-offs,[203] the burden of proof,[204] and questions of locus standi for third parties where a person other than the individual who actually enjoys the EU

---

[196] Case C-271/91 *Marshall v Southampton and S.W. Hampshire Area Health Authority* [1993] E.C.R. I-4362.

[197] Case C-66/95 *R. v Secretary of State for Social Security Ex p. Sutton* [1997] E.C.R. 2163 at 2190–2192, [28]–[35].

[198] [1997] E.C.R. 2163 at [87] of the judgment.

[199] [1997] E.C.R. 2163 at 2187–2189, [21]–[27].

[200] [1997] E.C.R. 2163 at 2190–2192, [28]–[35].

[201] Case 54/81 *Fromme v BALM* [1982] E.C.R. 1440.

[202] See the formulation used in Joined Cases C-397 and 410/98 *Metallgesellschaft Ltd v Inland Revenue Commissioners* [2001] 1 Ch. 620 at [86], [95] and [96] of the judgment.

[203] Case 68/79 *Just v Danish Ministry of Fiscal Affairs* [1980] E.C.R. 501 but see also Case C-309/06 *Marks & Spencer v Commissioners of Customs and Excise* [2000] 2 C.M.L.R. 42.

[204] Cases 205-215/82 *Deutsche Milchkontor GmbH v Germany* [1984] 3 C.M.L.R. 586.

law right seeks to have European Union law observed.[205] In one area, the directives giving effect to the Aarhus Convention on access to information and public participation in relation to environmental matters, there is an additional obligation to ensure that access to judicial procedures to enforce the directives shall not be "prohibitively expensive".[206] The Court of Justice has ruled that national law must ensure that the costs of bringing proceedings are not prohibitively expensive viewed both from the perspective of the resources of the individual claimant and also objectively.[207] Furthermore, the practice of requiring cross-undertakings from claimants, whereby they undertake to make good any damage caused if it subsequently transpires that the interim injunction should not have been granted, also contravenes the directive.[208]

Additional restrictions on national law

There are certain additional restrictions on the extent to which national law (and national courts) are free to determine the substantive and procedural conditions. In addition to ensuring respect for the principles of effectiveness and equivalence, the Court of Justice also prohibits rules of national law which make it impossible in practice or excessively difficult to enforce European Union law rights. Much of the substance of this principle now overlaps with or is subsumed within the principle of effectiveness. On occasions, the Court of Justice does refer to the principle as a separate reason for holding that a rule of national procedural rule contravenes EU law. Thus, Italian legislation placing the burden of proof on a taxpayer bringing an action for the repayment of taxes levied contrary to EU law and excluding all evidence other than documentary evidence to prove that the tax had not been passed on to the consumer was held to be contrary to EU law.[209] An ouster clause stating that a ministerial certificate was conclusive evidence that certain action was necessary for reasons of national security was contrary to European Union law as it prevented a woman from establishing a claim of unlawful discrimination.[210] In *Factortame*,[211] the Court of Justice considered that any requirement of English law making liability in damages depend upon proof of misfeasance in a public office would be such as to make it impossible in practice or excessively difficult to enforce the EU right and so was incompatible with European Union law for that reason.

17–084

---

[205] Case 158/80 *Rewe Handelsgesellschaft Nord mbH v Hauptzollamt Kiel* [1981] E.C.R. 1805. It is for national law to ensure an appropriate means whereby an individual can obtain judicial protection of his own Community law rights. Community law does not require that any particular remedy be made available or that new remedies be created, provided that the remedies available satisfy the principle of effectiveness and equivalence: see Case C-432/05 *Unibet (London) Ltd v Justitiekanslern* [2007] E.C.R. I-2271.

[206] Council Directive 85/337/EEC of 27 June 1985 as amended; Council Directive 96/61/EC of 24 September 1996.

[207] Case C-260/11 *R (Edwards) v Environment Agency (No.2)* [2013] 1 W.L.R. 2914, and subsequent decision of the Supreme Court at [2014] 1 W.L.R. 55. The rules governing costs awards in such cases are now contained in CPR 45 rr.41–44: see Chapter 9 above.

[208] Case C-530/11 *Commission v United Kingdom* judgment of the Court of Justice of 13 February 2014.

[209] *Amministrazione delle Finanze dello Stato v San Giorgio* [1983] E.C.R. 3595.

[210] Case C-222/84 *Johnston v Chief Constable of the Royal Ulster Constabulary* [1987] Q.B. 129.

[211] *R. v Secretary of State for Transport Ex p. Factortame Ltd* [1996] E.C.R. I-1029 at 1154, [73].

I. REMEDIES IN THE LAW OF ENGLAND AND WALES

17–085 The role of the domestic court is to determine whether there is a domestic law right which is analogous to the European Union law right. Then the national court must ensure that the remedies available to enforce the EU law right are not less favourable than those available to enforce that analogous domestic law right and must ensure that the remedies afford effective protection of the EU law right. The process of classification is simple in principle but often difficult to apply in practice.[212] This is due in part to the wide variety of situations in which EU law rights arise and in part to the tendency of English law to concentrate on remedies rather than defining the nature of rights in the abstract.

Public law remedies

17–086 One of the most frequent situations to arise is the exercise of statutory or other discretionary power by public authorities in a way that contravenes a directly effective provision of EU law. In such circumstances, judicial review will be available to challenge the legality of the acts of the public body. The judicial review procedure is, in principle, capable of providing an effective remedy and national law.[213] Public law remedies are available to invalidate the unlawful act[214] or to compel the performance of a duty imposed on a public body by EU law[215] will be available. European Union law may also require the provision of a remedy in damages where the breach is a sufficiently serious breach of a superior rule of EU law intended to confer rights on individuals which causes loss.[216] The award of damages is regarded in English law as a private law remedy and is considered below.[217] The following are examples of the types of situations where public law remedies may be granted in cases with a EU law dimension.

Decisions contrary to EU law

17–087 Administrative decisions taken by public authorities exercising statutory powers which contravene directly effective provisions of EU law will generally be regarded as void. Judicial review may be brought for a declaration that a decision is void as it contravenes EU law, or for a quashing order to quash the decision. A declaration has been granted, for example, declaring a decision by a minister, altering the basis of reimbursement of pharmacists for drugs imported from other EU states, as unlawful as it violated what is now Art.34 TFEU.[218] A decision of the Inland Revenue to adopt a particular approach to valuation in assessing taxation on oil sales was declared void, as the method adopted contravened EU

---

[212] See, e.g. *Matra v Home Office* [1999] 1 W.L.R. 146; *Preston (No. 2)* [2001] A.C. 455; *Levez* [1999] I.C.R. 521.

[213] *T-Mobile (Uk) Ltd. v Office of Communications* [2009] 1 W.L.R. 1565; *TN (Afghanistan) v Secretary of State for the Home Department* [2014] 1 W.L.R. 2095.

[214] e.g. a quashing order (see Chapter 6 above) or a declaration of invalidity (see Chapter 7 above).

[215] A mandatory order (see Chapter 6 above) or a declaration that a duty is owed (Chapter 7 above).

[216] See above at para.17–065.

[217] See at para.17–016.

[218] *R. v Secretary of State for Social Services Ex p. Bomore Medical Supplies Ltd* [1986] 1 C.M.L.R. 228.

law.[219] A quashing order has been granted to quash a deportation order on the grounds that the order violated EU law.[220]

Public law powers and EU law

Judicial review may be sought to compel public authorities to exercise statutory **17–088** powers in order to ensure compliance with EU law. A declaration has been granted requiring a minister to designate certain ports as authorised ports of entry for the import of milk from Ireland, in order to ensure compliance with Art.34 TFEU.[221] Judicial review may also be used to require public authorities to refrain from exercising statutory powers in a way that would contravene EU law. The Divisional Court granted a declaration that the Inland Revenue was under a duty not to implement a particular approach to valuation for tax purposes until the European Commission approved the actions of the Revenue, as these contravened EU law on State subsidies.[222] Although the courts granted declarations in these two cases, the courts could have issued a mandatory order and a prohibiting order respectively.

Powers and duties derived from EU law

EU legislation may directly confer powers and duties on public authorities. Such **17–089** powers are regarded as public law powers, and in the exercise of these powers national authorities are subject to judicial supervision by way of judicial review. The question of whether a public authority was required, under an EU regulation dealing with a common organisation of the market in fish, to make certain compensation payments was dealt with by judicial review.[223] The validity of EU legislation may be challenged indirectly by a claim for judicial review of decisions taken in the exercise of powers conferred by EU law,[224] or of national measures adopted to implement EU law.[225]

Primary legislation and EU law

Judicial review may be used to determine the compatibility of national legislation **17–090** with EU law, at least where the provisions of EU law are capable of conferring

---

[219] *R. v Att-Gen Ex p. I.C.I. Plc* [1987] 1 C.M.L.R. 72.
[220] *R. v Secretary of State for the Home Department Ex p. Dannenberg* [1984] Q.B. 766. See also *R. v Secretary of State for the Environment Ex p. Kingston-upon-Hull CC* [1996] C.O.D. 289.
[221] *R. v Minister of Agriculture, Fisheries and Food Ex p. Bell Lines Ltd* [1984] 2 C.M.L.R. 502.
[222] *R. v Att-Gen Ex p. I.C.I. Plc* (see above, fn.93).
[223] In *R. v Intervention Board for Agricultural Produce Ex p. Fish Producers' Organisation Ltd* [1987] 3 C.M.L.R. 473, MacPherson J. granted a declaration that the sums were payable. The matter was referred by the Court of Appeal to the European Court which has gave its ruling: [1991] 2 C.M.L.R. 853.
[224] Case C-181/84 *R. v Intervention Board for Agricultural Produce Ex p. E.D. & F. Man (Sugar) Ltd* [1986] 2 All E.R. 115.
[225] e.g. *R. (ABNA Ltd) v Secretary of State for Health and the Food Standards Agency* [2004] Eu.L.R. 88; *R. v Minister of Agriculture, Fisheries and Food Ex p. FEDESA* [1988] 3 C.M.L.R. 207. In such a case the court should refer the matter to the European Court under Art.267 TFEU as only the European Court may declare a Community instrument invalid; Case C-314/85 *Foto-Frost v Hauptzollanmt Lubeck-Ost* [1987] E.C.R. 4199 and see para.18–003.

directly effective rights. The courts have, for example, considered whether the Merchant Shipping Act 1988 was compatible with directly effective rights conferred upon individuals by the EC Treaty.[226] The House of Lords held that the Equal Opportunities Commission could seek a declaration by way of judicial review that certain provisions of domestic legislation were contrary to what is now Art.157 TFEU and the Directive on equal treatment.[227] There the applicant, the Equal Opportunities Commission, was the statutory body responsible for promoting equal opportunity. It had no directly effective rights itself but the provisions of the directive were capable of conferring directly effective rights on individuals. In cases involving directly effective rights, once there is a binding ruling that national law is in breach of European Union law, those with directly effective rights should have no difficulty in enforcing them. They will be able to obtain appropriate remedies in any case brought by them as any court or tribunal will have to disapply the incompatible provisions of national law. Judicial review will be available to quash any decisions taken on the basis of the incompatible legislation. Interim relief can be granted to prevent the application of the national legislation, as happened in *Factortame*[228] where the House of Lords granted an injunction to prevent the application of certain provisions of the Merchant Shipping Act 1988 as these appeared to contravene the directly effective rights conferred by provisions of the Treaty of Rome.

17–091   A different situation may prevail where no directly effective rights are in issue. It is at present uncertain whether the courts have jurisdiction to grant a declaration that domestic legislation is incompatible with European Union law where that EU law is not directly effective. That possibility may occur in two situations. First, it may be claimed that domestic legislation is incompatible with a provision of EU law which is not directly effective because it is insufficiently precise or unconditional to be directly enforceable in the national courts. In one case, the applicant sought a declaration that the increases in the excise duty on beer were incompatible with what is now Art.4(3) TEU, read with Art.113 TFEU. Article 4(3) TEU[229] and Art.113 TFEU[230] are not directly effective. The Court of Appeal considered that there was no breach of the Articles and left open the question of whether they could have granted a declaration that the domestic legislation was incompatible with European Union law if there had been a

---

[226] The Divisional Court considered the issue and referred the questions of compatibility to the European Court in *R. v Secretary of State for Transport Ex p. Factortame Ltd* [1988] 2 C.M.L.R. 353; the decision of the European Court is at Case C-221/89 [1992] Q.B. 680. The House of Lords also granted interim relief disapplying part of the provisions of the Act in *R. v Secretary of State for Transport Ex p. Factortame (No.2)* [1991] 1 A.C. 603.

[227] *R. v Secretary of State for Employment Ex p. Equal Opportunities Commission* [1995] 1 A.C. 1. The House of Lords held that a person who was actually claiming directly effective rights under Art.141 EC or the relevant directive ought normally to assert those rights against the employer before an employment tribunal and not by way of judicial review. Exceptionally, an individual was allowed to proceed by judicial review in *R. v Secretary of State for Employment Ex p. Seymour-Smith* [1997] 1 W.L.R. 473.

[228] *R. v Secretary of State for Transport Ex p. Factortame (No.2)* above, fn.214.

[229] Case 44/88 *Hurd v Jones* [1986] E.C.R. 29 at 85, [46]–[49]. Quaere if Art.4 TEU, read with other articles of the TFEU, may be sufficiently precise in particular contexts so as to have direct effect: see Lewis, *Remedies and the Enforcement of European Community Law* (1996), pp.28–29. See also *R. (Bancoult) v Secretary of State for Foreign and Commonwealth Affairs (No.3)* [2014] 3 W.L.R. 2921 at [142]–[143] (Art.4(3) TEU, read with Arts 198 and 199 TFEU not directly effective).

[230] Case 6/64 *Costa v ENEL* [1964] E.C.R. 585.

breach.[231] Secondly, additional problems arise in connection with directives. These are only capable of being directly effective as against an emanation of the state. In many cases, particularly in the employment field, an individual is primarily concerned with the actions of a private person, not an emanation of the State, and cannot rely directly on the directive as against that other person. In those circumstances, the question is whether the individual can claim a declaration that domestic legislation is incompatible with a directive. Even if a declaration was granted, it would not enable the individual to enforce his rights against a private individual.[232] The courts only have jurisdiction to grant a declaration that primary legislation is incompatible because it fails to comply with the directive. They cannot quash the national legislation or set it aside. The declaration would simply recognise the fact that the domestic law is incompatible with the directive (i.e. it recognises that national legislation is defective as it fails to confer the relevant rights in domestic law). It would not enable an individual to enforce that directive as against a private person. Positive legislation would still be required to implement the directive and to confer the rights on the individual. The fact that the government has failed to implement the directive may give rise to a claim for damages. The courts will not, however, allow a claim for a declaration simply as the means of founding a *Francovich* claim for damages against the government for failure to implement the directive. The individual will need to bring an action for damages to achieve that result.[233] On the current state of the authorities, it is possible that the courts might grant a declaration for the purpose of establishing that domestic law was incompatible with European law and so draw the matter to the attention of the government. Such a declaration would serve an essentially similar purpose to that served in the *EOC* case. A person with a sufficient interest would be establishing that the provisions of domestic law are incompatible with European Union law.

Subordinate legislation and EU law

Subordinate legislation which contravenes EU law may also be declared **17–092** invalid,[234] at least to the extent of the inconsistency.[235] Alternatively, the courts may declare that an individual is not to be subjected to those parts of the subordinate legislation which contravene EU law.[236] Public authorities may adopt decisions on the basis of an interpretation of such measures that does not conform

---

[231] *R. v HM Treasury Ex p. Shepherd Neame Ltd* (1999) 11 Admin. L.Rep. 517. See also *R. (Bancoult) v Secretary of State for Foreign and Commonwealth Affairs (No.3)* [2014] 3 W.L.R. 2921.
[232] *R. v Secretary of State for Employment Ex p. Seymour-Smith* [1997] 1 W.L.R. 473.
[233] [1997] 1 W.L.R. 473 at 480D–F. *R. v Secretary of State for Employment Ex p. EOC* [1995] 1 A.C. 1 at 32.
[234] See e.g. *R. (Partridge Farms Ltd) v Secretary of State for the Environment, Food and Rural Affairs* [2008] EWHC 1645 (order fixing compensation for cattle slaughtered because they had tuberculosis declared invalid as it breached the principle of equality laid down in EU law).
[235] See comments of Lord Clyde in *Brown v Secretary of State for Scotland* [1988] 2 C.M.L.R. 836 (for the report of the subsequent judgment of the Court of Justice see [1988] 3 C.M.L.R. 403).
[236] *MacMahon v Department of Education and Science* [1983] Ch. 277. This may be useful if only part of the subordinate legislation contravenes EU law but it is not possible to sever and quash the offending parts, e.g. if a regulation lays down conditions for EU and non-EU nationals, the regulations may only be invalid as far as EU nationals are concerned. The court may not wish to quash the whole of the subordinate legislation in such circumstances.

with the requirements of EU law. In such cases, it may be sufficient for the courts to construe the measure in conformity with European Union law and grant a declaration as to the true meaning of the measure, rather than invalidating the measure. Decisions taken by applying the incorrect interpretation could be declared unlawful or quashed.

17–093 Regulations may be made under s.2(2) of the European Communities Act 1972, for the purpose of giving effect to obligations imposed by EU law. Judicial review will be available to declare void any regulations made to implement a directive if the directive is subsequently declared void by the Court of Justice, as there is no European Union obligation to give effect to, and so no power to make regulations.[237] The precise extent of the powers conferred by s.2(2) of the European Communities Act 1972 remains unresolved. Section 2(2)(a) empowers the making of regulations for implementing an EU obligation including the making of transitional arrangements which may provide for the retention of national legislation. Section 2(2)(b) further empowers the making of regulations for the purpose of dealing with matters arising out of or related to the implementation of the EU obligation. The Divisional Court has held that the words "relating to" and "arising out of" should be given their natural meaning and that the regulation making power is a wide one.[238] The Court of Appeal has considered but left undetermined the precise scope of the powers conferred by s.2(2)(b).[239] Waller LJ indicated that the subsection empowered the making of measures which "naturally arise from or closely relate to" the EU obligation.[240] Jacob LJ provisionally considered that s.2(2)(a) covered all forms of implementation and that s.2(2)(b) was intended to go further but how much further depended on what the particular statutory instrument purported to do and the overall context. Jacob LJ accepted that s.2(2)(b) would not empower the making of regulations which had only a tenuous relationship with an EU obligation.[241] Where regulations go further than is permitted under s.2(2) of the European Communities Act 1972, and assuming there is no other power enabling such regulations to be made, then the regulations may, to that extent, be invalid.[242] An Order in Council under s.1(3) of the European Communities Act 1972, declaring that an ancillary Treaty is a Community Treaty may be challenged by way of judicial review if the Treaty is incapable in law of being regarded as an ancillary Treaty within s.1(3).[243]

Challenges to EU legislative measures

17–094 Judicial review may be used to challenge the validity of an EU legislative measure such as a regulation or directive. National courts have no jurisdiction to declare an act of the EU institution invalid; they must either refer the question of the validity of the act to the European Court for a preliminary ruling under Art.267 TFEU or they may dismiss the claim if they consider that the grounds of

---

[237] *R. v Minister of Agriculture, Fisheries and Food Ex p. FEDESA* [1988] 3 C.M.L.R. 661.
[238] *R. v Secretary of State for Trade and Industry Ex p. Unison* [1996] I.C.R. 1003 at 1014.
[239] *Oakley International Inc. v Animal Ltd* [2006] Ch. 273.
[240] [2006] Ch. 373 at [39].
[241] [2006] Ch. 373 at [68]–[81]. May LJ left the issue of the scope of s.2(2)(a) of open: see [47].
[242] per MacKay L.C. in *Hayward v Cammell Laird Shipbuilders (No.2)* [1988] A.C. 894.
[243] *R. v HM Treasury Ex p. Smedley* [1985] Q.B. 657.

alleged invalidity are unfounded.[244] Challenges to the validity of EU legislation are frequently brought via this route as individuals and other legal persons only have standing to bring direct actions in the Court of Justice alleging the invalidity of an EU measure in limited circumstances, i.e. if they are directly and individually concerned by the measure.[245] Consequently, national courts are required, so far as possible, to interpret and apply national procedural rules in a way that enables natural and legal persons to challenge the validity of any decision or national measure which applies a European legislative measure to that person.[246] The normal method of challenge is to seek judicial review of any national subordinate legislation implementing the EU measures or any individual decision applying the provisions of an EU Regulation to an individual. The domestic courts have held that they have jurisdiction to entertain challenges to a Directive even before implementing measures have been adopted and to refer the question of the validity of the Directive to the Court of Justice.[247] In principle, as an EU Regulation is directly applicable within a Member State, an individual could bring a challenge alleging that the Regulation itself is unlawful without the need to identify any individual national implementing measures.[248]

Time limits

A claim for judicial review in a purely domestic law matter must be brought   **17–095**
promptly and within three months of the date when the grounds for judicial review first arose although there is a discretion to extend the time for bringing the claim.[249] In cases where the challenge is based on EU law, the principle of effective protection requires that the period be sufficiently precise, clear and foreseeable and start from the time when the claimant knew, or ought to have known, of the alleged breach of EU law.[250] The courts will, therefore, operate the domestic law provisions in a way that, effectively, allows a claim alleging an EU law ground of challenge to be brought within months of the date when the claimant knew or ought to have known of the alleged breach of EU law.[251]

Interim relief in public law

Interim injunctions and stays are available in judicial review proceedings against   **17–096**
all public bodies and ministers.[252] The Court of Justice has held that rules of national law which prevented the grant of interim relief in appropriate cases to

---

[244] Case C-314/85 *Foto-Frost v Hauptzollamt Lubeck-Ost* [1987] E.C.R. 4199.

[245] Case C-50/00P *Union de Pequenos Agricultores v Council of the European Union* [2003] 2 W.L.R. 795.

[246] [2003] 2 W.L.R. 795 at [42] of the judgment.

[247] *R. v Secretary of State for Health Ex p. Imperial Tobacco Ltd* [1999] Eu. L.R. 582 and *R. (Intertanko) v Secretary of State for Transport* [2007] Env. L.R. 9 at [4].

[248] *R. v Secretary of State for Transport Ex p. Omega Air Ltd*, November 25, 1999.

[249] CPR r.54.5 discussed in fn.265 above.

[250] Case C-406/08 *Uniplex (UK) Ltd.) v NHS Business Authority* [2010] P.T.S.R. 1377 (dealing with the former provisions of the Public Contracts Regulations 2006 where the time limit was the equivalent to CPR r.54.5).

[251] *R. (Berky) v Newport City Council* [2012] L.G.R. 592; *SITA (UK) Ltd. v Greater Manchester Waste Disposal* [2011] L.G.R. 419 discussed in detail above in Chapter 9.

[252] See now *M v Home Office* [1994] 1 A.C. 377 and see above at para.8–012.

ensure the full and effective protection of rights claimed under EU law must be set aside.[253] The House of Lords has held that the domestic courts do have jurisdiction in appropriate circumstances to grant interim relief and even to suspend the operation of an Act of Parliament to protect EU law rights.[254]

17–097 The test for deciding whether it is appropriate in a particular case to grant interim relief is considered at present to be a matter of domestic, not European, law. The English courts will therefore apply the *American Cyanamid*[255] test, bearing in mind that interim relief in cases involving public authorities will require consideration of the wider public interest and not merely the private interests of the parties in deciding whether to grant interim relief.[256] Thus, the applicant will first have to establish that there is a serious issue to be tried. Then the courts will consider whether damages would be an adequate remedy if interim relief were refused. Frequently in public law cases, damages will not normally be relevant or adequate. In considering the balance of convenience, the courts will have regard to the wider interest in determining whether interim relief is appropriate. Similar principles are likely to be applied in determining whether to grant a stay.[257] Interim relief may be directed in form at a public body, but may in substance be aimed at preventing the activities of a third party (for example, by preventing the third party from acting on a planning permission). In those circumstances, a court has in the past usually required the person seeing interim relief to give a cross-undertaking that he will compensate the claimant for any damage caused as a result of the grant of interim relief, should the claim ultimately fail.[258] Now, in matters falling within the scope of the Aarhus Convention on access and public participation in environmental matters, the relevant EU directive provides that proceedings must not be prohibitively expensive. The Court of Justice has held that requiring the claimant to give a cross-undertaking in damages contravenes that provision.[259] As a result, the likelihood is that the domestic courts will no longer require a cross-undertaking in damages in claims falling within the scope of the Aarhus Convention.

17–098 There are occasions when a national court refers a question as to the validity of European Union legislation to the Court of Justice. The national court has a limited jurisdiction to grant interim relief suspending the operation of the European Union measure. The national court must have serious doubts about the

---

[253] *R. v Secretary of State for Transport Ex p. Factortame (No.2)* [1991] 1 A.C. 603.

[254] [1991] 1 A.C. 603.

[255] *American Cyanamid Co. v Ethicon Ltd* [1975] A.C. 396.

[256] *R. v Minister of Agriculture Fisheries and Food Ex p. Monsanto Plc* [1998] 4 All E.R. 321; see also *R. v Secretary of State for National Heritage Ex p. Continental Television* [1993] 3 C.M.L.R. 387 and see also paras 8–024 to 8–036 above.

[257] *R. v Inspectorate of Pollution Ex p. Greenpeace Ltd* [1994] 1 W.L.R. 570 and see above at para.6–028.

[258] *R. v Secretary of State for the Environment Ex p. Royal Society for the Protection of Birds* (1995) 7 Admin. L.Rep. 434.

[259] Case C-530/11 *Commission v United Kingdom* judgment, 13 February 2014.

validity of the measure, there must be urgency in the sense that interim relief is needed to avoid serious and irreparable harm being caused and account must be taken of the EU interest.[260]

The position is less clear in relation to interim relief to suspend national measures which are intended to implement a Directive which is alleged to be invalid but where the time-limit for implementing the Directive has not yet passed. In *R. v Secretary of State for Health Ex p. Imperial Tobacco Ltd,*[261] the Court of Appeal held by a majority that an application for interim relief to prevent the UK government acting to implement a Directive pending the outcome of a challenge to the validity of the Directive was to be determined in accordance with the principles developed by the European Court in the *Zuckerfabrik* case and not the domestic law principles governing interim relief. By the time that the case reached the House of Lords,[262] the matter had become academic as the government had undertaken not to make any national regulations implementing the Directive in question given the opinion of the Advocate General in the Court of Justice proceedings that the Directive was invalid. Three members of the House of Lords held that it was at least arguable that the appropriate test was that laid down in the jurisprudence of the Court of Justice, not the domestic law test, and would have referred the matter to the Court of Justice under Art.267 TFEU for a preliminary ruling on what was proper test to apply in considering the grant of interim relief. Two of their Lordships considered that the appropriate test was the domestic law test and, further, that that was acte clair and no reference was required. The Court of Justice has subsequently held that where it is alleged that national legislation is incompatible with provisions of EU law, it is a matter for national law to determine the criteria for deciding on the grant of interim relief to suspend the national law.[263]

Role of the court

The approach of the court in a judicial review application involving only questions of domestic law may well differ from its approach in cases involving an EU law element.[264] In considering a judicial review application, the court is traditionally limited to reviewing the legality of a decision and cannot substitute its view of the merits of a case for that of the decision-maker. The court may only consider whether the decision is ultra vires the powers conferred on the public body on the *Wednesbury* grounds of review—relevancy of considerations, improper purpose, misdirection of law, and so on. The role of the court in cases involving EU law rights may be different. The court may be required to formulate its own view of the merits of a particular administrative decision. This is

17-099

17-100

---

[260] Case C-92/88 *Zuckerfabrik Suderdiltnarschen A.G. v Hamptzellant Itzenhue* [1991] E.C.R. I-415; Case C-456/93 *Atlanta Fruchthandelsgesellschaft mbH v Bundesamt fur Ernahrung und Forstwirtshaft* [1995] E.C.R. I-3761 and see *R. (ABNA Ltd) v Secretary of State for Health and Food Standards Agency* [2004] Eu. L.R. 88 and Case C-453/03 *R. (ABNA Ltd) v Secretary of State for Health* [2005] E.C.R. I-10423.

[261] [2000] 2 W.L.R. 834.

[262] [2001] 1 W.L.R. 12.

[263] Case C-432/05 *Unibet (London) Ltd v Justitiekanslern* [2007] ECR I-2271 at [79]–[81].

[264] See, generally, Lewis, "Judicial Review and the Role of the English Courts in European Community Disputes" in *European Community Law in the English Courts* (Andenas and Jacobs edn, 1998).

particularly true where EU law permits Member States to derogate from general principles of European law in certain limited circumstances. Article 34 TFEU, for example, permits Member States to impose restrictions on imports on certain limited grounds, providing that the restrictions do not constitute arbitrary discrimination or a disguised restriction on trade. The national court is responsible for determining whether the measures constitute an impermissible restriction and, in particular, whether the measure is proportionate. This may lead a court to rule that measures are invalid as a contravention of EU law, even though the measures would not be invalidated on the narrower *Wednesbury* approach to judicial review.[265] The precise role of the court, even when considering proportionality, is not always clear as, depending on the context, the courts may give a greater margin of appreciation.[266] The role of the court may also draw it into the process of fact-finding. This may require a greater use of cross-examination and disclosure than is usually the case in judicial review.[267] Additional problems arise in connection with determining whether legislation contravenes EU law. In one case, Hoffmann J. had to deal with the question of whether the Shops Act 1950 had imposed greater restrictions on trade than were necessary to achieve the legitimate goal of regulating working hours on Sunday. Hoffmann J. took the view that that involved a balancing exercise which was properly the role of the legislature and the courts could only intervene if the view adopted by the legislature was not reasonably tenable.[268] The Advocate General expressly criticised the test adopted by Hoffmann J. when the matter was referred to the Court of Justice. He indicated that the court could not automatically accept the view of the legislature nor simply limit itself to considering the reasonableness of the view of the legislature.[269] In a subsequent case,[270] the House of Lords had to consider whether domestic legislation laying down different qualifying requirements for eligibility for certain employment rights for part-time workers as compared with full-time workers was objectively justified. The House of Lords therefore considered whether the measures adopted were suitable and necessary to achieve the aim of promoting part-time work. The House considered the written evidence but held that it did not provide any factual material justifying the correctness of the view that differing qualifying thresholds for part-time workers led to an increase in the amount of part-time work available. They therefore held that, on the material before them, the Secretary of State had not demonstrated that the national legislation was objectively justified and consequently ruled that it was incompatible with European law.

---

[265] *R. v Minister of Agriculture, Fisheries and Food Ex p. Bell Lines Ltd* [1984] 2 C.M.L.R. 502; *R. v Secretary of State for Social Services Ex p. Schering Chemicals Ltd* [1987] 1 C.M.L.R. 277; *R. v Minister of Agriculture, Fisheries and Food Ex p. Roberts* [1991] 1 C.M.L.R. 555.

[266] See, e.g. *R. (Sinclair Collis Ltd.) v Secretary of State for Health* [2012] 2 W.L.R. 304.

[267] See comments of Forbes J. in *R. v Minister of Agriculture, Fisheries and Food Ex p. Bell Lines Ltd* (see above, fn.249) at 511.

[268] *Stoke-on-Trent City Council v B & Q Plc* [1991] Ch. 48. See also *Smith (W.H.) Do It All Ltd v Peterborough City Council* [1991] 4 All E.R. 193.

[269] See Case C-169/91 *Stoke-on-Trent v B & Q Plc* [1993] A.C. 900 at 939, [27].

[270] *R. v Secretary of State for Employment Ex p. EOC* above, fn.70. Quaere if the approach of the House of Lords was unduly restrictive given the subsequent judgments of the European Court in Case C-317/93 *Nolte v Landesversicherunganstalt Hannover* [1996] I.R.L.R. 325 and Case C-444/93 *Megner and Sheffel v Innungkrankenkasse Vorderpfalz* [1996] I.R.L.R. 236.

Discretion

The remedies available on judicial review are discretionary. The courts have on occasions indicated that they continue to have a discretion to refuse remedies even where the case involves a EU law right.[271] Much may depend on the particular discretionary ground that is relied upon. The principle of legal certainty, for example, is a recognised concept in EU law. The refusal of permission to bring judicial review or the refusal of a remedy because of delay will, therefore, be consistent with EU law.[272] A remedy may be refused in English law because of the effect on the rights of others or because of the impact on the administration.[273] It is less likely that refusal of a remedy on this ground would be consistent with the obligation to give full and effective protection to an individual's directly effective EU law rights. On one occasion, the House of Lords held that they should not refuse a remedy on the grounds that compliance with EU law would not, in fact, have affected the decision reached.[274] There had been planning permission had been granted without an environmental impact assessment first having been carried out and the House of Lords quashed the decision. However, that decision should be read in context as it involved a complete failure to carry out an environmental impact assessment and the sole ground upon which it was said that the court should refuse a remedy as a matter of discretion was that the decision would have been the same in any event. That decision should not be read as prohibiting any exercise of discretion to refuse a remedy.[275]

17–101

Habeas corpus

Issues of EU law have been raised by way of applications for habeas corpus. Reliance has, unsuccessfully, been placed upon the provisions governing freedom of movement of persons as restricting the ability of Member States to extradite EU nationals.[276] The legality of detention pending the implementation of deportation orders could also raise questions of EU law which could be raised on an application for habeas corpus.

17–102

---

[271] See dicta of May LJ in *R. v Secretary of State for the Home Department Ex p. Tombofa* [1988] 2 C.M.L.R. 609 at 618–619.

[272] See, e.g. *R. (Gavin) v Haringey LBC* [2004] 2 P. & C.R. 13 (where there had been delay in bringing a challenge to the grant of planning permission the court refused to grant a quashing order as that would cause hardship to a third party and granted a declaration instead that procedural requirements had not been met).

[273] See above at para.12–035.

[274] *Berkeley v Secretary of State for the Environment* [2001] 2 A.C. 603 (dealing with statutory applications to quash but similar principles apply to judicial review).

[275] See dicta in *R. (Edwards) v Environment Agency* [2008] Env. L.R. 34; *Brown v Secretary of State for the Environment, Transport and the Regions* [2004] Env. L.R. 509. For discussion of the decision in *Berkeley*, see also *R. (Horner) v Lancashire CC* [2008] 1 P & C.R. 74 at [81]–[101]; *R. (Richardson) v North Yorkshire CC* [2004] 2 All E.R. 31 at [40]–[42] and *R (Jones) Mansfield DC* [2003] All E.R. (D) 277.

[276] See, e.g. *R. v Secretary of State for the Home Department Ex p. Launder* [1997] 1 W.L.R. 839; *Re Habeas Corpus Application of Carthage Healy* [1984] 3 C.M.L.R. 575; *R. v Governor of Pentonville Prison Ex p. Budlong* [1980] 1 W.L.R. 1110. The great majority of immigration cases are dealt with by the Immigration Appeals Tribunal or by way of judicial review.

Appeals

17–103 Judicial review may not be the only means by which issues of EU law come before the courts. Inferior courts and tribunals may have jurisdiction to deal with challenges to certain decisions and they may, therefore, have to determine issues of EU law in the exercise of their jurisdiction. It is now established that where an inferior court or tribunal has jurisdiction in an area where EU law rights are relevant it is under a duty to apply European law.[277] An individual may, usually should, bring a claim or an appeal involving questions of European law before such a tribunal.[278] The appellate machinery may not always provide an appeal against the particular decision under challenge. In those instances, the appropriate remedy for the individual seeking to enforce an EU law right is to bring a claim for judicial review. The judicial review procedure is, in principle, capable of providing an effective remedy although national law may, but is not required to, provide an appeal to a specialist tribunal.[279]

17–104 Statute may also provide rights of appeal on points of law from a particular tribunal to the courts. Questions of European Union law are, by virtue of s.3(1) of the European Communities Act 1972, questions of law not fact. Consequently, such issues may arise on appeal on a point of law or by way of case stated. The Divisional Court has quashed a forfeiture order made by a magistrates' court and upheld by the Crown Court, on the grounds that the order constituted a restriction on the free movement of goods contrary to what is now Art.34 TFEU.[280] Appeals from tribunals raising questions of EU law have been frequent.[281] A decision of a statutory arbitrator on the allocation of milk quotas was appealed on the grounds that the arbitrator had misconstrued relevant EU regulations.[282]

Private law remedies

17–105 Private law remedies may be available to enforce a EU law right. Some directly effective provisions of European law only impose obligations on individuals—most notably Arts 101 and 102 TFEU which bind undertakings and do not apply to public authorities acting in a public capacity.[283] Judicial review is only available against public authorities, so these obligations can only be enforced by

---

[277] See, e.g. *Autologic Holdings Plc v Inland Revenue Commissioners* [2006] 1 A.C. 118. *Worringham v Lloyds Bank Ltd* [1982] 1 W.L.R. 841; *Jensen v Corp. of Trinity House* [1982] 2 C.M.L.R. 218. Statute confers jurisdiction on tribunals to determine specific matters. In the course of exercising that statutory jurisdiction, they must disapply any provision of the statute that conflicts with European Union law. Such tribunals do not have a general discretion to apply European Union law.

[278] Claims should normally be brought via the statutory mechanism rather than judicial review: see *Autologic Holdings Ltd v Inland Revenue Commissioners* [2006] 1 A.C. 118.

[279] *T-Mobile (UK) Ltd. v Office of Communications* [2009] 1 W.L.R. 1565; *TN (Afghanistan) v Secretary of State for the Home Department* [2014] 1 W.L.R. 2095.

[280] *Conegate v HM Customs and Excise* Case 121/85 [1987] Q.B. 254. Similar issues may arise in judicial review proceedings: see *R. v Bow Street Magistrates' Court Ex p. Noncyp Ltd* [1989] 3 W.L.R. 467.

[281] See, e.g. *Yoga for Health Foundation v Customs and Excise Commissioners* [1985] 1 C.M.L.R. 340.

[282] *Puncknowle Farms Ltd v Kane* [1986] 1 C.M.L.R. 27.

[283] Case 136/86 *B.N.I.C. v Aubert* [1988] 4 C.M.L.R. 331. The articles do apply to the activities of nationalised industries: Case 41/83 *Re British Telecommunications: Italy v Commission* [1985] 2

way of an appropriate private law remedy for damages.[284] Other provisions of EU law—notably those on sex discrimination[285] and employment[286]—bind both private individuals and public authorities. Private law remedies need to be available in relation to the former, and may be available as against the latter in addition to, or instead of, judicial review. Finally, provisions of EU law which bind only public authorities may still, in certain circumstances, give rise to a right to claim compensation or damages from a public body.

Damages against a public authority

In the light of the decisions in *Francovich*[287] and *Factortame*[288] and others,[289] an **17–106** individual may in certain circumstances be able to claim compensation from a public body which has breached EU law in addition to claiming a public law remedy to have the unlawful action quashed or national legislation declared to be incompatible with European law. Previously, the Court of Appeal had held that the EU law right was akin to a right not to be subjected to an ultra vires measure.[290] It was held that the appropriate remedy was therefore a public law remedy which would set aside or quash the domestic action that was incompatible with EU law. Damages would not normally be available in cases of breach of European Union law unless the public authority was liable for the tort of misfeasance in a public office. That required proof that the public body had acted in breach of EU law and done so either knowingly or maliciously. That approach cannot now prevail in the light of the decision of the Court of Justice in *Factortame*. A public body will be liable in damages if it has committed a sufficiently serious breach of a provision of European law which was intended to confer rights on an individual and that individual has suffered loss as a result. It will not be necessary to prove misfeasance.[291]

C.M.L.R. 368. The English courts have assumed that the activities of the Milk Marketing Board, then a statutory body, fell within Arts 81 and 82: *Garden Cottage Foods v Milk Marketing Board* [1984] A.C. 130.

[284] See, e.g. Case C-453 *Courage Ltd v Crehan* [2002] Q.B. 507. The claimant ultimately failed to establish that there had been a breach of Art.81: see *Crehan v Inntrepeneur Pub Co.* [2003] Eu. L.R. 663. That judgment was upheld by the House of Lords in [2007] 1 A.C. 333. The remedy where a breach is established is compensatory damages: *Devenish Nutrition Ltd v Sanofi-Aventis SA* [2008] 2 W.L.R. 637.

[285] See, e.g. Art.157 TFEU (ex Art.119) on equal pay and Dir.76/207 EEC on equal treatment.

[286] See, e.g. Art.39 TFEU (ex Art.48) and Case 36/74 *Walrave v Association Union Cycliste Internationale* [1974] E.C.R. 1405.

[287] Joined Cases C-6/90 and C-9/90 *Francovich v Italian Republic* [1990] E.C.R. I-5357.

[288] Joined Cases C-46/93 and C-48/93 *Brasserie du Pecheur SA v Germany* and *R. v Secretary of State for Transport Ex p. Factortame Ltd* [1996] E.C.R. I-1029 and see above at 17–063 to 17–073. See generally Craig, "Once More Unto the Breach: The Community, the State and Damages Liability" [1997] 113 L.Q.R. 67.

[289] See cases in previous footnote.

[290] *Bourgoin SA v Ministry of Agriculture Fisheries and Food* [1986] 1 Q.B. 716 (the claim was eventually settled: [1988] 1 C.M.L.R. 716).

[291] If the breach is not sufficiently serious, EU law does not require national law to make damages available as part of the need to ensure an effective remedy. As English law does not yet generally recognise damages as a remedy for unlawful action, damages would not generally be required for a breach of EU law by a public body by reason of the principle of equivalence: see the dicta of the Court of Appeal in *R. v Secretary of State Ex p. Factortame (No.5)* [2001] A.C. 524.

17–107   The domestic courts accept that there is an obligation to compensate individuals who have suffered loss as a result of a sufficiently serious breach of EU law which conferred rights on the individual. The Court of Justice has identified a number of factors that a national court should take into account in determining whether there has been a sufficiently serious breach, including the clarity and precision of the EU law that has been breached, the measure of discretion left to national authorities, whether the infringement and the damage caused was voluntary or involuntary, whether any error was excusable or inexcusable and whether the position adopted by the EU institutions may have contributed to the adoption or retention of national measures contrary to EU law.[292] In addition, the Court of Justice held that requiring a claimant to satisfy certain rules of national law would undermine the full and effective protection of the EU law right to damages and so those rules of national law had to be disapplied. In particular, national law could not require the claimant to establish misfeasance in a public office or an element of fault on the part of the authorities over and above that already encapsulated in the concept of a sufficiently serious breach of EU law.[293] The approach of the domestic courts has been to apply the principles set out by the Court of Justice, and to take account of the factors identified by it, whilst recognising that the test requires a value judgment by the national court.[294]

17–108   Against that background, the House of Lords held that the UK was liable in damages for loss caused to Spanish fishermen by the enactment of the Merchant Shipping Act 1988 which prevented them fishing against the British quota. The House of Lords proceeded by applying the considerations identified in the Court of Justice to the particular facts of the case. The House considered that the legislation was clearly discriminatory on the grounds of nationality and therefore involved a breach of a fundamental Treaty obligation. It was likely to have grave consequences for the individuals affected. The legislation had been deliberately adopted as a matter of policy to remove the rights of the fishermen concerned. The legislation was not shown to be excusable. The European Commission had been consistent in its view that the legislation was incompatible with EU law. In those circumstances, the House of Lords held that there had been a sufficiently serious breach for the purposes of establishing state liability in damages.[295]

17–109   In determining the substantive conditions for liability in damages, the domestic courts have not sought to equate the right to compensation with any particular domestic law tort or other form of civil action. The courts have, however, considered what is the equivalent or similar domestic law right to the EU law right in determining the procedural rules and conditions that govern the enforcement of the right to compensation. The courts have tended to equate a claim for damages for loss caused by a sufficiently serious breach of EU law to a

---

[292] Joined Cases C-46/93 and C-48/93 *Brasserie du Pecheur SA v Federal Republic of Germany and R. v Secretary of State for Transport Ex p. Factortame Ltd* [1996] E.C.R. I-1029. See also Case C-63/01 *Evans v Secretary of State for the Environment, Transport and the Regions* [2003] E.C.R. I-1447.

[293] See above paras 17–063 to 17–068.

[294] *Byrne v Motor Insurers' Bureau* [2008] 3 C.M.L.R. 4 at [45].

[295] *R. v Secretary of State for Transport Ex p. Factortame (No.5)* [2001] A.C. 524. The German courts, in the companion case of *Brasserie du Pecheur SA v Germany*, held that Germany was not liable on the grounds of lack of causation: see [1997] 1 C.M.L.R. 971.

claim in tort for breach of statutory duty and have applied the procedural rules applicable in such tort claims to the damages claim. In *Factortame (No.7)*, for example, the High Court had to consider the nature of a claim for damages for breach of EU law in the context of limitation periods and the availability of damages for distress and aggravated damages.[296] The High Court held that the claim did amount to an action founded on tort within the meaning of s.2 of the Limitation Act 1980 and was subject to the six-year time-limit for bringing the claim set out in that section. A tort was a breach of a non-contractual duty which gives rise to a private law right to recover compensation from the party causing the injury. In the present case, the liability in damages imposed by EU law was such a liability. The combination of the breach of what is now Art.49 TFEU and s.2(1) of the European Communities Act 1972 (which was the means by which duties under EU law had force in the domestic law of the UK) amounted to a breach of statutory duty and that breach fell within the scope of an action founded on tort within s.2 of the Limitation Act 1980. The High Court also held that damages for injury to feelings and aggravated damages were not available for a breach of the rights of establishment under Art.49 TFEU. The rights conferred by Art.49 TFEU were intended to secure economic freedoms for individuals and were only intended to lead to damages for economic loss. Damages for injury to feelings and aggravated damages were only available under domestic law in relation to those torts where the claimant's self-esteem is an integral part of the damage for which compensation is awarded. A breach of Art.49 TFEU was not equivalent to such torts and, therefore, liability for such loss did not need to be extended to breaches of Art.49 TFEU as those torts were not similar or equivalent causes of action to rights derived from Art.49 TFEU.

17–110 Certain of the claims under EU law will involve a claim that other EU nationals have been treated less favourably than UK nationals either by reason of direct discrimination on grounds of nationality or indirect discrimination whereby rights or benefits are tied to residence conditions which are more difficult for EU nationals who are not British citizens to satisfy. The provisions of the Equality Act 2010 does makes racial discrimination unlawful in certain specific respects. It is unlikely, however, that a claim under the Equality Act 2010 will be a similar domestic action for the purposes of the equivalence rule in relation to breaches of provisions of the TFEU.

17–111 In *Factortame (No.7)*, the High Court held that breach of the Race Relations Act 1976 (the predecessor to the Equality Act 2010) was not a comparator cause of action to a claim for discrimination on grounds of nationality contrary to Art.49 TFEU. The concept of discrimination on grounds of nationality did not have the same connotations of hatred, ridicule or contempt on ethnic grounds which underlay the Race Relations Act 1976. Rather, Art.49 TFEU was intended to be used widely to enforce economic rights to free movement of persons and the right of establishment in a variety of circumstances by removing barriers that

---

[296] *R. v Secretary of State for Transport Ex p. Factortame (No.7)* [2001] 1 W.L.R. 942. See also *Nabadda v Westminster City Council* [2000] I.C.R. 951 and *Phonographic Performance Ltd v Department of Trade and Industry* [2004] 1 W.L.R. 1.

might otherwise exist. Consequently, a claim for breach of Art.49 was not comparable or similar to a claim for discrimination under the provisions of the then Race Relations Act 1976.[297]

17–112   Although damages are a private law remedy, a claim may be attached to a claim for a public law remedy in a claim for judicial review.[298] In practice, the court will first determine whether there has been any breach of EU law and whether the claimant is entitled to any remedies in public law, such as a quashing order to quash an unlawful decision or a declaration. Then the court will deal with the question of damages.

Remedies against private individuals

17–113   Provisions of EU law may give rise to directly effective rights enforceable against individuals. Only private law, not public law, remedies are available against individuals. A EU law right may therefore need to give rise to a private law cause of action. Alternatively, statute may confer particular rights on an individual, as is common in the field of employment, and EU law rights may take effect through those statutory provisions.

Private law causes of action: damages for breach of statutory duty

17–114   In actions against private individuals, the courts have regarded the tort of breach of statutory duty as an appropriate means, absent any other mechanism for giving effect to a directly effective EU right. The House of Lords has held in interlocutory proceedings in *Garden Cottage Foods v Milk Marketing Board*[299] that a breach of what is now Art.102 TFEU (which prohibits abuses of monopolistic power) gives rise to a civil action akin to a breach of statutory duty which is remediable by way of damages. Not every breach of a statutory duty in English law gives rise to a right of action on the part of an individual. Where, however, a statute is intended to confer a right of action on an individual against another individual, but the statute includes no specific statutory machinery for that purpose, the only available remedy is a civil action for damages for breach of statutory duty.[300] Similarly, where a provision of EU law confers rights on an individual intended to be enforceable in the national courts against another individual, the appropriate categorisation is to regard a breach as giving rise to a civil cause of action for damages akin to a breach of statutory duty in English law.[301] The Court of Justice has held that the need to ensure the full effectiveness of such rules requires that an individual may claim damages for loss caused to him by a contract or conduct liable to distort competition.[302] The Court also held that national law cannot prevent a party to such an unlawful contract bringing a claim solely on the grounds that he is a party to the contract and is, therefore, seeking to rely on his own wrongful acts, although national law may prohibit this

---

[297] See *R. v Secretary of State for Transport Ex p. Factortame (No.7)* [2001] 1 W.L.R. 942 at [251]–[256] and *Nabadda v Westminster City Council* [2000] I.C.R. 951.
[298] s.31(7) of the Senior Courts Act 1981 and CPR, r.54.3 and see above at para.2–180.
[299] [1984] A.C. 130.
[300] [1984] A.C. 130.
[301] [1984] A.C. 130.
[302] Case C-453/99 *Courage Ltd v Crehan* [2002] Q.B. 507.

where the party bears significant responsibility for the distortion of competition.[303] The issue arose in the context of a claim by party to the lease of a pub that the provisions of the lease violated what is now Art.101 TFEU.

Injunctions

Injunctions, including interlocutory injunctions, are available where an individual can maintain an action for damages for breach of statutory duty.[304] Difficulties arise if the courts are not prepared to classify a breach of EU law in this way. The courts have been reluctant in the past to allow an individual to maintain an action for an injunction, to restrain conduct prohibited by statute, unless the statute confers a right on the individual to recover damages in tort for the breach, or the individual has suffered special damage.[305] For that reason Lord Diplock in *Garden Cottage Foods*[306] was adamant that it was not possible to maintain an action based on a contravention of Art.102 TFEU, which gives rise to a remedy by way of injunction alone to restrain a defendant from causing loss in the future. If Art.102 TFEU entitled an individual to maintain a cause of action in private law, then that cause of action must entitle the individual to a remedy in damages as well as an injunction. According to this approach, the choice lies between either recognising provisions of EU law as giving rise to private law rights which must necessarily sound in damages (or an injunction where damages would not be an adequate remedy), or providing no positive remedy at all. There is no halfway house whereby an individual may enforce his European Union law right by way of an injunction even though a remedy in damages is not available. **17–115**

Subordinate legislation implementing EU law may also provide specifically for the grant of injunctions.[307] There may occasionally be remedies other than breach of statutory duty available, or the courts may determine that, in certain instances at least, the requirements of direct effect may be satisfied by allowing an individual to rely on EU law as a defence.[308] Injunctions in public law cases have been discussed above.[309] **17–116**

---

[303] The claimant ultimately failed to establish that there had been a breach of Art.81: see *Crehan v Inntrepeneur Pub Co.* [2003] Eu. L.R. 663. That judgment was upheld by the House of Lords in [2007] 1 A.C. 333. The remedy where a breach is established is compensatory damages: *Devenish Nutrition Ltd v Sanofi-Aventis SA* [2008] 2 W.L.R. 637.

[304] See, e.g. *Cutsforth v Mansfield Inns Ltd* [1986] 1 W.L.R. 558; an interlocutory injunction was refused in *Garden Cottage Foods v Milk Marketing Board* [1984] A.C. 130 as damages were an adequate remedy. See also *Holleran v Daniel Thwaites Plc* [1989] 2 C.M.L.R. 917 (injunction granted to restrain exercise of contractual rights where purpose of exercise was to procure a breach of European law).

[305] *Lonrho v Shell Petroleum Co. Ltd (No.2)* [1982] A.C. 173; *R.C.A. v Pollard* [1983] Ch. 135; *R. v Liverpool Daily Post and Echo Newspapers Plc* [1991] 2 A.C. 370.

[306] *Garden Cottage Foods v Milk Marketing Board* [1984] A.C. 130.

[307] See, e.g. *Director General of Fair Trading v Tobyward Ltd* [1989] 1 W.L.R. 517.

[308] See para.17–132, 17–115.

[309] See paras 15–092 to 15–095.

Declarations

17–117 The courts may make binding declarations of right.[310] Thus, the court may grant declarations declaring the rights of individuals under EU law in the private law field,[311] or in the public law field.[312]

Negligence

17–118 An action for negligence at common law is a possible but unlikely remedy for breach of EU law. No reliance has so far been placed on negligence in actions against public authorities.[313] To be successful, an individual would need to show that a public authority owed a duty of care not to enact subordinate measures, or take decisions which conflicted with EU law. This would be difficult in the light of the current approach of the courts to analogous situations in domestic law.[314]

Economic torts

17–119 There are a group of economic torts, such as conspiracy,[315] intimidation,[316] inducing breach of contract,[317] interfering with trade or business[318] and interfering with statutory duties, including duties imposed by EU law,[319] which may be relevant to some breaches of European Union law. The essential element of all these torts is an unlawful act and the intentional infliction of harm.[320] A contravention of EU law would probably be an unlawful act for the purpose of these torts, although the matter is not entirely free from doubt as a breach of an English statute is not always an unlawful act for these purposes.[321]

Miscellaneous torts

17–120 It is possible that the actions of a public authority, which are subsequently held to be invalid as the contravene of EU law, may involve the commission of various torts. The detention of goods contrary to Art.28 TFEU may involve a claim for

---

[310] CPR r.40.20.

[311] See, e.g. *Worringham v Lloyds Bank (No.2)* [1982] 1 W.L.R. 841.

[312] See, e.g. *R. v Minister of Agriculture, Fisheries and Food Ex p. Bell Lines Ltd* [1984] 2 C.M.L.R. 502.

[313] Reliance on negligence was expressly disclaimed in *Bourgoin SA v Ministry of Agriculture, Fisheries and Food* [1986] Q.B. 716. But see *Cato v Minister of Agriculture, Fisheries and Food* [1989] 3 C.M.L.R. 513 (action for negligent misstatement; duty of care owed but no breach).

[314] See, e.g. *Rowling v Takaro Properties Ltd* [1988] A.C. 473.

[315] *Crofter Hand Woven Harris Tweed Co. Ltd v Veitch* [1942] A.C. 435.

[316] *Rookes v Barnard* [1964] A.C. 1129.

[317] *Lumley v Gye* (1853) 2 E. & B. 216.

[318] *Merkur Island Shipping Corp. v Laughton* [1983] 2 A.C. 570.

[319] See *Barretts & Baird (Wholesale) Ltd v Institution of Professional Civil Servants* [1987] I.R.L.R. 3 and see Napier, "Breach of Statutory Duty and Unlawful Means in Strike Law" [1987] C.L.J. 222.

[320] For the definition of intention see *Lonrho v Al-Fayed* [1991] 3 W.L.R. 188.

[321] *Lonrho v Shell Petroleum Co. (No.2)* [1982] A.C. 173.

unlawful interference with goods.[322] Detention of EU nationals contrary to EU law on the free movement of workers could raise issues of false imprisonment.

Innominate tort

There is little judicial or academic support for the view that provisions of the EC Treaty create new or innominate torts. Lord Denning M.R. suggested that what are now Arts 101 and 102 TFEU created new torts which could be named "undue restriction of competition in the Common Market" and "abuse of dominant position in the Common Market".[323] This view was criticised by Lord Diplock in *Garden Cottage Foods*,[324] who regarded the creation of new torts as unnecessary given the potential availability of a cause of action based on a breach of statutory duty. A claim in *Bourgoin* that a breach of what is now Art.34 TFEU constituted an innominate tort was withdrawn, and was the subject of unfavourable comment in the Court of Appeal.[325] It is now generally accepted that the proper approach is to determine which of the existing remedies in English law should be available rather than creating new or innominate torts.   **17–121**

Statutory remedies for discrimination in employment

Specific statutory rights have been given by domestic law in the field of discrimination in relation to employment including in such matters as pay, contractual benefits and to other non-contractual benefits. Statute has provided specific remedies by way of complaint to an employment tribunal and set out procedural rules governing the various remedies.[326] EU law also seeks to ensure that individuals are guaranteed equal pay for equal work under Art.157 TFEU and are not discriminated against in other respects.   **17–122**

The employment tribunals have jurisdiction to enforce the rights conferred by statute on individuals. In exercising their statutory jurisdiction and enforcing those rights, the tribunals also have to apply and give effect to the directly effective provisions of EU law. If provisions of the relevant domestic law conflict with EU law, they must therefore disapply those inconsistent national   **17–123**

---

[322] See Case C-121/85 *Conegate Ltd v HM Customs and Excise* [1987] Q.B. 254 where Conegate undertook not to seek damages for the detention of the goods unless the goods had suffered physical damage.

[323] In *Application des Gaz SA v Falks Veritas* [1974] Ch. 381 at 396.

[324] *Garden Cottage Foods v Milk Marketing Board* (see above, fn.306) at 144–145.

[325] [1986] Q.B. 716.

[326] Equality Act 2010, s.120.

provisions.[327] Such tribunals do not have a general discretion to apply EU law. They do not, for example, have a general jurisdiction to hear and determine *Francovich* claims for damages.[328]

Equal pay

17–124   Both national law and EU law seek to ensure equal pay for equal work for men and women. The Equal Pay Act 1970 should be read in a way that is consistent with Art.157 TFEU. If that is not possible, limits or restrictions on the availability of the right to equal pay will be disapplied.[329] The Court of Justice has held that the provision in s.2(5) of the Equal Pay Act 1970 which provided that arrears of pay or compensation was limited to the two years prior to the institution of proceedings was not, as such, a breach of the principle of effectiveness.[330] The Court held that the question of whether the two-year rule was compatible with the principle of equivalence, i.e. that a claim derived from Art.157 TFEU should not be treated less favourably than similar domestic law rights, was a matter for the national court. The Employment Appeal Tribunal subsequently held that the rule did breach the principles of equivalence as s.2(5) was less favourable than the provisions applying to other comparable actions, including breach of contract, unlawful deductions from wages, race and disability discrimination.[331] Those claims had six-year time-limits not two years. Consequently, the EAT held that the claim for equal pay derived from Art.157 TFEU should be subject to a six-year time-limit.

17–125   Exceptionally, the Court of Justice has held that it was incompatible with the principle of effectiveness for the UK to adopt a procedural rule which provided that part-time workers who successfully demonstrated that their exclusion from a pension scheme constituted unlawful sex discrimination were limited to calculating their pensionable service only by reference to the two years prior to the institution of proceedings (together with subsequent years of service). That

---

[327] See, e.g. the decision of the Employment Appeal Tribunal in *Benkharbouche v Embassy of the Republic of Sudan* [2014] ICR 169 (provisions of domestic law preventing enforcement of rights derived from EU law disapplied; the provisions were not disapplied in respect of purely domestic law rights unconnected with EU law). See also *Biggs v Somerset CC* [1995] I.C.R. 811 at 830 approved by the Court of Appeal in [1996] I.C.R. 364 (employment tribunal would have had jurisdiction to disapply limits on the right to claim for unfair dismissal if those limits were contrary to European law). The approach of the EAT in *Biggs* was specifically endorsed by the Court of Appeal in *Barber v Staffordshire CC* [1996] 2 All E.R. 748 at 754c–755c.

[328] *Potter v Secretary of State for Employment* [1997] I.R.L.R. 21. The point was not argued in the House of Lords: see [1999] I.R.L.R. 566. Member States are entitled to determine which courts or tribunals are to have jurisdiction to hear certain matters: see above at para.17–077.

[329] See, e.g. *Scullard v Knowles* [1996] I.R.L.R. 344. Cases such as *Macarthys Ltd v Smith* [1979] 1 W.L.R. 1189 where the Court of Appeal considered that the English legislation did not provide a right to equal pay with a predecessor in the employment but that Art.141 EC did, would now probably be understood as a case where the restriction in the Equal Pay Act 1970 limiting the right to claim to persons engaged contemporaneously ought to be disapplied so that the statutory right to equal pay applied, unhindered, to previous employees as well as contemporaneous employees.

[330] C-326/96 *Levez v T.H. Jennings (Harlow Pools) Ltd* [1999] I.C.R. 521. Exceptionally, the Court of Justice held that the employer could not rely on the time-limit in that case as the woman had been told by her employer that she was receiving equal pay and enabling the employer to rely on the time-limit would, therefore, have made it impossible in practice for the claimant to have enforced her right to equal pay.

[331] [1999] I.R.L.R. 36.

procedural rule prevented the whole record of service from being taken into account when calculating the benefits that would be payable on retirement and after the date of the claim.[332]

The courts have also had to consider s.2(4) of the Equal Pay Act 1970 which provides that any claim for equal pay must be brought within six months of the end of the employment to which it relates. In the context of a claim concerning exclusion of part-timers from a pension scheme, the Court of Justice held that the imposition of a six-month time-limit did not breach the principle of effectiveness. The House of Lords subsequently held that the six-month limit, in the context of access to pensions, was not less favourable than the six-year limit applied to claims for breach of contract. The six-year limit applied from each breach of contract, i.e. from each time when the employer should have admitted the employee to the pension scheme and paid the contributions that would ultimately secure pension benefits. Once six years had passed from that specific failure to admit the employee and pay the periodic contributions required, no claim could be brought. The six-year limit, if it had applied, would not have run from the end of the employment. A six-month limit running from the end of the employment (but permitting claims to be brought in respect of all periods of employment) was therefore not less favourable than the rules applying to a breach of contract.[333]

17–126

Discrimination

National and EU law prohibits discrimination on grounds such as gender, race, age, or sexual orientation in relation to access to employment and the terms and conditions of employment other than pay. Section 124 of the Equality Act 2010 provides three remedies; a declaration of rights, damages, or a recommendation that certain action be taken. The remedies are available in relation to complaints of discrimination rendered unlawful by Pt 5 of the 2010 Act. There is no statutory limit on the amount of compensation payable in cases of sex discrimination and interest is also available on such awards. This follows the decision of the Court of Justice in *Marshall (No.2)*[334] that such limits were incompatible with European law as they undermined the effectiveness of EU law. A claim for discrimination must be brought within three months of the date of the act of discrimination complained of, although the tribunal has jurisdiction to extend that if it is just and equitable to do so. The employment tribunal may have regard amongst other matters to the fact that the claimant, or the claimant's lawyers, were unaware that a claim lay or because a decision of the Court of Justice alters the previous understanding of what the law was.[335]

17–127

---

[332] Case C-78/98 *Preston v Wolverhampton NHS Trust* [2001] 2 W.L.R. 408 and Case C-246/96 *Magorrian v Eastern Health & Social Services Board* [1998] I.C.R. 979.

[333] *Preston v Wolverhampton NHS Trust (No.2)* [2001] 2 W.L.R. 448.

[334] Case C-271/91 *Marshall v Southampton and South West Hampshire Area Health Authority* [1993] E.C.R. I-4367.

[335] *Mills v Marshall* [1998] I.R.L.R. 494; other limitation periods either do not allow for extension (such as s.2(4) and (5) of the Equal Pay Act 1970) or the discretion to extend time is narrower, such as that relating to claims for unfair dismissal under the Employment Rights Act 1996 where the complaint must be presented within three months unless that was not reasonably practicable; the fact that a person did not know of the right to claim or that there was a change in the understanding of the law did not mean that it was not reasonably practicable to make a claim: see *Biggs v Somerset CC* [1996] I.C.R. 364.

Restitutionary remedies

17–128 The Court of Justice has held that the right not to be subjected to national measures levying charges contrary to EU law carries with it the right to seek repayment of sums already levied.[336] The fact that a charge is contrary to EU law is both a defence to an action for payment *and* a basis for a claim for restitution.[337]

17–129 Charges and taxes levied by national authorities in the exercise of statutory powers may contravene EU law. They may constitute customs duties or charges having equivalent effect, and so violate Art.30 TFEU.[338] They may violate the provision on non-discrimination in Art.18 TFEU if they are applicable only to EU nationals other than UK nationals, or are fixed at a higher rate for EU nationals.[339] Provision imposing taxation may breach the provisions governing freedom of establishment.[340] Taxes levied under national law in the field of indirect taxation may contravene specific directives on the harmonisation of value added tax.[341] The House of Lords has held that taxes or charges levied pursuant to an ultra vires demand are recoverable as of right[342] or on the basis that it was money paid under a mistake of law.[343] Taxes, charges or other monies levied contrary to EU law may be recovered by way of a claim for restitution or, it seems, breach of statutory duty.[344] Interest, including compound interest, may be awarded.[345] The individual could also resist making payment on the grounds that the charges were not lawfully due.

17–130 There may also exist statutory machinery for the repayment of money unlawfully levied. Such machinery could be used to repay money levied contrary to EU law. In *Commissioners of Customs and Excise v Fine Arts Developments*

---

[336] Case C-199/82 *Amministrazione dello Finanze dello Stato v San Giorgio SpA* [1983] E.C.R. 3595.

[337] Case C-222/82 *Apple and Pear Development Council v Lewis* [1983] E.C.R. 4083 at 4125, [39]. See also Joined Cases C-397/98 and C-410/98 *Metallgesesllschaft Ltd v Inland Revenue Commission* [2001] Ch. 620 and Case C-446/04 *Test Claimants in FII Group Litigation v Inland Revenue Commissioners* [2006] E.C.R. I-11753.

[338] See, e.g. Case C-39/73 *Rewe-Zentral Finanz v Landwirtschaftskammer Westfalen-Lippe* [1973] E.C.R. 1039.

[339] See, e.g. Case C-309/85 *Barra v Belgium State and The City of Liège* [1988] E.C.R. 355 (charges for education for non-Belgian EEC nationals contrary to Art.7).

[340] C-362/12 *Test Claimants in Franked Investments Group v Commissioners of Inland Revenue* [2014] 2 C.M.L.R. 33.

[341] Case C-5/84 *Direct Comestics Ltd v Commissioners of Customs and Excise* [1985] E.C.R. 617.

[342] *Woolwich Building Society v Inland Revenue Commissioners (No.2)* [1993] A.C. 70.

[343] *Kleinwort Benson v Lincoln City Council* [1999] 2 A.C. 349. The claimant may seek to recover the ground on the basis of whichever rule is more favourable to him. In *Deutsche Morgan Grenfell Group Plc v Inland Revenue Commissioners* [2007] 1 A.C. 558, the taxpayer sought to recover money on the basis of mistake as that provided, at that stage, for a longer time limit for bringing claims before they came statute barred: see Limitation Act 1980 s.32. The law in relation to claims for recovery of tax has now been amended by the Finance Act 2004 s.320 which provides that the extended time limit for bringing claims on the grounds of mistake does not apply to claims relating to taxation. That provision was held to be incompatible with EU law as it failed to provide adequate transitional arrangements for existing claims: see C-362/12 *Test Claimants in Franked Investments Group v Commissioners of Inland Revenue* [2014] 2 C.M.L.R. 33.

[344] *Deutsche Morgan Grenfell Group Plc v Inland Revenue Commissioners* [2007] 1 A.C. 558 at [7].

[345] *Sempra Metals Ltd (formerly Metallgesellschaft Ltd) v Inland Revenue Commissioners* [2008] 1 A.C. 561.

Plc,[346] the House of Lords held that the relevant VAT legislation enabled overpayments of tax in one quarter to be deducted from a payment of tax in subsequent quarters, so that tax levied contrary to EU law could be deducted from tax payable in subsequent quarters. The House of Lords has held that where a statutory code is intended to provide an exhaustive code for the recovery of particular types of payment, that statutory code should normally be used as a means of seeking the recovery of monies paid at least in the first instance. The statutory regime may not, however, apply to a particular payment of tax mistakenly made by a taxpayer or the statutory procedure may not be available for particular reasons. In those circumstances, the taxpayer remains free to bring a restitutionary claim for the recovery of tax levied unlawfully or paid under a mistake of law.[347]

Subsidies paid by national authorities may violate the prohibition on providing state aid in Art.107 TFEU.. The Commission has power to order national authorities to recover such subsidies from the recipient.[348] Money paid out without the authority of Parliament is recoverable.[349] This principle could embrace money paid contrary to the provisions of the TFEU, on the basis that Parliament has not authorised national authorities to act in a way contrary to the TFEU as incorporated by the European Communities Act 1972.   **17–131**

EU law as a defence

Civil actions

EU law may be raised as a defence to an action. Actions to enforce industrial property rights may be met with the claim that the statutory provisions creating such rights contravene Arts 34 and 35 TFEU. The House of Lords has refused an injunction to enforce a patent for this reason.[350] Article 101 TFEU, prohibiting anti-competitive agreements, has been raised as a defence in an action for royalties,[351] and a claim for an injunction to enforce a market-sharing agreement.[352] A variety of Treaty provisions have been unsuccessfully pleaded as a defence to an action for a statutory debt.[353] A defendant sought, unsuccessfully, to resist a claim by a local authority to enforce its market rights on the ground that the enforcement of such rights involved a breach of what are now Arts 101 and 102 TFEU.[354]   **17–132**

---

[346] [1989] A.C. 914.
[347] *Deutsche Morgan Grenfell Group Plc v Inland Revenue Commissioners* [2007] 1 A.C. 558.
[348] Case C-52/84 *Re State Equity Holding: EC Commission v Belgium* [1987] 1 C.M.L.R. 710.
[349] *Auckland Harbour v The King* [1924] A.C. 318.
[350] Case C-434/85 *Allen & Hanburys v Generics (U.K.) Ltd* [1989] 1 W.L.R. 414 (the provisions of English law discriminated against EEC nationals. The national remedies, including injunctions, are available so long as English law goes no further than is permitted by Community law and does not discriminate against EEC nationals: see Case 35/87 *Thetford Corp. v Fiamma SpA* [1988] 3 C.M.L.R. 549).
[351] *Dymond v Britton (G.B.) & Sons (Holdings) Ltd* [1976] 1 C.M.L.R. 133.
[352] *Sirdar v Les Fils de Louis Mulliez* [1975] 1 C.M.L.R. 378.
[353] *Potato Marketing Board v Drysdale* [1986] 3 C.M.L.R. 333; *Potato Marketing Board v Robertson* [1983] 1 C.M.L.R. 93.
[354] *Leeds City Council v Watkins* [2003] Eu.L.R. 490.

Criminal law

17–133 EU law may provide a defence to a criminal offence. The Court of Justice has ruled that where a person is charged with an offence under a national law which is contrary to EU law, a conviction based on that national law is also contrary to EU law.[355] Subordinate legislation creating criminal offences which violate EU law will be regarded as invalid. Statutes enacted before 1972 creating criminal offences which violate subsequent EU law will be regarded as impliedly repealed to that extent.[356] Statutes enacted after 1972 would have to be construed according to European Union law or held inapplicable to the extent that they conflict with European Union law. Defences based on EU law raise issues of law to be determined by the court, not issues of fact for the jury.[357] Such defences may be raised as a defence in the criminal proceedings and the claimant is not restricted to challenging the allegedly invalid measure by way of judicial review.[358]

---

[355] Case C-269/80 *R. v Tymen* [1982] 2 C.M.L.R. 111; Case C-194/94 *CIA Security International SA v Signalson SA* [1996] E.C.R. I-2201 (provisions of national law, required to be but not notified to the Commission, could not be enforced against individuals); see discussion in *Interfact Ltd. v Liverpool City Council* [2011] 2 W.L.R. 396 (at [55]).

[356] See, e.g. Case C-63/83 *R. v Kirk* [1985] 1 All E.R. 453; *Procurator Fiscal, Stranraer v Marshall* [1988] 1 C.M.L.R. 657; Case 145/88 *Torfaen BC v B & Q Plc* [1990] 2 Q.B. 19.

[357] *R. v Goldstein* [1983] 1 W.L.R. 151.

[358] *Searby and Re Searby Ltd v R* [2003] Eu. L.R. 819.

CHAPTER 18

References to the Court of Justice for a Preliminary Ruling under Article 267 of the Treaty on the Functioning of the European Union

A. INTRODUCTION

Article 267 TFEU provides for a mechanism for co-operation between national courts and the Court of Justice whereby national courts and tribunals may, and in some instances must, refer certain questions of EU law to the Court of Justice for a preliminary ruling before the national court proceeds to give judgment. A reference is not a remedy in itself but is a step in the proceedings leading to the final determination of the case by the national court. The primary purpose behind Art.267 TFEU is to ensure that one supra national body, the European Court, has jurisdiction to provide definitive interpretations of EU law. This is designed to ensure the uniform interpretation of EU law throughout the EU and to prevent divergences between national courts on matters of EU law.

18–001

Article 267(1) TFEU provides the jurisdiction of the Court of Justice to give preliminary rulings and defines the questions that may be referred to the Court of Justice. Article 267(2) TFEU confers a power on national courts and tribunals to refer such questions to the European Court. Article 267(3) TFEU imposes an obligation on certain national courts and tribunals to refer such questions.

18–002

B. QUESTIONS THAT MAY BE REFERRED

The Court of Justice has jurisdiction to give preliminary rulings on the interpretation of the TEU and the TFEU,[1] the validity and interpretation of acts of the institutions of the EU[2] and, much less importantly, the interpretation of statutes of bodies offices and agencies of the European Union. Rulings on

18–003

---

[1] Article 267 TFEU refers to "the Treaties" which Art.1 TFEU defines as the Treaty on European Union ("TEU") and the Treaty on the Functioning of the European Union (TFEU"), those being the Treaties on which the European Union is founded. On references, see, generally, Anderson and Demetriou, *References to the European Court* (2nd edn, 2002).

[2] This covers regulations, directives and decisions and any sui generis acts of the institutions. Questions arising from treaties entered into by the Community may be referred (Case 12/86 *Demirel v Stadt Schwabisch Gmund* [1987] E.C.R. 3719), but not from agreements concluded by Member States outside the framework of the EU (Case 44/84 *Hurd v Jones* [1986] Q.B. 892).

interpretation extend to rulings on the effect of provisions of EU law, and in particular whether a provision of the Treaties or an act of the institutions is directly effective. The Court of Justice alone has jurisdiction to rule that an act of an institution is invalid.[3] A national court cannot declare an act of the institutions to be invalid. A national court may reject arguments that an act of an institution is invalid. If the national considers that the arguments are well-founded, the appropriate course is to refer the question of the validity of the measure to the Court of Justice.[4] "Well-founded" is understood by the domestic courts as meaning more than arguable and meaning that the contentions that the act of the institutions is invalid have a reasonable prospect of success.[5] The Court of Justice has held that a national court may grant interim relief suspending the operation of an administrative act of the national authorities based on European secondary legislation where the validity of that legislation is in doubt and the question of its validity is being referred to the Court of Justice.[6] In such circumstances, the national court may only grant interim relief if it has serious doubts about the validity of the measure and if it is necessary to grant interim relief to prevent serious and irreparable harm to the party seeking relief.[7] Furthermore, the national court has to safeguard the interest of the EU and if the grant of interim relief would lead to a financial risk to the EU, the national court must require the applicant to provide sufficient guarantees such as the payment of a deposit.

C. QUESTIONS OF FACT AND NATIONAL LAW

18–004 The jurisdiction of the Court of Justice on a reference is confined to providing definitive interpretations of EU law. It is the responsibility of national courts to find the relevant facts, and to apply EU law as interpreted by the Court of Justice to those facts.[8] Similarly, the Court of Justice has no jurisdiction to give interpretations of national law or to rule on the compatibility of national law with EU law.[9] Where a reference asks the Court of Justice to act in this way, the Court will usually re-formulate the question so that it does raise a question of EU law. The Court of Justice will then provide an interpretation of the relevant EU law which will enable the national court to determine the compatibility of national

---

[3] Case C-314/85 *Foto-Frost v Hauptzollamt Lubeck-Ost* [1987] E.C.R. 4199 (individual challenging validity of a regulation); Case C-408/95 *Eurotunnel SA v Sea-France formerly Sociètè Nouvelle d'Armement Transmanche SA (SNAT)* [1997] E.C.R. I-6315; an individual may not, however, challenge the validity of a decision of an institution of the EU in the national courts when he had standing to challenge its validity directly in the European Court under Art.230 (ex Art.173), as the decision was of direct and individual concern to that individual, as that would enable the individual to circumvent the two-month time-limit provided for by Art.230 (ex Art.173): see Case C-188/92 *TWD Textilwerke Deggendorf Gmbh v Germany* [1994] E.C.R. I-833.

[4] Case C-344/04 *R. (IATA and ELFA) v Secretary of State for Transport* [2006] E.C.R. I-403.

[5] *R. (Intertanko) v Secretary of State for Transport* [2007] Env. L.R. 8 at [46].

[6] Case C-456/93 *Atlanta Fruchthandelsgesellschaft mbH v Bundesamt fur Ernahrung und Forstwirtschaft* [1995] E.C.R. I-3761.

[7] See *R. (ABNA Ltd) v Secretary of State for Health and Food Standards Agency* [2004] Eu. L.R. 88 and the subsequent judgment in the Court of Justice in case C-453/03 *R. (ABNA Ltd) v Secretary of State for Health and Food Standards Agency* [2005] E.C.R. I-10423.

[8] *Salgoil S.p.A. v Italian Ministry for Foreign Trade Case* 13/68 [1968] E.C.R. 453.

[9] See, e.g. Joined Cases C-37/96 and C-38/96 *Sodiprem SARL v Direction Generale des Douanes* [1998] E.C.R. I-2039 at [22] of the judgment.

law with EU law.[10] Exceptionally, however, the Court of Justice may rule that it has all the factual material necessary to rule on the compatibility of national law with European Union law or to determine the outcome of the case and proceed to do so, even though, strictly, that is not a matter for the Court of Justice. It seems that the Court of Justice will do this when it is concerned at the variation in national decisions applying European Union law[11] or when it wishes to clarify how a new and potentially far-reaching of principle of European Union law ought to be understood.[12]

D. HYPOTHETICAL QUESTIONS

The Court of Justice only has jurisdiction under Art.267 TFEU if there is a genuine dispute between the parties.[13] The purpose of the preliminary ruling procedure is to enable the Court of Justice to assist in the administration of justice and, to that end, to give rulings which are of use to the national court dealing with the dispute before it and not to provide advisory opinions on general or hypothetical questions.[14] It is a matter for the national court to determine the need for a reference and the relevance of the questions to the dispute before it. The Court of Justice regards itself as bound, in principle, to give a preliminary ruling when the questions submitted concern the interpretation or validity of EU law.[15] The questions referred by a national court are presumed to be valid.[16] Exceptionally, however, the Court of Justice will refuse to give a ruling where it is manifest that the interpretation of EU law sought by the national court has no relevance to the actual facts of the main action or where the problem is hypothetical and the Court of Justice does not have before it the factual or legal material necessary to give a useful answer to a question.[17] The Court of Justice will generally seek to reply to the questions other than in the exceptional cases where it is clear that the interpretation of EU law can bear no relationship to the facts or the purpose of the main action.[18] The Court of Justice may also decline to answer the questions when the national court fails to provide the legal and factual

18–005

---

[10] See, e.g. Case C-98/86 *Minister Public v Mathot* [1987] E.C.R. 809.

[11] See, e.g. Case C-312/89 *Union departmentale des syndicats CGT de l'Aisne v SIDEF Conforama* [1991] E.C.R. I-997 and C-332/89 *Marchandise* [1991] E.C.R. I-1027 (where the Court resolved the question of whether national laws limiting Sunday trading were compatible with European law).

[12] Case C-392/93 *R. v HM Treasury Ex p. British Telecommunications Plc* [1996] E.C.R. I-1631 at [41] (whether failure to implement a directive properly gave rise to liability in damages).

[13] Case C-104/79 *Foglia v Novello* [1980] E.C.R. 745, and *Foglia v Novello (No.2)* Case 244/80 [1981] E.C.R. 3045.

[14] See, e.g. case C-116/02 *Erich Gasser Gmbh v MISAT Srl* [2005] 1 Q.B.1 [24]; Case C-458/93 *Criminal Proceedings Against Saddik* [1995] E.C.R. I-511 at [17].

[15] See case C-318/00 *Bacardi-Martini SAS and Cellier des Dauphins v Newcastle United Football Company Ltd* [2003] E.C.R. I-905 at [41] of the judgment.

[16] See, e.g. C-300/01 *Re Salzmann* [2003] E.C.R. I-4899 at [31].

[17] Case C-318/00 *Barcadi-Martini SAS and Cellier des Dauphins v Newcastle United Football Company Ltd* [2003] E.C.R. I-905. See Case C-105-94 *Celestini v Saar-Sektkellerei Faber GmbH & Co KG* [1997] E.C.R. 2971 at [21]–[22]; Case C-415/93 *Union Royale Belge des Societes de Football Association v Bosman* [1995] E.C.R. I-4921, at 5059, [59]–[61].

[18] See, e.g. Case C-267/99 *Urbing v Administration des Domaines* [2003] 2 C.M.L.R. 1021 at [23]–[31]; Case C-300/01 *RE Salzmann* [2003] E.C.R. I-4889 at [32]–[33].

information necessary to enable it to give a preliminary ruling.[19] In relation to the first category, the Court of Justice will, in particular, decline jurisdiction if the reference is the result of an artificial procedural device designed by the parties to obtain a preliminary ruling. The Court of Justice will be particularly vigilant to ensure that there is no abuse of the Art.267 TFEU procedure where the purported dispute is an attempt to persuade the national courts of one Member State to rule on the validity of the legislation of another Member State.[20] The Rules of Procedure provide for the national court to explain the relevant findings facts, the tenor of the relevant national legal provisions and a statement of the reasons prompting the reference and the national court should identify the provisions of EU law which it says require to be interpreted.[21]

E.   COURTS AND TRIBUNALS WHICH MAY REFER UNDER ARTICLE 267 TFEU

18–006   Article 267(2)TFEU provides that where a question within the scope of Art.267(2) TFEU is raised before any court or tribunal of a Member State, that "… court or tribunal may, if it considers that a decision on the question is necessary to enable it to give judgment, request the Court to give a ruling thereon". The definition of "court or tribunal" for this purpose is itself a question of EU law, as it involves interpreting Art.267 TFEU. The classification of the body in domestic law does not therefore determine whether the body has a power to refer.

18–007   The Court of Justice has highlighted two features which indicate whether a body is a court or tribunal for the purpose of Art.267 TFEU. First, there must be an element of public or State involvement in the composition or workings of the body so that it can be regarded as exercising official authority. Secondly, the body must exhibit judicial characteristics.

18–008   The Court of Justice has drawn attention to the following factors as indicating a sufficient connecting a link between the State and the tribunal:

---

[19] See, e.g. Case C-448/01 *EVN AG v Austria* [2004] 1 C.M.L.R. 739 at [78]–[83] of the judgment (no information on reasons for one of the questions referred; European Court declined to answer that question); Case C-318/00 *Bacardi-Martini SAS and Cellier des Dauphins v Newcastle United Football Company Ltd* [2003] E.C.R. I-905 (no explanation for reasons for needing a ruling provided, despite written request from the European Court; no preliminary ruling given). See also Case C-116/00 *Criminal Proceedings against Laguillaumie* [2000] E.C.R. I-4979; Case C-101/96 *Criminal Proceedings against Testa* [1996] E.C.R. I-381 and Joined Cases C-320/90 and C-322/90 *Telemarsicabruzzo SpA v Circostel and Minister delle Poste e Telecomunicazioni and Ministero della Difesa* [1993] E.C.R. I-393.
[20] *Foglia v Novello (No.2)* ([1981] E.C.R. 3045) and Case C-318/00 *Barcadi-Martini SAS and Cellier des Dauphins v Newcastle United Football Company Ltd* [2003] E.C.R. I-905. The European Court has accepted references even in these circumstances provided there is a genuine dispute: see Case 261/81 *Rau Lebensmittelwerke v De Smedt PvbA* [1982] E.C.R. 3961 and Case C-150/88 *Eau de Cologne & Parfumerie-Fabrik Glockengasse No.4711 v Provide Srl* [1991] 1 C.M.L.R. 715.
[21] See Rule 94 of the Rules of Procedure of the Court of Justice of 2012. See also Case C-318/00 *Bacardi-Martini SAS and Cellier des Dauphins v Newcastle United Football Company Ltd* [2003] E.C.R. I-905 at [44] of the judgment. See also Case C-116/00 *Criminal Proceedings against Laguillaumie* [2000] E.C.R. I-4979 at [15]–[16].

(a) the fact that members of the body are appointed by ministers[22];
(b) a requirement that the procedural rules be approved by a minister[23];
(c) the fact that the body is established by public law[24];
(d) the fact that the body has a compulsory jurisdiction so that individuals are required to take disputes to the body, suggesting that the body was an integral part of the machinery of justice within the Member State.[25]

The Court of Justice has drawn attention to the following factors as indicating that the body does exhibit "judicial characteristics": 18–009

(a) the fact that a body is bound to apply rules of law and operates on an adversarial basis[26];
(b) that its decisions are binding;
(c) that a tribunal is a permanent body charged with the settlement of disputes and not merely an ad hoc tribunal set up to resolve the instant case[27]; and
(d) it is independent.[28]

These are all relevant factors but the absence of one or more would not prevent a body qualifying as a court or tribunal.[29] In the case of professional disciplinary bodies, the Court of Justice has been influenced by the fact that there was no right of appeal from the body to the ordinary courts. If the individual was to be able properly to invoke his rights under EU law, that body must be able to make references to the Court of Justice.[30] 18–010

The body must also be acting in a judicial capacity in the particular case in which it seeks to make a reference. The Court of Justice declined a reference from the Council of the Bar Association of the Court of Appeal of Paris, raising questions on the rights of a French lawyer to provide services as an advocate before other courts in the EU. The Council was not dealing with a law-suit which it had a statutory duty to determine, and was not called upon to give a decision in proceedings intended to result in a decision of a judicial nature and so could not make a reference.[31] A body which is not seised of any dispute but is making an administration decision such as deciding whether conditions for registration are 18–011

---

[22] Case C-61/65 *Vaasen v Beambtenfonds Mijnbedrijf* [1966] E.C.R. 261; Case C-246/80 *Broekmeulen v Huitsarts Registratie Commissie* [1981] E.C.R. 2311 (one-third of members appointed by minister) and see Case C-54/96 *Dorsch Conslt Ingenieurgesellschaft mbH v Bundesbaugesells-chaft BerlinmbH* [1997] E.C.R. I-4961.

[23] *Vaasen* [1966] E.C.R. 261; *Broekmeulen* [1981] E.C.R. 2311 (rules could only be altered with ministerial consent).

[24] *Vaasen* [1966] E.C.R. 261. This is not a necessary requirement; in *Broekmeulen* [1981] E.C.R. 2311 the body was set up by private law but could make a reference.

[25] *Vaasen* [1966] E.C.R. 261. See also Case C-92/00 *Hospital Ingenieure Krankenhaustechnik Plannungs-Gesesellschaft mbh (HI) v Stadt Wien* [2002] E.C.R. I-5553 at [26].

[26] *Vaasen* [1966] E.C.R. 261. See also Case C-92/00 *Hospital Ingenieure Krankenhaustechnik Plannungs-Gesesellschaft mbh (HI) v Stadt Wien* [2002] E.C.R. I-5553 at [26].

[27] *Vaasen* [1966] E.C.R. 261.

[28] Case C-54/96 *Dorsch Conslt Ingenieurgesellschaft mbH v Bundesbaugesellschaft BerlinmbH* [1997] E.C.R. I-4961. See also Case C-92/00 *Hospital Ingenieure Krankenhaustechnik Planungs-Gesesellschaft mbh (HI) v Stadt Wien* [2002] E.C.R. I-5553 at [27].

[29] [1997] E.C.R. I-4961.

[30] *Broekmeulen* [1981] E.C.R. 2311.

[31] Case 138/80 *Re Borker* [1980] E.C.R. 1975.

satisfied is not exercising a judicial function.[32] The Court of Justice, however, has entertained a reference from the Italian Pretore, when acting in a preliminary capacity as public prosecutor in deciding whether to discontinue legal proceedings. Although that decision was not a judicial act, the Court of Justice held it had jurisdiction where the reference emanated from a court or tribunal which has acted in the "... general framework of its task of judging ... even though certain functions ... are not, strictly speaking, of a judicial nature".[33] The Court of Justice has similarly held that a court of one Member State could refer the question of the compatibility of charges imposed by another Member State for examining witnesses as the examination of witnesses occurred in the context of judicial proceedings intended to lead to a decision of a judicial nature.[34] The body must in essence be acting as a third party dealing with a dispute between two other parties. In the case of a government decision, it means some body acting in relation to a dispute between the administrative decision-maker and the individual. A government official responsible for taking the original decision cannot himself refer a question to Court of Justice as the official is not a court or tribunal within the meaning of Art.267 TFEU.[35]

Arbitration tribunals

18–012   One group of tribunals which cannot make references are arbitrators appointed pursuant to an arbitration clause in a contract. Such arbitrators exhibit many of the features discussed above. There is, however, no link between such arbitrators and the State, and parties are not obliged by law to refer disputes to such a body but do so as a matter of choice instead of leaving disputes to be dealt with by the ordinary courts. Consequently, they may not refer matters to the Court of Justice.[36] The ordinary courts in the national legal system have a duty to ensure that these arbitrators observe EU law.[37] The Court of Appeal has held that the fact that an arbitration award raises questions of EU law that are "capable of serious argument" is a relevant consideration in deciding whether to grant leave to appeal against the arbitration award.[38]

UK courts and tribunals

18–013   The broad interpretation given to Art.267(2) TFEU ensures that a very wide range of courts and administrative tribunals set up under English law have the power to refer questions to the Court of Justice. In addition to references from the High

---

[32] Case C-178/99 *Salzmann* [2003] E.C.R. I-4889; Case C-111/94 *Job Centre s.r.l.* [1995] E.C.R. I-3361 and see Case C-96/04 *Niebull* [2006] E.C.R. I-3561.

[33] Case C-14/86 *Pretore di Salo v Persons Unknown* [1987] E.C.R. 2545 at 2567, [7].

[34] Case C-283/09 *Werynski v Mediatel 4B spolkazoo* [2011] 3 W.L.R. 1316 at [45].

[35] Case C-24/92 *Corbiau v Administration des Contributions du Grand-Duche de Luxembourg* [1993] E.C.R. I-1277.

[36] Case C-102/81 *Nordsee, Deutsche Hochseefischerei GmbH v Reederei Mond Hochseefisherei Nordstern AG & Co. KG* [1982] E.C.R. 1095. See also Case C-125/04 *Denuit v Transorient-Mosaiques Voyages et Culture* [2005] E.C.R. I-923.

[37] [1982] E.C.R. 1095.

[38] *Bulk Oil (Zug) AG. v Sun International Ltd* [1984] 1 W.L.R. 147.

Court, Court of Appeal, the Supreme Court and courts such as the Crown Court,[39] county court[40] and magistrates' courts[41] there have been references from the Upper Tribunal,[42] the Employment Appeal Tribunal,[43] and an employment tribunal[44]. There is a possibility that professional disciplinary bodies such as the Law Society or the General Medical Council may have the power to refer. It has been suggested that as there is recourse from these bodies to the ordinary courts, either by judicial review or appeal on a point of law, these bodies will not be brought within Art.267 TFEU and the making of references would be left to the courts hearing appeals from such bodies. The absence of such recourse has certainly been influential in persuading the Court of Justice to bring bodies within Art.234 to ensure that EU law is properly observed; the presence of such recourse should not necessarily prevent a body exhibiting the other characteristics from being able to refer.[45]

F. COURTS AND TRIBUNALS WHICH ARE OBLIGED TO REFER UNDER ARTICLE 267(3) TFEU

Article 267(2)TFEU confers a discretionary power to refer on a wide range of bodies. Article 267(3)TFEU imposes a duty on certain courts to refer and provides that where a question of European law: **18–014**

> "... is raised in a case pending before a court or tribunal of a Member State against whose decisions there is no judicial remedy under national law, that court or tribunal shall bring the matter before the Court."

The idea underlying this obligation is to ensure that, at some stage, questions of European Union law are referred to the Court,[46] and to prevent a body of case law growing up in a Member State which is at variance with European Union law as interpreted by the Court of Justice. **18–015**

The Supreme Court and the Court of Appeal

The Supreme Court is subject to the obligation in Art.267(3) TFEU and must refer questions of EU law unless one of the exceptions to the duty discussed below applies. **18–016**

The Court of Justice has held that a court is not a final court within Art.267(3) TFEU if there is the possibility of an appeal to another court, even though that **18–017**

---

[39] See, e.g., Case C-63/83 *R. v Kirk* [1985] 1 All E.R. 453.
[40] See, e.g. Case C-222/82 *Apple and Pear Development Council v Lewis* [1984] 3 C.M.L.R. 733.
[41] See, e.g. Case C-145/88 *Torfaen BC v B & Q Plc* [1990] 2 Q.B. 19.
[42] See, e.g. case C-279/12 *Fish Legal v Information Commissioner* [2014] 2 W.L.R. 568 (reference from the Upper Tribunal (Administrative Appeals Chamber)).
[43] See, e.g. *Newstead v Department of Transport* [1986] 2 C.M.L.R. 196.
[44] See, e.g. *Smith, v Avdel Systems Ltd* [1993] 1 C.M.L.R. 534.
[45] The European Court accepted jurisdiction in a reference by the appellate committee of the Belgian Association of Architects: see Case C-166/91 *Bauer v Conseil National de l'Ordre des Architectes* [1992] E.C.R. I-2797.
[46] See Collins, *European Community Law in the United Kingdom* (4th edn, 1990), p.110.

right is not automatic and is dependent on the higher court accepting the appeal.[47] The higher court, however, will be obliged under Art.267(3) TFEU to refer any question of EU law either when considering whether to accept the appeal or when considering the merits at a later stage.[48] On that basis, Court of Appeal hearing a substantive appeal[49] is not a final court of appeal for the purposes of Art.267(3) TFEU. Even if the Court of Appeal refuses permission to appeal to the Supreme Court, there is still a judicial remedy available as the Supreme Court may grant permission to appeal.[50]

18–018   There is still the question of the approach that the Supreme Court should adopt to petitions for leave to appeal. In the light of the decision in *Lyckeskog*,[51] if a case raises a serious question of European Union law, the Supreme Court should arguably grant permission to appeal and then at some stage make the reference itself to ensure that the Court of Justice is given the opportunity to consider the question of EU law.[52] Failure to grant leave could result in a breach of Art.267(3) TFEU and could place the UK in breach of its Treaty obligations.

The High Court in criminal cases

18–019   In criminal cases involving challenges to a decision of a magistrates' court, the appropriate avenue of challenge (either directly from the magistrates' court or following an appeal to the Crown Court) is to the High Court on appeal by way of case stated or by judicial review. Appeal from the High Court is to the Supreme Court not the Court of Appeal. Appeals can only occur where the High Court certifies that a point of law of general public importance is involved, *and* either the High Court grants leave to appeal or the Supreme Court grants permission to appeal. Only the High Court may grant a certificate.

18–020   Where a certificate is granted, then the possibility of permission to appeal being given by either the High Court or the Supreme Court would, by analogy with the position in relation to the Court of Appeal,[53] be a judicial remedy and would prevent the High Court becoming a final court within Art.267(3) TFEU. Different considerations apply where the High Court refuses to grant a certificate, as then leave to appeal cannot be given by either the High Court or the Supreme Court. The point arose in *SA Magnavision NV v General Optical Council (No.2)*.[54] There, the High Court, sitting as a Divisional Court, had given judgment and refused to certify the point of law arising. It was only after judgment had

---

[47] Case C-99/00 *Criminal proceedings against Lyckeskog* [2003] 1 W.L.R. 9 at [16]–[19] of the judgment.

[48] [2003] 1 W.L.R. 9 at [18].

[49] If the Court of Appeal refuses permission to appeal to it, then, arguably, it is a court of final instance as there can no appeal to the Supreme Court against a refusal of permission to appeal to the Court of Appeal: see discussion at 9-000.

[50] See *R. v Pharmaceutical Society of Great Britain Ex p. Association of Pharmaceutical Importers* [1987] 3 C.M.L.R. 951.

[51] Case C-99/00 *Criminal proceedings against Lyckeskog* [2003] 1 W.L.R. 9.

[52] See Anderson and Demetriou, *References to the European Court* (London: Sweet & Maxwell, 2002) para.6–018. See also the discussion in *Cooper v Attorney-General* [2011] Q.B. 976 at [127] emphasising the importance of counsel drawing the attention of a court to EU law issues when there is no appeal against that court's decision.

[53] See para.18–017.

[54] [1987] 2 C.M.L.R. 262.

been given that the argument was made that the Divisional Court, by refusing to certify, had turned itself into a final court and was obliged by Art.267(3) TFEU to refer. The Divisional Court accepted that there was no appeal against its decision. It refused to refer, partly because one of the recognised exceptions to the obligation applied (these are discussed below) and partly because, as the court had already given judgment, there was no need for a preliminary ruling and nothing to which such a ruling could be applied. This leaves unanswered the question of what the High Court should do if the matter is raised before it has given judgment, and where the exceptions to the obligation do not apply. There is a strong case that where an arguable question of EU law arises, the High Court must either make a reference or at least certify the point as one of general public importance, so that the possibility of an appeal to the Supreme Court remains open.

Administrative tribunals

There may be a statutory right of appeal from an administrative tribunal to the courts. The Act setting up the tribunal may provide for a right of appeal on a point of law to the courts, or the tribunal may be one to which s.11 of the Tribunals and Inquiries Act 1992 applies and provides a right of appeal or to apply by way of case stated to the High Court on a point of law. Section 3(1) of the European Communities Act 1972 provides that questions of EU law are to be regarded as law (not fact, as is the case with questions of foreign law). Therefore, in relation to a tribunal where there exists an appeal on a point of law, there can be no doubt that a judicial remedy against the decision of a tribunal exists, and the tribunal is covered by Art.267(2) not Art.267(3) TFEU.   **18–021**

    Judicial review will also be available in relation to statutory tribunals, and errors of EU law would normally be reviewable by way of judicial review. There is no right to judicial review, but the claimant must apply for permission. Where permission is granted, there is clearly an adequate judicial remedy available against the decision and there can be no question of the tribunal being obliged to refer under Art.267(3) TFEU. In any event, the possibility of applying for permission will almost certainly be regarded by the domestic courts as an adequate judicial remedy, just as the possibility of applying for permission to appeal against decisions of the Court of Appeal is considered an adequate remedy.[55] It would certainly be inconvenient if every decision of a tribunal against which there was no right of appeal, simply the prospect of judicial review, had to be referred to the Court of Justice.   **18–022**

G.   EXCEPTIONS TO THE OBLIGATION TO REFER IN ARTICLE 267 TFEU

The Court of Justice has recognised three exceptions to the obligation to refer imposed by Art.234(3) EC. First, a court which takes a decision in interlocutory proceedings is not obliged to refer, even if its decision in those interlocutory proceedings is final, provided that the decision on the European Union law point   **18–023**

---

[55] See para.18–017.

does not bind the court that subsequently hears the main action, and that either party to the dispute can ensure that proceedings in the main action are actually instituted.[56] The House of Lords was not therefore obliged to make a reference to the Court of Justice when refusing an interlocutory injunction in a case involving European Union law.[57] Although there is no obligation to refer, a court retains a power to refer at the interlocutory stage.

18–024　Secondly, a court will not be obliged to refer where the question raised is materially identical to a previous question already the subject of a preliminary ruling of the Court of Justice.[58] The national court may apply the previous ruling to the question it is asked to decide. The national court retains a power to refer the question to the Court of Justice. As the Court of Justice is not bound by a rule of stare decisis, it is free to depart from its earlier judgment.[59] In the absence of new factors, the Court of Justice will usually answer the question by referring to the previous ruling.[60]

18–025　The third and most controversial exception to the obligation in Art.267(3) TFEU is the acte clair doctrine. The Court of Justice has held that where the correct application of EU law is so obvious as to leave no scope for any reasonable doubt as to the manner in which the question of European Union law is to be resolved, a national court is not obliged to make a reference.[61] The Court of Justice cautioned national courts against coming to such a conclusion too readily. National courts should be sure that the answer would be equally obvious to the courts of other Member States and to the Court of Justice, bearing in mind that EU law is drafted in several equally authentic languages using terminology peculiar to it, and must be set in the context of the objectives and state of evolution of European Union law.

18–026　The approach of the Supreme Court (and, previously, the House of Lords) reflects the approach advocated by the Court of Justice. It has referred questions where the answer is not obvious.[62] It has warned against too ready an assumption that the proper interpretation of EU law is so obvious that no reference is necessary, where there is no clear and consistent body of case law of the Court of Justice dealing with the provision of EU law that is in issue.[63] It has, in the past, referred questions to the Court of Justice even when it had no real doubt as to the answers that would be given.[64] They have refused to assume that the case law of

---

[56] Cases C-35-36/82 *Morson and Jhanjan v Netherlands* [1982] E.C.R. 3723.

[57] *Garden Cottage Foods v Milk Marketing Board* [1984] A.C. 130.

[58] Cases C-28-30/62 *Da Costa en Shaake NV v Nederlandse Belastingadministratie* [1963] E.C.R. 31.

[59] See Case C-466/00 *Kaba v Secretary of State for the Home Department (No.2)* [2003] 1 C.M.L.R. 1103; Case C-69/85 *Wunsche Handeslgesellschaft v Germany* [1986] E.C.R. 947.

[60] [1986] E.C.R. 947.

[61] Case C-283/81 *C.I.L.F.I.T. Srl v Ministry of Health* [1982] E.C.R. 3415.

[62] See, e.g., *Information Commissioner v Office of Communication* [2010] Env. L.R. 20 (reference on issue of general principle where answer not obvious); *R (Clientearth) v Secretary of State for Environment and Rural Affairs* [2013] 3 C.M.L.R. 29 (position on one issue clear but guidance required on others).

[63] *Apple and Pear Development Council v Commissioners of Customs and Excise* [1987] 2 C.M.L.R. 634.

[64] *Henn and Darby v DPP* [1981] A.C. 850; *Garland v British Rail Engineering* [1983] 2 A.C. 751. But see *Leverton v Clwyd Council* [1989] A.C. 706 (House of Lords interpreted both the relevant English and European Union law and concluded that both required the same approach even where the relevant European law had not been considered in that particular context by the Court of Justice).

the Court of Justice developed on one aspect of patent rights would automatically be applicable to another aspect, and made a reference.[65] Where the Supreme Court is satisfied, however, that the previous case law of the Court of Justice is clear on a particular point, they may decide that they are not obliged to refer.[66] It may also seek to decide a case on the basis of national law rather than European Union law where this may properly be done, thereby avoiding the necessity for a reference. So, where a claim is based on both domestic law and EU law, and the Supreme Court can decide in the claimant's favour on the domestic grounds, it will not go on to consider the European Union law issues.[67] The case may also involve the application of EU law to the facts which is a matter for the national courts, not the Court of Justice, and no reference need be made in those circumstances.[68]

H. DISCRETION TO REFER UNDER ARTICLE 267(2) TFEU

The decision to refer, by a court or tribunal to which Art.267(2) TFEU is ultimately a matter for the discretion of the national court in the particular case. The Court of Justice has offered guidance on the approach to be adopted. The Court of Justice has stated that, for an interpretation of EU law to be useful to a national court, it is essential that the national court define the legal context in which the reference is made. To that end, it is desirable for the facts of the case to be established and questions of national law settled before the reference is made.[69] The Court of Justice has stressed that these considerations do not restrict the discretion of the national court, which alone has knowledge of the facts of the case and is best placed to decide at what stage a reference should be made.[70]   **18–027**

The rules of procedure of the Court of Justice now require a reference from a national to set out a summary of the subject-matter and the relevant facts, the tenor of the relevant national provisions, a statement of the reasons prompting the reference and identifying the provisions of EU law considered to be relevant.[71] The guidance issued by the Court of Justice also encourages references to be drafted simply, clearly and precisely, in about ten pages, including that information and an explanation as to why the ruling sought is necessary to enable the national court to give judgment.[72]   **18–028**

---

[65] *R. v Comptroller of Patents Ex p. Gist-Brocades* [1986] 1 W.L.R. 51 (the caution was vindicated as the European Court did adopt a different approach; see *Allen & Hanburys Ltd v Generics (U.K.) Ltd* [1989] 1 W.L.R. 414).

[66] See, e.g. *British Fuels Ltd v Baxendale* [1998] 4 All E.R. 609 at 631e-g. If the previous case law is not clear, or appears to be contradictory, it may refer: see, e.g. *Preston v Wolverhampton Healthcare NHS Trust* [1998] 1 W.L.R. 280.

[67] *R. v Secretary of State for Social Services Ex p. Wellcome Foundation* [1988] 1 W.L.R. 635 and see also *British Leyland Motor Corp. v Armstrong Patents Co. Ltd* [1986] A.C. 577.

[68] *Bloomsbury International Ltd. v Sea Fish Industry Authority* [2011] 1 W.L.R. 1546 at [51].

[69] Cases C-36 & 71/80 *Irish Creamery Milk Suppliers Association v Irish Government* [1981] E.C.R. 735; *Celestini* [1997] E.C.R. I-2971and see paras 18–004 to 18–005 above.

[70] Case C-72/83 *Campus Oil v Minister for Industry and Energy* [1984] E.C.R. 2727.

[71] Rule 94 of the Rules of Procedure 2012.

[72] Recommendations to National Courts in relation to the institution of preliminary ruling proceedings 2012/C/338.

I. APPROACH OF THE UK COURTS

18–029 An attempt to provide a comprehensive set of guidelines was made by Lord Denning M.R. in *Bulmer v Bollinger*,[73] shortly after the UK joined the European Community as it then was. In the light of experience, the approach advocated there, particularly in so far as it expressed a preference for national courts determining issues of EU law themselves, has been shown to be unduly restrictive. The factors to which Lord Denning drew attention are, however, in substance the factors that courts do consider in exercising their discretion.

Decision on question of EU law must be necessary

18–030 A decision on the question of EU law must be necessary to enable a national court to give judgment before it can exercise its discretion under Art.267 TFEU to make a reference. This requirement is strictly speaking, a jurisdictional requirement rather than a factor relevant to the discretion to refer. Unless a decision is necessary, no power to refer exists. A national court must be satisfied that EU law is not only relevant to the dispute but that a decision on the point of European law will be "substantially determinative" of the case,[74] or is "reasonably necessary" in order to enable the case to be determined.[75]

18–031 The clearest situation where a decision on a question of EU law will be necessary arises where the outcome of a case depends solely on the question of EU law. Where the sole issue in a case was the validity of a European directive, a decision on that point of EU law was necessary.[76] In *EMI v CBS*,[77] Graham J. considered that the whole issue turned on EU law. If the defendant succeeded on that issue, he had a complete defence to the action; if the plaintiff succeeded on that issue, he would on the facts admitted be entitled to relief. Similarly, a reference was appropriate where the issue would substantially be determined by the interpretation given to a provision of an EU Regulation.[78]

18–032 A decision may be substantially determinative, even where some issues may be outstanding after the ruling is given. In *R. v Plymouth Justices Ex p. Rogers*,[79] the substantive issue in the case was the validity of certain UK regulations which allegedly contravened EU law. A decision on EU law was therefore necessary, even though one issue of fact remained to be determined. In *Samex*,[80] the issues of EU law might be substantially determinative in that an answer that was adverse to the defendants would dispose of the case, whereas a favourable answer

---

[73] [1974] Ch. 401.

[74] *R. v Plymouth Justices Ex p. Rogers* [1982] Q.B. 863; *Customs and Excise Commissioners v A.P.S. Samex* [1983] 1 All E.R. 1042.

[75] per Ormerod LJ in *Polydor Records v Harlequin Record Shops* [1980] 2 C.M.L.R. 413 at 428. The view of Lord Denning M.R. expressed in *Bulmer v Bollinger* [1974] Ch. 401, that the point of European law must be conclusive, has not been followed.

[76] *R. v Minister of Agriculture, Fisheries and Food Ex p. FEDESA* [1988] 3 C.M.L.R. 661.

[77] *EMI Records v CBS United Kingdom* [1975] 1 C.M.L.R. 285. See also *Van Duyn v Home Office* [1974] 1 W.L.R. 1107.

[78] *R. (Newby Food Ltd.) v Food Standards Agency* [2013] EWHC 1966 (Admin).

[79] [1982] Q.B. 863.

[80] *Customs and Excise Commissioners v A.P.S. Samex* [1983] 1 All E.R. 1042. See also *Erich Gasser Gmbh v MISAT Srl* [2005] 1 Q.B. and *Karen Murphy v Media Protection Services Ltd* [2008] EWHC 1666 (Admin) at [62](iv).

for the defendant might, depending on the answers received, still necessitate the trial of some short issues. A reference has been made where it could assist in isolating the issues before the court, and possibly rendering it unnecessary to consider certain complex factual issues.[81] Where the case can be determined on grounds of purely national law a decision on EU law will not be necessary. In *Bulmer v Bollinger*,[82] for example, a defence to a passing off action was based on EU law. A decision on that question was not yet necessary as the plaintiff had not yet established his claim under domestic law so the question of a defence did not arise at that stage. Similarly, where a point of EU law arises which would justify a reference but, even assuming that the point was decided in favour of the claimant, he would still lose on other grounds of EU law, a reference will not be necessary or appropriate.[83]

General approach to the exercise of discretion

The exercise of the discretion to refer is ultimately a matter for the particular court dealing with the case in the light of all the relevant factors. Those factors are discussed below. The Master of the Rolls has, however, described the general approach to the exercise of discretion as follows[84]:   **18–033**

> "I understand that the correct approach in principle of a national court (other than a final court of appeal) to be quite clear: if the facts have been found and the Community law issue is critical to the court's final decision, the appropriate course is ordinarily to refer the issue to the Court of Justice unless the national court can with complete confidence resolve the issue itself. In considering whether it can with complete confidence resolve the issue itself the national court must be fully mindful of the differences between national and Community legislation, of the pitfalls which face a national court venturing into what may be an unfamiliar field, of the need for uniform interpretation throughout the Community and the great advantages enjoyed by the Court of Justice in construing Community instruments."

Need to determine the facts

As a general rule, national courts should determine the facts before making a reference to the Court of Justice. Until the facts are established it may not be clear that a question of EU law does arise for determination.[85] Equally importantly, it may not be possible to formulate precisely the questions that are appropriate to the particular case.[86] Where an action is based on domestic law and a defence is based on EU law, it may become unnecessary to consider the defence if the   **18–034**

---

[81]   *Thetford Corp. v Fiamma S.p.A.* [1987] 3 C.M.L.R. 266.

[82]   [1975] Ch. 1.

[83]   *R. v Ministry of Agriculture, Fisheries and Food Ex p. British Pig Industry Support Group and Ward* [2000] Eu. L.R. 724 at [66].

[84]   *R. v International Stock Exchange Ex p. Else* [1993] Q.B. 534 at 545 (although, there the Court of Appeal allowed an appeal against a decision to refer as the issue of EU law could be resolved by the Court of Appeal).

[85]   *Church of Scientology of California v Commissioners of Customs and Excise* [1981] 1 All E.R. 1035; *Lord Bethell v SABENA* [1983] 3 C.M.L.R. 1 and see *South Pembrokeshire DC v Wendy Fair Markets Ltd* [1994] 1 C.M.L.R. 213 at 223–224.

[86]   *Lord Bethell v SABENA* [1983] 3 C.M.L.R. 1.

plaintiff fails to establish the facts necessary to support his action.[87] In criminal cases, magistrates' courts have been urged not to make a reference until there can be no question of an acquittal on the facts, and even then to do so only rarely.[88] The House of Lords expressed the view that in criminal trials on indictment it can seldom be an appropriate exercise of discretion to make a reference before the facts have been established, thereby delaying the trial, when the evidence may turn out differently from that anticipated.[89]

18–035   In the majority of cases where references have been made the facts have been found or have not been in dispute. On occasions where the substantial issue clearly raises a question of EU law, a reference may be made notwithstanding that technically an issue of fact remains to be determined.[90] There are also exceptions to the general rule that facts should be found first. If a ruling could isolate the issues which need to be addressed and could, depending on the answers given, render it unnecessary to engage on a complex and expensive fact finding exercise, then an early reference might be desirable. In *Thetford Corporation v Fiamma SpA*,[91] the Court of Appeal referred the question of whether a patent which lacked novelty constituted industrial property which was protected by Art.36 TFEU. A decision in favour of the plaintiffs would automatically entitle them to relief to protect their patent, and would avoid the considerable and expensive task of investigating whether or not the patent did lack novelty. The Divisional Court referred the validity of a directive prohibiting the administration of certain hormones to livestock, before making conclusive findings of fact.[92] The evidence in the case was considerable and a ruling from the Court of Justice could assist in determining the criteria by which the evidence ought to be assessed, and could render it unnecessary to review some evidence altogether. One area where a reference may be appropriate at an early stage without the need to find facts are challenges based on the validity of a EU legislative measure such as a directive or regulation. The validity of such a measure can only be determined by the Court of Justice and generally raises issues of law not fact. References have, accordingly, been made at the stage when permission to apply for judicial review is granted and before any substantive hearing takes place.[93]

18–036   Pleadings should clearly set out the factual issues that will be relevant to the questions that it is anticipated may be referred.[94]

---

[87] *Bulmer v Bollinger* [1974] 1 Ch. 401.

[88] *R. v Plymouth Justices Ex p. Rogers* [1982] Q.B. 863 (essential facts not in dispute and the essential issue was the extent to which the English subordinate legislation was compatible with Community law); see also Case 157/79 *R. v Pieck* [1981] 1 Q.B. 571 (reference by Pontypridd Magistrates' Court: facts not in dispute and sole issue one of Community law).

[89] *Henn and Darby v DPP* [1981] A.C. 850. But see *R. v Lomas* [1990] 1 C.M.L.R. 513 (issue was validity of Community regulation which could only be determined by European Court not a jury and so reference appropriate).

[90] *Polydor Records v Harlequin Record Shops* (see above, fn.68).

[91] [1987] 3 C.M.L.R. 266. See also Case C-116/02 *Erich Gasser Gmbh v MISAT Srl* [2005] 1 Q.B. 1.

[92] *R. v Minister of Agriculture, Fisheries and Food Ex p. FEDESA* [1988] 3 C.M.L.R. 661. In *R. v Pharmaceutical Society of Great Britain Ex p. Association of Pharmaceutical Importers* [1987] 3 C.M.L.R. 951 a submission that no reference could be made where there was a conflict of evidence one issue was rejected.

[93] See, e.g. *R. (ABNA Ltd) v Secretary of State for Health and Food Standards Agency* [2004] Eu.L.R. 88.

[94] *Hagen v Moretti* [1980] 3 C.M.L.R. 253.

Need to formulate questions

Courts should formulate the questions to be referred before making a reference. Courts may not be in a position to do this until the facts are established and it becomes clear what questions arise for determination, or until the issues have emerged in the course of argument.[95]

18–037

Need to determine questions of national law

The courts have on occasions indicated the desirability of determining any questions of national law before making a reference.[96] A determination of the national law points may render the EU law issues redundant, for example, where a claim based on both national and EU law succeeds on national law, or where a claim fails on national law grounds thereby rendering it unnecessary to consider a European law defence.[97] A national court should identify relevant provisions of national law which might conflict with EU law, so that the Court of Justice is better placed to determine which issues of EU law need to be determined to enable a national court to resolve a potential conflict.[98]

18–038

Previous ruling of the Court of Justice

The Court of Justice may already have given a ruling on the interpretation of the particular provision of EU law or the validity of EU legislation. A national court may simply apply that ruling to the case before it rather than making a reference.[99] A national court retains the power to make a reference if it considers the earlier ruling was incorrect, or where new circumstances suggest that the earlier ruling needs to be modified, or where clarification on the meaning or effect of the earlier ruling is sought.[100] The absence of a previous ruling of the Court of Justice is a factor in favour of making reference.[101]

18–039

Acte clair

The extent to which the interpretation of a provision of EU law is obvious is relevant to the exercise of the discretion to refer. Courts often refer to acte clair in this context, although strictly speaking the acte clair doctrine applies to courts

18–040

---

[95] *Lord Bethell v SABENA* [1983] 1 C.M.L.R. 1; *Wychavon DC v Midland Enterprises* [1988] 1 C.M.L.R. 397, at 409; *Prince v Secretary of State for Scotland* [1985] S.L.T. 74.

[96] *Lord Bethell v SABENA* ([1983] 1 C.M.L.R. 1; *Newstead v Department of Transport* [1986] 2 C.M.L.R. 196 (reference appropriate as matter fell to be decided solely on European law, no issue of domestic law to be decided).

[97] See, e.g. *R. v Secretary of State for Social Services Ex p. Wellcome Foundation* [1988] 1 W.L.R. 635 and *British Leyland Motor Corp. v Armstrong Patents Co. Ltd* [1986] A.C. 577.

[98] See *Irish Creamery Milk Suppliers Association v Irish Government* [1981] E.C.R. 735.

[99] See, e.g. *R. v Secretary of State for Social Services Ex p. Bomore Medical Supplies Ltd* [1986] 1 C.M.L.R. 228.

[100] See Case C-466/00 *Kaba v Secretary of State for the Home Department (No.2)* [2003] 1 C.M.L.R. 1103; Case 69/85 *Wunsche Handeslgesellschaft v Germany* [1986] E.C.R. 947.

[101] *Newstead v Department of Transport* [1986] 2 C.M.L.R. 196); *R. v Intervention Board for Agricultural Produce Ex p. Fish Producers' Organisation Ltd* [1988] 2 C.M.L.R. 661; *R. v HM Treasury Ex p. Daily Mail and General Trust Plc* [1987] 2 C.M.L.R. 1.

who are bound by Art.267(3) TFEU to refer, and relieves them of the obligation to refer. Courts against whom there is an appeal as of right, or where the case proceeds on the basis that leave to appeal will be given, may be readier to conclude that a question of interpretation is obvious as any doubt as to the correctness of the interpretation may be dealt with by the higher court.[102]

18–041   The Court of Appeal has warned that courts "... should exercise great caution in relying on the doctrine of *acte clair* as a ground for declining a reference".[103] Courts have referred questions when a point of EU law is arguable and not free from doubt,[104] even where they have formed a clear view themselves as to the likely answers to the questions raised.[105] Courts have, on occasions, applied the acte clair doctrine and interpreted provisions of EU law, or extrapolated principles from the existing case law of the Court of Justice, where the case law indicates a clear general approach to a particular provision of EU law.[106] The danger in following this course is illustrated by the fact that the Court of Appeal has on occasions concluded that a matter is acte clair and not ordered a reference where their view on the interpretation of the particular provision has not subsequently been vindicated in the Court of Justice.[107] The distinctive nature of EU law, the dynamic approach of the Court of Justice to the interpretation of EU law, and the fact that EU law can be said to be in a state of evolution reinforces the conclusion that courts should be extremely cautious in declining to refer solely on the ground that the interpretation of EU law is obvious.

Advantages enjoyed by the Court of Justice

18–042   The advantages enjoyed by the Court of Justice have been comprehensively summarised by Bingham J. as he then was[108]:

> "... [The Court of Justice] has a panoramic view of the Community and its institutions, a detailed knowledge of the treaties and of much subordinate legislation made under them, and an intimate familiarity with the functioning of the Community market which no national judge ... could hope to achieve. Where questions of administrative intention and practice arise the Court ... can receive submissions from the Community institutions. ... Where the interests of Member States are affected they can intervene to make their views known. ... Where comparison falls to be made between Community texts in different languages, all

---

[102] See *Barkworth v Customs and Excise Commissioners* [1988] 3 C.M.L.R. 759 at 768; the Court of Appeal seemed to proceed on the basis that any reference would be more appropriately made by the House of Lords in *Allen & Hanburys Ltd v Generics (U.K.) Ltd* [1986] 1 C.M.L.R. 101 at 124, [82] and 137, [144].

[103] per Kerr LJ in *R. v Pharmaceutical Society of Great Britain Ex p. Association of Pharmaceutical Importers* [1987] 3 C.M.L.R. 951 at 971. See also *R. v HM Treasury Ex p. Daily Mail and General Trust Plc* [1987] 2 C.M.L.R. 1.

[104] See, e.g. *Thetford Corp. v Fiamma S.p.A.* [1987] 3 C.M.L.R. 266; *Macarthys Ltd v Smith* [1979] 1 W.L.R. 1189.

[105] *Polydor Records v Harlequin Record Shops* [1980] 2 C.M.L.R. 413); *Customs and Excise Commissioners v A.P.S. Samex* [1983] 1 All E.R. 1042.

[106] This is particularly true of the Court of Appeal in certain areas such as sex discrimination; see, e.g. *Leverton v Clwyd CC* [189] A.C. 706 (affd. by the House of Lords partly on different grounds).

[107] As happened, e.g. in *Henn and Darby v DPP* [1981] A.C. 850 and *Allen & Hanburys Ltd v Generics (U.K.) Ltd* [1985] F.S.R. 610 (the House of Lords granted leave to appeal and made a reference to the Court which came to a different conclusion: see [1989] 1 W.L.R. 414).

[108] In *Customs and Excise Commissioners v A.P.S. Samex* [1983] 1 All E.R. 1042 at 1055–1056.

texts being equally authentic, the multinational Court ... is equipped to carry out the task in a way which no national judge ... could rival. The interpretation of Community instruments involves very often not the process familiar to common lawyers of laboriously extracting the meaning from words used but the more creative process of supplying flesh to a spare and loosely constructed skeleton. The choice between alternative submissions may turn not on purely legal considerations, but on a broader view of what the orderly development of the Community requires. These are matters which the Court ... is much better placed to assess and determine than a national court."

The fact that the Court of Justice will be in a position to receive submissions from the European Commission and the Council and Member States is relevant where the questions raised involve the interpretation of European legislation,[109] or where the practice of Member States is likely to be relevant in determining the point of EU law.[110] A reference to the Court of Justice may be appropriate where a provision has to be interpreted in the light of other complex provisions of European Union law and European policy as a whole.[111]

Delay and cost

A reference to a court will inevitably involve delay and cost. The average period **18–043** between making the reference and obtaining a ruling is about 18 months.[112] Such factors are relevant to the decision to refer, and are sometimes said to point against making reference.[113] Where, however, it is very likely that a reference will have to be made at some stage, there may well be a saving in both time and costs if the reference is made sooner, by a lower court, rather than later, by an appellate court. Such considerations have influenced the Employment Appeal Tribunal,[114] the Divisional Court,[115] and the Court of Appeal,[116] to make an immediate reference rather than deciding the matter themselves and leaving an appellate body to make a reference. The Court of Appeal has also made a reference where a decision in favour of one party on the EU law point would render unnecessary a time-consuming and expensive fact-finding exercise, and therefore could save time and cost overall.[117]

If the real motivation of a party in seeking a reference is merely to delay final **18–044** judgment before a national court, that may influence a court against making a reference. A court refused to make a reference on the compatibility of the UK

---

[109] *R. v Pharmaceutical Society of Great Britain Ex p. Association of Pharmaceutical Importers* [1987] 3 C.M.L.R. 951.

[110] *R. v Intervention Board for Agricultural Produce Ex p. Fish Producers' Organisation Ltd* [1988] 2 C.M.L.R. 661.

[111] *R. (Newby Foods Ltd.) v Food Standards Agency* [2013] EWHC 1966 (Admin) at [67].

[112] *R. v Dairy Produce Quotas Tribunal Ex p. Hall & Sons (Dairy Farmers) Ltd* [1988] 1 C.M.L.R. 592 (interpretation of regulation on dairy quotas involved considerations of provisions relating to common agricultural policy as a whole).

[113] *Bulmer v Bollinger* [1974] 1 Ch.401.

[114] *Newstead v Department of Transport* [1986] 2 C.M.L.R. 196.

[115] *R. v Dairy Produce Quotas Tribunal Ex p. Hall & Sons (Dairy Farmers) Ltd* [1988] 1 C.M.L.R. 592.

[116] *R. v Pharmaceutical Society of Great Britain Ex p. Association of Pharmaceutical Importers* [1987] 3 C.M.L.R. 951.

[117] *Thetford Corp. v Fiamma SpA* [1987] 3 C.M.L.R. 266.

Sunday trading laws where the real concern of the party seeking a reference was to obtain a two-year delay so that he could continue trading.[118]

Difficulty and importance of point of law

18–045 In the early years, lower courts refused to make reference when the point was considered to be obvious, as in *R. v Governor of Pentonville Prison Ex p. Budlong*; where the Divisional Court thought it was "common sense" that the EC Treaty was not intended to restrict a Member State's powers of extradition.[119] In *Bulmer v Bollinger*,[120] Lord Denning M.R. urged lower courts not to refer unless the point of law was really difficult or important, but rather to decide the point themselves. Subsequent cases have, however, stressed that the European Court is often better suited to decide issues of European law rather than national courts.[121] More recently, the courts have begun to emphasise again that where the difficulty is applying the principles of EU law to the facts of a particular case, rather than identifying what the principles are, a reference is not appropriate.[122]

18–046 Conversely, a court may be influenced in favour of making a reference by the fact that a point of law in issue is a genuinely novel and difficult one,[123] or one of great importance where it is desirable to obtain a decision from the Court of Justice which would be binding throughout the EU.[124]

Position of the court in the judicial hierarchy

18–047 Lower courts and tribunals should bear in mind the fact that their decisions may be appealed or reviewed. It may be more appropriate for a higher court to determine whether a reference is desirable and, perhaps more importantly, what precise form the questions to be referred should take. Magistrates' courts have been encouraged to exercise "considerable caution" before making a reference, even if this involves them deciding issues of European law themselves.[125] Their decision on the point of European Union law may be appealed or reviewed, and a higher court would be the suitable forum for deciding whether and what questions should be referred. The House of Lords also counselled presiding judges in trials on indictment not to refer but decide the question of European

---

[118] *Wychavon DC v Midland Enterprises (Special Event)* [1988] 1 C.M.L.R. 397. See also *Commissioners of Customs and Excise v APS Samex* [1983] 1 All E.R. 1042. In making a reference, the court took into account the fact that the party seeking a reference had nothing to gain by delay.

[119] [1980] 1 W.L.R. 1110.

[120] [1974] Ch. 401.

[121] See, especially, the comments of Bingham J. in *Customs and Excise Commissioners v A.P.S. Samex* [1983] 1 All E.R. 1042 at 1055.

[122] See, e.g. *R. v IRC Ex p. Professional Contractors' Group* [2002] Eu.L.R. 329 and *Trinity Mirror Plc v Commissioners of Customs and Excise* [2001] 2 C.M.L.R. 759 at 783–785.

[123] *R. v Intervention Board for Agricultural Produce Ex p. Fish Producers' Organisation Ltd* [1988] 2 C.M.L.R. 661.

[124] *Ex p. Fish Producers' Organisation Ltd* [1988] 2 C.M.L.R. 661. See also *R. v Pharmaceutical Society of Great Britain Ex p. Association of Pharmaceutical Importers* [1987] 3 C.M.L.R. 951. See also *London Borough of Harrow v Ibrahim* [2008] 2 C.M.L.R. 30 (reference where issues of general importance concerning the proper interpretation of recent EU law).

[125] *R. v Plymouth Justices Ex p. Rogers* [1982] Q.B. 863. In this instance a reference was, exceptionally, appropriate.

Union law themselves, and have the point considered on appeal if necessary.[126] The Employment Appeal Tribunal also takes into account the fact that they are the lowest tier in the appellate stage and, other things being equal, it would be more appropriate, for the reference to be left to the Court of Appeal or Supreme.[127] It must be said that this fact has not deterred the Employment Appeal Tribunal from making a reference when it considers it desirable, and it has also expressed the view that precisely because the matter is going to be appealed, costs will be saved by an immediate reference.[128]

Desire not to overburden the Court of Justice

The desire not to overburden the Court of Justice, and the corresponding need for a degree of restraint on the part of national courts in deciding to refer, particularly when the real issue is not the proper interpretation of EU law but its application to the facts, has been emphasised periodically in the case law as a relevant factor in deciding whether to refer.[129] In addition to references from national courts, the European Court hears direct actions against Member States and institutions of the EU. The workload of the European Court has increased as the number of Member States has increased (from the original six to 28), and the quantity of legislation has increased. A court of first instance has been created. This court does not have jurisdiction to give preliminary rulings under Art.267 TFEU, but hears staff cases and appeals against fines imposed for anti-competitive practices and some direct actions. The removal of these classes of cases from the Court of Justice gives the Court of Justice more time to deal with its case load, including references under Art.267 TFEU. Nonetheless, the caseload of the Court of Justice has increased considerably over recent years.

18–048

Wishes of the parties

The decision to refer is one for the court, not the parties. A court may decide to refer of its own motion or at the invitation of either party. The wishes of the parties, particularly in view of the delay and additional cost likely to be incurred, is a factor to be given some weight by the court in determining whether to make a reference.[130] Clearly, if both parties consider that a reference is required and are willing to bear the costs, that may influence a court in making a reference.[131]

18–049

---

[126] *Henn and Darby v DPP* [1981] A.C. 850.
[127] *Newstead v Department of Transport* [1986] 2 C.M.L.R. 196.
[128] [1986] 2 C.M.L.R. 196. See also *Burton v British Railways Board* [1982] Q.B. 1080.
[129] See, e.g. *R. v IRC Ex p. Professional Contractors' Group* [2002] Eu. L.R. 329; *Trinity Mirror Plc v Commissioners of Customs and Excise* [2001] 2 C.M.L.R. 759 at 783–785 and *Bulmer v Bollinger* [1974] Ch. 401.
[130] *R. v Pharmaceutical Society of Great Britain Ex p. Association of Pharmaceutical Importers* [1987] 3 C.M.L.R. 951; *Bulmer v Bollinger* [1974] Ch. 401. The court in *Maxim's Ltd v Dye* [1977] 1 W.L.R. 1155 was troubled at the thought of making a reference where the parties did not agree to a reference because of the expense that would entail. As a reference is a step in the national proceedings, legal aid may be available: *R. v Marlborough Street Stipendiary Magistrates Ex p. Bouchereau* [1977] 1 W.L.R. 414.
[131] *R. v Fishing Department Minister of Agriculture, Fisheries and Food Ex p. Agegate Ltd* [1987] 3 C.M.L.R. 939.

References cannot, however, be made by consent.[132] The decision remains that of the court, and the Court of Appeal has refused to make a reference even when both parties have requested one.[133] The courts have also been prepared to make a reference against the wishes of the parties.[134]

The presence of similar actions before the Court of Justice

18–050 Courts have not been dissuaded from making a reference because similar issues are already before the Court of Justice. The presence of other references raising the issue of the compatibility of the Sunday trading laws with European law has not deterred the High Court from referring essentially the same question.[135] The Court of Appeal was not deterred from making a reference raising the compatibility of certain measures taken by the Secretary of State with EU law, even where the Commission had begun a direct action in the Court of Justice against the UK under alleging that the UK action contravened the Treaty.[136] Nor has the fact that the validity of a directive has been challenged by the UK Government by way of a direct action in the Court of Justice deterred the Divisional Court from referring the question of the validity of the directive to the Court.[137] The presence of another action before the Court of Justice has actually been regarded as a factor pointing in favour of making a reference, rather than against.[138] If the issues are materially identical, it may be that a sensible approach would be to stay subsequent cases rather than make a reference.[139] If additional issues arise, or if the same issue arises but in a different factual context, a reference may be appropriate.

Stage at which the reference is sought

18–051 References may be sought at any stage in the proceedings before the national court, including preliminary and interlocutory stages.[140] The Court of Justice will accept references made at any stage of proceedings, and has emphasised that the precise stage at which a reference is to be made is a question for the national court.[141] The considerations discussed above apply equally to the exercise of the discretion to refer at a preliminary stage. Frequently, a reference will not be

---

[132] *Portsmouth City Council v Richards* [1989] 1 C.M.L.R. 673.

[133] *R. v Secretary of State for Social Services Ex p. Bomore Medical Supplies Ltd* [1986] 1 C.M.L.R. 228.

[134] *Newstead v Department of Transport* (see above, fn.118); *R. v Intervention Board for Agricultural Produce Ex p. Fish Producers' Organisation Ltd* [1988] 2 C.M.L.R. 661.

[135] *Rochdale BC v Anders* [1988] 3 C.M.L.R. 431.

[136] *R. v Pharmaceutical Society of Great Britain Ex p. Association of Pharmaceutical Importers* (see above, fn.43).

[137] *R. v Minister of Agriculture, Fisheries and Food Ex p. FEDESA* [1988] 3 C.M.L.R. 207.

[138] [1988] 3 C.M.L.R. 661.

[139] See, e.g. *ABNA Ltd v Scottish Ministers* [2004] 2 C.M.L.R. 967 (validity of EU directive already referred so no further reference required).

[140] See also CPR r.68.2(1) which makes specific provision for the High Court and Court of Appeal to refer at any stage in the proceedings.

[141] Case C-107/76 *Hoffman-La Roche v Centrafarm* [1977] E.C.R. 957; Case 14/86 *Pretore di Salo v Persons Unknown* [1989] C.M.L.R. 71.

appropriate at a preliminary stage in proceedings, as the facts will not be known and it may be unclear whether a question of European Union law arises.[142]

Courts have been prepared to make references at early stages in the proceedings where the facts are agreed and a decision on a point of law is necessary. References have been made on an application for interlocutory relief[143]; for a stay of proceedings[144]; to strike out proceedings as disclosing no cause of action.[145] References have been ordered on the grant of permission to apply for judicial review.[146] This may be particularly appropriate where the substance of a challenge is to the validity of an EU legislative measure such as a directive or regulation.[147] Only the Court of Justice can determine such questions and they frequently turn on questions of law rather than facts. In criminal cases, a reference may be made at the close of the prosecution case on a submission by the defendant of no case to answer, for example where it is alleged that the legislation creating the offence is contrary to EU law.[148] Issues of EU law and hence the question of whether it is appropriate to refer may arise on a preliminary point. In one case,[149] the claim sought judicial review of a preliminary ruling by magistrates in proceedings for the condemnation of certain books, that the defence that the books were for the public good was not available. In such cases, the courts, however, ought to be cautious about making a reference.[150] **18–052**

J. PROCEDURE BEFORE NATIONAL COURTS OR TRIBUNALS

High Court and Court of Appeal

References from the High Court and Court of Appeal are governed by CPR Part 68. An order referring a question to the Court of Justice may be made by the court on its own motion at any stage in the proceedings, or on application by either party before or at the trial.[151] The reference is made by the court itself, not by the parties, and the court is responsible for the order making the reference and may give directions as to the manner and form in which the schedule is to be prepared.[152] There is a Practice Direction[153] dealing with references and that **18–053**

---

[142] *An Bord Bainne Co-operative (Irish Dairy Board) (No.2) v Milk Marketing Board* [1985] 1 C.M.L.R. 6; *London Borough of Waltham Forest v Scott Markets* [1988] 3 C.M.L.R. 773.

[143] *Polydor Records v Harlequin Record Shops* [1980] 2 C.M.L.R. 413; *EMI Records v CBS United Kingdom* [1975] 1 C.M.L.R. 285.

[144] *Rochdale BC v Anders* [1999] 3 C.M.L.R. 673.

[145] *Thetford Corp. v Fiamma S.p.A.* [1987] 3 C.M.L.R. 266.

[146] *R. v Minister of Agriculture, Fisheries and Food Ex p. FEDESA* [1988] 3 C.M.L.R. 207 and *R. (Intertanko) v Secretary of State for Transport* [2007] Env. L.R. 8.

[147] See, e.g. *R. (ABNA Ltd) v Secretary of State for Health and Food Standards Agency* [2004] Eu. L.R. 88; *R. v Secretary of State for Health Ex p. Imperial Tobacco Ltd* [1999] C.O.D. 138.

[148] *R. v Plymouth Justices Ex p. Rogers* [1982] Q.B. 863.

[149] *R. v Bow Street Magistrates' Court Ex p. Noncyp Ltd* [1988] 3 W.L.R. 827 (affd. by CA: [1989] 3 W.L.R. 467). The Divisional Court suggested that it would be preferable for the proceedings to continue to the end and then seek judicial review of the magistrate's order.

[150] See para.18–047.

[151] CPR r.68.2.

[152] CPR r.68(2)(3).

draws attention to the Rules of Procedure of the Court of Justice and guidance from the Court of Justice.[154] The practice direction requires the courts to identify as clearly and succinctly as possible the question on which the court seeks a preliminary ruling.[155] Article 94 of the Rules of Procedure of the Court of Justice now require a reference from a national court to set out, in addition to the questions, a summary of the subject-matter and the relevant facts, the tenor of the relevant national provisions and a statement of the reasons prompting the reference, identifying the provisions of EU law considered to be relevant and explaining the relationship between those provisions and the provisions of national law. The guidance issued by the Court of Justice also encourages references to be drafted simply, clearly and precisely, in about ten pages, including the information referred to and an explanation as to why the ruling sought is necessary to enable the national court to give judgment[156]. Ideally, in order to comply with the Practice Direction and the rules and guidance, the order for a reference should identify the parties and summarise briefly the history of the proceedings. It should set out the relevant facts and the relevant provisions of national law. It should summarise the contentions of the parties and explain the reasons why a ruling from the Court of Justice is sought, identifying the EU law provisions in issue and it should formulate the questions clearly and precisely. The court may direct one of the parties to draft the reference and submit to the other party for comments,[157] or require the parties to prepare a draft in consultation.[158] The court may then adopt or vary the draft as it considers appropriate.[159]

18–054 The proceedings in which the order is made will be stayed until the Court of Justice has given a preliminary ruling on the questions referred, unless the court orders otherwise.[160] Following the making of an order, the Senior Master will transmit a copy of the order to the Registrar of the Court of Justice.[161] The Senior Master will not transmit the order until the time for appealing against the order has expired, or if an appeal is entered within that time, until the appeal has been determined.[162] There is provision for requesting that the hearing of the preliminary ruling procedure be expedited or dealt with urgently.[163]

---

[153] Practice Direction 68 – References to the European Court.

[154] Rules of Procedure of the Court of Justice 2012 and Recommendations to national courts on the initiation of preliminary rulings proceedings of 6 November 2012 (2012/C/3008).

[155] [1.2] of Practice Direction 68 – References to the European Court.

[156] See [20]–[28] of Recommendations to national courts on the initiation of preliminary rulings proceedings of 6 November 2012 (2012/C/3008).

[157] See, e.g. *Boots Co. Plc v Commissioners for Customs and Excise* [1988] 1 C.M.L.R. 433 at 439 where McPherson J. ordered the applicants to draft relevant questions within 14 days and the respondents to consider and propose amendments within 14 days whereafter the matter could be brought back to the court. See also *R. v HM Treasury Ex p. Daily Mail and General Trust Plc* [1987] 2 C.M.L.R. 1 at 7–10 and *Generics (U.K.) Ltd v Smith Kline & French Laboratories Ltd* [1990] 1 C.M.L.R. 416.

[158] See *Thetford Corp. v Fiamma S.p.A.* (see above, fn.32) at p.275.

[159] CPR r.68.2(3). See, e.g., the description of the process in *Teixiera v Lambeth London BC* [2009] H.L.R. 9 at [10]–[12].

[160] CPR r.68.4.

[161] CPR 68 r.3(1).

[162] CPR r.3(3).

[163] See rr.105 and 107 of the Rules of Procedure of the Court of Justice respectively and CPR r.68.2A.

Other courts and tribunals

Domestic rules of procedure have been laid down for some other courts and tribunals[164] but not for all courts and tribunals. The reference should now include the information required by Art.94 of the Rules of Procedure of the Court of Justice and the recommendations to national courts discussed above. The Court of Justice has not in the past refused to deal with a reference that fails to meet the guidance but has extracted from the information supplied on the reference the questions of EU law that arise for determination.[165] The failure to give the information required, however, increases the prospects that either the Court of Justice will not be in a position to give a preliminary ruling or may find that, exceptionally, a ruling is not necessary.

18–055

Costs and legal aid

Costs incurred before the national court may, and usually will, be reserved for the national court to decide when it has applied the ruling of the Court of Justice and gives final judgment in the case.[166] Costs will be in the discretion of the court, and will usually follow the event in that the unsuccessful party will normally pay the costs of the successful part.

18–056

Appeals against decisions to refer or refusals to refer

Appeals against a decision to refer or a refusal to refer are permitted under EU law.[167] An order of the High Court referring or refusing to refer a question may, with permission be appealed to the Court of Appeal.[168] Notice of appeal must be served within 21 days.[169] Appeal from the Court of Appeal to the Supreme Court against either a refusal or a decision to refer is available only with permission of either the Court of Appeal or the Supreme Court. The decision of a lower court on whether to refer or not will involve an exercise of discretion, and the Court of Appeal will only interfere with an exercise of judicial discretion where the decision: "… exceeds the generous ambit within which reasonable disagreement is possible and is, in fact, plainly wrong".[170]

18–057

There may also be the possibility of an appeal from a decision to make a reference by an inferior court or tribunal to the High Court or Court of Appeal.

18–058

---

[164] See, e.g. Crown Court Rules 1982 (SI 1982/1109).

[165] In Case C-83/78 *Pigs Marketing Board* (*Northern Ireland*) *v Redmond* [1978] E.C.R. 2347 the European Court abstracted the relevant questions of Community law from the questions referred and the covering letter sent by the resident magistrate of Armagh.

[166] There are a large number of cases where this has been done; see, e.g. *R. v HM Treasury Ex p. Daily Mail and General Trust Plc* [1987] 2 C.M.L.R. 1; *The Boots Co Plc v Commissioners for Customs and Excise* [1988] 1 C.M.L.R. 433. But see *Generics* (*U.K.*) *Ltd v Smith Kline & French Laboratories Ltd* [1990] 1 C.M.L.R. 455 where an order as to 80% of costs was made, with the remaining 20% reserved until after the ruling from the European Court. See also [1999] 1 W.L.R. 260 at 262H.

[167] Case C-146/73 *Rheinmühlen-Dusseldorf v Einfuhr- und Vorratsstelle für Getreide und Futtermittel* [1974] E.C.R. 139.

[168] CPR r.52.3.

[169] CPR r.52.4.

[170] per Stephenson LJ in *Bulmer v Bollinger*[1974] 1 Ch. 401 at 431.

Where an appeal is limited to an appeal on a point of law, an appeal will involve a point of law if it involves a misconstruction of Art.267 TFEU, such as misinterpreting the types of questions which may be referred or, possibly, in defining when a decision on EU law is necessary to give judgment. It also is probable that a court would regard an exercise of the discretion to refer which was plainly wrong or produced manifest injustice as involving an error of law. Decisions by inferior courts or tribunals on whether or not to refer are also subject to judicial review.[171] It is unlikely that a decision involving the exercise of the discretion to refer would be quashed, so long as the inferior court or tribunal had not misdirected itself or acted unreasonably.[172]

Withdrawal of references

18–059   The Court of Appeal,[173] the High Court[174] and in principle,[175] other courts or tribunals, have jurisdiction to order the withdrawal of a reference to the Court of Justice. In general, the courts should be reluctant to withdraw a reference and should only do so when it is manifest that a reference will not serve any purpose. One situation where this may be appropriate is where the Court of Justice has determined the point raised in the reference in other proceedings. Thus, the High Court ordered that a reference be withdrawn where the question of whether the Equal Treatment Directive prohibited discrimination on grounds of sexual orientation had been referred to the Court of Justice and that question was subsequently answered in the negative in a different reference.[176] In considering a reference, regard should be had to any indication from the Court of Justice, itself, that one of its decisions has rendered the matter acte clair.[177] A second situation where withdrawal may be appropriate is where the proceedings have become academic due to events occurring since the date of a reference. Thus, where the High Court referred various questions on free movement in relation to an order excluding a particular individual from the mainland, and that exclusion order was subsequently revoked by the government, the High Court ordered the withdrawal of the reference.[178] The Court of Justice retains jurisdiction in a case and will proceed to give a preliminary ruling unless and until, however, the referring court formally makes an order withdrawing the reference.[179]

---

[171] *R. v Plymouth Justices Ex p. Rogers* [1982] Q.B. 863.

[172] *R. v Plymouth Justices Ex p. Rogers* [1982] Q.B. 863.

[173] See *Royscott Leasing Ltd v Commissioners of Customs and Excise* (1998) 11 Admin. L.Rep. 251.

[174] See, e.g. *R. v Secretary of State for Defence Ex p. Perkins* [1998] I.R.L.R. 508.

[175] The Supreme Court has inherent jurisdiction. Other tribunals are, however, masters of their own procedure. They may make a reference if they consider that a decision on a question of EU law is necessary; there is no reason why they cannot decide that a reference is no longer necessary and order that it be withdrawn.

[176] See *Ex p. Perkins* [1998] I.R.L.R. 508 (withdrawing the decision to refer, reported in [1997] I.R.L.R. 297, following the decision of the European Court in *Grant v South-West Trains Ltd* [1998] I.R.L.R. 206).

[177] *Royscott* (1998) 11Admin. L.Rep. 251.

[178] *R. v Secretary of State for the Home Department Ex p. Adams, Independent*, April 28, 1995.

[179] Cases C-2/82 and C-4/82 *SA Delhaize Freres "Le Lion" v Belgian State* [1983] E.C.R. 2973.

K. PROCEDURE BEFORE THE COURT OF JUSTICE

Article 23 of the Statutes of the Court of Justice provides that, in cases involving preliminary references, the national court or tribunal shall notify the Court of Justice of its decision to make a reference. The Registrar of the Court will then notify the parties, the Member States and the Commission and, where an interpretation or ruling on the validity of an act of an institution is sought, the institution. The parties are those determined as such by the national court in accordance with the relevant national rules.[180] In judicial review claims, they will be the claimant, defendant, interested parties and those permitted to intervene pursuant to CPR 54. 17. In private law proceedings, it will be the claimants and defendants and those added as a party for the purpose of the reference.[181]

18–060

The Court of Justice comprises one judge for each of the 28 Member States.[182] The Court is divided into Chambers of three judges or five judges. The Court may assign the case to one of the Chambers if the difficulty and importance of the case or the particular circumstances are not such as to require the Court to sit in a Grand Chamber of 13 judges (or in certain circumstances a full Court comprising 15 judges).[183] The Court will also sit in a Grand Chamber when a Member State or an EU institution that is a party to the proceedings so requests.[184] The parties notified of the reference are entitled, although not obliged, to make written submissions within two months of the notification.[185] The Court may order a preparatory inquiry, where issues of fact need to be resolved. In the case of preliminary rulings, the facts underlying the litigation will normally be determined by the national court, not the Court of Justice. Where the validity of an act of an EU institution is in issue, then it may be necessary for the Court to determine facts.

18–061

After the written submissions, the next stage is the oral procedure before the Court. This will consist of the report of the Judge-Rapporteur, the oral argument of the parties, the Member States, the Commission, and other EU institutions if appropriate. The Court may dispense within an oral hearing if it considers that it has sufficient information to deal with the case.[186] There then follows the opinion of the Advocate-General unless the Court decides that the case can be determined without a submission form the Advocate-General.[187]

18–062

After deliberation, the Court then delivers its judgment. A copy of the judgment is served on the parties, and on the national court making the reference. The Court normally orders that the costs of the Member States and the Commission and any other EU institution which participate are not recoverable, and that the costs as between the parties in the proceedings is a matter for the national court, since the reference is a step in the action before the national court.[188] Following the ruling, the matter returns to the national court. That court

18–063

---

[180] Article 97 of the Rules of Procedure of the Court of Justice.
[181] Pursuant to CPR 19.2. See *Football Premier League Ltd. v QC Leisure* [2009] 1 W.L.R. 1603.
[182] Article 19 TEU.
[183] Statute of the Court of Justice Art.16.
[184] Statute of the Court of Justice Art.16.
[185] Statute of the Court of Justice Art.23.
[186] Rule 76 of the Rules of Procedure of the Court of Justice.
[187] Statutes of the Court Art.20.
[188] See, e.g. Case 434/85 *Allen & Hanburys Ltd v Generics (U.K.) Ltd* [1989] 1 W.L.R. 414.

then applies the ruling to the case before it. The ruling is binding as to the interpretation given but it is for the national court to find the facts and apply the ruling to the facts.[189] The normal rule that costs usually follow the event applies. The unsuccessful party will therefore have to pay the other side's costs prior to the reference, the costs of the reference itself, and the costs of the final proceedings where the national court applies the ruling.[190]

Effect of a preliminary ruling on questions of validity

18–064 A preliminary ruling of the Court of Justice is binding on the national court making the reference, which must then apply the ruling to the case before it. The Court of Justice has also held that the existence of a preliminary ruling that an act of an EU institution is invalid is sufficient reason for any other national court to regard the act as invalid in any other case in which the validity of the act is an issue.[191] A ruling that an EU act is invalid is declaratory, and the act is regarded as invalid from its inception.[192] The Court of Justice has held that it has the power to limit the temporal effect of a finding of nullity, and simply hold the measure invalid as for the future. All acts done in reliance on the measure before judgment was given will, therefore, continue to be regarded as valid. Thus, in one case the Court held that an EU act was invalid but ruled that money paid pursuant to an obligation imposed by the invalid regulation prior to the date of its judgment could not be recovered.[193] Where the Court of Justice rules that an EU act is invalid, a national court may refer further questions on the grounds, scope and the consequences of invalidity.[194]

Effect of a preliminary ruling on a question of interpretation

18–065 A ruling on the interpretation of a European Union provision is to be followed and applied by all national courts.[195] A preliminary ruling is declaratory in effect; that is, the ruling declares what EU law is and always has been. The interpretation as given by the Court of Justice should, therefore, be applied to all situations arising before the interpretation was given as well as situations arising after the ruling was given.[196] The Court of Justice has held that it has the power to limit the temporal effects of its rulings, in exceptional circumstances, to situations arising after the date of its judgment. In such circumstances, the ruling would have prospective effect only. In *Blaizot v University of Liège*,[197] for example, the

---

[189] See *Arsenal Football Club Plc v Reed* [2003] Eu. L.R. 641 on the approach national courts should adopt to applying rulings of the Court of Justice.

[190] See, e.g. *R. v Intervention Board for Agricultural Produce Ex p. Fish Producers' Organisation Ltd* [1993] 1 C.M.L.R. 707.

[191] Case C-66/80 *International Chemical Corp. v Amministrazione Delle Finanze delle Stato* [1981] E.C.R. 1191.

[192] [1981] E.C.R. 1191.

[193] Case C-145/79 *Roquette Freres SA v Administration des Douanes* [1980] E.C.R. 2917. See also Case c-112/83 *Societe des Produits de Mais SA v Administration des Douanes et Droits Indirects* [1988] 1 C.M.L.R. 459.

[194] *International Chemical Corp. v Amministrazione Delle Finanze Delle Stato* [1981] E.C.R. 1191.

[195] Case C-24/86 *Blaizot v University of Liège* [1989] 1 C.M.L.R. 57.

[196] Case C-309/85 *Barra v Belgium State and The City of Liège* [1988] 2 C.M.L.R. 409.

[197] Case C-24/86 [1989] 1 C.M.L.R. 57.

Court extended the interpretation given to "vocational studies" to include university education, so that discrimination on the grounds of nationality in relation to university would therefore be contrary to what is now Art.18 TFEU. The Court of Justice exceptionally limited the temporal effects of its ruling and provided that discriminatory fees charged to EU nationals before the date of its judgment could not be recovered unless legal proceedings had already been commenced before that date, largely because of the financial effects on universities of allowing retrospective claims. The Court of Justice alone can determine whether to limit the temporal effects of its rulings; neither national courts nor national law may do so.[198] The Court has held that the effect of a judgment can only be limited in the very judgment in which the interpretation is given; it is not possible to limit the effect of an earlier ruling on a question of interpretation in a subsequent case.[199]

---

[198] *Barra v Belgium State and The City of Liège* [1988] 2 C.M.L.R. 409.

[199] *Barra v Belgium State and The City of Liège* [1988] 2 C.M.L.R. 409. Quaere whether the same limitation applies in relation to rulings on the validity of EU Acts as well as interpretation of them. The ability of a national court to refer for a second time the consequences of a ruling of invalidity would seem wide enough to encompass a later reference asking the European Court to limit the effects of an earlier ruling. Yet the ruling in *Barra*, although dealing with a question of interpretation, would seem equally applicable to cases involving invalidity.

INDEX

This index has been prepared using Sweet and Maxwell's Legal Taxonomy. Main index entries conform to keywords provided by the Legal Taxonomy except where references to specific documents or non-standard terms (denoted by quotation marks) have been included. These keywords provide a means of identifying similar concepts in other Sweet and Maxwell publications and online services to which keywords from the Legal Taxonomy have been applied. Readers may find some minor differences between terms used in the text and those which appear in the index. Suggestions to *sweetandmaxwell.taxonomy@thomson.com*.

All references are to paragraph number

INDEX

Judicial Remedies in Public Law